CRITICAL SURVEY OF

Poetry

Fourth Edition

British, Irish, and Commonwealth Poets

CRITICAL SURVEY OF

Poetry

Fourth Edition

British, Irish, and Commonwealth Poets

Volume 2
Sir Richard Fanshawe—Nuala Ní Dhomhnaill

Editor, Fourth Edition
Rosemary M. Canfield Reisman
Charleston Southern University

S<small>ALEM</small> P<small>RESS</small>
Pasadena, California
Hackensack, New Jersey

Editor in Chief: Dawn P. Dawson

Editorial Director: Christina J. Moose　　*Research Supervisor:* Jeffry Jensen
Development Editor: Tracy Irons-Georges　　*Research Assistant:* Keli Trousdale
Project Editor: Rowena Wildin　　*Production Editor:* Andrea E. Miller
Manuscript Editor: Desiree Dreeuws　　*Page Des ign:* James Hutson
Acquisitions Editor: Mark Rehn　　*Layout:* Mary Overell
Editorial Assistant: Brett S. Weisberg　　*Photo Editor:* Cynthia Breslin Beres

Cover photo: Lord Byron (Archive Photos/Getty Images)

Copyright ©1983, 1984, 1987, 1992, 2003, 2011, by SALEM PRESS

All rights in this book are reserved. No part of this work may be used or reproduced in any manner whatsoever or transmitted in any form or by any means, electronic or mechanical, including photocopy, recording, or any information storage and retrieval system, without written permission from the copyright owner except in the case of brief quotations embodied in critical articles and reviews or in the copying of images deemed to be freely licensed or in the public domain. For information, address the publisher, Salem Press, at csr@salemspress.com.

Some of the essays in this work, which have been updated, originally appeared in the following Salem Press publications, *Critical Survey of Poetry, English Language Series* (1983), *Critical Survey of Poetry: Foreign Language Series* (1984), *Critical Survey of Poetry, Supplement* (1987), *Critical Survey of Poetry, English Language Series, Revised Edition*, (1992; preceding volumes edited by Frank N. Magill), *Critical Survey of Poetry, Second Revised Edition* (2003; edited by Philip K. Jason).

∞ The paper used in these volumes conforms to the American National Standard for Permanence of Paper for Printed Library Materials, X39.48-1992 (R1997).

Library of Congress Cataloging-in-Publication Data

Critical survey of poetry. — 4th ed. / editor, Rosemary M. Canfield Reisman.
　　v. cm.
Includes bibliographical references and index.
ISBN 978-1-58765-582-1 (set : alk. paper) — ISBN 978-1-58765-588-3 (set : Brit., Irish, Comm. poets : alk. paper) — ISBN 978-1-58765-589-0 (v. 1 : Brit., Irish, Comm. poets : alk. paper) — ISBN 978-1-58765-590-6 (v. 2 : Brit., Irish, Comm. poets : alk. paper) — ISBN 978-1-58765-591-3 (v. 3 : Brit., Irish, Comm. poets : alk. paper)
1. Poetry—History and criticism—Dictionaries. 2. Poetry—Bio-bibliography. 3. Poets—Biography—Dictionaries. I. Reisman, Rosemary M. Canfield.
　PN1021.C7 2011
　809.1'003--dc22

2010045095

First Printing

CONTENTS

Complete List of Contents xxix
Pronunciation Key xxxiii

Sir Richard Fanshawe 481
James Fenton 487
Anne Finch 491
Edward FitzGerald 495
Roy Fuller 500

George Gascoigne 505
John Gay 512
Oliver Goldsmith 520
John Gower 525
Robert Graves 534
Thomas Gray 542
Robert Greene 548
Fulke Greville 555
Thom Gunn 560
Ivor Gurney 568

Arthur Henry Hallam 575
Thomas Hardy 579
Tony Harrison 588
Seamus Heaney 594
Anne Hébert 605
Felicia Dorothea Hemans 609
Robert Henryson 612
George Herbert 617
Robert Herrick 626
John Heywood 635
Geoffrey Hill 641
Thomas Hood 650
A. D. Hope 660
Gerard Manley Hopkins 666
A. E. Housman 677
Ted Hughes 686
Leigh Hunt 694

Samuel Johnson 700
David Jones 707
Ben Jonson 711
James Joyce 719

Patrick Kavanagh 726
John Keats 731
Henry King 743
Thomas Kinsella 751
Rudyard Kipling 760

Charles Lamb 768
Walter Savage Landor 774
William Langland 780
Philip Larkin 786
D. H. Lawrence 795
Layamon 803
Irving Layton 808
Edward Lear 812
Thomas Lodge 817
Christopher Logue 823
Richard Lovelace 827
John Lydgate 832

George MacBeth 841
Hugh MacDiarmid 846
Louis MacNeice 854
James Clarence Mangan 866
Christopher Marlowe 870
Andrew Marvell 877
John Masefield 885
George Meredith 890
Charlotte Mew 894
Christopher Middleton 898
John Milton 905
John Montague 914
William Morris 924
Edwin Muir 933
Paul Muldoon 937
Les A. Murray 946

Thomas Nashe 953
Margaret Cavendish, duchess of
    Newcastle 958
Nuala Ní Dhomhnaill 964

COMPLETE LIST OF CONTENTS

Volume 1

Publisher's Note v
Contributors ix
Contents xiii
Complete List of Contents xv
Pronunciation Key xix

Dannie Abse 1
Joseph Addison 7
Æ 13
Richard Aldington 17
William Allingham 23
Matthew Arnold 30
Margaret Atwood 37
W. H. Auden 47

Thomas Lovell Beddoes 56
Patricia Beer 60
Aphra Behn 66
Hilaire Belloc 73
John Betjeman 80
Earle Birney 86
William Blake 91
Edmund Blunden 104
Eavan Boland 108
William Lisle Bowles 119
Nicholas Breton 124
Robert Bridges 131
Emily Brontë 137
Rupert Brooke 144
Elizabeth Barrett Browning 149
Robert Browning 158
Basil Bunting 168
Robert Burns 173
Samuel Butler 180
Lord Byron 186

Cædmon 197
Thomas Campion 202
Thomas Carew 208

Lewis Carroll 213
Anne Carson 225
George Chapman 228
Thomas Chatterton 235
Geoffrey Chaucer 243
John Clare 254
Austin Clarke 261
Arthur Hugh Clough 266
Leonard Cohen 272
Samuel Taylor Coleridge 276
William Collins 287
Padraic Colum 292
William Congreve 296
Henry Constable 301
Charles Cotton 306
Abraham Cowley 312
William Cowper 320
George Crabbe 327
Richard Crashaw 337
Cynewulf 344

Samuel Daniel 352
George Darley 359
Sir William Davenant 362
Donald Davie 367
Sir John Davies 375
Cecil Day Lewis 384
Thomas Dekker 390
Walter de la Mare 398
John Donne 405
Michael Drayton 417
William Drummond of Hawthornden 424
John Dryden 433
William Dunbar 442
Lawrence Durrell 451

T. S. Eliot 458
William Empson 468
Sir George Etherege 476

VOLUME 2

Contents xxvii
Pronunciation Key xxxiii

Sir Richard Fanshawe 481
James Fenton 487
Anne Finch 491
Edward FitzGerald 495
Roy Fuller 500

George Gascoigne 505
John Gay 512
Oliver Goldsmith 520
John Gower 525
Robert Graves 534
Thomas Gray 542
Robert Greene 548
Fulke Greville 555
Thom Gunn 560
Ivor Gurney 568

Arthur Henry Hallam 575
Thomas Hardy 579
Tony Harrison 588
Seamus Heaney 594
Anne Hébert 605
Felicia Dorothea Hemans 609
Robert Henryson 612
George Herbert 617
Robert Herrick 626
John Heywood 635
Geoffrey Hill 641
Thomas Hood 650
A. D. Hope 660
Gerard Manley Hopkins 666
A. E. Housman 677
Ted Hughes 686
Leigh Hunt 694

Samuel Johnson 700
David Jones 707
Ben Jonson 711
James Joyce 719

Patrick Kavanagh 726
John Keats 731
Henry King 743
Thomas Kinsella 751
Rudyard Kipling 760

Charles Lamb 768
Walter Savage Landor 774
William Langland 780
Philip Larkin 786
D. H. Lawrence 795
Layamon 803
Irving Layton 808
Edward Lear 812
Thomas Lodge 817
Christopher Logue 823
Richard Lovelace 827
John Lydgate 832

George MacBeth 841
Hugh MacDiarmid 846
Louis MacNeice 854
James Clarence Mangan 866
Christopher Marlowe 870
Andrew Marvell 877
John Masefield 885
George Meredith 890
Charlotte Mew 894
Christopher Middleton 898
John Milton 905
John Montague 914
William Morris 924
Edwin Muir 933
Paul Muldoon 937
Les A. Murray 946

Thomas Nashe 953
Margaret Cavendish, duchess of
    Newcastle 958
Nuala Ní Dhomhnaill 964

VOLUME 3

Contents xli
Complete List of Contents. xliii
Pronunciation Key xlvii

John Oldham 969
Michael Ondaatje 973
Wilfred Owen 977

Coventry Patmore 983
Pearl-Poet 991
Harold Pinter 1001
Alexander Pope. 1005
E. J. Pratt 1016
F. T. Prince 1021
Matthew Prior. 1026

Francis Quarles 1031

Sir Walter Ralegh 1037
Henry Reed 1043
John Wilmot, earl of Rochester. 1048
Isaac Rosenberg 1055
Christina Rossetti. 1060
Dante Gabriel Rossetti 1065

Thomas Sackville. 1074
Siegfried Sassoon. 1080
Sir Walter Scott. 1087
Sir Charles Sedley 1094
Robert W. Service 1099
William Shakespeare 1105
Percy Bysshe Shelley. 1112
Sir Philip Sidney 1126
Sir Robert Sidney. 1135
Jon Silkin 1141
Edith Sitwell 1145
John Skelton 1153
Christopher Smart 1159
Stevie Smith 1164
Robert Southey 1171
Robert Southwell 1178
Stephen Spender 1183
Edmund Spenser 1191

Robert Louis Stevenson 1201
Sir John Suckling 1206
Henry Howard, earl of Surrey 1212
Jonathan Swift 1218
Algernon Charles Swinburne. 1227

Alfred, Lord Tennyson 1236
Dylan Thomas 1245
Edward Thomas 1252
R. S. Thomas 1257
James Thomson. 1260
James Thomson. 1264
Charles Tomlinson 1268
Thomas Traherne 1277

Henry Vaughan 1284

Edmund Waller 1290
Isaac Watts 1297
Oscar Wilde. 1303
William Wordsworth 1310
Sir Thomas Wyatt. 1322

William Butler Yeats 1330
Edward Young 1349

RESOURCES
Explicating Poetry 1357
Language and Linguistics 1366
Glossary of Poetical Terms. 1378
Bibliography 1391
Guide to Online Resources 1401
Time Line. 1405
Major Awards. 1408
Chronological List of Poets 1415

INDEXES
Geographical Index of Poets 1421
Categorized Index of Poets. 1425
Critical Survey of Poetry Series:
 Master List of Contents 1437
Subject Index 1448

PRONUNCIATION KEY

To help users of the *Critical Survey of Poetry* pronounce unfamiliar names of profiled poets correctly, phonetic spellings using the character symbols listed below appear in parentheses immediately after the first mention of the poet's name in the narrative text. Stressed syllables are indicated in capital letters, and syllables are separated by hyphens.

VOWEL SOUNDS

Symbol	Spelled (Pronounced)
a	answer (AN-suhr), laugh (laf), sample (SAM-puhl), that (that)
ah	father (FAH-thur), hospital (HAHS-pih-tuhl)
aw	awful (AW-fuhl), caught (kawt)
ay	blaze (blayz), fade (fayd), waiter (WAYT-ur), weigh (way)
eh	bed (behd), head (hehd), said (sehd)
ee	believe (bee-LEEV), cedar (SEE-dur), leader (LEED-ur), liter (LEE-tur)
ew	boot (bewt), lose (lewz)
i	buy (bi), height (hit), lie (li), surprise (sur-PRIZ)
ih	bitter (BIH-tur), pill (pihl)
o	cotton (KO-tuhn), hot (hot)
oh	below (bee-LOH), coat (koht), note (noht), wholesome (HOHL-suhm)
oo	good (good), look (look)
ow	couch (kowch), how (how)
oy	boy (boy), coin (koyn)
uh	about (uh-BOWT), butter (BUH-tuhr), enough (ee-NUHF), other (UH-thur)

CONSONANT SOUNDS

Symbol	Spelled (Pronounced)
ch	beach (beech), chimp (chihmp)
g	beg (behg), disguise (dihs-GIZ), get (geht)
j	digit (DIH-juht), edge (ehj), jet (jeht)
k	cat (kat), kitten (KIH-tuhn), hex (hehks)
s	cellar (SEHL-ur), save (sayv), scent (sehnt)
sh	champagne (sham-PAYN), issue (IH-shew), shop (shop)
ur	birth (burth), disturb (dihs-TURB), earth (urth), letter (LEH-tur)
y	useful (YEWS-fuhl), young (yuhng)
z	business (BIHZ-nehs), zest (zehst)
zh	vision (VIH-zhuhn)

CRITICAL SURVEY OF
Poetry
Fourth Edition

British, Irish, and Commonwealth Poets

F

SIR RICHARD FANSHAWE

Born: Ware Park, Hertfordshire, England; June,
1608
Died: Madrid, Spain; June 16, 1666

PRINCIPAL POETRY

*"Il pastor fido," "The Faithful Shepherd," with an
Addition of Divers Other Poems*, 1648
(translation and original poetry)
The Shorter Poems and Translations, 1964
*The Poems and Translations of Sir Richard
Fanshawe*, 1997, 1999 (2 volumes; Peter
Davidson, editor)

OTHER LITERARY FORMS

With the exception of one essay and English versions of two Spanish plays, the published writings of
Sir Richard Fanshawe (FAN-shaw) are all poems: either original verse or translations from Latin, Italian,
Spanish, and Portuguese. Both the essay and the plays
are undistinguished. No collected edition of Fanshawe's works exists, but most of the poetry is available in modern texts. Geoffrey Bullough edited *The
Lusiad* (1963), N. W. Bawcutt collected both printed
and manuscript material in *The Shorter Poems and
Translations* (1964), and J. H. Whitfield's *Il pastor fido*
prints the original Italian and Fanshawe's English on
facing pages. *The Cyclopedia of English Literature*
(1847) reprints two poems found nowhere else.

Two extraliterary works throw considerable light
on the man and his times: *The Memoirs of Anne, Lady
Fanshawe*, written in 1676 and edited by John Loftis
(1979), gives a fond wife's view of her husband's private and public life, and *Original Letters and Negotiations of His Excellency Sir Richard Fanshawe*, published in two volumes (1724), records his years as
ambassador to Spain.

ACHIEVEMENTS

Sir Richard Fanshawe's reputation as a poet is small.
He wrote only a few poems in English; they demonstrate
a good ear for sound and a good eye for images, but the
canon is too small to be of major importance. Fanshawe
put more effort into translations, which in the 1640's
and 1650's expanded English literary horizons by introducing European classics and by prompting poetic
experimentation. Besides translating Latin poets such
as Horace and Vergil, Fanshawe rendered into English
many poems and plays from the Italian, Spanish, and
Portuguese. He translated authors (such as Luis de
Góngora y Argote, Luis de Camões, and Giambattista
Guarini) who, like himself, were courtiers, soldiers,
and diplomats as well as poets. He preferred the genres
that appealed to an aristocratic audience: the sonnet, the
epic, pastoral verse drama, and plays of intrigue.

Translation, however, is a sandy foundation for literary fame. If one translates works that later lose international stature, the translator's fame declines as well.
If one renders acknowledged classics, translators of the
next generation will offer more "modern" versions.
Fanshawe's translations suffered both fates. His well-
done translations of Guarini's *Il pastor fido* (1590; *The
Faithful Shepherd*) and Camões's *Os Lusíadas* (1572;
The Lusiads) are little remarked because the originals
are now scarcely read. Fanshawe did fine versions of
Horace's odes and Vergil's *Aeneid* (c. 29-19 B.C.E.),
but modern readers of these Roman poets can easily
find equally adept translations in contemporary idiom.
No wonder, then, that Fanshawe's name appears only
in the most thorough literary histories and anthologies.

If Fanshawe lacks a popular reputation, he preserves
one among period specialists. They acknowledge his
importance in helping open English literature to foreign influence. They also point out that Fanshawe began a new emphasis in translating the spirit more than
the literal sense of a work. Finally, they testify to the
fluidity and grace of Fanshawe's verse, which maintains a measure of Elizabethan lyricism amid the bombast and brittleness of much interregnum literature.

BIOGRAPHY

Sir Richard Fanshawe would have made the perfect
hero for a nineteenth century historical novel. His life

Sir Richard Fanshawe (©Michael Nicholson/CORBIS)

was shaped by the events of the English Civil War (1640-1660). King Charles I's disputes with the Puritans over church ritual and with Parliament over taxation brought two decades of rebellion, a regicide, and a Commonwealth government under Oliver Cromwell. Fanshawe's social class and ideals ensured that he would remain faithful to the Royalist cause and that he would spare neither expense nor energy in defense of monarchy. The war years brought Fanshawe dramatic and romantic adventures, a courageous and ardent wife, and a series of important political posts. He was, in Alfred Harbage's phrase, "royal quixote and married lover."

Fanshawe was born in 1608, the son of Sir Henry Fanshawe, third remembrancer to James I. At fifteen, Fanshawe entered Jesus College, Cambridge, where he excelled at classical languages. Three years later, he went to the Inner Temple to study law but found it a less agreeable subject. Two early poems record his fidelity to the Muse of poetry and to aristocratic ideals. A tour of France and Spain in the early 1630's allowed Fanshawe to indulge his love of languages and to pre-

pare for a diplomatic career. The tour was rewarded: From 1635 to 1638, he served as secretary to the English ambassador in Spain.

The eruption of civil war in 1640 brought Fanshawe into the Royal Army. Quartered at Oxford in 1643, he met Anne Harrison, seventeen years younger and the daughter of an impoverished knight. Fanshawe married her in 1644 and was appointed secretary of war to Prince Rupert. For the next two years, the newlyweds followed the prince's court around England and to the Channel Islands.

When the Puritan capture of Charles led to a lull in the fighting, the Fanshawes settled in London. In 1648, Fanshawe brought out his translation of *Il pastor fido* and other poems. Soon thereafter, the imprisoned Charles asked Fanshawe to carry letters to the queen in France. Back now on active service, Fanshawe became treasurer of the navy and recruited Royalist soldiers in Ireland. When Cromwell invaded Ireland after the execution of Charles, the Fanshawes barely escaped. Entering the service of Charles II, Fanshawe led an embassy to Spain to seek financial aid. In 1651, Fanshawe was captured at the Battle of Worcester and imprisoned at Whitehall. Two months later, Anne successfully petitioned for her husband's release on grounds of his ill health.

Fanshawe's enforced leisure in prison and on parole allowed him to turn his attention to literature. In the next six years, he produced the rest of his major works: translations of Horace's odes, Camões's epic, and two Spanish plays; he also rendered John Fletcher's *The Faithful Shepherdess* into Latin. The death of Oliver Cromwell (1658) and the restoration of Charles II (1660), however, turned Fanshawe's energies to politics again. Knighted in 1660 and elected to Parliament in 1661, Fanshawe rapidly received a series of major appointments: ambassador to Portugal, 1662; privy councillor, 1663; and ambassador to Spain, 1664. Fanshawe served in Madrid for two years before being recalled after a controversial negotiation of a commercial treaty. While preparing to return, Fanshawe was stricken with a fever and died. Anne took him on a final European crossing, bringing his body back to Hertfordshire for burial.

Fanshawe's life is vividly recorded in Anne's memoirs. She obviously loved her husband dearly and admired his every action, from his reading poetry as he walked to his sacrificing of his personal fortune for the Royalist cause. Her book describes Fanshawe as a brave soldier, a worthy courtier, the "tendrest husband imaginable," and a reserved man who revealed "the thought of his heart" only to his wife. Together they had survived battle, imprisonment, exile, and shipwreck as the winds of war blew them around England and across Europe. Anne's devotion to her husband more than matched his loyalty to the Stuart kings. The Fanshawes remain one of the remarkable couples in English literary history.

ANALYSIS

Sir Richard Fanshawe's reputation rests almost entirely on his translations, but he did write some creditable original poems, published in 1648, including "An Ode upon Occasion of His Majesty's Proclamation in the Year 1630" (1630), "The Saint's Encouragement" (1643), and "The Royalist" (1646). These three poems' topicality almost consigns them to social history, though they are charming pieces, skillfully contrived. Two poems, one of advice for Prince Charles "Presented to his Highness, *in the West*, Ann. Dom. 1646" and "The Rose," are among his better adaptations—translations so free as to be arguably Fanshawe's own, although acknowledged as translations. In all these poems, one sees traits that make him a dedicated and successful translator rather than a memorable original poet. His success as translator can best be seen in *The Faithful Shepherd* and *The Lusiad*.

"AN ODE UPON OCCASION OF HIS MAJESTY'S PROCLAMATION IN THE YEAR 1630"

In "An Ode upon Occasion of His Majesty's Proclamation in the Year 1630," the collegiate Fanshawe responds to a 1630 edict in which Charles I urged gentlemen to mind their rural estates and stop migrating to an overcrowded London. A survey of European countries torn by wars leads to one central image: England is like that "blest isle" to which Jove had chained the dove of peace while he fought to take over the heavens. What follows paints a picture of England's gentlemen and beautiful ladies healthfully at home in their natural country environment. The poem, as John Buxton points

out in *A Tradition of Poetry* (1967), is written in one of Fanshawe's peculiar stanzaic adaptations, the Sapphic. The classical Sapphic was a quantitative stanza consisting of three eleven-syllable lines followed by one of five syllables. The Sapphic tended to stay off balance, with a concentration of long syllables near the center of the lines and the short final line heightening the impression of asymmetry. The effect resembles sprung rhythm. Fanshawe adapts Sappho by using accentual rhythm and by shortening and regularizing the lines; three tetrameters precede a dimeter. In "An Ode upon Occasion of His Majesty's Proclamation in the Year 1630," the tetrameters of the early stanzas are as predictably regular as the wars that plagued Europe. Only the dimeters preserve the effect of syncopated rhythm. When, however, he comes to the four stanzas imaging England as Jove's blest isle, he "springs" the rhythm so that the most energetic and original rhythms of the poem coincide with its celebration of England's dynamic peacefulness. As a translator, Fanshawe habitually adapted stanzaic patterns in this way, not duplicating the original but finding an appropriate English analogue.

Young Fanshawe's metrical insights proved to be more acute, however, than his political ones. Within the decade, his country's "White Peace" had changed to war. However, the national pride evident in his support for Charles's proclamation remains as a crucial factor in two other original poems, "The Saint's Encouragement" and "The Royalist." Although both evidence the Cavalier spirit of Royalists whose king had not yet been defeated, the earlier song has a lighter tone than the latter.

"THE SAINT'S ENCOURAGEMENT"

In "The Saint's Encouragement," written early in the war, Fanshawe's speaker is a Puritan "saint" addressing his fellow rebels and urging them to fight on. The poem's nine stanzas undercut his encouraging words in heavy-handed ways. Fanshawe's Puritan promises to maintain liberty by "prisonments and plunders," brags of victories that were historical defeats, and indirectly indicates that Puritan fears are well founded. Fanshawe thus derides the motives the Puritans used to justify the war, but the poem shows little thematic growth. What makes it memorable are two technical devices—its meter and its refrain. Ostensibly, each eight-line stanza consists of two ballad stanzas butted together. The effect of the doubling is to rush one through alternating three- and four-stress lines at a pace no balladeer could maintain. What Fanshawe has done is re-create the helter-skelter tempo of the medieval poulter's measure, a meter in which lines of twelve and fourteen syllables alternate in couplets. The sing-song clumsiness of poulter's measure had been mocked from Geoffrey Chaucer's "The Tale of Sir Thopas" on, and thus the poem's very meter mocks the Puritan cause. The refrain, "the clean contrary way," enhances the fun. The rebels successively "fight for the king," frighten cavaliers, "stand for peace and truth," and get carried to heaven, "the clean contrary way."

"THE ROYALIST"

"The Saint's Encouragement" employs techniques of ridicule that only a cavalier sure of impending victory would dare use. By 1646, however, when Fanshawe wrote "The Royalist," the situation had changed. Four years of civil war had proven the parliamentary armies a real danger to Charles, now "distressed" and "beggared." Fanshawe's drinking song captures the tension with which Charles's loyalists lived. Its four eight-line stanzas eschew the metrical jokes of the earlier war poem; iambic tetrameter lines rhyme alternately. Its singer concentrates his energy fighting off grief with bowls of potent sack: "A sorrow dares not show its face/ When we are ships and sack's the sea." The ship image need not be apt, only feisty. "Pox on this grief, hang wealth, let's sing," the speaker continues. For more than half the poem such rebellious outbursts alternate with sentimental reminders that Royalists share the poverty of their king. Gradually, the singer's rebelliousness settles into the wistful, fantastic cast of alcoholic euphoria.

Although Fanshawe's Royalist found reality hard to accept in 1646, the poet profited from war's challenges. "An Ode upon Occasion of His Majesty's Proclamation in the Year 1630" succeeds because it concentrates a naïve patriotism in one exquisite image; "The Saint's Encouragement" succeeds because it cleverly expresses an oversimple political faith. "The Royalist," however, succeeds precisely because it does not simplify the tensions which Charles I's followers endured.

"PRESENTED TO HIS HIGHNESS" AND "THE ROSE"

In these original poems, Fanshawe relies on popular thinking for themes and images but creates his own pattern and situation. In poems such as "Presented to His Highness" and "The Rose," this reliance borders on translation. In "Presented to His Highness," Fanshawe notes the source "out of which this is taken," Robert Buchanan's poem honoring James I, then virtually translates the Latin, adapting whatever needs changing to fit England's current civil "self-hurt." The poem is the sort of advice disguised as praise that modern psychologists call "positive reinforcement" and that Renaissance handbooks called courtesy—tactful encouragement that a Royalist owed his prince.

"The Rose" differs from the poems previously discussed in treating love instead of politics. Its two versions so freely adapt such a conventional theme that editors and critics variously list it as original, translated from Guarini, or translated from Góngora. Fanshawe takes Góngora's sonnet "Vana Rose" and embroiders it with strange bright images from Guarini and other Renaissance writers. "Blushing," "virgin," "wardrobe," and "perfume" image the rose as a lovely young girl to whom the poem teaches a sober lesson: "Thou'rt wondrous frolic being to die so soon." "The Rose" shares the strengths of Fanshawe's original poems: metric sensitivity, colorful diction, a graceful central image. In its short eighteen lines (or fourteen lines in the alternate version), however, Fanshawe embeds images that work oddly with the central one. "Some clown's course lungs" can "poison thy sweet flower" by tearing it with a "careless plough." The image of ploughing as impregnating underlies the conceit, but the mixed metaphor gets even more eccentric when Fanshawe identifies those who would pluck the rose as "Herods." Most of these images do not occur in Góngora's stark sonnet. Whether such changes make the poem luxuriant translation or multilevel allegory is arguable. Fanshawe's translations of love themes do tend to heighten the sensual elements.

TRANSLATING GUARINI

In original poems and adaptations, Fanshawe was not a strongly original thinker. He was, however, a polished metrist with an eye for an image and an ear for the distinctive music of each language—qualities ideal in a translator. He had a personal affinity for Horace's genial wit and his Vergil sparkles with sensuous detail, but his translations of Guarini's pastoral and Camões's epic are his most impressive works, the first for grace and melody, the second for boldness. Guarini and Camões provided thoughts, images, sounds, and structures which Fanshawe transposed into English, preserving the very different characters of the original yet heightening elements important to his countrymen.

Guarini's *The Faithful Shepherd* offered his sophisticated Italian audience the excitement of a good soap opera and the psychological comforts of an analyst's couch—both in six thousand lines of melodious verse. It is fine closet drama, designed not for the stage but for leisurely reflection. Delicate characters who prize each other more than life face separation, jealousy, the decrees of an apparently malignant deity, and the machinations of more worldly characters, while the audience shares their emotional stretchings and remains secure that all will come out right. What occupies Guarini most is the array of psychological questions rising out of the situations. These range from the effectiveness of cosmetics to the meaning of dreams, from the pleasures of the hunt to the purpose behind obscure divine commands. The lengthy set speeches of closet drama allow him to present different perspectives on such questions, especially those concerning love. These speculations run through his pale, pastel landscape in bright little spills and waterfalls of poetry.

For "royal quixote and married lover" such poetry's appeal must be immediate. Fanshawe's dedication claims that *The Faithful Shepherd* relates to the exiled Prince Charles's situation. To Royalists, dialogues such as those of old Montano and Titiro, who counsel each other to preserve faith in impossible dreams, would be as memorable as subtle insights into the psychology of romantic love.

To capture the spirit of Guarini's melodious language, Fanshawe used five devices. He changed meter, added a rhyme scheme, condensed, modernized some references, and transposed decorative figures much as one might rearrange knickknacks on a shelf. Geoffrey Bullough, in "Sir Richard Fanshawe and Guarini," adds that Fanshawe tended to replace abstractions with concrete images. This tendency was perhaps Fanshawe's personal quirk, perhaps his judgment that Guarini's pastels needed more color for English tastes. Each of the other devices, however, brought the English closer to the spirit of the Italian than duplication could have done. As a translator, Fanshawe passed beyond competence into genius.

His choice of rhyme and meter, for example, minimizes differences between the two languages. An inflected language such as Italian is so naturally rich in rhymes that Guarini could achieve small ripples of rhyme without establishing a formal scheme. Since uninflected English is relatively rhyme-poor, Fanshawe accentuates what rhymes it has by ending lines with them. To achieve the sense of a rush of words, Guarini avoided a set metrical pattern and limited end-stops. Fanshawe chose to discipline English's relatively rougher sounds by using a definite meter: the iambic pentameter line that his audience's ear expected in high drama. He managed the effect of a rush of words, however, by varying the placement of his pauses:

> for he
> Who is still wrangling with his Destinie
> And his malignant fortune, becomes hoarse,
> And loses both his singing and discourse.

Fanshawe further enhances the effect of a rush of song by freely moving to passages of rhymed octometer or even shorter lines.

His other adaptations of Guarini evidence a similar care for the spirit of the original. An inflected language inevitably translates into more words in an uninflected one. Judicious cutting, especially of repetitious rhetorical figures, keeps Fanshawe's *The Faithful Shepherd* close to the original's length. Fanshawe was ready to abandon those figures which had gone out of fashion. Though his contemporaries admired a plainer, less ornamented style than some flamboyant predecessors had, to abandon ornament altogether would have suited neither Fanshawe, Guarini, nor their audiences. In fact, one is struck by Fanshawe's ability to reproduce the Italian poet's figure in passages of stichomythia and in the Echo passage, which relies upon puns. At times, Fanshawe moves rather than abandons a rhetorical device; he may cut a catalog from one of Mirtillo's set speeches, then insert a similar catalog into his next speech. The result is a beautifully naturalized piece of poetry: rich but not cloying, smooth and melodious, tighter and more concrete than the original but wide enough for the psychological and philosophical musings of its charming hero and heroine or of its mild villain and villainess. Fanshawe's verse is like a muted verbal watercolor rather than an oil on canvas.

TRANSLATING CAMÕES

When one compares *The Faithful Shepherd* with Fanshawe's translation of *The Lusiads*, one sees the justice of Voltaire's assertion that the Portuguese epic comes from Fanshawe's hand "bold, harsh, and unpoetical." The difference, however, may not be a sign of carelessness in the translator but rather of the fineness of his ear. In adapting Camões, Fanshawe used an approach different from that which he took with Guarini.

The Portuguese epic describes Vasco da Gama's epochal voyage around the Cape of Good Hope and on to Calicut (modern Calcutta), India. En route, da Gama stops at various ports and details much of the history of brave and adventurous Portugal, especially the wars by which it drove the Moors from Iberia. *The Lusiads* is a thoroughly masculine epic, a nine-thousand-line exercise in the passionate patriotism of a small but courageous country. Da Gama possesses all the virtues of a military leader and some of a diplomat's tact—traits necessary for peacefully expanding trade and coexisting more or less respectfully with alien cultures. Camões's narrative, however, unlike Guarini's pastoral, has little room for reflectiveness. What there is instead, Camões conveys in three ways. First, he uses a machinery of pagan gods (apparently under the rule of the Christian God) who fight for or against da Gama's success. Venus and Bacchus serve more often to tie *The Lusiads* to classical tradition than to justify God's ways to man. Second, Camões sometimes juxtaposes episodes whose political-science lessons are contradictory—leaving the reader to wrestle with implicit ambiguity. Third, Camões himself steps into the narrative to reflect upon the significance of a political maneuver, to hold Portugal up to other nations as an example, and to complain about bad government—or pray for better. More frequent than poetic musings, however, are judgments; instead of imagination's pale washes, the reader

sees logic's black-and-white and bright primary colors. These qualities Fanshawe chooses to heighten in his translation.

Thus, he retains the ottava rima of the original; its natural split into sestet and couplet are ideally suited for describing a situation or painting a picture, then making a brief transition to another situation or picture. Fanshawe does not cut down the pale flowers of rhetoric; rather, he creates newer, more exotic ones. He does not explain historical background but instead leaves the non-Portuguese reader struggling—at times, drowning—in da Gama's ocean, without the explanatory rafts that would keep him afloat during certain obscure episodes. Fanshawe is often metrically rough and grammatically awkward, simply omitting the small words which English substitutes for inflections.

Claiming in his dedication that history teaches, Fanshawe seems to have expended considerable energy on Camões's political commentaries. Otherwise, his best passages are those describing martial splendor, color, and pageantry, lamenting the fate of poets, predicting the glory of a small nation's future, or judging the rightness of causes. Fanshawe also devotes much attention to a purely physical—although married—sensuality with which Venus, in canto 9, rewards patience, obedience, and uncommon bravery.

Fanshawe's poems, original or translated, are rarely read today. His political science has become obsolete, and his Royalism looks naïve in the twentieth century. However, his loyalty, his personal love of color, his attention to sound and image—and the sweet humility that enables him to capture spirits as diverse as Camões and Guarini—remain as models for minor poets and major translators of any day.

OTHER MAJOR WORKS

NONFICTION: *Original Letters and Negotiations of His Excellency Sir Richard Fanshawe*, 1724 (2 volumes).

TRANSLATIONS: *Selected Parts of Horace*, 1652; *The Lusiad*, 1655 (of Luís de Camões's epic); *Fida pastora*, 1658 (of John Fletcher's play *The Faithful Shepherdess*); *Querer por solo querer, To Love Only for Love Sake*, 1670 (of Antonio de Mendoza's play); *Fiestas de Aranjuez*, 1671.

BIBLIOGRAPHY

Cordner, Michael. "Dryden's 'Astraea Redux' and Fanshawe's 'Ode.'" *Notes and Queries* 31 (September, 1984): 341-342. An examination of Fanshawe's "An Ode upon Occasion of His Majesty's Proclamation in the Year 1630." Cordner studies this work as it relates to Fanshawe's Royalist politics, the political situation in seventeenth century England and, in particular, Oliver Cromwell's achievements and England's political relations to France. Of interest to the Fanshawe scholar only.

Davidson, P. R. K., and A. K. Jones. "New Light on Marvell's 'The Unfortunate Lover'?" *Notes and Queries* 32 (June, 1985): 170-172. A discussion of a newly discovered collection of Fanshawe's miscellaneous letters, papers, and literary notes probably originally compiled in Madrid in the 1660's. Among the findings examined are verses presumed to be from his later "Latin Poems" and several epigrams. The "Prophetic Epigram" of 1648 is presented in its original Latin and translated. This work is of interest to the Fanshawe scholar only.

Fanshawe, Anne, and Anne Halkett. *The Memoirs of Lady Anne Halkett and Lady Ann Fanshawe*. Edited by John Loftis. New York: Oxford University Press, 1980. Lady Anne Fanshawe's memoirs offer exceptional insights into the life and work of her husband. Sir Richard's diplomatic duties to the court of James I and James II are well chronicled as is the couple's life during Sir Richard's tenure as England's ambassador to Spain and Portugal. Loftis includes comprehensive chronologies, annotated bibliographies, and an index.

Graham, Judith Hanson. "Sir Richard Fanshawe's Works as Public Poetry." *Dissertation Abstracts International* 46 (July, 1985): 157A. This is the first work to explore the relationship between Fanshawe's literature and his fierce Royalist politics. Graham carefully examines the content, form, and style of Fanshawe's poetry and convincingly argues that Fanshawe intended to affect the politics of the age through his poetry. Graham offers a new and valid approach to understanding Fanshawe.

Martindale, Charles. "Unlocking the Word-Hoard: In Praise of Metaphrase." *Comparative Criticism: A Yearbook* 6 (1984): 47-72. This dense, complex work applies various translation theories to the literary forms utilized by Fanshawe and such contemporaries as John Milton and John Dryden in their translations of classical literature. Martindale's study is best appreciated by the advanced Fanshawe scholar.

Pugh, Syrithe. *Herrick, Fanshawe and the Politics of Intertextuality: Classical Literature and Seventeenth Century Royalism*. Burlington, Vt.: Ashgate, 2010. Examines Royalistic polemics and classical allusion in the poetry of Robert Herrick and Fanshawe.

Robert M. Otten; Elizabeth Spalding Otten

JAMES FENTON

Born: Lincoln, Lincolnshire, England; April 25, 1949

PRINCIPAL POETRY

Our Western Furniture, 1968
Put Thou Thy Tears into My Bottle, 1969
Terminal Moraine, 1972
Vacant Possession: Poems, 1978
A German Requiem, 1980
The Memory of War: Poems, 1968-1982, 1982
Children in Exile: Poems, 1968-1984, 1983
Out of Danger, 1993
The Love Bomb, and Other Musical Pieces, 2003
Selected Poems, 2006

OTHER LITERARY FORMS

James Fenton is almost as well known as a journalist as he is as a poet. He began work in 1970 as a freelance writer, and in 1971, he joined the British weekly journal *New Statesman*. He went to Vietnam and Cambodia in 1973, and his account of the turmoil was published in poetry as *The Memory of War* and in prose as *All the Wrong Places: Adrift in the Politics of Asia* (1988). In 1983, he published *You Were Marvelous*, an account of his life as a journalist in Germany and as a theatrical critic in London. He continued to contribute to the press, discussing literary subjects and sometimes political matters. His collection of essays, *The Snap Revolu-*

tion, appeared in 1986, and *The Strength of Poetry*, his lectures while professor of poetry at Oxford University from 1995 to 1999, were published in 2001. From September, 2006, to May, 2008, he wrote a series of essays, "Things That Have Interested Me," for *The Guardian*.

ACHIEVEMENTS

James Fenton's greatest contribution to the world of letters may lie in the fact that he has shown that art and the real world of politics are not separate from each other, and that the artist can be an important public commentator on the world. In 1968, Fenton's first year at Oxford, he won the Newdigate Prize, the most important literary award available to undergraduates. His first collection, *Terminal Moraine*, won a Gregory Award. He became a fellow of the Royal Society of Literature in 1983. In 1984, he won the Geoffrey Faber Memorial Prize. In 1994, he became the Oxford Professor of Poetry. He is a fellow of the Royal Society of Literature and, in 2007, was awarded the Queen's Gold Medal for Poetry. Known as a leading poet in Great Britain, he also contributes regularly to *The New York Review of Books* and other magazines and journals.

James Fenton (©Joyce Ravid)

BIOGRAPHY

James Martin Fenton was born to an Anglican theologian and priest, John Charles Fenton, and Mary Hamilton Fenton; he was born in Lincoln in northern England and educated in part at the famous boys' school Repton in Derbyshire. He went to Magdalen College, Oxford, in 1967. Wanting to broaden his knowledge, he switched his course of study from English to philosophy, psychology, and physiology, and this interest in scientific subjects shows up occasionally in his poetry.

Although Fenton had distinguished himself as a poet at Oxford, he graduated with a third-class degree. However, he was able to find work as a journalist in London, where he soon joined the important leftist journal *New Statesman*. In 1972, he published his first volume of poems, *Terminal Moraine*. He won a Gregory Award for the book and used the money to finance a freelance writing trip to the Cambodian war zone. In Vietnam and Cambodia, he reported for British newspapers on the Vietnam War but also began to write poetry about this Eastern world of exotic beauty and nightmarish violence.

In 1976, Fenton returned to England and became a political correspondent for the *New Statesman*. In 1978, his work in Germany led to his poem "A German Requiem." In 1979, he became the drama critic for the London *Sunday Times* but continued to write poetry, if sparingly, throughout his periods of journalistic employment. In 1982, he had his greatest success with *The Memory of War*, a series of poems set mostly in the Far East. However well known he became as a war poet, he had another side to his art, which he showed in *Children in Exile*, in which many of the poems read like nonsense, with touches of the comic and the sinister.

In the mid-1990's, Fenton became the Oxford Professor of Poetry. He had traveled to interesting and sometimes dangerous parts of the world and had written poetry about his times abroad. Living just outside Oxford, he continued to involve himself in journalism, in serious literary criticism, and public broadcasting, with a steady, if modest, pursuit of poetry, often directly related to politics and public life in general.

ANALYSIS

James Fenton's public reputation is firmly connected to his occasional poems based in twentieth century political chaos. The occasional poem is a form with a long history in English literature, in which a historical incident is used as a basis for the work; John Dryden (1631-1700) was a master of the form. Fenton's use of a historical event, however, is less formal and more emotional than that of Dryden, and there is a strong sense of humanizing the occasional, making those works attractive to a contemporary audience. Fenton does, however, have several other distinct and attractive subjects for his art.

"IN A NOTEBOOK"

Three poems from *The Memory of War* are examples of Fenton's reaction to war in Cambodia: "In a Notebook," "Cambodia," and "Dead Soldiers." "In a Notebook" is in two sections, the first describing the idyllic village life before the war reaches the Cambodian people. *"There was a river overhung with trees/ With wooden houses built along its shallows/ From which the morning sun drew up a haze."* These passages are printed in italics and juxtaposed against the brutal truth of a later time: Some of the lines are the same, picked out of the earlier passage; again, "There was a river overhung with trees" but with a difference: "The villages are burnt," and the speaker is "afraid, reading this passage now,/ That everything I knew has been destroyed," and "most of [his] friends are dead." Fenton does not judge but simply reports the facts of disaster.

"CAMBODIA"

"Cambodia" is even more terse and uncommitted, a short poem of five sets of couplets: "One man shall smile one day and say goodbye./ Two shall be left, two shall be left to die./ One man shall give his best advice./ Three men shall pay the price." The numbers laconically mount until "One man to five. A million men to one./ And still they die. And still the war goes on."

"DEAD SOLDIERS"

"Dead Soldiers" is distanced from the slaughter, as the poet recalls a drunken meal "When His Excellency Prince Norodom Chantaraingsey/ Invited [him] to lunch on the battlefield." The tension between the ambition of the narrator, a correspondent eager to get a good interview, and the political cynicism of the partic-

ipants involves the "Jockey Cap," the brother of the infamous Pol Pot, who caused the murder of millions of his fellow Cambodians. Jockey Cap is proud to show that he is in "the know:" "did they show you the things they do/ With the young refugee girls?" Time passes, and the correspondent begins to realize that the war is simply a business; "It was a family war," and "there were villains enough." It is a sour, frank exploration of the higher levels of political corruption, indifference, and cruelty, ripe with irony and punning asides.

"A GERMAN REQUIEM"

The exploration of twentieth century political disasters is not always expressed in the hard-boiled language of the war correspondent; it can look quite innocent. "A German Requiem" is a poem about forgetting as a way to survive after World War II. A group of German widows, once or twice a year, takes a bus, the "Widow's Shuttle," to visit the graves of their war dead. In nine short sections, the women are viewed, picking and choosing with great care what they want to remember. "It is not your memories which haunt you./ It is not what you have written down./ It is what you have forgotten, what you must forget." Some of the memories have lugubrious twists to them. The town suffered so much destruction, so much death that the women "unscrewed the name-plates from the shattered doorways/ And carried them away with the coffins." Some memories elicit self-pity; "Oh, if I were to begin, if I were to begin to tell you/ The half, the quarter, a mere smattering of what we went through!" This is a guilty nation, perhaps, but there is a limit: "But come. Grief must have its term? Guilt too, then." Germany's responsibility for the war is never mentioned. "Nothing more need be said, and it is better that way—." This interest in commenting upon the cruelties of twentieth century politics is a constant in Fenton's career. It can also be seen in "Jerusalem" and "Tiananmen" in the volume *Out of Danger*.

"GOD, A POEM"

Always enthusiastic about the poetry of W. H. Auden, Fenton has been called the "second Auden," in large part because of his poetry of enormous sophistication, wit, and charm. He is most like Auden in his poems of whimsical, surrealistic angst, in which the metaphors, the similes, and the general settings strike a slightly manic comic frenzy. "God, a Poem" from *Children in Exile*, counts upon the novelty of a god who is sufficiently present to comment upon the narrator's concerns but not much help otherwise. Indeed, the language used by this questionable deity makes his powers somewhat suspect: "Oh he *said:* 'If you lay off the crumpet/ I'll see you alright in the end./ Just hang on until the last trumpet./ Have faith in me, chum—I'm your friend.'" This intimate, slangy salesman of salvation is a long way from the God of Christian forgiveness, and when pressed too far about his promise of eternal life, his demotic dismissal of responsibility is very clear. "'I'm sorry, I must have been pissed—/ Though your name rings a sort of a bell. You/ Should have guessed that I do not exist.'"

"THE EMPIRE OF THE SENSELESS"

"The Empire of the Senseless," section 5 of *The Memory of War*, consists of five poems of nonsense, reminiscent not only of Auden but also of Lewis Carroll, often at his most aggressive. Much of it is simply fun, with the pleasure coming from the singular freshness of the oddly skewed descriptions, as in "The Kingfisher's Boxing Gloves": "The alligator yawns and heaves a sigh./ Between its teeth, black as an upright grand,/ The mastik bird performs its dentistry."

This kind of edgy horseplay is only part of a piece of Fenton's improvisational flair in poetry. He includes some "found" poetry, arbitrary bits of prose found in odd places, and in "Exempla" (from *The Memory of War*) flirts with the idea of bringing science and scientific language into poetry. This sort of experiment is not always successful aesthetically, but it makes for lively interludes in his books.

"NOTHING" AND "OUT OF DANGER"

Fenton is not simply a clever poet; he is also a lyric poet of considerable power. If he seems to write more of failed love than triumph, he does it with intense, if reluctant, reticent feeling. "Nothing" (from *Children in Exile*) is plangent acceptance of failed love: "I take a jewel from a junk-shop tray/ And wish I had a love to buy it for./ Nothing I choose will make you turn my way." The desperation of the situation makes the lover unable to work, read, or write: "Nothing I am will make you love me more." It is reminiscent of the depressed love laments of Sir Thomas Wyatt and Henry Howard, earl of Surrey, seventeenth century English courtier poets.

"Out of Danger" displays Fenton's sexual passion. It is a love poem, after the fact, of reassurance to the loved one that all is over, and that no longer is she subject to the dangers of the love affair, the jealousy, the excesses of love: "I was cruel, I was wrong—/ Hard to say and hard to know./ You do not belong to me./ You are out of danger now—."

THE LOVE BOMB, AND OTHER MUSICAL PIECES

The Love Bomb, and Other Musical Pieces is a volume of two libretti and the text of an oratorio written in Fenton's characteristic lyrical verse. The musical pieces "The Fall of Jerusalem," "Haroun and the Sea of Stories," and "The Love Bomb," were written by Fenton as much for "the page" as for staged performance, and they share the theme of "fanaticism."

SELECTED POEMS

Selected Poems is a collection of works that exemplify the range of Fenton's writings, from light verse, to political and love poems, to opera libretti. It includes early and later published work, some of his verse work for the stage, and later unpublished poems.

OTHER MAJOR WORKS

NONFICTION: *You Were Marvelous*, 1983; *The Snap Revolution*, 1986; *All the Wrong Places: Adrift in the Politics of Asia*, 1988; *Leonardo's Nephew*, 1998; *The Strength of Poetry*, 2001; *A Garden from a Hundred Packets of Seed*, 2002; *An Introduction to English Poetry*, 2002; *School of Genius: A History of the Royal Academy of Arts*, 2006.

TRANSLATION: *Rigoletto*, 1982 (of Francesco Maria Piave's libretto).

EDITED TEXTS: *The Original Michael Frayn: Satirical Essays*, 1983; *Cambodian Witness: The Autobiography of Someth May*, 1987; *Underground in Japan*, 1992; *The New Faber Book of Love Poems*, 2006; *Selected Poems*, 2008 (of D. H. Lawrence).

BIBLIOGRAPHY

Grant, Damian. "The Voice of History in British Poetry, 1970-1984." *Etudes-Anglaise* 38, no. 2 (April-June, 1985): 158-179. A commentary on Fenton's historical poems and the various kinds thereof in the context of similar themes in other British poetry of the period.

Hulse, Michael. "The Poetry of James Fenton." *Antigonish Review* 58 (Summer, 1984): 93-102. A general commentary on Fenton's poetry up to the early 1980's.

Kerr, Douglas. "James Fenton and Indochina." *Contemporary Literature* 35 (Fall, 1994): 476-491. A discussion of the nature of Fenton's experience in the Far East and the poetry and prose arising from that experience.

Metcalf, Stephen. "Informal Menace." Review of *Selected Poems*. *The New York Times Book Review*, February 11, 2007, p. 9. Metcalf provides a brief but helpful review of Fenton's 2006 *Selected Poems*.

Parker, Ian. "Auden's Heir." *The New Yorker*, July 25, 1994, 62-68. Fenton has been able to make use of certain elements in Auden's work; a discussion of how he does it with success without being accused of imitation by critics.

Robinson, Alan. "James Fenton's Narratives: Some Reflections on Postmodernism." *Critical Quarterly* 29 (Spring, 1987): 81-93. Fenton's poems often have a strong narrative shape; Robinson examines that aspect of his work in the light of contemporary critical definitions.

Stark, Ellen-Kreger. "An American's Confession: On Reading James Fenton's *Out of Danger*." *Critical Quarterly* 36 (Summer, 1994): 106-110. A discussion of Fenton's use of the narrator and the nature of the confessional aspect in some of the poems in *Out of Danger*.

Charles H. Pullen

ANNE FINCH
Countess of Winchelsea

Born: Sydmonton, Hampshire, England; April, 1661
Died: London, England; August 5, 1720

PRINCIPAL POETRY

Miscellany Poems, on Several Occasions, 1713
The Poems of Anne, Countess of Winchelsea, 1902
Selected Poems of Anne Finch, Countess of Winchelsea, 1979
The Anne Finch Wellesley Manuscript Poems, 1998

OTHER LITERARY FORMS

On the rare occasions when Anne Finch worked in other genres, she wrote in verse, such as in her two plays, the unproduced closet dramas *The Triumphs of Love and Innocence* (pb. 1902) and *Aristomenes: Or, The Royal Shepherd* (pb. 1713). The former is a tragicomedy, the latter a tragedy. She also wrote an epilogue to Nicholas Rowe's 1714 *The Tragedy of Jane Shore*, which was spoken by the actress playing the title role.

ACHIEVEMENTS

When Anne Finch's *Miscellany Poems, on Several Occasions* appeared in 1713 ("Written by a Lady," according to the title page of the first printing, though later printings gave her name), it was only the third volume of poetry by a woman to have been published in the eighteenth century, and she was one of the first women to devote a lifetime to writing poetry. Contemporary social strictures and prejudices notwithstanding, Finch was acknowledged by London's male literary circles, many of her poems were included (albeit usually anonymously) in leading publications, and Alexander Pope and Jonathan Swift celebrated her in commendatory verses.

During her long career, she wrote in a variety of poetic forms, including elegies, pastorals, satires, verse epistles, beast fables, ballads, and occasional poetry, and though her output was mainly in the Restoration and Augustan neoclassic traditions, the poems often transcended prevailing conventions of subject, form, and theme. In her nature poems, for example, she anticipated the Romantic movement, and in many works she introduced a feminine sensibility, giving voice to a socially and educationally marginalized gender and presenting, perhaps for the first time, portraits of love and marriage from a woman's perspective.

BIOGRAPHY

Anne Finch was born in southern England to Sir William and Anne (Haslewood) Kingsmill, whose families were landed gentry with royal connections. Both parents died before Anne was three, and she and two siblings lived, at various times, with a stepfather, uncle, and grandmother. Unusual for the time, Sir William in his will set aside money for the support and education not only of his son and heir but also of his daughters. Young Anne thus had a substantive education in English poetry and drama, and also in the classics and foreign languages. She benefited, too, from living in London with her paternal grandmother, a wealthy, strong-willed woman (who twice brought Chancery suits in behalf of Anne and her sister).

In 1683, at age twenty-one, Anne joined the household of the duchess of York (Mary of Modena, Italian second wife of the duke of York, heir to the throne) and the next year wed Colonel Heneage Finch, a soldier who was part of the duke of York's retinue. By all accounts, this was a happy and loving marriage. Her husband through the decades actively supported her writing, requesting that she write poems for him, editing and transcribing them, and compiling manuscripts for private circulation.

In 1685, when the duke of York became King James II, the couple remained part of the court circle, but when James was deposed three years later, Colonel Finch stayed loyal to the Stuart cause and refused to swear allegiance to the new monarchs, William and Mary. Thus estranged from court and politics, Anne and Heneage Finch retreated to the country seat—Eastwell Park in Kent—of his nephew, the earl of Winchelsea, where they lived a kind of self-imposed exile for many years, though occasionally visiting London or the spa at Tunbridge Wells, where Anne sought relief from her unremitting neurotic complaints.

While in Kent, Finch continued to write poems (using the pseudonym Ardelia), and whereas she kept her work secret at court, in her country exile, she circulated poems in manuscript among acquaintances. She first appeared in print in 1701, when her Pindaric ode "The Spleen" was published. After his nephew died, in 1712, and Colonel Finch succeeded to the title, the couple moved permanently to London. There the countess, though still suffering from melancholy and depression, continued to write poetry and came to know leading writers of the period, including Pope, Rowe, and Swift, as well as John Gay, Matthew Prior, and Thomas Warton. In 1719, Swift in "Apollo Outwitted" praised her poetry and at the same time teased her for being so modest, playfully urging her to publish more often. At the age of fifty-nine, Finch died at her London home.

ANALYSIS

During the eighteenth century, after her death, Anne Finch was recalled primarily as the author of "The Spleen," widely admired as an exemplar of the then popular Pindaric ode form. In the nineteenth century, attention shifted to her nature poetry, primarily as a result of William Wordsworth's 1815 remark in his supplementary essay to the preface of *Lyrical Ballads* (originally published 1798):

> Excepting the nocturnal "Reverie of Lady Winchelsea," and a passage or two in the "Windsor Forest" of Pope, the poetry of the period intervening between the publication of the "Paradise Lost" and "The Seasons" does not contain a single new image of esteemed nature, and scarcely presents a familiar one from which it can be inferred that the eye of the Poet had been steadily fixed upon his object, much less that his feelings had urged him to work upon it in the spirit of genuine imagination.

As a result of this praise, Finch was regarded for more than a century almost solely as a pre-Romantic nature poet, but in the mid-twentieth century critics started to consider her as more of a mainstream neoclassical writer. Still another canonical shift occurred late in the twentieth century, when Finch was recognized as an early feminist voice.

"THE INTRODUCTION"

This poem, with which Finch opened manuscripts of her work that circulated among friends, is a poignant presentation in heroic couplets of the subservient place of women, particularly the plight of one who sought recognition and acceptance as a poet. Anticipating the censure she could expect by so-called Witts—men who achieved their reputations "only by finding fault"—Finch says they would call her lines "insipid, empty, uncorrect." They would condemn them simply because "they're by a Woman writt," and because "a woman that attempts the pen" is "an intruder on the rights of men." Such men tell women that they should desire just "Good breeding, fassion, dancing, dressing, play." Finch argues that women are not innately inferior, but rather are "Education's, more than Nature's fools" and recalls Old Testament women who functioned as public poets. At the end, she stoically withdraws "with contracted wing," determining to be content sharing her work with "some few friends." Two other poems in which Finch also deals with the obstacles confronting a woman poet are "The Appology" and the fablelike "Mercury and the Elephant."

"THE PETITION FOR AN ABSOLUTE RETREAT"

In the lengthy, discursive "The Petition for an Absolute Retreat," one of her two major nature poems, Finch's indebtedness to other seventeenth century poets is apparent: Andrew Marvell's view of the natural world as a haven, Henry Vaughan's mysticism, and Robert Herrick's straightforwardly simple style. Finch's poem is dedicated to the countess of Thanet (called Arminda in the poem), a country friend whose presence in a work celebrating rural privacy and seclusion as means of spiritual renewal suggests that Finch requires female companionship, perhaps an alter ego, to sustain her muse.

The poem also expresses her desire for a husband to share the retreat, a "*Partner* suited to my Mind," who will eschew "Fame and Splendor, Wealth and Pride" and will not let business, wars, or other matters separate them. Despite the opening paean to an "Absolute Retreat" in a remoteness "That the World may ne'er invade," Finch is not calling for a permanent, solitary, spartan isolation in her halcyon Eden, and she recognizes that retreat cannot halt the debilitating passage of time. The plethora of classical allusions, an idealized rather than a realistic portrayal of nature, and the elegiac rather than descriptive style place the poem firmly in the Augustan tradition, with only slight pre-Romantic qualities.

"A NOCTURNAL REVERIE"

Of Finch's more than two hundred poems, fewer than ten are principally about external nature, and the best of these are "The Petition for an Absolute Retreat" and "A Nocturnal Reverie." The latter, whose fifty lines make up one sentence, is noteworthy for its descriptive concreteness and specificity, from an opening that echoes the start of the fifth act of William Shakespeare's *The Merchant of Venice* (pr. c. 1596-1597) to the close, when dawn comes and "Our Cares, our Toils, our Clamours are renew'd," bringing the speaker's respite to an end. Like animals, the poet feels freer at night, but this is a "shortliv'd Jubilee," for "Morning breaks, and All's confused again." Whereas her con-

Anne Finch (The Granger Collection, New York)

temporary poets engage mainly in vague generalizing, Finch in this poem evokes the senses: She describes a returning stray horse coming so close that "torn up Forage in his Teeth we hear" and refers to cattle "unmolested" and other animals also at peace while "Tyrant-Man do's sleep," establishing a typically Romantic rivalry between man and nature. On the other hand, stereotypical epithets, a tribute to a friend midway through the poem, and a reflective, almost gothic melancholy make "A Nocturnal Reverie" closer to such eighteenth century standards as John Pomfret's "The Choice" (1700) and Thomas Warton the Younger's *Pleasures of Melancholy* (1747) than to James Thomson's *The Seasons* (1730, 1744), an Augustan Age touchstone for nature poetry.

"THE TREE"

Because the tree provides her with "delightful Shade" and "cool Shadows," the poet is indebted to it. She notes that birds, which it shelters, reward it with their music; travelers, who use it for protection from storms, thank it with their praise; and the shepherd, whom it shields from scorching sun, "Tunes to thy dancing Leaves his Reed." The poet pays her debt by wishing that the tree will stand for ages, "Untouch'd by the rash Workman's hand" until it dies naturally, when "fierce Winds," not an ax, will fell the dead tree, after which it will "like ancient Heroes, burn,/ And some bright Hearth be made thy Urn." By not naming any species, Finch universalizes the tree, so it exemplifies the Arcadian nature-versus-man theme that is central to the poem, which feminist critics also interpret as presenting a feminized landscape menaced by masculine intrusion.

"TO THE NIGHTINGALE"

"To the Nightingale," in Finch's 1713 *Miscellany Poems, on Several Occasions* along with "A Nocturnal Reverie," "The Tree," and "The Spleen," uses the bird as an emblem of lyric poetry, which had been a common practice among Renaissance writers, including Thomas Dekker, John Lyly, Thomas Middleton, and Sir Philip Sidney. Beginning by invoking the bird as muse, the speaker wants her song to be as free as the bird's, because poets are at their best "when unconfin'd" by tradition and rules. However, "Cares," presumably the world around her, weigh her down and their "Thoughts molest," so she decides that escape to the bird's lyric world is a futile hope, and like her peers she must be satisfied writing poems that "Criticize, reform, or preach," that is, embrace the prevailing neoclassical poetic practices. Because she is a woman, Finch knows that she faces even greater obstacles than do her male counterparts, and the realization is part of her problem. This poem of unrequited aspirations anticipates structurally as well as thematically John Keats's "Ode to a Nightingale" (1819) and Percy Bysshe Shelley's "To a Skylark" (1820).

"THE SPLEEN"

In her occasional poems, Finch usually utilizes neoclassical poetic devices that obscure the contemporary autobiographical elements. Among these works are "A Letter to Dafnis April: 2d 1685," a brief verse epistle to her husband; "To Mr. F. Now Earl of W.," also about her marriage; and the epistle "To My Sister Ogle, Decbr 31, 1688" and "A Poem for the Birth-day of the Right Honble the Lady Catherine Tufton." Primary in this group is "The Spleen," which was first published in 1701 and remained popular for a century, in large part

because of its subject: Finch's lifelong struggle with melancholy, depression, and other neuroses, which at the time were collectively called "the spleen," an affliction somewhat more common among women than among men.

Widespread attention first focused on the illness when Robert Burton's *The Anatomy of Melancholy* was published in three volumes in 1621, and poems dealing with melancholy proliferated, including John Milton's "Il Penseroso" (1629-1632), Matthew Green's "The Spleen," Robert Blair's "The Grave" (1743), and Thomas Gray's "Elegy Written in a Country Churchyard" (1751). However, "The Spleen"—a Pindaric ode in an irregular strophic pattern of 150 lines—is the most detailed treatment, so precise and accurate in its details that it was used as a text by eighteenth century medical practitioners.

Finch starts by describing the protean quality of the ailment's manifestations: "A Calm of stupid Discontent"; rage; "Panick Fear." She then laments how "On Sleep intruding dost thy Shadows spread," causing terror, bad dreams, and delusions. She recalls that Brutus "Was vanquish'd by the *Spleen*" and tells of how it changes an "Imperious *Wife*" into a servile woman and affects fools as well as "Men of Thoughts refin'd." Turning to herself, she laments its destructive force on her poetry ("I feel my Verse decay, and my crampt Numbers fail"). Following her clinical examination of the illness, she tells of how people pretend to suffer from the affliction to excuse wayward behavior and concludes with a grudging stoic recognition of the futility of attempting to conquer the debilitating illness.

OTHER MAJOR WORKS

PLAYS: *Aristomenes: Or, The Royal Shepherd*, pb. 1713 (wr. c. 1688-1691); *The Triumphs of Love and Innocence*, pb. 1902 (wr. c. 1685-1690).

BIBLIOGRAPHY

Brower, Reuben A. "Lady Winchelsea and the Poetic Tradition of the Seventeenth Century." *Studies in Philology* 42 (1945): 61-80. In this influential article, Brower places Finch's poetry firmly in the eighteenth century tradition and distances her from the Romantics. He considers her nature poems as products of her early years and demonstrates their similarity to seventeenth century Metaphysical poetry.

Hinnant, Charles H. *The Poetry of Anne Finch: An Essay in Interpretation.* Newark: University of Delaware Press, 1994. In this first comprehensive study of Finch's poetry, Hinnant examines her work in relation to that of Augustan contemporaries and nineteenth century Romantics, and also considers her as an early feminist writer. He provides detailed explications of many poems, usefully balancing his interpretations with those of others.

McGovern, Barbara. *Anne Finch and Her Poetry: A Critical Biography.* Athens: University of Georgia Press, 1992. This first full-length life of Finch focuses on her "historical place" and "displacement" (as McGovern puts it) among her contemporaries, "and particularly on the methods by which she developed a poetic identity for her own artistic liberation." Of value is an appendix of twelve uncollected poems from a manuscript at Wellesley College in Massachusetts.

McGovern, Barbara, and Charles H. Hinnant, eds. *The Anne Finch Wellesley Manuscript Poems.* Athens: University of Georgia Press, 1998. Fifty-three previously unpublished Finch poems from a manuscript at Wellesley College in Massachusetts are printed in this volume with useful critical commentary and annotations. Because Finch wrote many of these poems in the last two decades of her life, their availability makes possible a reevaluation of her career.

Mallinson, Jean. "Anne Finch: A Woman Poet and the Tradition." In *Gender at Work: Four Women Writers of the Eighteenth Century*, edited by Ann Messinger. Detroit: Wayne State University Press, 1990. A consideration of Finch as one of the first English women poets to surmount the barriers of sexual prejudice and forge a career that was accepted and applauded by contemporary male counterparts.

Parini, Jay, ed. *British Writers: Supplement IX.* New York: Charles Scribner's Sons, 2004. Contains a critical essay on Anne Finch describing her life and works.

Reynolds, Myra, ed. *The Poems of Anne, Countess of Winchelsea.* Chicago: University of Chicago Press, 1902. This volume, with a useful introduction, reprints what is included in the 1713 *Miscellany* as well as some works from manuscript sources. Though supplemented by the publication of the Wellesley manuscript poems, it remains a standard source.

Rogers, Katharine, ed. *Selected Poems of Anne Finch, Countess of Winchelsea.* New York: Ungar, 1979. The first collection of Finch poems since the 1902 edition edited by Myra Reynolds, this selection of almost seventy representative poems is prefaced by an introductory essay that explicates the poems, places them in their eighteenth century context, and considers Finch as an early woman poet of consequence.

Gerald H. Strauss

EDWARD FITZGERALD

Born: Near Woodbridge, Suffolk, England; March 31, 1809
Died: Merton, Norfolk, England; June 14, 1883

PRINCIPAL POETRY

Salámán and Absál, 1856
Rubáiyát of Omar Khayyám, 1859 (translation of Omar Khayyám's poetry; revised 1868, 1872, 1879)

OTHER LITERARY FORMS

Although Edward FitzGerald's reputation as a poet rests on the *Rubáiyát of Omar Khayyám*, he was a gifted writer in other forms. In 1851, FitzGerald published a philosophical dialogue called *Euphranor: A Dialogue on Youth*, and in 1852, he produced a collection of aphorisms titled *Polonius: A Collection of Wise Saws and Modern Instances.* FitzGerald's *Six Dramas of Calderón* in 1853 began his series of free translations of drama, which included his *Agamemnon* of 1865, *Oedipus Rex* in 1880-1881, and *Oedipus at Colonus* in 1880-1881.

ACHIEVEMENTS

Edward FitzGerald's essential achievement is unique in the history of English literature. His *Rubáiyát of Omar Khayyám* is nominally a translation, but out of hundreds of separate short poems by a relatively minor Persian poet of the twelfth century (Omar Khayyám), FitzGerald fashioned a beautifully unified poem in English. It is written with such power of expression, splendor of diction, and perfection of poetic music that it has long been recognized not only as an essentially original contribution to English poetry but also as one of the greatest poems in the language. FitzGerald's contemporary Charles Eliot Norton expressed the view that the *Rubáiyát of Omar Khayyám* had all the merits of a great original poem and that it was unique among translations for its value as English poetry. This view has come to be universal, and the distinguished scholar Cecil Y. Lang wrote in 1968 that FitzGerald's *Rubáiyát of Omar Khayyám* was "surely the most popular poem in the English language."

BIOGRAPHY

Edward FitzGerald was born in a Jacobean mansion in rural Suffolk, England. His parents were cousins and came from what was then one of the wealthiest families in Great Britain. As FitzGerald grew up, he developed a great dislike for the arrogance, ostentation, and formality of manners that he associated with wealth, but his part of the family fortune allowed him to live life on his own eccentric and creative terms throughout most of his adult years. FitzGerald's mother, Mary Frances FitzGerald, was a proud and dominating woman, and FitzGerald's relations with her were always difficult.

If FitzGerald's character was in part shaped by wealth and a troubled relationship with his mother, his early years also gave him a love for the quiet scenery of Suffolk, which would stay with him throughout his life. In 1818, FitzGerald was sent to the King Edward VI Grammar School in Bury St. Edmunds. There, he received a fine classical education and developed a number of important friendships. In 1826, FitzGerald went to the University of Cambridge, where he was an undisciplined but happy student who showed again his great gift for making friends. Among his many friends at Cambridge was the future novelist William Makepeace Thackeray.

After graduating from Cambridge in 1830, FitzGerald traveled briefly to Paris, spent time in London, Southampton, and Cambridge, and eventually made his way back to Suffolk. His family's wealth made it unnecessary for him to pursue a career, and for the next two decades or so FitzGerald mostly lived the quiet life of a country gentleman, developing his serious interests in art, music, literature, and gardening. He also became and would remain throughout his life a prolific and brilliant correspondent. During these years, FitzGerald was friends with and corresponded with a broad range of distinguished writers, including Thomas Carlyle; Thackeray; Alfred, Lord Tennyson; Frederick Tennyson; the scholar James Spedding; and the poet Bernard Barton.

Although FitzGerald's letters during this period show him to be a writer of great accomplishment, and it is evident that men of Carlyle's and Thackeray's stature respected his intellect and taste, he contributed nothing official to English literature between 1830 and 1850. In 1844, however, he met a young scholar of Eastern languages named Edward Cowell, who, by late 1852, was teaching FitzGerald Persian. In 1856, Cowell found a fifteenth century manuscript of Omar Khayyám in the Bodleian Library at Oxford. Cowell sent FitzGerald a transcript of this manuscript, and in 1859, appeared the first version of FitzGerald's *Rubáiyát of Omar Khayyám*.

Before the *Rubáiyát of Omar Khayyám*, FitzGerald's publications had been few, eccentric, and unsuccessful. Despite its beautiful prose, his *Euphranor* of 1851 went mostly unnoticed. His book of aphorisms, *Polonius*, fared little better. His very free versions of the dramas of Pedro Calderón de la Barca as well as his highly original translation of the Persian *Salámán and Absál* had little critical or popular success. At first, the *Rubáiyát of Omar Khayyám* did little better. By 1861, however, it began to be recognized in literary circles, and eventually it would be published in three more editions during FitzGerald's lifetime.

FitzGerald remained preoccupied with the *Rubáiyát of Omar Khayyám* throughout the rest of his life, but he also produced important, if very personal, versions of the works of Aeschylus and Sophocles. FitzGerald's quiet later years were marked by a constant stream of wonderful letters, increasing (though lovable) eccentricity of behavior, and a great interest in sailing and the simple life of the fishermen of his home county. He died while visiting friends in Norfolk on June 14, 1883. He was seventy-four.

ANALYSIS

Edward FitzGerald's place in English poetry is based on his *Rubáiyát of Omar Kháyyám*. Despite this poem's nominal status as a translation, it has long been recognized as an essentially original contribution to English literature. Whatever may be the merits of the original Persian poems from which the *Rubáiyát of Omar Khayyám* derives, the structure, diction, prosody, music, and movement of FitzGerald's poem belong to the English language and to FitzGerald himself. Moreover, even the ideas of the poem are given a unity, force, character, and application that have much more to do with FitzGerald than with Omar Khayyám.

FITZGERALD AS "TRANSLATOR"

During his literary career, FitzGerald produced translations of Greek tragedies, Spanish plays, and Persian poems. In all these works, his approach is the same: He leaves out what he wishes to leave out. He conflates and changes originals as it suits him. He dresses the altered frames of his materials in his own highly personal style, and he emphasizes that which interests him and dismisses or changes that which does not. FitzGerald was always completely honest about this. When the publisher of the *Rubáiyát of Omar Khayyám* spoke of the translation as being faithful, FitzGerald insisted that it was anything but that. In fact, FitzGerald always treated the works from which his translations derive as "sources" rather than "originals." He was little more concerned with being faithful to Omar Khayyám than William Shakespeare was worried about being faithful to his sources.

FitzGerald's freedom and originality in dealing with Omar Khayyám's poetry may best be seen in the fact that there is actually no coherent work called the *Rubáiyát* written by the Persian poet. The word *rubáiyát* in Persian is simply the plural form of the word for short poem or epigram. What Omar Khayyám

actually wrote—or was credited with—were roughly 750 individual short poems, each of which was a poem unto itself. Indeed, in Persian manuscripts, Omar Khayyám's quatrains or epigrams are arranged merely alphabetically, based on the first letter in the first line of each quatrain poem. FitzGerald's earliest version of the *Rubáiyát of Omar Khayyám* contains 75 stanzas, while his last version contains 101 stanzas. In all five versions of the poem, Omar Khayyám's epigrams have become true stanzas in a highly structured and unified whole. Thus, FitzGerald chose only those poems that he wanted to use and then imposed a unity on them that never existed in the original. Moreover, FitzGerald was very free with the original individual poems of Omar Khayyám. In his final *Rubáiyát of Omar Khayyám*, FitzGerald has 49 stanzas that roughly paraphrase actual Omar Khayyám poems; his other 52 stanzas are composites of more than one Omar Khayyám poem, or they do not derive from Omar Khayyám at all.

THEMES AND MEANINGS

FitzGerald's *Rubáiyát of Omar Khayyám* is a powerful meditation on and passionate questioning of the

Edward FitzGerald (The Granger Collection, New York)

meaning of human life and the nature of the cosmos. For FitzGerald's Omar Khayyám, the essential fact of life is life's brevity. Human beings are surrounded by darkness and death. There is great pathos in this, but the shortness and essential sadness of human life make momentary joy all the more important and cherishable. Also, it is only in such joys as love, retirement into gardens, flowers, poetry, and most of all, wine that the essence of true life is known. For FitzGerald's Omar Khayyám, neither worldly greatness nor religious doctrine has any real value or meaning. Worldly greatness is an illusion, and religious doctrine is futile. The universe is ruled by a dark, unknowable force, perhaps a god, but if this god exists, it moves and acts in deeply mysterious ways, without regard for humans and beyond human understanding.

In FitzGerald's *Rubáiyát of Omar Khayyám*, human beings exist only for a brief moment, and it is crucial that this moment be spent in vital, sensuous life rather than in empty speculation. In certain sections of the poem, FitzGerald makes Omar Khayyám question a very Christian-sounding religion in a sharply sardonic and even satiric spirit. These sections were both shocking and stimulating to FitzGerald's contemporaries, and perhaps they will always have that sort of power for many readers. It is tempting to describe the vision of the *Rubáiyát of Omar Khayyám* as a kind of hedonistic epicurean nihilism, but that is too simple. Somehow, the poem is neither so dark nor so grim as its themes would suggest. This is in part because of the sheer verbal and musical beauty of the poem, but it is also because basic human life and momentary joy are treated in the poem as having great value and pathos precisely because they are surrounded by death, unknowable mystery, and cosmic darkness.

STRUCTURE AND STYLE

One of the most outstanding features of FitzGerald's *Rubáiyát of Omar Khayyám* is its essential unity. FitzGerald achieves this by organizing his poem so that it begins with morning, the new year, and life and moves toward night, the close of the year, and death. Also, the stanzas of the poem are connected by repeated imagery, themes, and even grammar and syntax in such a way as to create a sense of movement within coherent unity. Moreover, the various sections of the poem, each

composed of several stanzas, form coherent arguments that are then linked by logic and rhetoric so as to form a powerful whole.

The imagery of the poem is at once simple, exotic, and effective. FitzGerald's wine cups, roses, moons, gardens, taverns, deserts, lovers, birds, and wine all combine in such a way as to communicate with passionate directness, while creating an exotic sense of an imaginative Persia that haunts the mind. The *Rubáiyát of Omar Khayyám* is a remarkably easy poem to read, but it creates a sense of richness and resonance.

The diction and general style of the *Rubáiyát of Omar Khayyám* are a remarkable combination of simplicity and sensuousness. FitzGerald's mode of expression often has an almost eighteenth century clarity and compactness:

> Myself when young did eagerly frequent
> Doctor and Saint, and heard great argument
>   About it and about; but evermore
> Came out by the same door where in I went.

However, this directness is combined with a tenderness and richness of music that are equally typical of FitzGerald:

> I sometimes think that never blows so red
> The Rose as where some buried Caesar bled;
>   That every Hyacinth the Garden wears
> Dropped in her Lap from some once lovely
>   Head.

Finally, in addition to structure, imagery, and diction, there is the distinctive stanza of the poem. FitzGerald's stanza, very loosely derived from Omar's quatrain form, consists of four lines of iambic pentameter, rhyming *aaxa*. This stanza was new to English, and FitzGerald's mastery of it created a distinctive prosodic and musical effect that accounts for much of the *Rubáiyát of Omar Khayyám*'s magic.

RECEPTION AND HISTORICAL IMPORTANCE

When FitzGerald first published the *Rubáiyát of Omar Khayyám* in 1859, it went almost totally unnoticed. By 1861, however, the poem was beginning to find readers among Pre-Raphaelite writers and artists. Dante Gabriel Rossetti, Algernon Charles Swinburne, and John Ruskin praised the poem, and it soon became popular in both England and the United States. By 1900, it was an acknowledged classic of English poetry, and it was published in hundreds of editions between 1870 and 1920.

Its historical importance lies in two spheres, one intellectual, the other poetic. Intellectually, FitzGerald's *Rubáiyát of Omar Khayyám* was a compelling expression of religious doubt in a great age of religious doubt. FitzGerald raised many of the same questions that poets such as Matthew Arnold, James Walter Thomson, Thomas Hardy, and A. E. Housman raised, but he invested those doubts with a pathos and tenderness that were uniquely attractive. Poetically, FitzGerald's poem spoke a sensuous, rich, and exotic language that appealed to and influenced not only the Pre-Raphaelite poets between 1860 and 1880 but also the aesthete and Decadent poets at the end of the nineteenth century.

OTHER MAJOR WORKS

NONFICTION: *Euphranor: A Dialogue on Youth*, 1851; *The Letters of Edward FitzGerald*, 1894 (revised 1960).

TRANSLATIONS: *Six Dramas of Calderón*, 1853 (of Pedro Calderón de la Barca); *Agamemnon*, 1865 (of Aeschylus' play); *Oedipus at Colonus*, 1880-1881 (of Sophocles' play); *Oedipus Rex*, 1880-1881 (of Sophocles' play).

MISCELLANEOUS: *Polonius: A Collection of Wise Saws and Modern Instances*, 1852.

BIBLIOGRAPHY

Alexander, Doris. *Creating Literature Out of Life: The Making of Four Masterpieces*. University Park: Pennsylvania State University Press, 1996. This excellent book contains a fascinating account of how FitzGerald created the *Rubáiyát of Omar Khayyám*. Emphasizes the psychological crises in FitzGerald's life that created the energies necessary to turn a "translation" into a work of original genius.

Bloom, Harold, ed. *Edward FitzGerald's the "Rubáiyát of Omar Khayyám."* Philadelphia: Chelsea House, 2004. Presents an introduction to FitzGerald's infamous study and chapters that consider the "fin de siècle cult" of FitzGerald's work, comparisons with poets such as Tennyson, "forgetting" Fitzgerald's study, and more. Bibliography, index.

FitzGerald, Edward. *Rubáiyát of Omar Khayyám: A Critical Edition*. Edited by Christopher Decker. Charlottesville: University Press of Virginia, 1997. Decker provides a scholarly critique of Omar Khayyám's life, FitzGerald's translations of the *Rubáiyát*, and the merits of the various editions of this famous set of poems. Decker's book is a useful tool for serious students looking for the definitive edition of FitzGerald's *Rubáiyát of Omar Khayyám*.

France, Peter, ed. *The Oxford Guide to Literature in English Translation*. New York: Oxford University Press, 2000. Provides an invaluable account of all of FitzGerald's translations, in which the *Rubáiyát of Omar Khayyám* and his other works are compared with other translations of the same originals and placed within the history of translation.

Heron-Allen, Edward. *Edward FitzGerald's "Rubáiyát of Omar Khayyám" with Their Original Persian Sources*. Boston: L. C. Page, 1899. A study of FitzGerald's stanzas paralleled with the Persian texts of possible sources, demonstrating that, although FitzGerald was inspired by Khayyamic and other Persian quatrains, the *Rubáiyát of Omar Khayyám* is an original English poem and not a translation.

Martin, Robert Bernard. *With Friends Possessed: A Life of Edward FitzGerald*. New York: Atheneum, 1985. The standard biography of FitzGerald, a brilliant account of his life and work; particularly strong on his psychological character, his friendships, his literary achievement, his life in Suffolk, and his letters.

Razavi, Mehdi Amin. *The Wine of Wisdom: The Life, Poetry, and Wisdom of Omar Khayyám*. Oxford, England: Oneworld, 2006. This biography of the poet discusses his works and places him in the world of Persian poetry.

Richardson, Joanna. *Edward FitzGerald*. London: Longman's, 1960. A brief but very useful study of FitzGerald. Contains a good overview of his life, a balanced and reliable account of the *Rubáiyát of Omar Khayyám*, and an especially strong section on FitzGerald as letter writer.

Teimourian, Hazhir. *Omar Khayyám: Poet, Rebel, Astronomer*. Stroud, England: Sutton, 2007. Biography that examines the various roles of Omar Khayyám, as well as his writings.

Wells, John, W. H. Martin, and Sandra Mason. *Edward FitzGerald and His Rubáiyát, 1809-2009*. Cambridge, England: University Library, 2009. A catalog of an exhibition celebrating two hundred years since the birth of FitzGerald.

Phillip B. Anderson

ROY FULLER

Born: Failsworth, Lancashire, England; February 11, 1912

Died: London, England; September 27, 1991

PRINCIPAL POETRY

Poems, 1939
The Middle of a War, 1942
A Lost Season, 1944
Epitaphs and Occasions, 1949
Counterparts, 1954
Brutus's Orchard, 1957
Collected Poems, 1936-1961, 1962
Buff, 1965
New Poems, 1968
Off Course, 1969
To an Unknown Reader, 1970
Song Cycle from a Record Sleeve, 1972
Tiny Tears, 1973
An Old War, 1974
From the Joke Shop, 1975
The Joke Shop Annexe, 1975
An Ill-Governed Coast, 1976
Poor Roy, 1977
Re-treads, 1979
The Other Planet, 1979
The Reign of Sparrows, 1980
More About Tompkins, and Other Light Verse, 1981
House and Shop, 1982

The Individual and His Times: Selected Poems, 1982
As from the Thirties, 1983
Upright Downfall, 1983 (with Barbara Giles and Adrian Rumble)
Mianserin Sonnets, 1984
New and Collected Poems, 1934-1984, 1985
Subsequent to Summer, 1985
Outside the Cannon, 1986
Consolations, 1987
Available for Dreams, 1989
Last Poems, 1993

OTHER LITERARY FORMS

Roy Fuller was a competent novelist and may well be considered a poet-novelist, much like Thomas Hardy. His principal novels are *The Second Curtain* (1953), *The Perfect Fool* (1963), *My Child, My Sister* (1965), and *The Carnal Island* (1970). He wrote several children's novels, including *Savage Gold: A Story of Adventure* (1946) and *With My Little Eye: A Mystery Story for Teenagers* (1948). He also edited *Byron for To-day* (1948) and *Fellow Mortals* (1981), an anthology of animal verse. His autobiography was issued in a number of volumes: *Souvenirs* (1980), *Vamp Till Ready: Further Memoirs* (1982), and *Home and Dry: Memoirs III* (1984), reissued in complete form as *The Strange and the Good: Collected Memoirs* (1989).

ACHIEVEMENTS

Roy Fuller was honored for his literary accomplishments, becoming a fellow of the Royal Society of Literature and a Companion of the Order of the British Empire in 1970. In that year, he won the Queen's Gold Medal for Poetry. Two years previously, he had won the Duff Cooper Memorial Prize for his *New Poems*, and in 1980, he received the Society of Authors Cholmondeley Award. In 1990, he was awarded an honorary doctorate of letters by the University of Kent at Canterbury.

BIOGRAPHY

Roy Broadbent Fuller was the elder son of Leopold Charles Fuller of Oldham, England, an industrial town in Lancashire, in the northwest of England, and of

Nellie Broadbent. His father was manager of a rubber-proofing mill but died when Roy Fuller was only eight. Two years later, his mother and her two sons moved to Blackpool, a nearby seaside town, where Fuller received his education at Blackpool High School. He left there at age sixteen, the minimum leaving age then being fourteen, and was articled (apprenticed) to a local firm of solicitors (attorneys). He became briefly involved in left-wing politics and always retained left-wing sympathies. His northern upbringing, with its culture of wry, antiestablishment humor, became one of the distinguishing features of his poetic voice.

He completed his articles in 1934, passing the necessary exams to qualify him as a lawyer. He moved south for his first post, at a law firm in Ashford, Kent, in the southeast of England. There he met Kathleen Smith, whom he married in 1936. Their only child, John, was born January 1, 1937. Later John was to become a well-known poet and academic in his own right. Just before the outbreak of World War II in 1939, the family moved to London, where Roy Fuller joined the Woolwich Building Society, one of the largest mortgage lending societies in the United Kingdom.

In 1941, he enlisted in the Royal Navy, in which he served until 1946. He was one of the first technicians to work with the recently installed systems of radar. In 1942, he was posted to Kenya, an experience that propelled him into writing poetry in a much more systematic way than before, though he had published a largely unnoticed volume of poems in 1939. His two volumes written during the war, *The Middle of a War* (1942) and *A Lost Season* (1944), brought him to public attention. In 1944, he was relocated back to London, becoming a lieutenant in the Royal Navy volunteer reserve. He worked at the Admiralty as a technical adviser to the director of naval air radio.

Fuller then resumed his legal career with the Woolwich, remaining with it until his retirement. He wrote several legal volumes on Building Society law and from 1958 to 1969 served as chairman of the legal advice panel of the Building Societies Association. On his retirement in 1969, he was made director of the Woolwich, a post he held until his death, and vice president of the Building Societies Association.

Fuller was thus one of the few modern poets who have systematically and successfully pursued a career outside the academic or artistic world. His commercial role did not prevent him from writing profusely or from becoming a respected poet, novelist, essayist, and reviewer. Between 1945 and 1969, he wrote seven adult and two children's novels, produced six volumes of poetry, and edited three volumes of other people's poetry. Shortly before his retirement, he was voted Professor of Poetry at Oxford University, a post he held until 1973.

He continued to be extremely active after his retirement, not only writing poetry and another novel and producing a lengthy series of memoirs, but also serving as a governor of the British Broadcasting Corporation (BBC) and as a member of the Arts Council as chairman of its literature panel. He also was chairman of the Poetry Book Society. He continued to live in London until his death in 1991.

ANALYSIS

Roy Fuller was respected as an accomplished poet and man of letters, who sought not only to raise the technical standards of poetry in his day but also to reinstate its moral voice and significance in a culture that he saw as constantly betraying itself. As a poet he fought against cultural sloppiness, using a voice typical of the great British ironists such as Alexander Pope and Lord Byron, but perhaps with more self-deprecation and sensitivity than most ironists.

THE WAR POET

Fuller's first volume of verse, titled merely *Poems*, attracted little notice. Two poems in it, however, are worthy of note: "To M. S. Killed in Spain" and "To My Brother." Both reflect the growing sense of war in the Europe of the late 1930's, his friend killed in the Spanish Civil War, and his brother touring Nazi Germany. The latter poem's central image is an edition of Alexander Pope's poems his brother had given him, Pope becoming symbolic of the ordered world Fuller feels is now shattering. Its influence is that of W. H. Auden, a poet he continued to admire for his intelligence, discipline, and formal skills.

It is in his war poetry that Fuller first found his true voice, ironically, as World War II produced very few British poets of note. In contrast to World War I, World

War II was not shocking. Fuller's depiction of it reflects personal boredom, the squalid world of military quarters and docks, and good-byes. The experience that really opened him was his being drafted to East Africa. The impact of a foreign culture and landscape forced his poetry to assume a new directness, as did the experience of living in close quarters with very ordinary young men, with the need to communicate in terms of their concrete realities.

"The Green Hills of Africa" depicts both a native village in striking detail and the debilitating effect of modern civilization. A similar pessimism informs "The Plains." Again, a masterful ability to depict a scene with a few vivid images is followed by a train of thought on the tawdriness of the cycle of killing and being killed. In the wake of the lion come the jackals and vultures. His concern for the animals is paralleled by his concern for the Africans. The narrative "Teba" shows the contradictions of a rapidly evolving society. Fuller's anti-idealism is again reflected in "The Petty Officers' Mess," possibly the most accomplished poem in the two volumes of war poetry. Fuller proceeds with an image of caged monkeys, through sailors' arguments to wider political questions, then ironically reduces these back again to the level of the monkeys' own scrapes and fights.

THE 1950'S

Returning to civilian life, Fuller wrote his next volume, *Epitaphs and Occasions*. His "Dedicatory Epistle" shows a new, easy ironic tone and verse form using iambic tetrameter couplets influenced by Pope and Auden. For all its lightness of tone, however, there is a note of purpose:

> The poet now must put verse back
> Time and again upon the track
> That first was cut by Wordsworth when
> He said that verse was meant for men.

This mixture of tautness, technical brilliance, ironic tone, and yet artistic seriousness was shared by a number of younger poets in the 1950's, particularly Donald Davie and Philip Larkin. The group came to be known as the Movement, representing a reaction to the florid Romanticism and gesturing of Dylan Thomas and other poets of the 1930's and 1940's.

Similar poems are "Meditation," often anthologized with its throwaway ending:

> . . . perhaps we shall, before
> Anything really happens, be safely dead.

In "Obituary to R. Fuller," actually quoted at his memorial service forty-two years later, his self-deprecation is comic. "The Divided Life Released" talks of the reality of wartime life and the unrealities of postwar suburban life, a dichotomy parallel to that of the poet and the lawyer, which Fuller managed to come to terms with creatively.

Counterparts and *Brutus's Orchard* followed, both containing powerful poems that break through the typical understatement, self-deprecating irony, and avoidance of emotion typical of the Movement style. "Rhetoric of a Journey" continues the theme of the uprooted, divided poet, but anchors it far more autobiographically in a moving statement. "Ten Memorial Poems," on Fuller's mother's death, is a confessional series, in places reminiscent of Alfred, Lord Tennyson's *In Memoriam* (1850). The feeling is that of the poet coming to full maturity in his control, depth, and focus.

"Images of Autumn" expresses Fuller's feeling of cultural helplessness. Poetry is no longer a public art form; the public no longer can hear the poet, who is now unheard and invisible. What is particularly difficult is that the poet is not writing just out of personal need but because he desires revelation of some "social truths." "Poet and Reader" closes with:

> All art foresees a future,
> Save art which fails to weigh
> The sadness of the creature,
> The limit of its day,
> Its losing war with nature.

Such rejection forces him into self-regarding stances: "Poem out of Character" is typical. It finishes by deconstructing his own poetry as gesture in the face of universal truth.

In "Elementary Philosophy," the despair of a godless philosophy is heard in tones that echo Thomas Hardy. Another of Hardy's themes, and also of William Butler Yeats, is the growing dichotomy of body and mind. From the middle of *Brutus's Orchard*, Fuller becomes much more aware of his own sexuality as he feels his body aging. "The Perturbation of Dreams" and "Mythological Sonnets" are powerful expressions of midlife angst.

THE 1960'S

"Faustian Sketches," the final section of Fuller's *Collected Poems, 1936-1961*, continues this awareness. In "On the Mountain," his own failing physical powers are symbolized by the decline and fall of the Roman Empire. The ironic surface tones of the earlier poems give way to deeper and more tragic ironies, with the poet's full range of emotions being engaged. The sonnet sequence *Meredithian Sonnets*, which closes the *Collected Poems*, well illustrates this.

Buff contains Fuller's third sonnet sequence, *The Historian*, which contains thirty-five sonnets, ranging over the ironies of history. "All history is the history of pain," he wrote elsewhere. "To X" is another sequence, of roundels this time, a difficult traditional form.

The decade began for Fuller with a recognition of his pivotal place in modern British poetry, with his *Collected Poems*; it closed with his *New Poems*, published shortly before his retirement from his business duties. Many of the poems in this volume are concerned with art and the artist. "Those of Pure Origin" is a striking, long philosophical poem, inspired by a quotation from the German poet Friedrich Hölderlin. Its clear, relaxed voice and well-controlled stanzaic free verse seem a model for philosophic discussion in verse.

LATER YEARS

Fuller's retirement merely released him into a prolific old age, although not adding unduly to his reputation. The same self-deprecating tone is heard in "To an Unknown Reader" in *Tiny Tears*: "a whole lifetime's remorseful exposure/ Of a talent falling short of its vision?" He continues to experiment in verse form; "At T. S. Eliot's Memorial Service" is written in couplets first used by Tennyson in "Locksley Hall."

From the Joke Shop probably illustrates best how prolific Fuller continued to be. It contains sixty-three poems written between late summer and early spring. Every poem is composed of three-line iambic stanzas, but the run-on lines and verses annul any sense of a mechanical form. The collection contains many poems reminiscent of "In Memoriam" and shows Fuller as a man of culture, not breaking any new territory in terms of what he has to say, but very stimulating in the flexibility of his poetic voice. "The Joke Shop" is his poetic imagination, with its need to "amuse" an audience.

If poems are jokes, they are also sparrows. Fuller sees himself as a minor poet in *The Reign of Sparrows*. What is striking here is the technical brilliance he has achieved, from cinquains to elegiac pindarics, as well as the ability to find significance in the most trivial everyday event. *Subsequent to Summer* (1985) continues the formal brilliance in this sequence of forty-nine quasi sonnets, each poem consisting of seven unrhymed couplets. It is effortless verse, philosophical poetry at its best. This fascination with the sonnet is akin to Robert Lowell's. In *Available for Dreams*, there is a tremendous variety of sonnet forms, becoming almost free verse, just as in Lowell's diary-like *Life Studies* (1959).

After Fuller's death, his son John discovered a large number of unpublished poems, which he edited as *Last Poems*. The American poet Wallace Stevens features prominently: Fuller's autumnal flowering has often been compared to that of Stevens, as to Yeats and Hardy. The final section, *Later Sonnets from the Portuguese* (echoing Elizabeth Barrett Browning's sequence), consists of some forty-four sonnets.

Fuller is praised for sustaining the quality of British poetry during the relatively lean period of 1950-1960. He went on to outwrite all the other Movement poets, using his intelligence, wit, and formal skills to make significant comments on the cultural and everyday life of the later part of the twentieth century. He may not take the reader out of that life, but he does fully engage with it in significant detail.

OTHER MAJOR WORKS

LONG FICTION: *The Second Curtain*, 1953; *Fantasy and Fugue*, 1954 (pb. in U.S. as *Murder in Mind*, 1986); *Image of a Society*, 1956; *The Ruined Boys*, 1959 (pb. in U.S. as *That Distant Afternoon*, 1957); *The Father's Comedy*, 1961; *The Perfect Fool*, 1963; *My Child, My Sister*, 1965; *The Carnal Island*, 1970; *Stares*, 1990.

NONFICTION: *Owls and Artificers: Oxford Lectures on Poetry, 1969-1970*, 1971; *Professors and Gods:*

Last Oxford Lectures on Poetry, 1973; *Souvenirs*, 1980; *Vamp Till Ready: Further Memoirs*, 1982; *Home and Dry: Memoirs III*, 1984; *The Strange and the Good: Collected Memoirs*, 1989; *Spanner and Pen: Post-war Memoirs*, 1991.

CHILDREN'S LITERATURE: *Savage Gold: A Story of Adventure*, 1946; *With My Little Eye: A Mystery Story for Teenagers*, 1948; *Catspaw*, 1966; *Seen Grandpa Lately?*, 1972; *The World Through the Window: Collected Poems for Children*, 1989.

EDITED TEXTS: *Byron for To-day*, 1948; *New Poems*, 1952 (with Clifford Dyment and Montagu Slater); *Supplement to New Poetry*, 1964; *Fellow Mortals*, 1981.

MISCELLANEOUS: *Questions and Answers in Building Society Law and Practice*, 1949; *The Building Societies Acts: Great Britain and Ireland, 1957-1961*, 1962.

BIBLIOGRAPHY

Austin, Allan E. *Roy Fuller*. Boston: Twayne, 1979. This compact volume contains chapters on early, middle, and late poetry up to *From the Joke Shop*. An excellent, comprehensive volume.

Hamilton, Ian. *Against Oblivion: Some Lives of the Twentieth-Century Poets*. London: Viking, 2002. Contains a chapter on Roy Fuller, describing his life and poetry.

Orr, Peter, ed. *The Poet Speaks*. London: Routledge & Kegan Paul, 1966. Fuller proves forthright in talking both about himself and his work.

Powell, Neil. *Roy Fuller: Writer and Society*. Manchester, England: Carcanet Press, 1995. A full biographical account of Fuller's life and writings with a lengthy bibliography.

Smith, Steven E. *Roy Fuller: A Bibliography*. Aldershot, England: Scholar Press, 1996. A good bibliography with a full index.

Tolley, A. T., ed. *Roy Fuller: A Tribute*. Ottawa, Ont.: Carleton University Press, 1993. A far-ranging collection of biographical pieces celebrating Fuller's life and assessing his contribution to modern literature.

David Barratt

G

GEORGE GASCOIGNE

Born: Cardington, England; c. 1539
Died: Stamford, England; October 7, 1577

PRINCIPAL POETRY

*A Hundreth Sundrie Flowres Bounde Up in One
    Small Poesie*, 1573 (poetry and prose; revised as
    The Posies of George Gascoigne Esquire, 1575)
The Fruites of Warre, 1575
The Complaynt of Phylomene, 1576 (a companion
    piece to *The Steele Glas, a Satyre*)
The Grief of Joye, 1576
The Steele Glas, a Satyre, 1576

OTHER LITERARY FORMS

The first two volumes of the poetry of George
Gascoigne (GAS-koyn) also contain many of his most
popular prose works. Among these is "Certayne Notes
of Instruction Concerning the Making of Verse" (1575,
also found in *A Hundreth Sundrie Flowres Bounde Up
in One Small Poesie*), an important work of literary
criticism that is said to be the first of its kind in the English language. Also found in the early volumes are a
number of full-length plays, all types never before presented in English, as well as some interesting masques
and royal entertainments.

Gascoigne also experimented with fictional and
nonfictional narrative. One of these works, *The Spoyle
of Antwerpe* (1576), is a rare example for the times of
detailed and honest journalistic reporting about the
war. *The Discourse of the Adventures Passed by Master F. J.* (1573; revised as *The Pleasant Fable of Ferdinando Jeronimi and Leonora de Valasco*, 1575) is a
work of prose fiction that has received considerable attention from scholars and critics. Also among these
works are several long didactic prose pieces that are
moralistic in tone.

ACHIEVEMENTS

George Gascoigne tried his hand at many forms of
literature, with an innovator's quick eye for literary
forms not used before in England or in English. Writing
as a gifted amateur at the court of Queen Elizabeth and
turning near the end of his life toward writing as a profession, Gascoigne presented a notable list of first
achievements. He wrote the first work of English literary criticism and presented in England the first ancient
Greek tragedy and the first translation from Italian
prose comedy. His verse satire *The Steele Glas, a
Satyre*, itself an important early example of social satire, was the first English poem (not including translations) that employed nondramatic blank verse.

Gascoigne was also innovative in narrative modes,
presenting in *The Discourse of the Adventures Passed
by Master F. J.* what many call the first work of prose
fiction in English. For a time he was followed by a
school of imitators, including George Whetstone and
Nicholas Breton. Gascoigne seldom brought his work
to a fine polish, however, and this lack of finish together with an archaic style in diction and meter have
produced a modern assessment that his works are valuable merely for their innovative literary attempts, rather
than their actual achievements.

This opinion has undergone some revaluation. Later
critics have stressed Gascoigne's serious commitment
to moral themes, his patriotic determination to form a
distinctively English practice in poetry (analogous to
the contemporary French movement sponsored by the
poets of the Pléiade), and his verve for realistic detail
and psychologically valid observation of human nature. Gascoigne is a transitional figure whose work
helped to extend English poetic resources and so led
to the "flowering" of the New Poetry of the 1580's
and 1590's. This fact was recognized to some extent by
his own age: The preface to Edmund Spenser's *The
Shepheardes Calender* of 1579 refers to Gascoigne as
"the very chief of our late rymers." In addition, Gascoigne offers many Elizabethan poetic "voices," selecting his own preferred emphases among the range of
options in style and convention available to poets during the Tudor period from Sir Thomas Wyatt through
John Donne (Gascoigne presents interesting points of
comparison with both of these poets). A reassessment

suggests a moral poetry of strength, verve, and self-perception; an amatory and social poetry of frankness, witty playfulness, and realism; an adroit and sensitive portrayal of first- and third-person personas; and a commitment throughout to extend the formal and linguistic resources of the English poetic medium.

BIOGRAPHY

A common mode of discussing personal lives in medieval and Renaissance literature is the exemplum, a device whereby figures from history or literature typify human virtues or vices such as heroism, devotion, or greed. As if conditioned by a habitual way of reading experience, many lives of actual sixteenth century literary figures fulfilled a seemingly fictionalized pattern, glossed by Richard Helgerson in his book *The Elizabethan Prodigals* (1976). The life of George Gascoigne provides a fine example of this "pattern of prodigality," in which youthful folly is coupled with writings in such "vain" literary forms as amatory verse. Gascoigne discusses his wasted youth and later reformation in many prefaces and poems, and although his efforts to reform were aimed at very practical financial goals, they were

George Gascoigne (Hulton Archive/Getty Images)

doubtless also sincere. Among Gascoigne's most important poems, in fact, are introspective accounts of his poor record of worldly successes.

Gascoigne began life from a secure position in a wealthy if litigious family of landed gentry. Like many other young Elizabethan gentlemen of means, he discontinued his formal education (in law) to pursue advancement at court, where he soon exhausted his patrimony and yet found no position. In addition, his reputation was sullied by various legal disputes and by a series of troubles over the legality of his marriage in 1561, as a man in his early years, to Elizabeth Bacon Breton, a much older widow with attractive property. By 1565, with friends at court but no chance of success there, the poet began to search for a means of making a living. He renewed his legal studies at Gray's Inn, where he spent most of his time in literary efforts; soon he had relocated in the country for an unsuccessful try at farming.

Gascoigne turned in 1571 to a new project for recouping his fortunes: He volunteered as a soldier in the Netherlands' campaign to aid William, Prince of Orange, against the Spanish. He returned briefly in 1572 to oversee the publication of an anonymous version of his collected writings, *A Hundreth Sundrie Flowres Bounde Up in One Small Poesie*. In mid-term of the same year, he was unexpectedly named a member of parliament from Midhurst (aided by the well-timed presentation of a dramatic masque at a wedding for a member of the family of Lord Montagu). In an anonymous letter, however, his creditors appealed to prevent his being seated, charging him with manslaughter, spying, and atheism, as well as with being "a common Rymer and a deviser of slaunderous Pasquelles againste divers personnes of greate callinge." Gascoigne returned quickly to the Holland wars, where he proved to be a capable leader but found little advancement of his fortunes, and where he learned the grim realities of war, expressed effectively in his poem "Dulce Bellum Inexpertis" ("War Is Sweet to Those with No Experience of It").

Gascoigne returned to England in 1574, to face the disastrous reception of *A Hundreth Sundrie Flowres Bounde Up in One Small Poesie*: Copies had been confiscated because of charges of libel and immorality.

Gascoigne undertook an entire change in his manner of life and his career as a writer, and finally his fortunes began to turn. A cleaned-up and reorganized version of his writings, *The Posies of George Gascoigne*, was a success, helped by the poet's repentant and revealing prefaces. Concurrently, he published his other serious, moralistic writings; gained important patronage; and found a promising position with William Cecil, minister to the queen. While his career was on the mend, he fell ill in 1576. He died in October, 1577, probably not quite forty years of age and, for the first time in many years, in good hopes for worldly comfort and a secure reputation as an Elizabethan writer, civil servant, and gentleman.

If the poet's difficulties benefited him, they did so by stimulating a vein of honest introspection. In addition, they urged the poet to consciously create his literary career. Gascoigne posed successfully as an aspiring Renaissance man, a virtuoso equally skilled in arms or letters. Gascoigne is certainly not the most important or the most successful of the Elizabethan poets. The critic John Buxton has rightly observed of him that "when greatness was within his reach he allowed himself to be distracted." However, Gascoigne is not the dull moralist and clumsy love lyricist of received literary-historical opinion. In poetic technique, he has the verve of an experimentalist and the skill of a virtuoso, although without achieving the final polish of succeeding poets. His lasting achievement, however, may rest in his sensitive but tough-minded portrayals of a series of personas, all expressing in one way or another his own effort to interpret, for himself as much as for others, a meaning for his life.

ANALYSIS

Linked to the pattern of reformed prodigality that shaped the poet's life, two personas are often reflected in George Gascoigne's writings, one a young courtier and the other a newly reformed moralist, "a man of middle-yeares, who hath to his cost experimented the vanities of youth, and to his perill passed them: who hath bought repentence deare, and yet gone through with the bargaine." The brash, witty young writer of society verse is interesting in comparison with and contrast to other Elizabethans writing in Italianate modes

of amatory poetry. In the best poems, the middle-aged moralistic persona is interesting, too. Gascoigne made a lifelong profound study of his "master," Geoffrey Chaucer (as he calls him in "Certayne Notes of Instruction Concerning the Making of Verse"). Gascoigne's ability to portray interesting and subtle personas most likely derives from his study of the first important vernacular poet in English.

Elizabethan poets were creators of artifice. Gascoigne intensified the efforts of his generation of poets—notably Barnabe Googe, Thomas Howell, George Turberville, and others—to extend the stylistic and linguistic potential of English as a poetic medium. A confirmed patriot in diction, Gascoigne preferred older, native words, striving for a Chaucerian effect, as Vere Rubel has shown in her *Poetic Diction in the English Renaissance* (1941). Similarly, as Rubel also shows, Gascoigne sought vigor and range in his vocabulary and made extensive use of figurative language from contemporary rhetoric, to create new or startling effects. He does not, however, often achieve the well-wrought and compressed effects of a more careful stylist such as Sir Philip Sidney; his rather loose syntax and conversational narration seem also to have been borrowed from Chaucer.

For Gascoigne, the key to a poem's effectiveness (and the first point in his "Certayne Notes of Instruction Concerning the Making of Verse") is "to grounde it upon some fine invention." The poet means here a clever, new, or indirect idea of how to accomplish the poem's aim—an invented story, an unusual comparison, or a studied hyperbole, but never anything trite or obvious. This emphasis on "invention" points to another feature of Gascoigne's poetry, especially his social and amatory poetry: These poems were written in response to quite specific circumstances, daily occasions calling for social dialogue or for personal expression. Poetry was a favored medium of social exchange in Elizabethan high society.

Following a seminal article by Yvor Winters, many modern critics have found that Gascoigne reacted against much Elizabethan poetry. Such critics rightly note in him a preferred speaker who is a somewhat rustic, folksy fellow, honest and direct. In presenting studied personas and enjoying conscious artifice, however,

Gascoigne places himself in the main current of Elizabethan poetic practice. Actually, the poet's opposition to styles current in his age is more apparent than real. Especially for modern readers, who are suspicious of elegance in poetry, Gascoigne's effect of forthright, direct speech seems "natural," obscuring the degree of artifice and mannerism underlying its creation.

Similarly, in his love poetry Gascoigne is often described as opposing the popular currents of Italianate Petrarchism that produced the "golden" New Poetry of the 1580's and 1590's. Indeed, many Elizabethan sonneteers borrowed from Petrarch and other Italian poets an elevated, passionate tone, a language of superlatives, and an idealistic devotion to the beloved. Italian poetry also offered other choices, however, and Gascoigne, like Wyatt before him, found in Italian models clever, witty indirectness, worldly-wise or Cavalier compliment, and a tone sometimes boastful, sometimes insulting, but seldom simply refined. Where Wyatt's persona expresses a high-minded moral resolve and rejects the amatory mores that ensnare him, however, Gascoigne's attitudes in the amatory poems are less moral. In his youthful poetry, he delights in verbal and social play for its own sake. In a slightly cynical, worldly way, he portrays the very real court society in which he lived—with such flair, in fact, that commentators in his age and in the twentieth century have read him as writing romans à clef, relating actual events involving real personalities of the day.

Gascoigne also sought to extend the range and power of vernacular poetry by exploring a variety of poetic lines and stanzas. His "Certayne Notes of Instructions Concerning the Making of Verse" describes many verse forms, identifying their characteristic uses and effects. Here Gascoigne shows sound judgment; for one, he opposes the common use of the term "sonnet" to mean any short, songlike poem, preferring the meaning that has come to be accepted in modern times. On the other hand, some less forward-looking aspects of Gascoigne's practices in form and meter require comment. As other poets of the generation before Spenser and Sidney did, Gascoigne often uses the long line of twelve or fourteen syllables, with obvious, unmodulated meters. Long verses had first become popular for their handiness in translating Latin epic me-

ters; they gave what was thought to be a stately effect and allowed for ease of line-for-line translation. The main forms are the "fourteener," rhymed iambic couplets of fourteen syllables each, and "the commonest sort of verse which we use now adayes," a couplet made of a twelve-syllable line followed by a fourteen-syllable line. (Gascoigne calls this "Poulter's measure," after the dairyman's habit of giving two extra eggs when a second dozen was bought.) Long verses resist compression of language and, moreover, tend to pause heavily in mid-line, with a sing-song effect. The jog-trot of these meters was increased by the preference of the poets of Gascoigne's generation for monosyllabic words and for a regularized iambic stress, with the heavy stresses evenly strong and the light stresses evenly light. The old-fashioned, obvious effects of these meters have obscured Gascoigne's other poetic values for many readers. As he matured, his metrical touch lightened, and he used the longer lines less frequently.

"GASCOIGNES MEMORIES"

Gascoigne's virtuoso talent is strikingly shown in five poems grouped together as "Gascoignes Memories." Upon his return in 1566 to Gray's Inn, five friends had challenged him to a verse-writing contest. Each was assigned a different theme, a proverb or a familiar Latin saying, for expansion and comment. In one weekend, Gascoigne produced five poems, 258 lines in all. Each has a unique verse structure, and all were composed on horseback without pen and paper—indeed a feat of memory. The most difficult verse form is seen in the poem on the theme *Sat cito, si sat bene* ("No haste but good," as the poet translates it), written in seven sonnets linked by repeated lines. In addition, the poems vary in tone and style, showing here the conversationality of proverbs, there an urbane polish. Each of the five poems meditates on the youthful poet's wasted time at court; they predict his later, mature voice of didactic seriousness that, without self-pity, works toward honest self-perception. In these same poems, however, Gascoigne performs a feat of brilliant poetic improvisation.

POETRY AS SOCIAL EXCHANGE

The young writer of society verse similarity took delight in his skill at verse making, which was closely tied to actual uses in court society. In Gascoigne's amatory poetry, one senses specific, real events, real lovers, and real affairs. In Elizabethan high society, fashionable amatory play did not necessarily imply actual *affaires d'amour*. Poems of amatory praise could gain remunerative recognition for their aspiring authors from quite proper court ladies—including the queen. Men and women typically paired off for a variety of social interactions, playing at pleasant amatory fictions. It is precisely these conventional social exchanges that Gascoigne manipulates with zest and skill.

One poem discusses the ill chance of the loser in a contest with another man for a woman's kiss. "Three Sonnets in Sequence" was written in a woman's copy of Lucius Apuleius's *Metamorphoses* (second century; *The Golden Ass*, 1566), a copy given by "her David" to "his Berzabe." Riddles in verse are propounded (but not solved). An amusing exchange of poems is made on the occasion of a dinner attended by a woman, her husband, her brother, her old lover, and a hopeful new suitor (the poem's speaker).

"Invention" is at the heart of these poems. A clever "invention" is analogous in poetic content (that is, in the poem's concept of what to say in order to respond effectively to a given social or amatory occasion) to the skillful realization of poetic language and form. The amatory poems praising court ladies strikingly show this element. Indeed, the poems "In Prayse of Brydges, Nowe Lady Sandes" and "In Prayse of a Gentlewoman Who Though She Were Not Very Fayre, Yet Was She as Hard Favored as Might Be" follow precisely the poet's suggestions in the "Certayne Notes of Instruction Concerning the Making of Verse" to "finde some supernaturall cause whereby [one's] penne might walke in the superlative degree" or "to aunswere for any imperfection that shee hath." The poem praising Bridges explains a birthmark on the lady's forehead as the scar of a wound made by jealous Cupid.

Gascoigne handles the Petrarchan amatory conventions with verve and with something of a showman's skill. Italianate verse supplied rich material for his own independent uses, pulled out of any original context, although the poems reproduce neither Petrarch's idealism nor his refined tone. Thus, in "Gascoignes Anatomie," the poet describes a lover's physical appearance feature by feature. The unkempt hair, hollow eyes, wan

cheeks, and trembling tongue are familiar, stereotyped details, but piled on with a characteristic exuberance. Another poem, "Gascoignes Passion," plays cleverly on Petrarchan contradictions, finding opportunity for unusual comparisons and inventive wordplay ("I live in love, even so I love to live"). One of the cleverest amatory poems is "Gascoignes Araignement," in which the speaker is accused of unjust flattery by Beauty in a court of law. The poem is Cavalier in tone and very successful in its use of a shorter, eight-syllable line.

The amatory poems tend to hint at underlying stories. This tendency is heightened by the many prose headnotes that give the occasions of their composition. (Probably to disguise his own participation in many social events—or to display his facility in creating personas—Gascoigne presented the first short poems in *A Hundreth Sundrie Flowers Bounde Up in One Small Poesie* anonymously.) This potential for narrative is inherent in Petrarchan conventions and may indeed have been consciously adapted by Gascoigne from similar headnotes in sixteenth century editions of Petrarch's sonnets—Gascoigne's autograph appears on the title page of a copy of an edition by Giovanni Gesualdo. Since Petrarch's poems trace his love for Laura *in vito* and *in morte*, these explanatory notes serve to narrate the story of the poet's love.

Gascoigne twice tried his hand at an extended linking of amatory poems to tell a story. The less complex attempt is "The Delectable History of Sundry Adventures Passed by Dan Bartholomew of Bathe." The affair opens with three poems of "triumph" at the protagonist's attaining "the bathe of perfect blisse" in love. Immediately, however, there follow his "Dolorous Discourses" on being jilted, then a series of increasingly despairing poems culminating in "His Last Wyll and Testament" and "His Farewell." The narrative success of these poems is heightened by the use of "the Reporter," a third-person narrator whose interspersed verse comments add an objective yet sympathetic context for the poet-persona's writings.

THE DISCOURSE OF THE ADVENTURES PASSED BY MASTER F. J.

The Discourse of the Adventures Passed by Master F. J. refines this technique. Here the place of "the Reporter" is taken, in prose, by a friend who tells the circumstances of the protagonist's writing a series of love poems considerably after the time when they were written. This narrator's commentary on the young poet's inexperience creates the sort of rich context which the Dan Bartholomew sequence lacks. The tale tells of the first love affair of F. J., with an experienced married woman, in a country house in the north of England. F. J. learns something of society and a good deal about himself. The narrator relates all this with sympathy and humor from the knowing perspective of a man who has rejected amatory folly but understands its pathos, idealisms, and delusions. He is, presumably, Gascoigne himself, looking back on his days of writing love poetry.

Although *The Discourse of the Adventures Passed by Master F. J.* is usually cited as prose fiction, it contains some of Gascoigne's most interesting amatory poems. The narrator's commentary includes critical assessments of the poems and explains poetic devices and intentions. Many of the poems are frankly adulterous—for example, F. J.'s "Frydayes Breakefast," which tells of a morning's lovemaking. The poems are "inventive"; the daring poem opening "Beautie shut up thy shop" claims that the mistress's beauty excels all others, leaving other men's ladies to seem like painted and trussed-up shopwares left behind once the genuine article has been sold. Such poems are questionable from any point of view requiring propriety or seriousness of content. Characteristically, however, Gascoigne defends them, including them among the "pleasant" poems of *The Posies of George Gascoigne* on the grounds of their "rare invention and Method before not commonly used."

In sum, Gascoigne's amatory *vers de société* is characterized by virtuoso display and clever, unusual content. The poet evokes a real world of social interplay and witty poetic exchanges. The narrative of *The Discourse of the Adventures Passed by Master F. J.* also suggests what Gascoigne can do when writing introspectively, as he often does on moral topics. In spite of the conservatism of his preferred theme of reformed youthful folly, Gascoigne handles it in his best poems with a perception and honesty that modern readers can appreciate. Although this reformed persona is of-

ten profoundly disillusioned, he still respects important values that are rare in a society whose snares have led him astray. In the important poem "Gascoignes Wodmanship," for example, this recognition leads to a double vision that balances the poet's sense of his own failings against those of his world, which in many ways has failed him. Such a persona makes an effective medium for satire.

THE STEELE GLAS, A SATYRE

It is thus significant to observe that Gascoigne's long satirical commentary on the corruptions of his times, *The Steele Glas, a Satyre*, is not merely objective. Its opening compares the speaker himself to the nightingale of myth, its tongue (his art) silenced by detractors and by worldly obstacles. This unusual opening frames the poem in the context of personal experience. Moreover, it helps the poet define his genre for his reader: His voice, like the bird's, is mournful and halting; like the bird "closely cowcht" in a thicket, he is a covert observer of men. Gascoigne also observes himself, in a well-known passage of self-description explained by this marginal gloss: "He which wil rebuke other mens faults, shal do wel not to forget hys owne imperfections."

As a central device, the satirist presents images in two mirrors, one of steel that cannot falsify and one of crystal that sees into the soul. The social satire is conveyed by an immense variety of examples of abuses of human potential or social responsibility; yet Gascoigne intersperses visionary descriptions of an ideal political state to counter an all-critical attitude. The ideas here are traditional, urging renewal of a hierarchical social order and attributing social corruptions to such cardinal sins as lust and greed. The Chaucerian language and vivid heaping of details from contemporary life create a distinctive English flavor. As Ronald Johnson comments, "At no one place is Gascoigne's perception unusually keen; breadth of vision rather than depth recommends the poem to us."

The most perceptive of the poems of personal analysis is "Gascoignes Wodmanship." As mentioned above, the poem mixes a satirist's awareness of society's faults with an introspective man's recognition of personal failings. The speaker's follies are portrayed with humor and sympathy. Thus the tone is at once serious, ironic, and bemused. Like many of the amatory poems, this one is based on a controlling "invention" supplied by an event in the poet's experience. While a guest of Lord Grey of Wilton, Gascoigne has poor luck in hunting, which he seeks to excuse by describing how "he shoots awrie almost at every marke" which he aims at in life. The metaphor of hunting is suspenseful and significant as well, because skill at hunting was a distinguishing accomplishment for an Elizabethan gentleman. The poem's main theme is the fleeting value of the goals for which the poet has aimed—favor at court, amatory pleasures, soldierly reputation. Something deeper is also suggested: In part, the poet has failed because his own morality prevents him from playing the games of society; ironically, his own codes of behavior make him unlikely to enjoy the world's rewards. "Gascoignes Wodmanship" is didactic and yet metaphorically and technically innovative, combining social satire with personal introspection and achieving an exemplary economy of style and control of tone.

A Hundreth Sundrie Flowres Bounde Up in One Small Poesie

A final type of poetry with which Gascoigne had success is the lyrical, songlike short poem. The maker of heavy fourteeners could also write lyrics for music: A tailnote to "Gascoignes Good Nyghte" in *A Hundreth Sundrie Flowres Bounde Up in One Small Poesie* lists eight poems that "have verie sweete notes adapted unto them." Among the most attractive of his writings is an original psalm, "Gascoignes Good Morrow," which expresses the pleasure of simple piety in direct language and a subtle stanza form. For a song with amatory content, "Of all the byrds that I do know," a charming melody was given in John Bartlett's *Booke of Ayres* (1606). This song was composed to praise a lady named "Phillip"—clearly a pseudonym, for "Phillip" was a stock name for a sparrow, as "Tom" is for a male cat. Likening the woman to a pet bird is lightly amusing, though teasingly salacious in its implication; for example, she is always on call for sexual play. In his songs, as in other forms, Gascoigne shows a virtuoso's talent for evoking a range of themes and effects; he handles the deceptively simple language of the form with skill.

Also in the form of a song is "Gascoignes Lullabie," the one among his short poems that has received, as it deserves, the most attention. Renouncing love, the speaker sings "as women do" to lull to sleep the lusts of youth. In an order assigned by the Elizabethan psychology of desire, they are his vanished youth itself and then his "gazing eyes" (which seek out feminine beauty), his "wanton will" (which impels him to desire), and his "loving boye" (a euphemism for his male potency). The poem's rich meaning results, in part, from the disarming music of the lullaby itself, which makes accepting the rigors of age seem ironically easy. Moreover, the central metaphor is significantly inappropriate in one sense, as babies, not old men, are to be sung to sleep; within the older man there remain, hidden, "full many babes" of youth's impulses that are not easily stilled. By the end, singing the poem serves as a frail distraction for the old man from still-active youthful urges. Treasuring what he must abandon, then, with some grimness, the speaker resolves to "welcome payne, let pleasure passe." This poem shows Gascoigne at his best. A governing metaphor, used as an "invention" around which the poem is built, provides richness of meaning and depth of feeling, accomplished with an ease that renders unobtrusive the artifice of the poem's language and verse form.

Other major works

LONG FICTION: *The Discourse of the Adventures Passed by Master F. J.*, 1573 (revised as *The Pleasant Fable of Ferdinando Jeronimi and Leonora de Valasco*, 1575).

PLAYS: *Jocasta*, pr. 1566 (with Francis Kinwelmershe; translation of Lodovico Dolce's play *Giocasta*); *Supposes*, pr. 1566 (translation of Ludovico Ariosto's *I suppositi*); *A Devise of a Maske for the Right Honorable Viscount Mountacute*, pr. 1572; *The Glasse of Governement*, pb. 1575; *The Princely Pleasures at Kenelworth Castle*, pr. 1575 (with others); *The Tale of Hemetes the Heremyte*, pr. 1575.

NONFICTION: "Certayne Notes of Instruction Concerning the Making of Verse," 1575; *A Delicate Diet, for Daintiemouthde Droonkardes*, 1576; *The Droomme of Doomes Day*, 1576; *The Spoyle of Antwerpe*, 1576.

BIBLIOGRAPHY

Austen, Gilliam. *George Gascoigne*. Woodbridge, Suffolk, England: D. S. Brewer, 2009. A thorough biography of Gascoigne that examines his major works, including his early and later poetry, including *The Grief of Joye*. Contains a chronological list of his works.

Hughes, Felicity A. "Gascoigne's Posies." *Studies in English Literature, 1500-1900* 37, no. 1 (Winter, 1997): 1-19. Argues that in *The Posies of George Gascoigne*, Gascoigne did not correct his writings in conformity with the wishes of censors who found his writing offensive. Rather, Hughes says, his "revised" edition of 1575 is no cleaner than the first edition, and it represents an attempt to brazen it out with the censors rather than placate them.

Johnson, Ronald C. *George Gascoigne*. New York: Twayne, 1972. An ample discussion of Petrarch and Gascoigne precedes separate chapters on the love lyrics and the other poems. *The Steele Glas, a Satyre* is discussed for its satire, *The Discourse of the Adventures Passed by Master F. J.* for its variety of narrative devices, and the three plays for their relationship to dramatic traditions. Includes a brief biography and a short annotated bibliography.

May, Steven. "Early Courtier Verse: Oxford, Dyer, and Gascoigne." In *Early Modern English Poetry: A Critical Companion*, edited by Patrick Gerald Cheney, Andrew Hadfield, and Garrett A. Sullivan. New York: Oxford University Press, 2007. Compares the poetry of Gascoigne, Sir Edward Dyer, and Edward, earl of Oxford.

Pincombe, Mike, and Cathy Shrank, eds. *The Oxford Handbook of Tudor Literature, 1485-1603*. New York: Oxford University Press, 2009. Contains three essays on Gascoigne, one on *The Steele Glas, a Satyre*.

Prior, Roger. "Gascoigne's Posies as a Shakespearian Source." *Notes and Queries* 47, no. 4 (December, 2000): 444-449. Gascoigne wrote a masque to celebrate the 1572 double wedding of a son and daughter of Anthony Browne, first Viscount Montague, and two children of Sir William Dormer. Prior draws many parallels between this masque, published in Gascoigne's collection *The Posies of George Gascoigne* and William Shakespeare's *Romeo and Juliet* (pr. c. 1595-1596).

Skura, Meredith Anne. *Tudor Autobiography: Listening for Inwardness*. Chicago: University of Chicago Press. 2008. Contains a look at Gascoigne's reinvention of himself in the chapter "Erasing an Author's Life: George Gascoigne's Revision of *One Hundredth Sundrie Flowres* (1573) in His *Poesies* (1575)."

Richard J. Panofsky

JOHN GAY

Born: Barnstaple, North Devonshire, England; June 30, 1685

Died: London, England; December 4, 1732

PRINCIPAL POETRY

Wine, 1708
Rural Sports, 1713
The Fan, 1714
The Shepherd's Week, 1714
Trivia: Or, The Art of Walking the Streets of London, 1716
Poems on Several Occasions, 1720, 1731
To a Lady on Her Passion for Old China, 1725
Fables, 1727, 1738
Gay's Chair: Poems Never Before Printed, 1820
The Poetical Works of John Gay, 1926 (G. C. Faber, editor; includes plays)

OTHER LITERARY FORMS

John Gay's early reputation was based on his poetry, but he produced several dramatic pieces of note between 1712 and 1731. In fact, three of his plays were not published until after his death. His claim to lasting fame, however, was *The Beggar's Opera*, which opened at the Theatre Royal in Lincoln's Inn Fields, London, on the night of January 29, 1728. It ran for sixty-two performances between January and June of that year, thirty-two of which were consecutive. Produced under the direction of John Rich, manager of

Lincoln's Inn Fields, the play supposedly made "Gay rich and Rich gay." Financial success aside, the piece wove together a number of popular modes: sarcasm against Italian opera, political satire, and social criticism that dared to compare the court circle with the then-current underworld network. There is some evidence to support the contention that the opera was prompted by Jonathan Swift's suggestion to Alexander Pope (by way of a letter dated August 11, 1716) that Gay should write a series of "Newgate pastorals"—burlesques of the pastoral tradition that had succeeded so well in *The Shepherd's Week*. The problem with that theory, however, is that it seems unreasonable that Gay would have allowed the suggestion to remain in limbo for twelve years. Perhaps a more plausible source for *The Beggar's Opera* is the career of the famous highwayman Jonathan Wild, who died at Tyburn Hill on May 4, 1725. Certainly, curiosity about Wild may well have motivated Gay to explore more deeply the workings of the London criminal element.

Polly (pb. 1729), a sequel to *The Beggar's Opera*, never graced the London stage during its author's lifetime. Sir Robert Walpole, the prime minister, had quickly recognized the assaults against himself and his party in *The Beggar's Opera*; thus, he ordered the duke of Grafton, as Lord Chamberlain, to deny a license for the production of *Polly*. Obviously, he feared more of the same. Gay published his play, however, and sales were brisk because of the Whig ministry's refusal to permit a stage production—an event that did not take place until 1777. Shortly after Gay's death, his last opera, *Achilles* (pr., pb. 1733), appeared on the stage for eighteen performances. However, its reception was cool, and general opinion held the piece to be hardly deserving of serious attention. The eight remaining plays published by Gay received varying degrees of critical response.

In May, 1711, Gay had published a two-penny pamphlet titled *The Present State of Wit, in a Letter to a Friend in the Country*, an account of contemporary periodical literature in England, with emphasis upon *The Tatler* and *The Spectator*.

ACHIEVEMENTS

John Gay's prominent stature within the literary and social circles of eighteenth century England requires no complex explanation. Indeed, his associations with his literary peers, especially among the outspoken Tory satirists of the early years of Walpole's ministry, were far deeper than mere political or professional ties. Pope, Swift, and John Arbuthnot regarded him with the utmost love and respect. Even Walpole, whom he attacked, appointed him to the post of commissioner of lotteries, granted him an apartment at Whitehall Palace, and influenced Queen Caroline to offer him a household post. Lewis Melville, who fairly early in the twentieth century compiled a collection of Gay's letters and surrounded it with biographical bits and pieces, maintained that Gay's friends—Lord Burlington, Lady Suffolk (Henrietta Howard), the duke and duchess of Queensberry—all placed their houses and their purses at the poet's disposal in an effort to compete for the pleasure of his company. Never, noted Melville, was a man of letters so pampered and petted.

Gay was, however, more to the Augustans than simply another social ornament or intellectual gadfly with a superficial talent for conversation and letters. Consider the degree to which his works held the interest of English readers and English theater audiences after his death in 1732. There were productions and revivals of his operas and recurrent editions of the *Poems on Several Occasions*, the *Fables, Trivia, The Shepherd's Week*, and even *The What D'ye Call It* (pr., pb. 1715). Throughout the century, readers of his poems and plays realized the timelessness of his social criticism. What those same readers may have forgotten, however, is that as a poet Gay remained carefully within the outward conventions of his day, never extending his art beyond his interest or his ability. He turned his back on the epic and focused, instead, on burlesque—on minute descriptions, light satire, and jocular song. He seemed more interested in following contemporary caricaturists than in emulating the strict Latin models of the first Augustan Age.

Gay gathered strength from the wit, the sparkle, and even the venom of his friend's personal dislikes and distastes, all of which helped him to refine his realistic humor. Thus, *The Shepherd's Week* reflects the bite of Pope's attack against Ambrose Philips's *Pastorals*, while there are more than coincidental associations between *Trivia* and Jonathan Swift's ultrarealistic "Description of the Morning" and "A Description of a City Shower," as well as some *Tatler* and *Spectator* fragments on the same general topic from Sir Richard Steele and Joseph Addison. Nevertheless, Gay never achieved intellectual or even poetic and satiric equality with Pope or Swift, principally because of his own poetic temperament. There are scholars of the period who maintain that he was only a songster—a very good one, to be sure, but still not a poet. Such a reaction may be too harsh, for he did hold his own among his contemporaries who sought to portray everyday life; he could harness current coffeehouse rumor and drawing-room gossip into readable poetry—with much the same success as the skilled novelists did later in the century. He knew the temper of the times: the city, its people, and its activities. He read the weekly gazettes and news sheets that graphically reproduced the sounds, smells, and irrational moments of a supposedly rational age.

Gay thus catered to and transcribed the Augustan era. His poetry—as did that of Swift, Pope, Matthew Prior, John Dennis, and Thomas Parnell—provided a mirror for society; but his particular glass was polished bright and clear, perhaps not as prismatic as those of his colleagues. His poetry caught hypocrisy in midair and hurled it back in the face of his reader: the flattery, the filth, the amusement, the exaggeration. Again, he sought not the higher grounds of epic and lyric for his work, but chose to remain at eye level—to write verse about town, club, street, tavern, coffeehouse, theater, bear pit, and drawing room. As a poet, Gay was genuine, and the degree to which society accepted his verse indicates that he met the criteria for art and satisfied the demands of the intellect.

Biography

John Gay was born at Barnstaple, North Devonshire, on June 30, 1685. His father, William Gay, died in early 1695, while his mother, a Hanmer (and a relative of the speaker of Parliament and editor of William Shakespeare, Sir Thomas Hanmer), had preceded her husband in death by only a few months (1694). An uncle, Thomas Gay (died 1702), took charge of both house and family, sending young John to the free grammar school at Barnstaple. There the boy received more than competent instruction in the classics and poetry

from the Reverend Robert Luck, a young High Churchman from Westminster School, newly graduated from Christ Church, Oxford. After the death of his uncle, the boy set out for London to become an apprentice to a silk mercer, a vocation that quickly lost its appeal for him. In fact, he became so depressed that his health suffered, and so he returned, in 1706, to Barnstaple and the house of another uncle, the Reverend John Hanmer, a Nonconformist and a sincere Calvinist who died in July, 1707.

Upon Hanmer's death, Gay once more set his course for London, where he served his former schoolmate and fellow poet, Aaron Hill, as a transcriber and general secretary. His first poem, *Wine*, came forth shortly thereafter; Gay announced that its sources were Miltonic, but the piece shows a strong influence of Ambrose Philips's most noteworthy labor of verse, *The Splendid Shilling*. Interestingly enough, the poem did not appear in the first edition of his *Poems on Several Occasions*.

At any rate, *Wine* sent Gay into the profession of letters. He formed an acquaintance with Alexander Pope, and his reputation rose when, in 1712, Bernard Lintot's *Miscellany* included his translation of one of Ovid's narrative poems from *The Metamorphoses* in close proximity to the first version of Pope's *The Rape of the Lock*. Early in 1713, *Rural Sports*, his georgic dedicated to Pope, appeared, followed, in the fall of that year, by a clever essay on the art of dress for Sir Richard Steele's *Guardian*.

Although Pope tried his hand at improving Gay's next major poetic effort, *The Fan*, the piece failed to engage the interest of its readers. Undaunted, Gay published *The Shepherd's Week*, a series of eclogues in which Pope also played a prominent role. Apparently the bard of Twickenham required some assistance in his attack upon Ambrose Philips and that poet's parodies of the pastoral form; Philips and Pope had published their separate volumes of pastoral poems in the same year (1709). Gay's part in the conflict was to depict rustic life without the usual classical ornamentation; in other words, Pope wanted something in which cattle would be milked and pigs would stray from their sties. To his credit, however, Gay went beyond mere ridicule and managed to produce a series of eclogues containing interesting elements of pastoral folklore and accurate descriptions of rural scenes.

Shortly after the publication of *The Shepherd's Week*, Gay obtained a position as secretary to Lord Clarendon, probably as a result of Swift's influence; the poet then accompanied his employer to the court of Hanover in 1714. However, the death of Queen Anne within the same year terminated Clarendon's mission as well as his need for a secretary. Returning to England in September, 1714, Gay, acting on the advice of Pope and Arbuthnot, took to publishing poetry that would secure him some favor at court. The most obvious of these pieces was an "Epistle to a Lady, Occasion'd by the Arrival of Her Royal Highness," written for the Princess of Wales, who came to England in mid-October, 1714. In that poem, he appealed directly for patronage and bemoaned the fact that he had been obliged to appeal for any type of employment.

The following year witnessed an upturn in the poet's fortunes. Lord Burlington sent him to Devonshire, and that journey found its way into a verse epistle titled "A Journey to Exeter." Then, in January, 1716, *Trivia* was published; Lintot paid him £43 for the effort, and he received at least £150 more from the sale of paperbound copies. Gay continued to serve the needs of the nobility and to compose verses in their honor. In July, 1717, William Pultney, soon to become earl of Bath, chose him as a companion for a trip to Aix. In 1718, he ventured to Cockthorpe, Oxfordshire, the seat of Lord Harcourt—which placed him near Pope, then hard at work on his translation of Homer's *Iliad* (c. 750 B.C.E.). Within two years, Lintot and Jacob Tonson published Gay's poems in two quarto volumes; more important to Gay at that point than the actual poems was the impressive subscription list, bearing witness to the extent of the nobility's willingness (at least at that moment during the reign of the first Hanoverian) to support its favorite men of letters. Gay allegedly earned in excess of £1000 from the two volumes, then lost it all (and much more, perhaps) in the disastrous South Sea speculation (1720).

Fortunately, Gay was rescued from both spiritual and financial failure by two of the more prominent subscribers to his 1720 *Poems on Several Occasions*, Catherine Hyde and her husband Charles, third duke of

John Gay (Library of Congress)

Queensbury. They took him into their home and into their circle of influential friends, thus easing Gay's financial difficulties. He even managed to secure the post of lottery commissioner, for which he received £150 yearly from 1722 to 1731. His health continued to pose a problem, although his successful career as a dramatist was just beginning. By early 1728, with *The Beggar's Opera* ready for production, he had already gained a foothold with his tragedy *The Captives* and by nomination as gentleman-usher to the small Princess Louisa (which he declined to accept). By the time that *The Beggar's Opera* was halfway through its run of sixty-three days, Gay had already earned between £700 and £800. After the London season, the opera was performed widely throughout England and Scotland—and in Ireland, where it was given twenty-four times consecutively. Even the sequel, *Polly*, although it never reached the stage during Gay's lifetime, brought the playwright between £1100 and £1200 from publication—far more than he could have achieved from actual performances.

Affluence, however, could not insulate Gay from sickness. In December, 1728, he suffered a serious at-

Critical Survey of Poetry

tack of fever, and the duke and duchess of Queensbury took him to their country seat of Amesbury, in Wiltshire. There he remained, working on an expanded version of his *Fables* and producing several pastoral dramas, operas, and comedies that contributed little to his literary reputation. Late in November, 1732, he came to London to arrange for the production of his *Achilles*; he suffered an attack of inflammatory fever and died on December 4, 1732, attended by his friend and physician, Arbuthnot. He lay in state at Exeter Exchange and then was carried for burial to Westminster Abbey, where Queensbury had erected a handsome monument to his memory. The juvenile quality of the epitaph, written by Gay himself—"Life is a jest, and all things show it./ I thought so once, and now I know i"—hardly rises to the level of the writer's status in life and the fact that his personal fortune, at his death, was in excess of £6000.

ANALYSIS

To understand John Gay's poetry—both individual poems and the entire poetic canon—one must understand the role of the Augustan satirist: the persona, the mask, the complex writer-character that Swift developed so naturally but so carefully and with such intensity in *Gulliver's Travels* (1726) and *A Modest Proposal* (1729). Of all Augustan prose writers and poets who flitted in and out of the persona, either to obscure or to sharpen their satiric bites, Gay employed the technique with the greatest variety. In his early poetry—*Wine, The Fan, Rural Sports, The Shepherd's Week*—he donned the mask of sophistication and tradition, of the highly literate, classical, rural Vergilian, of the suburban citizen of the world. At the height of success—the 1727 *Fables* and *To a Lady on Her Passion for Old China*—he assumed an air of quiet but intense morality. Finally, in the later pieces added to the *Poems on Several Occasions* and the second version of the *Fables*, Gay donned the garb of directness and obvious simplicity, trying very hard to press home the moral of a tale or to meet at least halfway the intellectual and artistic tastes of his readers. Gay succeeded as a poet and a satirist, according to Patricia Meyer Spacks, when he learned to manipulate his persona rather than hide behind it.

WINE

Gay's first published poem, *Wine*, written when the poet was only twenty-two years old, proved that he knew something about his subject and that he could at least imitate with the best of poets and imbibers. The blank verse, as well as the subject, reflects the influence of John Philips's *Cyder* (1708); the poem also demonstrates Gay's familiarity with the mock-heroic form and his early command of humorous exaggeration. Most important, though, *Wine* suggests the potential of better poems to come. The reader recognizes that Gay has abandoned the traditional elegance of his more mature colleagues, turning instead to common scenes of lower-class life. Additionally, of course, the comic operas that would come later show the degree to which he sympathized with the poorer elements of London society. To the surprise of modern readers who take their poetry seriously (and perhaps fail to appreciate eighteenth century tastes), the authorized version of 1708 was pirated on no less than two occasions by one Henry Hills, a London bookseller, which meant that the young poet's graphic descriptions of the seedier sides of London life proved attractive to more than a handful of his contemporaries. As all mere imitations (especially the immature ones) must fail, however, so did *Wine* fail to rise above the level of a schoolboy exercise.

THE SHEPHERD'S WEEK

The perils of imitation are still evident in a more accomplished work, *The Shepherd's Week*. Writing under the influence of Pope, Gay had to keep a sharp eye on Pope's suggestion that he ridicule Ambrose Philips's pastoral poems, while at the same time expressing his own devotion to rural England and displaying his knowledge of the rustic aspects of English life. If he had had a third eye, Gay certainly would have attended more carefully to his model, Edmund Spenser's *The Shepheardes Calender* (1579). At any rate, the result of his effort was a hodgepodge of all three influences. Gay must have realized what was happening, for the introductory "Proem to the Courteous Reader" stands as an apology for the entire set of pastorals, wherein the poet asserts that no English versifier heretofore has successfully produced a proper and simple eclogue after the true form of Theocritus. He then attacks Philips's outrageous conceits and proceeds to his own definition of the pastoral—an accurate imitation of the nature and manners of rustic life. In other words, Gay needed to tell his readers what he had done before they actually read the poem.

FABLES

Gay did not always have to apologize. In the fifty-one fables in verse composed for the five-year-old Prince William, duke of Cumberland, and published a year before *The Beggar's Opera*, his performance was quite authentic and more than satisfactory. In fact, both for his own generation and for posterity, the *Fables* may well be Gay's most important poetic work. True, he had an adequate number of predecessors whom he could (and did) imitate—particularly Jean de La Fontaine, whose *Fables choisies, mises en vers* (1668-1694; *Fables Written in Verse*, 1735) was first published in 1668. He managed, however, perhaps for the first time as a poet, to generate an air of worldly wisdom and to give it substance through expressions of wit and lively verse. Obviously, Gay knew the state of the polite world—the same world that he had seen and felt during his "trivial" tour throughout London; but he also envisioned a moral world that might someday overcome the triteness and false elegance of his own age. The fables are light, genial, and even gay—of the stuff that would both interest and instruct a five-year-old child. Such pieces as "The Elephant and the Bookseller," "The Lion and the Cub," "The Two Owls and the Sparrow," "The Two Monkeys," and "The Hare and Many Friends" continue to make sense for today's young and old alike.

TRIVIA

The unfortunate aspect of Gay's most characteristic poem, *Trivia*, and his most important poetic work, the *Fables*, is that they leave the impression of a gentle, good-natured, and lovable man whose spiritual age never exceeded twenty-two. In a sense, the titles of the two works established forever Gay's reputation as the poet of the trivial and the fabled, sufficiently lacking in intellectual acumen to compete with his seriously motivated contemporaries. Such impressions are gleaned while reading Gay's poems together with Samuel Johnson's conclusion that Gay never went beyond the trivial; with Joseph Warton's contention (in his 1782 essay on Pope) that Gay was merely neat and terse; and with

the correspondence of Pope and Swift, implying that Gay was a dear friend who needed to be loved and advised but whose poetry had little effect upon anyone. Consequently, not until recently has Gay's poetry been seen for what it is: a formal attack upon and a reshaping of the ideas, the values, and the very scenes of early eighteenth century England. In that sense, he stands pen-to-pen with his contemporaries, really no different in purpose from Prior, Pope, or Swift. Thus, in *To a Lady on Her Passion for Old China*, he joins ranks with those who lashed out at grave philosophers poring over spiders and butterflies in the name of human contemplation; like moles, they dig for information known to and appreciated only by themselves. In criticizing the outwardly absurd, however, Gay departed slightly from his fellows in that he rarely became upset or overly bitter at what he knew and saw. Instead, he adopted the language and the tone of a civilized man who is rarely open in his criticism, but prefers detachment and only sufficient mockery to hold the attention of his reader.

MORAL CONDITION

If Gay can stand beside his fellow satirists and Tory comrades, he can also, on occasion, rise above them as a poet seriously concerned with the moral state of the world—the universal world, rather than the limited sphere of Augustan London. For example, in "A Thought on Eternity," he contrasts infinity to the pettiness of his own times, in which actions and events are measured in terms of specific chronological periods. The virtuous soul, he concludes, regards life as a fleeting dream whereby the soul longs for freedom from earth and a flight into the wider span of eternity. In "A Contemplation on Night," published by Steele in his *Miscellany* of 1713, Gay looks to the heavens, a pure Newtonian sky, and enjoys the workings of an all-powerful Providence that nature has forced him to recognize. Even when the stars and the sun have passed from his view, he will, as a deeply moral man, understand the presence, the light, of the Creator. Even in the fairly early *Rural Sports*, in which Gay again takes advantage of the Augustans' drift toward Newtonianism, he does more than introduce countryside recreation into the georgic framework. The strength of the piece lies in his ability to combine vivid nature description with pure religious feeling; but the religious aspects aside, he still manages to create a poem that gives moral credence to the beauty of nature. He contemplates the sunset while also contemplating God, thus allowing the poetic soul to overflow with praise and declaration.

The same elements and combinations appear again in "Panthea" (1713), when a disappointed lady turns from the hateful town toward what she terms "some melancholy cave," a living grave in which she can cry and mourn forever. There she hopes to lose all sense of natural and human-contrived divisions of time. Another form of eternity emerges in "Araminta" (1713), a pastoral elegy set in a melancholy shade with such items as a croaking raven and an old ruin contributing to an atmosphere of human repentance.

Serious students of Gay's poetry may wonder why he never developed with more realism or intensity his respect for the creative power of God. Had he done so, he might have managed to contribute something to the growth and development of English hymnody. Gay, however, had little interest in and even less commitment to congregational worship. He evidenced little of the religious conviction demonstrated, for example, by Joseph Addison in the five *Spectator* hymns published in 1712. The religious and moral elements that do appear in Gay's poetry are always rather ambiguous. For example, in the fable of "The Ravens, the Sexton, and the Earth-Worm," the ravens believe they smell a dead horse; however, the sexton informs them that the local squire has died and will be buried on this night. The sexton is obviously put out because of the ravens' inability to distinguish human from beast, although the birds reply that a dead horse smells as good as a dead human being. Upon the scene crawls an earthworm, the expert on carrion, to mediate. The worm essentially sides with the birds, but he does offer the advice that the essence of a human is the soul, not the flesh. True virtue is seated in the immortal mind, the worm claims; thus, "Different tastes please different vermin."

The ambiguity of Gay's moral pronouncements takes the form of earnestness and cynicism combined. As an intellectual—or at least a member of an intellectual group of poets, dramatists, and aristocrats—he hid behind an intellectual hardness that he wanted very much to temper. Within his own moral composition,

there was a struggle between the strong rustic and provincial elements to which he had originally belonged and the influence of those intellectuals whom he chose to join and whom he emulated in his art. Again, Gay could never be considered a religious person or a religious poet; nevertheless, he could not totally conceal the enjoyment and the legitimate spiritual uplift that came to him (as it certainly comes to all persons of sensitivity) when he saw the actual workings of a God-created and God-ordered nature.

LEGACY

It is interesting to note that Gay's reputation as a poet has held firm throughout almost two centuries of critical comment. Johnson, in 1781, could not rank Gay very high because he thought his subject failed to achieve a significant degree of genius. In 1959, Bonamy Dobrée thought that Gay lacked a "capacity for thought," which prevented him from treating the substance of his poems with any depth. Perhaps both of those observers placed too much emphasis on the surface content of what still remains Gay's most characteristic poem, *Trivia*. Certainly, the poem may be marred by the rapidity of a walking tour through too many disconnected (thematically as well as geographically) parts of town; and equally certain is Gay's imperfect command of the mock-epic style. Nevertheless, Gay could pump life into the trivial, cramming his scenes with more facts than the naked eye could perceive at a single glance: thirty-five separate localities, at least sixty different ways of earning a living, the signs of the weather, the accoutrements necessary for walking the streets. Gay, indeed, lacked originality and depth, but no scholar can ever accuse him of lacking versatility; he applied his pen to anything that he thought might gain him a patron or a pound.

Gay the poet never quite achieved the intellectual power or the substance of the first-rate Augustan minds and artists. There is even some merit to the argument that, during his lifetime, his friends, not his published works, were actually responsible for the establishment of his literary reputation. His charming and witty songs certainly contained sufficient depth and unity to merit recognition, and the same may be said for the operas. The remainder of his verse is readable, but it is also too imitative to be distinctive. His interest as both poet and dramatist centered upon everyday life, and the novelists, dramatists, and poets of the late Hanoverian period surely benefited from the force and the action of his descriptions and characterizations. There will always be, no doubt, some challenge even to that contribution, for Gay has long been attacked for superficiality. Still, literary history will continue to provide a place for Gay's poetry, for he contributed, if nothing else, a sharp engraving of his times. If readers cannot appreciate Gay as a poet, they can at least learn from him and envision the Augustan Age because of him.

OTHER MAJOR WORKS

PLAYS: *The Mohocks*, pb. 1712; *The Wife of Bath*, pr., pb. 1713 (revised pb. 1730); *The What D'ye Call It*, pr., pb. 1715; *Three Hours After Morning*, pr., pb. 1717 (with Alexander Pope and John Arbuthnot); *Dione*, pb. 1720 (verse tragedy); *The Captives*, pr., pb. 1724 (verse tragedy); *The Beggar's Opera*, pr., pb. 1728 (ballad opera); *Polly*, pb. 1729 (ballad opera); *Acis and Galatea*, pr. 1731 (libretto; music by George Frederick Handel); *Achilles*, pr., pb. 1733 (ballad opera); *The Distress'd Wife*, pr. 1734; *The Rehearsal at Goatham*, pb. 1754; *Plays*, 1760; *The Plays of John Gay*, 1923 (2 volumes).

NONFICTION: *The Present State of Wit, in a Letter to a Friend in the Country*, 1711; *A Letter to a Lady*, 1714; *The Letters of John Gay*, 1966 (C. F. Burgess, editor).

MISCELLANEOUS: *Poetical, Dramatic, and Miscellaneous Works of John Gay*, 1795, 1970 (6 volumes); *Poetry and Prose of John Gay*, 1974 (2 volumes; Vinton A. Dearing, with Charles E. Beckwith, editors).

BIBLIOGRAPHY

Brant, Clare, and Susan E. Whyman, eds. *Walking the Streets of Eighteenth Century England: John Gay's "Trivia."* New York: Oxford University Press, 2007. In addition to the text of Gay's *Trivia*, the work contains a collection of essays that look at areas such as poverty, gender, street fashion, and pollution in the work and help provide a full picture of England at the time.

Dobrée, Bonamy. *William Congreve: A Conversation Between Swift and Gay.* 1929. Reprint. Folcroft, Pa.: Folcroft Press, 1969. A conversation between Jonathan Swift and Gay recorded at the house of the duke of Queensberry near London in 1730. They discuss Congreve's work with vigor, forthrightness, and wit. Of interest to scholars of both Gay and Swift.

Dugaw, Dianne. *Deep Play: John Gay and the Invention of Modernity.* Cranbury, N.J.: Associated University Presses, 2001. A critical and historical analysis of Gay's works. Includes bibliographical references and index.

Lewis, Peter, and Nigel Wood, eds. *John Gay and the Scriblerians.* New York: St. Martin's Press, 1988. These ten essays, the result of the tercentenary of Gay's birth, are important in presenting later trends in the analysis and criticism of Gay's work. They focus on the dichotomies found in Gay's life and writings, the perplexing contradictions that now seem to have been purposefully and carefully constructed. Includes notes and index.

Melville, Lewis. *Life and Letters of John Gay.* London: Daniel O'Connor, 1921. Reprints of Gay's letters, providing insight into the man and his life. Among Gay's correspondents were such notables as Jonathan Swift, Alexander Pope, John Arbuthnot, and the duchess of Queensberry. Includes previously unpublished letters that reside in the British Museum.

Nokes, David. *John Gay, a Profession of Friendship.* New York: Oxford University Press, 1995. A comprehensive biography with some previously unpublished letters. Nokes presents Gay as a complex character, torn between the hopes of court preferment and the assertion of literary independence. Includes bibliographical references and index.

Richardson, John. *Slavery and Augustan Literature: Swift, Pope, Gay.* New York: Routledge, 2004. An examination of how Jonathan Swift, Alexander Pope, and Gay viewed slavery in their writings. Gay's *Polly* is examined.

Spacks, Patricia Ann Meyer. *John Gay.* 1965. Reprint. New York: Twayne, 1984. A basic biography of Gay.

Walsh, Marcus. *John Gay: Selected Poems.* Manchester, England: Carcanet Press, 1979. The introduction gives some critical commentary and background information on Gay's poems in this selection, noting that Gay has been in the shadow of Alexander Pope and Jonathan Swift. Argues that his neglect is partly due to his being an "ironist rather than a satirist." A brief but insightful criticism of Gay's works.

Samuel J. Rogal

OLIVER GOLDSMITH

Born: Pallas, County Longford(?), Ireland; November 10, 1728 or 1730
Died: London, England; April 4, 1774

PRINCIPAL POETRY

"An Elegy on the Glory of Her Sex: Mrs. Mary Blaize," 1759

"The Logicians Refuted," 1759

The Traveller: Or, A Prospect of Society, 1764

"Edwin and Angelina," 1765

"An Elegy on the Death of a Mad Dog," 1766

The Deserted Village, 1770

"Threnodia Augustalis," 1772

"Retaliation," 1774

The Haunch of Venison: A Poetical Epistle to Lord Clare, 1776

"The Captivity: An Oratoria," pb. 1820 (wr. 1764)

OTHER LITERARY FORMS

Like Joseph Addison, Samuel Johnson, and other eighteenth century writers, Oliver Goldsmith did not confine himself to one genre. Besides poetry, Goldsmith wrote two comedies, a novel, periodical essays, a collection of letters, popular histories of England and Rome, and several biographical sketches. By the 1760's, literature had become a commercial enterprise, and successful authorship meant writing what the public would read. Goldsmith could write fluently on a wide variety of subjects, even when his knowledge of some of them was superficial. He was especially skillful at adapting another's work to his audience's interests: Many of his short poems are imitations of foreign models, and the collection of fictional letters, *The Citi-*

zen of the World (1762), is an adaptation of Montesquieu's *Persian Letters* (1721). Both his collected works and his letters are available in modern editions.

ACHIEVEMENTS

Oliver Goldsmith used his fluent pen to write himself out of obscurity. Like many other eighteenth century writers, he progressed from hackwork to authorship—and along the way did something to raise the level of hackwork. His life and career demonstrate the transition that occurred in British literature as commercial publishing gradually replaced patronage as the chief support of writers.

Goldsmith is both one of the most characteristic and one of the best English writers of the late 1700's. His *The Vicar of Wakefield* (1766), for example, both reflects the taste of the period for sentimental fiction and maintains itself as a minor classic today. His *The Deserted Village* is likewise a typical pastoral of the period and a landmark of English poetry. In his own time, Goldsmith reflected an important new sensibility in English culture: an awareness of Britain as part of a European community with which it shared problems and attitudes. This new view is evident in *The Traveller*, which contrasts the great states of Europe to understand the character of each nation more than to trumpet British superiority; this cosmopolitan spirit also shapes the letters of *The Citizen of the World*, which analyze English society through a Chinese visitor's eyes.

Even without a historical interest, many readers still find Goldsmith enjoyable for his style and his comedy. Goldsmith is one of the masters of the middle style; no reader has to work hard at his informal, almost conversational prose and poetry. Although his pieces are often filled with social observation, Goldsmith's human and humorous observations of people make his work accessible and pleasurable even to those who never met a lord or made the Grand Tour. His characters and perceptions are rooted in universal experiences.

BIOGRAPHY

Although David Garrick's epigrammatic remark that Oliver Goldsmith "wrote like an angel, but talk's like poor Poll" exaggerates his social awkwardness, it does contain an important indicator. Before Goldsmith discovered authorship, his life had been all trial and mostly error.

As the second son of an Irish clergyman, Goldsmith could not look forward to independent means; most of the family resources went to increase the dowry of a sister. Nature seems to have been equally parsimonious toward him: Childhood disease, natural indolence, and physical ungainliness left him prey to his classmates' teasing and his schoolmasters' scorn. His later days at Trinity College in Dublin were no better: He got into trouble with administrators, ran away, but returned to earn a low bachelor's degree in 1749.

For the next ten years, Goldsmith seemed at a complete loss for direction. He toyed with the idea of running away to America, but instead applied for ordination in the Church of England. Emphatically rejected by the local bishop, Goldsmith went in 1751 to study medicine at the University of Leyden. After mild attention to his studies, Goldsmith toured Europe, sometimes with the dignity of a "foreign student" and sometimes with the poverty of a wandering minstrel. Returning to London in 1756, he successively failed at teaching and at getting a medical appointment in the navy. He found work as a proofreader for the novelist-printer Samuel Richardson and as a hack writer for the bookseller Griffiths. To raise money, Goldsmith began writing *An Enquiry into the Present State of Polite Learning in Europe*, for which he found a publisher in 1759.

This lively account of the contemporary intellectual world won him attention from two literary entrepreneurs, Tobias Smollett and John Newbery, who gave him regular work on a variety of periodical papers writing essays, biographies, and a few poems. These labors brought him important acquaintances and the opportunity for greater success.

The year 1764 was a watershed for Goldsmith. First, he was admitted to the Literary Club, which brought together such luminaries as the actor David Garrick, the painter Joshua Reynolds, the politician Edmund Burke, and the writer Samuel Johnson. Second, he published *The Traveller*, which established him in the public's mind as one of the foremost poets of the day.

The success of *The Traveller* brought Goldsmith the first substantial income of his career, but because he

never was capable of careful financial management, he continued to do piecework as well as to engage in serious projects. The last decade of his life saw a remarkable output of rapidly written general works, haphazardly compiled anthologies, as well as his best poem, a novel, and two plays. Whatever effort he put into a project, his name on the title page enormously increased chances for a brisk sale.

Goldsmith wrote practically until the hour of his death. His last effort was the poem "Retaliation," a verse response to Garrick's teasing epigram. Goldsmith died on April 4, 1774, the victim of both a fever and the remedy prescribed to cure it.

ANALYSIS

Eighteenth century poets viewed themselves primarily in relation to their audience. They acted as intermediaries between the audience and some higher truth: divine providence, the majesty of state, or the ideal world described by art. In his verse, Oliver Goldsmith made two self-appointments: first as arbiter of literature for a society that had largely lost its ability to appreciate poetry and second as commentator on social changes. Arbitrating poetic ideals and offering social

Oliver Goldsmith (Library of Congress)

commentary were not separate activities, Goldsmith thought, because readers who could not discriminate real feeling in poetry were likewise not likely to observe the world around them accurately. Again, like other eighteenth century poets, Goldsmith expressed his concerns in both comic and serious works. The comic efforts tease readers back from excesses; the serious ones urge them to return to the norm. These trends are clearest in Goldsmith's best poems, two mock elegies, the didactic *The Traveller* and the pastoral *The Deserted Village*.

COMIC ELEGIES

Thomas Gray's "Elegy Written in a Country Churchyard" (1751) had started a fashion in poetry for sentimental reflections on occasions of death. This impulse, although quite natural, found further expression in lamenting the end of persons and things not traditionally the subjects of public mourning. (Gray himself parodied the fashion he had started with an ode on the death of a favorite cat who drowned while trying to snare a goldfish.) Goldsmith attacked this proliferation of laments in the *Critical Review* in 1759. Citing the corruption of the elegy, Goldsmith judged that his peers thought flattery, bombast, and sorrow sufficient ingredients to compose a moving poem. He also teased the popular mode of elegies with several mock versions; the best of these are "An Elegy on the Glory of Her Sex: Mrs. Mary Blaize" and "An Elegy on the Death of a Mad Dog." No other poems so well illustrate Goldsmith's comic ability.

Adapted from an older French poem, "An Elegy on the Glory of Her Sex: Mrs. Mary Blaize" laments with tongue in cheek the passing of a one-time strumpet turned pawnbroker. The poem's narrator strives hard to attribute conventional virtues of charity and probity to her, only to admit in the last line of each stanza to some qualification of the lady's virtue:

> She strove the neighbourhood to please,
> With manners wondrous winning,
> And never follow'd wicked ways,—
> *Unless when she was sinning.*

"An Elegy on the Death of a Mad Dog," which first appeared as a song in *The Vicar of Wakefield*, makes a similar point about the perversion of elegiac conven-

tions by telling of a "kind and gentle" man who befriended a dog "of low degree." At first they get along well, then the dog, "to gain some private ends," goes mad and bites the man. The townspeople lament that this good man must die a wretched death, betrayed by the ungrateful cur that he has trusted. In the final stanza, however, the poet twists the reader's sentimental expectation of a tragic ending: Instead of the man, it is the dog that dies.

THE TRAVELLER

Goldsmith had more serious issues to lay before his audience. His first major poem, *The Traveller*, attempts a philosophical survey of European life, showing, he declared in the dedication, that "there may be equal happiness in states that are governed differently from our own; that every state has a particular principle of happiness, and that this principle in each may be carried to a mischievous excess."

Condensing observations made on his trip to Europe into one moment, Goldsmith describes himself seated on a mountaintop in the Alps, from which he can look across to the great states of Europe: Italy, Switzerland, France, Holland, and Britain. Each land reveals to the poet's eye its special blessing—and its liability.

Italy, bountifully supplied by Nature and once the seat of empire, has been exhausted by the pursuit and burden of wealth; now peasant huts arise where once imperial buildings stood. Switzerland, less endowed by Nature, produces a self-reliant and hardy race that has few wants but cannot develop "the gentler morals" that are a hallmark of a refined culture. France, dedicated to the graces of civilized life, has developed the most brilliant society in Europe but one which is prey to ostentation and vanity. Holland, claimed from the sea by an industrious people, devotes its energies to commerce and trade that now accumulates superfluous treasure "that engenders craft and fraud." England, which Nature has treated neither too richly nor too miserly, is the home of Liberty and Freedom, which allow people to rule themselves; but self-rule in excess becomes party strife and colonial ambition.

Because every human society is imperfect, Goldsmith concludes, people must remember that human happiness is seldom regulated by laws or royal edicts. Since each of us is "to ourselves in every place consigned," the constant in life must be the "smooth current of domestic joy."

The Traveller echoes Goldsmith's favorite poets of the preceding generations and of his own time. Like Joseph Addison's "A Letter from Italy" (1703), it comments on England's political state by contrast with that of other European powers. Like Alexander Pope's *An Essay on Man* (1733-1734), it enunciates a philosophic principle in verse. Like Samuel Johnson's *The Vanity of Human Wishes* (1749), it concludes with the assertion that human happiness is determined by individual, not social experience. As derivative as *The Traveller* is, however, Goldsmith's poem is still his own. Less nationalistic than Addison's, less systematizing than Pope's, and less tragic than Johnson's, Goldsmith's poem possesses the graceful ease of the periodical essay whose tone is conversational and whose form mixes personal observation with public pronouncement. *The Traveller* is cast as an epistle to the poet's brother and as an account of the years of wandering that have led the poet to this meditation on human experience. The interest moves easily and naturally from the poet's wanderings to his social meditations, observations, and finally to philosophic insight. In the dedication to *The Traveller*, Goldsmith also laments the decay of poetry in a society verging on the "extremes of refinement." By echoing the themes and forms of earlier poets, Goldsmith offers his readers a return to the poetry of an age that brought the "greatest perfection" of the language. As he observed in *An History of England in a Series of Letters from a Nobleman to His Son* (1764), modern poets have only added finery to the muse's dress, not outfitted her anew.

THE DESERTED VILLAGE

The Deserted Village, 430 lines long, repeats the mixture of personal observation and public utterance. This time the topic is closer to home, the depopulation of the countryside because of a series of Enclosure Acts that turned formerly common village lands into private farms worked only for well-to-do landlords. Goldsmith observes that enclosure drives "a bold peasantry, their country's pride" into the city or away to the colonies. The poem is at once a lament for a lost way of life and a call to society to awaken to a danger.

The first 114 lines describe the poet's relationship to Auburn, the "loveliest village of the plain," an abstract, idealized version of Goldsmith's boyhood home. The poet recalls Auburn as a place of innocence where his youth was so happy that work and play were scarcely distinguishable. Now, like other villages, Auburn is "to hastening ills a prey"; these ills are trade, the growth of wealth, and the peasantry's departure from the land. The decline of Auburn darkens not only the poet's memory and civic pride but his hopes as well. Auburn was to be his place of retirement from life's cares where he might "die at home at last."

In the next 140 lines, the narrator surveys the buildings and inhabitants of Auburn: the church and the parsonage where the minister, "unpracticed he to fawn, or seek for power," kept a refuge to feed a hungry beggar, talk with an old soldier, and comfort the dying; the schoolhouse where the master, "a man severe and stern to view," shared with his pupils "the love he bore to learning"; and finally, the inn whose neat and trim interior played host to "greybeard mirth and smiling toil."

An equally long section then describes the present sad condition of Auburn. Imagining the village as a beautiful girl who turns increasingly to fashionable dress and cosmetics as her natural bloom fades, Goldsmith recounts how the "sons of wealth" force the peasantry off the land to build splendid estates with striking vistas. The displaced villagers trek to the cities, where pleasure seduces them from innocence or crime overcomes their honesty, or to the colonies, where a fiercer climate than England's threatens their lives. The section ends with a poignant description of families uprooted and friends or lovers separated as the people depart the village. With them "rural virtues leave the land."

The final section of the poem invokes "Sweet Poetry," which, like the inhabitants of Auburn, is being driven from the land. The poet hopes that poetry will nevertheless continue "to aid truth with [its] persuasive train" and teach humanity the age-old lesson that wealth ultimately destroys the simple virtues that bind people to the land and to one another.

The Deserted Village emphasizes that moral by a striking departure from literary convention. As a pastoral, the poem ought to persuade readers of the countryside's charms and goodness; as a pastoral it should express the ideals of peaceful virtue, harmony with nature, and productive use of the land that were commonplaces since classical Greek poetry. Goldsmith's poem presents these familiar ideas, but as a lament and a warning that the pastoral ideal is slipping away. Bound by tradition to use the conventions but unable to disguise the truth, the poet seeks to arouse rather than soothe the reader's imagination.

One of Goldsmith's most moving poetic devices in *The Deserted Village* is the catalog. At four crucial places, the narrative slows to allow leisurely description; these descriptive catalogs are composed of grammatically and metrically similar lines. The device is an elaboration of the neoclassical practice of balancing and paralleling couplets; its effect is to intensify the emotional impact of the passage. The catalog of the inn's furnishings is the most vivid of these passages and illustrates Goldsmith at his best.

FLAWED EXPERIMENTS

Trying his hand at many different styles and pieces, Goldsmith inevitably failed at some. "Threnodia Augustalis," for example, a poem mourning the death of the princess dowager of Wales, falls victim to the bombast and pomposity that Goldsmith laughed at in other elegiac poems. It shows how increasingly difficult had become the task of making poetic praise of the aristocracy sound convincing in an age when middle- and lower-class life was providing rich materials for the essay and the novel.

Another flawed poem is "Edwin and Angelina," a ballad of the type becoming more popular as the century progressed. Readers were drawn to this genre of folk poetry for its mysterious happenings in remote and romantic locations. Goldsmith tried to mix these qualities with the didactic strain of *The Traveller* and *The Deserted Village*. He tells of young lovers, separated by a cruel parent, who later meet while both are in disguise. The joy of their reunion is delayed while each delivers a long moral dissertation on the necessity of steadfast virtue and trust in Providence.

"The Captivity: An Oratorio" is a more ambitious treatment of the same theme but equally unsuccessful. Goldsmith makes a promising start by using the Israelite bondage in Babylon—a subject hardly ever treated in the literature of the age—as the frame for his moral,

but he simply does not have a poetic vocabulary capable of describing spiritual anguish. When, early in the poem, a prophet urges the Israelites to repent and "offer up a tear," the poem has reached its deepest point of profundity.

OTHER MAJOR WORKS

LONG FICTION: *The Vicar of Wakefield*, 1766.

SHORT FICTION: *The Citizen of the World*, 1762 (collection of fictional letters first published in *The Public Ledger*, 1760-1761).

PLAYS: *The Good-Natured Man*, pr., pb. 1768; *She Stoops to Conquer: Or, The Mistakes of a Night*, pr., pb. 1773.

NONFICTION: *The Bee*, 1759 (essays); *An Enquiry into the Present State of Polite Learning in Europe*, 1759; *The Life of Richard Nash of Bath*, 1762; *An History of England in a Series of Letters from a Nobleman to His Son*, 1764 (2 volumes); *Life of Henry St. John, Lord Viscount Bolingbroke*, 1770; *Life of Thomas Parnell*, 1770; *An History of the Earth, and Animated Nature*, 1774 (8 volumes; unfinished).

MISCELLANEOUS: *The Collected Works of Oliver Goldsmith*, 1966 (5 volumes; Arthur Friedman, editor).

BIBLIOGRAPHY

Dixon, Peter. *Oliver Goldsmith Revisited*. Boston: Twayne, 1991. An updated introduction to the life and works of Goldsmith.

Hopkins, Robert H. *The True Genius of Oliver Goldsmith*. Baltimore: The Johns Hopkins University Press, 1969. Hopkins interprets Goldsmith not in the traditional view as a sentimental humanist but as a master of satire and irony. The chapter "Augustanisms and the Moral Basis for Goldsmith's Art" delineates the social, intellectual, and literary context in which Goldsmith wrote. Hopkins devotes a chapter each to Goldsmith's crafts of persuasion, satire, and humor.

Kazmin, Roman. "Oliver Goldsmith's *The Traveller* and *The Deserted Village*: Moral Economy of Landscape Representation." *English Studies* 87, no. 6 (December, 2006): 65. A critical study of Goldsmith's view of England's social problems.

Lucy, Séan, ed. *Goldsmith: The Gentle Master*. Cork,

Ireland: Cork University Press, 1984. This short but useful collection of essays provides interesting biographical material on Goldsmith, as well as critical comment on his works.

Lytton Sells, Arthur. *Oliver Goldsmith: His Life and Works.* New York: Barnes and Noble, 1974. This volume is divided into two sections on Goldsmith's life and works, respectively. Individual chapters focus on particular facets of Goldsmith's work ("The Critic," "The Journalist," "The Biographer") and also feature more detailed studies of major works. Contains an extended discussion of Goldsmith as dramatist and poet.

Mikhail, E. H., ed. *Goldsmith: Interviews and Recollections.* New York: St. Martin's Press, 1993. Contains interviews with Goldsmith's friends and associates. Includes bibliographical references and index.

Quintana, Richard. *Oliver Goldsmith: A Georgian Study.* New York: Macmillan, 1967. This work incorporates biography and criticism in a readable account of Goldsmith's colorful life and his development as a writer. Goldsmith's many literary genres are discussed in depth, with chapters on his poetry, drama, essays, and fiction. A lengthy appendix offers notes on Goldsmith's lesser writings, such as his biographical and historical works.

Rousseau, G. S., ed. *Goldsmith: The Critical Heritage.* London: Routledge & Kegan Paul, 1974. A record of critical comment on Goldsmith, this volume is organized by particular works with an additional section on Goldsmith's life and general works. This anthology extends only as far as 1912, but pieces by Goldsmith's contemporaries, such as Sir Joshua Reynolds's sketch of Goldsmith's character, and by later critics such as William Hazlitt and Washington Irving, offer interesting perspectives on Goldsmith's place in literary history.

Swarbrick, Andrew, ed. *The Art of Oliver Goldsmith.* Totowa, N.J.: Barnes and Noble, 1984. This excellent collection of ten essays offers a wide-ranging survey of the works of Goldsmith. Essays treat individual works (*The Citizen of the World*, *The Deserted Village*, *The Traveller*), as well as more general topics such as the literary context in which Goldsmith wrote, the elements of classicism in his works, and his place in the Anglo-Irish literary tradition.

Worth, Katharine. *Sheridan and Goldsmith.* New York: St. Martin's Press, 1992. Worth compares and contrasts the lives and works of Goldsmith and Richard Brinsley Sheridan. Bibliography and index.

Robert M. Otten

JOHN GOWER

Born: Kent(?), England; c. 1330
Died: Southwark, England; October, 1408

PRINCIPAL POETRY
Cinkante Ballades, probably before 1374
Mirour de l'Omme, 1376-1379
Vox Clamantis, 1379-1382
Confessio Amantis, 1386-1390
Traitié pour Essampler Les Amantz marietz, 1397
Cronica Tripertita, 1400
In Praise of Peace, 1400
The Complete Works of John Gower, 1899-1902, 1968 (G. C. Macaulay, editor)
The Major Latin Works of John Gower: The Voice of One Crying and the Tripartite Chronicle, 1962 (Eric W. Stockton, translator)
The Minor Latin Works, 2005 (R. F. Yeager, editor and translator)

OTHER LITERARY FORMS
John Gower (GOW-ur) is remembered only for his poetry. A fine craftsperson, he holds a secure place in English poetry even when compared to his friend and the major poet of his time, Geoffrey Chaucer.

ACHIEVEMENTS
In his own lifetime and in the generations immediately following, John Gower's reputation as one of England's primary poets, second only to Chaucer himself, was secure and unquestioned. Gower wrote, and wrote competently, major poetic works in three languages: French, Latin, and English. With Chaucer, Gower was

instrumental in adapting the polished French style to English poetry, and his preeminence is recognized by his successors from John Lydgate to Sir Philip Sidney.

Gower's critical reputation began to decline sharply, however, in the seventeenth century, and it has never completely recovered. There were at least three major reasons for this decline. First, because of certain revisions in his works reflecting the political situation of the late fourteenth century, Gower has often been considered a political opportunist and sycophant. Second, it has been conjectured that another revision in his *Confessio Amantis* is evidence that Gower had a bitter and unresolved quarrel with his friend Chaucer. Third, Gower's works have been considered to be rather dull. The first two of these charges have nothing whatever to do with the quality of Gower's poetry and, in fact, are probably unfounded. The third charge is much more difficult to answer. It is certainly true that the *Mirour de l'Omme* and to some extent the *Vox Clamantis* are for the most part unpalatable to modern readers, though this is chiefly the result of a shift in taste away from the popular medieval mode of the *complaint*, which was generalized in content and moralistic in purpose. Gower's great English work, *Confessio Amantis*, is less overtly didactic and reveals the poet's real talent for imaginative storytelling.

Although Gower no longer receives the undeserved high praise of being placed second only to Chaucer, he is nevertheless recognized today as a poet of no small talent, though perhaps without Chaucer's genius. He was a superb craftsperson, whose verses in both French and English have a smoothness and a polish that Chaucer never achieves, although the regularity may at times become monotonous. Furthermore, Gower the craftsperson had a keen interest in unity and form. For example, he imposed a careful and rigid structure, whether based on the seven deadly sins or the three estates, upon his *complaint* material. There is also reason to believe that the many revisions he made in his major works during his lifetime were at least in part an attempt to forge them into a single, unified whole: John H. Fisher (*John Gower*, 1964) sees them as a three-part discourse on the nature of humankind and of society, and the need for each individual, but particularly the king, to follow reason and natural law for the common profit.

BIOGRAPHY

John Gower was born about 1330. That he was a Kentishman is indicated by several aspects of his English verse that were characteristic of the fourteenth century Kentish dialect. It has been suggested that he was descended from the Gower family of Langburgh, Yorkshire, and that he moved to Kent at an early age. This must remain conjecture, however, since no documentation exists, and little is known of Gower's early life. He was almost certainly a member of an upper-middle-class family and perhaps was a retainer in some noble house.

During the period 1365 to 1374, Gower was involved in a number of speculative real estate transactions in Kent. He may have been a lawyer, since his works display a keen knowledge of the legal profession. Probably about this time Gower was writing the short love poems in French that would later be collected in the *Cinkante Ballades*. Gower could have become familiar with French courtly poetry had he been connected in his youth to a noble household. However, the ballades show little influence of the contemporary school of French poetry, and Fisher has conjectured that he may have written the poems for the London *Pui*, a semireligious middle-class fraternal organization that held poetical contests at its feasts.

By the mid-1370's, Gower's literary career reached a turning point, as he became at once more ambitious and more sober. One influence could have been his association with Chaucer, which may have begun about that time, since by 1378, when Chaucer left for Italy, they were close enough for Chaucer to have given Gower his power of attorney. Gower now set his mind on a very moralistic and very long French poem, the *Mirour de l'Omme*. He followed this almost immediately by another moralizing poem, this time in Latin, called *Vox Clamantis*. In the first book of this poem, Gower presents a vivid and frightening picture of the Peasant's Revolt of 1381, from the perspective of a conservative, upper-middle-class landholder. He sees in the revolt the concrete epitome of the abstract evils of the world that he describes at length in the *Mirour de l'Omme* and the remainder of the *Vox Clamantis*.

By the late 1370's, Gower seems to have already begun his relationship with the Priory of St. Mary

Overeys in Southwark. He was a major benefactor of the priory, and he possibly contributed largely to its restoration in 1377. He is known to have lived in a personal apartment in the priory by the late 1390's and may have been living there for years, having been granted the living space in return for his charitable contributions. There is a strong possibility that many of the Gower manuscripts, which suggest authorial supervision in their excellence, may have been produced at the priory under Gower's watchful eye.

About 1386, King Richard II requested that Gower write something in English, and this marked a second turning point in his literary career, since in writing *Confessio Amantis* Gower was able to develop his real talent as a storyteller. But the different versions of *Confessio Amantis* also provide a good indication of Gower's relationship with the king. In the first version of *Vox Clamantis*, Gower had excused the young king from blame for the state of affairs in England, and exhorted him to follow after the example of his father, the Black Prince. The first version of *Confessio Amantis* in 1390 still presents the king in a good light. It also makes a flattering allusion to Chaucer as a poet of Venus. Later that year, Gower revised the poem, leaving out his earlier praise of Richard's rule, and in 1393, he revised it again, rededicating the work to Henry, earl of Derby (later to become Henry IV), and, incidentally, leaving out the praise of Chaucer. This latter action has caused some to speculate that a quarrel had occurred between the two poets, perhaps over Chaucer's good-humored jibes in the Man of Law's prologue at the "moral" Gower's shameful stories of incest in *Confessio Amantis*. However, the dropping of the Chaucer allusion may be explained in other ways. Gower may have left it out simply because he wanted to eliminate exactly the same number of lines as he was adding with his new dedication. He may even have dropped the lines because he knew that Richard would not like the revisions he had made, and Gower did not want to jeopardize Chaucer's favorable position with the king. On the other hand, Henry seems to have appreciated the dedication, for in 1393, he gave Gower a gift of a ceremonial collar.

Gower's opinion of Richard seems to have continued to deteriorate, for he also revised the *Vox Cla-*

mantis and replaced the passages excusing the king's youth with lines of stern admonition about the state of affairs in England. Gower welcomed the deposition of Richard and ascension of Henry IV in 1399 and wrote in the *Cronica Tripertita* a rather distorted history justifying Henry's assumption of royal power. Henry recognized Gower's loyal support, granting him an annuity of two pipes of wine on November 21, 1399.

By this time, Gower's health was failing. On January 25, 1398, nearly seventy years old, he married Agnes Groundolf, who was almost certainly his nurse. Perhaps Gower had been married before, but there is no record of it. During his final years while Agnes took care of him at St. Mary's, Gower was unable to do much writing, for he went totally blind in about 1401. Gower's will was attested on August 15, 1408, and proved on October 24 of that year. In it, he generously remembered Agnes and the canons of the priory, and gave his body to be buried in the churchyard there. The effigy can still be seen at Southwark Cathedral. It depicts Gower's head resting on three large volumes—the *Speculum Meditantis* (another name for the *Mirour de l'Omme*), the *Vox Clamantis*, and *Confessio Amantis*—upon which he wanted his posthumous reputation to rest.

ANALYSIS

Anyone who reads only a few lines of John Gower's poetry cannot help being struck by its intentional didacticism. Imaginative writing was typically didactic during the medieval age, but Gower's moralistic streak was so pronounced that it prompted his good friend Chaucer to apply the adjective that has been inseparable from the poet's name since it first appeared in *Troilus and Criseyde* (1382): "the moral Gower."

Since it seems clear that Gower thought of himself first as a moralist and only secondarily as a poet, any examination of Gower's poetry must concentrate chiefly upon theme. With Gower, the theme was nothing new or unusual; he was not an original thinker, but spoke with a voice rooted in tradition and mirroring the attitudes of the conservative, upper middle class to which he belonged. What is remarkable is the persistence of Gower's chief theme through his three major works, the *Mirour de l'Omme*, *Vox Clamantis*, and

Confessio Amantis; with almost monotonous consistency Gower stresses the degeneracy of the contemporary world because of the perversion and distortion of love. The love of which Gower speaks is the universal, divine love that in medieval thought (particularly as popularized in Boethius's *De consolatione philosophiae*, 523; *The Consolation of Philosophy*, late ninth century; and Ambrosius Theodosius Macrobius's *In somnium Scipionis* (c. 400, *Commentary on the "Dream of Scipio,"* 1952) was regarded as binding the universe in an ordered harmony. This universal order is divine law; thus law and love are immutably connected.

It is society in which Gower is chiefly interested. The laws governing society—human or "positive" law—should reflect the love and order of natural law, which humanity's reason should recognize. Fisher, who was first to realize the importance of this concept of nature and human law in Gower's three major works, calls those works a trilogy that takes its entire structure and meaning from this law/love idea. Thus Gower stresses the importance of individual reason and virtue in conjunction with legal justice that preserves the moral order for the common profit. For Gower, this meant preservation of the social order as well, and so the Peasants' Revolt of 1381, for example, becomes in the *Vox Clamantis* an illustration of humans rebelling against reason and natural law.

In addition, this preservation of law and order meant that the king occupied a uniquely vital position. Gower constantly stresses the importance of the principle of kingship in an ordered society. The king is charged with the responsibility of preserving legal justice and order among all three estates (clergy, nobility, and peasantry) and maintaining the moral integrity of the entire nation. This belief goes far in explaining Gower's shifting attitude toward Richard II and his ultimate allegiance to Henry IV as a king more likely to fulfill this obligation. Important in Gower's evaluation of Richard was his absolute insistence on humans' responsibility for their own actions. He consistently attacks fatalism and the idea of the "wheel of Fortune," stressing instead the responsibility of every individual, particularly the ruler, to follow the dictates of reason.

Gower's revisions of his main works reflect this disintegrating opinion of Richard and link the three works

to form a complete and systematic commentary on humanity and society. The encyclopedic nature of such an undertaking was typical of the Middle Ages, but Gower's concern for unity and form was rare. His moral theme and the influence of other didactic treatises of his day suggested to him two particular organizing formulas: the seven deadly sins and the three estates. While it may be argued that such formulas provide arbitrary and artificial patterns of organization, it cannot be denied that Gower's preoccupation with order and unity is strong; it may, in fact, reflect the theme of order so loudly proclaimed in the three works: form matches content.

Miroir de l'Omme

Gower's earliest major work is the *Miroir de l'Omme*, which he refers to in later life as the *Speculum Hominis* and, finally, the *Speculum Meditantis*, the alterations being an attempt to bring the earlier poem's title into harmony with *Vox Clamantis* and *Confessio Amantis* to suggest the close relationship of the three works. The *Miroir de l'Omme* survives in a single manuscript discovered in the Cambridge University Library in 1895 by Gower's great editor, G. C. Macaulay. The manuscript consists of 28,603 octosyllabic lines of French verse, although the absence of several leaves at the beginning and end indicate that the complete poem must have been some two thousand lines longer. The verse form is a twelve-line stanza known as a Héliland strophe, popular among French moral writers of the period. The lines rhyme *aabaabbaabaa*, and the stanzas generally contain a pause in the middle and a moral tag or summing up at the end, in the last two or three lines. Macaulay describes Gower's verse as strictly syllabic, while at the same time displaying a distinct English rhythm. He also stresses the uncanny regularity of the lines, finding only twenty-one of the more than 28,000 lines in the poem to be metrically imperfect.

Gower's main concern in the *Miroir de l'Omme* is his constant theme of the decay of the world and society because of humanity's turning from reason. He begins by calling sin the cause of all evils in the world, and in the first main section of the poem, Gower presents a manual of vices and virtues and delineates the efforts of the Devil and Sin to conquer man. Sin, it is said, was conceived by the Devil, who, enamored of his own creation, engendered upon her Death. Death, following his father's lead, likewise intermarried with Sin and produced the seven deadly vices. The Devil then held a conference with his whole brood and with the World to plan how they might best defeat God's plan and circumvent man's salvation. The parallel between this and John Milton's *Paradise Lost* (1667, 1674) is of course striking, although it seems unlikely that Milton could have read the *Mirour de l'Omme*: As far as is known, there was no manuscript available in his time. Still, no common source has been found, so the problem of the relationship of the two works is unresolved.

In Gower's work, the Devil is unsuccessful in his first attempt to win man over, since after much debate man follows the dictates of Reason. The Devil, however, increases his forces. After the seven daughters of sin marry the World, each has five daughters of her own, so that for some nine thousand lines, Gower delineates the five branches of each of the seven deadly sins. The entire progeny of vices then violently attack man, who comes completely under the power of Sin. God retaliates by sending seven virtues to marry Reason, and each of these has five daughters, to counter the thirty-five vices already described.

In the second main section of the poem, the next eight thousand lines, the author proposes to examine human society to determine whether the vices or the virtues are winning. Thus, Gower begins a complaint on the estates of man, reviewing every class of human society, beginning with the clergy, and moving through secular rulers, to the common people. Every rank of society is corrupt, according to Gower. The tone here is unrelentingly somber, yet this is probably the most interesting section of the *Mirour de l'Omme* because of the picture it gives modern readers of life in fourteenth century England. The descriptions are generally stock, but not necessarily untrue, and may be worth reading for the sake of comparison with Chaucer's estates satire in the general prologue to *The Canterbury Tales* (1387-1400): Here Gower describes a gluttonous monk who loves hunting, a venal friar who abuses the office of the confessional by taking advantage of young women, a physician in collusion with the apothecary to bilk his patients, and shopkeepers who engage in any number of tricks to cheat customers—such as the tavern keeper

who is able to get all the wines of Europe from a single cask. In Gower's world view, the order of society reflected the divinely ordained harmony of the universe. Reason and the law of love kept all in order. Thus rebellion was tantamount to revolt against God and, because it perverted reason, turned men into beasts.

Having described the origin of sin and the effect of sin on society, Gower ends with a discussion of what man must do to be reconciled with God. Man must reform and pray to the Virgin to intercede for him; thus the poem ends with a Life of the Virgin. What is thematically most important in this section is Gower's insistence upon man's responsibility for his own actions. The condition of the world and society cannot be blamed on the stars, says Gower, nor are plants, birds, and fish at fault, since they follow the law of nature. Man is to blame: He is a microcosm and the chaotic state of the world reflects his sin.

In the final analysis, the *Mirour de l'Omme* is not a great poem. It is not even, by most standards, a very good poem. Its organization and versification are admirable, and it gives a useful picture of its age, and there are flashes of good poetry in the complaint on the estates, but the unity is destroyed by the poem's inordinate length and monotony. Perhaps its relation to Gower's other major works is of chief interest: written in French, the *Mirour de l'Omme* was intended as a "mirror" in which one of the cultivated French-speaking laity might examine his conscience. Personal virtue and individual responsibility are the themes, and from here Gower could expand into the areas of legal justice and royal responsibility.

VOX CLAMANTIS

Gower's second major work, the *Vox Clamantis*, is a poem in seven books, consisting of some 10,265 lines of Latin elegiac verse. Gower's Latin lacks the smoothness and regularity of his French and English compositions, and the style is further muddled by his extensive wholesale borrowings from other Latin poems. Eric Stockton, the poem's modern translator, enumerates thirteen hundred lines that were appropriated chiefly from Ovid, the *Aurora* (started c. 1170) of Petrus Riga, and *De Vita Monachorum*; nevertheless, in spite of the patchwork of sources, Gower keeps the train of thought coherent, and the fact that the poem survives in ten manuscripts, four produced in Gower's lifetime, attests to the work's popularity.

This popularity, in contrast with the *Mirour de l'Omme*, is due in part to the more public nature of the *Vox Clamantis*. The subject matter—a critique of the three estates—is essentially the same as the second part of the *Mirour de l'Omme*, but the use of Latin suggests that Gower's concern is now not so much with the individual virtue stressed in the French poem as with the consequences of individual morality in human society. Thus he uses the universal language, and by aligning himself through his title with the messianic prophets Isaiah and John the Baptist, he implies that his words are divinely inspired.

The poem begins with what has been justly praised as the most powerful part of the *Vox Clamantis*: a vivid allegorical description of the Peasant's Revolt of 1381. The revolt is seen as a concrete manifestation of the consequences of individual sin for society as a whole: disintegration and chaos, a society rushing madly toward its own apocalyptic destruction. This first book begins as a dream vision. The narrator, after a fearful night, has a dream in which he sees moving across the fields bands of people suddenly changed, through God's wrath, into the forms of beasts. Here Gower graphically pictures how the failure of man to follow the dictates of reason degrades him and makes him bestial. The men turn into asses, swine, frogs, and flies, and oxen who refuse to eat straw or to be subject to the yoke—a description corresponding closely to Gower's condemnation of the peasantry at the end of the *Mirour de l'Omme*. Wat Tyler is pictured as a jay skilled in speech, inciting the peasants, who bring chaos to society by upsetting the ordered hierarchy that reflects the harmony inherent in natural law.

Book 1 continues with a description of the ferocious sacking of London, called "New Troy," and the murder of the archbishop of Canterbury, Simon Sudbury. Although the historical accuracy of Gower's account may be questionable, it does present a clear picture of the horror that a middle-class Londoner must have felt at the time. The narrator flees to the forests but can find no refuge until he escapes aboard a ship, apparently the ship of faith. He lands in the isle of Britain, whose inhabitants have through violence done away with law

and justice, though they could be the greatest people on earth if they could learn love. Gower again stresses love, the binding force of the universe, as the glue to hold society together.

How did society fall so low? Gower begins book 2, apparently the original opening of the poem, by emphasizing once again man's moral responsibility: Men like to blame Fortune for their problems, but this is merely shirking responsibility. Man is to blame for all evil in the world. This Gower follows by four books criticizing the three estates (clergy, nobility, and peasantry) in a manner similar to that of the *Mirour de l'Omme*. Again, Gower presents an interesting picture of the age, but one that lacks the realistic detail of Chaucer's satire or Langland's. Lechery and avarice are the most common vices. The two most vivid sections are, first, the description of the smaller merchants and artisans of London—the bakers, butchers, jewelers, and the like, all in the service of fraud that make the bustle of the city real for the reader—and, second, the vehement condemnation of all connected with the law, for law is turned into a device to make money, rather than a reflection of divine order.

In book 6, Gower specifically addresses the duties of the king, which are seen chiefly in terms of legal justice: The king should avoid sin and protect all laws and should rule peaceably and with love. It has been noted how Gower excused King Richard in the first version of the *Vox Clamantis* but indicts him in the second; in the final version, to which Gower appended the *Cronica Tripertita*, the fall of the king is portrayed as the direct consequence of the evils of his reign. Thus, Gower's conviction of the moral responsibility of the king for preserving the order of the state seems to have grown stronger as time went on.

After his address to the king, Gower returns to the general degeneration of the world from its former state. The theme of a golden past is brought out by a series of biblical and historical allusions that illustrate the world's decay. Book 7 begins with a description of the statue of Nebuchadnezzar's dream: The statue's golden head, representing the golden age, has been chopped off, and only the feet of iron and clay remain, symbolizing the ironlike hearts of the avaricious and the weak flesh of the lustful in the degenerate present.

The theme is not unlike that of Chaucer's "The Former Age." In fact, several of Chaucer's philosophical "Boethian" lyrics parallel parts of the *Vox Clamantis*: In book 6, chapter 14, Gower reminds the king that true nobility comes from virtue rather than birth—the theme of "Gentilesse." At the end of chapter 18, Gower begs the king to restore the laws and banish evil, in lines recalling the envoy to "Lak of Stedfastnesse." Since Chaucer translated Boethius in 1380, when Gower would have been writing this poem, it is interesting to speculate upon an exchange of ideas between the two poets.

The entire *Vox Clamantis* ends with a striking memento mori. Asserting again how man, the microcosm, perverts all creation when he sins, Gower gives the notion a gruesome twist by describing how the forms of putrefaction suffered by the flesh after death parallel the seven deadly sins: The avaricious man has now no coffer but a coffin; the wrathful man cannot now frighten away the worm devouring his heart. "As ye sin, so shall ye rot" seems to be the rule. Death comes to all; therefore, it is time now to repent. Gower ends by lamenting the condition of England, which not only is full of sin but also as a result lacks justice. An apocalypse is in store unless the nation repents and finds its way back to justice.

Thus, the *Vox Clamantis* ends as it began—with a clear emphasis upon the social consequences of the individual sins enumerated in the complaint on the estates. Reform is needed in society from the top down and in each person, but particularly in the king himself. Gower now needed to elaborate upon royal responsibility and its relation to love, and that is the theme of Gower's last and greatest work.

CONFESSIO AMANTIS

When Gower began to write in English, he also changed his approach to his theme and made it more subtle. According to the prologue to *Confessio Amantis*, Richard II gave Gower a commission for the poem, so Gower decided to write "in oure englissh." Since the audience was the court, Gower took the fashionable courtly love tradition as his starting point. In the "religion of love" vein, Gower structured his book as a confessional manual for a lover, full of tales illustrating the various sins against love, in the framework of the

seven deadly sins with Genius, priest of Venus, as confessor. Chaucer's *The Legend of Good Women* (1380-1386), a courtly love parody of the *Golden Legend*, may have sprung from the same royal command and may have been intended as a companion piece to *Confessio Amantis*. Gower, however, showed much more enthusiasm for the task, compiling a work of thirty-three thousand lines. The less moralistic approach and more accessible English language made this Gower's most popular work: Some forty manuscripts survive, and the book was printed by Caxton.

However, *Confessio Amantis* is apparently only a retreat from moralism. That it is deliberately intended to begin where the *Vox Clamantis* leaves off is apparent when the statue of Nebuchadnezzar's dream that ended the *Vox Clamantis* reappears in the prologue to *Confessio Amantis*. Also in the prologue, Gower again stresses his favorite themes: the decay of society and the world because of moral corruption and the destruction of reason; the corruption of the three estates, for which man must take full responsibility; and the disorder in creation mirroring the disorder in the microcosm, man. It is further asserted that society is chaotic because love, the creative principle that brings unity, is gone.

Most readers have seen this prologue as irrelevant to the love theme of the confession itself. The intended connection, however, is obvious: The world is in decay because of a lack of love, of *caritas*. The confessor, through his exemplary tales, instructs the lover in governing his passion through reason. Even the casual reader cannot help noticing that most of the tales do not take romantic love as their theme. In the "Tale of Constantine and Sylvester" (book 2), for example, Constantine recognizes that the urging of natural law, that universal principle of love, calls for pity—treating others as you would have them treat you. This has nothing to do with courtly love but reveals Gower's larger purpose. In the conclusion of *Confessio Amantis*, the lover is revealed to be too old for love—a poignant reminder of the transience of earthly love, *cupiditas*—and is advised to pursue instead the love (*caritas*) that does not end and that leads to the common profit.

The implication is that reason, in the end, has triumphed over blind passion and set the lover on the true course of love. This implies another of Gower's chief themes, delineated at length in the tales of *Confessio Amantis*: individual moral responsibility. Because man is endowed with reason, he must use it to direct his will to the good and not be overcome by passion, for this is disorder and sin. Derek Pearsall has shown that Gower's characters move in a world where human behavior has definite meaning, and where they are morally responsible for the consequences of their actions. Thus Gower's revisions of his sources often take the form of providing motives, or relating cause to effect. In the "Tale of Constantine," for example, Gower declares that charity never goes unrewarded, so Constantine's leprosy is cured. In the "Tale of Tereus" (book 3), from Ovid, Tereus becomes enamored of Philomene "with all his hole entente," and when he rapes her "he no reson understod." He is compared to a wolf, a lion, a hound—Gower depicts the bestiality of man without Reason. Clearly Tereus is morally culpable, and Gower also adds Philomene's prayer to Jupiter, in which she states that the god suffers many wrongs to be done, but that the evil is not his will. The point Gower makes is that man, specifically Tereus, is responsible for the evil. Thus what in Ovid is a tale of blind lust and barbarism is in Gower a tale of moral retribution.

The general theme of the tales is humanity's moral responsibility for the world's disorder, but it must be remembered that the original audience was the king. More than anyone else, the king must be a responsible moral agent, since he is accountable for the stability of the whole realm. Thus Gower adds book 7, on the education of Alexander. G. C. Macaulay and C. S. Lewis both considered this a digression; its central importance, however, is clear, given the whole corpus of Gower's poetry. *Confessio Amantis* moves from a look at the chaos in the world because of the absence of love, to an indictment of individuals through the exemplary tales, to a specific exhortation to the king to be himself a morally responsible being and so return the discordant realm to harmony. A king should learn chiefly five points of policy: truth, largess, justice, pity, and chastity. Central to these is justice: The king must be subject to God and follow the law, and he must ensure that legal justice prevails. Most edifying in book 7 is the tale of

Lygurgius, prince of Athens, who, having obtained his subjects' promise never to change the laws in his absence, left the city never to return, having established laws "only for love and for justice" to further "the comun profit."

Gower's concern with universal love and the common profit is presented rather abstractly in the *Mirour de l'Omme* and *Vox Clamantis*. In *Confessio Amantis*, however, where Gower must use exempla to illustrate different virtues and vices, his deep human compassion is manifest in his treatment of characters. Even in extreme cases, such as the "Tale of Canace" and her incestuous relationship with her brother (book 3), Gower can be sympathetic: He excuses the lovers because they simply follow natural law—incest is forbidden only by positive (human) law. It is the father, King Eolus, whose wrath kills Canace and her child, and who must be seen as morally culpable. Gower's addition to the story of Canace's address to her brother and the pathetic detail of the baby playing in his mother's warm blood serve to sentimentalize the tale and win the reader's sympathy for the victims.

This streak of compassion in the moral Gower is what makes *Confessio Amantis* so appealing. Not only the characters in the tales, but also those of the frame story are treated with sympathetic understanding. The lover, for instance, is very sympathetic: He is a pathetic and very human character who will obviously never win his love. He seems eminently real in his envy of his rivals, his eagerness to do little things for his lady, his practical aversion to going abroad to win fame in arms to impress his lady and possibly losing her to someone else while he is gone, and in the lover's humorous confession that he has never been late for a date with his love since she has never given him one.

Confessio Amantis, then, can be read for its own sake; one need not look in it only to find in the "Tale of Florent" (book 1) or the "Tale of Constance" (book 2), analogues of Chaucer's "The Wife of Bath's Tale" and "The Man of Law's Tale," or to read "Apollonius of Tyre" as the source of William Shakespeare's *Pericles, Prince of Tyre* (pr. c. 1607-1608). It may be in the end that Gower turns out to be an artist in spite of himself. His verse is neither ornate nor ambiguous nor complex; he was rather a consummate craftsperson whose English octosyllabic couplets are almost monotonously smooth and regular. Lewis called him England's first master of the "plain style," and Peter Fison noted that the verse deliberately avoids calling attention to itself. Perhaps Gower's aim was not to detract from the moral, which for him was poetry's most important aspect, but in *Confessio Amantis*, this style serves very well to focus attention on the action of the tale. Furthermore, Gower's concern for cause and effect, for the consequences of moral actions, leads to well-plotted tales, even as his concern for charity as a motivating factor in human actions helps to make his characters sympathetic. Thus, the techniques that Gower cultivated to further his primary moral purpose contributed ultimately to his secondary, aesthetic ends. As a result, when Gower is read today, it is for his skill as a storyteller as demonstrated in some of the tales of *Confessio Amantis*, and not for the very conscious morality of that or any other work.

BIBLIOGRAPHY

Bakalian, Ellen Shaw. *Aspects of Love in John Gowers' "Confessio Amantis."* New York: Routledge, 2004. The four chapters of this work examine the struggle between nature and reason, marriage and the four wives, the forsaken women, and lovesickness.

Bullón-Fernández, María. *Fathers and Daughters in Gower's "Confessio Amantis."* Rochester, N.Y.: Brewer, 2000. This volume in the John Gower Society's monograph series examines Gower's works from a feminist perspective. Bibliographical references, index.

Echard, Siân, ed. *A Companion to Gower.* Rochester, N.Y.: D. S. Brewer, 2004. This work examines all aspects of Gower, presenting a chronology of criticism about him and examining his legacy.

Kendall, Elliot Richard. *Lordship and Literature: John Gower and the Politics of the Great Household.* Oxford, England: Clarendon Press, 2008. Looks at Gower's political position and how it affected his poetry.

Nicholson, Peter. *Love and Ethics in Gower's "Confessio Amantis."* Ann Arbor: University of Michigan Press, 2005. Nicholson helps the modern reader understand the work and discusses it as both a poem and work of moral instruction.

Urban, Malte. *Fragments: Past and Present in Chaucer and Gower.* New York: Peter Lang 2009. The works of Geoffrey Chaucer and Gower are compared and contrasted, and their relationship is discussed.

Watt, Diane. *Amoral Gower: Language, Sex, and Politics.* Minneapolis: University of Minnesota Press, 2003. Discusses the themes of sex, language, and politics in Gower's works, particularly in *Confessio Amantis*.

White, Hugh. *Nature, Sex, and Goodness in a Medieval Literary Tradition.* New York: Oxford University Press, 2000. A thematic and historical examination of thirteenth and fourteenth century English and European literature, including, along with Gower, Guillaume de Lorris, Alanus de Insulis, Geoffrey Chaucer, and Jean de Meung.

Yeager, R. F., ed. *On John Gower: Essays at the Millennium.* Studies in Medieval Culture 46. Kalamazoo, Mich.: Medieval Institute Publications, 2007. A collection of more than ten essays covering the various works by Gower. Topics include holy fear and poetics in *Confessio Amantis*.

_____. *Re-visioning Gower.* Asheville, N.C.: Pegasus Press, 1998. A collection of essays presented at the meetings of the John Gower Society at the International Congress on Medieval Studies, Western Michigan University, 1992-1997. Includes bibliographical references.

Yeager, R. F., and A. J. Minnis, eds. *John Gower's Poetic: The Search for a New Arion.* Rochester, N.Y.: Boydell and Brewer, 1990. Presents the idea that Gower was a serious student in the matter of language. To reinforce this claim, Yeager offers chapters that include studies of Gower's stylistics and transformations. Contains extensive footnotes and a complete index. This work offers a refreshing perspective of interest to any student of the literature of Gower.

Jay Ruud

ROBERT GRAVES

Born: Wimbledon, Surrey, England; July 24, 1895
Died: Deyá, Majorca, Spain; December 7, 1985
Also known as: John Doyle; Barbara Rich (with
  Laura Riding)

PRINCIPAL POETRY

Goliath and David, 1916
Over the Brazier, 1916
Fairies and Fusiliers, 1917
Treasure Box, 1919
Country Sentiment, 1920
The Pier-Glass, 1921
The Feather Bed, 1923
Whipperginny, 1923
Mock Beggar Hall, 1924
The Marmosite's Miscellany, 1925 (as John Doyle)
Welchman's Hose, 1925
Poems, 1914-1926, 1927
Poems, 1914-1927, 1927
Poems, 1929, 1929
Ten Poems More, 1930
Poems, 1926-1930, 1931
To Whom Else?, 1931
Poems, 1930-1933, 1933
Collected Poems, 1938
No More Ghosts: Selected Poems, 1940
Work in Hand, 1942 (with others)
Poems, 1938-1945, 1946
Collected Poems, 1914-1947, 1948
Poems and Satires, 1951, 1951
Poems, 1953, 1953
Collected Poems, 1955, 1955
Poems Selected by Himself, 1957
The Poems of Robert Graves Chosen by Himself,
  1958
Collected Poems, 1959, 1959
The Penny Fiddle: Poems for Children, 1960
Collected Poems, 1961
More Poems, 1961, 1961
*The More Deserving Cases: Eighteen Old Poems
  for Reconsideration*, 1962
New Poems, 1962, 1962

Ann at Highwood Hall: Poems for Children, 1964
Man Does, Woman Is, 1964
Collected Poems, 1965, 1965
Love Respelt, 1965
Seventeen Poems Missing from "Love Respelt,"
  1966
Colophon to "Love Respelt," 1967
Poems, 1965-1968, 1968
Beyond Giving, 1969
The Crane Bag, 1969
Love Respelt Again, 1969
Poems About Love, 1969
Advice from a Mother, 1970
Poems, 1969-1970, 1970
Queen-Mother to New Queen, 1970
The Green-Sailed Vessel, 1971
Poems: Abridged for Dolls and Princes, 1971
Poems, 1968-1970, 1971
Deyá, 1972 (with Paul Hogarth)
Poems, 1970-1972, 1972
Poems: Selected by Himself, 1972
Timeless Meetings, 1973
At the Gate, 1974
Collected Poems, 1975, 1975 (2 volumes)
New Collected Poems, 1977

OTHER LITERARY FORMS

Robert Graves published fifteen novels, including
one (*No Decency Left*, 1932) written in collaboration
with Laura Riding. His novels are usually based on historical events or mythology. *I, Claudius* (1934) and
Claudius the God and His Wife Messalina (1934) borrow heavily from Suetonius's *Lives of the Caesars* (c.
120 C.E.). *Count Belisarius* (1938) concerns the brilliant general of the Byzantine emperor Justinian. *Sergeant Lamb of the Ninth* (1940; also known as *Sergeant
Lamb's America*) and *Proceed, Sergeant Lamb* (1941)
fictionalize the life of an actual English soldier in the
American Revolution. *The Story of Marie Powell, Wife
to Mr. Milton* (1943; also known as *Wife to Mr. Milton,
the Story of Marie Powell*) elaborates imaginatively on
John Milton's marital problems. *The Islands of Unwisdom* (1949; also known as *The Isles of Unwisdom*) is
based on the abortive attempt by the Spanish in the sixteenth century to colonize the Solomon Islands. *They*

Hanged My Saintly Billy (1957) is a minor work about the notorious career and execution of Dr. William Palmer for poisoning his friend, John Parsons Cook.

Biblical topics inspired two novels: *My Head! My Head!* (1925), about Elisha and Moses, and *King Jesus* (1946), his most significant attempt to fuse his ideas about the Triple Goddess with Christian and Hebrew myth. Greek mythology inspired *The Golden Fleece* (1944, also known as *Hercules, My Shipmate*) and *Homer's Daughter* (1955), while *Watch the North Wind Rise* (1949; also known as *Seven Days in New Crete*) is an entertaining fantasy about a mythological future when the worship of the Goddess is reestablished in Crete, the ancient stronghold of the Goddess cult.

Graves published more than fifty works in the non-fiction category, including literary criticism, books about writing and language, an autobiography, a biography of T. E. Lawrence, social commentaries, and studies in Greek and Hebrew myths. In addition, he translated such writers as Suetonius, Homer, Hesiod, Lucius Apuleius, Lucan Pharsalia, and Manuel de Jesus Galvan. He was one of the most versatile writers of the twentieth century, a persistent maverick often embroiled in intellectual arguments with other scholars because of his sometimes eccentric views.

ACHIEVEMENTS

The White Goddess: A Historical Grammar of Poetic Myth (1948), and Robert Graves's other studies in mythology, *The Greek Myths* (2 volumes; 1955), *Hebrew Myths: The Book of Genesis* (1964, with Raphael Patai) and *The Nazarene Gospel Restored* (1953, with Joshua Podro), together with his novels and poetry based on myth, have undoubtedly had a subtle and pervasive influence on modern literature. Their impact cannot be distinguished precisely from that of other writers, such as James Frazer, T. S. Eliot, Joseph Campbell, and others, who have contributed to the renewed interest in mythology and ancient patterns of belief. With the passing of the enthusiasm for social realism, the old patterns of myth reasserted themselves with a surprising vigor—perhaps in direct proportion to current discomfort with the demythologized, purely practical bent of technological society. Graves contributed significantly to this rediscovery of the past.

For the novel *I, Claudius*, Graves received the Hawthornden Prize, the oldest of the famous British literary prizes, and the James Tait Black Memorial Prize, administered through the University of Edinburgh for the year's best novel. Collections of his poetry gained the Russell Loines Award (1958), the William Foyle Poetry Prize (1960), the Arts Council Poetry Award (1962), and the Queen's Gold Medal for Poetry (1968).

Graves held only one full-time salaried position in his life—in 1926, when he taught for one year at the Egyptian University of Cairo. He was Clark Lecturer at Trinity College, Cambridge, in 1954, however, and Arthur Dehon Little Memorial Lecturer at the Massachusetts Institute of Technology in 1963. He also lectured in California, Hungary, Israel, and Spain. In 1970, he became an Honorary Member of the American Academy of Arts and Sciences.

BIOGRAPHY

Robert Graves was born July 24, 1895, in Wimbledon, near London, to Alfred Percival Graves and Amalie von Ranke Graves. His father was an inspector

Robert Graves (©Washington Post/Courtesy, D.C. Public Library)

of schools, a Gaelic scholar, and a writer of poetry of a conventional sort. His German mother was related to the historian Leopold von Ranke. Robert was one of ten children, five of them from his father's first marriage. The Graves household was conventionally religious, a tradition that Graves dispensed with in his maturity, but that left him, according to his autobiography, *Goodbye to All That* (1929), with "a great capacity for fear . . . a superstitious conscience and a sexual embarrassment." To the age of twelve, Robert and the other Graves children sometimes visited their German relatives, including their aunt, Baronin von Aufsess, who lived in a medieval castle in the Bavarian Alps. These romantic environs undoubtedly colored his early poetry.

When Graves attended Charterhouse, where he was listed as R. von R. Graves, his German connections were an embarrassment because of the anti-German sentiment developing in England. Graves did not find his schoolmates particularly congenial until he won their respect by becoming a competent boxer. He did find one prominent friend in George Mallory, a famous mountaineer who later died climbing Mount Everest. Mallory introduced Edward Marsh, then secretary to Winston Churchill, to Graves's poetry. Marsh, a patron of the contemporary Georgian school of poetry, encouraged Graves in his writing; but, he said, Graves should modernize his diction, which was "forty years behind the time."

Graves joined the Royal Welsh Fusiliers when World War I began and went to France as a nineteen-year-old officer. He became a close friend of the well-known war poet Siegfried Sassoon. Graves's autobiography, *Goodbye to All That*, written when he was thirty-five, includes one of the best accounts of trench warfare to come out of the war. Both Graves and Sassoon survived the war, though they suffered physical and mental wounds in the process. Graves received multiple wounds from an exploding shell and was, in fact, listed among the casualties, but eventually someone noted that the "corpse" in the hospital . . .tent had moved and Graves lived to fight again. One lung was seriously damaged, however, and he was soon brought back to England to serve in a training role.

The more lasting damage that Graves suffered from trench warfare however, was psychological, and helped to determine the nature of his poetry for nearly ten years. He suffered from war neurasthenia; he was prone to nightmares, obsessed with military strategy even in peaceful surroundings, and had waking hallucinations about comrades who had died in the war. He became acquainted with W. H. R. Rivers, a Freudian psychologist who was an expert in war neurasthenia and also interested in the role of the subconscious in poetic creativity. Under his influence, Graves became fascinated with dreams and developed a theory about poetry as a way of expressing and resolving mental conflicts. His poetry of this period was haunted by images of guilt, despair, and entrapment. Though he seldom wrote specifically about war experiences, he translated the emotions aroused there into more Gothic visions. Only years later, after he had achieved some distance from combat, could he treat it in both poetry and prose with a certain gritty objectivity.

In 1918, Graves married Nancy Nicholson, a painter, socialist, and ardent feminist who kept her maiden name. The couple had four children. Although it had seemed positive, the marriage failed in a shattering domestic crisis in which the American poet, Laura Riding, who had been staying with the Graves family, made a dramatic exit from a fourth-story window. She survived with a broken back and gradually recovered over a period of months. Graves and Riding were companions for the next thirteen years. They established the Seizin Press and later moved to Majorca, where Graves lived until his death in 1985 except when lecturing at universities or when political conditions forced the evacuation of British nationals. On one such occasion while Graves and Riding were living temporarily in the United States, Riding fell in love with and married the American poet Schuyler Jackson. Graves went back to England and eventually married Beryl Hodge, with whom he lived in Majorca until his death. He had four children from this marriage.

Riding had a considerable influence on Graves's writing. She was more obsessed with "truth" than with emotional expression in poetry and was fascinated with word-meanings. She encouraged Graves to forgo the gothic effects he was using when he looked on poetry as emotional therapy. She insisted on more rigorous thinking and verbal precision. Perhaps she merely supported a development that was already under way in Graves's writing; in any case, his poetry became more philosophic and ironic. After Riding severed her association with Graves, he developed his fascination with the mythological White Goddess, which provided a pattern of images for almost all his subsequent poetry.

Some critics suggest that the White Goddess mythology universalized Riding's personality, though Graves claimed that he simply discovered, and did not invent, the great Triple Goddess of Moon, Earth, and underworld who dominated preclassical religion. He became interested in the concept while doing research for a novel about Jason and the Golden Fleece, and studied such anthropologists as James Frazer, J. J. Bachofen, Jane Harrison, and Margaret Murray as well as recent archaeological studies. He finally worked out his theory while examining thirteenth century Welsh minstrel poems. These investigations culminated in *The White Goddess*, a unique combination of esoteric lore and inspired speculation. He was convinced (or claimed to be, at least) not only that the goddess cult once dominated the Western world, but also that most of the social evils of civilization stemmed from her overthrow and the subsequent domination by the male. The mythology of the goddess inspired much of Graves's subsequent writing.

ANALYSIS

Robert Graves was perhaps the most significant inheritor of the Romantic tradition in twentieth century poetry. After articulating his devotion to the White Goddess, he specialized in love poetry. He wrote significant poetry, however, at every stage of development, sometimes dealing with psychological or philosophical ideas as well as with mythological themes.

According to Graves, the art of poetry requires long experience with and attention to the meanings of words, a carefully developed craftsmanship, and an intuitive openness to what he called the poetic trance. He explained this process lucidly in one of his Oxford lectures, "The Poet in a Valley of Dry Bones" (published in *Mammon and the Black Goddess*, 1965):

A poet lives with his own language, continually instructing himself in the origin, histories, pronunciation, and peculiar usages of words, together with their latent powers, and the exact shades of distinction between what Roget's *Thesaurus* calls "synonyms."

The use of the English language depends largely on precedent. One needs to know the precedents and when to deviate from them. Graves says that "The exact rightness of words can be explained only in the context of a whole poem: each one being related rhythmically, emotionally, and semantically to every other."

"THE NAKED AND THE NUDE"

This meticulous sense for shades of meaning is demonstrated in an ironic poem called "The Naked and the Nude." "Nude" is associated with sly seduction, showmanship, and mock-religious poses, while the state of nakedness is appropriate in contexts of love, medicine, and "true" religious devotion: "naked shines the Goddess when/ She mounts her lion among men." The poet warns that though the brazen nude may defeat the naked in life, in the world of the dead they shall be pursued by Gorgons with whips. There, in a final play on meaning, "How naked go the sometime nude!" Here, of course, "naked" means exposed in its actuality. Thus, in the poet's personal lexicography, "nude" implies exploitation and prostitution, while the term "naked" fuses connotations of love, beauty, and truth.

"THE COOL WEB"

Graves has other poems that explore in a more serious tone the function of language. One of the most perceptive is "The Cool Web," in which language serves as a buffer between the speaker and the intensity of raw experience. It is one of the best poems written on the theme of language as a cocoon that protects but also embalms:

> There is a cool web of language winds us in,
> Retreat from too much joy or too much fear:
> We grow sea green at last and coldly die
> In brininess and volubility.

This state of insulation from the stark reality of experience contrasts with the clearer perception that he attributes to children: "Children are dumb to say how hot the day is . . . How dreadful the black wastes of evening sky. . . ." The poet suggests that one must either smother in a sea of words or throw off language and die of madness, "Facing the wide glare of the children's day." Besides being a unique expression of the function of language in controlling emotional reaction to experience, the poem also suggests a view of alternative fates somewhat analogous to Achilles' dilemma in Homer's *Iliad* (c. 750 B.C.E.; English translation, 1611). Achilles was supposed to have two possible destinies: a short life of violent action in obedience to his passions that would bring him everlasting fame, or a long, uneventful life if he chose to return home. Of course, the romantic traditionally prefers the short, intense life to the long, dull, conventional existence. Graves, however, gives a new turn to the screw: The ferocious quality of reality is not a romantic illusion, but its true color. It is the dull, conventional life that is an error—an illusion of order conceived and perpetuated by language.

"THE PHILOSOPHER"

Although Graves had the romantic's distrust of cold reason uninformed by the heart, the poem called "The Philosopher" seems to entertain at least the possibility of some benefit derivable from logic—given a suitable environment. The ideal housing for the logical mind is, unfortunately, a barren prison cell where the mind might be "free" of all the usual distractions of living. There one might weave a more perfect web of thought, "Threading a logic between wall and wall,/ Ceiling and floor more accurate by far/ Than the cob-spider's." In this paradoxically ideal situation, one might attain "Truth captured without increment of flies." The poet imagines the cell becoming a

> spacious other head
> In which the emancipated reason might
> Learn in due time to walk at greater length
> And more unanswerably.

The poem achieves an ironic fusion of contradictory attitudes—although, only persons quite dead to the world are in a position to form a logically consistent philosophy. This may suggest an outright parody of philosophers, but one fancies that the poet would really like to reconcile the worlds of experience and thought if he could. Perhaps Graves was struggling with Riding's rather obscure requirement that poetry express "truth."

Graves meticulously avoided schools and movements in poetry. Having emerged from the Georgian school popular in his early youth, he deliberately disregarded T. S. Eliot and Ezra Pound, who were dictating poetic taste somewhat later. Graves maintained that one does not write good poetry by imitating popular fashions or even recognized geniuses in the genre. The style should always be one's own and the idea or experience itself should determine form, diction, and rhythm. He despised what he saw as the tendency in modern poetry to cultivate obscurity for its own sake or to throw out rhyme or rhythm simply to rebel against nineteenth century Romanticism. He did, however, modernize his diction, as Edward Marsh once told him to do, weaning himself away from all decorative elaboration that served no function in the poem. When the cult of Eliot and Pound was on the wane, Graves became a model to many younger poets for his craftsmanship and his ability to match rhythm and diction with content.

"THE PIER-GLASS" AND "THE LEGS"

Graves repeatedly displayed this versatility of language. During the time when he was haunted by his war experiences, he became adept at the gothic mode. The collection called *The Pier-Glass* contains some of his best poems of that period. The title poem uses the ambience of a haunted house to convey the acute emotional trauma of its female persona, who returns obsessively to a deserted bedroom, "Drawn by a thread of time-sunk memory." She gazes at her pale reflection in a cracked pier-glass and at the curtained bed that is likened to a "puppet theatre where malignant fancy/ Peoples the wings with fear."

In spite of the gothic touches of such poems as "The Pier-Glass," Graves was soon writing other poems in an altogether different mode, as cool and ironic as anyone could wish. "The Legs," for example, is entirely original in subject matter, though surrealism may have inspired the wry humor and absurdity of the scene:

> There was this road,
> And it led down-hill,
> And round and in and out.
>
> And the traffic was legs,
> Legs from the knee down,
> Coming and going,
> Never pausing.

The persona is apparently feeling rather smug because he is standing firmly in the grass by the roadside, clearly self-possessed in the midst of this mindless activity of legs. Suddenly, his feeling of superiority becomes slightly clouded with doubt:

> My head dizzied then:
> I wondered suddenly,
> Might I too be a walker
> From the knees down?
>
> Gently I touched my shins.
> The doubt unchained them.
> They had run in twenty puddles
> Before I regained them.

The simplicity of diction, the clarity of the symbolic action, and the delicately modulated tempo make this poem delightful.

ORIGINS OF THE WHITE GODDESS

Graves became increasingly objective in his poetry as the urgencies of war and domestic upheavals receded, abandoning his notion of poetry as therapy, and writing more and more in a philosophic or ironic vein. With the disappearance from his life of Riding and his subsequent fascination with ancient myth, he found a reservoir of symbols and metaphors that contributed to a burst of creative activity during which he wrote some of the best love lyrics of his age. As he affirmed in "To Juan at the Winter Solstice," one of the best-known of the poems inspired by the White Goddess mythology, "There is one story and one story only/ That will prove worth your telling." That is the love story between the Great Goddess of Moon, Earth, and the underworld (or a woman who embodies her) and her champion, who represents in ancient myth the Sacred King (the god of the waxing and waning year)—or, by extension, the poet inspired by his muse. As he explains his discovery in *The White Goddess*:

> The Theme, briefly, is the antique story, which falls into thirteen chapters and epilogue, of the birth, life, death and resurrection of the God of the Waxing Year; the central chapters concern the God's losing battle with the God of the Waning Year for love of the capricious and all-powerful Threefold Goddess, their mother, bride and layer-out. The poet identifies himself with the God of the

Waxing Year and his Muse with the Goddess; the rival is his blood-brother, his other self, his weird.

The God of the Waxing Year is, of course, a variation of the primitive vegetation god. He suffers death in the fall but revives in the spring, like the Egyptian Osiris, murdered by his brother Set, god of desert and drought, only to be restored to life by his wife, Isis. The poet sees himself in both creative and sacrificial roles, alternately inspired by the love of the Goddess Muse and suffering ritual death when her love grows cold.

The historical and religious origins of the goddess, nevertheless, have some purely literary precedents in the numerous fatal women of Romantic poetry—John Keats's supernatural "La Belle Dame sans Merci," and Samuel Taylor Coleridge's weird women who dice with Death for the life of the Ancient Mariner. This is exactly the guise in which Graves often meets her, stressing her more frightening implications over her occasional gentleness. In "Darien," the poet tells his son about the Muse. "Often at moonrise I had watched her go./ And a cold shudder shook me/ To see the curved blaze of her Cretan axe." The Cretan axe is an emblem of the ancient Moon Goddess, having both convex and concave surfaces, suggesting different stages of the moon. The axe forebodes the price of being her chosen lover, for it is an instrument of sacrifice.

In the poem titled "The White Goddess," the persona also hints at the price of seeking the favor of the goddess. Spring, the poet suggests, always celebrates the Mountain Mother;

> But we are gifted, even in November
> Rawest of seasons, with so huge a sense
> Of her nakedly worn magnificence
> We forget cruelty and past betrayal,
> Heedless of where the next bright bolt may fall.

In ancient times, certain animals were associated with the Goddess, particularly the cat, bitch, cow, sow, owl, dove, and crane. (Her consort had other animal forms, such as the snake, bull, or the white roebuck.) In Graves's poem "Cat-Goddesses" the triad expands to nine (like the powerful ninefold-mountain mother of Parnassus whom Apollo reduced to nine little nymphs, the Muses). The poem speaks of the "perverse habit of cat-goddesses" who, "With coral tongues and beryl eyes like lamps/ Long-legged, pacing three by three in nines," offer themselves indiscriminately to "tatter-eared and slinking alley-toms." They do this simply to provoke jealousy. They promptly desert the "gross-headed, rabbit-coloured litters" that result from such casual unions. None of these careless offspring is the sacred child whom the Goddess bears to her chosen Sacred King, symbolizing the rejuvenation of spring and the fertility of the land.

"RETURN OF THE GODDESS" AND "THE SWEET SHOP AROUND THE CORNER"

In "Return of the Goddess," the Queen appears as a crane, reclaiming errant frogs who had unwisely crowned a king of their own devising. "The log they crowned as king/ Grew sodden, lurched and sank"; the frogs, "loud with repentance," await the Goddess's judgment day. At dawn, the Goddess returns as a "gaunt red-legged crane" to claim them, "Lunging your beak down like a spear/ To fetch them home again." This clever fable perhaps suggests that men, too, erred in transferring their allegiance to a male deity. Sooner or later, the impostor will sink, and the immortal Goddess will return.

Sometimes the Goddess is invoked only indirectly in a more realistic context. The excellent short poem "The Sweet Shop Around the Corner" tells of a little boy who, losing track of his mother in a crowd, grabs a strange woman's hand and drags her boisterously into a sweet shop, demanding candy. Only gradually does he realize with dread that something is wrong:

> Were Mother's legs so lean, or her shoes so long,
> Or her skirt so patched, or her hair tousled and grey?
> Why did she twitter in such a ghostly way?
> *O, Mother, are you dead*?
>   What else could a child say?

It is, of course, unnecessary for the appreciation of this poem to realize the mythic quality of Mother turned Crone. The poem is a model of clarity and brevity, yet achieves a striking revelation. The child, so confident in himself and his world of indulgent Mother and animal joys, looks suddenly on the face of old age and death.

Although Graves's long love affair with the White Goddess inspired many good poems, such exclusive at-

tention to this mythic framework ultimately limited his further development. It was hard for even so expert a craftsperson to go on telling the "one story only" in fresh and exciting ways. The change or deepening of perspective that one might expect from age never appeared. Moreover, sometimes the reader may yearn for a real woman with a distinctive personality to emerge from the repeated avowals of love. Nevertheless, Graves wrote some very good poetry at almost every stage of his long and devoted career. Through his investigations in mythology and his celebration of it in poetry, he reactivated a past that makes the present richer.

OTHER MAJOR WORKS

LONG FICTION: *My Head! My Head!*, 1925; *No Decency Left*, 1932 (as Barbara Rich; with Laura Riding); *Claudius the God and His Wife Messalina*, 1934; *I, Claudius*, 1934; *"Antigua, Penny, Puce,"* 1936 (also known as *The Antigua Stamp*, 1937); *Count Belisarius*, 1938; *Sergeant Lamb of the Ninth*, 1940 (also known as *Sergeant Lamb's America*); *Proceed, Sergeant Lamb*, 1941; *The Story of Marie Powell, Wife to Mr. Milton*, 1943 (also known as *Wife to Mr. Milton, the Story of Marie Powell*); *The Golden Fleece*, 1944 (also known as *Hercules, My Shipmate*, 1945); *King Jesus*, 1946; *The Islands of Unwisdom*, 1949 (also known as *The Isles of Unwisdom*); *Watch the North Wind Rise*, 1949 (also known as *Seven Days in New Crete*); *Homer's Daughter*, 1955; *They Hanged My Saintly Billy*, 1957.

SHORT FICTION: *The Shout*, 1929; *¡Catacrok! Mostly Stories, Mostly Funny*, 1956; *Collected Short Stories*, 1964.

NONFICTION: *On English Poetry*, 1922; *The Meaning of Dreams*, 1924; *Contemporary Techniques of Poetry: A Political Analogy*, 1925; *Poetic Unreason, and Other Studies*, 1925; *Another Future of Poetry*, 1926; *Impenetrability: Or, The Proper Habit of English*, 1926; *The English Ballad: A Short Critical Survey*, 1927; *Lars Porsena: Or, The Future of Swearing and Improper Language*, 1927; *Lawrence and the Arabs*, 1927 (also known as *Lawrence and the Arabian Adventure*, 1928); *A Survey of Modernist Poetry*, 1927 (with Riding); *Mrs. Fisher: Or, The Future of Humour*, 1928; *A Pamphlet Against Anthologies*, 1928 (with Riding; also known as *Against Anthologies*); *Goodbye to All That: An Autobiography*, 1929; *T. E. Lawrence to His Biographer Robert Graves*, 1938; *The Long Week-End: A Social History of Great Britain, 1918-1938*, 1940 (with Alan Hodge); *The Reader over Your Shoulders: A Handbook for Writers of English Prose*, 1943 (with Hodge); *The White Goddess: A Historical Grammar of Poetic Myth*, 1948; *The Common Asphodel: Collected Essays on Poetry, 1922-1949*, 1949; *Occupation: Writer*, 1950; *The Nazarene Gospel Restored*, 1953 (with Joshua Podro); *Adam's Rib and Other Anomalous Elements in the Hebrew Creation Myth: A New View*, 1955; *The Crowning Privilege: The Clark Lectures, 1954-1955*, 1955; *The Greek Myths*, 1955 (2 volumes); *Jesus in Rome: A Historical Conjecture*, 1957 (with Podro); *Five Pens in Hand*, 1958; *Greek Gods and Heroes*, 1960; *Oxford Addresses on Poetry*, 1962; *Nine Hundred Iron Chariots: The Twelfth Arthur Dehon Little Memorial Lecture*, 1963; *Hebrew Myths: The Book of Genesis*, 1964 (with Raphael Patai); *Majorca Observed*, 1965 (with Paul Hogarty); *Mammon and the Black Goddess*, 1965; *Poetic Craft and Principle*, 1967; *The Crane Bag and Other Disputed Subjects*, 1969; *On Poetry: Collected Talks and Essays*, 1969; *Difficult Questions, Easy Answers*, 1972.

TRANSLATIONS: *Almost Forgotten Germany*, 1936 (with Riding; of Georg Schwarz); *The Transformation of Lucius, Otherwise Known as "The Golden Ass,"* 1950 (of Lucius Apuleius); *The Cross and the Sword*, 1954 (of Manuel de Jesús Galván); *Pharsalia: Dramatic Episodes of the Civil Wars*, 1956 (of Lucan); *Winter in Majorca*, 1956 (of George Sand); *The Twelve Caesars*, 1957 (of Suetonius); *The Anger of Achilles: Homer's "Iliad,"* 1959; *The Rubáiyát of Omar Khayyám*, 1967 (with Omar Ali-Shah).

CHILDREN'S LITERATURE: *The Big Green Book*, 1962; *The Siege and Fall of Troy*, 1962; *Two Wise Children*, 1966; *The Poor Boy Who Followed His Star*, 1968.

EDITED TEXTS: *Oxford Poetry: 1921*, 1921 (with Alan Porter and Richard Hughes); *John Skelton: Laureate*, 1927; *The Less Familiar Nursery Rhymes*, 1927; *The Comedies of Terence*, 1962; *English and Scottish Ballads*, 1975.

MISCELLANEOUS: *Steps: Stories, Talks, Essays, Poems, Studies in History*, 1958; *Food for Centaurs: Stories, Talks, Critical Studies, Poems*, 1960; *Selected Poetry and Prose*, 1961.

BIBLIOGRAPHY

Bloom, Harold, ed. *Robert Graves*. New York: Chelsea House, 1987. Essays on Graves's historical novels, autobiography, and major themes. Includes chronology and bibliography.

Graves, Richard Perceval. *Robert Graves: The Assault Heroic, 1895-1926*. New York: Viking Press, 1986. Written by Graves's nephew. Though primarily concerned with Graves's life, this book delineates the conditions that led the poet to write his autobiography and leave England. The effect of World War I and his rejection of conventional morality appear largely in this study.

_____. *Robert Graves: The Years with Laura, 1926-1940*. New York: Viking Press, 1990. The second volume of Graves's three-volume study. Looking closely at the relationship between Graves and the American poet Laura Riding, this volume provides information concerning the respective contributions of the collaborators. Richard Perceval Graves is concerned with literary matters, though his fascination with the sensational aspects of the years Robert Graves and Riding spent together is evident. Of much interest, as in the first volume, are the notes, which indicate the breadth of the poet's friendships and the variety of places in which his papers have been placed.

_____. *Robert Graves and the White Goddess, 1940-1985*. London: Weidenfeld & Nicolson, 1995. This concluding volume to Graves's three-volume biography lacks the savor and drama of the second volume because it covers the relatively sedate life of an aged, lionized poet. Robert Graves had by age forty-five settled into life with Beryl Hodge, his second wife. They took up residence in Majorca, where he was visited by an unending succession of disciples and young women whom Graves adopted as lovers and muses.

Kernowski, Frank L. *The Early Poetry of Robert Graves: The Goddess Beckons*. Austin: University of Texas, 2002. A portrait of Graves and his work that benefits from the author's own interviews with his subject and input from Graves's daughter.

McPhail, Helen, and Philip Guest. *On the Trail of the Poets of the Great War: Robert Graves and Siegfried Sassoon.* Barnsley, South Yorkshire, England: Leo Cooper, 2001. Describes the wartime friendship between these two poets and their experiences on the battlefield, as well as their poetry.

Quinn, Patrick J., ed. *New Perspectives on Robert Graves.* Selinsgrove, Pa.: Susquehanna University Press, 1999. A thoughtful, updated volume on the works of Graves. Includes bibliographical references and index.

Seymour, Miranda. *Robert Graves: Life on the Edge.* New York: Henry Holt, 1995. Study relates Graves's experiences in World War I and his relationships with women to his theory of inspiration.

Seymour-Smith, Martin. *Robert Graves: His Life and Work.* New York: Paragon House, 1988. Intimate, fascinating glimpse of Graves the man. Seymour-Smith had known Graves since 1943 and has written extensively on him since 1956. Excellent introduction to Graves's remarkable life and literary career.

Katherine Snipes

THOMAS GRAY

Born: London, England; December 26, 1716
Died: Cambridge, England; July 30, 1771

PRINCIPAL POETRY

"Elegy Written in a Country Churchyard," 1751
Six Poems by Mr. T. Gray, 1753
Odes, by Mr. Gray, 1757
Pindaric Odes, 1758
Poems by Mr. Gray, 1768

OTHER LITERARY FORMS

Thomas Gray did not write a great deal of poetry, but he was a most prolific writer of letters. In the eighteenth century, the personal letter became so refined as an exercise in wit, description, and intellect that modern critics and literary historians now regard the letter as a minor art form of the period. Among the very greatest eighteenth century letter writers are Gray and his close friend Horace Walpole. The Gray of the letters sounds different from the poet. As he addresses his personal friends on a remarkably broad range of topics, there is a refreshing clarity and ease that his concept of poetry as an expression of ideals excluded from his verse. Especially famous are his descriptions of the Alps, which foreshadow the Romantic appreciation of nature's wilder aspects, but whatever the subject, the letters reveal that Gray was as much an artist in prose as in poetry.

ACHIEVEMENTS

Thomas Gray is usually viewed as the least significant major writer in an age that included such giants as Jonathan Swift, Alexander Pope, and Samuel Johnson, or as the most significant of such minor figures as James Thompson and William Cowper. That he enjoys such stature is the more amazing when it is remembered that, in his lifetime, he published less than one thousand lines of verse. Gray's immortality results from the quality of his work or, more accurately, the fine craftsmanship apparent in his every line. Poetry was only one of many subjects that interested Gray; indeed, critics and literary biographers often place him with John Milton and Johnson as one of the most learned poets in English literature. This is not to say that his poetry was not important to Gray. He was sensitive to the critical response to what he allowed to be published, and he brought to his composition all the learning and love for precision characteristic of the scholar. He wrote about things that mattered to him, things that moved him, and like William Wordsworth, he recollected in tranquillity his overflow of powerful feelings before beginning to write. Because some of the things that moved him— Gothic castles, wild mountain vistas, the annals of the poor—were subjects that later moved the poets of the early nineteenth century, he has often been called a "pre-Romantic." This epithet, however, is less useful than usual when it comes to characterizing Gray, for Gray did not share the Romantic concern with everyday speech, nor was he moved to self-revelation. Gray intruded into his work only inasmuch as he did not hesitate to use his profound scholarship; thus, he spoke with complete intelligibility to a rather select audience. It is the achievement of this careful, intellectual, and most perfect poet that the final products of his craftsmanship manage to transcend the intellect to communicate feelings that move his readers regardless of place or time.

BIOGRAPHY

Thomas Gray was born in Cornhill (London) on December 26, 1716. Of twelve children born to Philip and Dorothy Gray, only Thomas survived childhood. The family was fairly prosperous; Philip was a scrivener and exchange broker, and Dorothy operated a millinery. Dorothy was a loving parent, but Philip was an ill-tempered wife-beater who was responsible for making young Thomas's childhood less than happy. It may well have been to remove the child from his father's influence that Dorothy arranged for her eight-year-old son to go off to school at Eton, where her brothers were masters. At Eton, Gray met Richard West and Horace Walpole, who became his closest friends, but with the exception of the happiness resulting from these friendships, the studious and solitary Gray found little pleasure in the company of the rowdy young men of Eton. In 1734, Gray and Walpole left Eton for Cambridge University. The death of his aunt, Sarah Gray, provided an income sufficient for his modest needs. Gray left Cambridge in 1738 with the intention of studying law at the Inner Temple. In 1739, however, his friend Walpole was ready to put the finishing touch on his own education by taking the traditional Grand Tour of Europe. Walpole's father, the famous prime minister Sir Robert Walpole, believed that his son might benefit from the company of a good, sober companion and offered to pay all of Gray's expenses to take the Tour with Horace. For two years, Gray and Walpole traveled through France, Italy, and Switzerland. Gray was fascinated by the culture of Europe and vividly recorded his experiences and feelings in letters that are considered among the finest written in English. While touring Italy in May, 1741, Gray and Walpole quarreled. The reason for the disagreement is not clear—years later, after Gray's death, Walpole assumed the blame—but Gray returned to London alone and was not reconciled with

Thomas Gray (Archive Photos/Getty Images)

his friend until 1745. In 1742, he settled again at Cambridge and, except for a brief residence in London (1759-1761), stayed there for the rest of his life.

On June 1, 1742, West died; Gray never forgot the loss of his dearest friend. This same time marks a period of increased literary productivity as Gray turned from Latin to English as his poetic medium. He had long been a writer of Latin poetry but now began to work with classical forms, such as the ode, in English. Gray's first major poems, "Ode on the Spring," "Ode on a Distant Prospect of Eton College," and "Hymn to Adversity," were composed in 1742, but the Eton ode was not published until 1747; the Spring ode and "Ode on the Death of a Favorite Cat" appeared in an anthology in 1748. In the meantime, Gray was awarded a bachelor of civil law degree in 1743 and settled into the life of a Cambridge scholar. His appetite for study was insatiable. His notebooks attest to his extensive knowledge of natural history as well as art, philosophy, and languages. The famous "Elegy Written in a Country Churchyard" was published on February 15, 1751. It was immediately popular, and Gray's printer had to produce five editions that year to meet the demand. In December, 1757, four months after the publication of the *Odes, by Mr. Gray*, he rejected an offer to be poet laureate; it was an office that politics and poor poetry had caused to fall into low repute. The next decade was spent quietly at Cambridge, with frequent trips to London, Scotland, and Wales. In 1768, Gray was made Regius Professor of Modern History at Cambridge. His final years were plagued by attacks of gout, and he endured considerable pain until his death on July 30, 1771. He was buried beside his mother in the village of Stoke Poges.

ANALYSIS

In the spring of 1742, Thomas Gray turned his attention from writing Latin verse to composing in English. His first effort, "Noontide," later renamed "Ode on the Spring," was included with a personal letter to West, his dear friend. The letter came back unopened, and soon Gray's fear was confirmed; the companion of his Eton days had died. Ironically, that poem that West never saw dealt with the brevity of life. Certainly, Gray had reason to ruminate on such a theme; eleven of his siblings had died in infancy, leaving him the sole survivor. Now, the death of West intensified his feeling of loss. The purpose of mortal existence became the theme that Gray was to address from a variety of points of view in nearly all the major poems of his career.

"ODE ON THE SPRING"

While "Ode on the Spring" is an early effort, it is not unaccomplished. Gray simply did not produce careless or unrefined poetry; he labored long and thoughtfully to achieve a precise result. Some critics, including the great Johnson, have attacked "Ode on the Spring." In his *Lives of the Poets* (1779-1781), Johnson objects that "the language is too luxuriant, and the thoughts have nothing new," and fundamentally, Johnson is correct. The language is indeed luxuriant, and the content is by no means original. The poem is largely descriptive of the Buckinghamshire country where the poet, seated under a tree near the water, considers the brief lives of the insects as they frolic in the spring sun. The insects are a metaphor for the segment of humanity that, unlike the reclusive and scholarly poet, enjoys the sportive life

of temporal pleasures. As the poet meditates on his *sic transit* theme, the insects are suddenly allowed to interrupt and "in accents low" answer the sober poet. They tell him that from their point of view it is he who is wasting his life: He is alone, without a beautiful female companion; he has hoarded no treasures to give him pleasure, and his being adds nothing to the beauty of the countryside. Moreover, the poet's spring flees as quickly as that of the insects. Gray allows the poet no rebuttal to the insects' argument; their last words, "We frolic, while 'tis May," end the poem. Talking insects are unusual, but what they and the poet have to say is not. The figure of the poet as the detached observer who prefers to remain isolated from the affairs of humanity stretches back into antiquity. While "Ode on the Spring" is admittedly composed of highly conventional elements, it can be argued that the composition of those elements is unusually sophisticated and uniquely characteristic of Gray.

The persona in "Ode on the Spring" is very close to Gray himself: reclusive, scholarly, an observer more than a participant. The luxuriant language serves a double purpose. It creates an ideal nature, lavish and beautiful beyond reality, a nature before the fall in which the reader is not unduly shocked to find that humans can still talk to animals. Against this ideal, where beautiful May follows beautiful May without worry about time, is presented the fate of both the poet and the insects. Their concern, mortality, is very real; indeed, it is more real because it still exists despite the context of an unreal nature. The language, however, in addition to clarifying the external message of the reality of death, also satirizes. The poet, speaking in the first person, creates through his elaborate language this beautiful, ideal nature, although he would prefer to remain divorced from the mortal humanity he contrasts with his creation. He would be unique and pompously states,

> With me the Muse shall sit, and think
> (At ease reclin'd in rustic state)
> How vain the ardours of the crowd,
> How low, how little are the Proud,
> How indigent the Great!

The Muse, however, refuses to cooperate, and the poet's ideal nature with its ideal talking insects includes him with the rest of mortal humanity. Not only do his insects remind him that "On hasty wings thy youth is flown," but they also challenge his very style of life and argue that contemplation and detachment are most wasteful of spring. Thus, "Ode on the Spring," while conventional and luxuriant, as critics have said, is still a very skillful handling of conventions and an accomplished example of how poetic language can communicate more than one message simultaneously.

The news of West's death motivated Gray to explore more deeply the theme of human mortality that "Ode on the Spring" had introduced. During the summer of 1742, a season of intense sorrow and intense creative energy for Gray, he produced two important poems: "Hymn to Adversity" and "Ode on a Distant Prospect of Eton College."

"HYMN TO ADVERSITY"

"Hymn to Adversity" is less concerned with mortality than it is with the quality of existence. Like the spring ode, this poem is also voiced in the first person, but the element of parody is gone, and there is no reason to suspect that the voice in the poem is not that of Gray himself honestly attempting to cope with his own unhappiness. The theme is simple. Adversity visits everyone, but realizing this, humans can be led to forgiveness, generosity, and love for their fellows, with whom they are united by the common bond of affliction. The poet invites adversity to come to him, not in its more horrible form of disease, poverty, or death, but in the benign form of a teacher who can instruct him in what it means to be human. The critic and biographer of Gray, Morris Golden, has stated that to a modern reader "Hymn to Adversity" is perhaps "the chilliest poem written by Gray." This seems to be an excellent description, for the piece represents precisely those poetic conventions that delighted eighteenth century audiences but that modern taste has discarded. The poem teaches a moral, an excellent Christian moral: Humanity should endure and strive to profit from whatever is given to it and not rage against fate. The message is clarified by an extensive use of personification. Adversity is a definite, intelligent, and feminine entity. She is even given family relationships; she is "Daughter of Jove," sister and nurse to Virtue, companion of Wisdom (who dresses in sable), Melancholy (a silent maid), warm Charity, severe Justice, and weeping Pity. Her band includes screaming Horror, Despair, Disease, and Poverty; Laughter, Noise, and Joy flee from her frown. This is certainly an impressive cast for a poem of only forty-eight lines. While a modern reader might complain that personification can diminish the subtle ambiguities necessary for the reader's creative participation in the poem, the neoclassical reader would applaud the clarity of the lesson. Even Johnson was so impressed by the "moral application" of the ideas found in "Hymn to Adversity" that he refused to mention his "slight objections"—unusual for Johnson. Of course, Johnson himself frequently employed personification, and he must have recognized that "Hymn to Adversity" is a thematic cousin to his own *The Vanity of Human Wishes* (1749).

"ODE ON A DISTANT PROSPECT OF ETON COLLEGE"

The most enduring accomplishment of that fruitful summer of 1742 was "Ode on a Distant Prospect of Eton College." The theme is still the same: mortality and its consequences. Here, however, the poet relates his observations of the landscape without remarking on the quality of lifestyles as he did in "Ode on the Spring" and without preaching the Christian lesson of "Hymn to Adversity." In the Eton College ode, wisdom, the desired companion of Adversity in the hymn, is something that should not be courted but left to wait until its inevitable time. Likewise, happiness, which the poet of "Hymn to Adversity" made flee before the welcomed approach of Adversity, is here lamented: "And happiness too swiftly flies." It is not surprising that, next to "Elegy Written in a Country Churchyard," the Eton College ode has survived as Gray's most popular poem. It does not trouble the reader with pompous poets and talking insects, nor does it try to persuade the reader to enjoy the taste of bitter medicine. The poet who watches the children at play on the fields of Eton is surely no less lofty in his diction or elaborate in his constructions than the poets who sang of spring and adversity. The Eton poet, however, appears more natural in this elevated stance. In relation to the children he is observing, he really is a voice of wisdom, and it is clear that he takes no special pleasure in his relatively elevated state; he manages to avoid sounding pompous despite the baroque language. What does emerge is a sense of very deep and sincere sorrow, the more sincere to the reader familiar with Gray's life when it is remembered that he had been a student at Eton, and the writing of this ode in 1742 marked the severing of the last tie with those innocent days. He had lost the friendship of one school friend, Walpole, and now the last Eton friend, West, was gone too. Johnson objected to this ode because the subject "suggests nothing to Gray that every beholder does not equally think and feel." Actually, the same comment might be made to the poem's credit, but what is missing, and what an eighteenth century moralist would have expected, is a clearer statement of the lesson suggested by the subject being described. Gray, however, seems too personally affected to allow his meditations on the Eton landscape to follow to the expected lesson of Christian optimism, and he abruptly cuts himself off and concludes with one of the most famous lines in English poetry: "No more; where ignorance is bliss,/ 'Tis folly to be wise."

Viewed together, these three products of 1742, "Ode on the Spring," "Hymn to Adversity," and "Ode on a Distant Prospect of Eton College," make an interestingly unified trilogy. The spring ode introduces the two most obvious approaches to life: tranquil meditation and active pursuit of pleasure. No clear advantage is given to either, for one attitude is given to insects and the other to a pompous poet. "Hymn to Adversity" returns to explore in greater detail the life devoid of insect pleasures and steeled by trouble. In turn, the Eton ode focuses on the alternative, the life of innocent pleasure without the burdens of thought and hardship. None of these early works is distinguished by profundity or originality of thought, and while the adversity hymn and Eton ode do argue for particular lifestyles, clearly the trilogy of 1742 finally shows a Gray who has discovered no satisfactory answer to his questions.

"ELEGY WRITTEN IN A COUNTRY CHURCHYARD"

Gray's concern for the questions of human mortality and the proper conduct of life continued beyond the very productive year 1742. The poems written at that traumatic time clarified some of the questions but ultimately resolved nothing for the poet. Four years later, after Gray had had the opportunity to recollect in tran-

quillity the problems that West's death had forced on his attention, he returned to his theme in a poem that continues to be admired as a masterpiece of world poetry. "Elegy Written in a Country Churchyard" was probably begun in 1746, but like all of Gray's efforts, it was carefully reworked many times, even after its first publication in 1751. Indeed, Gray allowed publication only after he learned that a copy of the poem had been obtained by the editors of the *Magazine of Magazines*, a journal of which Gray had a low opinion, and that that magazine was about to publish the verses without permission. Gray's edition, published on February 15, 1751, by Robert Dodsley, beat the *Magazine of Magazines* by only one day. The poem was immediately popular; since the first hurried printing, it has gone through countless editions and numerous translations. In fact, some literary historians have claimed that it is the most famous poem in all English literature.

Like Gray's earlier efforts, the elegy is a product of its author's wide reading and knowledge of conventions. The poem is an excellent example of landscape poetry, a versified description of a rural scene incorporating the poet's reflections on the moral significance of what is observed. More specifically, Gray's elegy represents a then-popular species of landscape verse called graveyard poetry. These gloomy exercises, set in cemeteries and crypts, invariably reflected on the inevitability of death. While the ostensible purpose of the graveyard school was moral instruction, clearly some students of that school allowed sensational, grisly description to become an end in itself, with the moral lesson serving as little more than an excuse for cataloging every mortuary horror imaginable. Compared to such morbid works as James Hervey's *Meditations Among the Tombs* (1745), a prose piece that went through several editions in the eighteenth century, Gray's elegy is mild stuff indeed. "Elegy Written in a Country Churchyard" is genuinely concerned with mortality and the quality of life, and its gothic trappings exist only to establish the appropriate somber mood for the first-person ruminations of the poet. That mood owes much to the great care that Gray took with the sound of his poem. Onomatopoeia and alliteration are expertly employed with a diction that includes a great many long vowel sounds in order to communicate the mood of the poet. "Elegy Written in a Country Churchyard" does not merely tell the reader about the dead; it allows each reader to share in the experience of thinking about them.

Again, those thoughts are not memorable for their originality; rather, the achievement of the poem is its sensitive collection of the reactions that thoughtful people have always had to the awareness of their mortality. "The 'Church yard' abounds with images which find a mirror in every mind, and with sentiments to which every bosom returns an echo," said Johnson. Perhaps the principal message of the poem is the effect of death as a reminder of the unity of the human species and, indeed, the unity of the species with all of nature. The social conditions that distinguish one person from another in life are, finally, superficial. Talent, sensitivity, love of knowledge, and of course death, are common to the human community and ignore the fleeting borders set up by temporal wealth and power. The poet is saddened that the poor are restricted in their ability to develop and share their talents, but finds comfort in the ultimate erasure of all differences by death.

"THE PROGRESS OF POESY" AND "THE BARD"

With "Elegy Written in a Country Churchyard," Gray reached an understanding of the human condition, but he did not stoically accept the tragedy of poverty and stifled talent brought about by misuse of power. The old theme of the quality and style of life appears once more in the two great Pindaric odes, "The Progress of Poesy" and "The Bard." Unlike the previous elegy, the Pindarics were written in anticipation of successful publication. Gray intended them as his crowning achievement and poured into them all his skill as a master of poetic diction and classical forms, together with all his vast knowledge of history. Unfortunately, even the well-educated poetry readers of the eighteenth century were unprepared for so learned a poet as Thomas Gray. The poems were greeted with charges of obscurity and unintelligibility, and in later editions, Gray grudgingly provided notes to explain the references and allusions.

Both odes deal with poetry. "The Progress of Poesy" glorifies the art and demonstrates that poetry supports and contributes to political liberty. When tyranny

establishes itself, poetry and the beauty and order it creates leave, for oppression and beauty cannot coexist. "The Bard" is a specific example of the idea expressed in "The Progress of Poesy." Here, the last Welsh bard to escape the purge ordered by the invading Edward I confronts the king with a historically accurate prophecy of the downfall of his royal line. The bard's words, his poem, actually create a reality; the prophecy will come about, and then poetry will have destroyed tyranny. Gray composed this poem with considerable enthusiasm and later declared: "I felt myself the Bard." The statement is significant in relation to the theme first introduced by "Ode on the Spring." The noblest life, that of the creating bard who combats oppression and levels the social barriers in the community of humanity, was Gray's own, and those carefully crafted poems that so elegantly explored what to do with life were themselves the best answer.

OTHER MAJOR WORKS

NONFICTION: *The Correspondence of Thomas Gray*, 1935 (Paget Toynbee and Leonard Whibley, editors); *Thomas Gray's Journal of His Visit to the Lake District in October, 1769*, 2001 (William Roberts, editor).

BIBLIOGRAPHY

Bloom, Harold, ed. *Thomas Gray's "Elegy Written in a Country Churchyard."* New York: Chelsea House, 1987. Gray's elegy is probably the eighteenth century's single most celebrated poem, and it remains the subject of much critical debate. This study brings together a number of important essays on the elegy, spanning several decades.

Curr, Matthew. *The Consolation of Otherness: The Male Love Elegy in Milton, Gray, and Tennyson.* Jefferson, N.C.: McFarland, 2002. Examines male friendship in Gray's "Elegy Written in a Country Churchyard," John Milton's "Epitaphium Damonis," and Alfred, Lord Tennyson's "In Memoriam."

Downey, James, and Ben Jones, eds. *Fearful Joy: Papers from the Thomas Gray Bicentenary Conference at Carleton University.* Montreal: McGill-Queen's University Press, 1974. These essays, presented at Carleton University in 1971 (the two hundredth anniversary of Gray's death), provide an excellent sourcebook for students of Gray. All aspects of Gray's life, times, and poetry are addressed. Included is a handsome series of early illustrations of his work, many by the great artist-poet William Blake.

Garrison, James D. *A Dangerous Liberty: Translating Gray's "Elegy."* Newark: University of Delaware Press, 2009. Gray's most famous poem has been translated into many languages, including Greek, Latin, German, Italian, and French. Garrison looks at the poem in its various translations, thereby shedding light on the original.

Ketton-Cremer, R. W. *Thomas Gray: A Biography.* 1955. Reprint. London: Longmans, Green, 1966. A solid, well-written biography, very much in the "life and works" tradition. Clearly written and well researched, this remains one of the best accounts of Gray's life. Contains an impressive set of illustrations.

McCarthy, B. Eugene. *Thomas Gray: The Progress of a Poet.* Madison, N.J.: Fairleigh Dickinson University Press, 1997. Critical interpretation of selected works by Gray. Includes bibliographical references and index.

Mack, Robert L. *Thomas Gray: A Life.* New Haven, Conn.: Yale University Press, 2000. Incorporates recent revisionary scholarship on Gray as well as original archival research on the poet's family and formative years. Casts new light on Gray's personality and on the psychological and sexual tensions that defined his compelling poetry.

William J. Heim

ROBERT GREENE

Born: Norwich, Norfolk, England; c. July, 1558
Died: London, England; September 3, 1592

PRINCIPAL POETRY
A Maiden's Dream, 1591
The Poetry of Robert Greene, 1977

OTHER LITERARY FORMS

Robert Greene is known primarily for his comedies, prose romances, and pamphlets of London rogue life. Four plays are definitely his: *Orlando Furioso* (pr. c. 1588), *Friar Bacon and Friar Bungay* (pr. c. 1589), *James IV* (pr. c. 1591), and *A Looking Glass for London and England* (pr. c. 1588-1589; with Thomas Lodge). A fifth, *John of Bordeaux* (pr. c. 1590-1591), has been attributed to Greene because of its close similarity to his known work in theme, diction, and structure. *Alphonsus, King of Aragon* (pr. c. 1587), a *Tamburlaine*-type tragedy, has also been attributed to him, but it bears little resemblance to his known plays.

Greene's romances made him England's most popular writer of prose fiction in the 1580's. Early works, showing Italian influence, include, among others, *Mamillia: A Mirror or Looking Glass for the Ladies of England* (1583, 1593), *Morando: The Tritameron of Love* (1584, 1587), *Planetomachia* (1585), and *Penelope's Web* (1587). His pastoral romances, including *Ciceronis Amor* (1589, also known as *Tullies Love*), *Pandosto: The Triumph of Time* (1588), and *Menaphon* (1589), developed themes and forms popularized by Sir Philip Sidney's *Arcadia* (1590, 1593, 1598). Mantuanesque pastoral, with repentance as a major theme, predominates in later works, among them *Greene's Never Too Late* (1590), *Francesco's Fortunes* (1590), and *Greene's Mourning Garment* (1590).

In his last two years, Greene turned to another form, the rogue, or "connycatching," pamphlet, thereby creating a literary fashion. His *A Notable Discovery of Cozenage* (1591), *A Disputation Between a Hee Conny-Catcher and a Shee Conny-Catcher* (1592), *The Black Book's Messenger* (1592), and other small books in this series combined London street argot with satire of middle-class greed to produce a form that appealed to all levels of society.

Greene's death in 1592 sparked the publication of two alleged "deathbed" pamphlets, *Greene's Groatsworth of Wit Bought with a Million of Repentance* and *The Repentance of Robert Greene*, both usually attributed to him, but neither closely resembling his known prose, and thus probably spurious. The one surely authentic posthumous work, *Greene's Vision* (1592), follows the pastoral-penitent style of 1590 and was therefore likely written in that most fruitful year of his brief career.

ACHIEVEMENTS

The works for which Robert Greene is best known, his romances and his comedies, are largely poetic achievements, as well as milestones in the development of English prose and drama. What sets even his early fictions apart from those of his contemporaries (mainly translations of Continental stories) is his concern for the carefully crafted, rhythmic sentence, its meaning conveyed through striking images and comparisons. Though following English writer John Lyly to some extent in the development of this "euphuistic" style (after Lyly's *Euphues, the Anatomy of Wit*, 1579), Greene quickly learned to vary his forms, changing pace and tone to suit the demands of scene and character. By 1584, four years after the appearance of his first work, Greene was experimenting with other poetic modifications of his prose; he began to insert songs and emblematic poems to heighten description and further illuminate his characters. The songs, in particular, became a trademark of Greene's romances, achieving a remarkable variety of verse forms and moods in such works as *Ciceronis Amor*, *Menaphon*, and *Greene's Never Too Late*. These and other later romances by Greene are so dense with verse, especially love songs, poetic love letters, and introspective lyrics, that it can be said that here Greene's primary vehicle of story development is poetry. This style made Greene England's most popular prose writer in the years 1588 to 1592, the year of his death.

To make his verse achieve both illumination and individuation of his characters, Greene was more or less forced to break ground untouched by any previous English poet. Particularly vivid in this regard are two poems from *Menaphon*: "Sephestia's Song to Her Child" and "Doron's Eclogue Joined with Carmela's." The first, a lullaby about the forced separation of a noble family, and the second, a humorous love poem, are written in low style, their images drawn from English domestic life; both violate poetic conventions of the time by achieving a pastoral mood in deliberate avoidance of the conceits and heightened atmosphere of works such as Edmund Spenser's *The Shepheardes Calender* (1579) or the eclogues of *Arcadia*.

Greene's great influence on English dramatic comedy is principally owing to this same originality, this same enlivening and varying of mood through poetic device. Although his contemporaries appear to have thought most highly of him as a "maker of plots," Greene's plays immediately impress the modern reader by their verse. His best-known comedies, *Friar Bacon and Friar Bungay* and *James IV*, gain their power from that varying of image and verse form from character to character, scene to scene, that marks the romances. The same serious use of English rural imagery that Greene used in his later prose to create pastoral tones pervades his comedies as well and gives them those qualities that critics have called distinctly "festive" and "romantic." These qualities make Greene's plays as important in the development of comedy as are Christopher Marlowe's in the growth of tragedy.

Though poetry is a vital element throughout Greene's work, his influence as a poet has been far less great than his influence on the other genres, primarily because almost all his poems are incidental to his romances. In his time, several pieces were anthologized in collections of pastoral verse, but no scholar has detected in other poets' work the kind of influence that Greene's comedies exerted on William Shakespeare or his pamphlets on Ben Jonson and Thomas Dekker. This influence notwithstanding, the fact is that some of his poems, such as "Doron's Description of Samela" (also from *Menaphon*) and "Sephestia's Song to Her Child," are now recognized as being the best of their type from the period.

It may be that Greene's poetic influence has merely been overlooked: Little systematic study of his poetry has been made; Greene's complete verse was not collected and published until 1977. Nevertheless, his influence was significant. It is clear that in taking comedic lessons from Greene, Shakespeare followed his practice of varying structure (using rhyme, blank verse, prose, or song) to suit a speaker's rank or the tonal demands of a scene. The matching of verse to sense that is found in *As You Like It* (pr. c. 1599-1600) or *The Winter's Tale* (pr. c. 1610-1611) is an idea first embodied in English comedy in the plays of Greene. Likewise,

Robert Greene

Cambridge records reveal his baccalaureate degree and his M.A. from Clare in 1583, but neither his contemporaries nor Greene himself has left an account of his life there, notwithstanding the great practical importance Greene attached to his degrees, particularly the master's (and his second master's, from Oxford, in 1588); the words "Master of Arts in Both Universities" are prominently displayed on his title pages. Who exactly Greene was or what he did besides write and publish is not known. Most of the available quasi-biographical remarks come from a friend, Thomas Nashe, a notorious exaggerator, from an enemy, Gabriel Harvey, even less trustworthy, and from pamphlets of spurious attribution, *Greene's Groatsworth of Wit Bought with a Million of Repentance* and *The Repentance of Robert Greene*. Of Greene's appearance and character, Nashe wrote:

. . . a iolly long red peake, like the spire of a steeple, he cherisht continually without cutting, whereat a man might hang a Iewall, it was so sharp and pendant.

A good fellowe hee was . . . and in one yeare he pist as much against the walls as thou and thy brothers [speaking to Harvey] spent in three.

He made no account of winning credite by his works . . . ; his only care was to haue a spel in his purse to coniure up a good cuppe of wine with at all times.

Harvey, incensed over an inferred insult in Greene's last work, *A Quip for an Upstart Courtier* (1592), vented his anger in the following exercise of his poetic talent: "a rakehell, a makeshift: a scribbling foole:/ a famous bayard, in City, and Schoole." Harvey went on to say that Greene had had a whore as mistress and by her a son, Fortunatus, who died in infancy. Certainly, no corroborating evidence has been found. Nevertheless, the posthumous pamphlets, both in the repentance mode, stress the supposed degradation of Greene's life by putting into the deceased writer's mouth self-accusations similar to those made by Greene characters in several romances.

Mitigating somewhat these views are remarks by

Greene's poetic experiments with rural vernacular in his romances led to his cultivation of street talk in the conny-catching pamphlets, their popularity inspiring the city-based works of Jonson, Dekker, and all those who followed them.

BIOGRAPHY

According to the most widely accepted speculation, Robert Greene was born to a saddler and his wife in Norwich, Norfolk, in 1558. There is no reliable evidence for this speculation, since the only mention of Norwich as his birthplace is found in the posthumous pamphlet *Greene's Groatsworth of Wit Bought with a Million of Repentance*, its attribution to Greene probably spurious. Nevertheless, since it is known that Greene took his B.A. from St. John's (Cambridge) in 1580, the speculated birth date is a likely one. Moreover, since Greene held a sizar's appointment at Cambridge—a type of work-study position in which middle-class students kept their places by serving students from noble houses—it is also likely that Greene came from the home of an artisan.

Nothing is known about Greene's life before he entered Cambridge and little is known of it after he left.

poet "R. B." (probably Richard Barnfield), who wrote *Greene's Funeralls* (1593): "For iudgment *Ioue*, for Learning deepe, he still *Apollo* seemde:/ For fluent tongue, for eloquence, men *Mercury* him deemde./ His life and manners though I would, I cannot half expresse." Although this praise helps to balance the record, it provides no further fact. The only certain information about Greene's later life is the month and year of his death, September, 1592, the cause of death being a protracted illness, probably *not* brought on, as Nashe claimed, by a banquet of rhenish wine and pickled herring.

This veil over Greene's life is ironic in that he achieved great contemporary fame as a writer: Indeed, his popularity was so great that the titles of his works included his name. In fact, for ten years after his death, "Greene" continued to appear as a character in pamphlets and stories, his protean identity in these works reflecting the elusiveness of his actual biography.

ANALYSIS

To understand Robert Greene as a poet requires distinguishing among the three main categories of his verse: the ninety poems incidental to his romances, his memorial poem about Sir Christopher Hatton (*A Maiden's Dream*), and his verse comedies. The first illustrates the use of verse in the service of characterization in prose narrative; the third shows varied verse structure as the vehicle of character and mood. The second is Greene's only self-contained work in a conventional verse genre.

POEMS INCIDENTAL TO THE ROMANCES

The reader of Greene's incidental poems is doubly struck: first, by Greene's concentration on a single theme, the workings of romantic love; second, by the sheer diversity of Greene's forms, voices, and conceits. Whereas Sir Philip Sidney, William Shakespeare, and the other Elizabethan sonnet-cyclists explored the potential of a single form and voice to express the nuances of love, Greene's personas vary with his many character types, male and female, who "spoke" or "sang" poems of from four to eighty lines, in blank verse, ballads, quatrains, couplets, rime royal, and Petrarchan sonnet rhyme. Although rarely straying from English iambics, Greene did experiment with feminine endings and

quantitative verse. His lines are predominantly pentameter, but his many songs frequently call for use of tetrameter and the alternation of line lengths. He even composed several hexameters.

Despite his numerous ventures into different meters and lengths, Greene favored the six-line stanza (*ababcc*, *abbacc*, or *abcbdd*), the tetrameter couplet (particularly in his pastoral songs from 1588 onward), and the ballad. These forms, combined with his almost exclusive use of end-stopped lines, make it clear that Greene intended his verse to be sung—at least to be songlike. His usual introduction to a poem is typified by the following from *Greene's Never Too Late*: ". . . whereupon sitting downe, she [Isabella] tooke her Lute in her hand, and sung this Ode." In these introductions, Greene frequently calls his poems "ditties," "dumpes" (sad songs), "madrigals," and "roundelays," to emphasize their tunefulness. When he calls his poems "odes" or "sonnets," he does not use such terms to signify specific verse forms. "Ode" implied to Greene's readers a serious, measured expression of emotion; "sonnet" merely meant "song." The "ode" sung by Isabella is classical only in its mythological imagery; it is written in rhymed tetrameter couplets. Greene's sonnets range in length from twelve to more than thirty lines and are almost all balladlike, some with refrains.

Whether Greene actually intended his poems to be set to music is not known. Since most of his pieces are "written through" (without refrains) and contain a fairly complex image structure, it seems more likely that he meant them to remain on the page, to be considered at a more leisurely pace than music allows. A clear case in point is "Melicertus' Eclogue" from *Menaphon*. Influenced by Edmund Spenser, Sidney, and other contributors to the pastoral tradition, Greene here uses a song form to work out a complicated conceit that does not lend itself to singing. In the poem, Melicertus, a nobleman disguised as a shepherd, describes the beauties of his love, Samela. As Melicertus proceeds to show how the various features of his mistress were created to satisfy particular fancies of the gods, the poem proceeds in ballad form; but the number of images in even one line, "And mounts to heauen on ouer leaden wings," demands a reader's slower pace, enabling one to review a stanza to gather missed ideas.

Sometimes, however, a Greene poem is fully suited to musical setting. One of these is "Sephestia's Song to Her Child"; the strong pauses in each line mark this "dittie" as intended for the voice and the lute. Like Thomas Campion's airs, it moves the reader by invoking a familiar mood through a few definite images within a simple narrative.

In terms of imagery, most of Greene's songlike poetry from his early romances (1583-1588) displays a self-conscious classicism, conforming to his early use of such settings as Olympus, Ithaca, and Troy, and his explicit following of such learned models as John Lyly and Baldassare Castiglione. From 1588 on, most of Greene's verse comes closer to what might be called the English folk spirit, as exemplified in Sephestia's lullaby. Greene's imagery in these poems tends to spring from the same native source as his rhythms and stanza forms. Ironically, this shift is first seen in a romance titled *Ciceronis Amor*, a work outwardly classical in setting and character, since it deals with the courtship of Cicero and the patrician lady Terentia. This romance even includes a Vergilian pastoral setting, the "vale of Love"; nevertheless, the genius of this vale is distinctly English, almost Chaucerian.

ROMANTIC LOVE

Thematically, most of Greene's poems, like the romances in which they are contained, are about the workings of love, usually painful, in young men and women. As expressions of his characters' emotional states, the poems can be compared to soliloquies or set speeches in drama. What each poem says about love depends on the character's personality, station in life, and situation at the moment. Thus, the title character of *Menaphon*, a shepherd in love with a princess, joyfully proclaims his love in one poem and woefully exclaims on his rejection in another; his fellow shepherd, Doron, also sings about the lady, but his description is platonic, since he admires Samela, but does not dote on her affection. Greene creates love poems to fit an amazing array of character types: prostitutes, icy virgins, betrayed wives, arrogant princes, love-scarred travelers, love-starved rustics, and many others. Philomela's ode reveals the mind of the chaste wife of a jealous husband; in a completely different spirit is the song of Infida, the whore who inveigles the hero of *Greene's Never Too*

Late: "Thine eyes like flames of holie fires,/ *N'oseres vous, mon bel amy*, Burnes all my thoughts with sweete desires."

Because most Greene romances lead to a main character's remorse for wrongs done in the name of love, many of his poems dwell on either the overwhelming power of the emotion or the horrors of infatuation. Greene frequently handles this allegorically, in narratives about Cupid, Venus, and other mythological figures, as in "Radagon in Dianem," from *Francesco's Fortunes*. At other times, he comes at the issue directly, as in Philomela's ode, or in Francesco's sonnet on his infidelity. The two approaches differ with the characters' differing moods and motives: where the unscrupulous Radagon wants to seduce the innocent Mirimida by impressing her with his inventive wit, Francesco, ravaged by such schemes, creates verse that exhibits his newly found peace of mind. The second poem, while less showy, presents a more fully elaborated image, that of the prison, within a form that demands more control than does that chosen by Radagon. These two poems typify the marriage of form and dramatic function that Greene achieves in his best incidental poetry.

DRAMATIC VERSE

Even casual scrutiny of Greene's work suggests a connection between his stage writing, which began in 1588, and the change in his poetic style that took place the same year. Certainly, his many poetic experiments in the romances before 1588 had made Greene a fluent versifier before he began writing for the stage. His first known play, *Orlando Furioso*, of which only a partial text remains, shows Greene's ease in spinning long iambic sentences dense with mythology. Conversely, the more personal, vividly descriptive poetry in *Greene's Never Too Late* and *Francesco's Fortunes* owes something to the fast-paced, richly sensual dialogue of *Friar Bacon and Friar Bungay* and *James IV*.

Greene's plays probably had deeper influence on his incidental verse than did the verse on the dramatic style. Playwriting gave Greene a broader, generally less educated audience; drama also demanded greater diversity of diction and tone to suit the greater range of character types. The ephemerality and comparative informality of spoken verse demanded images that were vivid, yet simple enough to fit conversational discourse. That Greene learned these lessons quickly is shown by *Friar Bacon and Friar Bungay*, one year after *Orlando Furioso*. The later play features crisp dialogue interrupted infrequently by the long set speeches of which the earlier play had largely consisted. Of particular note is Greene's brand-new imagery, drawn from the English countryside, not from the courts of Venus. When Greene's aristocrats declaim in this play, they use hyperboles drawn from the contemporary world of commerce, not from Ovid. The most immediate impact of this new technique on Greene's incidental verse is found in *Menaphon*. One year later, the pastoral story of Mirimida, which concludes *Francesco's Fortunes*, shows even more strongly the influence of this play, as characters of different ranks speak verse amazingly different in diction and style; most of these poems are invigorated by images of English country life.

A different type of influence, but equal to that of *Friar Bacon and Friar Bungay*, was exerted on Greene's incidental poems by *James IV*. Written substantially in rhymed verse of various schemes, *James IV* tested Greene's ability to compose in a highly demanding poetic form a work for the popular stage. This form allowed Greene to imbue with a songlike tone this semihistorical tale of an English lady married to, betrayed by, and reunited with a Scots king. Like the tetrameter narratives contained in his romances of 1590, the rhymed verse in *James IV* gives the play a folk quality that softens and distances the often harsh events. The "feel" of the play is similar to that of Shakespeare's late romances. *James IV* also influenced the meditative "odes" in such romances as *Philomela: The Lady Fitzwater's Nightingale* (1592), *Francesco's Fortunes*, and *Greene's Vision*. The most striking traits of these poems—the single, integrated image and the perspective of melancholy wisdom—appear in numerous passages in the play.

The quiet lyricism of many of the speeches in *James IV* rehearses the tone of the "odes"; the emphasis on "I" and on the image of the speaker's performing a simple act, whether playing the lute or embroidering, even as the poem proceeds, makes them highly personal. At the same time, each speaker moralizes on a familiar theme, thus making the emotions available to all. Since the moral reflects explicitly back on the speaker, not on the reader, the "odes" have a quietly salutary effect, neither accusing nor warning. The sprightly tempo of the ballad form of these "odes," influenced by *James IV*, helps the romances containing them to convey that gentle optimism that is the hallmark of Greene's art.

A MAIDEN'S DREAM

Greene's only extended, self-contained work in a traditional poetic genre is *A Maiden's Dream*, his eulogy for Lord Chancellor Sir Christopher Hatton, who died November 20, 1591. The 389-line poem holds a strange place in the Greene chronology, as it comes at the end of a year in which he may have published no other verse, either dramatic or incidental. In 1591, Greene had turned from the romance to the conny-catching pamphlet, its characters being crooks and tradespeople, its setting the streets and haunts of London, its language slang and trade talk. How surprising, in this context, to read *A Maiden's Dream*, its rhyme-royal stanzas setting forth a young woman's vision of Hatton on his bier, "all in armour clad . . . a crown of Oliues on his helme . . ."; weeping Astraea holds his head in her lap, while tearful nymphs surround them. It is the sort of scene that Greene had not painted since his romance *Alcida: Greene's Metamorphosis* (1588), which had featured three pairs of emblematic poems adorning the tombs of fallen lovers. After the allegorical stage is set and the characters introduced, however, *A Maiden's Dream* proceeds in a different manner from that of the earlier work. Whereas the *Alcida* poems had piled up mythological parallels to the miseries of the lovers in the story, *A Maiden's Dream* presents allegorical figures: Justice, Temperance, Religion, and so on, who speak about affairs of state in England and Hatton's record of service. The gods are mentioned once or twice, for atmosphere, but Greene's intent is to recount the dead chancellor's deeds and, by so doing, present his own vision of an ideal England.

Within the series of eulogies presented in turn by each of the arrayed Virtues, Greene comments on other issues: religion, foreign wars, and the conflicts of classes; his views are typically moderate, his tone unembittered. As readers of the pamphlets or the plays might expect, his principal causes are charity and mercy, and Hatton becomes a convenient symbol of them both. Like his incidental poems from 1588 on, *A Maiden's Dream* was clearly influenced by Greene's playwriting. The later plays, particularly *James IV*, gave Greene fluency in composing dramatic rhymed verse, while his playwriting experience as a whole enabled him to present an idea graphically and concisely; thus, the allegorical frame. The plays also taught him to intensify emotion and change mood through the use of vivid images from everyday life, rather than through mythological hyperbole.

Although Greene would not again publish verse, whether extended, dramatic, or incidental, *A Maiden's Dream* gave him practice with a framework—the dream vision—and a mode—allegory—that he would employ the following year in another patriotic work, *A Quip for an Upstart Courtier*. This prose work is one more example of Greene's ability to apply in one genre the lessons learned in another.

OTHER MAJOR WORKS

LONG FICTION: *Arbasto: The Anatomy of Fortune*, 1584; *Euphues His Censure to Philautus*, 1587; *Penelope's Web*, 1587; *Alcida: Greene's Metamorphosis*, 1588; *Greene's Mourning Garment*, 1590; *Philomela: The Lady Fitzwater's Nightingale*, 1592.

SHORT FICTION: *Mamillia: A Mirror or Looking Glass for the Ladies of England*, 1583, 1593 (2 parts); *The Mirror of Modesty*, 1584; *Morando: The Tritameron of Love*, 1584, 1587 (2 parts); *Planetomachia*, 1585; *Pandosto: The Triumph of Time*, 1588; *Perimedes the Blacksmith*, 1588; *Ciceronis Amor*, 1589 (also known as *Tullies Love*); *Menaphon*, 1589; *Francesco's Fortunes*, 1590; *Greene's Never Too Late*, 1590; *Greene's Farewell to Folly*, 1591; *A Notable Discovery of Cozenage*, 1591; *The Black Book's Messenger*, 1592; *The Defense of Conny-Catching*, 1592; *A Disputation Between a Hee Conny-Catcher and a Shee Conny-Catcher*, 1592; *Greene's Vision*, 1592; *A Quip for an Upstart Courtier*, 1592.

PLAYS: *Alphonsus, King of Aragon*, pr. c. 1587; *Orlando Furioso*, pr. c. 1588 (verse play); *A Looking Glass for London and England*, pr. c. 1588-1589 (with Thomas Lodge; verse play); *Friar Bacon and Friar Bungay*, pr. c. 1589 (verse play); *John of Bordeaux*, pr. c. 1590-1591 (fragment); *James IV*, pr. c. 1591 (verse play); *Complete Plays*, 1909.

NONFICTION: *The Spanish Masquerado*, 1589; *The Royal Exchange*, 1590; *The Second Part of Conny-Catching*, 1591; *Greene's Groatsworth of Wit Bought with a Million of Repentance*, 1592; *The Repentance of Robert Greene*, 1592; *The Third and Last Part of Conny-Catching*, 1592.

MISCELLANEOUS: *Life and Complete Works in Prose and Verse*, 1881-1886 (15 volumes).

BIBLIOGRAPHY

Alwes, Derek B. *Sons and Authors in Elizabethan England*. Cranbury, N.J.: Associated University Presses, 2004. Contains two chapters on Greene, one on his romances and the other on his defense of poetry.

Crupi, Charles W. *Robert Greene*. Boston: Twayne, 1986. Crupi's publication addresses Greene's life based on relevant biographical and historical research printed since 1960. Contains extensive notes and references, a chronology, and a select bibliography of primary and secondary sources.

Hoster, Jay. *Tiger's Heart: What Really Happened in the Groat's-Worth of Wit Controversy of 1592*. Columbus, Ohio: Ravine Books, 1993. Attempts to separate fact from fiction as to the authorship of *Greene's Groatsworth of Wit Bought with a Million of Repentance*. Includes bibliographical references and index.

Jordan, John Clark. *Robert Greene*. 1965. Reprint. Charleston, S.C.: BiblioLife, 2009. Jordan's book is considered a main source for critics concerned with Greene's work. He presents Greene as a man of letters, who was an expert at narrative. The text includes a discussion of Greene's poetry, plays, and nondramatic work. A bibliography and appendixes are included. The appendices contain a framework for Greene's tales, misconceptions about Greene's life and career, as well as accounts of early allusions to Greene.

Melnikoff, Kirk, and Edward Gieskes, eds. *Writing Robert Greene: Essays on England's First Notori-*

ous Professional Writer. Burlington, Vt.: Ashgate, 2008. A collection of essays that examine the works of Greene and how he contributed to Elizabethan culture. Contains an annotated bibliography of research on Greene.

Wilson, Katharine. *Fictions of Authorship in Late Elizabethan Narratives: Euphues in Arcadia*. New York: Oxford University Press, 2006. Wilson looks at writers such as Greene, John Lyly, and Thomas Lodge, who blended high and low culture in their prose and were sources of Williams Shakespeare's comedies. She deals extensively with Greene's work.

Christopher J. Thaiss

FULKE GREVILLE

Born: Beauchamp's Court, Warwickshire, England; October 3, 1554

Died: Brooke House, London, England; September 30, 1628

PRINCIPAL POETRY

Caelica, 1633
An Inquisition on Fame and Honour, 1633
A Treatie of Humane Learning, 1633
A Treatie of Warres, 1633
A Treatise of Monarchy, 1670
A Treatise of Religion, 1670
Selected Poems, 1990

OTHER LITERARY FORMS

Fulke Greville (GREHV-ihl) wrote three verse dramas modeled on Seneca: *Mustapha* (pb. 1609), *Alaham* (pb. 1633), and *Antony and Cleopatra*. He destroyed *Antony and Cleopatra* because he feared that it contained material "apt enough to be construed, or strained to a personating of vices in the present Governors, and government." *Mustapha* exists in three different versions: one published without Greville's permission in 1609, two identical manuscripts that seem to have been written before the printed edition, and the 1633 version,

which appeared along with *Alaham* in the collection of Greville's works titled *Certain Learned and Elegant Workes of the Right Honourable Fulke, Lorde Brooke*. It was probably the translation of Robert Garnier's *Marc Antoine* (1592) by Sir Philip Sidney's sister, Mary, the countess of Pembroke, that initiated the fashion of the "French Seneca" to which Greville's plays were a contribution.

Of Greville's titled prose works, the two most important are *A Letter to an Honourable Lady* (1633) and *The Life of the Renowned Sir Philip Sidney* (1652), containing a survey of international relations in the 1580's and a history of Elizabeth's reign as well as an account of Sidney's life. Of particular interest to the literary historian is Greville's discussion of the difference between his view of poetry and that of Sidney.

ACHIEVEMENTS

Fulke Greville's reputation as a poet has grown appreciably. In *Poetry* (1939), Yvor Winters announced that Greville was "one of the two great masters of the short poem." Commenting on the great lyrics of the sixteenth century, Winters described them as "intellectually both profound and complex . . . restrained and direct in style, and . . . sombre and disillusioned in tone." While more recently critics have questioned the appropriateness of using the term "plain style" to describe Greville's verse, the poems in *Caelica*, his sonnet sequence, are now highly regarded.

His verse treatises, with the exception of G. A. Wilke's perceptive and informed comments (*Fulke Greville, Lord Brooke, the Remains: Being Poems of Monarchy and Religion*, 1965, G. A. Wilkes, editor), have received little attention. Didactic in tone, they are sententious and restrained in diction, but their very austerity can be moving to a reader interested in intellectual verse. Summarizing his own aesthetics in *A Treatie of Humane Learning*, Greville describes poetry and music as "things not pretious in their proper kind," but he adds that they can function "as pleasing sauce to dainty food . . . [c]ast upon things which in themselves are good" (stanza 12).

Greville has found some appreciative readers among men of letters and poets: Charles Lamb surprised his friends at a dinner party by selecting Greville and Sir Thomas Browne as the two writers whom he would most have liked to meet; Algernon Charles Swinburne, T. S. Eliot, and Theodore Roethke have praised Greville's works, but Samuel Taylor Coleridge paid him an especially high tribute when he imitated *Caelica*, "LXXXIV" in "Farewell to Love."

BIOGRAPHY

Fulke Greville, First Lord Brooke, supplied a structure for his own biography by having an epitaph engraved on his tomb at Warwick Castle that sums up his life in exemplary brevity: "Fulke Greville/ Servant to Queen Elizabeth,/ Councillor to King James,/ And Friend to Sir Philip Sidney,/ Trophaeum Peccati [Trophy of Sin]." His father, also named Fulke, married Anne Neville, who came from a family with landed wealth and a titled past. The relationship to which Greville gave most prominence on his tombstone, his friendship with Sidney, began when they entered Shrewsbury grammar school on the same day, October 17, 1564. Before he was fourteen, Greville matriculated at Jesus College, Cambridge. Sidney went to Oxford, but they were reunited when they were introduced

Fulke Greville (Archive Photos/Getty Images)

to Elizabeth's court in the late 1570's. Both young men joined the political party of Robert Dudley, the earl of Leicester, Sidney's uncle and an old friend of the Greville family.

Leicester's radical Protestant party thought that religion should determine domestic and foreign policy and opposed the more conservative faction led by William Cecil, Baron Burghley, and his son Robert Cecil. Both Sidney and Greville wanted to engage in more adventurous activities than Elizabeth was willing to sanction. In their early thirties, they ran away from court to join Sir Francis Drake on a voyage to the West Indies, but the Queen sent after them. After Sidney ignored the first messenger, the second messenger brought with him an offer of employment for Sidney under Leicester in the Low Countries. Greville remained in England, and Sidney's appointment ended tragically.

Sidney was wounded at Zutphen on October 12, 1586, and died three weeks later. The entire court went into mourning. Greville was overwhelmed. Later, he took upon himself the task of protecting his friend's reputation as an author. Rather than let an inferior version of *Arcadia* be made public, Greville interested himself in which manuscript was to serve as the source for William Ponsonby's 1590 quarto edition of the first two books and a part of the third. The chapter divisions, chapter summaries, and the arrangement of the eclogues were supplied by an "over-seer" who may have been Greville himself.

By 1594, Greville had joined the Essex circle, led by Robert Devereux, the earl of Essex, nephew to Leicester and political heir of Sidney. Essex had both married Sidney's widow, Frances Walsingham, and established himself as the leader of the radical Protestant faction. The influence of Essex assisted Greville in obtaining his first important political appointment as treasurer of the navy in 1598. By 1601, Essex had rebelled against the Queen and had been executed for treason; the death of Essex and disgrace of his party enabled Robert Cecil, Greville's great antagonist, to solidify his power. It was probably in 1601 that Greville destroyed his copy of *Antony and Cleopatra* because it might be interpreted as a political commentary on Elizabeth, Essex, and Cecil.

Prior to Elizabeth's death in 1603, Greville expected to be appointed to the Privy Council, but when James came to the throne, he lost his position as treasurer of the navy. Because Cecil regarded him as a dangerous political opponent, it was not until after his death in May, 1612, that Greville was able to enter the phase of his life that he himself labeled "Councillor to King James." Following Cecil's death, Greville shrewdly sought (and bought) the favor of all the leaders of the important political factions at court. On October 1, 1614, he became chancellor and under-treasurer of the Exchequer and Privy Councillor. After a decade of retired life, Greville entered the politically corrupt Jacobean court to serve for seven years as a prominent and powerful official. In 1621, an aging man, he lost his position as chancellor and under-treasurer, but the king created him Baron Brooke of Beauchamp's Court on January 29, 1621. Greville had requested two baronies so that he could leave two heirs, but the second, which he claimed on the basis of descent from Robert, Lord Willoughby de Broke, was denied.

Greville died on September 30, 1628, after having been stabbed by his servant Robert Hayward a month earlier. The servant's motives remain in doubt, but Greville's contemporaries speculated that Hayward might have felt angered by Greville's will. He left Hayward only twenty pounds a year for life. Greville gave orders that if his assailant had escaped, no one should pursue him: He desired that no man "should lose his life for him." The doctors replaced the "kell," a fatty membrane around the intestines, with "fat thrust into the wound of his belly . . . which putrifying, ended him." Ronald A. Rebholz, Greville's modern biographer, has suggested that his "temperamental incapacity for a prolonged relationship with a woman" might have resulted from a "homosexual bias which he controlled or could not admit" (*The Life of Fulke Greville: First Lord Brooke*, 1971). A contemporary, Sir Robert Naunton, however, describes him as "constant courtier of the ladies." His descendants quarreled over his property, taking opposite sides in the Civil War that was to divide England during the reign of Charles I. The last phrase that Greville caused to be placed on his tombstone, "sin's trophy," suggests the degree to which his youthful idealism had given way in his last years to a grim disillusionment.

ANALYSIS

At the age of fifty-eight, Fulke Greville wrote to Sir John Coke his much-quoted statement: "I know the world and believe in God." Critics have interpreted this comment as emblematic of Greville's thought. He is described as a worldly man whose experience led him gradually to reject this world as vain; these feelings of *contemptus mundi* are also supposed to have led him to attack human learning as a preparation for divine revelation. C. S. Lewis has described him as having the intellectual orientation of an Existentialist, the cast of mind of Søren Kierkegaard or Blaise Pascal (*English Literature in the Sixteenth Century Excluding Drama*, 1954). Greville's pessimism, however, may have been influenced by things external as well as internal. He outlived most of his contemporaries, but those who lived well into the seventeenth century shared his nostalgia for the Elizabethan court of their youth.

Greville's own analysis of his aesthetic intentions deserves careful attention:

> For my own part, I found my creeping Genius more fixed upon the Images of Life, than the Images of Wit, and therefore chose not to write to them on whose foot the black Oxe had not already trod, as the Proverbe is, but to those only, that are weather-beaten in the Sea of this World, such as having lost the sight of their Gardens, and groves, study to saile on a right course among Rocks, and quicksands.

His readers, then, will be those who want instruction and who do not need to be engaged by "the images of wit." The fiction or feigning that Sir Philip Sidney regards as the essential feature of poetry was not important to Greville. He wanted to present his ideas in restrained diction, preferring plain statement to the ornateness that was popular earlier in the sixteenth century.

It is misleading to speak of Greville's development as a poet because, except for a pirated version of the verse drama *Mustapha*, none of his work appeared during his lifetime. Since the Warwick manuscripts demonstrate that he revised his poetry and prose repeatedly, it is difficult to establish a reliable system of dating. Ronald Rebholz and G. A. Wilkes have each proposed plausible chronologies for composition and revision, but it is impossible to draw final conclusions because of the complexity of the manuscript evidence. Without suggesting that Greville moved from one phase to another, it is possible to differentiate three somewhat distinct literary styles: (1) the meditative style that Greville uses in *Caelica*, (2) the strenuous, involuted manner of the verse dramas, which led Swinburne to compare Greville's work to that of George Chapman, and (3) the analytical and discursive verse of his poetical treatises, poetry containing some of Greville's most profound thoughts. Rather than viewing Greville's literary career as a progression from *Caelica* to the treatises, or, conversely, as a movement from success with the lyric to failure with the philosophical poem, one should assess each of these styles in terms of its own literary objectives.

CAELICA

Although frequently included in discussions of the sonnet sequences that became popular in the 1590's, *Caelica* might be more accurately described as a collection of short lyrics. In forty-one poems, Greville uses the English sonnet form of three quatrains followed by a couplet, rather than the Italian form favored by Sidney, but he often breaks the poems before the sestet, as was customary in the Italian sonnet tradition. His other poems are usually composed of stanzas of four or six lines. Some evidence exists that the first seventy-six poems were composed prior to Sidney's death in 1586, and most scholars think that the sonnets are now arranged in the order in which they were composed.

Rebholz has described *Caelica* as evolving into a "series of anti-love poems." A large number of poems attack the inconstancy of women and men in a tone reminiscent of John Donne at his most cynical. The latter part of Greville's sequence is dominated by religious themes and images. His philosophical insights can be as moving as they are profound. In Sonnet LXXXVII, which Lewis singles out for special praise, Greville describes the soul as having fled the body: "To see it selfe in that eternall glasse/ Where time doth end and thoughts accuse the dead,/ Where all to come is one with all that was." Sonnets LXXXIV and LXXXV are companion poems that present a contrast between earthly love governed by Cupid and the heavenly love

governed by a "Nature by no other nature knowne." These two contrasting poems illustrate the conflicting themes and unresolved tensions in *Caelica*.

MUSTAPHA AND ALAHAM

Greville's two surviving verse dramas, *Mustapha* and *Alaham*, both use plots derived from Eastern sources. In *Mustapha*, Soliman the Magnificent (1520-1566) murders his loyal and virtuous son Mustapha because Rossa, a freed bondwoman for whom he feels a destructive sexual passion, persuades him that his son is plotting against him. Rossa wants to make her own son the sultan's heir. Her daughter Camena tries to warn Mustapha, but he will not save himself if it means causing disorder in the state. Ironically, the people almost rebel over the murder, but Achmat, Soliman's chief adviser, decides that order must be preserved in the state even if it means allowing Soliman's wicked act to go unpunished.

Alaham, like *Mustapha*, examines sexual lust and lust for power within a political context. Alaham is the second son of a sultan, but he is so consumed by a lust for power that he is willing to burn his father, brother, and sister alive on a funeral pyre in order to seize the throne. Hala, his unfaithful wife, decides to revenge herself on Alaham for murdering her lover and plots a violent revenge. She contrives a suitable punishment for him by devising a poisoned crown and cloak. She tortures him further by killing their child in front of him while he writhes in agony. After murdering the child, she realizes that she has killed the baby she had by her lover, not by her husband. Then she kills her other child and rejoices that she is going to hell, where she can indulge her passion for excess.

TREATISES

Rebholz has suggested the following chronology for the composition of the treatises: *A Treatise of Monarchy* (1599-1604, pb. 1670), *An Inquisition on Fame and Honour* (1612-1614, pb. 1633), *A Treatie of Warres* (1619-1621, pb. 1633), *A Treatie of Humane Learning* (1620-1622, pb. 1633), *A Treatise of Religion* (1622-1628, pb. 1670). Greville, however, seems to have intended to print first the treatise on religion, then the one on humane learning, the one on fame and honor, and finally the one on war. The order is given in Greville's hand in a manuscript of the treatises. The problem of chronology is complicated also by the omission of *A Treatise of Monarchy* and *A Treatise of Religion* from the first posthumous collection in 1633; these two treatises were published separately in 1670 as *The Remains of Sir Fulke Greville, Lord B*. In the case of *A Treatise of Religion*, Greville's antiprelatical stance probably led authorities to suppress the work.

The poems' titles accurately reflect their content. Greville the statesman and thinker presents his arguments in unadorned but powerful simplicity. As he observes in *A Treatie of Humane Learning*, he regards music and poetry as "ornaments to life," but only "whiles they do serve, and not possess our hearts." To interest oneself in art for art's sake would lead to a "disease of mind." Greville acknowledges that arts, like music and poetry, if they are used in church or military ceremonies, can "enlarge the mind" and suppress "passions of the baser kind." He, however, remains skeptical about the value of any knowledge other than the knowledge of God's grace.

By the end of his life, Greville felt the world to be so corrupt that reform was impossible. He had abandoned his faith in two of the basic tenets of Christian humanism: confidence that rational inquiry might result in the reform of institutions and conviction that each man was obligated to serve the state in order to promote the common good. In the last poem printed in *Caelica*, he prays for an apocalypse: "Rather, sweet Jesus, fill up time and come/ To yield the sin her everlasting doom."

OTHER MAJOR WORKS

PLAYS: *Mustapha*, 1609 (verse play); *Alaham*, 1633 (verse play).

NONFICTION: *A Letter to an Honourable Lady*, 1633; *The Life of the Renowned Sir Philip Sidney*, 1652; *Prose Works*, 1986 (John Gouws, editor).

MISCELLANEOUS: *Certain Learned and Elegant Workes of the Right Honourable Fulke, Lorde Brooke*, 1633; *The Remains of Sir Fulke Greville, Lord B.*, 1670.

BIBLIOGRAPHY

Alexander, Gavin. "Fulke Greville and the Afterlife." *Huntington Library Quarterly* 62, nos. 3/4 (2001): 203-231. Alexander discusses Greville's preoccupation with his posthumous influence. It is characteristic of Greville to look back to the dead, but it is equally his habit to think forward beyond his own death.

Greville, Fulke, Baron Brooke. *The Complete Poems and Plays of Fulke Greville, Lord Brooke (1554-1628)*. 2 vols. Edited by G. A. Wilkes. Lewiston, N.Y.: Edwin Mellen Press, 2008. This collection, edited by a prominent Greville scholar, presents a detailed examination of Greville's sonnets, verse plays, and treatises.

Hannay, Margaret P. *Philip's Phoenix: Mary Sidney, Countess of Pembroke*. New York: Oxford University Press, 1990. Greville regarded his close friendship with Sir Philip Sidney as a major influence on his life. This biography of Sidney's sister, Mary Sidney Herbert, countess of Pembroke, comments upon Greville and his contributions to and participation in the literary interests of the Sidney circle.

Klemp, P. J. *Fulke Greville and Sir John Davies: A Reference Guide*. Boston: G. K. Hall, 1985. Presents a chronological bibliography of works by and about Greville from 1581 to 1985. Each entry in the bibliography has been annotated. General studies of the political and literary contexts are also included in this useful bibliography.

McCoy, Richard C. *The Rites of Knighthood: The Literature and Politics of Elizabethan Chivalry*. Berkeley: University of California Press, 1989. This study of Greville and Sir Philip Sidney concentrates on the impact of chivalric codes and models of behavior on Elizabethan and Jacobean courtiers. McCoy offers insights into the philosophical issues that underlie courtly entertainments and pageants.

Norbrook, David. *Poetry and Politics in the English Renaissance*. Rev. ed. New York: Oxford University Press, 2002. This work on the connection between politics and poetry during the Renaissance contains a chapter on Greville.

Rebholz, Ronald A. *The Life of Fulke Greville, First Lord Brooke*. Oxford, England: Clarendon Press, 1971. The standard biography, this scholarly volume is thorough and meticulous. Rebholz divides Greville's life into four parts: "Friend to Sir Philip

Sidney" (through Greville's youth); "Servant to Queen Elizabeth" (middle life, through his loss of office); "Councillor to King James"; and "Trophaeum Peccati" (in which the death of hope, Christian humanism, and Greville's own death are addressed). Appendixes treat the dating of Greville's works, provide a foldout genealogical table, and reprint letters. The volume ends with a bibliography listing both primary and secondary sources, and an index.

Waswo, Richard. *The Fatal Mirror: Themes and Techniques in the Poetry of Fulke Greville.* 1972. Reprint. Charlottesville: University Press of Virginia, 1996. This full-length study of Greville's life and works contrasts the poetics of Greville and Sir Philip Sidney. Major emphasis is given to *Caelica.* Waswo comments upon the Platonic and Petrarchan elements in Greville's sonnet sequence and analyzes the rhetorical texture of what is frequently described as his "plain style."

Wilkes, G. A. "'Left . . . to Play the Ill Poet in My Own Part': The Literary Relationship of Sidney and Fulke Greville." *Review of English Studies* 57, no. 230 (2006): 291-310. Greville scholar Wilkes examines how Greville refashioned Sir Philip Sidney's literary identity after his death in two well-known letters and a biography.

Jeanie R. Brink

THOM GUNN

Born: Gravesend, Kent, England; August 29, 1929
Died: San Francisco, California; April 25, 2004

PRINCIPAL POETRY
Fighting Terms, 1954, 1962
The Sense of Movement, 1957
My Sad Captains, and Other Poems, 1961
Selected Poems, 1962 (with Ted Hughes)
A Geography, 1966
Positives, 1966 (with photographs by Ander Gunn)
Touch, 1967

The Garden of the Gods, 1968
The Explorers, 1969
The Fair in the Woods, 1969
Poems, 1950-1966: A Selection, 1969
Sunlight, 1969
Last Days at Teddington, 1971
Moly, 1971
Moly and My Sad Captains, 1971
Poems After Chaucer, 1971
Mandrakes, 1973
Songbook, 1973
To the Air, 1974
Jack Straw's Castle, 1975
Jack Straw's Castle, and Other Poems, 1976
The Missed Beat, 1976
Bally Power Play, 1979
Games of Chance, 1979
Selected Poems, 1950-1975, 1979
Talbot Road, 1981
The Menace, 1982
The Passages of Joy, 1982
Undesirables, 1988
The Man with Night Sweats, 1992
Collected Poems, 1993
In the Twilight Slot, 1995
Boss Cupid, 2000
Site Specific: Seventeen "Neighborhood" Poems, 2000

OTHER LITERARY FORMS
Thom Gunn was best known for his poetry as well as his essays that present criticism and autobiographical information. *The Occasions of Poetry: Essays in Criticism and Autobiography* (1982) collects Gunn's reviews and essays on poets from Fulke Greville and Ben Jonson to Robert Creeley and Robert Duncan. It also contains four valuable essays on the composition and inspiration of Gunn's own poetry, including the autobiographical sketch "My Life up to Now" (1977).

ACHIEVEMENTS
Thom Gunn was richly honored for his work during his lifetime. He won the Levinson Prize in 1955, the Somerset Maugham Award in 1959, the Arts Council of Great Britain Award in 1959, a National Institute of

Arts and Letters Award in 1964, and a Rockefeller Foundation award in 1966. He won a Gold Medal in poetry from the Commonwealth Club of California in 1976 for *Jack Straw's Castle*. *The Passages of Joy* earned the W. H. Smith Award (1980), two Northern California Book Awards in poetry (1982, 1992), and the PEN/Los Angeles Prize for poetry (1983). In 1988, he won the Robert Kirsch Award for body of work from the *Los Angeles Times* as well as the Sara Teasdale prize. He was honored with the Shelley Memorial Award of the Poetry Society of America and the Lila Wallace-*Reader's Digest* Writers' Award in 1990. *The Man with Night Sweats* earned him the Lenore Marshall Poetry Prize and the PEN Center USA West Poetry Award, both in 1993. He received a Lambda Literary Award in 1994 and the Award of Merit from the American Academy of Arts and Letters in 1998. He held a Guggenheim Fellowship in 1971 and a MacArthur Fellowship in 1993. In 2001, he received the Thom Gunn Award for Gay Poetry for *Boss Cupid*.

Thom Gunn (©Ander Gunn/Courtesy, Farrar, Straus and Giroux)

BIOGRAPHY

Born Thomson William Gunn, Thom Gunn grew up in the London suburb of Hampstead Heath, "forever grateful" that he was "raised in no religion at all." During the Blitz, he read John Keats, Alfred, Lord Tennyson, and George Meredith, who have all influenced his verse in various ways. His parents—both journalists, although his mother had stopped working before his birth—were divorced when he was eight or nine. After two years in the British army, Gunn went to Paris to work in the offices of the Metro. He attended Trinity College, University of Cambridge, during the early 1950's; there he attended the lectures of F. R. Leavis and began to write poetry in earnest, publishing his first book, *Fighting Terms*, in 1954, while still an undergraduate. He worked briefly on the magazine *Granta* and, as president of the English Club, met and introduced Angus Wilson, Henry Green, Dylan Thomas, and William Empson, among others. Here he also became a pacifist, flirted with socialism, hitchhiked through France during a summer vacation, and met Mike Kitay, his American companion, who influenced his decision to move to the United States.

After graduation, Gunn spent a brief period in Rome and Paris. At the suggestion of the American poet Donald Hall, Gunn applied for and won a creative writing fellowship to Stanford University, where he studied with the formalist poet and critic Yvor Winters. After a short teaching stint in San Antonio, Texas, where he first rode a motorcycle ("for about a month"), heard Elvis Presley's songs, and saw James Dean's movies, Gunn accepted an offer to teach at the University of California, Berkeley, in 1958.

Gunn returned to London for a year (1964-1965) just as the Beatles burst on the scene. Back in San Francisco, he gave up tenure in 1966, only a year after it was granted, and immersed himself in the psychedelic and sexual revolution of the late 1960's. While teaching at Princeton University in 1970, Gunn lived in Greenwich Village when the first art galleries began to appear in SoHo. He moved to San Francisco and began his tenure at University of California, Berkeley, first as a lecturer and then, beginning in 1973, as an associate professor of English. He continued to teach on a part-time basis to allow him, as he says, to write relatively unfettered by academic demands. Gunn died in San Francisco on April 25, 2004.

ANALYSIS

Thom Gunn first achieved notoriety in England, as part of what was called the Movement, an unofficial tag applied to some poets of the 1950's who were, in Gunn's words, "eschewing Modernism, and turning back, though not very thoroughgoingly, to traditional resources in structure and method." Poets of the Movement included Philip Larkin, Kingsley Amis, and Donald Davie, among others. Gunn continued to achieve critical acclaim by approaching a diverse number of subjects previously excluded from poetry, with a similar regard for structure and meter.

Having moved to the United States in the late 1950's, Gunn is somewhat of an amphibious poet. One might say that while his poetry has its formal roots in the English tradition, his subject matter has been taken largely from his American experience. He is known particularly for his exploration of certain counterculture movements from the 1950's to the 1980's. He is comfortable on the fringes of society, where popular culture thrives; rock music, motorcycle gangs, leather bars, and orgies have been his milieu. He is also considered one of the poets who deal most frankly with gay subject matter and themes. What distinguishes Gunn from other poets working with the same material is that he has refused to abandon structure and meter, preferring to impose form on chaotic subjects. Since the mid-1960's, however, Gunn has been increasingly influenced by American poets, notably William Carlos Williams; he turned first to the flexible meters of syllabic verse and subsequently to free verse, without sacrificing his demanding sense of form.

A poet interested in the possibilities of identity, Gunn is best known for his explorations into the existential hero, who takes many guises in his poetry, including the soldier and the motorcyclist. The greatest influence on his thought in these matters has been the existentialism espoused by Jean-Paul Sartre in his philosophical treatise *L'Être et le néant* (1943; *Being and Nothingness*, 1956). For Sartre, humanity is condemned to freedom to make its own meaning in an absurd universe. For Gunn, poetry has been the vehicle of this creation.

FIGHTING TERMS

Gunn began his poetic career while still at Cambridge, with the publication of *Fighting Terms*. The im-age of the soldier is first of all, Gunn has written, "myself, the national serviceman, the 'clumsy brute in uniform,' the soldier who never goes to war, whose role has no function, whose battledress is a joke," but it is also the "attractive and repellant" real soldier, who kills but also quests, like Achilles and Odysseus. Above all, the soldier is the poet, "an existential conqueror, excited and aggressive," trying to make sense of his absurd situation.

These poems show Gunn's propensity to try, not always successfully, to make meaning of action in the intervals between action. "The Wound" is a good example. While recuperating, a soldier remembers the engagement of battle. As "the huge wound in my head began to heal," he remembers the Trojan War, but it is unclear whether this was his actual experience or only a hallucination. It could be that he is a contemporary soldier reverting to myth in the damaged and "darkened" valleys of his mind. When he rises to act again, his wound "breaks open wide," and he must again wait for "those storm-lit valleys to heal." His identity is thus never resolved.

Similarly, in "Looking Glass," the narrator is a kind of gardener who observes his life under glass. He compares it to a Garden of Eden in which "a fine callous fickleness" sent him in search of pleasure, "gratification being all." Yet there is no God present in this world to give the world an a priori meaning: "I am the gardener now myself. . . . I am responsible for order here." In the absence of God, "risks are authorized"—a theme that imbues Gunn's later poems of experience. He is also alienated from society and does not "care if villagers suspect" that his life is going "to seed." He takes a kind of pride in his status as outsider: "How well it goes to seed." The act of observing the wild garden of his life is a pleasure in itself, even though he is an outcast, "damp-booted, unemployed."

In "The Beach Head," the narrator is a would-be conqueror planning a campaign into his own society: "I seek a pathway to the country's heart." Again the alienated outsider ("I, hare-brained stranger") is heard making sense of his life, wondering whether to enter history through a fine gesture, "With little object other than panache/ And showing what great odds may be defied." His alternative to action is to watch and "wait and calculate my chances/ Consolidating this my inch-square base." This conflict is at the heart of Gunn's poetry, early and late: whether to risk the heroic act or succumb to the passivity of contemplation. Yet the latter too has its risk—namely, that his failure to act may cause society's "mild liking to turn to loathing."

THE SENSE OF MOVEMENT

The Sense of Movement continues Gunn's exploration of the active versus the contemplative existential hero. Here the pose, poise, or panache of the hero is more important than the goal of the action, the movement constituting its own meaning. The volume introduces Gunn's idealized "American myth of the motorcyclist, then in its infancy, of the wild man part free spirit and part hoodlum"; his motorcyclist series is based on Andrew Marvell's mower poems. Gunn admits that the book is largely derivative ("a second work of apprenticeship"), partaking of Yvor Winters's formalism, William Butler Yeats's theory of the mask, and Jean-Paul Sartre's existentialist philosophy of engaged action.

The opening poem of the volume, "On the Move," explores the conflict between "instinct" and "poise." This is a key dichotomy in Gunn's work. The natural world of instinct is largely unavailable to thinking human beings, who, unlike birds, must create a kind of surrogate impetus for the meaningful movement. The motorcyclists become the focus for this conflict because of their assumed pose of wildness; yet it is a pose, a posture that is only "a part solution, after all," to the problem. Riding "astride the created will," they appear "robust" only because they "strap in doubt . . . hiding it." The doubt has to do with their destination, as they "dare a future from the taken routes." The absurdity of action (a notion central to existential thought) is emphasized in that the person can appeal neither to natural instinct nor to metaphysics for the meaning he must himself create: "Men manufacture both machine and soul." Unlike "birds and saints," the motorcyclists do not "complete their purposes" by reaching a destination. The movement is its own excuse: "Reaching no absolute, in which to rest,/ One is always nearer by not keeping still."

"In Praise of Cities" affirms the disorderly evolution of human attempts to create meaning in the cityscape, which is personified as a woman, "indifferent to the indifference which conceived her." She withholds and offers herself to the one who wants to discover her secrets. "She wanders lewdly, whispering her given name,/ Charing Cross Road, or Forty-Second Street." Yet the city is really a mirror in which the narrator sees his "own designs, peeling and unachieved" on her walls, for she is, finally, "extreme, material, and the work of man." As in "On the Move," however, the narrator does not so much comprehend as simply embrace the city, with "a passion without understanding." His movement is its own excuse, but the communion with humankind, through his created cityscape, is real.

MY SAD CAPTAINS, AND OTHER POEMS

My Sad Captains, and Other Poems marks a turning point in Gunn's career, a border crossing that is evident in the book's two-part structure. The first half is concerned with the conflict between the "infinite" will and the "confined" execution, and the meter is suitably traditional. The epigraph from William Shakespeare's *Troilus and Cressida* (pr. c. 1601-1602) suggests that while "desire is boundless," "the act is a slave to limit." Limit is represented by the formalist quality of the poems in this first part of the book.

The second half of the book is much less theoretical, more concerned with direct experience, as its epigraph from F. Scott Fitzgerald suggests: "It's startling to you sometimes—just air, unobstructed, uncomplicated air." This thematic quality is reflected in the breathy technique of syllabic verse, in which the line is determined by the number of syllables rather than accents; the rhymes are random or, when regular, slant. The syllabic form is well suited to the direct apprehension of experience in such poems as "Light Among Redwoods," where "we stand/ and stare—mindless, diminished—/ at their rosy immanence."

Thematically, the volume continues to develop Gunn's "existential conqueror" motif in poems such as "The Book of the Dead" and "The Byrnies," while expanding his poetic repertoire to include snails and trucks as well as some more exotic familiars: tattoo parlors in "Blackie, the Electric Rembrandt" and gay and leather bars in "Modes of Pleasure" (two poems, one title) and "Black Jackets."

"A Map of the City" is perhaps even more successful than "In Praise of Cities" in affirming the human chaos of the city by its treatment of the theme within a traditional form. The speaker stands on a hill at night, looking at the "luminous" city like a map below. Like William Blake's "London," Gunn's city is a maze of drunks, transients, and sailors. From this vantage point, he can "watch a malady's advance," while recognizing his "love of chance." He sees the city's concrete boredom and suffering but also its abstract "potential" for both satisfaction and danger. From this perspective, he can, if only for a moment, get his bearings in relation to the city as a whole, as a map, so that when he descends into the maze again, he will be able to navigate his way through its dangers and flaws. He embraces the "crowded, broken, and unfinished" as the natural concomitants to the riches of city life, as he concludes: "I would not have the risk diminished."

The title poem, "My Sad Captains," is a tribute to all those friends who have inspired the poet, "a few with historical/ names." These men who were immersed in experience once seemed to him to have lived only to "renew the wasteful force they/ spent with each hot convulsion"; yet now they exist "apart" from life, "winnowed from failures," and indeed above life, "and turn with disinterested/ hard energy, like the stars."

Though this poem closes the volume, it can be profitably read together with any number of poems from the book, but especially the opening poem, "In Santa Maria del Popolo," which describes a painting of the "one convulsion" of "Saul becoming Paul" by the sixteenth century artist Caravaggio (Michelangelo Merisi). Here Paul becomes "the solitary man," "resisting, while embracing, nothingness." Yet it is to Caravaggio that Gunn looks for this revelation, the artist being one of his "sad captains."

Although Gunn did not do much more with syllabic verse after *My Sad Captains, and Other Poems*, it was, he said, a way of teaching himself about "unpatterned rhythms," or free verse. From this point onward, he worked in both traditional and "open" forms.

POSITIVES

Positives is written entirely in open forms. These poems were written to accompany his brother Ander's photographs of life in London. Poems about other works of art are common, especially in modern poetry.

W. H. Auden's "Musée des Beaux Arts" (1939) and John Ashbery's "Portrait in a Convex Mirror" (1964) are examples of poems that interpret paintings from a distant time and place, as is Gunn's own "In Santa Maria del Popolo." In *Positives*, however, the collaboration is very much contemporary. The poems are written with the photographs, which seem to have taught Gunn to pay attention to the details of street life, pubs, construction sites, abandoned houses, and bridges in a way he never had before. As a result, Gunn gives up the symbolism of Yeats for luminous realities: "It is not a symbolic/ bridge but a real bridge;/ nor is the bundle/ a symbol." This quality makes *Positives* the least philosophical of his early works, even though the theme is large: the progress from birth and "doing things for the first time" to old age and "the terror of full repose." Written to face the photographs, the poems are freed of the burden of description, so that they have a transparent quality, a light touch, and, on the whole, a positive tone.

The poems and photographs depict the "memoirs of the body" in the lines of a face or a stance or gesture. In most cases, "an ambiguous story" can be read there: either as "the ability to resist/ annihilation, or as the small/ but constant losses endured/ but between the lines/ life itself!" These moments of activity in the present—human beings absorbed in the space between past and future—are Gunn's subjects: a child bathing, boys waiting to grow up, motorcyclists riding, a bride overwhelmed by the weight of lace, an old woman balancing a bundle on her head. Each has a history and a destiny, but these are components of their present hopes and fears.

TOUCH

Touch similarly reaches out to a real humanity. By making choices one may cut off other possibilities, but one also affirms a commitment to the individual experience. In "Confessions of the Life Artist," the narrator is "buoyant with the sense of choice." Having chosen, one finds that the death of possibilities unchosen only fortifies "one's own identity."

The opening poem addresses the "Goddess" of loneliness—Proserpine, the fruitful goddess confined away from human touch in the underworld. When she arises in a park, one of Gunn's ever-present soldiers is waiting for "a woman, any woman/ her dress tight across her ass/ as bark in moonlight." The final line seems to reject the idea that myth can enrich human lives; rather, it is persons, "vulnerable, quivering," who lend to myth their own "abundance."

The movement explored in previous volumes here becomes not linear motion through time but the spatial, encircling movement of the imagination wedded to emotion. In the "turbulence" of "The Kiss at Bayreuth," there is a paradoxical moment in which two "may then/ be said to both move and be still." The egotism of the "inhuman eye" of contemplation is overcome in the moment that two are able to "not think of themselves."

Similarly, in the title poem, touch is what Gunn's narrators seem to have been gravitating toward all along. As the narrator slips into the familiar space of a shared bed, he discovers an "enclosing cocoon . . . where we walk with everyone." This personal communion implies a larger community of sleepers who partake in the "continuous creation" of humanity.

There is not room here for a full discussion of the long poem "Misanthropos," but it is in this poem of seventeen sections that the theme of *Touch* is most fully explored. The protagonist is the last man on Earth after a great holocaust, or at least he seems to be. The problem of identity in the absence of others to validate one's existence is explored as the man sheds old values, memories, and emotions as he sheds his former clothes. When he at last loses the distinctions of language, he encounters other survivors, and direct sensation, experienced anew, is shocking.

MOLY

The background informing *Moly* is Gunn's experience with lysergic acid diethylamide (LSD), which, he said, "has been of the utmost importance to me, both as a man and as a poet." Although he recognized the acid trip to be "essentially non-verbal," it was important and "possible to write poetry about any subject that was of importance to you." Unlike other drug-induced poetry, which tends to mimic the diffusion and chaos of the raw experience in free verse, the poems in *Moly* attempt to present "the infinite through the finite, the unstructured through the structured." These poems are highly controlled by structure and meter, while dealing with strange transformations.

The title poem, "Moly," is a dramatic monologue in the voice of one of Odysseus's men who has been turned into a pig by the witch Circe. Its rhymed couplets underscore the dual nature of man, part human and part beast, in search of the essential and magical "root" that will restore his humanity: "From this fat dungeon I could rise to skin/ And human title, putting pig within." The herb he is seeking is moly ("From milk flower to the black forked root"), which rhymes with "holy." The influence of Yeats's "Leda and the Swan" (1924) is evident, yet the swine-man of Gunn's poem is a typically contemporary twist on the mythological theme of the beast-god of Yeats's modernist poem.

Gunn's 1973 essay "Writing a Poem" discusses the conception and composition of "Three," but it is illuminating as a more general discussion of how a poem comes to be. Gunn says that he encountered a naked family on the beach and wanted to preserve them on paper as a kind of "supersnapshot," to find "an embodiment for my haunting cluster of concepts" about them. He calls his desire to preserve this feeling a sense of "decorum"—that is, a description that would be true to his direct experience of them, not the "pat" theme of "innocence and repossession."

JACK STRAW'S CASTLE, AND OTHER POEMS

This idea of decorum seems to dominate the poems in *Jack Straw's Castle, and Other Poems*. Here there is a kind of easy humor and simplicity of emotion only glimpsed in the earlier poems. In "Autobiography," perhaps influenced by Robert Creeley, the speaker desires (and achieves) "the sniff of the real." "Last Days at Teddington" tells of a return to a house that "smelt of hot dust through the day," and all sensation is clear and complete, like the garden that "fell back on itself."

The title poem, however, is a nightmarish version of a fairy tale, in which Gunn confronts his own worst enemy, himself: "I am the man on the rack/ I am the man who puts the man on the rack/ I am the man who watches the man who puts the man on the rack." Yet by confronting the demons of the imagination in this way, he seems to clear the air for a renewed apprehension of experience, to recognize that the "beauty's in what is, not what may seem." In this way, "Jack's ready for the world."

THE PASSAGES OF JOY

The Passages of Joy is the world the poet of "Jack Straw's Castle" has readied himself for. In "The Menace," the speaker discovers "the stifling passages" of the mind, where "the opposition lurks" not outside himself, but within: "I am, am I,/ the one-who-wants-to-get-me." The joys seem less simple, more problematic after the decades of easy sex and drugs. This volume, in fact, contains Gunn's frankest expression of gay concerns in the era of acquired immunodeficiency syndrome (AIDS), although its focus shifts away from leather bars and orgies to long-standing relationships of shared domesticity.

The title is taken from Samuel Johnson's *The Vanity of Human Wishes* (1749), a satire on the tragic and comic elements of human hopes and errors. One of the poems ("Transients and Residents") bears an epigraph from Johnson's poem:

> Time hovers o'er, impatient to destroy,
> And shuts up all the Passages of Joy.

The very personal poems of this volume show Gunn, now past fifty, dealing with the effects of age—in a person, in a generation, and perhaps in the race.

The three parts of the book show Gunn in a range of moods, from what might be called the meditative poems of the first and third parts to the hip pop-culture poems of part 2. Part 2 begins with a poem for Robert Mapplethorpe, the controversial photographer of the more dangerous elements of the gay scene. Another poem features a "dead punk lady," the murdered girlfriend of Sid Vicious of Sex Pistols fame.

The poet of "A Map of the City" still "would not have the risk diminished," for in the risks are to be found certain "passages of joy." In addition to the literal underground passages of "Another All Night Party," in which orgies occur, there are also the symbolic rites of passage of "Adultery" and "Talbot Road."

"Talbot Road" is a poetic treatment of Gunn's "year of great happiness" in London during the Beatles era, when, according to his almost-identical prose account in "My Life up to Now" (1977), "barriers seemed to be coming down all over." One of these barriers had to do with Gunn's own sexuality. The centerpiece of the five-part poem is a return to Hampstead Heath, where he meets "my past self" in the form of a nineteen-year-old. "This was the year," he says, "the year of reconciliation," but it is unclear whether he means his own nineteenth year of 1964-1965; the ambiguity is intentional, for he means both. Hampstead Heath had been for him the scene of childish play and vague adolescent longings, where by day he "had played hide and seek/ with neighbor children"; in 1964, however, he could see the dark side that had always been there, since by night the Heath had long been a notorious venue for promiscuous sexual encounters, and there he now "played as an adult/ with troops of men whose rounds intersected/ at the Orgy Tree."

The central poem of the volume, however, is "Transients and Residents," in which these literal and figurative passages give way to the real passage of time. The four poems that make up this sequence stand in their own right as powerful and timely meditations on the passage of joy in the age of AIDS. Subtitled "An Interrupted Sequence," these four portraits of gay men in different roles explore the passing of a time of carefree sexual awakening and put the reader in the midst of sickness and death. The last portrait is of the poet himself at his desk, catching a glimpse of himself writing—which interrupts the sequence. This interruption perhaps provides a clue into the poet's view of the other portraits he has been drawing, for like the drug dealer in "Crystal," "he puts his soul/ Into each role in turn, where he survives/ Till it is incarnation more than role."

On the streets of "Night Taxi," a cabdriver takes his "fares like affairs/ — no, more like tricks to turn:/ quick, lively, ending up/ with a cash payment." As in the earlier motorcycle poems, Gunn remains obsessed with movement. The cabdriver is intent on maneuvering his way gracefully through the maze of the city, one with his machine. There is still a sense of independence, yet there is also a sense of community; the driver's movement depends on others, even is subservient to the wishes of others: "It's all on my terms but/ I let them think it's on theirs." It is an appropriate poem to end this book that focuses mostly on the importance of other people.

UNDESIRABLES

Gunn's later poems, such as those in *Undesirables*, return to the gritty side of city life in the 1980's, observing characters and situations with an edge of black humor, like scenes reflected in a switchblade. He has not given up his preoccupation with Yeats—"Old Meg" is an incarnation of Yeats's Crazy Jane—but all sense of imitation is gone. Gunn has renounced the Yeatsian pronouncement for the rabbit punch and the belly laugh. "Punch Rubicundus," for example, is a ribald poem about an aging gay man, in which the satire is all self-directed. The host, Mr. Punch, enters one of his "vaudeville of the sexual itch" parties, riding on a donkey, and says, "But this *can't* be Byzantium. (Though/ they do say Uncle Willie's ghost got an invite)." The irreverent reference to Yeats's "Sailing to Byzantium" (1927) and "Byzantium" (1932) is clear: Uncle Willie is William Butler Yeats, whose spirits were supposed to ride "astraddle on the dolphin's mire and blood" to "the holy city of Byzantium."

The poetry of Gunn continued to develop as an up-to-the-minute report on the contemporary scene. Yet his roots in the tradition of poetry were deep, and his dialogue with the poets and forms of the past was as much a part of his evolution as a poet as was his keen eye for the realities of his time.

THE MAN WITH NIGHT SWEATS

Gunn received critical acclaim for *The Man with Night Sweats*, recognized for its unsentimental examination of AIDS, death, and neglected members of contemporary American society. He wrote the poems during 1982 to 1988, a period when the AIDS epidemic was devastating the gay community and the global community shared widespread homophobia and concerns over its transmission. Here the topic of AIDS seemed a theme to which Gunn could attach a particular passion and poetic craft, a place to offer heartbreaking poems of young men struggling with a disease that consumes them with fear and its cruelty. The skepticism of his past poetry here gives way to elegy and lament, lyrical meditation, and a form of rage that is finely tooled with his poetic balance.

In this collection, Gunn acts as both a witness to the devastation of AIDS as well as one deeply involved with it. He writes in "The Renaissance," "You came back in a dream./ I'm all right now you said." His witnessing of the suffering also takes on a ferocity, a compulsion to attest to the wreckage of AIDS, almost as a way to provide a kind of defense:

I shall not soon forget
. . . .
The angle of his head,
Arrested and reared back
On the crisp field of bed, . . .

One of the strongest poems of the collection is "Lament," an elegy of more than one hundred lines in which the speaker describes in great detail the slow dying of a close friend in a hospital ward. Rather than elevate the dying friend with praise and abstraction as does traditional elegy, this piece repeats that death is a "difficult enterprise" and chronicles the tedium and pain experienced by his friend—the "clumsy stealth" that has "distanced" him "from the habits of health." "Lament" is a perfect example of Gunn's tightly channeled, yet deeply felt elegies that form this collection.

BOSS CUPID

Boss Cupid echoes the elegiac style of *The Man with Night Sweats*, its three sections examining the loss of friends, lovers, and even, in one case, a lifestyle. Rather than focusing entirely on loss, however, the collection also explores the sexual allure of youth, and renewal and recovery. Frank references to "the sexual New Jerusalem" of Gunn's younger years are here, and in "Saturday Night," he writes a genuinely affecting lament for the sex and drugs scene of the mid-1970's. It moves beyond the endpoints referenced in *The Man with Night Sweats* and his subsequent *Collected Poems* by pushing the boundaries of his poetry to include, in one loose whole, the makings of legend, myth, phantasmagoria, and autobiography. Historic, mythic figures such as Arachne and King David make appearances here, as well as the homeless, college students, and social deviants (as in his five "songs for Jeffrey Dahmer" grouped under the title "Troubadour"). His edgy wit, lyric versatility, and adept caricatures of personas help make this collection a powerful reminder that every life is "dense/ with fine compacted difference."

OTHER MAJOR WORKS

NONFICTION: "My Life up to Now," 1977; *The Occasions of Poetry: Essays in Criticism and Autobiography*, 1982, 1985 (Clive Wilmer, editor); *Shelf Life: Es-*

says, Memoirs, and an Interview, 1993; *Thom Gunn in Conversation with James Campbell*, 2000.

EDITED TEXTS: *Poetry from Cambridge 1951-52: A Selection of Verse by Members of the University*, 1952; *Five American Poets*, 1963 (with Ted Hughes); *Selected Poems of Fulke Greville*, 1968; *Ben Jonson*, 1974; *Ezra Pound*, 2000; *Selected Poems*, 2003 (by Yvor Winters).

MISCELLANEOUS: *Thom Gunn at Seventy*, 1999.

BIBLIOGRAPHY

Brown, Merle E. *Double Lyric: Divisiveness and Communal Creativity in Recent English Poetry*. New York: Columbia University Press, 1980. Brown argues that poetry is the result of the dialectic between the poet's thinking and speaking selves, the poem being a communal expression of that double consciousness. The theory bears fruit in the two chapters devoted to Gunn's work. The first explores the idea of "inner community" in the long poem "Misanthropos," the second the idea of "authentic duplicity" in Gunn's poetry up to *Jack Straw's Castle, and Other Poems*.

Gunn, Thom. "Thom Gunn." Interview by Christopher Hennessy. In *Outside the Lines: Talking with Contemporary Gay Poets*, edited by Hennessy. Ann Arbor: University of Michigan Press, 2005. Gunn explores his works, technical and emotional development, and the links between his sexuality and verse.

Guthmann, Edward. "A Poet's Life, Part 1: Reserved but Raw, Modest but Gaudy, Thom Gunn Covered an Enormous Amount of Ground in His Exquisite Work and His Raucous Life." *San Francisco Chronicle*, April 25, 2005, p. C1. On the one-year anniversary of Gunn's death, Guthmann wrote a two-part profile of the poet that described his life largely through conversations with friends and colleagues.

_____. "A Poet's Life, Part 2: As Friends Died of AIDS, Thom Gunn Stayed Healthy—Until His Need to Play Hard Finally Killed Him." *San Francisco Chronicle* April 26, 2005, p. E1. The second installment in a profile of the deceased Gunn reveals much about his life in San Francisco with partner Mike Kitay.

King, P. R. *Nine Contemporary Poets: A Critical Intro-duction*. London: Methuen, 1979. The chapter devoted to Gunn, "A Courier After Identity," discusses five distinct personas in Gunn's poetic development: the "embattled" stance of *Fighting Terms*, "a life of action and of pose" in *The Sense of Movement*, the "divided self" of *My Sad Captains, and Other Poems*, the striving for "contact" with humankind and nature in *Touch*, and the "widening sympathies" of *Moly* and *Jack Straw's Castle, and Other Poems*. An excellent overview.

Leader, Zachary, ed. *The Movement Reconsidered: Essays on Larkin, Amis, Gunn, Davie, and Their Contemporaries*. New York: Oxford University Press, 2009. A collection of essays on the Movement poets, including one on Gunn and one discussing Gunn and Donald Davie.

Michelucci, Stefania. *The Poetry of Thom Gunn: A Critical Study*. Jefferson, N.C.: McFarland, 2009. Michelucci finds a desire for freedom in Gunn's early poetry that leads to his vindication of his closeted sexuality.

Weiner, Joshua, ed. *At the Barriers: On the Poetry of Thom Gunn*. Chicago: University of Chicago Press, 2009. A collection of critical essays examine Gunn's poetry, including "Meat," "Considering the Snail," and "Duncan."

Richard Collins
Updated by Sarah Hilbert

IVOR GURNEY

Born: Gloucester, England; August 28, 1890
Died: Dartford, England; December 26, 1937

PRINCIPAL POETRY
Severn and Somme, 1917
War's Embers, 1919
Poems, 1954 (Edmund Blunden, editor)
Poems of Ivor Gurney, 1890-1937, 1973 (Leonard Clark, editor)
Collected Poems of Ivor Gurney, 1982 (P. J. Kavanagh, editor)

Eighty Poems or So, 1997
*Rewards of Wonder: Poems of Cotswold, France,
London*, 2000

OTHER LITERARY FORMS

Besides being a poet, Ivor Gurney (GUR-nee) is recognized as a gifted songwriter and composer of instrumental music. Of special interest are fine settings of poems by William Shakespeare, William Butler Yeats, Sir Walter Raleigh, Ben Jonson, John Clare, A. E. Housman, Wilfred Owen, John Masefield, and Edward Thomas. Gurney's musical work often exhibits the same erratic genius that distinguishes his poems, but this promising career was cut too short by the debilitating effects of military service and mental illness.

ACHIEVEMENTS

Ivor Gurney considered himself unjustly neglected and "one of Five War Poets." Both judgments are gradually being accepted by students of early twentieth century literature. His reputation is benefiting from the general recovery in critical esteem and cultural interest of the World War I poets. His work is associated with that of Wilfred Owen, Rupert Brooke, Siegfried Sassoon, Robert Nichols, Isaac Rosenberg, and others, as part of a significant chapter in modern literary history: the terrible interlude in which a conventional Georgian quietism was being replaced by new virtuosities of shock and disillusionment born in the trenches of war-ravaged Europe. Gurney's own poetry shares in that transformation of thought and technique. In many ways the most enigmatic and inconsistent of those soldier-poets and still the least known, he forged out of his own waywardness innovations in diction, rhythm, and tone that often surpass the others in interest and effect. None evokes more intricately the modernist pathos of "two ditches of heart-sick men;/ the times scientific, as evil as ever, again."

Gurney is also important as the first twentieth century writer to exhibit strongly the influence of Gerard Manley Hopkins, whose vigorous and technically daring verse appeared posthumously in 1916 and 1918. Specific resemblances of theme, language, and style suggest that Gurney responded immediately to the qualities in Hopkins now acknowledged as that Victo-

rian poet's most energizing contribution to the voice of modern literature.

Since Edmund Blunden's 1954 edition of the poems, including many previously unpublished pieces of great merit, Gurney has been discussed in several studies of the war poets and represented in anthologies of modern verse. What more Gurney might have achieved were it not for his rapid psychological disintegration is not certain. There is justice, however, in William Curtis-Hayward's estimate that in Ivor Gurney "what we have is the ruins of a major poet."

BIOGRAPHY

The two pressing facts of Ivor Bertie Gurney's life and poetry were his grisly experiences as a signalman and gunner in the trenches during World War I and his subsequent (though not necessarily consequent) decline into insanity. He was already suffering "beastly nervousness" before the war and actually hoped that the rigors of military life might stabilize his mind. The conditions he endured in the battlefields of Europe would have shaken the steadiest constitution, yet Gurney's vivid poems and letters of this period are remarkably poised and ironic. There was even a kind of jauntiness about his amused image of himself as a "neurasthenic musician" in soldier's garb. He resorted seriously to poetry at this time as a substitute for music and as a therapeutic outlet for troubled feelings and observations. Some of these verses appeared in English magazines, and two small volumes, *Severn and Somme* and *War's Embers*, were published. After being gassed in 1917, however, Gurney went home disabled and soon began to be sporadically afflicted by the melancholic derangement that would haunt the rest of his life. Following several generally shiftless years of unhappiness and encroaching mental disorder, he was sent permanently to the asylum in Dartford, Kent. There he continued to compose poems and verse fragments of eccentric brilliance, mostly expressing baffled resentment and spiritual anguish or intensely reliving grim wartime experiences.

Counterpointing the fierce inspirations of war and madness were two other important influences in Gurney's life: natural beauty and music. His heart was always in the delightful rural byways of his native

Gloucestershire, where his elemental need for country beauty and for rich associations rooted deep in local history was nourished. Nevertheless, it took the refining crucibles of battle and mental torment to transform the Severn and Cotswold landscape in Gurney's poetry into a sustained metaphor of joy and timeless sanity. Likewise, it was war and then psychological debility that turned his hand to poetry from his first love, music. He left the Royal College of Music to enlist in a Gloucestershire infantry regiment, and after the war was ultimately unable to resume the career that had been expected of him. Still, Gurney's accomplishment in music remains impressive. When he died of tuberculosis at Dartford in 1937, it was just a month too soon to see the tribute to his music in a special issue of *Music and Letters*. Nature and music, then, had formed his determination to "let beauty through" in the face of all that seemed ugly, brutal, and discordant in the world. Both recur as subjects in his poetry.

Among Gurney's acquaintances were many familiar names from the literary and musical circles of the day: Walter de la Mare, Ralph Vaughan Williams, Lascelles Abercrombie, John Masefield, Sir Edward Marsh, Herbert Howells, and others. Neither his sufferings nor his work was neglected by influential friends during his lifetime, although sad petitioning verses and letters from the asylum years sometimes accused "England" of shameful ingratitude. Altogether, it was Gurney's fate to make poetry out of the sorrows and rare consolations of a stricken consciousness.

ANALYSIS

Ivor Gurney's most interesting poetry falls generally into three types or styles. In two of these his accomplishment is often of the highest quality. To some extent, the three modes represent a development in his manner and technique, though the trend toward increasing originality, urgency, subjectivity, and disruptiveness is far from consistent. If there is any chronological pattern, it perhaps reflects the emergence and then the fragmentation of a unique artistic personality.

SPARE LYRICS

The first category of poems consists of lucid lyrics notable for a spare and laconic modernity of expression. Usually short, these terse, cool pieces demon-

strate a precise control of form and tone. Typical verses in this sardonically beautiful vein include "The Love Song," "Generations," "Old Tale," "The Songs I Had," "When I Am Covered," "To His Love," and even the sinister "Horror Follows Horror." As some of these titles suggest, Gurney's style here is songlike—a reflection of his strong musical talents and disposition. His thought, however, almost always has an elusive quality.

"GENERATIONS"

In the Blakean parable "Generations," for example, "The plowed field and the fallow field" alike sing a "prudent" song of fatalistic indifference to life's vicissitudes. The method of this poem is both unromantic and economical, with a disarmingly steady naturalness of idiom. Its amoral vision nevertheless seems to be slyly undermined by the poet's use of ambiguous connotative diction ("prudent," "reckoning," "power," and "brooding"), together with shifting values of the word "best." Rhythmic regularity reinforces this ambivalence of tone, and of course the relation of inanimate to human destinies remains an unasked question. Gurney's other poems of this type have much the same redolent simplicity. He achieves on these occasions the ironic distance that has since been considered the predominant perspective of twentieth century verse.

"TO HIS LOVE"

One of the finest war poems of this sort is the elegiac "To His Love," addressed with subtle but bitter irony to a dead comrade's beloved. It is ostensibly a nostalgic reminiscence and a conventional tribute to the commemoration of patriotic sacrifice. This poem too, however, is discreetly ambivalent. The phrasing and imagery actually signal bleak indignation at the untruths about war and death that are perpetrated by sentimental attitudes and rituals. In particular, attention is increasingly focused on the soldier's shattered body itself ("You would not know him now . . .") and on the significance of burying as quickly as possible ("Cover him, cover him soon!") what is left of their friend ("that red wet/ thing").

The real meaning of those sickeningly dehumanized remains is obviously not what the state and customary sentiment demand. Hence the compulsion to conceal the ghastly evidence under "violets of pride" in memorial rites that transmute the soldier's memory into a romantic glorification of war. Without openly offending the bereaved, the sustained ironic potential of words such as "pride" illustrates Gurney's ability to let tone control the fury underlying a placid surface. A similar duality is expressed in the off-handedness and coy enjambment of "But *still* he died/ *Nobly*." Here the tone captures and undermines the cavalier outlook of those who pass over the ugliness of death in battle by summarily glamorizing it. The same effect is achieved in the brusque logic of the immediately following clause ("so cover him over/ with violets . . ."), which dismisses the victim by automatically according him the standard "poetic" formalities of interment amidst royal purple violets. Burial deep under "thickset/ Masses of memoried flowers" removes and idealizes a gruesome reality that, the poem implies, should in fact be confronted. Moreover, habitual sentiments and ceremonial gestures tend to supplant authentic personal expression of grief and dissipate any sense of official responsibility. The flowers must be especially "thickset" in "Masses" (a pun on the eucharistic service) to conceal sufficiently the horror beneath from anyone who might rightly be angered or disillusioned by it. The unusual adjective "memoried" is richly connotative, hinting that the violets bring memories of happier days, are commemorative of military honor, reminding one of death, and perhaps capable themselves of remembering generations of other soldiers misrepresented and exploited even in death for the sake of pride.

Memory is indeed the poem's dominating idea. What impression of the dead should be retained? One possibility is the pastoral image of blithe youth in Gurney's opening stanzas, but that seems "useless indeed." Likewise, to make the soldier's death an instrument of nationalistic propaganda or romantic self-delusion is to perpetuate falsehoods that have, as his embittered fellows know, no connection with what really happened to him. The poem's final irony is the realization that even those aware of the truth yearn to escape it. A better use for a profusion of memorial flowers, it is urged, would be to hide from the poet himself "that red wet/ Thing I must somehow forget." It is nevertheless strongly implied that such immediate, excruciating knowledge cannot, and hence must not, be

forgotten or betrayed. This complex and poignantly developed theme, found in other Gurney poems too, suggests the unsettling insights that England was being afforded by the war poets.

PERSONAL NARRATIVES

The second strong vein in Gurney's verse is much more personal, tumultuous, and distinctive. The poems of this sort tend to be descriptive narratives that powerfully realize scenes, events, or sensations—usually stirring impressions connected with battle or with nature. Emphatic irregular rhythms and densely packed language show the influence of Hopkins and, to some extent, of Walt Whitman. Gurney first read these poets in the trenches, where, inevitably, his own manner was already being reforged into a more vigorous utterance.

The result was the emergence of a dramatic diction and syntax suited to the emotions and violent physicality of his new experiences: "wading/ Three feet of water past fire to the bones/ For Hell cold east of snow-sleeting Chaulness." The language energetically struggles with and overleaps grammar and traditional usage. It abounds in compound words, alliteration, striking inversions, breathless rhythms, onomatopoeia, and strikingly compacted visual and sensory effects. In many of the war poems, raw, brutal, shocked action and feeling are reenacted with physical and psychological realism.

Sometimes it is sound that the thickly textured language indicates ("the thud of boots/ On duck-board wood from grate on rough road stone"); elsewhere it is a visual image ("Moonlight lying thick on frost spangled fleet foot sward"), and still elsewhere a terrible revelation of mental anguish. Occasionally, Gurney juxtaposes styles, as in the black drollery of "The Silent One." There the "finicking accent" of an officer in the trenches is incongruous amid battle's "flashes" and "bullets whizzing." The poet-soldier is politely invited by his superior to crawl ahead to almost certain death. "Darkness, shot at: I smiled, as politely replied—/ 'I'm afraid not, Sir.'" Instead he keeps flat, thinking about music and swearing "deep heart's deep oaths/ (Polite to God)."

"CANADIANS"

In general, the war poems seek to catch directly the feel and mentality of battlefield life itself—the hours of waiting, the marching, the brief respites, and of course the squalor and violence. More than anything else, Gurney captures the pity and degradation. In "Canadians," the reader keenly senses the "infinitely grimed" faces, numbed weariness, and brutalization of "slouching" men "Dead past dead from the first hour" in a desolate place. A fifteen-line sentence of especially elliptical and interrupted syntax suggests the jumbled association of ideas raised in a fellow soldier's mind by such "iniquity of mere being," and biblical echoes and other religious allusions extend the situation's moral significance and lead the speaker to a bitter final reflection. He concludes that these Canadian volunteers, supposedly having come "finely" and freely and recklessly, must actually be victims that "Fate had sent for suffering and dwelling obscenely/ Vermin eaten, fed beastly, in vile ditches meanly."

The disillusionment felt by the poem's evidently Christian speaker enhances the force of the protest; to suggest that only a malevolent impersonal Fate could contrive such misery is to deny the right of Europe's Christian nations to make war in this fashion. That does not, of course, necessarily reflect Gurney's own view. As in the case of "Generations," discussed earlier, ideas different from the writer's own opinions may sometimes be dramatized in this way. In any event, the poem depicts one witness's emotional and intellectual reaction to the sordidness of modern mechanical warfare. The effect, as in other verses on related topics, is to deglamorize utterly a species of conflict that, ironically and ominously, makes men seem "Cave dwellers last of tribes."

NATURE POEMS

Gurney employs the same densely textured style for other subjects—notably in poems evoking "the love of Earth in me." What distinguishes those nature poems is an extraordinary fidelity to concrete particulars. Again like Hopkins, he is fascinated with specificity—real things that can be seen and named in catalogs of precise images. Poems such as "Cotswold Ways," "The Dearness of Common Things," "The Escape," and "Looking Up There" are typical. In such verses, Gurney is drawn especially to creation's counterpointing of "strange" and "queer" beauties. He works at "breaking to sight" the hidden richness of "small trifles,/ Real, beautiful" and even of sensually tactile things such as

the fabric of clothing. "How hard beauty hurts men," he cries, "with commonness and pangs and hurts them!"

There is also a dynamic vitalism, as in lines such as "The stars are sliding wanton through trees" or "The line of blue faint known and the leaping to white." The nature poems also express a personal devotion born of the need for engrossing antidotes to the distresses of battle and psychological suffering. Music figures similarly in the poems, occasionally being linked to the harmonies of nature; in one moment of dark humor, moreover, Gurney describes how he "learnt the machine gun, how it played/ Scales and arpeggios."

The poetry of this second type, then, divides Gurney's admirers from his detractors. The style is often undeniably knotted and cryptic—here and there virtually to the point of unintelligibility. Punctuation is haphazard, grammar deliberately tortured, allusions cryptic, and psychological impressionism pursued with such verisimilitude as to defy confident interpretation. The effect is to concentrate wonderfully Gurney's strenuous dramatization of consciousness, however, and to capture with distinctiveness what Hopkins would have called the "inscapes" of objects, action, or feeling. The peculiarity is not just the price paid for visual, aural, and semantic richness; it actually inheres in what Gurney is determined to elicit from the difficult materials of his experience. Success with such techniques is bound to be erratic, and there is a limit to what the power of suggestion by itself can express, but there are some splendid achievements in Gurney too. Indeed there is more than enough to justify the trouble of attending patiently to the poems—reading them aloud wherever possible—and perhaps valuing them as much for what they bravely attempt as for their relatively few sustained, unquestionable triumphs.

FLEXIBILITY IN VERSIFICATION

In formal versification, Gurney shows the flexibility that might naturally be expected of a musician. This is true of both the generally early simpler poems and the more rhetorically emphatic idiom of his second style. There is little inclination toward free verse or even blank verse and extraordinary versatility in rhyme patterns and cadences. Gurney's rhymes are usually rigid, yet remarkably unobtrusive—except when he attempts audacious pairings such as "coolish" with "foolish" or, within one line, "clangour" with "anger." Successful half-rhymes contribute to this effect of naturalness. The finely modulated poem "When I Am Covered," which may be Gurney's own epitaph, has four tercets that repeat twice an *aba bab* arrangement, while the following stanza from "To Crickley" shows the cumulative effect of more forceful rhyming:

> Then to you—deep in Hells now still-burning
> For sleep or the end's peace—
> By tears we have not saved you; yearning
> To accusation and our hopes loss turning.
> What gods are these?

The poet's rhythms, on the other hand, mark a decisive break from tradition. They tend toward the irregularity of passionate speech rather than the more or less consistent stress patterns of metrical law. Like Hopkins, he strove for the authentic accents of "speaking in high words," and wrote few pieces in standard rhythm that do not have a rather trivializing sing-song quality. The "To Crickley" stanza may serve also to illustrate Gurney's irregular cadence; each of the five lines is rhythmically different, only the last being standard, and the remaining stanzas of the same poem exhibit still other variations.

A MIND AT WAR WITH ITSELF

In turning to the third of the characteristic types of poem written by Gurney, technical analysis is difficult and perhaps out of place. Fascinating and moving as these strange poems are, they are bound to be incidental to the development of Gurney's critical reputation. Their form can be described as a peculiarly loose and discursive soliloquy sometimes reminiscent of William Wordsworth's procedure in *The Prelude: Or, The Growth of a Poet's Mind* (1850). Most of these poems date from the asylum years and are in fact repetitive and fragmentary. They tend also to be obsessive autobiographical laments in which Gurney strives courageously to make sense of his pain, disappointment, and shame. One or two, such as "The Lock Keeper," are more even and detached, though they do not surpass in power and pathos the ungainly personal utterances.

All the poems of this type do contain occasional lines or passages with the lucid beauty or Hopkinsesque strength of Gurney's other work, but the main interest of these pieces lies in their curiously gripping revelation of a sensitive mind at war with itself. For example, in "Chance to Work," addressed to the police authorities, Gurney begins with fervid recollections of a youthful joy in books, in music, in poetry, in love, and especially in natural beauty. Then come lines about strange illness, war, hospital, "evil forces," broken hopes, and the desperate therapy of hard physical exertion. Finally, there are the dreadful loneliness, suicidal longings, and complex recriminations of the asylum ward. The litany of real and imagined horrors concludes ruefully with the recurrent plea of Gurney's last years: "O if such pain is/ Not of account—a whole life's whole penalties/ To cancel . . . Grant pity, grant chance of Work." This poem, and others like it, are probably artistic failures, but they portray with unforgettable authenticity the hell of what is too readily called maddened consciousness.

A few excellent representative poems that have not already been cited are "Memory, Let All Slip," "Half Dead," "Darkness Has Cheating Swiftness," "Moments," and "What Evil Coil." Taken as a whole, Gurney's best poetry represents an imaginative and technical accomplishment at least comparable to that of the better-known war poets. Doubtless he is less consistent, and much more often confusingly idiosyncratic. At the same time, his is in certain ways a more sensitive and stylistically original voice. One cannot help responding to what he called "the making's eager pain"—his urgent impulse to find adequate forms of utterance for thoughts and feelings that customary poetic modes would not accommodate. Admired more by fellow poets—Blunden, de la Mare, Jon Silkin, and others—than by academic critics, Gurney's verse is probably too frequently singular, febrile, disorderly, and experimental (and too notoriously that of a madman) for the popular or scholarly taste. He may have been right to cry with ghastly candor, "There is nothing for my Poetry, who was the child of joy./ But to work out in verse crazes of my untold pain." Yet Blunden is also correct in having said of him,

> He perished, one may say, war and consumption apart,
> from the merciless intensity of his spirit both in watching
> the forms of things moving apace in the stream of change

and in hammering out poetic forms that should remain as their just representation and acclamation.

OTHER MAJOR WORK

NONFICTION: *Collected Letters*, 1991.

BIBLIOGRAPHY

Blevins, Pamel. *Ivor Gurney and Marion Scott: Song of Pain and Beauty*. Rochester, N.Y.: Boydell Press, 2008. This double biography looks at the life of the poet Gurney, who met Marion Scott while studying music and formed a partnership with her. Describes their lives separately and intertwined.

Gray, Piers. *Marginal Men: Edward Thomas, Ivor Gurney, J. R. Ackerley*. Houndmills, Basingstoke, Hampshire: Macmillan, 1991. An examination of Gurney, along with Edward Thomas, and J. R. Ackerley, that looks at his marginalized life and poetry.

Gurney, Ivor. *Collected Letters*. Edited by R. K. R. Thornton. Manchester, England: Carcanet Press, 1991. Invaluable source of biographical details of Gurney's life and friendships.

Hill, Geoffrey. "Gurney's 'Hobby.'" *Essays in Criticism* 34 (April, 1984): 97-128. Hill explores Gurney's poetry and music, oddly enough finding his poetry to be his self-proclaimed "hobby." Examines Gurney's irony as evidenced in his poetry, the same irony that Gurney claimed he detested, much like Walt Whitman, the poet Gurney considered to be his mentor.

Hipp, Daniel. *The Poetry of Shell Shock: Wartime Trauma and Healing in Wilfred Owen, Ivor Gurney, and Siegfried Sassoon*. Jefferson, N.C.: McFarland, 2005. This examination of three poets of World War I contains a section on Gurney and his works.

Hooker, Jeremy. "Honoring Ivor Gurney." *Poetry Nation Review* 7, no. 17 (1980): 16-19. Emphasizes the fact that Gurney's world was one of madness and incarceration, deeply affecting his poetry. Hooker honors Gurney as a poet and a man who, through a disintegrating life, managed to enliven the language with verse and was not fully appreciated in his period or in modern times.

Hurd, Michael. *The Ordeal of Ivor Gurney*. New York: Oxford University Press, 1978. The most quoted of all Gurney's sources, this book is an exhaustive study of his life and writings. In the course of the text, Hurd analyzes dozens of Gurney's poems while maintaining a chronological perspective. Supplemented by indexes and notes.

Moore, Charles Willard. *Maker and Lover of Beauty: Ivor Gurney, Poet and Songwriter*. Introduction by Herbert Howelles and decorations by Richard Walker. Rickmansworth, England: Triad Press, 1976. Although issued in a limited edition, this biographical volume on the poet-musician is one of the few sources available.

Pilkington, Michael. *Gurney, Ireland, Quilter, and Warlock*. Bloomington: Indiana University Press, 1989. A reference guide to the songs of Gurney and three other songwriters of these turn-of-the-century composers.

Waterman, Andrew. "The Poetic Achievement of Ivor Gurney." *Critical Quarterly* 25 (Winter, 1983): 3-19. Waterman's primary focus is to show how Gurney modernized himself and his perspectives in his poetry between the war years and his incarceration in a lunatic asylum. Not only is Gurney's poetry analyzed, but his musical talent is also critically explored.

Michael D. Moore

H

ARTHUR HENRY HALLAM

Born: London, England; February 1, 1811
Died: Vienna, Austria; September 15, 1833

PRINCIPAL POETRY

Poems, 1830

Remains, in Verse and Prose, 1834 (Henry Hallam, editor)

Poems of Arthur Henry Hallam, 1893 (Richard Le Gallienne, editor)

The Writings of Arthur Hallam, 1943 (T. H. Vail Motter, editor; poetry and prose)

OTHER LITERARY FORMS

In addition to his poetry, Arthur Henry Hallam (HAL-uhm) also wrote essays. Expository prose was probably more congenial to him than verse, and his most promising efforts were in that area.

ACHIEVEMENTS

Arthur Henry Hallam died at the age of twenty-two without having written any major poetry, yet he left behind unmistakable evidence of literary ability that, had he lived, might well have developed into lasting eminence (though probably in criticism rather than in poetry). While his verse displayed promise, none of his poems proved to be immortal; and his work does not appear in standard literary anthologies. For all its tantalizing possibility, Hallam's surviving literary output has interest chiefly as a revelation of the mind and personality valued by Alfred, Lord Tennyson above all others. Besides their relevance to Tennyson, however, Hallam's apprentice verses are still a minor literary achievement in their own right.

BIOGRAPHY

Arthur Henry Hallam, the son of a famous historian, was born in London on February 1, 1811. He spent the summer of 1818 abroad with his father, Henry, learning French. After two years of preparatory school at Putney, Hallam again traveled throughout the summer and then entered Eton, remaining for five years. While there, he was an active participant in debates on issues such as Catholic emancipation, the disarming of the Highlanders after Culloden, the merits of Thomas Jefferson, John Milton's political conduct, ancient versus modern writers, the character of Augustus, Greek accomplishments in history and drama, and many similar topics. Hallam left Eton, properly confirmed, in July, 1827, and then went on to Italy, where he remained for nine important months. Returning to England by way of Switzerland, he entered Trinity College, Cambridge, in October, 1828, and was soon recognized as an erratic but brilliant student who was already showing promise as a poet. In April, 1829, Hallam met Tennyson, thereby beginning the most eloquently celebrated friendship in English literature, and incidentally inviting a comparison of poetic talents that has never been to Hallam's advantage.

On May 9, 1829, Hallam was elected to membership in the Apostles, a debating society at Cambridge that included most of those whose fellowship and intellectual stimulation would be important to him, including Tennyson, for a time. Though Tennyson was relatively indifferent to the club and its disputations, Hallam relished this further opportunity for debate, and he presented several excellent essays to its members. Perhaps the most decisive addition to his own outlook gained from the Apostles was an appreciation for the poetry of Percy Bysshe Shelley, which quickly became a passion.

After illness, poetic defeat (by Tennyson), and summer travel in France and Switzerland, Hallam returned to Trinity in the fall of 1829 and arranged for the first English edition of Shelley's *Adonais: An Elegy on the Death of John Keats* (1821). His friendship with Tennyson also deepened considerably. During Easter vacation in 1830, Hallam visited the Tennysons at Somersby in Lincolnshire and fell in love with Alfred's sister Emily. That May, a collection of his verses (*Poems*) circulated privately. Some of its lyrics had originally been intended to appear jointly with Tennyson's, but this plan was quashed by Henry Hallam; so when

Arthur Henry Hallam (The Granger Collection, New York)

Poems, Chiefly Lyrical appeared in June, 1830, it contained Tennyson's work only. That summer Hallam and Tennyson were off to Spain on behalf of rebels opposing the Spanish monarchy. Tennyson always retained fond memories of this exciting and scenic venture, which he recalled in a poem of 1864.

In 1831, however, Hallam and Tennyson were together less often, for when the latter's father died in February, Alfred left Cambridge immediately. In March, Hallam's father forbade his seeing Emily Tennyson for a year. By that time, Hallam was beginning to relinquish his poetic ambitions, having been regularly overshadowed by his more promising friend. He acknowledged this disparity implicitly with a perceptive review of Tennyson's poetry, which was published that August in the *Englishman's Magazine*. It is Hallam's most important literary criticism. (A second essay by him on Tennyson, intended for the *Edinburgh Review* in 1832, has disappeared.) On October 29, Hallam read to the

Apostles a striking review of his own religious opinions called "Theodicaea Novissima" that lastingly impressed and influenced Tennyson.

In January, 1832, after some confusion over residency, Hallam graduated from Cambridge. By March, his father's prohibition had expired and Arthur (now of age) was free to announce his year-old engagement to Emily Tennyson, though the immediate result was only a tedious series of unsatisfactory financial negotiations between the Hallam and Tennyson families. Arthur, despairing and in bad health, was forced to work in a London law office copying documents. He spent much of his literary energies that year translating poems from Dante's *La vita nuova* (c. 1292; *Vita Nuova*, 1861; better known as *The New Life*). There was a short journey up the Rhine with Tennyson in July, a visit to Somersby in August, and an ecstatic Christmas there at year's end. Just when Hallam's life promised some fulfillment, however, he became seriously ill, went abroad for one last summer with his father, and died unexpectedly from a brain hemorrhage in Vienna on September 15, having attained the age of twenty-two years, seven and one-half months. In an episode that Tennyson would later versify, his body was then brought back to England and buried at Clevedon, on the Bristol Channel, on January 3, 1834.

Remains, in Verse and Prose, edited by his father, appeared later that spring, circulating privately (the first public edition was in 1862). Tennyson himself then spent almost seventeen years meditating upon the significance of his brilliant friend's death and writing the poems that would eventually comprise *In Memoriam* (1850); he also named his son for Hallam. A selection of Hallam's poems, together with his essay on the poetry of Tennyson, were edited with an appreciative introduction by Richard Le Gallienne in 1893. An invaluable edition of *The Writings of Arthur Hallam* (1943) by T. H. Vail Motter has been superseded in part by the texts and notes in Jack Kolb's edition of Hallam's letters, containing many poems.

ANALYSIS

Arthur Henry Hallam's chief contribution to English poetry lies in his influence upon Tennyson, including their rivalry and friendship, their mutual literary and intellectual reflections, and the tragic questioning of Hallam's loss that resulted in Tennyson's *In Memoriam*. Both were aspiring poets prior to their meeting, but Hallam's kindred mind almost certainly deepened Tennyson's in certain respects and helped him to some liberating influences, those of Shelley and Italy in particular. Tennyson's lifelong commitments to political and religious freedom, scenic travel, and poetic concern with landscape and geology probably owed a great deal to Hallam. Anyone familiar with Tennyson's poems, moreover, is aware that Hallam inspired not only *In Memoriam* but also some shorter poems, such as "Ulysses," which was in large part a heroic response to the news of Hallam's death, and "Vastness," which was in part a poignant reminiscence of it. Tennyson's longest poem, *Idylls of the King* (1859-1885), an epic of King Arthur, is thought to reflect the idealized humanity that Hallam might well have achieved. Full discussion of Tennyson's poetry, then, would deal at length with Hallam as a literary influence.

POETRY AS BIOGRAPHY

The poems that Hallam left are especially valuable as biography. While still at Eton in 1827, he published some verses on a story connected with the Lake of Killarney in the *Eton Miscellany*, but these were not reprinted by his father. His nine-month stay in Italy that year resulted in a flourish of poetry, much of it inspired by a young woman of twenty-six named Anna Wintour, whose dark eyes and floating hair he found irresistible. Several of his poetic tributes to her were in Italian (as some letters between Emily Tennyson and himself would later be). Other poems concerning Italy celebrated *objets d'art* in the Pitti Palace in Florence and the graves of John Keats and Shelley in Rome. After returning to England in 1828, Hallam continued to think of Wintour and wrote for her a long poem, full of Dante and William Wordsworth, titled "A Farewell to the South," which was published in 1830 but suppressed in 1834. It compares favorably with what other poets have written at the age of seventeen.

MEDITATIVE FRAGMENTS

In 1829, Hallam wrote (and published the next year) a series of "Meditative Fragments in Blank Verse," as he called them, which attest to his struggles not only with spiritual questions but also with desperate fears of approaching insanity, as his letters of that year attest.

Another poem, called "Lines Written in Great Depression of Mind" (March, 1829), even expresses his wish for death. That April, in the first of three vain tries, Hallam attempted to win the Chancellor's Medal at Cambridge with a long poem on the required topic, "Timbuctoo"; it was published separately as a pamphlet in 1828, reprinted in *Poems*, and appeared again in the *Remains, in Verse and Prose*. In three important footnotes, Hallam cited Plato, Samuel Taylor Coleridge, and Shelley (whom he praised) as sources. The prize was awarded to Tennyson's poem instead. Though naturally disappointed not to have won himself, Hallam (who had written a sonnet "To A. T." in May) was ever afterward a firm admirer of Tennyson's poetry and preferred it to his own.

TRAVEL POEMS

Hallam's French and Scottish travels of 1829 resulted in further poems, some of which are little more than exercises in versification and dialect. Two poems from July, "Sonnet Written in the Pass of Glencoe" and another "Written in View of Ben Lomond," evince Hallam's interest in geology; they have been compared with similar passages in *In Memoriam*. That same month Hallam visited Glenarbach, formerly the seat of Lord Webb Seymour (a geologist and friend of Henry Hallam), the home of Ann Robertson, who had been born in Italy and was there to rival Wintour (unsuccessfully) when Hallam was there in 1827. Seven of Hallam's poems were addressed to Robertson and her family, especially "A Farewell to Glenarbach," which reveals the influence of Wordsworth and several other predecessors upon Hallam, who was then eighteen.

POETIC INFLUENCES

Many of the verses written by Hallam throughout 1829 (his most prolific year) are those of an aspiring young poet who was learning to expand his capacities by studying and imitating more accomplished predecessors. Thus, his Scottish poems were frequently Wordsworthian, including "Written on the Banks of the Tay," "Stanzas Written in a Steam-boat," "Sonnet Written at Fingal's Cave, on the Island of Staffa" (compare Wordsworth's) and, more obviously, "Sonnet Written in the Pass of Killiecrankie, and Alluding to That Written by Mr. Wordsworth in the Same Place." Hallam's "Stanzas Written After Visiting Melrose Abbey in Company of Sir Walter Scott" commemorated an aged author and his hospitality without fully realizing what a favor had been received, while "The Burthen of Istambol" revealed that Lord Byron's influence on Hallam was still active.

At Malvern in September, 1829, Hallam wrote "Lines Addressed to Alfred Tennyson," the first clear indication of their intimacy. He also attempted "Wordsworth at Glenarbach: An Episode," recalling a conversation with Robertson about the poet; strongly indebted to Shelley's "Julian and Maddalo," it suggests that Hallam was experimenting further with poetic diction and forms. Thus, in "To One Early Loved, Now in India"— for which read Italy—he tried nine-line Spenserian stanzas (rather than his more frequent eight-line ones) in a final poetic tribute, the last of eleven poems in all, to Wintour. In December of the same year, Hallam wrote a less experimental but biographically significant sonnet full of his rapture at meeting Emily Tennyson.

POETIC DECLINE

Thereafter, the Tennysons were prominent in Hallam's poetry, but its volume was decreasing. During the Easter vacation visit to Somersby in 1830, Hallam wrote one sonnet to Alfred Tennyson and three to Emily. There were then two further poems addressed to Emily and her sister Mary, love poems for Emily alone, a lament for the death of the Reverend George Clayton Tennyson, and one more sonnet for Alfred's brother Charles, who was also a poet worthy of attention. "Stanzas," one of the poems addressed to Emily, was published in the *Englishman's Magazine* in August, 1831, together with Hallam's review of Tennyson's poems.

By 1832, Hallam's poetic ambitions had subsided, largely unfulfilled; he wrote only a handful of poems thereafter. "Scene at Rome," in 155 lines of blank verse, is a dialogue (imitating Walter Savage Landor) between Raffaelle and Fiammetta in the former's studio; it is very much like prose. "Lines Spoken in the Character of Pygmalion" are better, anticipating Robert Browning; they were actually spoken by Hallam as part of a charade. In September, he offered a sonnet "on an old German picture of the three kings of Cologne" to *Fraser's Magazine*, where it was published five months later. Finally, in "Long hast thou wandered," a poem of uncertain date, Hallam bade farewell to poetic

composition; with few exceptions, all his important literary work after October, 1831, was in prose.

OTHER MAJOR WORK

NONFICTION: *The Letters of Arthur Henry Hallam*, 1981 (Jack Kolb, editor).

BIBLIOGRAPHY

Brown, John. *Arthur H. Hallam*. Philadelphia: R. West, 1978. A basic biography dealing with the short life and works of Hallam.

Chandler, James. "Hallam, Tennyson, and the Poetry of Sensation: Aestheticist Allegories of a Counter-Public Sphere." *Studies in Romanticism* 33, no. 4 (Winter, 1994): 527. An examination of late Romantic aestheticism in the works of Hallam and Alfred, Lord Tennyson.

Clausen, Christopher. "Arthur Henry Hallam and the Victorian Promise." *Sewanee Review* 101, no. 3 (Summer, 1993): 375. A discussion of the differences between Alfred, Lord Tennyson's *In Memoriam* and William Gladstone's essay "Arthur Henry Hallam."

Hallam, Arthur Henry. *The Letters of Arthur Henry Hallam*. Edited by Jack Kolb. Columbus: Ohio State University Press, 1981. This selection of Hallam's voluminous correspondence includes many responses from personages such as Alfred, Lord Tennyson, his sister Emily, William Gladstone, and Richard Monckton Milnes. Kolb's introduction argues for the importance of the correspondence as Hallam's means "to keep pure and limpid," in Hallam's own words, "the source of all generous emotions."

_____. *The Poems of Arthur Henry Hallam*. Edited by Richard Le Gallienne. London: Elkin Mathews & John Lane, 1893. Contains a selection of poems, as well as the essay "On Some of the Characteristics of Modern Poetry, and on the Lyrical Poems of Alfred Tennyson." Le Gallienne's introduction provides a biographical sketch that explores the basis of Hallam's aesthetic writings. The poetry remains largely unanalyzed.

_____. *The Writings of Arthur Hallam*. Edited by T. H. Vail Motter. London: Oxford University Press,

1943. Collects Hallam's poems, essays, reviews, and translations, as well as juvenilia, an evaluation of the critical writings, and a note on Hallam's voluminous correspondence. Also contains a useful chronology of Hallam's life. Motter explains in his preface that the collection attempts to correct the perception of Hallam as a "mere shadow" of Alfred, Lord Tennyson.

Kolb, Jack. "Hallam, Tennyson, Homosexuality, and the Critics." *Philological Quarterly* 79, no. 3 (Summer, 2000): 365-396. Kolb, the editor of Hallam's letters, examines how the critics have viewed the relationship between Hallam and Alfred, Lord Tennyson, as portrayed in Tennyson's *In Memoriam* over the years, and what it shows about the critics' biases.

Mansell, Darrel. "Displacing Hallam's Tomb in Tennyson's 'In Memoriam.'" *Victorian Poetry* 36, no. 1 (Spring, 1998): 97-112. Mansell argues that Tennyson's poem "In Memoriam A. H. H." is in error concerning some facts about Hallam's death.

Martin, Robert Bernard. *Tennyson: The Unquiet Heart.* Oxford, England: Clarendon Press, 1983. This authoritative and brilliant biography of Alfred, Lord Tennyson is equally excellent on his friendship with Hallam. While hardly a chapter fails to mention Hallam, three chapters are devoted to him and his influence on Tennyson. These focus on student life at Cambridge, Hallam's influence on Tennyson's publications, and Hallam's death.

Dennis R. Dean

THOMAS HARDY

Born: Higher Bockhampton, Dorset, England; June 2, 1840
Died: Dorchester, Dorset, England; January 11, 1928

PRINCIPAL POETRY

Wessex Poems, and Other Verses, 1898
Poems of the Past and Present, 1901
Time's Laughingstocks, and Other Verses, 1909
Satires of Circumstance, 1914
Selected Poems of Thomas Hardy, 1916
Moments of Vision and Miscellaneous Verses, 1917
Late Lyrics and Earlier, 1922
Human Shows, Far Phantasies, Songs, and Trifles, 1925
Winter Words in Various Moods and Metres, 1928
Collected Poems of Thomas Hardy, 1943
The Complete Poetical Works, 1982-1985 (3 volumes; Samuel Hynes, editor)

OTHER LITERARY FORMS

Besides his eight substantial volumes of poetry, Thomas Hardy published fourteen novels, four collections of short stories, two long verse plays, and a variety of essays, prefaces, and nonfiction prose. Although Hardy directed before his death that his letters, notebooks, and private papers be burned, much interesting material has survived in addition to that preserved in *The Early Life of Thomas Hardy* (1928) and *The Later Years of Thomas Hardy* (1930), both of which were dictated by Hardy himself to his wife, Florence Hardy. A definitive seven-volume edition of Hardy's letters (1978-1988) was edited by Richard Little Purdy and Michael Millgate. In addition, Ernest Brennecke has edited *Life and Art* (1925). *An Indiscretion in the Life of an Heiress* appeared serially in 1878 and as a book in 1934; it is a story based on scenes from Hardy's rejected first novel, *The Poor Man and the Lady*, which he later destroyed.

ACHIEVEMENTS

Although Thomas Hardy's poetic reputation has grown steadily since his death, critics seem unable to agree on the exact nature of his poetic achievement or even on a list of his best poems. Aside from a small group of frequently anthologized pieces, the bulk of Hardy's poetry goes unread. Part of the problem is the immense amount of his verse—nearly a thousand poems in eight substantial volumes. The other problem is the inevitable comparison between his poetry and his fiction and the tendency to prefer one or the other, instead of seeking continuities in his work. This is an unavoidable problem with a poet-novelist, particularly with a novelist as accomplished as Hardy, whose fiction is better known than his poetry.

Hardy began his career as a novelist rather than as a poet. He turned to poetry later in life, publishing little before 1898. Here, however, chronology can be misleading. Hardy began composing verse early in life and continued to write poetry throughout the years when he was publishing his Wessex novels and tales. To a certain extent, economic pressures early led him to relegate poetry to a secondary place in his career. Once he had abandoned architecture, he turned to fiction to earn a livelihood. Had the means been available to him, he might have remained primarily a poet.

Yet even during his most productive years as a novelist, Hardy was putting aside verse that he would later publish. Sometimes these poems develop a lyrical twist to a scene or episode given fuller treatment in his novels, as in the case of "Tess's Lament," "In a Wood," or "At Casterbridge Fair." Moreover, Hardy was a lyrical prose stylist as well as a contemplative or meditative poet. The genres were fluid to him, and he moved easily from one to the other. Florence Hardy wrote in *The Later Years of Thomas Hardy* that "he had mostly aimed at keeping his narratives close to natural life and as near to poetry in their subjects as the conditions would allow, and had often regretted that these conditions would not let him keep them nearer still." Indeed, the same themes often appear in both the poems and the fiction: the capriciousness of fate, the cruelty of missed opportunities, and the large role of chance, accident, and contingency in human affairs.

Nor does chronology help much in understanding Hardy's development as a poet, since his verse shows only subtle variations in theme, subject matter, style, or treatment over more than six decades. There is a timeless quality in his verse, both early and late, with no discernible falling off in his creative power even in the late poems. Between 1898 and 1928, Hardy published eight volumes of lyrical poetry and two lengthy verse plays, which—even without the prior achievement of his fiction—would have made for an impressive literary career. That his poetry appeared after midcareer is a tribute to Hardy's undiminished creative imagination, especially when one remembers that the bulk of his poetry was published after he was sixty, with more than

half of his lyrical poetry appearing after he turned seventy-four. *The Dynasts: A Drama of the Napoleonic Wars* (pb. 1903, 1906, 1908, 1910) alone would have been a major accomplishment for a writer of his age. For his last volume, *Winter Words in Various Moods and Metres*, published posthumously, he wrote an unused preface in which he boasted that he was the only English poet to bring out a new volume of verse on a birthday so late in life. His ambition was "to have some poem or poems in a good anthology like the Golden Treasury." Thus the poems, though they are the work of a lifetime, are in their final form the product of Hardy's late career.

Yet these poems are not the serene and mellow harvest of a successful literary career. Hardy turned to poetry in mid-career after the hostile critical reception of *Jude the Obscure* (1895); after that, he resolved to write no more novels. Instead, his poems extend and concentrate the often bitter and fatalistic tone and mood of his fiction. His verse reflects the weariness and discouragement of his Wessex characters, who have faced the worst that life can offer and cherish no illusions about what the future may bring. Many deal with love entanglements and marital difficulties. Others are cynical poems about human failings or brooding meditations on aging, loss, and death. Even his nature poems are elegiac in tone, presenting a Darwinian view of harsh competition for survival in a brutal and indifferent world. One critic has remarked that Hardy's vision reflects "his sense of the irreconcilable disparity between the way things ought to be and the way they are: the failure of the universe to answer man's need for order."

Although Hardy may have lacked the buoyant optimism of Robert Browning or the sturdy faith of Alfred, Lord Tennyson, there is no lack of emotional depth in his poems. Hardy had an instinctive sense of the emotional basis of all good poetry. Temperamentally, he found the Wordsworthian formula of "emotion recollected in tranquillity" a continual source of creative inspiration. He had a keen emotional memory, and even late in life, he could recall the poignancy of incidents that had occurred a half century earlier. His range of topics may have been limited to a purview of Wessex, but he selected his poetic incidents or anecdotes on the basis of their emotional appeal and concentrated on evoking the essence of a mood or feeling. His wife recalled his remark that "poetry is emotion put into measure. The emotion must come by nature, but the measure can be acquired by art."

Hardy served his apprenticeship in Gothic architecture, and the same careful attention to detail that marked his church designs is evident in his subtle metrical variations. Although he experimented with a variety of stanzaic forms—the villanelle, triolet, and sapphic—he was partial to the ballad form and the common measure of hymn stanzas. He affected simplicity in his verse, favoring a subtle irregularity and practicing "the art of concealing art." Florence Hardy wrote:

> He knew that in architecture cunning irregularity is of enormous worth, and it is obvious that he carried on into his verse, perhaps in part unconsciously, the gothic art-principle in which he had been trained—the principle of spontaneity, found in mouldings, tracery, and such like—resulting in the "unforseen" . . . character of his metres and stanzas, that of stress rather than of syllable, poetic texture rather than poetic veneer.

Hardy is thus paradoxically the last of the great Victorians and the first of the moderns—at once traditional in style and modern in thought, attitude, and feeling. He laments the passing of the timeless relation of the countryman to the soil in his native Wessex and anticipates the confusion and bewilderment of the characters in his poems, who think in new ways but continue to feel in the old ways. Like Robert Frost, he writes of a diminished world, in which science has undercut traditional ways of thinking and believing. He shares much with the Georgian poets, who were younger than himself; their subdued lyricism, their dread of the Great War, their nostalgic pastoralism, and their sense of undefined loss and privation. What is unique in his vision is the compassion that he expresses for the victims of this changed world: his deep sense of their human plight and their loss of traditional sources of consolation. Hardy described himself once as less of a doubter or agnostic than "churchy" in an old-fashioned way: a person for whom the traditional sources of faith had disappeared yet who dreamed of "giving liturgical form to modern ideas." It is ironic that, when asked late in life whether he would have chosen the same career again,

Hardy replied that he would rather have been "a small architect in a country town," so deep was his love of church architecture and the grace and ornateness of the gothic style.

BIOGRAPHY

Thomas Hardy was born on June 2, 1840, in a rambling, seven-room cottage in Higher Bockhampton, on the edge of Bockhampton Heath, near Dorchester. He was the eldest of four children, with a sister, Mary, born in 1841, a brother, Henry, in 1851, and a sister, Kate, in 1856. His father, also named Thomas, was a master builder and mason with a love of church music and violin playing, and his mother Jemima (née Hand) Hardy was a handsome, energetic woman of country stock who loved books and reading. At birth, their first child was so frail that he was supposed dead; but an attending nurse rescued the baby, and his mother and aunt nursed him back to health, although Thomas remained a small, delicate child, physically immature in appearance until well into adulthood. Despite his frail appearance, Thomas was a vigorous, active boy who relished village life and freely roamed the heath behind his home. As a child, he so enjoyed the country dance tunes and melodies his father played that he was given a toy accordion at the age of four and was taught to play the fiddle as soon as he could finger the strings. The Church of England service strongly moved him and sometimes on wet Sunday mornings he would enact the service at home, wrapping himself in a tablecloth and reading the morning prayer to his cousin and grandmother, who pretended to be the congregation.

At the age of eight, Hardy began his schooling at the local school in Bockhampton, recently established by the lady of the manor. The boy was a quick pupil, and after a year, he was transferred to Isaac Last's Nonconformist Latin School near Bockhampton. There he continued until the age of sixteen, when he was apprenticed to the ecclesiastical architect John Hicks. During this time, he played at country dances with his father and uncle and taught Sunday school at the local parish. After his formal schooling ended, Hardy continued to study Latin and Greek with his fellow apprentices. Hardy also began writing verses about this time, being especially impressed with the regional dialect poetry of

Thomas Hardy (Library of Congress)

the Reverend William Barnes, a Dorset poet. After continuing his apprenticeship in church architecture for almost six years, Hardy finally left Bockhampton for London at the age of twenty-one.

In the spring of 1862, Hardy arrived in London with two letters of introduction in his pocket, having decided to continue his study of architecture there. Through good fortune, he found temporary work with a London friend of Hicks, who was able to recommend Hardy to the noted ecclesiastical architect John Blomfield, with whom Hardy began work as an assistant in the drawing-office. Hardy persevered in his architectural training, and within a year he won a prize offered by the Royal Institute of British Architects for his essay on the uses of glazed bricks and terra cotta in modern architecture. Blomfield's office was within walking distance of the National Gallery, and Hardy soon began spending his lunch hours there, studying one painting carefully each day. He especially admired the landscapes of J. M. W. Turner and the Flemish masters.

Work was light under Blomfield, and young Hardy found time to write his first sketch, "How I Built Myself a House," which he published in *Chambers's Journal* in 1865. He also continued writing poetry during this time, although little of his juvenilia has survived. In the evenings, he continued his education at King's College in London, studying French. For a brief time, he even considered applying to Cambridge to study for the ministry, but he gave up the idea as impractical.

The confinement of life in London gradually sapped Hardy's health, and within five years, he was advised to return to Bockhampton to recuperate. There he assisted his former employer John Hicks with church restorations and soon regained his health. With time on his hands, Hardy turned to fiction and began working on his first novel, *The Poor Man and the Lady*. In 1870, he sent the manuscript to a London publisher, whose editor, George Meredith, praised the young writer but urged him to try something else with more plot ingenuity and suspense. This Hardy did, and ten months later finished his second novel, *Desperate Remedies*, which unfortunately was also initially rejected before it was published in 1871.

In the meantime, Hicks had sold his firm to another architect, G. R. Crickmay, who engaged Hardy to complete some church restorations in Cornwall. Hardy moved with the firm to Weymouth and, in March, 1870, set off to Cornwall to inspect a dilapidated gothic church at St. Juliot. There he met Emma Gifford, the young sister-in-law of the rector, who was eventually to become his first wife. At this time Hardy was already engaged to his cousin Tryphena Sparks, a young schoolteacher, but their engagement was broken after he met Gifford.

Although Hardy did complete his supervision of the church restoration at St. Juliot, his interest was gradually shifting from architecture to literature, and he began writing fiction in earnest. *Under the Greenwood Tree* was published in 1872, followed by *A Pair of Blue Eyes* (1872-1873) and *Far From the Madding Crowd* (1874). He was now sure enough of his future to marry Gifford in London on September 17, 1874, and after their honeymoon in France, he settled down to begin *The Return of the Native* (1878).

The next ten years saw the publication of five more

novels and a number of short stories, strengthening his reputation as a major writer. He also continued to write poetry but withheld most of it from publication until after 1897. As their means grew, the Hardys moved back to Dorchester and built their permanent home, Max Gate. Hardy began making notes for an epic treatment of the Napoleonic Wars, eventually to become *The Dynasts*. Unfortunately, the Hardys had no children. This may have put a strain on their marriage, for although Emma Hardy continued to serve as her husband's secretary, making fair copies of his manuscripts for publication, she gradually drew apart from him and became embittered, perhaps resenting his success. Their marriage became a cold formality of two people living in separate rooms and seeing each other only at meals. The difficulties of this first marriage may have been reflected in the bleakness of Hardy's outlook.

After the Hardys moved into Max Gate in June, 1885, he embarked on his last decade of fiction writing. This period saw the publication of another five novels and approximately fifty short stories. *The Mayor of Casterbridge* (1886) was followed by *The Woodlanders* (1886-1887), *Tess of the D'Urbervilles* (1891), *Jude the Obscure*, and *The Well-Beloved* (1897). The multivolume edition of the Wessex novels also appeared in 1895-1896. During this time, Hardy was writing virtually a novel a year.

Hardy had ventured to treat new material in *Jude the Obscure*, and the uniformly hostile critical reception accorded the novel led him to put aside fiction after 1897 and embark on a second literary career as a poet. For the next thirty-one years, he would write only poetry. During that time, he published eight volumes of poetry, at least some of it early work, and the epic-drama *The Dynasts*. Hardy began to be recognized as a major English writer and received a number of awards, including honorary degrees from Aberdeen, Cambridge, and Oxford.

Emma Hardy died at Max Gate on November 27, 1912, and during his bereavement, Hardy visited the scenes of their courtship. Two years later, he married Florence Emily Dugdale, a young admirer who had served as his personal secretary after his wife's death. By this time, he was universally recognized as the last great Victorian writer and the preeminent English man

of letters, although his lack of reputation abroad prevented him from receiving a Nobel Prize. Despite personal misgivings, he spoke out patriotically for England during World War I. After the war, he lived quietly with his second wife at Max Gate during the last decade of his life. In 1923, he published a second verse play, *The Famous Tragedy of the Queen of Cornwall*, based on the romance of Tristan and Iseult. After a brief illness, Hardy died on January 11, 1928. His heart was buried in the grave of his first wife in their parish churchyard in Stinsford, and his ashes were installed in the Poets' Corner, Westminster Abbey. After his death, Florence Hardy published a two-volume biography that her husband had dictated to her. She died on October 17, 1937.

ANALYSIS

More than one critic has called the lyrics in *Satires of Circumstance* Thomas Hardy's finest achievement, although his most notable poems are probably distributed evenly among his eight volumes. Since there was no period of peak creative achievement for him—rather, a steady accumulation of poems over a long and productive career—the reader must search among the collected verse for those poems in which Hardy's style, vision, and subject matter coincide in a memorable work. Given the strength and originality of his vision, it is difficult to speak of influences on Hardy's poetry, although in many respects he carries forward the Romantic tradition of William Wordsworth and Percy Bysshe Shelley and the homey realism of George Crabbe. An obscure Dorset poet, William Barnes, whose poetry Hardy edited in 1908, may have first introduced him to the possibilities of writing regional poetry. Barnes was a clergyman and philologist with a keen interest in local dialects who introduced vivid scenes of Wessex life into his verse. Hardy read and admired Algernon Charles Swinburne and paid tribute to him on numerous occasions, notably in "A Singer Asleep," although his influence on Hardy appears to have been slight. Hardy's poetry is perhaps most akin in tone and spirit to Wordsworth's pastoral lyrics and odes, particularly "Michael," although Hardy's characters often lack the simple heroism and nobility of spirit of Wordsworth's protagonists.

WESSEX POEMS, AND OTHER VERSES

The appearance of Hardy's first volume of poetry, *Wessex Poems, and Other Verses*, was greeted by the critics with scarcely more understanding than that which had been accorded to *Jude the Obscure*. The fifty-one selections are a mixture of lyrics, sonnets, and ballads illustrated by the poet with thirty-one "Sketches of Their Scenes," designed to accompany the poems. The volume includes five historical poems in a ballad sequence about the Napoleonic Wars that anticipate *The Dynasts*; a series of four "She, To Him" love sonnets written in the Shakespearean manner; a number of lyrics on disillusioned love, of which "Neutral Tones" is probably the best; and a set of meditative nature poems, including the sonnet "Hap" and "Nature's Questioning." An additional group of lyrics enlarges on scenes from the novels, including the lovely "In a Wood," which echoes a nature description from *The Woodlanders*, and "The Ivy Wife," a figurative portrait of a possessive wife that borrows its metaphor from a description in that same novel.

"Neutral Tones" is the most frequently anthologized of Hardy's *Wessex Poems, and Other Verses*, and deservedly so. This four-quatrain lyric, rhyming *abba*, employs a series of muted winter images and a pondside meeting to describe the death of a love affair. The implied confession by the beloved that she is no longer in love creates the dramatic occasion, and although the pronoun employed is "we," the point of view is clearly that of the forsaken lover. The poem possesses that haunting quality of a painful moment forever etched on one's memory: The colorless imagery of the setting suggests an impressionistic painting of two lovers meeting against a dreary December landscape in which nature's barrenness ("starving sod," "greyish leaves") serves as a counterpoint to the death of love. Even the negations of Hardy's poetic syntax combine with the winter imagery and the bitter dramatic occasion to sustain the mood of "Neutral Tones." This poignant lyric about the failure of a love relationship was written, interestingly enough, just before Hardy's engagement to his cousin Tryphena Sparks was broken, perhaps because he discovered her infatuation with his friend Horace Maule. This theme of love's betrayal is of course also found often in Hardy's novels, although it achieves

greater intensity and concentration in poems such as "Neutral Tones."

"Hap," a sonnet about the forces that shape events unpredictably, records Hardy's troubled response to evolutionary theory, with its view of natural selection operating impartially, without purpose or direction. The speaker would prefer a personalized universe, even with "some Vengeful god," who wills and controls the course of events, rather than "Crass Casualty," "dicing Time," and "These purblind doomsters" who mete out bliss and pain alike without reason. "Hap" is thematically related to "Nature's Questioning," which implies that the author of the universe is "some Vast Imbecility" unconscious of human pains. This poem was so often quoted against him as evidence of his alleged atheism and hostility to religion that Hardy finally decided to write a preface for his second volume explaining that his poems taken individually did not necessarily reflect his personal philosophy. He later restated this disavowal in the preface to *Winter Words in Various Moods and Metres*; still, many of his poems did seem to invite speculation about his personal views. "Heiress and Architect," for example, is a philosophical allegory cast in terms of a dialogue between two speakers representing romantic and realistic views of life. The heiress finds her elaborate plans diminished in each succeeding stanza as she submits them to the cold scrutiny of the architect. Her house designs progressively shrink in this allegory of human dreams crushed by realities, a theme familiar to Hardy's novels.

POEMS OF THE PAST AND PRESENT

Hardy's second volume, *Poems of the Past and Present*, comprising a hundred poems, is nearly twice as long as *Wessex Poems, and Other Verses*. Two major sections include "War Poems," dealing with the Boer War, and "Poems of Pilgrimage," about notable historical and literary shrines in Italy and Switzerland, where the Hardys had traveled in the spring of 1882; a third section was composed of "Miscellaneous Poems." The "War Poems" record Hardy's deep reservations about British imperialism and the cost of war to ordinary men; "Drummer Hodge" is about a boy drafted from Dorset and fated to lie after his death under southern constellations. Among the "Miscellaneous Poems," "The Last Chrysanthemum" and "The

Darkling Thrush" are incomparably the best. The first describes a perennial blooming out of season, into the winter, past the time when it should have flowered. This curious natural event becomes the occasion for a lyrical meditation on the mysteries of growth and change that regulate the life of each organism. Hardy continues the English tradition of the nature lyric, although in a much more subdued form than, for example, Wordsworth's "I Wandered Lonely as a Cloud." Instead of drawing inspiration from a simple vernal scene, Hardy records a more complex response to a post-Darwinian natural world that can no longer be identified with a beneficent Creator. In the final stanza of "The Last Chrysanthemum," however, he seems unwilling to discard entirely the notion of a deliberate, shaping purpose, even though the poem's affirmation is tentative at best.

This metaphor of unseasonableness is carried forward in "The Darkling Thrush," perhaps Hardy's finest lyric. Here tone, mood, theme, subject, and setting coincide to shape a nearly flawless meditation on the dawning of a new century. Hardy's thrush is his solitary singer, the projection of the speaker's hopes and the spirit of his age, which in the midst of a bleak winter landscape, an image of the times, finds reason to fling his song against the gathering darkness of the coming age. Hardy employs the traditional formula of the romantic inspirational lyric: the speaker's despondency, the corresponding gloom of the natural landscape, then the sudden change of mood within the lyric, in this case in the third octave, after the glimpse of a seemingly trivial natural event, the sight of a single thrush singing in a copse against the winter twilight. Yet this poem does not achieve the triumphant resolution of Percy Bysshe Shelley's "To a Sky-lark" or John Keats's "Ode to a Nightingale"; instead, the concluding octave is curiously equivocal, even subversive of traditional consolations. The speaker still finds little cause for rejoicing; he simply pauses to marvel at the anomaly of the thrush's song against so bleak a setting. There is something so casual and disarming about the country setting, with the speaker leaning musingly on a "coppice gate" and quietly reflecting on the starkness of the December landscape, that readers may at first miss the implicit irony in his response to the thrush's "caroling." Was it

merely an illusion to find cause for hope in the bird's song? The poem's deliberate ambiguity resists any easy interpretation, but it would be unlike Hardy to offer glib reassurances.

TIME'S LAUGHINGSTOCKS, AND OTHER VERSES

Time's Laughingstocks, and Other Verses includes ninety-four poems in four groupings: "Time's Laughingstocks," "More Love Lyrics," "A Set of Country Songs," and "Pieces Occasional and Various." Most of the selections are rustic character sketches and ballads of uneven quality, although Hardy considered one of the ballads, "A Trampwoman's Tragedy," to be perhaps "his most successful poem." It is a country tale of jealousy, murder, and a hanging that leaves the speaker alone in the world, without her "fancy-man," to haunt the hills and moors in which the deeds took place.

SATIRES OF CIRCUMSTANCE

Satires of Circumstance continues the pattern of Hardy's earlier volumes of poetry, with 106 poems in four sections: "Lyrics and Reveries," comprising religious and philosophic meditations; "Poems of 1912-13," recollections of his courtship of Emma Gifford; "Miscellaneous Pieces"; and "Satires of Circumstance in Fifteen Glimpses." Two of the poems in the first section, "Channel Firing" and "The Convergence of the Twain," are among his most popular poems. Written three months before the outbreak of World War I, "Channel Firing" contains an ironic premonition of the impending conflict. The poem is narrated from the point of view of the dead in their coffins in a country churchyard, suddenly awakened by the "great guns" at sea. The nine stanzas in common measure present an ironic view of the futility and inevitability of war, with even God unable to prevent the ensuing bloodshed. All he can do is to reassure the frightened souls that "judgment-hour" is not at hand; the noise comes only from the naval guns practicing in the English Channel off the Dorset Coast.

Hardy wrote "The Convergence of the Twain" to commemorate the sinking of the luxury liner *Titanic* on April 14-15, 1912, after the ship collided with an iceberg on its maiden voyage across the Atlantic. He uses eleven stanzas of triplet rhyme with an extended third line to develop the theme and counterpoint of the human vanity ("Pride of Life") that boasted of building an unsinkable ship and "The Immanent Will" that prepared an iceberg to meet it by "paths coincident" on the night they were fated to collide. A retrospective narration in the first five stanzas pictures the sunken ship with its jewels and elegant furnishings now the home of grotesque sea-worms and "moon-eyed fishes." The final six stanzas recount the inevitable steps toward the final encounter as the two "mates"—ship and iceberg—move inexorably toward each other. A grim determinism seems to stalk this symbol of human arrogance and pride as the ship that even God "could not sink" goes down on its first voyage.

After the death of his first wife, Hardy wrote a series of elegies to Emma Gifford in his "Poems of 1912-13." The best of these may be "Voices," with its poignant recall of his first impressions of her as a young woman in Cornwall, its haunting dactylic tetrameters, and its lovely refrain. Here also Hardy projects much of his sadness and regret for their embittered relationship later in their marriage and for the series of misunderstandings that drove them apart. In "The Voice," he tries to recapture the joy of his earliest memories of his wife as she was during their courtship.

Perhaps the harshest portrait in *Satires of Circumstance* is Hardy's depiction of the hypocritical clergyman, who, "In Church," is discovered after the service by one of his Bible students, practicing before a mirror the flourishes and gestures that "had moved the congregation so."

MOMENTS OF VISION AND MISCELLANEOUS VERSES

Moments of Vision and Miscellaneous Verses, with 159 poems, is Hardy's largest volume, including a substantial body of reflective personal poems and an additional seventeen selections about World War I titled "Poems of War and Patriotism." Several of these lyrics are worth mentioning: "Heredity," with its glimpse of family traits that leap from generation to generation; "The Oxen," a frequently anthologized poem narrating a common folk legend about how the barnyard animals were said to kneel in adoration of the nativity on Christmas Eve; "For Life I Had Never Cared Greatly," a confession of Hardy's personal disillusionment; and "In Time of 'The Breaking of Nations,'" about how life, work, and love continue despite the ravages of war.

LATER POETRY

Two more volumes were yet to appear during Hardy's lifetime. Now in his eighties, he published *Late Lyrics and Earlier*, a collection of 151 lyrical incidents and impressions; three years later *Human Shows, Far Phantasies, Songs, and Trifles* appeared, with 152 poems. His last volume, *Winter Words in Various Moods and Metres*, was published posthumously by Florence Hardy. There is a sameness about these late poems that makes it difficult to select particular ones for discussion. A few show sparks of creative novelty, but many are recapitulations of earlier themes or material gleaned from notebooks or recollections during the time that Hardy was dictating his two-volume biography to his wife.

In *Late Lyrics and Earlier*, "A Drizzling Easter Morning" records a skeptic's response to the Easter resurrection on a day when rain falls and rural life continues unabated. "Christmas: 1924" from *Winter Words in Various Moods and Metres* draws a stark contrast between humankind's perennial hopes for peace on Earth and its use of poison gas in modern warfare; "He Never Expected Much" sums up the poet's personal philosophy; and "He Resolves to Say No More" expresses a tired old man's farewell to life, in which he refuses to offer any last words of insight. Perhaps this mood simply reflected his age and illness, but Hardy's last poem lacks the resoluteness of, for example, William Butler Yeats's "Under Ben Bulben."

THE DYNASTS

At one time, *The Dynasts* was hailed as Hardy's major achievement, although critics have since revised their judgment of this massive verse drama, "in three parts, nineteen acts, and one hundred and thirty scenes," of the Napoleonic Wars. Hardy subtitled his work "A Drama of the Napoleonic Wars," although he meant to glorify the British role in checking the French emperor's dynastic ambitions. In the play, he presents an allegorical view of history as a relentless, deterministic pageant in which human beings, mere automatons, enact the designs of the Immanent Will. Ever since his youth, Hardy had been planning a literary project involving the Napoleonic Wars, although he was unsure what form the work would eventually take. The final epic-drama, which he undertook in his sixties, is conceived on the grand scale of Shelley's *Prometheus Unbound: A Lyrical Drama in Four Acts* (pb. 1820), with the historical sweep of Leo Tolstoy's *War and Peace* (1865-1869), and though the work is unevenly executed, in places flawed by excessive allegory, and perhaps even inaccessible to the modern reader, it contains many impressive scenes.

From his early plans for an "*Iliad* of Europe from 1789 to 1815," Hardy evolved a dramatic form flexible enough to allow rapid panoramic shifts in scene that traced the paths of marching armies across the map of Europe and recorded the plots and intrigues of Napoleon as he schemed to strengthen his military domination. A chorus of Spirits or Phantom Intelligences introduce and conclude the scenes and interweave their comments with the human action below. What is most impressive, however, is Hardy's historical knowledge of the Napoleonic period, combined with his innate repugnance for war and his deep compassion for the victims of the clash of nations. His controlling vision, here and throughout his poetry, was of the continuity and sameness of the human spirit everywhere. As he observed about *The Dynasts*: "The human race [is] to be shown as one great network or tissue which quivers in every part when one point is shaken, like a spider's web if touched."

OTHER MAJOR WORKS

LONG FICTION: *Desperate Remedies*, 1871; *Under the Greenwood Tree*, 1872; *A Pair of Blue Eyes*, 1872-1873; *Far from the Madding Crowd*, 1874; *The Hand of Ethelberta*, 1875-1876; *An Indiscretion in the Life of an Heiress*, 1878 (serial), 1934 (book); *The Return of the Native*, 1878; *The Trumpet-Major*, 1880; *A Laodicean*, 1880-1881; *Two on a Tower*, 1882; *The Mayor of Casterbridge*, 1886; *The Woodlanders*, 1886-1887; *Tess of the D'Urbervilles*, 1891; *Jude the Obscure*, 1895; *The Well-Beloved*, 1897.

SHORT FICTION: *Wessex Tales*, 1888; *A Group of Noble Dames*, 1891; *Life's Little Ironies*, 1894; *A Changed Man, The Waiting Supper, and Other Tales*, 1913; *The Complete Short Stories*, 1989 (Desmond Hawkins, editor).

PLAYS: *The Dynasts: A Drama of the Napoleonic Wars*, pb. 1903, 1906, 1908, 1910 (verse drama); *The Famous Tragedy of the Queen of Cornwall*, pr., pb. 1923 (one act).

NONFICTION: *Life and Art*, 1925 (Ernest Brennecke, editor); *The Early Life of Thomas Hardy*, 1928; *The Later Years of Thomas Hardy*, 1930; *Personal Writings*, 1966 (Harold Orel, editor); *The Collected Letters of Thomas Hardy*, 1978-1988 (7 volumes; Richard Little Purdy and Michael Millgate, editors).

BIBLIOGRAPHY

Armstrong, Tim. *Haunted Hardy: Poetry, History, Memory*. New York: Palgrave, 2000. An attempt to elevate Hardy as poet within the Western tradition.

Gibson, James. *Thomas Hardy*. New York: St. Martin's Press, 1996. An introductory guide to Hardy's art, focusing on how Hardy used his own experience in his writing and tracing his development from fiction back to his first love, poetry.

Kramer, Dale, ed. *The Cambridge Companion to Thomas Hardy*. New York: Cambridge University Press, 1999. An essential introduction and general overview of all Hardy's work and specific demonstrations of Hardy's ideas and literary skills. Individual essays explore Hardy's biography, aesthetics, and the impact on his work of developments in science, religion, and philosophy in the late nineteenth century. The volume also contains a detailed chronology of Hardy's life.

Lanzano, Ellen Anne. *Hardy: The Temporal Poetics*. New York: Peter Lang, 1999. An examination of Hardy's poetics in the light of the temporal context out of which he wrote more than nine hundred poems. To a large extent, Hardy's struggle with the forms of time is a record of the nineteenth century engagement with the relationship of consciousness to the new science and the loss of traditional beliefs.

Mallett, Phillip, ed. *The Achievement of Thomas Hardy*. New York: St. Martin's Press, 2000. A study of the literary achievements of Hardy that also examines his depiction of Wessex. Bibliography and index.

Maynard, Katherine Kearney. *Thomas Hardy's Tragic Poetry: The Lyrics and "The Dynasts."* Iowa City: University of Iowa Press, 1991. This study examines the question of tragic literature's vitality in a secular age and explores the philosophical underpinnings of Hardy's tragic vision in his lyric poetry and in *The Dynasts*. It also examines Hardy's efforts within the context of nineteenth century poetry.

Millgate, Michael. *Thomas Hardy: A Biography Revisited*. New York: Oxford University Press, 2004. This biography enhances and replaces Millgate's 1982 biography, considered to be one of the best and most scholarly Hardy biographies available.

Page, Norman, ed. *Oxford Reader's Companion to Hardy*. New York: Oxford University Press, 2000. An encyclopedia devoted to the life and literary works of Hardy. Bibliography.

Ray, Martin, ed. *Thomas Hardy Remembered*. London: Ashgate, 2007. A collection of interviews with Hardy and recollections of him by his friends and acquaintances offer readers a fresh perspective on the writer. Also contains observations by Hardy on his writing and his contemporaries' opinions about his life.

Tomalin, Claire. *Thomas Hardy*. New York: Penguin, 2007. This thorough and finely written biography by a respected Hardy scholar illuminates the poet's drive to indict the malice, neglect, and ignorance of his fellow human creatures. Tomalin nicely brings Hardy's poetry to the fore in discussing aspects of his life that are apparent in his literary works.

Andrew J. Angyal

TONY HARRISON

Born: Leeds, Yorkshire, England; April 30, 1937

PRINCIPAL POETRY
Earthworks, 1964
The Loiners, 1970
From "The School of Eloquence," and Other Poems, 1978
Continuous: Fifty Sonnets from "The School of Eloquence," 1981
Selected Poems, 1984

The Fire Gap: A Poem with Two Tails, 1985
Selected Poems, 1987
V., and Other Poems, 1990
The Gaze of the Gorgon, 1992 (verse film)
Black Daisies for the Bride, 1993 (verse film)
Permanently Bard: Selected Poetry, 1995
The Shadow of Hiroshima, and Other Film/Poems, 1995
Versus Verse: Satirical Rhymes of Three Antibodies in Opposition to Practically Everything, 1995 (with Geoffrey B. Riddehough and Geoffrey A. Spencer)
Prometheus, 1998 (verse film)
Laureate's Block, and Other Occasional Poems, 2000
Under the Clock, 2005

OTHER LITERARY FORMS

Tony Harrison has strong, continuing connections with the theater and opera. His version of Molière's *Le Misanthrope* (1666; *The Misanthrope*, 1709) was produced by Great Britain's National Theatre in 1973, and his radical adaptation of Jean Racine's *Phèdre* (1677; *Phaedra*, 1701)—whose title, *Phaedra Brittanica*, suggests how far he took it away from its source—appeared in 1975. His adaptation of Aeschylus's *Oresteia* (458 B.C.E.; English translation, 1777) came in 1981. He has also worked in opera, both as a librettist (with Harrison Birtwistle in *Bow Down* in 1977) and as a regular translator and adaptor for the Metropolitan Opera in New York. He provided the English lyrics for Mikis Theodorakis's songs for the film *The Blue Bird* (1976).

Harrison has a wide range of interests as a translator, and the occasional translation often shows up in his volumes of poetry, but he also addresses himself to more substantial translation projects. While a lecturer in English in Nigeria, he collaborated with James Simmons on a translation of Aristophanes' *Lysistratē* (411 B.C.E.; *Lysistrata*, 1837) into the Pidgin English of a native tribe. He is also the translator of the work of the fourth century C.E. Greek epigrammatist Palladas, and the selection *Poems* appeared in 1975. In 1988, he wrote his first play, *The Trackers of Oxyrhynchus*, which was published in 1990.

ACHIEVEMENTS

Unusual in actually being able to make a living as a poet, albeit by adapting his talents to the theater, Tony Harrison is a major spokesperson for that peculiarly British phenomenon, the educated, working-class intellectual, nostalgically loyal to the class from which he came while committed without hypocrisy to the primarily middle-to-upper-middle-class world of the arts with all its comforts and civilities.

In 1969, Harrison won the Cholmondeley Award for Poetry, and in the same year the UNESCO (United Nations Educational, Scientific, and Cultural Organization) Fellowship in Poetry allowed him to travel as a representative of the international world of poetry to South America and Africa. Those journeys through several countries were to be used as subjects of several poems in his later publications. In 1972, *The Loiners*, his first full-length collection, won the Geoffrey Faber Memorial Prize. Other awards include the European Poetry Translation Prize (1983) for his translation of Aeschylus's *Oresteia*, the Whitbread Prize for Poetry (1992) for *The Gaze of the Gorgon*, the Prix Italia (1994) for the film *Black Daisies for the Bride*, the Heinemann Award (1996) for *The Shadow of Hiroshima, and Other Film/Poems*, the Northern Rock Foundation Writer's Award (2004), the Wilfred Owen Poetry Prize (2007), and the first PEN/Pinter prize (2009).

He has held numerous fellowships, having been named a Northern Arts Fellow in Poetry at Universities of Newcastle and Durham in 1967-1968 and 1976-1977; a Gregynog Arts Fellow at University of Wales in 1973-1974, a UK/US Bicentennial Arts Fellow, New York, in 1979-1980; and a fellow of the Royal Society of Literature in 1984.

BIOGRAPHY

Tony Harrison was born in Leeds, Yorkshire, in 1937 to a working-class family, and his primary education was in the Cross Flatts County Primary School. A promising student, he moved from there to the Leeds Grammar School. (At the secondary school level, English education clearly differentiates between students with academic inclinations and talents and students likely to terminate their education in their teens, a sepa-

ration that often has serious class implications.) Harrison went on to Leeds University, where he earned a degree in classics and a diploma in linguistics.

Harrison was married to Rosemarie Crossfield Dietzsch in 1962; they had a daughter and a son but were later divorced. He began his first career in 1962 as an itinerant university lecturer, teaching for four years in Nigeria, and in Prague, Czechoslovakia, for one year. In 1967, he became the first Northern Arts Fellow in Poetry at the Universities of Newcastle-upon-Tyne and Durham. Between 1973 and 1978, he had close connections as a translator and adaptor of European dramas with Great Britain's National Theatre and served as resident dramatist with them in 1977-1978. He also developed a continuing relationship as translator and librettist with the Metropolitan Opera, while maintaining his personal connections with northern England by living in Newcastle.

In the late 1980's, Harrison became directly involved as a theater director and as a playwright. He became a stage director at the National Theatre in London and was given the responsibility of bringing his first play, *The Trackers of Oxyrhynchus*, into performance, first at the ancient stadium at Delphi in Greece and then in London, with further presentations in Yorkshire and in Denmark. The play was originally written for one performance, but it proved to be strong enough for a major run. In 1984, he married Teresa Stratas, an opera singer. He is widely known as a poet and commentator on poetry in countries as far apart as Cuba, Brazil, Senegal, and Gambia.

ANALYSIS

It is generally accepted that Tony Harrison is not quite like his contemporaries in English poetry. That is true in more ways than one, although at the same time, seen from another angle, he is clearly aligned with many of the poets of postwar Great Britain. On the obvious level, he can be distinguished because of his use of his poetic gifts in the service of the theater. The role of translator and adapter is difficult to assess and is often unheralded. Indeed, it might be argued that the least obvious intrusion of the translator is the best indication of how successful that act of necessary manipulation of another's text is, since what is desired is a mirror image (in another language) of the original act of creation. Harrison, however, has not always confined himself to such gentle tumbling of art into another language, and it is of some value, when speaking of him as a writer, to look at a work such as *Phaedra Britannica* to see just how "creative" he can be in the face of a foreign text, using a flexible, almost unhinged couplet to turn Racine's *Phèdre* into a play about the English and their personal and political involvement in India. The result is not Racine, and it would be silly to suggest that it is, but it is an interesting example of how a late twentieth century poet can make verse drama despite its unfashionableness, and make it without ascending to fulsome, pumped-up afflatus, which would be risible, at the least, and pompously inappropriate in an age of deliberately flattened rhetoric.

THE LOINERS

It is not, however, simply a matter of Harrison's ability to turn his poetic gifts to the theater that is meant in distinguishing him from other poets. There is, for various reasons, a tendency in British poets to confine themselves, with some considerable success, to a narrow thematic line. This is not always true, and it should not be taken as necessarily debasing the quality of their work. Harrison, on the other hand, perhaps partly because of his travels as an educator, itinerant poet, and theatrical journeyman, has a very wide range of interests in his poems. *The Loiners*, his first collected volume, is the best example of that breadth and includes poems not only about his native north of England but also about Africa, America, South America, Europe, and the once-called Iron Curtain countries—states that fell under the control of the former Soviet Union. In those poems his liberal-leftist political inclinations are joined to his mischievous enthusiasm for sexual high jinks in poems that set out to smash the linguistic and political barriers with some considerable sophistication and impropriety. The poem "The Bedbug" puts it succinctly:

> Comrade, with your finger on the playback switch,
> Listen carefully to each love-moan,
> And enter in the file which cry is real, and which
> A mere performance for your microphone.

Along the way, in a manner consistent with his education in the classics and linguistics, he plants elegant, teasingly relaxed translations of European poets from the classical period forward; he surprises with the economy with which he intrudes metaphysical tendencies into poems, seemingly without effort. In "The Nuptial Torches," men burning at the stake are seen thus: "Their souls/ Splut through their pores like porridge holes./ They wear their skins like cast-offs. Their skin grows/ Puckered round the knees like rumpled hose."

The high-spirited cleverness of such imagery and the wit and sophistication with which Harrison interpolates allusions of intellectual (and technical) complexity into *The Loiners* bring him closer to American poets than one might expect of a writer who comes from the working class of Yorkshire, and at his deliberately flashy, improper best (see "Flying Down to Rio: A Ballad of Beverly Hills" in *From "The School of Eloquence," and Other Poems*), there are touches of James Merrill. Harrison knows that he has this sweet tooth for being naughty, and he sometimes makes poetry out of it.

"BRINGING UP"

In *Continuous*, the poem "Bringing Up" allows him to talk of his mother's reaction to some of the poetry in *The Loiners*: He ruefully remembers, at her death, his desire to put a copy of his poems in her hands before her cremation. "You'd've been embarrassed though to meet your God/ clutching those poems of mine that you'd like banned." He retrieves himself for a moment with the wry idea that they could both have their way: "I thought you could hold my *Loiners*, and both burn!" The poem continues, with Harrison determined to follow the idea with metaphysical doggedness in which he mingles (as he often does) wit with tenderness:

> And there together in the well wrought urn
> what's left of you, the poems of your child,
> devoured by one flame, unreconciled,
> like soots on washing, black on bone-ash white.
>
> May be you see them in a better light!
>
> But I still see you weeping, your hurt looks:
>
> *You weren't brought up to write such mucky books!*

TRACES OF METAPHYSICS

Perhaps something ought to be said about this word "metaphysical," which is usually applied to a group of late sixteenth and early seventeenth century poets including John Donne and Andrew Marvell, and is taken to mean that style of poetry, sometimes of philosophical theme (hence the word "metaphysical"), in which metaphors, images, and ideas, while often deliberately inappropriate, not only are used but also are explored rigorously to wring every association out of them, sometimes to a wildly ridiculous extent. There is a touch of swagger, of showing off, about this kind of poetry, even when it is tonally serious and thematically profound; when it is neither, it can still be aesthetically exciting. Harrison often attaches metaphysical structures to the most innocent metaphors, and his "riding" them with relentless enthusiasm is seen as informally connecting him to the "Martian" group (if it can even be called that), whose most obvious and successful practitioner is the British poet Craig Raine.

"THE SCHOOL OF ELOQUENCE" SERIES

Harrison is, however, much more formidable than such improvisatory zest for the startling image might suggest, and it is in his "The School of Eloquence" series that much of his best work has been done, and indeed may continue to appear, since the concept is open-ended. Appropriating a prosodic oddity that had previously been employed by George Meredith in his *Modern Love* (1862), a sonnet consisting of sixteen rhyming pentameter lines, Harrison has provided himself with a flexible form (with which he often deliberately tampers, committing "errors" to achieve spontaneity and tonal densities), and which serves as an ideal vehicle for his worldly-wise comments on modern society. Most important, the form provides him with a supple shape in which he can explore the dilemma of his worldly success with considerable range of feeling. Caught between his working-class background (which is still a potent force in British society), for which he has considerable affection, and his enviable position as an educated traveling man with reputation and connections in the glamorous world of the arts and the theater, he believes that he has, albeit innocently, betrayed his family. Educated out of his "clothed-capped" background and possessing artistic gifts far beyond the ambitions that his parents had for him, he uses these sonnets to try to make sense of what happened, as in "Breaking the Chain":

> The mams, pig-sick of oilstains in their wash,
> wished for their sons a better class of gear,
>   wear their own clothes into work 'but not go posh,
> go up a rung or two but settle near.

The poems come together, a few at a time, and develop into a small autobiographical novel, ranging from memories of childhood to rueful anecdotes about his fragile relationship with his parents before their deaths. Sometimes the poems deal with the difficult times of the parents' last illnesses, attempting to discover why so much love was so ineptly expressed. Despite his determination to write simply and to use working-class and regional dialect when appropriate, the poems are not simplistic. The last verse of "Breaking the Chain" deals with the expensive draftsman's instruments that his father bought for him, hoping that he might end up close at hand: "This meant the 'drawing office' to the dads,/ same place of work, but not blue-collar, white." It ends in a way that ought to remind the reader of Harrison's metaphysical bent, and perhaps of Donne's use of the compass image in "A Valediction: Forbidding Mourning." Harrison uses the idea with the lightest touch so that the smartness will not breach the plangent feeling:

> Looking at it now still breaks my heart!
> The gap his gift acknowledged then 's wide as
> eternity, but I still can't bear to part
> with these never passed on, never used, dividers.

There is some danger in this fusion of metaphysical imagery and deep feeling, the former threatening to fall into "cuteness," as it does occasionally (disastrously so in "Guava Libre," *From "The School of Eloquence," and Other Poems*), and the latter always a possible danger in the sonnets dealing with his family. Usually Harrison knows how far to go, and his good taste allows him to decide what the mix of high intelligence, clever allusions, deliberately awkward usages, and native dialect ought to be and how far he can dare take them. The danger is most apparent when the poems get into the area of private feeling, where he chooses to divest himself of sophistication for simple tale-telling, where the flatness of the language and the lines teeters on the edge of sentimental excess as in "Continuous":

> James Cagney was the one up both our streets
> His was the only art we ever shared.
> A gangster film and choc ice were the treats
> that showed about as much love as he dared.

That "choc ice" may be a bit too cunning, a bit too much total recall of the language of the cinema house of his childhood. However, a poem such as "Marked with D" gets much of its power from the way in which he strides into danger, taking his father's past job as a baker and indecorously describing his father's cremation in metaphysical images and puns baldly related to the baking of a loaf of bread:

> The baker's man that no-one will see rise
> and England made to feel like some dull oaf
> is smoke, enough to sting one person's eyes
> and ash (not unlike flour) for one small loaf.

In context, this kind of impropriety works not so much because it is so outrageously smart, but because, in a peculiar way, it enforces the simplicity of this working-class life, a world in which only the sparseness, the paucity of aspiration, exists in the crudest metaphor: The poetry comes out of its unpoetic rejection of appropriately sonorous language.

The family poems allow Harrison to enter into the continuing problems of the British working classes, the continuing limitations and disappointments of stunted lives, seemingly destined to be similarly confined in the future as the country goes on its inexorably threadbare way. The intrusion of the black and brown Commonwealth refugees into the working-class neighborhoods, already run-down and overcrowded, is the subject of a series of poems in which the wariness, the sense of the despair and helplessness of the lower class, seeing themselves as the victims of other people's problems, at and on the edge of racial prejudice that they hardly understand, is expressed through the eyes of his father. In these poems, Harrison can be most clearly identified as a working-class poet.

PASTORAL POEMS

Harrison is, however, always more than one kind of poet, and he often uses the sonnet form to explore his continuing fascination with language and how it can be used, misused, and sometimes betray, not simply within a community but also on the wider scale of political chicanery and indifference. He is a poet of considerable range; the open-ended nature of "The School of Eloquence" series, both thematically and tonally, allows for personal intimacies, political comment, scholarly puzzles, and arcane jokes about high and louche lowlife. Harrison is a cosmopolitan poet in the very best and widest sense of that word: intelligent, lettered, witty, skeptical, and, sometimes, cheerfully rude. It is also interesting to see Harrison reacting to America, not only in his obviously satiric poems about urban excess but also in his pastoral mode, which was not strongly represented in his work until the early 1980's. Harrison has two lovely long poems, set in the rural fastness of central Florida, "The Fire-Gap: A Poem with Two Tails" and "Cypress and Cedar," which extend his range into thoughtful apprehension of humanity's relation to the natural world in ways that are reminiscent of Samuel Taylor Coleridge's conversation poems on one hand and haunting reminders of Robert Frost on the other.

V., AND OTHER POEMS

In 1987, Harrison was shocked into writing a major poem, *V.* (included in *V., and Other Poems*), by his discovery that his parents' gravestones as well as those of many others in the cemetery on Beeston Hill in Leeds, Yorkshire, had been desecrated, not simply by being knocked about but also by the addition of obscene graffiti. The letter *v* appeared with some regularity in the sign-painting, indicating to Harrison that at least one of the vandals had an enthusiasm for football contests in which *v.*, standing for versus, signified team competition: Leeds *v.* Derby or, more seriously, black *v.* white, man *v.* wife, class *v.* class, or any of the other polarized conflicts that make life uncivilized. It is a disturbing poem, looking with considerable pessimism on the way in which young urban men in particular have descended to animalistic behavior, gratuitous violence, and aimless destruction. Given the nature of the usual market for poetry, the poem might well have been anthologized and forgotten, except for the fact that an English television program allowed Harrison to read the poem on prime-time television. The dismay expressed in the poem was understood, but Harrison had not restrained himself in the use of the language of the streets in the poem, and the flow of four-letter words caused considerable criticism of the television company and of the poet. It was, however, an interesting exception to the usual fate of poetry, since it not only articulated a public concern in art of considerable quality but also provoked the usually indifferent public, for perhaps the wrong reasons, into paying attention to an art form that it rarely, if ever, chooses to contemplate.

"LAUREATE'S BLOCK"

In the 1990's, Harrison merged a number of his talents to produce works that blended poetry with drama, film, and world news. His three filmed poems, *The Gaze of the Gorgon*, *The Shadow of Hiroshima, and Other Film/Poems*, and *Prometheus* attempted to explain the atrocities of the twentieth century: Nazism, nuclear war, imperialism, the unevenness of capitalism. However, the poet also made an obvious turn from his stand-by themes of politics and issues of class to his personal life. His work seemed to center on settling old scores with figures in the literary establishment, as well as an apparent obsession to convey a message— whether personal or political—to the public at large. In a very public quarrel and debate, played out in his poem titled "Laureate's Block" (in his 2000 collection of the same name), Harrison openly defended his staunch refusal to be appointed Britain's poet laureate while publicly quarreling with British poet Andrew Motion: "I'd sooner be a free man. Free not to have to puff some prince's wedding," he wrote in the poem, and specifically attacked "toadies like Di-deifying Motion"—a reference to an elegy, "Mythology," that Motion had written on Princess Diana's death.

In addition to his literary feuds, Harrison seemed to relish trumpeting details of his domestic life. Again in "Laureate's Block," he ends the poem with this quatrain:

> A poet's death fills other poets with dread,
> a king's death kings,
> but under my duvet is Queen Elizabeth,
> and off our bed slide these quatrains and all of
>   Thomas Gray.

Harrison alludes to his bedding of the Queen, both literally and metaphorically, while also making reference to the status of his marriage: the lover in the poem is not his wife, Stratas, but the actress Sian Thomas. Here, Harrison's messy personal life is held out for public display, a remarkable event given that Harrison is a notoriously private man.

OTHER MAJOR WORKS

PLAYS: *Aikin Mata*, pr. 1965 (with James Simmons; adaptation of Aristophanes' play *Lysistratē*); *The Misanthrope*, pr. 1973 (adaptation of Molière's play *Le Misanthrope*); *Phaedra Britannica*, pr. 1975 (adaptation of Jean Racine's play *Phèdre*); *Bow Down*, pr., pb. 1977 (libretto; music by Harrison Birtwistle); *The Passion*, pr., pb. 1977 (adaptation of the York Mystery Plays); *The Bartered Bride*, pr., pb. 1978 (libretto; adaptation of Karel Sabrina's opera; music by Bedřich Smetana); *The Oresteia*, pr., pb. 1981 (libretto; music by Birtwistle; adaptation of Aeschylus' play); *Dramatic Verse, 1973-1985*, pb. 1985; *Plays*, 1985-2002 (4 volumes; volume 1 published as *The Mysteries*); *The Trackers of Oxyrhynchus*, pb. 1990 (based on Sophocles' play *Ichneutae*); *The Common Chorus: A Version of Aristophanes' "Lysistrata*,*"* pb. 1992; *Square Rounds*, pb. 1992; *The Prince's Play*, pr., pb. 1996 (adaptation of Victor Hugo's play); *Fram*, pb. 2008.

TELEPLAYS: *The Big H*, 1984 (libretto; music by Dominic Muldowney); *The Blasphemers' Banquet*, 1990; *Prometheus*, 1998.

TRANSLATION: *Poems*, 1975 (of Palladas of Alexandra).

BIBLIOGRAPHY

Astley, Neil, ed. *Tony Harrison*. London: Bloodaxe Books, 1989. Astley has done a great service in bringing together the best academic journal articles written about Harrison, who has emerged as a major subject for scholars and poetry critics.

Byrne, Sandie, ed. *H, V., and O: The Poetry of Tony Harrison*. New York: St. Martin's Press, 1998. Critical interpretation of Harrison's poetry focusing on the three poems of the title. Includes bibliographic references and an index.

_____. *Tony Harrison: Loiner*. New York: Oxford University Press, 1997. Commemorates the sixtieth birthday of Harrison through an exploration of his work, including that of his best-known poem, "The

Loiners." Includes personal recollections of working with Harrison and critical analyses of his techniques and themes.

Kelleher, Joe. *Tony Harrison*. Plymouth, England: Northcote House, 1996. A brief critical introduction to Harrison's work.

Merriman, Emily Taylor, and Adrian Grafe, eds. *Intimate Exposure: Essays on the Public-Private Divide in British Poetry Since 1950*. Jefferson, N.C.: McFarland, 2010. Two essays look at Harrison's poetry, examining the divide between his public poetry and his more personal verse.

Rowland, Anthony J. *Tony Harrison and the Holocaust*. Liverpool, England: Liverpool University Press, 2001. Argues that while some of Harrison's poems are barbaric, they can be evaluated as committed responses to the worst horrors of twentieth century history.

Sheehan, Sean. *The Poetry of Tony Harrison*. London: Greenwich Exchange, 2008. Provides a book-length analysis of Harrison's poetry.

Thurston, Michael. *The Underworld in Twentieth-Century Poetry: From Pound and Eliot to Heaney and Walcott*. New York: Palgrave Macmillan, 2009. Contains a chapter analyzing Harrison's *V*.

Charles H. Pullen
Updated by Sarah Hilbert

SEAMUS HEANEY

Born: Mossbawn, County Derry, Northern Ireland; April 13, 1939

PRINCIPAL POETRY

Death of a Naturalist, 1966
Door into the Dark, 1969
Wintering Out, 1972
North, 1975
Stations, 1975
Field Work, 1979
Poems, 1965-1975, 1980 (pb. in England as *Selected Poems, 1965-1975*, 1980)

Sweeney Astray: A Version from the Irish, 1983 (revised as *Sweeney's Flight*, 1992)
Station Island, 1984
The Haw Lantern, 1987
The Cure at Troy: A Version of Sophocles' "Philoctetes," 1990 (verse play)
New Selected Poems, 1966-1987, 1990
Seeing Things, 1991
The Spirit Level, 1996
Audenesque, 1998
Opened Ground: Selected Poems, 1966-1996, 1998
The Light of the Leaves, 1999
Electric Light, 2001
The Burial at Thebes: A Version of Sophocles' "Antigone," 2004 (verse play)
District and Circle, 2006
Human Chain, 2010

OTHER LITERARY FORMS

Preoccupations: Selected Prose, 1968-1978 (1980) is a collection of memoirs, lectures, reviews, and essays in which Seamus Heaney (HEE-nee) accounts for his development as a poet. *The Government of the Tongue: The T. S. Eliot Memorial Lectures, and Other Critical Writings* (1988) similarly gathers reviews and lectures that elaborate on his views on the relationship between society and poetry.

ACHIEVEMENTS

Seamus Heaney's work has been recognized with some of the most prestigious honors in literary circles. Perhaps his most impressive award came in 1995, when he won the Nobel Prize in Literature. For *Death of a Naturalist*, he won the Eric Gregory Award in 1966, the Cholomondeley Award in 1967, and both the Somerset Maugham Award and the Geoffrey Faber Memorial Prize in 1968. He also won the Poetry Book Society Choice citation for *Door into the Dark* in 1969, the Irish Academy of Letters award in 1971, the Writer in Residence Award from the American Irish Foundation and the Denis Devlin Award (both for *Wintering Out*) in 1973, the E. M. Forster Award, election to the American Academy and Institute of Arts and Letters in 1975, and the W. H. Smith Award, the Duff Cooper

Memorial Prize, and a Poetry Book Society Choice citation, all in 1976 for *North*.

In 1982, Heaney was awarded honorary degrees by Fordham University and Queen's University of Belfast; the two universities noted particularly that his reflection of the troubles of Northern Ireland in his poetry had universal application. He then received a Los Angeles Times Book Prize nomination in 1984, as well as the PEN Translation Prize for Poetry in 1985, both for *Sweeney Astray*. He won the Whitbread Award in 1987 for *The Haw Lantern*, the Lannan Literary Award for Poetry in 1990, a Premio Internazionale Mondello in 1993, the Whitbread Award in 1996 for *The Spirit Level*, and the *Irish Times* Award in 1999 for *Opened Ground*. In 1999, he won the Whitbread Award for poetry and book of the year for his translation of the epic Anglo-Saxon poem *Beowulf*, which was considered groundbreaking in its use of the modern idiom. He received the Truman Capote Literary Award in 2003, the T. S. Eliot Prize for Poetry in 2006 for *District and Circle*, and the David Cohen Prize in 2009.

BIOGRAPHY

Seamus Justin Heaney was born into a Roman Catholic farming family in rural Country Derry, Northern Ireland (Ulster), the predominantly Protestant and industrial province of the United Kingdom on the island of Ireland. Much of his boyhood was spent on a farm, one border of which was formed by a stream that also divided Ulster from Eire, the predominantly Catholic Republic of Ireland. As a schoolboy, he won scholarships, first at the age of eleven to St. Colomb's College, a Catholic preparatory school, and then to Queen's University, Belfast, from which he graduated in 1961 with a first class honors degree in English. There he joined a group of young poets working under the direction of creative writers on the faculty.

He began his professional career as a secondary school English teacher, after which he went into teacher education, eventually joining the English faculty of Queen's in 1966. In 1965, he married Marie Devlin; they would have two sons and a daughter. When civil dissension broke out in Ulster in 1969, eventually leading to martial law, Heaney, as a Catholic-reared poet, became increasingly uncomfortable. In 1972, he relo-

Seamus Heaney (AP/Wide World Photos)

cated to a manor in the Eire countryside to write full time, although he also became a faculty member of a college in Dublin. Beginning in 1979, he adopted the practice of accepting academic appointments at various American universities and spending the rest of the year in Dublin. In 1986, he was appointed Boylston Professor of Rhetoric and Oratory at Harvard University, and in 1989, he became professor of poetry at Oxford University. To accommodate both positions, he split his time between a home in Dublin and one in Boston. In August, 2006, he suffered a stroke but has recovered.

ANALYSIS

Almost from the beginning of his poetic career, Seamus Heaney gained public recognition for poems rooted deep in the soil of Northern Ireland and flowering in subtle rhythms and nuanced verbal melodies. In many respects, he pursues a return to poetry's foundations in Romantic meditations on nature and explorations of the triple relationship among words, emotions, and the imagination. Heaney's distinctive quality as a poet is that he is at once parochial and universal, grounded in particular localities and microcultures yet branching out to touch every reader. Strangely, this unusual "here and everywhere" note remains with him even when he changes the basic subject matter of his poetry, as he has done frequently. His command of what William Blake called "minute particularity" allows him to conjure up a sense of the universal even when focusing on a distinct individuality—to see "a world in a grain of sand." He makes the unique seem familiar. Because his success at this was recognized early, he was quickly branded with the label "greatest Irish poet since Yeats"—an appellation that, however laudatory, creates intolerable pressure and unrealizable expectations. Neo-Romantic he certainly is, but not in William Butler Yeats's vein; Heaney is less mythic, less apocalyptic, less mystical, and much more material and elemental.

In many respects Heaney's art is conservative, especially in technique. Unlike the forms of the iconoclastic leading poets of the first half of the twentieth century—T. S. Eliot, E. E. Cummings, Wallace Stevens, Ezra Pound, William Carlos Williams, and Dylan Thomas—Heaney's meters, figures, diction, and textures are all relatively straightforward. Also in contrast, his poetry is not "difficult" as theirs was; his sentences generally employ standard syntax. Nevertheless, he is a master technician with an ear for fine and subtle verbal melodies. Instead of breaking with the past, his poems much more often depend on forging links; his music often harks back to that of William Wordsworth, John Milton, or Edmund Spenser. However, his diction is common and Irish as well as formal and English. Colloquial speech patterns of the brogue often counterpoint stately cadences of British rhetoric. The combination produces a varied music, blending the different strains in his personal history and in the history of his people and his region. His best poems ring in the memory with echoes of modulated phrase and evocative sound patterns. He has probed the Irish conscience and discovered a way to express it in the English language, to render the Irish soul afresh.

DEATH OF A NATURALIST

Heaney's first book, *Death of a Naturalist*, laid the groundwork for his achievement. Centered firmly in the country scenes of his youth, these poems declare both his personal heritage from generations of Irish farm laborers and his emancipation from it, acquired by the mastery of a foreign tradition, the literature of the English. His art is Irish in origins and inspiration and English by training. The result is a surprisingly uniform and rich amalgam that incorporates much of Ulster's complex mix of cultures. The poems become what Heaney at the time hoped was possible for his region: the preservation of both Irish and English traditions by a fusion that transcended either of them separately.

"Digging," a celebrated poem from this volume, illustrates this idea. It memorializes the typical work he associated with his father's and grandfather's generations (and, by implication, those of their ancestors): cutting turf, digging. He deliberately contrasts their tool of choice, the spade, with his, the pen: "I've no spade to follow men like them." By his instrument, he can raise their labor into art, in the process ennobling them.

"Follower" similarly contrasts his labor with his father's. It captures in paced phrases and exact images his father's skill at and identification with plowing. This was the ancestral craft of the Heaneys; it makes his father what he is. As a result, it serves as the model of what young Seamus believed he should grow up to become. Sent instead to school, however, he was not reared to the plow and could never do more than hobble in his father's wake. The poem ends in a complex and disturbing image:

> But today
> It is my father who keeps stumbling
> Behind me, and will not go away.

The meaning is clear and manifold. His father stumbles intellectually—because the son has climbed beyond him—and culturally, for he will never be able to reach this point or even appreciate it. His father also stumbles merely physically, as the older generation does, and he must be cared for by his son when he cannot care for himself. Finally, his father is a clog at Heaney's heels, hindering him by his heritage: The poet will never be able to evade his father's influence.

DOOR INTO THE DARK

Three years later, *Door into the Dark* found Heaney continuing to explore this material from his upbringing, but it also showed him expanding his range and developing new moral insights. Increasingly he began sensing that the various pasts in his heritage—of family, race, and religion—were reincarnating themselves in the present, that the history of the people was recapitulating itself. This insight bound present and past indissolubly together. What unfolded in the here and now, then, became part of a gradually evolving theme and variations, revealing itself in event and place.

Some of the poems in this volume accordingly focus on events and occupations illustrating continuity in the Irish experience. "Thatcher," for example, celebrates an ancient Irish craft: thatching roofs out of by-products and discards. The fabric of the poem beautifully reflects and incorporates its subject, for its rhythms and rhymes form parallel patterns that imitate one another and interlock, although the dovetailing is not exact. Left unstated in the poem is an implied theme: The craft of the poet is equally ancient and equally intricate. A similar interweaving of past and present occurs in "The Wife's Tale," in which the persona—a farm woman—re-creates simply the routine of laying out a field lunch for laborers during threshing. The narrative is matter-of-fact and prosaic, detached and unemotional, and unspecific in time: It could be almost anytime, a reiterative action. Her action thus binds the generations together, suggesting the sameness of human life regardless of time. The poem also subtly depicts the interdependence of husband and wife—he fights and plants, she nourishes and supports—and their failure to merge completely: "And that was it. I'd come and he had shown me,/ So I belonged no further to the work."

A number of the poems in this volume are simply musings on travels in Ireland and on the Continent. At first it is easy to pass over these pieces because the simple, undramatic language and quiet tone do not attract much attention. In fact, however, these meditations are extremely important in the evolution of Heaney's poetic orientation, for they document his growing awareness of place as a determinant of sensibility. For Heaney, a person's surroundings, particularly the environment of his or her growing-up years, become the context to which he or she instinctively refers new experiences for evaluation. They become the norms of consciousness, the images from which the individual forms values. In "The Peninsula," for example, the persona spends a day touring the scenes of his youth. He discovers upon return that he still has "nothing to say," but he realizes that henceforth he will "uncode all landscapes/ By this." In "Night Drive," the speaker, driving through France and thinking of his love in Italy, finds his "ordinariness" renewed by simple things such as signposts and realizes that the same thing is happening to her. Environment forms and frames consciousness.

More important, it also frames historical consciousness, the intersection of the past with the present in the individual. In the poems that first document this idea, Heaney announces what is to be a major theme: the inescapable presence of the past. This emerges in "Requiem for the Croppies," a long-after-the-fact elegy for the insurrectionist Catholic peasants—designated "croppies" because in the 1790's they cropped their hair to indicate their support of the French revolutionaries—who were slaughtered by the thousands at Vinegar Hill at the end of the uprising of 1798.

The poem, a simple sonnet, quietly recalls the mood of that campaign, in which unarmed, uneducated plowboys terrorized the great estates of the absent English overlords until they were hemmed in and mowed down by cavalry and cannon. At first, the rebellion was a romp; finally, it became a nightmare and a shame. The poem documents this in one encircling image: The ultimate harvest of the battle is the spilled barley, carried for food, which sprouts from the mass graves the following summer. A better symbol of futility and helplessness could hardly be found. Written in 1969, the year of the recurrence of the Troubles (ethnic conflicts in Ulster between Protestant unionists and Catholic secessionists), the poem both marks Heaney's allegiances—he was reared Catholic—and records his dismay over the renewal of pointless violence. Significantly, Heaney left Belfast for good in that year, although his major motive was to devote himself to writing full time.

"BOGLAND"

In the same year, Heaney encountered the book *The Bog People* (1969) by the ethnologist and anthropologist P. V. Glob. This account of a race of Iron Age peoples who inhabited the boglands of northern Europe in the dark past, before the Indo-European migrations of the first millennium B.C.E., was based largely on excavated remains of bodies that had been preserved by immersion in bogs. The photographs of these bodies particularly fired Heaney's imagination, especially because many of them had been ritualistically sacrificed.

Since the newspapers and magazines had recently been saturated with atrocity punishments and murders, often involving equally primitive rituals, Heaney postulated a connection between the two, forged by the history of terrorism between clans and religions in Northern Ireland: Modern Ulster, despite centuries of alterations in its facade and supposed progress in its politics and civilization, was populated by a race different only in accidentals from its Iron Age progenitors. The same elemental passions and atavistic fears seethed beneath a deceptively civilized surface. Furthermore, those ancient dark mysteries that precipitated the superstitious sacrifices had not been superseded by civilization; they had merely receded into the background. Unsuspected, they continued to be inherited in the blood. Although he nowhere uses the Jungian terminology, Heaney seems to subscribe to the idea of the collective unconscious, the reservoir of instinctive, intuitive behavior acquired genetically.

These ideas bear first fruit in "Bogland," in which he invents a powerful metaphor for another of his central themes. He visualizes his kind, his culture, as centered on a bog: "Our unfenced country/ Is bog that keeps crusting/ Between the sights of the sun." The bog simultaneously buries and preserves, destroys and reconstitutes. Through it, the past becomes continuous with the present, represented in it. The bog records all generations of humanity that have grown up alongside it, disclosing continuous occupation: "Every layer they strip/ Seems camped on before."

The bog is also an analogue of the human mind, which similarly buries and preserves, and which inherits the entire weight of the past. Furthermore, both have fathomless depths, brooding pools, and nameless terrors bubbling up from unplumbed regions. The bog becomes the perfect image of the inexplicable in the self

and in society as a whole. Further, it provides Heaney with a device for illustrating the force behind the violence and a means of distancing himself from it. The bog becomes a link with humankind's preconscious, reptilian past: "The bogholes might be Atlantic seepage./ The wet centre is bottomless."

WINTERING OUT

Heaney's third book, *Wintering Out*, secured his early reputation. Like his first two books, it is rooted in his homeland, but it also includes poems of departure. Places precisely realized play a large part in it; in particular, these places declare themselves through their ancient names. Heaney spins music out of them:

> *Anahorish*, soft gradient
> of consonant, vowel meadow,
>
> after-image of lamps
> swung through the yards
> on winter evenings.

Brough, Derrygarve, Ballyshannon voice related melodies, weaving together past and present, counterpointing also with English names: Castledawson, Upperlands. The two languages together stitch the present out of the past.

The volume opens with "Bog Oak," which Heaney makes into a symbol for his bog world: It is a relic from the past, wood preserved in a bog where no oaks now stand, excavated to make rafters for new buildings. Furthermore, it is saturated with the bog, so that images of past centuries may be imprinted in it, as on film, to be released as the wood is used and thus to redirect the present. In one more way, then, the past is reincarnated. Dreaming that the oak images will bring him contact with the spirits of past poets, Heaney reminds his readers that the history of poetry is also a means of realizing the past in the present.

Other species of the Irish environment also participate in this process of continuity. "Gifts of Rain," for example, memorializes the omnipresent threat of rain in the Irish weather, but it also makes the rain into a stream flowing through everything, a liquid voice from the past: "Soft voices of the dead/ Are whispering by the shore." It becomes a solvent of the Irish experience.

This awareness of and openness to all aspects of life,

especially the dark and the violent, leads Heaney to treat some topics in this volume that are quite different from his past choices. Among them is one of the more inexplicable incidents of human cruelty: infanticide by mothers, or maternal rejection of infants. "Limbo" considers an infant drowned shortly after birth and netted by salmon fishermen. Heaney dispassionately records the ironies, beginning with the simple suggestion that this child's baptism was in fact murder, the most extreme sacrilege, although he fully sympathizes with the mother's agony. Still, the child died without baptism; hence, it is ineligible for Heaven and must be relegated to Limbo, a place of painless exile, according to orthodox Catholic doctrine. Such a conclusion, however, is so unjust that it seems incompatible with any God who claims to incarnate love: "Even Christ's palms, unhealed,/ Smart and cannot fish here."

Similarly, "Bye-Child" re-creates the perspective of a child shut up by his mother in a henhouse, without vital human contact. The inscription states that he could not speak. Heaney seems astounded that anyone could deny a human the possibility of communication: to be human is to communicate. This child, as a result, becomes in turn a curiosity, a rodent, an alien, a "moon man"—nothing human. Still, his response to his rescuers reveals an attempt to communicate, to reach "beyond love."

The experience that apparently enabled Heaney to contemplate such events took place through Glob's *The Bog People*. He was so struck by the images of some of the recovered bodies—particularly those sacrificed in earth mother rites and those punished for crimes—that he wrote poems about them. The first, the three-part "The Tolland Man," first published in *Wintering Out*, has become one of his most widely reprinted poems. Heaney first describes the body, now displayed at the Natural History Museum at Århus, Denmark, and briefly alludes to his fate: Given a last meal, he was hauled in a tumbril to the bog, strangled, and deposited as a consort to the bog goddess, who needed a male to guarantee another season of fertility. In the second section, Heaney suggests that the ritual makes as much sense as the retaliatory, ritualistic executions of the Troubles; the current practice is as likely to improve germination. The third section establishes a link between survivors and victims, past and present. It implies that all humans are equally involved, equally responsible, if only by complicity or failure to act. Heaney suggests that senseless violence and complacent acceptance of it are both parts of human nature.

STATIONS

Heaney's next book, *Stations*, marked both an advance and a setback. The advance was compound, both formal and topical. Formally, the book consists of a series of prose poems; topically, they all deal with the experience of growing up rural and Catholic in an industrialized, Protestant-dominated culture. The title *Stations* alludes to this: The events detailed here constitute the contemporary equivalent of the Stations of the Cross, the sufferings Christ endured in his passion and death; moreover, they are the way stations of modern education, the stopping points of the soul. The poems show Heaney returning to his childhood to identify and document his indoctrination into the complicity he finds unacceptable in *Wintering Out*. In all these ways, the book celebrates gains.

The individual poems of *Stations* are less successful and less uniform than his earlier work. They disclose an artificiality, a staginess, a contrived quality formerly absent. They also depend on a good bit of private information for comprehension. In some respects, this is curious, because Heaney managed to avoid any hint of these weaknesses elsewhere, either in his poetry or in the retrospective prose that also dates from around this time. To an extent, this uneasiness must be associated with his private uncertainty during this period, when he was trying to justify his leaving Ulster rather than staying to take a stand. Whatever the reason, it left the poetry of the same time intact.

NORTH

His second book of 1975, *North*, capitalized on his previous successes; significantly, the title indicates that all these poems still focus on the poet's Ulster experiences. The book includes more meditations on place and place-names, such as "Mossbawn"; there are also a few more nature pieces and reminiscences. Far and away the majority of the collection, however, deals with the cultural conflict of the North, the pagan heritage of Ireland, and the continuity of past and present through the mediation of the bog people. A series based on bone fragments from the past supplements the bog material. Practically all of Heaney's best-known poems are found in this volume.

This is the first of Heaney's books that is more than a mere collection. The order and arrangement are designed to create an integrated reading experience; groupings reflect, refract, and diffuse patterns and themes. The basic structure of the book is twofold, with each part using distinctive verse forms. Part 1 focuses on the "North" of northern Europe from the time of its first population to the present. The basic verse is the taut, unrhymed or off-rhymed quatrain developed for *Wintering Out*; much of the diction is formal or archaic, and the atmosphere is solemn and austere. Part 2 takes "North" as contemporary Ulster. The root verse is the standard pentametric rhymed quatrain; the diction and tone are informal and playful. The polarity seems to reflect the two kinds of poetry Heaney describes repeatedly in *Preoccupations*: poetry that is "made" and poetry that is "given."

Some of the poems in part 1 actually fall partly outside this overly neat division. "Funeral Rites," an often-praised poem, joins the urgency of funerals during the Troubles with the legacy of pagan burials. The theme of the poem is that the frequent occurrence of funerals today has cheapened them: they lack the impact of ancient funerals, when death still meant something, still could be beautiful, and still could give promise of resurrection. The title poem also crosses the established border of the book. It centers on the imagination of the poet in the present, where he must work with what he finds—which falls far short of the epic standards of the past. Voices out of the water advise him to search the past of the race and express it through the roots of his language.

The center of part 1 is the past. Here the bog poems take precedence. There are six of them, all powerful. "The Grauballe Man" depicts another victim of the bog mother cult, this one written as if the persona were in the presence of the body. Heaney arranges a series of metaphors drawn from biology to create the image of the body, then inserts the line "The head lifts"—and the body seems to come alive before the mind's eye. The persona explicitly denies that this can be called a "corpse." Previously, seen only in photographs, the

man seemed dead, "bruised like a forceps baby." Now he is "hung in the scales/ with beauty and atrocity"—he has taken on the life of enduring art yet also testifies to humanity's eternal and ongoing depravity. Violence creates beauty, and vice versa.

"Punishment" portrays another category of victim among the bog people. According to the Roman historian Tacitus, the ancestral Germans punished women taken in adultery by shaving off their hair and immersing them naked in the bog, weighed down with stones and logs, until they drowned. This barely postpubescent girl of Heaney's poem illustrates the practice: undernourished, shaved, and blindfolded, she has no visible wounds. The persona sees her as a "scapegoat," a figure of terror: "her shaved head/ like a stubble of black corn." However, she was also "beautiful," one who could arouse love. Nevertheless, he recognizes that had he been present, he "would have cast . . ./ the stones of silence," in an allusion to the New Testament story of the woman taken in adultery. Heaney asserts that all human beings comply with the practices of their tribe, and then he finds the perfect modern parallel. In the early 1970's, young Catholic women who consorted with British soldiers were punished similarly by the Irish Republican Army: They were shaved, tarred, feathered, and chained to public railings. Again all spectators comply, and the past, the primitive past, is present.

In "Strange Fruit," Heaney borrows the metaphor in the title from an African American civil rights protest song, in which "strange fruit" refers to the bodies of lynched blacks hanging from gallows. The fruit in the poem is ancient: an accidentally preserved severed head of a young woman. Here there is no justification in ritual; the woman is simply the victim of random violence or tribal conflict. Heaney, as before, suggests that exhuming the head from its bog grave is equivalent to restoring it to life and beauty. This time, however, he finds the consolation of art itself disturbing. He adds a new note, alluding to another Roman historian: "Diodorus Siculus confessed/ His gradual ease among the likes of this." Multiple atrocities generate complacency as well as complicity. Thus this girl stops short of beauty; far from attractive, she has "eyeholes blank as pools in the old workings." This is an image of the forlorn, the abandoned. These black eyeholes—lacking eyes—still outstare "what had begun to feel like reverence." Tolerating atrocities may not be the state human beings finally want to reach.

FIELD WORK

Heaney's next book, *Field Work*, poses a series of questions, mostly dealing with the relationship between art and social conscience. The questions cast doubts on both the attitude he had adopted toward contemporary violence and the resolution to which he had come about his life. Still, the answers he finds basically confirm his decisions. He chooses here the path of civilization, of art, the "field work" of the practicing artist. At the balancing point of this book rest the Glanmore sonnets, a series of ten sonnets reflecting his life at the country estate of Glanmore, County Wicklow, his retreat after Belfast. In terms of subject matter, he returns overtly to the natural settings and homely ways of his first two books. In this work, however, he is much more concerned with the poetic temperament, its influences, and its relation to society.

Accordingly, several of the sounds trace the parallels between Heaney and other figures who used rural solitude to comment on society: the Roman poets Horace and Vergil, the mythical Irish hero Sweeney, and the English poet Wordsworth. The sonnets themselves are the densest, most intricate poems he had written to this point, rich and finely fashioned, delicate and subtle. Typical is sonnet 5, which commemorates the elderberry bush that served as refuge for the poet as a boy; he shapes it and his reminiscences about it into a symbol of his searches into the roots of language and memory.

Another major section of the book is devoted to elegies—three for victims of civil violence, three for fellow poets, and one for a relative killed in World War I. These are more conventional poems of mourning than his earlier meditations, which lamented but also accepted. They reflect a sense of absolute and final loss, the senseless wasting away that the pace of modern life leads people to take for granted, anger that so much good should be squandered so casually. Still, death is relentless and undiscriminating, taking the small with the great: "You were not keyed or pitched like these true-blue ones/ Though all of you consort now underground."

SWEENEY ASTRAY

After *Field Work* Heaney moved for a while in a different direction. *Sweeney Astray* is an adaptation of the medieval Gaelic epic *Buile Suibhne*. Heaney had long been fascinated by the character of Sweeney, at once king and poet, and had used him as one of the persona's alter egos in *Field Work*. In the poem, Sweeney fails in a quest and suffers the curse of Saint Ronan, the peacemaker, after repeatedly violating truces and killing one of the saint's clerics. Already nicknamed "Mad" because of his battle rages, Sweeney is now transformed into a bird and driven into the wilderness, doomed to be hunted by humans and beasts alike and to suffer delusions. The poem is more an anthology of rhapsodic songs and laments made by Sweeney in his exile than the standard heroic quest-poem. It is easy to detect the sources of Heaney's fascination, which include the easily overlooked rhyme of Sweeney's name with his own—the kind of thing he would spot immediately. Like Heaney, Sweeney is driven out of a violent society, though given to violence himself; he feels a natural kinship with animals, birds, trees, plants, and the things of the wild; he identifies with the places of his exile; and he senses the elemental divine pulse beating in and unifying everything. Furthermore, he represents the wounded imagination, in love with and repelled by the ways of humans in the world.

Although widely praised and honored, *Sweeney Astray* seems to have fallen short of Heaney's expectations. It did receive some hostile reviews, from Irish critics who did not really believe that English is a suitable medium for anything Gaelic and English critics who viewed Irish writers as plotting a hostile takeover of things British. The extent of Heaney's disappointment appears in the layout of *New Selected Poems, 1966-1987*, in which this book is the most scantily represented of his major works, being given only sixteen pages as against sixty-six for *Station Island* and forty-four for *North*. Clearly, it is more difficult to cull from a continuous sequence than from a collection; yet it is also true that ever since the publication of *North*, Heaney had paid considerable attention to the organization of his books, so that, theoretically at least, excerpting should be difficult from any of them.

STATION ISLAND

Station Island is Heaney's amplest, most diversified, and most highly integrated book of poems. It consists essentially of three parts: a collection of separate lyrics, many family-centered and some combined into mini-sequences; the title sequence, centered on Station Island, also called St. Patrick's Purgatory, in west Ireland, a favorite Irish pilgrimage site; and a series named "Sweeney Redivivus," in which he creates new poems through the persona of the poet-hero brought back to life in himself and committed to reveal what remains of the past in the here and now. The lyrics show Heaney experimenting with new line lengths, new forms, and new approaches. They include meditations reminiscent of W. H. Auden, such as "Chekhov on Sakhalin," and a series on found objects called "Shelf Life"; both provide him with occasions for discovering unexpected epiphanies.

Similarly, the Sweeney poems disclose Heaney deepening his vision. The identification with his mythic predecessor required by the translation brings him to a new vantage point: He realizes that perceptive and imaginative as Sweeney was, deeply as he penetrated to the soul of things, he still remained alien from the bulk of the people, and he had not changed much. Heaney writes out of a new humility and also now out of relief. He concludes that he need not blame himself for having abandoned his people in the Troubles. They were not really his people, in retrospect; his values were not theirs. He could not accomplish much for them that would last, thus it was better to pursue his poetry.

The title series also teaches him that lesson, though in a different way. It is Heaney's major triumph, consolidating and drawing on strengths he had been establishing since early in his career. It is the quintessential place-poem, for Station Island has many places and provides multiple occasions for poetry. Situated on Lough Derg in County Tipperary, Eire, the island was originally a primitive settlement; in the eighth or ninth century it became a locus of pilgrimage, renowned as a place of penitence. A number of foundation rings remain, the relics of either monastic cells or primitive dwellings. Devotees complete the act of repentance by making a circuit of these, kneeling and praying at each in turn, and by this act gaining remission of punishment for past sins.

Heaney bases his cycle on the persona's return to the island in middle age. Although by this point in his life he was an unbeliever, he finds the island well populated with souls eager to establish common ground with the living. For the devout, St. Patrick's Purgatory is a place of personal repentance, expiation, and rectification. For the literary, as a purgatorial site it has a forerunner in Dante's *Purgatorio* (in *La divina commedia*, c. 1320; *The Divine Comedy*, 1802). Heaney uses the experience as a poetic examination of conscience, a Catholic devotional exercise: He reviews his career as a poet, attempting to determine once again the proper relationship between poetry and society. In this process, he gains assistance and insight from the attendant ghosts, who include a number of figures from his private and literary past, notably including James Joyce. Heaney records their conversations, often weaving their voices together in terza rima, the verse form used by Dante. In the twelfth and last poem, Joyce advises Heaney to follow his lead in concentrating on art and ignoring the politics of the moment.

THE HAW LANTERN

The Haw Lantern continues in the direction mapped out in *Station Island*. It is among the slightest of Heaney's collections: thirty-one poems in fifty-two pages. His topics, too, are rather commonplace: hailstones, alphabets, fishing lures, a peacock's feather, and (in the title poem) the fruit of the hawthorn. Heaney transforms this brilliant red winter fruit metaphorically into a lantern, an instrument for seeing and for measuring human values. Commonly used for hedging in the British Isles, this thorny shrub becomes a means of testing human integrity in the daily situations that finally count. The book also contains another of Heaney's trademark sequences. "Clearances," a set of eight sonnets written to commemorate the death of Heaney's mother, moves him to another stage in the definition of his poetic character. Symbolically, this constitutes Heaney's prayer at his mother's deathbed, bonding him to the past and committing him to the future. It also sets him apart from Joyce, his spiritual mentor, who made his refusal to pray at his mother's bedside a pivotal scene in *A Portrait of the Artist As a Young Man* (1916) and *Ulysses* (1922).

SEEING THINGS

Despite being an active writer and continuing to produce published collections, Heaney seemed to move toward poetry that had a decidedly "later" feel about it beginning in the 1990's, as if the poet were consistently revisiting old scenes, revising opinions, refining thoughts once had, and critiquing versions of self presented in previous poems. In *Seeing Things*, Heaney appears to reach for a lightness, moving away from the thickets of alliteration and sensuality found in the early work or the harsh minimal realities of the bog period or even the casual sublimities of daily life found in both *Field Work* and, to a lesser extent, *The Haw Lantern*.

THE SPIRIT LEVEL AND OPENED GROUND

The Spirit Level explores the themes of politics, humanism, and nature. It includes in its composition a plea for hope, innocence, and balance, and to seek eventually that "bubble for the spirit level." Here he balances the personal with the universal, as well as the process of life to death, in an attempt to seek an equilibrium. *Opened Ground* provides a comprehensive overview of his poetry from 1966 to 1996, with works from the 1990's heavily represented: Much of *The Spirit Level* is reproduced here. By chronologically following his progression as a poet, readers can discern Heaney's peculiar wistful and earthy mixture of rural reverie and high public speech and see how his interests broaden in the middle and later poems when the poet seeks out Greek myths, Irish epics, and Scandinavian archaeological digs to look for correlatives appropriate for his meditations.

ELECTRIC LIGHT

Perhaps Heaney's most reflective collection during this period is *Electric Light*. Using a compilation of poetic genres and styles—including eclogue, elegy, epigram, yarn, meditation, and ecstatic lyric—Heaney meditates on the origins and inevitable ending of his life and art. His array of verse styles showcases Heaney's will and ability to speak of many kinds of experiences to many kinds of reader. Above all, his awareness of his aging, from which he turns away in memory and looks past in poems about death, gives the collection special coherence and expression. In "The Gaeltacht," modeled on a poem by Dante, he examines his literary fame, his desire for release from it, and a return to primal things. Heaney wishes he were in the Gaeltacht, a Gaelic-speaking region of northwestern Ireland, with one of his old pals "and that it was again nineteen sixty." Then other friends now old or dead would also be with them "talking Irish."

He also celebrates nature with a range of poems that explore landscapes, such as his birthplace of Northern Ireland, imprinted by human life, its meanings and violence handed down through the generations. Heaney's use of dialect and feeling-laden place-names distinctly help convey this theme. Notable literary figures make appearances here as well: He elegizes the Russian poet Joseph Brodsky, offers translations of Vergil and the Russian poet Alexander Pushkin, and has memorial poems for the Polish poet Zbigniew Herbert and American translator Robert Fitzgerald.

DISTRICT AND CIRCLE

District and Circle contains forty-four poems and several short prose pieces, including "One Christmas Day in the Morning" and "Fiddleheads." The poems differ significantly in structure and topic, and Heaney's poetic rhythms vary widely between the classical and contemporary. The poet employs many familiar themes evident in his previous work, such as remembrances of his rural Irish childhood, the lives of country folk, and Catholicism and the Catholic rites, but the poems all relate to the collective theme of memory.

The opening poem, "The Turnip-Snedder," a relatively short poem about an ancient turnip-mashing machine, is constructed as ten unrhymed couplets. The rhythm within the poem varies between and against the two-beat line and extends even further by Heaney's pairing of phrases throughout. The exact year of the poem is not noted, but the nostalgia-infused image of rural life and farmwork suggests a time when the agrarian lifestyle involved hard physical labor. Farmwork is the topic of several other poems in this collection.

"District and Circle," the title poem, has a more urban setting, involving train stations and rail travel. The poem is constructed as five stanzas of fourteen lines, except the third stanza, which is thirteen lines. This use of the fourteen-line stanza could be seen as Heaney's modern interpretation of a sonnet since he also combines the fourteen-line stanza with iambic pentameter. "District and Circle" places the speaker of the poem in an underground train station, waiting along with other travelers, and evokes an image of the jostle inherent in mass transit. The poem also addresses themes of identity and of isolation, even while in a familiar setting such as a crowded train station.

Heaney's tendency to retool the sonnet form also is evident in the poem "In Iowa," which depicts an old Mennonite mowing machine covered with snow. This poem consists of three unrhymed quatrains and a final couplet, which serves as the turn, or volta. Like other contemporary poets, Heaney incorporates the Petrarchan form in a modern narrative poetic structure. Within "In Iowa," Heaney takes certain artistic liberties that are not restricted by the strict metrical or rhyme schemes associated with the traditional Petrarchan form.

In this collection, Heaney recalls the people and sights of the rural Ireland of his childhood. Some of the poems within are overtly nostalgic, while others are imbued with a more subtle message elevating the agrarian lifestyle.

OTHER MAJOR WORKS

NONFICTION: *Preoccupations: Selected Prose, 1968-1978*, 1980; *The Government of the Tongue: The T. S. Eliot Memorial Lectures, and Other Critical Writings*, 1988 (pb. in U.S. with the subtitle *Selected Prose, 1978-1987*, 1989); *The Redress of Poetry*, 1995; *Homage to Robert Frost*, 1996 (with Joseph Brodsky and Derek Walcott); *Seamus Heaney in Conversation with Karl Miller*, 2000; *Sounding Lines: The Art of Translating Poetry*, 2000 (with Robert Hass); *Finders Keepers: Selected Prose, 1971-2001*, 2002; *Stepping Stones: Interviews with Seamus Heaney*, 2008 (with Dennis O'Driscoll).

TRANSLATIONS: *The Midnight Verdict*, 1993 (of Ovid and Brian Merriman); *Beowulf: A New Verse Translation*, 1999; *Diary of One Who Vanished*, 1999 (of song cycle by Leos Janáček of poems by Ozef Kalda).

EDITED TEXTS: *The Rattle Bag: An Anthology of Poetry*, 1982 (with Ted Hughes); *The Essential Wordsworth*, 1988; *The School Bag*, 1997 (with Hughes).

BIBLIOGRAPHY

Brandes, Rand, and Michael J. Durkan, eds. *Seamus Heaney: A Bibliography, 1959-2003*. London: Faber and Faber, 2008. Bibliography of the poet's works provides a good starting point for research.

Cavanagh, Michael. *Professing Poetry: Seamus Heaney's Poetics*. Washington, D.C.: Catholic University of America Press, 2009. Provides extensive analysis of the critical essays written by Heaney to discern his theory of poetics.

Collins, Floyd. *Seamus Heaney: The Crisis of Identity*. Newark: University of Delaware Press, 2003. A fine introduction to the poet's expertise and style.

Crowder, A. B., and Jason David Hall, eds. *Seamus Heaney: Poet, Critic, Translator*. New York: Palgrave Macmillan, 2007. These twelve essays address not only Heaney's poetry but also Heaney's criticism and translations.

Hall, Jason David. *Seamus Heaney's Rhythmic Contract*. New York: Palgrave Macmillan, 2009. An examination of Heaney's poetry that focuses on its structure and place it in the context of mid-twentieth century theories of meter and rhythm.

McCarthy, Conor. *Seamus Heaney and Medieval Poetry*. Rochester, N.Y.: Boydell & Brewer, 2008. Examines how Heaney translated medieval poetry and otherwise incorporated it into his poetry.

Moloney, Karen Marguerite. *Seamus Heaney and the Emblems of Hope*. Columbia: University of Missouri Press, 2007. An extensively researched study of Heaney's poetry and his theme of the Celtic fertility myth of kings marrying goddesses. Informative and easy to read.

O'Brien, Eugene. *Seamus Heaney and the Place of Writing*. Gainesville: University Press of Florida, 2002. Analyzes Heaney's attitude toward place and home and its relevance to Irish identity.

O'Donoghue, Bernard, ed. *The Cambridge Companion to Seamus Heaney*. New York: Cambridge University Press, 2009. A collection of essays that cover the life and works of Heaney, examining topics such as the Irish influence, the poet and medieval literature, and the poet as a critic.

Vendler, Helen Hennessy. *Seamus Heaney*. Cambridge, Mass.: Harvard University Press, 2000. Whereas other books on Heaney have dwelt chiefly on the biographical, geographical, and political aspects of his writing, this book looks squarely and deeply at Heaney's poetry as art.

James Livingston; Sarah Hilbert
Updated by Andy K. Trevathan

ANNE HÉBERT

Born: Sainte-Catherine-de-Fossambault, Quebec, Canada; August 1, 1916
Died: Montreal, Quebec, Canada; January 22, 2000

PRINCIPAL POETRY

Les Songes en équilibre, 1942
Le Tombeau des rois, 1953 (*The Tomb of the Kings*, 1967)
Mystère de la parole, 1960 (*Mystery of the Verb*, 1975)
Poèmes, 1960 (*Poems*, 1975, includes *Tomb of the Kings* and *Mystery of the Verb*)
Anne Hébert: Selected Poems, 1987 (bilingual edition)
Le Jour n'a d'égal que la nuit, 1992 (*Day Has No Equal but the Night*, 1994)
Œuvre poètique, 1950-1990, 1992
Poèmes pour la main gauche, 1997

OTHER LITERARY FORMS

Anne Hébert (AY-behr) wrote novels, plays, short stories, and screenplays in addition to her poetry collections. In most of her fiction, Hébert depicts the culture of rural Quebec, where she spent her childhood and adolescence. She explores the lives of the Québécois who dwell in the small towns, controlled by a religious and repressive society. In her novels, she portrays characters in the act of freeing themselves both physically and psychologically. Topics include witchcraft, vampires, and sorcery, and predominant themes are isolation, alienation, repression, violence, and revolt. *Kamouraska* (1970; English translation, 1973) and *Les Fous de bassan* (1982; *In the Shadow of the Wind*, 1983) retell events drawn from Québécois history. Her historical novels are part of the literary tradition of Quebec, but she radically alters the tradition with the addition of elements of the French New Novel and of Symbolism. Her plays also deal with murder and violence.

ACHIEVEMENTS

Anne Hébert achieved recognition as a major Canadian poet and novelist. She played an important role in the development of Canadian writing because her works brought elements of Surrealism and the New Novel, as well as realistic violence and rebellion, into Canadian literature. She won numerous awards for both her poetry and her fiction. Her first collection of poetry, *Les Songes en équilibre* (dreams in equilibrium), won the Prix Athanase-David in 1942. She received the Governor-General's Award in 1960 for *Poems*, in 1975 for *Les Enfants du sabbat* (1975; *Children of the Black Sabbath*, 1977), and in 1992 for *L'Enfant chargé de songes* (1992; *Burden of Dreams*, 1994). *Kamouraska* won the Prix des Libraires de France and the Grand Prix of the Académie Royale de la Langue Françaises de Belgique. The novel, which was also made into a motion picture and has been translated into seven languages, is considered a classic of both Québécois and Canadian literature. *In the Shadow of the Wind* was awarded the Prix Fémina in 1982. Her novel *Est-ce que je te dérange?* (1998; *Am I Disturbing You?*, 1999) was a finalist for the Giller Prize in 1999. Her final novel *Un Habit de lumière* (1999; *A Suit of Light*, 2000) was awarded the Prix France/Jean Hamelin.

BIOGRAPHY

Anne Hébert was born in Sainte-Catherine-de-Fossambault, Quebec, Canada, on August 1, 1916. She spent her childhood and adolescence in her family's home in the country. From a young age, she was encouraged to write poetry by her father Maurice-Lang Hébert, a poet and literary critic, and her cousin Hector de Saint-Denys Garneau, also a poet. She began writing poetry as a teenager. She received her education at Collège Saint-Cour de Marie in Merici, Quebec, and at Collège Notre Dame in Bellevue, Quebec. Hébert became involved in the film industry in Canada in 1940 and was affiliated with the government film bureau for a short period of time. She wrote for television and the theater as well as for radio. In 1942, she published her first collection of poetry *Les Songes en équilibre*. The work was very well received, and she was awarded the Prix Athanase-David.

In 1943, Hébert's cousin Saint-Denys Garneau died of a heart attack. His death was to have a significant impact on her poetry and her later fiction. In 1950, she began working for Radio Canada. That same year, with the financial help of novelist and television writer Roger Lemelin, she privately published *Le Torrent* (1950, 1962; *The Torrent: Novellas and Short Stories*, 1973), a collection of short stories. She had been unable to find a publisher for the collection because of its violent themes and descriptions. Death had already become a main theme after her cousin's death, and her sister Marie's death in 1952 further affected her poetry. Consequently, Hébert once again met with resistance

from Canadian publishers when she attempted to publish her second collection of poetry, *The Tomb of the Kings*. She published this volume at her own expense with a loan from Lemelin. From 1953 to 1954, she worked for the National Film Board of Canada.

In 1954, having received a grant from the Royal Society of Canada, she moved to Paris, where she hoped to find publishers for her works. Her move proved successful, as the Editions du Seuil became her publisher. In 1960, the firm published *Poems*, which won the Governor-General's Award. Hébert lived in Paris for most of the rest of her life but maintained strong ties with Quebec. She frequently visited there and, from 1959 to 1960, served again on the National Film Board of Canada.

After moving to Paris, Hébert turned to writing fiction. From 1958 to 1992, she published seven novels. For her novels, she primarily drew on her Québécois experience; five of these novels are set in Quebec, and only two in Paris. In 1992, she published the poetry collection *Day Has No Equal but the Night*. In 1993, she published *Œuvre poètique, 1950-1990*, which included all of her poetry except the early *Les Songes en équilibre*. In 1997, she published her final volume of poetry *Poèmes pour la main gauche* (poems for the left hand). That same year, she moved back to Canada and took up residence in Montreal. She published her final novel, *A Suit of Light*, in 1999. She died of bone cancer in Montreal on January 22, 2000.

ANALYSIS

Anne Hébert published five major collections of poetry, *Les Songes en équilibre*, *The Tomb of the Kings*, *Mystery of the Verb*, *Day Has No Equal but the Night*, and *Poèmes pour la main gauche*, from 1942 to 1997, spanning her life. Two of her collections, *Mystery of the Verb* and *Day Has No Equal but the Night*, begin with an essay on poetry. She defines poetry as an escape from solitude, as the poet releasing the self into the world. The poet, she says, lives twice: Once in the everyday reality of normal human exis-

Anne Hébert (Ulf Andersen/BOA Editions)

tence and a second time in the retelling of the world that both surrounds and exists within the poet. For Hébert, poetry comes from a mysterious combination of the poet's life experiences and the poet's surroundings, which insist on being voiced and being expressed cloaked in the poet's emotions. These beliefs are reflected in her poems.

Hébert's poetry is written in free verse; she employs unexpected juxtapositions of adjectives and nouns and creates images that have much in common with those of Surrealism. Images drawn from nature dominate her poetry. Her verse is filled with images of sun, gardens, birds, and especially water—rain, sea, rivers, and fountains. Other important images include night versus day, silence, noises, death, dead people, souls, hands, and cities.

LES SONGES EN ÉQUILIBRE

Written when Hébert was still living at her parents' country home in rural Quebec and before the death of her cousin Saint-Denys Garneau, the poems of *Les Songes en équilibre* reflect both her happiness in the company of her family and the sadness and loneliness brought about by the isolation and inertia of her life. They are the expression of a self not wishing to escape what is possessed but desperately in need of expansion, of discovery of something new and different. The poems also show the strong influence of Saint-Denys Garneau. There is a soft melancholy about the verse, which was replaced by a sharper, harder, more intense feeling in her later poetry.

The poems of *Les Songes en équilibre* are traditional and even conservative in comparison to her later ones. There is a strong religious overtone and an emphasis on suffering that leads to joy. Although the style and themes of these poems evidence external influences, especially her religious upbringing and Saint-Denys Garneau, in the final section, "L'Oiseau du poète," she is beginning to investigate the poet's inspiration, purpose, and role in society. These concerns are the subjects of her two essays on poetry that preface *Mystery of the Verb* and *Day Has No Equal but the Night*.

THE TOMB OF THE KINGS

The poems in *The Tomb of the Kings* were written and published before and after the deaths of her cousin

and her sister and the refusal of Canadian publishers to publish *The Torrent*. The poems reflect a very different Hébert, an individual in revolt against death, suffering, and oppression. The poems are filled with dark surrealist images of salty eyelids, burned hands, hands adorned with pain or sorrow, a dead bird's voice, small towns held in hands and up-ended, heavy echoes of silence, the day that rots, and hands cut off and planted in a garden. The poems mirror her despair at the loss of loved ones and in the shattering of her life and her ever-growing need to escape from the suffocating isolation and stagnation of her life.

The poems also deal with Hébert's struggle to move forward from her continuing connection with her childhood and to embrace fully her vocation as a poet. In the poems, she uses images of water, closed rooms, silence, death, and dead birds who sing in order to address her struggle. Day, night, death, and the unknown, which is complete commitment to the role of the poet, are the fields of existence in the poems. Day represents contact with human reality, with the mundane and repetitive. It is safe but unsatisfying. Night provides the escape of solitude but is also the field of another reality, that of dreams, which contains surprises and uncertainties. In the poems, she is attracted to death because it joins her to what she has lost and releases her from agony. However, she is also drawn to thoughts of death as a means of liberation from the past. She must face the realm of death to be released from its painful hold on her. She must also free herself from the solitude of closed rooms and silence. Through images of pure water and sheltering rain, she speaks poetically of the washing away of the past. The images of water and fountains also express the release of the poet's voice. Water conceals an unknown under its surface, an unknown that is the adventure of the poet who releases the poetry within the self and retells life's experiences and the world.

MYSTERY OF THE VERB

Mystery of the Verb is a collection of poems retelling the world and the human experience of the world. The poems represent Hébert's escape from solitude; she has chosen to release herself into the world. The title poem that opens the collection poetically describes the creation of the world through charity, the gift of fire, the genesis of mortal life, the binding of humans to Earth, and the gift of the word. This introductory poem is followed by poems about Earth, the seasons, nature, and its beauty. Hébert then includes a series of poems describing destruction, conflict, hatred, and earthly destruction, interspersed with poems of a religious nature. The final poem ends with the rebirth of Earth. The poems, written in long free verse, draw much of their force and beauty from the rhythm of the verse and the repetition of sounds and words.

OTHER MAJOR WORKS

LONG FICTION: *Les Chambres de bois*, 1958 (*The Silent Rooms*, 1974); *Dialogue sur la traduction: À propos du "Tombeau des rois,"* 1970 (with Frank R. Scott); *Kamouraska*, 1970 (English translation, 1973); *Les Enfants du sabbat*, 1975 (*Children of the Black Sabbath*, 1977); *Héloïse*, 1980 (English translation, 1982); *Les Fous de bassan*, 1982 (*In the Shadow of the Wind*, 1983); *Le Premier Jardin*, 1988 (*The First Garden*, 1990); *L'Enfant chargé de songes*, 1992 (*Burden of Dreams*, 1994); *Est-ce que je te dérange?*, 1998 (*Am I Disturbing You?*, 1999); *Un Habit de lumière*, 1999 (*A Suit of Light*, 2000).

SHORT FICTION: *Le Torrent*, 1950, 1962 (*The Torrent: Novellas and Short Stories*, 1973); *Aurélien, Clara, mademoiselle et le lieutenant anglais*, 1995 (*Aurélien, Clara, Mademoiselle and the English Lieutenant*, 1996).

PLAYS: *Le Temps sauvage*, pr. 1966 (*The Unquiet State*, 1983); *Les Invités au procès*, pb. 1967 (*The Guests on Trial*, 1988); *La Mercière assassinée*, pb. 1967 (*The Murdered Shopkeeper*, 1984); *La Cage*, pb. 1990; *L'Ile de la demoiselle*, pb. 1990.

SCREENPLAYS: *Saint-Denys Garneau*, 1960; *Kamouraska*, 1973 (with Claude Jutka); *Les Fous de bassan*, 1987.

MISCELLANEOUS: *Saint-Denys and Anne Hébert*, 1962.

BIBLIOGRAPHY

Corcoran, Patrick, ed. *The Cambridge Introduction to Francophone Literature*. New York: Cambridge University Press, 2007. In its section on Canadian writers, this volume contains a short biography of Hébert, with substantial critical analysis.

Gibson, Robert, ed. *Modern French Poets on Poetry: A Connected Anthology of Pronouncements on Poetry by the Poets Themselves—An Introduction to French Poetry from Baudelaire to the Surrealists*. New York: Cambridge University Press, 1979. A good overview of the theories of poetics that influenced Hébert's poetry and her use of surrealistic images.

Hacht, Anne-Marie, ed. *Poetry for Students*. Vol. 20. Detroit: Gale, 2004. Contains an in-depth analysis of Hébert's "The Alchemy of Day."

Pallister, Janis L., ed. *The Art and Genius of Anne Hébert: Essays on Her Works—"Night and the Day Are One."* Madison, N.J.: Fairleigh Dickinson University Press, 2001. Includes essays by the major critics of Hébert's work. Excellent extensive bibliography of her work.

Russell, Delbert W. *Anne Hébert*. Boston: Twayne, 1983. A basic biography of the poet, with analysis of her works.

Shallerup, Lee, ed. *Anne Hébert: Essays on Her Works*. Montréal: Guernica Editions, 2009. These essays deal extensively with Hébert's connection to rural Quebec. Includes an interview with the writer.

Willging, Jennifer. *Telling Anxiety: Anxious Narration in the Work of Marguerite Duras, Annie Ernaux, Nathalie Sarraute, and Anne Hébert*. Buffalo, N.Y.: Toronto University Press, 2007. Although the chapter on Hébert in this work examines *In the Shadow of the Wind*, a prose work, it discusses her use of language and her themes, which is informative for understanding her poetry.

Shawncey Webb

FELICIA DOROTHEA HEMANS

Born: Liverpool, England; September 25, 1793
Died: Dublin, Ireland; May 16, 1835

PRINCIPAL POETRY

England and Spain: Or, Valour and Patriotism,
    1808
Poems, 1808
The Domestic Affections, and Other Poems,
    1812
The Restoration of the Works of Art to Italy:
    A Poem, 1816
Modern Greece: A Poem, 1817
The Meeting of Wallace and Bruce on the Banks of
    the Carron, 1819
Tales and Historic Scenes in Verse, 1819
Wallace's Invocation to Bruce: A Poem, 1819
The Sceptic: A Poem, 1820
Stanzas to the Memory of the Late King, 1820
Dartmoor: A Poem, Which Obtained the Prize of
    Fifty Guineas Proposed by The Royal Society of
    Literature, 1821
A Selection of Welsh Melodies, 1822
The Siege of Valencia: A Dramatic Poem; The Last
    Constantine, with Other Poems, 1823
The Vespers of Palermo: A Tragedy, in Five Acts,
    1823
The Forest Sanctuary, and Other Poems, 1825
The League of the Alps, the Siege of Valencia, the
    Vespers of Palermo, and Other Poems, 1826
Poems by Mrs. Hemans, 1826 (2 volumes)
Hymns for Childhood, 1827, 1834
Hymns on the Works of Nature, for the Use of
    Children, 1827
Records of Women, with Other Poems, 1828
A Set of Original Songs, 1830
Songs of the Affections, with Other Poems, 1830
National Lyrics and Songs for Music, 1834
Scenes and Hymns of Life, with Other Religious
    Poems, 1834 (also known as *Hymns and Scenes*
    of Life, and Other Poems)
Poetical Remains of the Late Mrs. Hemans,
    1836

OTHER LITERARY FORMS

Felicia Dorothea Hemans (HEHM-uhnz) translated
works from Luis de Camões, Petrarch, Francisco
Gómez de Quevedo y Villegas, and others in *Transla-
tions from Camoens, and Other Poets, with Original
Poetry* (1818). Her verse drama, *The Vespers of
Palermo*, failed in London, but fared better in Edin-
burgh, where it was supported by Sir Walter Scott and
Joanna Baillie, and starred Sarah Siddons.

ACHIEVEMENTS

Noted as one of the best-selling and most widely
read British poets of the nineteenth century, along with
Sir Walter Scott and Lord Byron, Felicia Dorothea
Hemans was celebrated as the perfection of English
womanhood—upholder and defender of hearth, home,
and nation—and as founder of a school of sentimental
poetry. Current criticism is reevaluating her place in
English letters, assessing thematic cross-currents in her
work that undermine the more obvious themes, those
beloved by the Victorians yet denounced by the modernists. Critics are also recontextualizing her work and
reexamining the persona of Mrs. Hemans, as well as the
actual woman and poet.

BIOGRAPHY

Felicia Dorothea Hemans was born Felicia Dorothea Browne in Liverpool, England, the fifth of seven
children. When she was six years old, her family
moved to northern Wales, where Felicia spent her
childhood. Educated at home by her mother, with access to the Browne family's extensive library, she knew
Italian, French, Spanish, Portuguese, German, and,
most likely, Latin and Welsh. She began writing poetry
by the age of eight and published her first volumes in
1808: The first, *Poems*, contained poems of birds,
flowers, fairies, and the seaside, and the second, *England and Spain*, contained patriotic poems influenced
by her brothers' service in the Peninsular Wars.

By 1812, she was publishing regularly in magazines
and annuals, and she frequently brought out new verse
collections. In 1812, she married Captain Alfred Hemans, but in 1818, he left for Italy, leaving her to care
for five sons. However, it was an age when a woman
could earn an income by writing poetry. Unlucky in the

Critical Survey of Poetry

Felicia Dorothea Hemans (The Granger Collection, New York)

failure of her marriage, she was nevertheless fortunate in other matters: A wide circle of family and friends were supportive of her career. In addition, she was published by John Murray and by William Blackwood, two of the most significant publishers of her time. By 1825, an edition of her poems had been proposed in the United States, and she was invited to move to Boston to edit a periodical, but she declined this offer.

These professional successes were soon followed by personal losses, however, and she lost first her elder brother, and next her mother in January, 1827, after which she began to display the physical symptoms of the illness that rendered her an invalid and from which she eventually died. She continued her literary work and, in 1828, published *Records of Women, with Other Poems*, which reflects her personal losses. After her death, she was best known for this volume.

By the summer of 1828, her sister and a brother had moved away, and her two eldest sons had moved to Rome to live with their father. Her own health was becoming increasingly delicate, so she and her three younger sons moved to Liverpool, where she became

friends with many people, including William Wordsworth and Scott. She moved to Dublin in 1831, where one of her brothers lived, hoping for better opportunities for her sons. Her health continually worsened; she was able to compose only in a reclining position. She turned to writing mostly sacred pieces, many of which were collected in her *Scenes and Hymns of Life, with Other Religious Poems*. Her death in 1835 was attributed to a weak heart, possibly the result of rheumatic fever.

ANALYSIS

The reputation of Felicia Dorothea Hemans's works over the years has fluctuated because of changes of taste from the Romantic era to the present; critical reassessment is continuing. Her early works were hailed as "masculine," but she soon created a persona for herself as the poetess of hearth and home, of queen and country, the image beloved by the nineteenth century and remunerative for her and her family.

She was heir to two streams of poetics: one, the Romantic mode of Byron and Percy Bysshe Shelley, and the other, the sentimental mode of Samuel Richardson. In addition, she looked back to her female literary predecessors, including Baillie and Madame de Staël. From the example of Byron and Shelley, she learned to employ the dramatic impact of sound and image, and she developed a feminized romantic protagonist. The Byronic hero manifests in her stalwart yet isolated women who rise above their circumstances, while Shelley's soaring images of antimonarchical Promethean liberty transform into her resounding songs of the British patriot's imperial pride and hymns of apparent religious certainty. Her employment of the sentimental mode worked well for her throughout the nineteenth century, but it drew censure from the modernists, who insisted on impersonal poetry devoid of "excesses" of feeling. Although she was celebrated for songs and hymns published and sung in nineteenth century parlors, her works fell into near eclipse during the twentieth century until the late 1980's and early 1990's. The only work that kept her from total obscurity was "Casabianca," which was included in grade-school readers and recited on both sides of the Atlantic until the middle of the twentieth century. A significant voice during the literary "interregnum" between the deaths of the younger Romantics and the early works of the emerging Victorian era, Hemans is regarded by some as a literary progenitor of Alfred, Lord Tennyson.

An avid reader of history, Hemans followed Scott's example, exploring the psyche in remote times and places as well as examining universal human emotions. Along with her contemporaries, Hemans suited her form to content, delivery, and effect, writing ballads, closed heroic couplets, couplets in tetrameter, blank verse, and Spenserian stanzas. Her cadences were always mellifluous, sonorous, and regular, and her images were drawn in feminized versions of those of the Satanic school (formed around Shelley and Byron), but were used in service of more traditional religious tropes.

Typical characteristics of her work include the use of the affective mode, depictions of historical moments, a maternal focus on a stereotypically masculine situation, and the probing of the psyche in extreme situations. In the last two decades of the twentieth century, critics began to explore the idea that often, while Hemans writes one story in a poem, the very story undermines its own meaning.

THE SIEGE OF VALENCIA

The Siege of Valencia is a historical romance in verse: An imagined attack referencing El Cid serves as a medieval story against which universal themes and contemporary issues could be played out. The Moors are invading Valencia, taking hostage the sons of Gonzalez and Elmina, and setting the surrender of the city as the terms of their release. Elmina is caught between her love for her children as a mother and her civic responsibilities as Gonzalez's wife, thus setting up the personal/political dilemma as well as the stereotyped feminine/masculine gender dichotomy, also evident in the shifting character traits of their daughter Ximena.

LAYS OF MANY LANDS

Lays of Many Lands, published in *The Forest Sanctuary, and Other Poems*, ranges over the world and time, taking as its subjects historical figures and imagined characters in historical situations, and observing the individual in a state of alienation, expatriation, and exile. At once, Hemans adulates and critiques war, by referring to funeral chants and, as she often does, clos-

ing poems with death from war wounds, self-immolation, and other causes.

CASABIANCA

"Casabianca," first published in the *Monthly Magazine* in August, 1826, is by far the most famous of Hemans's poems. Known to countless by its first line, "The boy stood on the burning deck," the ballad-stanza exemplifies many of characteristics of her poems. Giacomo Casabianca, a Corsican boy aboard the French battleship *L'Orient* under the command of his father, has promised his father that he will remain at his post until his father releases him. The boat is burning, but the boy, unaware that his father is dead below deck, remains at his post and goes down with the ship in the midst of explosions and shooting flames. "Casabianca" has been celebrated for its portrayal of filial loyalty and youthful steadfastness and valor, as well as Hemans's ability to elicit sympathy, but it also has been derided as excessively sentimental. Later critics have begun to ask whether Hemans is actually subtly critiquing war and militarism rather than simply creating a message of loyalty and patriotism.

RECORDS OF WOMEN, WITH OTHER POEMS

Records of Women, with Other Poems was the best-selling volume by the best-selling poet at the time, containing many of the works for which Hemans was most loved. In this volume, Hemans translates the historical moment into a female idiom. She gives voice to women who persevere in the face of crushing adversity and devastating separations, who support the tortured and the dying in threatening situations, often without failing or fading, although their hearts and spirits are broken by unrequited love, separation, death, or a combination of these. In "Gertrude, or Fidelity till Death," Gertrude remains with her husband, the alleged assassin of Emperor Albert, through his torture on the wheel until his death, wiping his brow and wetting his lips. Her closing religious note thanks God for giving her the strength to minister to her husband's last days. "Juana," known to history as "Juana la Loca," sat by the corpse of her husband, Philip the Handsome, refusing to allow it to be clothed in a shroud, insisting that it remain in its monarchical robes and crown, and believing he would awaken and acknowledge the intensity of their love. Her vigil ended only when the corpse was significantly disfigured by death. The female protagonist of "The Switzer's Wife" grows momentarily faint on hearing that their home and freedom are threatened, but she summons courage and power as she declares that, for the sake of their son, her husband must fight for freedom. Her husband departs for war, and she is left to pray, rocking their child and singing him to sleep with a hymn.

Among the poems of bereavement, abandonment, and separation in *Records of Women, and Other Poems* is "Properzia Rossi," which voices the pain of unrequited love. The eponymous sculptor sculpts a bas-relief of Ariadne from a painting by Louis Ducis. As the sculptress watches the art object take shape under her hands, she meditates on love and fame, wanting to imbue her marble Ariadne with a voice that, after her own death, could so affect her beloved that it would elicit from him at least one emotional response. Stating that love was never hers, she declares that without it, fame is meaningless. Although in this poem, Hemans expresses a preference for love over fame, some modern critics are suggesting that as a poet and person, Hemans may have been quite pleased with her fame.

Many of the poems in this collection were adulated by Hemans's Victorian readers. Although poems such as "The Homes of England" earned her a reputation as the patriotic poet of hearth and home, in the twentieth century, these same poems were dismissed as jingoistic by critics and readers. In this poem, Hemans describes homes ranging from the great houses of the wealthy landed classes to the cottages of the working classes, ending with a patriotic paean to childhood love of country and God. Some are now questioning the Victorian reading as too facile, observing that the poem's subtext undermines its apparent theme.

OTHER MAJOR WORK

MISCELLANEOUS: *Translations from Camoens, and Other Poets, with Original Poetry*, 1818.

BIBLIOGRAPHY

Harding, Anthony John. "Felicia Hemans and the Effacement of Woman." In *Romantic Women: Voices and Countervoices*, edited by Paula R. Feldman and Theresa M. Kelley. Hanover, N.H.: University Press of New England, 1995. Discusses Hemans's

work in the context of writing with or against expected gender roles and social convention.

Mason, Emma James. *Women Poets of the Nineteenth Century*. Tavistock, England: Northcote House, 2004. Contains a section on Hemans and her work.

Sweet, Nanora, and Julie Melnyk, eds. *Felicia Hemans: Reimagining Poetry in the Nineteenth Century*. New York: Palgrave, 2001. Collection of articles on Hemans and changing critical assessments of the poet.

Wolfson, Susan J. "Domestic Affections and the Spear of Minerva: Felicia Hemans and the Dilemma of Gender." In *Re-visioning Romanticism: British Women Writers, 1776-1837*, edited by Carol Shiner Wilson and Joel Haefner. Philadelphia: University of Pennsylvania Press, 1994. Wolfson examines work by and about Hemans, maintaining that the lack of resolution of gender role conflicts supplies creative tension.

_____, ed. *Felicia Hemans: Selected Poems, Letters, Reception Materials*. Princeton, N.J.: Princeton University Press, 2010. Collects poetry and other materials not otherwise readily available.

Donna Berliner

ROBERT HENRYSON

Born: Place unknown; c. 1425
Died: Near Dunfermline, Scotland; c. 1505

PRINCIPAL POETRY

Tale of Orpheus, 1508
The Testament of Cresseid, 1532
The Morall Fabillis of Esope, the Phrygian, 1570 (also known as *Fables*; twelve shorter poems of uncertain attribution)
The Poems of Robert Henryson, 1906-1914 (3 volumes)
The Poems of Robert Henryson, 1981 (Denton Fox, editor)
The Poems of Robert Henryson, 1997 (Robert L. Kindrick, editor)

OTHER LITERARY FORMS

Robert Henryson most likely did not write in any genre other than poetry.

ACHIEVEMENTS

For centuries, the reputation of Robert Henryson rested on a mistake. His poem *The Testament of Cresseid*, which concludes or rounds out the events of Geoffrey Chaucer's *Troilus and Criseyde* (1382), was mistakenly credited to Chaucer and printed as Chaucer's (in an "Englished" version, smoothing out the Scottish dialect) for several generations. Thus, although his work drew admiration, the poet himself was little known.

Henryson was rediscovered by antiquarians in the eighteenth century, and for about one hundred years was a subject of interest among the Scottish literati, leading to editions of his poetry by David Laing (1865) and G. G. Smith (1906-1914). Today, Henryson is regularly studied, along with Gavin Douglas and William Dunbar, as one of the Scottish Chaucerians. Both Chaucer and John Lydgate can be seen to have influenced Henryson greatly. Although his own direct influence extends, perhaps, only to the English and Scottish lyricists of the early sixteenth century, he is now generally admired as a witty and learned man whose response to his sources (Aesop, Chaucer, and classical myth) reveals an interesting mind at work and earns him the right to be included among early Renaissance humanists. He vies with Dunbar for the distinction of being the preeminent Scottish poet before Robert Burns.

BIOGRAPHY

Very little is known about Robert Henryson's life. Dunbar, listing dead poets in "Lament for the Makaris" (c. 1508), indicates that Henryson predeceased Stobo, who died in 1505. The other scant biographical evidence suggests that Henryson came from the area of Dunfermline (notable for its Benedictine abbey and site of one of the king's favorite homes); that he was admitted as a licentiate at the University of Glasgow in 1462; and that he served as a notary public and possibly as a schoolmaster. So little is certain about Henryson's life that scholars do not agree on the probable chronology of his works or even on the dates when he was most active as a poet. Nothing at all is known about Henryson's family life.

The range of knowledge displayed in the poems confirms that Henryson knew, at the least, a little about many subjects—law, medicine, astronomy, myth, and music—and at least a few books very well. His *Fables* adapt Aesop, whom Henryson read in Latin; his *Tale of Orpheus* is based on a passage from Boethius's *De consolatione philosophiae* (523; *The Consolation of Philosophy*, late ninth century); he refers often to the Bible and frequently alludes to Chaucer.

ANALYSIS

Robert Henryson's work is often compared to Geoffrey Chaucer's and although he does not have the sweep and range of his English predecessor, Henryson does mirror, consciously or not, some of Chaucer's characteristics. Like Chaucer, he is interested in astrology, and in both *The Testament of Cresseid* and the *Tale of Orpheus*, the planets determine the fates of characters. In the *Fables*, his speaking animals sometimes have the comic and colloquial range of the Eagle in Chaucer's the *House of Fame* (1372-1380) or the birds in his *Parlement of Foules* (1380).

Henryson's most Chaucerian invention, however, is the narrative voice in *The Testament of Cresseid*. This narrative persona allows Henryson to present a morally complex situation with a degree of sophistication unmatched by his other works. Since the dates of Henryson's poems are uncertain, it would be wrong to view *The Testament of Cresseid* as a culmination of his narrative technique. However, in this brief work, he not only tells a story but also offers a series of moral perspectives on the action by allowing different characters, including the narrator, varying degrees of objectivity.

In the *Fables* and the *Tale of Orpheus*, he uses a more conventional method of achieving a mixed perspective. Each of the thirteen fables concludes with a separate section, labeled *moralitas*, which spells out the allegorical and moral implications of the fable itself. Similarly, the *Tale of Orpheus* concludes with an analytical *moralitas*, pairing each character and event with a specific allegorical function. Perhaps because formal allegory has long been an acquired taste, these two works show to a disadvantage beside the freshness and seeming modernity of *The Testament of Cresseid*.

FABLES

Henryson's longest work, *The Morall Fabillis of Esope, the Phrygian*, also known as *Fables*, is a collection of thirteen Aesopic fables, each consisting of a beast tale followed by an explicating *moralitas*. Unanimity has not been reached on the question of the sources for Henryson's versions of the traditional fables, but most scholars agree that he depended on the Latin verse *Romulus* of Gualterus Anglicus for seven of the tales. He may also have used a French translation of Gualterus known as *Isopet de Lyon*, John Lydgate's *Translation of Aesop* (wr. c. 1400, pb. 1885; the first Aesopic collection in English), and William Caxton's *Fables of Aesop*.

Some editors, borrowing phrases from early manuscripts, call Henryson's fables the *Morall Fabillis of Esope, the Phrygian*, but Denton Fox, pointing out that Henryson evidently thought Aesop was a Roman, doubts the authenticity of the title and prefers simply *Fables* (see Fox's 1981 edition).

Henryson provides a prologue to his tales that echoes the Horatian dictum about delight and instruction. In general, the fables themselves are lively tales in a colloquial style, featuring anthropomorphic beasts wandering into error. Some of the errors are more blatantly human than others, but all are corrected in the *moralitas*, which often have a more formal level of diction than do the tales. The relationship between fable and moral is not always what the modern reader expects; sometimes the highbrow stiffness of the moral does not do full justice to the human (or bestial) complexity of the tale. The key word in the preceding sentence is "bestial," for clearly the animals of the stories, like Eurydice and Cresseid, represent aspects of human beings' appetitive nature.

An example of the gap between fable and *moralitas* may be taken from the first fable, "The Cock and the Jasp," in which a rooster, scrounging in a dunghill for food, comes upon a precious stone. Realizing that he, a cock, can have no use for a jewel, he casts it aside and continues the search for food. Now, to the reader, the rooster seems to have made a wise choice. Is it not better to attend to basic needs, like that for food, and ig-

nore the useless material items? The *moralitas*, however, turns this perception inside out. Based on biblical tradition, the jewel is glossed as wisdom; suddenly, the cock can be seen as foolishly preferring dungy food to the intangible riches of knowledge. Henryson's intention, it would seem, is to shock the reader into recognizing his own similarity to the foolish cock.

The fables, then, are explicitly didactic, and they work by creating a gap between the formal "correct" view of a situation and the partial human/animal view. The tidy structure of "The Cock and the Jasp" is not, however, precisely paralleled by all the other fables. In fact, as the sequence progresses, the fables themselves become harsher and bleaker, and the morals less pleasant. In the first seven, only blatantly evil characters are punished; in the latter six, however, the innocent begin to suffer. For example, in "The Wolf and the Lamb," the twelfth fable, a pathetic lamb argues for its life but, without any hope of justice, is killed and eaten. The *moralitas* compares the lamb to "the pure pepill" and the wolf to "fals extortioners and oppresouris" and warns powerful men not to be like the wolf. A moral universe divides fable 12 from fable 1; Henryson has moved from questions of personal governance, as in "The Cock and the Jasp," to address his fears about the contemporary political situation.

The thirteenth and final fable has a religious dimension; here a greedy mouse and a predatory paddock (toad) end up in a life-or-death water fight, and both are killed by a passing bird of prey. The mouse is allegorized by Henryson as man's soul, the paddock as man's body, and the whole tale as a parable for the difficulty of reconciling the two. Man is warned that unless he can reconcile body and soul he may become the victim of external predators. Henryson does not, however, offer a plan for effecting such a reconciliation. Although the early fables often surprise the reader, they do offer moral advice. The later fables, much darker, offer cautionary tales without explicit directions about how to avoid pitfalls oneself.

THE TESTAMENT OF CRESSEID

By far Henryson's best-known work, *The Testament of Cresseid* owes its popularity and vitality both to its link to Chaucer's *Troilus and Criseyde* and to its own conciseness, originality, and sincerity. The entire poem consists of 616 lines, in contrast to the eight thousand lines of the Chaucerian inspiration.

In *The Testament of Cresseid*, Henryson abandons the fable-moral structure characteristic of his other works. Instead, the poem itself stands as a suitable *moralitas* to *Troilus and Criseyde* itself. Henryson takes the events of Chaucer's poem, particularly the actions of Criseyde, and carries them out to what he sees as their morally logical conclusion. The justice meted out to Cresseid (as Henryson spells her name) is swift and cruel: Diomed abandons her, she contracts leprosy (generally then considered to be a venereal disease), and Troilus, resurrected by Henryson despite his death in Chaucer, kindly gives her alms, although her disease makes her unrecognizable. She dies willing her spirit to the goddess of chastity, Diana.

What was Henryson's intention in following Cresseid after Chaucer's poem ends? Some readers have accused him of a puritanical streak, seeing in him a fierce desire to punish the wicked. He may also have been playing into the hands of an interested public, who had known the legend of a promiscuous Cresseid before Chaucer ever took up the subject. Even if tradition had already branded Cresseid a whore, Henryson's treatment of her does seem, at first, to smack of moral judgment. He seems to want people to receive their just rewards in this world, rather than in Heaven or Hell. In his poem, Troilus, for example, is still alive, graciously donating alms and cutting a dashing figure. The reader is left with no doubt about the relative wages of sin and fidelity. Cresseid rots and dies; Troilus prospers.

The poem as a whole is admirably structured and has often been praised for its concision. It begins with a variation on the conventional medieval opening reference to spring. A Scottish spring, apparently, is a cold and "doolie" affair, an apt setting for the sorrowful tale. Henryson follows Chaucer in creating a kind of naïve narrator for the tale, one who is hopelessly sympathetic to Cresseid—a sympathy that neither Chaucer nor Henryson necessarily shares. Thus while Henryson the poet assigns Cresseid leprosy, Henryson the narrator weeps for her. The narrator, much like the narrators in Chaucer's dream visions, stays up one night reading *Troilus and Criseyde*, then turns to "another quair," another book, for the rest of the tale, seeking to answer the question of what happened to Cresseid when she left Troy and deserted her lover Troilus for the Greek Diomed.

The new story begins as Cresseid, cast off by Diomed, decides to come home to her loving father Calchas, whom Henryson depicts as the keeper of the temple of Venus. In this very temple, Cresseid, on her knees in despair, blasphemes against Cupid and his mother by regretting that she ever sacrificed to them. The response to this blasphemy is swift; Cresseid has a dream vision in which "the sevin planetis" descend from their spheres. Earthly action is suspended while the planets debate Cresseid's punishment, with melancholy Saturn, "the hiest planet," being given responsibility for formulating the verdict. The narrator, true to his subjective affection for Cresseid, spends a stanza lamenting the "to malitious" judgment against Cresseid. The fate of the gods is nevertheless final, and the newly diseased Cresseid, after consultation with her father, moves into a nearby "spittail hous" to await death. At this point, Henryson includes an inset poem (made up of nine-line stanzas as distinct from the poem's rime royal) in which Cresseid laments her fate, wishes for death, and warns other ladies not to forget the pitfalls of sin and the fickle passage of time. This is her testament. Before Cresseid dies, she sends Troilus a ring. He suffers for her sake but stoically asserts that she brought her fate upon herself by her falseness.

The reader is left then with at least three verdicts on Cresseid: that of the planetary council, which condemns her for both her deed and her blasphemy of love; that of the narrator, who seems to see her (as she initially sees herself) as a wronged victim; and that of Troilus, who will always care for her but who accepts the inevitability of her fate. In the end, Henryson finds a way to offer multiple perspectives on a given action without resorting to the formal juxtaposition of fable and moral. The surprise of *The Testament of Cresseid* comes instead at the beginning, when readers realize that the apparently closed case of *Troilus and Criseyde* is suddenly subject to new evidence. Still, despite the resurrection of Troilus and the spectacular invention of Cresseid's leprosy, *The Testament of Cressied* offers no final word on Cresseid's fate. She remains as lovable, and as wrong, as she was for Chaucer.

TALE OF ORPHEUS

The *Tale of Orpheus* is a poem in rhyme royal of about the same length as the *Troilus and Criseyde*. It is solidly based on a passage in Boethius's *The Consolation of Philosophy* (III, metrum xii) and on Nicholas Trivet's commentary on that passage. Despite its relative concision, Henryson's poem is encyclopedic and ambitious, containing, like Chaucer's *House of Fame*, a supernatural journey and an explanation of music based on the harmonious proportions of the universe.

Of Henryson's major works, the *Tale of Orpheus* is the least popular, perhaps because of the number of lines given over to a theoretical discussion of music and the genealogy of the gods. Modern readers, however, also find uncongenial the strange gap between the myth of the *Tale of Orpheus* and the *moralitas* offered, in which Eurydice, glossed as sinful affection, is said more or less properly to belong in Hell.

The poem opens with the genealogy of Orpheus, tracing his descent from the mating of Calliope, "of all musik maistresse," and Phebus Appollo, god of poetry and intellect. When Orpheus grows up, Eurydice, queen of Thrace, woos and marries him (the role reversal here will prove significant). He loves her dearly, and when she is snatched to Hell, furiously pursues her. Why does she "die"? While frolicking in a meadow, she flees from a would-be attacker, the shepherd Arystyus, and is bitten by a snake. To understand why this series of events leads her to Hell, the reader must turn to the *moralitas*, which reveals that Orpheus, as "intellect," mates with Eurydice, "affection," at his peril. After all, Eurydice, rather than Orpheus, initiated the marriage. More oddly, Arystyus, who attacked Eurydice, is said to represent virtue, and in fleeing him, she exposed herself to sin, symbolized by the snake. Eurydice, then, represents a low passion for an intellectual creature like Orpheus and by implication all worthy human beings. Does Henryson rule out all human love? No, humans may have it on one condition, the same condition on which Orpheus is allowed to lead Eurydice out of Hell: He must not look back, or downward, but always keep his eyes fixed on the celestial spheres.

Human love, then, is always in danger of backsliding, always on the verge of failure. This may seem like a dark message, akin to the darkness of Cresseid's fate, especially since Orpheus ultimately fails to win back Eurydice. The poem, however, offers some hope: Reason and affection can be brought together by the "harp of eloquence," the power of poetry. This power immobilizes Cerberus and the three fates; frees Tantalus, Ixion, and Ticius from their hellish punishments; and earns Orpheus the right to try to free Eurydice. Love depends on poetry (a cousin of celestial harmony) for survival.

Henryson's poem is itself an eloquent voice, both showing tender affection between Orpheus and Eurydice and hinting, with a touch of *contemptus mundi*, that human beings ought to focus primarily on higher things. With luck, one can have both affection and intellect; in this poem, however, poor Orpheus ends up with only his eloquence, his sad ballads. Bereft of affection, he does not seem to profit from his intellect.

In terms of overall technique, the *Tale of Orpheus*, like some of the fables, shows Henryson achieving a complex point of view by juxtaposing the vision of his essentially human lovers with the stern voice of the *moralitas*, in which they become the abstractions intellect and affection. If he is fierce about the wages of sin, he is also a persuasive portraitist of the appeal that the sin of human love inevitably holds.

SHORTER POEMS

The twelve shorter poems attributed to Henryson range across a variety of standard genres and include "Robene and Makene," a comic *pastourelle* (a dialogue between lovers); "Sum Practysis of Medecyne," a satire on doctors; and poems in which age debates youth and death debates man. The poems exhibit the variety of contemporary stanza forms, and do not, for the most part, speak in a voice that particularly echoes that of Henryson's three major works. Aside from the titles given above, the twelve include "The Annunciation," "The Abbey Walk," "The Bloody Serk," "The Garmont of Gud Ladeis," "Against Hasty Credence," "The Praise of Age," "Ane Prayer for the Pest," "The Ressoning Betuix Aige and Yowth," "The Ressoning Betuix Deth and Man," and "The Three Dead Pollis." A thirteenth poem, "The Want of Wise Men," sometimes attributed to Henryson, has been rejected by Fox on the ground that no plausible proof of attribution exists. Indeed Fox suggests that proof of authorship is tentative for all the shorter poems.

BIBLIOGRAPHY

Gray, Douglas. *Robert Henryson*. Leiden, the Netherlands: E. J. Brill, 1979. This study begins with a background chapter on Henryson's world, but the bulk of the book (three chapters) is a detailed reading of the *Fables*. Contains separate sections on *The Testament of Cresseid*, "Orpheus and Eurydice," and the shorter poems. Includes illustrations and a good basic bibliography.

Henryson, Robert. *The Complete Works*. Edited by David J. Parkinson. Kalamazoo: Medieval Institute Publications, Western Michigan University, 2008. Contains a lengthy introduction that provides information about Henryson. The shorter poems are divided into two groups, those with stronger and weaker attributions.

_____. *The Poems of Robert Henryson*. Edited by Denton Fox. Oxford, England: Clarendon Press, 1981. This fine collection is accompanied by a full introduction that reviews Henryson's life and reputation, the texts, the manuscripts, and the individual works. The poems are given extensive commentary and an excellent Middle Scots glossary makes reading easy and enjoyable.

Kindrick, Robert L. *Henryson and the Medieval Arts of Rhetoric*. New York: Garland, 1993. A rhetorical study of Henryson's work that details Henryson's use of the *ars poetria*, *ars dictiminis*, *ars notaria*, and *ars praedicandi*. Provides an overview of medieval rhetorical traditions.

_____. *Robert Henryson*. Boston: Twayne, 1979. This analytic survey covers Henryson's personality as a writer, his times, and his literary tradition. He is characterized as a master of "wisdom literature," a brilliant stylist in both allegorical descriptions and realistic portrayals, as well as a possessor of a keen sense of humor. Such traits as his love and understanding of his fellow human beings, his portrayal of the dignity of the lower classes, his blunt yet clear diction, and his influences from rationalism and classical sources are discussed and examples are given. Includes a handy chronology and a short bibliography.

McDiarmid, Matthew P. *Robert Henryson*. Edinburgh: Scottish Academic Press, 1981. A biographical chapter dealing with the facts and speculations of Henryson's life is followed by a portrait of his times and the literary tradition he inherited. Detailed analyses of the three major poems as well as the shorter ones are accompanied by notes and a select bibliography.

McKenna, Steven R. *Robert Henryson's Tragic Vision*. New York: Peter Lang, 1994. A critical analysis of the rhetoric used in selected works by Henryson. Includes bibliographical references and index.

MacQueen, John. *Complete and Full with Numbers: The Narrative Poetry of Robert Henryson*. New York: Rodopi, 2006. Part of the Scottish Cultural Review of Language and Literature series, this volume examines Henryson's works, particularly the fables.

Diane M. Ross

GEORGE HERBERT

Born: Montgomery, Wales; April 3, 1593
Died: Bemerton, near Salisbury, Wiltshire, England; March 1, 1633

PRINCIPAL POETRY
Musae Responsoriae, 1620, 1662 (printed)
Lucus, 1623
Passio Discerpta, 1623
Memoriae Matris Sacrum, 1627
The Temple, 1633
Poems, 1958, 1961
Sundrie Pieces: A New Selection of George Herbert's Poetry, with Samples of His Prose, 2003 (illustrated by Sarah van Niekerk)

OTHER LITERARY FORMS
George Herbert's most important work besides *The Temple* is his prose treatise *A Priest to the Temple: Or,*

The Country Parson His Character and Rule of Holy Life, written when he was in fact a country parson at Bemerton during the last years of his life, though not published until 1652. However idealized it may be, *A Priest to the Temple* gives a good picture of the life of humble service that Herbert offered to his God and his parishioners. The volume of *Outlandish Proverbs Selected by Mr. G. H.*, published in 1640, testifies to Herbert's lifelong interest in the proverb, a form of literary and moral expression that is prominent throughout the poems in *The Temple*. Other minor works include a translation of *A Treatise of Temperance and Sobrietie of Luigi Cornaro* (1634), and a series of "Briefe Notes" appended to, but indicating various disagreements with, *The Hundred and Ten Considerations of Signior Iohn Valdesso* (1638).

ACHIEVEMENTS

George Herbert has always been and perhaps will continue to be read somewhat in the shadow of John Donne, arguably the greatest and most influential of the seventeenth century Metaphysical poets. At the same time, however, Herbert has rarely lacked an audience well aware of his remarkable poetic abilities and unique voice. During his lifetime, Herbert's English poems were most likely circulated in manuscript, no doubt within a rather restricted circle of friends, and were evidently highly regarded. Upon publication in 1633, the year of his death, *The Temple* began to reach an ever-widening group of readers, the number and variety of whom say something about Herbert's appeal. It is not enough to note that Herbert was extremely popular, though he certainly was that: At least eleven editions of *The Temple* came out in the seventeenth century.

Perhaps more interesting is the fact that unlikely bedfellows shared an interest in Herbert and claimed him as their own. Members of the so-called High Church party found Herbert's deep attachment to Anglican ceremonial beauty particularly congenial, and they read *The Temple* as a record of how spiritual conflicts might evaporate in the face of simple faith, humility, and conformity. Several important poets, including Henry Vaughan and Richard Crashaw, along with a host of minor poets, including Christopher Harvey,

Ralph Knevet, and Henry Colman, looked to Herbert as a guide in their devotions and a model for their poems. Other aspects of Herbert, however, appealed to many readers who could be called, for lack of a better term, Puritans. Though the Puritans are often criticized for a disinterest in, if not hostility to, art as an enemy of truth, Herbert's characteristic plainness, simplicity, and sincerity, coupled with his constant stress on the Bible as the center of the holy life, made him attractive to readers who were otherwise not greatly devoted to poetry. Richard Baxter and, later, John Wesley were extremely fond of Herbert, and it is no surprise that many poems from *The Temple* were subsequently adapted as hymns.

That Herbert could be appropriated so easily by such divergent readers indicates the richness of *The Temple*. Modern writers as varied as Gerard Manley Hopkins, T. S. Eliot, Dylan Thomas, Elizabeth Bishop, and Simone Weil have each in his or her own way learned from Herbert: as a poet who has a distinctive voice that nevertheless does not exclude other voices, particularly from the Bible and the Book of Common Prayer; as a man of purity and simplicity who is yet rarely naïve and often painfully sensitive to the intricacies of sin and self-deception; as a Christian, indeed a priest, wedded to humility but well aware that the resources of art can serve as resources of devotion.

BIOGRAPHY

George Herbert was born on April 3, 1593, into one of the most distinguished families of Montgomeryshire, active both in local politics and court service. The fifth son in a family of seven sons and three daughters, he was reared principally by his mother (his father died in 1596), by all reports a remarkable woman who left a deep impression on her children. Magdalene Herbert not only shrewdly managed an extremely large household—unlike the modern-day nuclear family, the upper-class household of the seventeenth century might contain upward of a score of children, relatives, servants, and visitors—but also supervised the education of her children. Perhaps more important, as Donne relates in his commemorative sermon on her, she was a model of piety and took a great interest in the spiritual development of her family. Herbert's early childhood thus well prepared him for a life of distinction and devotion, two clusters of values that he later spent much time trying to reconcile.

Herbert's formal education began at Westminster School, and upon entering Trinity College, Cambridge, he soon established himself as a young man of great promise. Moving quickly through A.B. and A.M. degrees and positions as a minor, then a major fellow, Herbert became the university orator in 1620. Such an appointment not only indicates the great verbal and oral skills that Herbert must have demonstrated, skills that he would later use to great advantage as both a poet and a preacher, but also testifies to the high regard in which he was held. The orator was in some respects the public spokesperson for the university, constantly communicating with government officials and dignitaries, and it was only a small step to graduate from this office to a more prestigious position at court or in state service.

This was not, however, to be Herbert's path. Perhaps his attendance at two particularly troubling terms of Parliament (in 1624 and 1625) discouraged him from a life of secular employment. Perhaps the death of King James and the accession of Charles I left him without a strong group of supporters to back any possible ambitions. Perhaps as he grew older, passed through several serious illnesses, and deepened his devotions, he came to see that a secular career did not, in the long run, have nearly as much to offer as a life of holy service. For whatever reason, Herbert chose to be ordained as a deacon by 1626, and four years later, he became a priest. With his wife, whom he married in 1629, Herbert lived the remaining years of his life at Bemerton, a small parish near Salisbury. He died on March 1, 1633.

Herbert's poetry is often deeply personal, so that many readers insist on looking at *The Temple* as a kind of veiled autobiography. Surely the major themes of his life are indeed the major themes in his poetry: On one level, *The Temple* dramatizes Herbert's conflicting drives toward secular achievement and religious retreat, his search for a satisfying vocation, and his apparently constant self-doubts and worries about his unworthiness to be a lowly servant of God, let alone a priest. *The Temple* is ultimately, however, far more than autobiographical, and the reader should not assume that every statement made by Herbert the poet is literally true of Herbert the man. The persona who narrates and undergoes a variety of experiences in *The Temple* is very much like Herbert but also very much like the readers of *The Temple*. Herbert's purpose in writing his poems was not so much to express his personal concerns as it was to clarify and perhaps resolve certain important problems that all Christians—some would broaden this to include all thoughtful readers—share. The details of Herbert's life thus figure largely in his poems, but as part of a design that is much more inclusive.

ANALYSIS

The Temple is unquestionably one of the most inventive and varied collections of poems published in the seventeenth century, and a reader can go a long way toward appreciating George Herbert by studying this inventiveness and variety. At the same time, though, the full range of Herbert's intentions and impact may be missed if his technical virtuosity is seen as an end in

George Herbert (Hulton Archive/Getty Images)

itself. Everything known about Herbert suggests that he would not want to be described as a master craftsman or skilled technician of poetry unless it was also stressed that every effort of his artistry served a central purpose: helping him to know, love, and praise God, and to understand better his place in a world filled with sin but governed and redeemed by Christ. Such poems as "Jordan" (I) and (II) and "The Posie" are in fact critical of certain styles of poetry and show that Herbert is more than occasionally impatient with the subterfuge, indirection, and even pride that seem inevitable in producing a well-written work. Ultimately, however, poetic creativity and devotion are welded together in *The Temple*. As the title suggests, Herbert imagines himself to be a builder, and nearly all the details, both large and small, of the structure he raises show it to be a place of intricate beauty as well as sacred worship.

THE TEMPLE

Understanding the design of *The Temple* as a whole is no easy matter, in part because Herbert's natural inclination seems to be to "play" with structure, rather than to adopt a fixed schema as the pattern for the entire work. *The Temple* is divided into three parts, as though the reader is going to be led step-by-step through a physical temple. "The Church-porch," by far Herbert's longest single poem, offers a great deal of advice on moral matters to prepare a youth who is otherwise not yet ready for more serious devotions. After such an initiation, the reader is ready to enter the section called "The Church," a collection of lyrics that continues to describe various places or objects in the church (the altar, stained glass windows, and so on) but that in doing so dramatizes the spiritual conflicts of a believer trying to secure his faith. The final section, "The Church Militant," turns from the life of the individual believer to the corporate body of the church, which, like each individual, must endure a series of successes and failures throughout its history. While the tripartite structure of *The Temple* thus has a certain obvious coherence, there are limits to the usefulness of such a scheme. Though Herbert never completely drops his theme of tracing out the contours of the physical temple, he quickly shows that his main interest is in exploring the temple within the heart and mind of the worshiper.

Herbert's flexible and open-ended play with structure, his ability to make patterns that are stable enough to support a great weight of meaning but loose enough to avoid dull predictability, is seen to a great advantage in the way he arranges the poems of "The Church." Far from being a random miscellany, "The Church" is a carefully ordered collection in which the individual poems are placed in sequences and other kinds of groups, sometimes with poems that stand nearby in the volume, at other times with ones located many pages away. Although even a superficial reading of the poems soon advises the reader that he must watch closely how they relate to one another, Herbert provides a good description of his method and a clue to where he learned it in his poem "The H. Scriptures" (II). Despite its many parts, the Bible, he suggests, has a basic unity, and in order to understand any particular story the reader needs to trace how "This verse marks that, and both do make a motion/ Unto a third, that ten leaves off doth lie." Like the Bible, "The Church" has a basic unity, and the reader understands the poems fully only when he or she takes into account how they comment on and echo one another.

Sometimes the patterns and sequences of the poems are rather straightforward. "The Church" opens with a series that moves through the events celebrated during Easter Week, and the cumulative effect of such poems as "The Sacrifice," "The Agonie," "Good Friday," "Easter," and "Easter-wings" is to reinforce a sense of the importance of this part of the Christian calendar. In another group, the typical progress of a Christian life is reflected in the succession of titles: "Affliction," "Repentance," "Faith," "Prayer," and "The H. Communion." Even when Herbert does not fully develop a sequence, there are many examples of paired poems, where one answers, corrects, or otherwise responds to another. "Church-monuments," one of Herbert's most impressive poems even though its theme is the body's inevitable decay, is immediately followed by "Church-musick," which focuses on the high-flying freedom of the soul once it is released from the body. The desperate pleas that fill "Longing" are short-lived; by the first line of the next poem, "The Bag"—"Away despair! My gracious Lord doth heare"—the pleas have been answered.

Toward the end of "The Church," the speaker in the poem "The Invitation" calls out to God, inviting him to a feast; the following poem, "The Banquet," shows not only that the invitation has been accepted but also that the feast is far more glorious than the speaker had imagined. The more the reader follows the many links drawing the poems closer and closer together, the more apparent it becomes that one aspect of Herbert's design in "The Church" is to use the entire collection to trace a believer's gradual attainment not only of wisdom but also, more important, of peace. Read as one long, continuous sequence, the poems of "The Church" do seem to have a general plot, as the tribulations so much in evidence early in the work gradually give way to a more subdued questioning and heightened moments of bliss. Many commentators have noted that Herbert marks out this general plot very clearly for his reader: At the beginning of "The Church" the reader is invited to "approach, and taste/ The churches mysticall repast," and the final poem in the section, "Love" (III), concludes quite simply—"So I did sit and eat"—showing that this task has been completed.

Without disregarding the broad movement in "The Church" from immaturity to maturity, pain to comfort, it is equally important to note that Herbert by no means presents a simple tale of easily achieved spiritual progress. The plot traced out by the lyrics in "The Church," while ultimately a hopeful one, is at the same time densely textured, complicated, filled with moments of weakness, backsliding, and lessons improperly learned. Numerous short sequences suggest that humanity's needs are answered by Christ, who is always nearby; for example, the momentary sense that Christ has vanished, and that even when he is near he is unapproachable, expressed in "The Search," "Grief," and "The Crosse," gives way to the blooming of joy in "The Flower"—joy that is both surprising and expected: "How fresh, O Lord, how sweet and clean/ Are thy returns! ev'n as the flowers in spring."

If comfort is predictable, though, so is despair, and many short sequences show how quickly people move back again from wonder to worry; the exhilaration of "The Temper" (I), for example, is extremely precarious, over and done with, even by the time the next poem, "The Temper" (II), begins: "It cannot be. Where is that mightie joy,/ Which just now took up all my heart?" As confusing and frustrating as these constant oscillations may be, Herbert's purpose is not to undermine the reader's security. By linking his poems in a variety of ways, often teasing and challenging his reader, Herbert expands the limits of the lyric form, setting the entire collection up to do what no one lyric possibly could: to dramatize and analyze the various moods and rhythms of a faithful believer.

POETIC STRUCTURE

Herbert's structural skill is evident not only in the overall plan and order of *The Temple* but also in the individual poems. His playful sense of poetic structure, though, has often been misunderstood and held against him. Such obviously patterned poems as "The Altar" and "Easter-wings," both of which are typographically shaped to resemble the objects named in the title, often strike some readers as quaint at best. Eighteenth century critics, for example, viewed these poems rather condescendingly as typical of Herbert and did not hesitate to consider him as a "false wit," incapable of more noble and creative effects.

Looked at more sympathetically, though, "The Altar" and "Easter-wings" are typical of Herbert only in suggesting how important poetic form is for him. Besides being a statement and a dramatization, a poem by Herbert is also an artifact, whose structure, sometimes simply, at other times subtly, reinforces a particular theme. At one end of the scale, there are directly imitative poems such as "Paradise," a poem about pruning in which the rhyme words are, in fact, pruned; "Heaven," in which the last word of the speaker's questions echoes in a following line as an answer; and "Trinitie Sunday," composed of a trinity of three-line stanzas. Other poems show more subdued but nevertheless effective pictorial designs: The shape of the stanzas in "The Agonie" suggests the image of the winepress mentioned in the poem, which calls to mind the association between Christ's sacrificial blood and sacramental wine; and each stanza in "The Bag" seems to contain an open space, literally like the bag mentioned in the poem used to take messages from humans straight to God.

Such directly imitative devices help to prepare the reader for Herbert's far more challenging uses of poetic form in other places in *The Temple*. The structure of "Church-monuments," for example, is meant not so much to imitate a gravestone, as the title seems to suggest, as to help the reader imagine the decay described in the poem that will sooner or later overcome gravestones, bodies, and the entire physical world. Because the lines are only occasionally end-stopped, the rhythm becomes somewhat unsettling, even ominous, and since the word "dust" is repeated again and again, the entire poem momentarily becomes like the hourglass mentioned in the last few lines, "which holds the dust/ That measures all our time; which also shall/ Be crumbled into dust."

Similarly, the theme and mood of the speaker in "The Collar" are powerfully and immediately conveyed by its structure: The poem is apparently unshaped, with irregularly alternating lines of different length to suggest the disordered mind of a man who has lost all control. By the concluding lines, though, the structure of the poem communicates the achievement of order. As the speaker exhausts himself to a moment of calmness, "normal" poetic form also surfaces in the relatively stable *abab* rhyme scheme of the last four lines: "But as I rav'd and grew more fierce and wilde/ At every word,/ Me thoughts I heard one calling, *Child!/* And I reply'd, *My Lord.*" Because he so often shapes his poems to have a visual impact, Herbert is compared with the emblem writers of his time, whose verses were either appended to illustrative plates or were at least meant to call to mind and interpret such illustrations. Such poems as "Church-monuments" and "The Collar," however, show that one of Herbert's particular skills is an ability to use the structure of his poems to imitate not only objects and static scenes but also dramatic processes.

LANGUAGE

Herbert's attention to structure is matched by his loving care for the language of his poems. Especially when compared with other works of his period, *The Temple* seems remarkably simple and direct, with little of the straining against meaning that characterizes so many of William Shakespeare's sonnets, and with hardly any of Donne's self-conscious roughness and almost inconsiderate obscurity.

As many critics have noted, though, Herbert's simplicity marks the triumph, not the abandonment, of art. The language of *The Temple* is that of the Bible (especially in the King James or Authorized Version, published in 1611) and the Book of Common Prayer: austere but resonant and multileveled. Herbert's delight in language reflects not only the deep influence of God's words, the Holy Scriptures, but also his awareness that human words, returned to God in prayer, praise, song, and poetry, are at least an acceptable celebration of God's Word made flesh in Christ.

Throughout "The Church," Herbert struggles with the dilemma that humans in poetry, as in all things, can give to God only what God has already given them; but though this undermines any pretense of human self-sufficiency, it is an arrangement in which Herbert ultimately finds a great deal of comfort. The heartfelt simplicity of the three poems titled "Praise" and the two titled "Antiphon," among many others in "The Church," signifies not only a poetic choice but also an acceptance of humanity's subservient place in God's world.

At the same time, however, Herbert's humility allows him to exploit the richness of the English language. Modern readers who consider puns to be at best a low form of wit need to be reminded that Herbert, like most other seventeenth century poets, used puns and wordplay not only for comic effects but also for much more serious purposes: to indicate deep correspondences between various things in the world, between language and reality and between different levels of experience.

In "The Sonne," Herbert confesses "I like our language well," in part because it lends itself so easily to one especially significant pun: The reader is led quickly through the multiple meanings of the title word, from "son" to "sun," and finally to Christ, who combines these meanings as Son of Man, Son of God, and the guiding and warming light of Christians: their sun. There may well be even another concealed pun here; "The Sonne" is written in the form of a sonnet. The title "The Holdfast" is also a pun that takes the reader into the central conflict of the poem: A "holdfast" is something one can cling securely to, in this case God; in addition, "holdfast" is a term for a stingy, self-reliant man, such as the speaker of the poem, who must first relax his hold on himself before he can truly understand "That all things were more ours by being his," that is, Christ's.

Though it is sometimes difficult to determine where Herbert's wordplay leaves off and the reader's invention begins, the title "The Collar" sets off a series of associations that are relevant to the lines that follow: The collar is perhaps first and foremost the Christian's yoke of discipline and obedience from which the speaker flees; this word also suggests "choler," the anger and distress of the speaker as he raves on and on; finally, by a slight adjustment it also sounds like the "caller," alluding not only to the situation of the speaker calling out in anguish but also to the infinitely patient God who calls even his unruly servant "Child."

Herbert occasionally uses puns and wordplay to construct a puzzle, the explanation of which points the reader toward a comforting observation. In "Jesu," for example, the title word is "deeply carved" in the speaker's heart. When his heart is broken by "A great affliction," the letters become scattered, but even so they spell out an important message: the fragments *J* (often printed as *I* in the seventeenth century), *ES*, and *U* form the statement "I ease you," a welcome affirmation of the power of Christ. Not all Herbert's poems are puzzles, but his constant reliance on puns keeps his otherwise short and compact lyrics from one-dimensional simplicity. Even the smallest details in a poem are liable to expand into several important meanings. In "Christmas," for example, when he describes the "glorious, yet contracted light" of the Christ child, he not only marvels at how the greatness of God has taken the diminutive form of a baby, but also celebrates the fact that humanity is bound, by legal contract or covenant, to God.

When Herbert questions, in the ominously titled poem "Discipline," "Who can scape his bow?" the various interpretations of the last word provide comforting associations. Besides being a weapon of war and traditional instrument of justice and wrath, the "bow" also calls to mind Cupid's bow and arrow, which are instruments of love; the rainbow, the sign after the Flood that God will change his ways of wrath; the bowlike cross, a common comparison found in many biblical commentators; and Christ's "bowing," taking human form to save humankind. Throughout *The Temple*, Herbert carefully avoids the two most common dangers of the pun—he is rarely ostentatious or ridiculous—and as a result his wordplay almost always adds a great deal of allusiveness and depth to his poems.

"THE CHURCH"

What makes Herbert an enduring poet is not simply his structural and stylistic expertise but also the application of these technical skills to themes of great importance. The general subject of *The Temple* is, in Herbert's own words as reported by Izaak Walton, his seventeenth century biographer, "the many spiritual Conflicts that have passed betwixt God and my Soul." Knowing this, it should be no surprise to see that the poems in "The Church" are constantly dramatic, most often revolving around a dual focus: humanity's inevitable sins and misunderstandings, and the processes through which humanity is comforted, instructed, and corrected.

Before telling humanity's tale, however, Herbert places human life within the frame of one larger event, the Crucifixion. Christ's drama must be told first, and, accordingly, the poem on "The Sacrifice" is placed near the beginning of "The Church." Although this poem is in many respects unusual for Herbert—it is very long, and uses Christ not only as the subject but also as the speaker—its pattern recurs in many other places: Unlike such poets as Donne and Crashaw, who often try to sustain a high dramatic pitch for an entire poem, Herbert, here and elsewhere, normally works with quick, unexpected, striking dramatic moments. "The Sacrifice" has a startling immediacy as Christ narrates the humiliating events of his crucifixion, and yet the reader also senses a curiously triumphant detachment. Even though Christ's repeated refrain is "Was ever grief like mine?" his voice is calm and ironic as he lists in obsessive detail the incongruities of his situation, the Son of God tortured by the people he offers to serve and save. After more than two hundred lines showing Christ's rather impassive power, Herbert breaks his carefully established format: Christ suddenly cries out in anguish *My God, my God—,* a broken, unfinished line that the reader presumably completes by adding, "why has thou forsaken me?" The refrain then changes in this stanza to the simple statement, "Never was grief like mine." Because of this sudden breakdown, the reader is drawn more surely into a fuller understanding of the sacrifice: Christ is not only serene and all-powerful but also, at least for one moment, vulnerable, human. Once "The Sacrifice" establishes to what extent Christ, despite his torment, is humanity's benefactor, the reader can realize more fully that the "spiritual Conflicts" in Herbert's poems are not truly between humanity and God but between humans and themselves.

Throughout "The Church," the focus is on the many ways that people find to resist God. Like Donne, Herbert is convinced of humans' basic and inescapable sinfulness, and some of his poems, like Donne's Holy Sonnets, explore arrogant intellectual pride ("Vanitie" [I] and [II]), disobedience ("Affliction" [I], "The Collar"), and the general blackness of the human soul ("Sinne" [I] and [II]). Beyond these themes, however, and in a manner that distinguishes him from Donne, Herbert is primarily interested in dramatizing far more intricate modes of self-deception and far less obvious subtleties of pride. The speaker in "The Thanksgiving," for example, seems genuinely moved by his meditation on Christ, and his exuberant plant to dedicate his life to charitable works probably strikes every reader as praiseworthy. In a turn that is characteristic of Herbert, however, the last two lines suddenly undermine all that has come before. At the height of his confident offering to Christ, the speaker stumbles: "Then for thy passion—I will do for that—/ Alas, my God, I know not what." Herbert is by no means ridiculing the speaker or banishing exuberance and charity from the devotional life, but he dramatizes very effectively how evasive one can be even when trying to dedicate oneself to following Christ's example.

A similar reversal occurs in "Miserie." Here the speaker clearly abhors sin and spends most of his time criticizing humanity's foolishness in choosing a filthy life of "strange pollutions" over the moral purity that might have been within reach. The accusations are extreme but compelling, and it takes little arguing to convince the reader that humanity is "A lump of flesh, without a foot or wing/ To raise him to a glimpse of blisse:/ A sick toss'd vessel, dashing on each thing." The last line, however, changes the focus of the poem entirely: After seventy-seven lines describing the "strange wayes" around him, the speaker suddenly realizes that "My God, I mean my self." In this way, Her-

bert shows that abhorrence of sin, while perhaps admirable, may be a mode of pride unless one includes oneself in the indictment.

"The Thanksgiving" and "Miserie" are also good examples of how Herbert typically includes the reader in his dramatic revelations and reversals. Although it might be overstating the case to say that Herbert traps his readers, many assent to and often identify with his speakers from the start of a poem. Because they accept their premises—the statements in both "The Thanksgiving" and "Miserie" seem plausible, if not praiseworthy, until the very end—they also share in their fall. The self-deception and pride of the speakers in many of Herbert's lyrics are thus, in a certain sense, duplicated in the reader, and as the speakers are dramatized, explored, and corrected, so is the reader.

LYRICS OF COMFORT

Throughout *The Temple*, Herbert's subject is not merely the correction of humanity's numerous flaws: Equally dramatic are the lyrics of recovery and comfort where the speaker overcomes not pride but feelings of unworthiness, uselessness, and weakness. For all his moments of self-scrutiny and criticism, Herbert is a remarkably gentle poet, and he knows when to remind his readers how securely he feels that they are ground in God's mercy. Without God, he explains, human beings are nothing—a premise that many modern readers find extremely discouraging—but he goes on to add that human beings need not be without God. For Herbert, humans are constantly cheered and renewed by God's presence: In "Aaron," feelings of worry about being a priest give way to calm confidence as soon as one sees that Christ "is not dead,/ But lives in me while I do rest"; in "The Flower," sadness about the fragility of life and poetry turns into a heightened sense of joy and beauty, truly "thy wonders"; and in "The Elixir," all human effort, as long as it is done "for thy sake," becomes "drudgerie divine," pleasant and ennobling.

"LOVE"

God's voice and presence appear throughout the volume, but nowhere so movingly as in the last poem of "The Church," "Love" (III). Here God and man meet face to face, and though a lesser poet might not have been able to withstand the temptation to overembellish the scene, Herbert's dramatic lyric is as understated as it is powerful. God is love, "quick-ey'd Love," whose every word and movement is meant to comfort an extremely shy human guest who is humbly aware that he is "Guiltie of dust and sinne." Humanity's unworthiness, however, is finally beside the point: Stated in its simplest possible terms, God knows, forgives, accepts, and redeems humanity.

Simple words of paraphrase, however, can never tell the whole story. "Love" (III) is not a statement but an enactment, not a bit of theological argument or explanation but a dramatization of a devotional gesture. From the beginning of "The Church," as he notes at the conclusion of "The Reprisall," one of Herbert's main tasks is to show how "In thee [Christ] I will overcome/ The man, who once against thee fought." The particular action and quiet tone of the last lines of "Love" (III)— "You must sit down, sayes Love, and taste my meat:/ So I did sit and eat"—confirm that the battle, against God and against himself, is over, celebrated by a meal that is simultaneously a lover's banquet, a communion service, and his first true taste of heavenly joy.

OTHER MAJOR WORKS

NONFICTION: *A Treatise of Temperance and Sobrietie of Luigi Cornaro*, 1634 (translation); *Outlandish Proverbs Selected by Mr. G. H.*, 1640 (also known as *Jacula Prudentum*, 1651); *A Priest to the Temple: Or, The Country Parson His Character and Rule of Holy Life*, 1652 (wr. 1632; also known as *The Country Parson*).

MISCELLANEOUS: *The Works of George Herbert*, 1941, 1945 (F. E. Hutchinson, editor).

BIBLIOGRAPHY

Blythe, Ronald. *George Herbert in Bemerton*. Salisbury, England: Hobnob Press, 2005. This biography of Herbert examines his later years, which were spent in Bemerton.

Clarke, Elizabeth. *Theory and Theology in George Herbert's Poetry: Divinitie, and Poesie, Met*. Oxford, England: Clarendon Press, 1997. Explores the relationship between Herbert's poetry and the notion of divine inspiration rooted in devotional texts of his time. Includes bibliographical references and indexes.

Cruickshank, Frances. *Verse and Poetics in George Herbert and John Donne*. Burlington, Vt.: Ashgate, 2010. This study of Herbert's poetry compares it with that of Donne and pays extra attention to the techniques used.

Hodgkins, Christopher. *Authority, Church, and Society in George Herbert: Return to the Middle Way*. Columbia: University of Missouri Press, 1993. A critical analysis in which Hodgkins demonstrates that Herbert's poetry is predominantly nostalgia for old English social, political, and religious customs. Identifies the changes in his poetry as reflections of the changing times.

_____, ed. *George Herbert's Pastoral: New Essays on the Poet and Priest of Bemerton*. Newark: University of Delaware Press, 2010. This collection of essays present critical analysis of Herbert's work, particularly his pastoral poems.

Malcolmson, Cristina. *George Herbert: A Literary Life*. New York: Palgrave Macmillan, 2003. A reconsideration of Herbert, his poetry and his politics. This insightful biography sheds new light on the poet's intentions and his contemporary audience.

Miller, Greg. *George Herbert's "Holy Patterns": Reforming Individuals in Community*. New York: Continuum, 2007. Examines Herbert's religious beliefs as they influenced his poetry and how Herbert's verse can be seen as moving people toward faith.

Stewart, Stanley. *George Herbert*. Boston: Twayne, 1986. In this brief study, Stewart surveys Herbert's life and writings in both poetry and prose and counters emphasis on Herbert's Protestantism by emphasizing his close connection with medieval Catholicism and High Anglican devotion. He concludes with a fine chapter on Herbert's influence on other seventeenth century poets and a helpful annotated list of key critical works on Herbert.

Strier, Richard. *Love Known: Theology and Experience in George Herbert's Poetry*. Chicago: University of Chicago Press, 1983. Offers penetrating critical readings of many of the key poems of *The Temple*, examining in particular how they confirm Herbert's deep debt to Protestant theology, especially that of Martin Luther. For Strier, Herbert's poems focus repeatedly on the unreliability of reason and the drama of human unworthiness rendered inconsequential by divine love.

Vendler, Helen. *Invisible Listeners: Lyric Intimacy in Herbert, Whitman, and Ashbery*. Princeton, N.J.: Princeton University Press, 2007. Vendler, who focuses on close readings that stress poetic and emotional complexity, compares and contrasts the writings of Herbert, Walt Whitman, and John Ashbery.

Sidney Gottlieb

ROBERT HERRICK

Born: London, England; August 24, 1591 (baptized)
Died: Dean Prior, Devonshire, England; October, 1674

PRINCIPAL POETRY

Hesperides: Or, The Works Both Humane and Divine of Robert Herrick, Esq., 1648 (includes *Noble Numbers*)
The Complete Poetry of Robert Herrick, 1963

OTHER LITERARY FORMS

The vast majority of the poetic works of Robert Herrick (HEHR-ihk) are included among the approximately fourteen hundred pieces contained in *Hesperides*, Herrick's only known published book of verse. There are about forty poems from contemporary manuscripts and poetic miscellanies that have at various times been attributed to Herrick, but their authorship is not certain and has been the subject of much editorial speculation.

Herrick is known exclusively for his poems. All that survives of his writing apart from his poetry are some fifteen letters he wrote when he was a student at Cambridge University (1613-1620) and a few pieces of official correspondence. The only other piece of writing with which he has been linked is a manuscript of poems and prose of topical interest, part of which has been said to be in his handwriting; his role in its authorship and compilation, however, is not yet firmly established.

ACHIEVEMENTS

In the more than three and a half centuries during which Robert Herrick's poems have circulated, his reputation has fluctuated widely. The earliest reference to him places him as a young poet in the company of the much esteemed Ben Jonson and Michael Drayton. One of his editors, J. Max Patrick, argued in *The Complete Poetry of Robert Herrick* (2d ed., 1968) that there is evidence to believe that Herrick was sufficiently well regarded in certain circles to warrant a relatively copious first printing of his collected works in 1648. What does not seem in doubt, however, is the oblivion into which his poems appear to have fallen within fifty years of their publication. References to Herrick are scant in the eighteenth century, and it was only in 1796 that an inquiry about him in a literary magazine began to stimulate the interest that would lead to his poetic exhumation. In 1810, an edition of about three hundred of his poems restored Herrick to public attention, providing a preview of the public response that his work would generate throughout much of the nineteenth century. Herrick came to be read and extolled for his numerous delicate and euphonious lyrics, while his satiric and "gross" epigrams proved offensive to Victorian sensibilities and went largely unpublished.

Modern critics have attempted to assess Herrick's achievements in a more balanced and integrated way; if they have generally been less rhapsodic over the "prettiness" and "sweetness" of his lyrics than the Victorians, they have also paid closer attention to the technical virtuosity and poetic acumen at work in the numerous forms and modes that *Hesperides* exhibits. In the modern "rediscovery" of the excellences of seventeenth century poetry, Herrick has fared well, ranking with John Donne, George Herbert, Andrew Marvell, and John Milton, as among the most widely read poets of the period; his "To the Virgins, to Make Much of Time," "Corinna's Going A-Maying," and "Delight in Disorder" are among the most often anthologized seventeenth century poems. At the same time, comparisons with his prominent poetic contemporaries—although occasionally invidious—have not only confirmed Herrick's stature but also helped to define the nature of his poetic achievement and appeal. To be sure, Herrick's poems do not have the dramatic intensity and immediacy of Donne's, and his one published volume may appear to lack the polyphonic self-scrutiny and structural rigor at work in Herbert's *The Temple* (1633). Still, from the concerns and images that recur throughout the *Hesperides*, there emerges a sense of a unifying poetic sensibility molding and transforming the disparate materials of the real world to reflect a coherent aesthetic vision. This vision is of sufficient strength and lucidity to suggest precisely what T. S. Eliot once claimed that Herrick's verse lacked: the "continuous, conscious *purpose*" characteristic of all major poets. Moreover, in his intermingling of ostensibly sensuous and erotic poetic experiences with religious, elegiac verse and political poems on the English Civil War, Herrick is increasingly coming to be seen not as a poetic trifler of exquisite sensibilities and superficial concerns but as a man very much of his war-torn, "troublesome" times. His "book" forms a significant poetic testament to a critical period in the evolution of English society and poetic art.

BIOGRAPHY

What is actually known and documented of Robert Herrick's life forms a rather skeletal outline and can be readily summarized. Christened in London on August 24, 1591, Herrick appears to have been the seventh child of Nicholas and Julian Herrick. Nicholas, a goldsmith, fell to his death from an upper story of his house on Goldsmith's Row on November 9, 1592, just two days after he had recorded his will. Obvious questions were raised concerning the possibility that Herrick's father had committed suicide, and they appear never to have been resolved. The nature of Herrick's boyhood education is not known, but in 1607, he was apprenticed for ten years to his uncle, Sir William Herrick, a wealthy goldsmith and merchant. The venture, however, was aborted, when, in 1613, at the relatively old age of twenty-two, Herrick was enrolled with his uncle's consent in St. John's College, Cambridge. It was during his years at Cambridge that Herrick wrote a series of letters to his uncle, all of which are variations on the timeless theme rehearsed by innumerable students: Send more money. Herrick received his A.B. degree in 1617, his A.M. in 1620, and in 1623, he was ordained an Anglican priest, serving in 1625 as chaplain in the

Robert Herrick (Hulton Archive/Getty Images)

duke of Buckingham's abortive military expedition to the Isle of Rhe. In 1630, Herrick left London and its cultural life to assume the vicarage of Dean Prior in rustic Devon, a position he held until 1647, when, because of his loyalties to the king and the Church of England, he was expelled, an event that was the catalyst for his return to London and the publication of his works in the following year. Nothing else is known of him until the restoration of the monarchy in 1660, when he successfully petitioned the Crown to be reinstated as vicar of Dean Prior, where, with no evidence of strife, he resided until his death in 1674 at the age of eighty-two.

That the documentary detail of Herrick's life is so easily reducible to a thumbnail sketch has made the task of relating Herrick's biography to his writings a difficult one. Indeed, early commentators tended, understandably, to approach Herrick's poems as if they were authorized and unexpurgated autobiography, attempting to fill in the gaps in what was known of his life from the evidence of his works. Such a modus operandi runs the obvious risk of confusing the poetic persona that

Herrick creates in his verse with the person whom the persona masks, ultimately doing little to elucidate either the works or his life. Here is one example of this kind of mythobiography: In his poetry, Herrick projects himself as a discriminating analyst of feminine charms addressing a great number of meditations on beauty to personages such as Corinna, Perilla, Julia, and Dianeme. This projection, however, does not in itself suggest that Herrick necessarily led the life of a libertine during his years in London or that indeed Corinna, Perilla, Julia, and Dianeme ever existed. In addition, there is no evidence to suggest that Herrick wrote such poems to while away the idle moments he supposedly endured after leaving the high life of London for the rustic seclusion of Dean Prior.

Still, invalid as it may be to take Herrick's poetry as the true mirror of his life, one can see, even from the sketchy biographical information available, how he wove the richly textured tapestry of his verse from the diverse strands of his background. His poems bespeak the deep immersion in the classics that he would have experienced at Cambridge, along with a full acquaintance with the poetic conventions current in the poetic circles of London in the 1620's. At the same time, his verses are steeped both in the biblical learning that any moderately educated person at the time would have imbibed and in the tenets of Anglican doctrine with which an Anglican cleric—especially one eager to demonstrate his steadfast affiliation with the Church of England—would have been conversant.

More important, Herrick draws upon the various elements of his life to create a complex and engaging poetic persona. The Herrick one meets in the poems is a character who bestrides different and potentially opposed worlds, seeking to reconcile them in the alembic of his verse. Classicist and divine, he pretends to be not merely the priest of both Apollo and the Christian God but also their poetic priest who aspires to serve the interests of both with one poetic vision and one poetic vocabulary—"Part Pagan," as he puts it in "The Fairie Temple: Or, Oberons Chappell," and "part Papisticall." Poetic priest of Bacchus and Eros as well, Herrick celebrates sensual experience for its physical value and for its intimations of a higher truth. Portraying himself as a votary of urban delights, Herrick asserts his contempt

for the unrefined elements of country life but labors to articulate the ways in which country customs—like urban refinements—have their part to play in his poetic universe.

Above all, Herrick's poetic persona would have his readers believe that his life is embodied in his volume of verses, that his "book" is all that he has been and all that he hopes, in the face of encroaching mortality, "Times trans-shifting," to be. In that fictive sense, his works are, indeed, "autobiography." In fact, though the literary record of the turbulent mid-seventeenth century is far from closed, there is no more eloquent testimony to the degree to which Herrick appears to have made his "book" his "Pillar" than the total literary silence into which he seems to have fallen after the publication of his verse, and in which the final twenty-five years of his life are enveloped. Vexing as this silence has been to critics and biographers trying to learn more about the man, it has had the effect of underscoring the point of one of Herrick's epigrams: "Seldome comes Glorie till a man be dead."

ANALYSIS

Robert Herrick is a poet of numerous modes and moods, whose poetic pleasure it appears to have been to present his readers with a world of abundance and variety. One need look no further than the opening poem in *Hesperides*, "The Argument of His Book," to get a sense not only of the dimensions of this plenitude but also of the underlying concerns that give Herrick's world its coherence, as well as of the style in which his poetic vision is mediated.

"THE ARGUMENT OF HIS BOOK"

Ostensibly, "The Argument of His Book" is a mere inventory, a poetic table of contents to the diverse "topics" treated in the hundreds of poems to follow, from the simple things of nature, "Brooks, Blossomes, Birds, and Bowers," to the grand themes of divinity, heaven, and hell. In its construction, the poem bespeaks simplicity, with the various categories to be treated in Herrick's ensuing poems neatly itemized in a series of seven rhymed, end-stopped couplets, each beginning with the unpretentious declaration "I say" or "I write." The incantatory power that builds with the sonorous reiteration and skillful alternation of "I sing" and "I write" gives aural hints of an art that merely counterfeits artlessness and transforms a "simple" and potentially monotonous list into something like a litany, a ritualized—some have said liturgical—chant. As a result, the overtly commonplace and profane subjects, the things of nature, the country customs, the affairs of youth and the heart, acquire a heightened significance and a semblance of parity with the explicitly spiritual themes. The things of this world and those of the next, "The Argument of His Book" would suggest, do not entail essentially opposed visions of experience but, when apprehended with the heightening power of art, are revealed to be complementary constituents of one coherent universe. In "The Argument of His Book," Herrick brings together the contrarieties of existence but does so to reveal their intrinsic harmony and point to their ultimate reconciliation.

What art heightens, it changes; and so "metamorphosis," both as theme and as the image of art's heightening power, is central to "The Argument of His Book" and remains so throughout Herrick's verse. Thus, the "Blossoms" to which Herrick alludes in the opening lines of "The Argument of His Book" are of interest not only as flowers but also as emblems of a continuous process of mythopoeic creation and transformation, as parts of the story of "How Roses first came Red, and Lillies White." In this way, nature heightened by art becomes art. The liquids of nature, the "Dewes" and "Raines," are fused and merged within the closure of one of Herrick's couplets with liquids refined by art "piece by piece" into cosmetic artifacts: "Balme," "Oyle," "Spice," and "Amber-Greece." In the sensual delights "of Youth, of Love," the poet finds the "access" to sing, not of sensuality or wantonness, but rather, in the phrase that has come to be synonymous with Herrick's personal signature, "cleanly-Wantonnesse."

What is "cleanly-Wantonnesse"? At once a figure of oxymoron, or paradox, and pleonasm, it is nothing less than the seminal conceit of Herrick's verse. On one hand, it evokes a wantonness in all its pejorative senses of lasciviousness, unruliness, and extravagance rendered "cleanly," chaste, and orderly; on the other hand, it suggests a "wantonnesse" in the less opprobrious sense of innocent playfulness that by its very definition

must be "cleanly." In the very "play" of the conceit, Herrick suggests the way in which nature unrefined and base can be redeemed and shown to be "cleanly" by the power of poetic language.

"Cleanly-Wantonnesse," however, denotes not only nature heightened by art but also nature preserved by art from the destructive forces to which it is subject: time, decay, and dissolution. For all their sensuous appeal and connotations of fecundity, the "Dewes" and "Raines" that Herrick includes in his poetic repertoire are also conventional metonyms of transience and mourning and anticipate the presence in his verse of a strong elegiac impulse. Indeed, in Herrick's poetic world, of which "The Argument of His Book" is an epitome, the metamorphosis of art and the mutability of nature are inseparably linked, the former arising from and responding to the latter, even as the stories of "How Roses first came Red, and Lillies White" are immediately preceded in the same couplet by the theme of "Times trans-shifting." As natural phenomena, the sensual delights "of Youth, of Love" are as ephemeral as blossoms; yet the "cleanly-Wantonnesse" that Herrick envisions in these experiences is proof against mortality and, in the world of his verse, as enduring as the "Heaven" that Herrick hopes to have, "after all."

"THE AMBER BEAD"

The images and issues introduced in "The Argument of His Book" recur in much of Herrick's verse and are particularly conspicuous in the works for which he is best remembered. One thinks immediately, for example, of "The Amber Bead," Herrick's delicately terse four-stanza, four-line adaptation of one of Martial's epigrams. Its very size a reflection of the theme it articulates, "The Amber Bead" affirms the victory of art over the corruptive processes of nature. By being "cleanly" encased within a bead of amber, a common fly acquires a permanence and significance in death that it could never have attained in life. In turn, the congealed amber becomes a medium of art that derives its function from the heightening it imparts to a thing of nature. Within the metamorphosis of the poem, the bead becomes a chamber, and, as if to accentuate the triumph of art over decay, the poet notes in the closing distich that though as "Urne," as an emblem of death, the bead may be "little," as "room," a place more often associated with living things, it is "More rich than Cleopatra's Tombe."

THE JULIA POEMS

The dialectic encapsulated in "The Amber Bead" is explored in varying tonalities and degrees of resolution over a wide range of Herrick's poems and is evident even in the many ostensibly frolicsome compliments that Herrick pays to his poetic mistresses, chief among whom is Julia. Most of these unfold as celebrations of some particular part or aspect of the lady's person: "Julia's Clothes," "Julia's Ribbon," "Julia's Breath," "The Candor of Julia's Teeth," to name a few. All are exercises in synecdoche and in extolling the part they celebrate the personage the part adorns. Each, in turn, is a piece of hyperbole, investing the item in question with miraculous properties, the reader is led to believe, simply because the item is an extension of Julia. Heightened in the process, then, are Julia herself and all that belongs to her, and nature as well, which is at once surpassed and enriched by Julia's very presence.

Were all these poems on Julia straightforward variations on this formula, they would not have engendered and sustained the interest they have. Instead, they are exercises in discovery, and by indirection and implication lead the reader to infer what is never explicitly stated. Consider, for example, the distich on Julia titled "Another upon her weeping." At a glance the poem would appear to belabor the obvious and in none too artful a manner. Told merely that Julia "by the River sate; and sitting there,/ She wept, and made it deeper by a teare," the reader wonders why it need be said twice in one line that Julia was sitting by the river and may ask why, if the consequence of Julia's weeping is merely the addition of one tear to the river, the poem needed to be written at all. It is only when one considers the secondary sense of "deeper" that the experience of the poem and the game of the poet become clearer. The dropping of a tear has made the river not merely physically deeper but also metaphysically deeper, more significant. The poet does not know, or, at least, does not say how this change has been accomplished; it is a mystery, and mysteries, as supernatural phenomena, are not to be solved but contemplated as manifestations of a higher power. Hence the deliberation with which the poet twice mentions where Julia was sitting: By pro-

tracting the line, he prolongs the experience and calls attention to the nub of the mystery, that Julia's mere presence enhances the value of the river. The poet has stated nothing of the kind; indeed, he could insist slyly that he was only describing a physical occurrence. Rather, it is Herrick's art here, as elsewhere, to immerse his reader in the process of discovery and permit the reader to recognize firsthand the power of poetic art to transform the commonplace into something extraordinary and imperishable.

"JULIA'S PETTICOAT"

Herrick's success in implicating the reader in the experience and interpretation of a poem is very much in evidence in another work involving Julia, the longer and more prominent "Julia's Petticoat." An apt illustration of "cleanly-Wantonnesse," the poem makes it clear that "cleanliness" and "wantonnesse" are in the eye of the beholder, both the poet who observes and describes the movements of Julia's gown and the reader who observes the poet and participates vicariously in the poet's experience.

From the very outset, however, it would appear that the experience in which the reader is invited to participate vicariously is itself vicarious and rather disingenuous. Unlike "Another upon her weeping," this piece is explicitly addressed to Julia, and by exploiting the rhetorical figure of synecdoche, the poet can hide, as it were, behind Julia's petticoat and pay her compliments without being so bold as to address them to the person herself. In this way, the interests of both parties are served: Julia can be flattered without blushing or having her modesty impugned, and the poet has license to fantasize as sensually as he pleases while feigning detachment.

The poem opens with the poet making an effort in good faith to keep his mind on "cleanly" things. Julia's garment is not merely any common blue petticoat, but an "Azure," therefore, heavenly blue, "Robe." Lest anyone suspect that the poet is paying more attention to Julia herself than to the gown she is wearing, he describes the notion of the garment as "ayrie," as if to suggest that it is animated either by its own power or by some force independent of Julia. However, the poet's efforts to maintain a distinction between the movements of the petticoat and the movements of its wearer seem less and less successful, and the more "wanton," the more playful and unruly the motions of the skirts, the more "wanton," the more lasciviously suggestive grows the language of the poet. In the space of only two lines, the poet applies the words "erring," "wandring," and "transgression" to the undulations of the gown, all words associated with moral levity and sufficiently synonymous to suggest that the poet may find their suggestions delectable enough to linger over them and turn them over in his mind. Moreover, the animation of the skirts becomes more and more like personification, as the gown is said to "pant, and sigh, and heave," with obvious sensual connotations.

Still, who is finding titillation in the petticoat, the poet or the reader? After all, the poet could claim that those questionable words "erring," "wandring," and "transgression" are in their root meanings simply words of motion and direction and can be taken to imply moral lapse only by those susceptible sorts who would read such meaning into them. As for the poet, the more sensually and erotically suggestive the gyrations of Julia's petticoat grow, the more energetic he becomes in finding images for the experience that transcend the physical and carnal. Thus, when at one point the gold-spangled gown moves with especial freedom and makes "a brave expansion," the poet likens it to a "*Celestiall* Canopie," leaving it to the more corrupted mind of his reader to ponder the perspective from which the unfurling of a canopy is normally viewed.

In fact, the poet would lead the reader to view the experience with dual vision, if the reader has the imagination to transcend his own "wantonnesse." On one hand, the poet lets the reader take in every sensual nuance the scene evokes; on the other, he asks the reader to celebrate the poetic vision that has brought the petticoat so suggestively to life. This is evident in what could be called, in more than one sense of the word, the climax of the poem, when the petticoat swirls so "wildly" that it clings to Julia's "thighs," thus forcing the poet to acknowledge for the first time the body beneath the garment that he has pretended to ignore all along. The poet responds very much as other poetic voyeurs of the period do, by being melted down, "As Lovers fall into a swoone." Here, though, the word "as" and the simile it introduces are significant. For ulti-

mately, though the poet may be "like" a lover and feel "as" a lover might, he is not a lover. Unlike his poetic contemporaries, though he may lie "Drown'd in Delights," he could not "die," in the Renaissance sense of attaining sexual consummation. Nor was it sensual rapture that melted the poet down, but a "conceit," an idea, a fancy, a "conceitedness."

In short, what Herrick celebrates in "Julia's Petticoat," more than the petticoat itself, more than Julia herself, is the poetic apprehension, the "conceit," that makes the petticoat so seductive. Nor is this to suggest that the physical experience in the poem has been nullified or minimized. Rather, the poet insists, the physical experience has been perfected because as aesthetic vision it will always yield pleasure and never be consumed. Such is the sense conveyed in the poet's closing declaration that were the vision of Julia's petticoat to move, like the cloud guiding the Israelites in the desert, to "Life Eternal," he could still love. He could love because his sensual experience has been refined and made imperishable by art, and will endure long after Julia and her petticoat have ceased to move so enchantingly.

"DELIGHT IN DISORDER"

The ascendancy of art over nature, the making "cleanly" by art of what is "wanton" in nature, is virtually formalized as an aesthetic principle in what is probably Herrick's most familiar poem, "Delight in Disorder." Another of Herrick's meditations on feminine attire, the poem owes much to the song, "Still to be neat, still to be dress'd," from Jonson's *Epicœne: Or, The Silent Woman* (pr. 1609); even so, in the particular terms and style in which it delineates the relationship of art and nature, "Delight in Disorder" is distinctly Herrick's poetic credo and a centerpiece of his verse.

On the face of it, the poem would appear to illustrate without qualification what its title professes: delight in disorder, preference for the unruliness of nature unregulated and unrestrained by art. Assuming the part of voyeur he had played in "Julia's Petticoat," the poet takes obvious delight in enumerating the various possibilities of "disorderliness" in a lady's attire, in envisioning a ribbon out of place, a cuff undone, a shoelace only loosely knotted. Moreover, the language in which these traces of untidiness are couched is of that suggestive sort that either reveals in the poet or elicits from the reader questions prompted by decidedly libertine impulses. These deviations from order and art are seductive, and when the poet concludes that they "bewitch" him more than when art is "too precise in every part," it would seem that for once Herrick permits the claims of nature to hold sway. A closer look at the texture and language of the poem, however, suggests that the poet himself is being quite precise when he objects not to art but to an art that is "too precise," too rigid, too artificial, too obviously artful, and that the "disorder" so esteemed in the poem is but a sensuously alluring illusion kept under firm control by a poetic art "neatly" disguised.

A hint of this control lies in the care with which the poet casts the experience in the form of a tightly structured argument, inscribed within one fourteen-line rhymed couplet sentence. Its central premise is stated in the opening couplet and illustrated by a series of five examples presented in the next five couplets, followed by a summation in the final two lines. Each example of disarray is introduced as if it were one more item on a checklist: "A Lawne," "An erring Face," "A Caffe neglectfull," "A winning move" in the "tempestuous" petticoat, "A careless shoe-string." The orderliness with which these items are listed seems modified by the sensuous turbulence that they arouse in the poet, but the more one perceives the excitation these examples produce, the more one is compelled to acknowledge the logical validity of the poet's main point and the rhetorical artistry with which he has presented it: Disorder, at least when packaged this way, is, indeed, delightful.

The last qualification is crucial. It is not just any kind of "disorder" that pleases, but a certain kind, a "sweet disorder," even as the "distraction" produced when the lady's "Lawne" is thrown errantly about her shoulders is a "fine distraction." Such phrases as "cleanly-Wantonnesse" and, for that matter, the title of the poem, are rhetorical figures, oxymora, coupled antitheses, suggesting that what pleases the poet most about the carelessness he describes is the reconciliation it embodies of the abandon of nature and the purposefulness and girding control of art.

This "girding" control is literally evident in the fact that the seemingly uninhibited play of the various pieces of the lady's clothing does not prohibit them

from performing the binding and restraining functions for which they are designed. The "Lawne" cast into "distraction" still envelops the shoulders "about" which it is "thrown." The "Lace" errs, strays, only to "Enthrall" yet another girdling item, the stomacher. The cuff, though "neglectfull," still encircles the wrist within it, while the "winning wave" produced by the "tempestuous" petticoat provides but a passing hint of expression and freedom in a garment intended to conceal and bind. Lastly, the shoestring is not so "carelesse" as to be unknotted, and in that "tye," that final reconciling of disparates, the poet transforms the "sweet disorder" he had set out to elucidate into its inverse, a "wilde civility," as the spontaneity of nature ultimately finds its most eloquent expression as a triumph of art.

"To the Virgins, to make much of Time"

Herrick's best art is a playful art but not escapist. In celebrating the virtues of artful playfulness, of "cleanly-Wantonnesse," Herrick does not avert his eyes—nor does he allow his readers to do so—from the darker side of nature, particularly the issues of transience and mortality. What gives Herrick's greatest poems their force is their sense of urgency in the face of temporal encroachment.

One familiar form assumed by urgency is that of the invitation or petition, an exhortation to participate in the poet's artfully playful world before it vanishes. Herrick is the foremost English poetic heir to the classical elegists and their recurrent theme, carpe diem, or "seize the day." This theme is the sole message of "To the Virgins, to make much of Time," best known for its opening line, "Gather ye Rose-buds, while ye may." A wholly unambiguous piece, the poem drives its point forcefully home through the poet's dexterous exploitation of rhyme. Using a feminine rhyming pattern in alternate lines, the poet creates an illusion of constant motion to persuade the virgins whom he is exhorting to marry, that their prime cannot endure, and that the only constant in life is the relentless motion of time and decay. Hence, time's "flying" today is coupled with "dying" tomorrow, while the closer to its apex the sun seems to be "getting," the nearer, in fact, it is to its "setting." To resist the opportunity to "marry" now is inevitably, the poet tersely concludes, to "tarry" forever.

"CORINNA'S GOING A-MAYING"

The carpe diem theme so succinctly intoned in "To the Virgins, to make much of Time" acquires a much fuller resonance and richness in "Corinna's Going A-Maying," one of the greatest of "invitational" poems, and Herrick's most profound scrutiny of the relationship between "cleanly-Wantonnesse" and transience, "Times trans-shifting." As it is in so many of Herrick's poems, the "wantonnesse" of "Corinna's Going A-Maying" is readily apparent. Cast in the conventional form of an aubade, a dawn song of a lover to his beloved, the poem presents a numinously sensual landscape and a speaker who has obviously thought of a wide array of rhetorical ploys with which to tease and cajole his mistress into going out with him to frolic and "fetch in May." Obviously of the persuasion that the best defense is a good offense, the poet anticipates any objections Corinna might raise about the moral propriety of what he is asking by impugning the morality of her reluctance. Corinna is a "sweet Slug-a-bed" for being so indolent as to stay in bed when all of nature has already risen and commenced its daily tasks. Nor can Corinna hide behind her virgin innocence when "A thousand Virgins on this day,/ Spring sooner than the Lark, to fetch in May." Is it not immoral to engage in such sensual delights? It is sacrilege not to; the birds have already said matins and sung hymns. Hence, Corinna is urged to "put on your Foliage" and join the rest of creation, for to do so is natural, and to do what nature ordains is holy.

That "cleanliness" is inherent in the "wantonnesse" in which the poet wishes Corinna to participate is, then, the central premise of the poet's argument. To be sure, that sensual pleasure is a sacred duty may seem an argument born of expediency and self-interest, and that the poet has to elaborate on this theme for four of the poem's five stanzas may suggest that Corinna, for one, has not been readily persuaded. Still, one comes to admire not only the ingenuity of the poet's reasoning but also the scope of his vision. The workings of the entire world are cited as proof that the sacred and profane respond to the same laws. The universe he describes is one in which country and city are interpenetrated with the same divinity to form one all-encompassing temple in which each porch and door, "An Arke or Tabernacle is/ Made up of white thorn neatly enterwove." All hu-

manity, the poet would have Corinna believe, participates in the same sacred rites of love, both those who formalize their love in the religiously and legally sanctioned customs, plighting their troth and finding a priest, and those who proceed directly to consummation. In the face of such evidence, can Corinna possibly maintain that the poet's invitation to go "A-Maying" is anything worse than "harmless follie"?

The poet does not wait for Corinna's reply—poets who issue such invitations, it seems, rarely do. Rather, as if to imply that enough time has been spent on polite discussion, the poet turns urgently in the last stanza of the poem to the carpe diem argument to confront Corinna with the imminence of their dissolution. Harsh and jarring as this concluding picture of existence is, it only follows logically from the vision of nature presented in the preceding parts of the poem. Corinna had been urged to partake of the sensual rites enjoyed by all of creation because she is part of that creation, but as a part of it she must share both in its joys and in its inevitable decay and disintegration.

Had Corinna been paying close attention to the poet's imagery, she might have anticipated this turn in the argument. The flowers with which the poet had exhorted her to bedeck herself flourish and fade with the seasons. The "gemmes" that, near the beginning of the poem, the poet had promised Corinna would be strewn "in abundance" upon her if she came forth, were but crystallized dewdrops, the illusion they conveyed of time standing still lasting only until the sunbeams melted them away. By the end of the poem, the solidified dews have evanesced and liquefied in the poet's imagination into a vast sea in which "All love, all liking, all delight/ Lies drown'd with us in endless night." His sportiveness turned somber, the poet renews his appeal to Corinna to enjoy the "cleanly-Wantonnesse" of nature's rites while there is still time, "and we are but decaying," an ambiguous phrase that could be taken to mean not only that the poet and Corinna have not fully decayed yet, and so still have some time, but also that life itself is "but" a process of decay, which makes the injunction to seize the moment all the more imperative.

NOBLE NUMBERS

The elegiac apprehension of mortality that dominates the ending of "Corinna's Going A-Maying" informs much of Herrick's verse and recurs even in his explicitly Christian devotional verse. Found in *Hesperides*, this grouping of "divine" poems is referred to as his *Noble Numbers*. These poems present the idea that theological belief in an everlasting spiritual life is not forceful enough to dispel the emotional certainty with which Herrick ponders the dissolution of nature. Thus, in the poem titled "Eternitie," the poet thinks of how all "times" are "lost i'th Sea/ Of vast Eternitie," and if Corinna and her poetic lover had had to look forward to being drowned in "endless night," the poet in "Eternities" defines spiritual immortality as being "Drown'd in one endlesse Day."

"To Blossoms"

The hope to which Herrick always returns is art and the celebration of artistic vision. Art alone can freeze or at least arrest the processes of natural decay to prolong and preserve sensual beauty. Such is the lesson of one of the loveliest and most thoughtful of Herrick's meditations on mortality, "To Blossoms." Opening with the central question of all elegies, the poet looks at some falling leaves and asks simply, "Why do yee fall so fast?" Consolation comes only when the poet looks again and sees the leaves as pieces of art, as leaves of a book in which one can "read" a valuable lesson: "How soon things have/ Their end, though ne'r so brave." The recognition that even falling leaves, if viewed artfully, have a lesson to teach permits the poet to see the dropping of the leaves in a new way; instead of "falling fast," they now "glide," their descent softened, the pleasure they afford prolonged.

"The Pillar of Fame"

The hope that reposes in Herrick's verses is epitomized in the poem that stands at the end of *Hesperides*, "The Pillar of Fame." A figure poem, its lines are arranged in such a way as to form the shape of a funereal monument, "Charm'd and enchanted" to endure all the ravages of mortality. If the evidence of time has any weight, Herrick's art has not betrayed its maker's confidence.

Bibliography

Coiro, Ann Baynes. *Robert Herrick's "Hesperides" and the Epigram Book Tradition*. Baltimore: The Johns Hopkins University Press, 1988. Argues for the structural integrity of *Hesperides*, insisting that the collection of poems be read as a whole. After exploring the cultural, political, and generic implications of the title of the book, Coiro provides a history of the epigram tradition and concludes with chapters on the epigrams of praise, mocking, and advice. Copious notes provide a rich bibliography to Herrick's criticism.

Guibbory, Achsah. *Ceremony and Community from Herbert to Milton: Literature, Religion, and Cultural Conflict in Seventeenth-Century England*. New York: Cambridge University Press, 1998. Offers new and original readings of Herrick, George Herbert, Thomas Browne, and John Donne in an examination of the relationship between literature and religious conflict in seventeenth century England.

Hammons, Pamela. "Robert Herrick's Gift Trouble: Male Subjects 'Trans-shifting' into Objects." *Criticism* 47, no. 1 (Winter, 2005): 31-65. Discusses how Herrick's portrayal of gift giving involves the male persona of the poem becoming absorbed into the item being given.

Landrum, David. "Robert Herrick and the Ambiguities of Gender." *Texas Studies in Literature and Language* 49, no. 2 (Summer, 2007): 181-208. Landrum argues that Herrick's attitude toward women varied from the predominant view that women were subordinate to men and was instead revisionist.

Marcus, Leah S. *The Politics of Mirth: Jonson, Herrick, Milton, Marvell, and the Defense of Old Holiday Pastimes*. Chicago: University of Chicago Press, 1986. Marcus devotes a chapter to Herrick's *Hesperides*, which she discusses in terms of their relationship to the revelry and holiday moods associated with the monarchy. Marcus regards Herrick as the Cavalier poet-priest and finds in *Hesperides*, particularly in "Corinna's Going A-Maying," the sexual energy associated with her thesis.

_____. *Robert Herrick*. Rev. ed. New York: Twayne, 1992. Updated in the light of later scholarship. A comprehensive critical study of Herrick's work. Includes bibliographic references and index.

Prestwich, Natalie K. "Ghostly Metaphysicality: A Manuscript Variant of Robert Herrick's 'The Apparation.'" *Notes and Queries* 52, no. 2 (June,

2005): 232-234. This discussion of metaphysicality in Herrick's poetry revolves around a manuscript variant of "The Apparation."

Pugh, Syrithe. *Herrick, Fanshawe and the Politics of Intertextuality: Classical Literature and Seventeenth Century Royalism.* Burlington, Vt.: Ashgate, 2010. Examines Royalistic polemics and classical allusion in the poetry of Herrick and Sir Richard Fanshawe.

Rollin, Roger B., and J. Max Patrick, eds. *"Trust to Good Verses": Herrick Tercentenary Essays.* Pittsburgh, Pa.: University of Pittsburgh Press, 1978. Contains an introductory essay concerning trends in Herrick's criticism as well as essays on the love poetry, on visual and musical themes, on the political poetry, and on the evolution of Herrick's literary reputation. A welcome feature is the inclusion of a selected, thoroughly annotated bibliography of Herrick's criticism.

Thomas Moisan

JOHN HEYWOOD

Born: London(?), England; c. 1497
Died: Louvain(?), Spanish Netherlands (now in Belgium); October, 1578

PRINCIPAL POETRY

A Dialogue of Proverbs, 1546, 1963 (Rudolph E. Habenicht, editor)
The Spider and the Fly, 1556

OTHER LITERARY FORMS

In addition to writing poetry, John Heywood wrote dramatic works that can be divided into two groups: debates and farces. The four debates include *The Play of Love* (pr. c. 1528-1529), *Witty and Witless* (abridged pb. 1846, 1909), *The Play of the Weather* (pb. 1533), and *Gentleness and Nobility* (1535, attributed to Heywood). The farces include *The Pardoner and the Friar* (pb. 1533), *Johan Johan the Husband, Tyb His Wife, and Sir Johan the Priest* (pb. 1533, commonly known

as *Johan Johan*), and *The Playe of the Foure P.P.: A Newe and a Very Mery Enterlude of a Palmer, a Pardoner, a Potycary, a Pedler* (pb. 1541-1547, commonly known as *The Four P.P.*). Two other plays, *Calilsto and Melibaea* (1530) and *Thersites* (1537), have been ascribed to Heywood but with insufficient evidence. Although Heywood was known in his own day primarily as the author of witty epigrams, modern criticism has tended to focus on his contributions to the evolution of English drama.

ACHIEVEMENTS

Many elements of John Heywood's work—comedy, bawdry, wordplay, and lyricism—reflect the various ways poetry was developing during the Renaissance in England. Heywood experimented with all these poetic devices, although his contemporaries saw him mainly as a "mad wit."

BIOGRAPHY

John Heywood's date of birth can only be calculated by a remark he made in a letter to Lord Burghley on April 18, 1575. He then claimed to be seventy-eight years old, which would place his birthday before April 18, 1497. There are even fewer direct indications of his birthplace. Bishop Bale and John Pitts, a friend of Heywood's son, both claim that he was born in London, and this is generally accepted for lack of any evidence to the contrary. Because of his long associations with the court, biographers often assume that as a boy Heywood entered the Chapel Royal as a chorister, but this is mere speculation. Nor is much known about his education. Anthony à Wood claimed that Heywood was a student at Broadgates, Oxford, for a short time, "But the crabbedness of logic not suiting with his airy genie, he retired to his native place, and became noted to all witty men." Broadgates did not begin to keep records until 1570, so this statement cannot be verified.

The first direct reference to Heywood's stay in Henry VIII's court occurs in 1515 when the *King's Book of Payments* records the payment of eight pence a day to a "John Heywoode." Even this reference raises more questions than it answers: It does not indicate what the money was payment for, and since the next reference to Heywood does not appear until 1519, some critics even assume that the first entry is for a different Heywood entirely. In June, 1519, however, Heywood received an allowance of one hundred shillings, and in August he is listed as a singer in the court. His association with the court continued throughout Henry's reign, although his duties are not always listed in the payment book. Presumably, he was involved in court entertainments of some sort. In 1526, he is referred to as a "player of the virginals," and in 1528, he was made steward of the royal chamber, a post he also held under Edward and Mary.

Thomas More entered Henry's court in 1519 and Heywood's association with More's circle is well known: Sometime in the 1520's, he married Eliza Rastell, the daughter of John Rastell and More's sister, Elizabeth. Heywood's strong Catholicism, in fact, almost led him to the same fate that More met at Henry's hands; he was imprisoned in 1543. The cause was an accusation made by Heywood and others against Archbishop Cranmer, a Protestant. They charged that Cranmer was not reporting violations of the Six Articles that were issued in 1539 and that were strongly Catholic. Heywood escaped death by recanting, although it is indicative of his reputation as a wit that Sir John Harington attributed Heywood's release to his "mirth" even though no direct evidence appears to support the contention. Heywood's political associations were better documented than his personal life: He had two sons (Ellis and Jasper) and one daughter, who later married John Donne and became the mother of the poet; yet in William Rastell's will there is mention of two more daughters, Johanna Stubbs and Elizabeth Marvin, about whom nothing is known. It is perhaps appropriate that an artist whose life revolved around the court should be remembered primarily through his relations with that court.

When Henry died in 1547 with Edward as his heir, Heywood's position did not change: He continued to present plays in court. Mary's accession in 1553 would have seemed to assure Heywood a bright future. As a good Catholic himself, he had always admired the young princess, even writing a poem praising her in 1534, a year when Mary's Catholicism put her out of Henry's favor. Heywood gave a Latin and English oration during Mary's coronation and later celebrated her

marriage to Philip in a poem. Mary, in turn, kept Heywood as steward of the queen's chamber and, when he resigned this post in 1555, granted him a forty-year lease on a manor and some lands in Yorkshire.

Heywood's associations with the court after Mary's death are not entirely clear. Although he died in exile in Louvain, he appears in records of Elizabeth's court during the first year of her reign. A comment made by Thomas Wilson is especially intriguing: He reports that he saw Heywood when he was in exile in Malines and brought him Elizabeth's forgiveness, saying that "the Queen was never so precise that she could not bear with men's weaknesses for their conscience in religion, and only misliked overt acts and rebellious practices." The phrasing of this message raises the possibility that Heywood might have been driven into exile because of a plot to restore Catholicism to the English throne. In any case, Heywood finally fled to Antwerp, where his son Ellis was in religious exile and, from there, went to Louvain, where he died in October, 1578.

It would be difficult to overestimate the influence that his years at court had on Heywood. As a dramatist, he must have benefited from the court masques and interludes that he directed. As a poet, he would have been in a position to benefit from as well as influence the development of English as a vehicle for poetic expression. He also found subject matter for his longest poem, *The Spider and the Fly*, in the enclosure laws and religious questions that would have been talked about in court at various times.

ANALYSIS

John Heywood's contemporaries knew him mainly as a writer of witty epigrams: John Florio, William Camden, and Gabriel Harvey comment on his skill in using this literary form. One of Heywood's epigrams opens with the question "Art thou Heywood with the mad merry wit?" and this wit emerges in the wordplay of which Heywood is so fond. His poems abound with puns and verbal quibbles and in this way he anticipates euphuism; in fact, John Lyly's work uses many of the proverbs that Heywood collected in his *A Dialogue of Proverbs*.

In addition to wordplay, there is a minor substratum of lyricism in Heywood that antedates the sonnets and lyrics of later Renaissance poetry. "Green Willow" most obviously illustrates this strain in Heywood, introducing the typical despondent Petrarchan lover and using alliteration to lend smoothness to the lines. Alliteration also became a hallmark of euphuism.

Another important aspect of Heywood's work is his comic realism and bawdy humor. He constantly provides a dramatic context for his poems, and this context, be it the mock-heroic descriptions of warfare in *The Spider and the Fly* or the fast-paced marital arguments of *A Dialogue of Proverbs*, usually provides comic overtones to his work. When describing people—the old wife in *A Dialogue of Proverbs*, for example—he focuses on their imperfections to provide comedy. This comic realism, along with the bawdry found in many of Heywood's poems, has prompted critics to place him in the Chaucerian tradition of English poetry, a tradition carried on through the Renaissance by poets such as John Skelton.

A DIALOGUE OF PROVERBS

Heywood's first poetry to appear in print was *A Dialogue of Proverbs*, an attempt to bring together "the number of the effectual proverbs in the English tongue" within a dramatic context. That context is a dialogue between the narrator and a young friend concerning the latter's marriage: He must choose between marrying a beautiful but destitute young woman and an ugly and old but wealthy widow. Collecting proverbs was by no means an innovation in the sixteenth century. William Caxton's *The dictes or sayengis of the philosophres* (1477), Desiderius Erasmus's *Adagia* (1500; *Proverbs or Adages*, 1622), and Nicholas Udall's *Apophthegmes* (1542), to name just a few, are all collections of proverbial lore. That Heywood worked specifically with English proverbs and attempted to provide a plot for them shows him to be a poet concerned with exploring the possibilities of the English language while giving a dramatic framework to his poem. Heywood was, after all, a playwright as well as a poet.

The strengths of *A Dialogue of Proverbs* are twofold—dramatic and verbal—and its weaknesses emerge in Heywood's inability to sustain the high standards that his best writing achieves. The dramatic structure of the work is complex, and such complexity does much to alleviate the tedium that a dialogue consisting mainly of proverbs might produce. Thus, after listening to his friend's dilemma and debating with him his marriage choices (part 1, chapters 1-6), the narrator proposes to tell the young man about two unions he has known: one a marriage of young people for love and one a December-May marriage between a rich woman and a poor young man. The first story takes up the rest of part 1 and chronicles the various ways the couple try to rise above their poverty; it ends when the wife and husband must part to make their separate ways in the world. The history of the December-May match takes up part 2 and shows the gradual deterioration of a marriage undertaken on the young man's part only for money. The introduction of these two stories within the frame of the debate between the narrator and his friend shows Heywood's fondness for elaborate plot structure.

He also delights in providing detailed descriptions of the secondary characters of the narrator's two stories, and often these descriptions are humorous. When the poor young wife goes to her aunt's house to beg forgiveness for her rash marriage, she meets another "kinswoman," Alice, whose "dissimulation" frightens the young wife. Alice is described in broadly humorous terms: "She is *lost with an apple, and won with a nut*;/ Her *tongue is no edge tool, but yet it will cut*./ Her cheeks are purple ruddy like a horse plum;/ And *the big part of her body is her bum*." While the wife is begging at her aunt's house, her husband is trying his luck with his family. After being refused aid by one uncle, he goes to another only to find him out and his wife leery of indigent relatives: "She was within, but he was yet abroad./ And straight as she saw me she swelled like a toad,/ *Pattering the devil's Pater noster* to herself:/ God never made a more crabbed elf!"

Unfortunately, descriptions such as these are the high points of the work and are by no means common. Much of part 2 is devoted to arguments between the old woman and her young husband, and while some of these are humorous, others are simply weighted down with proverbs. In addition, there are some strange lapses in dramatic structure for a poet who is also a playwright. Halfway through part 2, the December-May couple invite the young couple described in part 1 to dine with them. During the dinner, the two husbands think to solve their emotional and financial problems by changing wives: As the young man in the December-May marriage begins to "cast a loving eye" on the young wife, her husband casts a loving look "to his plate," bought with the old wife's money. This comic dramatic situation, suggestive of a fabliau, is never developed by Heywood, and the young couple passes out of part 2 with no effect on the story. It seems odd that Heywood went to the trouble of developing this dramatic situation only to leave it unresolved.

A similar ambiguity surrounds the narrator. In many ways, his presence lends drama—and occasionally dramatic irony—to the work. His steadiness contrasts with his young friend's impulsiveness: After hearing the tale of the first two lovers, the young man would immediately hasten off to marry the old wealthy woman before even hearing about the December-May marriage. When he finally agrees to listen to the story of the second couple, he is so impatient that he will scarcely let the narrator pause for supper. Within the stories he tells, the narrator's role as confidant to both the young husband and the old wife provides humor as both come to him to complain of their marriage: "Out of doors went she herewith; and hereupon/ In at doors came he forthwith, as she was gone." The split-second timing of these entrances and departures shows Heywood's dramatic sense translated into comedy.

The narrator by no means provides a consistent focal point for the work, however, and his attitudes toward the December-May couple are not well defined. When the wife complains about her husband's numerous adulteries, she notes that they are not even necessary since "To tick and laugh with me he hath lawful leave." The narrator remarks that "To that I said nought, but laughed in my sleeve." If the narrator's callousness is used by Heywood to show the humor of the wife's predicament, he seems to change in the next chapter when he upbraids the husband for his behavior. Heywood seems to change the narrator's character as dramatic—or comic—propriety demands; in many ways, then, the narrator remains a cipher.

Heywood's verbal skill emerges in his play on words, a style that anticipates euphuism. Thus, when the uncle of the poor young man in part 1 upbraids him for marrying against his family's wishes, he plays elab-

orately on the word "will." Heywood often uses earthy images in his poetry, and this is true of *A Dialogue of Proverbs*. At one point there is a play on the words "purse," "purgation," and "laxative." The arguments between the young husband and the old wife are especially rich in bawdy humor.

EPIGRAMS

Heywood's contemporaries saw him primarily as a writer of epigrams, and his output in this genre is enormous: He published collections of epigrams in 1550, 1555, 1560, and 1562. If, by an epigram, one means a short poem with a witty turn, then some of Heywood's epigrams do not even qualify as such. Epigram 92 of his first hundred, for example, is a long comparison of books and cheese, the point being that people differ in their tastes in both; it is hardly a startling display of wit. Similarly, he has several epigrams that are simply miniature sermons on some moral maxim.

At their best, however, Heywood's epigrams are lively examples of jest-book humor, drawing on animal fables, flytings, and colloquial dialogue for their effectiveness. Many of them involve invective between husband and wife; in fact, one almost suspects that Heywood considers marital arguments intrinsically amusing. Many of these colloquies, however, do contain humor in the form of puns and verbal quibbles. Occasionally one feels that, had Heywood worked in a longer form, he could have been a first-rate satirist. Epigram 30 of the first hundred is called "A Keeper of the Commandments" and is a relatively long epigram— forty-four lines—in which the narrator addresses a young rake and congratulates him on how well he "obeys" the Ten Commandments: For example, he has no more gods than one "for God thou hast none." The ironic play on the meaning of the Ten Commandments continues throughout the epigram, providing sardonic humor.

THE SPIDER AND THE FLY

If Heywood's canon may be judged by the amount of time he put into composing his poems, then surely *The Spider and the Fly* is his most important work: It did not appear until 1556, but Heywood says at the end that he had been working on it for more than twenty years. This time span may help to explain some of the ambiguity of the poem's allegory, for Heywood explicitly tells his audience in the preface that it is a parable. The story concerns a fly who wanders into a spider's web and is captured. This first leads to a debate between the spider and the fly as to the fly's legal rights and finally to an all-out war between the nations of spiders and flies. At the end of the poem, all the forces having been spent, a maid comes into the room and brushes down the remaining cobwebs and kills the spider.

Finding a sustained allegory in this plot is difficult. The first part of the poem, setting forth the legal haggling of the two opponents, seems to be only a generalized satire on the legal practices of the day. In chapter 27, however, the spider argues that "kings and peers" can be identified with spiders and flies. Obviously, Heywood has some topical reference in mind. Later, in chapter 44, the fly and the spider talk heatedly about rents, and the whole issue of the fly's right to be on the windowpane seems to hint at the enclosure laws. If the poem is in part about those laws, then the spider would have to represent the nobles and the fly the peasants. This seems out of keeping, however, with the spider's earlier assertion that he and the fly represent kings and peers. Furthermore, the ending of the poem seems to shift ground toward religious allegory. In the conclusion of the poem, Heywood identifies the maid as Queen Mary. Most critics, therefore, see the spiders as representing Protestants and the flies Catholics: The maid's killing of the spider may be a reference to the execution of Archbishop Cranmer. The problem is that the conclusion, in which Heywood supposedly explains the poem's meaning, offers only generalized praise of Mary as a monarch "whose sword, like a broom . . . sweepeth out filth clean." Even Heywood's near contemporaries had trouble with the poem's meaning: William Harrison, in his *Description of England* (1587), discusses "One [who] hath made a booke of the *Spider and the Flie*, wherein he dealeth so profoundlie, and beyond all measure of skill, that neither he himself that made it, neither anie one that readeth it, can reach unto the meaning thereof."

In a sense, the allegory of the poem is unimportant, for Heywood is at his best describing his characters on a very human level: He shows the mother spider's obvious pride in her "babe," who, at only eight weeks, wants to eat "some part of that flesh fly's brain." Simi-

larly, the battle scenes define the mock-heroic nature of the poem as ants and flies prepare for glorious combat. Heywood also uses the witty puns and verbal quibbles of which he is so fond, especially in the legal debates between the spider and the fly. The fact remains, however, that the poem is simply too long: Once the reader has savored the initial incongruities that give the poem its mock-heroic tone, the speeches of the spiders and flies become tedious. There is also a curious lack of shaping in the plot, since after the long war between the spiders and flies, the reader is left exactly where he or she was as the poem opened: Chapter 83 begins with the spider and the fly again debating the fly's fate. Perhaps this stalemate is necessary for the introduction of the maid (Queen Mary), whose wisdom finally solves the conflict, but it makes the main events of the poem seem curiously superfluous.

SHORTER POEMS

Heywood's shorter poems are strikingly different in content and poetic skill. Some are merely didactic, with little aesthetic leavening: "I desyre no number of manye thinges for store"; "Man, for thyne yll life formerly"; and "The harme that groweth of idlenes." However, the short emphatic lines of "A ballad against slander and detraction" give the poem a vigor and forcefulness lacking in many of Heywood's other moralizing works. His most striking poems either commemorate a specific person or event or are on less serious themes.

Of the first group, the poems about Queen Mary, while uneven in quality, do have some excellent lines. The imperative that opens "A song in praise of a Ladie" imparts an energy to the poem that some of the later rather tame compliments seem to undermine. His metrical craftsmanship is also noticeably lacking: The stanzas vary markedly in their metrics and the two extant versions of the poem show Heywood making changes in phrasing that seem to disregard the meter of his lines. The poem celebrating Mary's marriage to Philip relies mostly on heavy alliteration to achieve its effects, while the central metaphor of lamb (Mary) and eagle (Philip) seems strained and awkward.

The poem "A breefe balet touching the traytorous takynge of Scarborow Castell" contains individual lines that are striking: "Ye thought ye tooke the castell at your landyng,/ The castell takyng you in the selfe whyle." The didactic element perhaps keeps the poem from achieving what it might otherwise have done. The second stanza, for example, opens with a labored explanation that Scarborow Castle is simply a symbol of all royal lands, as if Heywood fears that an unobservant reader might be led by the poem to attack other property of the Crown. Furthermore, although the poem opens with an almost sympathetic picture of the gallant invaders, it does not go on to explore the ambiguity of seemingly heroic men caught in an ill-conceived venture: By the end of the poem they have become total villains. Heywood's most successful lyric, "All a grene wyllow is my garland," contains some lovely lines, while others occasionally fall flat. Nevertheless, its lyricism and Petrarchan conventions make it a fine example of early Renaissance love poetry.

Although Heywood is rather limited in poetic form—doing most of his work in epigrams or narrative poems—and is not always totally successful even in those forms, his work does show the sort of wit that later writers would develop more fully. His love of puns, wordplay, and alliteration seems to foreshadow writers such as Lyly, while his bawdry and comic realism align him with Skelton and others. Thus his writing shows, in embryo, the beginnings of two very different—but typically Renaissance—types of writing. In this sense, his wit was certainly eclectic.

OTHER MAJOR WORKS

PLAYS: *The Play of Love*, pr. c. 1528-1529; *Johan Johan the Husband, Tyb His Wife, and Sir Johan the Priest*, pb. 1533 (commonly known as *Johan Johan*; adaptation of *Farce nouvelle et fort joyeuse du pasté*); *The Pardoner and the Friar*, pb. 1533 (possibly based on *Farce nouvelle d'un pardonneur, d'un triacleur, et d'une tavernière*); *The Play of the Weather*, pb. 1533; *Gentleness and Nobility*, 1535 (attributed to Heywood); *The Playe of the Foure P.P.: A Newe and a Very Mery Enterlude of a Palmer, a Pardoner, a Potycary, a Pedler*, pb. 1541-1547 (commonly known as *The Four P.P.*; possibly based on *Farce nouvelle d'un pardonneur, d'un triacleur, et d'une tavernière*); *Witty and Witless*, abridged pb. 1846, 1909 (wr. c. 1533; also

known as *A Dialogue on Wit and Folly*); *The Dramatic Writings of John Heywood*, 1905 (John S. Farmer, editor).

MISCELLANEOUS: *Works*, 1562 (epigrams and poems); *Works and Miscellaneous Short Poems*, 1956 (Burton A. Milligan, editor).

BIBLIOGRAPHY

Bolwell, Robert G. W. *The Life and Works of John Heywood*. 1921. Reprint. New York: AMS Press, 1966. An early biography of Heywood written with extensive reference to his works and including transcriptions of several important texts from Heywood and the court of Henry VIII.

Henderson, Judith Rice. "John Heywood's *The Spider and the Flie*: Educating Queen and Country." *Studies in Philology* 96, no. 3 (Summer, 1999): 241-274. Heywood's *The Spider and the Fly* has been one of the least appreciated of many neglected poems of mid-Tudor England. Henderson claims that Heywood's purpose for writing the poem was not only to instruct but also to exhort commoners, professionals, magistrates, and the monarch to fulfill their obligations to the commonwealth.

Holstun, James. "The Spider, the Fly, and the Commonwealth: Merrie John Heywood and Agrarian Class Struggle." *ELH* 71, no. 1 (Spring, 2004): 53-90. Holstun argues that Heywood's *The Spider and the Fly* praises an ideal state that never came to pass, one in which a benevolent Catholic ruler implemented agrarian reforms. Contains a lengthy analysis of the poem.

Johnson, Robert Carl. *John Heywood*. New York: Twayne, 1970. A critical biography of the author including a chronology, list of publications, details about his life and career, as well as an index and an annotated bibliography.

Walker, Greg. *The Politics of Performance in Early Renaissance Drama*. 1998. Reprint. New York: Cambridge University Press, 2006. Although this work is about drama rather than poetry, it does contain a chapter on Heywood's political and social views, which are also evident in his poetry.

Carole Moses

GEOFFREY HILL

Born: Bromsgrove, Worcestershire, England; June
  18, 1932

PRINCIPAL POETRY

  For the Unfallen: Poems, 1952-1958, 1959
  King Log, 1968
  Mercian Hymns, 1971
  Somewhere Is Such a Kingdom: Poems, 1952-1971,
    1976 (includes previous 3 collections)
  Tenebrae, 1978
  The Mystery of the Charity of Charles Péguy, 1983
  Collected Poems, 1985
  New and Collected Poems, 1952-1992, 1994
  Canaan, 1996
  The Triumph of Love, 1998
  Speech! Speech!, 2000
  The Orchards of Syon, 2002
  Without Title, 2006
  A Treatise of Civil Power, 2007
  Selected Poems, 2009

OTHER LITERARY FORMS

Geoffrey Hill published *Lords of Limit: Essays on
Literature and Ideas* (1984), a collection of literary
criticism and essays, including work on rhythm in poetry, George Eliot, and Tory radicalism. *The Enemy's
Country: Words, Contexture, and Other Circumstances of Language*, (1991), a revision of Hill's 1986
Clark Lectures at Trinity College, Cambridge, is a
monograph on the language of judgment, focused
chiefly on the seventeenth century English poet John
Dryden. Hill also translated Henrik Ibsen's *Brand*, in
1978.

ACHIEVEMENTS

Since his attendance at Oxford in the early 1950's,
Geoffrey Hill has won recognition as a significant poet;
in the late 1960's and 1970's many critics, notably
Donald Hall, Christopher Ricks, and Harold Bloom,
championed him as a major poet of the twentieth century. Mastery of difficult rhyme patterns and allusions
to historical and literary figures characterizes his verse.

He portrays his most frequent themes, religion and tradition, in complex, often-contradictory ways. Some
critics attack his verse as obscure; others defend its density as perfectly suited to the difficulty of the thought
conveyed. Awards won include the Eric Gregory
Award for Poetry (1961), the Geoffrey Faber Memorial
Prize (1970), the Whitbread Award (1971), and the
Russell Loines Award (1983). In 1996, he became a
fellow of the American Academy of Arts and Sciences.
He won the Kahn Award for *Canaan* in 1998. *The Triumph of Love* won the Royal Society of Literature's
Heinemann Award in 2000. Hill received the Ingersoll
Foundation's T. S. Eliot Award for Creative Writing
(2000) and the Levinson Prize from *Poetry* magazine
(2006). In 2009, his *Collected Critical Writings* (2008)
won the Truman Capote Award for Literary Criticism.

BIOGRAPHY

Born on June 18, 1932, in the small market town of
Bromsgrove, in Worcestershire, England, Geoffrey
William Hill grew up in a nearby village, Fairfield,
where his father worked as a police officer. A lonely,
introspective child who often went for solitary walks,
he sometimes recited to himself poetry from Oscar
Williams's *A Little Treasury of Modern Poetry, English and American* (1946), a popular collection stressing such modernists as Ezra Pound, T. S. Eliot, and
William Carlos Williams.

Hill's devotion to poetry continued after his enroll-
ment at Keble College, Oxford, in 1950. Though not
among the most active members of the young Oxford
literary set, he concentrated on his English studies, ac-
quiring a thorough knowledge of English literary and
intellectual history. Under the aegis of Hall, a well-
known poet and translator of Japanese literature, Hill
published a few poems that at once attracted attention,
but this success did not sway him from his intention to
become a university teacher and scholar of English.

After graduation, he accepted a post in the English
department of Leeds University, where he benefited
from contact with G. Wilson Knight, generally regarded as the foremost twentieth century Shakespeare
critic. Knight, like Hill, was a polymath interested especially in the religious and symbolic aspects of poetry.
Under the stimulus of Knight, among others, Hill con-

Geoffrey Hill (Alice Goodman/Courtesy, Houghton Mifflin)

tinued to write verse while earning a reputation as a difficult, immensely learned lecturer.

Hill married Nancy Whittaker in 1956, and the couple had four children. His career since the 1950's has in essence continued the pattern laid down in his early adulthood, though the success of his verse has transformed him from an academic who writes poetry into a poet who also works as a scholar. In 1980, he was elected fellow of Emmanuel College, Cambridge, a college famous for its English faculty, like F. R. Leavis, one of the most formidable, controversial twentieth century critics. In 1987, he married Alice Goodman; the couple had one daughter. In 1988, he became university professor and professor of literature and religion at Boston University and later codirector of the Editorial Institute. In 2006, Hill moved back to Cambridge.

ANALYSIS

From his earliest work, religion and history have dominated Geoffrey Hill's poetry. As a religious poet,

he defends no particular orthodoxy but instead explores various positions, often incorporating later poems in a sequence to reject positions upheld earlier. He often meditates on World Wars I and II, concentrating especially on Adolf Hitler's murder of the Jews.

Hill's work since *For the Unfallen* has rung changes on a few constant themes: bitter criticism of the modern world, in particular the power and might that produced senseless slaughter and culminated in the Nazis' mass murder of Jews; his futile search for solace in premodern society and religion; and the inability of Christianity to provide consolation. His difficult rhymes and obscure diction mirror his pessimistic frame of mind.

FOR THE UNFALLEN

Such themes surfaced in Hill's first major collection, *For the Unfallen*. The book begins with "Genesis," one of the few poems Hill kept from a small pamphlet published while he was in college. The poem describes a series of walks taken in Worcestershire. In part 1, Hill dreams of creating a godlike language through poetry. Just as Adam was given authority to name all the animals of creation and thus to rule over them, so the poet can bring his own world into existence through verbal artifice.

Hill makes this suggestion only to withdraw it in part 2, where his poetic persona is a skeptic withdrawn from the world. However, Hill has not pictured the poet as creator in order to denounce this view for undue pride. Instead, he proves elusive, hinting that a poet who acknowledges humanity's lapse from perfection can return strengthened from a confrontation with sin and disillusion to then create a harmonious world evocative of Eden before the Fall; the difference from the initial claim to mastery is the poet's realization of the precarious nature of his vision.

For the Unfallen also includes a six-part sequence, "Of Commerce and Society," a pessimistic view of history critical of the development of European society since the Renaissance. Commercial values have gained control of the major European states. The pursuit of money and power is inimical to art. The last poem in the sequence, "The Martyrdom of Saint Sebastian," describes a Jamesian artist whose devotion to high artistic standards leads to conflict with the public and a rejection of his work comparable to Christian martyrdom.

The attitude so far described fits with Hill's devotion to the Tory Radicals of the nineteenth century. The "Young England" movement rejected the business values of the Industrial Revolution. Instead, figures such as Benjamin Disraeli preached a return to the standards of medieval England. The Oxford philosopher T. H. Green, the subject of an essay in Hill's *Lords of Limit*, criticized capitalism for its undue accent on the separation of individuals, as did the Christian socialist F. D. Maurice, another key figure in this antibusiness tradition.

One might expect Hill to support a return to tradition, but the poet refuses to be pinned down. In "The Lowlands of Holland" he declares Europe dead because of paralysis wrought by tradition. Folk songs, used throughout the sequence, do not support a return to "Merrie Old England"; they instead suggest the weight of the past. Holland, the earliest center of European capitalism and a great center of art and culture, lacks sufficient achievement to stave off decay. Like Pound, Hill dislikes finance with savage intensity.

Perhaps the artist can redeem society, as another poem in the sequence, "The Death of Shelley," suggests. Throughout most of his short life, Percy Bysshe Shelley was devoted to the French Revolution. He thought that the overthrow of superstition and barbarous customs would inaugurate a new era for humanity. The biblical promises of a new world would be fulfilled by human effort alone, with no supernatural intervention needed. In this hoped-for transformation, poets, the "unacknowledged legislators of mankind," would play a key role.

Hill treats Shelley's hopes with sympathy, yet rejects them. The sequence makes evident Hill's belief that twentieth century events make millenarian optimism impossible. In particular, Hitler's murder of several million Jews, as well as other horrors of the twentieth century, compel Hill to reject a belief in progress. Even a society run by artists cannot blot out the historical record of world wars.

KING LOG

Hill's next major collection, *King Log*, appeared nearly a decade later, in 1968. It included the contents of a beautifully printed pamphlet, *Preghiere*, issued four years previously, as well as other poems.

Since *Preghiere* is an Italian word for "prayers," the poems in this sequence suggest that the artist as priest can overcome political oppression through ascetic devotion to art. For example, "Men Are a Mockery of Angels" is spoken in the voice of the sixteenth century poet and philosopher Tommaso Campanella, a Platonist who believed in the rule of an intellectual and artistic elite. He devised an elaborate utopia, described in *La città del sole* (1623; *City of the Sun*, 1880). Hill depicts Campanella as a joyous person in spite of his imprisonment during the Spanish Inquisition. While jailed, he contemplates his philosophy and thus gains a certain detachment, so that his grim physical surroundings do not drag him into despair.

Hill's endorsement of this view of the artist is at best equivocal, as becomes clear in a later poem in the sequence, "Domaine Publique," which commemorates the death of Robert Desnos, a French poet who perished at the Nazi death camp of Terezin. Hill imagines Desnos mocking the Christian practice of asceticism. The charnel house the Nazis created was not a means of spiritual purgation. When millions are murdered, asceticism loses its significance. At any rate, so Desnos contends in the poem; although Hill seems largely in agreement, his undertone of detachment hints that perhaps the case for asceticism has not been altogether overcome.

The poems in *King Log* not included in the 1964 pamphlet center on two sequences: "Funeral Music" and "The Songbook of Sebastian Arrurruz." The first consists of eight sonnets in blank verse about the English Wars of the Roses. The initial sonnet describes the execution of John Tiptoft, earl of Worcester, at Pomfret Castle in 1470. Tiptoft, a Christian, welcomed death as the means of attaining a higher spiritual state. (Christian doctrine forbade suicide, so the initiative had to come from others.) Tiptoft arranged the details of his own execution: three blows of the executioner's ax to symbolize the three figures in the Trinity.

Hill finds the ascetic ideal appealing, even in the extreme form Tiptoft practiced. The flesh-and-blood world, in this view, conceals reality: like the cave in Plato's *Politeia* (fourth century B.C.E.; *Republic*, 1701), from which one must escape to gain genuine knowledge. However, the poet suggests that an attitude like

Tiptoft's may conceal a strong will to power, so that far from seeking to exit the world, Tiptoft might instead seek fame for his discipline through the acclaim others accord him.

Hill does not claim that this reduction of spirit to power is true; he merely suggests the possibilities, leaving the reader caught amid ambiguity. Hill's main assertion is that human beings are incapable of penetrating the world.

The two positions sketched in the initial sonnet remain locked in struggle throughout "Funeral Music." Several of the poems show strong interest in Averroës, an Arab philosopher whose work influenced Thomas Aquinas and other Christian philosophers of the Middle Ages. Averroës, following the teaching of Aristotle, emphasized contemplation as the highest aim of life, a doctrine taught in book 10 of Aristotle's *Ethica Nicomachea* (n.d.; *Nicomachean Ethics*, 1797). More controversially, Averroës came down firmly on one side of a famous Aristotelian dispute. According to Averroës, Aristotle thought that human minds are not really distinct. The "active intellect"—that is, the power of thought—is a single entity. Only will, emotion, and perception belong to individuals.

Hill finds this view congenial. The aim of ascetic discipline is to sink the person into the Universal Mind: One's individual personality does not count and is sloughed off. What prevents Hill from full commitment to this position, besides his liking for ambiguity? The answer lies in the subject matter of the sequence dealing with the Wars of the Roses. The violence and destruction of the wars, among the bloodiest in English history, prevent him from affirming humanity's goodness. Human beings are rapacious animals, according to Hill's sonnet on the Battle of Towton, the most destructive engagement of the wars. Much of the poem consists of diary entries by a soldier who believes that the real world lies elsewhere and that death in battle is a means to enter a higher realm. Hill's ironic language suggests that the soldier has not grasped the reality of the battle. Far from a spiritual exercise, the struggle is an evil display of lust for power and plunder. The soldier has used philosophy and asceticism to conceal what is taking place, both in the world and in his own soul.

Death and the destruction of war form the principal subject of another poem in *King Log*, "Ovid in the Third Reich." An artist living in Hitler's Germany claims that the pursuit of spiritual values will keep him immune from the horrors of the Third Reich and its führer. The speaker's clichés make apparent Hill's firm stand here and his repudiation of the standpoint of the artist. The artist's alleged withdrawal is in fact complicity with the Nazis, since it turns a blind eye to crime and disguises the pursuit of physical safety under the mantle of ascetic withdrawal from the world. Hill's poem does not deal with a "made-up" attitude. Many writers and artists responded to the Third Reich by practicing "inner emigration." Although Hill strongly sympathizes with asceticism, he thinks that the position just sketched is an untenable dualism. "Ovid in the Third Reich" is probably Hill's most unequivocal political statement.

The reader will by now have the impression that Hill paints a grim, sour picture of the human race. While this is to a large extent true, Hill yet again cannot be easily captured by formula. The second major sequence of *King Log*, "The Songbook of Sebastian Arrurruz," manifests a different mood.

Arrurruz is an imaginary Spanish poet who lived at the end of the nineteenth and beginning of the twentieth century. The years of his maturity coincide with a period of foment among Spanish intellectuals, resulting from Spain's disastrous defeat by the United States in 1898. Although Arrurruz does not directly concern himself with Spanish politics, he faces a sadness of his own. His wife has recently died, and he mourns her death. What should he do? He considers asceticism: Perhaps he ought now to abandon sexual desire as a vain thing. This solution appeals to Arrurruz, but cheerfulness keeps breaking in, and the Spanish poet finds that he cannot abandon women. He remembers his wife not only with sorrow but also with delight, and the poem ends in a witty rather than an elegiac stance. Poetry itself has erotic force, and indulgence in wordplay is a form of sexual pleasure. The sequence differs in style as well as content from Hill's usual practice. It is direct and easy to read, rather than complicated and historically allusive. It won high praise from critics like Martin Dodsworth who are normally inclined to criticize Hill's obscurity.

MERCIAN HYMNS

The poet had not abandoned his difficult style, as his next book, *Mercian Hymns*, made evident. The thirty poems in this book are written in a ritualistic language meant to be chanted as much as read. The "versets" of which the work is composed manifest Hill's knowledge of Anglo-Saxon bardic rhythms. The entire work constitutes an epic describing the reign of King Offa, an eighth century ruler from Mercia and the first Anglo-Saxon monarch to bring most of England under unified control. Not coincidentally, Hill is himself from Mercia, and the epic is also an account of his childhood.

Although the verse forms imitate a typical Anglo-Saxon song of praise for a king, *Mercian Hymns* is by no means a celebration of King Offa. Quite the contrary, Hill satirizes the king's vanity and lust for power. The name "Offa" suggests "offal," a parallel Hill is not slow to exploit.

Naturally, a poet of Hill's depth has much more in mind than pricking the boasts of a fatuous monarch. Hill intends the poem to be an analysis of a certain type of power. As a boy, the king dreamed of being in command, and his attitude when he gains the throne reflects his youthful preoccupations. His subjects are like a child's toys, to be played with and manipulated as he wishes. He lacks a genuine sense of the reality of others.

The indictment extends beyond King Offa. The poet himself views words as his creation: He too seeks power, though of a less immediately destructive kind than that of the king. A leitmotif of Hill's work is that rejection of the real world for a spiritual or aesthetic quest cannot entirely succeed; one cannot respond to the dangers of political power by aesthetic retreat. All human beings bear the burden of original sin, and escape from this dire condition cannot come from human effort.

One of the poems in *Mercian Hymns*, "Crowning of Offa," reveals more fully Hill's attitude toward the past. Hill notes the splendor of the coronation and the church; he does not view these altogether ironically and in fact genuinely admires them. He points out, however, that eighth century Anglo-Saxon society rested on *wergild*. If someone was killed, his family or retainers were expected to avenge him. If the killer paid

wergild, he could save himself and end the feud. The amount paid depended on whether the killing was accidental or deliberate and on the rank of the victim.

Hill's point is that this practice shows the degree to which Anglo-Saxon society was based on money. The worth of individuals varied, with a peasant having almost no value compared with a noble. Thus, he considers contrasting the modern capitalistic world with an idealized medieval past in which money was kept in its place inaccurate since medieval society was as mercenary as modern society.

Hill's jaundiced view of the Anglo-Saxon world is in part directed at an unlikely target. In *Notes Toward the Definition of Culture* (1948), T. S. Eliot called for a return to an organic society. In Eliot's view, twentieth century society encouraged unlimited pluralism and toleration, and society needed to share a common way of life founded on religion. Hill does not altogether reject this view but suggests that Eliot has oversimplified the relation between present and past. By accenting the commercial elements of King Offa's realm, Hill indicates that salvation cannot be found in a return to a premodern utopia.

"Hymn XXV," the last of the "Opus Anglicanum" series, takes aim at another critic and artist, John Ruskin, a leading Victorian social critic and authority on painting, who denounced the nineteenth century for abandoning craftsmanship. Ruskin argued that workers who lived before the Industrial Revolution took pride in their work, as for example, did nail makers. He noted in a famous letter in *Fors Clavigera* (1871-1884) that nails are not a purely utilitarian product but instead the product of immense skill.

While not denying Ruskin's point that this craft requires great skill, Hill indicts Ruskin for romanticizing it, recalling his own grandmother, who spent her life as a nail maker, practicing her trade in appalling poverty, her life a struggle to survive, not the pursuit of a skill undertaken for its own sake. Just as in the poems about King Offa, Hill lays bare the dark side of precapitalist society.

Another of the poems of *Mercian Hymns* sums up Hill's attitude to the state. In an imaginary meeting between King Offa and Charlemagne, Charlemagne gives Offa a sword as a present. (Although the two kings never actually met, Charlemagne did send Offa presents, including several swords, in 786.) The gift, an instrument of slaughter, epitomizes the nature of kingship.

Hill makes himself a character in the poem, imagining himself driving his car in an area where Offa and Charlemagne might have met, and mingling World War I battles in his mind with those Charlemagne fought in the same area. This fantasy self also thinks of Emperor Theodoric torturing and executing the philosopher Boethius. However dubious Hill may be about the merits of asceticism, clearly he believes political power to be much worse.

TENEBRAE

After *Mercian Hymns* was published, Hill spent several years translating Ibsen's *Brand*. As a result, he did not publish his next volume of poetry, *Tenebrae*, until 1978. As the title suggests, this volume offers no respite from Hill's customary dark brooding. Here he takes over certain forms used in Spanish Baroque poetry and uses a principal subject of that era as the work's theme. Spanish mystics such as Saint John of the Cross and Saint Teresa of Ávila often used sexual imagery to depict their religious struggles and visions; Hill does so as well, extending his portrayal of the struggle between flesh and spirit to other historical periods. Among the persons depicted in *Tenebrae* are William Butler Yeats, the French religious thinker Simone Weil, and the German theologian Dietrich Bonhoeffer.

Tenebrae is a Roman Catholic ceremony that commemorates the "harrowing of Hell," Christ's descent into the underworld after his burial and prior to the resurrection. The rite is rarely performed, but attraction to the obscure is Hill's hallmark. He composed the poems in *Tenebrae* in a ritualized language intended to evoke Catholic ceremony.

The first series in the book, "The Pentecost Castle," consists of fifteen short poems modeled on Spanish Baroque lyrics. One, based on a lyric by the poet Juan del Encina, pictures a heron pierced by the blade of physical love. The bird uses the experience to rise to a higher spiritual level.

Although Hill imitates the forms and themes of the Spanish Baroque, his attitude differs from the views of his Spanish exemplars. Though strongly attracted to mysticism, he is doubtful about the reality behind visions. He believes it very difficult to distinguish between true and false mysticism, and he thinks of God not as a savior but as a power that has withdrawn from the world, leaving humankind to its own devices. In "The Pentecost Castle," Hill's attitude toward the mystics about whom he writes is detached. He believes in a principle of compensation: A loss in sexual interest becomes a gain in spiritual insight, and vice versa. What spiritual insight means, however, is not a matter on which he feels able to pronounce.

Another section of *Tenebrae*, called "Lachrimae: Or, Seven Tears Figured in Seven Passionate Pavans," takes a more negative attitude toward mysticism than does the Pentecost sequence. Hill describes techniques of contemplation in detail, claiming that they have been deliberately designed to inflict pain and offer no compensatory rewards. One of his poems imitates an anonymous Spanish lyric; in contrast to the original writer, however, Hill denies that he has ever had contact with Christ. The final poem in "Lachrimae" is a translation of a verse by Lope de Vega Carpio, a sixteenth century playwright strongly inclined to skepticism. Hill's version closely parallels his model without altering its meaning: He finds Lope de Vega's doubt more congenial than the affirmations of mystics.

Hill's challenge to conventional piety goes further. He does not think Christ himself immune from hostile questioning. One poem pictures Christ on the cross; rather than gaze at him with wonder and praise, Hill would like to question Jesus, perhaps with the horrors of the world wars on his mind.

Hill's jaundiced view of Christ does not indicate conversion to atheism. Instead, he explores a perspective to which he is attracted but not fully committed. "Christmas Trees," a tribute to the German pastor and theologian Bonhoeffer, adopts a quite different point of view. Bonhoeffer, a Lutheran pastor from a well-connected German family with ties to the aristocracy, had achieved fame at a young age for a brilliant doctoral dissertation and had the potential to be a leading academic theologian. The rise of Hitler to power in 1933, however, changed Bonhoeffer's plans, for he strongly opposed the Nazis and led the faction of the

Protestant church that refused to recognize the leadership hand-picked by Hitler's minions. Involved in the failed July, 1944, plot to assassinate Hitler, Bonhoeffer was arrested, imprisoned, and eventually executed.

Hill treats Bonhoeffer with unreserved admiration, likening his willingness to risk his life to overthrow Hitler to Christ's sacrifice, a comparison herein inherently favorable. Though in the other poems he is uncommitted, Hill here displays no doubts about the meaning of Christ's redeeming death. Bonhoeffer, a true Christian, had imitated the life and works of his Master. However, perhaps the idea that Bonhoeffer's participation in the plot and his resulting death were a sacrifice for the secular community, not for the church, carries an undertone of religious skepticism. Bonhoeffer believed that if Hitler survived, Germany would face ruin; it is his attempt to act on this belief that earns Hill's praise. Further, while in prison, Bonhoeffer wrote a number of letters that teach "religionless Christianity," in which God no longer intervenes in the world but requires people to act for themselves. His assertions echo Hill's own belief.

The Mystery of the Charity of Charles Péguy

Hill's next major work, the last to appear in the 1980's, moves more in the direction of orthodox religion, although his characteristic ambiguity is fully present. The work in question is *The Mystery of the Charity of Charles Péguy*, a poem of one hundred quatrains.

Péguy, a Frenchman of unusually forceful personality, was both an ardent Catholic and a socialist. During the Dreyfus Affair, the controversy involving a Jewish army officer falsely convicted of treason in 1894, Péguy championed Captain Alfred Dreyfus and allied himself with the socialist leader Jean Juarès. He broke with the position of Juarès, however, after France entered World War I in August, 1914, for Juarès had sought a peaceful resolution, while Péguy was firmly anti-German. Too old for the draft, Péguy enlisted in the French army and was killed in the first months of the war.

Through most of the poem, Hill expresses unfeigned admiration for Péguy, even though many of Péguy's views differ sharply from ones Hill has supported elsewhere. As Hill shows, Péguy created a myth of the French peasant before the depredations of capitalism as devoted to the soil and part of an ideal rural community. Although this view seems quite like the one Hill excoriated when professed by Ruskin, he presents it in straightforward fashion, without his usual ambiguity or irony.

Péguy's devotion to the French nation went hand in hand with religion. For him, church and state were not separate entities but a united amalgam deserving his allegiance. The foremost expression of this union of throne and altar was his cult of Joan of Arc, whom he portrayed as the heroine of the nascent French nation, and it was largely Péguy's efforts, and those of other French nationalists, that caused Pope Benedict XV to elevate Joan to sainthood in 1920. Hill views saints with much less enthusiasm than does Péguy, but he presents Péguy's activities on Joan's behalf fully and fairly, possibly admiring not his particular religious stance but his selfless devotion to what he considered right, the "charity" of Hill's title.

Hill wholeheartedly endorses Péguy's criticism of the power of the machine. In doing so, Hill does not reverse the position of his earlier work, disagreeing with Eliot, Ruskin, and Péguy that an ideal world existed before the rise of capitalism. However, it does not follow from Hill's rejection of premodern nostalgia that he disagrees with these writers' criticism of the modern world. Like Péguy, Hill believes that machines endlessly repeat motion without purpose. People are forced to adjust themselves to a fixed routine and sooner or later fall victim to the implacable rhythm of industrialism. The philosopher Henri Bergson strongly influenced Hill's views, and Bergson's doctrine of time receives considerable attention in the poem.

The Triumph of Love

Like *The Mystery of the Charity of Charles Péguy*, *The Triumph of Love* is one long "poem" comprising a large number (150) of smaller items, a structure echoing the 150 psalms of the Psalter. Like *Mercian Hymns*, the poem's locale is Hill's West Midland childhood home, and its focus is the events of World War II. However, where *Mercian Hymns* uses the figure of King Offa, a secular ruler, as a focal point, *The Triumph of Love* focuses on the figure of Saint Kenelm, also a member of ancient Mercia's royal family renowned not for his rule but for his martyrdom, and underneath, a repeated return to the figure of the Virgin Mary, to whom the poem is dedicated. Perhaps the most significant departure from Hill's previous work, however, is the extent and degree of satire, even of farce, in *The Triumph of Love*.

Hill's poetic voice switches tone and mood often and abruptly throughout the poem, at one point commenting of another poet, "Rancorous, narcissistic old sod what/ makes him go on? We thought, hoped rather,/ he might be dead," and elsewhere characterizing the poetic form *Laus et vituperativo* ("praise and opposition") as

> . . . public, forensic,
> yet with a vehement
> private ambition for the people's
> greater good—Joannis
> Miltoni, Angli, pro Populo Angli-
> cano Defensio: this and other tracts,
> day-laboured-at, under great imposition
> Laus et vituperatio, lost, rediscovered,
> renewed on few occasions this century.

Veering from the colloquial to the Latinate, Hill also puns, excoriates, and inserts editorial comments and mock "errata" into his verse. This chorus—or cacophony—of voices echoes a new tolerance of disorder in Hill's poetry, a millennial embrace of postmodernism that nonetheless continues to express Hill's ongoing concerns with the aftermath of World War II's destruction of landscapes and peoples: "What is he saying;/ why is he still so angry?"

THE ORCHARDS OF SYON

The Orchards of Syon is the fourth and final collection in a series that began with *Canaan* and includes *Speech! Speech!* and *The Triumph of Love*. When read as a unit, the four collections are reminiscent of Dante's *La divina commedia* (c. 1320; *The Divine Comedy*, 1802). *The Orchards of Syon* consists of seventy-two blank-verse soliloquies structured in the autumnal tradition of the classical eclogue. The work thematically intertwines the idea of *La vida es sueño* (pr. 1635; *Life Is a Dream*, 1830) from Pedro Calderón de la Barca and the dark forest of the mind from Dante, as well as

Dante's *La vita nuova* (c. 1292; *Vita Nuova*, 1861; better known as *The New Life*). These dark forests may at times also be golden orchards, with a Frostean progression from green to gold to candescent red; at other times they may also be a "*Wood of the Suicides*" and "murderous fantasy." The progression is biographical as well; an old man looks back at his golden youth in the Goldengrove of his Worcestershire childhood and traces his memories through the historical events of his life (the world wars, the burned Zeppelin, the Holocaust, gutted tabernacles, the Blitz, and people fleeing through the Warsaw sewers) to create a chaotic, meandering spiritual biography in which Nebuchadnezzar gnaws grass and Cain's brood are busy at Heorot.

The poems range from verbose, self-indulgent, and clearly unrealized stanzas (the poet as "*Vox clamans in deserto*" telling us "I believe this has been done. . . ./ . . . I may be mistaken./ Don't look it up this time. . . .") to the dense and cryptic, full of Eliot-like allusions and Pound-like compression. There are truly elegiac images of birds and countryside and references to Petrarch, Vergil, Cassandra, King Lear, Tom Wyatt, Gustave Flaubert, Guy de Maupassant, Gerard Manley Hopkins, Alfred, Lord Tennyson, Wilfred Owen, Søren Kierkegaard, and Melchizedek.

Hill's theme may well be the reconciliation of the romantic love of nature with the violence of war and of modern life with the otherworldliness of Christianity. Hill has always been interested in the Romantics' question of the relationship of poetry to truth, hence his repeated references to Samuel Taylor Coleridge. Hill takes readers down blind alleys and leaves them there. At times the poet's prosaic voice dominates; at other times, he engages in wonderful lyricism. In ". . . *Beam/ us up, Asrael* . . . ," popular culture, in the form of a popular phrase from the television program *Star Trek*, mingles with the religiously esoteric in his use of the dark angel Asrael instead of *Star Trek*'s Scottie. Los Angeles is a holy place and Glastonbury is "mislodged on its mud lake."

There are images of staging, acting, and shutter play, including a shadow-play, wind machines off camera, handheld or swivel cameras, Shakespearean voices, Spanish drama from the Golden Age, the light fantastic, a production of Jean Cocteau's *Orphée* (pr.

1926; *Orpheus*, 1933) that Hill saw six times in one week, and the camera taking low-level shots of a reduced city and gutted towers. Much as Samuel Beckett mocked language, Hill plays with words: ". . . Oh my sole/ sister, you, little sister-my-soul"; ". . . no due season. Do not/ mourn unduly . . ."; ". . . Strophe after strophe/ ever more catastrophic. Did I say/ strophe? I meant salvo, sorry." The references to William Shakespeare's *The Tempest* (pr. 1611) and "Prospero's Farewell" suggest Hill's self-vision. An old man, reviewing his past and envisioning the end of his career, tries to remind himself of action to take with commands: ". . . Cite EMMANUEL:/ the man of sorrows whose blood burns us./ *Le misericordieux qui nous brûle le sang.*"

A Treatise of Civil Power

A Treatise of Civil Power echoes the title of English poet John Milton's 1659 polemic, *A Treatise of Civil Power in Ecclesiastical Causes*, and thereby prepares readers to consider the question of poets' involvement in issues of civic justice through the ages. In keeping with its stark title is the volume's direct style, illustrated in Hill's praise of George Frideric Handel's tightly organized music as "a treatise of civil power," deliberate and harmonious ("G. F. Handel, Opus 6"). The opening poem, "The Minor Prophets," describes the prophecies—including "scorched earth" and a "scorpion king"—of Joel and the other minor prophets of ancient Israel. Another poem, "Citations I," describes poetry as "*a means of survival*" that helps one regain one's self amid war and therefore is "*a mode of moral life.*" It urges readers to preserve democracy and respect the intelligence of citizens—in effect, to get back to basics.

The poems in this collection reflect Hill's obsession with aging, with the assertion that his ". . . lyric mojo/ atrophied at around ninety . . . " ("Citations II"), his self-description as ". . . an old body// its mouth working" ("On Reading *Blake: Prophet Against Empire*") and as ". . . a babbler/ in the crowd's face—" ("Nachwort"), and poem titles ("Before Senility"), but, in "Citations II," he also asserts that ". . . invention reinvents itself/ every so often in the line of death" and that he might even stroll through "a city of emerald" as promised in Revelations or at least a city of "zircon."

As usual, in poems such as "On Reading *Milton and the English Revolution*," Hill echoes the phrasing of his

sources, switches disconcertingly from the serious to the comic ("Fix your own tail to the Jerusalem donkey"), plays word games (". . . Idiolect/ that could be idiot dialect . . ."), and tosses out modern allusions and personal commentaries ("H. Mirren's super"). At times, as in "On Reading *Blake: Prophet Against Empire*," he admits his borrowings: ". . . (I've/ cribbed Whitman, you stickler—short of a phrase)." His topics range from poets (Sir Thomas Wyatt; Henry Howard, the earl of Surrey; William Blake), dramatists (Ben Jonson), and politicians (Oliver Cromwell, Edmund Burke) to representations of classical music in poetry (Handel and Johannes Brahms) and famous works of literary criticism to memorials for Gillian Rose, Ernest Barlach, and Aleksander Wat. Titles reflect their bookish topics: "On Reading *Crowds and Power*," "On Reading The *Essayes or Counsels, Civill and Morall*," "On Reading *Burke on Empire, Liberty, and Reform*." In "On Reading The *Essayes or Counsels, Civill and Morall*," Hill commingles the personal and modern ("my parents never owned a house") with the historical (seventeenth century issues), the sentimental with the realistic, and morality with quests for power.

"Masques" toys with Jonson's visions expressed through Inigo Jones's "great arches," then wallows in the "dung and detritus" of the streets, deflating the sublime with reminders of ordinary people on ordinary streets (as Hill does in other poems with reminders of his own resentments). In "Coda," Hill writes of his own great-grandfather who was a "Welsh iron-puddler," with his "penny a week insurance cum burial fund,/ cashing in pain itself . . . ," a common man suffering from the rules and regulations of civil power. At different points, Hill speaks with different voices, sometimes as Blake, sometimes as Milton or even the English Puritan conqueror Cromwell, who might well have "an unfinished psalm" echoing in his skull ("To the Lord Protector Cromwell"). He calls Burke a "realist" ("On Reading *Burke on Empire, Liberty, and Reform*"); rejects the Turing machine ("A Cloud in Aquila"); contemplates an "unsatisfactory tomb" in Framlingham Church, with its unfinished Hans Holbein sketch and "inaccurate pietas" ("In Framlingham Church"); and finds that, in fifty years of the Federal Republic of Germany and Willy Brandt kneeling at the Ghetto memorial in Warsaw, words fail and "Justice is in another world" ("On Looking Through *50 Jahre im Bild: Bundesrepublik Deutschland*").

Throughout the collection, Hill purposely creates obtuseness, even in his most exciting verses. For example, the title "Holbein" would seem to indicate a verse on the famous portrait artist, but instead it is about "the other Cromwell, the strange muse of Wyatt," and even for people versed in history, it takes a moment to connect the Renaissance poet Wyatt with Thomas Cromwell (not Oliver), who lost his head to a sharp axe for encouraging what proved to be Henry VIII's failed marriage with Anne of Cleves. Cromwell's "trim wit on the scaffold" refers to the Renaissance tradition of a final speech before execution; Hill's verse imitates Wyatt's meter. Similarly, the poem "Parallel Lives" becomes more meaningful if readers know that Plutarch's *Ethika* (after c. 100; *Moralia*, 1603) was translated into English by Wyatt as *Plutarckes Boke of the Quyete of Mynde* (1528).

OTHER MAJOR WORKS

NONFICTION: *The Lords of Limit: Essays on Literature and Ideas*, 1984; *The Enemy's Country: Words, Contexture, and Other Circumstances of Language*, 1991; *Style and Faith*, 2003; *Collected Critical Writings*, 2008.

TRANSLATION: *Brand*, 1978, 1981, 1996 (of Henrik Ibsen's dramatic poem).

BIBLIOGRAPHY

Ingelbein, Raphaël. *Misreading England: Poetry and Nationhood Since the Second World War*. Atlanta: Rodopi, 2002. An analysis of Hill along with Philip Larkin, Ted Hughes, and Seamus Heaney that considers the way in which each poet "misreads" his predecessors' visions of England during the nineteenth and early twentieth centuries, and also assesses the contrast between Heaney's Northern Irish nationalism and the Englishness of the other three.

McDonald, Peter. *Serious Poetry: Form and Authority, from Yeats to Hill*. New York: Oxford University Press, 2002. Looks at the interaction of their roles as critics as well as poets in William Butler Yeats, T. S. Eliot, W. H. Auden, Louis MacNeice, Seamus Heaney, and Hill.

McNees, Eleanor Jane. *Eucharistic Poetry: The Search for Presence in the Writings of John Donne, Gerard Manley Hopkins, Dylan Thomas, and Geoffrey Hill*. Cranbury, N.J.: Associated University Presses, 1992. Includes an analysis of some of Hill's poetry with an emphasis on the religious symbolism that it contains.

Milne, W. S. *An Introduction to Geoffrey Hill*. London: Bellew, 1998. Critical analysis of Hill's poetry with bibliographic references.

Roberts, Andrew Michael. *Geoffrey Hill*. Tavistock, England: Northcote House, 2002. This clear but subtle introduction to the poet and his work combines a close reading of Hill's poems with an overview of the critical debate they engender. Roberts captures the uniqueness of and the controversy aroused by Hill's work and ties it to contemporary issues.

Wainwright, Jeffrey. *Acceptable Words: Essays on the Poetry of Geoffrey Hill*. New York: Manchester University Press, 2006. A comprehensive critical study of Hill's work. It provides an introduction to Hill for new readers as well as in-depth analyses aimed to contribute to the understanding of Hill's poetry by those familiar with his work.

Bill Delaney; Leslie Ellen Jones
Updated by Gina Macdonald

THOMAS HOOD

Born: London, England; May 23, 1799
Died: London, England; May 3, 1845

PRINCIPAL POETRY

Odes and Addresses to Great People, 1825 (with John Hamilton Reynolds)
Whims and Oddities: In Prose and Verse, 1826-1827
"The Plea of the Midsummer Fairies," "Hero and Leander," "Lycus the Centaur," and Other Poems, 1827

The Epping Hunt, 1829

The Comic Annual, 1830-1839, 1842 (poetry and prose)

The Dream of Eugene Aram, the Murderer, 1831

Hood's Own: Or, Laughter from Year to Year, 1839

Miss Kilmansegg and Her Precious Leg, 1840

Whimsicalities: A Periodical Gathering, 1844

OTHER LITERARY FORMS

As a journalist, Thomas Hood contributed prose as well as poetry to such periodicals as the *London Magazine*, *The New Monthly Magazine*, and *Hood's Magazine and Comic Miscellany*. He also wrote drama criticism for *The Atlas* for several months in 1826, before trying to write dramatic pieces of his own. In 1828, he wrote an ill-fated farce, *York and Lancaster: Or, A School Without Scholars*, for the theater manager Frederick Henry Yates, and followed this unsuccessful attempt with at least two more burlesques that have been lost in whole or in part. He wrote two closet dramas that were not published until after his death: *Lamia: A Romance* (pb. 1852) based on John Keats's poem of the same title, and *Guido and Marina: A Dramatic Sketch* (pb. 1882), a romantic dialogue.

Hood did numerous etchings and drawings for his publications and had others executed under his direction. His best-known engraving, "The Progress of Cant," a large Hogarthian-style work published in 1825, shows a rag-tag parade of Londoners bearing signs and banners to proclaim their favorite causes and philosophies, meanwhile exhibiting their contrary actions.

Encouraged by the early success of his first volumes of comic verse, Hood published a two-volume collection of short stories titled *National Tales* in 1827; unfortunately, just as his attempts to write drama demonstrated his lack of dramatic skill, the stories exhibited that he had no real talent for prose fiction. Hood imitated the Italian novella form used by the Elizabethans, without writing a single story of literary value. He also wrote two novels—*Tylney Hall* (1834) and *Up the Rhine* (1840)—with somewhat better popular success, although the novels were nearly as lacking in literary merit. *Tylney Hall* went through numerous printings in England and America, but owed its success to the humorous portions; the serious plot and major characters are rather insipid, manifesting the same contrivance and shallowness that afflicted his short stores. *Up the Rhine* was a success in the bookstalls—in England, America, and, predictably, in Frankfurt. A travelogue-novel similar to Mark Twain's *Innocents Abroad* (1869), *Up the Rhine* draws upon Hood's "exile" years in Germany (1835 to 1839). It is light and enjoyable reading, but far from "quality" fiction. In both novels, Hood gave free vent to his punning genius, which adds humor but detracts from the overall temper of both stories. Another novel, *Our Family*, remained incomplete at Hood's death, although several chapters were published serially in *Hood's Magazine* (it was eventually published in 1861). There is no evidence that Hood's aspirations to be a novelist would have produced a better book. His many letters, though often delightful and always sparkling with wit and humor, are difficult to read. Hood's main difficulty as a prose writer was his inability to sustain a smooth, readable text that is not chopped up by distracting wordplay; in addition, he was simply not a good storyteller. Both problems greatly handicapped his ability to write long poetic narratives as well.

ACHIEVEMENTS

Thomas Hood's position in the generally overlooked period between the end of the Romantic movement and the beginning of the Victorian era has caused his true importance to be greatly underestimated. Although he can scarcely be called one of the giants of English poetry, his achievements are far from insignificant. His primary contributions to English letters have been fourfold: the refinement of English poetic humor, the popularization of poetry, the sympathetic portrayal of common English domesticity, and the arousal of humanitarian sentiments on a popular level.

Hood's comic verse—of which the amount is greater than and the quality superior to the work of any other English or American poet—evolved into what J. C. Reid calls "a highly individual amalgam of the farcical and the sinister, the pathetic and the ghoulish, that has few ancestors but many heirs." Hood's peculiar style did not preclude his diverse experimentation, whereby he often imitated and improved on earlier comic techniques. He remains without rival in the use of the pun. He left a legacy of humorous poetry so varied that it not only provides a smooth transition from the often acrimonious wit of the eighteenth century—with none of the acrimony—but also often anticipates comic techniques and themes that died with Hood until they were resurrected in the twentieth century, especially in the dark or grotesque humor of writers such as Franz Kafka.

Because Hood made poetry relevant to everyday life and wrote in a highly entertaining style, verse once more became something that the common people could enjoy. Since the death of William Shakespeare, who also catered in his drama to popular tastes, poetry had become an almost purely academic art form. The neoclassical movement isolated poetry from the common person to a great extent through various formulary restraints and elevated diction. The Romantic movement sought to reestablish the language of life as the language of poetry, but the philosophy and ideals of many Romantics were inaccessible to the masses. Hood popularized poetry by brilliantly expressing commonplace ideas in common words.

Writing for a popular audience meant being free to explore popular themes. Hood's treatment of domestic scenes merits special attention. Ordinary housewives and mothers, with their squalling babes in arms, domestic servants, husband-wife or parent-child relations, all the accoutrements of home and hearth (especially cookery) receive sympathetic treatment from the pen of this devoted family man. Hood takes the reader into mansions, but through the servant's entrance, and takes the butler's perspective or leaves the reader in the kitchen. What William Hogarth did with engraving, Hood did with poetry. Not afflicted by pretension or ambition, but sensitive to both, he remained the poet of the common folk throughout his career.

In his later years, this sympathy for the proletariat led to some of the first and finest advocacy of basic human rights ever to be expressed in verse. Hood echoed the faint cries of social protest sounded by William Blake, amplified them, and added his own passionate appeals for reform. Never a revolutionary, Hood sought to inspire the upper middle class to extend a hand of true charity and compassion to the needs of the poor, to influence industrialists to pay a decent wage, and to influence a notoriously competitive society to reassess its values. Hood was a voice crying somewhat in vain in the wilderness, but those he inspired were able to induce many notable social reforms in the second half of the nineteenth century.

BIOGRAPHY

Thomas Hood's father, also named Thomas, was a partner in the book-selling and publishing firm of Vernor and Hood, which produced *Poetical Magazine*, *Lady's Monthly Museum*, and the *Monthly Mirror*. His mother, Elizabeth Sands, was the daughter of an engraver. Both occupations determined the future career of Thomas Hood, one of six children in the Hood family to survive infancy. Hood's early education was at an Islington preparatory school, then at the Alfred House Academy at Camberwell Green. The deaths of his father and elder brother in 1811 left Thomas the man of the family, so he took a job clerking to supplement the family income. Poor health forced him to move from clerking to engraving for his uncle, but because his constitution continued to suffer, he was sent in 1815 to live with relatives in Dundee, Scotland, where he continued his apprenticeship in the engraving trade. At Dundee, Hood began writing seriously. His health improved, and he returned to London in the autumn of 1817, where he worked as an engraver until he was hired in 1821 by John Taylor, a former employee of Hood's father and then editor of the *London Magazine*. Within a few months, his mother died, leaving Hood the responsibility of providing for four sisters, one of whom also died a short time later.

At the *London Magazine*, Hood was plunged into the company of many of England's prominent writers—Charles Lamb, Allan Cunningham, T. G. Wainewright, and John Hamilton Reynolds. Hood's friendship with Reynolds brought him into close contact with the circle and work of the recently deceased Keats, and Hood strove for several years to imitate the great Romantic's lush and effusive style. Indeed, he was thought by many (including Cunningham) to be the logical successor of Keats, but Hood's collaboration with Reynolds on a book of comic verse in 1825 did more to further his literary career than any of his attempts to imitate the Romantics. During the same year, Hood married Reynolds's sister Jane and settled into the domestic life that would later inspire much of his poetry. Since he had ceased to edit the *London Magazine* during the previous year, Hood was obliged to publish in earnest for an income.

Hood's first daughter was born and died in May, 1827, inspiring Lamb's famous elegy "On an Infant Dying as Soon as Born." Hood's repeated exposure to the death of those closest to him was having a profound impact on his poetry, in which death figures so prominently. The following year an attack of rheumatic fever left Hood in the weakened condition that plagued him for the rest of his life. Hood continued writing, even while ill, since it was his sole means of support. He produced the first of his *Comic Annuals* in 1830, the year that his daughter Frances Freeling was born. Although his comic verse was popular, the Hood family never advanced beyond a lower-middle-class lifestyle. In 1832, they moved into their own home—Lake House in Wanstead—but the failure in 1834 of an engraving firm in which Hood had heavily invested, together with his own financial mismanagement, forced them to relinquish the house and accept the more economical life of the Continent. After the birth of his only son, Tom, Hood moved his family to Coblentz, Germany, to begin an "exile" that lasted until 1840.

In 1841, Hood assumed the editorship of *The New Monthly Magazine*. In and out of illness, financially struggling, and changing residences almost annually, Hood began to write his poems of social conscience. In 1843, he ceased editing *The New Monthly Magazine* to found *Hood's Magazine*, which he edited until early in 1845, although he was seriously ill during the entire period. A Civil List pension was granted his wife in November, 1844, when Hood was confined to what would be his deathbed. He continued writing almost to the very end. He died in May, 1845, and is buried at Kensal Green, London. Perhaps the finest tribute to his poetry is found in a letter from Hood to Frederick Ward, written in the summer of 1844: "Though I may not have reflected any very great honour on our national literature, I have not disgraced it." Such humility was typical of Hood.

Thomas Hood (Archive Photos/Getty Images)

ANALYSIS

Primarily because he lived to write and wrote to live, Thomas Hood managed to publish a staggering amount of poetry in a relatively short time. Unfortunately, the pressure to keep the creditors at bay and the bacon on his table rendered much of his poetry unworthy of regard; he often failed to edit poems for which he could hardly afford enough time to write. He was seldom more than a hack writer, churning out journalistic doggerel and meanwhile maintaining an apparently voluminous correspondence, editing his annuals and magazines, executing his engravings, and trying to establish a reputation as a novelist. The mystery of his life is that he accomplished all this as a frequently bedridden invalid.

As a consequence of his need to offer original and entertaining poetry to the public on a regular basis, Hood wandered widely through the realm of possibilities to produce a profusion of experiments in form and content, in theme, rhythm, and rhyme—perhaps covering a wider range than any other English poet. In Hood, one can find examples of such peculiarities as initial rhyme, various metrical arrangements of anapests and dactyls, all the major English stanza forms, and imitations of numerous styles—from those of Geoffrey Chaucer, Edmund Spenser, John Milton, Alexander Pope, Percy Bysshe Shelley, Lord Byron, Keats, and Shakespeare, to a host of lesser lights. Hood's imitations are often well-executed; his originals are even better. Omitting what is merely topical, trivial, childish, or deplorable, one finds that the remainder of Hood's canon contains a considerable quantity of poetry, some of it brilliant.

Hood began writing poetry as a pastime about 1814, during the period when he supplemented the family income by working as a clerk. In "Literary Reminiscences" (1833), Hood recalls how he stole moments from his employer, uninformatively identified as "Bell & Co.," to "take stray dips in the Castalian pool." A year later, after removing to Dundee, Scotland, to improve his health, Hood started writing a satirical *Dundee Guide*, the manuscript of which was unfortunately lost by 1820, although enough lines survived in a letter to show that it was nothing brilliant. As early as 1816, however, Hood began making anonymous contributions to Dundee periodicals, and thus first began to see his work in print. This fired him with a thirst to sell himself to "that minor Mephistopheles, the Printer's Devil." Hood was at this time being influenced by William Wordsworth and Samuel Taylor Coleridge, Byron, and Shelley; to a lesser extent by Lamb, George Crabbe, Robert Southey, and Leigh Hunt; and most of all by Sir Walter Scott, "The Great Unknown." The narrative manner of Byron's *Childe Harold's Pilgrimage* (1812-1818, 1819), *The Giaour* (1813), *The Bride of Abydos* (1813), *The Corsair* (1814), and *Lara* (1814), tempered by the influence of Scott's *The Lay of the Last Minstrel* (1805), *Marmion: A Tale of Flodden Field* (1808), *The Lady of the Lake* (1810), *Rokeby* (1813), and *Waverley: Or, 'Tis Sixty Years Since* (1814), combined to foster Hood's first major poem, *The Bandit*, probably written between 1815 and 1817 but not published until forty years after his death.

THE BANDIT

The Bandit is a relatively long poem (some 820 lines divided into three cantos), a narrative about Ulric, the earl of Glenallen, who, as a result of treacherous circumstances, has been forced into the role of "Chief-

tain" to a band of outlaws. Although a cunning and brave leader, Glenallen secretly despises the mischievous deeds he has done, yet "Repeated wrongs had turned his breast to steel,/ And all but these he had forgot to feel." In the first canto, Glenallen discloses the plans of his final act as chief of the bandits, "To 'venge the wrongs he suffered from the world!" Heedlessly, he discloses to the outlaws his true identity as earl of Glenallen, proclaimed a traitor to the throne of Scotland. All the bandits except Wolf, Glenallen's rival, depart with the chieftain to take revenge on Glenallen's former friend, Arden, at the latter's wedding to Glenallen's former betrothed, Adelaide. In the second canto, Glenallen disrupts the wedding and announces his intention of murdering Arden before he can consummate the marriage; but after the pitiful pleadings of "trembling Adelaide," he repents and orders his bandits to disperse. Just at this moment, Wolf arrives with another band to take Glenallen for the reward on his head. In the ensuing swordplay, Arden makes several attempts to save the life of Glenallen, who is finally wounded into unconsciousness after killing Wolf. Before the bandits can deal with the wedding guests, however, the castle is mysteriously set afire. The bandits take up the unconscious Glenallen and flee. Canto 3 opens with Glenallen already in the custody of the authorities, locked away in a tower and awaiting execution. In his bitterness of soul, he eagerly awaits the release that death will bring him. The keeper enters and proves to be a former confederate: "Is it Donald! or a mocking dream?/ Are these things so, or do they only seem?/ Am I awake?" Donald, after failing to convince Glenallen to escape, and in haste for what seems to be the sound of an approaching guard escort, lends his dagger to the captive so that he might dispatch himself honorably. Glenallen perishes just as "Pardon! Pardon!" echoes on the walls and Arden rushes into the cell.

The puerility of the plot and the verse fails to disguise the influences of Romanticism. Glenallen is a typical Romantic hero, arraigned in a stock melodramatic situation, pausing at the appropriate times to brood over his cruel alienation from humanity and life, more ready to die than to live. His is the childish fantasy of "after I'm dead and gone, then they'll be sorry they hurt me," but, after all, it is the same childishness of vision that pervades much of Byron and Shelley. The significance of *The Bandit* lies in Hood's ability to use language well and to exercise a healthy imagination in verse that accommodates at least the superficial elements of Romanticism at a time before he has seriously devoted himself to writing poetry.

KEATS'S INFLUENCE

Although there were Romantic tendencies in Hood's own writing before Keats's death, one can find in his verse a pronounced identification with the style of Keats that extends about five or six years after 1821, beginning with Hood's introduction to the Reynolds family through his work at the *London Magazine* that same year. Reynolds and his sisters had enjoyed a close friendship with Keats and entertained fond memories of the young Romantic. Hood entered an atmosphere in the Reynolds household suffused with intimacies from the life and work of the relatively unknown Keats. To this period belongs most of what is often called Hood's "serious" poetry.

The Romantic movement had peaked and already begun to decline into the commonplace sentimentality and melodrama from which Robert Browning and Alfred, Lord Tennyson were destined to rescue it momentarily. Shelley and Byron's best works had already been published; indeed, Shelley died soon after Keats. Coleridge had graduated to philosophy, Wordsworth had defected to the establishment. Keats's final volume—*"Lamia," "Isabella," "The Eve of St. Agnes," and Other Poems*—had appeared in 1820 (Hood's closet drama *Lamia*, based on Keats's poem, was written in 1824 but not published until after Hood's death). With friendly critics encouraging and applauding the growing likeness of Hood's poetry to that of Keats, it was an easy time for Hood to begin imagining himself to be Keats's successor.

"THE SEA OF DEATH"

Perhaps a sense of identification with Keats's illness and death led Hood to give death such a preeminent place in his serious and even in his comic verse. Hood seems to accord death a place of passive acceptance, at times even to embrace it. For example, "The Sea of Death," which appeared first in the *London Magazine* (March, 1822) and later in *"The Plea of the*

Midsummer Fairies," "Hero and Leander," "Lycus the Centaur," and Other Poems, makes the somewhat trite comparison of death to an "oceanpast" that erases the sand tracks of life "like a pursuing grave." This idea, however, is developed into a passively beautiful scene, where "spring-faced cherubs" also are asleep in "the birth-night of their peace." For contrast, Hood adds "neighbour brows scarr'd by the brunts/ Of strife and sorrowing"; and with the dead, Time itself "Slept, as he sleeps upon the silent face/ Of a dark dial in a sunless place." It is a typical Romantic eschatology; death is a place of silence and repose, a dreamlike eternity. Although Hood's view of death acquired a more theologically sound dimension during the next twenty years, his attitude of resignation to the inevitable did not change. His awareness of the closeness of death permeates all his poetry; death, dying, and corruption tinge nearly every poem with sobriety and cause his humor to wax dark. Living in continual ill health as he did, this could hardly be called a Romantic affectation.

SONNETS

Hood's important poems from this period include a number of sonnets, many deserving more attention than they have received. The sonnets also reflect the influence of the Romantic poets. "Midnight," the two-sonnet "On a Sleeping Child" (all three in the *London Magazine*, December, 1822), and the eulogistic "Sonnet: Written in Keats's 'Endymion'" (the *London Magazine*, May, 1823) are among his very best. Another, beginning "It is not death . . . ," reveals not only Romantic, but also direct Shakespearean influence. It was included, along with most of his other "serious" poetry, in the volume *"The Plea of the Midsummer Fairies," "Hero and Leander," "Lycus the Centaur," and Other Poems*.

"THE PLEA OF THE MIDSUMMER FAIRIES," "HERO AND LEANDER," "LYCUS THE CENTAUR, AND OTHER POEMS"

Most of the poems in this book (twenty-two of thirty-seven) had been previously published, many in *London Magazine*. The book constitutes the evidence offered by many that Hood was a thwarted Romantic because of the pervasive influence of Keats. The title poem consists of 126 Spenserian stanzas (except that the final lines are pentameters), celebrating, "by an allegory, that immortality that Shakespeare has conferred on the Fairy mythology by his *Midsummer Night's Dream*."

Hood had previously written a fairly long Romantic allegory, "The Two Swans" (1824), and so had prepared himself to create what he no doubt hoped would be considered his masterpiece. Lamb, to whom the poem was affectionately dedicated, likened the poem to "the songs of Apollo," but few others have felt it to be so. Although the poem abounds in the lush sensual imagery characteristic of Keats, it sags hopelessly throughout, mainly because the story is too skimpy and the monologues too substantial for a narrative of that length. The narrator, who happens on a circle of accommodating but unhappy fairies (including Titania, Puck, Ariel, and Queen Mab), learns from Titania that they are unhappy because their "fairy lives/ Are leased upon the fickle faith of men." Her complaint lasts through nearly eight stanzas, after which the "melancholy Shape" of time (Saturn, Mutability) appears with "hurtful scythe" to harvest the wee folk. After an argument between the fairies and Saturn that lasts seventy-five stanzas (nearly 60 percent of the poem), the ghost of Shakespeare arrives just in time to save the fairies, who express their affectionate gratitude by crowning the Bard with a halo "Such as erst crown'd the old Apostle's head." As an allegory defending the importance of imagination (fancy) above reason in poetry, the significance of human feeling, the allurements of nature, and the mysterious, "The Plea of the Midsummer Fairies" fails; seeking to establish the principles of the Romantic movement, Hood offended through employment of its excesses.

The second poem in the volume, *Hero and Leander*, while certainly not lagging as a narrative, nearly approaches *The Bandit* in its tendency toward melodrama. Written in the sestina form of Shakespeare's *Venus and Adonis* (1593), the poem has a loveliness of its own but it is not brilliant. By far the better is the third poem, *Lycus the Centaur*, first published in 1822. Dedicated to Reynolds, it employs the strikingly unusual rhythm of anapestic tetrameter couplets that give the impression of fast-paced narrative; it is a galloping rhythm, suitable to horses and centaurs. The 430 lines of the poem are rich in sensuous detail, a feature that

lies nearly dormant in poetry from Keats to Algernon Charles Swinburne. *Lycus the Centaur* must be read aloud to be thoroughly appreciated. Admittedly, Hood's poetry did not achieve anything near perfection. The poem has flaws, as when Lycus complains of his loneliness: "There were women! there men! but to me a third sex/ I saw them all dots—yet I loved them as specks"; or when several successive closed couplets begin to give the feel of "The Night Before Christmas," but *Lycus the Centaur*, for all its faults and its Keatsian imagery, is original and beautiful.

Most critics agree that the best poems in *"The Plea of the Midsummer Fairies," "Hero and Leander," "Lycus the Centaur," and Other Poems* are the lyrics, most of which are definitely Keatsian. Hood's "Ode: Autumn" at times provides an interesting contrast to Keat's "Ode to Autumn," but there is more to compare than to contrast. Two other short poems on autumn are included in the volume, as are three poems on the loss of innocence ("Retrospective Review," "Song, for Music," and "I Remember, I Remember"), a decent "Ode to Melancholy," and some of Hood's best sonnets. Pervasive throughout the book is the awareness, without terror, of death and corruption. Although the volume of serious poems caused some readers to see Hood as a worthy successor to Keats, *"The Plea of the Midsummer Fairies," "Hero and Leander," "Lycus the Centaur," and Other Poems* met with a generally poor critical and public reception and failed to sell out even a single printing.

ODES AND ADDRESSES TO GREAT PEOPLE AND WHIMS AND ODDITIES

The apparent cause of this cool reception to *"The Plea of the Midsummer Fairies," "Hero and Leander," "Lycus the Centaur," and Other Poems* is that during the years immediately preceding its publication Hood had captured the public's attention as a writer of comic verse. In 1825, he produced *Odes and Addresses to Great People* (in collaboration with Reynolds) and, in the following year, the first series of *Whims and Oddities*. The time for humor in poetry had come—not the incisive, often caustic wit of the eighteenth century, but an inoffensive, wholesome humor to help people laugh their way through the oppressively industrial times at the beginning of the nineteenth century. The reading public wanted a humor that appealed to people of low estate without being vulgar. It found in the humorous verse of Hood exactly what it sought, and came to expect nothing more nor less than that from him.

The success of Hood's early comic publications depended heavily on his skill as a punster, examples of which are so abundant that they need not be dwelt on at length. Most commonly cited in this regard are the two ballads, "Faithless Sally Brown" and "Faithless Nelly Gray." In the first, two lovers go out for a walk that is interrupted by an impress gang from the Royal Navy; "And Sally she did faint away,/ While Ben he was brought to." After Ben's tour of duty is finished, he returns to find Sally is another man's sweetheart; he laments, "I've met with many a breeze before,/ But never such a blow." In the opening stanza of the second poem, "Ben Battle was a soldier bold,/ And used to war's alarms:/ But a cannon-ball took off his legs,/ So he laid down his arms!" Although these are not the best examples of his craft, there is no question that Hood was the best punster of his century (perhaps the best in English letters); most of his puns are exceptional. Unfortunately, much of Hood's humor is topical; many of his puns and jokes cannot be grasped by the modern reader without an understanding of the times and a knowledge of the idiom of the 1820's and 1830's. Even so, many of Hood's poems retain an appreciable humor for today because they present general observations on the human condition. The most notable include "An Address to the Steam Washing Company" in *Odes and Addresses to Great People*; "A Valentine," "The Fall of the Deer," "December and May," "She Is Far from the Land," "Remonstratory Ode: From the Elephant at Exeter Change . . . ," "The Sea-Spell," and the darkly humorous "The Last Man," all in *Whims and Oddities* (First Series); and "Bianca's Dream," "A Legend of Navarre," "The Demon-Ship," and "Tim Turpin" in *Whims and Oddities* (Second Series). In "The Demon-Ship," Hood does a masterful job of creating a terrifying situation that is reversed in the humor of the closing lines. In "The Last Man," the wry ending cannot shift a much longer poem into the comic mode, so that the overall effect is far from humorous. As a serious poem, "The Last Man" offers a brilliant description of a postapocalyptic world.

A SERIOUS TURN

Hood continued writing "serious" poetry during the remainder of his life, but until the last few years, his comic verse claimed the limelight. With the failure of the engraving firm in 1834 and the subsequent "exile" to Germany, however, financial and physical hardship weighed heavily on Hood and his family, and his comic verses began to acquire a certain note of sobriety. There had always been a loosely didactic element, a flexible moralizing, in his humor. Without gross distastefulness, Hood amused his audience by good-naturedly ridiculing people and institutions that were newsworthy or offensive to the public—in a way that often seemed to "teach a lesson." One of the most consistent objects of his humor was human greed; another was impoverishment. Employee displacement caused by unjust laws or advancements in technological efficiency also provoked his satirical wit. Since Hood no longer entertained hopes of succeeding Keats, his "serious" poetry began to develop an originality and power of its own, as Hood became a voice of the people's protest against those institutions. Hypocrisy and ambition became primary targets of his comic verse, which also developed a morbid, often sadistic, grotesqueness. Poems such as "Death's Ramble," from *Whims and Oddities*, in which a morality play is effected through pun after pun, led to "Death in the Kitchen" (1828), in which the puns are ingenious but the philosophizing about death unhumorous; to "Gog and Magog" (1830), with its hints of judgment and violence; to "Ode to Mr. Malthus" (1839), wherein the double standard of the well-to-do is satirized; and, finally, to *Miss Kilmansegg and Her Precious Leg*. Each poem outdoes the last in taking a more caustic, albeit humorous, view of humanity or some of its elements.

MISS KILMANSEGG AND HER PRECIOUS LEG

Beginning with *Miss Kilmansegg and Her Precious Leg*, the serious side of Hood sought to reassert itself again, this time with a vigor and force of wit that it had manifested only in comic verse, but with a simplicity of expression unencumbered by flowery Romantic or Elizabethan rhetoric. During the final years of his life, Hood produced his greatest impact on English poetry in the songs of social protest—*Miss Kilmansegg and Her Precious Leg*, "The Song of the Shirt," "The Bridge of

Sighs," and others—and his artistic masterpiece, "The Haunted House," which alone, said Edgar Allan Poe, "would have secured immortality for any poet of the nineteenth century."

Miss Kilmansegg and Her Precious Leg is a long satirical narrative of almost 2,400 lines. The central character is born into a family of great wealth:

> When she saw the light—it was no mere ray
> Of that light so common—so everyday—
> That the sun each morning launches—
> But six wax tapers dazzled her eyes,
> From a thing—a gooseberry bush for size—
> With a golden stem and branches.

After separate passages dealing in detail with her pedigree, birth, christening, childhood, and education, the reader learns that one day, while riding, Miss Kilmansegg lost control of her horse, which bolted at the sight of a ragged beggar, and in the ensuing accident "Miss K" lost her leg. Because she had been educated to a life-style of conspicuous consumption and hatred for the ordinary, she insists fanatically on replacing her natural leg with a golden one: "All sterling metal—not half-and-half,/ The Goldsmith's mark was stamped on the calf." (The pun on "golden calf" is intentional.) After she receives the expensive leg, the poem pursues her through her career as a fashionable debutante, her courtship, and her subsequent marriage to a foreign count of questionable origin. Their honeymoon is spent at a country estate, where she learns that her husband's sole interest is gambling. After several years of tumultuous living that exhausts all of "Miss K's" resources, the count murders her in the night, using her expensive leg as a bludgeon. Hood concludes the poem with a moral reminiscent of the "Pardoner's Tale" from Chaucer: "Price of many a crime untold;/ Gold! Gold! Gold:/ Good or bad a thousand fold!" The poem is very funny throughout, but the humor is accompanied by an undercurrent of bitterness against the rich, and the moralizing stanza at the poem's conclusion seems to affirm its serious didactic intention.

"THE SONG OF THE SHIRT"

Eight months later, *The New Monthly Magazine* published Hood's "A Tale of a Trumpet," another satirical poem, this time about a deaf woman to whom the devil supplies a trumpet through which she can hear all manner of scandalous gossip. Again, the poem ends in a moral against rumormongering. In November, 1843, *Punch* published Hood's "A Drop of Gin," a poem reminiscent of Hogarth's famous engraving "Gin Lane." The following month, *Punch* published "The Pauper's Christmas Carol" and "The Song of the Shirt," poems of social protest that probably better express Hood's mind than any other poems of his last fifteen years.

"The Song of the Shirt," with its driving, mechanical rhythm, is based on the plight of a poor widowed woman with starving infants who was arrested while trying to pawn some of her employer's garments to obtain money for food (she was a seamstress for seven shillings a week). Touched by the newspaper accounts and always sensitive to the exploitation of the poor, Hood wrote what his wife considered to be his finest poem. In it, a woman sits sewing, and as she sews she sings the "Song of the Shirt": "Work! work! work!/ While the cock is crowing aloof!/ And work—work—work,/ Till the stars shine through the roof!" The poem calls to mind the protest movements and revolutions that were soon to plague Europe in the wake of the Industrial Revolution—and the publication of Karl Marx's *Manifest der Kommunistischen Partei* (1848; with Friedrich Engel; *The Communist Manifesto*, 1850) and *Das Kapital* (1867, 1885, 1894; *Capital: A Critique of Political Economy*, 1886, 1907, 1909; better known as *Das Kapital*). The woman's lament is a desperate appeal born of the most abject misery: "Oh! God! that bread should be so dear,/ And flesh and blood so cheap!"

"THE HAUNTED HOUSE"

"The Haunted House" (*Hood's Magazine*, January, 1844), over which Poe became ecstatic, is indeed a powerful artistic creation: a descriptive, camera-eye narrative that builds an atmosphere of terror—which dissipates in the absolute meaninglessness of the poem. The reader can learn nothing of the source of the mystery, other than that a murder has apparently been committed, and that the house is haunted. The conclusion of the poem could be transplanted to any other part of the poem without disrupting the internal logic. It is as if Hood had left "The Haunted House" unfinished, perhaps to add to the sense of mystery and terror, but more likely through a lack of inspiration.

THE LAST YEARS

The artistic achievement represented by "The Haunted House" notwithstanding, Hood's heart in these last years was more concerned with the suffering of others. Having spent so many years in sickness and pain, laboring feverishly to meet endless deadlines, striving in spite of his own sufferings to make others laugh, he had acquired a true compassion for the poor and unfortunate that sought to be expressed in his verse. His last years of writing produced "The Lady's Dream" (February, 1844), a song of regret for a life not spent ministering to the needs of others; "The Workhouse Clock" (April, 1844), an "allegory" that fires its blistering sermon at a leisurely middle class: "Christian Charity, hang your head!"; and "The Lay of the Labourer" (November, 1844), a panegyric to the working class.

A final volume of comic verse—*Whimsicalities*—appeared in 1844, but besides "The Haunted House," Hood's most regarded publication of that year is "The Bridge of Sighs." Often anthologized or cited as an example of dactylic verse, it concerns a young woman who commits a desperate suicide by leaping from a city bridge. Journalistic, as most of Hood's verse was, "The Bridge of Sighs" is based on an actual case; whatever the circumstances of the original suicide were, however, Hood turns the incident to good use in expounding a favorite theme:

> Alas! for the rarity
> Of Christian charity
> Under the sun!
> Oh! it was pitiful!
> Near a whole city full,
> Home she had none!

Hood continued to write even as he lay upon his deathbed, where, among other poems and letters, he produced "Stanzas" (March, 1845): "Farewell, Life! My senses swim;/ And the world is growing dim;/ . . . Strong the earthy odour grows—/ I smell the Mould above the Rose!" Hood's farewell to life concludes with the same homely, cheerful philosophy that infused so much poetry written in pain, the same positive outlook that inspired him to ask for reform rather than revolu-

tion: "Welcome, Life! the Spirit strives!/ Strength returns, and hope revives;/ . . . I smell the Rose above the Mould!" The juxtaposition of the stanzas intimates that Hood's source of hope and strength was his willingness to embrace death without terror. Nine years after his death, a monument was erected over his grave, paid for by public subscription. Beneath the bust of Hood is engraved a simple coat of arms: on the shield is a heart pierced by a sewing needle; under it, the scroll reads, at Hood's request, "He sang the Song of the Shirt."

OTHER MAJOR WORKS

LONG FICTION: *Tylney Hall*, 1834; *Up the Rhine*, 1840.

SHORT FICTION: *National Tales*, 1827.

PLAYS: *York and Lancaster: Or, A School Without Scholars*, wr. 1828; *Lamia: A Romance*, pb. 1852; *Guido and Marina: A Dramatic Sketch*, pb. 1882.

MISCELLANEOUS: *Hood's Magazine*, 1861; *The Works of Thomas Hood*, 1869-1873 (Thomas Hood, Jr., and Mrs. Frances Freeling Broderip, editors; 10 volumes; 1882-1884, 11 volumes; 1972, 8 volumes).

BIBLIOGRAPHY

Brander, Laurence. *Thomas Hood*. London: Longmans, Green, 1963. Discusses Hood's early and later poems, as well as the public poems, for which Hood is remembered the most.

Clubbe, John. *Victorian Forerunner: The Later Career of Thomas Hood*. Durham, N.C.: Duke University Press, 1968. A scholarly and important contribution to the literary criticism available on Hood's later poems. Clubbe asserts that Hood wrote many of his most memorable poems in the last decade of his life.

Edgecombe, Rodney Stenning. *A Self-Divided Poet: Form and Texture in the Verse of Thomas Hood*. Newcastle-upon-Tyne, England: Cambridge Scholars, 2007. This in-depth examination of the poetry of Hood looks at his style in both the serious and lighter poems.

Jeffrey, Lloyd N. *Thomas Hood*. New York: Twayne, 1972. This introduction to Hood's poetry argues for the intrinsic value of his work despite his being overshadowed by the Romantics. Views the study

of Hood's poems as an important lead into nineteenth century literature. Discusses his poetry selec-
tively and devotes one chapter to the macabre and
grotesque in his works.

Jerrold, Walter. *Thomas Hood: His Life and Times.*
1907. Reprint. New York: Greenwood Press, 1969.
A full account of Hood's life with critical commentary of his poems. An important work for Hood
scholars.

Lodge, Sara. *Thomas Hood and Nineteenth-Century
Poetry: Work, Play and Politics.* New York: Manchester University Press, 2007. A biography of
Hood that looks at his life and writings, with a chapter on the grotesque and one on humour.

Reid, J. C. *Thomas Hood.* London: Routledge & Kegan
Paul, 1963. A full-length biographical and critical
study of Hood. Well researched and sympathetic in
its approach to this poet.

Larry David Barton

A. D. HOPE

Born: Cooma, New South Wales, Australia; July 21,
1907

Died: Canberra, Australian Capital Territory,
Australia; July 13, 2000

PRINCIPAL POETRY

The Wandering Islands, 1955
Poems, 1960
A. D. Hope, 1963
Collected Poems, 1930-1965, 1966
New Poems, 1965-1969, 1969
Dunciad Minor: An Heroick Poem, 1970
Collected Poems, 1930-1970, 1972
Selected Poems, 1973
The Damnation of Byron, 1973
A Late Picking: Poems, 1965-1974, 1975
A Book of Answers, 1978
Antechinus: Poems, 1975-1980, 1981
The Age of Reason, 1985
Selected Poems, 1986

Orpheus, 1991
Selected Poems, 1992
Selected Poetry and Prose, 2000

OTHER LITERARY FORMS

A. D. Hope distinguished himself as poet, critic, and
editor. His collections of lectures, essays, and reviews
addressed English and Australian literature, and he also
edited anthologies. He wrote one play, *Ladies from the
Sea* (pb. 1987).

ACHIEVEMENTS

While Australia has yet to produce a poet with a lasting influence on world literature, A. D. Hope has perhaps come closest to attaining an international reputation. Since the publication of his first collection in
1955, he emerged as the dominant figure in Australian
poetry.

Hope stands outside the mainstream of much modern poetry in his strict formalism and outspoken disdain
for much of the poetry and critical theories of his contemporaries, or what he called in *The New Cratylus:
Notes on the Craft of Poetry* (1979) "Heresies of the
Age." In his carefully balanced wit and in the lucidity
of his use of such neoclassical forms as the heroic couplet, he seemed much closer in his attitudes and manner
to Alexander Pope than to T. S. Eliot. While early compared to W. H. Auden in his sometimes scathing denunciations of twentieth century life, Hope possessed a distinctive voice with a wide range; his satirical poems
have been no less admired than his passionate love poetry. In all his work, the notion of poetry as a learned
craft is preeminent. Unlike many of his contemporaries, he remained content to express his vision in the
traditional patterns of accentual-syllabic meter and
rhyme.

Hope's first collection was published when he was
nearly fifty; thereafter, his reputation grew rapidly. He
was the recipient of numerous awards, including the
Grace Leven Prize (1956), the Arts Council of Great
Britain Award for Poetry (1965), the Britannica Award
for Literature (1965), the Myer Award for Australian
Literature (1967), the Ingram Merrill Award for Literature (1969), the Levinson Prize (1969), the *The Age*
Book of the Year Award (1976) for *A Late Picking*,

the Robert Frost Prize (now the Christopher Brennan Award) from the Fellowship of Australian Writers (1976), a New South Wales Premier's Literary Award Special Award (1989), and an ACT Book of the Year Award (1993) for *Chance Encounters*. He was elected Ashby Visiting Fellow of Clare Hall, Cambridge, and honorary fellow of University College, Oxford. In 1972, he was named Officer, Order of the British Empire, and Companion of the Order of Australia in 1981. He traveled and lectured extensively, especially in the United States.

BIOGRAPHY

Alec Derwent Hope was born in Cooma, New South Wales, Australia, on July 21, 1907, the firstborn of the family. His father, Percival Hope, a Presbyterian minister, moved the family to Tasmania when Hope was four years old. In the rural area where Hope's father's new congregation was located, school was rudimentary at best, often being held in the local sheepshearing shed. Hope, like many middle-class children, received much of his primary instruction at home. His mother, who had been a schoolteacher, taught him to read and write, and his father later instructed him in Latin. The family library was large, and the parents took turns reading classics of English literature aloud to the five children. Hope began to write poems in ballad stanzas when he was seven or eight, and by the time he was in his early teens, he had published his first poem, a translation of Roman poet Catullus's *Phasellus ille quem videstis, hospites.*

When Hope was fourteen, he was sent to the Australian mainland for his secondary education, first at Bathurst High School and later at Fort Street High School, one of the best schools in Sydney. Upon graduation, he was awarded a scholarship designated for sons of Presbyterian clergymen and matriculated at St. Andrew's College of the University of Sydney. He had originally intended to study medicine, but low science marks forced him to read for an arts degree instead. During his undergraduate years, he published poems in university magazines and in the Sydney *Bulletin*. He graduated in 1928. Hope distinguished himself in his undergraduate work in philosophy and English and won a scholarship for further study in England.

He entered University College, Oxford, in the fall of 1928, shortly after the graduation of Auden, Louis MacNeice, and Stephen Spender. Poor and underprepared, Hope had difficulty with the tedious Oxford English curriculum, which at that time leaned heavily toward philological studies. Despite his admiration for such notable scholars as C. S. Lewis, he managed no better than a third-class degree, which he completed in 1930.

He returned to Sydney just as the Depression was deepening and became a public-school teacher and vocational psychologist for several years before obtaining a position as a lecturer in education at Sydney Teachers' College in 1937. In 1938, he married Penelope Robinson and was appointed lecturer in English at Sydney, where he remained until 1944. In 1945, he became the senior lecturer in English at the University of Melbourne, where he taught courses in English and European literature. In 1951, he became the first professor of English at Canberra University College (now the Australian National University), a chair that he held until 1968, after which he was Library Fellow for three years and later professor emeritus. Hope, who long suffered from poor health, passed away on July 13, 2000, in Canberra.

ANALYSIS

In his introduction to a selection of his poems in 1963 as part of the Australian Poets series, A. D. Hope stated that "all theories about poetry are inadequate and that good poetry has been written on many assumptions that actually appear to be incompatible with one another." That claim notwithstanding, Hope did admit to several "comfortable prejudices" that allowed him to ignore poetical practices with which he had no sympathy. "The chief of these," he said, "is a heresy of our time which holds that by excluding those things which poetry has in common with prose, narrative, argument, description, exhortation and exposition, and that, depending entirely on lyric impulse or the evocative power of massed imagery one can arrive at the pure essence of poetry." This remark is central to any understanding of Hope's work, for he consistently lamented the impoverishment of twentieth century poetry when comparing it to the "great variety of forms practised in the past." The remark also reveals the strong influence of Latin studies on Hope's work, for his list includes most of the common topics of classical rhetoric. Of those he mentions, narrative and argumentation are important techniques that he consistently employed in his best poems.

Hope's second complaint was with "the notion that poetry can be improved or its range extended by breaking down the traditional structure of English verse by replacing its rhythms by those of prose." Hope, who studied at Oxford with C. L. Wrenn, editor of *Beowulf*, wrote learnedly on the origins of English poetic meter, particularly on the transition from accentual meters to accentual syllabics, which took place in the century after Geoffrey Chaucer's death (the 1400's), and on the metrical practices of John Dryden and Pope. Like Robert Frost, Hope credited the tension between meter and sentence rhythm as the key to the successful iambic pentameter line, of which Hope was a master. Given his mastery of meter, Hope had little patience with theories of "open form" or "projective verse" that were forwarded in defense of free verse.

According to Hope, another of the modern "heresies" stemmed from "that irritable personalism which is partly a heritage of the Romantics, the view that poetry is primarily self-expression." Even though Hope stated his disagreement with the poetical theories of Edgar Allan Poe, he would seem to agree with the primacy of a poem's effect on its audience: "The poem is not a feeling, it is a structure of words designed, among other things, to arouse a certain state of feeling." Similarly, Hope seems to have agreed with Eliot ("a poet whose poetry I cannot bring myself to like at all") in the need for a poet to find "an 'objective correlative' for the transmission of the poet's state of heart and mind to his readers."

It should be apparent from these comments that Hope had little sympathy for the confessionalist tendencies of much modern poetry, which, according to Hope, provide many poets with "an adoring cannibal audience waiting for the next effusion of soul meat." He added that the emotions in poems should not necessarily be equated with the emotions of poets: "The delight of creation and invention is their proper emotion and this must be in control of all other feelings."

Finally, Hope's personal preferences in the language of poetry were that it be "plain, lucid, coherent, logically connected, syntactically exact, and firmly based in current idiom and usage." To a large degree, Hope remained true to this dictum; his poetry is remarkable for its avoidance of needless obscurity and ambiguity. As he said, "A poem which can be parsed and analysed is not necessarily a good poem, but a poem which cannot is almost certainly bad." He did, however, allow himself the option of a certain elevation of language, what has been disparaged in recent decades as "poetic diction." With William Wordsworth, Hope agreed that "a poet should certainly be a man speaking to men in a language common to all," but that does not mean that the debased vocabulary of conversational speech should be the poet's sole resource. For Hope, whose learning and therefore vocabulary were far-ranging, the "word-hoard" of the poet should be ample enough to include terms from a great range of interests that, in his own case, included numerous historical and literary references, classical allusions, and scientific terms.

AUSTRALIAN COLONIAL LITERATURE

Australian literature, like all colonial literatures, including that of the United States, has been throughout much of its short history in search of an identity. During the nineteenth century, Australian poets fell into two general classes: those who imitated the poetic styles of the English Romantics and Victorians, and those who carried on a lively body of "bush poetry," largely anonymous balladry derived from the folk traditions of Great Britain. Of the first group, Oscar Wilde, reviewing an 1888 anthology of Australian writing, could find "nothing but echoes without music, reflections without beauty, second-rate magazine verses, arid third-rate verse for Colonial newspapers, . . . artless Nature in her most irritating form." Hope made two revealing comments regarding the situation of the Australian writer of his generation: The first was that his father's library, while amply supplied with the classics of English literature, contained no Australian poets; the other was that, as late as the early 1950's, Hope had to struggle to obtain credit status for the course in native literature that he instituted and taught at Canberra University College. Thus, Australian poets are caught in an uncomfortable dilemma: They may wish to create a truly "national" poetry, but they lack a tradition on which to build it.

Hope himself identified, in *Native Companions: Essays and Comments on Australian Literature, 1936-1966* (1974), the three main stages of a colonial literature. In the first, the work of colonial writers is simply part of the literary tradition of the homeland. In the second, writers born in the new land but educated in the tradition of the mother country attempt to create a literature of their own. In the final stage, this self-consciousness disappears, and writers emerge who can influence the whole literary tradition, including that of the mother country. Though Hope believed that Australian literature was in the middle stage, one could argue, with the publication of Judith Wright's *The Moving Image* and James McAuley's *Under Aldebaran* in 1946, the publication of Hope's first collection, *The Wandering Islands*, in 1955, and the novelist Patrick White's winning of the Nobel Prize in Literature in 1973, that Australian writing had moved into its maturity.

THE WANDERING ISLANDS

Though Hope had been publishing poetry and criticism since the late 1930's, *The Wandering Islands*, which appeared when he was forty-eight, was his first full collection. In a cultural climate that was still marked by parochialism and censorship, Hope's first book was something of a *succès de scandale*. The sexual explicitness of the title poem, his lightly worn learning, and his unsparing satire caused many critics to accuse him variously of academism, obscurity, misogyny, and even anti-Australian sentiments. Certainly, "Australia" would not have pleased the nationalistic poets of the Jindyworobak movement, at whose expense Hope had on occasion been mercilessly critical in his reviews. In this outwardly bitter poem, Hope sees his homeland as "without songs, architecture, history." Despite the fact that Hope later characterizes himself as one who turns "gladly home/ From the lush jungle of modern thought" to a country that has not yet been overwhelmed by "the chatter of cultured apes," the poem gave his early critics an abundant supply of ammunition with which to attack him.

In the book's title poem, Hope also delineates another constant theme of his work: the attractions and disappointment of love. For Hope, "the wandering islands" are the isolations of individual sexual identities, which are always, like the sundered beast in Plato's analogy of the two sexes, frustrated in their attempts at complete union:

> An instant of fury, a bursting mountain of spray,
> They rush together, their promontories lock
> An instant the castaway hails the castaway,
> But the sounds perish in that earthquake shock.

In these brief seconds of orgasmic loss of self lies "all that one mind ever knows of another,/ Or breaks the long isolation of the heart."

Commenting on Hope's recurrent motifs in a review of *The Wandering Islands*, S. L. Goldberg notes that "the attitude from which his themes arise is Dionysian or tragic, disturbed, romantic, existentialist at least in its premises; on the other hand, the sense of tradition and order implicit in his art . . . is decidedly Apollonian or classical, and intellectual rather than freely organic." In this sense, Hope seems closest to the tradition of the English Metaphysical poets, John Donne in particular, who saw no divorce between passion and intellect, the "dissociated sensibility," to borrow Eliot's phrase.

SEXUAL IMAGERY

A significant number of Hope's best poems deal with the sexual theme, by turns satirically and seriously. In "Conquistador," he sings "of the decline of Henry Clay/ . . . a small man in a little way," who is mashed flat in a sexual encounter with a "girl of uncommon size," who uses "him thereafter as a bedside mat." The poem, which is not without its darker side, bears comparison with Auden's "Ballad of Miss Gee." In "The Brides," Hope, in an impressive piece of social satire, works an extended conceit, for the smartest model in the sexual showroom is lured to the altar by promises of

> every comfort: the full set
> Of gadgets; knobs that answer to the touch
> For light or music; a place for his cigarette;
> Room for his knees; a honey of a clutch.

That the majority of contemporary marriages last not much longer than a new car's extended warranty period is at least implicit in this witty poem.

"IMPERIAL ADAM"

In other poems, Hope expands the sexual theme to include larger observations of nature and human history. "Imperial Adam," one of his most widely reprinted poems, retells the story of the Fall as a sexual fable. Having partaken of the "delicious pulp of the forbidden fruit," Adam and Eve immediately experience the awakening of sexual desire:

> Sly as the snake she loosed her sinuous thighs.
>
> And waking, smiled up at him from the grass;
> Her breasts rose softly and he heard her sigh—
> From all the beasts whose pleasant task it was
> In Eden to increase and multiply
>
> Adam had learned the jolly deed of kind:
> He took her in his arms and there and then,
> Like the clean beasts, embracing from behind
> Began in joy to found the breed of men.

In lines that are reminiscent of William Butler Yeats's "A shudder in the loins engenders there/ The broken wall, the burning roof and tower . . . ," Hope foreshadows the whole violent future of humanity in the "sexual lightning stroke" of the first embrace. The poem closes with Adam witnessing the consequences of his act:

> Adam watching too
> Saw how her dumb breasts at their ripening wept,
> The great pod of her belly swelled and grew,
>
> And saw its water break, and saw, in fear,
> Its quaking muscles in the act of birth,
> Between her legs a pigmy face appear,
> And the first murderer lay upon the earth.

RESISTING ROMANTICISM

It is significant that Hope, in a later poem titled "The Planctus," offers "another version of the Fall" in which Eve escapes the Garden and is provided with another helpmate, "While Adam, whose fellow God had not replaced,/ Lived on immortal, young, with virtue crowned,/ Sterile and impotent and justified." In Hope's view, a purely hermetic retreat from the moral perplexities of life is equivalent to a living death.

One other early poem comments, at first satirically, on those who see the "standardization" of the modern age as somehow unnatural, in particular the typical "Nature Poet" who "from his vegetable Sunday School/ Emerges with the neatly maudlin phrase" to protest the "endless duplication of lives and objects" that the American poet Theodore Roethke decried in "Dolor." Against this romantic assumption, Hope weighs the evidence of Earth herself, whose procreative fecundity "gathers and repeats/ The cast of a face, a million butterfly wings." Hope argues persuasively that such "standardization" is, in fact, the essence of the reproductive forces that rule nature and human life. As he says, it is love that "still pours into its ancient mould/ The lashing seed that grows to a man again."

Even in those poems that seem purely lyrical, Hope resists the romantic temptation to find in love any easy solutions. In one of his finest short poems, "As Well as They Can," he combines the twin demands of art and love in lines that ironically echo the conceit of Donne's "The Bait":

> As well as he can, the poet, blind, betrayed
> Distracted by the groaning mill, among
> The jostle of slaves, the clatter, the lash of
>   trade,
>   Taps the pure source of song.
>
> As well as I can, my heart in this bleak air,
> The empty days, the waste nights since you
> went,
> Recalls your warmth, your smile, the grace and
>   stir
>
>   That were its element.

DIALECTICS AND HISTORY

Hope's poetry is founded on dialectical premises—between the sexes, between assertion and counterargument, between art and life, even between the living poet and his predecessors. In "Moschus Moschiferus," which is on first glance conventional in its subtitle, "A Song for St Cecilia's Day," he contrasts "the pure, bright drops of sound" of Tibetan hunters' flute music with the ends to which it is put, ensnaring the hapless mouse-deer of the title, hunted almost into extinction for their precious musk glands. As a footnote to the twentieth century that has seen, in Nazi Germany to cite only one example, the powers of music set to evil uses, Hope can offer the saint little more than a sardonic gift:

> Divine Cecilia, there is no more to say!
> Of all who praised the power of music, few
> Knew of these things. In honor of your day
> Accept this song I too have made for you.

Similarly, in carrying on a continuing debate with the writers and literature of the past, Hope takes a revisionist view of personalities and characters that must now be seen from a contemporary perspective. In "Man Friday," he writes a sequel to Daniel Defoe's *The Life and Strange Surprizing Adventures of Robinson Crusoe, of York, Mariner, Written by Himself* (1719; commonly known as *Robinson Crusoe*) in which Friday, having had his fill of life in a country where

> More dreadful than ten thousands savages,
> In their strange clothes and monstrous mats of hair,
> The pale-eyed English swarm to joke and stare,
> With endless questions round him crowd and press
> Curious to see and touch his loneliness

makes his escape home by a last, suicidal swim. "Faustus," informed by the devil that "Hell is more up-to-date than men suppose" and that his soul has long since been in hell, "reorganized on the hire-purchase plan," avoids living further in his purely material world by killing both Helen and himself. Lord Byron, who boasted of thousands of seductions, in "The Damnation of Byron" is condemned to a "Hell of Women" where, at last satiated by endless "wet kisses and voluptuous legs agape// He longs for the companionship of men, their sexless friendliness."

In all these poems, as well as in many others from *A Book of Answers* and *The Age of Reason*, Hope's collection of verse epistles and narratives concerning leading figures, both historical and fictional from the Augustan Age, one is always aware of an intellect passionately involved in a dialogue with the past.

ORPHEUS

When Hope's wife died, his dialogue with the past took final form as a five-part conversation with her shade. These "Western Elegies" immediately follow the title poem in Hope's last collection of verse, *Orpheus*. They are written in classical hexameter, a measure rarely used to good effect in English verse. They climax in a vast meditation on language and time, "The Tongues," in which Hope celebrates the flowering of Indo-European languages, then reviews his personal acquaintance and love for tongues as diverse as Latin, Norse, and Russian:

> The man who has only one tongue lives forever alone
>   on an island
> Shut in on himself by conventions he is only dimly
>   aware of,
> Like a beast whose mind is fenced by the narrow
>   extent of its instincts.

At the end of "The Tongues," Hope anticipates his own imminent translation, in the other sense of that word:

> How shall I tell her the world is simpler than men
>   imagine,
> For those set apart by God speak a tongue used
>   only by angels;
> That the distance from East to West is no more
>   than its word for "I love you"?
> And perpetual pentecost springs and renews itself
>   in that message,
> Which blesses the gifts of tongues and crowns, the
>   venture of Babel.

Even though Hope has stressed, perhaps ingenuously, that his own poems are "hardly ever 'confessions' and [are] usually written in a spirit of 'as if' highly misleading to any unwary commentator or putative biographer," it would be a mistake to assume that his poetry is impersonal in any sense. Eliot, who said that poetry should be "an escape from personality," went on to add that one must first have a personality to be able to escape from it. In "Hay Fever," a late poem that is one of the few clearly autobiographical works in Hope's oeuvre, the gentle memory of an Edwardian summer spent mowing hay in rural Tasmania moves the mature poet to speculate on the abundant harvest of a life's work:

> It is good for a man when he comes to the end
> of his course
> In the barn of his brain to be able to romp
> like a boy in the heap . . .
> To lie still in well-cured hay . . . to drift
> into sleep.

A. D. Hope's voice, so distinctive in its ability to match the orchestra's full range, is truly remarkable.

OTHER MAJOR WORKS

PLAY: *Ladies from the Sea*, pb. 1987.

NONFICTION: *The Structure of Verse and Prose*, 1943; *The Study of English*, 1952 (lecture); *Australian Literature, 1950-1962*, 1963; *The Cave and the Spring: Essays on Poetry*, 1965; *The Literary Influence of Academies*, 1970 (lecture); *A Midsummer Eve's Dream: Variations on a Theme by William Dunbar*, 1970; *Henry Kendall: A Dialogue with the Past*, 1971; *Native Companions: Essays and Comments on Australian Literature, 1936-1966*, 1974; *Judith Wright*, 1975; *The Pack of Autolycus*, 1978; *The New Cratylus: Notes on the Craft of Poetry*, 1979; *Poetry and the Art of Archery*, 1980 (lecture); *Chance Encounters*, 1992.

TRANSLATION: *The Shorter Poems of Catullus: A New Translation*, 2007.

EDITED TEXTS: *Australian Poetry, 1960*, 1960; *Henry Kendall*, 1973 (with Leonie Kramer).

BIBLIOGRAPHY

Brissenden, R. F. "Art and the Academy: The Achievement of A. D. Hope." In *The Literature of Australia*, edited by Geoffrey Dutton. Rev. ed. New York: Penguin Books, 1976. Through the analysis of several poems, Brissenden concludes that Hope invokes through his poetry the entire history and culture of Western civilization, thus making him far more than an Australian poet.

Brooks, David, ed. *The Double Looking Glass: New and Classic Essays on A. D. Hope*. St. Lucia, Qld.: University of Queensland Press, 2000. An essay collection covering Hope's entire career.

Darling, Robert. *A. D. Hope*. New York: Twayne, 1997. Reviews the whole of Hope's poetic work in the context of modernist and contemporary poetry, particularly Australian poetry.

Hart, Kevin. *A. D. Hope*. New York: Oxford University Press, 1992. Brief biography and critical interpretation of Hope's work. Includes bibliography.

McCulloch, A. M. *Dance of the Nomad: A Study of the Selected Notebooks of A. D. Hope*. Canberra, A.C.T.: Pandanus Books, 2005. While this study focuses on Hope's notebooks rather than his poetry, it reveals the man behind the poetry.

Martin, Philip. "A. D. Hope: Nonconformist." *Journal of Popular Culture* 23, no. 2 (1989): 47-54. Starting from the Nonconformism of Hope's religious upbringing, Martin analyzes Hope's career through his eightieth year as a variation on the theme of personal nonconformism.

Mathur, Malati. *A. D. Hope: Merging Meridians—Poetic Vision*. New Delhi: Creative Books, 2006. Malthus examines the themes in the poetry of Hope.

Morse, Ruth. "A. D. Hope: Australian Poet Whose Erotic Work Outraged Local Opinion but Drew International Acclaim." *Guardian*, July 25, 2000, p. 22. Obituary describes his life and notes how his poems were learned, erotic, and often humorous. Notes that he made enemies of Australian writers Patrick White and Max Harris.

R. S. Gwynn
Updated by Alan Sullivan

GERARD MANLEY HOPKINS

Born: Stratford, England; July 28, 1844
Died: Dublin, Ireland; June 8, 1889

PRINCIPAL POETRY

Poems of Gerard Manley Hopkins, Now First Published, with Notes by Robert Bridges, 1918
Poems of Gerard Manley Hopkins, 1930, 1948, 1967
The Poetical Works of Gerard Manley Hopkins, 1990

OTHER LITERARY FORMS

Gerard Manley Hopkins's letters and papers were published in six volumes that appeared between 1935 and 1959: *The Letters of Gerard Manley Hopkins to Robert Bridges* (1935, 1955; C. C. Abbott, editor), *The Correspondence of Gerard Manley Hopkins and Richard Watson Dixon* (1935, 1955; Abbott, editor), *The Notebooks and Papers of Gerard Manley Hopkins*

(1937; Humphry House, editor), *Further Letters of Gerard Manley Hopkins* (1938, 1956; Abbott, editor), *The Journals and Papers of Gerard Manley Hopkins* (1959; House and Graham Storey, editors), and *The Sermons and Devotional Writings of Gerard Manley Hopkins* (1959; Christopher Devlin, editor). A selection of letters from the three volumes edited by Abbott, *Gerard Manley Hopkins: Selected Letters*, was published in 1990. Edited by Catherine Phillips, the letters include many analyses of the work of other poets and artists; they also reveal his bouts of "melancholy," or depression, and implicitly show his internal struggles between his religion and his work as a poet. In addition to the published material, there are significant unpublished lecture notes and documents by Hopkins at the Bodleian Library and the Campion Hall Library at Oxford University.

ACHIEVEMENTS

Although Gerard Manley Hopkins saw almost none of his writings published in his lifetime, he is generally credited with being one of the founders of modern poetry and a major influence on the development of modernism in art. Many of his letters reflect a sense of failure and frustration. "The Wreck of the *Deutschland*," which he considered to be his most important poem, was rejected by the Jesuit magazine *The Month*. As a professor of classical languages and literature, he was not a productive, publishing scholar. As a priest, his sermons and theological writing did not find popular success. Yet in 1918, some thirty years after his death, his friend Robert Bridges published a collection of his poems. By 1930, when the second edition of this volume appeared, Hopkins had begun to attract the attention of major theoreticians of modernism: Herbert Read, William Empson, I. A. Richards, and F. R. Leavis. They acclaimed Hopkins as a powerful revolutionary force in poetry. Interest in his poetry led scholars to unearth his scattered letters and papers. Here, too, modern readers found revolutionary concepts: inscape, instress, sprung rhythm, underthought/overthought, counterpoint. Since about 1930, an enormous amount of scholarly analysis has combed through Hopkins's poetry and prose, establishing beyond doubt that he is one of the three or four most influential forces in modern English literature.

BIOGRAPHY

Gerard Manley Hopkins was the first of eight children born to Manley Hopkins, a successful marine insurance agent who wrote poetry and technical books. The family was closely knit and artistic. Two of Hopkins's brothers became professional artists, and Hopkins's papers contain many pencil sketches showing his own talent for drawing. He was devoted to his youngest sister, Grace, who was an accomplished musician, and he tried to learn several musical instruments as well as counterpoint and musical composition. The family was devoutly Anglican in religion. When Hopkins was eight years old, they moved from the London suburb of Stratford (Essex) to the more fashionable and affluent Hampstead on the north edge of the city.

From 1854 to 1863, Hopkins attended Highgate Grammar School. Richard Watson Dixon, a young teacher there, later became one of Hopkins's main literary associates. Hopkins studied Latin and Greek intensively, winning the Governor's Gold Medal for Latin Verse, as well as the Headmaster's Poetry Prize in 1860 for his English poem "The Escorial." His school years seem to have been somewhat stormy, marked by the bittersweet joy of schoolboy friendships and the excitement of a keen mind mastering the intricacies of Greek, Latin, and English poetry. He was such a brilliant student that he won the Balliol College Exhibition, or scholarship prize. Balliol was reputed to be the leading college for classical studies at Oxford University in the 1860's. Hopkins attended Balliol from April, 1863, until June, 1867, studying "Classical Greats," the philosophy, literature, and language of ancient Greece and Rome. The first year of this curriculum required rigorous study of the structure of the Latin and Greek languages. This linguistic study terminated with a very demanding examination, in which Hopkins earned a grade of "first" in December, 1864. The remaining years of his program involved the study of the philosophy and literature of ancient writers in their original tongues, concluding with the final honors examination. Hopkins concluded his B.A. (Hons.) with a "first" in June, 1867. A double first in "Classical Greats" is a remarkable accomplishment. Benjamin Jowett, the Master of Balliol and himself a famous classical scholar, called Hopkins "The Star of Balliol" and all who knew

Gerard Manley Hopkins (Library of Congress)

him at this period predicted a brilliant career for him. Hopkins loved Oxford—its landscapes and personalities, the life of culture and keen intellectual striving—and always looked back to his college days with nostalgia. His schoolmate there was Robert Bridges, who was to be his lifelong friend and correspondent.

These years were not peaceful, however, for the promising young scholar and poet. The colleges of Oxford University were then religious institutions. Only Anglicans could enroll as students or teach there. For some thirty years before Hopkins entered Balliol, Oxford University had been rocked by the Oxford Movement. A number of its illustrious teachers had questioned the very basis of the Anglican Church, the way in which the Church of England could claim to be independent of the Roman Catholic Church. Many of the leading figures of the Oxford Movement had felt compelled to leave Oxford and the Church of England and

to convert to Roman Catholicism. Among the converts was Cardinal John Henry Newman, whose *Apologia pro Vita Sua*, or history of his conversion from the Anglican to the Roman Church, was published in 1864, the year Hopkins was preparing for his Moderations at Balliol. To follow Newman's lead meant to give up hope of an academic career at Oxford, and perhaps even the hope of completing his B.A. Nevertheless, by 1866 Hopkins was convinced that the only true church was the Roman. In October, 1866, he was received into the Roman Catholic Church by Newman himself. It is hard for modern readers to imagine the pain and dislocation this decision caused Hopkins. His family letters reveal the anguish of his father, who believed that his son's immortal soul was lost, not merely his temporal career. Hopkins was estranged from his family to some degree ever after his momentous conversion. After he had completed his B.A. at Oxford, Hopkins taught in 1867 at Newman's Oratory School, a Roman Catholic grammar school near Birmingham. There he decided to enter a religious order. In May, 1868, he burned all manuscripts of his poems, thinking that poetry was not a fit occupation for a seriously religious person. Fortunately, some of his early writing survived in copies he had given to Robert Bridges. He wrote no further poetry until "The Wreck of the *Deutschland*."

In the summer of 1867, he went on a walking tour of Switzerland. In that September, he entered the Jesuit Novitiate, Manresa House, London, for the first two years of rigorous spiritual training to become a Jesuit priest. There he followed the regime of the *Ejercicios espirituales* (1548; *The Spiritual Exercises*, 1736) of Saint Ignatius of Loyola (1491-1556), taking vows of poverty, chastity, and obedience. From 1870 to 1873, he studied philosophy at St. Mary's Hall, Stonyhurst, in the North of England. Although Hopkins had been a brilliant student of classical philosophy at Oxford, he seems not to have pleased his Jesuit superiors so well. Perhaps part of the problem was an independence of mind that could be disconcerting. At Stonyhurst, he first read the medieval philosopher John Duns Scotus, who had an unusually strong influence on Hopkins. He then returned to Manresa House for a year as professor of rhetoric. From 1874 to 1878, he studied theology at St. Bueno's College in Wales. There he began to write poetry again when he heard of the wreck of a German ship, the *Deutschland*, and the death of five Catholic nuns aboard.

It is the custom in the Jesuit order to move priests from one location to another frequently and to try them out in a variety of posts. In the next few years, Hopkins tried many different kinds of religious work without remarkable success. He was assigned to preach in the fashionable Farm Street Church in London's West End, but he was not a charismatic or crowd-pleasing performer. Parish work in the Liverpool slums left him depressed and exhausted. When he was assigned temporarily to the Catholic parish church in Oxford, he seemed to have had trouble getting along with his superior. Finally, he was appointed professor of Greek and Latin literature at University College, Dublin, Ireland. He held this post until his death in 1889. The Catholic population of Ireland at that time was in near-revolt against English oppression. Hopkins felt a conflict between his English patriotism and his Catholic sympathies. Although he had been a brilliant student as a young man, the University College duties gave him little opportunity to do gratifying scholarly work. Much of his time was spent in the drudgery of external examinations, grading papers of hundreds of students he had never taught. His lectures were attended by only a handful of students. He projected massive books for himself to write, but never was able to put them together. In this period, he wrote many sonnets that show spiritual desolation, unhappiness, and alienation. He died of typhoid in 1889 at the age of forty-five. Not until a generation later did the literary world recognize his genius.

ANALYSIS

In 1875, a number of Roman Catholic religious people had been driven out of Germany by the Falck Laws. In the winter of that year, five exiled nuns took passage on the *Deutschland*, which ran aground in a snowstorm near the Kentish shore of England. The ship gradually broke up in the high seas and many lives were lost, including those of the nuns. Their bodies were brought to England for solemn funeral ceremonies and the whole affair was widely reported in the newspapers. At this time, Gerard Manley Hopkins was studying theology at

St. Bueno's College in Wales. He read the reports in the press, and many details in his poem reflect the newspapers' accounts. He seems especially to have noticed the report that, as passengers were being swept off the deck into the icy seas by towering waves, the tallest of the five nuns rose up above the others just before her death and cried out for Christ to come quickly to her. Hopkins discussed this fearful catastrophe with his rector, who suggested that someone should write a poem about it. Taking that hint as a command, Hopkins broke his self-imposed poetic silence and began to write again. The experience of the tall nun at her moment of death captured his imagination. How frightening and cruel it must have been to be on the deck of the shattered ship! Yet she was a faithful Catholic servant of God. How could God torment her so? What did she mean when she cried out for Christ to come to her as the fatal waves beat down on her?

"THE WRECK OF THE DEUTSCHLAND"

"The Wreck of the *Deutschland*" is a very difficult poem. Unlike the smooth sentences of Tennyson's *In Memoriam* (1850), for example, Hopkins's elegy is contorted, broken, sometimes opaque. When Robert Bridges published the first volume of Hopkins's poems in 1918, he warned readers that "The Wreck of the *Deutschland*" was like a great dragon lying at the gate to discourage readers from going on to other, more accessible poems by Hopkins. The thread of the occasion, however, can be traced in the text. The dedication of the poem to the memory of five Franciscan nuns exiled by the Falck Laws drowned between midnight and morning of December 7, 1875, gives the reader a point of reference. If readers skip to stanza 12, the story goes ahead, following newspaper accounts of the events reasonably clearly. Stanza 12 relates that some two hundred passengers sailed from Bremen bound for the United States, never guessing that a fourth of them would drown. Stanza 13 explains how the *Deutschland* sailed into the wintry storm. Stanzas 14 and 15 tell how the ship hit a sandbank and people began to drown. Stanza 16 depicts an act of heroism in which a sailor tries to rescue a woman, but is killed; his body dangles on a rope for hours before the eyes of the sufferers. Stanzas 17 through 23 are about the tall nun. In stanza 24, the poet contrasts his own comfortable setting under a safe roof in Wales with that of the nuns who were in their death struggle on the stormy sea. He has no pain, no trial, but the tall nun is dying at that very moment. Rising up in the midst of death and destruction, she calls, "O Christ, Christ, come quickly." Stanzas 25 through 35 contemplate that scene and ask, "What did she mean?" when she called out. What was the total meaning of her agony and life? The poem therefore can be divided into three sections: Stanzas 1 to 10 constitute a prologue or invocation, stanzas 11 through 25 depict the agony of the shipwreck and the tall nun, and stanzas 25 through 35 contemplate the meaning of that event. The middle section, describing the shipwreck and the tall nun's cry, is reasonably clear. Difficult details in this section are mostly explained in the notes to the revised fourth edition of *Poems of Gerard Manley Hopkins*. There are some additional perspectives, however, which are helpful in grasping the total work.

"The Wreck of the *Deutschland*" is related to the Jesuit contemplative "composition of place" and "application of the senses." As a member of the Society of Jesus, Hopkins's daily life and devotions were shaped by the *Ejercicios espirituales* (1548; *The Spiritual Exercises*, 1736) of Saint Ignatius of Loyola. Moreover, at certain times in his career, he withdrew from the world to perform the spiritual exercises in month-long retreats of an extremely rigorous nature. One objective of the spiritual exercises is to induce an immediate, overwhelming sense of the presence of divinity in our world. The contemplative is directed by the *Spiritual Exercises* to employ the technique of "composition." For example, to get a sharper sense of the divine presence, one might contemplate the birth of Christ. First one must imagine, or compose, the scene of the Nativity in all possible detail and precision. When Christ was born, how large was the room; what animals were in the stable; where was the holy family; were they seated or standing; what was the manger like? The imagination embodies or composes the scene. The contemplative then applies his five senses systematically to the composition. What did it look like, sound like, smell like, feel like, and taste like? Such a projection of the contemplative into the very situation induces a very powerful awareness of the religious experience. "The Wreck of the *Deutschland*" is similar to such a contemplative

exercise. Hopkins is trying to experience the religious truth of the nuns's sacrifice. The middle of his poem is a composition of the scene where the tall nun died. It is constructed systematically to apply the five senses. Stanza 28 depicts the struggle of the poet to put himself in the nun's place, to feel what she felt, to suffer as she suffered, to believe as she believed. At her death, she saw her Master, Christ the King. The poet tries to participate in her experience. The poem should be read in comparison with other poems of the religious meditative tradition—for example, the poetry of George Herbert, Richard Crashaw, and Henry Vaughan. Louis L. Martz in *The Poetry of Meditation: A Study in English Religious Literature of the Seventeenth Century* (1962) is the best introduction to this aspect of Hopkins's work.

COMPLEXITIES OF SPRUNG RHYTHM

In addition to the religious complexities of the poem, there are aesthetic complexities. Hopkins claimed to have discovered a new poetic form, "sprung rhythm," which he employed in "The Wreck of the *Deutschland*." Despite intense scholarly investigation of Hopkins's metrics, there is no clear agreement as to what he means by "sprung rhythm." "The Wreck of the *Deutschland*" contains thirty-five stanzas, each with eight lines of varying length. If one counts the syllables in each line, or if one counts only the accented syllables in each line, there is a rough agreement in the length of a particular line in each of the stanzas. For example, line 1 has four or five syllables in almost all stanzas. Line 8 is much longer than line 1 in all stanzas. What makes lines of varying length metrical?

It is sometimes thought that Hopkins was isolated in the Jesuit order and did not know what he was doing when he created unusual poetic forms. That is absurd, for he was a professor of classical literature and in correspondence with leading literary scholars. The best way to look at sprung rhythm is to see what Hopkins's associates thought about meter. Robert Bridges, his college friend and lifelong correspondent, studied the iambic pentameter of Milton and wrote a major book on the prosody of Milton. Bridges thought that Milton built his lines out of iambic feet, units of two syllables with the second syllable pronounced more loudly than the first. An iambic pentameter line therefore had five iambic feet, or ten syllables with the even-positioned syllables stressed more loudly than the odd-positioned ones. Lines in Miltonic pentameter that do not fit this pattern follow a few simple variations defined by Bridges. Bridges's study appears to be accurate for Milton, but clearly Hopkins is not writing poetry of this sort. The number of unstressed syllables differs widely in his lines, a condition that Bridges shows never occurs in Milton.

Another of Hopkins's correspondents, Coventry Patmore, was a leading popular Catholic poet who wrote a study of English metrics based on time, similar to the prosody of hymns. Hopkins's sprung rhythm seems more consistent with such a musical time-based pattern than with the accentual-syllabic pattern of Milton as defined by Bridges. Hopkins, as a professor of classical languages, knew the advanced linguistic work going on in that area. Greek poetry was thought to be quantitative, based on the length of vowel sounds. As a schoolboy, Hopkins had to practice translating an English passage first into Latin, then into Greek poetry, arranging the long and short vowels into acceptable feet. (Some of his Latin and Greek poetry is collected in *Poems of Gerard Manley Hopkins*.) Modern readers are not often trained to understand these models in classical languages and so do not appreciate how important they are to Hopkins's patterns in English verse. In Hopkins's unpublished papers, there are lines of Greek poetry interlined by drafts of his English poems, sometimes with arrows and doodles matching up the English and Greek phrases. It seems possible that Hopkins based his distinctive rhythms on Greek models, especially the odes of Pindar. Essentially, however, the key to sprung rhythm remains to be discovered.

PRIEST VS. POET

"The Wreck of the *Deutschland*" was submitted to the Jesuit magazine *The Month* and, after some delay, rejected for publication. Hopkins said that they "dared not" print it, although there is no need to imagine a dark conspiracy among the Jesuit authorities to silence Hopkins. It is likely that the editors of *The Month* simply found "The Wreck of the *Deutschland*" baffling in form and content. The rejection dramatizes, however, a peculiar condition in Hopkins's life. His unquestionable genius for poetry found almost no encouragement

in his immediate surroundings as a Jesuit priest. His poetry is, of course, shaped by Roman Catholic imagery and is mainly devotional in nature. Without his Church and his priestly calling, he never could have written his poems. On the other hand, what he wrote was largely unappreciated by his closest associates. Ironically, this highly religious poet became famous in the twentieth century because of the praise of readers who were frequently anti-Roman Catholic. There was a central anguish in Hopkins's life, a conflict between his priestly duties and his artistic creativity. Many scholars have tried to explain how Hopkins's poetry and his priesthood fit together. Roman Catholic critics usually tend to say that the Catholic faith made Hopkins a great writer. Readers who are hostile to Catholicism tend to think that Hopkins was a serious writer in spite of extreme discouragements and restraints placed on him by his faith. The truth is probably somewhere in the middle. If Hopkins had not been severely troubled, he would have had little motivation to write. His poems show all the commonplaces of religious imagery found in much less powerful Catholic poets, such as his friend Coventry Patmore. Hopkins rises above the average religious versifier because of his origial genius, yet this originality is what the Jesuit editors of *The Month* did not understand.

"THE WINDHOVER"

Stung by the criticism of his major poem, not only by the Jesuit editors but also by his friend Robert Bridges, Hopkins never again tried to write something so long and elaborate. He retreated into the most traditional form in English prosody, the sonnet. After "The Wreck of the *Deutschland*," Hopkins's most famous work is the sonnet "The Windhover." More has been written about these fourteen lines than about any other piece of poetry of comparable length in English. All of Hopkins's sonnets are related to the Petrarchan model, but he alters the tradition to fit his peculiar genius. The poem employs line-end rhymes *abba abba cdcdcd*. In addition to the repetition of sound at the end of each line, there is also thickly interwoven alliteration and assonance within each line. This internal rhyme is related to the *cynghanedd* or consonant chime of Welsh poetry. Hopkins tried to learn Welsh when he was a student at St. Bueno's College in Wales and he actually wrote a bit of Welsh poetry in the form called *cywydd*. The meter of "The Windhover" is the so-called sprung rhythm, allowing great variation in the length of lines. The Petrarchan sonnet uses its rhyme scheme to define two parts of the poem: *abba abba* is the octave or exposition in the opening eight lines, *cdcdcd* is the sestet or commentary in the concluding six lines. Hopkins explained in his letters that the essence of a sonnet is balance and proportion. The octave asserts a situation or condition and then a surprising commentary comes back in the sestet to reply to the octave. Since the sestet has only six lines, it must be correspondingly "sharper" or more forceful if it is to balance the initial statement. The key to the sonnet is this proportion. Hopkins wrote some sonnets longer than the usual fourteen lines and a few shorter, "curtail" or cut-short, sonnets. In all his sonnets, however, he maintains the proportion of octave to sestet, eight to six, and forces the shorter conclusion to a higher pitch of intensity.

In its octave, "The Windhover" describes the flight of a hawk of a kind commonly used in falconry or hunting circling against the dawn sky. The sestet begins with the description of the hawk diving, plummeting earthward, as it "buckles." The sure, steady circling of the hawk in the octave is astonishing, but the sudden buckling downward is even more thrilling. It is beautiful and breathtaking. In the sestet, the increased beauty of the hawk as it dives is compared to a plough made to shine as it is driven through sandy soil, and to an ember coated with ashes that sparkles when it falls and breaks.

"The Windhover" illustrates one of the key terms in Hopkins's aesthetic vocabulary: "inscape," a word he coined for the inner nature of a thing that distinguishes it from everything else in creation. Hopkins's reading of Franciscan philosopher John Duns Scotus is pertinent to his concept of inscape. *Qualis* in Latin means "what." When people look at the qualities of things, they examine what these things have in common with other members of their class. The qualities of a good racing horse are those features that it has in common with other good horses. Duns Scotus imagines that there is an opposite to quality. *Haec* means "this" in Latin. Duns Scotus coins the word *haecceitas*, the "thisness" of a thing, which sets it apart from every-

thing else, making it unique and different—the principle of individuation. Hopkins frequently celebrates the rare, unusual, or unique in nature. He turns away from the universal quality and toward the individual. The octave of "The Windhover" can be seen as the poet's description of a natural event: the flight and dive of a falcon. In that movement, he seeks to find the inscape, the innermost shape as evidence of God's presence in the created world. He tries to see into the form of the thing, to find what makes it original, unique, special, strange, striking. Like the sacrifice of the tall nun in "The Wreck of the *Deutschland*," the act of the hawk is "composed" so as to be the object for a religious meditation.

Paradoxically, the only way to grasp the unique inscape of a thing is to compare it with something else. The tension of this paradox is evident in the striking, surprising comparisons that Hopkins employs in "The Windhover," comparing the dive of a hawk with a plough shining in use and a burning coal sparkling as it collapses. The poem says that these three events are comparable or analogous in that in each case when the object buckles it becomes brighter and more glorious. When the hawk buckles in its dive, it is a thousandfold more lovely than in its stately circling. When the rusty plough buckles to its work, the abrasion of the sandy soil makes the ploughshare shine in use. When the ash crumbles or buckles, its inner brightness shows through the gray, outer ash-coating. Hopkins gave "The Windhover" the dedication, "To Christ Our Lord." The Jesuit order sees itself as the chivalry or the Knights of Christ. Ignatius advises the novice to buckle on the armor of Christ. To become a Jesuit, to buckle on the armor of a true Christian knight, is the proper and glorious activity of a man who would follow his nature, or unique calling. In like manner, a hawk follows its true nature, it is what it was made to be, when it sails in the wind and dives. A plough was made to work the earth, a coal to burn, and these things do what they were intended to do when they buckle. The activity of buckling may be painful or dangerous, but it produces glory, brilliance, grace, and beauty. The discipline of accepting the vows of the Jesuits may be painful in some earthly way, but it brings the glory of Christ's service. Christ, too, accepted the pain and duty of his earthly incarnation. He was buckled to the cross. He did what he had to do and so was brought to glory through pain and humiliation. The structure of "The Windhover" appears to be a set of analogies or comparisons all coming together in the word "buckle." Such a strucure is also to be found in the odes of the Greek poet Pindar, which Hopkins studied intensely in school. Pindar's poems praise a great athlete or hero by linking together a series of seeming digressions in one key image or figure, sometimes called a "constellation," such as the "golden lyre," a "beacon fire," a "horse," or a "tree." Hopkins's poetry unites the Christian tradition of anagogical interpretation of the created world and the classical Greek tradition of the Pindaric ode.

THE SONNET FORM

Most of Hopkins's shorter poems are sonnets, yet within the confines of this form, Hopkins displays great originality in his metrical structure, his repetition of sound in alliteration and internal rhyme, and his changes in the length of the sonnet while maintaining the crucial eight-to-six proportion of the octave/sestet division. Like the form of the sonnet, the subjects of most of Hopkins's poems are extremely traditional: elation at the sight of some particular bit of nature; personal dejection, desolation, and despair; celebration of the inner worth of an outwardly ordinary human being. These three topics are commonplaces of Romantic and post-Romantic literature. Hopkins's originality lies in treating these subjects with unusual power and perception. Romantic poets such as William Wordsworth and Percy Bysshe Shelley often looked at nature and said that they felt their hearts leap up to behold the beauty of spring or autumn. For Hopkins, every little corner of nature was evidence of the divine presence of God. His Christianity reinforces the Romantic sentiment. The confluence of the Romantic and the Christian tradition produces unusually powerful statements.

Consider, for example, the sonnet "Hurrahing in Harvest." Like "The Windhover," this poem is an Italian sonnet, rhymed *abba abba cdcdcd*. Lines 6 and 7 end with an unusual rhyme device. "Saviour" is rhymed with the next line, but in order to hear the complete rhyme, one must continue to the "r" sound that begins line eight: "gave you a/ Rapturous." This extended rhyme is common in Hopkins and illustrates his predilection for unusual twists within the framework of rigid

traditional expectations. The subjects of "The Windhover" and "Hurrahing in Harvest" are also similar. In both poems, the speaker looks up at the sky and finds nature breathtakingly beautiful. "Hurrahing in Harvest" declares that the summer is now ending. The stooks, or shocks of bundled grain, are now stacked in the fields. The technical and regional term stooks is characteristic of Hopkins's vocabulary. The word is not commonly known, but it is exact. The speaker looks up at the autumnal skies and sees the clouds. With the bold verbal comparisons that the poet prefers, he compares the skies to "wind-walks"—they are like alleyways for the winds. The clouds are like "silk-sacks"; they are soft, dainty, and luxurious. The movement of the clouds across the sky is like "mealdrift" or flour pouring across the heavens. In that soft, flowing beauty, the speaker walks and lifts up his eyes. He sees the glory of the natural scene and then recognizes that beyond the heavens, behind all the created universe, there stands the Savior. He at first rejoices in the sheer beauty of nature, but such earthly beauty leads him to the unspeakable inner beauty of Christ's immediate presence in the natural world. In the sestet, the speaker sees the azure hills of autumn as strong as the shoulder of a stallion, majestic and sweet with flowers, like the shoulder of God bearing the creation in all its glory. The speaker realizes that all this is here for him to see, and the realization makes his heart leap up as if it had wings; his spirit hurls heavenward.

NATURE SONNETS

Hopkins wrote many poems celebrating nature in sonnet form. "God's Grandeur" states in the octave that the grandeur of God's creating has been obscured by the Industrial Revolution, trade and toil. The sestet replies that there is a spark of freshness deep in nature that will spring up like the sun at dawn because God broods over Earth like a bird over its egg. "The Starlight Night" begins with a powerful octave describing the beauty of the stars in the night sky. The sestet replies that the stars are like a picket fence separating us from heaven through which we can glimpse a bit of what is on the other side. "Spring" typically gives an excited picture of the juice and joy of the earth stirring in springtime and compares it to the youthful, primal goodness of children, a hint of sinless Eden.

"PIED BEAUTY"

"Pied Beauty" is one of Hopkins's most important philosophical poems on nature. It reflects his study of Duns Scotus and his notion of inscape. The poem is a "curtail" or cut-short sonnet, only ten and a fraction lines long. Hopkins explained that this poem maintained the eight-to-six ratio, which he felt was the key to the sonnet form. The exposition, which occupies the first six lines, states that God is especially to be praised for the irregular, dappled, serviceable parts of creation. The sestet generalizes that whatever is contradictory, strange, or changeable originates in God.

In Platonic thought, a material thing is beautiful insofar as it approaches its unchanging ideal. For example, a beautiful circle is one that approaches—as nearly as possible in our world—the perfection of an ideal circle. Because the things of the world are always struggling to become like their perfect forms, the material world is always changing. It is sometimes called the mutable world of "becoming." The ideal world cannot change, however, because when something is perfect, any change would make it imperfect. The world of Platonic ideals is therefore unchanging. It is sometimes called the world of permanent "being."

"Pied Beauty" makes a striking statement about the nature of beauty. It asserts that things are not beautiful because they approach the perfect type, but because they are various, changing, contradictory. Hopkins seems to be praising the very aspect of the material world that Platonic philosophy connects with degeneration and decay. Somehow God, who is perfect and unchanging, has fathered a universe of imperfection, contradiction, and decay. Nevertheless, this created world reflects his praise: Duns Scotus maintained that God's perfection must be manifest somehow in the constant change and variety of his creation.

"DUNS SCOTUS'S OXFORD"

Hopkins's admiration for Duns Scotus is expressed in "Duns Scotus's Oxford," which combines the nature-sonnet and the celebration of a famous man. Its octave depicts the ancient university town of Oxford. The sestet comments that this was the very city that Duns Scotus knew when the subtle doctor taught there in the thirteenth century. Now Hopkins finds Scotus to have the best insight into philosophical problems, even more

comforting to him than Greek philosophers such as Plato, or Italian philosophers such as Saint Thomas Aquinas. All the nature sonnets give an extremely sharp picture of some relatively common event or situation in nature: a hawk in flight, the landscape of Oxford, the rebirth of the countryside in springtime, the clouds and fields of autumn. The poet reflects on the source of all this beauty. The scene itself uplifts his spirits, but the awareness of God's creative force glimpsed behind the material world brings even more elation.

THE HEROIC SONNET

A second group of poems is in the tradition of the heroic sonnet. These poems examine a person's life and define what is noteworthy in an ordinary man's career. "The Lantern Out of Doors" is typical. The octave tells of seeing a lantern moving at night. There must be someone behind that light, but he is so far off that he passes in the darkness and all that can be seen is a little spark. Humans have trouble knowing other people, and they all die. The sestet replies that Christ knows every person; Christ is the first and last friend of every human.

"Felix Randal," one of Hopkins's best sonnets, is about a blacksmith who fell ill and died. The once powerful man wasted away, but he finally came to accept Christ. Paradoxically, in the weakness of his death he became more blessed than in the pagan power he was so proud of in the days when he forged and fitted horseshoes with his fellow workers.

"The Soldier," "Tom's Garland: Upon the Unemployed," and "Harry Ploughman" all fit into the category of poems celebrating the inner worth of ordinary people. Perhaps the pattern of this kind of sonnet is best displayed in "In Honour of Saint Alphonsus Rodriguez: Laybrother of the Society of Jesus." Alphonsus Rodriguez performed no noble deeds. For forty years, however, he faithfully carried out his duty and filled his station as doorkeeper. It is not his exploits, but his humanity, that Hopkins celebrates. Humility, obedience, and simple faith have their reward. The poem is in the tradition of Milton's theme of the faithful Christians: "They also serve who only stand and wait."

SONNETS OF TERROR

The third major theme of Hopkins's sonnets is spiritual desolation and terror. These poems constitute the dark, opposite side of Hopkins's view of reality. In the nature poems, the poet looks at some part of the created universe and feels that God is in every corner of the world. His joy, already aroused by the pure beauty of nature, rises to an ecstatic pitch when he realizes that God is behind it all. The poems of desolation, sometimes called the "terrible sonnets," on the other hand, imagine a world without God—all joy, freshness, and promise withdrawn. They depict the dark night of the soul.

Many readers think that these poems are directly autobiographical, indicating that Hopkins in the last years of his life was devastated by despair. This view is probably not sound. The sonnet is a highly dramatized form; sonnets are traditionally constructed like little plays. Thus the speaker of one of William Shakespeare's sonnets is no more Shakespeare, the man himself, than is Macbeth or Hamlet, and the persona or mask through which a sonneteer speaks is not to be confused with the real author. *The Spiritual Exercises* of Saint Ignatius, moreover, follows a spiritual progression that every Jesuit would imitate in his retreats and private worship. In a long retreat, lasting about a month, the exercitant is called on to drive himself gradually into a state of extreme desolation into which a renewed sense of God's presence finally bursts like Easter into the dormant world.

The sonnets of terror may be as artificial as Elizabethan love sonnets. They may be, to some degree, virtuoso exercises in imagining a world devoid of spirituality and hope. The real feelings of Hopkins may be quite separate from the imagined feelings of the persona who speaks these sonnets. On the other hand, one can hardly imagine that Hopkins could write these poems unless there were some wrenching personal feelings motivating his creative act.

The sonnets of terror appeal to readers today because they mirror a cosmic despair or alienation. The feeling that modern humans are strangers in a strange land, that they are alienated from the profit of their own productivity, that they are caught in a meaningless or absurd activity like Sisyphus rolling his stone endlessly up a mountain in Hell, is extremely widespread. It is doubtful that Hopkins felt alienated in exactly this way. His religious belief promised him a future life and salvation. When he speaks of despair, it is always hypothetical: Think how unbearable life would be if there were not hope.

"CARRION COMFORT"

"Carrion Comfort," among the best of Hopkins's dark sonnets, considers despair, which is itself a sin, depicting the struggle of the Christian with his own conscience. It begins a series of six sonnets of unusual power that treat the struggle of the soul. These poems should be read in sequence: (1) "Carrion Comfort," (2) "No Worst, There Is None," (3) "To Seem a Stranger Lies My Lot," (4) "I Wake and Feel the Fell of Dark, Not Day," (5) "Patience, Hard Thing" and (6) "My Own Heart Let Me Have More Pity On." Read in sequence, these sonnets constitute a short psychodrama or morality play.

The Christian speaker confronts his own doubt, weakness, and unworth, and is terrified of God. In five scenes, he is seen writhing and twisting in mental contortions of guilt and terror. At the conclusion of "My Own Heart Let Me Have More Pity On," the sestet provides the dramatic release, as God's smile breaks through, like sunlight on a mountain guiding the traveler. This sonnet sequence corresponds to the progress of the seeker through the final stages of his spiritual exercises. The same progress of the mind, through terror to elation at the Resurrection, is outlined in "That Nature Is a Heraclitean Fire and of the Comfort of the Resurrection." The first segment of this poem looks at the changing natural world. Like a bonfire, everything around humans is changing, decaying, being consumed. Humans seem so pitifully weak and vulnerable among these flames. The only hope is Christ's promise of salvation, which comes to humans like a beacon. People will pass through the fire and, even when all else is destroyed, their souls will endure like immortal diamonds.

HOPKINS'S VOCABULARY

A striking characteristic of Hopkins's poetry is his rich vocabulary. As he sought to find the inscape or unique form in the created universe, he also attempted to find in language the original, spare, strange, exactly right word. He was one of the best trained linguists of his age, working at the research level in Latin and Greek, while studying Anglo-Saxon and Welsh. His notes and journals show him repeatedly developing elaborate etymologies of words. He belonged to a widespread movement in the Victorian era, spearheaded by Robert Bridges and his Society for Pure English, which glorified the archaic elements in modern English. In his notes, he records dialect words and the special words used by workers for their tools or by country people for plants and animals. This attention to the texture of language pours forth in his poetry in an unusually rich, eccentric vocabulary.

LEGACY

Despite the orthodoxy of his religious views, Hopkins is known as one of the founders of modernism in literature. He is frequently compared with Walt Whitman, Emily Dickinson, and the French Symbolist poets as a great revolutionary who rebelled against the sterile forms of Victorian verse and brought a new urgency, freshness, and seriousness to poetry. He revolutionized the very basis of English meter with his experiments in sprung rhythm. He revitalized the bold metaphor in the manner of the English Metaphysical poets. He created a whole new lexicon, a poetic vocabulary constructed from dialect, archaic, technical, and coined words.

The critics who initially praised his work in the 1920's and 1930's tended to see him as a cultural primitive, a man isolated from the corruption of society and so able to return to a state of nature and get to the core of language more easily than writers such as Alfred, Lord Tennyson, who seemed corrupted by false traditions. Although Hopkins was undoubtedly a great innovator, he was certainly not a cultural primitive. He was a highly trained professor of Latin and Greek language and literature. In addition to his "Double First in Greats" from Oxford University, he undertook years of rigorous philosophical and theological training with the Society of Jesus. He was at the center of a group of correspondents who were as powerful intellectually as any group found in his era: Bridges, Dixon, Patmore, and other less frequent scholarly correspondents.

Hopkins was not a naïve writer; on the contrary, he was an extremely sophisticated writer. His poetry is revolutionary, not because he was ignorant of tradition, but because he brought together many powerful threads of tradition: the contemplative practice of the *Spiritual Exercises*, with their "composition of place" and "application of the senses"; the conventions of the Petrarchan sonnet; the complicated metrical studies of Bridges, Patmore, and the classical scholars; the classical philosophical background of Oxford University; and the medieval thought of the Jesuit schools, especially of John Duns Scotus. These traditions met, and sometimes conflicted sharply, in Hopkins. From that confluence of traditions he gave modern readers the unique gift of his poems.

OTHER MAJOR WORKS

NONFICTION: *The Correspondence of Gerard Manley Hopkins and Richard Watson Dixon*, 1935, 1955 (C. C. Abbott, editor); *The Letters of Gerard Manley Hopkins to Robert Bridges*, 1935, 1955 (Abbott, editor); *The Notebooks and Papers of Gerard Manley Hopkins*, 1937 (Humphry House, editor); *Further Letters of Gerard Manley Hopkins*, 1938, 1956 (Abbott, editor); *The Journals and Papers of Gerard Manley Hopkins*, 1959 (House and Graham Storey, editors); *The Sermons and Devotional Writings of Gerard Manley Hopkins*, 1959 (Christopher Devlin, editor); *Gerard Manley Hopkins: Selected Letters*, 1990.

BIBLIOGRAPHY

Bloom, Harold, ed. *Gerard Manley Hopkins*. New York: Chelsea House, 1986. Includes a number of significant essays on Hopkins, chronology, a bibliography, and index.

Brown, Daniel. *Gerard Manley Hopkins*. Tavistock, England: Northcote House/British Council, 2004. A biography of Hopkins that examines his life in relation to his poetic works and themes.

_____. *Hopkins' Idealism: Philosophy, Physics, Poetry*. New York: Oxford University Press, 1997. Offers new readings of some of Hopkins's best-known poems and is the first full-length study of Hopkins's largely unpublished Oxford undergraduate essays and notes on philosophy and mechanics.

Feeney, Joseph J. *The Playfulness of Gerard Manley Hopkins*. Burlington, Vt.: Ashgate, 2008. Feeney examines the poetry of Hopkins, from the early period to the late, looking at his sense of humor and playfulness.

MacKenzie, Norman H. *Excursions in Hopkins*. Philadelphia: Saint Joseph's University Press, 2007. Examines the poetry of Hopkins in detail. Includes two chapters on "The Wreck of the *Deutschland*."

_____. *A Reader's Guide to Gerard Manley Hopkins*. 2d ed. Philadelphia: Saint Joseph's University Press, 2007. This guide provides information about Hopkins that helps readers interpret his poetry.

Mariani, Paul. *Gerard Manley Hopkins: A Life*. New York: Viking, 2008. Mariani, a poet, integrates Hopkins's spiritual and literary life to portray the life and works of Hopkins.

Milward, Peter. *A Lifetime with Hopkins*. Ann Arbor, Mich.: Sapientia Press, 2005. Jesuit priest and literary scholar Milward looks at Hopkins's views on God, nature, the self, and people, and examines his place in literary tradition.

White, Norman. *Hopkins: A Literary Biography*. New York: Oxford University Press, 1992. This massive biography traces the life, career, and religious struggles of the brilliant but profoundly alienated Victorian poet.

Wimsatt, James I. *Hopkins's Poetics of Speech Sound: Sprung Rhythm, Lettering, Inscape*. Buffalo, N.Y.: University of Toronto Press, 2006. The author examines the poetic techniques used by Hopkins, including sprung rhythm, lettering, and inscape.

Todd K. Bender

A. E. HOUSMAN

Born: Fockbury, Worcestershire, England; March 26, 1859
Died: Cambridge, England; April 30, 1936

PRINCIPAL POETRY
A Shropshire Lad, 1896
Last Poems, 1922
More Poems, 1936
Collected Poems, 1939

OTHER LITERARY FORMS
A. E. Housman (HOWS-muhn) created a single work of prose fiction, *A Morning with the Royal Fam-*

ily, a youthful fantasy printed without his permission in 1882 in the *Bromsgrovian* and unpublished elsewhere. His translations total 102 lines from Aeschylus's *Hepta epi Thēbas* (467 B.C.E.; *Seven Against Thebes*), Sophocles' *Oidipous epi Kolōnōi* (401 B.C.E.; *Oedipus at Colonus*), and Euripides' *Alkēstis* (438 B.C.E.; *Alcestis*) and first appeared in A. W. Pollard's *Odes from the Greek Dramatists* in 1890. They have since been included in the *Collected Poems*. Henry Maas has collected more than eight hundred of Housman's letters, which, though not in the great tradition of English letter-writing, shed considerable light on the poet's enigmatic personality.

ACHIEVEMENTS
Although A. E. Housman's fame today rests on a handful of poems, it was to classical scholarship that he devoted most of his life. For nearly fifty years, he was a professor of Latin, first at University College, London, and later at Cambridge University. A profound and prolific scholar fluent in five languages, he published in that time approximately two hundred critical papers and reviews spanning the entire spectrum of classical literature from Aeschylus to Vergil. This work consists mainly of textual emendations of corrupt manuscripts and is highly technical, providing a stark contrast to the lucid simplicity of his poetry. Titles such as "Emendationes Propertianae," "The Codex Lipsiensis of Manilius," and "Adversaria Orthographica" abound in *The Classical Papers of A. E. Housman* (1972), collected and edited by J. Diggle and F. R. D. Goodyear in three volumes. In addition, Housman has left behind editions of Ovid, Juvenal, Lucan, and Marcus Manilius and several major lectures, including *The Confines of Criticism* (1969) and *The Name and Nature of Poetry* (1933).

Housman held no illusions either about the power of classical knowledge to influence human character or the extent of its appeal, but he nevertheless placed the highest premium on learning for its own sake and was a relentless seeker after truth using the method of textual criticism, which he defined in *The Application of Thought to Textual Criticism* (1922) as "the science of discovering error in texts and the art of removing it." This was for him "an aristocratic affair, not communicable to all men, nor to most men." The one thing most necessary to be a textual critic "is to have a head, not a pumpkin, on your shoulders, and brains, not pudding, in your head." He applied to others the same rigorous standards of scholarship that he set for himself, and he had no sympathy for incompetence in any form. He was particularly annoyed by the practice of modern criticism of following one manuscript whenever possible instead of weighing the relative merits of alternative manuscripts, a practice, he writes in his preface to Juvenal (1905), designed "to rescue incompetent editors alike from the toil of editing and from the shame of acknowledging that they cannot edit." His harshest words are reserved for self-complacent and insolent individuals masquerading as sane critics. His vituperative attacks on Elias Stoeber and Friedrick Jacob in his 1903 preface to Manilius may be taken as typical: "Stoeber's mind, though that is no name to call it by, was one that turned as unswervingly to the false, the meaningless, the unmetrical, and the ungrammatical, as the needle to the pole," and "Not only had Jacob no sense for grammar, no sense for coherency, no sense for sense, but being himself possessed by a passion for the clumsy and the hispid he imputed this disgusting taste to all the authors whom he edited." The extent of Housman's learning and the unbridled candor of his judgments made him a respected and feared polemicist and perhaps the most formidable classicist of his age. W. H. Auden called him "The Latin Scholar of his generation."

Throughout his career Housman repeatedly denied having any talent for literary criticism, and he turned down the Clark Lectureship in English Literature at Trinity College, Cambridge, on the ground that he did not qualify as a literary critic, who, he wrote in *The Confines of Criticism*, is rarer than "the appearance of Halley's comet." When he was at University College, London, he delivered papers on various English poets including Matthew Arnold, Algernon Charles Swinburne, and Alfred, Lord Tennyson, but he refused to allow them to be published and apparently resented the demands the Literary Society made on him, writing in his preface to Arthur Platt's *Nine Essays* (1927) that "Studious men who might be settling *Hoti*'s business and properly basing *Oun* are expected to provide amusing discourses on subjects of which they have no official knowledge and upon which they may not be titled even to open their mouths." Nevertheless, Housman's several excursions into literary criticism reflect a great sensitivity to such central concerns as the integrity of literary texts and the debasement of language. In its emphasis on the numinous intractability of great poetry, *The Name and Nature of Poetry* is an oblique repudiation of the intellectualism of T. S. Eliot and I. A. Richards. Housman's criticism shows the influence of Matthew Arnold, but the importance he attached to the undergirding of impressionistic judgments with sound scholarship goes beyond that Victorian sage.

As a poet, Housman was successful to the point of celebrity. *A Shropshire Lad* was initially slow to catch on with the reading public, but after Grant Richards took over as Housman's publisher, it became a great success on both sides of the Atlantic. Its moody *Weltschmerz* caught the fin de siècle state of mind, just as *Last Poems* captured the ennui of a war-weary generation. Today the inevitable reaction has set in, and Housman's poetry is not as highly regarded as it once was. The melancholy of his poems too often seems uninformed by spiritual struggle, but the plaintive lyricism of his best work has a universal and enduring appeal.

Biography

Alfred Edward Housman was born on March 26, 1859, in Fockbury, Worcestershire, into an ancient family of preachers and farmers whose English roots extended back to the fourteenth century. His great-grandfather on his father's side, an evangelical preacher who lived out his life with a wife and eight children in genteel poverty, was shy and unassertive in manner but inwardly tough, capable of bearing up under the hardships of life with manly fortitude. Housman was able to observe at first hand that stoicism, which informs so much of his mature poetry, in his own mother, Sarah, whose prolonged suffering and death after bearing seven children was a model of quiet courage. In the words of George L. Watson, "With his grimly stoical demeanor, Housman often recalled some ancestral farmer, glowering at the inclement weather" (*A. E. Housman: A Divided Life*, 1957). No such family precedent exists for Housman's career as a scholar unless it be a distant cousin on his father's side who was a lecturer in Greek and Divinity at Chichester College, and still less exists for the poet's rejection of the Church within a year of his mother's death.

The death of Housman's mother on his twelfth birthday brought a traumatic end to his childhood and left him with a profound sense of loss from which he never fully recovered. He had adored the witty, intelligent woman who took pride in her descent from Sir Francis Drake, and her death created a vacuum that could not be filled by his father, Edward, a lackluster solicitor who took increasingly to drink during Sarah's illness and who, two years after her death, married his cousin Lucy and began a long slide into poverty, dying after many years of broken health in 1894. Alfred was never close to his father. He regarded his drunkenness and general improvidence as intolerable weaknesses and held him in barely concealed contempt. He was, however, close to his six brothers and sisters during his early life and, as the oldest, conducted literary parlor games for them, taking the lead in writing nonsense verse, a practice that continued during summer vacations through his college years.

Sarah's death was not permitted to interrupt for long Housman's studies at nearby Bromsgrove School, where he had enrolled on a scholarship in the fall of 1870. Bromsgrove was an old and reputable public school and provided an excellent foundation in the classics, English, and French. As a student, Housman was introspective and shy and was known as Mouse by his classmates. Throughout his childhood, he was afflicted with a nervous disorder, and while a student at Bromsgrove, he had violent seizures that the headmaster attributed to Saint Vitus's dance (chorea). Later in life this nervous condition took the form of occasional facial contortions that might "incongruously reappear in the course of the most impersonal lectures, as he read aloud one of the odes of Horace, leaving his astonished students 'afraid the old fellow was going to cry,'" in the words of George L. Watson. His nervous affliction notwithstanding, Housman seemed to thrive on the rigorous eleven-hour-a-day regimen at Bromsgrove School. In 1874, he appeared for the first time in print with a poem in rhymed couplets about the death of Socrates

A. E. Housman (Time & Life Pictures/Getty Images)

for which he won the prize for composition in English verse and which he delivered on Commencement Speech Day. It was published in the *Bromsgrove Messenger* on August 8, 1874, much to his later chagrin. In adult life, Housman was always jealous of his reputation and forbade the publication of his juvenilia and occasional addresses, which he felt did not meet the high standards he set for himself.

Housman's career at Bromsgrove School ended in triumph as he won the Lord Lyttelton prize for Latin verse, the honorarium for Greek verse, and the Senior Wattell prize, along with a generous scholarship to St. John's College, Oxford. At least some of Housman's success at this time can be attributed to Herbert Millington, who became headmaster at Bromsgrove School in 1873. A man of keen intellect, Millington presented a formidable figure to the students, and Housman felt some hero-worship for him, referring to him much later as a good teacher for a clever boy. Millington was the most important role model of Housman's youth.

In the fall of 1877, Housman entered Oxford and, within a few days, was writing irreverently to his stepmother about the solemn Latin ceremony of matriculation. He joined the Oxford Union, and although he was inactive, he was "an avowed member and staunch champion of the Conservative faction" (Watson). Generally, however, Housman remained uninvolved in the life of the university. He was unimpressed by its professors and attended only one lecture by the illustrious Benjamin Jowett. Housman came away disgusted by Jowett's disregard for the "niceties" of scholarship. A lecture by John Ruskin also left Housman unimpressed. Housman later wrote that "Oxford had not much effect on me." This was not entirely the case, for it was at Oxford that he began to develop in earnest his capacity for classical scholarship. Passively resisting the conventional curriculum, Housman early in his Oxford career decided to devote his energies to the text of the Latin poet Sextus Propertius, whose garbled works required extensive editorial attention. He continued to work on Propertius for the remainder of his time at Oxford. Watson writes that Housman was already "embarking on those problems of conjectural emendation which are the acme of classical learning." It was also at this time that Housman began keeping a commonplace book of his favorite quotations, which tended toward the sepulchral, as one might expect of a young man whose only adornments for his college rooms were Albrecht Dürer's "Melancholia" and "The Knight, Death and the Devil." Housman's favorite poem during his early Oxford years was Arnold's "Empedocles on Etna" (1852), which he said contained "all the law and the prophets." He was attracted to Thomas Hardy's early novels for their gloomy stoicism. For a time, Housman flirted with the poetry of Swinburne and wrote an antiecclesiastical poem, "New-Year's Eve," modeled on Swinburne's style.

Clearly the most important thing that happened to Housman during these years was his friendship with Moses Jackson, which had a deep and lasting effect on him. Among the first people he met at Oxford were A. W. Pollard and Jackson. He liked them both, but he was especially attracted to the latter. Jackson was everything that Housman was not: sociable, handsome, athletic, and charismatic. A brilliant student of engi-neering, he excelled with ease at everything he did. The three became fast friends, and in 1879, Housman won a first class in Moderations but his failure to win either the Hertford Classical Scholarship or the Newdigate Prize for English verse was an omen of worse to come. In his last year at Oxford, Housman shared rooms with Pollard and Jackson, and according to Watson, this "was to be the most perturbed and momentous period of his life." There is convincing evidence that at this time Housman developed a passionate attachment for Jackson, which he kept hidden from everyone at great psychic cost to himself. He became irritable and moody, but his friends apparently suspected nothing. He failed his examination in Greats, and in the summer of 1881, he returned to his family in disgrace. Andrew S. Gow in his *A. E. Housman: A Sketch* (1936) attributes Housman's failure to the nature of the curriculum, which emphasized history and philosophy at the expense of literature, but the weight of later opinion places the blame on Housman's changed feelings for Jackson.

Housman returned to Oxford in the fall of 1881 to qualify for the lowly pass degree. He worked occasionally as a tutor in Greek and Latin at his old school and studied intensively for the Civil Service Examination. In December, 1882, he moved to London to share lodgings with Jackson and Jackson's younger brother, Adalbert, and went to work in the Patent Office, where he spent the next ten years registering trademarks. From this point until 1885, not one letter emerged from Housman, and not even a brother and sister could gain access to him when they came to live in London. In 1886, Housman, seeking the peace of solitude, took private rooms in Highgate, and from this time on, his "invariable mode of life," according to Watson, would be "monastic seclusion." Only the Jackson brothers were encouraged to intrude on his privacy.

In 1888, Housman broke on the scholarly world with an avalanche of brilliant critical articles that won for him an international reputation (and would secure for him the chair in Latin at University College, London, in 1892). Given that these early scholarly publications were researched in the evenings at the British Museum after a full day at the Patent Office, his accomplishment must be seen as nothing short of heroic. His *Introductory Lecture* (1937) was given on October 3, 1892, at University College and earned for him the lasting respect of his colleagues. Housman's scholarly writing continued unabated during his years there. He continued to work on the manuscripts of Propertius, edited works by Ovid and Juvenal, and in 1897 came out with a brilliant series of papers on the *Heroides*. In the meantime, Moses Jackson had gone to live in India and Adalbert had died, plunging Housman into near suicidal gloom that was to persist at intervals for the rest of his life and that could be relieved only by creative activity. In 1896, *A Shropshire Lad* appeared, published at his own expense, and 1899 saw the first paper on Manilius, the poet who was to become the object of Housman's most important work of scholarship. His edition of Manilius appeared in five books over a twenty-seven-year period, "a monument of incomparable skill and thankless labour."

The eventual success of *A Shropshire Lad* and Housman's recognized position as a scholar of the first rank made him something of a celebrity, and during his last ten years at University College, he would dine at the Café Royal with a select circle of friends that included his brother Laurence, his publisher Grant Richards, his faculty colleague Arthur Platt, and a few others. By now Housman was a connoisseur of fine food and wine and an accomplished dinner conversationalist. He remained aloof from the London literary scene, however, and had little appreciation for the serious writers of his day, including the poet William Butler Yeats. On a lesser level, he intensely disliked the novels of John Galsworthy, and when James Joyce's *Ulysses* (1922) was published, Housman sniffed, "I have scrambled and waded through and found one or two half-pages amusing." Nor did he display any interest in music or painting. About such composers as Ralph Vaughan Williams and Charles Butterworth, who set some of his poems to music, Housman remarked, "I never hear the music, so I do not suffer."

In October, 1911, Housman was elected Kennedy Professor of Latin at Cambridge University and a fellow of Trinity College. His brilliant inaugural lecture on *The Confines of Criticism* remained unpublished during his lifetime because he was unable to verify a

reference in it to Percy Bysshe Shelley. At the university, Housman became a member of a select group of the faculty known as The Family, which met twice a month for dinner. At these ritual banquets, Housman proved a good raconteur and was a well-accepted member of the group, but he held himself back from intimate friendships with his colleagues for fear of rejection or disappointment. He was equally distant toward his students; and his lectures, which he gave twice weekly in all three academic terms, were sparsely attended both because of the highly technical nature of his subject matter and the coldness of his demeanor on the platform. Throughout his twenty-five years at Cambridge, Housman continued to publish widely, directing his major efforts to the edition of Manilius. He was both respected as a great scholar and feared as a devastating polemicist. *Last Poems*, which appeared in 1922, was a great success. In the spring of 1933, Housman was prevailed on to give the Leslie Stephen Lecture. He delivered *The Name and Nature of Poetry* on the twenty-second anniversary of his inaugural lecture as Kennedy Professor of Latin. In the summer of 1935, an ill Housman rallied enough strength for one last trip to France, where he had vacationed regularly since 1897. Weakened by heart disease, he died in Cambridge on April 30, 1936. In the words of Watson, he "wore in absolute repose a look of 'proud challenge.'"

ANALYSIS

A. E. Housman once remarked, with that scathing condescension of which he was a master, that Swinburne "has now said not only all he has to say about everything, but all he has to say about nothing." Actually, when Housman was at Oxford he fell under Swinburne's powerful spell. His "New Year's Eve" (*Additional Poems*, 21), written about 1879, celebrates the death of the gods in a labored imitation of the "Hymn to Proserpine": "Divinities disanointed/ And kings whose kingdom is done." The poem is interesting but uninspired, and it is good that Housman early rejected Swinburne as a model. Still, one wishes that Housman had possessed more of the older poet's exuberance of imagination and richness of rhetoric, for it is in these qualities that his poetry is most deficient.

Practically all his poems are variations on the related themes of mortality and the miseries of the human condition; while a close reading reveals considerably more variety than at first appears, it is nevertheless true that the body of Housman's poetry is slighter than that of any other English poet of comparable reputation. The authorized canon consists of only three small volumes, which were published separately: *A Shropshire Lad*, *Last Poems*, and the posthumous *More Poems*. The twenty-three *Additional Poems* and three verse translations have been added to the *Collected Poems* for a total of 175 original poems. All are short, some no more than a stanza in length. The predominant form is the lyric. The tone is characteristically mournful and the mood elegiac. It is useless to look for any kind of development, either of substance or technique, in these poems, for most of them were written in the 1890's when Housman was under great psychological stress. They are intensely autobiographical inasmuch as they spring from the deep well of Housman's psyche, but few refer to specific events in his life. Housman's passion for privacy was as great as Robert Browning's, and he was attracted to the lyric as a verse form largely because of its essential impersonality. The emotion of his poems is usually general, an undifferentiated *Weltschmerz*, and such dramatic elements as may occur as persona and setting are characteristically undefined. The extremely personal and revealing "The world goes none the lamer" (*More Poems*, 21) and "Because I liked you better" (*More Poems*, 31) are exceptional.

DOOMED LOVE

In the world of Housman's poetry, which is more obviously consistent than that of more complex poets, youth fades into dust, lovers are unfaithful, nature is lovely but indifferent, and death is the serene end of everything. These great archetypal themes have given rise to some of the world's finest poetry, from Sir Walter Ralegh's "The Nymph's Reply to the Shepherd" to William Butler Yeats's "Sailing to Byzantium." What makes them interesting in Housman's poetry are the particular forms in which they are cast. "With rue my heart is laden" (*A Shropshire Lad*, 54), a poem sometimes set to music, may be taken as exemplary of his lyricism:

> With rue my heart is laden
> For golden friends I had,
> For many a rose-lipt maiden
> And many a lightfoot lad.
> By brooks too broad for leaping
> The lightfoot boys are laid;
> The rose-lipt girls are sleeping
> In fields where roses fade.

In this lyric of studied simplicity there is a classical blending of form and substance. The simple and inventive diction; the Latinate syntax, parallelism, and balance; the alternating seven- and six-syllable lines restrain still further the already generalized emotion; and while the poem is cold and artificial, it has a kind of classical grace. A comparison with William Wordsworth's "A Slumber Did My Spirit Seal" will reveal the power of a great sensibility working through the constraints of classical form to convey a sense of profound personal feeling.

In too many of Housman's lyrical poems, including the well-known "When I was one-and-twenty" (*A Shropshire Lad*, 13) and "When first my way to fair I took" (*Last Poems*, 35), the feeling is severely attenuated by a mannered flatness, and the passion that the poet undoubtedly experienced is swallowed up by the generalization of the emotion. At worst, the feeling degenerates into the bathos of "Could man be drunk for ever" (*Last Poems*, 10) or the histrionic posturing of "Twice a week the winter thorough" (*A Shropshire Lad*, 17), but at their best there is a genuine communication of feeling, as in "Yonder see the morning blink" (*Last Poems*, 11) and "From far, from eve and morning" (*A Shropshire Lad*, 32). There is a thin line between the expression of the poignancy of existence and sentimentality, and it is a tribute to Housman's tact that he so seldom crosses it.

Housman's poems work best when the emotion is crystallized by a dramatic context, as in some of the love pieces and the poems about soldiers in which the oracular pronouncements about the miseries of living that so easily lapse into an unacceptable didacticism are subordinated to more concrete situations. "Oh see how thick the goldcup flowers" (*A Shropshire Lad*, 5) is a clever and humorous dialogue between a young blade and a girl who spurns his advances, but beneath the surface gaiety there is the slightest suggestion of the mortality and faithlessness of lovers. In "Delight it is" (*More Poems*, 18) the youthful speaker addresses the maiden in words of reckless honesty—"Oh maiden, let your distaff be/ And pace the flowery meads with me/ And I will tell you lies"—and one is to assume that he is a prototype of all young lovers.

In "Spring Morning" (*Last Poems*, 16), the idyllic beauty of an April morning and the universal renewal of life in the spring place in ironic relief the "scorned unlucky lad" who "Mans his heart and deep and glad/ Drinks the valiant air of dawn" even though "the girl he loves the best/ Rouses from another's side." The speaker of "This time of year" (*A Shropshire Lad*, 25) is more fortunate, but only because the former lover of his sweetheart has died. "Is my team ploughing" (*A Shropshire Lad*, 27) dramatizes a similar situation in which the surviving youth has taken his dead friend's girl. In a dialogue that extends beyond the grave, the living lover tells his dead friend: "I cheer a dead man's sweetheart/ Never ask me whose." One of the most effective of Housman's love poems is "Bredon Hill" (*A Shropshire Lad*, 21), in which the sound of the church bells reminds the speaker of the untimely death of his sweetheart. The poem ends ambiguously with the distraught lover saying to the humming steeples: "Oh, noisy bells, be dumb/ I hear you, I will come." Also with death in mind is the speaker of "Along the field" (*A Shropshire Lad*, 26), who a year before had heard the aspen predict the death of his sweetheart. The prediction fulfilled, he now walks beside another girl, and under the aspen leaves he wonders if they "talk about a time at hand/ When I shall sleep with clover clad/ And she beside another lad."

In all these poems love is doomed to transience by infidelity or death. This, they say, is the human condition. In virtually all of them, death has supplanted sex as the major ingredient, making them unique in English love poetry.

DEATH

Death is also, less surprisingly, the main element in most of Housman's military poems. The poems about soldiers, with the exception of the frequently anthologized "Epitaph on an Army of Mercenaries" (*Last Poems*, 37), are not as well known as some of Housman's

other poetry. At first sight they may seem somewhat out of place, but it is not surprising that an introverted classical scholar of conservative convictions should glamorize the guardians of the empire. The attitude toward the soldier is consistently one of compassion and respect and the poems convey a depth of sincerity not always felt elsewhere. The prospect of young men going to die in foreign lands in the service of the queen takes on an added poignancy from the death of Housman's younger brother, Herbert, who was killed in the Boer War. On another level, a soldier's death is an honorable form of suicide and a way to attain lasting fame. "The Deserter" (*Last Poems*, 13) and "The Recruit" (*A Shropshire Lad*, 3) may be taken as typical. In the first, the lass, rejected by her lover so that he may rejoin his comrades, upbraids him and others like him for scouring "about the world a-wooing/ The bullet to their breast"; in the second, the lad is promised eternal fame either as a returning hero or as a slain comrade. In "Lancer" (*Last Poems*, 6), the speaker affirms his coming death with the ringing refrain of "*Oh who would not sleep with the brave?*" In these poems Housman succeeds in investing Thanatos, characteristically an enervated and sterile attitude, with a singular vitality. The placid stoicism of the soldiers makes these ultimately the least melancholy of all of Housman's poems.

The melancholy that permeates virtually every line of Housman's poetry is a matter of temperament more than of a well-wrought metaphysics. He affirms the existence of the soul in such poems as "The Immortal Part" (*A Shropshire Lad*, 43) and "Be still, my soul" (*A Shropshire Lad*, 48) even as he denies its immortality, the agnostic "Easter Hymn" (*More Poems*, 1) notwithstanding. Such monologues to the dead as "To an Athlete Dying Young" (*A Shropshire Lad*, 19) and "Shot? so quick, so clean an ending?" (*A Shropshire Lad*, 44) are intended as no more than poetic license. Death is seen as the final, desirable release from the Sisyphean exhaustion of living. Thanatos ultimately leads to suicide, which in several of the poems is prescribed as the best antidote for the illness of life. Other strategies for coping with the suffocating consciousness of "our long fool's-errand to the grave" are hedonism and, more logically, stoicism.

HEDONISM AND STOICISM

In Housman's hedonistic poems, the traditional sexuality of the carpe diem theme has been eliminated. In his most rousing invitation to pleasure, "Think no more lad" (*A Shropshire Lad*, 49), the lad is told to "be jolly/ Why should men make haste to die?" Such pleasures as "jesting, dancing, drinking" stave off the darkness, since "'tis only thinking/ Lays lads underground." The other exercises in hedonism are more subdued. The speaker of "Loveliest of trees" (*A Shropshire Lad*, 2), aware of his limited time, will go about the woodlands "To see the cherry hung with snow," and "The Lent Lily" (*A Shropshire Lad*, 79) invites anyone who will listen to enjoy the spring and gather all the flowers that die on Easter Day. In "Reveille" (*A Shropshire Lad*, 4), the lad is enjoined to rise and enjoy the morning, for "Breath's a ware that will not keep/ Up, lad: when the journey's over/ There'll be time enough to sleep." "Ho, everyone that thirsteth" (*More Poems*, 22) makes an effective use of the living waters of Scripture as a metaphor of fulfillment. The poem concludes that "he that drinks in season/ Shall live before he dies," but the "lad that hopes for heaven/ Shall fill his mouth with mold."

Stoicism is a more satisfying way of coming to grips with the human condition, and it provides the basis for several of Housman's most rewarding poems, including "The Oracles" (*Last Poems*, 25), "The Sage to the Young Man" (*More Poems*, 4), and "The chestnut casts his flambeaux" (*Last Poems*, 9). In this last poem, an embittered young man drinking in a tavern deplores the passing of another spring and curses "Whatever brute and blackguard made the world" for cheating his "sentenced" soul of all that it has ever craved. Then with dramatic suddenness, he sees that "the troubles of our proud and angry dust/ Are from eternity," and this leads to his stoic affirmation that "Bear them we can, and if we can we must." The idea here that human misery is both certain and universal is the central focus of such powerful poems as "The First of May" (*Last Poems*, 34), "Westward on the high-hilled plains" (*A Shropshire Lad*, 55), and "Young is the blood" (*More Poems*, 34). In "Young is the blood," the speaker identifies his own pain in a youth he espies whistling along the hillside highway and proclaims in the succession of the generations "that the sons of Adam/ Are not so evil-

starred/ As they are hard." This is the heart of Housman's stoicism, and this is one of his more honest and successful poems.

In a number of Housman's poems, the universalization of the existential predicament embodies a vision of the remote past that suggests the ultimate insignificance of everything. The speaker of "When I watch the living meet" (*A Shropshire Lad*, 12) is reminded by the moving pageant filing through the street of the dead nations of the past where "revenges are forgot/ And the hater hates no more," just as the speaker of "On Wenlock Edge" (*A Shropshire Lad*, 31) is put in mind by a storm of "the old wind in the old anger" threshing the ancient Roman city of Uricon. He knows the storm will pass even as "the Roman and his trouble," both now "ashes under Uricon." The perspective shifts to the future in "I wake from dreams" (*More Poems*, 43) and "Smooth between sea and land" (*More Poems*, 45), which present visions of apocalyptic dissolution.

The poetry of Housman is the poetry of negation. Most of it is shot through with a nameless melancholy and much of it is pessimistic. His lyrics invite comparison with Hardy's, with which they are often included in anthologies, but they reflect none of Hardy's moral depth. They are closer in spirit to those of Heinrich Heine, whom Housman mentioned as one of the three major influences on his work, along with the English ballads and the songs of William Shakespeare. Housman's *Weltschmerz* struck a deep chord in two generations of English readers, making *A Shropshire Lad* and *Last Poems* two of the most popular volumes of poetry of their period. Today, Housman's reputation is tempered by the knowledge that his poetry, though capable of creating haunting moods, neither expands nor deepens one's self-awareness nor one's awareness of life, despite his claim in "Terence, this is stupid stuff" (*A Shropshire Lad*, 62) that it prepares one for life's rigors. For this reason, Housman must be considered a minor poet.

OTHER MAJOR WORKS

LONG FICTION: *A Morning with the Royal Family*, 1882.

NONFICTION: *The Application of Thought to Textual Criticism*, 1922; *The Name and Nature of Poetry*, 1933;

Introductory Lecture, 1937; *Selected Prose*, 1961 (John Carter, editor); *The Confines of Criticism*, 1969; *The Letters of A. E. Housman*, 1971 (Henry Maas, editor); *The Classical Papers of A. E. Housman*, 1972 (J. Diggle and F. R. D. Goodyear, editors).

EDITED TEXTS: *M. Manilii Astronomicon Liber Primus*, 1903; *Ivnii Ivvenalis Satvrae*, 1905; *M. Manilii Astronomicon Liber Secundus*, 1912; *M. Manilii Astronomicon Liber Tertius*, 1916; *M. Manilii Astronomicon Liber Quartus*, 1920; *M. Annaei Lvcani Belli Civilis Libri Decem*, 1926; *M. Manilii Astronomicon Liber Quintus*, 1930.

BIBLIOGRAPHY

Bayley, John. *Housman's Poems*. New York: Oxford University Press, 1992. An analysis of the poetic works of Housman.

Bloom, Harold, ed. *A. E. Housman*. Philadelphia: Chelsea House, 2003. Collection of essays on Housman that covers topics such as masculine relationships and the gay subtext and Housman's divided persona. Contains considerable analysis of *A Shropshire Lad*.

Corcoran, Neil, ed. *The Cambridge Companion to Twentieth-Century English Poetry*. New York: Cambridge University Press, 2007. Contains a chapter discussing Housman's poetry and comparing it with that of Hardy, Charlotte Mew, and Edward Thomas Peter Howarth.

Efrati, Carol. *The Road of Danger, Guilt, and Shame: The Lonely Way of A. E. Housman*. Madison, N.J.: Fairleigh Dickinson University Press, 2002. This examination of Housman's life and works focuses on the effect of his presumed homosexuality on his poetry and lifestyle.

Graves, Richard Perceval. *A. E. Housman: The Scholar-Poet*. London: Routledge & Kegan Paul, 1979. A fine, balanced biography, drawing on material previously unpublished from public and private sources. Especially significant is Graves's reconciliation of Housman's romantic poetry and classical scholarship. Extensive notes and a bibliographical essay make this volume an especially useful study.

Holden, Alan W., and J. Roy Birch. *A. E. Housman: A Reassessment*. New York: St. Martin's Press, 2000. A collection of both biographical and critical essays that uncover the deceptive simplicity of Housman's poetry and life. Includes bibliographical references and index.

Leggett, B. J. *Housman's Land of Lost Content: A Critical Study of "A Shropshire Lad."* Knoxville: University of Tennessee Press, 1970. Contending that *A Shropshire Lad* contains most of Housman's enduring poems, Leggett provides a painstaking analysis of its structure and its theme ("the problem of change"). Leggett aims to shift discussion away from Housman's personality.

_____. *The Poetic Art of A. E. Housman*. Lincoln: University of Nebraska Press, 1978. A useful study divided by topics: the use of metaphor, nature poetry, structural patterns, Housman, T. S. Eliot, and "critical fashion in the thirties." Leggett devotes two chapters to Housman's theory and practice of poetry because this has been a contested point in literary criticism. Supplemented by extensive notes but no bibliography.

Naiditch, P. G. *Problems in the Life and Writings of A. E. Housman*. Beverly Hills, Calif.: Krown & Spellmam, 1995. A lucid and readable biographical account with lasting contributions to knowledge of a great and controversial scholar. Includes a bibliography and index.

Page, Norman. *A. E. Housman: A Critical Biography*. New York: Schocken Books, 1983. A succinct account drawing on published and unpublished sources, with separate chapters on Housman's classical scholarship and the development of his poetry. The introduction is especially helpful on the biographer's method, on his evaluation of previous biographies, and on his decision to separate discussions of the life and the work.

Robert G. Blake

TED HUGHES

Born: Mytholmroyd, Yorkshire, England; August
   17, 1930
Died: North Tawton, Devon, England; October 28,
   1998

PRINCIPAL POETRY

The Hawk in the Rain, 1957
Lupercal, 1960
Wodwo, 1967
Crow: From the Life and Songs of the Crow, 1970,
   1972
Selected Poems, 1957-1967, 1972
Cave Birds, 1975 (revised as *Cave Birds: An
   Alchemical Cave Drama*, 1978)
Gaudete, 1977
Moortown, 1979
Remains of Elmet, 1979
Selected Poems, 1957-1981, 1982
River, 1983
*Flowers and Insects: Some Birds and a Pair of
   Spiders*, 1986
The Cat and the Cuckoo, 1987
Wolfwatching, 1989
*Rain-Charm for the Duchy, and Other Laureate
   Poems*, 1992
Three Books, 1993 (includes *Remains of Elmet*,
   Cave Birds, and *River*)
Elmet, 1994
Collected Animal Poems, 1995
New Selected Poems, 1957-1994, 1995
Birthday Letters, 1998
Collected Poems, 2003 (Paul Keegan, editor)

OTHER LITERARY FORMS

Ted Hughes wrote many poems and tales for children, several stage and radio plays, nonfiction works on William Shakespeare and other writers, and translations of poetry from many languages. Hughes was also a prolific editor and anthologist, having edited several volumes by his wife Sylvia Plath and other poets.

ACHIEVEMENTS

Ted Hughes was undoubtedly one of the major British poets of the twentieth century, and probably the most influential English poet of the post-World War II era. His writing began as a reaction to the Movement poetry of the 1950's—a poetry marked by understatement, classical restraint, and a refusal to go beyond everyday reality. By contrast, Hughes signed himself as a poet who distrusted the intellect and the narrow conformity of ordinary activity. His poetry embraces the violent life of nature, particularly as exemplified by animals and birds, but also by people who allow instincts and drives to reveal a language of the heart. He thus returned English poetry to a romantic tradition, critical of the materialism and soullessness of contemporary society.

He produced poetry regularly, besides editing and dramatizing, particularly for radio. He also wrote extensively for children, in various genres. He became Britain's poet laureate on December 19, 1984—a largely honorary role, but one that carried considerable prestige, bespeaking his acceptance by the British literary establishment. He was awarded the Order of Merit by Queen Elizabeth II for his service to poetry. In 1998, *Birthday Letters* received the Whitbread Poetry Award the T. S. Eliot Prize for Poetry.

BIOGRAPHY

Ted Hughes was born Edward James Hughes in a small Yorkshire town on the edge of the moors, only a few miles from where the famous Brontë sisters (Charlotte, Emily, and Anne) had lived. His father, William, a carpenter, had been badly wounded in World War I during the Gallipoli landings. Hughes was the youngest of three children. His brother briefly became a gamekeeper; his sister, Olwyn, became an executor and literary agent for the estate of Sylvia Plath. When Hughes was seven, the family moved to a mining town in south Yorkshire called Mexborough. From the grammar school there, he won an scholarship to attend Cambridge University, and he went to Cambridge in 1951 after two years of national service in the Royal Air Force. Having changed his major from English to archaeology and anthropology, he graduated in 1954.

Hughes then worked at a number of jobs, including

teaching. Although he had been writing poetry from the age of fifteen, he wrote little at Cambridge and attempted to publish only locally at first. In 1956, he met Sylvia Plath, who was two years younger than he and was in Cambridge on a Fulbright Fellowship. At the time of their meeting, she was already a published poet. She began to send his poems to magazines and also entered him for a competition in New York for a first volume of poetry. He won with *The Hawk in the Rain*, and through its publication, his name quickly became known.

Plath and Hughes were married within four months of meeting. He returned with her to the United States in 1957, where they earned their living by teaching and writing prolifically together. In 1959, they returned to London, Hughes having completed *Lupercal*, helped by a Guggenheim Fellowship. The next year, their daughter, Frieda, was born, and the year after that, they moved to Devon, in the southwest part of England. Soon after the birth of their second child, Nicholas, in 1962, the marriage collapsed. Plath returned to London and filed for divorce, but during a bitterly cold winter she fell into a deep depression and committed suicide on February 11, 1963.

For some time after Plath's suicide, Hughes wrote only for children. In March, 1969, his new partner, Assia Wevill, and her child Shura both died tragically. Hughes dedicated *Crow*, a volume that marked a new direction in his poetry, to them. The volume also solidified his reputation as a writer and poet.

In 1970, he married Carol Orchard, the daughter of a Devon farmer whose farm he was leasing. *Moortown* includes many details about his experiences there and shows Hughes returning somewhat to the subject matter of his earlier poetry. Controversy over his relationship with Plath continued to dog him, especially in the United States, where his reputation was badly affected. He remained silent about the affair until the publication of *Birthday Letters* in 1997. Only after his death was the publication of Plath's journals allowed by their daughter, Frieda.

Apart from periods in London and Yorkshire, where he helped establish the Avron Foundation, which encourages creative writing, he continued to live in Devon until his death in 1998 from cancer. He was sixty-eight.

Ted Hughes (©1991, Jane Bown)

At his memorial service at Westminster Abbey, Hughes's close friend and fellow poet Seamus Heaney stated that Hughes was "a great poet through his wholeness, simplicity and unfaltering truth to his whole sense of the world."

ANALYSIS

Ted Hughes's poetic career was somewhat cyclical. His first volumes of verse contain individual poetic statements on the nature of the created world, focusing on particular animals, plants, people, and seasons. These poems are intended as explorations of identity, of the "thing in itself"—following closely the late Victorian poet Gerard Manley Hopkins, whose emphasis in much of his nature poetry was on the "this-ness" or "selfhood" of each created being.

Although Hopkins saw such creation as manifestations of the variety and infiniteness of the Creator, Hughes denied the existence of divinity. In the earlier poetry, his metaphysical claims are very limited; at most he acknowledges some sort of unconscious inspiration, in the manner of Robert Graves, whose concept of the "White Goddess" as poetic inspiration and creative spirit influenced him heavily, and also of Dylan Thomas, though at first Hughes lacked the exuberance of these poets.

Yet Hughes increasingly felt the need for some sort of philosophical expression for his romanticism. That expression, when it came, was as surprising as it was forceful. The themes of violence that characterize the early poetry are transformed in the cycle of mythological poems *Crow* and *Gaudete* to an anarchic energy that subverts the organizing institutional principles of humankind, as expressed in religion, culture, and rationality. Hughes's need for a mythology to advance his personal poetic development was akin to that of William Butler Yeats, a poet he much admired (he claimed that at Cambridge he knew all of Yeats by heart).

Again like Yeats, having established a mythology in the middle part of his career and having made some very powerful poetry out of it, Hughes felt free to leave it to one side. Thus, from *Moortown* onward, his poetry tended to return to a more specific focus, based on the natural life surrounding him. He also returned to poems of personal reminiscence and the ritualized violence of war, and as a last gesture, to the publication of poems over his failed marriage to Plath.

THE HAWK IN THE RAIN AND LUPERCAL

Most of Hughes's poetry was first published in various poetry magazines and in literary and other journals, although some was commissioned for specific projects. Critical work on Hughes has grown steadily since the publication of *The Hawk in the Rain*, which was widely recognized from the first as showing great promise. The poems in this volume can be taken alongside those of *Lupercal*, since their composition must be seen as overlapping. One volume contains forty poems, the other forty-one. Rather more from *Lupercal* find their way into Hughes's 1982 *Selected Poems, 1957-1981*.

ANIMAL POEMS

Many of Hughes's most anthologized poems are to be found here—for example, "The Thought Fox," "Hawk Roosting," "Esther's Tomcat," "Six Young Men," "View of a Pig," "An Otter," and "Pike."

Most of these are animal poems that in their specificity, brilliance of imagery, and originality of viewpoint are immediately striking and reasonably accessible. It has been pointed out, as a caution, that only a limited number of poems in *The Hawk in the Rain* are real animal poems. In fact, to believe that the animals presented are real is to misunderstand the poetry, epito-

mized in "The Thought Fox," which explicitly states that the place of such animals' existence is in Hughes's imagination, for which memory and observation have only provided the raw materials. The majority of his poems are in fact infused with animal imagery. For example, the protagonist of "Famous Poet" is a monster, the subject of "Secretary" is "like a starling under the bellies of bulls," and "A Modest Proposal" is built around the extended simile of two wolves.

Lupercal is perhaps more obviously about animals, and here the nearest influence is D. H. Lawrence. Lawrence, however, develops more moral sympathy for his creatures than does Hughes, whose attitude is far more ambivalent. Hughes frankly admits to terror at times—for example, in "Pike," whose pond he "fished/ With the hair frozen on my head/ For what might move." The pike, like the hawk and the thrushes, is a perfect killing instrument; this reality both fascinates and horrifies Hughes. He recognizes in these creatures depths of darkness that exist within himself. The Jungian idea of a personal shadow is never far distant. In a number of his poems, including "Pike," "An Otter," and "To Paint a Water Lily," the dualism of natural life is vividly portrayed in terms of the surface and depths of water.

In a more ambitious poem, "Mayday on Holderness," this idea is combined with a geographical image of concentric circles. Starting with "the furnace door whirling with larvae" on a pond, through the generating life of the country in springtime, he sees all such draining into the North Sea, beneath which the dead soldiers of Gallipoli lie still, crying, "Mother, Mother!" The "Mother" is profoundly ambiguous, since it is "motherly summer" that moves on the pond in the apparently endless cycle of regeneration ending in (violent) death.

Few of the other poems in these first two volumes—apart from "Pennines in April" and "Wind," in both of which the landscape is seen in terms of the sea—are what might be called regional. Nevertheless, the sense of a northern English countryside is very strong, especially in its bleakness, its mud, and the sheer struggle required to survive there. A number of poems deal with humans who can survive such conditions—"Roarers in a Ring," "Dick Straightup," and "Crag Jack's Apostasy." More significantly, other survivors are praised, though somewhat enigmatically, in "The Retired Colonel" and the powerful "The Martyrdom of Bishop Farrar." What the characters of these poems possess is a physical courage drawn from the deep wellsprings of natural life. Farrar's courage, therefore, is not so much religious or moral as spiritual, in the Lawrentian sense Hughes later developed.

The title poems of both volumes were omitted from *Selected Poems, 1957-1981*. "The Hawk in the Rain," perhaps too reminiscent of Hopkins's "The Wind-hover," contrasts the earthbound poet, drowning in "the drumming ploughland," to the hawk that "effortlessly at height hangs his still eye." The poet is aware of "the master-/ Fulcrum of violence where the hawk stands still," but the violence emanates not only from the hawk but also toward the hawk, which ultimately crashes to the ground. This awareness of the continuity of forces running through nature, destructive yet energy giving, is one of the central features of these two volumes. The other title poem, "Lupercalia," celebrates a Roman festival of fertility, Lupercus being a god of prophecy also. The poet perhaps sees himself as a priest celebrating both prophetically and ritualistically the mystery of the fertility of nature, giving birth by sacrificing.

WAR POEMS

Another group of poems is the war poems: not of World War II, as might be expected from a poet whose boyhood was spent in that period, but of World War I, in which his father fought (William Hughes was one of the few survivors of a regiment otherwise wiped out). Later poems, such as "Out" (*Wodwo*) and "Dust As We Are" (*Wolfwatching*), explain how the young boy heard his father reenacting these traumatic experiences. Clearly, he entered deeply into his father's sufferings, and the impact of the violence of humankind in war must have shaped his perceptions of universal violence.

WODWO

Between 1960 and 1967, Hughes concentrated on children's poetry and poetic drama. The births of his own two children during these years seem to have moved him to channel his creative effort into working his animal poetry into comic and fable-related material. Hughes did a number of school broadcasts, including a reworking of the Orpheus and Eurydice myth. This echoes poignantly Hughes's own personal tragedy at this time, the breaking up of his marriage and his wife's subsequent suicide. Undoubtedly, these sad events affected his poetic output immediately and in the longer term acted as catalysts for radical changes in style and manner.

The volume that collects Hughes's adult poetry of the period, *Wodwo*, reflects this upheaval. Some critics see it as a pivotal volume in Hughes's development; certainly it must be seen as transitional. In this, and in its overall layout, it is very similar to Robert Lowell's *Life Studies* (1959), published not long before. Like Lowell's volume, *Wodwo* contains two sections of poetry sandwiching several prose pieces, some of which are autobiographical. Although Hughes's stay in the United States had brought him into touch with such American poets as Wallace Stevens, Hart Crane, and Lowell, the differences remain striking. The open confessional style that Lowell (and John Berryman) developed is the very opposite of Hughes's private manner of creating poems from which autobiographical details must be excavated skillfully, fragment by fragment.

Wodwo contains some forty poems, to which a few others were added later. Although the poetry is transitional, Hughes selected a greater proportion of it for his 1982 selection than of any other volume. It moves toward a fabular, allegorical, or mythic approach to animals and plants, as in "The Bear," "The Green Wolf," and "The Howling of Wolves." Each creature in these poems manifests some aspect of a life force, certainly, but in a more ritualistic and metaphysical way than in earlier poems. The title poem tells of some legendary animal seeking its identity, full of questions, exploring the dualism of intention and instinct, of self and not-self. Though still in the romantic tradition, many of the poems seem explicitly antiromantic in sentiment; in "Skylarks," for example, Hughes denies the truth-beauty equation. Despite critical claims to unity, the volume is more a collection of parts: Hughes is still searching for a belief system for his poetics. The arrangement of poems within the volume seems somewhat random, and their internal logic appears arbitrary. The title of one poem, "You Drive in a Circle," is rather apt for the whole collection.

CROW

Nevertheless, a number of poems in *Wodwo* do point forward to Hughes's next volume, *Crow*. "Logos," "Reveille," and "Theology" reorder the Adam and Eve story in the simplistic, demotic comic style that typifies *Crow*. The powerful "Pibroch" suggests the medieval sense of the chain of being, while it denies medieval teleology—leaving a bleakness and pessimism caught also in "Wings" and "Gnat Psalm." Hughes's verse, too, is far more experimental in *Wodwo*, ranging from the tight balladlike form of "The Bear" to the loose "Wodwo," in which punctuation and line structures have almost collapsed. Particularly, Hughes is moving away from poetic rhetoric toward the direct speaking voice (as did Lowell), and the isolation of the single line or phrase is exploited as an alternative to stanza form. Thus, even if *Crow* did come as a shock, there had been hints of it previously.

The cycle of *Crow* actually began as a response to an invitation from the American artist Leonard Baskin to write poems to accompany his drawings of mythic animals, particularly a crow that was half bird, half human. Hughes was already aware of the crow in various Native American legends as a trickster figure, and he saw in this image an "object correlative" on which to construct the mythology he needed for his poetic. The volume is subtitled *From the Life and Songs of the Crow*, suggesting that the original intention was, as it had been for Yeats, to construct a full mythology. The complete mythology failed to materialize, however—possibly because of certain irresolvable contradictions in the enterprise—and thus there is very much of a provisional feel to the volume. Later editions added several more poems, and there seems to be no internal reason that other poems should not be added, deleted, or rearranged. Nevertheless, *Crow* came as a new, powerful, and quite shocking voice in British poetry in the early 1970's, a voice that most reviewers did recognize as once and for all establishing Hughes as a major poet, if not the major poet of his generation.

Hughes's need for myth springs from two explicit causes, with probably two unstated factors also involved. First is his stated rejection of Christianity, its account of creation and of the Creator, and the nature of its spirituality—a rejection arising from his encounter

with narrow fundamentalism in the village chapel of his boyhood. His rejection is in some sense reactionary: He still needs Christian myth, especially the account of the Fall. Many of his poems in *Crow* and elsewhere rework the figures of Adam, Eve, and the serpent, introducing Crow as a "wild card" element to suggest a creative principle separate from the God of the Genesis account (see, for example, "Crow's Theology," "Crow Communes," and "Crow's First Lesson").

Second is his rejection of demythologizing rational humanism and the preeminence of the word as logical utterance and rational discourse. In this he follows William Blake and Robert Graves, as he does stylistically. He sees modern Western civilization as having lost its primitive energies through its superficial materialism and its denial of the spirit. For him, though, the spirit is out of nature, not out of Christianity—there is nothing holy about it, nor any moral necessity to it ("A Disaster" and "Crow's Account of St. George" are illuminating in this regard).

These rejections are explicit. Not openly explored yet clearly influential in Hughes's life are the nuclear threat that hung heavily over the world in the 1960's and 1970's and the tragic deaths of two women close to him. There also seems to have been a difficult, unresolved relationship with his mother. At a psychological level, *Crow* could be interpreted as an attempt to exorcise these tragedies and to resolve his feelings toward the women involved (as in "Criminal Ballad," "Song for a Phallus," "Crow and Mama," and "Lovesong"). On a political level, the nuclear threat could be seen as a subtext, underlining for him the urgency for Western civilization to find new roots to draw on, however primitive or pagan.

A new influence on Hughes's style in this period was contemporary East European poetry, especially that of Vasko Popa, whose work he helped to make known in the West. Like Popa, Hughes was interested in colloquial, folktale-like myths as images of survival, and he used poem cycles to build up such mythology. The trickster figure is basically a survivor, although the central contradiction is that usually he stays unchanged, whereas Hughes wants Crow to develop and to take on different roles and guises—as victim, helper, rebel, humankind, even Hughes himself as poet.

Crow is anarchic; so is the verse form. Words mean what Hughes wants them to mean. His rejection of rational discourse is exhilarating, creative, and unpredictable; it is also arbitrary, exasperating, and sometimes sheer nonsense, a total poetic joke. Hughes at times seems bardic, the shaman, willing to be possessed by spiritual forces to speak wisdom or healing; at other times he seems a naughty boy writing rude words. Yet "the song was worth it," as he writes in the final enigmatic "Two Eskimo Songs." Here also water finishes up "utterly worn out utterly clear." The cycle is meant ultimately as a purification of the will to live: What it does not give is a purpose for living.

GAUDETE

Gaudete (meaning "rejoice") seeks to resolve some of the contradictions of *Crow* by positing a hero and his shadow (to use a Jungian term), or double. This double is, in fact, the protagonist—the Reverend Nicholas Lumb, acting as substitute vicar for a village (Lumb Bank is actually the name of Hughes's house in Yorkshire). In fact, he sets himself up as high priest of a pagan fertility cult and spends his time bringing to life the latent sexuality of the village women by making love to them. In a climactic scene, a young woman is ritually initiated into the pagan cult but is killed by its priestess (or witch), who is jealous of Lumb, since she suspects that he is human enough to want to elope with the girl. Meanwhile, the village men, out of jealousy and anger, pursue Lumb in a semiritual stag hunt and shoot him. The bodies of the girl, Lumb, and the priestess, who has stabbed herself, are then burned by the men to hide the evidence.

The main part of the narrative is told in some fifty-five sections of a new, flexible, and pulsating narrative verse, interspersed with passages of poetic prose. The narrative is enfolded by a prologue and an epilogue, which deal with the real vicar, abducted by dark forces out of a dead world to heal a woman. For his inability to do this, he is violently beaten in a purgatorial ritual and then resurrected. The fruits of his resurrection, which takes place on the west coast of Ireland, are some forty short, gem-like poems, centering on the theme of suffering and emptying self.

The whole volume is quite extraordinary. Unlike previous volumes, it must be read as a unity—it is impossible to extract, reorder, or add. It is clearly an achieved work: Response is one of purgation or catharsis. The mythic basis is Dionysus and his female followers, the Bacchantae, though ritualistic patterns from other fertility cults are also used. In an interview given in 1971, Hughes called his poetry "a war between vitality and death . . . [that] celebrates the exploits of the warriors on either side." In a reworking of Graves's White Goddess, he links Venus with Sycorax, a female figure turned by the Middle Ages into the figure of Mary, and now lost. Western humanism has served Adonis, the god of rationality. *Gaudete* then becomes the reinstatement of Dionysus—and Venus—as the new spiritual force, Adonis having brought a general death.

In this release, however, men and women become totally separated—the men into their violence, their killer instincts, and the women into their unconscious fertility. Normal men-women relationships necessarily break down. The end is destruction and harm, as damaging as anything Adonis brings. Yet by creating Lumb as a duality, Hughes is able to avoid the dichotomy that he elsewhere describes as possible responses to the energy "of the elemental power circuit of the Universe": Refusal brings death, but acceptance brings destruction. To escape the dichotomy, one needs the purgatorial experience—not the naked instinctual one, though it is necessary to recognize and embrace the shadow within oneself—and through it to come to some sort of resurrection of spirit. Both Lumbs undergo a death. Out of this comes, at the end, a Dickinsonian distillation of regenerative and intuitive wisdom, cryptically and allusively personal. It rounds off a poem that seeks a way forward (not merely a subversion), as an alternative to both Christianity and modern secularism.

CAVE BIRDS

Between *Crow* and *Gaudete*, Hughes produced a number of other volumes, two of which were done in close conjunction with Leonard Baskin. *Cave Birds* was based, like *Crow*, on a series of Baskin drawings of various fabular birds. Hughes then wrote further poems, for most of which Baskin did drawings—some thirty in all. The volume represents a reworking of *Crow* in a much more positive and orderly fashion. A bird—a cockerel to start with—is drawn into the underworld into a Kafkaesque trial scene. As it realizes the guilt of its rationalism, it takes on a series of shifting guises to reach its own hidden psyche. It refuses easy answers, going through execution, a dying to self, until finally it meets (in Jungian fashion) an anima, a female counterpart. Their marriage in "Bride and Groom Lie Hidden for Three Days" suggests renewal through love, reversing poems such as "Lovesong" and "The Lovepet," in which sexual love is shown as purely destructive and possessive. Finally comes resurrection— as a falcon, the Egyptian Horus, a sky god. Thus the book contains a complete cycle of dying and rising, showing the need to die in order to live spiritually. Hughes's final question is "But when will he land on a man's wrist?" At their best, the poems have a beautifully cadenced sensitivity; at worst, they are perhaps too tied to Baskin: Hughes's rhetoric begins to establish itself too easily.

SEASON SONGS

Season Songs was also done with Baskin, but this time Baskin was merely Hughes's illustrator. The pieces in this book were intended for children primarily, but they manifest a delightful marriage of traditional seasonal poetry and the vivid children's poetry of a few years earlier. A number of the poems seem assured of a place in the many anthologies produced for schools. Nature is not romanticized here, but neither is it full of the instinctual violence and bleakness of *Lupercal* or the chaos of *Crow*. "Swifts" and "The Harvest Moon" are good examples of the suppleness of style of which Hughes was now master, and also of his mixing of modern and traditional imagery.

REMAINS OF ELMET

Another volume, *Remains of Elmet*, was produced at this time, in conjunction with the photographer Fay Godwin. A later volume, *River*, was done in the same way. *Remains of Elmet* is a portrait of the region of Hughes's youth, whereas *Season Songs*, anticipating *Moortown*, reflects the Devon countryside and farm where he had settled.

MOORTOWN

Moortown is a mixed volume, almost an anthology in itself. It incorporates a large section of poems centering on the Devon farm, but written over a period of time as a "verse farming diary," and then several separate se-

quences or minicycles. One of these, "Prometheus on His Crag," had been published separately in 1973, the result of an invitation to take part in a drama festival in Persepolis, Iran. For this occasion Hughes had written a drama, *Orghast* (pr. 1971), centered partly on the Prometheus myth. The cycle of poems emerged indirectly from this play as a sort of meditation.

For inclusion in *Moortown*, several more were added, making a total of twenty-one. They trace the sufferings of Prometheus from his first awakening to his agony, chained to a rock, as part of his punishment for stealing fire from the gods (though he does not remember doing so), to his trying to identify the full suffering (the vulture pecking at his liver, the heat and the cold, the permanence of the enchainment), to his coming to terms with it. The vulture is even admired for its being a perfect instrument of punishment. The sequence ends with a poem as full of questions as "Wodwo," but also with a sense of acceptance that the poet's humanity is made up of pain and endurance. The poems themselves are in tightly controlled yet very flexible stanzas, with a typical disintegration at the end into isolated lines and phrases. The imagery, again typically, is startling, violent yet lyrical in its dramaticity.

The second sequence is "Adam and the Sacred Nine." Here again, an originally mythic figure holds this shorter cycle together. Each poem describes a different bird that comes to present itself to Adam—not for him to name, as in the Genesis account, but for him to learn from. One or two poems, such as "The Dove Came," are in the *Crow* style; each bird is symbolic or allegorical and all are far removed from the *Lupercal* treatment. Further sequences are titled "Earth-Numb" and "Seven Dungeon Songs."

The farming poems are more relaxed and personal, focusing largely on the sufferings and joys of the farm animals in creating new life; births and miscarriages are detailed, almost gratuitously at times, along with deaths and partings of mothers and infants. Certainly the treatment suggests that creation, even with human intervention, works poorly. Nevertheless, the quality of felt experience is powerfully portrayed. In this antipastoral, the reader comes to see Hughes as a compassionate, sensitive farmer.

FLOWERS AND INSECTS AND WOLFWATCHING

The farming poems, like *Season Songs*, show Hughes moving away from mythic statements toward more lyrical and personal ones. This tendency continues in *Flowers and Insects* and *Wolfwatching*. In the latter, myth remains in "Two Astrological Conundrums" and "Take What You Want But Pay for It," but "Wolfwatching" is a more orthodox zoo poem, and "The Black Rhino" has an ecological message. Perhaps the most attractive poems here are those of reminiscence, especially concerning his father. The violence of the war poems of *The Hawk in the Rain* is now counterbalanced by a small boy's watching of a shell-shocked father.

BIRTHDAY LETTERS

Fortunately, becoming British poet laureate did not have a negative impact on Hughes's creativity, as can sometimes happen. Although his laureate poems, collected in *Rain-Charm for the Duchy, and Other Laureate Poems*, were not particularly striking, what was striking was the publication of the deeply personal *Birthday Letters*. For the first time, Hughes allowed his account of the Plath marriage to be told, in eighty-eight poems written over a twenty-five-year period. The poems show Hughes as somewhat passive, even as a victim of Plath's instability and despair. The poems won for Hughes a posthumous Whitbread Award for Book of the Year in 1998.

OTHER MAJOR WORKS

SHORT FICTION: *The Threshold*, 1979; *Difficulties of a Bridegroom*, 1995.

PLAYS: *The Calm*, pr. 1961; *Epithalamium*, pr. 1963; *Seneca's Oedipus*, pr. 1968; *Eat Crow*, pb. 1971; *Orghast*, pr. 1971; *The Story of Vasco*, pr. 1974 (music by Gordon Crosse; adaptation of a play by Georges Schehadé).

RADIO PLAYS: *The House of Aries*, 1960; *A Houseful of Women*, 1961; *The Wound*, 1962; *Difficulties of a Bridegroom*, 1963; *Dogs*, 1964; *The House of Donkeys*, 1965; *The Head of Gold*, 1967.

NONFICTION: *Poetry Is*, 1970; *Shakespeare's Poem*, 1971; *Henry Williamson: A Tribute*, 1979; *Shakespeare and the Goddess of Complete Being*, 1992, 1993; *Winter Pollen: Occasional Prose*, 1994 (W. Scammel, editor).

TRANSLATIONS: *Selected Poems*, 1968 (with Yehuda Amichai; of Amichai); *Selected Poems*, 1976 (with Janós Csokits; of Janós Pilinszky); *Amen*, 1977 (with and of Amichai); *Time*, 1979 (with and of Amichai); *Blood Wedding*, 1996 (of Federico García Lorca); *Phèdre*, 1998 (of Jean Racine); *Alcestis*, 1999 (of Euripides); *The Oresteia*, 1999 (of Aeschylus).

CHILDREN'S LITERATURE: *Meet My Folks!*, 1961; *The Earth-Owl and Other Moon-People*, 1963; *How the Whale Became*, 1963 (stories); *Nessie the Mannerless Monster*, 1964 (also as *Nessie the Monster*, 1974); *Poetry in the Making: An Anthology of Poems and Programmes from "Listening and Writing,"* 1967 (revised as *Poetry Is*, 1970); *The Iron Giant: A Story in Five Nights*, 1968 (pb. in England as *The Iron Man*, 1968); *Five Autumn Songs for Children's Voices*, 1969; *The Coming of the King, and Other Plays*, 1970 (augmented as *The Tiger's Bones, and Other Plays for Children*, 1974); *Orpheus*, 1971 (play); *Spring, Summer, Autumn, Winter*, 1974 (revised as *Season Songs*, 1975); *Earth-Moon*, 1976; *Moon-Whales, and Other Moon Poems*, 1976; *Moon-Bells, and Other Poems*, 1978; *The Pig Organ: Or, Pork with Perfect Pitch*, 1980 (play; music by Richard Blackford); *Under the North Star*, 1981; *What Is the Truth? A Farmyard Fable for the Young*, 1984; *Ffangs the Vampire Bat and the Kiss of Truth*, 1986; *Tales of the Early World*, 1988; *The Iron Woman: A Sequel to "The Iron Man,"* 1993; *The Dreamfighter, and Other Creation Tales*, 1995; *The Iron Wolf*, 1995; *Shaggy and Spotty*, 1997.

EDITED TEXTS: *New Poems 1962*, 1962 (with Patricia Beer and Vernon Scannell); *Five American Poets*, 1963 (with Thom Gunn); *Here Today*, 1963; *Selected Poems*, 1964 (by Keith Douglas); *Ariel*, 1965 (by Sylvia Plath); *A Choice of Emily Dickinson's Verse*, 1968; *Crossing the Water*, 1971 (by Plath); *Winter Trees*, 1971 (by Plath); *With Fairest Flowers While Summer Last: Poems from Shakespeare*, 1971 (also as *A Choice of Shakespeare's Verse*, 1971); *Johnny Panic and the Bible of Dreams, and Other Prose Writings*, 1977, 1979 (by Plath); *New Poetry 6*, 1980; *The Collected Poems of Sylvia Plath*, 1981; *1980 Anthology: Arvon Foundation Poetry Competition*, 1982 (with Seamus Heaney); *The Journals of Sylvia Plath*, 1982 (with Frances McCullough); *The Rattle Bag: An Anthology,*

1982 (with Heaney); *Selected Poems*, 1985 (by Plath); *A Choice of Coleridge's Verse*, 1996; *By Heart: 101 Poems to Remember*, 1997; *The School Bag*, 1997 (with Heaney).

BIBLIOGRAPHY

Bentley, Paul, ed. *The Poetry of Ted Hughes: Language, Illusion, and Beyond*. New York: Longman, 1998. An introductory guide to Hughes that places him within the context of developments in poetic and literary theory during his lifetime.

Feinstein, Elaine. *Ted Hughes: The Life of a Poet*. New York: W. W. Norton, 2001. Feinstein attempts to clear away the "he said, she said" controversies that surround Hughes's life and offers a more complex depiction than has usually been presented.

Greening, John. *The Poetry of Ted Hughes*. London: Greenwich Exchange, 2007. A guide that provides analysis and criticism of the poetic work of Hughes.

Malcolm, Janet. *The Silent Woman: Sylvia Plath and Ted Hughes*. New York: Alfred A. Knopf, 1994. A provocative inquiry into the controversial lives of Plath and Hughes.

Middlebrook, Diane. *Her Husband: Hughes and Plath—A Marriage*. New York: Viking, 2003. Middlebrook brings insight and empathy to a probing examination of the literary marriage of the century.

Roberts, Neil. *Ted Hughes: A Literary Life*. New York: Palgrave Macmillan, 2006. Hughes is the focus of this biography, and while Roberts does address his marriage to Sylvia Plath, he treats Hughes as a talented and influential poet in his own right. He examines Hughes' unpublished letters and notebooks to glean information about his early life, his thoughts on his position as poet laureate, and the impact that his wife's suicide had on him and his writing. This is a well-written study of Hughes' life and his development at a poet.

Sagar, Keith. *The Challenge of Ted Hughes*. London: Macmillan, 1994. Sagar is a leading British writer on Hughes, having edited and written several other critical books on him. Includes a bibliography.

_____. *The Laughter of Foxes: A Study of Ted Hughes*. Liverpool: University of Liverpool Press, 2000. A thorough literary study.

Sagar, Keith, and Stephen Tabor. *Ted Hughes: A Bibliography, 1946-1995*. London: Mansell, 1998. A complete bibliography.

Scigaj, Leonard M. *Ted Hughes*. Boston: Twayne, 1992. Scigaj is one of the United States' leading exponents of Hughes and rightfully chosen to write this introductory volume in the well-known Twayne series of introductions to major authors.

_____, ed. *Critical Essays on Ted Hughes*. New York: G. K. Hall, 1992. One of the best collections of essays on Hughes. Some other collections are fragmentary or celebratory.

Wagner, Erica. *Ariel's Gift: Ted Hughes, Sylvia Plath and the Story of the Birthday Letters*. London: Faber & Faber, 2000. Offers a careful examination of the writings that detail the minds and relationship of poetry's most harrowing couple.

David Barratt
Updated by Barratt

LEIGH HUNT

Born: Southgate, England; October 19, 1784
Died: Putney, England; August 28, 1859

PRINCIPAL POETRY
Juvenilia, 1801
The Feast of the Poets, 1814
The Story of Rimini, 1816
Foliage, 1818
Hero and Leander and Bacchus and Ariadne, 1819
The Poetical Works of Leigh Hunt, 1923 (H. S. Milford, editor)

OTHER LITERARY FORMS

Leigh Hunt was a poet, familiar essayist, critic, political commentator, playwright, and translator. While he wrote well in all these genres and with occasional brilliance in some, his reputation as an essayist has best endured. The critical essays reveal a keen sense for what is good in literature; they quote extensively from the works being considered. The familiar essays are famous for their quiet good humor. They are seldom as polished as the essays of Charles Lamb or as perceptive as those of William Hazlitt; still, a few—such as "Getting Up on Cold Mornings" and "Deaths of Little Children"—continue to be anthologized as classics.

ACHIEVEMENTS

In his own time, the general reading public respected Leigh Hunt as an important literary figure, one whose opinions on literature and the political scene were both valid and influential. His role as editor of several periodicals afforded him an effective means of voicing those opinions to a great many readers, far more than expensive books could reach. Thus, Hunt was the great popularizer of the Romantic movement in England. Later critics, however, concluded that several of his contemporaries, though then of less influence and popularity, were actually better artists and more profound thinkers. The common twentieth century attitude has tended to ignore Hunt's individual achievements, instead viewing him as the comparatively less important hub of an illustrious literary circle: John Keats, Percy Bysshe Shelley, Lord Byron, Lamb, and Hazlitt, in particular. More recently, critics have again begun to assess Hunt's own achievements, and while few would allow that he was as fine a poet as Keats, as graceful an essayist as Lamb, or as profound a critic as Hazlitt, still his work does not merit oblivion. His translations are among the finest in English, and he must be credited with increasing the English-speaking world's awareness of Italian literature. His countless journalistic pieces reflect wide reading and high standards of scholarship, and he deserves recognition for his contribution to the quality of popular journalism. A fair assessment of Hunt's literary achievement would have to include his positive influence on the several young poets who went on to surpass their mentor, but that assessment should also not overlook the quality of his own work as a journalist and translator.

BIOGRAPHY

James Henry Leigh Hunt was the son of a Philadelphia lawyer who had returned to England at the time of the American Revolution. The father was a highly prin-

cipled if rather impractical man who changed his profession from lawyer to Unitarian minister and occasional tutor. At seven years of age, young Hunt was sent to school at Christ's Hospital, where Lamb and Samuel Taylor Coleridge had also been students. Hunt's *The Autobiography of Leigh Hunt* (1850) reveals that from his earliest years, he was instilled with a hatred of all that is evil. He detested violence, was shocked by profane language, and opposed tyranny by defending his weaker schoolmates with passive resistance of schoolyard bullies. Hunt stayed at Christ's Hospital until he was fifteen. At seventeen, he published a volume of juvenile verse.

In 1808, Hunt became the editor of a journal, *The Examiner*, owned by his brother John. *The Examiner* championed a number of liberal causes: abolition of slavery, freedom of the press, an end to imprisonment for debt. In their catalog of social evils, the Hunts did not hesitate to include even the Prince Regent of England. Their description of the prince as "a violator of his word, a libertine over head and ears in debt and disgrace, a despiser of domestic ties, the companion of gamblers" resulted in a libel case and two years' imprisonment for both brothers. Prison was not very hard on Leigh Hunt. He had a decent room, which he decorated with flowered wallpaper, and in which he received such notable visitors as Byron, Shelley, and Hazlitt. After his release, Hunt published his major poem, *The Story of Rimini*, and became the literary mentor to young Keats. The Tory critics, however, could not forgive the slandering of the prince and viciously attacked Hunt. In 1817, *Blackwood's Magazine* coined the term "cockney school" to describe Hunt's frequently colloquial style, and the appellation was to plague him for many years.

In 1822, Hunt and his family arrived in Italy. Shelley invited him to assume editorship of *The Liberal*, a periodical conceived by Byron and Shelley as a vehicle for their own writings. Shelley drowned soon thereafter, and when Byron, upon whom the Hunts had depended for financial support, left Italy, the family was stranded until 1825, when Hunt borrowed enough money to return to England. He naturally felt that Byron had done him an injustice, and in 1828, he published *Lord Byron and Some of His Contemporaries*, presenting a most unfavorable picture of Byron's personal fears and dishonesties. Hunt maintained in the face of widespread adverse criticism that he had included nothing that he did not believe to be entirely true. True or not, few considered it proper to write so about a man who had recently gone to a heroic death.

With the exception of the embarrassment resulting from his identification with the character Harold Skimpole in Charles Dickens's *Bleak House* (1852)—Dickens insisted that any similarity was unintentional—the remainder of Hunt's life was rather uneventful. He wrote voluminously in all literary forms and on countless topics. The concise *Cambridge Bibliography of English Literature* (1965) estimates that a complete edition of his prose works alone would fill forty volumes. He lived to see his liberal ideas become the popular thought of the day and himself a respected figure in the literary community. Hunt's productive life ended peacefully in 1859 while he was visiting one of his oldest friends, the printer Charles Reynell, in Putney.

ANALYSIS

Leigh Hunt's three-volume *The Autobiography of Leigh Hunt* has remained the single most important source of information on both the facts of his life and those personal attributes that influenced his writings. There is, in fact, comparatively little in *The Autobiography of Leigh Hunt* dealing exclusively with Hunt; it is more a series of recollections and examinations of his many literary friends. This fact is of some importance in understanding Hunt the man, for it reflects a total lack of selfishness and a genuine sympathetic concern for the many fortunate people who won his friendship. These friendships were treasured by Hunt, and in the accounts of his youthful infatuations is reflected the simple kindheartedness and romantic idealism that were noted by his contemporaries and by later critics. *The Autobiography of Leigh Hunt* does not follow a strict chronology but is rather a series of units. For example, he describes his parents' lives until their deaths before he discusses his own early years. In fact, Hunt's father lived to see his son a successful editor. This organizational method may well be a result of Hunt's reliance on personal taste. His taste of course was selective; he extracted from his experience what he considered excellent and showed little regard for the organizational coherence of the whole. His literary criticism, indeed even his poetry, displays the same fondness for selection found in his autobiography.

Most critics agree that Hunt's greatest contribution to poetry was not the poetry he himself wrote but rather his fine criticism of the poetry of others. Again, Hunt's criticism is based on his own excellent taste, but his taste was far more useful in recognizing good literature than in distinguishing what was specifically bad and forming a thoughtful critical opinion as to the nature of the faults. In practice, Hunt the critic was a selector; he chose those passages from a work that especially appealed to his taste and quoted them at length. Thus, he assumed that the works would speak for themselves. He did not conceive of a critic as one who thinks for the reader and locks literature into a single interpretation. If Hunt has survived as a critic, it is because his personal taste was so good. At the same time, his natural sensitivity to what is fine in literature may be said to have worked against his ever achieving a place among the very greatest critics. He had no need for detailed analysis to tell him what was fine in art, and he created no aesthetic concepts approaching the sophistication of some of his contemporaries, notably Coleridge. Thus, Hunt cannot be numbered among the important literary theoreticians. His reputation as a quite respectable critic is dependent on the fact that he was perhaps the greatest appreciator of literature in the history of English letters.

The same quality of taste that enabled Hunt to select what was best in the writings of others also influenced his own poetic compositions. That selective talent, however, did not serve Hunt the poet quite so well. In the composition of his own verse, he was inclined to combine lines and passages reflective of specific poetic principles without a view to the appropriateness of the principle in relation to the poem as a whole. For example, Hunt as the great popularizer of Romantic literary ideas did more than William Wordsworth to bring home to the nineteenth century reader the notion that poetry should reflect the language really used by people. Another aim of the Romantics was to make a place in literature for the experiences of the lower classes, comprising that whole stratum of society that neoclassical writers generally ignored. Hunt's conviction that it was the business of poetry to do these things led him, much more than Wordsworth, Coleridge, and his other illustrious contemporaries who shared these ideas, to overlook yet another major principle of composition that had so concerned the neoclassicist: decorum.

Decorum demanded that all the various elements of a work of art contribute to the unified effect of the work as a whole. Thus, diction must be appropriate to character and action; a king suffering tragedy should not speak like the common man in the street. Decorum made the poet responsible to the propriety of the particular work. Hunt too often forced the work to comply with principle, and while the principle of natural poetic language suited certain poems, lines such as "The two divinest things this world has got,/ A lovely woman in a rural spot" are jarring. The many critics who have viewed Hunt's poetry with disfavor have really played variations on a single theme: the unevenness of the work. The tone is inappropriate for the subject; good writing is not maintained throughout; the central idea is lost for the digressions. These are all pitfalls into which a reliance on personal taste might lead one, and though Hunt is guilty of all this, it must also finally be acknowledged that this same disregard for uniformity resulted in an important contribution to English poetry of the nineteenth century.

THE STORY OF RIMINI

The unfortunate couplet just quoted is from *The Story of Rimini*, a retelling of Dante's tragic story of Paolo and Francesca and Hunt's most ambitious poetic effort. At the time of its composition, Hunt found John Dryden "The most delightful name to me in English literature." In *The Autobiography of Leigh Hunt* he confesses that while *The Story of Rimini* was intended to reflect the vigor and music of Dryden's natural style, his personal taste produced some variations, such as a more simple diction and less vigorous versification. Obviously the results of these liberties were not always happy. The effect of *The Story of Rimini* on English poetry, however, was certainly positive. The poem contributed greatly to the breakup of the highly polished closed couplet perfected by Alexander Pope; Hunt called for a less rigid couplet structure making use of run-on lines and feminine endings. The poem had a

marked influence on the styles of several of his contemporaries. Some of Keats's most important early pieces, such as "I Stood Tip-toe Upon a Little Hill" and "Sleep and Poetry," show the influence of Hunt's couplet. Indeed, the motto for "I Stood Tip-toe Upon a Little Hill" was borrowed from *The Story of Rimini*.

Still, the vicious political critics from *Blackwood's Magazine* and the *Quarterly* who dubbed Hunt the leader of the cockney school of poetry were not completely wrong in their identification of the poem's faults. The freer couplet form resulted in an easy, almost conversational tone that was only aggravated by colloquial diction. Hunt simply did not recognize that some of the ingredients he selected to mix in this noble experiment were not appropriate to the dignity of the subject. Regardless of particular theories of poetic composition or the unique tastes of any age, a character such as Francesca deserves better than "She had strict notions on the marrying score."

Despite its several flaws, *The Story of Rimini* does contain passages of natural grace and elegance. Clearly Dryden's lesson was not completely lost on Hunt. Moreover, the canon of Hunt's poetry includes some astonishingly pure gems that prove the truth of the judgment of *The Cambridge History of English Literature* (1916) that Hunt's best poetry is better than his best prose. These best efforts are short—sonnets and brief narratives. The rigid structure of the sonnet seems to have provided the direction that Hunt was likely to lose sight of in his longer experiments, and brief narratives prevented those digressions that he was likely to engage in for their own sake and at the expense of the clarity of his theme. The sonnet on "The Nile" is an example of Hunt at his best. Critics have generally praised it over the sonnets on the same topic by Keats and Shelley. In this poem, Hunt achieves smooth versification with natural rhymes and diction reflective of the tranquil progress of the river through an ancient and glorious landscape. Very unobtrusively, in only the last one and a half lines, meditation on the river is allowed to slide gracefully into a metaphor for meditation on human experience. Had Hunt more often shown the sense of dignity and decorum obvious in "The Nile," his place as an important English poet would be secure.

"ABOU BEN ADHEM"

The best of the brief narratives is also Hunt's most famous poem. "Abou Ben Adhem" first appeared in Samuel Carter Hall's *The Amulet* (1835) and is certainly one of the most frequently anthologized poems in the English language. The poet relates a simple tale, and while an incident of angelic visitation might seem to demand the most heroic language, Hunt wisely understood that the point of the tale is not so much the magnificence of the angel as it is the intimacy that exists between a good person and the divine. The character of Abou Ben Adhem, then, is most important; that character had to be made to appeal to human readers. Thus, Abou Ben Adhem, secure in his knowledge of what he is, is not intimidated by the angel. His address is respectful but relaxed and touched by humor. He does not disagree with the angel's omission of his name from the list of those who love God but politely suggests an alternative: "I pray thee then/ Write me as one that loves his fellow-men." In this poem of only eighteen lines, Hunt successfully drew a quite sophisticated character and suggested a relationship between God and human beings more subtle than the implied message that God loves people who love their neighbors. In the hands of a lesser poet, "Abou Ben Adhem" might have been an undistinguished exercise in lofty language and baroque figures; the theme would allow such an approach. Indeed, in the hands of Hunt it might have been a hodgepodge of styles and words at war with themes, but in this poem and several others, he managed to keep his eye on the poem itself rather than on assorted notions about poetry.

In his *An Essay on Criticism* (1711), Pope describes two kinds of literary genius: the genius to create the material of poetry, the rhetorical figures, the variety of styles, and the genius to know how to arrange the material into a unified whole. In this latter respect, Hunt too often showed himself deficient. When he managed to overcome that deficiency, as he often did, he showed himself the worthy companion of Keats, Shelley, and the many immortal Romantics who loved him so well.

OTHER MAJOR WORKS

PLAY: *A Legend of Florence*, pr. 1840.

NONFICTION: *Lord Byron and Some of His Contem-*poraries, 1828; *Imagination and Fancy*, 1844; *Wit and Humour*, 1846; *Men, Women, and Books*, 1847; *The Autobiography of Leigh Hunt*, 1850; *Leigh Hunt's Dramatic Criticism, 1808-1831*, 1949 (Carolyn W. Houtchens and Lawrence H. Houtchens, editors); *Leigh Hunt's Literary Criticism*, 1956 (Houtchens and Houtchens, editors).

MISCELLANEOUS: *Selected Writings*, 1990.

BIBLIOGRAPHY

Blainey, Ann. *Immortal Boy: A Portrait of Leigh Hunt*. New York: St. Martin's Press, 1985. This biography adds further dimension to the usual perception of Hunt as a cheerful character by emphasizing the infuriating and melancholic sides of the man. Blainey's brief, well-written portrait focuses on Hunt's vulnerable, human qualities. Includes several illustrations, extensive bibliography, and index.

Edgecombe, Rodney Stenning. *Leigh Hunt and the Poetry of Fancy*. Cranbury, N.J.: Associated University Presses, 1994. Critical analysis of selected poetry by Hunt. Includes bibliographical references and index.

Holden, Anthony. *The Wit in the Dungeon: The Remarkable Life of Leigh Hunt*. New York: Little, Brown, 2005. A look at Hunt's personal life, literary achievements, and his relationships with other prominent writers of his time. Includes sixteen pages of black-and-white photos.

Hunt, Leigh. *Leigh Hunt: A Life in Letters, Together with Some Correspondence of William Hazlitt*. Edited and introduced by Eleanor M. Gates. Essex, Conn.: Falls River, 1998. A collection of correspondence that offers invaluable insight into Hunt's life and work.

Johnson, Brimley. *Leigh Hunt*. 1896. New York: Haskell, 1970. Examines Hunt's major works in great detail, assessing the writer's abilities separately as a journalist, poet, and critic. Johnson suggests that "gratitude" to Hunt for his service to liberalism and his "popularization" of taste should persuade critics to overlook his "shallow" intellect and weak style. Supplemented by an index.

Kendall, Kenneth E. *Leigh Hunt's "Reflector."* Paris: Mouton, 1971. Examines Hunt's first literary periodical as a reflection of contemporary thought and times. Although the short book looks at other contributors from the Hunt circle, Hunt receives most of the attention. Kendall suggests that *The Reflector* was very important to the literary development of Hunt. Complemented by a bibliography, index, and appendixes.

McCown, Robert A., ed. *The Life and Times of Leigh Hunt: Papers Delivered at a Symposium.* Iowa City: Friends of the University of Iowa Libraries, 1985. A collection of critical essays covering various aspects of Hunt's writings. Titles included are "Leigh Hunt in Literary History: A Response," "Inter Pares: Leigh Hunt as Personal Essayist," and "Leigh Hunt's Dramatic Success: A Legend in Florence." These essays marked the bicentennial of Hunt's birth.

Roe, Nicholas. *Fiery Heart: The First Life of Leigh Hunt.* London: Pimlico, 2005. A biography of Hunt's life and his achievements as a poet and journalist up until the death of his friend, Percy Bysshe Shelley, 1822.

William J. Heim

J

SAMUEL JOHNSON

Born: Lichfield, Staffordshire, England; September 18, 1709
Died: London, England; December 13, 1784
Also known as: Dr. Johnson

PRINCIPAL POETRY

London: A Poem in Imitation of the Third Satire of Juvenal, 1738
The Vanity of Human Wishes: The Tenth Satire of Juvenal Imitated, 1749
Poems: The Yale Edition of the Works of Samuel Johnson, 1965 (volume 6; E. L. McAdam, Jr., and George Milne, editors)

OTHER LITERARY FORMS

Samuel Johnson was a journalist, essayist, critic, scholar, lexicographer, biographer, and satirist. Early in his career, he wrote reports on the debates in Parliament for *The Gentleman's Magazine*. Until 1762, when he received a pension from the British government, Johnson was a professional writer and wrote what publishers would buy. The most important results of his efforts, in addition to his poetry, were his *A Dictionary of the English Language: To Which Are Prefixed, a History of the Language, and an English Grammar* (1755), his essays in *The Rambler* (1750-1752) and *The Idler* (1758-1760), and *Rasselas* (1759).

A Dictionary of the English Language remains one of the outstanding achievements in the study of language. Johnson contracted in 1746 with a group of publishers to write the first comprehensive dictionary of the English language. Nine years later, with the help of only six assistants, he produced a work that is notable for its scholarship and wit. Although scholars fault its etymological notes, its definitions are generally apt and often colored by Johnson's wit, biases, and sound understanding of English usage.

The Rambler and *The Idler* are composed of period-ical essays, which, when combined with those that Johnson wrote for *The Adventurer* (1753-1754), number more than three hundred. The essays discuss literature, religion, politics, and society. They were much admired in Johnson's day, but are less so in the modern era. They are often grave, but rarely dull, and represent some of the finest prose in English. Another important prose work, *Rasselas, Prince of Abyssinia*, is Johnson's major contribution to fiction. Like Voltaire's *Candide: Ou, L'Optimisme* (1759; *Candide: Or, All for the Best*, 1759; also as *Candide: Or, The Optimist*, 1762; also as *Candide: Or, Optimism*, 1947), *Rasselas, Prince of Abyssinia* features a naïve young protagonist whose adventures gradually strip away his illusions. Johnson's work is the less harsh of the two, but is similar in tone.

Johnson's work as a biographer and scholar began early. In 1740, he wrote biographies of Admiral Robert Blake, Sir Francis Drake, and Jean-Philippe Barretier. These works are unoriginal in content. In 1744, he published *An Account of the Life of Mr. Richard Savage, Son of the Earl Rivers* (better known as *Life of Richard Savage*), which was later included in *Prefaces, Biographical and Critical, to the Works of the English Poets* (1779-1781, 10 volumes; revised in 1781 as *The Lives of the Most Eminent English Poets*; best known as *The Lives of the Poets*), although it was often published separately. Savage was a bitter and angry man; Johnson emphasized with dramatic narrative the wrongs society had visited on him. Many years after *Life of Richard Savage*, Johnson agreed to write a series of prefaces to the works of English poets for a group of booksellers. The result was *The Lives of the Poets* (four volumes in 1779 and an additional six volumes in 1781). These essays are marked by Johnson's critical insight and immense knowledge of literature; many are still standard references. Johnson was also an editor, and produced an important edition of Shakespeare with commentary. Some critics have denigrated Johnson's lack of appreciation of Shakespeare's poetry, but his appraisal of the plays is well considered, and his defense of the plays against dogmatic neoclassical criticism is notable for its good sense.

Among Johnson's other significant writings are the political essays *Thoughts on the Late Transactions Re-*

specting Falkland's Islands (1771) and *Taxation No Tyranny: An Answer to the Resolutions and Address of the American Congress* (1775), and the account of his travels in Scotland with his young Scottish friend, James Boswell, titled *A Journey to the Western Islands of Scotland* (1775). In these works, Johnson displays his hatred of war and political profiteering and his acuteness of observation.

Achievements

The diversity of Samuel Johnson's writings can be daunting; he was a novelist, playwright, essayist, journalist, editor, critic, scholar, biographer, lexicographer, etymologist, moralist, social and political commentator, philosopher, and poet. His poem *London* was published at least twenty-three times during his lifetime, and the popularity of his poetry contributed much to his reputation as the quintessential man of letters. In his era, no one had read more of the world's literature than he, and few equaled his literary achievements. Johnson seems to have so dominated the literary life of England that the period from 1750 to 1784 is often called the Age of Johnson.

"Poet" was a term of honor in eighteenth century England. The poet was at the apex of literature, and Johnson took pleasure in being referred to as one. After his death, his reputation as a poet fell from the high esteem of his contemporaries to a level of near disregard. His best-known poetry is the product of intellectual work, not inspiration. The Romantics and their nineteenth century descendants valued emotional and inspirational verse. Johnson's verse is well organized, often satirical, filled with social commentary and moralizing, and more realistically observational than metaphorical; his poetry is well within the Augustan style. He was among the best poets of his day, his verse being dynamic and rich in thought. He believed that poetry should emphasize the contemporary language of the poet and be accessible to the poet's contemporary readers. In this belief, he is in the same tradition as John Donne, John Dryden, Alexander Pope, and even poets such as Karl Shapiro. The language of Johnson's verse is still accessible to readers; it is distinctive in its combination of precision, nearly explosive anger and contempt, and acute observation of the human condition.

Biography

Many writers have suffered, and many more have pretended to suffer, for their art. Samuel Johnson's own suffering in fact made his art necessary. He was born on September 18, 1709 to Michael Johnson, a bookseller, and Sarah (née Ford), who was then forty years old. The labor had been difficult, and Johnson was, by his own account, born nearly dead. While he was a child, he contracted scrofula and smallpox; he was horribly scarred by the diseases and became deaf in one ear and partially blind in one eye. Although his father was a respectable citizen and even gained a small degree of

Samuel Johnson (Library of Congress)

701

prominence in 1709 as sheriff of Lichfield, Johnson's ancestors were of humble background. His parents were unhappy with each other, and their mild mutual hostility contributed to the miseries of their son's life.

In spite of his ugliness, poor background, and unhappy family life, Johnson became a leader among his schoolmates. He was not an ideal student; he would neglect his studies, then in great bursts of energy apply himself to learning. He wrote much as he had studied; for example, *Life of Richard Savage* was written in as little as thirty-six hours, and it has been claimed that *Rasselas, Prince of Abyssinia* was completed in a week. He aspired to be almost anything but a writer. With a small savings, he paid for more than a year at Oxford, from October, 1728, to December, 1729, but lack of money forced him to leave. After his father's death in 1731, he tried teaching. He was temperamentally unsuited for teaching; he gesticulated wildly when lecturing, and his bizarre antics confused his students. David Garrick, the actor, was among his pupils, and later helped Johnson have the verse play *Irene: A Tragedy* produced in 1749. He married Elizabeth Jervis, the widow of Harry Porter, in 1735. She was nineteen years his senior, but provided him with love, a home, and companionship that helped to stabilize his passionate and explosive personality.

Johnson's next ambition was to become a lawyer, but his poverty and physical infirmities inhibited his studies and his ability to pursue strenuous professions. He turned to writing to support himself and his wife. Acutely aware of his responsibilities as a husband, Johnson took work where he could find it. He moved to London and persuaded the publisher of *The Gentleman's Magazine*, Edward Cave, to allow him to write for the periodical. During this period of his life, he wrote and sold the poem *London* and tried to interest theater owners in a rough version of *Irene*. As a professional writer who sought to meet the needs of publishers, Johnson wrote essays, reports, poetry, and biographies—whatever would earn him money. *London* was a success and greatly advanced his reputation, but he sold the copyright and profited little from it. His literary labors earned enough for food and a place to live, but he endured bitter poverty.

A group of London publishers contracted with him in 1746 for *A Dictionary of the English Language*; he completed its compilation seven years later and it was published in 1755. The loyal support of the syndicate of publishers provided him with some small financial security, although his life remained hard. While writing the dictionary with the help of six secretaries, Johnson wrote *The Rambler*, which was published twice weekly from 1750 to 1752. The periodical's reputation was great, but its sales were small. Such was the reputation of the dictionary and *The Rambler* that Johnson became known as "Dictionary Johnson" and "Author of *The Rambler*." In 1749, the poem *The Vanity of Human Wishes* was published. It has become probably the best known of Johnson's poetic works. Also in that year, Garrick, Johnson's onetime pupil, by then a famous actor, produced *Irene* at the Drury Lane Theatre. The play lasted for nine nights, a respectable run, and Johnson earned almost two hundred pounds from the production. Subject to depressions in the best of times, Johnson was greatly saddened by the death of his wife in 1752.

From 1755 to 1762, Johnson's most important literary efforts were *The Idler*, which was published from 1758 to 1760 in the *Universal Chronicle*, and *Rasselas, Prince of Abyssinia*. In 1759, Johnson's mother died. Perhaps her illness and death inspired Johnson to contemplate his youth and its disillusionments. The evident result was *Rasselas, Prince of Abyssinia*. Some biographers assert that *Rasselas, Prince of Abyssinia* was written to pay for his mother's funeral, but most scholars disagree. In 1762, Johnson was awarded an annual pension of three hundred pounds, enough to free him from the necessity of labor.

In 1763, Johnson met Boswell, a young Scot who would become a favorite companion. It is because of Boswell's *The Life of Samuel Johnson, LL.D.* (1791) that scholars know more about the last twenty years of Johnson's life than they know of the previous fifty-five. Free from financial cares and afflicted by a variety of physical complaints, Johnson did not write at the prodigious rate that he had when he was younger. His principal literary efforts were *The Lives of the Poets*, a series of prefaces to English poets written for a consortium of booksellers, and *A Journey to the Western Islands of Scotland*, an account of a tour in 1773 with Boswell. Johnson's poetry during his last years consisted primarily of parodies and burlesques written for friends and Latin verse, composed mostly for his own contemplation. Always a moody and introspective man, his poetry became private and contemplative in his last years. In public, of course, he sought companionship and good conversation, relishing his status as England's leading man of letters. In private, he had an almost morbid dread of death. He believed that people should, at the peril of their souls, fulfill all their talents; he was acutely aware of his own superior intellectual powers and believed that he had not properly made use of them. Once in February, 1784, the dropsy that afflicted him disappeared while he prayed, and he took the relief to be a sign from God and spent the last months of his life in spiritual peace. He died on December 13, 1784, and was buried on December 20 in Westminster Abbey, as befitted a poet.

ANALYSIS

Samuel Johnson wrote two major poetic works: *London* and *The Vanity of Human Wishes*. The remaining verse divides into the play *Irene*, poems in Latin, miscellaneous verse in English, and translations from Greek and Latin. *London* was the most popular of Johnson's poems during his life, and it remains the most accessible to modern audiences. Its language is clear and its images straightforward. Like *London*, *The Vanity of Human Wishes* is an imitation of the satires of Juvenal, a Latin poet of the first and second centuries. It is widely regarded as Johnson's poetic masterpiece and is Johnson's effort to convey the essence of the Christian ethos through verse and imagery. The density of its images and ideas makes *The Vanity of Human Wishes* difficult to interpret even for experienced critics. *Irene*, on the other hand, yields readily to interpretation through its strong plot, although its verse, while competent, is unremarkable.

LONDON

Johnson customarily composed his poems mentally before committing them to paper. *London* was composed in this manner; it was written on large sheets of paper in two columns—the left being for the first draft and the right for revisions. Johnson's poetry is firmly in the Augustan tradition, typified in the eighteenth century by the works of Pope, Jonathan Swift, and Joseph

Addison; *London* is characteristically Augustan in its dependence on a Latin model, in this case Juvenal's third satire. When the poem was published, the passages that were derived from Juvenal were accompanied by Juvenal's original lines, which were included at Johnson's request—a common practice at the time. A good edition of *London* will include the relevant Juvenalian passages.

Juvenal's third satire, Johnson's model for *London*, focuses on Rome. In general, Juvenal's satires attack what he perceived to be the immorality of Roman society. In his third satire, he cites particulars in the city of Rome itself. Johnson focuses his poem on the city of London and, like Juvenal, cites particulars. He also includes translations from Juvenal's poem and updated versions of some of Juvenal's sentiments. As the accompanying Latin verse shows, Johnson's borrowings are only part of the whole and tend to illustrate the universality of some of the poem's ideas. Too much of *London* is original for it to be simply a translation. For example, Juvenal writes from the point of view of a conservative Roman who believed that his countrymen had grown soft from lack of war and sacrifice, while Johnson writes from the point of view of an eighteenth century Christian who believed that the vices of his age stemmed from his countrymen's failure to recognize the importance of the soul. Johnson was a man of ideas, and his ideas make *London* his own work—a statement of his views of the city when he was a young man of twenty-eight.

London is written in rhyming iambic pentameter couplets. Johnson believed that blank verse could be sustained only by strong images; otherwise, verse needed clear structure and rhyme. His best poetry exemplifies his ideas about prosody; *London*'s heroic couplets follow the model established by Pope. The poem's language is lively and its ideas flow rapidly. Johnson's condemnations are sharply expressed:

> By numbers here from shame or censure free,
> All crimes are safe, but hated poverty.
> This, only this, the rigid law pursues,
> This, only this, provokes the snarling muse.

The city is portrayed as rife with crime, folly, and injustice. King George II is said to be more interested in

Hanover than England and London; learning is said to be unrewarded (a favorite theme of Juvenal); government is said to be grasping while the nation sinks; and the city is characterized as architecturally in bad taste. The satire makes London seem bleak and ugly, but the language is exuberant and makes London's faults seem exciting.

The poem's persona (the speaker) is named Thales, who intends to leave London for Cambria (Wales); he craves solitude and peace. Some scholars have identified Thales as the personification of Richard Savage, who had suffered poverty and indignities in London; he left London in 1739 for Wales. Other scholars maintain that Johnson had not yet met Savage, and that *London* was, after all, published in 1738, a year before Savage's migration. This dispute over seeming minutiae represents a major problem that infects much criticism of Johnson's works. Those who support the notion that Savage is the original for Thales sometimes cite Johnson's assertion that anyone who is tired of London is tired of life. They maintain that the poem's point of view is not representative of Johnson but of Savage. Even some critics who do not assert that Savage was the model for Thales dismiss *London* as insincere—as an exercise that does not reflect Johnson's true love for the city.

Students new to the study of Johnson should be wary of reasoning based on Johnson's views in Boswell's *The Life of Samuel Johnson, LL.D.* Boswell's work is monumental; it has helped to shape the modern view of eighteenth century England. Johnson's opinions as reported by Boswell are forcefully expressed and seemingly permanently set, and even knowledgeable scholars have sometimes read into Johnson's early works the views he held when he was a conservative old man. In fact, like most writers who have been fortunate enough to have long careers, Johnson changed his views as he matured, read new works, and gained new experiences. As a young man, Johnson was rebellious and angry. He was learned and poor, and he disliked the Hanoverian monarchy. The architecture of London in 1738 could be not only ugly but also downright dangerous—poorly built walls sometimes collapsed into the streets. The crowding, poverty, and crime of London would probably have shocked any young person from the country who was experiencing it for the first time; Johnson arrived in London in 1737, and the poem appeared in 1738.

THE VANITY OF HUMAN WISHES

The Vanity of Human Wishes, on the other hand, was written when Johnson was in his middle years. Juvenal's satires still interested him, as they did, according to Boswell, in his late years, and *The Vanity of Human Wishes* is an imitation of Juvenal's tenth satire. In this satire, Juvenal shows that people are unable to perceive their own best interests. Some people wish to be eloquent, even though Cicero was doomed by his own eloquence; others seek power, even though Alexander the Great was undone by power. Wise people, Juvenal says, would let the gods choose what is best for them. Typical of the Latin poet, the tenth satire expresses a conservative Roman's disgust with the foolishness of society in the empire. The dominant themes in the satire would have appealed to Johnson: anger at a people who neglect the ideals that made them great, dismay at the successes of fools at the expense of supposedly intelligent people, and the notion that society's values were distorted, with learning and wisdom ranking below ignorance and vice.

The ethos of *The Vanity of Human Wishes* is Christian. Johnson replaces Juvenal's notion that people do not choose to do what will do them good with the idea that people choose vainly when they choose material and worldly success. Johnson also replaces Juvenal's notion that wise people let the gods choose for them with the idea that wise people put their lives in God's hands. The tenth satire of Juvenal was popular during the Middle Ages because preachers could convert its criticisms of vice into homilies on the dangers of materialism, and it provides ready material for Johnson's portrait of human life gone astray. Nearly 350 lines of his poem are devoted to discussing how people who seek wealth, power, or other earthly pleasures and rewards fail to find happiness. The poem is thick with images and requires close reading; it is in large part depressingly negative. Much of human life seems hopeless. Even so, Johnson's scope is remarkable; he reaches beyond the range of *London* and beyond the range of Juvenal's satire; he discusses all human beings, everywhere. He cites Thomas Wolsey's power and wealth, Charles XII of Sweden's ambition, the miserable fates of John Churchill Marlborough, who was debilitated by strokes, and Swift, who suffered from a disease similar to senile dementia. Neither power, wealth, ambition, honor, nor intellect mean much in the great scheme of life, and none are proof against misery and humiliation.

Johnson leaps back and forth through time, and from one part of the world to another, in his effort to convey the vastness of his topic and universality of his theme. He asserts:

> Unnumber'd suppliants crowd Preferment's gate,
> Athirst for wealth, and burning to be great,
> Delusive Fortune hears th' incessant call,
> They mount, they shine, evaporate, and fall.

A host of examples are mustered to support Johnson's contention that all earthly human wishes are vain; a reader can feel overwhelmed by the images and arguments that Johnson presents. If one does not read the poem carefully, one might interpret it as a despairing depiction of human endeavors and of lives without hope. Some critics call the poem "stoic," as if the only response to the hopelessness of life as depicted by Johnson were withdrawal and endurance. Such a reading misses the poem's fundamental point and fails to recognize Johnson's rejection of stoicism: "Must helpless man, in ignorance sedate,/ Roll darkling down the torrent of his fate?" No, Johnson answers, because "petitions yet remain,/ Which heav'n may hear, nor deem religion vain." God is the solution to the vanities of humanity. Stoicism demands a retreat into one's self; Johnson advocates that one reach outside oneself. An important teaching of Christianity in Johnson's day was that one needed to seek beyond the material world for happiness—that unselfishness would bring enduring rewards. Johnson notes the "goods for man the laws of heav'n ordain," "love," "patience," and "faith." He says, "With these celestial wisdom calms the mind." Just as folly is universal, so too is the answer to folly. God responds to anyone who is devoted to him.

The Vanity of Human Wishes is grim; the poem reflects Johnson's personality and his concerns, and his unhappy view of the disorder of an unfair world is expressed in relentless images. He was also a Christian,

holding out hope for himself and the rest of humanity. His poetic skill is revealed in his shift from a lengthy account of the failures of even the best of people to the simple assertion of God's ability to ease the misery of anyone. He uses the heroic couplet, as in *London*, to give his poem a clear structure. Within that structure, he maneuvers ideas with seeming ease and resolves the complex problem of the vanity of human wishes with the poetically elegant answer of the Christian ethos.

IRENE

Johnson's play *Irene* was begun while he was still a teacher, before he moved to London in 1737, and he continued to work on it sporadically until 1749, when Garrick produced it under the title *Mahomet and Irene*. The primary source for the play was the *Generall Historie of the Turkes* (1603), by Richard Knolles. The story is filled with intrigue: Mahomet, the Turkish sultan, falls in love with Irene, a Greek Christian. He offers her wealth, power, and marriage if she will renounce Christianity and convert to Islam. His followers are unhappy that their leader, who has conquered Constantinople, would fall for a conquered infidel, and they plot his overthrow. Greeks join in the plotting as well. After some soul searching and passionate scenes, Irene yields to Mahomet and becomes a victim of the play's intrigues. The plot of *Irene* is surprisingly good, given its neglect by modern readers. Its weakness is in its blank verse, which, as Donald Greene notes in *Samuel Johnson* (1970), has a "sledgehammer monotony." Although the play made money during its run as Garrick's production and was reprinted three times while Johnson lived, it was not a critical success. Its verse is unimaginative and dull, unequal to the strengths of both plot and characters. However, Johnson reveals insight into his characters, particularly the spiritually struggling Irene, and an ability to present an interesting story.

PROLOGUES, EPITAPHS, ELEGIES

Although *London* and *The Vanity of Human Wishes* are justifiably rated by critics as his best poems, much of Johnson's lesser verse is rewarding. His *Prologue Spoken at the Opening of the Theatre in Drury-Lane* (1747), for example, discusses the merits of drama. In addition to writing superior prologues, Johnson was a master of the epitaph and elegy. His "Epitaph on

Hogarth" is representative of his ability to evoke pathos in a short poem with such lines as: "Here death has clos'd the curious eyes/ That saw the manners in the face." The poem on William Hogarth, the painter, was something of an exercise for Johnson, written as it was in response to Garrick's request for advice on an epitaph requested by Mrs. Hogarth.

His "On the Death of Dr. Robert Levet" comes more from his heart. The elegy was written in 1782 after the death of the friend and surgeon who had been living in Johnson's home. The poem presents a picture of a man who was "Officious, innocent, sincere,/ Of ev'ry friendless name the friend." Johnson makes the poem a comment on life in general, both its sorrows and glories, and makes the seemingly humble Levet a representative of the best virtues: sacrifice for others, modesty in material desires, and selfless working to improve the lot of humanity. The poem is united by metaphor ("mine" and "caverns") and theme.

WIT AND HUMOR

The somber themes of the elegy and epitaph and the weighty themes of the prologues and major poems might suggest that Johnson's verse is devoted exclusively to the unhappy aspects of life. Such a view, however, would be unbalanced. Even in the bitterness of *London*, there is witty wordplay, and Johnson had a remarkable taste for stinging humor. He sent to Mrs. Thrale in 1780 a poem about her scapegrace nephew, John Lade, titled "A Short Song of Congratulation." Lade had recently come into his inheritance, and Johnson lists the various ways that the young man could waste his money. The wit is pointed and accurate; Lade wasted his fortune. Most of Johnson's light verse is extemporaneous, being meant for his friends, rather than for the public, lacking the careful structure of Johnson's other poetry. His Latin poetry, on the other hand, is usually very well constructed.

CRITICAL RESPONSES

Johnson's stature as a poet has varied according to critical fashion. The critics of the Romantic and Victorian periods often dismissed his work as heavy-handed; they favored spontaneity and image over calculation and idea. Johnson was a man of ideas; he thrived on them and loved to toy with them, but his work was also emotional. The critics of the nineteenth century fa-

vored lyric poetry over satire and often missed the merits of the poetic tradition in which Johnson's best verse belongs. Twentieth century critics have, in general, rediscovered the virtues of Johnson's prosody. At his best, he fashions his verse with persuasive naturalness. His poetry conveys a powerful vision of the universality of the human condition. *The Vanity of Human Wishes* rightly ranks as one of the best and most important poems of world literature; with *London* and some of the minor poems, taken as a group, it argues powerfully for Johnson's status as a significant poet.

OTHER MAJOR WORKS

LONG FICTION: *Rasselas*, 1759 (originally pb. as *The Prince of Abissinia: A Tale*).

SHORT FICTION: Essays in *The Rambler*, 1750-1752; *The Adventurer*, 1753-1754; Essays in *The Idler*, 1758-1760.

PLAY: *Irene: A Tragedy*, pr. 1749.

NONFICTION: *A Compleat Vindication of the Licensers of the Stage*, 1739; *Marmer Norfolciense*, 1739; *The Life of Admiral Blake*, 1740; *An Account of the Life of John Philip Barretier*, 1744; *An Account of the Life of Mr. Richard Savage, Son of the Earl Rivers*, 1744 (better known as *Life of Richard Savage*); *Miscellaneous Observations on the Tragedy of Macbeth*, 1745; *The Plan of a Dictionary of the English Language*, 1747; *A Dictionary of the English Language: To Which Are Prefixed, a History of the Language, and an English Grammar*, 1755 (2 volumes); Preface and notes to *The Plays of William Shakespeare*, 1765 (8 volumes); *The False Alarm*, 1770; *Thoughts on the Late Transactions Respecting Falkland's Islands*, 1771; *The Patriot: Addressed to the Electors of Great Britain*, 1774; *A Journey to the Western Islands of Scotland*, 1775; *Taxation No Tyranny: An Answer to the Resolutions and Address of the American Congress*, 1775; *Prefaces, Biographical and Critical, to the Works of the English Poets*, 1779-1781 (10 volumes; revised as *The Lives of the Most Eminent English Poets*, 1781; best known as *The Lives of the Poets*); *The Critical Opinions of Samuel Johnson*, 1923, 1961 (Joseph Epes Brown, editor); *The Supplicating Voice: Spiritual Writings of Samuel Johnson*, 2005 (John F. Thornton and Susan B. Varenne, editors).

TRANSLATIONS: *A Voyage to Abyssinia*, 1735 (of Jerome Lobo's novel); *Commentary on Pope's "Essay on Man,"* 1738-1739 (of Jean Pierre de Crousaz).

MISCELLANEOUS: *The Works of Samuel Johnson*, 1787-1789; *The Yale Edition of the Works of Samuel Johnson*, 1958-1990 (16 volumes).

BIBLIOGRAPHY

Clingham, Greg, and Philip Smallwood, eds. *Samuel Johnson After Three Hundred Years*. New York: Cambridge University Press, 2009. This collection of essays covers various topics, including his writings and thought.

Hibbert, Christopher, and Henry Hitchings. *Samuel Johnson: A Personal History*. New York: Palgrave Macmillan, 2009. A biography that focuses on Johnson's personal life and how it affected his public self and his writings.

Lipking, Lawrence. *Samuel Johnson: The Life of an Author*. Cambridge, Mass.: Harvard University Press, 1998. In Lipking's terms, he has written a life of an author, not the life of a person—by which he means that he concentrates on the story of how Johnson became a writer and a man of letters.

McIntyre, Ian. *Hester: The Remarkable Life of Dr. Johnson's "Dear Mistress."* London: Constable, 2008. Hester Lynch Thrale (later Piozzi) was a diarist and patron of the arts and a friend of Johnson. She appears in his writings as Mrs. Thrale, and she published a book of Johnson's anecdotes and of her letters after his death.

Martin, Peter. *Samuel Johnson: A Biography*. Cambridge, Mass.: Harvard University Press, 2008. Martin attempts to reconcile the varying aspects of Johnson's life, including his depression. Contains a chapter on the poetry.

Meyers, Jeffrey. *Samuel Johnson: The Struggle*. New York: Basic Books, 2008. Meyers takes the position that Johnson's life was a struggle, physically, economically, mentally, and personally. Contains analysis of his poetry throughout.

Nokes, David. *Samuel Johnson: A Life*. New York: Henry Holt, 2010. Portrays Johnson as an active force in the Enlightenment rather than simply a recorder of events. Brings in the viewpoints of his wife, a black manservant, and Hester Lynch Thrale, who was a friend of Johnson and a biographer.

Reinert, Thomas. *Regulating Confusion: Samuel Johnson and the Crowd*. Durham, N.C.: Duke University Press, 1996. Reinert reexamines Johnson's views of human nature, urban culture, and individualism. "The crowd" of the book's title refers to Elias Canetti's theories of crowds and power, which Reinert applies to his reevaluation of Johnson.

Kirk H. Beetz

DAVID JONES

Born: Brockley, Kent, England; November 1, 1895
Died: Harrow, London, England; October 28, 1974
Also known as: Dai Greatcoat

PRINCIPAL POETRY

In Parenthesis, 1937
The Anathemata: Fragment of an Attempted Writing, 1952
The Tribune's Visitation, 1969
The Sleeping Lord, and Other Fragments, 1974
The Kensington Mass, 1975
The Roman Quarry, and Other Sequences, 1981

OTHER LITERARY FORMS

David Jones's other main creative outlet was painting, but he did write a number of essays and reviews connected to art and literature. A collection of these essays and reviews, many of which date back to the 1940's, appeared as *Epoch and Artist: Selected Writings* (1959), edited by his associate, Harman Grisewood. Other essays were collected after his death by Grisewood as *The Dying Gaul, and Other Writings* (1978).

ACHIEVEMENTS

David Jones's *In Parenthesis* gained instant recognition for the poet when it won the Hawthornden Prize in 1938. Before and immediately afterward, Jones's achievements had been in his modernist painting. Recognition of Jones as both artist and poet came with the award of a Civil List Pension in 1954 and the award of the Order of the British Empire in 1955. *The Anathemata* won the Russell Loines Award in 1954.

Further recognition came with the Bollingen Prize for Poetry in 1960, the Levinson Prize from *Poetry* magazine in 1961, and an award from the Society of Authors Travelling Fund in 1962. His *Epoch and Artist* won a Welsh Arts Council Award in 1959 and an honorary doctor of literature degree from the University of Wales in 1960. The next year, he was elected as a fellow of the Royal Society of Literature and to membership in the Royal Watercolour Society. In 1972, he won the gold medal of the Royal National Eisteddford on Wales in recognition of his promotion of Welsh culture and history. Perhaps his greatest honor came in 1974 (the last year of his life), when the Queen invited him to become a Companion of Honour, an order limited to just sixty-six notable men of letters and public figures.

Biography

Walter David Michael Jones was born in Brockley, Kent, the youngest of three children. His father, a printer who was also a lay reader in the Church of England, came from North Wales. His mother was a Londoner whose father was a barge builder at Rotherhithe on the River Thames. David attended the local parish church and was educated locally, early demonstrating a gift for drawing.

At the age of fourteen, he entered the newly formed Camberwell School of Art in south London, where he studied from 1909 through 1914. At the outbreak of World War I, despite his poor physique, he managed to enroll in the London Welsh Battalion of the Royal Welsh Regiment, which was made up of London Cockney boys and Welshmen. By this time, Jones had become interested in his Welsh roots, especially after visits to relatives in North Wales. During his service, Jones sustained wounds, contracted trench fever, and finished the war in a peacekeeping force in Ireland. He was demobilized in 1919. Many of Jones's war experiences found their way into his long poem *In Parenthesis*.

As a war veteran, Jones was granted a scholarship to the Westminster School of Art, a center of British modernism. He was particularly attracted to Eric Gill, a Catholic convert who was establishing a reputation as a modernist sculptor. When Jones left the school in 1921, he joined the Catholic arts community Gill had founded in southern England and became a Catholic, a move that created a breach between him and his father. He also fell in love with Petra, Gill's younger daughter. The couple got engaged but did not marry.

In 1924, Gill moved the community to mid-Wales, the first time Jones had actually lived in the country he had come to regard as his true home. Jones was developing his own style as a painter of both oils and watercolors. In 1928, Jones held his first exhibition in London. Gill moved the community to outside northwest London in the Chiltern Hills, where Jones met and fell in love with Prudence Pelham, an aristocrat. He also met Helen Sutherland, who became a much-needed patroness, even though he was painting prolifically from 1928 through 1932.

In 1932, he had a complete nervous breakdown. This began a series of depressive episodes that occurred throughout the rest of his life. He was not able to paint but instead worked on writing prose and poetry about his war experiences. He was again influenced by modernists, especially T. S. Eliot and James Joyce. By 1936, he presented the text of *In Parenthesis* to Faber & Faber, the publishing house where Eliot worked. The first print run of fifteen hundred copies enjoyed instant success, receiving praise from both Eliot and William Butler Yeats. Jones followed this work with a series of poetic meditations on the Catholic Mass.

During World War II, Jones stayed in London and continued writing and painting. Much of his writing consisted of essays on art and literature in which he sought not only Catholic insights, but also ways back into Celtic and Roman history to work out a cultural history of Western Europe. The poetic outcome was *The Anathemata*.

Before *The Anathemata* could be published, Jones had another nervous breakdown in 1947 and entered a nursing home in Harrow in north London. After his recovery, he remained in Harrow. In the 1950's, Jones began to receive wider recognition through prizes and exhibitions, culminating in being named to the Queen's Birthday Honours List in 1955. In the 1960's, he was writing rather more than painting, but he was also fighting to keep chronic depression in check. His last major painting, *Trystan ac Esseult*, was done in 1963. Recognition and honors continued to come in, though by now modernism was giving way to other literary and artistic movements. Jones died quietly in 1974.

ANALYSIS

David Jones's poetry is difficult to categorize, apart from saying that it is modernist and long. In some ways, it is not even poetry, as large sections are written in poetic prose and can be read more like a novel. Jones was inspired to use such a mix by medieval sources, in which the division between prose and poetry was more fluid than in the twentieth century. Like Eliot and Ezra Pound, he draws on whatever sources inspire him and quotes them, regardless of whether they are in English. Like Eliot, he relies on notes to explain the more private associations.

What is different is that Jones's poetry is much more grounded in his personal experiences as soldier and artist and in his identity as a Londoner, Welshman, and Catholic. His speech makes his poetry dramatic, and like other modernists, he writes much of his work as dramatic monologue. The voices are typically those of London Cockneys or Welsh bards. The matter is epic and mythic, his imagination having been grounded as much in Celtic and Germanic mythology as in Roman or Greek. Though never having been taught Latin, Greek, or Welsh, Jones is prepared to write in them. His knowledge of the traditional Latin rites of the Roman Catholic Church pervades all of his writing, and his is profoundly religious and spiritual poetry.

IN PARENTHESIS

It could be claimed that *In Parenthesis* is the greatest war poem to have come out of World War I, but it is long, difficult, and appeared well after the other war poets had published their poetry. In addition, it is not quotable, though it is eminently readable, demanding to be read out loud, hence its success as a radio poem.

In Parenthesis is divided into seven parts, covering a period from December, 1915, to the Battle of the Somme in the summer of 1916, which becomes its climax. At all stages, it seems autobiographical. At first, the poet's persona is Private John Ball, named after a rebel priest who led an uprising against Richard II. At the end of the poem, Ball appears to be dying of wounds. The poet at times stands back from Ball and seems closer to some of the Welsh soldiers. The poet's stance is thus made more ambiguous.

Part 1, "The Many Men So Beautiful," follows a battalion of soldiers from their base camp in England to their embarkation. Parts 2 to 4 follow their journey through France to the front lines, showing how they accustom themselves to their conditions and survive through the winter. Jones's minutely detailed descriptions of the front lines is akin to Robert Graves's war memoir *Goodbye to All That: An Autobiography* (1929).

Part 5, "Squat Garlands for White Knights," details the battalion's removal from winter quarters southward to an unknown destination. Parts 6 and 7 deal with their new deployment and the ensuing battle, in which most of the battalion are massacred. Ball survives with a few others but is critically wounded. The poem ends with his waiting to be carried off the battlefield by stretcher-bearers.

THE ANATHEMATA

By contrast, *The Anathemata* is not specific as to time or place. Its ambition is to trace the rise and nature of western civilization from a Christian, and especially Catholic, point of view. Its focus is on "the matter of Britain" and the Mass. However, it incorporates other spiritual traditions and sees Britain not as an amalgam of Celtic and Saxon traditions. It is a more difficult work than *In Parenthesis* because of its historical circularity, and it demands a great deal of work from its readers. They need to grasp some quite obscure Welsh mythology, for example, and to be able to converse in several languages.

However, Jones's own control and grasp of what he is doing is profound. Once the sense of the speaking voice is internalized, it creates a momentum that carries the reader through the difficult and obscure passages into an experience that is singularly rare in modern poetry: a sense of being involved with the past and the present as a continuity.

The name of the poem means "things devoted to a deity," and it is one of the most profoundly moving religious poems of the modernist movement, comparable to Eliot's *Four Quartets* (1943). It is divided into eight parts, from "Rite and Foretime," dealing with the Greeks' first discovery of Britain, to "Sherthursdaye and Venus Day," which deals with the crucifixion of Christ. Section 5, "The Lady of the Pool," is set in London's docklands and at times echoes Jones's grandfather, the Thames barge builder.

THE SLEEPING LORD, AND OTHER FRAGMENTS

The Sleeping Lord, and Other Fragments is a collection that gathers most of Jones's other poems, some of which are unfinished. The title poem, written 1966-1967, deals with a Welsh version of the Arthurian legend and shows how deeply immersed Jones became in Welsh myth and prehistory and how he was able to detect traces of its spirituality in Catholicism. Normally Welsh Christianity is seen as ineluctably Protestant, so Jones is revealing new insights.

"The Tribune's Visitation" is set in Roman Palestine at the time of Christ. Jones developed a great sense of the continuity of the Roman world, and the Roman soldiers are shown as similar to those of World War I. Other poems included are "The Tutelar of the Place" and "The Hunt," the latter a reworking of another Welsh legend.

OTHER MAJOR WORKS

NONFICTION: *Epoch and Artist: Selected Writings*, 1959 (Harman Grisewood, editor); *David Jones: Letters to Vernon Watkins*, 1976; *The Dying Gaul, and Other Writings*, 1978 (Grisewood, editor); *Dai Greatcoat: A Self-Portrait of David Jones in His Letters*, 1980 (Rene Hague, editor); *David Jones: Letters to a Friend*, 1980; *David Jones, a Fusilier at the Front: His Record of the Great War in Word and Image*, 1985; *Inner Necessities: Letters of David Jones to Desmond Chute*, 1985.

BIBLIOGRAPHY

Alldritt, Keith. *David Jones: Writer and Artist*. London: Constable, 2003. This biography of Jones covers both his artistic and poetic lives in detail and traces Jones's philosophical and religious changes. Includes black-and-white plates of paintings.

Blamires, David. *David Jones: Artist and Writer*. Manchester, England: Manchester University Press, 1971. This is not a biography, but rather a critical analysis of Jones's work, both artistic and poetic. It is still one of the definitive books on Jones's achievement.

Blissett, William. *The Long Conversation: A Memoir of David Jones*. New York: Oxford University Press, 1981. This is a detailed recording of all the conversations the author had with Jones, from their first meeting in 1959 until Jones's death in 1974. It contains biographical material as well as a sense of Jones's wide-ranging literary and artistic interests and concerns.

Dilworth, Thomas. *Reading David Jones*. Cardiff: University of Wales Press, 2008. Provides Jones's poetry along with commentary, explanations, and biographical information. Notes the influence of his painting on his poetry.

Hague, Rene. *A Commentary on "The Anathemata" of David Jones*. Wellingborough, England: Christopher Skelton, 1977. This is a detailed commentary on the complete text of Jones's greatest poem, written by a very old acquaintance, who had discussed the work with Jones.

Matthias, John, ed. *Introducing David Jones: A Selection of His Writings*. Boston: Faber and Faber, 1980. While this is mainly a selection of Jones's three major long poems, it does contain a valuable introduction by Stephen Spender, a contemporary of Jones, and a long introduction by the editor.

Miles, J., and D. Shiel. *David Jones: The Maker Unmade*. Cardiff, Wales: Poetry Wales Press, 1995. A full-length analysis of his poetry with a particular emphasis on its Welsh roots.

Robichaud, Paul. *Making the Past Present: David Jones, the Middle Ages, and Modernism*. Washington, D.C.: Catholic University of America Press, 2007. Examines Jones's treatment of medieval mythology in his poetry and how his poetry relates to modernism.

David Barratt

BEN JONSON

Born: London, England; June 11, 1573
Died: London, England; August 6, 1637

PRINCIPAL POETRY

Poems, 1601
Epigrams, 1616
The Forest, 1616
Underwoods, 1640
Ben Jonson, 1925-1952 (includes *Ungathered Verse*; C. H. Hereford, Percy Simpson, and Evelyn Simpson, editors)

OTHER LITERARY FORMS

Ben Jonson's fame has rested mainly on his comic drama, especially on the masterpieces of his maturity, *Volpone: Or, The Fox* (pr. 1605), *Epicœne: Or, The Silent Woman* (pr. 1609), *The Alchemist* (pr. 1610), and *Bartholomew Fair* (pr. 1614). Surviving earlier comedies are *The Case Is Altered* (pr. 1597), *Every Man in His Humour* (pr. 1598), *Every Man Out of His Humour* (pr. 1599), *Cynthia's Revels: Or, The Fountain of Self-Love* (pr. c. 1600-1601), *Poetaster: Or, His Arraignment* (pr. 1601), and *Eastward Ho!* (pr., pb. 1605, with George Chapman and John Marston). Later comedies are *The Devil Is an Ass* (pr. 1616), *The Staple of News* (pr. 1626), *The New Inn: Or, The Light Heart* (pr. 1629), *The Magnetic Lady: Or, Humours Reconciled* (pr. 1632), and *A Tale of a Tub* (pr. 1633). Jonson wrote two tragedies, *Sejanus His Fall* (pr. 1603) and *Catiline His Conspiracy* (pr., pb. 1611). Two uncompleted works date apparently from the end of his life: the pastoral *The Sad Shepherd: Or, A Tale of Robin Hood* (pb. 1640) and the tragedy *Mortimer His Fall* (only a few pages).

Jonson's court masques and entertainments may conservatively be said to number about thirty, differing tallies being possible depending on whether minor entertainments of various kinds are counted. Besides plays, masques, and original nondramatic verse, Jonson wrote and translated a few other works that help to place him in the Renaissance humanistic tradition; all were first published in *The Works of Benjamin Jonson* (1640-1641). As a vernacular humanist, Jonson wrote *The English Grammar* (1640); he translated Horace's *Ars poetica* (as *Horace His Art of Poetry*) in 1640; finally, he compiled and translated extracts from classical and modern authors, mostly having to do with ethics, education, and rhetoric; the collection is titled *Timber: Or, Discoveries Made upon Men and Matter* (1641).

ACHIEVEMENTS

Ben Jonson's achievements as a writer of verse can best be summarized by saying that he founded English neoclassicism. Jonson, of course, wrote several decades before what is usually thought of as the neoclassic age, but his work clearly foreshadows that of John Dryden and Alexander Pope. His, like theirs, was a mode of poetry generally imitative of ancient Roman forms, concerned, as important Roman writers had been, with behavior on a specifically human stage of action, and sometimes heroic, often satirical, in tone and stance.

BIOGRAPHY

Benjamin Jonson's father, a minister, died a month before his son's birth. Ben's mother remarried, apparently fairly soon thereafter, the stepfather being a master bricklayer of Westminster. A friend enrolled Jonson at Westminster School, but (as he told William Drummond) he was taken from school at about the age of sixteen and put to a "Craft," presumably bricklaying. Unable to endure this occupation, Jonson escaped briefly into the wars with the Netherlands. The next few years (roughly, his early twenties) are the most obscure of Jonson's life. At some point during this time, he married and began having children, although practically nothing is known about his wife or family.

Jonson reappears in the late 1590's in theatrical records as an actor and part-time playwright. In these years, Jonson was repeatedly at odds with the law, usually because of his involvement with satirical or political drama. He also attracted the authorities' hostility through his conversion to Roman Catholicism. (Eventually he returned to the Church of England and later in life expressed, above all, distaste for those who claimed complete theological certainty.) In the series of comedies of humours beginning with *Every Man in His Humour*, Jonson coined an original form of satirical comedy based on the caricature of psychological types. In 1600 to 1601, he temporarily abandoned the open-air public playhouses to present his comical satires at the more fashionable indoor private theater at Blackfriars. The move was part of the provocation of the stage quarrel, or war of the theaters, in which Jonson, Thomas Dekker, and John Marston traded plays lampooning one another. Jonson's earliest datable nondramatic poetry also belongs to these years. From the first, Jonson wrote occasional and panegyric verse addressed to the aristocracy, invoking their patronage.

The first decade and a half of the seventeenth century were the years of Jonson's superb creativity and greatest popularity as a playwright. During those years, he was in social contact with fellow playwrights such as William Shakespeare, and also with scholars such as William Camden and John Selden. Jonson's associations, however, were not limited to the theatrical and the learned; he was steadily employed as the writer of court masques throughout the reign of James I. Both

Ben Jonson (Library of Congress)

the king and the aristocrats at the court responded to Jonson's work for many years with notable offers of support. The years from 1616 through 1624 probably marked the height of his prestige. In 1616, he published *The Workes of Benjamin Jonson* in folio. A royal pension came in the same year and, in 1619, an honorary degree from Oxford. Also gratifying was the gathering around Jonson of the Tribe of Ben, a circle of poetic sons, including Thomas Carew and Robert Herrick, who adopted him as their mentor.

The accession of Charles I to the throne in 1625 ended Johnson's tenure as regular writer of masques for the court, and in other respects also, the last dozen years of Jonson's life contrast with the preceding successful decades. At some points during these last years, he was clearly in financial need, and he suffered a stroke in 1628. He was writing comedies again for the popular stage, but none of them won much acclaim. Against such bleak circumstances, however, stands a persistence of poetic energy, embodied in much outstanding verse attributable to these years. Jonson held the regard of his circle of poetic sons until his death in 1637, and beyond: One of them, Sir Kenelm Digby, finally assembled and published Jonson's later along with his earlier *Works* in 1640-1641.

ANALYSIS

Until the last few decades, attention to Ben Jonson's poetry focused largely on the famous songs and the moving epitaphs on children. Such choices were not ill-advised, but they are unrepresentative. The works in these modes certainly rank among Jonson's most successful, but they differ in tone from Jonson's norm.

Songs such as "Kiss me, sweet: the wary lover" and "Drink to me only with thine eyes" evoke emotions beyond the world of reason or fact, partly through reference to extravagant gestures and implausible experiences: hundreds and thousands of kisses, a wreath that will not die after the beloved has breathed on it. Through rhythms that are stronger and less interrupted than Jonson usually created, the songs activate the capacity to respond sensually and irrationally to language. Some of them create magical secret worlds where sense and emotion are to be experienced in disregard of troubling or qualifying context (the "silent summer nights/ When youths ply their stol'n delights" in "Kiss me, sweet: the wary lover"). Exactly such worlds are created, but also subjected to critique, in *Volpone* and *The Alchemist*.

The epitaphs, particularly those on Jonson's own children ("On My First Son," "On My First Daughter") are so effective because in them subjective emotions strain against rational conviction. Jonson's statement in each of these poems is doctrinal and exemplary, involving resignation to the will of God, but part of the power of the affirmation of belief arises from Jonson's undertone of grief over which faith has won out. Regret and despair have not been reasoned away but are being rationally controlled; consolation is not easy.

Such richly concentrated poems obviously deserve attention; that they should have received exposure to the virtual exclusion of Jonson's less lyrical or emotive verse, however, perhaps represents a holdover from Romantic or Victorian taste for rhapsodic expressions of feeling and imaginative vision in poetry. In fact, the renewal of contact with the Metaphysical sensibility achieved by T. S. Eliot and other critics in the 1920's and 1930's, which brought about the displacement of Victorian approaches to a number of seventeenth century writers, did not do so, immediately or directly, in the case of Jonson as a nondramatic poet. Some of Jonson's works are recognizably close to the secular reaches of John Donne's writing, but the speaker's psychological self-discovery through metaphor, so often the business of a Donne poem, is only occasionally Jonson's way. The contrast is especially clear between Jonson's poetic range and the realm of the meditative, intense, often all-but-private Metaphysical religious lyric. Jonson wrote very few strictly devotional poems; the ode "To Heaven" is probably the only strikingly successful work that could bear that label. In poems such as the ode to Sir Lucius Cary and Sir Henry Morison and the funeral elegies, where the afterlife is mentioned, the relation of humanity as such to divinity is not the real focus of attention. The poems involve tensions mainly between diverse human levels, between more ordinary experience on one hand and, on the other, an excellence or superiority of nature that Cary, Morison, Lady Jane Pawlet, and the other exemplary figures achieve.

At most, only on the peripheries of Jonson's nondramatic verse can it be seen to approximate pure emotive lyricism, or can it be cast in Metaphysical terms. Only in the late twentieth century did criticism achieve a modern reunderstanding of Jonson's achievement, involving a strongly positive evaluation of his central, typical poetic work. Jonson emerges in this criticism as decisively a neoclassic artist, the intellectual background of whose poetry is Renaissance humanism.

TIMBER

Jonson appears as a humanistic thinker in *Timber*, and his career reflected humanistic motivations and aspirations. Fundamentally, Jonson conceived of learning, thought, and language as phases of people's active life. Humanists conceived of education as the initiation of patterns of wise and effective behavior in the student's life. Humanistic education was largely linguistic because of the traditional importance of the persuasive linguistic act, the centrality of oratory (or, for the Renaissance, the counseling of the prince and nobles) in the repertory of practical, political skills. Patterns both of moral behavior in general and of speech specifically were normally learned through imitation of the deeds and words of figures from the past; for most humanists, and very definitely for Jonson, this did not mean that modern men were supposed to become mere apes of their predecessors, but rather that, through first following models, men should exercise and organize their own capacities to a point where they could emulate and rival the ancients, becoming effective on their own terms as the ancients were on theirs.

As a nonaristocratic humanist in a stratified society, Jonson essentially followed a pattern marked out since the time of Thomas More and Thomas Elyot early in the preceding century when he attached himself to noble households and the court. Debarred by birth from directly wielding the largest measure of power in his society, he engaged in action obliquely by speaking to the powerful, counseling and offering praise to encourage the elite in the wise conduct of life and authority. This was the light in which Jonson saw his masques, not only as celebrations, but also as reminders of ideals, such as justice, which should inform the court's activity. A great many of Jonson's moralizing poems addressed to noblemen and others also clearly exhibited actual hortatory intent.

Jonson's thought includes, as one might expect, special factors that set it off somewhat from humanism as it appears in other contexts. For one thing, while Jonson was not an unbeliever, it is certainly true that his humanism does not merge clearly and continuously into moralistic, pastoral Christianity, as had that of Desiderius Erasmus a hundred years before. The ethical universe of *Timber* is one of Roman, not obtrusively Christian, virtues; if anything, Jonson looks forward to later secular rationalism. Another characteristic of Jonson's humanism is the trace of influence from Seneca and Roman Stoicism, apparent in his writing, as elsewhere in early seventeenth century English expression. A main effect of Senecan influence on Jonson seems to have been to encourage a concern with and regard for what can best be called integrity; that is, the correlation of an individual's behavior with his inner nature rather than with outward circumstance. Such concern naturally belonged with the Senecan concept of specifically linguistic behavior that *Timber* expresses—a heightened awareness of style as emerging from and conveying an image of the "inmost" self.

Jonson's neoclassic verse is the poetic cognate of his quite secular, somewhat Senecan version of humanism. Splitting the relation into separate aspects only for the sake of analysis, one can say that in form Jonson's poems are above all linguistic acts, the talk of a persona to an implied (often, a designated) human audience. In content, the poems are orderings of levels or modes of human behavior.

EPISTLES

Jonson's "An Epistle answering to One that asked to be Sealed of the Tribe of Ben" is identified by its title in terms of the act of communication that it imitates, the letter. Relatively few of Jonson's titles actually include the word "epistle," but many of them involve, or even simply consist of, the designation of an addressee—"To Katherine Lady Aubigny," "To Sir Robert Wroth," and so on. Thus the reader is asked to be aware of many of Jonson's poems not primarily in terms of any myths they may relate or images they may invoke, but as linguistic action, the linguistic behavior of a human speaker toward a human audience.

The fiction of speaker and audience is not an inert element but has an impact on the poem's other aspects. Many qualities of style are conditioned by the character of the addressee and his relation to the speaker. In the "Epistle to Master John Selden," the speaker states that he feels free to use a curt, "obscure," at times almost telegraphic style because "I know to whom I write": He knows that Selden is not only intelligent but also at home with the speaker's ways of thinking. Generally, the grandiloquence, expansiveness, and elaborate structure of public oratory will rarely be appropriate for an epistle or other poem addressed by one person to another.

Jonson's style in "An Epistle answering to One that asked to be Sealed of the Tribe of Ben" is fairly typical of that in a number of his poems. His diction is generally colloquial; Edmund Bolton's characterization of Jonson's "vital, judicious and practicable language" (in Edmund Bolton's *Hypercritica*, c. 1618) is an excellent general description of the style. Syntactic units in Jonson's poems are by and large brief and stopped abruptly so that one jumps (or stumbles) from clause to clause rather than making easy transitions. Units are typically not paired or otherwise arranged symmetrically in relation to one another. The effect in "An Epistle answering to One that asked to be Sealed of the Tribe of Ben" is one of rather blurting, unpremeditated speech, propelled by some emotional pressure. Structurally, too, the poem seems unpremeditated, beginning with appropriate introductory comments to the would-be disciple to whom Ben is writing, then falling away into contemptuous griping about phony elements in Jonson's society, circling down into what reads like underlying anxiety about Jonson's personal situation—and coming through this human situation to a now almost heroic assertion of what it means to be Ben or one sealed of his tribe.

In other poems, the style varies, within a generally informal range. Jonson's meaning can in fact be obscure when the syntax is very broken or a great deal of meaning is concentrated in one phrase; the effect is often that of a rather impatient intelligence, not using more words than it needs to communicate meaning to its immediate addressee. In extreme cases, the reader may feel like an outsider reading a communication not meant for him (see, for example, the "Epistle to Sir Edward Sackville"). Such privacy, immured by style, sets Jonson off somewhat from Augustan neoclassic writers such as Alexander Pope, who usually engage in smoother and more public address.

Titling the poem an epistle, besides drawing attention to its character as a linguistic act, also of course associates it with a generic tradition. Seneca was the most influential classical practitioner of the moral epistle as a prose form, Horace of the form in verse. Jonson's epistles and many of his other poems evoke these authors' works in content and style, sometimes through specific allusion. Clearly related to classical tradition, yet utterly topical and personal (with its references to the politics of "Spain or France" and to Jonson's employment as a writer of masques), "An Epistle answering to One that asked to be Sealed of the Tribe of Ben" is a successful act of humanistic imitation. Overt reference to tradition reveals the moral statement of Jonson's poetry in relation to the whole body of classical moral wisdom—and implies that Jonson is not afraid of the juxtaposition.

The particular wisdom of this poem is conveyed most clearly in the description of the course of conduct Jonson has "decreed" for himself, which comes after the middle of the poem's descriptions of a social environment of indulgence of appetite, empty talk, and illusory "Motions." Jonson's resolve is to "Live to that point . . . for which I am man/ And dwell as in my Center as I can." The image is one of withdrawal from concern for meaningless external situations; it is also a picture of a life standing in relation to some firm, definite principle, as opposed to the poem's earlier images of unfounded judgments and groundless chatter.

The ideas of withdrawal and of a "Center" within the personality are clearly reminiscent of Seneca and Horace. The most characteristic aspect of the poem's meaning is that it consists of definitions not so much of the ideal principle itself as of the behavior that is or is not oriented to it. Jonson is not much concerned with describing the Center except as such, as a point from which surrounding space takes orientation. He is concerned with describing centeredness, and distinguishing it from shapeless and unfocused conditions; or, to return from geometry to humanity, with describing what it is like to operate on a firm moral basis, and distinguishing this from the "wild Anarchy" in which those outside the Tribe of Ben live.

The focus on behavior that is or is not guided, rather than on the available guiding transcendent principle, corresponds to the specifically secular emphasis of Jonson's humanism. There is an almost (though certainly not quite) agnostic quality in Jonson's almost interchangeable references to the "point," the "Center," "heaven," and "reason" as the source of his wisdom and strength. Clearly it is the exemplification of those qualities in life that interests him. Such an interest makes Jonson stand out as strikingly modern against the backdrop, for example, of the highly articulated ideal world of Edmund Spenser; it links Jonson forward to the essence of English neoclassicism, such as in Pope's ethically oriented satires and moral essays.

It should be noted that the movement toward the Center involves choice and effort: Jonson must decree it to himself, and even those who have been once sealed to the tribe of Ben have still to fear the shame of possibly stumbling in reason's sight. For good or evil, no destiny holds Jonson's human beings in place. The ideal principle is only vaguely defined; it is merely an available, not a controlling, factor.

EPIGRAMS

Like the epistles and other more or less epistolary longer poems, Jonson's epigrams are, in form, primarily linguistic acts. They are comments "on" or "to" someone. They are self-consciously brief remarks, aiming to capture the essence of a character—sometimes, implicitly, to reduce an object to its true dimensions (many of Jonson's epigrams are satirical).

The epigrammatic mode is closely related to the epistolary in Jonson's practice and in the tradition out of which he writes. Martial, the Roman epigrammatist whom Jonson regularly imitated, conceived of his works as epistles in brief. Jonson's style has the same constituents. The broken syntax sometimes seems part of epigrammatic compression; sometimes it promotes a casualness that is part of Jonson's reduction and dismissal of a satirized personality, as in epigram 21 ("On Reformed Gamester").

The pentameter couplets in which Jonson writes not only the epigrams but also the great bulk of his neoclassic verse are derived partly from normal English practice for nonlyric poetry going back through Geoffrey Chaucer. They are also, however, influenced by a classical form, the elegiac distich—a prosodic vehicle used by, among others, Martial. Readily recognizable and essentially symmetrical, the form tends to stand as a strong balancing, controlling, ordering presence in the poetry in which it appears. Part of its potential is as a structure for concentrated, gnomic, almost proverbial utterance, easy for the reader to carry away in his mind; this potential is best realized when the couplet is a tightly closed unit, as is normally the case in Pope.

Jonson uses the form in the several ways just mentioned. Couplet order underscores orderly, almost (for Jonson) patterned, praise of a firmly centered man in epigram 128 ("To William Roe"). Some epigrams consist of single gnomic couplets (epigram 34, "Of Death"), and others are memorable for neat, closed-couplet wit (epigram 31, "On Banck the Usurer"). Both Jonson's prestige and his virtuoso skill in testing the couplet's range of uses were important in establishing it as the standard neoclassic prosodic structure. Jonson's most characteristic way of exploiting the couplet, however, was not simply to employ, but simultaneously to violate, its order, to write across the prosodic structure as if in disregard of it. Actually, more often than not, in Jonson's verse, syntactic and phrasal breaks do not come at such points within a line as to facilitate the prosodic caesura, nor are they matched with line endings or even the ends of the couplets themselves (see, for example, epigram 46, "To Sir Luckless Woo-all"). The couplet may be opposed by meaning, along with grammar: Antitheses and other logical and rhetorical structures work at cross purposes with the prosody (epigram 11, "On Some-Thing, that Walks Some-Where").

In such circumstances, the couplet does not cease to be an obtrusive form. Jonson maintains the reader's awareness of it, precisely as a structure that is not managing to control or limit the autonomy of his grammar, rhetoric, and logic. The latter, of course, are the elements of the oratorical presence in the poetry—of Jonson's voice or speech. The net effect is to enhance the sense of the independent liveliness of the speaking persona, his freedom to move about, to understand and

to explain in his own way, on his own terms. Jonson's handling of the couplet implies through form a quite radical version of secular humanism, a sense of the detachment of linguistic action (and of man the linguistic actor) from any containing structure.

Many of the same kinds of content are present in the epigrams as in the epistolary writings. The epigrammatic image of William Roe's stable personality, mentioned earlier, is obviously cognate with Jonson's self-image in "An Epistle answering to One that asked to be Sealed of the Tribe of Ben," as are such portrayals as those of Sir Henry Nevil (epigram 109), William, earl of Pembroke (102), and Sir Thomas Roe (98). (The latter contains one of Jonson's more gnomic statements of the concept of the inner-directed and self-sufficient man: "Be always to thy gathered self the same/ And study conscience, more than thou would'st fame.") Satire, often a phase in the epistles, can fill entire epigrams. Something, that Walks Somewhere, Sir Voluptuous Beast (epigrams 35 and 36) and Don Surly (epigram 38) are incisively but fully realized satiric characters, clearly inhabitants of the same world as the "humour" characters Corbaccio and Epicure Mammon in Jonson's plays. Something, that Walks Somewhere, the lord who walks in "clothes brave enough," "buried in flesh, and blood," unwilling to do and afraid to dare, is one of Jonson's most powerful pictures of pointless, disorganized life—almost of disorganized protoplasm. Jonson suggested in many indirect ways that he regarded Horace as his mentor, and his work certainly has many Horatian traits, but his satire sometimes seems to belong less in the Horatian than in the harsher Juvenalian category.

"TO PENSHURST"

"To Penshurst," one of Jonson's most famous poems, celebrates a different kind of relatedness from the internal centering discussed so far. Here human life is benign because it stands within what people have recently learned to call an ecosystem: a web of connections between elements that feed and feed off one another and through interaction perpetuate one another's well-being. At Penshurst, the Sidney family's country estate, nature freely delivers its supply into the Sidneys' hands; fish and birds "officiously" serve themselves up; but here and even more in the very similar poem "To Sir

Robert Wroth," one feels that the humans could have a harvesting function, culling what sometimes seems almost like a glut of natural abundance. In any case, the human lords of Penshurst themselves stand as the basis of further relations, providing a social center to which neighbors from a whole community and guests from farther away "come in." The neighbors bring even more food, and the "provisions" of Penshurst's "liberal board" flow back to them. The system yields more than it can use, and the superflux passes to the unenvied guest and is there, ready to be offered to the king, the regulator of a larger system and community, when he happens into this particular sphere. The system, though nature flows through it, is not mindless. From Penshurst's lady's "huswifery" up through "The mysteries of manners, arms and arts" that the house's children are learning, specifically human roles and human activities have their place in this strong and ample natural and human network; in fact, the sophisticated culture of an ancestral figure of the house, Sir Philip Sidney, can be alluded to without seeming out of place here.

A close modern analog to "To Penshurst" is W. H. Auden's "In Praise of Limestone," where people also mesh with landscape in a perfect way; Auden's description of the limestone system, however, is interrupted by accounts of less pleasing, more technological adjustments of the relation. In "To Penshurst," on the other hand, contrasting satiric pictures or references have less share than in almost any of Jonson's works. Only a few lines, mainly at the poem's beginning and end, succinctly insert Jonson's usual distinctions. Penshurst is Edenic. One is left with the uneasy feeling that the poem's being so much anthologized may be bound up with its being, for Jonson, atypically untroubled.

ODES

Jonson's ode "To the Immortal Memory and Friendship of that Noble Pair, Sir Lucius Cary and Sir H. Morison" stands near the beginning of the history of English efforts to imitate Pindar's odes. It has a complex and stately stanzaic structure. Nevertheless, many traits are carried over from Jonson's epigrammatic and epistolary style, in particular the tendency toward syntax that is at odds with prosodic divisions, of which the poem contains egregious examples: For instance, a stanza break comes in the middle of the name "Ben/ Jonson."

An epic, "Heroologia," which Jonson planned, would probably have represented another extension to a new genre of his characteristic manner and ethical matter. The epic was to be in couplets and was to deal with "the Worthies of his country, roused by fame" (reports William Drummond). Like Pope, Jonson actually wrote a mock-epic rather than the serious one; Jonson's work is the "merdurinous" "On the Famous Voyage" (epigram 133).

The ode to Cary and Morison is extreme in imagery as well as in syntactic prosodic tension. It opens with a notorious image, that of the "infant of Saguntum" who retreated back to the womb before it was "half got out," appalled by the horror and devastation of wartime scenes into which it was being born. Jonson goes on to surprise conventional taste even further by suggesting that this vaginal peripety represents a "summ'd" "circle . . . of deepest lore, could we the Center find." References to circle and center of course bring along a whole train of important imagery and structure in Jonson, as well as alluding to the structure of the whole poem, with its repeated peripeteia of "Turn," "Counter-Turn," and "Stand."

The will to shock, or at least to write in uncompromisingly extraordinary ways, may indirectly express the speaker's grief and sense of loss (the poem's occasion is Morison's death). It is certainly connected with a larger demand to see life in an unconventional way, which is the poem's essential consoling strategy. (Jonson speaks of the "holy rage" with which Morison "leap'd the present age"; readers are asked to do the same thing, in the same mood.) The distinction that Jonson insists on is between visions of life as "space" and as "act." In terms of the former—sheer duration—Morison's life was indeed lamentably cut off: He lived barely into his twenties. In terms of "act," Morison's life was perfect:

> A Soldier to the last right end
> A perfect Patriot, and a noble friend,
> But most a virtuous Son.
> All Offices were done
> By him, so ample, full and round,
> In weight, in measure, number, sound
> As, though his age imperfect might appear,
> His life was of Humanity the Sphere.

This is, notably, purely secular consolation. There are later references to a "bright eternal day," but it has less to do with Christian Paradise than with a pagan heaven of commemoration, in which Morison (and Cary) may persist as an "Asterism," a constellation. The poem's contrast with "Lycidas" marks the distance between John Milton's more old-fashioned Christian humanism and Jonson's secular mind.

Jubilation, rather than lamentation, over Morison's perfection of "act" is, like most of Jonson's higher choices, not easy to maintain. The speaker's own "tongue" "falls" into mourning at one point. Cary, Morison's great friend who survives him and to whom the poem is at least in part addressed, is exhorted to "call . . . for wine/ And let thy looks with gladness shine"—and to maintain connection. Like the centered men of the epigrams and epistles, and like the Sidneys of Penshurst, Cary is to act in relation, to "shine" on earth in conjunction with Morison's now heavenly light. The function of the poem vis-à-vis Cary is to establish this relation for him, and the broken but single name of Ben Jonson bridges over precisely the two stanzas in which the relation of the two friends is most fully discussed.

The poem includes a satirical picture. Contrasting with the vital life of act, the vacuous life of space is personified as a futile careerist, "buoy'd . . . up" in the end only by the "Cork of Title." More than by alternation of satiric and positive images, however, the poem works by a tension constant throughout: the tension between the naturalistic sense of death as an end, which is never really lost, and the other vision on which Jonson is insisting. The poem is a celebration of secular heroism. It depicts that quality in its subjects ("Nothing perfect done/ But as a Cary, or a Morison"), enacts it in its language, and demands it of its readers. The tension and energy that the poem displays are the reasons for reading Jonson's verse.

OTHER MAJOR WORKS

PLAYS: *The Case Is Altered*, pr. 1597; *The Isle of Dogs*, pr. 1597 (with Thomas Nashe; no longer extant); *Every Man in His Humour*, pr. 1598, 1605; *Hot Anger Soon Cold*, pr. 1598 (with Henry Chettle and Henry Porter; no longer extant); *Every Man Out of His Humour*, pr. 1599; *The Page of Plymouth*, pr. 1599 (with Thomas Dekker; no longer extant); *Robert the Second, King of Scots*, pr. 1599 (with Chettle and Dekker; no longer extant); *Cynthia's Revels: Or, The Fountain of Self-Love*, pr. c. 1600-1601; *Poetaster: Or, His Arraignment*, pr. 1601; *Sejanus His Fall*, pr. 1603 (commonly known as *Sejanus*); *Eastward Ho!*, pr., pb. 1605 (with George Chapman and John Marston); *Volpone: Or, The Fox*, pr. 1605; *Epicœne: Or, The Silent Woman*, pr. 1609; *The Alchemist*, pr. 1610; *Catiline His Conspiracy*, pr., pb. 1611 (commonly known as *Catiline*); *Bartholomew Fair*, pr. 1614; *The Devil Is an Ass*, pr. 1616; *The Staple of News*, pr. 1626; *The New Inn: Or, The Light Heart*, pr. 1629; *The Magnetic Lady: Or, Humours Reconciled*, pr. 1632; *A Tale of a Tub*, pr. 1633; *The Sad Shepherd: Or, A Tale of Robin Hood*, pb. 1640 (fragment).

NONFICTION: *The English Grammar*, 1640; *Timber: Or, Discoveries Made upon Men and Matter*, 1641.

TRANSLATION: *Horace His Art of Poetry*, 1640 (of Horace's *Ars poetica*).

MISCELLANEOUS: *The Magnificent Entertainment Given to King James*, 1603 (with Dekker and Thomas Middleton); *The Workes of Benjamin Jonson*, 1616; *The Works of Benjamin Jonson*, 1640-1641 (2 volumes).

BIBLIOGRAPHY

Bloom, Harold, ed. *Ben Jonson*. Broomall, Pa.: Chelsea House, 2001. A collection of essays providing literary criticism of Jonson's major works.

Booth, Stephen. *Precious Nonsense: The Gettysburg Address, Ben Jonson's "Epitaphs on His Children," and "Twelfth Night."* Berkeley: University of California Press, 1998. Using three disparate texts, Booth demonstrates how poetics can triumph over logic and enrich the reading experience. Booth's presentation is playful yet analytical and his unique reading of "Epitaphs on His Children" is a valuable addition to critical thought on Jonson's work.

Cousins, A. D., and Alison V. Scott, eds. *Ben Jonson and the Politics of Genre*. New York: Cambridge University Press, 2009. Contains essays on Jonson and his writings, including one on his country house poems and another on epistles.

Dutton, Richard, ed. *Ben Jonson*. Longman Critical Readers. Harlow, England: Pearson Education, 2000. This study presents critical analysis and interpretation of Jonson's literary works. Bibliography and index.

Harp, Richard, and Stanley Stewart, eds. *The Cambridge Companion to Ben Jonson*. New York: Cambridge University Press, 2000. A companion to the writer and his works.

Loxley, James. *The Complete Critical Guide to Ben Jonson*. New York: Routledge, 2002. A handbook designed to provide readers with critical analysis of Jonson's works. Bibliography and index.

Miles, Rosalind. *Ben Jonson: His Life and Work*. London: Routledge & Kegan Paul, 1986. Miles's volume is a fine standard biography-study, especially for the literary background and Jonson's position in Jacobean courtly society. The scholarly apparatus is thorough: a chronology, an index, a select but extensive bibliography, notes, and an appendix.

Riggs, David. *Ben Jonson: A Life*. Cambridge, Mass.: Harvard University Press, 1989. This is a full-scale biography rather than a literary biography; the works illuminate the life rather than vice versa. The illumination is brilliant. Riggs reviews all the facts and assembles them in memorable order. He includes all the standard scholarly attachments, but the book deserves to be read simply for the revelations it contains for Jonson and his age, most of which are illustrated.

Summers, Claude J., and Ted-Larry Pebworth. *Ben Jonson*. Rev. ed. New York: Twayne, 1999. An introductory overview of Jonson's life and work. Includes bibliographical references and index.

Watson, Robert N., ed. *Critical Essays on Ben Jonson*. New York: G. K. Hall, 1997. A collection of previously published and new essays edited by an established authority on the life and work of Jonson. Includes an introduction that provides an overview of criticism of Jonson's work over his career. In addition, some previously unpublished interviews, letters, and manuscript fragments are included.

John F. McDiarmid

JAMES JOYCE

Born: Dublin, Ireland; February 2, 1882
Died: Zurich, Switzerland; January 13, 1941

PRINCIPAL POETRY
Chamber Music, 1907
Pomes Penyeach, 1927
"Ecce Puer," 1932
Collected Poems, 1936

OTHER LITERARY FORMS

Although James Joyce published poetry throughout his career (*Chamber Music*, a group of thirty-six related poems, was in fact his first published book), it is for his novels and short stories that he is primarily known. These works include *Dubliners* (1914), a volume of short stories describing what Joyce saw as the moral paralysis of his countrymen; *A Portrait of the Artist as a Young Man* (1916), a heavily autobiographical account of the growing up of a writer in Ireland at the end of the nineteenth century and the beginning of the twentieth; *Ulysses* (1922), a novel set in Dublin in 1904, recounting the day-long adventures of Leopold Bloom, a modern-day Odysseus who is both advertising man and cuckold, Stephen Dedalus, the young artist of *A Portrait of the Artist as a Young Man* now grown somewhat older, and Molly Bloom, Leopold's earthy wife; and *Finnegans Wake* (1939), Joyce's last published work, not a novel at all in the conventional sense, but a world in itself, built of many languages and inhabited by the paradigmatic Earwicker family.

ACHIEVEMENTS

James Joyce's prose works established his reputation as the most influential writer of fiction of his generation and led English prose fiction from Victorianism into modernism and beyond. To this body of work, Joyce's poetry is an addendum of less interest in itself than it is in relationship to the other, more important, work. At the same time, in the analysis of Joyce's achievement, it is impossible to ignore anything that he wrote, and the poetry, for which Joyce reserved some of his most personal utterances, has its place along with the play *Exiles* (pb. 1918)—now seen as more important than it once was—and the essays, letters, and notebooks.

BIOGRAPHY

The life of James Augustine Aloysius Joyce is interwoven so inextricably with his work that to consider one requires considering the other. The definitive biography of Joyce, by Richard Ellmann, is as strong in its interpretation of Joyce's work as it is of his life. If Joyce, as Ellmann suggests in that biography, tended to see things through words, readers must try to see him through his words—the words of his work—as well as through the facts of his life.

Joyce was born into a family whose fortunes were in decline, the first child to live in the match of a man who drank too much and accumulated too many debts and a woman whose family the Joyces considered beneath them. John Joyce, James's father, became the model for Stephen's father both in *A Portrait of the Artist as a*

James Joyce (Library of Congress)

Young Man and in *Ulysses*, where he is one of the most memorable characters, and also a model for H. C. Earwicker in *Finnegans Wake*. If Joyce's father seemed not to understand his son's work or even to show much interest in it during his lifetime, that work has become a surer form of immortality for him than anything he ever did himself.

Joyce was educated at Clongowes Wood College, a Jesuit school not far from Dublin that he memorialized in *A Portrait of the Artist as a Young Man*, and later at Belvedere College, also Jesuit, in Dublin. In 1898, on his graduation from Belvedere, he entered University College, Dublin. At this point in his life, increasingly rebellious against the values of his home and society, Joyce did his first writing for publication. He graduated from the university with a degree in modern languages in 1902 and then left Dublin for Paris to study medicine. That, however, quickly gave way to Joyce's real desire to write, and he entered a difficult period in which he turned to teaching to earn a living. The problems of the father had become the problems of the son, but during this period Joyce wrote some of his best earlier poems, including what is now the final piece in the *Chamber Music* sequence. With the death of his mother imminent in April, 1903, Joyce returned to Dublin, where, the following winter, he began to write the first draft of *A Portrait of the Artist as a Young Man* (known as *Stephen Hero*).

By far the most important event after Joyce's return to Ireland, however, was his meeting in June, 1904, with the woman who was to become his mate for the rest of his life, Nora Barnacle, whose roots (like those of the family Joyce) were in Galway, the westernmost county in Ireland. If Joyce's mother's family had seemed too low for the Joyces, Nora's family was even lower on the social scale, but Joyce, like Stephen Dedalus, was to escape the net of convention and take the woman he loved away from Ireland to live in a succession of temporary residences on the Continent while he established himself as a major writer. The model, at least in part, for Molly Bloom and also for Anna Livia Plurabelle, Nora, not Joyce's legal wife until 1931, was the mother of their two children—Giorgio, born in 1905, and Lucia, born in 1907—and Joyce's main emotional support for almost four decades.

From the time Joyce and Nora moved to the Continent until the outbreak of World War I, they lived chiefly in Trieste, a port city in northeastern Italy that in appearance seemed more Austrian than Italian; there Joyce taught English in a Berlitz School, and wrote; he returned to Ireland only twice, in 1909 and again in 1912, for what turned out to be his last visit. With the outbreak of the war, Joyce and his family moved to Zurich, which was neutral ground, and in 1920—after a brief sojourn once again in Trieste—moved to Paris, where they were to remain until the fall of France twenty years later.

Paris in the 1920's, Ernest Hemingway was to write years later, was a "moveable feast," but Joyce, as always, was a selective diner, an integral part of the literary life of Paris at that time, yet aloof from it, imaginatively dwelling in the Dublin of 1904, the year he had met Nora. Having published *Chamber Music*, *Dubliners*, *A Portrait of the Artist as a Young Man*, and *Exiles*, Joyce had embarked on his most ambitious project to date—a treatment in detail of one day in Dublin—June 16, 1904—and the adventures of a modern-day Odysseus, Leopold Bloom, ultimately to be his greatest single achievement in characterization. The serialization of *Ulysses* had begun in 1918; its publication in book form waited until Joyce's fortieth birthday, on February 2, 1922. Because of publication difficulties resulting from censorship, Joyce did not realize much financially from the book until later in his life, and remained dependent on a succession of patrons and subscribers not only for its initial publication but also for his livelihood. With its publication, however—difficult though it was to achieve—came the recognition of Joyce as the greatest living novelist in English, a master stylist who had managed (as such major figures as T. S. Eliot and Ezra Pound were quick to see) to give the modern experience a historical dimension that so many realistic novels had lacked.

As recognition of *Ulysses* came, Joyce characteristically moved on to something different (in a sense, in his published work he almost never repeated himself, in style or in form, though he dealt continuously with certain themes), publishing in 1924 the first portion of what for years was termed "Work in Progress" and then ultimately became *Finnegans Wake*. This novel broke new ground in the same way *Ulysses* did, in its rendering of unconscious universal experiences and in its use of language; but it took much longer for it to achieve general recognition as a masterpiece. Plagued throughout his lifetime by financial problems, health problems (especially with his eyes), and family problems (his daughter's mental health was always fragile, and she has lived most of her life in a sanatorium), Joyce remains the prime example of the artist as exile.

ANALYSIS

Chamber Music appeared in 1907, but James Joyce had been working on the poems that comprise the volume for some time before that date. As early as 1905, he had worked out a plan for the poems, different from the one finally devised for the 1907 version but perhaps more revealing of the thematic content of the poetry. With the addition of several poems not in the 1905 scheme, *Chamber Music* came to thirty-six poems of varying lengths and forms, the work of a young man who had already largely abandoned poetry in favor of prose fiction.

CHAMBER MUSIC

In many ways the poems of *Chamber Music* are typical of the period in which they were written. The poetry of the late nineteenth century in English has a hothouse quality; like the French Symbolists, who—next to the English Romantics—provided the chief inspiration throughout this period, the poets of the fin de siècle eschewed ordinary life in favor of an aesthetic ideal. This was in fact the final flowering of the ideal of art for art's sake so important to nineteenth century literature and art, an attitude that the young Joyce flirted with and ultimately abandoned, satirizing it in the pages of *A Portrait of the Artist as a Young Man*. In the poems of *Chamber Music*, however, the satire is less easy to detect, and fin de siècle themes provide the basis of many of the poems in the sequence. The dominant note of the poetry of the fin de siècle is one of weariness or sadness, the favorite time dusk or night, the favorite stance one of retreat; in Joyce's *Chamber Music* poems, as later in *A Portrait of the Artist as a Young Man*, such favorite attitudes are questioned but not totally rejected. If the final note is one of anger or bitterness rather than simply of sadness or despair, there is still a strong enough taste of the latter to mark the poems—even the celebrated number XXXVI—as the work of a young man who has grown up in the last important moment of aestheticism. Even so, the experience of the young man who is the principal speaker of the sequence of poems seems ultimately to toughen him in a way more typical of Joyce than of the poetry of the fin de siècle.

In Joyce's 1905 sequence, the personas of the poems are more easily perceived, the themes developed in them clearer, as William York Tindall was first to point out at length in his 1954 edition of *Chamber Music*. In that sequence there are thirty-four poems, designated first in the following list, with the numbers from the 1907 edition in Roman numerals in parentheses immediately after: 1 (XXI), 2 (I), 3 (III), 4 (II), 5 (IV), 6 (V), 7 (VIII), 8 (VII), 9 (IX), 10 (XVII), 11 (XVIII), 12 (VI), 13 (X), 14 (XX), 15 (XIII), 16 (XI), 17 (XIV), 18 (XIX), 19 (XV), 20 (XXIII), 21 (XXIV), 22 (XVI), 23 (XXXI), 24 (XXII), 25 (XXVI), 26 (XII), 27 (XXVII), 28 (XXVIII), 29 (XXV), 30 (XXIX), 31 (XXXII), 32 (XXX), 33 (XXXIII), and 34 (XXXIV).

This sequence has certain important features. Poem 1 (XXI) introduces the young man of the sequence, a sort of romantic rebel in the tradition of the Shelleyan hero, a "high unconsortable one" more in love with himself than with anyone else. This theme of aloofness and narcissism is struck in several poems following this one—in 2 (I), 3 (III), and 4 (II)—but by 5 (IV) the young man has not only become the speaker of the poem, but he has also found someone to love. Poem 6 (V) gives her a name—Goldenhair—and establishes the theme of the next group of poems: the young man in pursuit of Goldenhair, in the traditional rites of courtship. In 7 (VIII), he pursues her through the "green wood," and in 8 (VII), he sees her among the apple trees, vernal settings for these ancient rites. In 9 (IX), however, he cannot find her, and 10 (XVII) explains why: Here the third persona of the sequence is introduced—the rival who is a friend of the young man and who, at the same time, is threatening his relationship with Goldenhair: "He is a stranger to me now/ Who was my friend." Poem 11 (XVIII), addressed both to Goldenhair and to the rival, complains of the failure of friends and suggests that another woman may well give the young man succor. As the poems proceed, this other

woman takes on a variety of connotations, until finally, in 17 (XIV) the young man imagines his union with her in terms suggesting that she has combined characteristics, in Tindall's words, "of church, mother, muse, nation, and soul." After 17, the poems do variations on the themes of separation and lost love, ending in 33 (XXXIII) and 34 (XXXIV) on a decidedly wintry note: "The voice of the winter/ Is heard at the door./ O sleep, for the winter/ Is crying, 'Sleep no more.'"

This pattern of love challenged by a rival and ending in bitter or mixed feelings occurs elsewhere in Joyce's work, most notably in *A Portrait of the Artist as a Young Man* and in the play *Exiles*, where, as a test of a relationship, it provides the major theme. *Chamber Music* thus becomes an early working out of this theme, though Joyce ultimately agreed to an ordering of the poems (devised by his brother Stanislaus) different from the one of 1905—allowing for an ending on a much stronger note with poem XXXVI, beginning "I hear an army charging upon the land," which was not part of the 1905 sequence at all and which suggests an attitude that is more than simply passive or accepting on the part of the young man. These little poems, while carrying the weight of themes developed more completely in Joyce's later work, are also lyrics light and fresh enough to serve as the basis of songs. Joyce himself set a number of them to music, and over the years they have been set by many other composers as well.

Poem 16 (XI) illustrates the technique of the lyrics of *Chamber Music*. The diction is simple but frequently archaic—note the use of "thee" and "thy," "hast" and "doth," in keeping with much of the lyric poetry of the 1890's—and the tone light and songlike, with touches of irony apparent only in the last few lines of the second stanza. This irony is heralded in line 9 by the verb "unzone," which stands out in a poem of otherwise simple diction. Like many such words in these poems, "unzone" is unusual for the accuracy with which it is used (compare, for example, "innumerous" in poem 19 [XV]), Joyce returning to its original meaning of "encircle" or "surround," derived by way of the Latin *zone* from Greek *zona*, or "girdle." What is frequently most distinctive about Joyce's choice of words, in prose as well as in poetry, is their accuracy. In this context, the contrast between the formality of "unzone" and the "girlish bosom" of the next line, reinforced by the irony in other poems of the series dealing with the wooing of Goldenhair, makes the reader question her innocence if not the young man's intentions.

The repetition of the opening lines of 16 is another notable feature of the series. In 12 (VI) one can see the same quality on a somewhat larger scale, the final line pointing back to the beginning of the poem. If the poems of *Chamber Music* are relatively simply lyrics, they have their own complexities and ambiguities, as this poem shows. The "bosom" of the first stanza is conceivably Goldenhair's, but may also be interpreted as that of mother or church. "Austerities," like "bosom" used twice in the poem, in particular leads the reader to think so, the bosom or heart leading to an ascetic, not hedonistic, form of satisfaction for the young man. In this poem, the young man flees from the relationship with Goldenhair and seeks other means of satisfaction. The language of the poem creates irony through repetition, forcing the reader to reexamine the premises of the relationship described. If this technique is much simpler than the one Joyce employed in his prose masterpieces, it is certainly a technique of the same order.

POMES PENYEACH

In 1927, Joyce published a second volume of poetry with the unassuming title *Pomes Penyeach*. The occasion for the volume was largely negative; stung by criticism of "Work in Progress" from people such as Ezra Pound, who had been so supportive of *Ulysses*, Joyce wished to show that he could also produce a relatively simple volume of lyrics. However, the lyrics were too simple for the taste of the time, and the volume went largely ignored; Pound himself suggested that Joyce should have reserved the poems for the Bible or the family album. This criticism now seems unfair, or at least out of proportion. The thirteen poems of *Pomes Penyeach* do not in any sense break new ground in English poetry, but they provide a kind of personal comment on Joyce's private life that is not easy to find in the prose works, and some of them are also simply good lyrics in the manner of *Chamber Music*.

The poems represent work of a period of approximately twenty years, beginning with "Tilly," composed in 1903 just after Joyce's mother's death, and ending with "A Prayer" of 1923, though stylistically they are of a piece. In this poetry, Joyce favored a diction and tone that seemed archaic by the late 1920's, and he did so without any of the irony apparent or at least incipient in certain poems of *Chamber Music*. If the mood of these poems did not suit the times in which they appeared, neither did it seem to suit the style of the supreme punster of "Work in Progress." They provide the single instance in Joyce's published work of an anachronism—a work that looks back in style and tone, in this case to the poetry of Joyce's youth and young manhood, rather than forward in time—and this accounts in part for their unenthusiastic reception.

In *Pomes Penyeach*, the poems occur in roughly the order of their composition, and may be grouped according to subject matter. Some celebrate Joyce's feelings toward his children, as in "A Flower Given to My Daughter" or "On the Beach at Fontana," while others refer to feelings provoked in him by women he fancied himself to be in love with, either in the Trieste period or in Zurich during World War I. Some poems suggest certain of the prose works, such as "She Weeps over Rahoon" with its echoes of the long story "The Dead," written some five years before the poem. The final poem of the group, "A Prayer," returns to the mood of the darker poems in *Chamber Music* and to the image of woman as vampire that occurs so frequently in the poetry and art of the fin de siècle. It also suggests the strain of masochism that shows itself so often in Joyce's work in connection with sensuous pleasure. All in all, these lyrics provide an engaging record of various moods of Joyce as he passed into middle age, tempered by the public reputation he had acquired by that time.

"A Flower Given to My Daughter" and "A Prayer" illustrate the extremity of mood and variety of technique of these poems. In the first, the inverted word order and quaint diction of the poem—"sere" is the best example of the latter—do not keep the last line from being extremely touching, in part because it is so realistic a description. Joyce manages in the best of *Pomes Penyeach* to find just such a strong line with which to end, establishing a kind of contrast between the somewhat antique technique of the poem and conclusions remarkable for their simplicity and strength. "A Prayer" is far more dramatic in tone, but here the long lines and the rolling words ("remembering" followed by "pitying") also carry the reader into the joy become anguish of the final lines. In these poems as in others of the group, Joyce seems to be using the style and tone of another time with sometimes deadly effect—a conscious archaism rather than the more distanced irony of some of the poems of *Chamber Music*.

"ECCE PUER"

In 1932, Joyce published his last poem, "Ecce Puer," a touching commemoration of two occasions—the death of his father and the birth of his grandson and namesake Stephen James Joyce, the son of Giorgio and his wife, Helen. "Tilly," the first item of *Pomes Penyeach*, was written on the occasion of the death of his mother and is in many ways the strongest of the group; "Ecce Puer"—written just after the death of John Joyce—is even stronger. For felt emotion conveyed, it has no equal among Joyce's works in this form, and its concluding stanza is all the more touching for its echoes of the theme of paternity so important to *Ulysses*—"A child is sleeping:/ An old man gone./ O, father forsaken,/ Forgive your son!" In fact, the poem was completed not many days after the tenth anniversary of the publication of *Ulysses*, which provides yet a third occasion for its composition.

SATIRIC POEMS

In addition to *Chamber Music*, *Pomes Penyeach*, and "Ecce Puer," Joyce published occasional broadsides—satiric poems to express his unhappiness over various literary matters. These include "The Holy Office" (1904) (now the rarest of all the published works of Joyce), an attack on the Irish literary movement by a young writer who already knew that his work was to be essentially different from theirs, and "Gas from a Burner" (1912), an attack on the Dublin publisher who ultimately burned the proofs of *Dubliners* rather than print what he considered an indecent book.

Finally, in *A Portrait of the Artist as a Young Man*, one of the crucial moments occurs (in the final part of the book) when Stephen Dedalus composes a poem in the form of a villanelle. This poem, while technically not Joyce's, represents as sure a comment as Joyce ever made on the aestheticism of the 1890's, and thus stands in contrast with *Pomes Penyeach*, which echoes the themes and tones of that time.

Joyce's poetry was ultimately expressed most fully in his prose works, where the traditional distinctions between poetry and prose are effectively blurred. Perhaps in the end, his lyric poetry is best viewed as a minor expression—almost a form of relaxation—of a master stylist in prose.

OTHER MAJOR WORKS

LONG FICTION: *A Portrait of the Artist as a Young Man*, 1914-1915 (serial), 1916 (book); *Ulysses*, 1922; *Finnegans Wake*, 1939; *Stephen Hero*, 1944 (Theodore Spencer, editor).

SHORT FICTION: *Dubliners*, 1914.

PLAY: *Exiles*, pb. 1918.

NONFICTION: *Letters of James Joyce*, 1957-1966 (3 volumes); *The Critical Writings of James Joyce*, 1959; *Selected Letters of James Joyce*, 1975 (Richard Ellmann, editor); *The James Joyce Archives*, 1977-1979 (64 volumes); *On Ibsen*, 1999; *Occasional, Critical, and Political Writing*, 2000.

BIBLIOGRAPHY

Attridge, Derek, ed. *The Cambridge Companion to James Joyce*. New York: Cambridge University Press, 1990. A collection of eleven essays by eminent contemporary Joyce scholars. Surveys the Joyce phenomenon from cultural, textual, and critical standpoints. A valuable aid and stimulus, containing a chronology of Joyce's life and annotated bibliography.

Blades, John. *How to Study James Joyce*. Houndmills, England: Macmillan, 1996. An excellent study guide for students of Joyce. Includes bibliographical reference, outlines, and syllabi.

Bulson, Eric. *The Cambridge Introduction to James Joyce*. New York: Cambridge University Press, 2006. A work on Joyce that is divided into his life, his works, and the critical reception.

Ellmann, Richard. *James Joyce*. 1959. 2d ed. New York: Oxford University Press, 1984. The definitive biography, generally regarded as the last word on its subject's life and widely considered as the greatest literary biography of the twentieth century. Copiously annotated and well illustrated, particularly in the 1984 edition.

Jones, Ellen Carol, and Morris Beja, eds. *Twenty-first*

Joyce. Gainesville: University Press of Florida, 2004. This useful reference work collects thirteen scholarly essays written by Joyce experts. Part of the University Press of Florida James Joyce series.

McCourt, John. *James Joyce: A Passionate Exile*. New York: St. Martin's Press, 2001. Photos and sketches embellish this account of the life, times, relationships, and works of Joyce. Excellent introductory text, particularly for its illustrations.

Potts, Willard. *Joyce and the Two Irelands*. Austin: University of Texas, 2001. Potts aligns Joyce with Catholic nativists, arguing that, while the novelist rejected Catholicism, his treatment of independence and industrialization betrays a sympathy for Irish nationalism.

Stewart, Bruce. *James Joyce*. New York: Oxford University Press, 2007. A biography of Joyce that looks at his life and works.

Strathern, Paul. *James Joyce in Ninety Minutes*. Chicago: I. R. Dee, 2005. A biography of Joyce that attempts to explain his life and works in an easily understandable manner.

Theall, Donald F. *James Joyce's Techno-Poetics*. Toronto, Ont.: University of Toronto Press, 1997. Representative of a new wing of Joyce studies, Theall's work examines Joyce as a progenitor of today's cyberculture. Includes bibliography and index.

Archie K. Loss

K

PATRICK KAVANAGH

Born: Inniskeen, Ireland; October 21, 1904
Died: Dublin, Ireland; November 30, 1967

PRINCIPAL POETRY

Ploughman, and Other Poems, 1936
The Great Hunger, 1942
A Soul for Sale, 1947
Recent Poems, 1958
Come Dance with Kitty Stobling, and Other Poems, 1960
Collected Poems, 1964
The Complete Poems of Patrick Kavanagh, 1972 (Peter Kavanagh, editor)

OTHER LITERARY FORMS

Three fictional autobiographies—*The Green Fool* (1938), *Tarry Flynn* (1948), and *By Night Unstarred* (1977)—are based on the years Patrick Kavanagh (KAV-uh-nuh) spent in County Monaghan. The latter part of *By Night Unstarred* pursues his life into Dublin. Various prose essays and occasional pieces can be found in *Collected Prose* (1967) and *November Haggard: Uncollected Prose and Verse of Patrick Kavanagh* (1971). *Kavanagh's Weekly*, a magazine that published thirteen issues between April 12 and July 15, 1952, contains a variety of fiction, commentary, and verse that was written under various pseudonyms but is almost all Kavanagh's own work (reprinted, 1981). *Lapped Furrows: Correspondence, 1933-1967* (1969) and *Love's Tortured Headland* (1974) reprint correspondence and other documents between 1933 and 1967. After the poet's death, his brother Peter edited and published his work, and Peter's biography, *Sacred Keeper* (1980), contains a number of previously unpublished or unreprinted documents. Despite the claims of various titles, Kavanagh's work remains uncollected. A poem ("The Gambler") was adapted for

ballet in 1961, and *Tarry Flynn* was dramatized in 1966; each was performed at the Abbey Theatre.

ACHIEVEMENTS

Despite handicaps of poverty, physical drudgery, and isolation, Patrick Kavanagh became the leading figure in the "second generation" of the Irish Literary Revival. He practically reinvented the literary language in which rural Ireland was to be portrayed. Bypassing William Butler Yeats, John Millington Synge, and Lady Augusta Gregory, he returned for a literary model to a fellow Ulsterman, William Carleton, and to his own experience of country life as a subject. He invested his fiction and poetry with fresh regional humor that did not sentimentalize or condescend to its characters. His vision is fundamentally religious, imbued with a Catholic sacramental view of nature. His various criticisms of Irish life and institutions arise from an unrefined but genuine spirituality. The quality of Kavanagh's work is uneven, and his public attitudes are inconsistent. Even so, the sincerity of his best work, its confidence in its own natural springs, its apparent artlessness, its celebration of local character, place, and mode of expression, make him the most widely felt literary influence on the poets of contemporary Ireland, most significantly on those with similar backgrounds, such as John Montague and Seamus Heaney.

BIOGRAPHY

Patrick Kavanagh was the fourth of ten children of James Kavanagh, a shoemaker, and his wife, Bridget. The Kavanagh home was in Mucker, a townland of Inniskeen, County Monaghan, near the Armagh (and now Northern Ireland) border. The boy attended Kednaminsha National School until he was thirteen, when he was apprenticed to his father's trade. Later, he worked a small farm purchased in the nearby townland of Shancoduff. His first literary influences were the school anthologies that featured Henry Wadsworth Longfellow, Charles Kingsley, William Allingham, Alfred, Lord Tennyson, Robert Louis Stevenson, and Thomas Moore, and his earliest poems were written in school notebooks. As he worked on his small farm, he nurtured his taste on magazines picked up at fairs in the town of Dundalk. His keen observations of country life, its customs, characters, and speech patterns, together with his growing awareness of his sensitivity that set him apart from his peers, are well set forth in his account of his early life, *The Green Fool*. Many of his early poems appeared in the 1930's in *The Irish States-man*, whose editor, Æ (George William Russell), was the first to recognize and cultivate the peasant poet. Æ introduced him to modern world literature, providing him with books, advice, payment, and introductions to the Irish literary establishment. Of the books given him by Æ, *Gil Blas of Santillane* (1715, 1724, 1735), *Ulysses* (1922), and *Moby Dick: Or, The Whale* (1851) remained the classics most revered by Kavanagh.

After he moved to Dublin in 1939, he supported himself as a journalist. Throughout the 1940's, he wrote book and film reviews, a range of critical and human interest pieces, city diaries, and various pieces for *The Irish Press* (as "Piers Plowman"), *The Standard*, *The Irish Times*, and *Envoy*. During that time, the long poem *The Great Hunger*, his second poetry collection, *A Soul for Sale*, and the novel *Tarry Flynn* appeared, so that following the deaths of Yeats (1939) and James Joyce (1941), he emerged as the central figure in Irish literary life. His most ambitious journalistic venture was in 1952 when, with his brother's financial and managerial assistance, he produced *Kavanagh's Weekly*, which ran for thirteen issues (April 12-July 5). This production comprises the fullest expression of Kavanagh's "savage indignation" at the mediocrity of Irish life and letters. It is useful as a document of the Dublin ethos in the early 1950's and in reading Kavanagh's poetry of the same period. In October, 1952, *The Leader* responded—in a spirit typical of the infamous factionalism of Dublin's literary politics—with a malicious "Profile," which prompted Kavanagh to file suit for libel. Following a celebrated trial, which Kavanagh lost, he fell dangerously ill with lung cancer.

He made a dramatic physical recovery, however, which in turn revivified his creative powers. This second birth resulted in a group of poems—mainly sonnets—written in 1955 and 1956—set in and around the Rialto Hospital and by the Grand Canal, Dublin, and published in *Recent Poems* and *Come Dance with Kitty Stobling, and Other Poems*. Thereafter he went into a slow decline, physically and creatively. In April, 1967,

he married Katherine Moloney, but he died the following November. He is buried in Inniskeen.

His brother Peter (twelve years his junior) was Kavanagh's constant correspondent, financier, confidant, critic, and promoter. He edited and published many works arising from this fraternal collaboration, including *Lapped Furrows*; *November Haggard*; *The Complete Poems of Patrick Kavanagh*, which supersedes and corrects *Collected Poems*; a bibliography, *Garden of the Golden Apples* (1972); and a documentary biography, *Sacred Keeper*. Despite its title, *Collected Prose* contains only a sampling of Kavanagh's prose works.

ANALYSIS

Although he frequently and vehemently denied it, Patrick Kavanagh was a distinctively Irish poet. He had already formed his own voice by the time he discovered—or was discovered by—the Celtic Revival and became a leading figure in the second generation. Kavanagh was not a Celtic mythologizer such as William Butler Yeats, a conscious dialectician such as J. M. Synge, a folklorist such as Lady Gregory, an etymologist such as James Joyce, or a Gaelic revivalist such as Douglas Hyde. He felt and wrote with less historical or political consciousness than his progenitors. His gifts and temperament made him an outsider in Inniskeen, his lack of formal education and social grooming excluded him from Dublin's middle-class literary coteries, and his moral sensibility excluded him from Bohemia.

Yet in retrospect, Kavanagh emerges as the dominant Irish literary personality between 1940 and 1960. Although he admired each of the Revival's pioneers for particular qualities, he regarded the Irish Literary Revival in the main as an English-inspired hoax. The romanticized peasant, for example, he considered the product of Protestant condescension, and he felt that too many writers of little talent had misunderstood the nature of Yeats's and Joyce's genius and achievements, so that the quality of Irishness replaced sincerity.

Against a pastiche of literary fashions that misrepresented the peasant, attempted the revival of the Irish language, and promoted nationalism in letters and in politics, Kavanagh posited his own belief in himself, in his powers of observation, and his intimate knowledge of the actual lives of country people. Kavanagh's subsequent popular success in Ireland and his influence on the third generation are attributable to several distinct characteristics: his parochialism, which he defined as "confidence in the social and artistic validity of his own parish"; his directness, the apparent offhandedness of his work, and his freedom from literary posing; his deep Catholicism, which went beyond sentimentality and dogma; his imaginative sympathy for the ordinary experiences of country people; his comedy; his repose; his contemplative appreciation of the world as revelation; and his sincerity, his approval of feelings arising only from a depth of spirit. Although he has often been admired for one or more of these virtues, and although his manner often masked these qualities, they must be taken as a whole in accounting for his character as a poet. He disdained the epithet Irish poet, yet shares with each of the pioneers of the Revival one or more signally Irish characteristics.

Kavanagh's creative development followed three stages: first, the works of intimacy with and disengagement from the "stony grey soil" of parochial Monaghan; second, the works that show his involvements with Dublin or national cultural issues; and third, his "rebirth" in the post-1955 reconciliation of public and private selves, when rural parish and national capital find mutual repose.

Kavanagh's two most successful fictional works, *The Green Fool* and *Tarry Flynn*, provide a rich lode of documentation of their author's country background and the growth of his sensibility. Some of his finest lyrics come from this period, along with his magnum opus, *The Great Hunger*. All these works are set in the same few townlands, and the theme is the revelation of grace in ordinary things and tasks. Through these poems, and from *The Green Fool* to *Tarry Flynn*, the poet's confidence in his own visionary gifts progressively deepens, even though the expression is often uncertain. In a handful of lyrics, however, such as "Ploughman," "Inniskeen Road: July Evening," "A Christmas Childhood," "Spraying the Potatoes," "Shancoduff," and "Epic," Kavanagh's technique realizes his intentions. In each of these, the chance appearances belie the deft design, and the natural voice of the countryman is heard for the first time since Carleton in Irish literature.

"SHANCODUFF"

"Shancoduff" (In *The Complete Poems of Patrick Kavanagh*) is one of Kavanagh's most successful expressions of his parochial voice and is a representative early poem. The small farmer's pride in his bare holding is seemingly disquieted by a casual comment from passing strangers: "By heavens he must be poor." Until this uninvited, materialistic contrast with other places intrudes, this little world, although uncomfortable, has been endurable. Now it may not be so.

Before the cattle drovers assess the farm, the readers have seen it through the eyes of its owner, and they do not need to be told that he is a poet. With him they have first observed these hills' exemplary, incomparable introspection (lines 1-7). Even as his readers are being invited to contemplate the hills' ontological self-sufficiency, however, the poet, by necessity a maker of comparisons, introduces mythological and geographical allusions from the larger world. Even though these references—to Lot's wife, the Alps, and the Matterhorn—ostensibly imply his sympathy with his property's self-justification, their very statement admits some kind of comparison and betrays the principle it proposes. This and the irony in "fondle" arrange the scene for the dour pragmatism of the jobbers. Shancoduff is very poor land, poets do make poor farmers, or farmers make poor poets, and the eavesdropping owner-farmer-poet seems disconcerted. The question in line 16 is slyly rhetorical, however; the poet's evident disdain for the jobbers implies that his heart may not be quite so "badly shaken."

The poem operates by a set of contrasts that set the cold, wet, dark, ungainly native places against apparently more positive reflections from the outside. Earth and water oppose air and fire; Saint Patrick's see of Armagh (and/or ancient Ulster's adjacent capital of Emhain Macha) is a counterattraction to the foreign cities of dubious renown—Sodom, Rome, London, even perhaps Tokyo. The gauche place-names of Kavanagh's parish do not seem to invite tourists, yet they combine in shaping the poet's attitude to these humble townlands and the design of the poem (see also "Old

Black Pocket"; "Glassdrummond," "Streamy/Green Little Hill"; "Featherna," "Streamy"; with the "Big Forth" they compose an ancient, native estate).

"Shancoduff" uses seasonal, biblical, and religious images to suggest his parochial independence from urban cultures, while foreshadowing several motifs that run through Kavanagh's later works: his distrust of cities and critics, his investment of local dialect or commonplace phrases with larger, often mystical, reference, his disdain for positivist assessments, and his cutting irony. Yet, despite the representative nature of its content, it must be admitted that by its total coherence and clarity this poem stands out from most of his work.

THE GREAT HUNGER

The Great Hunger is Kavanagh's most ambitious poem and is one of signal importance in the literature of modern Ireland. First published in 1942, it is 756 lines long, in fourteen sections. It narrates the life of Patrick Maguire, a peasant farmer whose life is thwarted by physical poverty, Jansenism, and the lack of imagination. The poem is Kavanagh's most extensive rebuke to the idealization of the peasant: A report "from the other side of the ditch," it has great reportorial force. For just as it describes the degradation of the rural poor, it also projects Maguire sympathetically as a figure of keen self-awareness and spiritual potential. Maguire's anguish is muffled and extended by his procrastination, the dull round of gossip, gambling, and masturbation. The Church distorts his natural religious sensibilities into patterns of guilt, which, together with his mother's hold on the farm, conspire to justify his pusillanimity. Woman is the embodiment of life's potentialities, and Maguire's failure to marry is thus the social expression of his spiritual retardation.

The title recalls the potato famine of 1845 to 1847, when starvation and disease ravaged the population and caused long-term psychological and social harm. The mood of the people turned pessimistic as they accepted the disaster as a judgment from an angry deity, and they turned penurious. This historical catastrophe had a deeply depressing effect on rural life, enlarged the power of the Church, reduced national self-confidence, and led to the disuse of the native language and the loss of the gaiety and spontaneity for which the Irish

had been renowned. Kavanagh's poem reflects several of these effects with unflinching honesty.

The poem is a tour de force of descriptive writing, technical variation, and complex tonal control. In the modernist mode, it uses the rhythms and idioms of jazz, nursery rhymes, ballads, the Hiberno-English dialect, the Bible, the pastoral, and the theater, with only occasional lapses in momentum. The poet stands at very little distance from his subject; the tone is somber to bitter. Kavanagh shows compassion rather than condescension toward his protagonist; the humor is grim and restrained. *The Great Hunger* suffers by its occasional stridency, but its urgency and commitment do not diminish it as much as its author would have readers think when he later disowned it as "lacking the nobility and repose of poetry" (*Self-Portrait*).

By the time Kavanagh had made that statement, he had gone through some important changes in spirit. Even though *The Great Hunger* established his reputation in Dublin's literary life, he suffered from lack of patronage and managed to survive only by journalism. That activity he undertook with zest and courage— witness *Kavanagh's Weekly*—but it brought to the fore some of his insecurities that found expression in flailing abuse of his rivals and in sententious dogma on a range of public issues. As the objects of his satirical verses changed, the central vision began to disintegrate. The bitter libel suit against *The Leader* was a personal disaster. His bout with lung cancer took him close to death, and his creative energies had reached their nadir. His remarkable physical recovery, however, led to a spiritual revivification on the banks of the Grand Canal, Dublin, in the year following the summer of 1955.

RECENT POEMS AND COME DANCE WITH KITTY STOBLING, AND OTHER POEMS

This reinvigoration of spirit is reflected in a group of sonnets published in *Recent Poems* and *Come Dance with Kitty Stobling, and Other Poems*, notably the title poem of the latter, along with "Canal Bank Walk," "The Hospital," and "Lines Written on a Seat on the Grand Canal." As his various accounts (notably in *Self-Portrait*) of this experience testify, Kavanagh rediscovered his original capacities to see, accept, and celebrate the ordinary. In these poems, the original innocence of the Monaghan fields graces his experience of Dublin, mediated by his hospitalization and the repose offered by the environment of the Grand Canal. Kavanagh purged these poems of many defects that had marred his previous work—contentiousness, self-pity, shrill engagement in passing events, messianic compulsions—all of which arose from relative shallows.

In "Lines Written on a Seat on the Grand Canal," for example, there is a nicely balanced irony in the mock-heroic view of self, which is deftly subsumed by the natural grace observed in the setting. The artificial roar is drowned by the seasonal silence. The well-tempered voice of the poet commands original simplicities with easy assurance. The poet's memorial, "just a canal-bank seat for the passer-by," summarizes Kavanagh's testament: his acknowledgment of Yeats, his self-definition as observer, namer, and diviner, and his humility as no more than a "part of nature." The countryman, the poet, the visionary, the Irishman, and the citizen are finally reconciled to one another. Although the poem appears to mirror the persona's affection of indifference, its taut conclusion indicates that casualness has not been easily won.

The accomplishment of these late poems notwithstanding, Kavanagh retained a sense of defeat to the end of his career. He never overcame a defensiveness arising from his deprived youth. He rarely reconciled his feelings for his Monaghan sources and his need for a Dublin audience. His *The Complete Poems of Patrick Kavanagh* shows how small a proportion of his total production is truly successful. Nevertheless, his impact on Irish cultural life is large, and this is attributable to the color of his personality, the humor of his prose, and his unsentimental social criticism, as much as to his poetic oeuvre.

OTHER MAJOR WORKS

LONG FICTION: *The Green Fool*, 1938; *Tarry Flynn*, 1948; *By Night Unstarred*, 1977.

PLAY: *Tarry Flynn*, pr. 1966.

NONFICTION: *Lapped Furrows: Correspondence, 1933-1967*, 1969 (with Peter Kavanagh); *Love's Tortured Headland*, 1974 (with Peter Kavanagh and others); *A Poet's Country: Selected Prose*, 2003 (Antoinette Quinn, editor).

MISCELLANEOUS: *Kavanagh's Weekly*, 1952, serial (1981, facsimile); *Self-Portrait*, 1964; *Collected Prose*, 1967; *November Haggard: Uncollected Prose and Verse of Patrick Kavanagh*, 1971 (Peter Kavanagh, editor).

BIBLIOGRAPHY

Agnew, Una. *The Mystical Imagination of Patrick Kavanagh*. Blackrock, County Dublin, Ireland: Columba Press, 1998. A critical study of selected works by Kavanagh. Includes bibliographical references and indexes.

Garratt, Robert F. *Modern Irish Poetry: Tradition and Continuity from Yeats to Heaney*. Berkeley: University of California Press, 1986. The chapter devoted to Kavanagh is divided into four parts: his criticism of the Irish Literary Revival and revisionist reading of William Butler Yeats, his early poetic realism, his poetic rebirth in the "Canal Bank" poems, and the development of his influential poetics of the local and familiar, which influenced the next generation.

Heaney, Seamus. *The Government of the Tongue*. New York: Farrar, Straus and Giroux, 1988. This collection of prose by Kavanagh's most famous successor contains a lecture in which Kavanagh's poetry is seen in two stages: the "real topographical presence" of the early poems, followed by the "luminous spaces" of the late poems. The essay shows the importance of Kavanagh for younger Irish poets in the words of one of the best.

Kavanagh, Peter. *Sacred Keeper: A Biography of Patrick Kavanagh*. The Curragh, Ireland: Goldsmith Press, 1980. This partisan biography by the poet's devoted brother claims to avoid the lies and legends of "the eccentric, the drunkard, the *enfant terrible* of Dublin" in favor of the facts, lovingly recorded in a pastiche of letters, poems, photographs, articles, and reminiscences.

Nemo, John. *Patrick Kavanagh*. Boston: Twayne, 1979. Provides a useful overview of Kavanagh's life and work, along with a chronology and a bibliography. The examination of the poetry is thorough and authoritative.

Quinn, Antoinette. *Patrick Kavanagh*. Syracuse, N.Y.: Syracuse University Press, 1991. A critical assessment of Kavanagh's oeuvre. Includes bibliographical references and indexes.

Ryan, John. *Remembering How We Stood: Bohemian Dublin at Mid-century*. New York: Taplinger, 1975. A chapter of this colorful, if respectful, memoir captures "Paddy Kavanagh," the picturesque eccentric and pub crawler, in the local atmosphere of literary Dublin from 1945 to 1955. Entertaining and anecdotal but not thoroughly reliable.

Smith, Stan, ed. *Patrick Kavanagh*. Portland, Oreg.: Irish Academic Press, 2009. A collection of essays about Kavanagh that cover the reception of his early and later poetry and his identity as an Irish writer.

Warner, Alan. *Clay Is the Word: Patrick Kavanagh, 1904-1967*. Dublin: Dolmen Press, 1973. The first full-length study and the best introduction to Kavanagh, Warner's book is engaging in tone, discursive in method, and speculative in its conclusions. Makes use of reminiscences of those who knew the poet as well as literary analyses of the poems. Includes bibliography.

Cóilín Owens

JOHN KEATS

Born: Moorfields, London, England; October 31, 1795

Died: Rome, Papal States (now in Italy); February 23, 1821

PRINCIPAL POETRY

Poems, 1817

Endymion: A Poetic Romance, 1818

"Lamia," "Isabella," "The Eve of St. Agnes," and Other Poems, 1820

Life, Letters, and Literary Remains of John Keats, 1848

The Fall of Hyperion: A Dream, 1856

OTHER LITERARY FORMS

In *The Use of Poetry* (1933), T. S. Eliot referred to the letters of John Keats (keets) as "the most notable and the most important ever written by any English poet," primarily because "there is hardly one statement of Keats about poetry, which . . . will not be found to be true." The letters also offer an important gloss on specific poems and have thus become important for understanding Keats. Besides many passing comments of brilliance, the central concept of the letters is "negative capability." As defined by Keats, it is the capability to remain "in uncertainties, Mysteries, doubts, without any irritable reaching after fact & reason," which implies a disinterestedness that permits even competing ideas full play to reach their potential. In his letters, Keats often carried an idea to its extreme with extraordinary intellectual flexibility; another day, its opposite will surface to be worked out, as all things "end in speculation." The concept is also taken to include Keats's understanding of the poetical character, or the ability to surrender one's personal self to create characters and objects with independent life. Keats believed that the artist's first responsibility was to create beauty, which implies that the artist's personally held ideas and beliefs should be temporarily suspended or treated only partially so as to realize fully the work's aesthetic potential. Through the use of sympathetic imagination, Keats attempted to become the thing he was creating, to intensely identify with its life, not to find his personal life reflected in it. The standard edition of Keats's letters is *The Letters of John Keats, 1814-1821* (2 volumes; 1958, Hyder Edward Rollins, editor). Text citations are to that edition.

ACHIEVEMENTS

Without being facetious, one could identify John Keats's greatest achievement as becoming one of the greatest poets of the English language in twenty-five years, three months, and twenty-three days of life, for Keats died before the age of twenty-six. Douglas Bush has said that no other English poet would rank as high as Keats if he had died as young—not William Shakespeare, John Milton, or Keats's greatest contemporary, William Wordsworth. Whereas other poets, especially his Romantic contemporaries, have gone in and out of critical fashion, Keats's reputation has endured since shortly after his death.

Keats followed the Shakespearean model of impersonality in art; that is, the surrendering of self to the fullest development of character and object, and it is this impersonality, coupled with intensity, that makes his poetry readily accessible to a wide range of modern readers. The reader does not have to re-create Keats's time, empathize with Romantic norms and beliefs, or identify with the poet's unique biographical experiences to appreciate his poetry fully. Keats is sane, honest, and open; his art is varied, intense, and rich in texture and experience. As he said of his poetic model, Shakespeare, Keats was as little of an egotist as it was possible to be, in the Romantic period, at least, in the creation of art.

BIOGRAPHY

Though the events of John Keats's life are meager, his biography has fascinated many. Keats did not have a single physical, social, familial, or educational advantage in life, nothing to prepare for or enhance the development of his genius. Internally, however, he was afire with ambition and the love of beauty. Even at that, he did not discover his poetic vocation until late, given the

John Keats (Library of Congress)

fact that he died at the age of twenty-five and spent the last eighteen months of his life in a tubercular decline. His career lasted from 1816, when Keats renounced the practice of medicine, to the fall of 1819, when he stopped working on his last great, though incomplete, poem, *The Fall of Hyperion*. One almost has to count the months, they are so few and precious. In fact, in a single month, May, 1819, he wrote four of his great odes—"Ode to a Nightingale," "Ode on a Grecian Urn," "Ode on Melancholy," and ironically, "Ode on Indolence."

This remarkable and courageous poet, the oldest of four children, was born to keepers of a London livery stable. His father was killed in a fall from a horse when John was eight; his mother died from tuberculosis when he was fourteen. His relatives arranged for schooling and apothecary training so that he might make a living, but the year he received his certificate, 1816, he began to devote himself to poetry. He wrote some good, but mostly bad, poetry, or at least poetry that does not add much to his reputation, until the summer of 1818. His reward was a brutal review of his major early work, *Endymion*, in a leading magazine of the day. Keats was criticized so severely that Percy Bysshe Shelley speculated that the review began Keats's physical decline.

Actually, the truth was much worse. Keats was nursing his brother Tom, who was dying from tuberculosis, when the reviews came out. Though he was too strong in character to be deeply affected by criticism, especially when he was a more astute critic of his poetry than his readers, a contagious illness could hardly be thwarted with character. In the fall of 1818, Keats also fell deeply in love with Fanny Brawne. They intended to marry, but his illness soon made their future together impossible. Sadly, the futility of their love and passion offered important inspiration to Keats's poetry. By late fall, 1819, in the same year that he had written "The Eve of St. Agnes," the odes, *Lamia*, and *The Fall of Hyperion*, his illness was severe enough to arouse his deep concern. In July, 1820, his influential volume *"Lamia," "Isabella," "The Eve of St. Agnes," and Other Poems* was published. Keats, however, now separated from Fanny, ill, in desperate need of money, and unable to achieve his major ambition of writing a "few fine Plays" in the manner of Shakespeare, was utterly despondent. He later spent a few months under the care of the Brawnes, but left England for Italy in September, 1820, in an attempt to save his life in the milder Italian weather. Joseph Severn, a dear friend, nursed him until his death in Rome in February, 1821.

Forever thinking aloud in his letters about the central concerns of existence, Keats once found purpose in this earthly life as "a vale of soul-making"; that is, although every human being perhaps contains a spark of divinity called soul, one does not attain an identity until that soul, through the medium of intelligence and emotions, experiences the circumstances of a lifetime. Thus the world has its use not as a vale of tears, but, more positively, as a vale of becoming through those tears. Keats's soul flourished as rapidly as his genius, and the poetry is evidence of both.

ANALYSIS

To love and to work are, psychologists say, the principal concerns of early adulthood. In John Keats's case, they became, as well, the dominant themes of his most important poetry. The work theme includes both the effort and the love of creating beauty and the immortality Keats longed for as recompense. Once, perhaps exaggerating, Keats wrote that "the mere yearning and fondness" he had "for the Beautiful" would keep him writing "even if [his] night's labours should be burnt every morning and no eye ever shine upon them." Not passing, however, was the tenacity of his ambition: "I would sooner fail than not to be among the greatest." Keats's quest for immortality takes several forms: It appears openly, especially in the sonnets and in "Ode on Indolence" and "Ode to Psyche" as the anxieties of ambition—being afforded the time, maintaining the will and energy, and, not least, determining the topic, or territory, for achievement. It includes a metamorphosis fantasy, whereby the young poet becomes deified or capable of immortal poetry through absorption of divinely granted knowledge. The ambition/work theme also takes a self-conscious turn in *The Fall of Hyperion*, questioning the value to a suffering humankind of the dreamer-poet's life and work.

The love theme explores dreams of heterosexual bliss, but it also moves into the appropriate relationships to be had with art and nature. The imagination is the ally of love's desires; reality and reason are their nemeses. In "The Eve of St. Agnes," a better lover, in *Lamia*, a better place, are dreams that dissipate in the light of reality and reason. "Ode to a Nightingale" attempts a flight from reality through identification with beautiful song rather than through dream, but the result is an intensification of distress. "Ode on Melancholy," "To Autumn," and "Ode on a Grecian Urn," however, suggest perspectives on the human condition, nature, and art that can be maintained with honesty and deeply valued without recourse to dream. One could say that Keats's love theme moves toward the understanding and acceptance of what is.

Concomitant with the maturation of theme and perspective is Keats's stylistic development. Like most poets, Keats went through phases of imitation during which he adapted the styles and themes he loved to his own work and ambitions. Leigh Hunt, Edmund Spenser, John Milton, and always Shakespeare provided inspiration, stylistic direction, and a community of tradition. Regardless of origin, the principal traits of Keats's style are these: a line very rich with sound pattern, as in "with brede/ of marble men and maidens overwrought," which also includes puns on "brede" ("breed") and "overwrought" (as "delicately formed on" and as "overly excited"); synesthetic imagery, or imagery that mingles the senses ("soft incense," "smoothest silence"); deeply empathic imagery ("warmed jewels," "all their limbs/ Locked up like veins of metal, crampt and screwed"); stationing or positioning of characters to represent their dramatic condition (so Saturn after losing his realm, "Upon the sodden ground/ His old right hand lay nerveless, listless, dead,/ Unsceptered; and his realmless eyes were closed"); the use of the past participle in epithets ("purple-stained mouth," "green-recessed woods"); and, of course, as with every great writer, that quality that one can only describe as *Je ne sais quoi*—I know not what—as in the lines from the sonnet "Bright Star": "The moving waters at their priest-like task/ Of pure ablution round earth's human shores."

Themes of ambition and accomplishment inform many of Keats's sonnets. The claiming of territory for achievement is the focus of "How Many Bards Gild the Lapses of Time," "On First Looking into Chapman's Homer," "Great Spirits Now on Earth Are Sojourning," and the great "Ode to Psyche." In "On First Looking into Chapman's Homer," for example, Keats recounts the discovery of Homer's "demesne." The extended metaphor of the sonnet is narrator-reader as traveler, poet as ruler, poem as place. The narrator, much-traveled "in the realms of gold," has heard that Homer rules over "one wide expanse," yet he has never "breath[ed] its pure serene." During the oration of Chapman's translation, however, he is as taken as an astronomer "When a new planet swims into his ken" or as an explorer, such as "stout Cortez," when "He stared at the Pacific—and all his men/ Looked at each other with a wild surmise—/ Silent, upon a peak in Darien." The complementary images of the distant planet and the immense ocean suggest both the distance the narrator is from Homeric achievement and its epic proportions. His reaction, though, represented through the response of Cortez, is heartening: while lesser beings look to each other for cues on what to think, how to react, the greater explorer stares at the challenge, with "eagle eyes," to measure the farthest reaches of this new standard for achievement.

Following the lead of his contemporary William Wordsworth, though with a completely original emphasis, Keats's territory for development and conquest became the interior world of mental landscape and its imaginings. Wordsworth had defined his territory in his "Prospectus" to *The Recluse* (1798) as "the Mind of Man—/ My haunt, and the main region of my song." Whereas Wordsworth believed that mind, "When wedded to this goodly universe/ In love and holy passion," could create a vision of a new heaven and a new earth, Keats initially sought to transcend reality, rather than to transform it, with the power of the imagination to dream. "Ode to Psyche" explores Keats's region and its goddess, who was conceived too late in antiquity for fervid belief. While Wordsworth asserts in "Lines Composed a Few Miles Above Tintern Abbey" (1798)

that "something far more deeply interfused" could sanctify our experience with nature, Keats locates days of "holy . . . haunted forest boughs" back in a past that precedes even his goddess of mind. The only region left for her worship must be imagined, interior. As priest, not to nature, but to mind, the poet says he will be Psyche's "choir" to "make delicious moan/ Upon the midnight hours," her voice, lute, pipe, incense, shrine, grove, oracle, her "heat/ Of pale-mouthed prophet" dreaming in "some untrodden region of [his] mind." In the "wide quietness" of this sacred microcosm, "branchèd thoughts, . . ./ Instead of pines shall murmur in the wind"; a "wreathed trellis of working brain" will dress "its rosy sanctuary"; the goddess's "soft delight" will be all that "shadowy thought can win." In keeping with the legend of Cupid as lover of Psyche, a casement will remain open at night "To let the warm Love in!" Keats's topic becomes, then, how the mind is stimulated by desire to create imagined worlds, or dreams, rather than, as in Wordsworth's case, how the mind is moved by love to re-create its perception of the real world.

HYPERION

Besides finding his territory for achievement, Keats struggled as well with the existential issues of the artist's life—developing the talent and maintaining the heart to live up to immense ambitions. It is to be doubted whether poets will ever be able to look to Shakespeare or to Milton as models without living in distress that deepens with every passing work. The "writing of a few fine Plays," meaning Shakespearean drama, remained Keats's greatest ambition to the end. Yet the achievement of *Paradise Lost* (1667, 1674) haunted him as well, and *Hyperion* was an attempt in its mold. Keats became more critical of Milton's achievement during the course of composing *Hyperion*, however, for it was, "though so fine in itself," a "curruption [sic] of our Language," too much in "the vein of art," rather than the "true voice of feeling." In fact, Keats gave up *Hyperion* because Milton's influence weighed so heavily that he could not distinguish the poem's excessively self-conscious artistry from its true beauty derived from accurate feeling.

Aesthetic considerations aside, a recurring theme in Keats's works of epic scope was the fantasy of poetic metamorphosis. The sonnet "On Sitting Down to Read King Lear Once Again" introduces the wish for transformation that will enable the poet to reach Shakespearean achievement. The metaphor is consumption and rebirth through fire, as adapted from the Egyptian legend of the phoenix bird, which was said to immolate itself on a burning pile of aromatic wood every five hundred years to engender a new phoenix from its ashes. The narrator-poet lays down his pen for a day so that he might "burn through" Shakespeare's "fierce dispute/ Betwixt damnation and impassion'd clay." To "burn through" must be read two ways in the light of the phoenix metaphor—as reading passionately through the work and as being burned through that reading. He prays to Shakespeare and the "clouds of Albion" not to let him "wander in a barren dream" when his long romance, *Endymion*, is concluded, but that "when . . . consumed in the fire" of reading *King Lear*, he may be given "new phoenix wings to fly at [his] desire." Out of the self-immolating achievement of reading will arise a poet better empowered to reach his quest.

The transformation theme of *Hyperion* exceeds the passionate wishfulness of "On Sitting Down to Read King Lear Once Again" by stressing the need for "knowledge enormous," as befits the poem's epic ambitions. *Hyperion* is a tale of succession in which the Titans are supplanted by the Olympians as the reigning monarchs of the universe, with focus upon Hyperion the sun god being replaced by Apollo, the new god of poetry and light. It has been suggested that *Hyperion* becomes Keats's allegory for his own relationship with his poetic contemporaries, especially Wordsworth. Keats had said that Wordsworth was Milton's superior in understanding, but this was not owing to "individual greatness of Mind" as much as to "the general and gregarious advance of intellect." *Hyperion* embodies this hypothesis of progress in its succession and transformation themes.

The poem opens with Saturn, who was the supreme god of the Titans, in a position of perfect stasis—the stationing referred to above—stupefied by his loss of power—"His old right hand lay nerveless, listless, dead,/ Unsceptered." Thea, the bewildered wife of the as-yet-undeposed Hyperion, visits to commiserate. She informs Saturn that the new gods are wholly incompe-

tent; Saturn's "sharp lightning in unpracticed hands/ Scorches and burns our once serene domain." The question is: Why, with the world running perfectly, was there a need for change? Saturn, an image of pomposity and egotism, perhaps inspired by Wordsworth's character, knows only of his personal loss:

> I have left
> My strong identity, my real self,
> Somewhere between the throne, and where I sit
> Here on this spot of earth.

"Thea, Thea! Thea!" he moans, "where is Saturn?" Meanwhile, Hyperion is pacing his domain in the region of the sun, wondering: "Saturn is fallen, am I too to fall?" In his anxiety he overreacts, attempting to wield more power than he ever possessed by making the sun rise early. "He might not," which dismays him tremendously. The first book of this unfinished three-book epic ends with Hyperion sailing to earth to be with his fallen peers.

At the same time, Saturn and Thea also reach those "regions of laborious breath" where the gods sit

> Dungeoned in opaque element, . . .
> Without a motion, save of their big hearts
> Heaving in pain, and horribly convulsed
> With . . . boiling gurge of pulse.

The Titans receive their deposed king with mixed response—some groan, some jump to their feet out of old respect, some wail, some weep. Saturn, being unable to satisfy their need to know why and how they have fallen, calls on Oceanus, the former god of the sea, for not only does he "Ponderest high and deep," but he also looks content! Oceanus then reveals a law of succession particularly appropriate for the early nineteenth century: "We fall," he says, "by course of Nature's law, not force/ Of thunder, or of Jove." Blinded by sheer supremacy, Saturn has not realized that, as he was not the first ruler, so he will not be the last. Nature's law is the law of beauty. Just as heaven and earth are more beautiful than chaos and darkness, and the Titans superior in shape and will to heaven and earth, so the new gods signal another significant advance in being; "a fresh perfection treads,/ A power more strong in beauty, born of us/ And fated to excel us," Oceanus explains, "as we pass/ In glory that old Darkness." In short, the eternal law is that "first in beauty should be first in might."

On Apollo's isle, the important transformation is about to begin. Apollo, as a good Keatsian poet, can make stars throb brighter when he empathizes with their glory in his poetry; yet he is inexplicably sad. Mnemosyne the muse seeks to assist her favorite child, who aches with ignorance. She emits what he needs to know and he flushes with

> Names, deeds, gray legends, dire events, rebellions,
> Majesties, sovran voices, agonies
> Creations and destroyings, all at once
> Pour[ing] into the wide hollows of [his] brain.

Apollo shouts, "knowledge enormous makes a God of me" and "wild commotions shook him, and made flush/ All the immortal fairness of his limbs." It is like a death pang, but it is the reverse, a dying into life and immortal power. The poem ends incomplete with Apollo shrieking, Mnemosyne arms in air, and the truncated line—"and lo! from all his limbs/ Celestial * * *." No one has been able to conjecture to the satisfaction of anyone else where the poem might have gone from there, although the result of Apollo's transformation seems inevitable. He would replace Hyperion, effortlessly, in this pre-Darwinian, pre-Freudian, universe where sons, like evolving species, acquire power over the earth without conscious competition with their fathers. As Oceanus indicates, the Titans are like the

> forest-trees, and our fair boughs
> Have bred forth . . .
> . . . eagles golden-feathered, who do tower
> Above us in their beauty, and must reign
> In right thereof.

However timorously, it would follow that Keats, bred on Spenser, Shakespeare, Milton, and Wordsworth, would have to live up to, if not exceed, their accomplishments.

This myth of progress would necessarily still require the superior poem to be written to support its prophetic validity. Keats knew that he needed deeper knowledge to surpass Wordsworth, but there was not much he could do about it. Though it was an attractive imagining, no god was likely to pour knowledge into the wide hollows of his brain. "I am . . . young writing at random—straining at particles of light in the midst of a great darkness," he wrote with characteristic honesty, "without knowing the bearing of any one assertion of any one opinion." Ironically, his dilemma brought out the strength his modern readers prize most highly, his courageous battling with, to use his favorite phrase of Wordsworth's, "the Burthen of the mystery." Caught in this impasse between noble ambition and youthful limitation, Keats's spirit understandably failed in weaker moments. His self-questioning was exacerbated when he reflected on the frailty of earthly achievement. Such is the torment in "On Seeing the Elgin Marbles," the Grecian ruins brought to England by Lord Elgin.

The narrator opens feeling "Like a sick eagle looking at the sky" in the face of the magnificent architectural ruins. Ironically, they are only the "shadow of a magnitude" that once was, an insubstantial image emphasizing how much has been lost rather than how much was once achieved. Human achievement wasted by time brings the narrator a "most dizzy pain" born of tension between body and soul over committing one's life to mortal achievement. In "Ode on Indolence," Keats enjoys a temporary respite from his demons— love, ambition, and poetry—in a state of torpor in which the body temporarily overpowers spirit. One morning the shadows come to him: love the "fair Maid"; "Ambition, pale of cheek,/ And ever watchful with fatiguèd eye"; and, "the demon Poesy." At first he burns to follow and aches for wings, but body prevails: even poetry "has not a joy—/ . . . so sweet as drowsy noons,/ And evenings steeped in honeyed indolence." The victory is transitory outside the poem; within it, a respite from ambition, love, and work is accepted.

THE FALL OF HYPERION

All these issues—the quest for immortality; the region of quest as dream; the transformation essential to achieve the quest; the spiritual weakness inevitably felt in the face of the challenge to be immortal; and, beyond all these, an altruism that seeks to distinguish between the relative value of humanitarian works and poetry in behalf of suffering humanity—are melded in Keats's second quest for epic achievement, *The Fall of Hyperion*. Following a brief introduction, the poem moves to a dream arbor reserved for the dreamer, who "venoms all his days,/ Bearing more woe than all his sins deserve." Remnants of a feast strew the ground; the narrator eats, partakes of a draft of cool juice and is transported through sleep and reawakening to a second dream kingdom. He finds himself this time amid remnants of an ancient religious festival. These dream regions represent Keats's aspirations to romance and epic respectively. Off in the west, he sees a huge image being ministered to by a woman. The image is Saturn; the minister is Moneta, Mnemosyne's surrogate. Moneta's face is curtained to conceal the immense knowledge her eyes can reveal to those worthy of receiving her immortal knowledge. She challenges the narrator to prove himself so worthy by climbing the altar stairs to immortality, or dying on the spot. Cold death begins to mount through his body; in numbness he strives to reach the lowest step—"Slow, heavy, deadly was my pace: the cold/ Grew stifling, suffocating, at the heart;/ And when I clasped my hands I felt them not." At the last moment, he is saved; his "iced feet" touch the lowest step and "life seemed/ To pour in at the toes." He learns that he has been saved because he has felt for the suffering of the world, though he is only a dreamer, without hope for himself or of value to others. True poets, Moneta tells him, pour balm on the world; dreamers increase the vexation of humankind.

Although in his letters Keats gave precedence to "fine doing" over "fine writing" as "the top thing in the world," the poem does not clarify whether humanitarians are above the poets of humankind, though both are unquestionably above the dreamers. The poem then moves to the metamorphosis that will make the dreamer a poet through the acquisition of knowledge. Moneta's bright-blanched face reveals the immortal sorrow she has endured for eons; her eyes hold the narrator enthralled with the promise of the "high tragedy" they contain, for their light and the sorrowful touch of her voice reveal deep knowledge. He begs to know, and she relates the fall of the Titans. The revelation begins the narrator's transformation: "Whereon there grew/ A power within me of enormous ken./ To see as a God sees." His vision opens with the "long awful time" Saturn sat motionless with Thea at his feet. In anguish, the narrator sits on a tree awaiting action, but the pain must be endured, for knowledge does not come easily or quickly, not even in a dream. The narrator curses his prolonged existence, praying that death release him from the vale, until Saturn moves to speak and the narrator witnesses scenes of the beginning of things from Hyperion. The poem continues but this version also ends incomplete, with Hyperion flaring to earth.

It is a poignant fact that Keats never believed that his poetry, his work, had come to anything, his epic endeavors left incomplete, no "few fine Plays" written. Writing to Fanny Brawne in February, 1820, he said that he had frequently regretted not producing one immortal work to make friends proud of his memory. Now frighteningly ill, the thought of this failure and his love for Fanny were the sole two thoughts of his long, anxious nights. Quoting Milton's lines on fame from "Lycidas," Keats wrote to her: "Now you divide with this (may *I* say it) 'last infirmity of noble minds' all my reflection."

Their love had earlier spawned his most important love poems, though he refused his created lovers the bliss of unreflecting love. It would seem unfortunate that dreams do not outlast the act of dreaming, but Keats's romances, "The Eve of St. Agnes" and *Lamia*, approach wish-fulfillment more critically. "The Eve of St. Agnes" permits a love dream to become flesh to provoke a dreamer's response to the contrast between dream and reality, though they are, in person, the same; *Lamia* permits a too-ordinary mortal to enter the love dream of a lovely immortal to elicit the likely response of the nondreamer to the experience of continuous, in this case, carnal, perfection. Together the poems serve to show that lovers cannot have it either way: Either reality will not be good enough for the dreamer, or the dream will not satisfy the extra-romantic desires of the nondreamer.

"THE EVE OF ST. AGNES"

"The Eve of St. Agnes" presents an array of wish-fulfilling mechanisms that seek to alter, control, or purify reality—praying, suffering, drinking, music, ritual, dance, and, at the center, dreaming. This poem with a medieval setting opens with a holy beadsman, "meagre, barefoot, wan," praying to the Virgin in the castle's icy chapel. Though he is fleetingly tempted to walk toward the music dancing down the hall from a party within, he turns to sit among "rough ashes" in recompense for his and others' sins. Among others praying this frigid night is Madeline, who follows the ritual of Saint Agnes: If a maiden refrains from eating, drinking, speaking, listening, looking anywhere, except up to heaven, and lies supine when she retires, she will be rewarded with the vision of her future husband. The irony of the patron saint of virgins inspiring a heterosexual vision is lost on the young girl, panting as she prays for all "the bliss to be before to-morrow morn." Meanwhile, Porphyro, her love, is in reality racing across the moors to worship his Madeline. As Madeline works on her dream, Porphyro will act on his desired reality—getting into Madeline's bedroom closet where "he might see her beauty unespied,/ And win perhaps that night a peerless bride."

The lovers' stratagems provide a weird culmination, though they move in complementary pattern. While Madeline is undergoing her ritualistic deprivations, Porphyro is gathering, through the assistance of her wily old nurse, Angela, a banquet of delights to fulfill deliciously her sensual needs; while she undresses, he gazes, of course, unseen; while she silently sleeps, he pipes in her ear "La belle dame sans merci." When she awakens to find the man of her dream at her side, however, the seemingly perfect solution is shattered. Madeline's dream of Porphyro was better than Porphyro and she tells him so: "How changed thou art! how pallid, chill, and drear!" She implores that he return to her as the dream. Porphyro arises, "Beyond a mortal man impassioned far/ At these voluptuous accents" and

> like a throbbing star
>
> . . . .
>
> Into her dream he melted, as the rose
> Blendeth its odor with the violet—
> Solution sweet.

The moon of Saint Agnes, which has been languishing throughout the poem, sets as Madeline loses her virginity. Madeline, however, comes out of the experience confused; she wanted a dream, not reality, and apparently she could not distinguish between them at their climax. Now bewildered, and feeling betrayed and vulnerable to abandonment, she chides Porphyro for taking advantage. He assures her of his undying devotion

and the two flee the sleeping castle into the storm, for he has prepared a home for her in the southern moors. The drunken revelers from the party lie benightmared; Angela soon dies "palsy-twitched"; and the loveless beadsman, after thousands of Aves, sleeps forever among his ashes.

A skeptical reading of the poem has found Porphyro a voyeur and (perhaps) a rapist, Madeline a silly conjurer whose machinations have backfired; an optimistic reading has Madeline and Porphyro ascending to heaven's bourn. The language, imagery, and structure allow both interpretations, which is the way of complex ironic honesty. The dream experience, for example, has two parts: the first when Madeline awakens to find Porphyro disappointingly imperfect; the second when the two blend into "solution sweet." It would seem that dream and reality have unified in the second part, but the first part is not thereby negated. Rather, the lovers are lost in sensory intensity, which, according to Keats, makes "all disagreeables evaporate." Whether the moment of intensity is worth the necessary conjuration before or the inevitable disillusionment afterward is a judgment on the nature of romance itself, down to this very day.

LAMIA

Lamia provides the nondreamer, Lycius, with much more than the two ordinary lovers of "The Eve of St. Agnes" are permitted; but the question is whether more is better. T. S. Eliot wrote that humankind cannot stand very much reality; Keats suggests in *Lamia* that neither can people bear very much dreaming. Lamia, as imagination incarnate, provides her lover Lycius with a realized dream of carnal perfection that extends continuously until he tires of her adoration. When Lamia, once bound in serpent form, was capable of sending her imagination abroad to mingle among the mortals of Corinth, she saw Lycius in a chariot race and fell in love. After being released from her serpent prison house by another immortal, Hermes, in an exchange of wish fulfillments, she assumes a glorious woman's body to attract Lycius. She is successful, but a series of compromises must be made to win him and satisfy his desires. Those compromises are the record of imagination's degeneration. Because Lycius is so overwhelmed by her beauty, he believes she must be immortal and loses his confidence. She "throws the goddess off" to encourage his masculinity. When he tires of the carnal pleasure she provides in the "purple-lined palace of sweet sin," she begs on her knees that he might preserve the privacy of their dream, for she knows of her vulnerability to reason. The sight of her begging brings out the sadist in Lycius, who "takes delight in her sorrows, soft and new." His passion grown cruel, Lamia plays the complementary masochist, burning, loving the tyranny. She grants his wish that they should be married before all of Corinth, and creates a feast and a vision of palatial splendor for the "gossip rout." The philosopher Apollonius, tutor to Lycius, crashes the party to destroy the dream with his "keen, cruel, perceant, stinging" eye. Apollonius is reason to Lamia's imagination, and in the confrontation between them, Lamia dissipates; Lycius the scholar-lover dies because he is incapable of balancing reason and imagination; and Apollonius is left with a Pyrrhic victory, for he has lost his pupil whom he intended to save.

Ironically, the loss of the dream, the dreamers, and the battle is not even tragic because not one was worthy of salvation. Lycius risks his dream so that his friends will look with admiration, but his friends choke over his good fortune; Lamia concedes to this foolish vanity; and Apollonius, the brilliant sophist, mistakes the whole situation, feeling that Lycius has become the prey of Lamia. More than saying that dreams cannot mix with reality, *Lamia* warns that imagination cannot be prostituted to the pleasure principle. Dreams are pure and sensitive constructs inspired by love, created for the psyche by the imagination. The eye of self-consciousness; participation with others, including loved ones; the dictates of forces less pure than love—all cause dissolution of the ephemeral dream.

"ODE TO A NIGHTINGALE"

"Ode to a Nightingale" leaves the medium of the dream for empathic identification with a natural being that seems to promise transcendence of the human condition. Again, a transcendence of self is fleetingly achieved, leaving the poet, *in propria persona*, more isolated and bewildered thereafter. He opens the poem having returned from identification with the bird's "happiness" that causes and permits it to sing "of summer in full-throated ease." The poet, however, is now drowsy and numb, so far has he sunk from that high experience of unself-conscious joy. He wishes for any wine, human or divine, that might effect a dissolution of consciousness and a return to the bird; for among men, "but to think is to be full of sorrow/ And leaden-eyed despairs." The transience of the physical splendor of beauty, of the psychological heights of love; the tragedy of early death, the indignity of aging to death; participation in human misery—all have thwarted any love or hope he might feel for the human condition.

In the fourth stanza, the poet seems to join the bird, but ambiguously. After exhorting either his imagination or the bird (or both) to fly "Away! away!" where he will reach it on "the viewless wings of Poesy," he seems to achieve the connection: "Already with thee! tender is the night." The eighth and final stanza supports the interpretation of his extended identification, for it has the poet being tolled back from the bird "to my sole self." Before the identification in stanza 4, however, he has qualified the power of those viewless wings to keep him in stable flight, for "the dull brain perplexes and retards." Consequently, throughout the poem, he is neither entirely with the bird, nor entirely in his metaphysical agony, but rather in a state of mixed or split consciousness that leads to the poem's concluding questions: "Was it vision, or a waking dream?/ Fled is that music:—Do I wake or sleep?" In the sixth stanza, for example, as he sits in his "embalmèd darkness" in the arbor, he says, "Darkling I listen; and, for many a time/ I have been half in love with easeful Death." Shortly, he seems to be lost in the ecstasy of the bird's song. Yet immediately he retracts, for common sense tells him that, if he were dead, his ears would be in vain, and "To thy high requiem" of the bird, he would "become a sod."

The seventh stanza distinguishes the immortality of the bird's song from the mortality of the poet, and for another passing moment he seems to experience identification as he slips into empathy with those through time who have also heard the immortal song, especially Ruth of the Old Testament: "Perhaps the self-same song that found a path/ Through the sad heart of Ruth, when, sick for home,/ She stood in tears amid the alien corn." This song that flows through time sparks both the poet's identification with it and his empathy for fellow beings. He is not as explicit as Walt Whitman would be in defining immortality as empathy for all beings and experiences of all times, but his revealed feeling for others is the eternal human counterpart to the song that eternally elicits the feeling. Still, the great divider between the bird and poet is the poet's self-consciousness. The bird, unaware of its individuality and coming death, is more a medium of the song of its species than a being in its own right. The poet withdraws completely in the final stanza to his "sole self." The imagination cannot support the identification with a dissimilar being for very long. The bird's song fades until it is metaphorically dead to the poet, "buried deep/ In the next valley glades." The stimulus for experience now fled, the poet recognizes the division he has undergone between empathy and identity, being in and out of self, with neither strain coming to resolution. The bewilderment of the conclusion reflects perfectly the imperfect resolution of his experience.

"ODE ON MELANCHOLY"

The "Ode on Melancholy" offers perhaps the most positive perspective possible to one who appreciates this tragedy of the human condition. Its psychology is a variant of Satan's from *Paradise Lost*: "Evil, be thou my good." The poet advises that when the "melancholy fit shall fall," as fall it must, one should not seek to escape with "poisonous wine," "nightshade," or other agents that would "drown the wakeful anguish of the soul," for that very anguish is the catalyst for more intensely valuing transient beauty, joy, and love. Even the anger of a loved one will reach a value transcending relationship, if one should "Emprison her soft hand, and let her rave,/ And feed deep, deep upon her peerless eyes." The glow fired by her passion, the beauty, joy, and pleasure that accompany love, all must dwindle, die, depart, sour; but if one holds an awareness of their end while indulging in their prime, the triumph of deep inclusive response will reward the sensitive soul with ultimate mortal value. It will be among Melancholy's "cloudy trophies hung," which is to say, the "sadness of her might" will hold him forever sensitive to the richness of transience.

"TO AUTUMN"

In like manner, "To Autumn" offers a perspective on nature in the ultimate richness of its condition. It has al-

ways been difficult for poets to look on nature without moralizing its landscape for human edification. The Romantic period especially sought its morality from nature and its processes. Keats, however, describes nature without pressing metaphor out of it; his goal is to offer it as worthy in itself so that one might love it for itself. If there are analogues between human nature and nature, they are not the subject, concern, or purpose of the poem. As several critics have noted, the stanzas move from the late growth of summer to the fulfillment of autumn to the harvested landscape; correspondingly, the imagery moves from tactile to visual to auditory in an ascension from the most grossly physical to the most nonphysical. The sun and the season are in league to load and bless the vines with fruit, and in a string of energetic infinitives, the push of life's fulfillment is represented: "To bend with apples the mossed cottage trees," to "fill all fruit with ripeness to the core," "To swell the gourd, and plump the hazel shells," "to set budding more,/ And still more, later flowers for the bees." An image of surfeited bees, who think summer will never end, their "clammy cells" are so "o'er-brimmed," concludes the first stanza.

Stanza 2 presents the personification of autumn "sitting careless on a granary floor"; sound asleep "Drowsed with the fume of poppies" in the fields; "by a cyder press, with patient look," watching the "last oozings hours by hours." The harvested stubble plains of stanza 3 provoke the poet's question, "Where are the songs of spring?" Even so, the question is raised more to dismiss it as irrelevant than to honor its inevitability. Autumn has its own music and the poem softly presents it: as the stubble plains are covered with the rosy hue of the dying day, the "small gnats mourn," "full-grown lambs loud bleat," "Hedge crickets sing," "with treble soft/ The red-breast whistles from a garden-croft," and "gathering swallows twitter in the skies." The suggestion of animate life singing unconsciously in its joy, while just as unconsciously readying for winter, signals the end of the natural year. Unlike Shelley, however, who in "Ode to the West Wind" looks through the fall and coming winter to spring as an analogue of rebirth for humankind, Keats allows not more than a suggestion of what is to follow, and that only because it belongs to the sound and action of the season. Autumn is accepted for itself, not as an image, sign, or omen of spiritual value. Ripeness is all.

"ODE ON A GRECIAN URN"

As "Ode on Melancholy" and "To Autumn" established perspectives on the human condition and nature, so "Ode on a Grecian Urn" establishes a relationship with art. This ode begins and ends by addressing the urn as object, but the subject-object duality is dissolved in the third of the five stanzas. The experiential movement of the poem is from ignorance through identification to understanding. The poet addresses the urn as a "bride of quietness," "still unravished" by passing generations. It is a "foster child of silence and slow time." Once the child of the artist and his time, the urn belongs not to eternity, for it is vulnerable to destruction, but to the timeless existence of what endures. It is a sylvan historian, containing a narrative relief of the beings and scenes of its surface. The poet asks questions of it as historian; what gods, music, bacchanalian frenzy it images. All is silent; but that is best, we learn, for "Heard melodies are sweet, but those unheard/ Are sweeter," free to become as flawless as imagination can wish. The second stanza finds the poet moving close, addressing the urn's individuals. The "Fair youth" who pipes the song so softly that only the spirit hears, the "Bold lover" who has neared the lips of his maiden, both arouse the poet-lover's empathy.

In the third stanza, the poet participates fully in the urn's existence as he inspires scenery and youths with imaginative fervor. The "happy, happy boughs! that cannot shed/ [their] leaves, nor ever bid the spring adieu"; the "happy melodist, unwearied,/ Forever piping songs forever new"; and, above all, "more happy love! more happy, happy love!/ Forever warm and still to be enjoyed,/ Forever panting, and forever young"— none of it can pass. Nature, art, and love remain in the glow of their promise. The love on the urn arouses a special contrast with "breathing human passion . . ./ That leaves a heart high-sorrowful and cloyed,/ A burning forehead, and a parching tongue." The fourth stanza begins to pull out of intense identification, with questions on the urn's religious scene: "Who are these coming to the sacrifice?" To what "green altar" does the priest lead his sacrificial heifer? What town do they come from that will be emptied of its inhabitants for-

ever? Stanza 5 again addresses the urn as object, but with increased understanding over stanza 1. She is now "Attic shape! Fair Attitude! with brede/ Of marble men and maidens overwrought." The bride, though unravished and wed to quietness, has her breed of beings, themselves passionately in pursuit of experience. She is a "silent form" that "dost tease us out of thought/ As doth eternity: Cold Pastoral!" If her silence provokes participation so that viewers lose self-consciousness in her form, then truly they are teased out of thought, as the poet was in stanza 3. Why, though, is she a "Cold Pastoral!"

Critics have taken this to be the poet's criticism of the urn in her relationship with those who contemplate her; perhaps it is best, however, that the urn remain cold, if she is to encourage and reward the viewers' empathy. Stanza 3 criticized human passion for its torrid intensity in contrast with the urn's image of love "Forever *warm* and [thus] still to be enjoyed." The urn remains a cold object until it is kindled by the viewers' passion. When the mortals of the present generation have been wasted by time, the urn will continue to exist for others, "a friend to man," to whom it (or the poet) has this to say: "Beauty is truth, truth beauty—that is all/ Ye know on earth, and all ye need to know."

Much has been written about these final lines of the "Ode on a Grecian Urn," and the technicalities of this famous problem for criticism must be at least briefly addressed. The difficulty is in determining who is saying what to whom; the issue has a mundane origin in punctuation. According to the text of the *Lamia* volume, the lines should be punctuated with the quotation marks enclosing only the beauty-truth statement: "'Beauty is truth, truth beauty'—that is all. . . ." If the lines are punctuated thus, the urn makes the beauty-truth statement, and the poet himself offers the evaluation of it, either to the urn, to the figures on the urn, or to the reader. Many scholars, however, see the matter differently; they would place the entire aphorism within quotations, based upon manuscript authority: "'Beauty is truth . . . need to know.'" With this punctuation, the urn is talking to man. Both choices lead to problematic interpretations. In the former case, it does not make much sense for the poet to speak to the urn or to its images about "all ye know on earth," as if there were someplace else for the urn to know something. There might be an afterlife where things can be known, but not for the urn. It would be odd for the poet to speak to the reader in that way, too. The inconsistency in tone would be especially awkward. Several lines earlier, he had joined his reader in saying to the urn: "Thou . . . dost tease us out of thought." To refer now to "us" as *ye*, as in "that is all/ Ye know on earth," is out of tone. On the other hand, the argument against the urn speaking the entire aphorism is directed against its sufficiency. It has been argued that human beings need to know a great deal more than "Beauty is truth, truth beauty," no matter how one tries to stretch the meanings of the terms to make them appear all-inclusive. There is no way to resolve this critical problem with confidence, though trying to think through it will provide an exercise in Keatsian specuation at its best.

To agree that the experience the poet undergoes is entirely satisfactory might be enough, though there is not critical unanimity about this, either. Lovers about to kiss, rather than kissing; trees in their springtime promise, rather than in fruition; a song that has to be imagined; a sacrifice still to be made, rather than offered— all can suggest experience short of perfection. Yet, like Keats's dreams that surpass reality, these figures are safely in their imaginative prime. The kiss, after all, may not be as sweet as anticipated; the fruit may be blighted; the song may be tiresome or soon grow so; the sacrifice may be unacceptable.

In fact, a reader comes to Keats's poetry as the poet himself came to the urn. Like all great art, Keats's poetry is evocative; it leads its readers' emotions and thoughts into and then out of its formal beauty to teach and delight. One can stand back and examine its formal perfection; one can ask questions of it about human nature and its desires for being and loving. Yet only through the experience of it can one learn what it has to teach; only after one goes through the empathy of Keats's narrator in stanza 3 can one speak with confidence of its meaning.

OTHER MAJOR WORKS

NONFICTION: *The Letters of John Keats, 1814-1821*, 1958 (2 volumes; Hyder Edward Rollins, editor).

MISCELLANEOUS: *Complete Works*, 1900-1901 (5 volumes; H. B. Forman, editor); *Complete Poems and Selected Letters of John Keats*, 2001.

BIBLIOGRAPHY

Bloom, Harold, ed. *John Keats*. Rev. ed. New York: Chelsea House, 2007. Contains essays on the poetry of Keats. Includes essays on the *Hyperion*s, "La Belle Dame sans Merci," and "The Eve of St. Agnes."

Christensen, Allan C. *The Challenge of Keats: Bicentenary Essays, 1795-1995*. Atlanta: Rodopi, 2000. Contributors to this volume reexamine some of the criticisms and exaltations of Keats to find a new analysis of his achievement. Delivers an appraisal of the historical and cultural contexts of Keats's work and an in-depth discussion of the influences and relationships between Keats and other poets.

Cox, Jeffrey N. *Poetry and Politics in the Cockney School: Keats, Shelley, Hunt, and Their Circle*. New York: Cambridge University Press, 1998. This monograph in the Cambridge Studies in Romanticism series examines the "second generation" of Romantics (those associated with Leigh Hunt) and challenges the common idea that the original Romantics, including Keats, were solitary figures, instead postulating the social nature of their work. An entire chapter, "John Keats, Coterie Poet," is devoted to Keats.

Hebron, Stephen. *John Keats*. New York: Oxford University Press, 2002. A biography of Keats that delves into his life and works.

McFarland, Thomas. *The Masks of Keats: The Endeavour of a Poet*. New York: Oxford University Press, 2000. The well-known scholar of Romantic literature surveys the essence of Keats.

Motion, Andrew. *Keats*. Chicago: University of Chicago Press, 1999. A biography that emphasizes Keats's politics as well as his poetry and personality. Motion won a Whitbread Prize for his biography of Philip Larkin, but *Keats* is his first dealing with the Romantic period. Highlighting the tough side of Keats's character, Motion puts to rest the image of Keats as little more than a sickly dreamer.

Robinson, Jeffrey C. *Reception and Poetics in Keats: My Ended Poet*. New York: St. Martin's Press,

1998. Readings of other poets' poems addressed to or about Keats, followed by an examination of Keats as a precursor to the visionary, open-form poetry of some of the modern age's experimental poets.

Siler, Jack. *Poetic Language and Political Engagement in the Poetry of Keats*. New York: Routledge, 2008. Applies Peter Burger's aesthetic categories in an interpretation of the poetry of Keats.

Sitterson, Joseph C., Jr. *Romantic Poems, Poets, and Narrators*. Kent, Ohio: Kent State University Press, 2000. An examination of narrative and point of view in the poetry of the Romantic poets William Wordsworth, Samuel Taylor Coleridge, William Blake, and Keats. Close readings of the major poems, including *Lamia*, from various critical perspectives. Includes bibliographical references and index.

Whale, John. *John Keats*. New York: Palgrave Macmillan, 2005. Examines the poetry and letters of Keats with an emphasis on gender and sexuality as well as love and desire.

Richard E. Matlak

HENRY KING

Born: Worminghall, Buckinghamshire, England;
    January 16, 1592 (baptized)
Died: Chichester, Sussex (now West Sussex),
    England; September 30, 1669

PRINCIPAL POETRY

Poems, Elegies, Paradoxes, and Sonnets, 1657
Poems and Psalms, 1843
Poems, 1965 (Margaret Crum, editor)

OTHER LITERARY FORMS

Henry King's significant literary remains other than poetry are his Latin verses and his surviving sermons, which span almost a half-century and provide an excellent record of his ministerial concerns. They have not, however, been collected.

ACHIEVEMENTS

A full assessment of Henry King's poetic stature has been slow to evolve. It appears that among his contemporaries, King was renowned less as a poet than as a churchman, as an eminent preacher and respected bishop of Chichester, and there is no evidence to suggest that King would have preferred to be viewed in any other way. It was only in the period during which for political reasons he was forcibly denied his bishopric that King, at a rather advanced age, published his poetry, and his output is relatively modest—by the reckoning of his most modern editor, Margaret Crum (*Poems*, 1965), only eighty-six poems, exclusive of his little-read and little-esteemed metrical transcriptions of the Psalms. Though the widespread appearance of a number of King's poems in various manuscripts both during his life and for several decades after his death would attest to some popularity, King's poetic achievement as a whole was left to rest in oblivion throughout the eighteenth and much of the nineteenth centuries.

Newly edited and republished in 1843, King's poems attracted some of the attention paid in the late nineteenth and early twentieth centuries to England's poetic antiquities and seventeenth century divines, and when King's good friend and religious associate John Donne came to be "rediscovered" and reacclaimed as one of England's great poets, King's poetic canon began to receive its first sustained critical study. Comparisons with Donne's verse have been inevitable and not wholly to King's advantage. King's personal association with Donne and a general resemblance between the cerebral and sometimes recondite imagery that King employs and the ingeniously involved "conceits" made famous by Donne have led to King's being labeled one of the lesser disciples of Donne's "school," or what Samuel Johnson dubbed the Metaphysical mode of poetry. That King's imagery is less "knotty" and philosophically adventurous than Donne's and that King's verse lacks the dramatic impact so conspicuous in Donne's have made it easy to confuse difference with inferiority and to view King not as a poet with his own concerns and idiom but simply as Donne's unsuccessful imitator. Moreover, the high percentage of his verse that is occasional, that is, that was prompted by and composed for a particular event, may suggest that his poetry lacks the spontaneity and originality the modern reader demands of poetry.

With closer scrutiny, however, has come the recognition not only that King may owe as much to Ben Jonson as he does to Donne, but also, and more important, that, far from being anyone's servile imitator, King studied and emulated the example of older contemporaries such as Donne and Jonson, while fashioning a poetic style through which he spoke with his own distinctive, ever thoughtful, frequently meditative, voice. In the evolution of poetic techniques and tastes in the seventeenth century, King's volume of published verse is a valuable document, encompassing as it does a period of forty-five years (1612-1657), and at once reflecting the poetic practices of the Elizabethan period and presaging those of the Restoration and neoclassicism. To the epigrammatic plainness and conciseness of Jonson's iambic pentameter and tetrameter rhymed couplets, King brings a refinement of expression that heralds the lapidary smoothness cultivated by practitioners of the rhymed couplet form in the middle and later decades of the century, and if some of King's images recall the kind of imagery brought into vogue by Donne near the beginning of the century, the polished trenchancy of some of King's more satiric and polemical pieces foreshadows the great heroic verse satires of John Dryden near the end of the century.

Above all, King's poetry is of immense interest as a lucid record of a poet's response to a most turbulent and critical period in English history, a period that brought fundamental changes to England's political, social, and religious institutions, and that challenged the perceptive poet to examine the purposes and value of his art. Like the actors Hamlet so esteemed, King's poems are "the abstract and brief chronicles of the time," and King himself a diligent poetic chronicler of the significant literary-historical events of his lifetime: the deaths of great poets, the births and deaths of princes and heirs to the throne, the travails and deaths of monarchs. To these subjects, King brought the unifying perspective of a poet nurtured in the Renaissance view of the cosmos and disposed to see in the events of the world—no matter how great or small—the workings of a divinely ordered universe. Thus, side by side in King's poetic "Kalendar" stand poems on affairs of state and affairs

of the heart; and in the upheavals of the politic body and the death of a king, as in personal disruptions and the death of a wife, King is prepared to read the hints of a greater disorder and the portents of a world with, in Donne's words, "all cohaerance gone." It is in its power to illuminate these correspondences between the "greater" and "lesser" worlds, and between the poet's private self and his public role, that the signal achievement of King's poetry lies.

BIOGRAPHY

Even a cursory examination of the poet's background will suffice to show that Henry King's art is very much a reflection of the life that produced it. Born in 1592, King was the eldest of five sons of John King, scion of an aristocratic family and renowned Anglican divine and eventual bishop of London. Since John King intended each of his sons to enter the ministry, Henry received an education befitting a man of learning. As a youngster, he attended the Westminster School, where Jonson, among many other notables, had studied, and where, as part of his classical training, he became practiced in the techniques of versification. After he left Westminster, he proceeded to Oxford, where he took his B.A. degree in 1611, his M.A. in 1614, and his B.D. and D.D. in 1625.

The oldest son of an influential clergyman, King came into contact as a child and young man with some of the most distinguished churchmen and courtiers of the time, among whom was Donne. Donne was a good friend of John King and, according to Donne's early biographer, Izaak Walton, grew to be no less fond of Henry. In 1616, as a young student of divinity, King was named to the clerical office of Prebendary of St. Paul's Church, where several years later, Donne would become dean. Their relationship remained close, and shortly before his death in 1631, Donne made King his legal executor. King's final service for Donne came in the form of the funeral elegy he composed, "Upon the Death of my ever Desired friend Dr. Donne Deane of Pauls."

From the example of his father, from his formal education, and, not improbably, from his acquaintance with Donne would emerge the intellectual cast of mind and the religious and political propensities that would permanently shape King's life, his career, and, no less so, his poetry. From all that is known of it, King's life appears to have been a genuinely religious one, predicated on a belief that God's ordinances were embodied in two temporal institutions: the Church and the Crown. Thus, religious orthodoxy and political conservatism were the mainstays of his thought and colored almost everything he wrote. No personal loss—not even the death of his young wife in 1624—could overturn his religious convictions, and although in his verse he acknowledges the pain of loss most frankly, as he does in the celebrated elegy he wrote for his wife, "The Exequy," his affirmation of the triumph of the immortal soul over death is nonetheless assured.

Nor did the tribulations of the civil tumult weaken his adherence to either Church or monarch, despite the considerable privations his loyalty cost him. In 1643, a victory of the forces representing the Parliamentary and Puritan factions over the Royalist army led to the ejection of King from the bishopric of Chichester to which he had been elevated only a year before. Stripped of almost all his property and personal papers, King existed on rather modest means—apparently not without some harassment—for the next seventeen years, until, with the Restoration of the monarchy in the person of Charles II, King returned to his church in Chichester. In the years immediately following his ejection, King wrote his most staunchly partisan and pro-Royalist verse, culminating in by far his longest and most passionate pieces, the elegies written just after the execution of Charles I in 1648, "A Deepe Groane, fetch'd at the Funerall of that incomparable and Glorious Monarch," and "An elegy upon the most Incomparable King Charls the First."

As strong as King's personal convictions were, his best verse is curiously undogmatic. The depth of King's learning and belief manifests itself not in a welter of information to be presented as absolute truth, but in a self-assured spirit of inquiry. If King shares anything with Donne, it is the pleasure he takes in exploring an idea through the play of language and metaphor. Like Donne, King seems often to be probing, discovering the essential likenesses in things that have ostensibly little in common, between an emotional state or religious point, for example, and the physical properties

of the universe. Thus, when King takes a position on an issue, he does not presume its correctness but demonstrates it carefully and seriously, yet imaginatively. It is the depth of both his convictions and intelligence that leaves the reader with the sense of having shared or worked through with the poet the experience he presents in his verse. King's poetic corpus may be relatively small, but a survey of his poems gives one the impression of having learned a good deal about their author precisely because King shows so much, not only of what he thinks, but how he thinks as well.

ANALYSIS

Like most of the technically accomplished poets of his era, Henry King was proficient in a wide range of forms and styles. However, the form that seems to have been most congenial to his poetic temper, and in which he wrote his most memorable pieces, was the elegy. Constituting a significant part of his rather compact volume, elegies punctuate King's entire poetic career, accounting for his first datable poem, "An Elegy Upon Prince Henryes Death" (1612), and his last, "An Elegy Upon my Best Friend L. K. C." (Lady Katherine Cholmondeley, 1657). Indeed—though it is unlikely that King himself would have coveted this distinction—the list of notable personages memorialized so eloquently in his funeral poems might well give King claim to the title of elegiac poet laureate of the seventeenth century.

ELEGIES

That what King calls the "Elegiack Knell" peals so resonantly in his verse is in part a measure of the occasional and public character much of his poetry assumed. For King, as for many of his contemporaries, private experience and public events were not inimical as poetic subjects, but complementary; in both lay hints of universal significance for the discerning poet to interpret and elucidate. Thus, a poem called forth by a particular "occasion"—the birth of a child or the death of a celebrated war hero—could serve as a vehicle for recording, for solemnizing, the significance of an event for both the poet and the world at large. No "occasion," though, fulfills this purpose more ably than that of death, for no event is at once so private and so public, and when, in turn, death deprives the world of an individual of special importance, a "Matchlesse" wife, or a "most Incomparable" monarch, for example, the scope of the loss is all the more conspicuous, its implications all the more universal. The "weeping verse" and funeral rites invoked in King's elegies are in part, then, a literary convention by means of which King affirms and reaffirms the common basis of experience that he as a poet shares with the public about whom and for whom he writes.

Still, to suggest that the elegiac strain in King's verse is in some sense "conventional" is not to impugn or belittle what it may reveal about the innermost concerns of King's poetic psyche. In her seminal discussion of "The Laureate Hearse" in *Studies in Seventeenth Century Poetic* (1950), Ruth Coons Wallerstein persuasively argued that the response to death in the elegiac poems of the seventeenth century crystallized the deepest spiritual and poetic preoccupations of the era, a thesis to which King's elegies prove no exception. For King, the "occasion" of death subjected the aspirations of life and art to their most intense scrutiny. In metaphoric terms, King conceived of death as a literary text, the "Killing rhetorick" and "Grammer" of which contained lessons about human experience that King seems never to have tired of reading.

Just how tireless this reading was is suggested not only by the sheer frequency with which elegiac themes appear in King's verse but also by their appearance in poems that are not explicitly funereal pieces and have little ostensibly to do with the issues of death and mourning. A conspicuous example is the poem King wrote in honor of the newly born Prince Charles, titled "By Occasion of the young Prince his happy birth. May 29-1630." No subject, one would think, has less to do with death than does birth, and, in an ethos in which the divine right of kings was a respected principle, no birth would be a source of as much public rejoicing as would that of a prince and heir apparent. Yet, at the outset of the poem, the reader finds King laboring, not to express his joy but to explain why he has hesitated to write, why at first, in fact, he "held it some Allegiance not to write." What has tempered King's celebrative mood is the recognition that everything that makes the arrival of Prince Charles a welcome event entails a sobering reflection about his father, King Charles. In the advent of

a child abides the hope of immortality, along, unfortunately, with the acknowledgment of mortality. Hence, even a newly born child is a memento mori, and in that book of harsh lessons by which King metaphorically conceived of death, children form "The Smiling Preface to our Funerall." The arrival of a prince, connoting as it does the hope of a smooth succession and continuity in the royal line, underscores the inevitability of the death of the monarch; to acclaim the birth of Charles the Prince is, King fears, to anticipate and make seem all the more imminent the passing away of Charles the King.

Such insights bring King to something of a dilemma. As a loyal Englishman, he would like to use his poetic gifts to frame a compliment to the Crown. Yet his poetic vision enables, obliges, him to see the infant prince both for what he is and for what he represents. The apprehension of mortality and the rhetoric of death force King to see and say things inappropriate to the ostensibly complimentary occasion; but to excise his elegiac concerns, King implies, is to render his compliment hollow and poetically false.

King's solution, both in this poem and in many others, is to reconcile his elegiac presentiments with his religious convictions and to turn the occasion of paying a compliment into an opportunity for teaching a salutary lesson. True, the birth of an heir is a tacit intimation of mortality, but mortality itself is but a milestone on the soul's journey to immortality, and but the last instance of finitude before all time is transformed into the infinitude of life everlasting. To pretend to ignore death, to be obsessed with prolonging life on earth, is to repudiate a fundamental article of faith: "And wee in vaine were Christians, should wee/ In this world dreame of Perpetuitye." Rather deftly, King pays the royal father the ultimate compliment of eschewing flattery and appealing, instead, to wisdom and Christian humility to accept a wholesome truth: "Decay is Nature's Kalendar; nor can/ It hurt the King to think He is a Man." With these reflections articulated, and with the fullest implications of the Prince's birth understood, King can with more genuine enthusiasm acclaim the happy event and even look forward to that time when young Charles will "lead Succession's goulden Teame" and ascend to his father's throne.

"THE EXEQUY"

The poem on "the young Prince" exemplifies the pattern of argumentation that King pursues in much of his verse, wherein, with varying degrees of success and conviction, he strives to achieve a synthesis in which elegiac sadness and pessimism over the transience of this world is answered by religious belief in the permanence of the next. Nowhere, perhaps, is this religious elegiac vision more moving and more triumphant than in King's most frequently anthologized piece, the poem he wrote on the death of his young wife, Anne, "The Exequy."

What at first seems peculiar about this poem, which deals with so emotionally charged an experience, and which ultimately manages to be so moving, is that it at first appears so distanced, so oddly impersonal. Little is learned about Anne herself, and one wonders at first whether King is merely making use of the death of his wife as a pretext for a philosophical discourse. One has only to read a little way into the poem to discover that it is delivered as a meditation in which Anne is a rather abstracted presence. The title of the poem may promise that it is addressed "*To* his Matchlesse never to be forgotten Freind" [italics added], but the poem opens with the poet apostrophizing a burial monument, "Thou Shrine of my Dead Saint." To the extent that Anne herself is addressed at all within the first ten lines of the piece, it is not as a person but as "Deare Losse." It is this "Losse" that consumes all the poet's emotional energy, but that energy has been subsumed in study, in a commitment to do nothing but "meditate" on the loss itself. It is the "Deare Losse" that forms "the Book,/ The Library whereon I took."

Although the poet at first seems to be distanced from Anne, it is precisely this distancing that establishes the emotional tension and intensity within the poem. The poet must turn to the study of his loss because that is all that is left him; all that remains of Anne, after all, is the "Lov'd Clay" lying in the tomb. In the discipline of meditation, then, the poet finds a method of coping with death and a means by which he may explore the psychology of grief and "compute the weary howres/ With Sighes dissolved into Showres."

Initially, at least, meditation enables the poet not so much to allay his grief as to define its scope. The emotional void left by the death of Anne makes existence as a whole a desolation because it was Anne who gave existence its meaning. Here the influence of Donne on King becomes readily apparent, for in attempting to define the impact of his wife's loss, King employs the kind of imagery used by Donne to illustrate the experiences of separation and loss in poems such as "A Valediction: Forbidding Mourning" and "A Nocturnal upon Saint Lucy's Day." The extinction of Anne's life is like the extinction of the sun, since it was she who brought "Light and Motion" to the poet's now darkened "Hemispheare." Yet this is a "straunge Ecclipse," one "As ne're was read in Almanake," because it was not caused by the obstruction of the moon but by the earth itself, which in reclaiming Anne's "Lov'd Clay" has "interposed" itself between the poet and his sun.

What makes this "Ecclipse" especially "straunge" is not merely its provenance but its duration. Unlike a "normal" solar eclipse, this one is not transitory, but will endure as long as the earth endures. The eclipse of the poet's world is not an extraordinary phenomenon but a systemic and all too ordinary condition. With the recognition of this fact comes the realization of the immensity of the poet's loss. In depriving the poet of his wife, mortality has made earthly existence at once a void and a barrier to their reunion that can only be surmounted by the extinction of existence itself.

Still, implanted in the depths of King's sorrow are the very seeds of his remission, although King's recognition and articulation of this truth proceed as much from the promptings of his faith as from the workings of his intellect. If by dying, Anne has succumbed to the mortality inherent in her earthly nature, it follows that all things earthly, including the earth itself, must inevitably succumb as well. Thus, the onerous sentence of King's grief bears with it the promise of a terminus, and King can look forward to that apocalyptic "Day" when a "fierce Feaver must calcine/ The Body of this World," even as a more localized fever has already consumed the body of Anne, "My Little World."

The expectation of the world's dissolution would not be much of a source of comfort to the poet were it not coupled with his unqualified belief in a universal Resurrection. On this premise turns the argument—and the mood—of the latter parts of the poem. Death becomes, then, less a boundless condition than a transitional event: The death of the body brings about the liberation of the soul, while the death of earthly existence is the purificatory and regenerative mechanism by which "our Bodyes shall aspire/ To our Soules blisse." So it is that no hint of equivocation mars the confidence with which the poet envisions that endless day on which "wee shall rise,/ And view our selves with cleerer eyes/ In that calme Region, where no Night/ Can hide us from each other's sight." Moreover, that the poet begins to use pronouns such as "wee" and "us" suggests that the reunion with Anne to be attained in the general Resurrection is already under way, and that the gulf created by death that had so tormented the poet at the outset of the piece has already been bridged by the poetic process of meditation. Death becomes less an insuperable foe than a functionary accountable to a higher power. Anne's tomb is less a devourer of her flesh than a temporary custodian whose duty will be to return on the day of the Resurrection an accurate "reck'ning" of "Each Grane and Atome of this Dust." Nothing has been, or will be, lost.

At the same time, it is a measure of the complexity and artistry of King's vision that no matter how assured his faith leads him to be about the ultimate implications of death, its immediate reality remains no less horrid. Although King's quickened religious insight may enable him to think of Anne now, not as someone gone forever, but as his temporarily sleeping bride, there is something chillingly reminiscent of Juliet's entombment in the Capulets' charnel house in the picture of King's young wife, enfolded with "Black Curtaines," lying on "Thy cold bed/ Never to be disquieted." Death seems no less importunate, no less an interloper, and when the poet poignantly takes "My last Goodnight" he forcibly acknowledges that he is still very much wedded to the things of this world, "to that Dust/ It so much loves." Indeed, the poet's resounding triumph in the conclusion of the poem takes the form of a paradox: The more fully he affirms his mortality, the more clearly he beholds the date of his transcendence, the very rapidity with which mortality encroaches setting the pace by which immortality approaches. It is this image of mortality fused with immortality in one relentless motion that resonates in the cadences of King's

parting assurance to his wife that "My pulse, like a soft Drum/ Beates my Approach, Tells Thee I come," while the resolute stroke of eight monosyllabic words underscores the poet's final promise that "I shall at last sitt downe by Thee."

"SIC VITA"

Elegiac sadness for the human condition merges with religious conviction in King's poem to his wife to produce an illusion of poise and inner assurance that make the poem one of the great elegies of the language and, not surprisingly, his most highly esteemed work. In other poems, King's vision is more darkly elegiac, his remorse over the fragility of human existence less evenly tempered by the consolation of faith. One striking instance is the twelve-line epigram titled "Sic Vita," a poem very much in the memento mori tradition, the very compression and conciseness of which give dramatic immediacy to its familiarly elegiac theme that existence is transitory and all too peremptorily brief. In the first six lines of the poem, King presents a series of six exquisite and ephemeral natural phenomena whose exquisiteness, in fact, arises from their ephemeral character and from the teasing hope they engender that somehow they can be preserved, frozen in time. The space is very small, but King manages to select examples that are representative of the diverse operations of the natural world, both great and small: a falling star, a soaring eagle, the fecundity of spring, a gust of wind on the sea, some dewdrops, some bubbles on the surface of water. All these are introduced as terms of one extended simile, and in the seventh and eighth lines one discovers that what draws them together, besides their ephemeral attractiveness, is that they are emblems of humanity. Humankind is but one more image of transience, and, like the other entities of nature, people too have a life and "Light" that are "borrow'd" and will be "streight Call'd in, and Pay'd to Night."

If it took only one eight-line sentence to establish the common bond between humanity and the other elements of its universe, it takes only one four-line sentence to make the implications of this bond briskly and brusquely clear. Swept up in the annihilative rush of time, mortality, and King's swiftly paced iambic tetrameter verse are all the things of nature, including humanity and, worse, all traces of humanity's life: "The Dew dryes up: The Starr is shott:/ The Flight is past:/ And Man Forgott."

For King, the brevity of existence is, however, often only a catalyst for other, even more somber, ruminations about the human condition. Indeed, the importunity of death would hold little but terror for King did he not see it as the culmination of the sorrows that afflict and waste a person's life. "What is th' Existence of Man's Life?" King asks rhetorically at the outset of "The Dirge," only to answer the question immediately: "open Warr, or Slumber'd Strife," from which "Death's cold hand" alone provides a reprieve. What makes this "strife" most pernicious is that it arises from the disorders that Original Sin has wrought on the human soul and psyche, effectively making humans their own implacable foes, in whom "each loud Passion of the Mind/ Is like a furious gust of Wind."

"THE DIRGE"

It is this perception that makes King, at his most pessimistic, a satirist in the vein of the writer of Ecclesiastes, a scourge of vanity, of the delusions and emptiness that are the inveterate accessories of one's existence. Such is certainly the stance King assumes in "The Dirge," in which he concludes by employing one of William Shakespeare's recurrent metaphors, likening humanity's existence to a play, "a weary Enterlude," the acts of which are consumed by people's "vaine Hope and vary'd Feares," and the only fitting "Epilogue" to which is "Death." Even more stridently contemptuous is the assessment of humanity and its aspirations that King offers in "An Elegy Occasioned by Sicknesse." Here illness becomes a meditative device to turn one's attention inward and "Make Man into his proper Opticks look,/ And so become the Student and the Book." What this self-inventory reveals is rather deflating. From conception and birth, humanity is ordained to emerge as little else but "complicated Sin." At the height of people's pretensions, they are merely "Poore walking Clay," fated to be "a short-liv'd Vapour upward wrought,/ And by Corruption unto nothing brought."

In the face of these dour appraisals of the worth of humankind, the value and role that King allots in his poetry to meditation and the self-scrutiny entailed in

meditation become clear. Central to King's excoriation of human vanity is the premise that people's intellect is a casualty of their spiritual defects, that vanity prevents people, for all their apparent intellectual attainments, from knowing themselves and what conduces to their own good. Thus, the meditative strain so recurrent in King's poems has, in part, a hortatory function and invites people to lay aside the studies of the external world with which they are so preoccupied in order to study themselves, their "proper Opticks," the better to confront and dispel, if possible, the mists impairing their vision.

"THE LABYRINTH"

Such is the challenge posed in "The Labyrinth," which opens with the proposition that "Life is a crooked Labyrinth" in which humanity is "dayly lost" and then proceeds to draw the reader into a scrutiny of the conundrums that lie at the heart of human conduct. How can it be that humans can know what is good, resolve to do the good, and then lapse and relapse into wrong, ever erring, never extricating themselves from the labyrinth their will has created? "Why is the clearest and best judging Mind/ In her own Ill's prevention dark and blind?" What contrition can possibly be effective when the mind has become so practiced at begging forgiveness while rationalizing the commission of sin, when, like the usurper King Claudius in *Hamlet, Prince of Denmark* (pr. c. 1600-1601), the sinner cannot in good conscience seek to undo what he has done since he knows that he would do it again? The more thoughtfully readers ponder these questions, the more surely they are drawn into the labyrinth the poet is describing, for in posing these questions the poet has been appealing to the readers' intellects; and the more the readers acknowledge the intellectual validity of the questions, the more deeply they identify themselves as intellectuals and implicate themselves in the cycle of rationalization and recrimination that the labyrinth comprises.

Are there answers to these questions? None, King implies, that can be provided by human intellection, even as there are no strategies the intellect can devise on its own for coping with the experience of death. The intellect is part of the problem, and unaided, it cannot provide a solution to what King calls "this home-bred tyranny." Instead, King can only abjure his intellectual pretensions and appeal to God for the insight that the human mind lacks. With a nod to Ezekiel (11:19), King calls on God in his redemptive power to soften humankind's heart and "imprint" on the human "breast of flint" the marks of true contrition, for it is only through the genuine conversion of the heart that the mists clouding the mind will be dispersed. For King, as for his contemporaries, there was no inherent dichotomy between the mind and the emotions, the affections of the mind following directly from the disposition of the heart and soul. Thus, God is beseeched to provide not merely emotional reassurance but intellectual clarity, or "thy Grace's Clew," with which King, like some latter-day, Christianized Theseus, may aspire to thread his way through "this Labyrinth of Sinne/ My wild Affects and Actions wander in."

The skepticism with which King regards the powers of the human intellect very much affects the attitude he brings to the intellectual activity of writing poetry. If the intellect is impaired by its own frail mortality, then the verse that the intellect produces will be similarly inept, incapable of dealing satisfactorily with the experiences and paradoxes of the human condition. Indeed, in depicting the phenomenon of death, for example, as a text, as a book with its own lessons to impart, King explicitly calls attention to the deficiencies of his own text, his verse. Thus, in his early "Elegy Upon Prince Henrye's Death," King not only laments the passing of the young prince, but also wonders how his own verse can ever do justice to the occasion or presume to vie in eloquence with the succinctly "Killing rhetorick" of death, which manages to embody "Woe's superlative" in only two words: "Henry's dead." Again and again, King's poetry runs a poor second either to the experience to which it responds or to the emotion it is intended to express. "And think not," he hastens to assure his deceased friend in "The Departure: An Elegy," that "I only mourne in Poetry and Ink." Rather, the "melancholy Plummets" of his pen "sink/ So lowe, they dive where th'hid Affections sitt." So impatient does King ultimately profess to become with the inadequacy of his verse that in his last datable poem, "An Elegy Upon my Best Friend, L. K. C.," King announces his "long Farewell" from his poetry, "That Art, where with our Crosses we beguile/ And make them in Harmonious numbers smile"—a valediction in which King strives for that elusive fusion of art and life by burying his verse with his friend.

It is not to impugn King's sincerity to suggest that his insistence on the deficiencies of his poetry owes a good deal to convention. As an apt student of poetry and poetic tradition, King would have been quite aware of the innumerable writers of and before his time who displayed their eloquence by lamenting their lack of eloquence, who emblazoned the depth of their passion or sense of loss by artfully expressing their inability to express their passion or loss. With King, however, the convention acquires something of the force of a personal signature. Loath to divorce his poetic craft for his life, he was even less willing to excise his verse from the principles and beliefs that gave his life its purpose. Convinced of the contingency and vulnerability of human existence, King could not consider his poetic exercises as anything but reflections of his own limitations. King would not have minded very much the gentle irony that the very powers he denigrated in his verse helped to ensure the continued survival and appeal of that verse.

BIBLIOGRAPHY

Berman, Ronald. *Henry King and the Seventeenth Century*. London: Chatto & Windus, 1964. King is presented in this study as embodying some of the paradoxes of the seventeenth century. It includes a biography and an in-depth look at King's world, his political and social philosophies, as well as an analysis of his poetry. Examples are used extensively, and notes and bibliography follow the text.

Crum, Margaret, ed. *The Poems of Henry King*. Oxford, England: Clarendon Press, 1965. The introduction to this collection provides a biography, a short discussion of the poems, and notes on the original texts. The poems themselves are followed by notes and appendixes.

Keeble, N. H. Review of *The Sermons of Henry King (1592-1669), Bishop of Chichester*, edited by Mary Hobbs. *Notes and Queries* 40, no. 4 (December, 1993): 550. Keeble provides some biographical and historical information in an assessment of Hobbs's collection of King's sermons.

Tuve, Rosamund. *Elizabethan and Metaphysical Imagery*. Chicago: University of Chicago Press, 1947. This is a study of the imagery employed by the Elizabethan and Metaphysical poets of the English Renaissance. The analysis stresses the intellectual, sensual, and charming aspects of the imagery. King and other poets as recent as William Butler Yeats are covered in the discussion.

Wallace, John M., ed. *The Golden and the Brazen World: Papers in Literature and History, 1650-1800*. Berkeley: University of California Press, 1985. This collection contains an essay by Cleanth Brooks on King's "The Exequy" and "The Legacy" titled "Need Clio Quarrel with Her Sister Muses? The Claims of Literature and History" (pp. 1-15). The essayist takes a biographical approach and gives a close reading of "The Exequy." He discusses seventeenth century theological beliefs, burial customs, and King's life and literary career to illuminate the poem in the light of its historical roots.

Thomas Moisan

THOMAS KINSELLA

Born: Dublin, Ireland; May 4, 1928

PRINCIPAL POETRY

The Starlit Eye, 1952
Three Legendary Sonnets, 1952
The Death of a Queen, 1956
Poems, 1956
Another September, 1958, 1962
Moralities, 1960
Poems and Translations, 1961
Downstream, 1962
Six Irish Poets, 1962
Wormwood, 1966
Nightwalker, and Other Poems, 1968
Poems, 1968 (with Douglas Livingstone and Anne Sexton)
Tear, 1969

Butcher's Dozen, 1972
Finistere, 1972
Notes from the Land of the Dead, and Other Poems, 1972
A Selected Life, 1972
The Good Fight: A Poem for the Tenth Anniversary of the Death of John F. Kennedy, 1973
New Poems, 1973
Selected Poems, 1956-1968, 1973
Vertical Man, 1973
One, 1974
A Technical Supplement, 1976
The Messenger, 1978
Song of the Night, and Other Poems, 1978
Fifteen Dead, 1979
One, and Other Poems, 1979
Peppercanister Poems, 1972-1978, 1979
Poems, 1956-1973, 1979
One Fond Embrace, 1981, 1988
Her Vertical Smile, 1985
Songs of the Psyche, 1985
St. Catherine's Clock, 1987
Blood and Family, 1988
Poems from Centre City, 1990
Madonna, and Other Poems, 1991
Open Court, 1991
From Centre City, 1994
Collected Poems, 1956-1994, 1996
The Pen Shop, 1997
The Familiar, 1999
Godhead, 1999
Citizen of the World, 2000
Littlebody, 2000
Collected Poems, 1956-2001, 2001, 2006
Belief and Unbelief, 2007
Man of War, 2007
Selected Poems, Poems 1956-2006, 2007

OTHER LITERARY FORMS

In addition to his own poetry, Thomas Kinsella (kihn-SEH-luh) has published a large body of verse translated from the Irish. This work is most notably embodied in *The Táin* (1969), his celebrated version of the eighth century Irish epic *Táin bó Cuailnge*, and in *An Duanaire, 1600-1900: Poems of the Dispossessed*

(1981; with Sean O Tuama). ("An duanaire," literally translated, means "the poemery.") An appreciation of the significance that Kinsella attaches to the Irish-language tradition of Irish poetry and the magnitude of his commitment to it is crucial to an overall sense of his achievement. His introduction to *The New Oxford Book of Irish Verse* (1986), which he edited, provides convenient access to Kinsella's thinking on the subject of the Irish-language poetic tradition. The attitude expressed in that introduction recapitulates earlier statements contained in the poet's small but influential body of cultural criticism.

ACHIEVEMENTS

Thomas Kinsella is one of the most important Irish poets to emerge since the end of World War II. By means of a restlessly experimental formal and aesthetic sense, broadly conceived themes, and relentless self-scrutiny and self-exposure, his work has raised him above his contemporaries in the Republic of Ireland and placed him in the forefront of his generation of poets writing in English.

In the context of contemporary Irish poetry, his work has an unwonted syntactical density, complexity of imagery, and dramatic intensity. Since modern Irish poetry in English is noted more for lyric grace than for tough-minded plumbing of existential depths, Kinsella's poetry gains in importance because of its originality. Its essential inimitableness, in turn, commands respect by virtue of the tenacity of vision it embodies.

In recognition of his uniqueness and commitment, Kinsella has received widespread critical acclaim and has won the Guinness Poetry Award in 1958 for *Another September* and the Irish Arts Council Triennial Book Award in 1961 for *Poems and Translations*. He is a four-time winner of the Denis Devlin Memorial Award, in 1964-1966, 1967-1969, 1988, and 1994. He has also held two Guggenheim Fellowships. In 1983, along with Sean O Tuama, he received the American Book Award from the Before Columbus Foundation.

Thomas Kinsella (AP/Wide World Photos)

In 2007, he was awarded the rarely given Freedom of the City of Dublin. He has received honorary doctorates from the University of Turin and the National University of Ireland.

BIOGRAPHY

Thomas Kinsella was born in Dublin on May 4, 1928. His family background is typical of the vast majority of native Dubliners—Catholic in religious affiliation, left-tending Nationalist in politics and lower-middle class in social standing, the kind of background detailed with such loving despair by one of Kinsella's favorite authors, James Joyce, in the stories of *Dubliners* (1914). Kinsella's father worked at the Guinness brewery and was active in labor union matters.

Educated at local day schools, Kinsella received a scholarship to attend University College, Dublin, to read for a science degree. Before graduation, however, he left to become a member of the Irish civil service, in which he had a successful career as a bureaucrat, rising to the rank of assistant principal officer in the Department of Finance.

Kinsella left the civil service in 1965 to become artist-in-residence at Southern Illinois University. In 1970, he was appointed to a professorship of English at Temple University, a position he retained until 1990. In the end, he taught for one semester a year at Temple, spending the rest of the year in Dublin running the Peppercanister Press.

Founded in 1972, Peppercanister is the poet's private press. It was established, in the poet's own words, "with the purpose of issuing occasional special items." As well as being a notable addition to the illustrious private and small tradition of Irish publishing, Peppercanister has allowed Kinsella to produce long poems on single themes and to carry out fascinating exercises in the area of the poetic sequence. It has also allowed him to use it as a work in progress and to avoid using literary magazines to bring out new poems. He also has used it for critical and cultural statements in prose.

In 1976, Kinsella founded Temple University's School of Irish Tradition in Dublin, enabling him to continue dividing his time between the United States and Ireland. Since his retirement from teaching in 1990, he has continued his direction of Peppercanister Press, as well as the Dolmen and Cuala Presses, both in Dublin. He established a pattern of living part of the year in County Wicklow and the rest in Philadelphia.

ANALYSIS

From the outset of his career, Thomas Kinsella has shown an unremitting preoccupation with large themes. Love, death, time, and various ancillary imponderables are persistently at the forefront of Kinsella's poetic activity. Such concerns beset all poets, no doubt, as well as all thinking beings. More often than not, Kinsella grapples with these overwhelming subjects without the alleviating disguise of metaphor, and he confronts them without the consolations of philosophy. Their reality consists of the profundity of the poet's human—and hence, frequently baffled and outraged—experience of them.

Even in Kinsella's early love lyrics, it is impossible for the poet merely to celebrate the emotion. He cannot view his subject without being aware of its problematical character—its temporariness and changeability. Thus, to identify Kinsella's themes, while initially informative, may ultimately be misleading. It seems more illuminating to consider his preoccupations, which a reader may label time or death, as zones of the poet's psychic experience, and to recognize that a Kinsella poem is, typically, an anatomy of psychic experience, a rhetorical reexperiencing, rather than a particularly conclusive recounting. Such a view would seem to be borne out by the forms that his poems typically assume. Their fractured look and inconsistent verse patterns (unavoidably but not imitatively reproducing the prosody of T. S. Eliot and Ezra Pound) suggest an idea still developing. As Kinsella writes in "Worker in Mirror, at His Bench": "No, it has no practical application./ I am simply trying to understand something/ —states of peace nursed out of wreckage./ The peace of fullness, not emptiness."

An immediate implication of this approach to poetry is that it owes little or nothing to the poet's Irish heritage. His concerns are common to all humanity, and while the conspicuous modernism of his technique has, in point of historical fact, some Irish avatars (the unjustly neglected Denis Devlin comes to mind), these are of less significance for a sense of Kinsella's achievement and development than the manner in which he has availed himself of the whole canon of Anglo-American poetry. In fact, an interesting case could be made for Kinsella's poetry being an adventitious, promiscuous coalescence of the preoccupations of poets since the dawn of Romanticism. Such a case might well produce the judgment that one of the bases for Kinsella's general importance to the history of poetry in the postwar period is that his verse is a sustained attempt to inaugurate a post-Romantic poetic that would neither merely debunk its predecessor's fatal charms (as perhaps Eliot desired to do) nor provide them with a new repertoire of gestures and disguises (which seems to have been Pound's project). The effect of this judgment would be to place Kinsella in the company of another great Irish anti-Romantic of twentieth century literature, Samuel Beckett.

A more far-reaching implication of Kinsella's technique is that it provides direct access to the metaphysical core of those preoccupations. Often the access is brutally direct. Throughout, Kinsella repeats the refrain articulated in the opening section of "Nightwalker" (from *Nightwalker, and Other Poems*): "I only know things seem and are not good." This line strikes a number of characteristic Kinsella notes. Its unrelieved, declarative immediacy is a feature that becomes increasingly pronounced as his verse matures. There is a sense of the unfitness of things, of evil, of times being out of joint. The speaker is strikingly committed to his subjective view. The line contains a representative Kinsella ambiguity, depending on whether the reader pauses heavily after "seem." Is "are not good" entailed by, or opposed to, "seem"? Readers familiar with Kinsella will hear the line announce a telltale air of threat and of brooding introspection. There is also, perhaps, a faint suggestion of meditative quest in "Nightwalker," which occurs in other important Kinsella poems from the 1960's (such as "Baggot Street Deserta" from *Another September*, and "A Country Walk" and "Downstream" from *Downstream*). Such an undertaking, however, is hardly conceived in hope and does not seem to be a quest for which the persona freely and gladly volunteers. Rather, it seems a condition into which he has been haplessly born.

It is not difficult to understand Kinsella's confession that his vision of human existence is that of "an ordeal." In fact, given the prevalence in his verse of ignorance, darkness, death, and the unnervingly unpredictable tidal movements of the unconscious—all frequently presented by means of apocalyptic imagery—there is a strong indication that the poet is doing little more than indulging his idea of "ordeal," despite the prosodic virtuosity and furious verbal tension that make the indulgence seem an authentic act of soul baring. Such an evaluation, however, would be incomplete. Also evident is the poet's desire to believe in what he has called "the eliciting of order from experience." Kinsella's verse is a continuing experiment in the viability of the desire to retain such a belief and a commitment to negotiate the leap of artistic faith that alone is capable of overcoming the abyss of unjustifiable unknowing that is the mortal lot. The possibility of achieving that act of composed and graceful suspension is what keeps Kinsella's poetry alive and within the realm of the human enterprise.

Although Kinsella's oeuvre exemplifies, to a dauntingly impressive degree, persistence and commitment in the face of the virtually unspeakable abyss, it has gone through a number of adjustments and modifications. Taken as a whole, therefore, Kinsella's output may be considered an enlarged version of some of its most outstanding moments, a sophisticated system of themes and variations. In the words of the preface to *Wormwood*, "It is certain that maturity and peace are to be sought through ordeal after ordeal, and it seems that the search continues until we fail."

One of the most important adjustments to have occurred in the development of Kinsella's poetic career is his emergence from largely private, personal experience, primarily of love. His early poems, particularly those collected in *Another September* and *Downstream*, seem too often to conceive of experience as the struggle of the will against the force of immutable abstractions. While these poems respect the necessarily tense and tentative character of experience, they seem also to regard mere experience as a pretext for thought. These poems share with Kinsella's later work the desire to achieve distinctiveness through allegories of possibility. However, their generally tight, conventional forms have the effect of limiting their range of possibilities. In addition, the typical persona of these poems seems himself an abstraction, a man with only a nominal context and without a culture.

DOWNSTREAM

By *Downstream*, such isolation was being questioned. The concluding line of this collection's title poem—"Searching the darkness for a landing place"— may be taken (although somewhat glibly) as a statement emblematic of much of Kinsella's early work. However, the collection also contains poems that, while painfully acknowledging the darkness, consider it as an archaeological redoubt. One of the effects of this adjustment is that the poet's personal past begins to offer redemptive possibilities. In addition, and with more obvious if not necessarily more far-reaching effects, a generalized past, in the form of Irish history, becomes an area of exploration. It is not the case that Kinsella never examined the past prior to *Downstream* ("King John's Castle" in *Another September* is proof to the contrary). Now, however, to the powerful sense of the past's otherness that "King John's Castle" conveys is added a sense of personal identification.

The poem in *Downstream* that demonstrates this development in Kinsella's range is "A Country Walk." Here, the persona, typically tense and restless, finds himself alone, explicitly undomesticated, with nothing between him and the legacy of the past discernible in the landscape through which he walks. The poem does not merely testify to the influential gap between present and past (a crucial preoccupation in all modern Irish writing) but also enters into the past with a brisk openness and nonjudgmental tolerance. "A Country Walk" reads like a journey of discovery, all the more so since what is discovered is not subjected to facile glorification. The fact that the past is so securely embedded in the landscape of the poem suggests that history is in the nature of things and that there is as much point in attempting to deny its enduring presence as there is in trying to divert the river which is, throughout the course of the poem, never out of the poet's sight. The poem ends, appropriately, on a note of continuity: "The inert stirred. Heart and tongue were loosed:/ 'The waters hurtle through the flooded night. . . .'"

If anything, the present is circumvented in "A Country Walk." To ensure that the reader is aware of this, Kinsella daringly uses echoes of William Butler Yeats's "Easter 1916" to show how antiheroic is contemporary Ireland and to emphasize that the country is still, to paraphrase a line from Yeats's "September 1913," fumbling in the greasy till. This moment in "A Country Walk" prefaces the understandable admission "I turned away." The interlude, however, draws attention to a noteworthy feature of Kinsella's verse: its satire. From the outset, Kinsella's work was capable of excoriation. The addition of local, often contemporary, Irish subject matter has created the opportunity for some scalding satirical excursions.

NIGHTWALKER, AND OTHER POEMS

Perhaps the most notorious of these sallies is to be found in the long title poem of *Nightwalker, and Other Poems*, a poem that, in many ways, is an illuminating counterpart to "A Country Walk." Here, the setting is urban, contemporary Dublin, and the speaker, lacking the briskness of his opposite number in "A Country Walk," refers to himself as "a vagabond/ Tethered." The demoralizing spectacle of modern life is the poem's subject. Nothing is spared. In particular, Kinsella's years in the civil service are the basis for a damning portrait of national ideals stultified and betrayed. This portrait goes so far as to include figures from Irish public and political life who, although distorted by the poet's satirical fury, remain eminently recognizable and still occupy the highest positions in the land. Each of the poem's numerous scenarios is exposed as a hollow social charade, and in direct contrast to the sense of release felt at the end of "A Country Walk," this poem concludes on a note of anticlimax: The speaker fails to find anything of redemptive value in current conditions.

NOTES FROM THE LAND OF THE DEAD, AND OTHER POEMS

Although Kinsella has by no means forsaken the satirical mode (as *Butcher's Dozen*, Peppercanister's first publication, makes vividly clear), his career has developed more fruitfully through exploring the pretexts and presuppositions of his need that poetry be a salvage operation, acknowledging existence's many disasters and the intimacy of their wreckage and through acknowledgment saving face. Thus, in *Notes from the Land of the Dead, and Other Poems* and also in the later *New*

Poems, the past is personal and the poems seem like diagnoses of memory and origins. Just as the setting for many of these poems is the poet's childhood home, so the poems reveal what has to be internalized for the sake of comprehending one's native land. In these poems, the speaker is the absorbed witness of others' agony, not only the agony of the deathbed but also the equally unrelenting travail described in "Tear": "sad dullness and tedious pain/ and lives bitter with hard bondage."

The poems in *Notes from the Land of the Dead, and Other Poems* are also noteworthy for their degree of interaction with one another. Earlier, in *Wormwood*, Kinsella produced a strict yet supple poetic sequence. Now, the idea of sequence reemerges and takes more fluid form, a technique that can be seen embryonically in the interrelated sections of "Nightwalker" and that finds mature embodiment in many of the Peppercanister poems. This greater access to range and flexibility has enabled the poet to be less dependent on the singular effects of the dramatic lyric, where, as noted, there seemed to be a considerable degree of pressure to will experience to denote purpose. As a result of an increasing commitment to formal and metrical variety, Kinsella's voice has become more authentically meditative, its brooding habit engendering a measure of containment rather than disenchantment. This voice is present not only in such important Peppercanister collections as *One*, *A Technical Supplement*, and *Song of the Night, and Other Poems* but also in some of the superb individual poems these books contain, notably *Finistere* (*One*) and "Tao and Unfitness at Inistiogue on the River Nore" (*Song of the Night, and Other Poems*).

BUTCHER'S DOZEN

It is not clear, however, that Kinsella established Peppercanister with the expectation that such wonderful poems would result. On the contrary, the press came into being because of the need to publish an uncharacteristic Kinsella production, a poem written for a particular occasion. The poem in question, *Butcher's Dozen*, was written in response to the killing in the city of Derry, Northern Ireland, of thirteen civil rights demonstrators by British troops. This event took place on the afternoon of Sunday, January 30, 1972, a day that will live in infamy in the minds of Irish people. The poem's immediate occasion is the horrifying event, but its subtitle, "A Lesson for the Octave of Widgery," clarifies the line of attack taken by Kinsella. The subtitle names the Lord Chief Justice of the United Kingdom, Lord Widgery, chairman of the essentially whitewashing court of inquiry set up to examine the event. Thus, *Butcher's Dozen* is a critique not only of the troops' action but also of the mind-set such actions denote. The poem's incisive and abrasive couplets enact an alternative language and disposition to that of the Lord Chief Justice's report. While, from an aesthetic standpoint, *Butcher's Dozen* is hardly Kinsella's greatest poem, its significance as a cultural document is indisputable and is reinforced by the explanatory background notes that Kinsella wrote to accompany it.

A SELECTED LIFE AND VERTICAL MAN

The other occasional poems contained in the Peppercanister series also have to do with significant deaths. In order of appearance, the poems are *A Selected Life*, *Vertical Man*, *The Good Fight: A Poem for the Tenth Anniversary of the Death of John F. Kennedy*, and *The Messenger*. It has become standard practice to regard *A Selected Life* and *Vertical Man* together, two independent but intimately related treatments of the one event, the untimely death of the poet's friend, Seán Ó Riada. Again, the issue of cultural significance arises. Ó Riada, as well as being an accomplished composer of classical music (*Vertical Man* is the title of one of his compositions for orchestra), was also an extraordinary influence on Irish folk musicians. His conception of the rich tradition and important heritage of Irish folk music was the direct inspiration of the internationally acclaimed group the Chieftains. More relevant to the development of Kinsella's career, Ó Riada's scholarly, pleasure-giving rehabilitation of a dormant legacy is an important counterpart to the poet's explorations in Irish-language poetry. As the penultimate stanza of *Vertical Man* has it: "From palatal darkness a voice/ rose flickering, and checked/ in glottal silence. The song/ articulated and pierced."

THE GOOD FIGHT

In the light of the public demeanor assumed in *Butcher's Dozen* and the greater degree of interplay between textural openness and formal control contained in both Ó Riada poems, Kinsella undertook his most ambitious public poem, *The Good Fight*. Not only is the poem's subject matter ambitious, in particular given how rare it is for Irish poets to seek subjects outside the ambit of their own culture and tradition (a rarity that later Irish poets such as Derek Mahon would work to dismantle), but also, formally speaking, *The Good Fight* is one of Kinsella's more daring experiments.

As in the case of earlier Peppercanister poems on public themes, *The Good Fight* has an author's note attached, which begins with the remark, "With the death of Kennedy many things died, foolish expectations and assumptions, as it now seems." In a sense, the poem is a collage of contemporary desires, a view borne out by the numerous allusions to and quotations from Kennedy speeches and other sources from the period. However, such a view is contradicted by two other features of the poem. The most obvious of these are the various quotations from Plato's *Politeia* (fourth century B.C.E.; *Republic*, 1701) and *Nomoi* (fourth century B.C.E.; *Laws*, 1804), which are used to counterpoint the poem's development. This classical reference has the effect of measuring Kennedy's fate against some nominal yet conventionally uncontroversial standard of age-old wisdom. This feature in turn is seen in terms of the pervasive sense of unfulfilled aftermath that pervades the poem. It seems remarkable that this achievement is so little known.

THE MESSENGER

The significant death in *The Messenger* is not that of a well-known figure but of the poet's father. This immensely moving document testifies to Kinsella's growth as an artist. The poem's subject, death, has been a constant presence in his work since "A Lady of Quality," in *Poems*, and has been treated variously in such accomplished and representative poems as "Dick King" and "Cover Her Face" (both from *Downstream*). *The Messenger*, however, dwells more on celebrating the life that preceded its occasion than on the death of a man desiring to possess his culture: "The eggseed Goodness/ that is also called/ Decency." The poet's redemptive power and his cultural as well as personal responsibility to discharge it are seen to consummate effect in this powerful, moving work.

BLOOD AND FAMILY

Blood and Family, Kinsella's first publication from a major publisher since the 1979 *Peppercanister Poems, 1972-1978*, is a reprint of later Peppercanister publications. The volume contains *The Messenger*, *Songs of the Psyche*, *Her Vertical Smile*, *Out of Ireland*, and *St. Catherine's Clock*. The decision to open the volume with a reprint of *The Messenger* is a good one, given that it sets the cultural tone and prosodic idiom for the remainder of the poems. At the same time, it may be said that this volume consolidates rather than enlarges Kinsella's reputation, not merely because of the familiarity of some of its contents but also because of the tension that its title invokes. The sense of belonging to two disjunctive collectives, family and nation, is here articulated thematically but also in terms of form and metrics. The result is an emphatic, diverse restatement of themes of brokenness and incompleteness that have informed the poet's vision from virtually its inception. Although these themes are addressed and expressed with Kinsella's typical vehement, tight-lipped energy, the impression remains one of ground being reworked as worked anew, of a poet revisiting old preoccupations in search of unfamiliar nuances.

POEMS FROM CENTRE CITY

In *Poems from Centre City*, however, there is evidence of a slightly different Kinsella. The poems in this Peppercanister pamphlet address the state of contemporary Dublin in a much more direct way than hitherto, lacking the range and ambition of, for example, "Nightwalker," and presenting themselves more intimately, as more the products of occasions, than is customary with this poet. Metrically simple and verbally direct, they attempt to come to terms with the decay—physical, moral, and institutional—of Kinsella's native place. Decay as a subject is no stranger to Kinsella's imagination. However, despite the comparatively fresh perspective on the poet's concerns that *Poems from Centre City* provides, it should not be assumed that the collection is intended to be thought of as a polemic. The inclusion of a poem on W. H. Auden, one of Kinsella's most permanent influences, may be understood as a caution against the reader's comprehending *Poems from Centre City* as a narrowly activist set of statements on, for example, an environmental theme.

At the same time, the diagnostic—or at least exploratory—thrust of much of Kinsella's work is once again in evidence in this small sampling of his work. The formal range is restricted; the subject matter is largely drawn from the immediacy and adventitiousness of an attentive citizen's experience. A number of the poems are suggested by memory, though all succeed in avoiding either moralizing or sentimentality. In terms of accessibility and immediate effectiveness, *Poems from Centre City* is among the most appealing of Kinsella's later works.

THE PEN SHOP

The 1990's found Kinsella publishing a number of poetry collections, often slight in size but heavy in themes and recollections. *The Pen Shop*, a small volume consisting of two sections titled "To the Coffee Shop" and "To the Pen Shop," focuses on the renewal of a poetic career late in the poet's life. Readers find Kinsella strolling through the streets of Dublin, visiting favorite haunts—the General Post Office, Grafton Street, the Guinness brewery, Trinity College—and seeing the specter of his father in every turn. He meanders to Nassau Street for "some of their best black refills" from the pen shop, and then finds himself at Bewley's, the city's famed tea and coffee shop. Rather than partake in tea or coffee, he instead consumes pills from a tin, needing the black draft of medicinal inspiration to enter his system "direct" with its taste of death, "foreign and clay sharp"; for only in this way may he be jolted into imaginative life and become the grand instrument of his muse's spectral writing: "The long body sliding in/ under my feet." Only then may he no longer be, like the other old men in Bewley's, "Speechless." Indeed, only then may he, like the first voices, "rising out of Europe," become "clear in calibre and professional,/ self chosen,/ rising beyond Jerusalem."

THE FAMILIAR

In 1999, Kinsella issued two short books simultaneously. *The Familiar* consists of the longer title poem and three short poems, all erotically charged and intimate, a style familiar to Kinsella readers. However, here the familiarity is of the flesh, with some

mythical overtones. In the title poem, there are "demons over the door" and he has a "Muse on [his] mattress." When he goes to relieve himself during a night of lovemaking, he sees "three graces above the tank." The love scene ends with Kinsella invoking, in the volume's three short poems, a saint in "St. John's," a bride in "Wedding Night," and "Iris," the messenger of the gods.

GODHEAD

Godhead consists of two short poems and a longer title poem. It has little in common thematically with *The Familiar*, since the two short poems are American seascapes ("High Tide: Amagansett" and "San Clemente, California: A Gloss") and the title poem is an evocation of the Holy Trinity of Father, Son, and Spirit. However, both collections share a continuity in their terse, grainy, and stark poetic styles. His poems display a characteristic Irish style in their mythical and religious approach, yet at the same time are startlingly concrete and even irreverent. To speak of the crucifixion as "The Head hanging on one side,/ signifying abandonment" is gruesomely effective, while to end with the line "Dust of our lastborn" seems anticlimactic but haunting.

COLLECTED POEMS, 1956-2001

Toward the end of any poet's career comes the need to produce a complete works. Inevitably, earlier work will have gone out of print, and the poet may experience a need to revise and re-arrange early poetry in the light of later developments. In Kinsella's case, there had been attempts to produce selected works in 1973 and 1979, but by 1990, much of his earlier work had gone through a period of comparative neglect, as other Irish poets, most obviously Seamus Heaney and Paul Muldoon, came to the fore. This resulted in most of his earlier work being largely unavailable.

The production of *Collected Poems, 1956-1994* in 1996 was a major rehabilitation for Kinsella and made his work known to the general public for the first time in many cases. What was significant about the collection was the enormous revision that the earlier poetry had gone through at Kinsella's hand. This only emphasized what students of his writing always knew: that he regarded all his poetry as work in progress, as opposed to, say, Muldoon, who refused to revise his poetry, saying he had no more right to revise it than his readers did.

Kinsella had cut out many of the more Romantic, florid gestures from the earlier poetry, pointing toward the style he was now adopting of simpler, ungestured statement. He had also rearranged some of the poems, and a sense of unity about the oeuvre as a whole was beginning to emerge. Also incorporated were the more or less final version of many of the Peppercanister poems.

The 1996 edition was published by Oxford University Press, one of Kinsella's main publishers. However, in 1999, Oxford University Press decided to cut poetry from its publishing list. This meant little for Kinsella's new work, as the Peppercanister Press was handling that, but it left the *Collected Poems, 1956-1994* high and dry. After some negotiation, Carcanet Press, based in Manchester, England, agreed to produce *Collected Poems, 1956-2001*. It was published in 2001 in the United Kingdom, but copyright did now allow for distribution in the United States. In 2006, Wake Forest University Press published an American version.

Perhaps for the first time, the *Collected Poems, 1956-2001* clearly showed Kinsella's development as being in many ways parallel to that of his great predecessor Yeats. An initial lyrical period, full of imagery, was followed by periods of more political commitment and ironic statement and by more symbolic, very complex personal statements of belief, often drawing on Jungian psychology. Finally came a reversion to a more settled, simpler style, where any form of poetic pretentiousness was avoided.

The other development that can be traced is Kinsella's move to the United States, which resulted in a freeing from traditional bonds of expectation and expression; however, unlike with Muldoon, Kinsella's themes, imagery, and subject matter remain rooted in his Irishness. The depths found by fellow Irish writer James Joyce are mediated through such American poets as William Carlos Williams and in particular Robert Lowell. Kinsella's poetry thus becomes more and more Western mainstream and less and less stereotypically Irish, a move that did not meet the approval of all critics.

OTHER MAJOR WORKS

NONFICTION: *Davis, Mangan, Ferguson? Tradition and the Irish Writer*, 1970 (with W. B. Yeats); *The Dual Tradition: An Essay on Poetry and Politics in Ireland*, 1995; *A Dublin Documentary*, 2006 (poetry and prose); *Prose Occasions: 1956-2006*, 2009 (Andrew Fitzsimmons, editor).

TRANSLATIONS: *The Breastplate of Saint Patrick*, 1954 (revised as *Faeth Fiadha: The Breastplate of Saint Patrick*, 1957); *Longes mac n-Usnig, Being the Exile and Death of the Sons of Usnech*, 1954; *Thirty-three Triads, Translated from the Twelfth Century Irish*, 1955; *The Táin*, 1969 (of *Táin bó Cuailnge*); *An Duanaire, 1600-1900: Poems of the Dispossessed*, 1981 (with Sean O Tuama).

EDITED TEXT: *The New Oxford Book of Irish Verse*, 1986.

BIBLIOGRAPHY

Abbate Badin, Donatella. *Thomas Kinsella*. New York: Twayne, 1996. An introductory biography and critical interpretation of selected works by Kinsella. Includes bibliographical references and index.

Fitzsimmons, Andrew. *The Sea of Disappointment: Thomas Kinsella's Pursuit of the Real*. Dublin: University College Dublin Press, 2008. Produced to honor Kinsella's eightieth birthday, this book analyzes Kinsella's work and career, especially his thematic and structural developments.

Harmon, Maurice. *The Poetry of Thomas Kinsella*. Atlantic Highlands, N.J.: Humanities Press, 1974. The author provides an overview of many of Kinsella's achievements, as well as helpful background information. Kinsella's preoccupation with the Irish language is also dealt with, and close readings of the major poems are offered. In addition, the poet's prosodical originality is analyzed. A valuable introductory guide.

_____. *Thomas Kinsella: Designing for the Exact Needs*. Dublin: Irish Academic, 2008. This volume offers a comprehensive examination of Kinsella's works, looking at them chronologically and grouping them based on similar styles and attitudes. The themes of his poems are also discussed along with his focus on politics and life in Dublin.

Jackson, Thomas H. *The Whole Matter: The Poetic Evolution of Thomas Kinsella.* Syracuse, N.Y.: Syracuse University Press, 1995. A comprehensive overview of Kinsella's achievement.

John, Brian. "Irelands of the Mind: The Poetry of Thomas Kinsella and Seamus Heaney." *Canadian Journal of Irish Studies* 15 (December, 1989): 68-92. An analysis of the cultural implications of the two most important Irish poets of their generation. Kinsella's severe lyricism is contrasted with Heaney's more sensual verse. The two poets' senses of place, time, and history are also examined. The visions of Ireland produced are important evidence of the contemporary debate about Irish national identity.

_____. *Reading the Ground: The Poetry of Thomas Kinsella.* Washington, D.C.: Catholic University of America Press, 1996. A comprehensive study of Kinsella's poetry. John explores the poet's development within both the Irish and the English contexts and defines the nature of his poetic achievement.

Johnston, Dillon. "Kinsella and Clarke." In *Irish Poetry After Joyce.* Notre Dame, Ind.: University of Notre Dame Press, 1985. Kinsella's debt to his most important Irish poetic mentor is discussed. The origins and thrust of Kinsella's satirical tendencies are identified and analyzed. The poet's standing in the tradition of modern Irish poetry is also evaluated.

Skloot, Floyd. "The Evolving Poetry of Thomas Kinsella." Review of *Collected Poems, 1956-1994. New England Review* 18, no. 4 (Fall, 1997): 174-187. Skloot examines Kinsella's evolving style and themes. Offers a good retrospective look at Kinsella's body of work.

Tubridy, Derval. *Thomas Kinsella: The Peppercanister Poems.* Dublin: University College Dublin Press, 2001. A study of the poetry Kinsella has published with his own press.

George O'Brien; Sarah Hilbert
Updated by David Barratt

RUDYARD KIPLING

Born: Bombay, India (now Mumbai, India); December 30, 1865
Died: Hampstead, London, England; January 18, 1936

PRINCIPAL POETRY

Schoolboy Lyrics, 1881
Echoes, 1884 (with Alice Kipling)
Departmental Ditties, 1886
Barrack-Room Ballads, and Other Verses, 1892
The Seven Seas, 1896
An Almanac of Twelve Sports, 1898
Recessional, and Other Poems, 1899
The Five Nations, 1903
Collected Verse, 1907
A History of England, 1911 (with C. R. L. Fletcher)
Songs from Books, 1912
Sea Warfare, 1916
Twenty Poems, 1918
Rudyard Kipling's Verse, 1885-1918, 1919
The Years Between, 1919
Q. Horatii Flacci Carminum Librer Quintus, 1920 (with Charles L. Graves, A. D. Godley, A. B. Ramsay, and R. A. Knox)
Songs for Youth, 1924
Sea and Sussex from Rudyard Kipling's Verse, 1926
Rudyard Kipling's Verse, 1886-1926, 1927
Songs of the Sea, 1927
Poems, 1886-1929, 1929
Selected Poems, 1931
Rudyard Kipling's Verse, 1885-1932, 1933
Rudyard Kipling's Verse, 1940 (definitive edition)

OTHER LITERARY FORMS

Rudyard Kipling is best known for his short stories. His *Just So Stories* (1902), *The Jungle Book* (1894), and *The Second Jungle Book* (1895) are favorites with children and are among the most widely read collections of stories in the world. His novel *Kim* (1901) also ranks among the world's most popular books. Kipling's fiction, however, presents a critic with most

of the problems that his verse presents, making it difficult to discuss one without the other. The fiction is often thought to be barbaric in content and representative
of a discredited imperialistic point of view; too often,
critics discuss Kipling's political views (which are often misrepresented) rather than his literary merits.
Kipling's contempt for intellectualism makes him unfashionable in most critical circles, and those who admit to having admired him seem to be ashamed of their
affection. Not all critics, however, have been ambiguous in their admiration of Kipling's work; especially
since the 1960's, critics have made the short stories objects of serious study. In any case, Kipling's fiction has
remained immensely popular from the late Victorian
era to the present. It has been made into no fewer than
thirteen motion pictures, including *Captains Courageous* (1937) and *The Jungle Book* (1942, 1967, and
1998). Kipling's fiction has the vigor and passion that
appeal to the popular imagination, and a subtlety and
brilliant prose style that are worthy of careful study.

ACHIEVEMENTS

Henry James called Rudyard Kipling a genius; T. S.
Eliot called him a writer of verse who sometimes ascended to poetry. His *Departmental Ditties* brought
him extravagant praise and fame. Some scholars assert
that he was the world's best-known author from the
1890's to his death. However, even his admirers have
been uncertain of his achievement, particularly in poetry. Kipling often sang his poems while he composed
them; they are often ballads or hymns, and all feature
clear rhythms that urge a reader to read them aloud.
Their surface themes are usually easy to understand;
the language is clear and accessible to even casual
readers.

Perhaps the accessibility of Kipling's verse is the
source of the confusion; twentieth century critics have
all too often regarded poetry that is popular among the
common people as automatically bad; obscurity has
been the hallmark of much of the best of twentieth
century poetry. Kipling's verse is informed by the Victorian masters, such as Alfred, Lord Tennyson, and
Algernon Charles Swinburne. It is out of step with the
modernist school, which may be why many readers
think of Kipling as Victorian, even though he actively

wrote and published into the 1930's; his autobiography
appeared in 1937, the year after his death. His harsh
views of ordinary people; his angry polemics, political
conservatism, and lack of faith in so-called utopian societies; and the Cassandra-like prophecies of war that
fill much of his verse repel many aesthetes and political
liberals. Kipling has been portrayed as a philistine. The
truth is that he did not understand much of the social
change of his lifetime, but he understood people, and in
his verse, he preserves the thoughts, emotions, hopes,
and despairs of people usually ignored by poets. If one
approaches his verse with an open mind, one will likely
find brilliant prosody, excellent phrasing, surprising
metaphors, and a poetic ethos that transcends literary
and political fashion.

Kipling won the Nobel Prize in Literature in 1907.
The award was, in part, a recognition of Kipling's
worldwide appeal to readers; he touched more hearts
and minds than anyone else of his generation. His work
added phrases to the English language; few today realize that they paraphrase Kipling when they assert that
"the female is deadlier than the male" or that "East is
East and West is West."

BIOGRAPHY

Joseph Rudyard Kipling was born in Bombay (now
Mumbai), India, on December 30, 1865. His parents
were John Lockwood Kipling and Alice (née Macdonald) Kipling. His father was then a sculptor and designer and was principal and professor of architectural
sculpture of the School of Art at Bombay, and he later
became curator of the museum at Lahore. His mother
came from a family of accomplished women. John
Lockwood Kipling set many of the high standards for
literary skill that Rudyard endeavored to match in both
fiction and poetry. Both parents encouraged their son's
literary efforts and took pride in his achievements.

Except for a brief visit to England, Rudyard Kipling
spent his first five years in India. In 1871, he was taken
with his sister Alice to England and left with Captain
and Mrs. Holloway of Lorne Lodge in Southsea. After
several unhappy years in the ungentle care of Mrs. Holloway, he left Lorne Lodge in 1877. In 1878, he was
sent to United Services College in Devon. In 1882, he
traveled to Lahore, where his father had found him a

Rudyard Kipling (©The Nobel Foundation)

job as a reporter for the *Civil and Military Gazette*. He had seen little of his parents since 1871. Somewhat to his annoyance, he discovered that his parents had gathered the verses from his letters to them and had them published as *Schoolboy Lyrics* in 1881. In 1887, he joined the staff of the *Pioneer* of Allahabad, which he left in 1889. His experiences in England figure in many of his stories; his experiences as a journalist in India are reflected not only in his fiction but also in much of his best verse.

In 1888, Émile Édouard Moreau began the Indian Library, primarily to help Kipling and to capitalize on the young writer's talents. The first six volumes of the series consisted of Kipling's work. In 1889, Kipling traveled to Singapore, Hong Kong, and Japan; through the United States; and to England. His *Departmental Ditties* was printed in England in 1890, and the response to his poetry moved him from the status of a promising young writer to the forefront not only of English letters but also of world literature. His writing

from 1890 onward brought him wealth and lasting popularity. The initial praise of his work was extraordinary—in 1892, Henry James wrote to his brother William, "Kipling strikes me as personally the most complete man of genius (as distinct from fine intelligence) that I have ever known"—but by the 1900's, he would suffer extraordinary abuse at the hands of the critics. Kipling married Caroline Starr Balestier in 1892 and moved to Brattleboro, Vermont, where her relatives lived. While living in the United States, he had two daughters. Although he liked his home in Vermont, Kipling left the United States when his enmity with his brother-in-law became public and created a scandal. After some traveling, he returned to visit his mother-in-law; during a stay in New York, he and his family fell ill; his wife, younger daughter Elsie, and baby son recovered quickly, but he nearly died and his elder daughter Josephine did die.

He settled at Rottingdean in England in 1897. His wife took charge of much of his family and social affairs, and A. P. Watt, a literary agent, handled his literary and business affairs. His life in Rottingdean was productive but isolated; as the years passed, he saw less and less of his literary friends. In 1907, to the chagrin of his detractors, he won the Nobel Prize in Literature. His poetry at the time warned England of impending war and of England's unpreparedness. When war began in 1914, his son, with his father's help, enlisted in the army. In late 1915, John Kipling was killed in a British attack during the Battle of Loos. From the end of World War I to his death, Kipling worked to perfect his literary art and vigorously expressed his opinions on politics and society. At the end of his life, he wrote his autobiography and helped prepare the Sussex edition of his works. He died January 18, 1936, while embarking on a vacation. His ashes were buried in Westminster Abbey's Poets' Corner.

ANALYSIS

Rudyard Kipling's poetry is such a part of the culture of English-speaking people that one is hard put to approach his work without preconceived notions of its quality and content. In his own day, Kipling's poetry outraged many critics and provided handy epithets for politicians of many political leanings. Even today, scholars can be excited by his so-called racial and imperialistic topics. Myths thus abound. Kipling's verse is called racist; in fact, Kipling's verse repeatedly emphasizes that no one can rightfully be regarded superior to another on the basis of race or origin. "The White Man's Burden," he wrote, was to "Fill full the mouth of Famine/ And bid the sickness cease." Although imperialistic, the poem emphasizes not race but the obligations of Europeans and Americans to the oppressed peoples of the world.

"THE LAST OF THE LIGHT BRIGADE"

Kipling is said to glorify warfare by devoting much of his poetry to descriptions of the lives of soldiers; in fact, he shows war to be ugly and stupid. In "The Last of the Light Brigade," he portrays veterans of the Crimean War as destitute: "We leave to the streets and the workhouse the charge of the Light Brigade!" In the poem, Kipling calls attention to the differences between Tennyson's poetic description of the ill-fated charge and the degradation that characterized the soldiers' lives. Another myth is that Kipling's poetry is coarse and crude. The subject matter is, indeed, sometimes crude, but not the prosody. Even T. S. Eliot, who admired Kipling's work, asserted that Kipling wrote good verse that occasionally ascended to poetry but that in general Kipling did not write poetry.

CRITICISM, FOUNDED AND UNFOUNDED

Some of the sources of misconceptions about Kipling's poetic achievement seem obvious: Casual or careless readings might glean only the surface remarks of subtle poems; Kipling's political poetry was and remains unpalatable to many people who condemn it on no other grounds than political distastefulness; his aggressive dislike of academics and admiration for men of action alienate many of those who would be likeliest to write about his poetry. Some of the negative myths are Kipling's fault. If one writes on the politics of the moment, one invites political interpretations of one's work.

Nevertheless, too much of the criticism of Kipling's poetry is clearly biased. Many rationales for denigrating the poetry seem contrived, as if covering reasons that would not bear exposure. After all, portraits of the hard lives of working people, as well as soldiers, dominate novels from Émile Zola to the present; such novels

are often praised for their realism. One of the most highly regarded Anglo-American poets of the twentieth century, Ezra Pound, was a fascist who made propagandistic radio broadcasts from Italy during World War II. His avowed racism is well known and is as unpalatable to well-informed and compassionate people as anything to be found in the work of Kipling. Indeed, Kipling deplored Nazi Germany and dictatorships in general. Yet Pound was fashionable; Kipling was not.

Kipling's unfashionableness has its origins in two important aspects of his poetry: His versification was clear and usually unadorned, and his subjects were usually plain, working-class people. He began his career in the Victorian era, and his lyrical and narrative poetry has more in common with the styles of Tennyson, Robert Browning, and Swinburne than it has with the styles that have been predominant in a more modern age. One of the important aspects of modernism in poetry was the emphasis on metaphor; metaphors were used to make such works as Eliot's *The Waste Land* (1922) hauntingly remote from casual reading. Critics came to expect good poetry to demand close and sometimes prolonged reading for one to understand even the most basic meanings of the verse.

"LOOT"

Kipling's approach to his poetry was neither better nor worse than that of his later contemporaries; it was merely different, because he aimed for an audience other than the literary elite. Poetry had been a genre for popular reading; Kipling kept it such. His best poetry will reward close reading by perceptive readers; it will also reward the unskilled or casual reader with a basic surface meaning. For example, "Loot" provides a basic discussion of techniques for looting; the persona—the poem's speaker—says, "always work in pairs—/ It 'alves the gain, but safer you will find." A quick reading elicits the picture of a lowly soldier providing a description of an ugly but realistic aspect of war (and provides ammunition against Kipling for anyone who is determined to misread the poem as somehow glorifying looting). A close reading of the poem, however, reveals a careful use of language; Kipling uses his knowledge of soldiers and their ballads to give his persona an authentic voice. One will also discover a picture of the mindless violence and degradation of war at the level of the common foot soldier. Kipling's style was out of step with the literary movement of his day; it was judged by the wrong standards and often still is.

Victorians and common folk

Poetry has traditionally been regarded as the elite of literary genres. The term *poet* was reserved in the sixteenth, seventeenth, and eighteenth centuries for those who had excelled in literature; it was a term of honor to which writers aspired. Poetry has been thought of as appropriate to high aspirations and great ideas; it has been considered "elevating." The Victorians added the notion that poetry was morally uplifting and that a poet was obliged to discuss high topics in grand language; thus, biblical phrasing and high-sounding archaisms such as "thee" and "thou" lingered in nineteenth century poetry. No matter how much they were involved with the literary revolutions of their time, Kipling's contemporaries were children of the Victorians. Many of the most admired poems of the first three decades of the twentieth century focused on the Arthurian legends or revived Latin poetic traditions.

Kipling's poetry, in contrast, focuses on common people, the active people whose raw manner of dealing with the world most interested him. Soldiers, as the frequent vanguard of the British Empire and the products of the laboring classes, were often subjects of Kipling's poetry; laborers themselves were also often the subject of his verse. Kipling gave these people voices; his keen insight made his language strikingly acute. It is coarse, harsh, and elemental. In addition, the poetry by which he is best known is in the ballad form. The ballad is a lyrical folk song that grows and changes with use and custom; it is heard in bars, at country fairs, and in the barracks of soldiers. Kipling's use of the ballad explains in part Eliot's judgment that Kipling is a verse-writer instead of a poet; the form is believed by some scholars to be beneath poetry.

Thus, elitism has had much to do with negative responses to Kipling; critics seem to believe that Kipling has degraded verse. Even though he was a conservative with some Victorian notions of poetry, Kipling was ahead of his time. Egalitarianism became one of the significant movements in the twentieth century; literacy burgeoned, as did access to literature. Kipling wrote for the broad literate mass of people; he gave

voices to people who were generally left out of poetry, and he did not romanticize them. A soldier's achievement is to survive one more day; a laborer's achievement is to feed himself one more day. Their contempt for those who are not physically active fits well with Kipling's own disgust with aesthetes who are out of touch with much that is thought and done by those who provide the foundations for civilization.

"The Way Through the Woods" and "Cities and Thrones and Powers"

Kipling's verse is highly crafted poetry. It uses metaphors and prosody in unusual ways, but this is a strength, not a weakness. Kipling's mastery of metaphor is apparent, for example, in "The Way Through the Woods," which describes an eroded road that was closed some seventy years before. On its surface, the poem offers a wistful description of the encroachment by the wilderness on a road no longer used. It is more than that, however; there is an eeriness in its description of "coppice and heath," "ring-dove broods," and "trout-ringed pools," which all utterly hide a road that makes its presence felt only in echoes of the past. The lost road and the woods that have covered it are metaphors for the passage of time and the transitoriness of human works. The theme of the fragility of human achievements is an important one in poetry; in "The Way Through the Woods," Kipling makes the theme mystical and haunting.

The near futility of human endeavors when confronting time is a common motif of Kipling's work. Although "The Way Through the Woods" is remote in tone and metaphor, Kipling is perfectly willing to be blunt—and still metaphorical. In "Cities and Thrones and Powers" he uses flowers as metaphors:

> Cities and Thrones and Powers
> Stand in Time's eye,
> Almost as long as flowers,
> Which daily die:

The poem continues and turns tragedy into triumph:

> But, as new buds put forth
> To glad new men,
> Out of the spent and unconsidered Earth
> The Cities rise again.

Few readers would have trouble understanding the basic metaphor: Flowers die but leave seeds that grow into new flowers, and cities do the same. Even Kipling's eccentric phrase "Almost as long as flowers" is within easy reach of the unsophisticated reader: In the vastness of time, cities exist only briefly. The surface meanings of the central metaphor do not preclude subtlety. The transitoriness of "Cities and Thrones and Powers" is a melancholy topic, one that other poets have used to show the vanity of human achievements. Percy Bysshe Shelley's "Ozymandias" is the archetypal expression of the theme; a pedestal alone in the desert bears an almost meaningless inscription: "My name is Ozymandias, king of kings:/ Look on my works, ye Mighty, and despair!" Shelley adds: "Nothing beside remains." A city and civilization are reduced to desert. Kipling takes the same sad theme, attaches it to flowers, making the frail plants bear the weight of civilization, and in flowers he reveals that seeming transitoriness is in fact a cycle of renewal. "Time," he says, "Ordains . . . That in our very death,/ And burial sure,/ Shadow to shadow, well persuaded, saith,/ See how our works endure!" In the deaths of human works are the seeds of new works: One civilization begets another.

Kipling's interest in the passing and survival of civilizations also extended to current events. In "The Dykes" of 1902, he ponders the dangers to Britain posed by the militancy of Europe. "These are the dykes our fathers made: we have never known a breach," he says. The people of Britain have built protections against their enemies, but through neglect the "dykes" might be broken. "An evil ember bedded in ash—a spark blown west by the wind . . ./ We are surrendered to night and the sea—the gale and the tide behind!" Kipling the prophet uses metaphor to warn of war. "The Dykes" is dynamic and threatening; history has shown its warning to be apt.

"GUNGA DIN"

Kipling's narrative poetry is probably his best known. It includes "Gunga Din" and "The Ballad of East and West," both of which discuss British imperialism and cultural differences and are thus unfashionable. "Gunga Din" is as well known a poem as exists in English. In it Gunga Din, a water bearer for British soldiers in India, faithfully serves his masters and saves the life of the poem's narrator—giving up his own life in the process. Kipling uses the rhythm of the ballad form to create strikingly memorable phrases, including the last lines:

> You Lazarushian-leather Gunga Din!
> Though I've belted you and flayed you,
> By the livin' Gawd that made you,
> You're a better man than I am, Gunga Din!

The language is raw and the verse melodic; the combination is powerful. Gunga Din's life is shown to be miserable, and his masters are shown as beastly, but Gunga Din is revealed as having a noble quality that Kipling valued; Gunga Din cares enough for his fellow men to die for them. Thus, the last line summarizes the central theme of the poem; Gunga Din is the better man.

"THE BALLAD OF EAST AND WEST"

In a similar vein, "The Ballad of East and West" shows that all men can understand one another in the fundamental test of courage:

> Oh, East is East and West is West, and never the
> 　twain shall meet,
> Till Earth and Sky stand presently at God's great
> 　Judgment Seat;
> But there is neither East nor West, Border, nor
> 　Breed, nor Birth,
> When two strong men stand face to face, though
> 　they come from the ends of the earth!

Kipling admired men of action and physical courage. He asserted that men can communicate on fundamental levels that transcend the veneer of culture. In "The Ballad of East and West," two strong men are brought face to face, their differences seemingly beyond hope of peaceful resolution. They discover that they are alike and not as different as others would believe. Beginning as enemies, they part as friends.

"THE ABSENT-MINDED BEGGAR"

Kipling dealt with large metaphysical ideas, with the cycles of civilizations and the threats to Western civilization, yet for all his great themes, Kipling was at home with subjects no more lofty than the ordinary person's hope for a better future. In "The Absent-Minded Beggar," for example, Kipling reminds his readers of the hard lot of the dependents of the soldiers who fought in the Boer War. "When you've finished killing Kruger with your mouth,/ Will you kindly drop a shilling in my little tamborine/ For a gentleman in khaki order South?" The poem was written to help raise money for the needs of the families of the soldiers. The tone is sympathetic but honest. The British soldier has "left a lot of little things behind him!" The "little things" include his children—not necessarily legitimate—wives, lovers, girlfriends, and debts. The families will "live on half o' nothing . . . 'Cause the man that earns the wage is ordered out." The soldier is "an absent-minded beggar, but he heard his country call." Kipling's language demonstrates his understanding of his subject. The poem reveals the fundamental Kipling—not imperialist, not prophet, not poet playing with great poetic conceits—but a poet who understands people and cares about them. Few writers can be honestly said to have cared more about their subjects than Kipling.

Long after the politics of his day are forgotten and his polemics have become of interest only to literary historians, Kipling's essential efforts will still have meaning. Readers who approach Kipling's verse with a love for poetry can still declare, as did scholar David Masson to his students at Edinburgh in 1890, while holding a copy of "Danny Deever," "Here's Literature! Here's Literature at last!"

OTHER MAJOR WORKS

LONG FICTION: *The Light That Failed*, 1890; *The Naulahka: A Story of East and West*, 1892 (with Wolcott Balestier); *Captains Courageous: A Story of the Grand Banks*, 1897; *Kim*, 1901.

SHORT FICTION: *Quartette*, 1885 (with John Lockwood Kipling, Alice Macdonald Kipling, and Alice Kipling); *In Black and White*, 1888; *Plain Tales from the Hills*, 1888; *The Phantom 'Rickshaw, and Other Tales*, 1888; *Soldiers Three: A Collection of Stories*, 1888; *The Story of the Gadsbys*, 1888; *Under the Deodars*, 1888; *Wee Willie Winkie, and Other Child Stories*, 1888; *The City of Dreadful Night, and Other Places*, 1890; *The Courting of Dinah Shadd, and Other Stories*, 1890; *Life's Handicap*, 1891; *Mine Own People*, 1891; *Many Inventions*, 1893; *The Jungle Book*, 1894; *The Second Jungle Book*, 1895; *Soldier Tales*, 1896; *The Day's Work*, 1898; *Stalky and Co.*, 1899; *Just So Stories*, 1902; *Traffics and Discoveries*, 1904; *Puck of Pook's Hill*, 1906; *Actions and Reactions*, 1909; *Rewards and Fairies*, 1910; *A Diversity of Creatures*, 1917; *Land and Sea Tales for Scouts and Guides*, 1923; *Debits and Credits*, 1926; *Thy Servant a Dog*, 1930; *Limits and Renewals*, 1932; *Collected Dog Stories*, 1934.

NONFICTION: *American Notes*, 1891; *Beast and Man in India*, 1891; *Letters of Marque*, 1891; *The Smith Administration*, 1891; *A Fleet in Being: Notes of Two Trips with the Channel Squadron*, 1898; *From Sea to Sea*, 1899; *Letters to the Family*, 1908; *The New Army in Training*, 1914; *France at War*, 1915; *The Fringes of the Fleet*, 1915; *Sea Warfare*, 1916; *Letters of Travel, 1892-1913*, 1920; *The Irish Guards in the Great War*, 1923; *A Book of Words*, 1928; *Something of Myself: For My Friends Known and Unknown*, 1937; *Uncollected Prose*, 1938 (2 volumes); *Rudyard Kipling to Rider Haggard: The Record of a Friendship*, 1965 (Morton N. Cohen, editor); *The Letters of Rudyard Kipling*, 1990-2004 (6 volumes; Thomas Pinney, editor); *Writings on Writing*, 1996 (Sandra Kemp, editor); *Kipling's America: Travel Letters, 1889-1895*, 2003 (D. H. Stewart, editor).

MISCELLANEOUS: *The Sussex Edition of the Complete Works in Prose and Verse of Rudyard Kipling*, 1937-1939 (35 volumes).

BIBLIOGRAPHY

Adams, Jad. *Kipling*. London: Haus Books, 2005. This biography sheds light on Kipling's inspiration for his poetry and portrays sides of his character that are rarely seen.

Allen, Charles. *Kipling Sahib: India and the Making of Rudyard Kipling*. New York: Pegasus Books, 2009. A biography of Kipling that focuses on his childhood and later life in India and the country's influence on his works.

Bloom, Harold, ed. *Rudyard Kipling*. Philadelphia: Chelsea House, 2004. Essays on Kipling's major works, his views on art and life, and his vision of empire. Includes introduction, chronology, and bibliography.

Coates, John. *The Day's Work: Kipling and the Idea of Sacrifice*. Madison, N.J.: Fairleigh Dickinson University Press, 1997. Explores one of Kipling's favorite themes.

Dillingham, William B. *Rudyard Kipling: Hell and Heroism*. New York: Palgrave Macmillan, 2005. This biography offers a close look at some of Kipling's most noted works while exploring the complexities of his personality.

Gilmour, David. *The Long Recessional: The Imperial Life of Rudyard Kipling*. New York: Farrar, Straus and Giroux, 2002. An interesting account of Kipling's life and his complex and changing views of the British Empire, written with an awareness of the rise of terrorism emanating from the postcolonial developing world.

Lycett, Andrew. *Rudyard Kipling*. London: Weidenfeld and Nicolson, 1999. Lycett's exhaustive biography provides invaluable insight into the life and work of Kipling. Includes bibliographical references and index.

Mallett, Phillip. *Rudyard Kipling: A Literary Life*. New York: Palgrave Macmillan, 2003. Looks at how his unusual family background, the deaths of his children, and his relationship with critics affected his life and writings.

Pinney, Thomas. *In Praise of Kipling*. Austin: Harry Ransom Humanities Research Center, The University of Texas at Austin, 1996. A volume of criticism that is mostly positive.

Ricketts, Harry. *Rudyard Kipling: A Life*. New York: Carroll and Graf, 2000. In a detailed and lively account of Kipling's life, Ricketts also analyzes the literary works that emerged from that popular but controversial career.

Kirk H. Beetz

L

CHARLES LAMB

Born: London, England; February 10, 1775
Died: Edmonton, England; December 27, 1834

PRINCIPAL POETRY

Blank Verse, 1798 (with Charles Lloyd)
Poetry for Children, 1809 (with Mary Lamb)
The Works of Charles Lamb, 1818
Album Verses, 1830
Satan in Search of a Wife, 1831
The Poetical Works of Charles Lamb, 1836

OTHER LITERARY FORMS

Charles Lamb began his literary career writing poetry and continued to write verse his entire life. He tried his hand at other genres, however, and is remembered primarily for his familiar essays. These essays, originally published in the *London Magazine*, were collected in *Essays of Elia* (1823) with another collection appearing ten years later, *Last Essays of Elia* (1833). In addition to his poetry and essays, Lamb wrote fiction, drama, children's literature, and criticism. He wrote one novel, *A Tale of Rosamund Gray and Old Blind Margaret* (1798). In 1802, he published his first play, *John Woodvil: A Tragedy*, which was followed shortly by another attempt at drama: *Mr. H.: Or, Beware a Bad Name, a Farce in Two Acts* (pb. 1806). In addition to several prologues and epilogues, he published two other dramas: *The Pawnbroker's Daughter: A Farce* (pb. 1825) and *The Wife's Trial* (pb. 1827). In addition, he wrote (largely in collaboration with his sister Mary) several children's books: *The King and Queen of Hearts* (1805), *Tales from Shakespeare* (1807), *Adventures of Ulysses* (1808), *Mrs. Leicester's School* (1809), and *Prince Dorus* (1811). Lamb's criticism appeared in various periodicals but was never systematically collected and published during his lifetime. He did publish copious critical notes to accompany his vo-

luminous extracts from Elizabethan plays, *Specimens of English Dramatic Poets, Who Lived About the Time of Shakespeare, with Notes* (1808).

ACHIEVEMENTS

Much of Charles Lamb's literary career was spent in search of an appropriate genre for his particular genius. He wrote poetry, drama, fiction, and criticism, but of these he truly distinguished himself only in criticism. When he happened upon the persona of Elia and the familiar essay, however, these early efforts contributed to his success. As if he had been in training for years preparing to create the *Essays of Elia*, Lamb applied what he had learned from each of the earlier literary forms in which he had worked. Incorporating his knowledge of the importance of rhythm, dramatic context, characterization, dialogue, tone, and point of view, he placed it into the *Essays of Elia* collections and created masterpieces.

Today's literary critics value the essays of Lamb because they embody and reflect in prose the Romantic predisposition found in the great poetry of the day. These familiar essays have a biographical impulse, organic form, symbolic representation, syntactic flexibility, and occasional subject matter. The popularity of Lamb's essays, however, does not depend on their historical or theoretical relevance. The *Essays of Elia* collections were as celebrated in Lamb's day as they are in modern times and for the same reason: The character of Elia that Lamb creates is one of the most endearing personae in English literature. Elia's whimsical reminiscences may border on the trivial, but that is insignificant, because the character of the speaker preempts the content of his speech. The personality of Elia becomes the focal point of the essay. His sentimentality, tempered by irony, elevates these pieces to the status of art, conferring on them their timeless appeal.

Just as the character of Elia is essential to the success of the essays, Lamb's personality overwhelmed his accomplishments in his own day. No discussion of Lamb's achievements would be complete without mention of his many friends, who provided the essential ingredient for his famous nights at home and his fascinating correspondence. A list of his friends is a roster of the major figures of English Romanticism:

Samuel Taylor Coleridge, Robert Southey, William Wordsworth, William Godwin, William Hazlitt, Thomas De Quincey, George Dyer, and Benjamin Robert Haydon. His midweek parties from 1801 through 1827 assembled writers, artists, actors, and critics for both frivolous and serious discussion. Port, mutton, cards, and tobacco made the following workday the longest of the week for Lamb. What the success of his weekly gatherings suggests, his correspondence corroborates: Lamb was an honest critic, a sensitive friend, and a sympathetic confidant. When he mentioned his many friends, he assumed his usual tone of self-deprecation, claiming that they were "for the most part, persons of an uncertain fortune." When talking of Lamb, his friends were less diffident. Henry Crabb Robinson epitomizes the opinion of Lamb's friends when he characterized Lamb as "of all the men of genius I ever knew, the one the most intensely and universally to be loved."

BIOGRAPHY

Charles Lamb was born in London to poor parents. His father was a servant and clerk to Samuel Salt, Esquire, of the Inner Temple, and his mother was Salt's housekeeper. Like his older brother John, Lamb went to Christ's Hospital School when he was seven, sponsored by Salt. There he met Coleridge, who was to become his friend for life. Because of a stutter, Lamb did not follow Coleridge to Cambridge on scholarship. Instead, at the age of fourteen, with his education complete, he went to work. His first two apprenticeships came to nothing. In 1792, however, he took a position as an accountant in the East India House, where he remained until his retirement in 1825. Lamb often complained about his position at the East India House, claiming that the work was boring and unimaginative. In fact, the routine about which he complained was a setting and stabilizing influence that his temperament needed and his art exploited. Lamb received an adequate income for a modicum of work, and though not rich, he was comfortable by the standards of his day. Two other events in his life, however, diminished the happiness offered by this financial security.

Among celebrated bachelors, Lamb is one of the most famous. His unmarried status, however, was not of his own choosing. Sometime around 1792, he fell in love with Ann Simmons, a Hertfordshire neighbor of his maternal grandmother, Mrs. Field. Mrs. Field is said to have discouraged the relationship by pointing out that there was insanity in the Lamb family, and Ann married a London pawnbroker and silversmith named Barton. Lamb's poetry, letters, and essays testify to the sorrow he felt over his loss. Thirty years later in "Dream Children," Elia would fantasize about the woman he never married and the children he never fathered, who instead "call Bartram father." Mrs. Field's warning may have been a self-fulfilling prophecy. At the end of 1795, in despair over "another Person," Lamb committed himself to Hoxton Asylum for six weeks. In a letter to Coleridge dated May 27, 1796, he explains his condition: "I am got somewhat rational now, & *don't bite any one*. But *mad I was*—& many a vagary my imagination played with me."

The second unhappy event that crucially influenced Lamb's life was also related to madness. On September

Charles Lamb (Popperfoto/Getty Images)

22, 1796, his sister Mary went mad and fatally stabbed their mother with a kitchen knife. She was tried in the courts, found insane, and remanded to Lamb's custody for life, at his request. Because of his devotion to Mary, his life was altered permanently. Lamb and Mary had always been close, but now they became inseparable, except, that is, when Mary felt her madness coming on. Then the two could be seen walking hand in hand—crying and carrying Mary's straitjacket—to Hoxton Asylum where she would stay until she was well again. To make up for the family that neither of them had, they both cultivated a great number of friends. Stories abound concerning Lamb's remarkable personality, his charming wit, quick sallies, pointed puns, and clever ripostes. It was this engaging personality that Lamb managed to translate into his depiction of Elia. Elia first appeared in the *London Magazine* in August, 1820, with the essay "Recollections of the South-Sea House." Elia is however, a mask, but a mask sharing many of Lamb's traits and experiences.

In 1825, Lamb sent his last Elia essay to the *London Magazine* and retired from the East India House. His retirement, eagerly awaited, proved disappointing. He missed the routine, the motivation, the camaraderie of the office. Worse was the frequent illness of Mary that left him alone more and more often. Lamb was not a man able to cope with loneliness, and his drinking increased. With the death of Coleridge in July of 1834, Lamb seemed to lose interest in life. On Saturday, December 27, 1834, he died in his home at the age of fifty-nine. He is buried in Edmonton churchyard, outside London.

ANALYSIS

Charles Lamb's attitude toward poetry evolved as he matured. As a young man, he considered himself an aspiring poet. He experimented with rhythms, modeled his diction after Sir Philip Sidney and his sentiment after William Lisle Bowles, discussed theory with Samuel Taylor Coleridge, and took pleasure in criticizing his own and others' work. In his early verse, there is little of the humor, irony, or modesty that typify his later writing. Lamb is not only serious but also self-consciously so, dealing with weighty topics in an elevated style. His early poems are heavy with melancholy

and despair, even before Mary killed their mother. The poems are also personal and confessional and suggest an adolescent indulgence in emotion. Writing to Coleridge in 1796, Lamb explained, "I love my sonnets because they are the reflected images of my own feelings at different times."

Following Mary's disaster, Lamb's reality became as tragic as he had previously imagined. He wrote to Coleridge, "Mention nothing of poetry. I have destroyed every vestige of past vanities of that kind." This was the first of several renunciations of poetry made by Lamb throughout his life, but—like similar renunciations of liquor and tobacco—it was temporary. In a few months, he was sending Coleridge new verses, but the subject matter was altered. Lamb turned to poetry for solace and consolation, composing religious verse. His interest in poetry had revived, but the sensational occurrences that influenced the rest of his life encouraged him to become one of the least sensational of poets. From this new perspective, he counseled Coleridge to "cultivate simplicity," anticipating William Wordsworth's preface to *Lyrical Ballads* (1798). In his next letter to Coleridge, he praised Bowles and Philip Massinger and said he favored "an uncomplaining melancholy, a delicious regret for the past." Lamb's early sentimentality had been displaced by real tragedy, and his poetry changed accordingly.

With the healing passage of time, Lamb's literary interests shifted. In the years 1800 to 1805, he wrote several poems, but for the most part, these middle years of his literary career were spent as a journalist. Around 1820, Lamb again began to write poetry, but of a completely different sort. The last period of his poetic production had been spent writing album verse and other occasional poems. As he matured, Lamb outgrew his earlier confessional mode and turned to people and events around him for subjects. He used his imagination to a greater degree, coloring reality, creating fictions, and distancing himself from his subject. His poetry changed with him, and it came to reflect a fictitious personality similar to the Elia of the essays. Like the Elia essays, Lamb's later poetry contains many autobiographical elements, but they are cloaked and decorous. In place of self-indulgent confessions is a distance and control not found in the early verse.

Lamb wrote and published most of his serious verse—that which is most often anthologized—in the period between 1795 and 1800. His best and worst poems are among these efforts, which are autobiographical and despondent. They mourn the loss of love, of bygone days, and of happier times. They vary greatly in form, as Lamb experimented with different meters and structures. He was most successful in tight and traditional verse forms and least successful in blank verse. In fact, his blank verse is bad, a surprising situation since his strength in more structured forms is in the control and variation of meter and rhythm.

SONNETS

A favorite form of Lamb's throughout his life was the sonnet, which he began writing early in his career. Appropriately enough, two of his earliest and best poems are English sonnets, published in Coleridge's *Poems on Various Subjects* (1796). This first significant publication by Lamb shows the influence of the Elizabethans on his poetry. His syntax, imagery, and diction suggest the practice of two centuries earlier. One of these sonnets, "Was it some sweet device of Faery," mourns a lost love "Anna" and is clearly a response to the loss of Ann Simmons. The poem's sophisticated rhythm, with frequent enjambment and medial stops, transcends its commonplace subject. Here, as often in Lamb's poetry, the handling of rhythm turns what might be a mediocre effort into an admirable poem. His use of rhetorical questions in this sonnet is skillful, too. Unlike the stilted tone that such questions often provide, in this sonnet the questions actually help to create a sense of sincerity.

Another sonnet from the same volume, "O, I could laugh to hear the midnight wind," also treats the subject of lost love. The poem is nicely unified by the images of wind and wave, and it reflects the Romantic idea of the unity of human beings and cosmos. It also presents another Romantic concept, the value of the imagination and the powerful influence of memory. This poem is a reminder that much of Wordsworthian theory was not unique to Wordsworth. The ideas that the poem considers may be Romantic, but the style is that of an earlier day. The diction is antique, the imagery tightly unified, and the sonnet form itself conventionally developed. Lamb's prosody is pleasant but not novel.

In 1797, Coleridge's book of poetry went into a second edition, but with an amended title, ". . . to which are now added Poems by Charles Lamb." Lamb had already contributed four poems to the earlier edition, but now there appeared fourteen of his poems. The additional ones are, on the whole, inferior to the initial four; seven are sonnets written about the same time as those that Coleridge had already published. Of interest is one addressed to Mary and written before her tragedy, "If from my lips some angry accents fell." The closing lines give a sense of the personal nature of these verses:

> Thou to me didst ever shew
> Kindest affection; and would oft times lend
> An ear to the desponding love-sick lay,
> Weeping with sorrows with me, who repay
> But ill the mighty debt of love I owe,
> Mary, to thee, my sister and my friend.

The other poem of note in this volume was published in a supplement at the end of the edition. Lamb was signaling its inferiority, and his judgment was correct. "A Vision of Repentance" is an experiment in Spenserian stanza. It opens with a vision, "I saw a famous fountain, in my dream." The fountain turns out to be the waters of redemption that have attracted "Psyche" as well as the speaker. A dialogue between the two ensues, and Psyche reports that she has forsaken Jesus and given "to a treacherous WORLD my heart." After some further conversation, the speaker leaves Psyche with the wish "Christ restore thee soon." The poem is one of several by Lamb that deal with Christianity. Like his other religious verse, it is flawed: didactic, prolix, and unrhythmical.

BLANK VERSE

Lamb's failure with the Spenserian stanza is paralleled by his experiments in blank verse. In 1798, he and Charles Lloyd published a volume titled *Blank Verse*. Lacking the direction given by a tight form or a controlling convention, Lamb's blank verse is verbose, clumsy, and unsure. His autobiographical subject matter and confessional intent are uncomfortably couched in an elevated style reminiscent of John Milton. The two are not compatible. The volume, however, does contain one work by Lamb worthy of his talent.

"THE OLD FAMILIAR FACES"

"The Old Familiar Faces," though not in blank verse, is Lamb's best-known poem. The subject is typical of this period in Lamb's career; it is a lamenting revelation of intense personal grief and loss. Its power, however, lies not in its subject matter, but in the skillful way in which Lamb manipulates the prosody. The poem evokes humanity's essential isolation and loneliness in the dolorous tolling repetition of the phrase "All, all are gone, the old familiar faces."

The form of the poem creates the effect. Rather than blank verse or the thumping rhymed verse of which he was too fond, Lamb chose a three-line stanza that replaced rhyme with the repetition of the title line. In this way, he gained form without the convoluted syntax of the padded line that rhyme often demanded. The rhythm of the line is that used by Coleridge in "Christabel," and it is agreeable to think that it was Lamb who suggested this meter to his friend.

The poem is justly often anthologized; its rhythm is perfectly suited to the subject. Ian Jack in the *Oxford History of English Literature* (1963) suggests that the success of the meter conflicts with the other poems in the volume. He concludes, "It is hard to say how far the effect of the poem is due to metrical sophistication, and how far to a felicitous awkwardness."

"HESTER"

By 1800, the self-indulgent moroseness of Lamb's early verse was beginning to be displaced by a greater sense of reserve and control. These years saw less poetic activity by Lamb, but the poems he wrote are, on the whole, more able. An excellent example of the newfound discipline displayed by Lamb occurs in "Hester." The poem again deals with the subjects of loss, death, and despair, but he handles them with a new and previously uncharacteristic restraint. The tight rhyme scheme and the concluding hypermetrical iambic dimeter line provide Lamb with a form he uses well: a short line, a varied rhythm, and a regular stanza:

> A springy motion in her gait,
> A rising step, did indicate
> Of pride and joy no common rate
>   That flush'd her spirit

"Hester" is not one of the immortal poems in the English language, but it is a solid achievement worthy of a young poet. Ian Jack has compared it favorably with the lyrical ballads of Wordsworth.

"A FAREWELL TO TOBACCO"

Another poem from this period breaks the morbidity of Lamb's previous verse and prefigures the wit and urbanity found in *Essays of Elia*. Lamb wrote "A Farewell to Tobacco" in what he called "a stammering verse" because he used tobacco to retard his own stammering. Once again he turned to the short line, in this case an irregular eight-syllable trochaic line with rhyming couplets, and it well served his comic intent. Gone is the gross subjectivity; instead, the poem humorously indicts tobacco, while admitting that the habit is unbreakable. Good-natured wordplay and clever burlesque make the poem one of Lamb's most enjoyable. The comic tone established in "A Farewell to Tobacco" appears again in 1812 when Lamb composed one of his few political poems. "The Triumph of the Whale" gently ridicules the prince regent by comparing George with a leviathan. He satirizes the regent's girth, appetite, retinue, and failed constancy. The poem exists mainly, however, for the pun on which it ends: "the PRINCE of WHALES."

"WRITTEN AT CAMBRIDGE"

The last noteworthy poem of this period is a sonnet that illustrates Lamb's mature, relaxed, and personal style. "Written at Cambridge" is an autobiographical whimsy that details how the poet feels as he walks around the university. A note of disappointment begins the poem because the speaker regrets that he had been unable to attend such an institution. This sense of loss disappears, however, with the speaker's slightly foolish but nevertheless touching portrait of his imaginative usurpation of Cantabrigian wisdom while strolling its grounds. This poem is worthy of "gentle Charles."

THE POETICAL WORKS OF CHARLES LAMB

Of the original poems published in the posthumous collection *The Poetical Works of Charles Lamb*, almost half are from his last period, 1820 to 1834. Most of these are "album verse," a popular form in the 1820's. These occasional verses—written at the request of and about the album's owner—are humorous and light, built around epigrams, puns, and acrostics. Most of this album verse, while representative of the genre, is hardly memorable, with two exceptions. "On the Arrival in England of Lord Byron's Remains" is a good example of Lamb's mature tone, and it reveals his opinion of Lord Byron: "lordly Juan, damned to lasting fame,/ Went out a pickle, and came back the same." A more serious work that arrives at unpleasant conclusions is "In My Own Album," a poignant comparison of life to an album. The poem returns to the theme of self-reproach that colored so much of Lamb's early verse, but there exists a distance and a universality that was not at work before. Rhymed tercets provide Lamb the form in which he worked best, and his iambic hexameters are smooth and graceful. The music of his verse complements his rhythm and meter.

"ON AN INFANT DYING AS SOON AS BORN"

Two of Lamb's best poems, both products of this late period, nicely exemplify his mature serious and comic styles. Both were written after Lamb had won recognition as an essayist, when he no longer felt he had to prove himself as a poet. Freed from the necessity of competing with Edmund Spenser, John Donne, and Milton (not to mention Coleridge, Robert Burns, and Robert Southey), Lamb discovered his own rhythm and voice. These, his finest verses, are the products of his natural strengths, and not those borrowed from another time or another artist. Relaxed and self-assured, Lamb mastered the short line and the comic effect of rhyme. He cultivated forms that worked for him and his voice. "On an Infant Dying as Soon as Born" deals with loss and death in a poignant and moving way. The maudlin, pathetic tone is gone. In its place is an elegant lament for the state of all humans, an elegy that transcends the single occasion, a threnody whose language and figures are worthy of Andrew Marvell or Henry Vaughan. The dead child, addressed as "Riddle of destiny," presents to the speaker an insoluble problem, the suffering of innocent people. The speaker concludes that "the economy of Heaven is dark" and that even the "wisest clerks" are unable to explain why an infant dies while

> shrivel'd crones
> Stiffen with age to stocks and stones;
> And crabbed use the conscience sears
> In sinners of an hundred years.

The poem closes with a traditional, but guarded, optimism.

SATAN IN SEARCH OF A WIFE

Lamb's longest and last poem published during his life, *Satan in Search of a Wife* (1831), consists of two books of thirty verses each. It is usually said that Lamb never valued this poem because he wrote his publisher not to mention that the "damn'd 'Devil's Wedding'" was written by the author of the *Essays of Elia*. Nevertheless, he thought highly enough of the poem to have it published. The ballad is Lamb at his best: light, jocular, ironic, punning, occasional, and personal. It begins with an echo of Lord Byron's *The Vision of Judgment* (1822) in reverse. Instead of Saint Peter grown bored, the devil is out of sorts:

> The Devil was sick and queasy of late,
>   And his sleep and his appetite fail'd him;
> His ears they hung down and his tail it was clapp'd
> Between his poor hoofs, like a dog that's been rapp'd—
>   None knew what the devil ail'd him.

The tale continues, telling of the Devil's love for a tailor's daughter, his successful wooing of her, and the joyful wedding. Lamb's autobiographical propensity shows up even here, for lurking behind all the fun are serious complaints about bachelorhood, about women as lovers, women as mothers, and even women who murder, with the speaker concluding that "a living Fiend/ Was better than a dead Parent." The poem is, however, anything but maudlin. It is an energetic and fancy-filled romp that spoofs the devil, marriage, foreigners, and the Christian idea of Hell. It is vintage Lamb: genteel, a bit cynical, but kind and sincere. The essays of Lamb will continue to earn him fame, but poems such as *Satan in Search of a Wife* have been too long neglected.

OTHER MAJOR WORKS

LONG FICTION: *A Tale of Rosamund Gray and Old Blind Margaret*, 1798.

PLAYS: *John Woodvil: A Tragedy*, pb. 1802; *Mr. H.: Or, Beware a Bad Name, a Farce in Two Acts*, pb. 1806; *The Pawnbroker's Daughter: A Farce*, pb. 1825; *The Wife's Trial*, pb. 1827.

NONFICTION: *Specimens of English Dramatic Po-*

ets, *Who Lived About the Time of Shakespeare, with Notes*, 1808; *Essays of Elia*, 1823; *Last Essays of Elia*, 1833; *The Letters of Charles Lamb*, 1935 (3 volumes); *Miscellaneous Essays*, 2009.

CHILDREN'S LITERATURE: *The King and Queen of Hearts*, 1805; *Tales from Shakespeare*, 1807 (with Mary Lamb); *Adventures of Ulysses*, 1808; *Mrs. Leicester's School*, 1809 (with Mary Lamb); *Prince Dorus*, 1811.

MISCELLANEOUS: *The Works of Charles and Mary Lamb*, 1903-1905 (7 volumes; 1912, 6 volumes).

BIBLIOGRAPHY

Aaron, Jane. *A Double Singleness: Gender and the Writings of Charles and Mary Lamb*. New York: Oxford University Press, 1991. Argues that Lamb's close relationship with his sister Mary led to a feminism in his writing that was in contrast to the prevailing style.

Barnett, George Leonard. *Charles Lamb*. Boston: Twayne, 1976. This volume is an excellent introduction to Lamb. Barnett supplies a biography interwoven with an analysis of Lamb's major works. Supplemented by a chronology of Lamb's life and work, an index, and a bibliography. Suitable for all students.

Burton, Sarah. *A Double Life: A Biography of Charles and Mary Lamb*. New York: Viking, 2003. This biography looks at the relationship between Lamb and his sister, who became linked after her mental illness emerged.

Cecil, David. *A Portrait of Charles Lamb*. New York: Scribner, 1984. A standard biography of Lamb that also covers his writings.

Cornwall, Barry. *Charles Lamb: A Memoir*. Boston: Roberts Brothers, 1866. Serious students of Lamb will find this old book essential, as it was written only thirty-two years after Lamb's death, by a contemporary who knew him well. Lamb was astonishingly well loved, and his work held in high esteem by his contemporaries. It is interesting to see that the reputation of his work remains good today.

James, Felicity. *Charles Lamb, Coleridge, and Wordsworth: Reading Friendship in the 1790's*. New York: Palgrave Macmillan, 2008. Focuses on the relationship among Lamb, Samuel Taylor Coleridge, and William Wordsworth. Contains substantial analysis of Lamb's writings.

Lucas, Edward V. *The Life of Charles Lamb*. 5th ed. 2 vols. London: Methuen, 1921. This book remains the standard biography on Lamb. It is built on information gathered from Lamb's writings. Lucas provides a great many facts about Lamb's life but little critical analysis of his work. Valuable for all students.

Monsman, Gerald. *Charles Lamb as the London Magazine's "Elia."* Lewiston, N.Y.: Edwin Mellen Press, 2003. Although this work is primarily about Lamb's essays, it sheds light on the author and the themes of his poetry.

Riehl, Joseph E. *That Dangerous Figure: Charles Lamb and the Critics*. Columbia, S.C.: Camden House, 1998. An examination of criticism by Lamb's contemporaries of his works, with extensive bibliographic references.

John F. Schell

WALTER SAVAGE LANDOR

Born: Warwick, England; January 30, 1775
Died: Florence, Italy; September 17, 1864

PRINCIPAL POETRY

The Poems of Walter Savage Landor, 1795
Gebir: A Poem, in Seven Books, 1798
Poems from the Arabic and Persian, 1800
Poetry by the Author of Gebir, 1800
Gebirus, Poema, 1803
Count Julian, 1812 (verse drama)
Idyllia Nova Quinque Heroum atque Heroidum, 1815
Idyllia Heroica Decem Librum Phaleuciorum Unum, 1820
Andrea of Hungary, 1839 (verse drama)
Giovanna of Naples, 1839 (verse drama)
Fra Rupert: The Last Part of a Trilogy, 1840 (verse drama)

The Siege of Ancona, 1846 (verse drama)
The Hellenics Enlarged and Completed, 1847
Poemata et Inscriptiones, 1847
Italics of Walter Savage Landor, 1848
The Last Fruit off an Old Tree, 1853
Heroic Idyls, with Additional Poems, 1863
The Poetical Works of Walter Savage Landor, 1937
    (Stephen Wheeler, editor)

OTHER LITERARY FORMS

The reputation of Walter Savage Landor (LAHN-dawr) rests primarily on his poetry, but he was a skilled writer of prose as well. His political writings are notable for their anger and his criticism for its insight into the mechanics of writing. All his prose is witty; it is frequently satirical. As with his poetry, Landor's prose works are carefully phrased and sometimes more perfect in their parts than their wholes. Ranked as one of the most important practitioners of nonfiction prose in the nineteenth century, he is viewed by critics as one of the outstanding prose stylists of the English language.

ACHIEVEMENTS

Walter Savage Landor's poetry has never had a wide readership. Much of its appeal is in its near-perfect phrasing and versification; such an appeal of skill almost inevitably attracts admirers among other poets, the fellow practitioners of a demanding art. Landor remains admired for the variety of poetic forms that he mastered and for the clarity of his phrasing; he is often faulted for the detached tone of his work—for the lack of emotional response to his subjects. His poetry often seems crystalline and fragile, as if unable to withstand the burden of a large audience. Fine prosody and marvelously apt phrasing when combined with the distant tone of much of his verse makes ranking him among poets a difficult task. Compounding the difficulty are his poetry's classical characteristics, which seem in conflict with the Romantic and Victorian eras during which he wrote. His poetry lacks the emotional vigor of Percy Bysshe Shelley's work but compares well with the beauty of John Keats's odes and is superior to Lord Byron's verse in ingenuity. He cannot match William Wordsworth in importance to the history of poetry, although many poets have valued his

contributions to the understanding of prosody. Taken by itself, apart from its era and influence, Landor's poetry is equal in melodic beauty and economy of phrasing to much of the best in English poetry. As a poet, Landor might fairly be ranked behind Wordsworth and Robert Browning in overall achievement and behind Keats in imagery; he is second to none in phrasing and prosody.

BIOGRAPHY

Walter Savage Landor was a man given to fierce passions; he could burst out in either anger or generosity almost without warning. He was egotistical and given to romantic notions about life; this combination caused him much unhappiness and yet underlies much of his best writing. He was born on January 30, 1775, in Warwick. In 1780, he began his schooling at Knowle; in 1783, he was sent to study at Rugby. After eight years of annoying his teachers and antagonizing others with his satirical sense of humor, he was sent home. Landor, however, remembered Rugby fondly; while there, he developed his taste for poetry and demonstrated a precocious skill in composing verse. The Reverend William Langley, of Ashbourne, Derbyshire, became Landor's tutor in 1792. The next year, Landor entered Trinity College, Oxford. While at Oxford, he punctuated a political dispute by shooting at a neighbor's shutters; suspended from college for two terms, he left Oxford in 1794, never to return. He moved to London and had his poetry published under a grand title for a mere twenty-year-old, *The Poems of Walter Savage Landor* (1795). The volume brought him a small but loyal following among other writers and readers who had a taste for fine literature.

When his father died, Landor inherited a large fortune. This he spent on a large estate in Wales and on outfitting his own regiment to fight in Spain against the French. After the French left Spain, Landor's regiment disappeared, and he hastened home. In Wales, he tried to improve the lives of the peasants and to introduce enlightened methods of managing an estate. No one seemed to appreciate his efforts, and after losing much money, he abandoned the effort.

In 1811, in one of his grand gestures, he married an attractive woman who was beneath him in both wealth

Walter Savage Landor (Hulton Archive/Getty Images)

and social station. Far from being grateful, his bride, Julia Thuillier, repeatedly cuckolded Landor and made his life unpleasant. She did not appreciate her husband's generous nature, his intellect, or his interests. Although she is often portrayed as a nasty and cruel woman, she and Landor seem to have had enough truces to produce a daughter and three sons. In 1814, Landor toured the Continent, where he was eventually joined by his wife. From 1816 to 1818, he stayed in Como, Italy, and in 1818, his first son was born. His daughter followed in 1820, while he was in Pisa. From 1821 to 1828, he lived in Florence, where his second and third sons were born in 1822 and 1825. By 1835, his family life was unbearable; his wife dedicated herself to embarrassing him publicly and committing adultery privately. Landor had doted on his children and spoiled them; nevertheless, when he left his wife and returned to England, they chose to remain with her, although in the 1840's, his two eldest sons and his daughter visited him for months at a time. During the years of unhappy marriage, Landor continued to write, building a loyal following of admiring friends, including Ralph Waldo Emerson and John Forster.

Landor's trenchant wit and attacks on the misdeeds of public officials frequently involved him in trouble. In 1857, old but still fiery, he published attacks on a Mrs. Yescombe, whom he saw as a villainess because of an injustice visited on a young woman. Convicted of libel in 1858, he left England in 1859 to seek refuge from litigation in Fiesole, where he had maintained his family since 1835. Rejected by his family, he wandered to nearby Florence, where Robert Browning offered him a home. He died on September 17, 1864. He had wanted to be buried near Bath in England but was interred instead at Florence. He had wanted an epitaph that mentioned his closest friends but instead received one that mentions his wife and children.

ANALYSIS

The poems of Walter Savage Landor are like fragile crystals, the clarity of which disguises their masterfully crafted form. The meaning of Landor's verse often seems transparent; he believed in clarity as a poetic virtue. The seeming ease with which his verse can be understood belies the strenuous efforts Landor made to pare down his phrases and to present his ideas with near-perfect economy. Much of his success in economical phrasing comes from his mastery of a host of meters and poetic subgenres, chief among which were the verse drama, the dramatic scene, the heroic poem, and the Hellenic poem. Landor had a restless mind, requiring activity; he had a voracious appetite for ideas. Writing poetry provided him with relief from such intellectual demands. Poetry was thus more of a hobby than a career; Landor wrote verse for recreation, and the complexity of his prosody and the pureness of his language originate in part from this recreational aspect of his versifying. His poetry represented an effort to find peace of mind, to discharge some of his extraordinary intellectual energy. The literature of ancient Greece and Rome had a long history of amateur scholarly study and had inspired and informed the neoclassical period in England that was just ending when Landor was born, and he found ready materials for such agreeable study in a host of commentaries on form and style. The Greeks supplied him with ideas about life and human relationships; the Latin poets supplied him with high standards for poetic composition and style. He sometimes wrote in Latin, perhaps to capture the elegance and sense of sweet phrasing that typifies much of the best of the poetry of the classical Romans.

Landor's use of classical materials has long created problems for literary historians. His life spans the Romantic era and ends when the Victorian era was well under way. Although some Romantic poets—notably Percy Bysshe Shelley—used classical myths as subjects, they rarely employed classical forms. A classicist can be identified by his use of the standards of the ancient poets: an emphasis on phrasing, good sense, and logical order. A classicist restrains his emotions in favor of clarity of expression and tends to use classical works as models for his own. The Romantics, on the other hand, reacted to the preceding neoclassical age by emphasizing mysticism, nature, and traditional English poetic forms such as blank verse and the sonnet.

In his tastes and models, Landor was every inch a classicist and had more in common with Alexander Pope and Samuel Johnson than with Wordsworth or Shelley, but in his subjects, he turned to nature as an ideal, somewhat as Wordsworth did and even more as did the Renaissance poet Sir Philip Sidney, and he wrote blank verse with a facility that had been alien to many of his neoclassical forebears. He had in common with his contemporaries a vast enthusiasm for poetry, but, whereas his contemporaries lived for their art, Landor's art was his servant. Emotional outbursts were reined in; uncontrolled poetic fervor was not for Landor. His spirit was as restless as Lord Byron's, but where Byron turned his restlessness into a poetic ideal, Landor used poetry to subdue his own restlessness. Thus, the determined and hard self-control evident in Landor's verse sets him apart from the poets of his time. Some critics call him a Romantic, though seemingly more for the age in which he lived than for the qualities of his work. He actually was the son of the neoclassical age; he followed a poetic path that was a logical extension of what the neoclassicists had achieved, while Wordsworth and the Romantics followed a poetic path that was a logical reaction against the neoclassicists. Landor was a classicist in a Romantic age.

VERSE DRAMAS

As a good student of the classical authors, Landor believed in poetic simplicity. His verse dramas reveal at once the strengths and weaknesses of the simplicity that gives his poetry its crystalline character. Although not the best of his dramatic efforts, perhaps the best known of his dramas is the tragedy of *Count Julian*. The play resembles a child's perception of tragedy—all loud voices and grim visages. The characters exclaim instead of converse; each word seems meant for the ages. The welter of "Ohs!" and other short exclamations are sometimes more risible than dramatic. Even so, the subject of *Count Julian* has much potential for good drama. A Spanish warrior who has driven the Moors from Spain avenges the rape of his daughter by his king by leading the Moors back into his country, with disastrous consequences. The play's blank verse is austere, remote from the characters and their emotions. Landor had hoped that *Count Julian* might be performed, but its poetry is more important than its drama; it is now regarded strictly as a closet drama. *Andrea of Hungary* and its sequels *Giovanna of Naples* and *Fra Rupert: The Last Part of a Trilogy* are dramatically and poetically more successful. Blank verse and character blend well in these plays; the scenes between Andrea and Giovanna in the first of them are relaxed, revealing two interesting personalities. Landor cared little for plot, which he called "trick"; thus, the sequence of events in his trilogy of plays is predictable and has few twists. Andrea is murdered, probably at the instigation of the ambitious Fra Rupert; Giovanna remains a paragon of virtue through three marriages and is eventually murdered; Fra Rupert commits suicide, and his villainy is revealed. Landor uses the plot as a vehicle for some of his notions about power and politics, and his blend of apt phrase, characterization, and good verse is often moving.

Landor's dramatic scenes also feature blank verse, though they are only short conversations. In "Essex and Bacon," for example, Landor shows the earl of Essex meeting with Francis Bacon after the earl's condemnation to death for treason. Landor's interest in ambition and the abuse of power provides the scene's depth. Essex sees himself as greater than Bacon because he took a glorious chance by opposing Queen Elizabeth, and he cannot understand how his friend can call him "lower than bergess or than churl." Essex declares, "To servile souls how abject seem the fallen!/ Benchers and message-bearers stride o'er Essex." He dismisses Bacon with contempt. When alone, Bacon is allowed the last word, which, in summary, says that ambition is often mistakenly thought to be great by those who allow it to run their lives, when, in fact, it is arrogance. The dramatic scenes generally reflect Landor's concern with the abuse of power; "Ippolito di Este" perhaps makes Landor's feelings clearest. This short drama introduces the audience to the brothers Ferrante, Giulio, and the Cardinal Ippolito di Este. Ferrante has the misfortune to have his eyes admired by a woman whom his brother the cardinal desires; the cardinal has Ferrante's eyes removed. The dramatic scene is truly horrible, even if Ferrant is too saintly to be palatable.

GEBIR

Of Landor's heroic poems, his first (and his first important poem, written when he was perhaps twenty years of age), *Gebir*, is probably the best known. Gebir is king of Gades (Cádiz); he conquers Egypt and the heart of Queen Charoba, then is assassinated. The poem takes him through heroic adventures, including a trip to the underworld. *Gebir* reveals Landor's extensive scholarship, based as it is on Arabian history. The verse is spare, already featuring Landor's emphasis on succinct phrasing; its scenes are dramatic and resemble the tragedies in structure. Unfortunately, the language of the poem is too remote for successful characterization; Gebir, who is a strong, dynamic young man, talks like an ancient Greek god. His love, Charoba, is more accessible to readers, although she, too, often merely declaims. *Gebir* displays much fine poetry; it may not always succeed, but it is good enough by itself to establish Landor's claim to poetic importance. Admired by contemporary critics and poets, including Robert Southey, the poem established Landor as a significant poet.

HELLENIC POEMS

Landor's so-called Hellenics are poems that are informed by ancient Greek myths and history. They encompass blank verse, lyrics, sonnets, and conversations. The best of these, such as "Coresos and Callirhöe," "The Altar of Modesty," "Acon and Rhodope," "Pan," and "The Marriage of Helena and Menelaos," are exquisite gems of the poet's art. Each is representative of Landor's classical principles; the poems are simple in

form, their clarity of language being the result of much revision, and they reflect intelligent observation. They focus on characters and generally deliver homilies on love and life. In "Pan and Pitys," for instance, Pitys is loud in her derogation of Boreas, her suitor. Boreas hears her, and he drops a large rock on her. The exchanges between Pan and Pitys are loud and boisterous; her foolishness and insensitivity are also loud; perhaps she should have spoken more kindly of her suitor. In "Acon and Rhodope," a man loses sight of what is important in his life and loses all he cares for. The verse is thick with colors and odors that represent a mixture of life and death; apple trees have "freckled leaves" and oleanders have "light-hair'd progeny." The effect of the Hellenic poems is one of another world that is somehow part of the common one. The characters have thoughts, emotions, and problems, much like those that are common to humanity, but their world is richer, more intense than common experience. Such intensity is well evoked in "The Marriage of Helena and Menelaos," in which the sixteen-year-old Helena faces her husband-to-be and the prospect of adulthood for the first time. The gibes of siblings, the fears of appearing foolish, and the sense of losing youth too soon, condense into a poignant, short series of events. "The Marriage of Helena and Menelaos" is a product of the mature Landor; it is alive with ideas, focused on a dramatic moment, and deceptively simple on its surface.

THE SIEGE OF ANCONA

Although Landor strove to use elevated language and to create clear, often austere, verse, his poetry contains much variety and life. Works such as "Homer, Laertes, Agatha" and "Penelope and Pheido" not only feature Landor's classicism but also feature high poetry and are lively. Landor brings humanity to his poetry; he focuses on the difficulties people have when faced with problems larger than themselves. Like that of other poets who lived long lives, Landor's verse changed over the years; it began by being brash and noisy, as in *Gebir* and *Count Julian*; grew to reflect his thoughts on politics and power, as in *Fra Rupert*; and attained a blend of erudition and humanity that brings sensitivity to "The Marriage of Helena and Menelaos," written when Landor was eighty-nine years old.

Among his most sensitive and interesting works is

the verse drama *The Siege of Ancona*. Typical of Landor's work, it is known to only a few critics and admirers of poetry. Its verse is clear and its tone is heroic, without the declamatory faults of *Count Julian*; its psychology is subtle and its values those of a classicist who was nevertheless a part of the Romantic period. The Consul of Ancona asserts that "the air/ Is life alike to all, the sun is warmth,/ The earth, its fruits and flocks, are nutriment,/ Children and wives are comforts; all partake/ (Or may partake) in these." Like Wordsworth, Landor found a universal metaphor in nature; unlike Wordsworth, he made his natural world Arcadian in the manner of English Renaissance poets. He labored at the classical ideal of spare verse and detached tone; he yielded to the Romantic desire to express his innermost spirit. At its best, his poetry is clear and crystalline, maintaining a warmth and sensitive empathy for the common joys, miseries, and confusions that people face in their daily lives.

OTHER MAJOR WORKS

LONG FICTION: *Imaginary Conversations of Literary Men and Statesmen*, 1824-1829 (5 volumes); *The Pentameron and Pentalogia*, 1837.

SHORT FICTION: *Dry Sticks Fagoted*, 1858.

NONFICTION: *Citation and Examination of William Shakespeare*, 1834.

MISCELLANEOUS: *The Complete Works of Walter Savage Landor*, 1927-1936 (16 volumes; Thomas E. Welby and Stephen Wheeler, editors); *Walter Savage Landor: Selected Poetry and Prose*, 1981 (Keith Hanley, editor).

BIBLIOGRAPHY

Dilworth, Ernest. *Walter Savage Landor*. New York: Twayne, 1974. An excellent critical introduction for those unfamiliar with Landor's work. The author points out the poet's aims and achievements as well as his shortcomings in style and substance. Frequent quotations support the text, and a chronology, notes, references, and an excellent select bibliography are included.

Field, Jean. *Landor*. Studley, Warwickshire, England: Brewin Books, 2000. A biography of Landor with a selection of his works. Includes bibliographical references and index.

Hanley, Keith. Introduction to *Walter Savage Landor: Selected Poetry and Prose*. Manchester, England: Carcanet Press, 1981. Discusses Landor's role as a neoclassicist, the art of imitation, the classical structure of feeling, and his poetic style.

Hewitt, Regina. *Symbolic Interactions: Social Problems and Literary Interventions in the Works of Baillie, Scott, and Landor*. Lewisburg, Pa.: Bucknell University Press, 2006. This study of Landor, Joanna Baillie, and Sir Walter Scott contains a chapter on Landor's solution of political contention. Although focused on his long fiction, it sheds light on Landor's life and work.

Pinsky, Robert. *Landor's Poetry*. Chicago: University of Chicago Press, 1968. This analysis of about twenty poems explores, among other things, Landor's repeated use of subjects and gives a fair picture of his poetic artistry. The author defends Landor and makes a case for the intellectual content of the poems. Some of the lesser verse is shown to have real artistry behind it. Special attention is paid to an analysis of Landor's use of rhythms. Omitted in the discussion are Landor's tributes to other writers.

Super, Robert H. *Walter Savage Landor: A Biography*. New York: New York University Press, 1954. This lengthy, definitive biography replete with accurate detail includes material and documents hitherto ignored or undiscovered. The author corrects previous carelessness, errors in chronology, and other distortions. This fine example of biographical scholarship includes an index and an extensive system of notes and references displaying the meticulous accuracy seen throughout.

Kirk H. Beetz

WILLIAM LANGLAND

Born: Cleobury Mortimer(?), Shropshire, England; c.
1332
Died: London(?), England; c. 1400

PRINCIPAL POETRY

*The Vision of William, Concerning Piers the
Plowman*, c. 1362, A Text; c. 1377, B Text;
c. 1393, C Text (also known as *Piers Plowman*)
Richard the Redeless, c. 1395 (attributed)

OTHER LITERARY FORMS

William Langland (LANG-luhnd) is remembered
only for his poetry.

ACHIEVEMENTS

Apparently, in its own day, *The Vision of William,
Concerning Piers the Plowman* was a very popular
work. More than fifty manuscripts of the poem in its
various versions still exist. The poem's four printings
before 1561 are evidence of its continued popularity.
The audience of *Piers Plowman* was not, as it was for
most poems of the alliterative revival, a small group of
provincial nobles; rather, as J. A. Burrow has shown,
the poem would have been read by a broadly based national public of parish priests or local clergy whose
tastes favored purely didactic literature. In addition,
Burrow connects the poem with a growing lay public of
the rising bourgeoisie, whose tastes were still conservative and generally religious. The didactic content of
the poem, then, was its chief appeal in its own time.

By the sixteenth century, however, with the rise of
Protestantism, William Langland's poem became acclaimed for its aspects of social satire. This strain in the
poem had been underlined even in the fourteenth century, when John Ball, in a letter to the peasants of Essex
during the revolt of 1381, mentioned Piers the Plowman. Possibly because of this mention, the very orthodox Catholic Langland came, ironically, to be associated with Lollardy, and to be looked on as a bitter critic
of the Roman Church and a precursor of Protestantism.

By the late sixteenth century, Langland's western
Midland dialect had become too difficult for any but the
most ardent reader, and so no new edition of *Piers
Plowman* appeared until 1813. Though nineteenth century readers deplored Langland's allegory, they could
still, like the readers before them, admire *Piers Plowman* as social satire, and in addition, they could appreciate and admire the stark realism in such scenes as the
confession of the seven deadly sins in Passus 5 (B
Text). Their chief interest in Langland was historical:
They viewed the poem as a firsthand commentary on
the fourteenth century.

BIOGRAPHY

Virtually nothing is known of the poet who wrote
Piers Plowman. At one time, in fact, there was some
debate about whether a single author or perhaps as
many as five were responsible for the three separate
versions of the poem. That controversy has since
ended, and scholarship has established a single author
for all three versions.

That author's name was almost certainly William
Langland. Two fifteenth century manuscript notes attribute the poem to Langland, and there is a line in the B
Text that seems to be intended as a cryptogram of the
poet's name: "'I haue lyued in londe', quod [I], 'my
name is longe wille.'" One manuscript declares that
Langland was the son of a certain Stacey (Eustace) de
Rokayle, who later held land under the Lord Despenser
at Shipton-under-Wychwood in Oxfordshire; in all
likelihood, Langland's father was a franklin. It has
been conjectured that Langland was illegitimate, but
the difference in surname is no real reason to assume
this, such differences being common in the fourteenth
century. Langland was not born in Oxfordshire but
rather in Shropshire, at Cleobury Mortimer, some eight
miles from the Malvern Hills that serve as the setting
for the first two visions in *Piers Plowman*. Because the
B Text is dated with some accuracy c. 1377 and because the poet in the B Text declares himself to be
forty-five years old, the date of Langland's birth has
been set at about 1332.

Whatever else is "known" about the author's life is
conjectured from passages in the poem that describe
the narrator's life and is based on the assumption that
the narrator, "Will," and the poet Langland are one and
the same. In the C Text, the poet speaks of having gone

to school, and most likely he was educated at the priory of Great Malvern in Worcestershire. He would have gone through the usual training for the priesthood, but, according to evidence in the poem, the deaths of his father and friends left him without a benefactor and forced him to abandon his studies before taking holy orders. He would have been unable to advance in the Church, having left school with only minor orders, partly because of his incomplete education and because, as the poet writes, he was married—a right permitted only to clerks in orders below subdeacon.

Because of these apparent facts, E. Talbot Donaldson assumes that Langland was an acolyte, one of the poor, unbeneficed clergy who had no official way of making a living within the Church hierarchy. Certainly he was poor, but he seems to have claimed exemption from manual labor by virtue of his being a tonsured clerk. W. W. Skeat conjectures that Langland may have earned some money as a scribe, copying out legal documents, since the poem displays a close knowledge of the form of such documents. Perhaps he was able to pick up odd clerical jobs here and there in the city of London, where, according to an apparently autobiographical account in the C Text, he went to live at Cornhill with his wife, Kitte, and daughter, Callote. According to this passage, Langland seems to have earned money by going about singing the office of the dead or other prayers for the living and making regular monthly rounds to the homes of his wealthy patrons.

Langland describes himself, though perhaps with some ironic hyperbole, as a singular character, apparently very tall and lean (his nickname is "Long Will"), wandering about dressed as a beggar, showing little respect for the wealthy who liked to parade their own importance, and spending time scribbling verses. Some considered him mad. Certainly it is true that he spent a good deal of time writing and rewriting *Piers Plowman*. He seems to have labored some thirty years, refining the poem and perhaps was still revising it at his death; the last two passus of the C version show little change from those of the B Text, suggesting that Langland may have died before he finished the last revision. To be sure, the date of Langland's death is even less certain than that of his birth; it is unlikely that the poet survived his century. If, as has often been dis-

puted, Langland was the author of the poem *Richard the Redeless*, he was still alive in 1395.

ANALYSIS

Modern criticism has begun to concentrate, for the first time, on the artistry of *Piers Plowman*. With the return of so many modern poets to the free accentual verse similar to William Langland's, readers are now more able to respond to the verse of *Piers Plowman*. Further, with the contemporary conviction that everyday themes and language are valid subjects for poetry, readers have become more sympathetic to some of Langland's finest passages, which treat everyday experiences in the vocabulary of the common man.

However, it seems, ultimately, that the first readers of *Piers Plowman* were most correct: The poem's basic intent is didactic, and for Langland, all artistry was secondary to the message he was trying to convey. Perhaps his greatest achievement is the theme itself, which is at once as simple and as complex as any in literature. Beginning as the Dreamer's simple question in Passus 2 (B Text), "How may I save my soul?," the theme turns into a multilayered search for individual salvation, for the perfection of contemporary society, for a mystical union with God, and for a way to put mystical vision to practical use in perfecting society. These searches are set against varied landscapes ranging from the contemporary world to the inner world of the soul, across biblical history, through Hell to Armageddon. For contemporary critics concerned largely with structure in literature, Langland's most remarkable feat is his ability, in spite of real or apparent digressions and inconsistencies, to put a poem of the encyclopedic range and depth of *Piers Plowman* together into a structured whole.

Piers Plowman is a difficult poem. One is not likely to find a more complex poem, nor one that poses quite so many problems. An entrance to the poem might best be achieved by an examination of those problems—problems of text, of form, of structure, and of interpretation—one at a time.

First, the poem exists in three totally different versions. The earliest version, known as the A Text, must have been written, or at least begun, about 1362, since it alludes to such things as the plague of 1361 and a certain great windstorm known to have occurred in January, 1362. This first version is a poem of some 2,500 lines, consisting of a prologue and eleven books or "passus." In the second, or B Text, William Langland revised his poem and added nine new passus, expanding *Piers Plowman* to more than 7,200 lines. This version must have been written about 1377, since the fable of the cat and mice in the prologue seems to allude to events that occurred in the parliament of 1376-1377.

Langland thoroughly revised the poem one more time, increasing its length by another hundred or so lines, and this final version is known as the C Text. It contains no prologue but twenty-three passus. W. W. Skeat dated the C Text about 1393, believing that it reflected the differences that began in 1392 between the citizens of London and the king. An earlier date may be more accurate, however, since Thomas Usk seems to refer to the C version of *Piers Plowman* in his *Testament of Love* (1387), and Usk died in 1388. In the C version, the poet often attempts to clarify ambiguities and at times eliminates some of the social criticisms. He also eliminates some of the more dramatic scenes in B, such as Piers's tearing of Truth's pardon in Passus 7. Although the C Text may represent the author's ultimate intent, and although accurate critical texts of the C Text have made it more universally available, the vast majority of scholars and readers have preferred the B version, and so all references to the poem in this analysis are to George Kane and E. Talbot Donaldson's edition of the B Text.

A POEM OF THE ALLITERATIVE REVIVAL

Having established the B version as the poem, however, one is not at all sure what sort of poem it is. *Piers Plowman* falls simultaneously into several categories, none of which defines it completely. It is, first, a poem of the alliterative revival. Poetry in English had originally been alliterative and followed strict metrical rules. When English verse began to appear once more in the west and north in the mid-fourteenth century, poets attempted to follow this native tradition. The Middle English alliterative line, however, was much freer than it had been in Old English: Lines had no fixed syllabic content, the number of stressed syllables was not always four, as in classic alliterative verse, but might be three, five, or six, and the alliterated sound was not al-

ways governed by the third stressed syllable, as in classic alliterative verse. The alliterative poets did, however, tend to rely on a special poetic diction and to decorate their poetry with elaborate rhetorical figures recommended by the poetic manuals of the time, such as that of Geoffrey of Vinsauf.

Langland, however, differed markedly from other alliterative poets. Possibly because his audience was not the aristocracy, he had no interest in elaborate rhetoric or poetic diction but rather used simple vocabulary and employed only those figures of speech that involved repetition, since his goal was to get his message across clearly. Langland did, however, continue and even furthered the trend toward a freer alliterative line, employing various rhythmic patterns as they suited the tone of his poem, sometimes alliterating a different sound in the second half-line than he had in the first, sometimes not alliterating at all, and often tossing in Latin quotations as nonalliterating half-lines. The overall tendency of Langland's verse, despite the Latin, is toward a naturalness of vocabulary and rhythm.

PIERS PLOWMAN AS SERMON LITERATURE

Piers Plowman also has a great deal in common with sermon literature. G. R. Owst saw Langland as drawing primarily from the pulpits of England his message of social reform, justice for the poor, condemnation for those who pervert the great institution of the Church, and a recommendation of love and work as opposed to revolution. Elizabeth Salter sees Langland's emphasis on teaching rather than fine writing and his use of metaphors and imagery in a purely functional manner to illustrate his material as consistent with sermon literature; however, *Piers Plowman*, in scope and complexity, goes far beyond even the most elaborate sermons, so again the label "sermon in verse" is inadequate.

PIERS PLOWMAN AS A DREAM VISION

The poem also takes the form of a dream vision. For the Middle Ages, influenced as they were by the biblical stories of Joseph and Daniel and by Ambrosius Theodosius Macrobius's famous commentary of Cicero's "Somnium Scipionis" ("Dream of Scipio"), dreams were profoundly important and could often take on oracular significance. Thus, beginning with Guillaume de Lorris and Jean de Meung's thirteenth century *Le*

Roman de la rose (*The Romance of the Rose*, partial translation c. 1370, complete translation 1900), there arose a genre of poetry containing a dreamer-narrator who relates his vision, which may be full of signs that the reader must interpret. Once again, however, *Piers Plowman* transcends the bounds of the form, for Langland writes not of one vision but of many. There are, in fact, ten separate visions in the poem, two of which are represented as dreams within dreams. Moreover, in contrast with the more typical medieval love visions, Langland seriously presents the visions as divine revelations. Perhaps Morton Bloomfield is more accurate, then, in describing *Piers Plowman* as an *apocalypse*: a literary work in the form of a vision revealing a divine message and deeply criticizing contemporary society.

A knowledge of its genre may help to explain some of the confusion in the structure of the poem. Anyone reading *Piers Plowman* for the first time must be struck by the bewildering plunges into and out of scenes, the unannounced and unexpected comings and goings of a multitude of new characters, the apparently unrelated sequence of events that seem to follow no cause-and-effect relationships. It could be argued that a dream vision would follow the logic of dream—of association and symbol rather than induction and deduction; this may be a partial answer. One could also say that the poem is not intended to be a narrative, which would follow a cause-and-effect pattern. It has, rather (like a sermon), a thematic unity. The Dreamer asks in the beginning, "What must I do to save my soul?," and the theme that unites the poem is the answer to that question. Essentially, the unifying motif is the quest for the answer, a quest that becomes a pilgrimage of the individual to God. Significantly, Langland calls the divisions of his poem *passus*, or "steps"—each new incident is another step toward the goal of the quest.

THE VISIO

Structurally, *Piers Plowman* is divided into two sections, the *Visio* and the *Vita*. The *Visio* depicts the world as it is, introduces the main themes, and prepares the way for the search that follows in the *Vita*. The narrator, Will (a persona for William Langland, but also a personification of the human will), falls asleep and relates his dream of a "fair field full of folk"—the people of

Middle Earth as they work out their lives between heaven (a Tower of Truth) and hell (a dark dungeon). The Holy Church appears to Will as a lady and discourses on the fall of Lucifer and on love as the way to Truth. When the Dreamer asks how he may recognize falsehood, he is shown a series of scenes involving Lady Meed and her proposed marriage, first to Falsehood, then to Conscience. Lady Meed is the representation of *cupiditas*, the opposite of love: She is the love of earthly reward, and when she is driven out by Conscience and Reason, it represents the possibility of humans controlling their desire for worldly wealth by following the dictates of reason and conscience. In Will's second dream, Reason gives a sermon inspiring the people to repent, and there follows Langland's noted portrayal of the confession of the seven deadly sins. The people then begin a pilgrimage in search of Truth; here Piers the Plowman makes his first appearance, offering to guide them to Truth. First, however, Piers must plow his half-acre. The implied moral is that the needs of the body must be taken care of but that the will should desire no more than what is of material necessity.

The pilgrimage to Truth never takes place. Truth sends Piers a pardon, saying that those who do well will be saved. When a priest tells Piers that this is no pardon at all, Piers tears up the paper in anger. The point of this scene seems to be lost in obscurity. Robert Worth Frank considers the scene an attack on papal indulgences: The true "pardon" is God's command to do well. The priest, on the other hand, supports the idea of papal indulgences, which Piers angrily rejects by tearing the parchment, symbolically tearing up paper pardons from Rome. In a later interpretation, scholar Denise N. Baker denied that Piers's pardon is a pardon at all. The scene, according to Baker, reflects the Nominalist-Augustinian controversy of the fourteenth century, which concerned humanity's ability to do good works. The Augustinian position was that man was unable to do good works without God's grace, and Piers's tearing up of the pardon is Langland's emblem of man's dependence on God's gift of grace. Whichever interpretation is correct, Piers decides to leave plowing and begin a life of prayer and penance in order to search for Do-Well.

THE VITA

The *Vita* section of the poem is divided into three parts: the lives of Do-Well, Do-Better, and Do-Best. With the abandonment of the people's search for Truth, it is apparent that society cannot be reformed corporately but only on an individual basis. Will goes on an individual quest for the three degrees of doing well, for three grades of Christian perfection. The life of Do-Well is confusing: In the third dream, Will confronts his own faculties (Thought, Intelligence, Imagination), as well as guides such as Study, Clergy, and Scripture. In the meantime, Will has a dream-within-a-dream wherein he follows Fortune for forty-five years. After he wakes, Will falls asleep again, and in a fifth vision, led by Patience and Conscience, he meets Haukyn, the Active Man, whose coat (his soul) is terribly stained with sin.

The sixth vision, the life of Do-Better, begins with Will's discourse with Anima, who rebukes Will for vainly seeking knowledge and extols the virtue of charity. Will falls into another, deeper, vision, in which he sees Piers Plowman as guardian of the Tree of Charity; sees Abraham, Moses, and the Good Samaritan as the personifications of Faith, Hope, and Charity; and learns about the Holy Trinity. In the eighth vision, the climax of the life of Do-Better and of the poem, the Dreamer witnesses the passion of Christ, sees Christ jousting in the arms of Piers Plowman, witnesses the Harrowing of Hell, a debate between the four daughters of God, and the Resurrection.

The two final dreams present the life of Do-Best. Piers Plowman is now Christ's vicar on earth. The Holy Spirit descends, bestowing gifts on the Christian body, enabling Piers to plow the field of the world. Conscience, seeing the Antichrist preparing to attack, directs all Christians to build a fortress, the Church of Unity, but the Christians are unprepared for battle. In the final vision, the Antichrist attacks. Conscience makes the mistake of letting a Friar into Unity, whose easy confessions corrupt the Church, and the people lose all fear. Conscience then vows to become a pilgrim and search for Piers Plowman to help in the fight, and the quest begins anew as the Dreamer awakes.

The poem is unified by the repetition of various themes. Salter gives the example of the recurring themes of the nature and function of sin, which is introduced in the section on Lady Meed, expanded on in the confession of the seven deadly sins, restated in the picture of Haukyn's coat, and returned to again as the sins assist the Antichrist in the final attack on Unity. Even so, the nature and function of love in the universe, as it pertains to personal salvation and the reform of society, is the chief theme of the poem; and that theme is inextricably linked with the chief unifying motif of the poem, Piers the Plowman in his many incarnations.

ALLEGORICAL INTERPRETATIONS

Deciding precisely what Piers signifies is part of the last and largest problem of the poem, that of interpretation. It is obvious that Langland's chief vehicle of expression in *Piers Plowman* is allegory, but it is unclear precisely how to read the allegory. Scholar Robert Worth Frank calls the kind of allegory that is typical of Langland "personification-allegory," which, he says, generally involves a single translation of the character's name (such as "Study," "Reason," "Scripture") into the abstract quality that it denotes. In this sense, the characters are "literal." It is a mistake to read more into the allegory than the form allows. In practice, however, this does not seem to work. "Sloth," for example, is simply sloth—one need inquire no further—but the more important characters, such as Do-Well, Do-Better, and Do-Best, are obviously much more complicated and seem to have multiple meanings.

An alternative approach to the allegory is that of D. W. Robertson and Bernard Huppé, who, in applying medieval exegetical criticism to literary texts, see a fourfold interpretation of the allegory. In discussing the complex symbol of the Tree of Charity, for example, they say that it allegorically represents the just; anagogically, Christ on the cross; and tropologically, the individual Christian. The difficulty with this approach is its rigidity: Some things are simply meant to be taken literally, while others may have multitudes of meanings far beyond these four.

A more beneficial approach to the meaning of these symbols is Salter's, which emphasizes a more open and flexible reading; here the reader is receptive to various sorts of significations, not necessarily in any exact order or category. The two most puzzling and multifaceted allegorical symbols are the three lives and Piers himself.

Do-Well, Do-Better, and Do-Best have been most often identified with the active, the contemplative, and the mixed lives. This may make more sense to modern readers if they realize, as T. P. Dunning notes, that the active life in the Middle Ages denotes not manual labor but rather the active practice of virtue, the works of prayer and devotion to which Piers devotes himself at the end of the the *Visio*. This is the active life conceived of as the first stage of the spiritual life, and in the *Vita*, it involves, first, the Dreamer's search through his own faculties, the emergence from intellectual error and then, with the repentance of Haukyn, the rejection of moral disorder. Do-Better would then represent the contemplative life, in which the Dreamer actually experiences a kind of union with God in a firsthand vision of Christ's passion. Do-Best, however, represents the mixed life, in which the individual must return to life in the world and, with the assistance of the Holy Spirit, work for the reform of society: Charity is not limited to love of the individual for God but includes love for others as well.

At the same time, the three lives may suggest the mystical theme of the soul seeking God, where Do-Well represents the purgative state and Do-Better the stage at which the mystic, like the Dreamer, achieves his illumination in a direct vision of God. For the mystic, however, there is no final unity in this world; he, like Conscience in the end, must continue the search and work toward another partial union. Do-Best reveals the practical results of illumination, which are in the service of others.

The three lives, then, suggest at least these things, and more, but Piers's meaning is more obscure. He appears in the poem only occasionally, but his presence dominates the action at crucial points. In the *Visio*, after the confession of the sins, Piers steps in, announcing that he is a friend and servant of Truth, and offering to lead all on a pilgrimage to him. First, however, he must plow his half-acre, and he organizes all the people to help with the work, thus establishing an ordered society in this world. At the end of the *Visio*, he receives the pardon from Truth for himself and his followers, which he tears up, pledging to leave his plow and search for Do-Well.

In the Do-Well section, Piers is mentioned by Clergy

(Passus 13) as one who preaches the primacy of love as opposed to learning. In Do-Better (Passus 15), Anima identifies Piers with Christ by means of a cryptic Latin comment about "Peter, that is Christ." In Passus 16, Piers is warder of the Tree of Charity, which he explains to the Dreamer. The tree's fruit, identified as the patriarchs and prophets, is stolen by the devil, whom Piers chases, armed with a stave symbolizing Christ. Piers is then shown teaching Jesus the art of healing. At the climax, Christ fights for the souls of humankind, the fruit of Piers the Plowman, clad in Piers's arms.

In Do-Best, Piers returns to the poem. First the Dreamer sees a confused image in which Christ himself seems to be Piers, stained with blood and bearing a cross. The Holy Spirit then makes Piers the Plowman his vicar on Earth, and Piers founds the Church, dispensing grace in the form of the eucharist, behaves like God in his charity to all, and then disappears.

THE FIGURE OF PIERS PLOWMAN

All this presents a confused figure who seems at times to be the symbol of moral integrity, at times Christ himself, and at the end perhaps the ideal pope whom conscience searches for to restore the corrupt and divided Church of the fourteenth century. The eminent literary historian Nevill Coghill thought that Piers personified Do-Well, Do-Better, and Do-Best successively. Later, Barbara Raw showed that Piers's career in the poem depicts the restoration of the divine image in humankind, somewhat distorted with the Fall but still present and restored at Christ's incarnation. According to Augustine and Aquinas, the restoration of this image took place in three stages, which may parallel Do-Well, Do-Better, and Do-Best. In Do-Better, Piers becomes the image of Christ because Christ has taken human form, Piers's arms. In Do-Best, Piers embodies the restored image of God in humanity: He has become like God. Salter sees Piers similarly: When Piers describes the way to Truth in Passus 5, he declares that people will find Truth's dwelling in their own hearts. Piers represents this divine element in humankind, the Truth of God as it exists in humans, and as the poem reaches its climax, it is revealed that God is to be found in humans, as the man Piers becomes godlike. This, then, is Langland's ultimate message, which in spite of all the problems with *Piers Plowman* can still be stated with some certainty: Human beings bear the stamp of the image of God and can, through Christ, achieve Do-Best with Piers the Plowman.

BIBLIOGRAPHY

Benson, C. David. *Public "Piers Plowman": Modern Scholarship and Late Medieval English Culture*. University Park: Pennsylvania State University Press, 2004. In his analysis of the work, Benson treats the poem as a public work, anchored in its medieval world, rather than a personal or elite work.

Brewer, Charlotte. *Editing "Piers Plowman": The Evolution of the Text*. New York: Cambridge University Press, 2006. An account of the more than fifty editions of the poem that have appeared since 1550. Brewer examines the lives and motivations of the various editors and the relationships among successive editions.

Hewett-Smith, Kathleen M., ed. *William Langland's "Piers Plowman": A Book of Essays*. New York: Routledge, 2001. A collection of critical essays examining the relevance of Piers Plowman to contemporary literary theory and to fourteenth century culture and ideology. Includes bibliographical references and index.

Kelen, Sarah A. *Langland's Early Modern Identities*. New York: Palgrave Macmillan, 2007. Kelen uses cultural studies and the book's history to show how editors and scholars during the sixteenth through the early nineteenth century used their own concept of the Middle Ages to reshape the work.

Langland, William. *Piers Plowman: The Donaldson Translation, Select Authoritative Middle English Text, Sources and Backgrounds, Criticism*. Edited by Elizabeth Robertson and Stephen H. A. Shepherd. New York: W. W. Norton, 2006. This work, part of the Norton Critical Editions, combines the most authoritative version of the text, E. Talbot Donaldson's translation of *Piers Plowman* into modern English, with critical analysis and explanatory annotations.

_____. *Piers Plowman: A New Translation of the B-Text*. Translated with an introduction and notes by A. V. C. Schmidt. New York: Oxford University Press, 2009. Medieval scholar Schmidt, who earlier edited a parallel-text edition of the A, B, C, and Z versions of *Piers Plowman*, has produced a new, annotated translation of the work.

The Penn Commentary on Piers Plowman. Vol. 1 by Andrew Galloway; Vol. 5 by Stephen A. Barney. Philadelphia: University of Pennsylvania Press, 2006. The initial two volumes of the first full, line-by-line commentary on *Piers Plowman* is intended for readers of all three texts, who have some knowledge of Middle English.

Simpson, James. *Piers Plowman: An Introduction*. 2d ed. Exeter, England: University of Exeter Press, 2007. Simpson's introduction to *Piers Plowman*, part of the Exeter Medieval Texts and Studies series, examines topics such as mercy and justice and the cultural context of the poem.

Zeeman, Nicolette. *Piers Plowman and the Medieval Discourse of Desire*. New York: Cambridge University Press, 2006. Zeeman provides a different interpretation of *Piers Plowman* by linking it to medieval inquiries into the nature of intellectual and spiritual desire. She finds a narrative of desire rather than of an education of the will.

Jay Ruud

PHILIP LARKIN

Born: Coventry, England; August 9, 1922
Died: Hull, England; December 2, 1985

PRINCIPAL POETRY
The North Ship, 1945, 1966
The Less Deceived, 1955
The Whitsun Weddings, 1964
High Windows, 1974
Collected Poems, 1988
Early Poems and Juvenilia, 2005 (A. T. Tolley, editor)

OTHER LITERARY FORMS
　　Although Philip Larkin is thought of today primarily as a poet, his first literary successes were novels: *Jill*

(1946, 1964) and *A Girl in Winter* (1947). The two were widely acclaimed for their accomplished style, accurate dialogue, and subtle characterization. *Jill* was valued highly for its intimate look at wartime Oxford. The protagonist in each is an outsider who encounters great difficulty in attempting to fit into society, and the two novels explore themes of loneliness and alienation to which Larkin returns time and again in his later poetry. Larkin wrote comparatively little about literature and granted few interviews. His literary essays were collected into *Required Writings: Miscellaneous Pieces, 1955-1982* (1984). He also wrote extensively on jazz, chiefly in his reviews for the *Daily Telegraph*, and a number of those pieces appear in the volume *All What Jazz: A Record Diary, 1961-1968* (1970). His opinions of jazz works are frequently instructive for the reader who wishes to understand his views on poetry, particularly his comments on what he saw as the "modernist" jazz of Charlie Parker, which, like all modernism, concentrates on technique while violating the truth of human existence. True to his precepts, Larkin eschewed, throughout his career, technical fireworks in favor of a poetic that reflects the language of the people. He edited *New Poems*, 1958, with Louis MacNeice and Bonamy Dobrée, and he was chosen to compile *The Oxford Book of Twentieth-Century English Verse* (1973).

ACHIEVEMENTS

Few poets succeeded as Philip Larkin did in winning a large audience and critical respect for such a small body of poetry, and indeed his success may be attributable in part to the rate at which he wrote poems. Because he brought out, according to his own estimate, only three to five poems a year, he could give each one the meticulous attention required to build extremely tight, masterful verse. As a result, each of his slim volumes contains numerous poems that immediately catch the reader's attention for their precise yet colloquial diction.

His chief contribution to British poetry may well be his sustained determination to work in conventional forms and colloquial, even vulgar and coarse, language. In this attempt, as in his ironic self-deprecation and his gloomy outlook, he resembles Robert Frost.

Also like Frost, he worked consciously against the modernist poetics of Wallace Stevens, T. S. Eliot, Ezra Pound, and their heirs, the poetics of disjunction and image. Most of Larkin's poetry demonstrates a distrust of symbolic and metaphorical language, and a reliance instead on discursive verse. His insistence on plain language reflects a belief in the importance of tradition, a faith in the people who remain in touch with the land, and a suspicion of modern society, urban development, and technological advancement. Larkin stands as the chief example among his contemporaries of the line of counter-modernist poetry running not from William Butler Yeats and the Symbolists but from Thomas Hardy and Rudyard Kipling, for both of whom he had great admiration.

Larkin's popularity also results, in part, from his speaking not only as one of the people but for them as well. For all its bleakness and irony, or perhaps because of it, his poetry represents the attitudes of a segment of the British population that found itself with greatly diminished expectations following World War II; institutions were losing their traditional value and function, and the problems of empire (the crowning achievements of those institutions) were rushing home to roost. His poetry represents a search for meaning within the bewildering complexity of the twentieth century. His awards include the Queen's Gold Medal for Poetry (1965), the Russell Loines Award (1974), and the W. H. Smith Literary Award (1984).

BIOGRAPHY

The Englishness of Philip Arthur Larkin's poetry is decidedly provincial; his England does not revolve around London, and in fact, there is a marked suspicion of the capital and the cosmopolitan urbanity it represents. From his diction to the frequency with which his speakers are seated in cars or trains traveling through the countryside, his poems reflect the provincialism of his life. Larkin was born August 9, 1922, in Coventry, where his father served as city treasurer throughout his childhood. He described his childhood as a bore and not worth mentioning, suggesting that no biography of him need begin before he turned twenty-one. Although he was not a particularly good student at the King Henry VII School in Coventry, he matriculated at St. John's

College, Oxford, in 1940, hoping to get in a year of school before he was called into the military. As it eventually turned out, he failed his army physical and stayed in college, graduating with first-class honors in 1943. His time at Oxford had a profound effect on the youthful Larkin; in the introduction to *Jill*, he suggests that the war radically diminished the students' grand view of themselves, and this sense of reduced importance stuck with him in his poetry. Perhaps even more crucial to his development, though, were his friendships with budding writers Bruce Montgomery (Edmund Crispin) and Kingsley Amis. The Amis-Larkin friendship seems to have influenced both men, and their early writings share many attitudes and themes.

While at the university, Larkin published poems in the undergraduate magazines and in the anthology *Poetry in Wartime* (1942). (He had had one poem published in the *Listener* in 1940.) Fortune Press took notice and asked him to submit a collection; he did, and *The North Ship* was published in 1945. The poetry in that collection is heavily influenced by Yeats's work, to which he was introduced by the poet Vernon Watkins,

Philip Larkin

who read and lectured at the English Club at Oxford and with whom Larkin subsequently developed a friendship.

After graduation, Larkin took a post as librarian in Wellington, Shropshire. He claimed that while there he began to read Thomas Hardy's poetry seriously, which allowed him to throw off the Yeatsian influence. He subsequently worked as a librarian in Leicester, in Belfast, and, after 1955, as head librarian at the University of Hull. His attitudes toward his work vacillated, and that ambivalence is displayed in his poems, particularly in "Toads" and "Toads Revisited." Nevertheless, he remained at his position as librarian and eschewed the life of poet-celebrity. He died in Hull of cancer on December 2, 1985.

ANALYSIS

If Rudyard Kipling's is the poetry of empire, then Philip Larkin's is the poetry of the aftermath of empire. Having lived through the divestiture of England's various colonial holdings, the economic impact of empire building having finally come home, together with the ultimate travesty of imperial pretensions and the nightmare of Nazi and Soviet colonization in Europe, Larkin was wary of the expansiveness, the acquisitiveness, and the grandeur implicit in the imperial mentality. Many features of his poetry can be traced to that wariness: from the skepticism and irony, to the colloquial diction, to the formal precision of his poems.

Indeed, of all the writers who shared those ideals and techniques and who came to be known in the 1950's as the Movement, Larkin most faithfully retained his original attitude and style. Those writers—Kingsley Amis, Donald Davie, John Wain, Elizabeth Jennings, and Thom Gunn, among others—diverse though they were, shared attitudes that were essentially empirical, antimodernist, skeptical, and ironic. Most of those views can be understood as outgrowths of an elemental alienation from society and its traditional institutions. Amis's Jim Dixon is the outstanding fictional embodiment of these attitudes; although he desperately wants and needs to be accepted into university society and the traditional power structure it represents, his contempt for the institution and those in it, bred of his alienation, carries him into situations that border on both hilarity and disaster. *Lucky Jim* (1954) is *the* Movement novel.

Isolation and alienation figure prominently in both of Larkin's novels, as well; yet it is in his poems that they receive their fullest development. The speakers of his poems—and in the great majority of cases the speaker is the poet himself—seem alienated from their surroundings, cut off from both people and institutions. While that alienation normally shows itself as distance, as irony and wry humor, it can sometimes appear as smugness, complacence, even sneering judgment. Larkin turns his sense of isolation, of being an outsider or fringe observer, into a position of centrality, in which the world from which he is alienated seems to be moving tangentially to his own sphere. In his best poems, that distance works two ways, allowing the poet to observe the world in perspective, as if viewing it through the wrong end of a pair of binoculars, so that weighty matters seem less momentous, while at the same time reminding the poet that he, too, is a figure of little consequence. When his poems fail, the poet risks very little of his own ego as he sits back in safety, judging others across the frosty distance.

Larkin gains his perspective in large measure through his belief that nothing lies beyond this world, that this existence, however muddled it may be, is probably the only one. His skepticism is thoroughgoing and merciless; he rarely softens his tone. In some writers such belief might provoke terror or a compulsion to reform the world. In Larkin, it gives rise to irony. He examines the feeble inhabitants of this tiny planet surrounded by the void and asks if it can all be so important.

The resulting sense of human insignificance, including his own, leads him to several of the characteristic features of his work. He rejects "poetic" devices in favor of simpler, more mundane vehicles. His diction, for example, is nearly always colloquial, often coarse, vulgar, or profane. His distrust of a specialized diction or syntax for poetry reflects his distrust of institutions generally. Similarly, he shies away from the intense poetic moment—image, symbol, metaphor—in favor of a discursive, argumentative verse. Although he will occasionally resolve a poem through use of an image or a metaphor, particularly in *High Windows*, he more com-

monly talks his way through the poem, relying on intellect rather than emotion or intuition.

This rejection of the stuff of poetry leads him to a problem: If overtly poetic language and poetic devices are eschewed, what can the poet use to identify his poems as poems? For Larkin the answer lies in the external form of the poems: scansion, rhyme schemes, stanzaic patterns. The tension and the power of a Larkin poem often result from the interplay of common, unexceptional language with rigorously formal precision. "The Building," from *High Windows*, is an example of such tension. The poet meditates on the function of the hospital in modern society and the way in which it takes over some of the duties traditionally performed by the Church, all in very ordinary language. The poem, however, is stretched taut over not one but two sophisticated units: a seven-line stanza and an eight-line rhyme scheme (*abcbdad*). Rhyme pattern and stanzaic pattern come together at the end of the eighth stanza, but the poem does not end there; rather, the poet employs another rhyme unit, a stanza plus a line, as a means of resolving the poem. Even here Larkin's shrewd distrust of the intellectual viability of poetic forms displays itself: Ending neatly on the fifty-sixth line would be too neat, too pat, and would violate the poem's ambivalence toward the place. Similarly, although his rhyme schemes are often very regular, the same cannot be said for the rhymes themselves: speech/touch, faint/went, home/welcome. If Larkin recognizes his need for traditional forms in his poems, he recognizes also the necessity of altering those forms into viable elements of his poetry.

Finally, there is in Larkin a sense of an ending, of oblivion. For all his distrust of the "new apocalypse crowd," many of his poems suggest something similar, although with a characteristic difference. Where the "crowd" may prophesy the end of the world and everything in it, he, working out of his alienation, more commonly seems to be watching the string run out, as if he were a spectator at the edge of oblivion.

THE NORTH SHIP

Larkin's first volume of poetry, *The North Ship*, went virtually unnoticed at the time of its original publication and would be unnoticed still were it made to stand on its own merits. (It has few.) The poems are almost uniformly derivative Yeatsian juvenilia, laden with William Butler Yeats's imagery but shorn of its power or meaning; this is the verse of a young man who wants to become a poet by sounding like a known poet. No one has been more critical, moreover, of the volume than the poet himself, characterizing it as an anomaly, a mistake that happened when he did not know his own voice and thought, under the tutelage of Vernon Watkins, that he was someone else. That he allowed the republication of the work in 1966, with an introduction that is more than anything else a disclaimer, suggests a desire to distance the "real" poet from the confused adolescent.

Despite his objections, the book can be seen as representative of certain tendencies in his later verse, and it is enlightening to discern how many features of his mature work show themselves even when buried under someone else's style. A major difference between Larkin's poems and Yeats's lies in the use of objects: While the younger poet borrows Yeats's dancers, horses, candles, and moons, they remain dancers, horses, candles, and moons. They lack transcendent, symbolic value; objects remain mere objects.

There is also in these early poems a vagueness in the description of the phenomenal world. Perhaps that generality, that vagueness, could be explained as the result of the Yeatsian influence, but it is also a tendency of Larkin's later work. One often has the impression that a scene, particularly a human scene, is typical rather than specific.

One of the things clearly missing from this first work is a suspicion of the Yeatsian symbols, attitudes, and gestures, almost none of which the mature Larkin can abide. His assertion that it was his intense reading of Hardy's poetry that rescued him from the pernicious influence of Yeats may have validity; more probably, time heals youthful excess, and during the period when he was outgrowing the poetry of *The North Ship*, he began a salutary reading of Hardy.

THE LESS DECEIVED

A striking development in Larkin's second book of poems, *The Less Deceived*, is his insistence on the mundane, the unexceptional, the commonplace. In "Born Yesterday," a poem on the occasion of Sally Amis's birth, for example, he counters the usual wishes for beauty or brilliance with the attractive (for him) possi-

bility of being utterly unextraordinary, of fitting in wholly by having nothing stand out. This wish he offers, he says, in case the others do not come true, but one almost has the sense that he wishes also that the others will not come true, that being average is much preferable to being exceptional.

Larkin makes a similar case for the ordinary in the wickedly funny "I Remember, I Remember," which attacks the Romantic notions of the writer's childhood as exemplified in D. H. Lawrence's *Sons and Lovers* (1913). In other places, he has described his childhood as boring, not worthy of comment, and in this poem, he pursues that idea vigorously. In the first two stanzas, he comes to the realization that he does not recognize the Coventry station into which the train has pulled, although he used it often as a child. When his traveling companion asks if Coventry is where he "has his roots," the poet responds in his mind with a catalog of all the things that never happened to him that supposedly happen to writers in their youth, "the splendid family/ I never ran to," "The bracken where I never sat trembling." Through the course of that list, he recognizes that the place looks so foreign now because it never gave him anything distinctive, that there is nothing that he carries with him that he can attribute to it. Then, in a remarkable about-face, he realizes that the location has very little to do with how his childhood was spent or misspent, that life is largely independent of place, that the alienation that he senses is something he carries with him, not a product of Coventry.

The poem at first seems to be an honest appraisal of his youth in contradistinction to all those romanticized accounts in biographies and novels, but the reader is forced finally to conclude that the poet protests too much. There is no childhood in which nothing happens, and in insisting so strongly on the vacuum in which he grew up, Larkin develops something like the inverse of nostalgia. He turns his present disillusionment and alienation back against the past and views it from his ironic perspective. Larkin is often the victim of his own ironies, and in this poem, his victim is memory.

His irony, in this poem as in so many, is used defensively; he wards off criticism by beating everyone to the punch. Irony is in some respects safer than laying oneself open for inspection. In many of his finest poems, however, he drops his guard and allows himself to think seriously about serious subjects. The foremost example in *The Less Deceived* is "Church Going." The title turns out to be marvelously ambiguous, appearing at first blush to be a mere reference to attending church, but then becoming, as the poem progresses, an elliptical, punning reference to churches going out of fashion.

The first two stanzas are curtly dismissive in a manner often encountered in Larkin, as he describes his stop from a bicycle trip at a church that is apparently Ulster Protestant. Neither he (since he stops for a reason he cannot name and acts guilty as he looks around) nor the church (since it is not at all out of the ordinary) seems worthy of attention. He leaves, thinking the church "not worth stopping for." In the third stanza, however, the poem shifts gears in a way typical of Larkin's finest work: the dismissive attitude toward mundane existence, the wry observations give way to serious contemplation. "Church Going," in fact, contains two such shifts.

In stanzas 3 through 7, Larkin reflects on the fate of churches when people stop going altogether—whether they will become places that people will avoid or seek out because of superstition, or become museums, or be turned to some profane use—and wonders, as well, who will be the last person to come to the church and what his reasons will be. Larkin has a sense, conveyed in a number of poems, that he and his generation of skeptics will be the end of religion in England, and in this poem he wonders about the results of that doubting. The final stanza contains yet another shift, this one rather more subtle. As if the "serious house on serious earth" were forcing the poet to be more serious, he shifts away from his musings about its fate, which are after all only another kind of dismissal, and recognizes instead the importance of the place. He suggests, finally, that the shallowness and disbelief of modern people cannot eradicate the impulse to think seriously and seek wisdom that the Church, however outmoded its rituals, represents.

THE WHITSUN WEDDINGS

The two finest poems in Larkin's succeeding volume display similar movements of thought. In the title poem, "The Whitsun Weddings," the movement takes on further embellishment; not only does the poem

move from dismissiveness to contemplation, but also the language of the poem moves from specificity toward generality in a way that mirrors the theme. The poem also contains one of Larkin's favorite devices: the use of a train ride (occasionally a car ride) to depict the movement of thought.

The poem opens with the concern for specificity of someone who, like the speaker, is late; when the train leaves the station at "one-twenty," it is "three-quarters-empty." He catches glimpses of scenery along the way, none of it very interesting, much of it squalid and polluted. Not until the third stanza (suggesting the incompleteness of his detailed observation) does he notice the wedding parties at each station. Even then, it is with the dismissive attitude of someone who, as a professional bachelor and alienated outsider, rather scorns the tackiness of the families gathered on the platforms to see the couples off, as well as that of the unreflective couples with whom he shares the coach. His ironical, detailed description takes up most of the next five stanzas.

Toward the end of stanza 7, however, he undergoes a change, has a moment of vision in which the postal districts of London appear as "squares of wheat." That image leads him, in the final stanza, to see the couples as symbols of fertility, so that finally the slowing train inspires in him an image of arrows beyond the scope of his vision, "somewhere becoming rain." That he loosens the reins of his vision, so that he can describe not merely what he sees but also what he can only envision, is a major development in his attitude from the beginning of the poem. It demonstrates a breaking down, however slight or momentary, of his alienation from the common run of existence and of his resistance to recognizing his own relationship with these others. The poem may ultimately be judged a failure because of the brevity of that breaking down, but the image it spawns of fertility and life just beginning is magnificent.

"Dockery and Son" displays a similar movement and is a stronger poem because the poet is forced to lower his defenses much earlier and reveal himself more fully during the course of his meditation. An offhand comment by the Dean that a fellow student now has a son at school sets the speaker's mind in motion. His first musings on the train home are again mundane, dismissive, of the "you-never-know-do-you" sort, and so boring that he falls asleep. On reconsideration, though, the poet experiences the shock of being brought up hard against the reality of having missed, irrevocably, what is for most men a major part of life—familial relations. Even this reflection remains thin and unsatisfactory, and he moves on to explore the nature of unquestioned and unquestioning belief and its source, deciding that it results not from wisdom or truth but from habit and style grown sclerotic. Yet those beliefs are what a man's life turns on, producing a son for Dockery and nothing for the poet.

At this point, very late in the poem, Larkin develops one of his marvelous reversals on the word "nothing." For most, it connotes an absence, a negation, a nonentity, but for Larkin "nothing" is a positive entity, a thing or force to be reckoned with, "Nothing with all a son's harsh patronage." The line suggests that the poet has had to wrestle with this "nothing" he has created even as a father, such as Dockery, has had to wrestle with the problems brought on by having a son. The similarity, however, does not stop there; the poet goes on to recognize the common fate that awaits not only Dockery and himself but everyone as well. Most commentators read the final phrase, "the only end of age," as meaning death, and certainly that meaning is there. Nevertheless, to understand it as merely meaning death is to lose some of the force it holds for the speaker. Rather, it must be read back through the stanza and the poem as a whole, so that the emphasis on nothingness informs that certain knowledge of death. That the poet not only knows he will die but also has already tasted the nothingness he knows, as an unbeliever, that death entails, makes the experience of that knowledge the more poignant. As is so often true in Larkin's work, that poignancy, which could border on self-pity, is tempered by the understanding that he at least comprehends, and there lies behind the poem's ending an unstated irony aimed at those such as Dockery who engage life so fully as to obscure that reality.

Again, that constant strain of alienation insinuates its way into poem after poem. Throughout *The Whitsun Weddings*, the poet feels himself cut off from his fellow humans, often struggling to retrieve a spirit of community with them, sometimes simply wondering why it is so. The volume, while it represents little change from its predecessor, renders a picture of a man in middle age who feels life passing him by, and who sees more and more clearly the inevitable. Settings are close, small; lives are petty, insignificant; society is filled with graffiti and pollution. In "The Importance of Elsewhere," he finds comfort in being a foreigner in Ireland, since at least he can explain his estrangement from his fellow inhabitants there. In England, ostensibly at home, he has no such excuse.

HIGH WINDOWS

A number of the poems in *High Windows* display that estrangement, often in unsettlingly smug tones. "Afternoons," in the previous book, shows Larkin at his judgmental worst, picking out nasty little details of petty lives and common tastes. In this volume, "The Old Fools," a poem that is often praised for its unexpected ending, displays a similar attitude. After railing against the infirmity and senility of the elderly throughout the poem, the tag line of "Well, we shall find out" rings false, sounding too much like an attempt to dodge inevitable criticism.

"Going, Going" presents some of the same problems, yet it implicates the poet in his critique in a way that "The Old Fools" does not. What is going is England itself, and that entity, it turns out, is place, not people. People have ruined the landscape and the architecture, reducing everything to rubbish. The poem redeems itself through its linguistic implication of its creator. The piece remains polemical throughout, avoiding the impulse to resolve through metaphor, as if the misanthropic, gloomy sensibility demands a crabbed style distrustful of the richness of figurative language and, perhaps, mirroring the destruction of English literature: If "carved choirs," echoing as they do William Shakespeare's "bare ruined choirs where late the sweet birds sang," are ruined and replaced with "concrete and tyres," then this poem's language is the replacement for Shakespeare's. Everywhere the poet turns, he finds traditional institutions, including poetry, degraded into mundane modern forms.

A much finer expression of that discovery is to be found in "The Building," which brings together numerous themes and ideas from throughout Larkin's canon. Like "Dockery and Son," it is a meditation on the foretaste of death; like "Going, Going," a consideration of the degradation of institutions in the modern world;

like "Church Going," a questioning of what people shall do without churches.

The first two stanzas examine the ways the building in which the speaker sits resembles so many other modern buildings—high-rise hotels, airport lounges—although there is something disturbingly unlike them, as well. Not until the end of the second stanza does he reveal that it is a hospital. What unites people here is the common knowledge of their own mortality; even if they are not to die immediately, they are forced by the place to confront the fact that they will die eventually. The inescapability of that knowledge tames and calms the people in the building, as once the knowledge of death and its aftermath quieted them in church.

The recognition of this similarity grows slowly but steadily throughout the poem. The words keep insinuating a connection: "confess," "congregations," a "locked church" outside. The reaction people have in the hospital also suggests a function similar to that of the Church; outside they can hide behind ignorance or refusal to face facts, while inside the hospital those illusions are stripped away and reality is brought into the clear, sharp light, the unambiguous clarity of hospital corridors. This growing realization culminates in a final understanding that unless the modern hospital is more powerful than the traditional cathedral (and Larkin, suspicious of all institutions, does not think it is), then nothing can stop the ineluctable fate that awaits humanity, although (and now the similarities are overwhelming) every night people bring offerings, in the form of flowers, as they would to church.

A remarkable poem such as "The Building" can overcome a score of "Afternoons," and what is more remarkable about it is the way Larkin overcomes his initial alienation to speak not only at, but also to, and even for, his fellow humans and their very real suffering. His finest poems end, like this one, in benedictions that border on the "Shantih" of T. S. Eliot's *The Waste Land* (1922), giving the reader the sense that a troubling journey has reached a satisfying end.

COLLECTED POEMS

The publication of his *Collected Poems* in 1988 brought to light scores of poems previously uncollected, long out of print, or unavailable to the general reading public. These poems will not significantly alter Larkin's reputation, other than to expand the base on which it rests. For fans of his work, however, the additions prove quite valuable, showing as they do the movement from juvenilia to maturity. The early work displays even more clearly than, say, *The North Ship* the various influences on the young poet: Yeats and W. H. Auden. A work such as "New Year Poem" demonstrates a remarkable prescience, dated as it is the day before (and written an ocean away from) Auden's famous "New Year Letter" of 1941; both poems look at the future and consider the social and spiritual needs in a time of crisis.

Larkin, ever parsimonious, wrote very few poems during the last decade of his life: *Collected Poems* reveals a mere seventeen. Many of those concern themselves with his standard topics—the ravages of age, the sense of not being in step with the rest of society, the approach of death. In "The Mower," for example, he ruminates on having run over a hedgehog in the tall grass, killing it. From this experience, he takes away a feeling of responsibility for the death, a sense of the loss of this fellow creature, and the reflection that, given our limited time, we should be kind to one another. This slight poem (eleven lines) sums up much of Larkin's thought in his later years: Death is a complete cessation of experience, not a transmutation but a blankness, an end, while life itself is a vale of unhappiness, and people therefore owe it to themselves and one another to make the way as pleasant as possible.

In "Aubade," perhaps the most substantial of the late poems, Larkin writes of the approach of death, now another day closer because it is a new morning. He declares that we have never been able to accept death, yet are also unable to defeat it. Once religion offered the consolation of afterlife; for Larkin, that promise is no longer valid. What people fear most, he asserts, is the absence of sensation, of affect, that is death, as well as the absolute certainty of its coming. His "morning poem" is really a poem of the dark night of the soul. The fifth, and final, ten-line stanza brings the light of day and the unmindful routine of the workaday world, the routine that acts as a balm by taking our minds off our ultimate problem. Indeed, the poem's closing image presents those representatives of the mundane, postal carriers, going among houses like doctors, their daily rounds offering temporary solace.

These two poems present Larkin's typically ironic approach to the literary tradition. "The Mower" is a highly unconventional garden song. Although its title recalls Andrew Marvell's poems "The Garden" and "The Mower, Against Gardens," it shares none of their pastoral innocence or coyness. It finds death, not life, in the world of nature. Similarly, he subverts the traditional use of the aubade form to discuss not the coming day but also a coming night. In both cases, he undermines traditionally upbeat forms. Yet these poems also point to the playfulness of which Larkin was capable even in his bleakest moments, finding amusement in poems of abject despair. That may prove to be his great gift, the ability to face darkness fully, to take it in, and still to laugh, to be ironic even about last things.

OTHER MAJOR WORKS

LONG FICTION: *Jill*, 1946, 1964; *A Girl in Winter*, 1947.

NONFICTION: *Selected Letters of Philip Larkin, 1940-1985*, 1992 (Anthony Thwaite, editor); *Further Requirements: Interviews, Broadcasts, Statements, and Book Reviews, 1952-1985*, 2001 (Anthony Thwaite, editor); *Larkin's Jazz: Essays and Reviews, 1940-1984*, 2001 (Richard Palmer and John White, editors).

EDITED TEXTS: *New Poems*, 1958 (with Louis MacNeice and Bonamy Dobrée); *The Oxford Book of Twentieth-Century English Verse*, 1973.

MISCELLANEOUS: *All What Jazz: A Record Diary, 1961-1968*, 1970; *Required Writings: Miscellaneous Pieces, 1955-1982*, 1984.

BIBLIOGRAPHY

Booth, James. *Philip Larkin: The Poet's Plight*. New York: Palgrave Macmillan, 2005. Offers readers insight into the themes of Larkin's poetry and the histories behind them.

_____, ed. *New Larkins for Old: Critical Essays*. New York: St. Martin's Press, 2000. A collection of essays on Larkin's work by established commentators and younger critics. Individual essays examine Larkin's novels and poetry in the light of psychoanalytical, postmodern, and postcolonial theories.

Bradford, Richard. *First Boredom, Then Fear: The Life of Philip Larkin*. Chester Springs, Pa.: Dufour Editions, 2005. A biography of Larkin that delves into his youth, romances, and career as a poet.

Castronovo, David. *Blokes: The Bad Boys of English Literature*. New York: Continuum, 2009. Discusses the poets Larkin, Kinsley Amis, John Osborne, and Kenneth Tynan. Examines socialism and radicalism in their works.

Leader, Zachary, ed. *The Movement Reconsidered: Essays on Larkin, Amis, Gunn, Davie, and Their Contemporaries*. New York: Oxford University Press, 2009. This work on the Movement poets sheds light on their views and poetry. Contains three essays on Larkin.

Motion, Andrew. *Philip Larkin: A Writer's Life*. New York: Farrar, Straus and Giroux, 1993. This short work provides an introduction to the man and his work. The book offers thematic and literary-historical overviews, although only one chapter on the poems themselves.

Osborne, John. *Larkin, Ideology and Critical Violence: A Case of Wrongful Conviction*. New York: Palgrave Macmillan, 2007. Osborne sees Larkin as a poet of undecidability, part of the transition to postmodernist indeterminacy.

Palmer, Richard. *Such Deliberate Disguises: The Art of Philip Larkin*. New York: Continuum, 2008. Palmer examines the poetry of Larkin at length.

Rossen, Janice. *Philip Larkin: His Life's Work*. New York: Simon & Schuster, 1989. This intelligent and highly readable overview traces Larkin's development through the first two books, then looks at his lyric impulse, his firmly rooted Englishness, his sexual ambivalence, his use of vulgarity, and his struggle with mortality. The study ties in the poetry with the novels, jazz criticism, and literary criticism to develop a total view of the context of the poetry.

Stojkovic, Tijana. *Unnoticed in the Casual Light of Day: Philip Larkin and the Plain Style*. New York: Routledge, 2006. This comprehensive linguistic and historical study of plain style poetry examines Larkin's poetry from that framework.

Thomas C. Foster

D. H. LAWRENCE

Born: Eastwood, Nottinghamshire, England;
    September 11, 1885
Died: Vence, France; March 2, 1930
Also known as: Lawrence H. Davison

PRINCIPAL POETRY

Love Poems, and Others, 1913
Amores, 1916
Look! We Have Come Through!, 1917
New Poems, 1918
Bay, 1919
Tortoises, 1921
Birds, Beasts, and Flowers, 1923
The Collected Poems of D. H. Lawrence, 1928
Pansies, 1929
Nettles, 1930
The Triumph of the Machine, 1931
Last Poems, 1932
Fire, and Other Poems, 1940
Phoenix Edition of Complete Poems, 1957
The Complete Poems of D. H. Lawrence, 1964
    (Vivian de Sola Pinto and Warren Roberts,
    editors)

OTHER LITERARY FORMS

D. H. Lawrence's productions reflect his artistic range. Accompanying his considerable body of poetry, the eleven novels published during his lifetime include *Sons and Lovers* (1913), *The Rainbow* (1915), *Women in Love* (1920), *The Plumed Serpent* (1926), and *Lady Chatterley's Lover* (1928). He wrote almost continuously for literary periodicals in addition to publishing five volumes of plays, nine volumes of essays, and several short-story collections including *The Prussian Officer, and Other Stories* (1914), *England, My England* (1922), and *The Woman Who Rode Away, and Other Stories* (1928). His final works, including *Apocalypse* and *Etruscan Places*, appeared between 1930 and 1933, and more poetry, essays, and drafts of fiction have since been collected in *Phoenix: The Posthumous Papers of D. H. Lawrence* (1936) and *Phoenix II: Uncollected, Unpublished, and Other Prose Works* (1968).

Several of Lawrence's works, as well as Harry Moore's biography, *The Priest of Love*, have been adapted for the screen. The *Phoenix Edition of D. H. Lawrence* was published in 1957; Viking has printed *The Complete Short Stories of D. H. Lawrence* (1961) and *The Complete Plays of D. H. Lawrence* (1965).

ACHIEVEMENTS

D. H. Lawrence's work has consistently appealed to the adventurous and the perceptive. Ford Madox Ford, editor of the progressive *English Review*, printed Lawrence's earliest poems and short stories there in 1911, recognizing beneath their conventional surfaces potent psychological and emotional undercurrents previously unexplored in British letters. Before Freud's theories were widely known, Lawrence's *Sons and Lovers* daringly probed the dangerous multilayered mother-son-lover triangle he had experienced in his own life. After his elopement, itself a scandal, Lawrence produced *The Rainbow*, seized by Scotland Yard in 1915 and publicly condemned for obscenity. Lawrence's subsequent self-exile from England and his growing artistic notoriety came to a climax in the censorship trials of *Lady Chatterley's Lover*. Behind the alleged pornography, however, critics soon grasped Lawrence's genuine ability to convey what T. S. Eliot called "fitful and profound insights" into human behavior. Lawrence's admirers also included Edward Garnett, John Middleton Murry, Richard Aldington, Amy Lowell, and Rainer Maria Rilke, although Virginia Woolf perhaps illustrated her generation's ambivalence toward Lawrence most pungently: "Mr. Lawrence has moments of greatness, but he has hours of something quite different." Lawrence's own critical studies, particularly his pseudonymous *Movements in European History* (1921), and *Studies in Classic American Literature* (1923), reveal a singular blend of historical perspective and instinctive understanding appreciated only after his death. Once the laudatory memories and abusive denunciations had died out, Lawrence's artistic reputation grew steadily, attributed generally to the craftsmanship of his short fiction and the uncompromisingly honest investigations of sexuality in his novels. As readers young in spirit increasingly observe, however, Lawrence's greatest gift, his affirmation of life, shines most brightly in his poetry.

BIOGRAPHY

David Herbert Lawrence was born in Eastwood, Nottinghamshire, England, on September 11, 1885. His mother, Lydia Beardsall, had come from a fiercely religious middle-class family reduced in circumstances since the depression of 1837. Lydia, "a superior soul," as her third son called her, had been a schoolteacher, sensitive and musical, six years younger than her husband, to whom she was distantly related by marriage. His family had also lost money and position, and Arthur Lawrence, the proud possessor of a fine physique and a musical soul, had gone down into the mines as a child to work. Lydia's disillusion with her marriage, her husband's alcoholic degeneration, and the continual marital strife that haunted her son's childhood provided much of the conflict at the heart of Lawrence's work.

Out of hatred for her husband and a desperate resolve that her children should not sink to his level, Lydia used them as weapons against him. Much later,

D. H. Lawrence (Courtesy, D.C. Public Library)

Lawrence regretted and in part redressed the unfavorable portrait of his father in his autobiographical "colliery novel," *Sons and Lovers*, which exhibits his mother's domination and his own fragile opposition through his love for Jessie Chambers, the "Miriam" whom he loved and left in literature as well as life.

Obedient to his mother's demands, Lawrence took a teaching position at Croydon, near London, in 1908. He was devastated by the ugly realities of urban life, disgusted by his savage pupils, and frustrated by the young women in his life. His mother's lingering death from cancer in late 1910, not long after he had laid an early copy of his first novel, *The White Peacock* (1911), in her hands, sent him into a "heavy, bitter year," from which he emerged physically shaken by near-fatal pneumonia, unable to progress with his writing, and bent on leaving England. In the spring of 1912, he became smitten with "the woman of a lifetime," his former language professor's wife, the Baroness Frieda von Richthofen. Upon their elopement that May, they left behind them Frieda's children and Lawrence's England forever, except for a few brief and mostly unhappy intervals.

Lawrence then had to live by his pen, and he increased his output dramatically, pouring out not only fiction and poetry but also criticism and travel essays. After a painful stay in Cornwall during World War I, shunned because of Frieda's German connections and his own antiwar sentiments, Lawrence, shocked by British repression of *The Rainbow*, began the worldwide wandering that lasted the remainder of his life.

Lawrence almost realized his ambition of writing a major novel on each continent. After visiting Ceylon and Australia, he settled for a time with Frieda and a few friends near Taos, New Mexico, devoting himself to the idealization of primitivism as a vehicle for modern humankind's regeneration. Working on his novel *The Plumed Serpent* in Mexico in late 1924, he was struck simultaneously with harsh psychic and physical blows; he realized that his artistic position was untenable and went down "as if shot" with a combination of typhoid and the long-standing illness diagnosed then for the first time as tuberculosis.

Slowly recuperating on his ranch, Lawrence regained his creative equilibrium in a play, *David* (pb.

1926), and a lovely fragmentary novel, "The Flying Fish," written, he said, "so near the borderline of death" that its spell could not be recaptured "in the cold light of day." There he proclaimed the belief in "regenerate man" to which he dedicated the rest of his short life. He returned in thought at least to England with *Lady Chatterly's Lover*, written on a sunny hill in Italy, a "novel of tenderness" that awakened violent protests and lawsuits, driving him even further into his metaphysical contemplation of human destiny. Very ill, holding to life through the strange bond of creativity alone, Lawrence worked out his conclusions on personal immortality in his *Last Poems*, until on March 2, 1930, in a sanatorium on the French Riviera aptly called "Ad Astra," "once dipped in dark oblivion/ the soul ha[d] peace, inward and lovely peace."

ANALYSIS

D. H. Lawrence had written poetry all his creative life, but he did not set his poetic theory down until 1923. His poetry, as with nearly everything that he wrote, is uneven; and he knew it, distinguishing between his early self-conscious verse and the "real poems" that his "demon" shook out of him, poems he called "a biography of an emotional and inner life." In a preface to another man's poetry, Lawrence defined the process by which he himself transmuted "inner life," the core of his work, into art: "a bursting of bubbles of reality, and the pang of extinction that is also liberation into the roving, uncaring chaos which is all we shall ever know of God." Lawrence's poetry is thus best seen in the context of his life and through the painful paradox of his creativity, rooted in his most profound basic concept, the theory of human regeneration that he conveyed so often in the image of Paradise Regained.

As Richard Hoggart has observed, Lawrence's inner life spoke with both "the voice of a down-to-earth, tight, bright, witty Midlander" and "the voice of a seer with a majestic vision of God and life and earth." The Midlands voice first announced the major themes that Lawrence never abandoned: class, religion, and love. Lawrence very early felt the strictures of a working-man's life and the humiliation of poverty as keenly as he felt the happiness he shared at the Chambers' farm, among birds, beasts, and flowers threatened by encroaching industrialism. His "Rhyming Poems" also reflect his youthful love, quivering between the extremes of idealistic "spirituality" pressed on him by his mother and Jessie Chambers, so fatally alike, and a powerful sexual drive crying out for satisfaction. At sixteen, he abandoned his mother's harsh Congregationalism, though the "hymns of a man's life" never lost their appeal for him, and from 1906 to 1908, he was affected deeply by his experience of Arthur Schopenhauer's "Metaphysics of Sexual Love," which places sex at the center of the phenomenal universe, and Friedrich Nietzsche's works, probably including *Die Geburt der Tragödie aus dem Geiste der Musik* (1872; *The Birth of Tragedy out of the Spirit of Music*, 1909), which sees Greek tragedy as the result of creative tension between Apollonian rationalism and Dionysian ecstasy. Lawrence's prophetic voice had begun to whisper.

Although his mother's slow death gradually disengaged him from her domination, Lawrence tried to weave his early concerns of class, love, and religion into an organic whole. Once he recovered from his own severe illness late in 1911, he looked toward new physical and creative horizons, and after his elopement with Frieda, he at last was able to complete *Sons and Lovers* in a new affirmation of life. There were, however, characteristic growing pains. Frieda's aristocratic connections in Germany afforded him the social position that he, like his mother, had always envied while decrying its values, and he delighted in using his wife's baronial stationery at the same time that he was undergoing inevitable agonies at her cavalier disregard for sexual fidelity. The first book of Lawrence's "Unrhyming Poems," *Look! We Have Come Through!*, records the resolution of his complicated marital relationship in a form completely liberated from Georgian poetic convention. During World War I, Lawrence tried to locate humanity's vital meaning in a balance of power between love and friendship, replacing the God he had lost with the human values promised by his *The Rainbow* and the four-part sexual harmony of *Women in Love*.

After the debacle of *The Rainbow*, Lawrence's social message became more strident. From 1917 to 1925, rapt in his dream of human regeneration—now fixed on the figure of a patriarchal political leader—

Lawrence went to the ends of the civilized earth. The fiction that he produced during that period urges progressively more primitive reorganizations of society, culminating in a faintly ridiculous neo-Aztec pantheon imposed on Mexico in *The Plumed Serpent*, a novel embedding Lawrence's highest hopes in stubbornly incantatory verse and sometimes turgid prose.

At the midpoint of his career, a substantial conflict was brewing between Lawrence's urge for social reform and his prophetic sense of responsibility. The religious voice was clear in the poems of *Birds, Beasts, and Flowers*, where, as Vivian de Sola Pinto has observed, "the common experience is transformed and invested with mythical grandeur." Such a stirring transmutation proved incompatible with the "down-to-earth Midlands voice" calling for political answers to social questions. By 1923, possibly with memories of Nietzsche and Schopenhauer, Lawrence had defined his "simple trinity" as "the emotions, the mind, and then the children of this venerable pair, ideas." Lawrence also insisted that God's traditional position relative to human beings had changed, so that Christ could no longer serve as the pathway to the Father; the Holy Ghost would have to lead human beings to a "new living relation," nothing less than the spiritual regeneration that Lawrence hoped to bring to humankind from the wreckage of modern Western civilization.

When Lawrence collapsed on completing *The Plumed Serpent*, he was forced to abandon his old dream of social rebirth through politically enforced primitivism. In the poetic "The Flying Fish," he announced that the Indian's "primeval day" and the white man's mechanism "nullified each other." Now, as de Sola Pinto remarked, Lawrence's "ecstasy controlled by the rational imagination" produced memorable poetry in *Birds, Beasts, and Flowers*, foreshadowing the affirmation of life eternal that Lawrence finally was to achieve.

Lawrence's irritation with Western materialism erupted once more late in his life in the angry little poems that he called his *Pansies* and *Nettles*, glimpses of humankind's stupidity, conceit, and boorishness encapsulated in stinging doggerel. Hardly his finest poetic achievement, these poems nevertheless represent more than a sick man's impatience with human frailty.

They also demonstrate a quality of Lawrence's insight that he called "quickness," "the breath of the moment, and one eternal moment easily contradicting the next eternal moment."

By 1928, already gravely ill, Lawrence had turned almost completely to examining "the pang of extinction that is also liberation," the paradox, as he saw it, of physical death. His prophetic voice far outstripped the satiric note as he painted and wrote in the familiar archetypes of the Garden of Eden, regained, he felt now, through the apocalypse of death. His three original themes had coalesced into a great hymn of humankind's essential renewal, the "religion of wonder" that he had glimpsed in the Etruscans: "The whole universe lived; and the business of man was himself to live amid it all." Lawrence paid a heavy price for restoring humankind to Paradise, the unification of his Midlands voice and his prophetic voice in the acceptance of death as life's necessary other half. At last, he was able to create a convincing myth as he had created all his work, from the ideas born of his own mind and emotions. Lawrence's *Last Poems*, like Rainer Maria Rilke's terrible and beautiful angels, burst the bubbles of reality, and Lawrence closed his poems, like his life, on the noble vision of resurrection.

"RHYMING POEMS"

Lawrence's "biography of an emotional and inner life" begins with his "Rhyming Poems," written between 1904 and 1912. Those he called "imaginative or fictional," he reworked twenty years later, mostly in his Midlands voice, "to say the real say," because "sometimes the hand of commonplace youth had been laid on the mouth of the demon." The subjective poems of his early years, "with the demon fuming in them smokily," were unchangeable.

One of the lessons that Lawrence had to learn as a young poet was when to leave his "demon" alone. "Discord in Childhood," a pain-filled record of the elder Lawrences' marital combat, had originally been a long poem, and, he said, a better one. Frightened by his own creativity, Lawrence burned the first poem as a young man, although he later worked the scene into *Sons and Lovers*. Characteristically, even the preserved version connects violent human emotion with nature and its forces: "Outside the house an ash-tree hung its terrible whips," while within, "a male thong" drowned "a slender lash whistling she-delirious rage" in a "silence of blood."

A similar sensuous absorption in brutal natural forces appears in the "Miriam" poems, darkening the mood of "Renascence," which celebrates "The warm, dumb wisdom" that Lawrence learned from his "Eve." The woman was to provide his pathway to creativity, the means to his apprehension of nature, and the viewpoint of sensitivity, but for now, Lawrence received only "Strange throbs" through her, as when "the sow was grabbing her litter/ With snarling red jaws"; and, as in "Virgin Youth," "We cry in the wilderness."

Later, when he lived in Croydon, Lawrence saw violent urban deformation of nature, and it nearly shattered him; in "Transformations," beauty spills continuously into decay before him as men, "feet of the rainbow," are "twisted in grief like crumpling beech-leaves," and Lawrence is left to wonder at humanity's destiny: "What are you, oh multiform?"

He began to sense an answer looming in the growing recognition of his prophetic mission. In the poem "Prophet," he proposed "the shrouded mother of a new idea . . . as she seeks her procreant groom," using familiar biblical symbolism to stress the religious aspect of his utterance. Before the "shrouded mother," "men hide their faces," the fear bred of artificial social pressures forcing them to deny the powerful enriching role of sexuality in their lives. At last, in "Dreams Old and Nascent," Lawrence called for violent social action: "to escape the foul dream of having and getting and owning." For the first time, he attempted to define his affirmation of the vital impulse: "What is life, but the swelling and shaping the dream in the flesh?"

LOOK! WE HAVE COME THROUGH!

Lawrence shaped the dream of his own "crisis of manhood, when he marrie[d] and [came] into himself" in the cycle *Look! We Have Come Through!*, attempting in these highly personal poems a crucial connection between the lives of the flesh and the spirit. Greeting physical love in intimate Imagist lyrics like "Gloire de Dijon," he passed through "the strait gate of passion" in "Paradise Re-entered," in which his typically fierce human love must be "Burned clean by remorseless hate." His religious sense, too, had already departed materi-

ally from orthodox Christianity. In the same poem, he abandoned both God and Satan "on Eternity's level/ Field," and announced, "Back beyond good and evil/ Return we," with a distinctly Nietzschean echo suggesting his burgeoning preoccupation with spiritual evolution.

From the same nontraditional quarter came the promise that Lawrence incorporated into "Song of a Man Who Has Come Through," one of the closing poems of this cycle. Lawrence willingly yielded himself up to "the wind that blows through me," "a fine wind . . . blowing the new direction of Time." The wind of his prophetic aspect, to prove at times tempestuous, was the vehicle that Lawrence hoped to use "to come at the wonder" he sensed in the act of being, and with it he fashioned the personal experiences recorded in this set of poems into *The Rainbow* and *Women in Love*.

BIRDS, BEASTS, AND FLOWERS

The major poetic work of Lawrence's middle years was *Birds, Beasts, and Flowers*, which R. P. Blackmur called "a religious apprehension" and de Sola Pinto has described as an "exploration of what may be called the divine otherness of non-human life." The social criticism that Lawrence vented in this volume is chiefly directed at the United States, "lurking among the undergrowth/ of Many-stemmed machines." Lawrence plainly confirmed his simultaneous fascination with and repulsion for "Modern, unissued, uncanny America" in "The Evening Land": "And I, who am half in love with you,/ What am I in love with?" Although Lawrence distrusted the American reliance on the machine, he saw "Dark, aboriginal eyes" in the American "idealistic skull," a "New throb," which, like his dramatic character David, he finally concluded was "the false dawn that precedes the real." The aspect of humanity that had always most repelled him, inflexible will, was even less acceptable to him in the United States than it had been in Europe, as he noted in "Turkey-Cock," "A raw American will, that has never been tempered by life." In several pieces of fiction, including "The Woman Who Rode Away" and *The Plumed Serpent*, he attempted to subdue that will by sheer force of primitive emotion and even compulsive self-sacrifice. Reversing that position in "Eagle in New Mexico," Lawrence candidly acknowledged the necessity of opposition to bloodthirsty will, negating his own proposal of primitivism as a remedy for modern civilization: "Even the sun in heaven can be curbed . . ./ By the life in the hearts of men." Finally, Lawrence unleashed considerable venom at "The American Eagle," which he had come to consider the symbol of civilization's disaster, "The new Proud Republic/ Based on the mystery of pride." Contradicting the very concept of political dominance by an "aristocracy of the spirit" that he had advocated for so long, Lawrence denounced the "bird of men that are masters,/ Or are you the goose that lays the . . . addled golden egg?"

None of the rancor of Lawrence's American-directed diatribes is present in the finest poetry of *Birds, Beasts, and Flowers*, in which de Sola Pinto finds "an affirmation of the grandeur and mystery of the life of nature." Working from a mundane incident, a visit by a poisonous Sicilian snake to his water trough on "a hot, hot day," "Snake" illustrates Lawrence the poet at his most capable, commanding a deceptively simple style, ordinary speech, and a consummate adaptation of rhythm to meaning. The resulting interior monologue evokes a passionate mythopoeic response. The snake "had come like a guest in quiet," and Lawrence described himself as "afraid," but "honoured still more/ That he should seek my hospitality." In one of Lawrence's flashes of intuitive perception, the snake "looked around like a god" before retreating through a cranny in the wall. Lawrence's "voices . . . of accursed human education" impelled him to toss a log at the creature, a petty act that he shortly regretted profoundly: "And so, I missed my chance with one of the lords of life." "Snake" realizes a striking balance between mind and emotion, penetrating the mystery of civilized humanity's destruction of nature and eclipsing the conventional Christian symbolism of Evil Incarnate. In the snake's deathly potential, too, is the premonition that "the lords of life are the masters of death," an insight not developed fully until Lawrence had returned to Europe.

Still closer than "Snake" to expressing humanity's most archetypal need, the yearning after life renewed, Lawrence's "Almond Blossom" opens "a heart of delicate super-faith/ [in] . . . The rusty swords of almond-trees." Much of Lawrence's poetry has been assailed for

supposed incoherence of utterance and Whitmanesque repetitiousness, but in "Almond Blossom," de Sola Pinto notes, Lawrence is "thinking in images." Lawrence's old Christian path to God, "The Gethsemane blood," bursts now into "tenderness of bud," a splendid annunciation of "A naked tree of blossom, like a bridegroom bathing in dew." The "new living relation" of humankind with God that Lawrence was proclaiming in his philosophical essays now assumed fulfillment in an emboldened image that merged social consciousness, love, and religion: "Think, to stand there in full-unfolded nudity, smiling,/ With all the snow-wind, and the sunglare, and the dog-star baying epithalamion."

Pansies and Nettles

There is a marked shift in tone from *Birds, Beasts, and Flowers* to the following volumes of poems, *Pansies* and *Nettles*. In *Pansies*, Lawrence was immediately accused of obscenity for using "the *old* words [Lawrence's italics], that belong to the body below the navel." Those who knew him intimately, like Frieda, often referred to him as a puritan in sexual matters, and a purpose far different from obscenity motivated both his *Pansies* and *Nettles*; he had a stern, almost Calvinistic urge to destroy what he considered genuine pornography, "the impudent and dirty mind[s]" that had condemned *Lady Chatterley's Lover*. Lawrence had never been patient, and his introduction to *Pansies* is one of his most savage jeremiads: "In the name of piety and purity, what a mass of disgusting insanity is spoken and written." Such social "insanity" was his greatest enemy, and he fought the mob "in order to keep sane and to keep society sane." His chief weapon was a hard-edged Swiftian wit that did not shrink from the scatological to make a point. In *Pansies*, Lawrence assailed most of the sacred cows of his time: censorship, "heavy breathing of the dead men," "our bald-headed consciousness," "narrow-gutted superiority," the "Oxford cuckoos," "ego-perverted love," even "elderly discontented women."

Lawrence's short series of *Nettles* must have stung his detractors even more viciously. In "13,000 People," a poem on the public reaction to the brief exhibition of his paintings abruptly terminated by British police, he flailed the "lunatics looking . . . where a fig-leaf might have been, but was not." He even figuratively neutered his "little Critics": "brought up by their Aunties/ who . . . had them fixed to save them from undesirable associations."

Despite his ferocity when assaulting social "insanity," the unhealthy forces of repression and censorship, Lawrence was still approaching a positive solution for modern humankind's woes in both *Pansies* and *Nettles*. In the little poem "God" in *Pansies*, he declared: "Where sanity is/ there God is," linking his own beliefs to the Supreme Being. Lawrence also dedicated several of the longer *Pansies* (*pensées*, or even heartsease, he had suggested in the introduction) to the Risen Lord, the new subjective path to God by which humanity could serve as its own Savior: "A sun will rise in me,/ I shall slowly resurrect." In "More Pansies," a still later group, Lawrence came even nearer the mystery of human being, identifying the Holy Ghost as "the deepest part of our own consciousness/ wherein . . . we know our dependence on the creative beyond." Finally, as Lawrence struggled both in his poems and in his philosophic essays with the immensity of his apocalyptic vision, his satiric voice became only an overtone of the religious message he was attempting to enunciate. That message sprang from his "strange joy/ in a great [new] . . . adventure."

LAST POEMS AND APOCALYPSE

None of the poetry that Lawrence wrote during his life became him more than the *Last Poems*, which he wrote while leaving it. In his final prose work, *Apocalypse*, he was still clinging to the physical life he had celebrated so long and so rapturously, but in the *Last Poems*, Lawrence was setting out gladly into a new country whose borders he had glimpsed in *Etruscan Places*, his vivid sense of place even capturing the paradoxical "delight of the underworld" in ancient tombs, "deep and sincere honour rendered to the dead and to the mysteries."

In "Bavarian Gentians," Lawrence powerfully enlarged the mythic role of nature's archetypes of resurrection as he descended into the "new adventure": "Reach me a gentian, bring me a torch!" Previously concentrating on Eve as man's mediator with Paradise Regained, Lawrence now saw woman as symbolic Persephone, "a voice . . . pierced with the passions of dense gloom." The image of biblical mystical marriage could satisfy him no longer, and Lawrence now looked toward the mythic "splendour of torches of darkness, shedding darkness on the lost bride and her groom."

With the relatively minor exceptions of poems dealing with the symbols of his *Apocalypse* and a few more prickly observations on humanity's social vicissitudes, *Last Poems* represents the birth pangs of Lawrence's incomplete poetic masterpiece, "The Ship of Death." He had seen a little model ship in an Etruscan tomb, and it had carried his imagination toward the possibility of one long poetic testament, where, as Richard Aldington suggests, "suffering and the agony of departure are turned into music and reconciliation." The extant fragments of Lawrence's radiant vision center on a new concept in his stormy artistry, the peace of a soul fulfilled at last in its greatest adventure: "the long and painful death/ that lies between the old self and the new." Lawrence's long struggles with the nightmares of humankind's collective insanity were finally over, and he had "come through" his early preoccupations with the stresses of class and love and even religion, finding again within himself the possibility of a new dimension of human perception. At last body and mind, life and death had become one for him, "filling the heart with peace."

Lawrence's poetic development from conventional Georgian verse to mythopoeic vision spanned only the first thirty years of the twentieth century, yet his ultimate vision approaches the universal. In his "moments of greatness," far from a willfully obscene *Weltbild*, he opens a breathtaking vista of the potential of the human condition in its entirety, not only body, not merely soul, but also a creativity as vital as the Greek tragedy that Nietzsche had earlier proclaimed as the result of Apollonian-Dionysian tension. Lawrence's occasional Midlands lapses from literary propriety seem a small enough price to pay for the validity and vitality of his finest poetry, described best in the tenderly honest words of his fellow poet Rainer Maria Rilke: "act[s] of reverence toward life."

OTHER MAJOR WORKS

LONG FICTION: *The White Peacock*, 1911; *The Trespasser*, 1912; *Sons and Lovers*, 1913; *The Rainbow*, 1915; *The Lost Girl*, 1920; *Women in Love*, 1920; *Aaron's Rod*, 1922; *Kangaroo*, 1923; *The Ladybird*,

The Fox, The Captain's Doll, 1923; *The Boy in the Bush,* 1924 (with M. L. Skinner); *The Plumed Serpent,* 1926; *Lady Chatterley's Lover,* 1928; *The Escaped Cock,* 1929 (best known as *The Man Who Died*); *The Virgin and the Gipsy,* 1930; *Mr. Noon,* pb. 1984 (wr. 1920-1922).

SHORT FICTION: *The Prussian Officer, and Other Stories,* 1914; *England, My England,* 1922; *St. Mawr: Together with "The Princess,"* 1925; *Rawdon's Roof,* 1928; *The Woman Who Rode Away, and Other Stories,* 1928; *Love Among the Haystacks, and Other Stories,* 1930; *The Lovely Lady, and Other Stories,* 1933; *A Modern Lover,* 1934; *The Complete Short Stories of D. H. Lawrence,* 1961.

PLAYS: *The Widowing of Mrs. Holroyd,* pb. 1914; *Touch and Go,* pb. 1920; *David,* pb. 1926; *The Plays,* pb. 1933; *A Collier's Friday Night,* pb. 1934; *The Complete Plays of D. H. Lawrence,* 1965.

NONFICTION: *Study of Thomas Hardy,* 1914; *Twilight in Italy,* 1916; *Movements in European History,* 1921; *Psychoanalysis and the Unconscious,* 1921; *Sea and Sardinia,* 1921; *Fantasia of the Unconscious,* 1922; *Studies in Classic American Literature,* 1923; *Reflections on the Death of a Porcupine, and Other Essays,* 1925; *Mornings in Mexico,* 1927; *Pornography and Obscenity,* 1929; *À Propos of Lady Chatterley's Lover,* 1930; *Assorted Articles,* 1930; *Apocalypse,* 1931; *Etruscan Places,* 1932; *The Letters of D. H. Lawrence,* 1932 (Aldous Huxley, editor); *Phoenix: The Posthumous Papers of D. H. Lawrence,* 1936 (Edward McDonald, editor); *The Collected Letters of D. H. Lawrence,* 1962 (2 volumes; Harry T. Moore, editor); *Phoenix II: Uncollected, Unpublished, and Other Prose Works,* 1968 (Moore and Warren Roberts, editors); *The Letters of D. H. Lawrence,* 1979-2000 (8 volumes; James T. Boulton et al., editors); *Selected Critical Writings,* 1998; *Late Essays and Articles,* 2004; *Introductions and Reviews,* 2005.

BIBLIOGRAPHY

Balbert, Peter. *D. H. Lawrence and the Phallic Imagination.* New York: St. Martin's Press, 1989. This book is a well-reasoned response to feminist critics, who, especially since the 1970's, have accused Lawrence of misogyny. For "The Woman Who Rode Away," Balbert gives a revisionist study that shows the causes for misreadings in other works.

Bell, Michael. *D. H. Lawrence: Language and Being.* New York: Cambridge University Press, 1992. Discusses the development of Lawrence's metaphysics not only in terms of his emotional life but also in terms of philosopher Martin Heidegger's metaphysics.

Ellis, David. *D. H. Lawrence: Dying Game, 1922-1930.* New York: Cambridge University Press, 1997. The third volume of the Cambridge biography of Lawrence links his writings with the incidents of his life.

Ingersoll, Earl, and Virginia Hyde, eds. *Windows to the Sun: D. H. Lawrence's "Thought-Adventures."* Madison, N.J.: Fairleigh Dickinson University Press, 2009. This collection of essays on themes in Lawrence's writing and his thoughts contains an essay on his poetry.

Kinkead-Weekes, Mark. *D. H. Lawrence: Triumph to Exile, 1912-1922.* New York: Cambridge University Press, 1996. Volume 2 of this three-part biography covers Lawrence's life from his elopement with Frieda von Richthofen and the publication of *Sons and Lovers* through World War I. Highly detailed account based on newly available Lawrence letters; discusses Lawrence's relationships with Ezra Pound, T. S. Eliot, Wyndham Lewis, Ford Madox Ford, and others.

Maddox, Brenda. *D. H. Lawrence, the Story of a Marriage.* New York: Simon & Schuster, 1994. Examines Lawrence's life, focusing on his marriage and how it affected his writings.

Schneider, Daniel J. *The Consciousness of D. H. Lawrence: An Intellectual Biography.* Lawrence: University Press of Kansas, 1986. Tracing all the major works chronologically, Schneider treats Lawrence's religious nature at all stages of his life.

Squires, Michael. *D. H. Lawrence and Frieda: A Portrait of Love and Loyalty.* London: André Deutsch, 2008. Squires, who had access to Frieda's unpublished letters, writes of the relationship between Lawrence and Frieda, and how it developed.

Squires, Michael, and Keith Cushman, eds. *The Challenge of D. H. Lawrence.* Madison: University of

Wisconsin Press, 1990. This group of essays, which deal both with individual works and with broader literary contexts, supplies some interesting and provocative insights. Of particular note is the first article, by Wayne C. Booth, a self-confessed "lukewarm Lawrentian," who maintains that Lawrence's works are better appreciated upon rereading and reconsideration.

Worthen, John. *D. H. Lawrence: The Early Years, 1885-1912.* New York: Cambridge University Press, 1991. The first volume of the Cambridge biography of Lawrence covers his childhood in Nottinghamshire and his years as a teacher in a London suburb. Offers new insights into his relationships with his mother, Lydia, and with Jessie Chambers, Louie Burrows, Frieda Weekley, and other individuals who influenced his formative years.

_____. *D. H. Lawrence: The Life of an Outsider.* New York: Counterpoint, 2005. Written by a distinguished Lawrence scholar, Worthen, this compelling, readable biography is accompanied by several photos.

Mitzi M. Brunsdale

LAYAMON

Born: Probably in northern Worcestershire, England; c. 1200
Died: Place and date unknown
Also known as: Lawman

PRINCIPAL POETRY
Brut, c. 1205

OTHER LITERARY FORMS

Layamon (LI-uh-muhn, also LAY-uh-muhn) is known only as the author of the partially translated poetic chronicle known as Layamon's *Brut.*

ACHIEVEMENTS

Layamon's *Brut,* which John Strong Perry Tatlock describes as "the nearest thing we have to a traditional racial Epic," is the first major literary work in Middle English, and the first version in English of the stories of King Arthur and of King Lear. Assessing Layamon's achievement is difficult because his *Brut* is a much expanded translation of Wace's *Roman de Brut* (c. 1155), itself an Anglo-Norman translation and expansion of Geoffrey of Monmouth's *Historia regum Britanniae* (c. 1136; *History of the Kings of Britain,* variant version before 1155; vulgate version 1718). Consequently, it is necessary first to briefly describe these earlier versions and the influence they are known to have exerted.

Geoffrey of Monmouth, writing in Latin in the early twelfth century, constructed a pseudohistory of the British (as opposed to the Anglo-Saxon) kings of England, beginning with the legendary Brutus (a grandson of Aeneas), continuing through the celebrated reign of King Arthur, and ending with the last British kings in the seventh century. The primary effect of Geoffrey's *History of the Kings of Britain* was to stimulate international interest in the legends of Arthur, which previously had been well known only to the Welsh and Breton peoples. Geoffrey's *History of the Kings of Britain* and the *Prophetiae Merlini* (before 1135; *The Prophecies of Merlin,* 1966) were translated in places as far away as Iceland. Centuries later, in Elizabethan times, Geoffrey's *History of the Kings of Britain* would be rediscovered by the Tudor kings, who wished to stress their ancient Welsh claims to the throne. As part of this new interest, the *History of the Kings of Britain* would provide subject matter for Edmund Spenser and William Shakespeare. Spenser devotes canto 10 of book 2 of *The Faerie Queene* (1590, 1596) to a "Chronicle of British Kings," based on Geoffrey and derivative histories, such as Raphael Holinshed's *The Chronicles of England, Scotland, and Ireland* (c. 1577). For his tragedy of *King Lear* (pr. c. 1605-1606), Shakespeare consulted both Holinshed's and Spenser's versions. There he found the basic plot outline, including the opening love test, Lear's progressive humiliation by Goneril and Regan, and his eventual redemption (restoration in Geoffrey's *History of the Kings of Britain*) by Cordelia and the duke of France. To these elements, Shakespeare added the parallel subplots of Gloucester, Kent, and the Fool, and he rearranged the ending in a masterful fashion typical of his treatment of source materials.

The influence of Geoffrey's *History of the Kings of Britain* on medieval Arthurian literature was primarily by way of the Anglo-Norman translation by Wace. Wace's courtly version in octosyllabic couplets motivated and stylistically influenced his immediate successors, Chrétien de Troyes, Marie de France, and Thomas of Britain. More substantial use of his subject matter was made by fourteenth century prose romancers, in the French Vulgate *Merlin* and the stanzaic *Morte Arthur*. The latter work was a major source for Sir Thomas Malory's *Le Morte d'Arthur* (1485), and thus one can trace a circuitous route from the first to the last of the great Middle English Arthurians. Malory also made use of the alliterative *Morte Arthure*, perhaps the Arthurian work closest in spirit and substance to Layamon's *Brut*. Even this product of the alliterative revival, however, is thought to be based not on Layamon but on Wace, or perhaps on the fourteenth century translation of Wace by Robert Mannyng of Brunne. Among medieval works, only Robert of Gloucester's chronicle (in its later recension, c. 1340) can confidently be said to have made direct use of Layamon's *Brut*.

Even though Layamon's chronicle, which survives in only two manuscripts, represented something of a dead end in the development of Arthurian legend, Layamon was rediscovered in the nineteenth and twentieth centuries. Both Alfred, Lord Tennyson and Ezra Pound made demonstrable use of Layamon's poetic style. Linguists continue to study *Brut*'s early, more highly inflected dialect, and stylistic critics remain fascinated by its poetic form, which lies somewhere between the formulaic, alliterative meter of Anglo-Saxon poetry and the developing meter of the Middle English rhymed romances. The major modern contribution to Layamon scholarship, however, is the edition by G. L. Brook and R. F. Leslie.

BIOGRAPHY

All the known details concerning Layamon's life are derived from the opening section of his *Brut*, the first five lines of which read as follows (in Madden's translation, which includes the significant manuscript variants):

There was a priest on earth (or in the land) who was named Layamon; he was son of Leovenath (Leuca),—may the Lord be gracious to him!—he dwelt at Ernley, at a noble church (with the good knight) upon Severns bank (Severn),—good (pleasant) it there seemed to him—near Radestone, where he books read.

The author's name, which has been spelled in a number of ways, is Scandinavian in origin, and is cognate with modern English "Lawman." The recorded variant spellings of his father's name are less confusing when one realizes that the scribe often writes *u* for *v*; "Levca" can then be seen as a shortened form of "Leovenath." Tatlock hypothesizes, in the light of the familiarity with Ireland that Layamon exhibits in his poem, that perhaps Leovenath went to Ireland with the Norman invading force, married a Scandinavian Irishwoman (there having been a sizable Viking population in Ireland at that time), and later returned to England with his son. In any case, the only residence Layamon himself mentions is a church at "Ernley" on the banks of the Severn near "Radestone." These details accord well with a village variously referred to as Lower Areley, Areley Kings, and Areley Regis, not far from Worcester and the Welsh border. The books that Layamon mentions as having read (line 5) have usually been taken to be service books that he used in his role as a priest. Despite attempts to find the man behind these few details, however, Layamon remains little more than a name, an occupation (priest and translator), and a place-name. Even the time in which he "flourished" is derived from the supposed date of composition of the *Brut*, which is itself undergoing a reevaluation.

ANALYSIS

To analyze Layamon's *Brut*, it is first necessary to continue the discussion of his sources. As mentioned above, Layamon's main source was Wace's *Roman de Brut*, which in the edition that Madden consulted consisted of 15,300 lines, as opposed to the 32,350 lines in his edition of Layamon's *Brut*. Granted that Madden's lines (now termed half-lines) are shorter than the lines in Wace, it is still apparent that Layamon considerably expanded his main source. It has been suggested that Layamon may have used an already expanded version of Wace, which had been conflated with an earlier chronicle (now lost) by Gaimar. As this suggestion cannot be verified, however, most critics have looked elsewhere for supplementary sources. One recent modification in this matter of primary sources is the discovery that some of the material previously considered original in Wace derives instead from an extant "variant version" of Geoffrey. Furthermore, additions occurring in a Welsh version of Geoffrey are paralleled in Layamon.

Layamon in his preface mentions two works in addition to Wace: "the English book that Saint Bede made" and another book "in Latin, that Saint Albin made, and the fair Austin." Saint Bede the Venerable's best-known work, and the work potentially of the most use to Layamon, is his *Historia ecclesiastica gentis Anglorum* (731; *Ecclesiastical History of the English People*, 1723), written in Latin and later translated into Anglo-Saxon. Albinus of Canterbury (died 732) reportedly helped Bede gather source materials, and so a number of critics have assumed that Layamon erroneously attributed the Old English translation to Bede, and Bede's Latin original to Abbot Albinus (and to the great apostle to the English, "Austin" or Saint Augustine of Canterbury, died 604 or 605). Layamon claims both to have "compressed" these three books (including Wace) into one and to have used the latter two books "as a model." This second statement is closer to the truth, for Layamon did not in fact make any incontestable use of Bede. He was probably acting in a tradition of vague citation to a previous authority; Geoffrey before him had claimed access to a certain "most ancient" sourcebook. Nor can Layamon be shown conclusively to have drawn upon Geoffrey in the original Latin, upon classical authors, upon French Arthurians (besides Wace), or upon Welsh records. Evidence does suggest, however, that he was familiar with late Anglo-Saxon homiletic literature, and may even have read classical Anglo-Saxon verse in manuscript.

The best known of Layamon's additions are those that contribute new material to Arthurian legend. Wace had made the first recorded reference to the Round Table, to which Layamon adds an account of the quarrels over precedence that led to its institution (11360ff.) To Arthur's biography, Layamon adds an account of the

elvish gifts at his birth (9608ff.), a premonitory dream of his final misfortunes in the battle with Molred (13982ff.), and an expanded version of Arthur's mysterious departure to Avalon (14277ff.) Arthur as a character seems less a romance hero than a stern and successful king, feared and respected by all the kings and great knights of Europe. (Perhaps it should be noted that the better-known exploits of some of Arthur's knights, such as the Lancelot affair and the quest for the Holy Grail, do not appear in Geoffrey, Wace, or Layamon.) As for Merlin, Layamon reports more of his prophecies than Wace had done, and adds an account of his stay in the wilderness (9878ff.) that can be compared with the Welsh tales of Merlin Silvestris.

BRUT

Carolyn V. Friedlander discusses additions from other parts of Layamon's *Brut* in her examination of five of its longer episodes: those of Leir, those of the *Brut*, heroes and thanes. As an illustration, she cites an interesting Arthurian passage, in which Wace's knights ascend a tower and joke gaily about the relative merits of wartime and peace. Layamon, on the other hand, first characterizes the "ancient stonework" of the tower (12419), in a motif that recalls the older Anglo-Saxon elegies. The gay debate becomes a tense exchange or "flit" (12459) that recalls the "flytings" of Anglo-Saxon and Old Icelandic narrative verse. Another "Saxon echo" frequently alluded to is found in the description of Loch Ness (10848ff.), which is populated with the same sea-creatures ("nicors") mentioned in *Beowulf* (c. 1000).

C. S. Lewis also finds Layamon "fiercer but kinder" than Wace; Tatlock comments on a pervasive delight in crushing enemies, and sees therein echoes of Irish saga literature. Also suggestive of Irish influence is Layamon's greater emphasis on the marvelous and on appearances from the world of "faery." Layamon's additions concerning Arthur's weapons and the elvish smith who forged them evoke equally Anglo-Saxon and Irish legends. Finally, Tatlock also mentions Layamon's technical familiarity with matters of seamanship, which, together with other details from medieval life, contributes to the personal stamp that Layamon puts on his material.

Layamon achieves a further degree of originality

simply by virtue of the poetic form he employs. Geoffrey's *History of the Kings of Britain* is in prose, and Wace's *Roman de Brut* is in octosyllabic couplets; Layamon's *Brut* is written in a combination of alliterating and rhyming half-lines. The presence of alliteration suggests an inheritance from Anglo-Saxon verse, though not without some attendant changes. Metrically, Layamon's lines favor an iambic trochaic rhythm rather than the predominantly trochaic rhythm of Anglo-Saxon verse. This change leads to a greater proliferation of unstressed syllables at either end of the half-line. Furthermore, alliteration seems to be more an ornament than a strictly regulated requirement in Layamon's verse.

In these aspects of form, Layamon's *Brut* resembles a few other Early Middle English poems, including some late poetic entries in the Anglo-Saxon chronicle, the "Worcester fragments," "The Grave," and "The Proverbs of Alfred." Tatlock remarks how these poems also all lack the understatement, parenthesis, and periphrasis that characterized Anglo-Saxon verse. To account for these developments, scholars have hypothesized that a less strict, more popular form of alliterative verse may have existed alongside the more refined Anglo-Saxon compositions, such as *Beowulf*, which were committed to manuscript. It may be that the tradition degenerated (partially as a result of changes in the language itself), or, again, it may be that Layamon and the others, perhaps additionally influenced by the "rhythmic alliteration" of Anglo-Saxon prose, imperfectly revived the old forms. Such a revival (variously explained) did occur in the later Middle Ages, yielding, for example, the alliterative *Morte Arthure*.

Another feature that Layamon's *Brut* shares with the earlier Anglo-Saxon poetry is the presence of repeated lines and half-lines called formulas. Examples have been collected by Tatlock and Herbert Pilch, who also lists formulas that the *Brut* shares with Anglo-Saxon verse and with roughly contemporary verse. Formulas are present in much of the world's traditional narrative poetry, the recurrent epithets in Homer perhaps being the best-known examples. Early in the twentieth century, the Homeric scholar Milman Parry, supplementing his research with fieldwork on contemporary Yugoslavian oral epic, developed what is

known as oral-formulaic theory to account for this widespread appearance of formulas. According to Parry and his student Albert Lord, formulas are learned by apprentice poets as a means whereby they may improvise long oral narratives. This theory has since been applied to Old English and some Middle English verse, even though many of Parry's original statements have had to be modified considerably. For example, Layamon as a translator is not improvising but rather working in close conjunction with a written text (even if he probably worked more "in his head" than modern poets tend to do). Why, then, would he have a need for ready-made formulas? He may instead have been using formulas ornamentally, in imitation of the earlier models, or there may have been other factors at work that made formulas desirable. Layamon seems to have been constrained to avoid ending his sentence units with the first half-line (as had often been the case in the earlier poetry). Formulas, which are more frequent in his second half-lines, may have represented a useful way to "pad out" the whole line, acting somewhat like the "rhyme tags" in metrical romances. Layamon's use of formulas differs in other ways from Anglo-Saxon practice. Fixed epithets, such as "athelest kingen" for Arthur, are more common, as are formulas that recur in similar situations, such as "wind stod an willen," often used in sea voyage descriptions.

Rhyme was likewise employed ornamentally in the Early Middle English poems mentioned above, prompting some scholars to hypothesize that rhyme was developing independently in England, probably under influence from Latin hymns. Surely the example of Wace strengthened this tendency toward the couplet, which would become the norm in rhymed romances. There may also be an Irish influence at work in Layamon's unusual rhyming by consonant classes and on contrasting stresses. Here are some sample rhyme-pairs, modernized from the episode of Arthur's final dream (13971ff.): bestride/ride; tiding/king; son/welcome; fair knight/fare tonight. The first rhyme is exact; the second example rhymes an unstressed with a stressed syllable as does the third; yet here the consonants *m* and *n* do not match, but are related instead by way of a shared phonological class ("nasals"). The last example ingeniously interweaves homonyms and rhymes.

One final stylistic element distinguishing Layamon from his Anglo-Saxon predecessors is his use of the extended simile. Arthur's pursuit of Colgrim, for example, is compared (for eight lines, 10629ff.) to a wolf hunting down a mountain goat. Most of Layamon's extended similes, in fact, occur in this part of the Arthurian section, leading scholars to suppose that a single source may be responsible for this stylistic feature. Here, as elsewhere, however, the question of sources should not be allowed to overshadow Layamon's unique achievement. The *Brut* can and should be read for its own merits, as a poem and not simply as "Arthurian matter" divorced from its particular form.

BIBLIOGRAPHY

Bryan, Elizabeth J. *Collaborative Meaning in Medieval Scribal Culture: The Otho Layamon.* Ann Arbor: University of Michigan Press, 1999. Before print technology, every book was unique. Two manuscripts of the "same" text could present that text very differently, depending on scribes, compilers, translators, annotators, and decorators. The author questions whether it is appropriate to read such books, including *Layamon*, as products of a single author and finds cultural attitudes that valued communal aspects of manuscript texts: for example, a view of the physical book as connecting all who held it. Bibliographical references, index.

Donahue, Dennis. *Lawman's "Brut," an Early Arthurian Poem: A Study of Middle English Formulaic Composition.* Lewiston, N.Y.: Edwin Mellen Press, 1991. Examines the formulas and themes in the *Brut*, arguing that Layamon made artistic use of formulas, themes, and imagery in revising his Anglo-Norman source and creating darker portraits of Vortiger, Uther, and, especially, King Arthur.

Harford, Thomas J. *A Comprehensive Study of Lazamon's "Brut."* Lewiston, N.Y.: Edwin Mellen Press, 2002. Examines the poem in terms of its treatment of language, historical identity, and nationalism, and also looks at more than one hundred years of scholarship.

Layamon. *Layamon's Arthur: The Arthurian Section of Layamon's "Brut."* Edited by W. R. J. Barron and S. C. Weinberg. Austin: University of Texas Press, 2001. A fully edited version of the original text is accompanied by a close parallel prose translation, a substantial introduction, textual notes, and an updated bibliography. Sources are reviewed, as well as the social context of the poem and the structure. Includes a discussion of the Arthur character as hero and the *Brut* as a national epic.

_____. *Layamon's "Brut."* Translated by Donald G. Bzdyl. Binghamton, N.Y.: Center for Medieval and Early Renaissance Studies, 1989. Prose translation of the *Brut* is accompanied by an excellent bibliography that includes many articles and related studies. The introduction gives a good survey and appreciation of Layamon and the poem.

Le Saux, Francoise H. M. *Layamon's "Brut": The Poem and Its Sources.* New York: D. S. Brewer, 1989. This study characterizes Layamon as more than the simple parish priest, as he is so often seen. Le Saux looks at many possible sources and traditions that inform the poem. She sees Layamon as a mixture of Welsh and English cultures—the allies against the Norman invaders. Previous scholarship is reevaluated, and the thematic and stylistic relationship to the sources is examined. Includes bibliography.

Pilch, Herbert, ed. *Orality and Literacy in Early Middle English.* Tübingen, Germany: G. Narr, 1996. A collection of essays on Layamon and the *Brut*, presenting various theories, including Layamon's use of formulas.

Tiller, Kenneth Jack. *Lazamon's "Brut" and the Anglo-Norman Vision of History.* Cardiff: University of Wales Press, 2007. Applies critical thinking on twelfth century historiography to Layamon's *Brut*.

Paul Acker

IRVING LAYTON

Born: Tîrgu Neamț, Romania; March 12, 1912
Died: Montreal, Quebec, Canada; January 4, 2006
Also known as: Irving Peter Lazarovitch; Israel
Pincu Lazarovitch

PRINCIPAL POETRY

Here and Now, 1945
Now Is the Place, 1948
The Black Huntsman, 1951
Love the Conqueror Worm, 1951 (with Louis
Dudek and Raymond Souster)
Cerberus 1954, 1954
In the Midst of My Fever, 1954
The Long Pea Shooter, 1954
The Blue Propeller, 1955
The Cold Green Element, 1955
The Bull Calf, and Other Poems, 1956
The Improved Binoculars, 1956
Music on a Kazoo, 1956
A Laughter in the Mind, 1958
A Red Carpet for the Sun, 1959
The Swinging Flesh, 1961
Balls for a One-Armed Juggler, 1963
The Laughing Rooster, 1964
Collected Poems, 1965
Periods of the Moon, 1967
The Shattered Plinths, 1968
Selected Poems, 1969
The Whole Bloody Bird: Obs, Aphs, and Poems,
1969
The Collected Poems of Irving Layton, 1971
Nail Polish, 1971
Lovers and Lesser Men, 1973
The Pole-Vaulter, 1974
Seventy-five Greek Poems, 1974
The Darkening Fire: Selected Poems, 1945-1968,
1975
The Unwavering Eye: Selected Poems, 1969-1975,
1975
For My Brother Jesus, 1976
The Covenant, 1977
The Poems of Irving Layton, 1977

The Tightrope Dancer, 1978
Droppings from Heaven, 1979
The Love Poems of Irving Layton, 1979
For My Neighbours in Hell, 1980
Europe and Other Bad News, 1981
A Wild Peculiar Joy: Selected Poems, 1945-1982,
1982
The Gucci Bag, 1983
*The Love Poems of Irving Layton with Reverence
and Delight*, 1984
Dance with Desire: Love Poems, 1986
Final Reckoning: Poems 1982-1986, 1987
Fortunate Exile, 1987
Fornalutx: Selected Poems, 1928-1990, 1992
Raging Like a Fire, 1993

OTHER LITERARY FORMS

Irving Layton is known primarily for his poetry. He
edited several collections of Canadian poems and
wrote social and political essays and an autobiography,
Waiting for the Messiah: A Memoir (1985).

ACHIEVEMENTS

Irving Layton received numerous awards and honors
from the Canadian government and from universities in
Canada. He won Canada's Governor-General's Award
in 1959 for his collection *A Red Carpet for the Sun*. In
1976, he was made an Officer of the Order of Canada in
recognition for his literary achievements. Layton received honorary doctorates from three Canadian universities: Bishop's University in 1970, Concordia University in 1976, and York University in 1979.

Layton was honored internationally for his poetry.
He was nominated for the Nobel Prize in Literature for
two consecutive years (1982 and 1983) by admirers in
Italy and Korea. In 1993, he was inducted into Italy's
Institute Pertini and was the first non-Italian to win the
Petrarch Award, an Italian award that recognizes poetic
talent. Layton's works have been translated into nu-
merous languages.

BIOGRAPHY

Irving Peter Layton was born Israel Pincu Lazarovitch in Tîrgu Neamț, Romania, in 1912 and moved
at the age of one with his family to Montreal, Canada.

He graduated from Baron Byng High School, which the Canadian novelist Mordecai Richler also attended. In the early 1930's, Layton associated with many of Montreal's disaffected left-wing intellectuals whose Marxist ideology helped shape the political and social attitudes of his early poetry and prose. Later in the decade, he attended Macdonald College, graduating with a bachelor of science degree. In 1938, he married Faye Lynch. After a brief stint in the Canadian Army during 1942-1943, he attended McGill University in Montreal, where he received an M.A. in economics and political science in 1946.

For the next two decades, Layton earned his living teaching at Montreal high schools and at Sir George Williams University (now Concordia University). During this time, he became a member of a group of young poets in Montreal that included Louis Dudek and John Sutherland, who cofounded and edited *First Statement*, a periodical influential in the promotion of modern poetry in Canada. In 1945, Layton's first work of poetry, *Here and Now*, appeared. Throughout his early career, he wrote and published a new collection each year, largely at his own expense; however, his work remained generally unrecognized. In 1948, he divorced his first wife and married Sutherland's sister Betty, with whom he had a son and daughter. In the next decade, he began an extensive correspondence with the American poet Robert Creeley; this dialogue helped Layton formulate many of his ideas about poetry. The year 1956 marked a turning point in Layton's career when his collection *The Improved Binoculars* was published with a laudatory preface by the distinguished American poet William Carlos Williams. With the publication in 1959 of his award-winning work *A Red Carpet for the Sun* by the prestigious Canadian publisher McClelland and Stewart, Layton began to achieve commercial success and critical recognition in the literary world.

In 1957, Layton began a relationship with Aviva Cantor, with whom he had a son, David. He moved from Montreal with his new family and took a position as writer-in-residence at the University of Guelph in Ontario. Later that same year, he was appointed to the English department at York University in Toronto. With the publication of works such as *The Collected*

Poems of Irving Layton in 1971 and *Engagements: The Prose of Irving Layton* in 1972, Layton began to develop a national reputation not only for crafting groundbreaking and conscientious poetry but also for espousing forthright and controversial ideas that shocked Canadian readers and provoked reviewers and literary critics. In the late 1960's, after receiving the prestigious Senior Arts Fellowship from the Canada Council, Layton began to travel abroad extensively, visiting Israel, Asia, Australia, and Europe, and in 1974, his poetry was published in Italy with great success. At this time, Layton began to cultivate celebrity status in Canada and abroad, often to the detriment of real public appreciation for his poetic achievements. His vivacious personality, his provocative opinions, the erotic subject matter and imagery of his poetry, and his tumultuous relationship with his fourth wife, Harriet Bernstein, all contributed to his image as a member of the counterculture, which was the focus of many of his interviews and appearances in the media. Nonetheless, he undeniably influenced a new generation of Canadian poets such as Leonard Cohen and Seymour Mayne.

Layton's publication of several impressive collections throughout the 1980's drew numerous awards and honors, and in 1982 and 1983, he was nominated for the Nobel Prize in Literature by admirers in Italy and in Korea. In 1985, he married Anna Pottier, a young Acadian, and settled in Montreal. In response to Elspeth Cameron's *Irving Layton: A Portrait*, an unflattering biography published in 1985, Layton wrote *Waiting for the Messiah*, which described his early life in Montreal and his attempts to establish himself as a poet. Layton produced several more significant collections before 1994, when he was diagnosed with Alzheimer's disease. He died in 2006.

ANALYSIS

Irving Layton's significance as poet lies in his unique and complex articulation of the cultural, political, and social issues that preoccupied him during his lifetime. He is also important in Canadian literature as one of the country's first writers to focus on questions related to the identity and survival of Jews and Jewish culture throughout the world. Many of Layton's works give definitive proof to his own theories that poetry should be filled with vitality, subtlety, drama, and relevance to the real world. His poetry, with its erotically charged language and imagery, with its bold focus on new subject matter, and with its explosion of old myths and clichés, never failed to arouse both intense admiration and severe admonishment from critics, reviewers, and readers. In this respect, Layton followed the models of past writers who broke with tradition, such as the Romantic poets William Blake, Lord Byron, Percy Bysshe Shelley, and Walt Whitman. In the modern author D. H. Lawrence and the poet Williams, he found the inspiration to denounce bourgeois values, particularly through the use of shocking language and a focus on taboo themes.

Many of Layton's early works, such as *Here and Now* and *Now Is the Place*, focused on descriptive poetry and on social satire that denounced Canada's middle-class prudishness and philistinism. The latter theme permeated his collection *The Cold Green Element*. Once his reputation as poet and activist became firmly established after the critical and popular success of *A Red Carpet for the Sun*, Layton began to deal with topics encompassing a bolder vision in his poetry. Concern for the universal human condition became the major theme of collections written in the 1980's, especially *Europe and Other Bad News* and *A Wild Peculiar Joy*. In such works, Layton continually underscored the values of poetic truth, social concern, and an honest confrontation with history. Another leading and highly controversial theme that permeated Layton's writing was the importance of sexual love, which he equated with the act of writing poems. *The Love Poems of Irving Layton with Reverence and Delight* is his definitive collection on the topic. In it he explored his own responses to the various aspects of love through the numerous relationships he experienced throughout his lifetime. In the latter part of Layton's career, he focused more intently on Jewish concerns, while continuing to reject any forms of established religion, which he viewed as the source of man's inhumanity to man. Through his poetry, he began to articulate recognition of the Holocaust as a turning point in world history, much like other Jewish writers who bore witness to the effects of this event. In *For My Brother Jesus* and *The Covenant*, Layton used the prism of tragic history to explore the relationship between the survival of cultural heritage and the mission of the poet.

In the two decades before his death, Layton was nationally recognized as a preeminent writer for his role in broadening the limits of Canadian literature. Internationally, he was praised and acknowledged as a poet of global significance for his energetic artistry in exploring the individual's status in the contemporary world.

A RED CARPET FOR THE SUN

The award-winning *A Red Carpet for the Sun* brought Layton recognition as a leading Canadian poet, especially since it was his first work to be issued by a major publishing house, McClelland and Stewart. The work features more than two hundred of his best poems written between 1942 and 1958. Many of the basic themes that run throughout Layton's collections are represented here, such as the Western mythic ideas of death and rebirth and an exploration of how the twentieth century evil that is exemplified in the Holocaust and in nuclear war contributes to moral indifference and cultural atrophy. Layton's corrective vision for the ills of the modern age, such as social inequities and bourgeois materialism, is exemplified in one of his most famous poems in the collection. "The Birth of Tragedy" both describes the joy and value of poetry for Layton and also celebrates his hero Friedrich Nietzsche. Other notable poems in the book include many that explore universal experience through personal moments, such as "In the Midst of My Fever," "The Cold Green Element," and "Berry Picking." In the important preface to the collection, Layton reiterates his commitment, as a poet, to decry the inhumanity of the past and to help shape a better future for humankind.

BALLS FOR A ONE-ARMED JUGGLER

The poems of *Balls for a One-Armed Juggler* mark a turning point in Layton's vision of the past. The collection focuses on the destruction of European culture following World War II and on the consequent universal decay of values and morals. In "The Real Values," "Thanatos," and the much-praised "A Tall Man Executes a Jig," Layton demonstrates artistic complexity and control as he shapes a new perspective on the poet's confrontation of harsh truths. The collection is significant as an expansion of social awareness and protest in the history of Canadian poetry.

FOR MY BROTHER JESUS

For My Brother Jesus raised a storm of controversy in Canada because of the nature of its subject matter. In a reflection of Layton's harsh reactions to the evils of the twentieth century, the book's preface targets Christianity as the real source of anti-Semitism and as the destroyer of European culture. The collection underscores Layton's revised vision of his cultural role. His mission is to be a militant poet and an artistic activist, to change the world, and to enter what he describes as the pantheon of Jewish heroes, a group that includes Jesus, whom he reclaims for the Jews as a symbol of the Jewish nation. Ultimately, Layton integrates the history of persecuted Jewry with his conception of the unique role played by another cultural outsider, the "prophet-poet," who memorializes ways that cultural catastrophes have altered perceptions of God and humanity by all humankind in the twentieth century. In poems such as "The Haemorrhage," Layton explores the significance of the tragedy of the Holocaust and other incidents of Jewish persecution throughout history. However, this collection also has a mellow tone of nostalgia and remembrance. Poems such as "Art of Creation" describe how the poet discovers invigorating energy in the past that haunts him.

A WILD PECULIAR JOY

A Wild Peculiar Joy is a comprehensive collection of Layton's poetry that he and the Canadian poet Dennis Lee selected. It was republished in 2004 with a new introduction by Sam Solecki and excerpts from Layton's essays on poetry. Many of the selected poems reflect Layton's strong social and political conscience. Both the title of the book and the poems that it encompasses mirror the intense nature of his provocative artistry. Notable pieces such as "The Fertile Muck" and "Whatever Else Poetry Is Freedom" fully articulate his construct of poet as visionary.

OTHER MAJOR WORKS

NONFICTION: *Engagements: The Prose of Irving Layton*, 1972; *Taking Sides: The Collected Social and Political Writings*, 1977; *An Unlikely Affair: The Irving Layton-Dorothy Rath Correspondence*, 1980; *Waiting for the Messiah: A Memoir*, 1985; *Wild Gooseberries: Selected Letters of Irving Layton, 1939-1989*, 1989;

Irving Layton and Robert Creeley: The Complete Correspondence, 1990.

EDITED TEXTS: *Canadian Poems, 1850-1952*, 1953 (with Louis Dudek); *Pan-ic: A Selection of Contemporary Canadian Poems*, 1958; *Love Where the Nights Are Long: Canadian Love Poems*, 1962; *Anvil: A Selection of Workshop Poems*, 1966; *Anvil Blood*, 1973; *Shark Tank*, 1977.

BIBLIOGRAPHY

Francis, Wynne. "Irving Layton." In *Canadian Writers and Their Works*, edited by Robert Lecker, Jack David, and Ellen Quigley. Poetry Series. Vol. 5. Toronto: ECW Press, 1985. Includes a brief biography and an analysis of how Layton fits into the Canadian tradition and milieu. The author uses a detailed analysis of Layton's poetry to chronicle his struggle for acceptance.

Jason, Philip K., ed. *Masterplots II: Poetry Series*. Rev. ed. Pasadena, Calif.: Salem Press, 2002. Contains an in-depth analysis of the poem "Golfers."

Mandel, Eli. *The Poetry of Irving Layton*. Rev. ed. Toronto: Coles, 1981. A revised edition of the author's initial study published in 1969. Thoroughly analyzes the major thematic concerns of Layton's poetry and examines the reactions of the English-Canadian establishment to his work.

Mansbridge, Francis. *Irving Layton: God's Recording Angel*. Toronto: ECW Press, 1995. A biography of Layton based on extensive interviews with his friends, family, and colleagues. The author, who edited an edition of Layton's letters, underscores how his poetry and life overlapped.

Mayne, Seymour, ed. *Irving Layton: The Poet and His Critics*. Toronto: McGraw-Hill Ryerson, 1978. A collection of criticism on the major works of Layton's literary career that were published through 1975. Included are the opinions of critics and of poets from three generations. The reviews of American critics and poets are also represented.

Smith, Jennifer, and Elizabeth Thomason, eds. *Poetry for Students*. Vol. 12. Detroit: Gale Group, 2001. Contains analysis and criticism of Layton's "A Tall Man Executes a Jig."

Diana Arlene Chlebek

EDWARD LEAR

Born: Holloway, England; May 12, 1812
Died: San Remo, Italy; January 29, 1888

PRINCIPAL POETRY

A Book of Nonsense, 1846, enlarged 1861
Nonsense Songs, Stories, Botany and Alphabets, 1871
More Nonsense, Pictures, Rhymes, Botany, Etc., 1872
Laughable Lyrics: A Fourth Book of Nonsense Poems, Songs, Botany, Music, Etc., 1877
Nonsense Songs and Stories, 1894
Queery Leary Nonsense, 1911 (Lady Strachey, editor)
The Complete Nonsense of Edward Lear, 1947 (Holbrook Jackson, editor)
Teapots and Quails, and Other New Nonsenses, 1953 (Angus Davison and Philip Hofer, editors)

OTHER LITERARY FORMS

Edward Lear's verse collections include three prose stories and three prose recipes called "Nonsense Cookery." A few of his fanciful botanical drawings are accompanied by whimsical texts. Like his poems, these pieces show Lear at play with language, blithely disregarding common sense.

Two volumes of letters, most of them to Chichester Fortescue, were published in 1907 and 1911. Enlivened by riddles, cartoons, and bits of verse, they demonstrate Lear's fascination with the sound and meaning of words. He uses puns and creative phonetic spellings; he coins words and humorously distorts existing ones. A cold January day in Corfu is so "icicular" that it "elicits the ordibble murmurs of the cantankerous Corcyreans." He complains of the proliferation of tourists, especially "Germen, Gerwomen, and Gerchildren," around his property in San Remo. Although he often revealed his loneliness and depression, Lear characteristically found something to laugh about—if not in his situation, then in his response to it: He called himself "savage and black as 90,000 bears," and wished he were "an egg and was going to be hatched." In 1883, he

wrote, "I sometimes wish that I myself were a bit of gleaming granite or pomegranite or a poodle or a pumkin"; at seventy-one and in ill health, Lear's imperishable delight in wordplay pulled him out of self-pity.

He kept journals of his painting excursions; these were later published with his own illustrations. Lacking the warmth and spontaneity of the letters, these topographical and travel books are valuable to readers who relish pictorial description and wish to know the conditions of travel in the nineteenth century.

ACHIEVEMENTS

Edward Lear thought of himself as a topographical landscape painter, and his ornithological drawings are still highly regarded. Students of nineteenth century painting also admire his watercolor drawings—pen or pencil sketches executed outdoors and later elaborated and colored. Nevertheless, Lear's reputation as an author eventually overshadowed his painting, and he become famous as the founder of nonsense literature and today is best known for the verses and cartoons he created to entertain children. He popularized the form that came to be known as the limerick, and his innovative comic drawings have influenced many artists, notably James Thurber.

BIOGRAPHY

Edward Lear was the twentieth of twenty-one children born to Jeremiah and Ann (Skerrett) Lear. Financial difficulties led to the dispersal of the family; although the Lears were later reunited, from 1816, Edward was looked after by his oldest sister, Ann. She was devoted to him and encouraged his interest in reading and painting, but the nearsighted, homely, rather morbid child brooded over being rejected, as he saw it, by his mother. His diary alludes mysteriously to another early trauma, perhaps a sexual assault. His inclination to isolate himself grew after the onset of epilepsy (he called it his "demon") when he was five years old. He always felt that he was not like other people.

At fifteen, he was earning his own living as a draftsman. Within five years, his skill in drawing birds brought him to the attention of Lord Stanley (later the thirteenth earl of Derby), who invited him to Knowsley to make drawings of his private menagerie. There he made acquaintances who would become lifelong patrons and began to create comical verses and drawings to amuse his host's children.

In 1837, the earl sent him to Italy to recover his health and to study landscape painting. From that time, England was no longer his permanent home. Lear traveled throughout the Mediterranean world and lived in several places, explaining his wandering by saying that his health required a temperate climate, that he needed to make sketches as "studies" for his oil paintings, and that he must support himself by making his work available to wealthy tourists. His restlessness also suggests that he was searching for, and perhaps trying to avoid, something: an all-consuming interest.

Amazingly industrious even by Victorian standards, Lear generally spent most of his day sketching or painting; in leisure hours, he read widely and taught himself a half-dozen languages. Hard work seemed to help ward off depression and epileptic attacks but did not prevent his being lonely. For thirty years, his only constant companion was his Albanian servant, Giorgio Kokali, to whom Lear showed extraordinary kindness and loyalty. While busily preparing one set of illustrations for a travel book and another for a volume of natural history, he decided to publish the series of limericks he had begun at Knowsley. His painting gave him less satisfaction than his nonsense verse, which he wrote for the children of friends and for other youngsters he met in hotels and aboard ships. His verse became a vehicle for self-expression, while painting all too often meant drudgery and frustration. Upon receiving a legacy at the age of thirty-seven, he studied for a time at the Royal Academy, as if hoping to win recognition as a serious artist. Lear apparently had small regard for the watercolor drawings he produced by the hundreds: They were "pot-boilers" and "tyrants" that required much time yet brought little money. Although he sometimes sold large landscapes in oil and received modest sums for his books, he often worried about his finances and had to rely on the patronage of wealthy friends.

Lear tried to be independent, but he constantly suffered from loneliness. He maintained a voluminous correspondence with scores of friends, sometimes rising early to write as many as thirty-five letters before breakfast. Occasionally he expressed wonder that "this child," an odd, moody fellow, should have so many friends. He confided in a few—Chichester Fortescue, Franklin Lushington, and Emily Tennyson (his ideal woman)—but even to them he could not reveal his dark memories or speak of his "demon." More than once he considered marriage but could never bring himself to propose, despite evidence that Augusta Bethell would have accepted him. Terrified of rejection, this charming and lovable man told himself and his confidants that he was too crotchety, ugly, poor, and sickly to be a good husband. Another impediment of which he may have been conscious was his homosexuality. His response to Lushington, a kind but undemonstrative person, can only be called passionate; for several years, he fretted over Lushington's inability to give and receive affection. Emotional and spiritual intimacy were what he most craved, however, and his relationship with Lushington eventually became mutually satisfying. Throughout his adult years, Lear seems to have been happiest in the company of children.

Edward Lear (Hulton Archive/Getty Images)

Haunted by a sense of failure and determined to put an end to his wandering, in 1871, he moved into a house he had built in San Remo. Yet he traveled to India after his sixtieth birthday, making hundreds of drawings, and talked of going a second time. His last years were darkened by loneliness, illness, and a series of disappointments. He finally lost the will to work when his eyesight failed and he was near collapse. None of his friends was with him when he died.

ANALYSIS

Edward Lear is known as the founder of nonsense literature, and he has never been surpassed in that genre. Charles L. Dodgson (Lewis Carroll) had the opportunity to learn from Lear, and Lear may have learned from him; however, Carroll's nonsense verse is much different: funnier, more intellectual, and less musical. Lear was a true poet, keenly sensitive to the sounds and "colors" of words. His poems have lasted not only because they are amusing and melodious but also because they express the innocence, melancholy, and exuberance of Lear himself.

THE LIMERICK FORM

According to Lear himself, he adopted the form for his limericks—or "nonsense rhymes," as he called them—from "There was a sick man of Tobago," published in *Anecdotes and Adventures of Fifteen Gentlemen* (c. 1822). Most of them begin with this formula: "There was an Old Man [or Old Person, or Young Lady] of [place name]." The last line is nearly the same as the first, with Lear typically using an adjective (sometimes appropriate, sometimes whimsical) before the character's designation. Each limerick is accompanied by a cartoon of its main character in action—riding a goose, sitting in a tree, refusing to respond sensibly to a sensible question. More than three-quarters of the limericks concern old people; even some of those called "young" in the texts appear elderly in the drawing. Most of Lear's folk are eccentrics. One old man runs through town carrying squealing pigs; another will eat nothing but roots. Physical oddities such as very long legs or huge eyes are common. Several characters with noses even more prodigious than Lear's deal variously with that handicap: One hires an old woman to carry it, another allows birds to roost on it,

while a third adamantly denies that his nose is long. Lear's intended audience, children of the Victorian era, were surely amused not just by his characters' oddness but also by the fact that these laughable people were supposed to be "grown-ups."

FORMULAS FOR HUMOR

Lear often found humor in incongruity and arbitrariness. An old man of Dunrose, "melancholy" because his nose has been "seized" by a parrot half as large as himself, is said to be "soothed" on learning that the bird's name is Polly. A few characters suffer terrible ends—drowning, suicide, choking on food, death from despair, being baked in a cake. Yet even their situations are amusing; either the text indicates that these people somehow deserve their fate, or the poem or cartoon indicates that they are not distressed by it. For example, the "courageous" Young Lady of Norway, flattened by a door, asks, "What of that?"

Lear's avowed purpose was to write "nonsense pure and absolute" for the amusement of "little folks." Consciously or not, he also dramatized the conflict between the individual and society. Even children must have noticed how often the limericks' heroes and heroines were at odds with the people around them. In Brill, Melrose, Parma, Buda, Columbia, and Thermopylae, and other real-world settings specified by Lear, "they"—representatives of Respectable Society—stare, turn aside, express disapproval, offer unwanted advice, and punish. A man who "dance[s] a quadrille with a Raven" is "smashed" by his countrymen; so is the fellow who constantly plays his gong. A fat man is stoned by the children of Chester. The reader is not surprised that one old man has "purchased a steed, which he rode at full speed,/ And escaped from the people of Basing." Aldous Huxley called Lear a "profound social philosopher" for his portrayal of the consequences of nonconformity (*On the Margin*, 1928). Lear's touch, however, was always light; even the limericks containing violence or death are not sad or horrific.

The eccentrics are more likely to be friendly with animals than with other human beings. They live with birds, ride bears, play music for pigs, and try to teach fishes to walk—but they can also be attacked by insects, bulls, and dogs (Lear was terrified of dogs). Apparently, being truly alive is a lonely, risky affair. Accidents, physical and mental afflictions, and rejection by others, all in the nature of things, seem especially likely for the person who is different from his neighbors. Yet, unpredictably, "they" are sometimes solicitous and considerate, inquiring about the comfort of some irascible characters, warning others of imminent danger. "They" treat a depressed man by feeding him salad and singing to him; "they" glue together a hapless fellow "split quite in two" by a fall from a horse.

Lear's society, then, is committed to maintaining order and the general well-being—if necessary, at the expense of people who behave in ways "they" do not approve of and cannot understand. This is the world we know. Without the preachiness of much contemporary children's literature—or rather, literature written for the edification of children—the limericks convey that civil, mannerly behavior is expected. From Lear's perspective, as from the child's, adult judgments appear arbitrary. For some reason, or no reason, "they" are delighted with a girl named Opsibeena who rides a pig; "they" seem less likely to appreciate innovation than to encourage decorum, however meaningless: One man ingratiates himself with his neighbors by sitting in his cellar under an umbrella.

IMAGINARY SETTINGS

The nonsense songs are set in an imagined world in which animals and objects talk, sing, and dance with one another. Some of these characters are heroes; others are bored and lonely misfits. Like Lear, an early admirer of Lord Byron, they seek happiness in love, companionship, and travel. Odd friendships and courtships, mysterious events, and unexpected reversals abound. Lear has created a world in which anything wonderful may happen. The rules of decorum do not apply, do not exist. An owl marries a pussycat, and the Poker woos the Shovel. The title characters in "The Daddy Long-Legs and the Fly," unwelcome in polite society, sail away to "the great Gromboolian Plain," where they spend their days at "battlecock and shuttledoor." Disgusted with idleness, a Nutcracker and a Sugar-tongs ride off on stolen ponies, never to return—ignoring the protests of their household companions. Less adventurous, a perambulating table and chair ask some friendly animals to lead them safely home. Most successful in their quest are the Jumblies of the green heads and blue hands. Despite the warnings of "all their friends" (akin to the limericks' "they"), the Jumblies go to sea in a sieve, discover "the Lakes, and the Torrible Zone,/ and the hills of the Chankly Bore," and return home after twenty years to be lionized by their neighbors. Unlike most of Lear's songs, "The Jumblies" has no undercurrent of melancholy or dread.

MARRIAGE, FAMILY, AND FREUDIAN INTERPRETATIONS

A wanderer for most of his life, Lear often wished for (but doubted that he really wanted) a home with a wife and children. His "laughable lyrics," which sometimes poke fun at the conventional sex roles, courtship rituals, and marriage, reveal that he was ambivalent about committing himself to a woman. As George Orwell remarked in his essay "Nonsense Poetry," "It is easy to guess that there was something seriously wrong in [Lear's] sex life" (*Shooting an Elephant, and Other Essays*, 1950). More recent critics, reading nonsense literature as a manifestation of the author's repressed emotions, have noted that it is the pussycat, not the owl, who proposes matrimony; judging by Lear's cartoon, the owl is somewhat afraid of his bride. Again, a duck (a cigar-smoking female) talks a rather effeminate kangaroo into letting her ride around the world on his tail. Deserted by the girl he loves, the sorrowful title character in "The Dong with a Luminous Nose" wanders in lonely frustration; at night his great red nose, illuminated by a lamp "All fenced about/ With a bandage stout," is visible for miles. In pre-Freudian times, this poem was surely "laughable" in a simpler way than it is now.

"THE COURTSHIP OF THE YONGHY-BONGHY-BÒ"

The hero of "The Courtship of the Yonghy-Bonghy-Bò" proposes to a married woman; when she regretfully refuses him, he flees to "the sunset isles of Boshen" to live alone. Remaining in Coromandel, "where the early pumpkins blow," the lady "weeps, and daily moans." So romantic and comical an ending would have been impossible if the Bò had offered himself to a woman who was free to marry him. "The Courtship of the Yonghy-Bonghy-Bò," one of the songs for which Lear composed a piano accompaniment, uses the verbal music of repetition, assonance, and alliteration. Indeed, in this and other songs he achieves a lyricism reminiscent of the Romantic poets. Parodying the Romantic manner as he made verse out of personal concerns and fantasies, he was looking for a way to deal with his emotions. He once burst into tears while singing the song, written while he struggled to make up his mind about marrying "Gussie" Bethell.

"The Pelican Chorus"

To the Nutcrackers and Sugar-tongs, domesticity—perhaps the most sacred of Victorian ideals—is a "stupid existence." Home is sweet only to the timorous table and chair, the phobia-ridden Discobboloses, and the cautious Spikky Sparrows. Mr. and Mrs. Sparrow don human clothing, ostensibly to protect themselves from catching cold but actually, it seems, to "look like other people." Lear does portray some happy and admirable couples. In "The Pelican Chorus," King and Queen Pelican sing of their present joys and recall their daughter's courtship by the King of the Cranes. They are content, even though they realize that they will probably never see Daughter Dell again. A less skillful poet would have allowed the song to become maudlin or merely ridiculous, but Lear maintains a balance of melancholy, nostalgia, and humor. He reveals the singers' pride in their "lovely leathery throats and chins" and pleasure in the "flumpy sound" their feet make as they dance. (This kind of music is impossible for the crane, who, it is whispered, "has got no webs between his toes.") They complacently visualize Dell's "waddling form so fair,/ With a wreath of shrimps in her short white hair." The old pelicans' confusion—or fusion—of past and present is at once amusing and poignant; each stanza ends with this refrain:

> Ploffskin, Pluffskin, Pelican jee,
> We think no Birds so happy as we!
> Plumpskin, Ploshkin, Pelican jill,
> We think so then, and we thought so still!

"Mr. and Mrs. Discobbolos"

"Mr. and Mrs. Discobbolos," another poem about a family, ends with what must be described as an entertaining catastrophe. For twenty years, this couple lives in peaceful isolation atop a wall—because they are afraid of falling off. Then, quite suddenly, the wife begins to fret because their "six fine boys" and "six sweet girls" are missing the pleasures and opportunities of social intercourse. Disgusted, perhaps driven mad, Mr. Discobbolos slides to the ground and dynamites home and family "into thousands of bits to the sky so blue." One feels that he has done the right thing, even though his action is surprising and mysterious. Possibly he cannot endure mixing once again with conventional society or thinking that any of his children may marry such a "runcible goose" as his wife. Perhaps the poet is once again exploding the myth of the happy home. The attempt to make sense out of exquisite nonsense is part of the pleasure of reading Lear.

"Incidents in the Life of My Uncle Arly"

No doubt he exposed more of his hopes and fears than he intended. Some of the songs, especially those written late in his life, involve the emotions in a way that the limericks do not. Since the poet sympathizes with the pain and joy of these creatures of fantasy, so does the reader. Lear's last ballad, published posthumously, is clearly autobiographical. "Incidents in the Life of My Uncle Arly" is a formal imitation of "The Lady of Shalott," which tells of the wanderings and death of a poor and lonely man. At last "they" bury him with a railway ticket (representing Lear's freedom and rootlessness) and his sole companion, a "pea-green Cricket" (symbolic, perhaps, of the poet's inspiration to make music of his own experience). Lear, the "Adopty Duncle" of many children, states four times that the hero's shoes are "far too tight." Among the many afflictions of the poet's last years were swollen feet. Arly's tight shoes may represent any of the constraints on the poet's happiness. Thomas Byrom has pointed out that Lear, like UncLE ARly, was a homeless traveler for more than forty years before building a villa in Italy (*Nonsense and Wonder*, 1977). Sad without being pessimistic, the poem characterizes a man whose life was lonely yet rich in experience.

"Eclogue"

Lear's "Eclogue" is the product of his capacity for making fun of his sorrows and his tendency to self-pity and grumbling. In this parody of a classical genre, the singing contest between shepherds, Lear and John Addington Symonds catalog their woes; the latter's wife, Catherine, finally judges whose miseries are greater. The "Eclogue" is laughable, but the reader of

Lear's correspondence sees how truly it reflects his assessment of himself and his career; but *A Book of Nonsense* saw thirty editions in his lifetime.

"THE QUANGLE WANGLE'S HAT"

Lear's pleasure in his verse is expressed most clearly in "The Quangle Wangle's Hat." Wearing a beaver hat 102 feet wide, the title character sits sadly in a Crumpetty Tree, wishing (like Lear in San Remo) that someone would come to visit. Then he is approached by a series of exotic animals, some of them (like the Quangle Wangle himself) familiar from Lear's other writings. When they ask for permission to live on his hat, the hero welcomes each one. Enjoying a simple yet profound comradeship, an assembly of Lear's creatures blissfully dances "by the light of the Mulberry moon"—"and all [are] as happy as happy could be." Here in microcosm is Lear's imagined world, singularly free of conflict. The real world is not like this, but Lear persuades readers to imagine that it might be. Friendship and sharing of oneself offer the best hope of contentment in the fantasy world, as in the real one. The Quangle Wangle is Lear.

OTHER MAJOR WORKS

NONFICTION: *Illustrations of the Family of Psittacidae: Or, Parrots*, 1832; *The Birds of Europe*, 1832-1837 (5 volumes); *Views in Rome and Its Environs*, 1841; *Gleanings from the Menagerie and Aviary at Knowsley Hall*, 1846; *Illustrated Excursions in Italy*, 1846 (2 volumes); *Journals of a Landscape Painter in Albania, Etc.*, 1851; *Journals of a Landscape Painter in Southern Calabria, Etc.*, 1852; *Views in the Seven Ionian Islands*, 1863; *Journal of a Landscape Painter in Corsica*, 1870; *Letters of Edward Lear*, 1907; *Later Letters of Edward Lear*, 1911; *Indian Journal*, 1953 (Ray Murphy, editor); *Edward Lear in Southern Italy*, 1964; *Selected Letters*, 1988 (Vivien Noakes, editor).

MISCELLANEOUS: *The Complete Verse and Other Nonsense*, 2001 (Noakes, editor); *Nonsense Songs and Stories*, 2009.

BIBLIOGRAPHY

Byrom, Thomas. *Nonsense and Wonder: The Poems and Cartoons of Edward Lear*. New York: E. P. Dutton, 1977. Byrom attributes the idiosyncrasies of Lear's "nonsense" to his epilepsy.

Chitty, Susan. *That Singular Person Called Lear: A Biography of Edward Lear, Artist, Traveller, and Prince of Nonsense*. New York: Atheneum, 1989. This comprehensive bibliography contains eight pages of plates.

Colley, Ann C. *Edward Lear and the Critics*. Columbia, S.C.: Camden House, 1993. A history of the critical reception of Lear's work. Includes bibliographical references and index.

Lehmann, John. *Edward Lear and His World*. New York: Scribner, 1977. Relatively slim volume contains 137 illustrations as well as an index and a bibliography.

Levi, Peter. *Edward Lear: A Biography*. New York: Scribner, 1995. This biography of Lear describes his life as one of twenty-one children, his violent and secret struggle with epilepsy, his depression, and the inspiration for his works.

Noakes, Vivien, ed. *The Complete Verse and Other Nonsense*, by Edward Lear. London: Penguin, 2001. In this volume, Noakes renounces her guess that Lear may have been gay, which was the major premise of her earlier works, including *Edward Lear: 1812-1888* (1986).

_____. *Edward Lear: The Life of a Wanderer*. Rev. ed. Thrupp, Stroud, Gloucestershire: Sutton, 2006. Noakes rewrote this biography, originally published in 1969, in which she portrayed Lear as possibly gay, to reflect her changed opinion.

Mary De Jong

THOMAS LODGE

Born: London(?), England; 1558(?)
Died: London, England; September, 1625

PRINCIPAL POETRY

Scillaes Metamorphosis, 1589
Phillis with the Tragical Complaynt of Elstred, 1593
A Spider's Webbe, 1594
A Fig for Momus, 1595

OTHER LITERARY FORMS

Thomas Lodge wrote widely in genres other than poetry. His first prose work was *A Reply to Gosson* (1580), an answer to Stephen Gosson's *School of Abuse* (1579). His prose romances include *The Delectable History of Forbonius and Prisceria* (1584), *Rosalynde: Or, Euphues Golden Legacy* (1590), *Euphues Shadow* (1592), and *A Margarite of America* (1596). Other prose works encompass miscellaneous subject matter: a biography, *The Famous, True, and Historical Life of Robert Second Duke of Normandy* (1591); an invective in dialogue form, *Catharos* (1591); and a historical narrative, *The Life and Death of William Long Beard* (1593). *An Alarum Against Usurers* (1584), an exposé of contemporary money lenders, has the strong moral message of *A Looking Glass for London and England* (pr. c. 1588-1589), the play that Lodge wrote with Robert Greene. In about 1586, *The Wounds of Civill War*, another play he had written, was produced. His pamphlets on philosophical and religious topics include *The Diuel Coniured* (1596), *Prosopopeia* (1596), and *Wits Miserie and Worlds Madnesse* (1596). His later works are translations (*The Flowers of Lodowicke of Granado*, 1601; *The Famous and Memorable Works of Josephus*, 1602; *The Works, both Morall and Natural, of Lucius Annaeus Seneca*, 1614; *A Learned Summary upon the Famous Poem of William of Saluste, Lord of Bartas*, 1625) and medical works (*A Treatise on the Plague*, 1603; *The Poore Mans Talentt*, 1621).

ACHIEVEMENTS

Thomas Lodge's poetry displays a facility in versification that, by itself, would mark him as a poetic talent. His experiments with verse forms—quatrains and couplets in *Scillaes Metamorphosis*, sonnets of ten to thirty-two lines ranging from tetrameters to hexameters in the poems appended to *Scillaes Metamorphosis*, poems mixing long and short lines in the miscellanies, and iambic pentameter couplets in the satires—show him to be much concerned with the craft of poetry, even when his experiments are not successful. He shows the same eagerness in trying new types of poems and subject matter, and his works range from sonnets to verse epistles, complaints, satires, eclogues, lyrics, and Ovidian narrative. His debt to the Romans in his verse epistles, satires, and Ovidian narrative is one that later writers also incurred, and Lodge to a great extent introduced these literary forms into English. Not all his works are equally successful, and his facility at versification and image making sometimes produces trivial or precious poems; nevertheless, he did point the way to later poetic development in English literature.

BIOGRAPHY

Thomas Lodge's biography is sketchy. The existing evidence prompted early biographers to portray him as a dissolute rake—disinherited by his family and jailed for debts—but more recent writers have been kinder. Although his mother was apparently worried about Lodge's stability, she also favored him in her will above her other sons. Furthermore, even though there are ample records of suits and countersuits involving Lodge and various creditors, some of his problems seem to have been caused by naïveté, such as neglecting to get receipts and then being sued for ostensibly unpaid debts.

Lodge was born probably in 1558, since on taking his bachelor's degree in 1577 he would most likely have been eighteen or nineteen. Moreover, in a lawsuit with his brother William in 1594, he lists his age as being about thirty-six. In *A Treatise on the Plague*, he talks about London as if it were his birthplace, and presumably it was. His father was a prosperous grocer who became city alderman and, in 1562, Lord Mayor of London. As a child, Thomas Lodge may have been a page in the household of Henry Stanley, fourth earl of Derby: *A Fig for Momus* opens with a dedication to Stanley's son, William, and reminds him of the time his "noble father in mine infancie . . . incorporated me into your house." If this reference is to a lengthy period of time spent in Stanley's household, he surely would have met the famous people of his day and acquired the attributes—and education—of a gentleman.

Lodge's affluence, however, was not to continue. By the time his father had finished his term as Lord Mayor, he declared bankruptcy, a victim of financial problems caused by England's war with France and the 1563 outbreak of the plague. When Thomas Lodge entered the Merchant Taylor's School in 1571, he was one of a group of students who were admitted as the sons of poor men, paying reduced tuition. In 1573, Lodge entered Trinity College, Oxford. After taking his degree, he entered the Inns of Court in 1578.

His relationship with his parents at this period is problematical. When his father died in 1584, Thomas Lodge was not mentioned in his will. By this time, Lodge had written pamphlets—his *A Reply to Gosson*—and perhaps had converted to Catholicism. Trinity College, which had been founded during Mary's reign, still reflected strong Catholic influences, and Lincoln's Inn also had strong Catholic affinities, numbering among its members many recusants. In 1581, Lodge had been called before the Privy Council to answer charges, perhaps stemming from his religion. His literary activity and new religion might have displeased his father enough to cause him to disinherit his son; on the other hand, his mother's will, made in 1579, had already left him a large estate, which perhaps accounts for his father's reluctance to leave him any more. Yet even his mother's intentions are open to speculation. She stipulated that Lodge was not to receive his bequest until he was twenty-five, prompting some biographers to believe that she doubted her son's stability. She also included a proviso that Lodge would receive a yearly allowance only if he stayed at Lincoln's Inn and conducted himself "as a good student ought to do." If his behavior displeased her executors, they were to distribute his bequest among her other sons; Lady Anne seems to have felt the need to exercise special control over this particular son. Early biographers tended to see Lodge at this period as a profligate and debt-ridden young man. This view, however, is based partly on Gosson's attack on Lodge's character, which is hardly a credible source. Lodge's youthful degeneracy seems to have been exaggerated in early accounts of his life.

Sometime between 1585 and 1588, Lodge made a sea voyage, a venture he was to repeat in 1591 with Sir Thomas Cavendish. This latter voyage shows the perils to which the Elizabethan sense of adventure could lead: The expedition was plagued with bad weather, a mutinous crew, and widespread disease. Throughout his life, Lodge had published regularly, no matter what he did on a day-to-day basis; in 1597, however, he turned to the study of medicine and from then on produced only translations or works on medicine. He took his medical degree from the University of Avignon and probably practiced for a while in Belgium. He later returned to England and, in 1602, had his degree from Avignon registered at Oxford, a formality that would, perhaps, have attracted English clients. During the plague of 1603, Lodge worked tirelessly, even publishing a treatise on the disease with the intent of discrediting quack doctors who were profiting from people's fear and ignorance.

In 1604, Lodge married the widow of an Elizabethan spy who had formerly been a Catholic working for the pope. Although this man eventually became an atheist, his wife remained loyal to her religion, receiving a pension from Gregory XIII. Lodge's marriage to her—along with his own earlier conversion—apparently brought him under suspicion by the government, and the Royal College of Physicians denied him permission to practice in London. By 1605, Lodge was again practicing in Belgium. Finally, with the help of the English ambassador to France, he was allowed to return to England and, in 1610, entered the Royal College of Physicians. The plague again swept through London in 1625 and Lodge was made plague-surgeon. He died in 1625, presumably a victim of that disease.

In many ways Lodge's life exemplifies the variety of experience that a Renaissance man might have. While born to wealth, he was often involved in litigation over debts, whether incurred through real want or only through carelessness. A writer of delicate sonnets, he was also an adventurer who undertook two sea voyages. Although he was not persecuted for his religion as actively as some, his fortunes still rose and fell as his beliefs changed. Finally, the rather heedless young man acquired over the years a moral depth that caused him to work assiduously as a doctor throughout the plague years while others were fleeing London.

ANALYSIS

Perhaps Thomas Lodge's most famous work is the prose romance *Rosalynde*, the source for William Shakespeare's *As You Like It* (pr. c. 1599-1600) and a lively piece of writing by itself. Although the prose narrative of *Rosalynde* lies outside the bounds of this analysis, it does contain lyrical poems that, for their excellence, rival the best of Lodge's work. Their beauty was appreciated by Lodge's contemporaries, and many reappeared in *England's Helicon* (1600). Containing simple and even homely images and language, they explore the paradoxes of the Petrarchan lover without being excessive; as usual, Lodge is a master of metrics and many of these lyrics are presented as songs. "Rosalynds Madrigal" is an especially good example of Lodge's success as a lyricist. The poem alternates long and short lines in the first quatrain of each stanza; the stanzas close with four consecutive rhyming lines and a final line that may or may not rhyme with one of the lines in the first or second quatrain. Lodge's craftsmanship is evident in the way he can alternate long and short lines and use intermittently rhyming final stanza lines to achieve a musical effect. The homely images—love builds a "neast" in Rosalynd's eyes—also give the poem a certain lightness of tone. Many of the poems he wrote for the miscellanies show the same light touch and metrical skill:

> My bonnie Lasse thine eie,
> So slie,
> Hath made me sorrow so:
> Thy Crimsen cheekes my deere,
> So cleere,
> Hath so much wrought my woe.

PHILLIS WITH THE TRAGICAL COMPLAYNT OF ELSTRED

When Lodge's lyrics fail, they do so because they lack lightness and are not really profound enough to carry their serious, heavy tone; often they simply catalog the complaints of the Petrarchan lover and use balanced euphuistic lines to achieve a stately emphasis. Such emphasis seems misplaced, however, since the situations Lodge describes are often derivative. The sonnets in *Phillis with the Tragical Complaynt of Elstred* vary in quality. Some of them have the light touch of *Rosalynde*, although even in these Lodge is not consistent. Sonnet 13 opens by comparing Cupid to a bee: "If I approach he forward skippes,/ And if I kisse he stingeth me." The images describing love become more conventional as he goes along—tears, fire—and the poem ends with a conventional statement of constancy: "But if thou do not loue, Ile trulye serue hir,/ In

spight of thee, by firme faith deserue hir." Sonnet 37, containing heavy hexameter lines, lacks even the intermittently light tone of Sonnet 13.

The *Phillis with the Tragical Complaynt of Elstred* sequence closes with a long medieval complaint, "The Complaint of Elstred." Although hardly an inspired poem, it does show Lodge's affinities with pre-Renaissance verse. "Truth's Complaint over England" is also medieval in feeling and recounts Truth's lament over the condition of Lodge's England. Lodge's concept of satire seems mixed in his early works. "Truth's Complaint over England" achieves its social criticism through moralizing sentiments reminiscent of medieval complaint; Lodge's *A Reply to Gosson*, however, seems to show an awareness of different satiric possibilities. Confusing the etymology of *satire* and *satyr*—as most Renaissance writers did—Lodge gives a history of drama in which he asserts that tragedy evolved from satyr plays. The widely accepted Renaissance belief was that these plays allowed the playwright to scourge his audiences for their vices by having a satyr denounce them. In this way English writers came to think of satire as a harsh, uncouth form: Juvenal as opposed to the more urbane Horace. Lodge himself follows *Scillaes Metamorphosis* by a poem titled "The Discontented Satyr," a paean to discontent, the best emotion one can feel in a corrupt age.

A FIG FOR MOMUS

By the time he wrote *A Fig for Momus*, Lodge seems to have adopted this harsher Juvenalian mode of satire. This series of poems opens with a satire of flatterers and hypocrites, and Lodge is at his best in the imaginary characters and situations he evokes. Meeting an innkeeper with "a silken night-cap on his hed," the narrator is told that the man has had "An ague this two months." The narrator comments sardonically that "I let him passe: and laught to heare his skuce:/ For I knew well, he had the poxe by Luce." Lodge's second satire—incorrectly labeled the third—urges parents to set good examples for their children. The piece owes a special debt to Juvenal's Satire 14 on the same subject, and, if much of it seems simply moral preaching, the sheer number of vices that he catalogs keeps the poem moving. Perhaps Lodge's fourth satire offers his most memorable and bitter character study: a miser, old and decrepit, but still concerned with amassing a greater fortune. The gruesomely realistic description of the man shows Lodge at his best. His fifth satire opens with a paraphrase of Juvenal's Satire 10, although his debt to Horace is also apparent in his description of the contented life. If this satire is less bitter and harsh than his others, it is perhaps because of the influence of Horace. In addition to introducing Juvenal into English literature, Lodge made one other lasting contribution to English satire: He was the first to use the epigrammatic pentameter couplet.

If *A Fig for Momus* does not seem, as a whole, the bitter invective that the satiric elements might lead one to expect, it is because Lodge has interspersed other genres: eclogues and verse epistles. His eclogues offer little new to English literature—Alexander Barclay, Barnabe Googe, Edmund Spenser, and Michael Drayton had already worked in this form—and their general theme of human corruption is not developed in an interesting way. Furthermore, their poetry, compared to Spenser's masterpiece in this genre, is noticeably deficient, Lodge's verse epistles, however, were the first to appear in English and, although they are uneven, the best of them have a lightness and wit that are typical of Lodge. The epistle "To his Mistress A. L." opens with a buildup in the first two lines that the following ones humorously deflate: "In that same month wherein the spring begins,/ And on that day when Phoebe left the twinnes/ (Which was on Saturday, the Twelfth of March)/ Your servant brought a letter seal'd with starch." The letter turns out to be a request for information on how to lose weight, and the epistle cites various learned authorities on the subject, concluding that it is better to be "fat, slicke, faire" than "leane, lancke, spare." The epistle titled "In praise of his Mistris dogge" opens wittily enough with a request that his mistress "for a night . . . grant me Pretties place," and then proceeds to a canine history, ending with a pun: "Thus for your dog, my doggerell rime hath runne."

SCILLAES METAMORPHOSIS

If Lodge introduced the verse epistle into English, he was also one of the first to write Ovidian narrative, a literary type that would later appear in Christopher Marlowe's *Hero and Leander* (1598), Shakespeare's *Venus and Adonis* (1593), Drayton's *Endimion and*

Phoebe (1595), and John Marston's *The Metamorphosis of Pygmalion's Image and Certain Satires* (1598). Ovid had, of course, been known before Lodge: Arthur Golding's translation of the *Metamorphosis* (1567) was a standard Elizabethan treatment of the Roman poet. Yet Golding allegorizes Ovid to make his eroticism acceptable; Lodge is far from finding any allegory in his source.

Scillaes Metamorphosis is noteworthy for its elaborate images and conceits: Lodge has taken Ovid's 143 lines and expanded them to nearly 800. To the original story of Glaucus's love for the disdainful Scilla, Lodge adds an opening frame story in which the narrator, also a rejected lover, walks along the shore "Weeping my wants, and wailing scant reliefe." Finally, he meets Glaucus, the sea god, and hears his story. As Glaucus recounts Scilla's disdain to a group of nymphs, Venus appears with Cupid. Cupid cures Glaucus's lovesickness with an arrow and then shoots Scilla, who immediately falls in love with Glaucus, who now rejects her. Knowing her case to be hopeless, Scilla finally curses all men, whereupon she is beset by the personifications Furie, Rage, Wan-hope, Dispair, and Woe, who transform her into a flinty isle.

If one could sum up Lodge's handling of Ovid in one word, it would be "embroidery." Whenever Lodge can stop for a lengthy and sensuous description, he does. Some of these are very successful, such as the description of Venus after she has found the wounded Adonis: It ends with Lodge's touching lines "How on his senseless corpes she lay a crying,/ As if the boy were then but new a dying." The story of Venus and Adonis itself shows Lodge's leisurely narrative pace, since it is interpolated in the main story of Glaucus. Glaucus's description of Scilla is also leisurely and sensuous. Ovid simply says that she was *sine vestibus* when Glaucus saw her; Lodge's Glaucus minutely recounts her physical beauty, dwelling on her hair, cheeks, nose, lips, neck, breasts, and arms.

The flaws in Lodge's poem—and it is by no means of uniform quality—have to do in part with this massing of description and detail. Lodge does not seem to have any awareness that his poem cannot sustain the same high pitch stanza after stanza: Glaucus's laments, for example, all begin to sound alike. Lodge has partially dealt with this problem in the frame story at the beginning of the poem, the very place where the reader is unlikely to need a rest from the high pitch of the poem. Nevertheless, Lodge does offer an interesting double perspective on Glaucus that the rest of the poem might have done well to develop. After the narrator spends four stanzas crying and groaning over an unrequited love, Glaucus appears and berates the narrator's love-sickness in stanzas that almost bristle with moral advice. After counseling the narrator, however, Glaucus falls into exactly the same error and even faints while describing his own hopeless love. This humorous contradiction between Glaucus's words and actions lends an ironic perspective to the story that the rest of the poem does not explore. Indeed, the personifications from medieval allegory who transform Scilla seem totally out of place in Lodge's poem, as if he had not really decided what the dominant tone of Ovidian narrative should be.

His verse form is also ill-chosen, although he does the best he can with it. Composed of stanzas consisting of a quatrain (*abab*) and a couplet (*cc*), the poem has difficulty moving forward: The couplets are always stopping the flow of action. In one sense this hardly matters, since Lodge is more concerned with leisurely description than with fast-paced narrative action. The poem, nevertheless, is a narrative, however leisurely, and the recurring couplets do present a problem. Lodge almost seems to feel that this is so and usually manages to begin a new clause as the couplet begins, avoiding at least the awkwardness of the self-contained couplet having to continue the lines before it.

Hardly any of Lodge's long poems are unqualified successes, although they all have striking passages and show much facility of versification. That he was an experimenter is evident in the number of new poetic forms he introduced into English; experimenters cannot always produce perfect products. Nevertheless, music and lightness of tone mark many of Lodge's best works and make him a considerable figure in the development of Renaissance poetry.

OTHER MAJOR WORKS

LONG FICTION: *The Delectable History of Forbonius and Prisceria*, 1584; *Rosalynde: Or, Euphues Golden Legacy*, 1590; *Euphues Shadow*, 1592; *A Margarite of America*, 1596.

PLAYS: *The Wounds of Civill War*, pr. c. 1586; *A Looking Glass for London and England*, pr. c. 1588-1589 (with Robert Greene).

NONFICTION: *A Defence of Poetry, Music, and Stage Plays*, c. 1579; *A Reply to Gosson*, 1580; *An Alarum Against Usurers*, 1584; *Catharos*, 1591; *The Famous, True, and Historical Life of Robert Second Duke of Normandy*, 1591; *The Life and Death of William Long Beard*, 1593; *The Diuel Coniured*, 1596; *Prosopopeia*, 1596; *Wits Miserie and Worlds Madnesse*, 1596; *A Treatise on the Plague*, 1603; *The Poore Mans Talentt*, 1621.

TRANSLATIONS: *The Flowers of Lodowicke of Granado*, 1601; *The Famous and Memorable Works of Josephus*, 1602; *The Works, both Morall and Natural, of Lucius Annaeus Seneca*, 1614; *A Learned Summary upon the Famous Poem of William of Saluste, Lord of Bartas*, 1625.

MISCELLANEOUS: *The Complete Works of Thomas Lodge*, 1883 (4 volumes; Sir Edmund Gosse, editor).

BIBLIOGRAPHY

Donno, Elizabeth Story. "The Epyllion." In *English Poetry and Prose, 1540-1674*, edited by Christopher Ricks. New York: Peter Bedrick Books, 1986. A leading authority on Elizabethan narrative poetry, Donno illuminates the conventions and qualities that characterize the forms. Places Lodge clearly against his cultural background. The thorough index demonstrates Lodge's manifold activities, and the bibliography covers all major works.

Holmes, John. "Thomas Lodge's Amours: The Copy-Text for Imitation of Ronsard in *Phillis*." *Notes and Queries* 53, no. 1 (March, 2006): 55-58. In 1904, L. E. Kastner denounced Lodge as a plagiarist for similarities in his work to the sonnets of Pierre de Ronsard. Holmes examines what Lodge's debt is to Ronsard and compares their works.

Lodge, Thomas. *Rosalind: Euphues' Golden Legacy Found After His Death in His Cell Silexedra (1590)*. Edited by Donald Beecher. Ottawa: Dovehouse Editions, 1997. Beecher provides an informative introduction to the work that served as the basis for

Shakespeare's *As You Like It*. Bibliographical references, index.

Ostriker, Alicia, and Leslie Dunn. "The Lyric." In *English Poetry and Prose, 1540-1674*, edited by Christopher Ricks. New York: Peter Bedrick Books, 1986. Ostriker and Dunn divide the field here, the former taking verse written independently, the latter lyrics written for music—a division first made during the Elizabethan period. Lodge is covered in both categories. The index demonstrates more of his diversity, and the bibliography collects the primary sources.

Rae, Wesley D. *Thomas Lodge*. New York: Twayne, 1967. A critical biography of Lodge that includes a chronology, an index, and a detailed bibliography.

Ryan, Pat M. *Thomas Lodge, Gentleman*. Hamden, Conn.: Shoestring Press, 1958. Ryan's book is a study of Lodge's life and work, intended for students and general readers.

Walker, Alice. *The Life of Thomas Lodge*. Norwood, Pa.: Norwood Editions, 1978. A biography of the life of Thomas Lodge.

Carole Moses

CHRISTOPHER LOGUE

Born: Portsmouth, Hampshire, England; November 23, 1926
Also known as: Count Palmiro Vicarion

PRINCIPAL POETRY

Seven Sonnets, 1954
Count Palmiro Vicarion's Book of Limericks, 1955
Devil, Maggot, and Sons, 1956
The Man Who Told His Love: Twenty Poems Based on Pablo Neruda's "Los cantos d'amores," 1958
Count Palmiro Vicarion's Book of Bawdy Ballads, 1959
Patrocleia: An Account of Book Sixteen of Homer's "Iliad" Freely Adapted into English, 1959

Red Bird, 1959
Songs, 1959
Songs from the Lily-White Boys, 1960
Pax: Episodes from the Iliad, Book Nineteen, 1963
Logue's A.B.C., 1966
The Words of Christopher Logue's Establishment Songs Etcetera, 1966
The Girls, 1969
New Numbers, 1969
The Isle of Jessamy, 1971
Twelve Cards, 1972
Abecedary, 1977 (with Bert Kitchen)
War Music: An Account of Books Sixteen to Nineteen of Homer's "Iliad," 1980
Ode to the Dodo: Poems, 1953-1978, 1981
Lucky Dust, 1985
Kings: An Account of Books One and Two of Homer's "Iliad," 1991
The Husbands: An Account of Books Three and Four of Homer's "Iliad," 1994
Selected Poems, 1996
Logue's Homer—War Music, 2001
All Day Permanent Red: The First Battle Scenes of Homer's Iliad Rewritten, 2003
Cold Calls: War Music Continued, 2005

OTHER LITERARY FORMS

At the beginning of his literary career, while in Paris, Christopher Logue (lohg) did a certain amount of hack work for Olympia Press, including a pornographic novel, *Lust* (1954). On returning to London, he worked for the satirical magazine *Private Eye*, and a number of his pieces have been compiled in *Christopher Logue's True Stories from Private Eye* (1972) and *Christopher Logue's Bumper Book of True Stories* (1980).

Logue became engaged in writing film and theater scripts and in translating. His translation *The Seven Deadly Sins* (1986), unfortunately, did not gain the approval of the Bertolt Brecht estate. He also became interested in children's literature, writing children's verse and editing a number of anthologies of children's verse, including *The Children's Book of Children's Rhymes* (1986).

ACHIEVEMENTS

As an antiestablishment poet, Christopher Logue has probably found it more difficult to achieve recognition in the mainstream literary world of Britain. However, his experiments with public verse reading, including the first public poetry reading at the National Film Theatre in 1958, did create something of a stir in London in the 1950's, when new forms of drama were also beginning to gain a following. His main recognition came first from writing for *Private Eye* from the 1950's through the 1970's, when it became the leading British satirical magazine and much feared by politicians and establishment figures and before crippling libel cases tamed it.

Logue was a middle-aged man before he won any major awards. In 1990, he won the Bernard F. Conners Prize for Poetry from the *Paris Review* for his poem "Kings." In 2002, *Logue's Homer—War Music* was shortlisted for the Griffin Poetry Award. His reworking of Homer's *Iliad* (c. 750 B.C.E.; English translation, 1611) had caught the public eye, however, and for *Cold Calls*, the fifth volume of the enterprise, he received the Whitbread Poetry Prize for 2005 and was also nominated for the Whitbread Book of the Year. In 2007, he received national recognition by being made a Companion of the British Empire.

BIOGRAPHY

Christopher Logue was born to a middle-class Roman Catholic couple living in the port city of Portsmouth, in southern England. Their only son, he was sent away to a private Catholic school in Bath run by the Christian Brothers, then briefly attended Portsmouth Grammar School. In 1943, when Logue was seventeen, he joined the army as a paratrooper. After an accident in which he lost sight in one eye, he was transferred to the Black Watch. In 1945, he was sent to Palestine. While there, he served a sixteen-month prison term for possession of classified documents. Up until this time, he had shown no interest in books or writing, but in prison, he began reading.

After release in 1948, he drifted back to London, then moved on to Paris in 1951, finding himself in the literary world of Samuel Beckett, Henry Miller, and Alexander Tocchi, a Scottish novelist. To earn money, he wrote for the pornographic market under the pseudonym Count Palmiro Vicarion. Two novels and two volumes of poetry brought him his first earnings from publications. He also edited a new literary magazine, *Merlin*.

Returning to England in 1956, he found work as a scriptwriter and actor in the Royal Court Theatre of Kenneth Tynan and in British films under director Ken Russell. He also starting writing for *Private Eye*, then in its infancy as a satirical review of British cultural and political life. Satire was a main literary genre of the time, and Logue's antiestablishment stance fitted in perfectly.

However, Logue became drawn to poetry, especially poetry as performance and as poster art, which he saw as a main vehicle of the left-wing views he espoused. He helped reestablish the tradition of public poetry readings accessible to ordinary people in pubs, clubs, and theaters. He published small volumes of verse that gained a reputation among more avant-garde reviewers. He became very active in the Campaign for Nuclear Disarmament and was imprisoned several times on marches and demonstrations. In the 1970's, he suffered bouts of depression.

Logue had remained unmarried, despite developing an interest in children's literature, especially verse for children. However in 1985, at the age of fifty-eight, he met and married a somewhat younger woman, the critic and biographer Rosemary Hill, settling down in Camberwell, an inner suburb of south London.

He worked on a project that had long fascinated him. A British Broadcasting Corporation commission in 1956 got him interested in reworking the *Iliad*, the ancient epic poem by the Greek poet Homer. Logue's version, as it evolved, was not a translation, as Logue had never learned Greek and he added material. Although a pacifist, he focused on the battle scenes of the original text. The first volume in Logue's version was *Patrocleia*, from book 16 of Homer's epic. He followed this with numerous other titles. Together, these works earned him the title of Britain's best living war poet.

ANALYSIS

Christopher Logue's poetry has developed from its first Romantic-modernist beginnings under the inspiration of Ezra Pound, William Butler Yeats, and T. S. Eliot, to a fully fledged mock heroic. His first two volumes of poetry contain work that is by and large modernist but with occasional Romantic flashes. In this, it is not strikingly original in any way, but it does suggest someone trying to move away from the formalism of the Movement poets of the time, while refusing to get drawn into what he felt was the too comfortable Romanticism of the later Yeats. "For My Father" is one early poem in which the poet has struck an authentic voice. Real dialogue lies at its heart. The influence of Pablo Neruda can be seen in the collection *Red Bird* as well as *The Man Who Told His Love*.

As early as 1959, however, *Songs* shows the poet breaking away from the erudtion and allusiveness of his first poems. Logue was beginning to find the voice that made him famous as a public poet, declaiming in a popular style on the issues of the day in the idiom of the day, a voice that perhaps culminated in the 1969 Isle of Wight Festival, where he gave public poetry readings before some 100,000 people and singer-songwriter Bob Dylan performed. The biggest influence on these 1959 poems was German Marxist dramatist Brecht. Logue abandoned the academic style of poetry, and his language became dramatic, strident, racy, and satiric.

As time went by, Logue adapted this style to both comic and children's verse. He used some forms of children's verse in his poetry for adults; for example, he adapted the rhyming ABC for adult satiric verse as in *Abecedary*. At the same time, Logue had a developing interest in Homer's great epic poem, the *Iliad*. Early attempts to put this into English verse, not as a translation but as a new, culturally relevant version, include *Patrocleia* and *Pax*. These two attempts were reprised and enlarged in *War Music* in 1980. The volume dealt with the episodes in the *Iliad* in which Achilles reenters the war on the Greek side, enraged by the death of his partner, Patroclus. Two further volumes, *Kings* and *The Husbands*, were then packaged with *War Music* and reissued as one volume under the title *Logue's Homer—War Music* in 2001. Two further volumes followed: *All Day Permanent Red*, which got its title from a Revlon lipstick advertisement, and *Cold Calls*. The enterprise closely parallels that by the contemporary West Indian poet, Derek Walcott, whose *Omeros* (1990) is likewise based on a work by Homer but set in the Caribbean.

NEW NUMBERS

New Numbers is probably the most representative of Logue's populist poetry. Its opening poem is typical in that it brashly refuses to behave like a poem, challenging the audience with "This book was written to change the world." In other words, the volume is intended to be politically charged and dynamic, not merely of academic or aesthetic interest. It is absurdist in language and imagery. None of the poems have titles, and they are divided from each other only by small spaces, giving the sense of continuity and creating a cumulative effect.

One of the longer ones, "I have to tell you about Mr Valentine," is an allegory of the search for the ideal love preventing enjoyment of the real and actual grace of life as it is to be found in its fullness. The figures at times are cartoon-strip figures, grotesque, with fragments of dialogue thrown in. They capture the culture of the 1960's, with hippies, beatniks, and the search for Eastern mysticism. Each topic is treated with sympathetic absurdity. Many seem takeoffs of stories from the gutter press. The language is demotic, colloquial, and begging to be read aloud. This is the Brechtian ideal done in English.

SELECTED POEMS

Selected Poems, published in 1996, has become the most available collection of Logue's poetry, as many of the earlier volumes have gone out of print. The collection draws from earlier volumes but does not identify the collection in which each poem was originally published. However, the earliest poem, "Professor Tucholsky's Facts," is from *Songs*, the first of Logue's populist collections. Some poems were selected from *Ode to the Dodo* and *Songs from the Lily-White Boys*. Others have not been published anywhere else, including the last poem in the collection, "From Book XXI of Homer's *Iliad*," which was a discarded experiment for *War Music*. The collection also presents work from *Singles* (1973), a series of lyrics set to music. The final lyric contains the lines "Last night in Notting Hill// I saw Blake passing by. . . ." These poems are reminiscent of William Blake's *Songs of Innocence and of Experience* (1794) because of their lyric and ironic quality and also in that they comment on contemporary London.

Other selections are made from *New Numbers* and

The Girls. Urbanal (1975) is possibly the best poem of the volume, an urban elegy not unlike Robert Lowell's. It references Blake again, beginning with a lament for a thirty-year-old tree taken down because it is inconvenient to a neighbor. It takes on a tragic note, the poet/tree identification being deeply felt. The fact that there are very few poems representing the 1980's and 1990's show how much of Logue's creative writing was being put into the Homer project.

COLD CALLS

Cold Calls, billed as the penultimate volume of *Logue's Homer*, covers book 5 of the *Iliad*, going back before the original *War Music* to where Achilles, the great Greek hero, is still sulking in his tent, refusing to help his side. It covers the battle in the plains before Troy, where the Trojans sweep the Greeks back to their ships and threaten to burn them, despite suffering heavy losses themselves.

The style is clearly dramatic and, in fact, does better read aloud. Dialogue, commentary, and narrative mingle in a fast-paced, easily understandable style vastly different from traditional translations. There are detailed descriptions of the blood-thirstiness of the fighting, mingled with the gods' frequent interventions as they take sides. The volume is just forty-four pages long and needs almost no notes. The gods, especially Aphrodite, are made to seem very fallible, very human. However, it is difficult to see the poet as a pacifist. The soldiers are made to seem ridiculous at times, but only from a political point of view.

OTHER MAJOR WORKS

LONG FICTION: *Wand and Quadrant*, 1953; *Lust*, 1954.

SHORT FICTION: *Christopher Logue's True Stories from Private Eye*, 1973; *Christopher Logue's Bumper Book of True Stories*, 1980; *Private Eye's Oxford Book of Pseuds*, 1983 (with Kathryn Lamb).

SCREENPLAY: *Savage Messiah*, 1972.

TELEPLAYS: *Antigone*, 1962; *The End of Arthur's Marriage*, 1965.

NONFICTION: *Prince Charming: A Memoir*, 1999 (autobiography).

CHILDREN'S LITERATURE: *The Crocodile*, 1976 (of Peter Nickl; illustrated by Binette Schroeder); *Puss in Boots*, 1976 (illustrated by Nicola Bayley); *Ratsmagic*, 1976 (illustrated by Wayne Anderson); *The Magic Circus*, 1979 (illustrated by Anderson).

TRANSLATIONS: *Friday*, 1972 (of Hugo Claus); *The Seven Deadly Sins*, 1986 (of Bertolt Brecht).

EDITED TEXTS: *The Children's Book of Comic Verse*, 1979 (illustrated by Bill Tidy); *London in Verse*, 1982; *Sweet and Sour: An Anthology of Comic Verse*, 1983 (illustrated by John Glashan); *The Children's Book of Children's Rhymes*, 1986 (illustrated by Tidy).

BIBLIOGRAPHY

Bainbridge, Charles. "The War in Heaven." Review of *Cold Calls*. *The Guardian*, October 8, 2005, p. 18. Examines both *Cold Calls* and the entire *War Music* project, finding Logue's translation successful in part because of the vigor and energy he brings to the story.

Carne-Ross, D. S. *Classics and Translations: Essays*. Edited by Kenneth Haynes. Lewisburg, Pa.: Bucknell University Press, 2010. Contains an essay examining Logue's *Patrocleia* as a translation. Carne-Ross, a radio producer and classicist, helped Logue begin his work.

Leddy, Michael. "*All Day Permanent Red*: The First Battle Scenes of Homer's *Iliad* Rewritten." Review of *All Day Permanent Red*. *World Literature Today* 78, nos. 3/4 (September-December, 2004): 100-102. Praises the action in the poem and Logue's ability to make the reader see it happen.

Logue, Christopher. "Logue in Vogue." Interview by Liz Hoggard. *The Observer*, January 22, 2006. Logue gives a full-length interview after publication of *Cold Calls*, discussing his life and writing.

Ramsden, George. *Christopher Logue: A Bibliography, 1952-1997*. London: Stone Trough Books, 1997. The only fully annotated bibliography of Logue's many publications, small and large, and critical and journal articles.

Underwood, Simeon. *English Translators of Homer from George Chapman to Christopher Logue*. London: Northcote House, 1998. Fits Logue into the English tradition of Homer translation, comparing him to Alexander Pope especially.

David Barratt

RICHARD LOVELACE

Born: Holland or Woolwich, Kent, England; 1618
Died: London, England; 1656 or 1657

PRINCIPAL POETRY

*Lucasta: Epodes, Odes, Sonnets, Songs, &c. to
    Which Is Added Aramantha, a Pastorall*, 1649
*Lucasta: Posthume Poems of Richard Lovelace,
    Esq.*, 1659
The Poems of Richard Lovelace, 1925 (2 volumes;
    C. H. Wilkinson, editor)

OTHER LITERARY FORMS

Apart from the lyrics published in the two volumes of his poetry, Richard Lovelace wrote two plays, neither of which appears to be extant. The youthful *The Scholar* or *The Scholars*, a comedy, may have been produced at Gloucester Hall, Oxford, in 1636, and repeated later at Whitefriars, Salisbury Court, London. The prologue and epilogue appear in the first *Lucasta*. A second play, a tragedy titled *The Soldier* (1640), was written during the second Scottish expedition in 1640 but was never produced, according to Anthony à Wood, because of the closing of the theaters. Lovelace also wrote commendatory verses for a number of volumes published by friends or associates, versions of which appear in the collected editions of his poems. In addition, he wrote some lines, engraved under the portrait of Vincent Voiture, prefixed to the translation of the *Letters* by John Davies in 1657.

ACHIEVEMENTS

Although chiefly remembered for a handful of exquisite lyrics celebrating what Douglas Bush called the Cavalier trinity of beauty, love, and honor, Richard Lovelace has gradually risen to critical attention. Written for the most part against the somber landscape of England during the Civil War and Interregnum, Lovelace's poetry asserts more complex concerns and more authentic attitudes than those usually attributed to that "mob of gentlemen who wrote with ease." Lovelace was decidedly a literary amateur in the Renaissance tradition of the courtier, and his sensibilities were deepened and roughened by the calamities that befell him, his cause, and his king. "To Althea, from Prison," and "To Lucasta, Going to the Wars" are justly admired along with a few other frequently anthologized pieces, but the achievement is considerably larger than their slight number and scope might suggest. In his ode "The Grasshopper," for example, written to his friend Charles Cotton, Lovelace fashions from an emblematic examination of the fate of that "poor verdant fool" an affirmation of human friendship that transcends particular circumstance and achieves an authentic tragic tone. In the lines written "To my worthy friend Mr. Peter Lely, on that excellent picture of his Majesty and the Duke of York, drawn by him at Hampton Court," Lovelace evokes the "clouded majesty" of King Charles I, transforming a typical genre piece describing a painting into a somber elegiac on human dignity and courage in the face of adversity.

Like most of his fellow Cavalier poets, Lovelace was indebted to the poetry of Ben Jonson and John Donne. To Jonson, he owed what graciousness and form he achieved, especially in the choice of classical models. To Donne, he owed some degree of intellectual toughness and delight in what ingenious conceits he could master. To the limitations of both, in different ways, he was indebted for those infelicities of style that came with too much striving and too much care. Among his immediate contemporaries, he was no doubt influenced by his relative, the translator Thomas Stanley, who may have helped him in more substantial matters than verse. Other poets with whom Lovelace shared stylistic affinities and thematic concerns were Robert Herrick, Sir John Suckling, and Andrew Marvell.

BIOGRAPHY

The broad outlines of Richard Lovelace's life are easy enough to sketch, but when it comes to filling in the details, much remains conjectural. Born in 1618 either at the family manor of Bethersden, Woolwich, Kent, or in Holland, Lovelace was the eldest son of Sir William Lovelace and his wife, Anne (Barne). (The Woolwich church register does not commence until 1663.) His mother spent some time in Holland, where his father served under Sir Horace Vere and was later killed at the siege of Groll in 1627. Her references to her son Richard in her will make it seem likely that he was born while she was with her husband in the Low Countries.

Richard had four brothers, Thomas, Francis, William, and Dudley (the last of whom was responsible for seeing *Lucasta: Posthume Poems* through the press after his brother's death), and three sisters, Anne, Elizabeth, and Johanna. There are no records of Lovelace's childhood. In January, 1630, Lady Lovelace married Jonathan Brown or Browne of London, doctor of laws, and it may be presumed that the family's fortunes were enhanced as a result. The poet was educated at Charterhouse and entered Gloucester Hall, now Worcester College, Oxford, as a gentleman commoner in 1634.

By all accounts, the young scholar was handsome and amiable. In his second year, according to Anthony à Wood, a not very reliable authority in the case of Lovelace, he attracted the attention of an eminent lady of the queen, who prevailed on the archbishop of Canterbury, then chancellor of the university, to have him awarded a master of arts, though he was only of two years' standing. The following year, Lovelace was at Cambridge University, where he met several young men then in residence who were to contribute commendatory verses to *Lucasta* twelve years later; among them was Andrew Marvell.

Upon leaving the university, Lovelace joined the court, where he attracted the attention of George, Lord Goring, later earl of Norwich, and was sent by him as an ensign in the first expedition against the Scots in 1639, under the earl of Northumberland. During the second of these ineffectual campaigns, he was commissioned captain. Although he apparently wrote the tragedy titled *The Soldier* during the second campaign, the only direct reference to the Scottish campaigns is the drinking song "To General Goring, after the pacification of Berwick." Among those who rode northward with Lovelace was the poet Sir John Suckling, whose "Ballad upon a Wedding" is traditionally thought to address Lovelace, although there is little, if any, substantive evidence for the attribution.

Following the Scottish campaigns, Lovelace returned to Kent and took possession of the family estates. In late April, 1642, he helped deliver the Kentish Petition to the House of Commons, for which he was confined in prison for perhaps as long as two months. The petitioners could not have hoped for any response less severe, especially as a similar petition of the previous month on behalf of the bishops and the liturgy had been ordered burned by the common hangman. In June, Lovelace was released on bail from his confinement, provided he remain in close communication with the Speaker of the House. Although he was forbidden to take an active role in the struggle between the king and Parliament, he outfitted his brothers Francis and William with men and money to aid the royalist cause and arranged for his younger brother, Dudley, to study tactics and fortification in Holland.

Lovelace probably spent the greater part of the years 1643-1646 in Holland and France. His departure may have occasioned the lyric "To Lucasta, going beyond the seas." In Holland, he presumably learned the language and acquired an appreciation of the world of art then flourishing, with Rembrandt at the height of his powers. Lovelace was present at the siege of Dunkirk in 1646, where he was wounded. A year later, he was back in London and was admitted with the Dutch-born portraitist Peter Lely to the Freedom of the Painters' Company. In 1648, he and his brother were taken as prisoners to Peterhouse in London, possibly as a precautionary measure because of their past activities and the turbulent state of affairs in Kent at the time. It was during this second confinement, apparently, that he prepared his lyrics for publication in 1649. He was discharged on April 10, 1649, some ten months after his incarceration. During the year, Lovelace sold what remained of his family estates, including the family portraits, among which was one of himself by an unknown artist. These later came to Dulwich College.

Virtually nothing is known of Lovelace's activities in the years preceding his death, which occurred sometime before October, 1657, the date of the publication of Eldred Revett's *Poems*, which contained an elegy on Lovelace. Wood provides an account of Lovelace's last days and death. It has achieved popularity as suiting the legend of the man, but that Lovelace died a miserable death in utter poverty seems less than likely. Fifteen months before his death he wrote "The Triumphs of Philamore and Amoret" for the celebration of the marriage of his friend Charles Cotton. The poem, itself, may account for Wood's version of Lovelace's wretched end. Its references to Cotton's aid, however, "when in mine obscure cave/ (Shut up almost close prisoner in a grave)/ Your beams could reach me through this vault of night," would seem not to call for Wood's exaggerated description of the event. That Lovelace's fortune and fortunes were gravely reduced by the end seems clear. He would hardly have been alone in facing such hardships. There were friends to help, and it is unlikely that such abject poverty would not have been hinted at, had it occurred, in the various elegies occasioned by the publication in 1659 of *Lucasta: Posthume Poems*. The community of lettered friends was closely knit and evidence exists that discounts the implications of Wood's narrative. The poet Thomas Stanley, Lovelace's kinsman, had helped several needy and deserving poets and royalists, among them Sir Edward Sherburne, John Hall, and Robert Herrick. Cotton clearly assisted Lovelace in his time of need, and it is well known that Marvell tirelessly aided Milton in the early years of the Restoration. These are examples of the kind of support that surely would have been available to such an important gentleman and poet. Lovelace's place of burial, in Wood's account, was "at the west end of the Church of Saint Bride, alias Bridget, in London, near to the body of his kinsman William." The church was completely destroyed in the Great Fire of London in 1666 along with any records that could verify the place of burial.

ANALYSIS

Richard Lovelace's name has epitomized the supposed values of the world he inhabited, while its later link with Samuel Richardson's villain in *Clarissa* (1747-1748) has added guilt by association. The poet was, however, neither villain nor fop. Whatever glitter or romance touched his poems was incidental to a career dominated by darkness and despair, against which he strove with considerable stoicism. Indeed, although the themes of love, friendship, and retirement appear frequently in his poems (along with an informed and highly cultivated notion of the role of the arts of music, painting, and literature in relation to the good life), a pervasive sense of disillusionment and tragic isolation gives the best of them a keen edge. More than one critic has noted a claustrophobic sense of entrapment that is never far from the surface of his work. The traditional themes of what Earl Miner calls the "social mode of cavalier poetry" celebrate the good life, the ruins and remedies of time, the ordering process of art set against the disorder of the age, and the special values of love and friendship in the face of loss. Yet the Cavaliers were forced increasingly to survive in a winter world, like that characterized by Lovelace in "The Grasshopper," a poem that has received considerable critical attention in recent years.

"THE GRASSHOPPER"

In this poem, as in "The Snail," "The Ant," and "A Fly Caught in a Cobweb," Lovelace turns to the emblems of nature for lessons that bespeak the necessary fortitude of all life faced with the inevitable process of mutability. He shares his desire to fashion ethical and political statements of an allegorical kind by means of a microscopic examination of the natural world with other poets of his time, particularly Andrew Marvell, although the Anacreontic strain was most fully exploited by the royalist writers Thomas Stanley, Robert Herrick, and Abraham Cowley. Of the various reasons for examining the tiny creatures of the natural world, foremost was the wish to draw comparisons with the world of affairs amounting to little more than thinly veiled subversive propaganda. Although Lovelace and his fellow royalists were fascinated by the delicate craftsmanship that art shared with nature, "The Grasshopper" emerges as both a political and an ethical warning, as well as a pattern for refined artistry. The dual impulses in the poem, indeed, threaten its unity. In the end, it is only by recourse to paradox that Lovelace holds the disparate elements together.

In their enterprise to reinforce the royalist position by examples drawn from the world of nature, Lovelace and his fellow poets could not claim a monopoly on the material. Rebellion employed its own arguments from nature in support of human rights. When all else failed, the royalists found that their best alternative was a return to the nature found on what country estates were left to them, where they accepted a life of enforced retirement with whatever solace they could find. For

Lovelace, this last refuge from the political realities was no longer available.

LOVE, HONOR, AND TRUTH

The best known of Lovelace's lyrics are those that celebrate love, honor, and truth, especially "To Lucasta, Going to the Wars" and "To Althea, from Prison," the latter set by John Wilson for John Playford's *Select Airs and Dialogues* (1659). It is one of a number of royalist dungeon pieces that may be indebted to Vincent Voiture's *Dans la prison*, although prison philosophy was certainly something of a Cavalier convention. For all of Lovelace's asseverations that "iron bars do not a prison make," a sense of lost conviction lingers about the poem like Althea's whispering to her loved one "at the grates." While the poet extravagantly claims his right to lie "tangled" in his mistress's hair and "fettered to her eye," a feeling of suffocating doom weighs heavily on the poem. In comparison, the joyous, almost Elizabethan "Gratiana, dancing and singing," creates a world of exuberance, excitement, and courtly fascination, defining an atmosphere that exists, like Izaak Walton's trout-filled streams, in a world forever vanished. The theme of mutability sparkles through the verse like the golden tresses of Aramantha, that flower of another poem, which when loosened and shaken out will "scatter day."

In truth, for Lovelace it is sorrow that scatters his days, along with the realization that "joys so ripe, so little keep." Though the popular lyric "The Scrutiny" flaunted that brand of cynicism and masculine arrogance learned from John Donne through Thomas Carew and Sir John Suckling, the richer imaginative strain is the note that sounds touching true worth irretrievably lost. The general slightness of Lovelace's lyrics is, in one sense, a measure of what has vanished; and the brief attention span that shows itself in many of the poems, such as "Gratiana, dancing and singing," which disintegrates after the brilliance of the opening four stanzas, may be as much the result of distracted or shattered sensibilities as it is of limited poetic skills. The lyrics frequently end in fragments of broken vision or imaginative exhaustion. There are debts, as well, to the courtier poet Sir Thomas Wyatt, whose verse, like Lovelace's own, was often crabbed and tortured but could rise to take the measure of a tawdry world.

THE INFLUENCE OF GIAMBATTISTA MARINO

Perhaps because he was an amateur poet and a connoisseur of art, Lovelace saw very clearly the value of restoring the ruins of time. Like many of his contemporaries, particularly Stanley, an indefatigable translator, Lovelace went to continental as well as classical models for his verse, including that fantastic lyricist of the previous generation, Giambattista Marino. It may be assumed that the Petrarchan themes employed by Marino and his followers fascinated the royalist imagination, both by their sensuousness and by the brilliance of their metaphorical transformations. If poetry could change things, such linguistic strategies as the Marinisti presented in search of the marvelous might be enlisted by the Cavaliers in support of the royalist vision. After all, in the king they were accustomed to see poetically and politically the divinely linked agent of the miraculous. Beyond this, translation became for the poets of the time a means both to enrich their own meager gifts and to reinforce the realm of humane letters that was, they believed, the special preserve of the royalist writers.

From Marino, Lovelace borrowed the ideas and images for a number of his better poems. In "Elinda's Glove," working from Marino's *Il Guanto* (c. 1600's) "Gli occhi di foco e'l sen di ghiaccio armata," Lovelace developed the images of sexual passion and feminine cruelty into an emblem that combined its sexuality with a social statement, transforming the intensely private into the mode of social convention and sophisticated tolerance, with tinges of mockery. Lovelace's "Song: To Aramantha, that she would dishevel her hair" develops one of Marino's favorite themes, while the complimentary verses of "Gratiana, singing and dancing" paraphrase the sonnet of Giovanni Leone Sempronio, "La bella ballerina," and Lovelace's lyric "The Fair Beggar" employs a motif developed in the poem "Bellissima Mendica" by the Marinist Claudio Achillini.

Although much of his poetry written to celebrate friends and fellow artists was mere compliment, Lovelace often struck a note of sincerity that swept aside cant and allied human dignity with the longer life of art. On occasion these poems may owe something to models drawn from Marino's *La Galeria* (1619), but mere ingenuity gives way to the demands of authentic history and personal tragedy. In this regard, his poems written to Lely deserve a place in any appraisal of his accomplishments as a poet. In "Painture," he displays a fairly comprehensive understanding of painting and its particular fate in England, where the indifference of the average Englishman to anything but family portraits had troubled painters from Hans Holbein on. With Lely, Lovelace shares a sense of the importance of painting and seeks, by that bond, to establish an alliance against philistinism: "Now, my best Lely, let's walk hand in hand,/ And smile at this un-understanding land," where men adore merely their "own dull counterfeits."

LEGACY

Like his "Fly Caught in a Cobweb," as a poet and courtier Lovelace may seem to be a "small type of great ones, that do hum/ Within this whole world's narrow room." His vision as a minor poet, however, may display more clearly the age that produced him than do the more majestic tones of genius that rise above the humble chorus of voices from the land. In his "Advice to my best brother, Colonel Francis Lovelace," he counsels that "to rear an edifice by art so high/ That envy should not reach it," one must inevitably "build low." The lessons of humanity lie close to the surface of his poetry, more visible than the treasures of his wit. In the analysis of his poetry, that shallow part has satisfied most inquirers. Many have failed even to look that closely.

In his own day, Lovelace's poetry achieved little serious recognition. A few poems were known and recognized, but he did not enjoy a reputation such as Suckling did, for example. By the eighteenth century, he seems to have been almost forgotten. Had it not been for Bishop Thomas Percy, who reprinted his two most famous lyrics in his *Relics of Ancient English Poetry* (1765), he might easily have completely faded from sight. From his friend and benefactor Cotton, he received a suitable estimate in an elegy written for *Lucasta: Posthume Poems*:

> In fortune humble, constant in mischance,
> Expert in both, and both served to advance
> Thy name by various trials of thy spirit
> And give the testimony of thy merit;
> Valiant to envy of the bravest men
> And learned to an undisputed pen.

OTHER MAJOR WORKS

PLAYS: *The Scholar(s)*, pr. 1636?; *The Soldier*, wr. 1640.

BIBLIOGRAPHY

Allen, Don Cameron. "Richard Lovelace: 'The Grass-Hopper.'" In *Seventeenth-Century English Poetry: Modern Essays in Criticism*, edited by William R. Keast. New York: Oxford University Press, 1962. Examines the rich tradition embodied in the image of the grasshopper, at once the spendthrift, the poet-singer, and the king. Concludes that the indestructible kingdom created at the end of the poem is an inner one created by the poem.

McDowell, Nicholas. *Poetry and Allegiance in the English Civil Wars: Marvell and the Cause of Wit*. New York: Oxford University Press, 2008. This examination of Andrew Marvell looks at his associates, who include Lovelace. Several of Lovelace's poems are examined in detail.

Marcus, Leah S. *The Politics of Mirth: Jonson, Herrick, Milton, Marvell, and the Defense of Old Holiday Pastimes*. Chicago: University of Chicago Press, 1986. Couples Lovelace and Andrew Marvell, contemporaries whose poetry concerned cultural survival, and finds *Lucasta* a treasury of Cavalier political beliefs that Marvell later modified in his own poetry. Marcus accords only one of Lovelace's poems, "The Grasshopper," an in-depth analysis, but that discussion is followed by a treatment of Marvell's Mower poems, which rewrite Lovelace's original poem.

Robertson, Randy. *Censorship and Conflict in Seventeenth-Century England: The Subtle Art of Division*. University Park: Pennsylvania State University Press, 2009. A study of censorship in seventeenth century England that looks at authors such as Lovelace, John Milton, Andrew Marvell, and Jonathan Swift.

Semler, L. E. *The English Mannerist Poets and the Visual Arts*. Madison, N.J.: Fairleigh Dickinson University Press, 1998. Offers an introduction to the parallel history of the Mannerist poets and artists with specific attention to Lovelace, among others. Includes bibliographic references and an index.

Wedgwood, C. V. *Poetry and Politics Under the Stuarts*. New York: Cambridge University Press, 1961. Wedgwood traces the disintegration of the defeated Cavaliers through her reading of Lovelace's famous "To Althea, from Prison," a poem that prompted many imitations by other Cavalier poets.

Galbraith M. Crump

JOHN LYDGATE

Born: Lydgate, Suffolk, England; 1370(?)
Died: Bury St. Edmunds, Suffolk, England; 1451(?)

PRINCIPAL POETRY

Ballade at the Reverence of Our Lady, Qwene of Mercy, wr. c. 1430
The Temple of Glass, pb. 1477 (wr. c. 1403)
The Life of Our Lady, pb. 1484 (wr. c. 1409)
Fall of Princes, pb. 1494 (wr. 1431-1439)
The Siege of Thebes, pb. 1496 (wr. c. 1422)
The Secrets of Old Philosophers, pb. 1511 (wr. c. 1451)
The Hystorye, Sege, and Dystruccyon of Troye, pb. 1513 (wr. c. 1420; better known as *Troy Book*)
The Testament of J. Lydgate, pb. 1515 (wr. c. 1449)
The Life of Saint Albon and the Life of Saint Amphabel, pb. 1534 (wr. c. 1439)
The Dance of Death, pb. 1554 (wr. c. 1430)
Guy of Warwick, pb. 1873 (wr. c. 1426)
The Lives of Saints Edmund and Fremund, pb. 1881 (wr. c. 1433)
Complaint of the Black Knight, pb. 1885 (wr. c. 1400)
Translation of Aesop, pb. 1885 (wr. c. 1400)
The Pilgrimage of the Life of Man, pb. 1899-1904 (wr. c. 1426)
Queen Margaret's Entry into London, pb. 1912 (wr. c. 1445)

OTHER LITERARY FORMS

John Lydgate (LIHD-gayt) wrote only one significant piece of prose, *The Serpent of Division*. Scholars are uncertain as to its exact date of composition, but Walter Schirmer, in his *John Lydgate: A Study in the Culture of the Fifteenth Century* (1961), suggested the year 1422. Drawing on Lucan's *Pharsalia* (c. 80 C.E.) and Vincent of Beauvais's *Speculum Historiale*, Lydgate here presents the first comprehensive account of the rise and fall of Julius Caesar ever written in English. As in other writings, Lydgate uses this story as an *exemplum*, a story used to teach morality. Here Lydgate's lesson had to do with civil war.

Certain of Lydgate's poems are very intimately connected with later English dramatic forms, especially the *masque*. His "mummings" were meant to accompany short pantomimes or the presentation of *tableaux vivantes*. For example, in 1424, *Mumming at Bishopswood* was presented at an outdoor gathering of London's civic officials. A narrator presented the verses while a dancer portrayed the Goddess of Spring with various gestures and dance steps. The lesson of the poem is conveyed through allegory, where immaterial entities are personified. Here Spring represents civil concord, and Lydgate argues that just as the joy, freshness, and prosperity of Spring replace the heaviness and trouble of winter, so too the various estates, the nobles, the clergy, and the commoners, should throw off their discord and work together in their God-given roles. Success in these "mummings" probably helped prepare Lydgate for his part in the preparation of the public celebrations for the coronation of Henry VI in 1429, and for the triumphant entry into London of the same king with his new queen, Margaret, in 1445.

ACHIEVEMENTS

John Lydgate was one of the most prolific writers in English, with 145,000 lines of verse to his credit. To match this, one would have to write eight lines a day, every day, for about fifty years. Furthermore, almost every known medieval poetic genre is represented in the Lydgate canon.

For hundreds of years, the English literary public regarded Lydgate's achievement as equal to that of Geoffrey Chaucer or John Gower. Indeed, the three writers were generally grouped together into a conventional triad of outstanding English poets. George Ashby's praise in 1470 is typical:

Maisters Gower, Chaucer & Lydgate,
Primier poetes of this nacion,
Embelysshing oure Englisshe tendure algate
Firste finders to oure consolacion.

Furthermore, Lydgate was the glass through which his contemporaries understood and appreciated Chaucer, whom they considered a rhetorician, not a realist, the writer who finally formed English into a suitable vehicle for poetry, philosophy, and learning. In the end, perhaps Lydgate's greatest achievement was to consolidate this new status for his native tongue. Wholehearted monk, sometime administrator, and laureate versifier for kings and princes, Lydgate wrote poetry representative of his times and proper for someone of his position: sometimes prolix, often dull, but everywhere sincere, decorous, well crafted, and worthy of remembrance.

BIOGRAPHY

John Lydgate was born into turbulent times. His life spanned seventy years of the Hundred Years' War with France, and, when he died, the Wars of the Roses were about to begin. In 1381, he witnessed the Peasants' Revolt; in 1399, he saw Richard II deposed. The earlier years of his life were those of the Great Western Schism, with popes in both Avignon and Rome. At the same time, the anticlerical Lollards were stirring up trouble for the Church in England. Even nature seemed to conspire against the peace, for, beginning in 1349, the plague struck regularly, killing large portions of the English population.

Born of peasant stock, Lydgate was reared in the quiet village of Lydgate, far from the civil turmoil that raged elsewhere. He must have had a fairly normal childhood, for he later wrote: "Loth to lerne [I] loved no besyness,/ Save pley/ or merth . . . Folowyng alle appetytes longyng to childhede" (*The Testament of J. Lydgate*, 11). His serious side prevailed, however, and perhaps as early as 1385 he joined the Benedictine monastery at Bury St. Edmunds, about sixty-five miles northeast of London. Bury St. Edmunds was one of the richest of England's monasteries, with eighty monks, twenty-one chaplains, and 111 servants. Here Lydgate received much of his formal education, although it is

likely that he also spent a few years at Oxford, where he may have begun his literary career by writing his *Translation of Aesop*, the first book of fables written in Middle English. If Oxford was a good place to begin writing, however, the magnificent library of Bury St. Edmunds was just the place to nourish such a career, for it is thought to have contained about two thousand volumes, at the time making it one of the finest in England.

By the time he was ordained a priest in 1397, Lydgate probably had begun building a modest literary reputation. Indeed, John Bale, a sixteenth century biographer, suggests that Lydgate had already started a school of rhetoric for the sons of noblemen. Although some scholars are dubious about this, it is certain that Lydgate at this time began to make friends among the aristocracy, many of whom were later to become his literary patrons.

As a matter of fact, Lydgate soon came to the attention of Prince Hal, later Henry V, who in 1409 charged him with writing a life of the Blessed Virgin Mary. Thus Lydgate wrote his first saint's legend, *The Life of Our Lady*. This was to be the start of a long and fruitful relationship between Lydgate and the Lancastrian dynasty, a dynasty that both the poet and his brother monks saw as a strong bulwark of Catholic orthodoxy against the Lollards.

Henry V was more interested in battle, conquest, and deeds of chivalry than in piety, however, and by October, 1412, he conceived a different sort of project for Lydgate's talent: a retelling of the popular story of Troy. It took Lydgate eight years, relying mostly on Guido delle Colonne's *Historia Troiana* (c. 1285), to construct *The Hystorye, Sege, and Dystruccyon of Troye*, a long epic of thirty thousand lines. His taste for versifying history, however, was hardly sated by this massive work, for very soon after completing *Troy Book*, Lydgate set out on another long poem: *The Siege of Thebes*. He found the frame for this tale in Chaucer's works; he presents the work as a continuation of *The Canterbury Tales* (1387-1400). Thus the pilgrim "Daun John" Lydgate himself tells the Thebes story—at length. In the prologue, Lydgate shows his sense of humor, ironically contrasting his own appearance, "so pale, al devoyde of blode," to that of Chaucer's strong, lusty monk.

Lydgate's admiration for his master, Chaucer, knew no bounds; for Lydgate, Chaucer was the "lodesterre" of English letters. Although he probably never met the older poet, Lydgate was a very close acquaintance of Chaucer's son, Thomas, who was a wealthy country gentleman in Oxfordshire. A glimpse of the closeness of this relationship is seen in Lydgate's *Ballad to Thomas Chaucer* (1417).

In 1423, Lydgate moved closer to the circles of power at Windsor; he was given charge of the priory at Hatfield in Essex, a post that he retained, at least nominally, until 1434, when he was granted a *dimissio*, or formal written permission to return to Bury St. Edmunds "to seek the fruit of a better life." In fact, Lydgate probably resided at Hatfield only until 1426. It seems that in that year Lydgate was sent to Paris to take up a senior post on the staff of John of Lancaster, duke of Bedford. Here, among other things, he wrote *Guy of Warwick*, an adaptation of an old epic poem glorifying a mythical English hero who saves England from the Danes by overcoming their champion, Colbrand.

While in France, Lydgate met Thomas de Monta-

John Lydgate (Archive Photos/Getty Images)

cute, the fourth earl of Salisbury, who was the second husband of Alice Chaucer, the granddaughter of the poet. Montacute had a great interest in letters and commissioned Lydgate's translation of Guilliam de Deguileville's popular *Pèlerinage de la vie humaine* (1330-1331), a long allegorical romance concerning the "pilgrimage" of man through this earthly existence.

It can be assumed that in Paris, Lydgate mixed with people of the highest tastes and education, both English and French, for these years were productive ones for him, during which he wrote many of his satires and religious poems. He was inspired, for example, by one of the most popular themes of fifteenth century art, the *danse macabre*. Both in painting and in verse, this motif portrays the skeletons of men and women of all social classes dancing together as equals—in death. Lydgate's *Dance of Death* is a fairly close translation of verses that he discovered written on the colonnade surrounding the cemetery of the Église des Innocents in Paris.

In 1429, Lydgate returned to London for the coronation of the seven-year-old Henry VI. By this time, he was the premier poet of England, and thus he was commissioned to write an official *Roundel for the Coronation*, setting forth Henry's hereditary claim to the throne. Lydgate also had a hand in the planning of the official public celebrations for the event. He did the same in 1432 when Henry triumphantly returned to London from his coronation in Paris as king of France.

Fall of Princes, Lydgate's most important work, was commissioned in May, 1431, by Henry V's brother, Humphrey, duke of Gloucester, then warden of England. In some thirty-six thousand lines, the poet chronicles the continual movement of the Wheel of Fortune, raising up and then casting down men and women of power and wealth. It took him eight years to complete, while he increasingly felt his powers being drained by age.

In 1433, the king spent four months at Bury St. Edmunds, and in commemoration of the event, Lydgate was asked to write a life of the monastery's patron, Saint Edmund, for presentation to the monarch. Later, in 1439, Lydgate wrote his final piece of hagiography, *The Life of Saint Albon and the Life of Saint Amphabel*.

Lydgate received a lifelong pension from the king in

1439, but he was not left in peace at Bury St. Edmunds to enjoy it. In 1445, he was again given responsibilities for the planning of a public celebration, this time for the arrival in London of Henry VI's new queen, Margaret, daughter of King René of Anjou. For this occasion he wrote *Queen Margaret's Entry into London*, a work that no longer exists in its entirety.

In 1448, the poet, suspecting that his life was almost over, began his versified *The Testament of J. Lydgate*, perhaps his most intensely personal poem. In it, he denounces, somewhat conventionally, the levity of his youth, but he later proclaims in very moving terms his personal devotion to the name of Jesus. The tone and range of subject matter in *The Testament of J. Lydgate* are much different from those of the more famous *Testament* written less than a decade later by François Villon.

Lydgate must have passed his last few years with some sadness over his country's fortunes. The Hundred Years' War was winding down, but not in England's favor. Further, the internal political turmoil that would eventually lead to the Wars of the Roses was growing in England. Lydgate's final work, which he left unfinished, is another attempt to offer wise counsel to the country's leaders. *The Secrets of Old Philosophers* is a translation of the *Secreta Secretorum*, supposedly written by Aristotle for his pupil Alexander. Benedict Burgh, who completed the work, relates that just after Lydgate wrote verse 1,491, "deth al consumyth," the pen dropped from his hand, and the much-honored poet passed into history.

ANALYSIS

Once the uncrowned poet laureate of England, John Lydgate was appreciated by kings, princes, and nobility. In more modern times, he is often disparaged by literary scholars. Critics have charged that his poetry is dull, long-winded, and poorly wrought. Not all these charges will stand scrutiny, however, and one could argue that Lydgate's fall is due primarily to a shifting of tastes in poetry rather than to poor craftsmanship on his part.

It is true that Lydgate's poetry consistently frustrates the modern reader, who expects poetry to be compressed and concise; Lydgate's poems are generally voluminous. Instead of irony or ambiguity, Lydgate usually assumes a rather prosaic straightforwardness. On the other hand, instead of ordinary words in their natural order, Lydgate uses obscure terms in complicated syntax. Far from writing art for art's sake, Lydgate consistently insists on teaching sound doctrine and morality. Finally, in place of a uniquely personal vision and style, Lydgate always writes as a conventional public poet.

If one reads Lydgate through "medieval spectacles," however, these characteristics seem not only normal but praiseworthy as well. Lydgate saw himself as a rhetorician and thus felt it necessary to be both "sweet and useful" in his writing. Poetical art, to the medieval mind, was the application of rhetorical know-how to traditional themes and stories. Thus, he was first a craftsperson, not a prophet or seer. He would not have considered his personal emotions or insights worthy of remembrance.

It is ironic, therefore, that Lydgate the careful craftsperson has developed the reputation of being a poor versifier. If one assumes that his lines were supposed to be strictly iambic pentameter, this opinion may be justified. Fortunately, beginning with C. S. Lewis in 1939, certain scholars have suggested that Lydgate's line was based on a slightly different model, one that blends the French tradition of decasyllabic verse with the native tradition of balanced half-lines, thus allowing a variable number of stresses and syllables. In the light of these scholarly studies, Lydgate's verse seems consistently good.

Some critics argue that Lydgate is important as a poet of transition, since they find the seeds of Renaissance humanism in some of his work. Although it would be foolish to discount their insights completely, however, the more traditional reading is that Lydgate is a purely medieval writer.

COMPLAINT OF THE BLACK KNIGHT

Much of what can be said about John Lydgate's art in the *Complaint of the Black Knight* can be applied very readily to the bulk of his writings. The poem, written about 1400, is a conventional love complaint, a very popular genre of the age, of ninety-seven Chaucerian stanzas (stanzas of seven pentameter lines rhyming *ababbcc*). It begins with the poet, sick at heart, journeying out into the May morning to find some succor for his pain. He encounters birds singing, beautiful trees and flowers, a clear river, and a fountain that provides him water to refresh his spirits. All of a sudden, the poet discovers an arbor in which a handsome knight, dressed in black, sits moaning as if sick. After hiding, the poet discreetly listens to the lover's complaint.

The centerpiece of this poem is the highly artificial soliloquy that follows. Here the knight first confesses that he is tortured with overwhelming love; second, protests that his lady, because of false rumors about his conduct, disdains him; third, remonstrates with the God of Love, who, he claims, is unfair to honest lovers and rewards only the false; and fourth, offers his life to his lady: "My hert I send, and my spirit also,/ What so-ever she list with hem to do." Moved to tears by this complaint, the poet prays to the rising Venus, asking that she will have pity on this true lover. He then prays that all lovers will be true and that they will enjoy one another's embraces. Finally, he sends his poem off to his princess, hoping that this "little book" will speak eloquently of his pain in love.

The whole poem is borrowings, not only from Geoffrey Chaucer's *Book of the Duchess* (c. 1370), Lydgate's main source, but also from many of the poems of the French allegorical school. Borrowing, however, is normal procedure for medieval poets, for, as Robert Payne has shown in his *The Key of Remembrance* (1963), they considered their primary task to be not poetic invention but rather the reordering and the embellishment of traditional truths or literary works. Lydgate here is true to his times, and he works as a craftsperson, not a seer. His main talent, then, lies squarely within the confines of rhetoric.

The landscape in the *Complaint of the Black Knight*, for example, is not constructed from personal observation or experience but is taken directly from conventional descriptions of nature that Lydgate found in "old books." He tries to construct a *locus amoenus*, an idealized natural site fit for idealized lovers, both successful and frustrated. Thus, he uses all the details, the May morning, the flowers, the birds, the clear stream, that the sources stipulated. Moreover, Lydgate borrows not only descriptions of nature but also many other traditional themes, images, and literary postures, making the poem entirely conventional.

After selecting his genre, his themes, and his sources, Lydgate, working methodically, amplifying, contracting, or rearranging parts according to his own tastes, next fashions a fitting structure for them. Finally, he adds the embellishment, the literary "colors," such as alliteration, antithesis, chiasmus, echoing, exclamation, parallelism, or repetition. Thus, in lines 232 to 233, the Knight describes his woes with an elaborate chiasmus, reminiscent of Chaucer's *Troilus and Criseyde* (1382), book 1, 420: "Now hote as fire, now colde as asshes dede,/ Now hote for colde, now colde for hete ageyn." In lines 400 to 403, Lydgate adapts an exclamation from *Troilus and Criseyde*, book 5, 1828-1832:

> Lo her the fyne of loveres servise!
> Lo how that Love can his servantis quyte!
> Lo how he can his feythful men dispise,
> To sle the trwe men, and fals to respite!

Lydgate regularly protests that he has no literary "colors," but this too is a conventional literary pose. On the contrary, one finds "colors" used carefully and continuously throughout the Lydgate corpus.

In fact, Lydgate is so much interested in the surface decoration of his poetry that he sometimes seems to neglect its deeper significance. The elaborate descriptions of nature in the literature of courtly love, for example, were meant to have a purpose beyond that of mere ornamentation; they were supposed to carry an allegorical meaning. In Chaucer's *Romaunt of the Rose* (c. 1370), from which Lydgate borrowed some of his landscape, the fountain of Narcissus represents the Lady's eyes, the garden represents the life at court, and the rose-plot is the mind of the lady wherein personified fears and hopes do battle. C. S. Lewis discusses these allegorical meanings at length in *The Allegory of Love* (1936), but he could not do the same for Lydgate's version of the garden, for here the long description of the garden is not integrated with the rest of the poem. Once the Knight begins his soliloquy, Lydgate seemingly forgets the garden, whose description is thus solely a piece of rhetorical virtuosity. Indeed, that which is of most value in the poem is the part that is most intrinsically rhetorical: the formal complaint of the Knight. In Lewis's words, "The slow building up and decoration, niche by niche, of a rhetorical structure, brings out what is best in the poet."

In this context, Lydgate's famous predilection for florid Latinate diction makes sense. The poet himself coined the term *aureate* to describe both a highly wrought style and an elevated diction. In *Fall of Princes*, he describes his task in the following way: "Writing of old, with letters aureat,/ Labour of poetis doth hihli magnefie." The medium here fits the message, for Lydgate cannot resist twisting normal English word order. Moreover, the influence of Lydgate's style on his successors was great indeed, for the use of "aureat lettres" came to dominate fifteenth century verse. It was not until the nineteenth century, when William Wordsworth began to attack "poetic diction," that "aureate" came to have pejorative connotations.

BALLADE AT THE REVERENCE OF OUR LADY, QWENE OF MERCY

Lydgate, however, felt that, just as the host of the Holy Communion was encased in a highly decorated monstrance for public adoration, so too religious matter should be placed in a suitably ornate poetic vehicle. His invocations to Mary in the *Ballade at the Reverence of Our Lady, Qwene of Mercy*, are often cited as prime examples of this suitably ornate diction. After invoking the "aureat licour of Clyo" to enliven his dull wit, Lydgate compares Mary to the stars, precious jewels, various birds, a red rose, and many other things in a riot of exotic images expressed in extravagant terminology. Lines 36 through 39 are a good example:

> O closid gardeyn al void of weedes wicke,
> Cristallyn welle of clennesse cler consigned,
> Fructifying olyve of foilys faire and thicke,
> And redolent cedyr most derworthly ydyned.

These images certainly were not original with Lydgate; they are doubtless echoes of the *Song of Songs*, but Lydgate has presented them in fittingly sonorous language, filled with alliteration.

RELIGIOUS VERSE

Not surprisingly, a great body of Lydgate's verse is explicitly religious, and nowhere is he more representative of his times than when he writes his saints' lives. Christian saints were the heroes of the medieval Catholic Church, and there was a great thirst on all levels of

society for knowledge about them. Very early in the Christian era short narratives about the deaths of martyrs, *passiones*, or about the lives of confessors, *vitae*, began to be composed. These were meant to be read during the liturgy or the Divine Office. In the High Middle Ages, vernacular legends began to be written for the common folk, and, especially with the advent of the friars, these were used for public preaching. The legends, however, were viewed primarily as a literature of edification rather than as objective history or biography. Thus, "successful" structures, incidents, and even historical details were exchanged freely among the various legends. Generally speaking, then, medieval legend can be considered a type of popular formulaic literature.

THE LIVES OF SAINTS EDMUND AND FREMUND

In honor of the visit, in 1433, of Henry VI to Bury St. Edmunds, Abbott William Curteys commissioned Lydgate, who had written a number of *vitae* earlier, to write *The Lives of Saints Edmund and Fremund* for presentation to the king. Lydgate's response was an "epic legend," in which the life of Edmund, the former king of East Anglia (died 870), is retold in a suitably long (3,693 lines) narrative.

The work is divided into three sections. Books 1 and 2 recount the life, death, and burial of Edmund; book 3 treats the life of Fremund, the king's nephew and avenger; and, finally, an appendix records several of Edmund's posthumous miracles. Most of the work is in Chaucerian stanzas.

Lydgate, using the Latin *Vita et Passio cum Miraculis Sancti Edmundi*, Bodlian Ms. 240, as his primary source, incorporates many of the standard characteristics of the *passio*. Thus, Edmund's birth is miraculously foretold by a strange widow when Alkmund, his Saxon father, is on a pilgrimage in Rome. In his youth, Edmund is pious and mature well beyond his years, so much so that his distant relative, Offa, chooses him as his successor to the East Anglian throne. After Offa dies, Edmund governs wisely and moderately, but despite his ability as a warrior, he comes to realize that bloodshed is hateful in the sight of God and repudiates warfare. Therefore, to protect his people from the marauding Danes, he offers his own life in return for their safety. When brought before the violent Hyngwar, leader of the Danes, Edmund refuses apostasy in the standard interrogation. Hyngwar loses self-control, as is typical of "evil judges," at Edmund's aggressive retorts and orders the King's execution. After undergoing a sustained round of tortures with superhuman endurance, Edmund is finally beheaded, but not before he sings out a long panegyric to God in which he asks to die as God's "true knight." The head of the slain king, although hidden, is miraculously protected by a wolf until it is found by Edmund's subjects. Other miracles follow before Fremund is introduced in book 3.

In this legend, Lydgate uses his sources freely, carefully choosing incidents that serve his own purposes. The posthumous miracles, for example, are chosen to illustrate his theme that tyrants and other prideful people are eventually punished by God. His arrangement of those miracles indicates concern for symmetry, balance, and artistic control. In short, Lydgate's contribution to the history of the Edmund legend is that of a masterful rhetorician who fitted the legend into an elegant structure; added rhetorical flourishes such as prologues, prayers, and epilogues; and finished the surface with the appropriate sonorous diction.

FALL OF PRINCES

The literary cousin to the saint is the fallen prince, for one can fashion an *exemplum* from each. If medieval audiences could be edified by the courage of the former, they could be taught detachment and humility from the life of the latter: for example, from the lives of Priam and Saul, Alexander and Caesar, Arthur and King John of France.

The theme of the world's transitoriness was another medieval commonplace, but Giovanni Boccaccio's *De Casibus Illustrium Virorum* (1358) treated the theme in a systematic and comprehensive way for the first time. In this work, all the kings just mentioned, and many more besides, pass before the Italian poet and complain of their downfalls. Boccaccio's work became extremely popular and was translated into French in 1409 by Laurent de Premierfait. In 1431, Duke Humphrey of Gloucester commissioned Lydgate to translate it into English, and this free translation was titled *Fall of Princes*. The task took Lydgate eight years.

Working from the French translation, Lydgate expands Boccaccio's work even more, filling in abbreviated stories, adding missing ones, inserting exhortations, and writing envoys for the end of each chapter. The result is a massive medieval history book (36,365 lines), a mirror for princes, and an encyclopedia of world biography. Lydgate follows his medieval penchant for inclusion rather than concision, and thus the sheer bulk of the work is both a positive attribute—it contributes to an impression of weight and solemnity—and a fault—Boccaccio's fine structure seems completely lost.

Fall of Princes may be called a book of tragedies, for the medieval definition of tragedy was much simpler than Aristotle's: "For tragedie, as poetes spesephie,/ Gynneth with ioie, eendith with adversite:/ From hih estate [Men] caste in low degre." Lydgate follows both Boccaccio and Laurent in deprecating the blind goddess Fortune, a personification blamed as the fickle distributor of both tragedy and good luck. In the prologue to book 1, Lydgate describes her as "transitory of condicioun," "hasty & sodeyne," since "Whan men most truste, than is she most chaungable." One often encounters medieval representations of the "Wheel of Fortune," where one sees the blindfolded goddess spinning a wheel to which various men are attached. Those on the top, the rulers, enjoy the favors of good fortune, whereas those on the bottom, paupers or prisoners, are in misery. Figures on either side, however, the rising courtier or the falling prince, emphasize that the wheel is never static, and that both kingdoms and rulers pass away.

There were several common reactions to these lessons in mutability. First of all, they inspired sorrow over time's passing. Thus the *Ubi sunt?* (Where are they?) theme is found in much of medieval poetry, from the Anglo-Saxon *Wanderer* to the "Ballade des dames du temps jadis" ("Ballad of the Ladies of Bygone Times") of Villon. Poets using this theme complain that everything beautiful, noble, or great in this world eventually passes away. Lydgate repeats this theme often and at length in *Fall of Princes*. In the envoy to book 2, Lydgate ponders the fate of Rome. "Where be thyn Emperours, most sovereign of renown?" he asks. "Where is now Cesar"; where "Tullius?" His answer is not as poetic as Villon's "But where are the snows of bygone years?," for he states directly that "Off alle echon the odious ravyne of time/ Hath be processe the brought to ruyne."

If, on one hand, time brings everything to an end and princes are brought low by Fortune's variability, on the other hand, a good Christian ought to see God's Providence working through Fortune, punishing pride or arrogance. Thus, by pondering tragedy, men of power can learn meekness, detachment, and humility, and place the highest value on spiritual things. "Ley doun thi pride," cries Lydgate; "Cri God merci, thi trespacis repentyng!" For the Romans, of course, it is too late, but it is not too late for Lydgate's contemporaries.

One wonders how many medieval princes read completely through all nine books of Lydgate's *exempla*. Even the Knight from Chaucer's *The Canterbury Tales*, for example, could stand only so many of the similar tragedies told by Chaucer's Monk: "good sire, namoore of this!" he cries, for "litel hevyness/ Is right ynough to muche folke" (Prologue to the "Nun's Priest's Tale"). Even Lydgate himself grew tired of his forced march through the ruins of history, for he complains about his fatigue in the prologue to book 8. Moreover, Lydgate expanded on his sources less and less with each succeeding book.

All this has led scholars to speculate that perhaps the best way to read *Fall of Princes* would be to read only extracts of the best passages. The structure of the work is basically inorganic and encyclopedic, since Lydgate, again being true to the aesthetics of his age, seems to have expanded on his sources to include in his work all "useful knowledge" rather than critically selecting and editing his material to allow an organic structure to emerge. Moreover, Pearsall remarks that probably Lydgate's contemporaries more often read the poem in extracts than as a whole, since parts of the work often appear detached from the rest in surviving manuscripts. Practicality supports this view, for there is much repetition and dull elaboration in the poem that most people would rather avoid; but, on the other hand, more detailed work needs be done on the poem's structure before it can be said that here Lydgate completely lacked structural control.

VERSIFICATION

The versifying in *Fall of Princes*, as in most of Lydgate's work, has traditionally given critics prob-

lems. Although most of his lines can be scanned as rather regular iambic pentameter, a large number cannot, and these have in the past led certain writers to call Lydgate a bungling versifier. Later critics have been fairer to the poet, however, and for good reason. First, medieval scribes were notoriously free in "correcting" their copy, adding or deleting words or changing spelling according to regional pronunciations. Especially with regard to the final *-e*, the sounding of which had probably ceased by the fifteenth century, scribal practices varied widely. Second, for all the current philological sophistication, medievalists are still not sure how Lydgate's contemporaries would have pronounced their native tongue. In short, all scansion of Lydgate's poetry is tentative at best.

The best approach to Lydgate's line seems to be that of scholar Ian Robinson. He claims that Lydgate wrote a "balanced pentameter" line, a line that was meant to work both in half-lines and as a full line of five metrical feet. The English metrical line was in transition at the time, and this means that there were two sometimes conflicting traditions competing in the art not only of Lydgate but also of Chaucer. The first was the rather recently adopted French decasyllabic line, later to evolve into the English iambic pentameter of William Shakespeare. The oldest English tradition of verse, however, revived in the thirteenth and fourteenth centuries, constructed lines based on stress and alliteration rather than on syllable count. Thus the opening lines of *The Vision of William, Concerning Piers the Plowman*, a poem of the fourteenth century alliterative revival, run as follows: In a sómer séson// whan sóft was the sónne/ I shópe me in shróudes// as I a shépe wére." Although one generally finds four stressed syllables per line (the first three of which were usually alliterated), the total number of syllables per line, stressed and unstressed, varied widely. That is why it makes no difference, metrically speaking, whether the final unstressed syllables italicized above were pronounced or not. In either case these lines are good alliterative verse since both read smoothly in rhythmic half-lines.

So too with Lydgate. If his verse is read with a strong medial caesura, letting the stresses, whether two or three per half-line, fall where they are most natural, the lines hardly ever seem awkward. On the contrary, they are generally easy to scan. Some lines, especially the "broken-backed" variety—lines with only four stressed syllables—seem to fit the English side of the tradition a bit more, whereas others, being to the modern sensibility more "regular," favor the French side. Line 4,465 from book 2, for example, "Off slaúhtre, móordre// & outráious róbbyng," even offers a hint of alliteration in the stressed syllables. On the other hand, lines such as "Thĭ bĭldyng gán // ŏff fáls dĭscéncĭoún" can be seen as favoring the French side of the tradition, although it still breaks easily into two smooth half-lines.

OTHER MAJOR WORK

NONFICTION: *The Serpent of Division*, pb. 1559 (wr. 1422?).

BIBLIOGRAPHY

Cooney, Helen, ed. *Nation, Court, and Culture: New Essays on Fifteenth-Century English Poetry*. Portland, Oreg.: Four Courts Press, 2001. This collection of essays on poets of the fifteenth century discusses Lydgate as well as Thomas Hoccleye and John Skeleton.

Cooper, Lisa H., and Andrea Denny-Brown, eds. *Poetry and Material Culture in the Fifteenth Century: Lydgate Matters*. New York: Palgrave Macmillan, 2008. This work reevaluates Lydgate's work in the light of medieval material culture. Describes how poetry spoke to the increased relevance of material goods and possessions to late medieval identity and literary taste.

Ebin, Lois A. *John Lydgate*. Boston: Twayne, 1985. This concise yet thorough book-length study serves as a useful introduction to the Lydgate canon and contains chapters on his courtly poems, moral and didactic poems, and religious poems. Includes a chronology of Lydgate's life and complete notes, including a list of secondary sources, references, and an index.

Mortimer, Nigel. *John Lydgate's "Fall of Princes": Narrative Tragedy in Its Literary and Political Contexts*. New York: Oxford University Press, 2005. An extended discussion of the poem that features accounts of nearly five hundred mythological and historical figures who fell from fame into obscurity.

Nolan, Maura. *John Lydgate and the Making of Public Culture*. New York: Cambridge University Press, 2005. Argues that Lydgate, who wrote for an elite London readership, helped develop English public culture. Provides a new interpretation of Lydgate's relationship to Chaucer.

Pearsall, Derek Albert. *John Lydgate (1371-1449)*. Victoria, B.C.: University of Victoria Press, 1997. A bibliography of works by and about Lydgate with a brief biographical sketch.

Scanlon, Larry, and James Simpson, eds. *John Lydgate: Poetry, Culture, and Lancastrian England*. Notre Dame, Ind.: University of Notre Dame Press, 2006. This collection of essays examines topics such as Lydgate's syntax and his lives of saints as well as specific works, such as *The Temple of Glass*.

Gregory M. Sadlek

M

George MacBeth

Born: Shotts, Scotland; January 19, 1932
Died: Tuam, County Galway, Ireland; February 17, 1992

PRINCIPAL POETRY

The Broken Places, 1963
A Doomsday Book, 1965
The Colour of Blood, 1967, 1969
The Night of Stones, 1968
A War Quartet, 1969
The Burning Cone, 1970
Collected Poems, 1958-1970, 1971
The Orlando Poems, 1971
Shrapnel and a Poet's Year, 1973, 1974
In the Hours Waiting for the Blood to Come, 1975
Buying a Heart, 1978
Poems of Love and Death, 1980
Poems from Oby, 1982
Published Collections, 1982
The Long Darkness, 1983
The Cleaver Gardens, 1986
Anatomy of a Divorce, 1988
Collected Poems, 1958-1982, 1989
Trespassing: Poems from Ireland, 1991
Patient, 1992
Selected Poems, 2002

OTHER LITERARY FORMS

In addition to his numerous volumes of poetry, George MacBeth published poetry pamphlets, chapbooks, and limited-edition books. Many of these, initially published in small editions, became parts of larger books and have thus been incorporated into the mainstream of MacBeth's work. MacBeth also published children's books, novels, plays, and an autobiography, and he edited several volumes of poetry.

The sheer volume of MacBeth's production reveals his almost obsessive dedication to writing and the breadth of his interests. Among his publications other than poetry, the autobiography *My Scotland* (1973) probably holds the greatest interest for the reader of his poetry because of what it reveals about MacBeth's background and development. MacBeth himself described the book as a nonlogical, nonnarrative, massive jigsaw of autobiographical bits, a collection of about two hundred short prose pieces about being Scottish.

ACHIEVEMENTS

A corecipient of Sir Geoffrey Faber Award in 1964, George MacBeth was one of the most prolific poets of twentieth century Britain. Volume alone, however, did not account for his significance as a poet; rather, he earned his stature for the diversity of his writing. He was, in the best sense of the word, an "experimental" poet: absolutely fearless in his willingness to attempt new forms and take on unusual subjects, yet simultaneously fascinated by traditional meter and rhyme, as well as by material that has fueled the imagination of poets for centuries. *Poems of Love and Death* contains poems ranging from the dangerously romantic "The Truth," with its didactic final stanza that includes the lines "Happiness is a state of mind,/ And grief is something frail and small," to the satiric "The Flame of Love, by Laura Stargleam," which mocks the dime-novel story line that it exploits. MacBeth is as likely to write about a missile commander as about evening primroses, and the reader familiar with his writing is not at all surprised to find these disparate topics dealt with in a single book, in this case *Buying a Heart*. In fact, it is the sense of discovery and the vitality of MacBeth's imagination that continues to attract many readers.

BIOGRAPHY

Born in Scotland near Glasgow, George Mann MacBeth lived the greater part of his life in England. This circumstance had a substantial impact on his poetry, leading him to view himself as something of an exile. Although he felt comfortable in England, he did not regard himself as English and remarked on the sensation of detachment, of living and working in a foreign country. The Scotland he left as a child remained in his mind as a lost world, a kind of Eden that could never be regained, and his sense of loss helped make him, in his own evaluation, "a very retrospective, backward-looking poet." Perhaps more significantly, his detachment, or rootlessness, enabled him to embrace a larger part of the world than is available to most writers.

Another significant element of MacBeth's life was his long-term association with the British Broadcasting Corporation, where he worked as a producer of poetry programs. This position bought him into contact with the leading poets in England and around the world and exposed him to everything that was happening in poetry. MacBeth himself acknowledged that his close work with a broad variety of poets over the years influenced his writing, particularly in the areas of technique and structure. Always careful not to become too involved in purely "English" writing, he consciously tried to keep in touch with poetic developments in the world at large, and his accomplishments as a poet can be measured most accurately if they are considered in the context of that endeavor.

By the late 1980's, MacBeth had moved to Ireland, continuing to work there as a freelance broadcaster, a teacher, and a writer, and traveling frequently to give readings of his poetry abroad. His life was tragically cut short when, in 1992, he died of motor neuron disease, in Tuam, County Galway.

Analysis

George MacBeth once remarked that he considered the word "experimental," often used to describe his work, to be a term of praise. Although he acknowledged the possibility of failing in some of his excursions into new forms and new subjects, he obviously felt the risk to be justified. His strongest impulse as a writer was to test the bounds of poetry and, wherever possible, extend them.

This daring push toward the limits of his craft is nowhere better revealed than in the fourth section of his *Collected Poems, 1958-1970*, where MacBeth employs his no-holds-barred approach and enjoys doing it. Indeed, the sense of pleasure that MacBeth manages to communicate, his pure delight in the shape of language on the page, is essential to readers because it helps carry them through poems that at first glance may repel rather than attract.

"LDMN Analysis of Thomas Nashe's 'Song'" and "Two Experiments"

Two such forbidding poems that challenge the analytical mind in satiric fashion are "Two Experiments" and "LDMN Analysis of Thomas Nashe's 'Song.'" The first of these poems, divided into two sections, presents a "Vowel Analysis of 'Babylonian Poem' from the German of Friederike Mayröcker" and a "Numerical Analysis of 'Brazilian Poem' from the German of Friederike Mayröcker." If the ponderous and unlikely subtitles are not enough to warn the reader not to be too serious, the actual text should be sufficiently illuminating. The first section is a listing of vowels, ostensibly from the Mayröcker poem, presented in the following fashion: "U EE-EI A I AE-IIE-EIE UE EOE U EI; E." Thus runs the first line, and the second section begins in the following way: "(. .2 2 6 2 3 5: 2 3 3-6 3 8: 3." Clearly, these representations are meaningless, but they do make a point, not a very positive point, about the analytical approach to poetry: that critical analyses of poetry may make no more sense than these vowel and number analyses. A similar statement is made in "LDMN Analysis of Thomas Nashe's 'Song,'" which offers an arrangement of *L*'s, *D*'s, *M*'s, and *N*'s, presumably as they might be extracted from the Nashe poem.

As might be expected, the response to such experimentation has not been universally positive, and a number of readers have questioned whether such strategies can properly be called poetry. Ironically, this may be the very question that MacBeth wants the reader to ask, the ultimate critic's question: "What is poetry?" MacBeth himself is as sincere as any reader in his search for an answer, for he offers no dogmatic views of his own; he merely tosses out experiments in an effort to determine where the boundaries lie.

"Fin du Globe" and "The Ski Murders"

Other poems that are somewhat less eccentric but nevertheless experimental are "The Ski Murders" and "Fin du Globe." The first is an "encyclopaedia-poem" consisting of twenty-six individual entries, one for each letter of the alphabet. The entries themselves are written in a prose style that might have been taken from a spy novel, and the reader is invited to construct his own story by piecing the vignettes together in whatever fashion he wishes. The second poem is presented as a game containing fifty-two "postcards" and four "*fin du globe*" cards. The players (the readers) are instructed to deal out the cards as in an ordinary deck and to read, in turn, the brief postcard message printed on each. When a *fin du globe* card is turned up, the game is over. Again, the question arises—Is this poetry?—and once again MacBeth is challenging the reader while exploring the limits of his craft and trying to extend his artistic territory. Even the most skeptical readers can find pleasure in these and similar experiments, for they are clever and entertaining, and one can sense the pleasure that MacBeth himself must have experienced in giving free rein to his imagination.

"A POET'S LIFE"

Among MacBeth's most successful comic poems is "A Poet's Life," which first appeared in *In the Hours Waiting for the Blood to Come* and has since developed into a kind of serial poem published in various installments. In its original form, the poem consists of twelve episodes focusing on various aspects of the poet's life. The point of view is third person, to permit MacBeth as much distance as possible from his subject, himself. The result is a poem, which avoids the gloomy seriousness of typical introspection and yet focuses on some serious themes, showing the poet to be as human as anyone else. The first section of the poem is representative of MacBeth's technique; it shows the poet at home, trying to write and jotting down the following lines: "today I got up at eight, felt cold, shaved,/ washed, had breakfast, and dressed." The banality here reflects a larger tedium in the poet's life, for nothing much happens to him, except in his imagination. It is not surprising, then, when his efforts to write lead nowhere and he turns to the television for an episode of the *Avengers*, a purely escapist adventure show.

Viewed almost as a specimen or as a caged animal might be viewed, the poet is an amusing creature, sipping his "peppermint cream" and sucking distractedly on his pencil; and yet he is also pitiable. There is, in fact, something of the fool about the poet, something reminiscent of Charlie Chaplin's little tramp, for although he evokes laughter or a bemused smile there is something fundamentally sad about him. The poignancy comes from the realization that the poet, no matter how hard he tries to blend into the common crowd, must always remain isolated. It is the nature of his craft; writing poetry sets him apart. Consequently, when he goes to the supermarket, dressed in "green wranglers" to make himself inconspicuous, he still stands out among the old women, the babies, and the old men. He is "looking/ at life for his poems, is helping/ his wife, is a normal considerate man," and yet his role as poet inevitably removes him from the other shoppers and from the world at large.

Technically, "A Poet's Life" is rather simple and straightforward, but several significant devices work subtly to make the poem successful. The objective point of view enables MacBeth to combine the comic and the pathetic without becoming maudlin or self-pitying; this slightly detached tone is complemented by MacBeth's freewheeling, modernized version of the *Don Juan* stanza. It is typical of MacBeth to turn to traditional forms for inspiration, to borrow them and make them new.

"HOW TO EAT AN ORANGE"

Not a poet to break the rules without first understanding what the rules are, MacBeth is fascinated by traditional forms as well as by those that are new and experimental. It is a measure of his poetic temperament that he is able to take a traditional form and incorporate it into his general experimentation. The reader often encounters regular rhyme and meter in MacBeth's work and occasionally recognizes something like a sonnet or sestina. Invariably, though, the standard form is modified to conform to MacBeth's urge to experiment. "How to Eat an Orange" is as nearly a sonnet as it can possibly be without actually being one. It has fourteen lines and a Shakespearean rhyme scheme, including the final couplet; but it lacks the iambic pentameter. In fact, it has no regular meter at all, although the iambic does surface from time to time like a theme played in the background. Form, then, is not an end in itself but a means to an end, and MacBeth employs whatever forms he finds useful, including the traditional, in communicating his ideas.

"WHAT METRE IS"

MacBeth's attitude toward form is captured most provocatively in a poem titled "What Metre Is." A tour de force of technique, this poem stands as the poet's manifesto. The controlling idea is that the poem itself will provide examples of various poetic devices while they are being discussed. For example, when alliteration is mentioned, it appears in the context of the following passage: "leaping/ long lean and allusive/ through low lines." The uses of prose are considered in this fashion: "Prose is another possibility. There could be three/ sentences in the stanza. This would be an example of/ that." Other aspects of metrics discussed and illustrated in the poem are syllabics, free verse, word and interval counting, internal rhyming, rhythm, assonance, and finally, typography, "its mos/ t irrit/ ating (perhaps) manif/ estation." Irritating and mechanical it may be, representing the voice of the typewriter and the "abdic/ ation of insp/ iration," but still the poet feels compelled to say "I li/ ke it." He likes it because it is "the logica/ l exp/ ression o/ f itsel/ f." Having gone through his paces, the way a musician might play the scale or some well-known traditional piece just to prove he can, MacBeth turns finally to the experimental, which, despite its flaws, holds some irresistible attraction for him. He can manage traditional metrics, and he illustrates this ability in the poem, but he can also handle the riskier, less traditional devices. This poem, then, embodies on a small scale the range of poetic techniques one is likely to encounter in MacBeth's poetry: the traditional, often with modifications, and the experimental, always with MacBeth's own particular daring.

Childhood, war, and violence

If MacBeth takes chances with the form of his poems, he also takes considerable risks with the content. Many of his poems are violent or sexually explicit, and some readers have found his subject matter objectionable. Perhaps the chief characteristic of the content of his poetry is a fascination with fear and violence, which MacBeth feels can be traced to his childhood. As a boy during World War II, MacBeth lost his father and experienced the bombing of his house. He collected shrapnel in the streets after air raids, spent night after night in the shelters, and grew up surrounded by physical violence and the threat of death. This kind of environment affected him strongly, and MacBeth felt that it led ultimately to a kind of obsession with violence that finds an outlet through his poetry.

The connection between his childhood experience of the war and such poems as "The Sirens," "The War," and "The Passing Ones" is obvious because these poems are explicitly about that experience, about "those bombed houses where/ I echoed in/ The empty rooms." Other poems, such as "Driving West," with its apocalyptic vision of a nuclear war, are less concerned with the actual experiences of World War II than with the nightmare vision it instilled. MacBeth's childhood fear of bombs has been translated into an adult's vision of the end of the world: "There was nothing left,/ Only a world of scrap. Dark metal bruised,/ Flung soup of blood, anchors and driven screws." This is the inheritance of Hiroshima and Nagasaki, a vision of the potential that humanity has to destroy itself and the entire planet.

"The Burning Poem"

The same influences are operating, though less obviously, in "The Burning Poem," which ends with the following passage: "Burning, burning,/ and nothing left to burn:/ only the ashes/ in a little urn." Here the violence has been freed of its war context with only a passing reference to suggest the connection: "rice paper, cartridge-paper,/ it was all the same." The merging of art, as represented by the rice paper, and war, represented by the cartridge paper, suggests the relationship between MacBeth's experiences of the war and his poetry. He is, in effect, "Spilling petrol/ on the bare pages." There is a sense in which many of MacBeth's poems are burning with the effects of remembered violence.

"A Confession"

Inevitably, the violence loses its war context entirely and becomes associated with other things, just as it must have been absorbed into MacBeth's life. In "A Confession," for example, the topic is abortion, and the woman who has chosen to abort her child remembers the procedure as "the hard cold inrush of its killer,/ Saw-teeth, threshing fins, cascading water,/ And the soul spat like a bubble out of its head." The act was not clinical or antiseptic but personal and highly violent. The woman, in the course of her dramatic monologue, reveals an obsessive guilt and an inability to deal with what she has done. She wonders, finally, what her punishment might be "For crucifying someone in my womb." In this case MacBeth is somewhat removed from the poem because he uses the persona of the woman, but in "In the Hours Waiting for the Blood to Come" and "Two Days After," he approaches the topic of a lost or aborted child in a much more personal way, considering the impact of the death on the people involved in the relationship. In "Two Days After," the couple make love, but the act has less to do with love than with guilt and a kind of spent violence.

Often, MacBeth's images seem designed specifically to shock the reader, to jolt him or her out of complacency. It is important, however, to realize that MacBeth employs violent and sexually explicit passages for more than merely sensational purposes. He wants to consider the darker side of human nature; violence and fear are alive in the world, and acknowledging their existence is a first step toward coming to terms with them.

"THE RED HERRING"

It would be a mistake to regard MacBeth as merely a poet of sex and violence, for he has more dimensions than those. MacBeth himself seems bothered by the attention that has been given to the more sensational aspects of his poetry to the exclusion of other elements, and has remarked that he does not find his poetry any more violent than anyone else's. In terms of his total body of work, he is right, but the shocking and explicit poems inevitably call more attention to themselves than those that are more subdued in tone and subject matter, especially the very fine children's poems and MacBeth's engaging forays into the fantastic or surreal.

"The Red Herring" is a good illustration of MacBeth's poetry for children. The elements of the poem are a dried red herring, a bare wall, a ladder, and a man with a hammer, a nail, and a long piece of string. After the man has tied the red herring to the string suspended from the nail in the top of the wall and gone away, the poet addresses the question of why he would bother to make up such a simple story: "I did it just to annoy people./ Serious people. And perhaps also/ to amuse children. Small children." Undoubtedly, a child could take pleasure in this poem, but it is not entirely limited to the child in its appeal. The adult who is able to put off his seriousness for a moment or two will find himself smiling at the poem because of its saucy tone and at himself because he was probably gullible enough to enter the poem with a serious mind, even though the title itself warned him that things were not what they seemed. The playfulness here is characteristic of MacBeth's sense of humor, and, as usual, it is designed to make a serious point as well as to please.

"SCISSOR-MAN"

Related to the children's poems are MacBeth's trips into the fantastic, as reflected in "Scissor-Man." The speaker, a pair of scissors used to cut bacon rind, contemplates his position in life, grousing about being kept under the draining board rather than in the sink unit. Further, he worries about what might be going on between the nutcrackers and the carrot grater and vows that if he should "catch him rubbing/ those tin nipples of hers/ in the breadbin" he will "have his/ washer off." Clearly, this is not meant to be children's poetry, but it is, perhaps, a kind of children's poetry for adults, for it engages the imagination in the same way that nursery rhymes and fairy tales do. In this case, MacBeth's humor seems designed to be an end in itself, an escape into the purely fanciful.

If one were to compile a list of adjectives to describe MacBeth's poetry, it would include at least the following: experimental, traditional, humorous, serious, violent, compassionate. The fact that these adjectives seem to cancel one another out is significant, for MacBeth is possessed of a vital desire to encompass everything. In all his diversity, MacBeth is an original and important contemporary poet, a risk-taker who is continually trying to extend the boundaries of his art.

OTHER MAJOR WORKS

LONG FICTION: *The Samurai*, 1975; *The Transformation*, 1975; *The Survivor*, 1977; *The Seven Witches*, 1978; *The Born Losers*, 1981; *The Katana*, 1981; *A Kind of Treason*, 1982; *Anna's Book*, 1983; *The Lion of Pescara*, 1984; *Dizzy's Woman*, 1986; *Another Love Story*, 1991; *The Testament of Spencer*, 1992.

PLAYS: *The Doomsday Show*, pr. 1964; *The Scene-Machine*, pr., pb. 1971 (music by Anthony Gilbert).

NONFICTION: *My Scotland*, 1973.

CHILDREN'S LITERATURE: *Noah's Journey*, 1966;

Jonah and the Lord, 1969; *The Rectory Mice*, 1982; *The Book of Daniel*, 1986.

EDITED TEXTS: *The Penguin Book of Sick Verse*, 1963; *Penguin Modern Poets VI*, 1964 (with J. Clemo and E. Lucie-Smith); *The Penguin Book of Animal Verse*, 1965; *Poetry, 1900-1965*, 1967; *The Penguin Book of Victorian Verse*, 1968; *The Falling Splendour*, 1970; *Poetry for Today*, 1983; *The Book of Cats*, 1992 (with Martin Booth).

BIBLIOGRAPHY

Booth, Martin. *Travelling Through the Senses: A Study of the Poetry of George MacBeth*. Isle of Skye, Scotland: Aquila, 1983. A brief assessment of Mac-Beth's poetic work.

Dooley, Tim. Review of *Collected Poems, 1958-1982*, by George MacBeth. *The Times Literary Supplement*, January 26, 1990, p. 101. According to Dooley, the poems in the volume under review reveal a healthy development: "Formal scrupulousness replaces formal daring and self-examination replaces self-regard." Dooley praises the "new tenderness" that accompanied MacBeth's increasing attention to form.

Ries, Lawrence R. "George MacBeth." In *Poets of Great Britain and Ireland Since 1960: Part 2, M-Z*, edited by Vincent B. Sherry, Jr. Vol. 40 in *Dictionary of Literary Biography*. Detroit: Gale Research, 1985. A judicious appreciation that calls attention to MacBeth's black humor and dexterity as a "trickster." Some biographical facts are given, but the piece is primarily a survey of the achievements (and disappointments) of MacBeth's poetry through *Poems from Oby*.

Robinson, Peter. "Keep on Keeping On: Peter Robinson Salutes Two Collections by Poets Whose Stock May Have Fallen but Who Never Gave Up." Review of *Selected Poems*, by George MacBeth, and *Residues*, by R. S. Thomas. *The Guardian*, March 8, 2003, p. 25. In this review of two books of poetry, including the MacBeth collection by Anthony Thwaite, Robinson argues that MacBeth's poetry, while uneven, does not deserve to fade from memory.

Rosenthal, Macha Louis. *The New Poets: American and British Poetry Since World War II*. New York: Oxford University Press, 1967. Rosenthal discusses MacBeth in the context of all English language poets in the last half of the twentieth century. MacBeth, a prolific and experimental poet, defined his times as well as being a product of them. Contains a bibliography.

Schmidt, Michael, and Grevel Lindop. *British Poetry Since 1930: A Critical Survey*. Oxford, England: Carcanet Press, 1972. A useful overview that places MacBeth's poetry in context. MacBeth gave shape to the alienation of modern life by being one of the most fecund and experimental of modern poets.

Thwaite, Anthony. *Twentieth-Century English Poetry: An Introduction*. New York: Barnes & Noble, 1978. Discusses MacBeth as a member of the Group, with only a very brief characterization of his poetry itself but providing an overview of the twentieth century British poetry that can serve as a context for a student of MacBeth. Contains a bibliography and an index.

Neal Bowers

HUGH MACDIARMID
Christopher Murray Grieve

Born: Langholm, Scotland; August 11, 1892
Died: Edinburgh, Scotland; September 9, 1978

PRINCIPAL POETRY
A Moment in Eternity, 1922
Annals of the Five Senses, 1923 (as C. M. Grieve; prose sketches)
Sangschaw, 1925 (as Hugh M'Diarmid)
A Drunk Man Looks at the Thistle, 1926
Penny Wheep, 1926
To Circumjack Cencrastus: Or, The Curly Snake, 1930
First Hymn to Lenin, and Other Poems, 1931
Scots Unbound, and Other Poems, 1932
Selected Poems, 1934
Stony Limits, and Other Poems, 1934

Second Hymn to Lenin, and Other Poems, 1935

Selected Poems, 1944

Speaking for Scotland, 1946

A Kist of Whistles, 1947

In Memoriam James Joyce: From a Vision of World Language, 1955

The Battle Continues, 1957

Three Hymns to Lenin, 1957

Collected Poems of Hugh MacDiarmid, 1962

A Lap of Honour, 1967

A Clyack-Sheaf, 1969

More Collected Poems, 1970

The Hugh MacDiarmid Anthology: Poems in Scots and English, 1972

Complete Poems, 1920-1976, 1978 (2 volumes)

Selected Poetry, 1992 (Alan Riach and Michael Grieve, editors)

The Revolutionary Art of the Future: Rediscovered Poems, 2004 (John Manson, Dorian Grieve, and Riach, editors)

OTHER LITERARY FORMS

Hugh MacDiarmid (mak-DUR-mihd) wrote prolifically through most of his life. His more than seventy books include social criticism, political polemics, autobiography, and literary criticism. He edited earlier Scottish poets such as William Dunbar and Robert Burns and several poetry anthologies, and he founded and edited a number of Scottish periodicals.

ACHIEVEMENTS

Only slowly has Hugh MacDiarmid come to be recognized as a major twentieth century poet. He spent most of his life laboring in one way or another for Scotland and won his earliest acclaim there. He was a founder, in 1927, of the Scottish Center of PEN, the international writers' organization, and of the National Party of Scotland the following year, although his always radical political views led him into the Communist Party in the 1930's.

Despite his extreme social and political views, his friends were legion. He once observed that few other people could boast of friendships with William Butler Yeats, T. S. Eliot, and Dylan Thomas, and the circle of his admirers extended worldwide. After many years

of promoting, usually undiplomatically, Scotland and Scottish culture, he was awarded a Civil List pension in 1950, and although his criticism of Scottish education continued unabated, Edinburgh University awarded him an honorary doctor of laws degree in 1957.

Not until the 1960's, however, did MacDiarmid's poetry begin to appear in British and modern poetry anthologies. Despite a general awakening to his greatness since that time, reliable commentary of his work remains largely in the hands of Scottish critics. As an innovator in modern literature, MacDiarmid deserves to be ranked with Eliot, James Joyce, and Samuel Beckett.

BIOGRAPHY

Born Christopher Murray Grieve on August 11, 1892, in Langholm, Scotland, near the English border, Hugh MacDiarmid adopted his pen name in the early 1920's. His father's side of the family worked mostly in tweed mills, while his mother's people were farmers; throughout his life, MacDiarmid championed the working class. His father, who was a rural postman, died while MacDiarmid was still a teenager. Educated at Langholm Academy and Broughton Junior Student Center, Edinburgh, the young man worked thereafter as a journalist and became active in politics. In World War I, he served in the Royal Army Medical Corps in Salonika, Italy, and France.

In 1918, MacDiarmid was married, and he settled after the war in Montrose, Angus, where he continued as a reporter, local politician, and contributor to the Scottish Renaissance and Nationalist movements. Although MacDiarmid adopted his pen name in the early 1920's, he continued to write prose under his given name for years afterward. He lived in England most of the time between the years 1929 and 1932, working at temporary jobs, perfecting his antipathy to the English, and suffering the breakup of his marriage.

After being remarried in 1932, MacDiarmid returned to Scotland, worked briefly in Edinburgh, and from 1933 to 1941 lived in Whalsay in the Shetland Islands, where he developed the geological interest that permeates his poems of this period. He performed factory and merchant tasks during World War II, after which he traveled considerably, including trips to communist nations. As late as 1964, when he was seventy-

Hugh MacDiarmid (©Bettmann/CORBIS)

two, he stood as Communist candidate for Parliament in the district of Kinross and West Perthshire, insisting as always that his Communist and Nationalist commitments in no way conflicted. The publication of *Collected Poems of Hugh MacDiarmid* in the United States in 1962, while omitting many good poems, brought him to the attention of a wider reading public, and in his final years, he was acknowledged as one of Scotland's greatest poets. He died at the age of eighty-six on September 9, 1978.

ANALYSIS

When Hugh MacDiarmid began writing poetry seriously after serving in World War I, the Scots literary tradition had reached one of its lowest points. In the century following the deaths of Robert Burns, Sir Walter Scott, and Lord Byron, Scottish poetry consisted largely of enervated and sentimental effusions that imitated the surface mannerisms of Burns's lyrics. Under the circumstances, it is hardly surprising that MacDiarmid wrote his earliest poems in standard English.

Although his style was reminiscent of English Romanticism, it had from the start more vigor and individuality than the work of most of his contemporaries.

A MOMENT IN ETERNITY

The best of these early poems, *A Moment in Eternity*, establishes MacDiarmid's essentially Romantic disposition, "searching the unsearchable" in quest of God and immortality. Although his style and technique were to change radically, these ambitions remained with him, and "eternity" remained to the end of his career one of the most frequent words in his poetic vocabulary. His rhythms in this early poem are supple, varied, but basically iambic; his diction, pleasant but rather conventional.

SANGSCHAW AND PENNY WHEEP

It was not long, however, before he began to write under his pseudonym in a vocabulary forged from various local Scottish dialects and words from literary Scots dating as far back as the late medieval period of Scottish literary glory, when Robert Henryson, William Dunbar, Gavin Douglas, and others overshadowed the best English poets. He charged this "synthetic Scots" with a surprising vitality in two early books of lyrics, *Sangschaw* and *Penny Wheep*. The poems were about God, eternity, the Scottish countryside, love, and other subjects. Because he broke with the stereotypes of recent Scottish poetry and because he challenged his traditionally literate countrymen with a diction reaching back to a time of Scottish literary ascendancy, MacDiarmid was basing his strategy on an appeal to the best in his readers.

A DRUNK MAN LOOKS AT THE THISTLE

Before the publication of the second of these works, he was already shaping another book. *A Drunk Man Looks at the Thistle*, also issued in 1926, proved a much more ambitious work: a sequence of lyrics and meditative poems making up one long, symbolically unified poem. Although MacDiarmid was to write many long poems, he would never find a structural principle more effective than the one he used here. Although some critics have objected to the titles of the fifty-nine poems as interfering with the unity of the book, anyone reading through the sequence will have no trouble perceiving its integrity. The first title, "Sic Transit Gloria Scotia," signals the poet's concern with the cultural and literary decline of his native land and suggests his intention of arresting that decline personally. *A Drunk Man Looks at the Thistle* has come to be recognized as more than a regional achievement, though MacDiarmid took several risks that probably delayed recognition of the scope of his achievement.

In the first place, the title, while accurate, is an odd one for an ambitious literary work, as it seems to lack seriousness and in fact to cater to the common perception of the Scottish peasantry as whiskey-guzzling ne'er-do-wells. His employment of a Scots vocabulary also posed problems. The vocabulary threatened to repel English readers, who expected poets to clothe respectable verse in literary English. The numerous dialect words required heavy use of a specialized dictionary. Even if willing to wrestle with the words, however, such readers were likely to associate Scots with feeble imitations of Burns. MacDiarmid appeared unconventional and frivolous not only in choosing a drunkard as the poem's speaker but also in choosing the lowly thistle, rather than a more "worthy" flower such as a rose, as his central symbol. Who else had made anything of such a homely weed since the rhetorical question of Matthew 7:16: "Do men gather grapes of thorns, or figs of thistles?"

Nevertheless, MacDiarmid had reasons to hope for a harvest. His format permitted him a series of lyrical, comical, and satirical reflections in a variety of meters and stanzas, both rhymed and unrhymed, with the concomitant advantage of showing off his technical versatility. He could also expect that his more extravagant poetic flights, being merely the dreams of a drunken man, would not reflect on him. Apparent digressions were no problem, either, for everyone expects a drunken man to meander. Therefore, while his character indulged in a leisurely display of reactions to all that ailed him and Scotland, the poet could carefully guide his inebriated speaker along a purposeful path.

The drunkard begins by complaining of the difficulty of keeping up with his drinking partners, especially since the Scotch does not compare with the old-time variety, thereby establishing that everything Scottish now seems to be "destitute o'speerit," including the appalling poetry now produced by supposed devotees of Burns. An immediate dilemma presents itself: How can one be a good Scot yet shake off the Scottish lethargy and mediocrity? Interestingly, MacDiarmid's method involves the occasional incorporation of translations and adaptations from French, Belgian, German, and Russian poets, and two original lyrics addressed to Fyodor Dostoevski. MacDiarmid obviously considered the great Russian novelist a kindred spirit in the struggle to repossess imaginatively a stubbornly recalcitrant homeland. To be a good Scot meant, among other things, to accept competent assistance wherever available.

In a poem called "Poet's Pub," based on a poem by Aleksandr Blok, the drunkard resists the idea of going home to his wife, Jean, who is sure to nag him. Instead, he hopes to discover the truth said to be in wine, especially those truths ordinarily dark to him and to his cronies. He catches sight of a "silken leddy" in the pub, but she soon fades from sight, and eventually he stumbles outside to begin his homeward trek. The fourth poem of the sequence introduces the thistle and the image with which MacDiarmid customarily pairs it, the moonlight: "The munelicht's like a lookin'-glass,/ The thistle's like mysel," he observes, one of the resemblances being that he needs a shave.

In the poems that follow, the symbolic values of thistle and moonlight proliferate. A poem addressed to "The Unknown Goddess"—again adapted from Blok—presumably refers to the mysterious lady of the pub, who may represent his muse but is certainly the opposite of Jean. The drunkard's attention alternates between depressing reality ("Our Educational System," "The Barren Fig," "Tussle with the Philistines") and inspired visions ("Man and the Infinite," "Outward Bound," "The Spur of Love"). The drunken man is not sure of much: "And yet I feel this muckle thistle's staun'in'/ Atween me and the mune as pairt o' a Plan." He regards himself as his nation's "soul" and thus free to appropriate the humble thistle: In one of his flights he compares his homeward course to the wanderings of Ulysses; in another he sees himself "ootward boond" toward eternity. The thistle may serve to unite humans and the infinite, or it may simply take off on its own and leave humans nothing but the hole in which it was once rooted. Periodically his thoughts return to Jean, who "ud no' be long/ In finding whence this thistle sprang," for it is in her absence that the plant has grown for him.

The man's thoughts oscillate between Scotland—materialistic, Philistine, ill-educated, yet worth redemption—and himself as representative of the more general human condition—earthbound and mortal yet aspiring to eternity. The thistle has, despite its general ugliness, the capacity to flower, to put out at its tip a "rose" that permits MacDiarmid the traditional associations of that flower in a different context. In "The Form and Purpose of the Thistle," the speaker reflects on the "craft" that produced the odd, prickly stalk capable of breaking into flowers "like sudden lauchter," a craft of puzzling contrarieties. In "The Thistle's Characteristics," the poet ranges over humanity's illusions and presumptions. "For wha o's ha'e the thistle's poo'er/ To see we're worthless and believe 't?" Later he employs the Norse myth of Yggdrasill, the ash tree that binds together Earth, Heaven, and Hell; in this case, however, humanity is a "twig" on a giant thistle that, far from uniting creation, "braks his warlds abreid and rives/ His heavens to tatters on its horns." The Yggdrasill poem insists on humanity's suffering and ends by seeing humans as so many Christs, carrying their crosses "frae the seed," although as the drunkard slyly puts it, most feel it far less than he "thro' bein' mair wudden frae the stert!" Such satiric thrusts at his countrymen occur frequently in the work as a whole. However painful the life, the soul will soar in its "divine inebriety." Intoxication, then, is also a metaphor in this poem, standing for the poetic imagination that can rise above, and gain solace by reflecting on, humankind's common "Calvary."

The drunken man contemplates the oppressive English rule over an exhausted and often foolish Scotland, but even more often, his thoughts wind between Heaven and Earth, between the aspirations of the rose and the limitations of the rooted stalk. He longs for the mysterious lady, then is gripped by the recollection of practical Jean at home. Near the end of the work, he sees himself, God, the Devil, and Scotland all on a great cosmic wheel that sums up Scotland's and man's slow journeys through history. Pondering Scottish resistance to change and new ideas, he wonders if he must "assume/ The burden o' his people's doom" by dying heroically for his recalcitrant fellows. He falters over the decision, not exactly rejecting heroism but choosing to return to Jean's arms. The last lyric of the poem pays eloquent tribute to what he has left of his vision: silence. The conclusion is a joke, for he imagines what Jean will say to that: "And weel ye micht,/ . . . efter sic a nicht!"

The final lines of the poem are consistent with the whole work: Despite his insistence on the dignity of human imagination, the drunken man is always aware of the indignity of human circumstances and his inability to grasp the meaning of life. Only a drunk—that is, only a person intoxicated by life generally and the life of the mind particularly—would bother with such a spiritual quest.

To Circumjack Cencrastus

MacDiarmid's next book of poetry, *To Circumjack Cencrastus*, is more of a miscellany, but one stanza of the poem aptly titled "MacDiarmid's Curses" holds a particular irony:

> Speakin o' Scotland in English words
> As it were Beethoven chirpt by birds;
> Or as if a Board school teacher
> Tried to teach Rimbaud and Nietzsche.

Although these lines do not precisely deny the possibility of a shift to "English words," they scarcely foretell the fact that within a few years MacDiarmid would virtually cease to write in his Scottish amalgam, even when "speakin' o' Scotland." By the middle 1930's, he would be creating a very different sort of poetry using standard English.

Hymns to Lenin

In the meantime, MacDiarmid continued to employ Scots for his first two "hymns to Lenin." Many intellectuals of the time shared his hope, but few his enduring faith, in the efficacy of communism. It remains difficult to read objectively the "First Hymn to Lenin," in which the Soviet leader, Vladimir Ilich Lenin, is hailed as a successor to Christ, or to appreciate it as poetry. MacDiarmid seems to have traded metaphysical doubts for political assurance, and the exchange does not enhance his poetry. He was always extreme in his enthusiasms, but from this point on, his polemical voice invaded his poetry more frequently. Within *First Hymn to Lenin, and Other Poems*, however, is found "At My Father's Grave," with its eight lines of flexible blank verse meditating hauntingly on his father, as if from "across a valley."

STONY LIMITS, AND OTHER POEMS

With *Stony Limits, and Other Poems*, MacDiarmid moved into a new phase of his poetic career. He still included poems in Scots, notably a group called Shetland Lyrics, but he was now working in a literary English that differed markedly from that of his very early poetry. The English poems were at this point more discursive, somewhat less concrete, and considerably more formal. The title poem, in nine ten-line stanzas, pays tribute to Charles Doughty, a poet, geologist, and travel writer who delighted in the lonely occupation of studying the soil and rock formations of remote regions, his most famous book being about the Arabian desert. Gregarious himself, MacDiarmid could respond enthusiastically to Doughty's serenity, his indifference to the crowd, and his capacity for appreciating realms of silence. When this book appeared, MacDiarmid had retreated to the Shetland Islands, where, without ceasing his political involvements, he had begun to study the geology of this northern outpost. He created a new difficulty for his reader, for "Stony Limits" is peppered with terms such as "xenoliths," "orthopinacoid," "striae," and "microline." The geological terminology signals his camaraderie with Doughty and also a growing love of precision quite distinct from the passion for suggestiveness that created the thistle and moonlight images in *A Drunk Man Looks at the Thistle*. This elegy is quiet, almost reverent, but without the defiant tone of his hymns to Lenin.

"ON A RAISED BEACH"

He carries his scientific enthusiasm further in a longer poem in the same collection, "On a Raised Beach." The poem begins "All is lithogenesis—or lochia," a line hardly calculated to appeal immediately to the laity, but since the first term signifies rock formation and the second the discharge from the womb after childbirth, the line immediately juxtaposes the contrasting elements of the poem, stones and human life. Actually, the first twenty-four of the poem's more than four hundred lines teem with technical geological terms, most of which cannot be found in an ordinary desk dictionary. Anyone who braves this formidable initial barrier, however, discovers an arresting meditation on the human situation vis-à-vis that of the stones, which "are one with the stars."

MacDiarmid points out that specific terms can be given to scientific phenomena, but humankind finds more difficulty in expressing its convictions and preferences. The permanence of stone emphasizes the transience and impatience of humankind. Early in the poem, he compares humans unfavorably to the one other creature stirring on the beach, a bird whose "inward gates" are, unlike those of humans, "always open." MacDiarmid argues that the gates of stones stand open even longer. The poet's admiration for these enduring veterans of a world older than humanity can easily imagine resembles Henry David Thoreau's for living nature, and a number of the lines have a Thoreauvian ring to them—for example, "Let men find the faith that builds mountains/ Before they seek the faith that moves them." As in Thoreau, nature teaches the perceptive person humility. Life is redundant, says MacDiarmid, but not stones. Human culture pales before the bleak but beautiful sentinels of time on a scale beyond humankind's ordinary comprehension.

As the stately free verse moves on, MacDiarmid alludes to various stones with human associations: the missile that David hurled at Goliath, pebbles with which Demosthenes filled his mouth, the rock that guarded Christ's tomb. Human culture is like Goliath, doomed to fall, and no orator can hope to rival the lithic earth in eloquence. Stones not only draw humans back to their beginnings but also lead them on to their end. No stone can be rolled aside like the "Christophanic" one to release death, but death is not on that account to be feared, because dying is less difficult than living a worthwhile life.

Despite the weightiness of "On a Raised Beach," despite its rather sepulchral tone, the poem does not oppress but conveys a breath of caution, a salutary deflation of human arrogance. The poem might have benefited from a beach more specifically evoked, like Matthew Arnold's Dover Beach, but it nevertheless communicates effectively the "capacity for solitude" by which MacDiarmid strives to imitate the great stones.

LUCKY POET

The virtual disappearance of Scots lyrics after *Stony Limits, and Other Poems* seems to be not a repudiation of the poet's earlier theory but an acknowledgment that after several hundred poems in that medium, he needed to test the linguistic possibilities of English. Like Burns before him, MacDiarmid could sing best in Scots and create more comedy and humor than he ever seemed to have tried in literary English. Advocates of his poetry (many of whom are Scottish) have tended to prefer the Scots poems, but the best of his English poems have their own excellence, and it is of a sort appropriate to an older man. They are sober, thought-provoking, and reflective of the intensity of a poet deeply committed to his art and alert to the world about him. Like Yeats and Eliot, he changed his style in middle age to produce a kind of verse in sharp contrast to that which gained for him his initial audience.

Not until the publication of his autobiography, *Lucky Poet*, in 1943 did MacDiarmid formulate in detail his prescription for the poetry he had been attempting to practice for a decade. This book contains several previously unpublished poems, one of which, "The Kind of Poetry I Want," sets forth vigorously the theory that he had been developing. The diction and rhythms of this long poem are prosaic, and its topical allusions date it severely, but it rings with conviction. Probably no poem ever written realizes all its specifications. According to MacDiarmid, the poet must be a polymath who can base his or her work on "difficult knowledge" in many fields, including the sciences, and must be technically accomplished and equipped with "ecstasy." Poetry must reflect closeness to and knowledge of nature. The poet must know the countryside and the technological order and must deploy linguistic and historical learning. Poetry must be factual and still illuminate values, argues MacDiarmid; it must integrate the knowledge of its various sources and—as a crowning touch—must reflect a poet uninterested in personal success. At one point, MacDiarmid concedes that such poetry must await social reorganization, presumably along communistic lines.

MacDiarmid was better equipped than most to pursue his poetic ideal. By mid-career, his poetry bristled with learned allusions to Russian, Hebrew, Turkish, Chinese, Greek, and Gaelic poetry, to name a few. Not all the poems in *Lucky Poet* are learned, but they are all provoking. Two of them excoriate the cities of Edinburgh and Glasgow for their bourgeois sins, and the good humor of his earlier social criticism has vanished.

Clearly, he is less willing than ever to cater to merely conventional taste and expectations.

In Memoriam James Joyce

By the time of *In Memoriam James Joyce*, MacDiarmid was brewing a poetry in some ways like Joyce's prose, packed with recondite allusions, quotations in many languages, puns, technical vocabulary, and an often tortuous syntax. The tone was more likely to be oracular and insistent. How many of his poetic tenets he was then fulfilling is disputable, but he clearly was not integrating knowledge, and perhaps he was inadvertently demonstrating the impossibility of such integration in the second half of the twentieth century, with its myriad specialists. Reminiscent of his previous work is the poem "We Must Look at the Harebell." MacDiarmid is at his best when "looking" rather than persuading, and this poem has fresh observations not only of the harebell but also of the pinguicula or butterwort (a small herb), the asphodel, the parsley fern, and other flora to be found by a person willing to climb rocks and descend into bogs. The plants he observes are interesting, but even more interesting is his determination to reveal the prospects of nature.

A Lap of Honour

MacDiarmid appears to have written relatively little new poetry after the publication of *In Memoriam James Joyce*, but because *Collected Poems of Hugh MacDiarmid* omitted a number of his earlier poems, the volume *A Lap of Honour*, which appeared five years later, when the poet turned seventy-five, was an important addition. It contained some poems that had appeared only in periodicals and others from books difficult to obtain in 1967. One of the most important inclusions was "On a Raised Beach," only a short extract of which had appeared in the 1962 collection. There were several, by then welcome, Scots poems from an earlier day. Thus, this volume made accessible to many readers for the first time a sampling of MacDiarmid's work over the decades of his greatest vitality, the 1920's, 1930's, and 1940's.

Later poetry

The innovations of his later poetry have an importance beyond the success of individual poems. In an age when many poets knew little about science and even affected to despise it, MacDiarmid was trying to widen the range of the poet's expertise. Although the scientific knowledge of even an amateur such as MacDiarmid is bound to seem inadequate to a well-trained scientist, he was often able to enhance his subjects with metaphors drawn from science. Thus, in "Stony Limits," he compared his projected poem in praise of Doughty to the process of crystallization in rocks and to the growth of lunar formations, and in "Crystals Like Blood," he could liken the memory to the extraction of mercury from cinnabar. Such metaphors doubtless have very little effect on a scientifically illiterate reader, but his fear was of a poetry that failed by appealing only to the badly educated. His aspiration to the precision of the exact sciences was probably unrealistic, but he was doing his part to integrate the "two cultures" at a time when many intellectuals were dividing into mutually antagonistic and uncomprehending camps. His efforts to apply the discoveries of modern linguistics to poetry were unsuccessful, but there is no telling what they may have suggested to younger poets. He carried allusion and quotation beyond what many readers would consider tolerable limits, but he did not shrink from challenging those who were able and willing to follow him. Like Eliot, MacDiarmid was trying to use tradition creatively, and like Ezra Pound, he often moved outside the Western tradition favored by Eliot. Few poets have worked so diligently for so long to widen the possibilities of poetry.

By a curious irony, MacDiarmid's poems in English, because of their high density of technical words and obscure quotations and allusions, present greater difficulties than his earlier ones in Scots. Lacking the humor and lyricism of the early poems, his English poems often repay the reader's careful attention with their insight into the natural world and their challenge to conventional ways of looking at the world and of expressing the results of such observations. Nevertheless, his early mission to rescue Scottish poetry by creating a composite dialect out of folk and literary sources and to speak to a materialistic generation of the possibilities of a richer culture and authentic spiritual life was doubtless his greatest accomplishment. Even without consulting the glossary of *Collected Poems of Hugh MacDiarmid*, the English-speaking reader can take pleasure in the energy and lyrical buoyancy of *A Drunk Man Looks at the Thistle*, and with very little trouble, the full meaning is available to all. It has been suggested that this poem is the modern equivalent of the medieval dream vision. Undoubtedly, only a poet steeped in literary tradition could have written it. Taking advantage of a form that allows a comprehensive and uninhibited vision, MacDiarmid fashions a poem that is highly original because it reflects a modern, skeptical sensibility, and is readily understandable because it is made from the materials of everyday life. While aiming at universality in his later poetry, he achieved it most fully in his odyssey of a drunken cottager beneath the Scottish "mune."

OTHER MAJOR WORKS

NONFICTION: *Contemporary Scottish Studies*, 1926; *Albyn: Or, Scotland and the Future*, 1927; *The Lucky Bag*, 1927; *The Present Condition of Scottish Music*, 1927; *At the Sign of the Thistle: A Collection of Essays*, 1934; *Scottish Scene: Or, The Intelligent Man's Guide to Albyn*, 1934 (with Lewis Grassic Gibbon); *Scottish Eccentrics*, 1936; *The Islands of Scotland*, 1939; *Lucky Poet*, 1943 (autobiography); *Cunningham Graham: A Centenary Study*, 1952; *Burns Today and Tomorrow*, 1959; *David Hume: Scotland's Greatest Son*, 1961; *The Kind of Poetry I Want*, 1961; *The Company I've Kept*, 1966; *Scotland, 1968: Selected Essays of Hugh MacDiarmid*, 1969 (Duncan Glen, editor); *The Letters of Hugh MacDiarmid*, 1984 (Alan Bold, editor); *New Selected Letters*, 2002 (Dorian Grieve et al., editors).

EDITED TEXTS: *Northern Numbers, Being Representative Selections from Certain Living Scottish Poets*, 1920-1922 (3 volumes); *Robert Burns, 1759-1796*, 1926; *The Golden Treasury of Scottish Poetry*, 1940; *Robert Burns: Poems*, 1949; *Selected Poems of William Dunbar*, 1955; *Robert Burns: Love Songs*, 1962; *Henryson*, 1973.

MISCELLANEOUS: *Annals of the Five Senses*, 1923.

BIBLIOGRAPHY

Baglow, John. *Hugh MacDiarmid: The Poetry of Self*. Montreal: McGill-Queen's University Press, 1987. Somewhat academic in style but still effective as an effort to present MacDiarmid's writing beyond the context of his nationalist ambitions and his connections with ultra-leftist politics. Includes an appendix discussing critical responses to MacDiarmid and an extensive list of references.

Bold, Alan. *Hugh MacDiarmid, Christopher Murray Grieve: A Critical Biography*. London: John Murray, 1988. A solid discussion of the writer's life and work by a sympathetic but discerning biographer, with a thorough bibliography and a glossary of Scots words. Photographs and drawings nicely complement the text.

Glen, Duncan, ed. *Hugh MacDiarmid: Or, Out of Langholm and into the World*. Edinburgh: Akros, 1992. A short biographical study of MacDiarmid with bibliographic references.

Herbert, W. N. *To Circumjack MacDiarmid: The Poetry and Prose of Hugh MacDiarmid*. Oxford, England: Clarendon Press, 1992. A thorough, lucid, and knowledgeable consideration of MacDiarmid's poetry and its connections to other writers, social issues, and aesthetic strategies.

Lyall, Scott. *Hugh Macdiarmid's Poetry and Politics of Place: Imagining a Scottish Republic*. Edinburgh: Edinburgh University Press, 2006. This biography and literary criticism of MacDiarmid looks at his poetry and examines how the poet's views of Scotland pervade it.

O'Connor, Laura. *Haunted English: The Celtic Fringe, the British Empire, and De-Anglicization*. Baltimore: The Johns Hopkins University Press, 2006. This work on how Anglo-Celtic modernists William Butler Yeats, Marianne Moore, and Hugh MacDiarmid de-Anglicize their literary vernaculars contains an entire chapter on MacDiarmid's poetry, as well as many references to his work.

Oxenhorn, Harvey. *Elemental Things: The Poetry of Hugh MacDiarmid*. Edinburgh: Edinburgh University Press, 1984. An exploration of MacDiarmid's poetry from the perspective of political and cultural matters in Scotland. Somewhat uneven in terms of poetic analysis and a little too respectful of MacDiarmid's claims that there is a coherent philosophical position informing all the poetry.

Riach, Alan. *Hugh MacDiarmid's Epic Poetry*. Edinburgh: Edinburgh University Press, 1991. A well-known scholar of Scottish culture, and MacDiarmid

in particular, offers interpretations of the poetry. Bibliographical references, index.

Scott, P. H., and A. C. Davis. *The Age of MacDiarmid: Essays on Hugh MacDiarmid and His Influence on Contemporary Scotland*. Edinburgh: Mainstream, 1980. An important collection of essays from eminent scholars of MacDiarmid. The first group of essays is largely autobiographical in nature; the second group addresses themes such as MacDiarmid's nationalism, politics, and the language problem in his work.

Robert P. Ellis

Louis MacNeice

Born: Belfast, Ireland (now in Northern Ireland); September 12, 1907
Died: London, England; September 3, 1963
Also known as: Louis Malone

PRINCIPAL POETRY

Blind Fireworks, 1929
Poems, 1935
Poems, 1937
The Earth Compels, 1938
Autumn Journal, 1939
The Last Ditch, 1940
Poems, 1925-1940, 1940
Selected Poems, 1940
Plant and Phantom, 1941
Springboard: Poems, 1941-1944, 1944
Holes in the Sky: Poems, 1944-1947, 1948
Collected Poems, 1925-1948, 1949
Ten Burnt Offerings, 1952
Autumn Sequel: A Rhetorical Poem in XXVI Cantos, 1954
The Other Wing, 1954
Visitations, 1957
Eighty-five Poems, 1959
Solstices, 1961
The Burning Perch, 1963
The Collected Poems of Louis MacNeice, 1966 (E. R. Dodds, editor)

OTHER LITERARY FORMS

Although he was a poet first and foremost, Louis MacNeice (mak-NEES) published a number of important works in other genres. His only novel, *Roundabout Way* (1932), not very successful, was published under the pseudonym Louis Malone. MacNeice's only other venture into fiction was a children's book, *The Penny That Rolled Away* (1954), published in England as *The Sixpence That Rolled Away*.

An area in which he was no more prolific, but much more successful, was translation. The combination of his education in classics with his gifts as a poet led him to do a successful translation of Aeschylus's *Agamemnon* in 1936. E. R. Dodds, an eminent classics professor at Oxford and literary executor of MacNeice's estate, calls the translation "splendid" (*Time Was Away*, 1974, Terence Brown and Alec Reid, editors). W. B. Stanford agrees that in spite of the almost insurmountable difficulties of Aeschylus's text, MacNeice succeeded in producing an eminently actable version, genuinely poetic, and generally faithful to the original. MacNeice's translation of Johann Wolfgang von Goethe's *Faust: Eine Tragödie* (pb. 1808, 1833; *The Tragedy of Faust*, 1823, 1838) for radio presented very different problems—in particular, his not knowing German. The radio medium itself also produced problems in terms of what the audience could follow. MacNeice collaborated with E. L. Stahl on the project, and on the whole it was successful. According to Stahl, MacNeice succeeded in rendering the work's unusual combination of the dramatic with the lyric, producing excellent versions of the various lyrical passages.

MacNeice wrote several plays for the theater and nearly one hundred radio scripts for the BBC. Except for *The Agamemnon of Aeschylus*, his theatrical works are not notable, although *Station Bell* was performed by the Birmingham University Dramatic Society in 1937, and a similar play, *Out of the Picture*, was performed in 1937 by the Group Theatre in London, which had also done *Agamemnon*. The verse play was accounted a failure, while having its moments of very good poetry and wit. It was similar to the plays that W. H. Auden and Christopher Isherwood were producing for the Group Theatre in the 1930's: cartoonish parodies in the service of leftist political views. Mac-

Neice's play does, however, show a serious concern with love. Much later, in 1958, MacNeice wrote *One for the Grave* (pr. 1966), patterned on the medieval morality play. It exemplifies his growing interest in allegory, described in *Varieties of Parable* (1965). During World War II, MacNeice wrote documentary dramas for radio, contributing much that was original, though not of lasting literary value, to the genre. His later radio dramas, such as *Out of the Picture*, and his late poems tend toward allegory and quest motifs. *The Dark Tower* (published in *The Dark Tower, and Other Radio Scripts by Louis MacNeice*, 1947) is the most successful of these dramas in its equilibrium between realism and allegory.

MacNeice also wrote an unfinished prose autobiography, published posthumously as *The Strings Are False* (1965); several works of mixed poetry and prose, most notably *Letters from Iceland* (1937) with Auden; and several volumes of literary criticism. These works illuminate MacNeice's poetry, offering insight into the self-conscious relationship of one poet to his predecessors and his craft. *Modern Poetry: A Personal Essay* (1938) is significant as a manifesto of one of the new poets of the 1930's, who believed that poetry should speak directly to social and political issues. *The Poetry of W. B. Yeats* (1941), written before the major scholarly commentaries on William Butler Yeats, offers lucid insights into particular poems, as well as illuminating MacNeice's own goals as a poet. *Varieties of Parable*, a posthumous printing of MacNeice's Clark Lectures of 1963, elucidates his concern with writing poetry that operates on two levels simultaneously, the realistic and the symbolic, moral, or allegorical.

ACHIEVEMENTS

Louis MacNeice is most notable as an exemplar of Socrates' maxim that the unexamined life is not worth living. The major question surrounding his reputation is whether he ranks as a minor or a major poet, whether his poems show a progression of thought and technique or an essential similarity over the years. No one would deny that his craft, his mastery of prosody and verse forms, is of the highest order. Most critics agree that in his last three volumes of poems MacNeice took a new point of departure. Auden asserts in his memorial address for MacNeice (*Time Was Away*) that posterity will endorse his opinion that the later poems do advance, showing ever greater craftsmanship and intensity of feeling. Auden claims that of all his contemporaries, MacNeice was least guilty of "clever forgeries," or dishonest poems. This honesty, combined with an ingrained temperamental skepticism, is at the root of both his major contributions to poetry and what some people see as his flaws. MacNeice is a philosophical poet, Auden says, without a specific body of beliefs, except for a fundamental sense of *humanitas* as a goal and standard of behavior. He is a harsh critic of general systems because he is always faithful to the complexity of reality.

MacNeice's achievements as a poet are paradoxical: He combines an appeal to large audiences with highly learned allusions, and he focuses on everyday events and political issues while also exploring ultimate metaphysical questions. Most interesting is his transition from the 1930's view that the poet is chiefly a communicator, almost a journalist, to the belief that poetry should operate on two levels, the real and the allegorical. It is these contradictory qualities, along with the literary-historical value of recording a thoughtful person's ethical responses to the trials of modern life, that will ensure MacNeice's poetry a lasting reputation.

Biography

Louis MacNeice was born Frederick Louis MacNeice on September 12, 1907, in Belfast, the son of a well-respected Church of Ireland rector. Because his early childhood experiences inform the imagery and ideas of almost all his work, the details of MacNeice's early life are important. His father, John Frederick MacNeice, and his mother, Elizabeth Margaret, were both natives of Connemara in the west of Ireland, a bastion of wild tales and imagination. Both parents communicated to their children their strong attachment to the Ireland of their youth as opposed to the stern, dour, Puritanical atmosphere of Ulster. MacNeice's father was extraordinary among Protestant Irishmen in his outspoken support for Home Rule and a united Irish republic. Thus the young poet started life with a feeling of displacement and a nostalgia for a culture and landscape he had never seen. Life in the rectory was, of course, pervaded by religion and a sense of duty and social responsibility. MacNeice had a sister, Elizabeth, five years his elder, and a brother, William, in between, who had Down syndrome and therefore did not figure heavily in the other children's play. The children were fairly isolated and developed many imaginative games. Louis showed a tendency toward gothic preoccupations in his fear of partially hidden statues in the church and in the graveyard that adjoined his garden. Of special significance is his mother's removal to a nursing home and subsequent death when Louis was seven. She had provided comfort and gaiety in the otherwise secluded and stern life of the Rectory. Louis, the youngest, had been particularly close to her, and his poetry reflects the rupture in his world occasioned by her loss. Without their mother and intimidated by the misery of their father, the MacNeice children became particularly subject to the influences of servants. On one hand, the cook, Annie, was a warm Catholic peasant who spoke of fairies and leprechauns. On the other hand, Miss MacCready, who was hired to take care of the children when their mother became ill, was the antithesis of both Mrs. MacNeice and Annie, a puritanical Calvinist, extremely dour and severe, lecturing constantly about hell and damnation.

In 1917, MacNeice's father remarried. Though she was very kind and devoted, the new Mrs. MacNeice had a Victorian, puritanical outlook on life that led to further restrictions on the children's behavior. Soon after the marriage, MacNeice was sent to Marlborough College, an English public school, further confusing his cultural identity. From this point on, England became his adopted home, but the English always regarded him as Irish. The Irish, of course, considered him an Anglo-Irishman, while he himself always felt his roots to be in the west of Ireland. Both at Marlborough and later at Merton College, Oxford, MacNeice was in his milieu. At Marlborough he was a friend of Anthony Blunt and John Betjeman, among others. He flourished in the atmosphere of aestheticism and learning. At Oxford he encountered Stephen Spender and the other poets with whom he came to be associated in the 1930's. MacNeice studied the classics and philosophy at Oxford, and these interests are second only to the autobiographical in their influence on his poetry. He graduated from Oxford with a double first in Honour Moderations and "Greats."

Having rebelled against his upbringing by drinking heavily and rejecting his faith at Oxford, MacNeice in a sense completed the break by marrying a Jewish girl, Mariette Ezra. Together they moved to Birmingham, where he was appointed lecturer in classics at the University. In Birmingham, MacNeice encountered the working class and taught their aspiring children at the University. He had always been protected from the lower classes of Belfast and in English schools had lived among the upper classes. The new contact with working people led to a healthy respect for the ordinary man and a broadening of MacNeice's social awareness. At the same time, he was becoming recognized as a member of the "poets of the thirties," with Auden, Isherwood, Spender, and Cecil Day Lewis, whose sense of social responsibility led them to espouse Marxism. MacNeice never became a communist, but he did write about social issues and questioned the comfortable assumptions of traditional English liberalism. While at Birmingham, MacNeice became friendly with E. R. Dodds, who was later to become his literary executor. In 1934, he and his wife had a son, Dan, and in 1936, his wife abruptly left her son and husband to live with an American graduate student at Oxford, Charles Katzman. This abandonment, parallel to the death of his mother, haunted MacNeice for many years and is reflected in his poetry. In the later 1930's, MacNeice traveled twice to Spain, reporting on the Spanish Civil War, and twice to Iceland, the second time with Auden. In 1936, he became lecturer in Greek at Bedford College for women at the University of London. In 1939 and 1940, he lectured at colleges in the United States, returning to what he felt to be his civic responsibility to England following the outbreak of World War II.

From 1941, MacNeice worked for the British Broadcasting Corporation as a scriptwriter and producer, except for the year and a half in 1950-1951 that he served as director of the British Institute in Athens, Greece. In 1942, he married a singer, Hedli Anderson; they had a daughter, Corinna, the following year. In the 1940's and 1950's, MacNeice traveled extensively, to India, Greece, Wales, the United States, Africa, Asia, France, and Ireland. His premature death in 1963 was

Louis MacNeice (Hulton Archive/Getty Images)

the sort of paradoxical experience he might have used in a poem on the irony of life. He was going far beyond the call of duty for the BBC by descending a chilly manhole to check the sound transmission for a feature he was producing. He suffered from exposure, contracted pneumonia, and died. Such a death appears to represent the antithesis of the poetic, yet for MacNeice, poetry spoke about the ordinary as well as the metaphysical and it was intended to speak to the ordinary man. His death resulted from the performance of his ordinary human responsibility, his job.

ANALYSIS

Louis MacNeice was an extremely self-conscious poet. He wrote several books of literary criticism, gave lectures on the subject, and often reflected on the role of the poet in his poems. In an early essay, written in 1936, he reveals his allegiance to the group of poets represented by W. H. Auden, who believed their chief responsibility to be social rather than purely artistic. MacNeice divided art into two types: parable and escape. William Butler Yeats and T. S. Eliot, while unquestionably great, represent the latter, the less valid route. MacNeice always retained his belief in "parable-art," that is, poems that appear naturalistic while also suggesting latent moral or metaphysical content—although he came to realize in later years that journalistic or overly realistic art has its defects while "escape-art" often addresses fundamental problems. MacNeice's lasting conception of the poet's task is remarkably close to William Wordsworth's in the preface to the *Lyrical Ballads* (1798): The poet should be a spokesperson for and to ordinary men. To communicate with a large audience, the poet must be representative, involved in current events, interested in the news, sports, and so on. He must always place the subject matter and the purpose of his art above a pure interest in form. In *Modern Poetry*, he echoes Wordsworth's dictum that the poet must keep his eye on the object. A glance at the titles of MacNeice's poems reveals the wide range of his subjects; geographical locations, artists, seasons, classical and mythical figures, types of people, technological objects, and types of songs are a few representatives of the plurality embraced by his poems. Furthermore, like Wordsworth, MacNeice studies external objects, places, and events closely, though his poems often end up really being about human consciousness and morality, through analogy or reflection on the experience.

Telling vs. showing

Thus, MacNeice's fundamental approach to poetry also resembles Wordsworth's. Many of his poems are a modernized, sometimes journalistic version of the loco-descriptive genre of the eighteenth century, arising from the description of a place, object, or event, followed usually by a philosophical, moral, or psychological reflection on that event. Although MacNeice attempts to use a plain, simple style, his training in the classics and English literature tends to produce a rich profusion of allusive reverberations. The relationship between the topical focus of the poem and the meditation it produces varies from association to analogy to multiple parallels. In technique, MacNeice differs from the Imagistic, Symbolist thrust of T. S. Eliot, Ezra Pound, and the modern American poets influenced by them. The framework of MacNeice's poems is primarily expository; he tells rather than trying to show through objective correlatives.

Poet of ideas

As Terence Brown argues in *Louis MacNeice: Sceptical Vision* (1975), MacNeice is most notable as a poet of ideas. In his study of Yeats, he emphasizes the importance of belief in giving substance to a poet's work. Many critics have mistakenly criticized MacNeice's poetry on this basis, finding it superficial and devoid of philosophical system. Brown argues cogently that MacNeice is deceptively philosophical because he remains a skeptic. Thus the few positive beliefs underlying his poetry appear negative. Many of his poems question epistemological and metaphysical assumptions; depending on one's interpretation, MacNeice's "final" position may seem positive or negative. Many of his poems represent what might loosely be called an existentialist position. Although he never stops evaluating the validity of religion, MacNeice ceased to believe in God in his late teens, after being brought up in the home of a future Anglican bishop. The loss of God and Christianity left a huge gap in the metaphysical structure of MacNeice's thought, and he resisted replacing it with another absolute system such as Marxism. He retained a strong sense of moral and social duty, but he found no objective sanctions for value and order. In his poems, he explores the conflicting and paradoxical facts of experience. For example, he believes that a new social order will benefit the masses, but he is honest enough to admit his fondness for the privileges of the elite: good education, clothes, food, and art. He remains obsessed with the Heraclitean theory of flux, that we can never step into the same river twice. Yet when we face the absence of certainty, belief, and absolute value, we can celebrate plurality and assert ourselves against time and death. Brown distinguishes the modernity of MacNeice in "a sceptical faith, which believes that no transcendent reality, but rather non-being, gives being value."

Stylistics

The most striking technical features of MacNeice's poems evince his sometimes conflicting concerns with reaching a large audience of ordinary people and with reflecting philosophically on experience. In line with the former, he attempts to use colloquial, or at least plain, language, and often to base his rhythm and style on popular musical forms, from the folk ballad, nursery rhyme, and lullaby to modern jazz. His concern with contemporary issues, coupled with his classical training, makes irony and satire inevitable. Like the English Augustans (with whom he did not want to be identified), MacNeice cannot help contrasting reality with the ideals of past literature, politics, and belief systems. His satire of contemporary society tends to be of the urbane, gentle, Horatian type, only infrequently becoming harsh and bitter. Other stylistic features mark his concern with metaphysical issues. He uses analogy and paradox, accreting many resonances through classical and biblical allusions, usually simultaneously. Many poems pose unresolved questions and problems, circling back on their beginnings at the end. The endings that repeat initial statements or questions would seem to offer closure, or at least a definite structure, to the poems, but paradoxically they do not. Rather, they emphasize the impossibility of answering or closing the issue.

Another stylistic feature that recurs throughout MacNeice's work is the list, similar to the epic catalogs of Homer. Rather than suggesting greatness or richness as they usually do in epics, MacNeice's catalogs represent the irreducible plurality of experience.

EVOLUTION VS. STASIS

In addition to the question of his belief system or lack thereof, critics have disagreed over whether MacNeice's work develops over time or remains essentially the same. The answer to this question is sometimes viewed as a determinant of MacNeice's rank as a poet. An argument can be made for both positions, but the answer must be a synthesis. While MacNeice's appreciation of the complexity of life, its latent suggestions, grows as his poetry develops, certain interrelated clusters of themes and recurring images inform his work from beginning to end.

For example, the places and events of his childhood shape his problematic identity and worldview, including his obsessions with dreams and with Ireland as a symbol of the more gothic, mysterious, and mystical sides of experience. Connected with his upbringing in the home of an Anglican rector is a preoccupation,

mentioned above, with disbelief in God and religion, and faith in liberal humanism. The disappearance of God results in complex epistemological and moral questions that also pervade many poems. Another related thematic cluster is a concern with time, death, and Heraclitean flux. Closely related to this cluster is an increasing interest in cycles, in repetition versus renewal, reflected in many poems about spring and fall.

Although these themes, along with recurring images of train journeys, Ireland, stone, dazzling surfaces, and time represented as space, among others, continue to absorb MacNeice's attention, the types of poems and emphases evolve over time, particularly in response to changes in the political temper of the times. His juvenilia, written between 1925 and 1927, reflects the aesthetic focus of his student years, playing with sound and rhetorical devices, musing on sensation, death, God, and self-consciousness. MacNeice did not really emerge as a poet until the 1930's, when his teaching, marriage, and life among the workers of Birmingham opened his eyes to the world of social injustice and political reality. At that point he was influenced by Auden, Spender, and Lewis, and came to see the poet's role as more journalistic than purely aesthetic.

FROM POLITICAL TO PHILOSOPHICAL

The poems of the 1930's reflect his preoccupation with the disheartening political events in Spain and Germany and his belief that the existing social order was doomed. The poetry of this period is more leftist than at any other stage in MacNeice's career, but he never espouses the dogmas of Marxism. During World War II, his poetry becomes more humanistic, more positive in its treatment of man. MacNeice's faith in human nature was fanned by the courage and generosity he witnessed in his job as a fire watcher in London during the war.

After the war, his poems become at first more philosophical, reflecting a revaluation of the role of art and a desire for belief of any kind, not necessarily in God. At this point, the poems express an existential recognition of the void and a disgust with the depersonalization of England after the war; they also play with looking at subjects from different perspectives. His last three volumes of poems, published in 1957, 1961, and posthumously in 1963, represent what most critics consider to be the apotheosis of MacNeice's career. The lyrics of his latest poems are austere and short, often using tetrameter rather than pentameter or hexameter lines. Many of these poems are "parable-poems" in the sense that MacNeice described in his Clark Lectures of 1963, published as *Varieties of Parable*; that is, they use images to structure a poem that is in effect a miniature allegory. The poems appear to be topical or occasional, but they hold a double or deeper meaning.

"The Kingdom"

Because MacNeice was essentially a reflective, philosophical poet, his poetry records an ongoing dialectic between the shaping forces of his consciousness and the events and character of the external world. Thus certain techniques, goals, and preoccupations tend to recur, though they are different in response to historical and personal developments in MacNeice's life. Since he was a skeptic, he tends to ask questions rather than give answers, but the more positive values that he holds become clearer by the last years of his life. In particular, the idea of a kingdom of individuals, who lay claim to their freedom and create their lives, is implicit in many of the later poems, after being introduced in "The Kingdom," written around 1943. The members of this kingdom counteract flux and fear by their genuineness, their honest seeing and feeling, their incorruptibility. The Greek notion of *arête*, sometimes translated as virtue or excellence, but without the narrowly moral meaning usually attached to "virtue," comes to mind when one reads the descriptions of exemplary individuals in "The Kingdom." This kingdom is analogous to the Kingdom of Christ, the ideal Republic of Plato, and the Kingdom of Ends in Immanuel Kant's moral system. Yet it does not depend on absolutes and thus it is not an unattainable ideal but a mode of life that some people manage to realize in the ordinary course of life. Moreover, the members of this kingdom belong by virtue of their differentness, not because they share divine souls or absolute ideas of reason.

"Blasphemies"

MacNeice sees himself in terms of stages of development in such poems as "Blasphemies," written in the late 1950's, where he describes his changing attitude toward God and belief. The poem is a third-person narrative about his own feelings toward religion since his childhood. In the first stanza, he is seven years old, lying in bed pondering the nature of the unforgivable sin against the Holy Ghost. In the second stanza, he is seventeen, striking the pose of a blasphemer, parodying prayers. The middle-aged writer of the autobiographical poem mocks his earlier stance, seeing the hollowness of rebellion against a nonexistent deity. The third stanza describes how, at thirty, the poet realized the futility of protest against an absence and turned to a new religion of humanism and realism, facing facts. The mature MacNeice undercuts these simple new faiths by ending the stanza with a question about the nature of facts for a thirty-year-old. Stanza 4 finds the poet at forty attempting to appropriate the myths of Christianity for purely symbolic use and realizing that their lack of absolute meaning makes them useless to him. At the age of forty, he has reached a crisis of sorts, unable to speak for himself or for humankind. The final stanza sums up MacNeice's ultimate philosophical position: that there are no ultimate beliefs or postures. He finally throws off the entire issue of Christianity, finding divinity neither above nor within humankind.

The irreducible reality is that he is not Tom, Dick, or Harry, some archetypal representative of ordinary man. He is himself, merely fifty, a question. The final two lines of the poem, however, in typical MacNeice fashion, reintroduce the problem of metaphysics that he has just dismissed. He asserts that although he is a question, that question is as worthwhile as any other, which is not saying too much. He then, however, uses the word "quest" in apposition to the word "question," reintroducing the entire issue of a search for ultimate meaning. To complete the confusion, he ends with a completed repetition of the broken-off question that opens the poem: What is the sin against the Holy Ghost? The repeated but augmented line is an instance of the type of incremental repetition used in folk ballads such as "Lord Randall," and it suggests the kind of dark riddle often presented in such songs. The final question might be just idle intellectual curiosity or it might imply that ultimate questions of belief simply cannot be escaped by rationality.

"To Hedli"

MacNeice's dedicatory poem, "To Hedli," which prefaces the 1949 *Collected Poems, 1925-1948*, serves as a good introduction to his technique and themes. The poem is clearly occasional and autobiographical, using the first-person point of view that he often eschews in later poems. While employing fairly plain diction, the poem is a sestina, a highly restrictive verse form made up of six stanzas, each having six lines ending with the same six words throughout the poem. In addition, the final word of each stanza is repeated as the last word of the first line in the succeeding stanza. MacNeice takes a few liberties, adding a tercet, or half-stanza, at the end, and substituting the word "returning" for "turning" in stanza 4. The poem is typically self-reflective, calling into question the poetic efforts represented in the collected poems, regretting the unanswered question present in the volume. The content of the poem thus radiates out from a highly specific event, the collecting of MacNeice's poems from 1925-1948, and their dedication to the listener of the poem, his second wife, Hedli. From this focus the poem reaches back to the poet's past practices and beliefs and outward to suggest a broad metaphysical stance. The poem is therefore typically occasional, personal, and philosophical. Although the poem does not make explicit reference to World War II, its recent horror is implicit in the anger of those who believed they knew all the answers and the "grim past" that has silenced so many poets.

Two recurrent themes that pervade this poem are the need for belief and the motif of repetitive cycles, with the question of renewal. The sestina form, so highly repetitive, mirrors the concern with cycles. Stanza 1 calls the poetic moments in the collection "April Answers." In MacNeice's works, spring and fall always signal, on one level, the cycles of time and life. In "Day of Renewal," he says he has measured all his experience in terms of returning autumns. The answers that come in April are the positive side of cycles; they herald renewal if not rebirth. The poems, or answers, implicitly compared to perennial plants, seem to have "withered" off from their bulbs or roots, their questions. The questions, or sources of the poems, are akin to the frozen barrenness of winter, perhaps representing despair. Stanza 3 picks up the metaphor implicit in the word "withered" by comparing the "Word" to a bulb underground. MacNeice is writing this poem during the period when he began attempting to deal with religious

matters symbolically, so it is clear that "Word" has no literal Christian significance. It is rather the source of true poetry, informed by some body of belief. The cycles of renewal in MacNeice's past work are contrasted with a larger cycle in which this word is awaiting a new generation of poets who will produce "full leaf" and "bloom" of meaning and image.

The alternating stanzas, two and four, criticize more clearly what MacNeice sees as his own weaknesses as a poet. He has lived too much in the present, in a no-man's-land of belief, between unknown gods to come and the rejected gods of his ancestors. This position parallels, though without the defined system of belief, Yeats's prophecy in "A Second Coming." There is a milder sense than Yeats's of the crumbling of the old order in the outpouring of angry sound from those who knew the answers, perhaps enthusiasts for communism. Stanza 4 explains MacNeice's past contentment with "dazzle," the poetic mirroring of intense moments in the flux of life, and with chance gifts washed up by the sea of life. These gifts were fragments from older castaways who could never return. This statement suggests that while nature repeats its cycles endlessly, men die. The final half stanza suggests that the poet is growing older and has nothing but half answers; his end is in sight. Stanza 5 begins with the word "But," clearly contrasting the poet's past contentment with his present goals. He refers to the autumn in which he is writing this dedicatory poem (November, 1948) and parallels the leaves' turning brown with the gilt's flaking off his poetic images. The poem ends with a definite desire for some fundamental answers to metaphysical questions. Unlike later poems, "To Hedli" at least implies that such answers may exist.

"AN ECLOGUE FOR CHRISTMAS"

Among the earlier poems in the 1949 collection, "An Eclogue for Christmas" (December, 1933) marks an early point of departure, a turning toward serious poems of social commentary. In his fragmentary prose autobiography, *The Strings Are False*, MacNeice describes his absorption in his home life during the early 1930's. His sister, in "Trees Were Green" (*Times Was Away*), comments on the special pleasure Christmas always represented for her brother. MacNeice explains that when he had finished writing this poem he was taken aback by the depth of his despair over Western culture's decay. Like many of the poems of this period, "An Eclogue for Christmas" combines colloquial language with a classical form, the eclogue, which is a dialogue between shepherds, often on love or poetry, or the contrast between city and country life. The two speakers of MacNeice's poem, A. and B., represent the city and the country, the country in this case being the world of the landed gentry in England. There is no disagreement between the two speakers; they mirror each other's prophecies of doom in terms of the societies they represent. Neither city nor country escapes the horrors of the times. B., the representative of country life, tells A. not to look for sanctuary in the country. Both places are equally bad. The poem describes a time like that in Yeats's "A Second Coming," but in a more dominant way than "To Hedli." It seems that MacNeice could clearly see the coming of World War II. The poem satirizes contemporary upper-class British society as mechanistic, slick, and superficial. The rhythms of jazz pervade the hectic and chaotic life of the city, and people like A. become automatons. Rather than being individuals like those in MacNeice's later "The Kingdom," people are grotesque in their efforts to be unique.

The motif of cyclical return is what motivates the poem, the reflection on Christ's birth as represented by "old tinsel and frills." This is a hollow repetition, not a renewal or rebirth. The elaboration of technological "improvements" has alienated people from the genuine reality of life. The cyclicity of history is suggested in the metaphor of the Goths returning to silence the pneumatic drill. Yet MacNeice is such a skeptic that he is unable to make a wholesale condemnation of modern industrial society. He admits that a narcotic beauty can be perceived in the lights and bustle of the city, which he here calls an "organism" rather than a machine. B. attacks the country gentry in Marxist terms, as a breed whose time is about to end. He alludes to the destruction of the "manor wall" by the "State" with a capital "S," and also to private property as something that is turning to "poison and pus." Much of this part of the dialogue is carried on in questions, so it is difficult to assign a positive attitude to either speaker, let alone the author. A., who seems closer to MacNeice, counters the Marxist-inspired questions of B. with questions about the results of violent revolution. A. is clearly the skeptic who sees the problems inherent in capitalist society but cannot accept the Marxist solution. A. interrupts B., telling him not to "gloat" over his own demise, suggesting the irony of an upper-class communism. The poem ends with self-mocking assertions on the part of both speakers; they have no choice but to cling to the few good, real things they have in life.

Like so many of MacNeice's poems, this one circles back to its opening occasion, the significance of Christmas. The ending holds out a somewhat flippant hope for renewal, but it is extremely "ephemeral," like the few positive ideas in the last part of the poem. Thus, "An Eclogue for Christmas" shows MacNeice facing an "evil time," the discord and injustices of modern industrial society, but unwilling and unable to accept the premises of a new regime founded on violence and the subordination of the individual to the state. This skepticism sets him apart from the group of poet-friends surrounding Auden.

Autumn Journal

In the fall of 1938, MacNeice wrote *Autumn Journal*, a long poem in twenty-four cantos, commenting specifically on the depressing political events of the time: the Munich Pact and the Spanish Civil War. In a prefatory note, he categorizes the poem as half lyric and half didactic, hoping that it presents some "criticism of life" with some standards beyond the "merely personal." The poem, however, is a journal (as the title states) and its record of events is tinged by fleeting personal response. It is a huge, complex version of his shorter poems in its intertwining threads of autobiography, travel, politics, philosophy, morality, and poetics. The personal-ethical response to political events is the strongest of these threads, coloring the entire poem. Because it takes its impetus from the private and public events of the days and months of late 1938, from late August until New Year's Eve, it does not have an overall architectonic structure; each individual canto rounds itself out as a separate unity that is enhanced by its relationship to the whole.

The poem as a whole is given closure by the parallels between the dying summer at the beginning, the dying year at the end, and the threatened death of European civilization from the impending world war throughout. The narrative is basically chronological, following the poet's first day of the fall term, through trips to Oxford and finally to Spain. The narrative technique resembles stream of consciousness, the thoughts and memories of the poet creating the subject matter. The poem is more fluently lyrical than many of MacNeice's poems, which have been criticized as being "flat." It uses an alternating rhyme scheme like that of ballad stanzas (*abcbdefe* . . .), but the effect resembles terza rima.

As in most of MacNeice's works, the meditations are rooted in specific observations of actual times, places, and events. Canto 1 begins with a catalog of concrete images of summer's end in Hampshire, ordinary people leading ordinary lives, insulated within their families. The poet-narrator is in a train, as in so many of his poems. The train ride comes to symbolize the journey of life, the time line of each individual. In an ambiguous tone, MacNeice mentions his dog lying on the floor of the train, a symbol of lost order. This is picked up both more seriously and more ironically in canto 7 when the dog is lost while political treaties are dying and trees are being cut down on Primrose Hill to make an antiaircraft station. The loss of the dog is the close of the "old regime." In MacNeice's personal life, the "old regime" represents his marriage to Mariette, but in larger terms, it is the demise of traditional Western capitalist society. At the end of this canto, the speaker tries to work up enthusiasm for a war that he cannot romanticize. He realizes exactly what it is, yet he also realizes that he may have to become uncritical like the enemy, like Hitler propagandizing on the radio.

Canto 8 builds, through satirical popular song rhythms, to a climax of fear about the outbreak of war. At the end of the canto the poet learns that the crisis is averted through the sacrifice of Czechoslovakia. He does not explain his response directly except to say that he has saved his own skin as an Englishman in a way that damns his conscience. The poet-narrator feels a terrible conflict between a natural desire to avert war and a sense of duty, which might in earlier times have been called honor, to face up to the threat of Hitler and defeat him. This conflict is implicit until canto 12, in which he describes people, himself included, lacking

the heart to become involved in ethics or "public calls." In his private debate with his conscience, MacNeice recalls the soldiers training across the road from his home when he was a child during World War I. Having described the beginning of classes in canto 9, cynically and mockingly stating that *we* are safe (although the Czechs are lost), the poet is reading Plato in preparation for teaching his philosophy course. The ethical differences between Plato and Aristotle form an important context for the progress of MacNeice's feelings and thoughts in the poem. In canto 12, he rejects Plato's ideal forms as a world of capital initials, preferring instead the Heraclitean world of flux, of sensation. He admits at the end of canto 12 that his desire is to be "human," in the fullest sense, to live in a civilized community where both mind and body are given their due. He undercuts this desire by satirizing the professors of humanities who become "spiritually bankrupt" snobs, yet conceding his own willingness to take the comforts that such a profession provides. Though the connection is not explicitly made here, the reader must keep in mind the overwhelming threat to civilization that forms the background of these reflections. *Autumn Journal* traces MacNeice's emotional and moral journey from reluctant self-interest to reluctant determination to do his share to protect humanity in the impending war.

Canto 13 is a mocking, slightly bitter rejection of the elitist education, particularly in philosophy, that MacNeice has received. The bitterness arises from the disjunction between the promise and world of thought and the real world he must inhabit. He must be happy to live in the world of appearances and plurality, life in the particular rather than the eternal and ideal realm. The poet's synthesis between skepticism and moral and civic responsibility is revealed in the next canto where he describes a trip to Oxford to help drive voters to the polls. While he cannot commit himself to political ideologies, he does mobilize himself to act for a "half-believed-in principle." Imperfect though it is, the parliamentary system is England's only hope for political progress. Here MacNeice comes to the important realization that to shun politics for private endeavor is to risk the conditions that support or allow that private endeavor. As he drives back to London at the end of canto 14, MacNeice has a new understanding of the need for all Englishmen to unite against the threat of fascism. This new resolution allows the cheerful final image of the sun caressing the plurality of nature, wheelbarrows full of oranges and apples. This serenity is undercut in the following canto by a nightmarish effort to escape through drink the horrors that threaten, horrors associated in MacNeice's mind with his childhood fears and bad dreams.

In canto 17, at nine o'clock on a November morning, the poet savors a moment of almost Keatsian escape in a bath, allowing responsibility to die. Metaphorically he speaks of the ego merging into the bath, thus leading himself into a meditation on the need of man to merge, or at least interact, with those outside himself. Significantly, MacNeice affirms Aristotle's ethical notion that humankind's essence is to act, as opposed to Socrates' idea that humankind's crowning glory is to think. The canto ends with his refusal to "drug" himself with the sensations of the moment. This climactic decision to act is followed by cantos satirizing industrialized England, implying, as William Blake does in *Songs of Innocence* (1789) and *Songs of Innocence and of Experience* (1794), that church and state conspire to allow social injustice. While MacNeice is not a communist, he fairly consistently condemns *laissez-faire* economics as an instrument of evil. Although canto 18 is very bitter about England's social and political failure to act, it ends with the affirmative statement that the seeds of energy and choice are still alive. Canto 20, trying to sound bitter, relaxes into a nostalgic longing for Christmas, a week away, a "coral island in time." This beautiful image is typical of MacNeice's conflation of space and time. Any poem about consciousness exists in the stream of time, but to be comprehensible the passing of time must be anchored to spatial reference points. MacNeice frequently concretizes this space/time relationship by metaphorically imaging time as a geographical space. Christmas here is an ideal moment, described through an allusion to the lotus eaters of the *Odyssey* (c. 725 B.C.E.; English translation, 1614). The remainder of the canto speaks respectfully of Christ but ends on a satirical note about people exploiting the season to beg for money. This carries additional overtones, however, because if one remembers the spirit of Christmas rather than the self-

ish pleasures it brings, nothing is more appropriate than to celebrate Christ's birthday by giving money to beggars.

Canto 21 returns to the notion of canto 17, that one must live a life beyond the self, in spite of the wish to quit. The poem, like the year, ends with MacNeice's train journey through France to Spain. Significantly, the poem skips Christmas, implying that neither the hollow religion of Christianity nor the personal pleasures of the holiday have a meaningful place in the ethical and political events at hand. MacNeice goes to face the New Year in Spain, a place where metaphorically all Europe may soon stand in time. He goes to confront his duty as a man of action and a citizen of a free country. His New Year's resolutions, detailed in the penultimate canto, reveal his self-criticisms and determination to seek the roots of "will and conscience," to participate. The final canto is a sleep song, gentle in tone, allowing some peace after the hard-won resolutions of canto 23. MacNeice addresses himself, his parents, his former wife, and all people, to dream of a "possible land" where the individual can pursue his natural abilities in freedom and understanding. He tells of his hope to awaken soon, but of his doubts to sleep forever.

VISITATIONS, SOLSTICES, AND THE BURNING PERCH

Most critics agree that MacNeice's final three books of poems, *Visitations*, *Solstices*, and the posthumous *The Burning Perch*, achieve new heights of technical precision and depth of meaning. The themes of flux and renewal become even more prominent than in the past. According to his own statements in literary criticism, MacNeice was attempting to write more "parable-poems." The use of the train journey and of Christmas Day in *Autumn Journal* exemplifies the multiple layers of meaning he could achieve in describing an actual event, object, or place. In these later poems, there is more respect for the mysterious, the dark side of experience. The focus on life as a paradox is playfully yet darkly expounded in poems resembling folk ballad riddles, poems such as "A Hand of Snap-shots," "The Riddle," and parts of "Notes for a Biography." In particular, the poems of *The Burning Perch* give brief nightmare sketches of the gothic side of experience. Connected to the motifs of riddles and paradoxes is a new concern with perspective or various ways of knowing, as in Part I of "Jigsaws," "The Wiper," "The Grey Ones," and perhaps "Budgie."

"The Wiper," from *Solstices*, is a perfect example of the kind of "parable-poem" MacNeice sought to write in his later years. On the literal level, it starts with a concrete description of the driver's and passengers' perspective of the road from inside the car on a dark, rainy night. The first stanza portrays the glimpses of the shiny asphalt when the windshield wipers clear the window, only to blur it when they move back the other way. The focus shifts to the nature of the road and then to an outside view of the wet cars on the road. The fourth stanza turns to the memory of the car's passengers, to the relationship between past and present, while the final stanza looks not very invitingly to the "black future," literally the dark night ahead on the road. Only through subtle double meanings does MacNeice suggest the allegorical or symbolic nature of the poem. The words "mystery" and "always" in stanza 2 and "black future" in stanza 5 are the only obvious indicators of a level of meaning beyond the literal.

The poem symbolizes life as a journey with the potential of being a quest, a potential limited by the restrictions of partial blindness. The riders in the car can see only brief snatches of a black road, a mysterious road with unknown dimensions. The darkness of night, the meaningless void of existence, is broken intermittently by the lights of other people insulated and partially blinded in their own "moving boxes." Significantly, while each driver is able to see very little through the dark and rain, his or her car gives off light that illuminates the way for other drivers, if only transiently. The dials in the cars measure speed and distance covered. In Aristotle's terms, these are indicators of efficient causes, but the final cause, the destination and the daylight, is not indicated. The final line of the poem is highly characteristic of MacNeice in its qualified, pessimistically positive assertion. In spite of ignorance and clouded perceptions, living in a world of night and rain, the drivers manage to stay on the road.

MacNeice is a poet of contradictions, a learned classicist who sought to write in a colloquial idiom and appeal to a broad audience, a man who sought belief but was unable to accede to the dishonesty of systematiz-

ing. His poems are above all honest. They study life in the fullness of its antinomies and paradoxes.

OTHER MAJOR WORKS

LONG FICTION: *Roundabout Way*, 1932 (as Louis Malone).

PLAYS: *Out of the Picture*, pr., pb. 1937; *Station Bell*, pr. 1937; *One for the Grave*, pr. 1966; *Selected Plays of Louis MacNeice*, 1993.

RADIO PLAYS: *Christopher Columbus*, 1944; *The Dark Tower, and Other Radio Scripts by Louis MacNeice*, 1947; *The Mad Islands and The Administrator*, 1964; *Persons from Porlock, and Other Plays for Radio*, 1969.

NONFICTION: *Letters from Iceland*, 1937 (with W. H. Auden); *I Crossed the Minch*, 1938; *Modern Poetry: A Personal Essay*, 1938; *Zoo*, 1938; *The Poetry of W. B. Yeats*, 1941; *Astrology*, 1964; *The Strings Are False*, 1965; *Varieties of Parable*, 1965.

TRANSLATIONS: *The Agamemnon of Aeschylus*, 1936; *Goethe's Faust, Parts I and II*, 1951 (with E. L. Stahl).

CHILDREN'S LITERATURE: *The Penny That Rolled Away*, 1954.

BIBLIOGRAPHY

Brown, Terence. *Louis MacNeice: Sceptical Vision*. New York: Barnes & Noble, 1975. Concerned with the themes in MacNeice's poetry. Argues that the poet's real contribution is as a proponent of creative skepticism. The result is a dependable, authoritative study. Contains a good bibliography and notes.

Brown, Terence, and Alec Reid, eds. *Time Was Away: The World of Louis MacNeice*. Dublin: Dolmen Press, 1974. A collection including personal tributes, reminiscences, and evaluations of MacNeice's work. Several pieces are of interest, including one by MacNeice's sister that contains personal biographical information. Other selections look at MacNeice's Irishness, his poetry, and his reaction to his mother's death. Includes W. H. Auden's "Louis MacNeice: A Memorial Address."

Devine, Kathleen, and Alan J. Peacock, eds. *Louis MacNeice and His Influence*. New York: Oxford University Press, 1998. Essays by leading experts on MacNeice's work examine the range and depth of his achievement, including his influence on Michael Longley, Derek Mahon, Seamus Heaney, and Paul Muldoon. Includes bibliographical references and index.

Longley, Edna. *Louis MacNeice: A Study*. London: Faber & Faber, 1988. The first complete study after MacNeice's death. Explores the dramatic nature of MacNeice's poetry, stresses the importance of his Irish background, and credits William Butler Yeats's influence, hitherto downplayed. This piece of historical criticism moves chronologically, linking MacNeice's life and times. Special attention is given to his English, war, and postwar poems. Bibliography.

McDonald, Peter. *Louis MacNeice: The Poet in His Contexts*. New York: Oxford University Press, 1991. An examination of MacNeice in the context of Northern Ireland and its poets. W. J. Martz, reviewing for *Choice* magazine, notes the author's "need to see MacNeice as MacNeice . . . in his contexts rather than those that have hitherto been thought to be his." Bibliography, index.

Marsack, Robyn. *The Cave of Making: The Poetry of Louis MacNeice*. New York: Oxford University Press, 1982. This book looks at MacNeice as a poet of the 1930's and focuses on despair and disillusionment in his work. Contains commentary on the poet's craft and process based on papers, drafts, and notes made available to the author. Extensive notes and an excellent bibliography make this a helpful companion to reading MacNeice.

Moore, Donald B. *The Poetry of Louis MacNeice*. Leicester, England: Leicester University Press, 1972. This descriptive study traces the poet's development chronologically. Tracks themes such as self, society, and philosophy through MacNeice's work. The final chapter gives a retrospective and general critical overview. Includes a select bibliography with citations of related works.

O'Neill, Michael, and Gareth Reeves. *Auden, MacNeice, Spender: The Thirties Poetry*. London: Macmillan Education, 1992. A close analysis of the major works of three giants of 1930's English poetry.

Stallworthy, Jon. *Louis MacNeice*. New York: W. W. Norton, 1995. Stallworthy produces the first full-scale biography of MacNeice, a tour de force "not likely to be superseded," according to W. J. Martz of *Choice* magazine. Includes pictures and copies of manuscript pages, each dated. Bibliography, notes, index.

Wigginton, Christopher. *Modernism from the Margins: The 1930's Poetry of Louis MacNeice and Dylan Thomas*. Cardiff: University of Wales Press, 2007. The author looks at the poetry of MacNeice and Dylan Thomas, placing their works in the Auden-dominated 1930's and discussing their poetry in relation to modernism.

Eve Walsh Stoddard

JAMES CLARENCE MANGAN

Born: Dublin, Ireland; May 1, 1803
Died: Dublin, Ireland; June 20, 1849

PRINCIPAL POETRY

Poems, by James Clarence Mangan, with Biographical Introduction, by John Mitchel, 1859
Poems of James Clarence Mangan (Many Hitherto Unpublished), 1903 (D. J. O'Donoghue, editor)
Poems, 1996-1999 (4 volumes; Jacques Chuto, editor)
Selected Poems of James Clarence Mangan, 2003

OTHER LITERARY FORMS

James Clarence Mangan (MAN-gahn) is known primarily for his poetry and verse translations from more than twenty different languages, including Gaelic. However, he also wrote and translated witty, humorous prose works, articles, stories and essays, most of which appeared between 1832-1849 in different Irish periodicals, such as the *Comet, Irish Penny Journal, Dublin University Magazine, Vindicator, Nation*, and *Irish Monthly Magazine*. During the last year of his life, Mangan wrote a series of articles called "Sketches and Reminiscences of Irish Writers," published in *The Irishman*.

ACHIEVEMENTS

The biggest distinction any mid-nineteenth century Irish poet could hope to achieve was to be called a national poet. James Clarence Mangan, one of the Young Ireland poets, won this "title" through versatile and prolific poetic production. Although written in English, most of his poetry absorbed distinctly Gaelic patterns and rhythmical structures and effectively revived the tone and imagery of the ancient bardic verse. Mangan's work inspired a whole generation of Irish writers—among them William Butler Yeats and James Joyce—to find their own voice and, thus, continue the process of de-Anglicization of Irish literature and culture, which had been the goal of the first Celtic Revival at the end of the eighteenth century, by means of antiquarian explorations of the ancient Celts' heroic past. Haunted by a sense of cultural inferiority and lost identity caused by the country's colonial dependence on the British Empire, Mangan's poetry responded to the pressing demand in nineteenth century Ireland for a national literature. His authentic, powerful counter-images would help Ireland resist and repair the cultural rupture and discontinuity caused by the colonial intervention.

BIOGRAPHY

Remembered by his contemporaries as a bohemian, James Clarence Mangan was a victim of morbid melancholy, opium, and alcohol. He was prone to painful introspection, which, intensified by his Catholicism, led to frequent withdrawals from friends, family, and society. This, combined with his recurring financial difficulties and physical neglect, resulted in a troubled, though artistically intensive, life and an early death at the age of forty-six.

The poet was born in Dublin, where he spent his whole life. His father gave up his position as a schoolteacher to run the grocery business he had inherited through his wife. He sent James to a Jesuit school where the boy started learning Latin, Spanish, French, and Italian—languages that would determine to a great extent the course of his career. A rather eccentric child, he experienced severe difficulties dealing with the "outside" world and withdrew into an eight-year-long state of blindness, allegedly caused by excessive exposure to rain. His relatives found him hard to reach and considered him "mad."

Mangan was fifteen when he became the family's breadwinner—his father had gone bankrupt. The first job he took was at a scrivener's office. It was at this time that he started publishing his first poems in the *Grant*'s and *New Ladies'* almanacs and when his mysterious blindness disappeared. Two years later, however, in 1820, an illness and a severe emotional disturbance led to a diagnosis of hypochondriasis. His poetic apprenticeship ended in 1826, but his ill health persisted. By this time, Mangan had moved away from his family and had started publishing nationalistic poetry. He continued earning a meager living by doing clerical work. In 1833, he supported a parliamentary petition for repeal of the Act of Union between Ireland and Britain. His political activism motivated him also to start learning Gaelic and establish close contacts with Gaelic scholars.

In 1834, the *Dublin University Magazine*, Ireland's most prestigious periodical at the time, started accepting Mangan's poetry for publication. This marked the beginning of a long-term collaboration; in *Dublin University Magazine*, the twenty-two chapters of Mangan's *Anthologia Germanica = German Anthology: A Series of Translations from the Most Popular of the German Poets* (1845), as well as numerous other "translations" from various languages, would appear for the next twelve years. The following few years were also eventful: In 1836, Mangan met Charles Gavan Duffy, the future founder of the nationalist Young Ireland Party and its weekly magazine *The Nation*, both active advocates of physical-force politics as the only means to achieve Irish independence.

Two years later, Mangan was hired by George Petrie, a famous antiquarian, to work at the Ordinance Survey Office. The project involved surveying and remapping the whole of Ireland for the purposes of the British government. This was arguably the most enabling experience in Mangan's life as, on one hand, it strengthened his contacts with Gaelic scholars and, on the other hand, allowed him to get acquainted with numerous historical sources and manuscripts, and through them, with Ireland's ancient past. Touched by concrete visions of the glory of the ancient Celts,

Mangan began reworking Eugene O'Curry's prose translations of Irish bardic verse, gaining confidence in the strength of his own artistic voice. These poems, "translations" from the Irish, appeared in the *Irish Penny Journal*, founded in 1840 with the task of popularizing the country's Gaelic past.

Although the late 1830's marked a very fruitful period in Mangan's artistic life, they had detrimental effects on his health, which worsened to such an extent that friends started referring to him as "poor Mangan." They also realized that he had become addicted to opium (later to be substituted by alcohol) in an attempt to deal with his attacks of "intellectual hypochondriacism." He denied the fact, refusing to take an abstinence pledge. His finances worsened when the Ordnance Survey Office was closed in December of 1841. It took Petrie a few months to find Mangan a new job—this time at the Trinity College Library. The poet experienced relative financial stability for a few years, but the solitary nature of his work made it hard for him to publish. As biographers point out, his artistic production in *Dublin University Magazine* alone had declined from an average of one hundred pages annually, between 1835 and 1839, to about thirty during each of the following five years.

Having been unemployed for about six months, in 1845, Mangan resumed his job at Trinity Library. It was a half-time position, which meant increased financial difficulties for the poet. The years 1845-1846, however, were marked by remarkable creative achievements and the publication in *Nation* of his most passionate nationalistic verse. He declared his readiness, as his biographer Ellen Shannon-Mangan pointed out, "to devote [himself] almost exclusively to the interests of [his] country." However, his desire to join openly the physical-force politics led by Duffy was repeatedly thwarted by the latter's refusal to admit Mangan in the Irish Confederation. As the great Famine intensified in Ireland, so did Mangan's bad health. In December of 1847, ill and homeless, he took to drinking again, although he had tried to give it up for a number of years. The remaining year and a half of his life was characterized by bad health and poverty, despite the isolated attempts by few of his friends to help him. Still, Mangan continued to write and publish poetry.

In May, 1849, he contracted cholera. In June, having allegedly recovered from it, he was found dying in a street cellar. He was taken to a hospital, where he died a week later.

Analysis

As an Irish Romantic poet, James Clarence Mangan was aware of a loss of innocence, a feeling central to Romantic subjectivity in general, which was intensified by the poet's attempts to cope with the feeling of being trapped in a present corrupted by Britain's colonial power. The poet's search for an alternative, natural and pure self (individual, cultural, national) was therefore colored by a search for an appropriate medium for its expression. Until the beginning of his ardent nationalism in the mid-1830's, Mangan relied primarily on translation from various European and Middle Eastern languages as a means of escaping his oppressive environment, both personal and social. Through acts of imagination, translation transported him to various, often exotic lands. However, his biographers emphasize repeatedly that Mangan had no knowledge of most of the languages from which he "translated." He often transformed his originals by saturating them, especially Oriental verse and that of the minor German Romantics, with rhetorical and stylistic effects typical for his own nationalistic poetry. When Duffy criticized him once for a rather loose Moorish "translation," Mangan pointed out instead its relevance to the Gaelic Revival, responding in his own witty way: "Well, never mind, it's Tom Moorish."

There were also cases when Mangan attributed his own verse to foreign poets. "Twenty Golden Years Ago," he claimed, was originally a German poem by Selber (German for "himself"). Other works were attributed to a Persian poet by the name of Hafis ("half-his"). It is true that, in the absence of an Irish literary tradition in English, a poet like Mangan had greater chances to support himself by publishing translations from languages with rich and firmly established literary traditions, such as German, or from cultures that were distinctly non-English, such as Turkish, Persian, or even Serbian. Translation, therefore, offered Mangan a means of release from his personal anguish and a means of pulling himself away from English Romanticism, which represented for all Irish the culture of the colonizer. Poems such as "Siberia" demonstrate eloquently Mangan's idea of the devastating effects his country's colonial history had had on Irish consciousness. He translated the poem, which originally voiced Freiligrath's impressions of an Icelandic landscape, into a metaphor with distinct political overtones pointing to the inhuman conditions in Ireland during the Famine: "Blight and death alone./ No summer shines." The year was 1846:

> Pain as in a dream,
> When years go by
> Funeral-paced, yet fugitive,
> When man lives, and doth not live,
> Doth not live—nor die.

"O'Hussey's Ode to the Maguire"

Mangan never learned enough Gaelic to be able to translate Irish verse. Therefore, he relied primarily on the "translation" strategies he had already acquired. His wide access to old numbers of *Dublin University Magazine* allowed him to benefit from Samuel Ferguson's and other antiquarians' prose translations from the 1820's and 1830's. Mangan's creative imagination and acute ear for melody and rhythm completely transformed them into remarkable pieces of poetry. "O'Hussey's Ode to the Maguire" serves as a poignant example. Compare the opening stanzas of Ferguson's translation (1834) with Mangan's poem (1846). The speaker is Eochaidh Ó Heodhussa, chief bard of the Maguire Hugh. Hugh, himself, is in the Irish province of Munster, waging war against the colonizing enterprise of Queen Elizabeth I:

> Cold weather I consider this night to be for Hugh!
> A cause of grief is the rigor of its showery drops;
> Alas, insufferable is
> The venom of this night's cold.

> Where is my Chief, my master, this bleak night, mavrone!
> O, cold, cold, miserably cold is this bleak night for Hugh,
> Its showery, arrowy, speary sleet pierceth one through
>   and through,
> Pierceth one to the very bone!

Although Mangan preserved the four-line stanza of Ferguson's translation, his poem reveals a psychological intensity not readily audible in Ferguson's version.

Partly because each of the poets chose to emphasize different sides of the native Irish character— Ferguson stressed its profound sense of loyalty to a leader, while Mangan singled out its pure, natural force and strength— the two texts convey different political messages. Ferguson, representative of the Anglo-Irish Ascendancy, strives to bring England's attention to the respect and loyalty with which the Old Irish address their leader, a quality the Crown should value in its subjects if the prosperity of both England and Ireland is to be secured. By 1846, however, the physical-force politics as a means to achieve Irish independence had gathered considerable momentum. That is why Mangan's regular *abba* rhyme is opposed to variations in line length and beat, from iambs to dactyls or anapests, to produce a singular explosive power.

"Kathaleen Ny-Houlahan"

This poem of 1841 refers to an Irish sovereignty myth, very much like Mangan's most famous poem, "Dark Rosaleen." Ireland is personified as a beautiful young queen ("Ny" is the feminine equivalent of the masculine "O," as in O'Neill), whose beauty and youth fade in sorrow, while waiting for her land and people to be delivered from the distress the enemy has inflicted upon them. Only masculine strength and sacrifice can again transform the "ghostly hag" into a maiden-queen. Mangan based the poem on a literal translation from the Irish by O'Curry and, although its immediate context relates to a particular historical event, the eighteenth century Jacobite rebellions, it is beyond doubt that the contemporary readers saw it on another level: the pressing need for decisive action, if Ireland's prosperity was to be restored. In a subtle way, very much as in "Dark Rosaleen," the poem establishes a contrast between a glorious past and a rather bleak present carried across by the conditional in line four below:

> Think her not a ghastly hag, too hideous to be seen,
> Call her not unseemly names, our matchless Kathaleen:
> Young she is, and fair she is, and would be crowned a
>   queen,
> Were the king's son at home here with Kathaleen
>   Ny-Houlahan!

The poem contains another major theme—homelessness and wondering—introduced and elaborated upon by the framing effect of the first and last quatrains. The implicit comparison between the Irish and God's chosen people justifies the cause of Ireland's independence and renders distinctly optimistic both the end of the poem and the struggle against Britain.

"THE NAMELESS ONE"

Published in 1849, after Mangan's death, this ballad is often interpreted as the poet's farewell to his country. It is worth noting that it was one of Joyce's favorite poems, and it is not difficult to see why. In the very first stanza, the poet creates a host of images that are distinctly Irish and at the same time transcend the narrow, nationalistic notion of Irishness that Joyce found oppressive: The "song," like the salmon, one of Ireland's ancient symbols, has started its journey to the sea, mature and full of hope. The identity of the singer, his "soul," is no longer to be separated from the "song," his art. The restraining power of history and tradition, language and ideology—the name—means no more. All that matters is the cycle of life itself, encompassing both God (first stanza) and hell (last stanza), birth and death.

OTHER MAJOR WORKS

NONFICTION: *Autobiography*, 1968.

TRANSLATIONS: *Anthologia Germanica = German Anthology: A Series of Translations from the Most Popular of the German Poets*, 1845 (2 volumes); *The Poets and Poetry of Munster: A Selection of Irish Songs by the Poets of the Last Century, with Poetical Translations by James Clarence Mangan*, 1849.

MISCELLANEOUS: *The Prose Writings of James Clarence Mangan*, 1904 (D. J. O'Donoghue, editor); *Prose*, 2002 (2 volumes; Jacques Chuto, editor); *Selected Prose of James Clarence Mangan*, 2004.

BIBLIOGRAPHY

Chuto, Jacques. *James Clarence Mangan: A Bibliography*. Portland, Oreg.: Irish Academic Press, 1999. This bibliography, by an editor of Mangan's poems, lists the works of the poet, his contributions to magazines, as well as works written about him. Contains a index of titles and first lines.

Lloyd, David. *Nationalism and Minor Literature: James Clarence Mangan and the Emergence of Irish Cultural Nationalism*. Berkeley: University of California Press, 1987. Mangan's literary production is examined in terms of its "failure" (in the positive sense of "resistance") to comply with imperial narrative models of cultural development. Focus is on the political and cultural effects of colonialism on Irish nationalist ideology and the emerging Irish aesthetic culture.

MacCarthy, Anne. *James Clarence Mangan, Edward Walsh, and Nineteenth-Century Irish Literature in English*. Lewiston, N.Y.: Edwin Mellen Press, 2000. This study of nineteenth century Irish literature in English compares and contrasts the works of Mangan and Walsh.

Shannon-Mangan, Ellen. *James Clarence Mangan: A Biography*. Dublin: Irish Academic Press, 1996. Excellent, detailed study of Mangan's life and works, relying on extensive use of primary materials. Includes short analyses of Mangan's most significant work.

Welch, Robert. "James Clarence Mangan: 'Apples from the Dead Sea Shore.'" In *Irish Poetry from Moore to Yeats*. Irish Literary Studies 5. Totowa, N.J.: Barnes & Noble, 1980. Examines Mangan's literary achievements within the context of the emerging Irish national literature in English. Welch compares Mangan's Romantic nationalism with works of English and German Romantic poets. The chapter contains stylistic and rhetorical analyses of about twenty original poems, translations, and prose works.

Miglena Ivanova

CHRISTOPHER MARLOWE

Born: Canterbury, England; February 6, 1564
Died: Deptford, England; May 30, 1593

PRINCIPAL POETRY

Hero and Leander, 1598 (completed by George Chapman)

"The Passionate Shepherd to His Love," 1599 (in *The Passionate Pilgrim*)

OTHER LITERARY FORMS

Christopher Marlowe's literary reputation rests primarily on the following plays: *Tamburlaine the Great, Part I* (pr. c. 1587); *Tamburlaine the Great, Part II* (pr. 1587); *The Jew of Malta* (pr. c. 1589); *Edward II* (pr. c. 1592); *Doctor Faustus* (pr. 1588). Two unfinished plays, *Dido, Queen of Carthage* (pr. c. 1586-1587; with Thomas Nashe and the fragmentary *The Massacre at Paris* (pr. 1593), round out his dramatic canon. He produced two important translations: *Elegies* (1595-1600), which treats three books of Ovid's *Amores* (c. 20 B.C.E.; English translation, c. 1597), and *Pharsalia* (1600), which treats Lucan's first book *Bellum civile* (60-65 C.E.; *Pharsalia*, 1614), and was first entered in the Stationers' Register as *Lucan's First Book of the Famous Civil War Betwixt Pompey and Caesar* (1600).

ACHIEVEMENTS

Christopher Marlowe's plays established him as the foremost of the University Wits, a loosely knit group of young men, by reputation generally wild and rakish, that included Thomas Lodge, Thomas Nashe, George Peele, and the older, perhaps less unruly, John Lyly. Their work largely established the nature of the English drama that would reach its apogee in the work of William Shakespeare. Marlowe shares with Thomas Kyd the honor of developing the English conception of tragedy. Marlowe also developed the rather clumsy blank verse of the day into the flexible vehicle of his "mighty line," using it to flesh out his tragic characters as they fell from greatness. He shares the honor of reshaping the dramatically crude chronicle play into the mature and subtle history play. His *Edward II* bears comparison with William Shakespeare's *Richard III* (pr. c. 1592-1593) and anticipates Shakespeare's "Henriad."

Although Marlowe attracted much casual comment among his contemporaries, serious criticism of his work was rare until the nineteenth century. After the Puritan diatribe of T. Beard in *The Theatre of Gods* [sic] *Judgements* (1597) and W. Vaughn's consideration in *The Golden Grove* (1600), no serious criticism appeared until J. Broughton's article, "Of the Dramatic Writers Who Preceded Shakespeare" (1830). Beginning in 1883, with C. H. Herford and A. Wagner's article "The Sources of Tamburlaine," Marlovian criticism grew at an increasing rate. Two critics initiated the very extensive body of modern scholarship that began in the first decade of the twentieth century: Frederick S. Boas with his edition and commentary of the works (1901), and Brooke with an article, "On the Date of the First Edition of Marlowe's *Edward II*," in *Modern Language Notes* (1909). Boas's contribution culminated in the monumental *Marlowe: A Biographical and Critical Study* (1940). Although both writers concentrated on Marlowe's drama, they also began a serious examination of his poetry. From 1910 onward, the volume of criticism has been almost overwhelming.

Marlowe's nondramatic poetry has attracted an impressive, even a disproportionate, amount of critical attention, considering that it consists simply of one lyric poem, known in several versions, and one narrative poem, generally considered to be an 817-line fragment of a longer projected work. Had Marlowe's dramatic work been only middling, it is unlikely that his poetry, excellent as it is, would have been so widely noticed and esteemed. C. F. Tucker Brooke observes in his *The Works of Christopher Marlowe* (1964) that *Hero and Leander*, Marlowe's narrative fragment, was enormously popular with the Elizabethans and that the literature of the period is rich in allusions to the poem. His lyric poem "The Passionate Shepherd to His Love" also enjoyed an early and continuing popularity from its first appearance in *The Passionate Pilgrim* (1599) and *England's Helicon* (1600), two widely circulated collections of English verse. A version of the poem is included in Isaac Walton's *The Compleat Angler: Or, The Contemplative Man's Recreation* (1653).

While most of the criticism bears on concerns other than the poetry, criticism dealing with *Hero and Leander* and, to a lesser degree, with "The Passionate Shepherd to His Love," is more than respectable in quantity. Interest covers many aspects of the poems: the rhetorical and prosodic forms, with their implications for aesthetics and comedic intent; bibliographic matters dealing with publication history, textual variations, and their implications for questions about authorship; mythological bases and sources; possible autobiographical elements; and moral and ethical values, often centering on sexuality and implied homosexuality. The foregoing list is not exhaustive, and any given study is likely to include several of the aspects while using one of them to illuminate one or more of the others. Marlovian criticism boasts the names of many outstanding modern scholars; a sampling would include J. A. Symonds, T. S. Eliot, U. M. Ellis-Fermor, F. S. Tannenbaum, Mario Praz, J. Q. Adams, M. C. Bradbrook, J. Bakeless, L. Kirschbaum, W. W. Greg, Helen Gardner, F. P. Wilson, C. S. Lewis, and Louis L. Martz.

BIOGRAPHY

Biographical interest in Christopher Marlowe has been keen and perhaps too often controversial. Public records are relatively numerous, considering that he was a sixteenth century Englishman who died before he was thirty years old. His baptism, progress through school and university to the M.A. degree, and the details of his death are documented. Contemporary references to Marlowe and his works are likewise plentiful. The variety of interpretation placed upon this evidence, however, is truly astonishing. What is quite clear is that Marlowe was born into a relatively affluent family of

Christopher Marlowe (Hulton Archive/Getty Images)

tradesmen in Canterbury. His father was in the shoe trade, possibly as a shoemaker, possibly as an employer of shoemakers. In any case, in January, 1579, Marlowe entered King's School, an institution operating just beyond Canterbury Cathedral. In December, 1580, he enrolled in Corpus Christi College, Cambridge, on a scholarship. In 1584, Marlowe graduated with a B.A. degree but continued his studies, still on scholarship. Marlowe's attendance was, at least occasionally, irregular, and he was engaged from time to time upon some sort of secret work for the government, the nature of which remains unclear despite much speculation. It involved travel on the Continent; it may have involved spying at home or abroad. When, in 1587, the university determined to withhold the M.A. degree from Marlowe, the Privy Council intervened in the name of the queen and insisted that Marlowe's services to the Crown were sufficient grounds for granting the degree.

Upon leaving Cambridge, Marlowe immediately immersed himself in the political and intellectual life of London, on one hand, in the aristocratic circles of Sir Walter Raleigh and Sir Thomas Walsingham, and on the other, in the bohemianism of the London actors and playwrights. Both groups apparently contributed to the underworld contacts that tavern life and secret government service would suggest. As early as 1588, Robert Greene attacked Marlowe indirectly as an atheist, a charge that reappeared from time to time. In 1589, Marlowe was involved in a brawl with a certain William Bradley that ended with Bradley's death at the hands of one Thomas Watson. Both Marlowe and Watson were jailed temporarily because of the affair, which was finally adjudged to have been a case of self-defense.

By 1592, both *Tamburlaine the Great, Parts I and II*, and *Doctor Faustus* had been produced and published. Meanwhile, Marlowe's reputation as a dangerous fellow had grown. In that year, he had been bound over to keep the peace by a brace of frightened constables, and he appears to have been one of the atheist playwrights attacked in Robert Greene's *Groatsworth of Wit Bought with a Million of Repentance* (1592). On May 12, 1593, Marlowe's fellow University Wit, friend, and former roommate, Thomas Kyd, during or shortly after torture, wrote a letter to the Lord Keeper, Sir John Puckering, accusing Marlowe of ownership of papers, found in Kyd's room, which denied the divinity of Christ.

Whether or not Kyd's confession influenced them, the Privy Council issued a warrant for Marlowe's arrest and ordered him to report to them daily. On May 30, Marlowe spent the day at the Bull Inn in Deptford in the disreputable company of the double-agent Robert Poley and two other possible spies, Nicholas Skeres and Ingram Frizer. The coroner's report indicates that they had walked in the garden during the day and then had eaten supper together. Following a quarrel about the bill, Marlowe is said to have taken Frizer's dagger from his belt and beaten him about the head with it. Frizer managed to grasp Marlowe's arm, reverse the blade, and force it into Marlowe's head. The jury found that the stab wound was the cause of death and declared the death to be instant and accidental.

On the whole, the jury was composed of competent men, the sequence of events plausible, and the jury's conclusion sound. Short, then, of the discovery of more telling evidence, all theories of a plot of premeditated murder against Marlowe must be taken as only more or less interesting conjectures. Perhaps it was inevitable that the facts about a famous man whose life was both colorful and secretive would excite equally colorful speculation about the facts that lie beyond the official records and public accusations.

ANALYSIS

Christopher Marlowe's lyric poem "The Passionate Shepherd to His Love" is known in several versions of varying length. C. F. Tucker Brooke's 1962 reprint of his 1910 edition of Marlowe's works cites the six-stanza version of *England's Helicon*, with variant readings provided in the notes. Frederick S. Boas, in *Christopher Marlowe: A Biographical and Critical Study*, puts the case for holding that only the first four stanzas are certainly Marlowe's. Fredson Bowers, in the second volume of his monumental *The Complete Works of Christopher Marlowe* (1973), offers a "reconstructed" four-stanza version of the original poem printed alongside the six-stanza version of *England's Helicon*. All versions provide a delightful and innocuous exercise in

the pastoral tradition of happy innocent shepherds sporting in a bucolic setting. Simply put, a lover outlines for his sweetheart the beauties and pleasures she can expect if she will live with him and be his love. Nature and the rejoicing shepherds will provide the pair with entertainment, clothing, shelter, and all things fitting to an amorous paradise.

"THE PASSIONATE SHEPHERD TO HIS LOVE"

The stanza is a simple quatrain rhyming in couplets. While it is a fine example of Elizabethan taste for decoration and is very pleasing to the ear, it presents nothing especially clever in its prosody. A few of the couplets are fresh enough in their rhymes, such as "falls/ madrigalls," "kirtle/ Mirtle," and "buds/ studs," but the rest are common enough. The alliteration falls short of being heavy-handed, and it achieves neither clearness nor subtlety. The poem's appeal, then, seems to lie mostly in its evocation of young love playing against an idealized background, its simple language and prosody forming part of its overt innocence.

Sir Walter Ralegh's famous response, "The Nymph's Reply to the Shepherd," also published in *England's Helicon*, sets all the cynicism associated with the carpe diem poetry of a John Donne or an Andrew Marvell against Marlowe's pose of innocence. Ralegh's shepherdess argues that the world and love are too old to allow her to be seduced by "pretty pleasures." She speaks of aging, of the cold of winter, of the sweet appearance that hides bitterness and approaching death. She scorns his offers of beauty, shelter, and love as things that decay and rot. Were youth, love, and joy eternal, and old age well provided for, then she might love. Both poems are set-pieces and imply nothing except that both poets were makers working within established traditions. The innocence of Marlowe's poem argues nothing about his own personality and much about his ability to project himself imaginatively into a character and a situation. In doing this, he produced a gem, and that is enough.

HERO AND LEANDER

In contrast to the simple, single-leveled "The Passionate Shepherd to His Love," *Hero and Leander* is a more complex, more sophisticated poem. Whatever ultimate plans Marlowe may have had for the completed poem, the two completed sestiads are in the comic mode as they portray the fumbling yearnings and actions of two adolescents faced with passions with which they are totally unprepared to deal. The story of young love, then, is constantly undercut with one sort of comedy or another.

Perhaps the easiest clues to Marlowe's comic intention lie in his choice of epic style and heroic couplets, both of which lend themselves to witty parody because they are traditionally used seriously. The epic tradition allows Marlowe to pay his lovers elaborate, and obviously exaggerated, compliments through the use of epic similes and through comparison with the classical tales of gods and heroes. The heroic couplet allows him to emphasize the fun with variations of the meter and with comic rhymes, generally feminine ones.

The retelling of the famous tale of two ill-fated lovers—whose trysts require Leander to swim across the Hellespont to visit Hero in her tower—begins soberly enough, as a mock-epic should. By the ninth line, however, Marlowe begins a description of Hero's garments that is wildly ornate and exaggerated in style. Her dress, for example, is lined with purple and studded with golden stars; the sleeves are green and are embroidered with a scene of Venus, naked, viewing the slain and bloody Adonis; her veil reaches to the ground and is so realistically decorated with artificial vegetation that men mistake her breath for the odor of flowers and bees search it for honey. The picture, thus far, could pass as an example of Elizabethan taste for the gaudy, and becomes clearly comic only in retrospect.

The twenty-fifth line, however, presents a figure that sets the anticlimactic tone informing the whole piece. Hero's necklace is described as a chain of ordinary pebbles that the beauty of her neck makes shine as diamonds. Later on, her naked beauty causes an artificial dawn in her bedchamber, to Leander's delight. The improbabilities are piled on thickly: Her hands are not subject to burning because sun and wind alike delight in them as playthings; sparrows perch in her shell buskins; Cupid could not help mistaking her for his mother, Venus; and Nature itself resented having been plundered of its rightful beauty by this slip of a girl. Marlowe points up the comedy of the Cupid passage with a feminine rhyme: "But this is true, so like was one the other,/ As he imagined Hero was his mother." He

signs the comic intent of the Nature passage with an outrageous conceit and compliment: "Therefore in sign of her treasure suffered wrack,/ Since Hero's time, hath half the world been black." Throughout the two sestiads, similar tactics are employed, including much additional use of comic feminine rhyme (Morpheus/ visit us, cunning/ running, furious/ Prometheus, kist him/ mist him, and yv'ry skin/ lively in) and mocking versions of the epic simile.

The compelling argument for Marlowe's comedic intent, however, lies in this treatment of situation, theme, and character. Boas reflects a view commonly held by critics at the turn of the twentieth century when he argues that Marlowe's purpose was to tell the stories of the lovers, working in as much mythology as possible. He does not see the comedy as anything but incidental, and congratulates Marlowe on rescuing the grossness of Ovidian comedy with "delicate humor." Brooke, also an early twentieth century Marlovian, regards *Hero and Leander* as an essentially original work to be judged independently of George Chapman's continuation of the poem. Brooke treats the poem as an extended example of masterful heroic verse with no hint that such verse could be used here as an adjunct of comedy.

The French critic Michel Poirier comes nearer to Marlowe's comedic intent in his biography *Christopher Marlowe* (1951, 1968), in which he describes the poem as belonging to the genre of Renaissance hedonism. He sees the poem as a "hymn to sensuality, tastefully done." He too sees the poem as erotic, but argues that it avoids equally ancient crudeness and the rough humor of the medieval fabliaux. Philip Henderson's essay "Christopher Marlowe" (1966) points up the by-then-dominant view by observing that *Hero and Leander* is not only a parody but also a very mischievous one, written by a poet who is so disengaged from his poem that he is able to treat it wittily and with a certain cynicism. John Ingram in *Christopher Marlowe and His Associates* (1970) harks back to an earlier view in claiming that no other Elizabethan poem equals it for purity and beauty. He notes nothing of the ironist at work.

A. L. Rowse, an ingenious if not always convincing literary historian and critic, sees *Hero and Leander*, in

Christopher Marlowe: His Life and Work (1964), as a sort of rival piece to Shakespeare's *Venus and Adonis*. He goes so far as to suggest that Marlowe and Shakespeare read their poems to each other in a sort of combat of wit. However that may be, Rowse is probably right in seeing the poem as being carefully controlled, in contrast to the view, well-represented by Boas, that the poem is structurally a mere jumble. Rowse sees the poem as organically unified by the careful playing off of this mode and that technique against a variety of others.

In his essay "Marlowe's Humor," included in his most useful book *Marlowe: A Collection of Critical Essays* (1964), Clifford Leech rejects earlier criticism holding that the comic passages were the work of other writers and pits C. S. Lewis's denial, in his *English Literature in the Sixteenth Century* (1954), that *Hero and Leander* contains any humor at all against T. S. Eliot's assertion in *Selected Essays* (1950-1972) that Marlowe was at his best when writing "savage comic humor." Leech's position is that the poem is dominated by a humor at once gentle and delighting, not to say sly. He supports his position with a shrewd analysis of the subtle effects of tone and verse form. Louis L. Martz, in *Hero and Leander: A Fascimile of the First Edition, London, 1598* (1972), also sees Marlowe's tone as comic and as conveyed through the couplet, and he characterizes the poem as being carefully structured as a triptych, with the Mercury fable, usually viewed as a digression, as the central picture, flanked by tales depicting mortal love. He sees Marlowe's digression as intentional and Ovidian. Martz, as a whole, comes down firmly on the side of those who see the poem as a thoroughgoing comedy.

Philip Henderson keeps to the comedic interpretation but also brings boldly to the fore a factor in the story long recognized but generally treated as minor, incidental, and otherwise unaccountable—that of homosexuality as a theme. In *Christopher Marlowe* (second edition, 1974), he argues that the passage describing Leander's body is "rapturous," but that the element is reduced to farce by Leander's encounter with Neptune as he swims the Hellespont. At the same time, Henderson firmly denies that Rowse's description of Marlowe as clearly homosexual has any basis in fact.

On balance, Henderson concludes that the critics' urge to find irony and sensational undertones obscures recognition of the beauty properly belonging to *Hero and Leander*, and he notes further that the insistence upon seeing comedy throughout Marlowe's work is a modern one. William Keach, tracing Marlowe's intentions in "Marlowe's Hero as 'Venus' Nun" (*English Literary Renaissance*, Winter, 1972), argues that Marlowe is largely indebted for the "subtleties and complexities" of his poem to hints from his fifth century Greek source, Musaeus. Keach sees both poets as ironists and argues that Hero's activities as a priestess of love who is puritanically virginal are essentially silly.

John Mills, in his study "The Courtship Ritual of Hero and Leander" (*English Literary Renaissance*, Winter, 1972), sees Hero at the opening as a compound of innocence and sexuality, with all the confusions that such a compound can make, both in her own mind and in those of men who observe her. Mills's interest lies, however, not so much in this condition itself as in the web of classical elements and allusions in which it is contained. He argues, in effect, that the poem depends upon an overblown, stereotypical, and mannered attitude toward romantic sex that he compares to Vladimir Nabokov's theory of "poshlust." Mills concludes that Marlowe's "poshlustian comedy" arises out of the actions being played out in a physical and material world of sexuality in such terms that Hero and Leander, and innocent readers, are persuaded that their activities are really spiritual. In another essay, "Sexual Discovery and Renaissance Morality in Marlowe's 'Hero and Leander'" (*Studies in English Literature, 1500-1900*, XII, 1972), published immediately after that of Mills, William P. Walsh argues that Marlowe is ironic in basing the story on love at first sight and making his characters slaves of their irrational passion. His notion is that the lovers themselves, not sexuality, are the objects of humorous comment with which they are not entirely out of sympathy. His development of the theme is detailed and astute, and he points out, in discussing the invented myth of the Destinies' love affair with Mercury, the generally overlooked argument that Marlowe makes for reproduction as the true object of sex, as against pleasure for its own sake. Walsh suggests that the inability of Hero and Leander to see beyond their dream of a sexual paradise at once positions them for the eventual tragic ending traditional to their story, yet keeps them reduced to comic stature in Marlowe's portion of the poem.

In writing *Hero and Leander*, then, Marlowe displayed ingenuity and erudition by telling an ironically comic tale of the mutual wooing and seduction of a pair of inexperienced but lusty young lovers. The telling is intricately and objectively organized and describes a rite of passage that is neither sentimentalized nor especially brutalized. The result is a highly skilled tour de force in the tradition of the Elizabethan maker, cynical enough, perhaps, but confessional or autobiographical only tangentially, if at all. Coupled with "The Passionate Shepherd to His Love," *Hero and Leander* establishes Marlowe's claim to a high place in the select company of those British poets who have produced a slender but superior body of lyric poetry.

OTHER MAJOR WORKS

PLAYS: *Dido, Queen of Carthage*, pr. c. 1586-1587 (with Thomas Nashe); *Tamburlaine the Great, Part I*, pr. c. 1587 (commonly known as *Tamburlaine*); *Tamburlaine the Great, Part II*, pr. 1587; *Doctor Faustus*, pr. c. 1588; *The Jew of Malta*, pr. c. 1589; *Edward II*, pr. c. 1592; *The Massacre at Paris*, pr. 1593; *Complete Plays*, pb. 1963.

TRANSLATIONS: *Elegies*, 1595-1600 (of Ovid's *Amores*); *Pharsalia*, 1600 (of Lucan's *Bellum civile*).

MISCELLANEOUS: *The Works of Christopher Marlowe*, 1910, 1962 (C. F. Tucker Brooke, editor); *The Works and Life of Christopher Marlowe*, 1930-1933, 1966 (R. H. Case, editor); *The Complete Works of Christopher Marlowe*, 1973 (Fredson Bowers, editor).

BIBLIOGRAPHY

Bloom, Harold, ed. *Christopher Marlowe: Modern Critical Views*. New York: Chelsea House, 1986. This volume consists of thirteen selections, mainly excerpts of previously published books that are landmarks in Marlowe criticism. The bibliography at the end of the volume includes most of the major critical studies of Marlowe.

Blumenfeld, Samuel L. *The Marlowe-Shakespeare Connection: A New Study of the Authorship Question*. Jefferson, N.C.: McFarland, 2008. Blumenfeld argues that Marlowe faked his death and continued writing plays and poetry as William Shakespeare.

Downie, J. A., and J. T. Parnell. *Constructing Christopher Marlowe*. New York: Cambridge University Press, 2000. This scholarly study contains essays on Marlowe's life and works. Includes bibliography and index.

Grantley, Darryll, and Peter Roberts, eds. *Christopher Marlowe and English Renaissance Culture*. Aldershot, Hants, England: Ashgate, 1999. This collection of essays covers topics such as Marlowe and atheism and the staging of his plays and provides in-depth analysis of most of his plays. Bibliography and index.

Hopkins, Lisa. *Christopher Marlowe: A Literary Life*. New York: Palgrave, 2000. A study of Marlowe's career and what is known of his life. Hopkins focuses on Marlowe's skepticism toward colonialism, family, and religion.

Nicholl, Charles. *The Reckoning: The Murder of Christopher Marlowe*. New York: Harcourt Brace, 1992. Nicholl examines the Marlowe's life, as well as the circumstances of his death.

Riggs, David. *The World of Christopher Marlowe*. New York: Henry Holt, 2005. This rich study of the poet/playwright, including both biography and analysis of Marlowe's works, is an excellent source of information about Marlowe's historical and social context.

Simkin, Stevie. *A Preface to Marlowe*. New York: Longman, 2000. Provides comprehensive and full analysis of all Marlowe's dramatic and non-dramatic works, brings the texts to life, and emphasizes the performance aspects of the texts. A controversial and challenging reading that reopens debates about Marlowe's status as a radical figure and as a subversive playwright. Bibliographical references and index.

Trow, M. J., and Taliesin Trow. *Who Killed Kit Marlowe? A Contract to Murder in Elizabethan England*. Stroud, England: Sutton, 2001. This discussion focuses on Marlowe's mystery-shrouded death, providing both the evidence that is available and the many theories that exist. Bibliography and index.

B. G. Knepper

ANDREW MARVELL

Born: Winestead-in-Holderness, Yorkshire, England;
    March 31, 1621
Died: London, England; August 16, 1678

PRINCIPAL POETRY

*The First Anniversary of the Government Under
    His Highness the Lord Protector*, 1655
Miscellaneous Poems, 1681
Complete Poetry, 1968

OTHER LITERARY FORMS

In 1672, with the publication of *The Rehearsal Transpros'd*, Andrew Marvell (MAWR-vuhl) became a pamphleteer. In this animadversion on the works of Samuel Parker, Marvell vigorously supported King Charles II's stand in favor of religious toleration. No other work by Marvell was so widely received in his lifetime as this urbane, witty, slashing satire. According to Marvell's contemporary Gilbert Burnet, "From the King down to the tradesman, his books were read with great pleasure." Parker's counterattack quickly engendered Marvell's second pamphlet, *The Rehearsal Transpros'd: The Second Part* (1673). *Mr. Smirke: Or, The Divine in Mode* (1676), was Marvell's defense of Herbert Croft, the bishop of Hereford, against Francis Turner's pamphlet attack. His next pamphlet, *An Account of the Growth of Popery and Arbitrary Government in England* (1677), resulted in the government's offering a reward for the identity of the author. *Remarks upon a Late Disingenuous Discourse* was published posthumously in 1678. Some three hundred letters are also extant and available in Margoliouth's edition, as well as in those of Captain Edward Thompson and Alexander B. Grosart.

ACHIEVEMENTS

In his own century and for some time afterward, Andrew Marvell's reputation rested much more on his prose pamphlets, a few political poems, and his political activities, than on his achievement as a lyric poet. Most of his poems, including all the lyrics, remained unpublished until the posthumous edition of 1681. By

then the Metaphysical mode was no longer in fashion, and the book of Marvell's poems seems to have been desired more for its excellent engraved portrait of the politician and pamphleteer than for anything else. Appreciation of Marvell's poetry was increased by Charles Lamb's essay of 1818, but it remained sporadic until after the publication of T. S. Eliot's essay on the occasion of the tercentenary of Marvell's birth in 1921. Except for a quantity of imitations of his verse satires, some of which were attributed to him, his influence on other poets was slight. By far his widest poetic audience is in the present day. He has had a modest influence on some twentieth century writers, such as Marianne Moore.

Today Marvell is recognized as a lyric poet of the first rank, although how uniformly excellent his poems are, individually or collectively, remains a subject of debate. Certainly the quality is somewhat irregular. Nevertheless, with a rather small corpus he has been awarded at least three apt distinctions. That three-quarters of his work is in eight-syllable form and much of it is brilliant has earned him the title master of the octosyllabic. A few fine poems on a difficult subject have caused him to be called Cromwell's poet. Finally, while his work includes civic, pastoral, and georgic material, he is, more than any other poet in English, the garden poet.

BIOGRAPHY

Andrew Marvell was born on March 31, 1621, at Winestead-in-Holderness, Yorkshire. He was the fourth child and only surviving son of Andrew Marvell, Sr., a clergyman. In late 1624, the Reverend Marvell became lecturer at Holy Trinity Church in Hull, to which the family moved. The poet grew up there and was for the rest of his life associated with Hull, representing the city in Parliament for the last eighteen years of his life. On December 14, 1633, the young Marvell entered Trinity College, Cambridge. In 1637, Marvell was converted by Jesuits and ran away to London, whence his father retrieved him and returned him to Cambridge. Sometime in 1641, Marvell left Cambridge, having received the B.A. degree but without completing the requirements for the M.A.

Marvell may then have spent some time working in

Andrew Marvell (Library of Congress)

the commercial house of his brother-in-law, Edmund Popple, in Hull. His activities during the turbulent 1640's are not well recorded, but it is known that during that period he spent four years abroad, learning Dutch, French, Italian, and Spanish. He studied the gentlemanly art of fencing in Spain, and in Rome, he paid a visit to the impoverished English Catholic priest, Flecknoe, whom John Dryden would make the butt of a satiric poem. Engaged in this Grand Tour, Marvell seems to have avoided any direct part in the English Civil War. Marvell returned to England in the late 1640's, publishing a congratulatory poem (probably written in 1647) for a volume of Richard Lovelace's verse in 1649, and contributing one poem to a volume lamenting the death of the young Lord Hastings in June, 1649. From 1650 to 1652, Marvell was tutor to Mary Fairfax, daughter of the parliamentary general, Lord Fairfax, whose resignation in June, 1650, left Cromwell dominant. That same month, Marvell must have composed "An Horatian Ode upon Cromwell's

Return from Ireland," in which he applauds Cromwell's activities up to that point and anticipates his success in the coming campaign against the Scots. Because the poem also shows great sympathy and regard for the late King Charles in the brief passage dealing with his execution, a good deal of critical attention has been paid to the question of whether Marvell's praise of Cromwell is genuine, ironic, or intended to create an image toward which it might be hoped that the real Cromwell would gravitate. Marvell is elsewhere so prone to see more than one side of a question that it does not really seem remarkable that he may have recognized good qualities in both King Charles and Cromwell. "Upon Appleton House" and "Upon the Hill and Grove at Bill-borow," which describe two Fairfax estates, must be presumed to date from Marvell's days with the Fairfaxes; it is likely that a number of the lyrics, including "The Garden" and the Mower poems, also date from that period.

In 1653, Marvell left the Fairfax employ and sought, through John Milton, a position with the Commonwealth government. When his association with Milton began is uncertain, but it is known that they became and remained very close friends. In September, 1657, Marvell received a government post, becoming Latin Secretary, sharing (with Milton) responsibility for correspondence with foreign governments. He retained this post until the dissolution of the Commonwealth government. During the Cromwell years, Marvell wrote a number of poems in praise of Cromwell. These include "An Horatian Ode upon Cromwell's Return from Ireland," *The First Anniversary of the Government Under His Highness the Lord Protector*, 1655, and "A Poem upon the Death of His Late Highness the Lord Protector." Although Cromwell and his son, and perhaps close associates, presumably saw these poems, they seem not to have been widely circulated. Only *The First Anniversary of the Government Under His Highness the Lord Protector* was printed, and that anonymously.

In 1659, the Corporation of Hull chose Marvell to represent them in Parliament. He remained a member for the rest of his life, being twice reelected. He seems to have made the transition to the Restoration of Charles II with relative ease, and from his position in Parliament joined other friends of Milton in protecting that poet from serious harm under the new regime. During this period Marvell's satiric talents blossomed. His satiric verse included three "advice to a painter" poems parodying a poem by Edmund Waller and lampooning various influential persons and their policies. More important by far were his prose pamphlets, especially the first, *The Rehearsal Transpros'd*. This was an attack on the pamphlets of Samuel Parker, a rising Church of England divine, who strongly supported conformity and had tangled in print with the nonconformists, especially John Owen. The question of toleration versus conformity was a very important one in the politics of 1672, with Charles II, for his own reasons, trying to put through a policy of toleration. Marvell's powerful and witty book quickly went through multiple editions. Parker strongly counterattacked with a new pamphlet, causing Marvell (despite an anonymous threat to cut his throat) to reply with *The Rehearsal Transpros'd: The Second Part*. Parker did not reply further. Marvell's last three pamphlets are of considerably less importance. *Mr. Smirke: Or, The Divine in Mode* used with less success and for a less crucial cause the techniques of the two parts of *The Rehearsal Transpros'd*. Next, *An Account of the Growth of Popery and Arbitrary Government in England* evoked the government offer of a reward for the name of the author, who died before action was taken on an informer's report. The title of this work precisely indicates the concerns that Marvell voiced in it, suggesting that leading government figures were involved in a plot to make England Catholic again. By 1674, Marvell himself was involved in clandestine activities as a member of a pro-Dutch "fifth column," apparently operating under the name of "Mr. Thomas" and making secret trips to Holland. Marvell's death, on August 16, 1678, was the result of his physician's treatment of a fever and not, as was suspected by some, a political murder. His last pamphlet, *Remarks upon a Late Disingenuous Discourse* is his least readable work and is of little importance.

ANALYSIS

Andrew Marvell is firmly established today in the ranks of the Metaphysical poets, and there is no question that much of his work clearly displays the qualities appropriate to such a position. He reveals a kinship with the Metaphysical poets through his ingenious use of extended logic, even when dealing with emotions; his yoking of very dissimilar things, of the mundane (even profane) with the sublime, of large with small and far with near; and his analytic quality. His use of puns, often woven into intricate groups, may be added to the list. Like John Donne and the other Metaphysical poets, Marvell shapes his rhythm with careful attention to his meaning. Marvell's admiration for Donne shows not only in having written some strongly Donne-like poetry ("On a Drop of Dew," "Young Love," and parts of "Upon Appleton House," for example), but also in his gratuitously full use of one of Donne's poems in a pamphlet written late in Marvell's life. It might be added that Marvell's prose works, especially his most successful, show the same Metaphysical qualities.

Although Donne's best-known poetry (as well as Marvell's most Donne-like work) resembles puzzles from which attentive reading gradually extracts greater clarity, a similar approach to Marvell's best and most "Marvellian" passages (for example, "a green thought in a green Shade") causes them not to become more clear so much as more dazzling. Marvell has been called "many-sided," "ambiguous," "amphibian," "elusive," and "inconclusive." He is. He has been said to have a vision that is "complex," "double," or "ironic." He does.

Marvell's work often shows a remarkable ability to make opposites interdependent, to create a *concordia discors*. Such is the relationship of Cromwell and King Charles in "An Horatian Ode upon Cromwell's Return from Ireland," and of retirement and action in "Upon Appleton House" and "The Garden." Sometimes, no less remarkably, he achieves moments of what can only be called "fusion," as in the "annihilation of all that's made" in "The Garden," or in the last few lines of "To His Coy Mistress." He will at times surprisingly mix levity and gravity, as in "To His Coy Mistress" and parts of "Upon Appleton House." His use of qualifiers is unusual ("none, *I think*," or "*If* these the times").

Marvell employed decasyllabics for his last two Cromwell poems, inventing a stanza combining lines of eight and six syllables for the first. Three fourths of his work was in octosyllabics, however, and he has been rightly called the "master of the octosyllabic."

"To His Coy Mistress"

Certainly the most widely anthologized and best known of Marvell's poems is "To His Coy Mistress." It is not only a seduction poem, but also a deduction poem, in which the theme of carpe diem is presented as a syllogism: (1) If there were world enough and time, the lady's coyness would not be a crime; (2) There is not world enough and time; (3) therefore, this coyness may or may not be a crime. Marvell must have been aware that his poem depended on flawed logic; he may have meant it to be ironically typical of the desperate reasoning employed by would-be seducers.

In the first section of the poem, the speaker describes the vast amounts of time ("An age at least to every part") and space (from the Ganges to the Humber) he would devote to his love if he could. This apparently gracious statement of patience is then juxtaposed with the striking image of "Time's winged chariot hurrying near" and the resultant "Deserts of vast eternity." "Deserts," meaning "unpeopled places," is emphasized by the shift of the stress to the first syllable of the line. There follows the arresting depiction of the drawbacks of postmortem chastity, with worms "trying" the lady's "long-preserved virginity," as her "quaint honor" turns to dust.

Imagery of corruption was not unusual in carpe diem poems, and it also occurs (the memento mori theme) in visual arts of the period; Marvell's lines are, however, remarkably explicit and must have been devised to shock and disgust. The passage represents, as Rosalie Colie notes in *My Ecchoing Song* (1970), "sound psychology" in frightening the lady into the comfort of her lover's arms, an event that the next two lines suggest may indeed have occurred at this point, as the speaker rescues himself from the danger of excessive morbidity with the urbanely ironic comment, "The grave's a fine and private place,/ But none, I think, do there embrace." This makes the transition to the last section of the poem, wherein the speaker, having shown that however limitless time and space may intrinsically be, they are to mortals very limited, offers his solution. The answer is to take energetic action. The formerly coy mistress, now described (either in hope or in fact) as having a "willing soul" with "instant fires," is invited to join the speaker in "one ball" of strength and sweetness, which will tear "thorough the iron gates of life." This third section of the poem is an addition not typical of carpe diem poems, which usually suggest rather than delineate the consummation. The amorous couple, the speaker indicates, should enthusiastically embrace the inevitable and each other. Like the elder Fairfaxes in "Upon Appleton House," they should "make Destiny their choice" and devour time rather than waiting for time to consume them. In its three sections, "To His Coy Mistress" presents first a cheerful and generous offering of limitless time and space, then a chilling reminder that human life is very limited, and finally a frenzied but extraordinarily powerful invitation to break through and transcend all limits.

"The Garden"

If "To His Coy Mistress" makes the case for action versus hesitation, "The Garden," the best-known hortensial work of the "garden poet," considers the question of action versus contemplation. Like much of Marvell's work, it employs a rich texture of wordplay and classical and Christian allusions. It is a retirement poem, in which the speaker begins by celebrating his withdrawal from the busy world of human endeavor. This theme is one rich in tradition, and would have been attractive during the uncertain and dangerous times in which Marvell lived. In this poem, however, the speaker retires not merely from the world of men, but, in a moment of ultimate retirement, from the world of material things. As the poet contemplates the garden, his mind and his soul momentarily transcend the material plane.

In the first stanza, the speaker comments on the folly of seeking human glory. Men "vainly" ("from vanity," and also "in vain") "amaze" themselves (surprise themselves/trap themselves in a maze) in their efforts to achieve honors (represented by the palm, oak, and bay leaves used in classical victors' wreaths). Even the best such victory represents success in only one area of endeavor, for which the victor receives the decoration of a wreath woven from a single species, a wreath that in its singleness "upbraids" (braids up/rebukes) his "toyles" (coils of hair/efforts). In contrast, repose is rewarded by "all flowers and all trees." Addressing Quiet and Innocence personified, the speaker uses a typically Marvellian qualifier when he says that their sacred plants "if here below,/ Only among the plants will grow," suggesting that quiet and innocence may be really unobtainable on Earth. The solitude experienced by the lone visitor among the plants of the garden is nevertheless worth seeking, for, in comparison, "Society is all but rude"—society is nearly "coarse," or (an inversion and a pun) society is almost "rustic." The next three stanzas describe the physical, sensual values that the garden offers in contrast to those of the world. As the "society" of the garden is superior to that of men, so the sensuality of the garden is more intense than that of men: "No white or red was ever seen/ So amorous as this lovely green" (the colors of fleshly passion are less "amorous" than the green of the garden), and the beauties of the trees exceed those of any woman. The gods Apollo and Pan knew this, the speaker says, since they pursued the nymphs Daphne and Syrinx, not for their womanly charms, but in order to obtain their more desirable dendritic forms.

In the fifth stanza, the speaker reaches a height of sensual ecstasy as the various garden fruits literally thrust themselves on him, in what Rosalie Colie rightly calls a "climactic experience." It is powerfully sexual, yet the speaker is alone and in the garden, as Adam once was in Eden. And then the speaker, "stumbling" and "Insnared," falls, reminding the reader of the Fall in Eden. Marvell's speaker, however, is still alone and still—indeed, more than ever—in the garden. The next two stanzas describe what is occurring "Meanwhile" on the mental and spiritual planes. The mind withdraws from the lesser pleasures of the body to seek its own kind of happiness. Within the mind, an interior paradise, are the images of all things in the physical world, just as the sea was thought to contain creatures corresponding to all terrestrial species. Yet the mind, unlike the sea, can create, imaginatively, "Far other worlds and other seas," transcending the mundane, and "Annihilating all that's made/ To a green thought in a green shade," an image that R. I. V. Hodge in *Foreshortened Time* (1978) calls "arguably the most intriguing image

in Marvell's poetry or in the whole of the seventeenth century." Many explications have been offered for this couplet; the central notion seems to be that through the action of the mind in creating the far other worlds and seas, the physical world ("all that's made") is compacted, or by contrast appears to be compacted, into a single thought. It is, however, a "green" thought—a living, fertile thought that is the source, through the action of the mind, of the transcendent worlds and seas. Indeed, perhaps the thinker himself has almost been annihilated; "in a green shade" could indicate not only that the thinker is shaded by the trees, but also that he is (for the moment) a shade, an insubstantial shadow of his physical self. The green thought is, perhaps, the Platonic pure idea of garden from which all gardens derive. It could be suggested that this is the true garden of the poem.

In stanza 7, the soul leaves the body in a flight indicative of its later, final flight to heaven. In the next stanza, the garden is compared explicitly to Eden—not merely Eden before the Fall, but Eden before Eve. Three times, in successive couplets, the speaker states that Paradise enjoyed alone is preferable to Paradise shared. Such praise of solitude can hardly be exceeded, even in the considerable Christian literature on the subject, and perhaps Marvell, relying on his readers' knowledge that Adam had after all requested Eve's company, expected his readers to identify this stanza as a momentary effusion, not shared by the poet himself, on the part of the poem's persona. The reader is reminded, at least, that mortals in the fallen world can only approximate paradisical ecstasy, not achieve it, until they leave this world for a better one. The speaker, now quite recalled from his ecstasy, observes "this dial new." The term may indicate a literal floral sundial, in which small plots of different plants marked the hours around a circle; it clearly and more importantly indicates the entire renewed postlapsarian world, under the mercy of God the "skillful gardener," who provides the "milder sun" (the Son, Christ, God's mercy). The bee, who is industrious rather than contemplative, "computes its time [thyme] as well as we!" This is a typically Marvellian paradox. The bee's industry is reminiscent of the negatively viewed "incessant labors" of the men in the first stanza; the bee, however, is performing wholesome activity in the garden, reckoned with flowers. The situation is analogous to that of the speaker in stanza 5 who fell, but did not Fall, remaining in the garden.

The poem's persona at first rejected the world of action for the garden's solitude and the contemplative exercise thereby made possible. Contemplation has led to physical, then to mental, then to spiritual ecstasy, but the ecstatic moment is limited because the speaker, dwelling in a world that remains thoroughly fallen, is not yet "prepared for longer flight." Refreshed by his experience and noting that the "dial" is *new*, the speaker can accept the action of the bee and recognize action, as well as contemplation, as an appropriate part of human existence.

"Upon Appleton House"

Another poem dealing with the question of withdrawal versus action is "Upon Appleton House," which clearly raises the issue of involvement in the English Civil War and subsequent disturbances. The poem falls into two halves, each depicting both action and retirement, and builds toward a resolution in the form of Lord Fairfax's daughter Mary, who was under Marvell's tutelage. A genre of the time was the "country house" poem, in which a country estate was described, and its inhabitants and their way of life thereby praised. "Upon Appleton House" begins in this manner, with the first nine stanzas devoted to the house itself. Employing a variety of conceits, Marvell finds the modest size and decoration of the structure preferable to the overblown grandeur of other houses. It is on a human scale, with "short but admirable Lines" that "In ev'ry Figure equal Man." Nevertheless, it is less modest than its owner, Lord Fairfax. When he arrives, the house sweats, and from its square hall sprouts a "Spherical" cupola, outdoing the proverbially impossible task of squaring the circle.

A source of building material for the house was the ancient nunnery whose ruins were still evident, wherein had dwelt the nuns whose order had in former times owned the estate. By recounting a historical episode connected with the nunnery, Marvell shows how it is also a source of the estate's present occupants. An ancestral Fairfax had wooed the "blooming Virgin" Isabel Thwaites, "Fair beyond measure" and an heiress.

She was induced to enter the nunnery at Appleton, from which she could ultimately be extracted only by a Fairfacian raid. This tale, told in stanzas 11 to 35, falls into two distinct parts. The first (stanzas 11 to 28) is essentially a nun's eloquent invitation to Isabel to withdraw to the secluded life of the cloister. The joys of this "holy leisure," behind walls that "restrain the World without," are attractively and enthusiastically described, though Marvell would not wish to portray otherwise so Catholic an institution. The passage wherein Isabel is compared to the Virgin Mary, and the later picture of the nuns "in bed,/ As pearls together billeted,/ All night embracing arm in arm," may be meant to raise doubts in the reader's mind that would be confirmed when he is told that "The nuns smooth tongue has suckt her in." After debating what to do, the betrothed Fairfax decides to remove her from the nunnery by force. In a rather burlesque episode, the nuns, whose "loud'st cannon were their lungs," are dispossessed of their prize and, in the next stanza, which flashes forward to the Dissolution, of their nunnery.

Action in this case has been far superior to withdrawal. It leads ultimately, however, to another withdrawal, that of Sir Thomas Fairfax, son of the celebrated couple. After a heroic military career, he retired to Appleton House, but the flower beds there, which he shaped like the bastions of a fort, show that he was incapable of retiring fully. Stanzas 36 to 40 describe the flower-fort, wherein flower-cannons discharge salutes of scent and the bee stands sentinel. There follows (stanzas 41 to 45) a lamentation by the poet over the present unhappy state of England, "The garden of the world ere while," and praise of Fairfax, "Who, had it pleasèd him and God," could have prevented it. In this first half of the poem, then, Marvell has first described the house as an illustration of the greatness of its owner, then shown the virtue of action over withdrawal, then indicated that a man of great action can never fully retire. Finally, he has shown regretful acceptance of Fairfax's retirement, with the clear statement that England suffers without ameliorative action on someone's part. In the second half of the poem, the same ideas will be reiterated and enhanced, except in the last part, the focus will be not on Fairfax but on his daughter Mary ("Maria"), whose embodiment of the values of retirement and action will effect a resolution.

From the flower fort, the speaker can look down over the meadow (stanzas 46 to 60) onto the public world of action. It is a world capable of topsy-turvy, this "Abyss" of a meadow, from which it is a wonder that men rise alive. Men (seen from the hill) look like grasshoppers, but grasshoppers (perched on the tall grass) "are Gyants there." Cows look like beauty spots or fleas, and when the land is flooded, "Boats can over bridges sail" and "Fishes do the stables scale." It is a dangerous world, where the Mowers "massacre the grass," which is very tall, and the rail (humbly close to the ground) is accidentally killed: "Lowness is unsafe as hight,/ And chance o'retakes what scapeth spight." The earlier lamentation over England's condition in stanzas 41 to 43 invites the reader, if invitation were needed, to read this section as an allegory of England, although it may be carrying the allegory too far to see the hapless rail as Charles I, as has been suggested. The mowers who cause the carnage, leaving the field like a battlefield "quilted ore" with piles of hay that look like bodies, are not evil. As they dance in triumph, their smell is fragrant, and their kisses are as sweet as the hay. Marvell compares the meadow at the outset with stage scenery, constantly changing. Describing a series of scenes as the hay is harvested and piled and the cattle set loose in the field to crop the last few inches of grass, he ends with a flood. The flood is caused by the opening of sluices up-river, but the reader is meant to think of the biblical Flood.

Taking refuge from the drowned world, the speaker "imbarks" (embarks/encloses in bark) himself in the "green, yet growing ark" of an adjacent wood. The trees are as tightly woven together as are the families of Fairfax and Vere (Fairfax's wife's family). From without, the wood seems absolutely solid, but inside it is "passable" and "loose." The nightingale, a bird of solitude, sings here, and "highest oakes stoop down to hear,/ And listning elders prick the ear." The nightingale may represent Mary Fairfax, twelve years old when Marvell became her tutor, in which case the "Elders" would be her parents. At any rate, while the song of solitude is attractive, the "Sadder" sound of the stockdoves, whose necks bear "Nuptial Rings," is more

pleasing. This indication, even within the wood, that private withdrawal may not be desirable, prepares for the later part of the poem, when Mary herself appears. In a lengthy section very reminiscent of "The Garden," the speaker revels in the delights and the security of the wood, a place "where the world no certain shot/ Can make, or me it toucheth not." He wishes never to leave the wood, and requests, in a passage that reminds many readers of Christ's crucifixion, that the vines and brambles fetter him and the "courteous Briars nail [him] through."

Noticing that the flood has subsided, he finds the meadow equally attractive. It is "newly washt," with "no serpent new." The "wanton harmless folds" of the river attract the speaker, who abandons himself to the pleasures of angling, achieving in stanza 81 such harmony with the landscape that it is difficult to distinguish between him and it. The sedge surrounds his temples, his side is a riverbank, and his "sliding foot" may remind the reader of the "Fountains sliding foot" in "The Garden." The sudden arrival of Maria, however, extracts him from this reverie by means of an odd inversion wherein she, the pupil, reminds the presumably adult speaker of his responsibility. Calling himself a "trifling Youth," he hastily hides his fishing gear.

Essentially the rest of the poem is devoted to praise of Maria, a creature neither of withdrawal nor of action, but a fusion of both. Among the imagery giving her awesome power are echoes of the Last Judgment: She has "judicious" eyes, she "already is the Law," and by her the world is "wholly vitrifi'd." Nature collects itself in silence, and the sun blushingly conceals himself. As the halcyon, flying "betwixt the day and night," paralyzes nature and turns it blue, so Maria gives her surroundings the stillness of glass and imbues them with her (their) qualities: "Tis She that to these Gardens gave/ That wondrous beauty which they have," and so also with the woods, meadow, and river. Intelligent (learning languages to gain wisdom, which is "Heavens Dialect"), without vanity, and raised in the "Domestick Heaven" of Appleton House, she is not the new branch that a male heir would be on the "Farfacian oak." Instead, she is a sprig of mistletoe that will one day be severed "for some universal good." Presumably this will be her marriage, which will be of considerable political importance. The product of the seclusion of Appleton House, she is thus the ideal person to take action to affect the world at large; in her the apparent opposites of withdrawal and action are harmoniously fused.

The final stanza of the poem features a pattern of conceits reminiscent of the first stanza, and compares the fishermen carrying their boats to tortoises, echoing the tortoise in stanza 2. The fishermen are "rational amphibii," amphibians who can think; but they are also thinkers who can operate in two mediums: Human beings need both contemplation and action. This concord of opposites, which is more powerful than compromise and is presented with reason and wit, represents those characteristics central to Marvell's work.

OTHER MAJOR WORKS

NONFICTION: *The Rehearsal Transpros'd*, 1672; *The Rehearsal Transpros'd: The Second Part*, 1673 (for modern editions of the two preceding entries, see *The Rehearsal Transpros'd and The Rehearsal Transpros'd: The Second Part*, 1971; D. I. B. Smith, editor); *Mr. Smirke: Or, The Divine in Mode*, 1676; *An Account of the Growth of Popery and Arbitrary Government in England*, 1677; *Remarks upon a Late Disingenuous Discourse*, 1678; *The Prose Works of Andrew Marvell*, 2003 (Martin Dzelzainis and Annabel Patterson, editors).

MISCELLANEOUS: *The Poems and Letters of Andrew Marvell*, 1927, 1952, 1971 (H. Margoliouth, editor).

BIBLIOGRAPHY

Chernaik, Warren L. *The Poet's Time: Politics and Religion in the Work of Andrew Marvell*. New York: Cambridge University Press, 1983. For Chernaik, Marvell is a poet-prophet whose political ideas are consistent, militant, and rooted in his religion. Also discusses Marvell's later (post-1666) satiric poetry and his political polemics.

Hunt, John Dixon. *Andrew Marvell: His Life and Writings*. Ithaca, N.Y.: Cornell University Press, 1978. Hunt's intent is to provide a context against which some of Marvell's major poems ("Upon Appleton House," "An Horatian Ode upon Cromwell's Return from Ireland," and "Last Instructions to a Painter") can be read. Profusely illustrated.

Klause, John. *The Unfortunate Fall: Theodicy and the Moral Imagination of Andrew Marvell*. Hamden, Conn.: Archon Books, 1983. In his extensive analyses of the Cromwell poems, "The Garden," and "Upon Appleton House," Klause finds Marvell "adapting" to political realities. Complemented by an extensive bibliography of primary and secondary sources.

Murray, Nicholas. *World Enough and Time: The Life of Andrew Marvell*. New York: St. Martin's Press, 2000. Even with the information uncovered in the three decades since the last biography of Marvell was written, little is known about long stretches of Marvell's career. Murray's narrative takes full advantage of what is available and provides a clear portrait of Marvell and his life in the Cromwell era and the Restoration.

Patterson, Annabel. *Marvell: The Writer in Public Life*. New York: Longman, 2000. Focuses on the intersection of Marvell's political and literary views.

Ray, Robert H. *An Andrew Marvell Companion*. New York: Garland, 1998. A useful, comprehensive reference guide to the life and works of the poet and political satirist. Includes a chronology of the poet's life and works, a bibliography, and suggestions for further research.

Rees, Christine. *The Judgment of Marvell*. London: Pinter, 1989. Rees argues that Marvell's poetry concerns choice or the impossibility of choosing, and his choices involve the life of pleasure, as well as those of action and contemplation. Using this threefold division, she offers extensive commentary on approximately twenty-five well-known poems.

Stocker, Margarita. *Apocalyptic Marvell: The Second Coming in Seventeenth Century Poetry*. Athens: Ohio University Press, 1986. Stocker's book offers a corrective view of Marvell, a poet committed to an apocalyptic ideology that informs all his poems. Supplemented by an extensive bibliography.

C. Herbert Gilliland

JOHN MASEFIELD

Born: Ledbury, Herefordshire, England; June 1, 1878

Died: Near Abingdon, Berkshire, England; May 12, 1967

PRINCIPAL POETRY

Salt-Water Ballads, 1902

Ballads, 1903

The Everlasting Mercy, 1911

The Story of a Round-House, and Other Poems, 1912

The Widow in the Bye Street, 1912

The Daffodil Fields, 1913

Dauber: A Poem, 1913

Philip the King, and Other Poems, 1914

Good Friday, and Other Poems, 1916

Sonnets and Poems, 1916

The Cold Cotswolds, 1917

Lollington Downs, and Other Poems, 1917

Rosas, 1918

A Poem and Two Plays, 1919

Reynard the Fox: Or, The Ghost Heath Run, 1919

Enslaved, and Other Poems, 1920

Right Royal, 1920

King Cole, 1921

The Dream, 1922

Sonnets of Good Cheer to the Lena Ashwell Players, 1926

Midsummer Night, and Other Tales in Verse, 1928

South and East, 1929

The Wanderer of Liverpool, 1930 (poems and essay)

Minnie Maylow's Story, and Other Tales and Scenes, 1931

A Tale of Troy, 1932

A Letter from Pontus, and Other Verse, 1936

Ode to Harvard, 1937

Some Verses to Some Germans, 1939

Guatama the Enlightened, and Other Verse, 1941

Natalie Masie and Pavilastukay: Two Tales in Verse, 1942

Wonderings (Between One and Six Years), 1943

I Want! I Want!, 1944

On the Hill, 1949

Poems, 1953

The Bluebells, and Other Verse, 1961

Old Raiger, and Other Verse, 1961

In Glad Thanksgiving, 1967

Selected Poems, 1978

Sea-Fever: Selected Poems, 2005 (Philip W. Errington)

OTHER LITERARY FORMS

John Masefield (MAYS-feeld) wrote books of poems and verse plays, prose plays, novels, and other prose works, including histories.

ACHIEVEMENTS

John Masefield's poetry appealed to a very wide audience. His first book of verse, *Salt-Water Ballads*, sold out in six months, and his narrative poems were very popular. *The Everlasting Mercy* was a sensation in his day. Some of his lyric poems, including "Sea Fever," have become standards of English poetry. He received many honorary degrees from institutions including Oxford and Cambridge. In 1930, he was elected to membership in the American Academy of Arts and Letters, and he was president of the Society of Authors in 1937. In 1961, he was made a Companion of Literature by the Royal Society of Literature, and also in that year he won the William Foyle Poetry Prize. In 1964, the National Book League gave him a prize for writers older than sixty-five.

BIOGRAPHY

John Edward Masefield was born June 1, 1878, in Ledbury, Herefordshire. His very early years were happy ones, although the children in the family spent their time with their nurse and saw little of their parents; they saw their mother only between teatime and bedtime at six o'clock. She died a few weeks after giving birth to a sixth child when John was six-and-a-half years old. Their grandparents died a year after their mother, and the family, in reduced circumstances, moved into the grandparents' home. John occasionally visited his godmother, wrote his first poems when he was about ten, and went to boarding school. His father

John Masefield (Hulton Archive/Getty Images)

died at age forty-nine after suffering from mental disorders. Taking over as guardians, his aunt and uncle suggested that John be trained to go to sea in the merchant marine. Although he wanted to write or paint, he decided to pursue seafaring because the son of a governess whom he had liked enjoyed being a cadet on the school ship H.M.S. *Conway.*

Masefield joined that ship when he was thirteen and left it when he was sixteen, having learned a good deal of mathematics and navigation. He became an apprentice on a four-masted cargo barque sailing for Chile, which did not touch land for three months. During the voyage, he had some trouble with seasickness and experienced the fury of Cape Horn storms. He was released from service after he became seriously ill with sunstroke and a possible nervous breakdown. After a hospital stay in Valparaiso, he went home. His aunt nagged him into going to sea again; but he deserted ship in New York, causing his uncle to cut him off financially.

The seventeen-year-old Masefield could not find work in that depression year; thus, he and an acquaintance became vagrants, getting occasional work on farms and sleeping out, an experience that gave him great empathy for the down-and-out. After some months, he returned to New York City, living in Greenwich Village, almost starving but writing poetry. He finally obtained work with long hours at a bar and then moved to Yonkers to work in a carpet factory, reading the English poets in his spare time. At nineteen, he was suffering from tuberculosis and malaria. He returned to England (earning his way back on a ship) hoping to be a writer there. Poor and sick, he obtained a clerk's position in a London bank, which he held for three years. He regained his health, became reconciled with his aunt and uncle, and was especially close to his sisters. He managed to meet William Butler Yeats and to become part of the Yeats's circle. In 1901, he became exhibition secretary for an art show in Wolverhampton. His poems were being published regularly in magazines, and his first book of verse, *Salt-Water Ballads,* was very popular.

When he met Constance de la Cherois Crommelin, she was thirty-five and he was twenty-three, but despite the difference in their ages, they were married in 1903, after Masefield had obtained an editorial position. They took a house in Greenwich; then John left Constance and his baby daughter Judith for a nighttime editorial position in Manchester. He wrote articles and reviews and worked seven days a week for the publisher; yet, he still managed to write plays, one of which, written in 1907, was produced. (Curiously, also, one of his stories was pirated for the stage.)

About the time that his son Lewis was born, Masefield became infatuated briefly with Elizabeth Robins, an American actress and author who became a veritable goddess to him. He called her "mother" and wrote to her, sometimes many times a day. After she withdrew from his life, he had a burst of creativity that produced *The Everlasting Mercy,* a long narrative poem that caused a great stir.

After settling into a country house in Lollington, he became a Red Cross worker in a French hospital during World War I. In 1915, he visited Gallipoli for the Red Cross, an, in 1916, he traveled to the United States on a lecture tour, but also with the intention of enlisting Americans' sympathy with Britain in the war: He had been in touch with British intelligence. He also organized theatricals and verse reciting contests in his area.

When Masefield's wife, Constance, was recovering from an operation for a brain tumor, the family moved to the Cotswolds; later they lived in a village near Dorchester, called Clifton Hampden, in the upper valley of the Thames. Masefield died in 1967, after refusing to have his leg amputated when he developed gangrene from an infected toenail. He was cremated, as he had wished, and his ashes were deposited in the Poets' Corner in Westminster Abbey.

ANALYSIS

John Masefield's difficulties in life—his early poverty, ill health, and arduous labors—caused him to develop a reflective attitude toward the world. Although he is often thought of as a writer of rollicking sea and narrative poems, his poetry is usually concerned in some way with the tragedy of human life; it is seldom simply humorous. He seemed to value most highly his more formal philosophical poems, although his lighter pieces have been the most popular. Many of these poems seem simple because he chose to speak in the vernacular about common experiences. His own experiences, however, gave him great empathy with the downtrodden, and he deliberately chose to treat such matters, as he points out in "Consecration." He will not speak of the great, he says, but of the lowly and scorned; and he ends the poem with a heartfelt "Amen."

Masefield's poems about the life of the common sailor are firmly rooted in the ballad tradition. He makes use of a dramatic speaker as he skillfully interweaves narrative and lyrical material. A number of such poems deal with death at sea; some treat the subject lightly, in a manner of a sea chantey, but the harsh realities underlie the touches of humor. In "The Turn of the Tide" and "Cape-Horn Gospel I," the soul or ghost wants to continue working on the ship after death. Masefield's most famous work, "Sea Fever," is about these two realities, the harshness and the appeal of life at sea. The title suggests a disease; the sea can be a kind of addiction. Masefield's refrain repeatedly emphasized that the speaker "must go down to the seas again,"

while alliteration effectively evokes the rhythms of wheel and wind and sail. The speaker responds to a call; he has no choice in the matter. The life is like that of the vagrant gypsy, or, not so explicitly, like the gull's and the whale's. The life of the sea fascinates, but it is also lonely, gray, and painful. The middle stanza of the three, however, contains none of these negative images, suggesting that the very heart of the matter is the delight in the movement of the ship. In the last stanza, the wind no longer pleasantly makes the white clouds fly; it is as sharp as a "whetted knife." From this life, the speaker, in the last two lines, desires two things: "quiet sleep and a sweet dream when the long trick's over." The sea journey is suddenly the journey of life, with a final sleep at the end. According to the glossary that Masefield supplied for the *Salt-Water Ballads*, a trick is "the ordinary two-hour spell at the wheel or on the lookout," but the "long trick" suddenly suggests the trip itself and life itself, for Masefield has transformed the realistic situation into a symbolic one with a single word.

"CARGOES"

"Cargoes" is a different type of sea poem, without a speaker or story line. Three ships are described briefly, each in one short stanza. Masefield here is an imagist presenting only the pictures, with no explicit connections between them and no commentary on them. The inclusion of the last freighter, the British coaster, seems ironic, since it is less attractive than the ships of the past; it is actually dirty and sails in less attractive seas. Including it may also seem ironic because of its cargo: such humble items as coal and tin trays. It can scarcely be compared with the quinquereme from Nineveh with its glamorous apes and ivory, or with the Spanish galleon with its jewels and gold; yet it is the modern representative of a tradition that goes back to the ancients. A third irony is that it actually exists, whereas the others are gone, though, of course, it too will become a thing of the past. Here, Masefield makes skillful use of meter and stanza form, the unusual number of spondees imparting a feeling of strength, reinforced by the periodic use of two short lines rather than a single long one. Masefield made light of objections that a ship from Nineveh was not plausible because Nineveh was two hundred miles inland. As Constance Babington Smith notes in *John Masefield: A Life* (1978), he responded to a question of an Eton boy: "I can only suggest that a Ninevean syndicate must have chartered the ship; even so it was odd." The first line of the poem is musical in its repetition of sounds, including the *n*, short *i*, and *v*. It is not improbable that the poet chose Nineveh for its alliterative and evocative qualities.

As the modern freighter in "Cargoes" is less distinguished than its antecedents, the modern city in "London Town" is less pleasant than the country and the small town. Masefield is speaking in his own voice here, for in the last line he speaks of the land in which he was bred, and the countryside described is his homeland. The poet alternates stanzas in praise of London with stanzas in praise of the country, but all those in praise of London end with a defect or a deficiency, with a varied refrain in favor of leaving the place. In two of these stanzas, the deficiency is given in only a half line of contrast, as in the statement that the world is busy there, while the mind grows "crafty." The alternate stanzas praise the countryside without reservation and are prefaced with a joyous song like "Then hey" or "So hey." The poem is joyous in the delight of the poet in returning to the world of nature, but the criticism of the city is sobering. In the last stanza about London, it hardly matters that the tunes, books, and plays are excellent if "wretchedly fare the most there and merrily fare the few." The city is a tragic place, for beneath its artifice there is misery and poverty. The irony is somewhat like that of Masefield's long narrative poem *Reynard the Fox*, in which the hunters seek an exciting diversion, while the fox is only trying desperately to survive.

THE EVERLASTING MERCY

Masefield's homeland, described in the country scenes in "London Town" and other poems, includes the Malvern Hills mentioned at the beginning of *The Vision of William, Concerning Piers the Plowman* (c. 1362, A Text; c. 1377, B Text; c. 1393, C Text; also known as *Piers Plowman*), and the influence of that work is apparent in Masefield's long narrative poem *The Everlasting Mercy*. Masefield had resolved to write about the lowly, and some of the lowly are anything but perfect. Saul Kane bit through his father's hand and went to jail nineteen times, but he tells the

reader in a monologue that is part soliloquy and part public attestation that he regrets breaking his mother's heart. He says, "Now, friends, observe and look upon me" to see evidence of the Lord's pity; it is an address to the reader that is reminiscent of the medieval religious lyrics in which Christ tells the reader to look at how his side bleeds or in which the Blessed Virgin invites the reader to weep with her. The effect is that the figure, whether it be Christ or Saul Kane, becomes a static moral picture. It is short-lived here, however, as Saul plunges into his story of a poaching-rights argument, boxing, and celebration.

The otherworldly passages in the poem are instrumental in Saul's religious conversion to a different way of life, the first of them being Saul's remembrance on his way to the celebration of how the bell ringer had seen spirits dancing around the church at Christmas. The whole eerie scene becomes vivid to him, and he prays when he thinks of Judgment Day. After the party, he leans out the window and is tempted by the devil to throw himself down, even as Christ was tempted. He decides not to kill himself and feels exalted; he wants to excoriate the righteous, who would secretly like to be whores and sots and who "make hell for all the odd/ All the lonely ones of God." After this realization, he runs through the town and rings the fire bell. After he speaks out to the squire's parson for his actions toward the poor, he is upbraided by the mother of a lost child whom he had befriended; when she summons the mystical imagery of the Book of Revelation, he shrinks away. After he insults a Quaker woman who visits the bar and then leaves, exhorting him, he suddenly feels, in a mystical passage about tide, sun, moon, and bells ringing for someone coming home, that he has been converted. Feeling that he was born to "brother" everyone, he sees everything symbolically, from mole to plowman, and says that Christ will plow at the "bitter roots" of his heart.

First Christ and then Saul become plowmen, a transformation reminiscent of *Piers Plowman*. At the end of the work, where the meter changes from iambic tetrameter to a more lyrical trimeter, he seems to have awakened to the beauty of nature. The poem is enhanced by its many ironies, such as that Saul should experience the world of the spirit while he is drunk, and that Saul, of all people, could become a patient plowman and a Christlike figure. Some of the names in the story are symbolic: certainly Saul and Miss Bourne, the Quaker, and possibly Saul's last name, Kane (Cain). Although Saul is not exactly Everyman, his life in its aimlessness, belligerence, and unhappiness embodies a tragic pattern of human existence that is not uncommon. Masefield was not religious in the traditional sense, but he seems to have believed in reincarnation and to have been fascinated by religion, a number of his works being on religious themes. This poem was a sensation in its time; it was considered shocking for its direct language and crudity. Sir James Barrie, however, described it in the *Daily Chronicle* of November 29, 1912, as "incomparably the best literature of the year."

"CLM"

Because his story poems, sea poems, and songs are so vivid, Masefield's more subdued philosophical poems have been generally neglected. "CLM," a tragic work about women and motherhood, was written during his wife's second pregnancy, when he was romantically involved with Elizabeth Robins, whom he called Mother. The letters of the poem's title stand for the name of Masefield's actual mother. Speaking of his prenatal life, the poet sees the fetus as common earth and as a leech. Pregnancy is "months of birth," and birth itself is hell. His present life involves the death of "some of her," some cells he received from her; thus, the subject of death is first raised in connection with his own life. Not until the second stanza does the reader become aware that the speaker's mother is dead. Both the womb and the grave are dark.

There is a cluster of images associated with his desire to see her again, together with the uncertain nature of such an encounter: gates of the grave, knocking, "dusty" doors, her "dusty" beauty, and passersby in the street. He feels that he has not repaid his debt of life to her and to other women, and he uses the images of men triumphing over women, trampling on their rights and lusting after them, to convey men's selfishness and their subjugation of women. At the end of the poem, in an ironic and tragic reversal of his desire to see his mother again, he tells the grave to stay shut so that he will not be shamed. The shut grave image stands in strong contrast to the earlier image of its opening.

DAUBER

Much of Masefield's more philosophical poetry was concerned with beauty. Some of his ideas on this theme were embodied in the narrative poem *Dauber*, in which a young artist becomes a sailor because he wants to paint ships and sea life as they have never been painted before. His insensitive shipmates, however, destroy his paintings. When he dies in a fall from the yardarm during a storm, his last words are, "It will go on." Ironically, he is mourned not as an artist but as a fine sailor-to-be.

BEAUTY AND DEATH

The worship of beauty and the linking of beauty and tragedy in human life were recurrent themes in Masefield's sonnets. Beauty exists in nature and within the individual, despite the reality of death, and beauty exists in a life to come. Beauty and death are related, for, as he says in one sonnet, the life that was is "Pasture to living beauty." The beautiful may die, but Beauty will go on. The personified Beauty of many of his sonnets seems to be an amalgam of the goddess Nature, the world soul of Platonic philosophy, God, the Beatrice of Dante, and the women in the poet's life. "On Growing Old" asks Beauty to be with him as he sits amid the imagery of age and death: an old dog, his own coldness by the fire, the yellow leaves of a book, the embers. The word "her" indicates that Beauty possesses the seas and land where he is no longer able to go. Comparing himself to a beggar in the Strand, he asks Beauty for gifts—ironically, not youth, but wisdom and passion, which he compares to bread and to rain in a dry summer. They are necessities in the closing darkness of old age and death, for with them "Even the night will blossom as the rose."

Masefield, then, was a more philosophical poet than is generally realized. Beauty was a kind of goddess in his work, and a kind of quest as well; he was fascinated by the interrelationship of beauty with tragedy and death. It was also no accident that he chose to retell in his verse the tragic tales of Troy, of Arthur, and of Tristan and Isolt, for he dealt in many of his poems with the tragedies and ironies of human life.

OTHER MAJOR WORKS

LONG FICTION: *Captain Margaret*, 1908; *Multitude and Solitude*, 1909; *Lost Endeavour*, 1910; *The Taking of Helen*, 1923; *Sard Harker*, 1924; *Odtaa*, 1926; *The Hawbucks*, 1929; *The Bird of Dawning*, 1933; *Victorious Troy: Or, The Hurrying Angel*, 1935; *Basilissa*, 1940.

SHORT FICTION: *A Mainsail Haul*, 1905; *A Tarpaulin Muster*, 1907.

PLAYS: *The Campden Wonder*, pr. 1907 (one act); *The Tragedy of Nan*, pr. 1908; *Mrs. Harrison*, pb. 1909 (one act); *The Tragedy of Pompey the Great*, pr., pb. 1910; *The Witch*, pr. 1911 (adaptation of a Norwegian play); *Philip the King*, pr. 1914 (one act); *The Faithful*, pr., pb. 1915; *Good Friday: A Dramatic Poem*, pb. 1916; *The Locked Chest*, pb. 1916 (one act); *The Sweeps of Ninety-eight*, pr., pb. 1916; *Esther*, pr. 1921 (adaptation of Jean Racine's play); *Melloney Holtspur: Or, The Pangs of Love*, pb. 1922; *A King's Daughter: A Tragedy in Verse*, pr. 1923; *Tristan and Isolt: A Play in Verse*, pr. 1923; *The Trial of Jesus*, pb. 1925; *The Coming of Christ*, pb. 1928; *Easter: A Play for Singers*, pr. 1929; *End and Beginnings*, pb. 1933; *A Play of St. George*, pb. 1948.

NONFICTION: *Sea Life in Nelson's Time*, 1905; *On the Spanish Main*, 1906; *Shakespeare*, 1911; *Gallipoli*, 1916; *The Battle of the Somme*, 1919; *Chaucer*, 1931; *The Conway from Her Foundation to the Present Day*, 1933; *In the Mill*, 1941; *The Nine Days' Wonder*, 1941; *New Chum*, 1944; *So Long to Learn*, 1952; *Grace Before Ploughing*, 1966.

CHILDREN'S LITERATURE: *Martin Hyde*, 1910; *Jim Davis*, 1911; *The Midnight Folk*, 1927; *The Box of Delights*, 1935.

MISCELLANEOUS: *A Book of Both Sorts: Selections from the Verse and Prose*, 1947.

BIBLIOGRAPHY

Babington-Smith, Constance. *John Masefield: A Life.* New York: Oxford University Press, 1978. This full biography was prepared with the active cooperation of Masefield's family and friends. Includes a select list of books by Masefield and an index.

Binding, Paul. *An Endless Quiet Valley: A Reappraisal of John Masefield.* Woonton, England: Logaston, 1998. Binding provides a critical analysis of Masefield's works, examining them within their historical framework. Includes index.

Drew, Fraser. *John Masefield's England: A Study of the National Themes in His Work.* Rutherford, N.J.: Fairleigh Dickinson University Press, 1973. This work looks at the specific qualities of Masefield's Englishness through the corpus of his work. Includes bibliography and index.

Dwyer, June. *John Masefield.* New York: Frederick Ungar, 1987. This volume covers the whole corpus of Masefield's work. Includes a bibliography and an index.

Errington, Philip W. *John Masefield, the "Great Auk" of English Literature: A Bibliography.* New Castle, Del.: Oak Knoll Press, 2004. This bibliography of Masefield's works and works about him provides a good start for research on the writer.

Spark, Muriel. *John Masefield.* Rev. ed. London: Hutchinson, 1992. A biography and critical study of selected works. Includes bibliographic references.

Sternlicht, Sanford. *John Masefield.* Boston: Twayne, 1977. This volume covers both life and works in a clear, well-focused way. Contains bibliography and index.

Rosemary Ascherl

GEORGE MEREDITH

Born: Portsmouth, England; February 12, 1828
Died: Flint Cottage, near Box Hill, Surrey, England; May 18, 1909

PRINCIPAL POETRY
Poems, 1851
Modern Love and Poems of the English Roadside, 1862
Poems and Lyrics of the Joy of Earth, 1883
Ballads and Poems of Tragic Life, 1887
A Reading of Earth, 1888
Poems: The Empty Purse, 1892
Odes in Contribution to the Song of French History, 1898
A Reading of Life, with Other Poems, 1901
Last Poems, 1909

The Poetical Works of George Meredith, 1912
(3 volumes)
The Poems of George Meredith, 1978 (2 volumes;
Phyllis B. Bartlett, editor)

OTHER LITERARY FORMS

George Meredith wrote more than one dozen novels, including *The Ordeal of Richard Feverel* (1859), *The Egoist: A Comedy in Narrative* (1879), and *Diana of the Crossways* (1885). His novels attack egoism, or excessive self-importance, and sentimentality, or unfounded pride in fine sensibility. The characters and situations presented in Meredith's novels are fictions, but they are often drawn, sometimes closely, from real people and actual incidents. Meredith's novels have been praised for their descriptions of society and their characterizations, especially of women, and criticized for their excessive elaboration of incident and background and for their highly artificial style, which many readers find both tedious and distracting. Meredith, whose novels explore a vein of comedy marked by rueful self-recognition, articulated his ideas on comedy in *On the Idea of Comedy and the Uses of the Comic Spirit* (1877).

ACHIEVEMENTS

For much of George Meredith's career, his audience was small but select. Reviews of his work were mixed, yet he received praise from writers as varied as Alfred, Lord Tennyson, Robert Browning, Algernon Charles Swinburne, Thomas Hardy, and Robert Louis Stevenson. With the publication of *Diana of the Crossways* in 1885, Meredith's popular reception blossomed. His last years were full of honor. In 1892, on the death of Tennyson, he was elected president of the Society of Authors. Ten years later, he was made vice president of the London Library. He was honored several times in his last years by leading figures of the literary world. In 1905, Meredith received the Order of Merit.

BIOGRAPHY

George Meredith was the son and grandson of tailors of modest means whose good looks, social graces, and personal proclivities enabled them to move in higher social circles than most tradespeople did. When Meredith was about eighteen, he became a clerk to a solicitor who introduced him to a circle of writers and artists. Through his friend Edward Peacock, the son of novelist and poet Thomas Love Peacock, Meredith met Mary Peacock Nicolls, a widow six years older than he. She was beautiful, witty, sophisticated, and artistic, and Meredith fell passionately in love with her. He had his good looks to offer her, along with the promise of his talent—and poverty. He proposed, and she refused him several times. Finally, in 1849, they were married.

They had a son, Arthur, but the marriage was stormy. They were both strong-minded, and they were stressed by poverty. Mary was volatile and independent. After seven years, the marriage was failing, although the couple kept up appearances. Then she initiated an affair with Meredith's friend, the artist Henry Wallis, with whom she had a child. She abandoned her husband and Arthur to go with Wallis to Capri, Italy, in 1858. Soon Wallis abandoned her, and she returned to England in ill health. After she left him, Meredith never saw her again. She lived in poverty, loneliness, and misery until her death in 1861. Some of the emotion of his courtship is reflected in Meredith's "Love in the Valley" and *The Ordeal of Richard Feverel*, and the breakup of the marriage informs "Modern Love," although none of these works should be regarded as reliable autobiography.

Because Meredith's publications did not meet with great popular success, he supported Arthur and himself for a time as a political journalist, writing dutifully for a paper more conservative than he. In 1862, he became a reader for the publishers Chapman and Hall, considering a great many manuscripts, inevitably rejecting some that went on to be great successes for other publishers but also giving important early encouragement to such writers as Thomas Hardy, Olive Schreiner, and George Gissing. He continued with Chapman and Hall until 1894.

Meredith was physically vigorous for much of his life and a great walker, both in frequent short rambles and in longer walking tours. He enjoyed strong friendships. On September 20, 1864, he married Marie Vulliamy. This marriage led to an estrangement between Meredith and his son, but it was a stable and happy union until Marie's death in 1885.

George Meredith (The Granger Collection, New York)

Meredith continued to work actively through the turn of the twentieth century. As he aged, his health declined, but his temperament mellowed. Although many of the friends of his youth and middle age predeceased him, a new generation of friends supported him. On May 18, 1909, after a short illness, he died, widely revered and much honored.

ANALYSIS

George Meredith, a gifted conversationalist, once provoked playwright F. C. Burnand to exclaim, "Damn you, George, why won't you write the way you talk?" Meredith would not. In an age of conscious stylists, he was one of the most mannered, in both prose and poetry. He wrote a great deal of poetry, much of it flawed by strained, awkward, and overly elaborate figures of speech. His poems are sometimes frustratingly indirect in expression. The grammar of his lines can be extremely convoluted, often for the sake of rhyme. Many of his poems are rhythmically monotonous, and many are quite didactic. Meredith also wrote excellent poetry, however, pleasurable and rewarding to many

readers, who may make happy discoveries, particularly among his lyrics. Among his most rewarding poems are "Love in the Valley," "Lucifer in Starlight," and "Modern Love."

"LOVE IN THE VALLEY"

"Love in the Valley" is a much-admired long lyric, first published in 1851 and very extensively revised in 1878. The finished poem consists of twenty-six eight-line stanzas. The poem's pentameter lines have a fluid, seemingly spontaneous rhythm, sometimes mimetic and consistently effective.

The poem's narrator alternately celebrates the beauty, innocence, and freedom of his beloved and describes the rural valley that is her home. The descriptions of the valley are vivid and detailed, presenting images of moonlight, dusk, and dawn; of birds and the sky; of vegetation green and golden. The descriptions of the woman, "Pure from the night, and splendid for the day," are less specific but no less intense. To the censorious, the woman is not faultless; to the narrator of the poem, she is innocent, sensual, changeable, and elusive.

The poem develops in a series of mirror images: A swallow's wings are mirrored in the water, and the woman's mother "tends her before the laughing mirror." Throughout the poem the subject is mirrored metaphorically in nature, as nature is mirrored in her. When the lovers embrace, the narrator says, "our souls were in our names"—that is, each soul was mirrored in the name of the other.

In the last stanza the narrator says, "heaven is my need"—a heaven that is mirrored, by love, in the valley and in the woman. The poem is full of swift, elusive, mutable things: shy squirrels, swooping swallows and owls, winking minnows, the changing sky throughout the day, the cycle of the seasons, and the woman herself, "this wild thing." In all this change, there is constancy; whatever the time of day, whatever the season, the valley—with all its swift, elusive creatures—is still itself. For all her changeableness, the beloved is still herself. In transience is treasured, timeless truth.

"THE LARK ASCENDING"

"The Lark Ascending" (1883) is a poem of 120 lines. The generally regular iambic tetrameter lines rhyme in couplets. The poem describes and reflects on the prolonged and soaring song of the skylark, which sings as it flies, often so high that it is lost to the eye and can be followed only by the ear.

The first long stanza (sixty-four lines) describes the outpouring in song of a skylark at sunrise. The stanza is one long sentence, perhaps imitating the song it describes. Poets, notably Percy Bysshe Shelley, have found in the skylark's song an emblem of spiritual transcendence. Meredith, too, makes it a symbol. In the second stanza, he says that the swallow carries Earth with it and voices Earth in its song. In the third stanza, Meredith says that though humankind can hear the song, people lack the voice for such singing, spoiled as they are by the "taint of personality." In the last stanza, he corrects himself: Some people, through their life's struggles and self-forgetfulness, have souls great enough to be embodied in the skylark's song of transcendence.

The idea that Meredith struggled to express in "The Lark Ascending" is also expressed, more simply and more clearly, in "Song in the Songless" (1901), eight lines of alternating tetrameter and dimeter: "They have no song, the sedges dry/ And still they sing," the poem begins, and it concludes: "There is but sound of sedges dry/ In me they sing." In this eloquent lyric, the speaker, transcending age, inarticulateness, and personality, is united with nature.

"LUCIFER IN STARLIGHT"

"Lucifer in Starlight," one of Meredith's most widely read poems, is one of twenty-five sonnets Meredith published in 1883. Lucifer is the Prince of Darkness with the name of Light, and the poem plays throughout on imagery of light and dark: Lucifer's shadow on the arctic snow and stars against the dark sky. The poem is Miltonic in its agon, its diction, its imagery, and its stately rhythm appropriate to ponderous flight. Significantly, however, the cosmology of Meredith's poem is modern; rolling Earth is no longer the fixed center of the universe.

The imagery of the octave is easily visualizable and highly effective. The sestet, at first reading, is also readily comprehensible, although on reflection it may be less successful. The metaphors shift quickly from "the brain of heaven" to "the army of unalterable law," and neither metaphor is really visual. Nonetheless, the reader can grasp Meredith's point.

Prince Lucifer, the proud rebel, stands against order, which is embodied in military organization and the regular movement of the stars, in reason, in law, and, presumably, in the hierarchy that gives him his title. Lucifer is, in fact, an egoist. He is defeated in this poem not by the tangible force that cost him the scars he wears but by the force of an abstract idea. He surrenders not to God but to "unalterable law"—if unalterable, then presumably as immune to the will of God (whomever or whatever that might be) as to any initiatives of the proud rebel. Meredith, like other late Victorians, abandoned Christianity for the indistinctly defined religion of science. The strictly prescribed form of the sonnet is highly appropriate to this poem's subject, linking both poet and reader to the order it expresses, embodies, and imposes.

"MODERN LOVE"

"Modern Love" (1862), Meredith's most highly regarded poem, consists of fifty sixteen-line stanzas, which Meredith called sonnets. This sixteen-line form is more flexible than traditional sonnet forms, and Meredith's sonnet sequence differs from others in the detailed and coherent narrative that links the individual sonnets.

"Modern Love" tells the story of a failing marriage, partly through a third-person narrator but largely from the point of view of the husband. The sequence opens with the couple's estrangement. The wife has taken a new lover, and the husband, still in love with his wife as she was, vacillates between jealousy and physical desire for her. He recognizes her misery as they maintain the facade of marriage, yet he cannot bring himself to show her pity. To feed his wounded ego, he initiates a flirtation of his own, an affair that is eventually consummated but unrewarding. Husband and wife painfully attempt to reconcile. The wife does finally believe that she has won back her husband's love, but she commits suicide to leave her husband free to pursue his new love—which, ironically, he does not really want to do.

Among the most memorable sonnets in the sequence are the first, depicting the couple lying uncommunicative in their bed, "each wishing for the sword that severs all"; the thirteenth, in which Nature, who plays "for Seasons, not Eternities," brings both the growth and death of love; the forty-seventh, with its evocative nature imagery; and the last, with its sensitive and remarkably objective analysis of the process by which love dies.

"Modern Love" does not moralize. Many Victorians found this a shocking failure, but later generations have found that what the poem accomplishes instead is much more meaningful. "Modern Love" is remarkable for its subtly modulated presentation of conflicting emotions and for its unsparingly honest expression of the husband's motives, evasions, and perceptions.

OTHER MAJOR WORKS

LONG FICTION: *The Shaving of Shagpat*, 1855; *Farina*, 1857; *The Ordeal of Richard Feverel*, 1859; *Evan Harrington*, 1861; *Emilia in England*, 1864 (also known as *Sandra Belloni: Or, Emilia in England*, 1886); *Rhoda Fleming*, 1865; *Vittoria*, 1867; *The Adventures of Harry Richmond*, 1871; *Beauchamp's Career*, 1874-1875 (serial), 1876 (book); *The Egoist: A Comedy in Narrative*, 1879; *The Tragic Comedians*, 1880; *Diana of the Crossways*, 1885; *One of Our Conquerors*, 1891; *Lord Ormont and His Aminta*, 1894; *The Amazing Marriage*, 1895; *Celt and Saxon*, 1910 (unfinished).

SHORT FICTION: *The Case of General Ople and Lady Camper*, 1890; *The Tale of Chloe*, 1890.

NONFICTION: *On the Idea of Comedy and of the Uses of the Comic Spirit*, 1877; *The Letters of George Meredith*, 1970 (3 volumes; C. L. Cline, editor).

BIBLIOGRAPHY

Beer, Gillian. *Meredith: A Change of Masks*. London: Athlone Press, 1970. Attempts one of the first modern appraisals of Meredith's art, seeing him as a novelist anticipating twentieth century concerns and techniques, as well as questioning Victorian certitudes. Includes an index.

Heimstra, Anne. "Reconstructing Milton's Satan: Meredith's 'Lucifer in Starlight.'" *Victorian Poetry* 30 (Summer, 1992): 122-133. Explores at length Meredith's debt in this poem to John Milton's portrayal of Satan in *Paradise Lost* (1667, 1674) and goes on to analyze the implications of Meredith's wording and imagery.

Houston, Natalie M. "Affecting Authenticity: 'Sonnets from the Portuguese' and 'Modern Love.'" *Studies in the Literary Imagination* 35, no. 2 (Fall, 2002): 99-122. Examines Victorian poetic theory, with emphasis on the role of authenticity, in an analysis of Elizabeth Barrett Browning's *Sonnets from the Portuguese* and Meredith's *Modern Love*.

Kozicki, Henry. "The 'Unholy Battle' with the Other in George Meredith's 'Modern Love.'" *Papers on Language and Literature* 23 (Spring, 1987): 140-160. Contains a summary of the criticism dealing with conflict in "Modern Love." Kozicki then discusses the poem in detail. His references to the suppressed version of Sonnet 10 are especially interesting.

Muendel, Renate. *George Meredith*. Boston: Twayne, 1986. Chapters on Meredith's poetry, his early fiction, his novels of the 1870's and 1880's, and his last novels. A beginning chapter provides a brief biography. Includes chronology, notes, and an annotated bibliography.

Roberts, Neil. *Meredith and the Novel*. New York: St. Martin's Press, 1997. A good study of Meredith's long fiction. Includes bibliographical references and an index.

Williams, Ioan, ed. *Meredith: The Critical Heritage*. London: Routledge & Kegan Paul, 1971. A collection of reviews and essays showing the critical reception of Meredith's work from 1851 through 1911. Contains indexes of his work, periodicals, and newspapers.

David W. Cole

CHARLOTTE MEW

Born: London, England; November 15, 1869
Died: London, England; March 24, 1928

PRINCIPAL POETRY

The Farmer's Bride, 1916, 1921 (also known as *Saturday Market*, 1921)
The Rambling Sailor, 1929
Collected Poems of Charlotte Mew, 1953
Collected Poems and Prose, 1981
Selected Poems, 2008

OTHER LITERARY FORMS

Though primarily known for her poetry, Charlotte Mew (myew) also wrote short stories and essays. Her first story to appear in print was "Passed" (1894), published in John Lane and Elkin Mathews's *The Yellow Book*, which also published works by Henry James and Max Beerbohm and the drawings of Aubrey Beardsley. From 1899 to 1905, Mew was a regular contributor to *Temple Bar*, a magazine for middle-class Victorians, which published the stories "The China Bowl" (1899), "An Open Door" (1903), "A White Night" (1903), and "Mark Stafford's Wife" (1905), as well as the essays "Notes in a Brittany Convent" (1901) and "The Poems of Emily Brontë" (1904). "An Old Servant" (1913), Mew's tribute to her childhood nurse, Elizabeth Goodman, appeared in *The New Statesmen*. Mew rewrote "The China Bowl" as a one-act play, which was broadcast by the British Broadcasting Corporation posthumously in 1953. That same year, *Cornhill Magazine* published her story "A Fatal Fidelity."

ACHIEVEMENTS

Although Charlotte Mew's work never won any awards, her poetry did win accolades from major literary figures, including Virginia Woolf, Thomas Hardy, Siegfried Sassoon, Rebecca West, H. D., and novelist May Sinclair. In 1923, Hardy, John Masefield, and Walter de la Mare secured for her a Civil List pension of seventy-five pounds per year.

BIOGRAPHY

Charlotte Mew was born in 1869 in the Bloomsbury section of London, where she would live her whole life, much of it at 9 Gordon Street. She was the first girl born to Frederick Mew and Anna Maria Kendall. Originally from the Isle of Wight, Frederick Mew had been sent to London by his father to train as an architect. He became an assistant to architect H. E. Kendall, Jr. In 1863, he married Kendall's daughter, Anna Maria. Anna Maria, an invalid much of her life, saw her marriage as beneath her. Frederick's death in 1898 put the family into financial crisis. Of the seven Mew children, only Charlotte, her older brother, Henry, and two younger siblings, Anne and Freda, survived to adulthood. Henry and Freda were both institutionalized for mental illness, a situation that strained the family's limited resources and haunted Mew's poetry.

Following her father's death, Mew lived with her sister Anne and her mother at Gordon Street. Eventually they lived in the basement, having rented out the upper rooms for additional income. Mew was particularly devoted to Anne, a painter who attended the Royal Female School of Art and later rented a studio, 6 Hogarth Studios. In 1909, the year Mew published "Requiescat," her sister Anne had a painting accepted by the Royal Academy. As girls, they attended the Gower Street School and later lectures at University College, London.

At Gower Street, Mew developed a crush on Miss Lucy Harrison, the school's headmistress. Mew's unrequited love for Harrison anticipates her most important adult female relationships. Of particular importance were her relationships with Ella D'Arcy, assistant literary editor of *The Yellow Book*, whom she met in 1894, a year before composing "The China Bowl," and novelist and suffragette May Sinclair, whom she met in 1913 through Mrs. Dawson "Sappho" Scott, an arts patron and founder of International PEN. Sinclair brought Mew's work to the attention of Ezra Pound, who published "The Fête" in *The Egoist*. Mew wrote "Madeleine in Church," which many consider her best poem, during the years of her friendship with Sinclair. While in love with both D'Arcy and Sinclair, Mew repressed her desire because of a strict sense of sexual propriety. Perhaps for the same reason and out of fear that any offspring would suffer mental illness, Mew and her sister Anne decided to never marry.

In 1915, Mew met Alida Monro (née Klemantaski), whose husband, Harold, owned the Poetry Bookshop (Bloomsbury), where Mew read her work. After reading Mew's poem "The Farmer's Bride" in *The Nation* (1912), Monro convinced her husband to publish a collection of Mew's poetry. In 1916, the Poetry Bookshop printed five hundred copies of *The Farmer's Bride*. Five years later, it brought out a revised edition with eleven additional poems. Despite unflagging support from the Monros and positive reviews from H. D. and West, the book did not sell well. In 1929, the Poetry Bookshop posthumously published Mew's poetry collection, *The Rambling Sailor*.

In 1923, the same year Mew was awarded the Civil List pension, her mother died of bronchial pneumonia. Unable to continue paying rent on their house, now in Delancey Street, Mew and her sister Anne lived temporarily at Anne's studio. Anne's health was seriously declining, and in June, 1927, she died of cancer. On February 15, 1928, devastated by the loss of her sister and perhaps fearing for her own mental health (she had become obsessed with germs and the possibility that her sister had been buried alive), Mew agreed to enter a nursing home near the Baker Street Station. Less than one month later, on March 24, 1928, she committed suicide by drinking half a bottle of Lysol.

ANALYSIS

At times autobiographical, Charlotte Mew's poetry frequently takes the themes of longing, death, insanity, and loneliness. It often addresses passion, religious and sexual, as well as sin and the distance between a heavenly God and individual human suffering on Earth. Her work frequently contains tensions created through binaries of inside/outside, freedom/confinement, nature/society. Her deeply emotional verse contains jarring juxtapositions of images and is marked by irregular rhyme and meter. Writing in the last decade of the nineteenth century and the first decades of the twentieth, Mew's poetry straddles the fin de siècle and early modernist periods.

THE FARMER'S BRIDE

The poems in *The Farmer's Bride* reflect Mew's dominant themes. "Ken" and "On the Asylum Road" provide moving depictions of madness and the isolation that results from mental illness. "Ken" closes with the lines, ". . . when they took/ Ken to that place, I did not look./ After he called and turned on me/ His eyes. These I shall see—" The final dash suggests that the speaker remains haunted by Ken's gaze. In "The Narrow Door," death disrupts a game of "shop" as a coffin is carried out through the narrow door before which the "café children" play. Images of death appear in the partially autobiographical "The Changeling," in which "the little pale brother" has been "called away," and "The Quiet House," which opens with "the old Nurse" and concludes with the speaker's revision of the famous line from René Descartes, "some day I *shall* not think; I

shall not *be*!" In "Fame," Mew's speaker mediates on whether she could renounce her fame, represented by "the over-heated house," "Where no one fits the singer to his song,/ Or sifts the unpainted from the painted faces," and return to her previous life, symbolized in "The folded glory of the gorse, the sweet-briar air." Choosing Fame, the speaker fantasizes taking her "To our tossed bed." A still birth, "A frail, dead, new-born lamb," "The moon's dropped child," results from their union, a consequence of ambition and sexual passion.

The title poem, "The Farmer's Bride," tells of a young bride, who, having developed a fear of men, runs away. Chased after and returned by the villagers, she is locked away where she "does the work about the house" "like a mouse." The bride's imprisonment, symbolic of women's confinement in marriage, is contrasted against her natural self, which the narrator associates with "wild violets" and the "beasts in stall." In the lines "Sweet as the first wild violets, she,/ To her wild self. But what to me?," the break between "self" and "me," illustrates this broken and unconsummated union. The farmer laments that there are no children: "What's Christmas-time without there be/ Some other in the house than we!" The poem ends with the farmer overcome by his grief and sexual desire: "Oh! my God! the down,/ The soft young down of her, the brown,/ The brown of her—her eyes, her hair, her hair!"

The Farmer's Bride also contains the two-hundred-line free-verse poem, "Madeleine in Church," a dramatic monologue spoken by a woman who prefers to kneel not before Jesus, but rather a "plaster saint" ". . . more like [her] own clay,/ Not too divine." Too high on the cross, Jesus appears distant from the realities of her life, her marriage and divorce, the death of her child, her fading youth. She challenges him, "What can You know, what can You really see/ Of this dark ditch, the soul of me!" Unlike the traditional "fallen woman," Mew's Madeleine is unrepentant, insisting twice, "We are what we are" and that she will not be among the "broken things" held in God's "everlasting wings." The poem offers two versions of love through which Mew repeats the human/divine binary represented by the saint and Jesus. Mew invites readers to compare the perfect yet unattainable passion of Mary Magdalene for Jesus, "a passion" "so far from earthly cares and earthly fears" that one can only look "at it through tears," to the marriage of the speaker's mother, who was "yoked to the man that Father was." Looking to bridge this chasm between the heavenly and the earthly, the speaker longs for a human Jesus, who would notice or even speak to her: "If He had ever seemed to notice me/ Or, if, for once, He would only speak."

THE RAMBLING SAILOR

This posthumous collection of thirty-two poems was edited by Alida Monro and contains six of Mew's "Early Poems," including "Requiescat." While the collection continues themes of loss, loneliness, and death, particularly the death of children, these poems express resignation and a fragile hope. They are poems of remembrance, of things, places, and people lost. The speaker in "The Trees Are Down" observes the cutting down of "the great plane-trees at the end of the gardens," and in "Fin de Fête," the speaker recalls how she and an anonymous "you" "should have slept" together like children in a fairy tale, but now there is only the speaker's "lonely head."

Stylistically these poems are more restrained; there are more sonnets, and fewer free-verse lines overspill the page. In a mirroring of form and content, the sexual and religious passion, the grief and despair is also contained, though tentatively. The speakers in these poems appear less consumed with earthly desires, meditating instead on the afterlife. The speaker in "In the Fields," reflecting the "lovely things which pass," asks, "Can I believe there is a heavenlier world than this?," and "Not for That City" claims, "We strain our eyes beyond this dusk to see/ What, from the threshold of eternity/ We shall step into. . . ." Facing their own death or the death of someone they love, the speakers in these poems look to nature, particularly spring, for solace. Having previously ". . . liked Spring last year/ Because you were here," the speaker of "I So Liked Spring," decides, "I'll like Spring because it is simply Spring/ As the thrushes do," and the war poem, "May, 1915," assures its readers, "Let us remember Spring will come again."

BIBLIOGRAPHY

Dowson, Jane, and Alice Entwistle. "'I Will Put Myself, and Everything I See, upon the Page': Charlotte Mew, Sylvia Townsend Warner, Anna Wickham and the Dramatic Monologue." In *A History of Twentieth-Century British Women's Poetry*. New York: Cambridge University Press, 2005. Contains considerable analysis of Mew's poetry, finding the poet's hallmark to be an ability to summon "felt absence."

Fitzgerald, Penelope. *Charlotte Mew and Her Friends*. 1992. Reprint. London: Flamingo, 2002. In this book-length biography, Fitzgerald examines Mew's life in the context of her friendships with Ella D'Arcy, Mrs. Dawson Scott, and May Sinclair. Contains selected poems and bibliography.

Goss, Theodora, ed. *Voices from Fairyland: The Fantastical Poems of Mary Coleridge, Charlotte Mew, and Sylvia Townsend Warner*. Seattle: Aqueduct Press, 2008. Presents the poetry of Mew, Coleridge, and Warner, with some critical analysis.

Hamilton, Ian. *Against Oblivion: Some Lives of the Twentieth-Century Poets*. New York: Viking, 2002. Contains a biography essay on Mew that looks at her poetry. Hamilton edited a selection of Mew's poetry.

Katz, Jon, and Kevin Prufer, eds. *Dark Horses: Poets on Overlooked Poems—An Anthology*. Urbana: University of Illinois Press, 2007. Contains Mew's poem "The Trees Are Down," with a commentary by Molly Peacock.

Kendall, Tim. *Modern English War Poetry*. Oxford: Oxford University Press, 2006. The chapter on Mew compares her war poetry to that of Edward Thomas, analyzing the trope of spring in each.

Leighton, Angela. *Victorian Women Poets: Writing Against the Heart*. New York: Harvester Wheatsheaf, 1992. The chapter on Mew in this introduction to eight nineteenth century women poets provides a biography and analysis of her work, identifying her as a Victorian and drawing comparisons to writer and artist Christina Rossetti.

Rice, Nelljean McConeghey. *A New Matrix for Modernism: A Study of the Lives and Poetry of Charlotte Mew and Anna Wickham*. New York: Routledge, 2003. Rice views both Mew and Wickham, who both published through the Poetry Bookshop, to be modern poets.

Sarah Fedirka

CHRISTOPHER MIDDLETON

Born: Truro, Cornwall, England; June 10, 1926

PRINCIPAL POETRY

Poems, 1944

Nocturne in Eden, 1945

Torse Three: Poems, 1949-1961, 1962

Nonsequences/Selfpoems, 1965

Our Flowers and Nice Bones, 1969

The Lonely Suppers of W. V. Balloon, 1975

Pataxanadu, and Other Prose, 1977

Carminalenia, 1980

Woden Dog, 1981

111 Poems, 1983

Serpentine, 1985

Two Horse Wagon Going By, 1987

Selected Writings, 1989

The Balcony Tree, 1992

Intimate Chronicles, 1996

The Word Pavilion, and Selected Poems, 2001

Of the Mortal Fire: Poems, 1999-2002, 2003

Tankard Cat, 2004 (also pb. as *The Anti-Basilisk*, 2005)

The Tenor on Horseback, 2007

Collected Poems, 2008

OTHER LITERARY FORMS

In addition to collections of poetry and short prose, Christopher Middleton has published an impressive number of translations, edited volumes, and critical essays. His translations from German cover a wide variety of genres, including poems by Johann Wolfgang von Goethe, Friedrich Hölderlin, Eduard Mörike, Hugo von Hofmannsthal, Georg Trakl, Paul Celan, and Günter Grass. He has also translated Friedrich Nietzsche's letters and such major works of modern German prose as Robert Walser's *The Walk, and Other Stories* (1957), *Jakob von Gunten* (1969), and *Institute Benjamenta* (1995) Christa Wolf's autobiographical novel *The Quest for Christa T.* (1970), and Elias Canetti's critical study of Kafka's letters to his fiancé, *Kafka's Other Trial: Or, The Letters to Felice* (1974).

Middleton has also edited or coedited several an-
thologies of verse and prose in translation: *No Hatred and No Flag, Twentieth Century War Poems* (1958), which was published a year later in German as *Ohne Hass und Fahne*; *Modern German Poetry, 1910-1960: An Anthology with Verse Translations* (1962, with Michael Hamburger); and *German Writing Today* (1967). He has also published German translations of his own works, including two pieces from *Pataxanadu, and Other Prose*, "The Pocket Elephants" (1969; *Der Taschenelefant*) and "Getting Grandmother to Market" (1970; *Wie wir Grossmutter zum Markt bringen*). He is also the author of a libretto for a comic opera, *The Metropolitans* (1964, music by Hans Vogt).

Middleton's critical essays have appeared in numerous journals, and many have been collected in *Bolshevism in Art, and Other Expository Writings* (1978), *The Pursuit of the Kingfisher* (1983), and *Jackdaw Jiving: Selected Essays on Poetry and Translation* (1998).

ACHIEVEMENTS

Christopher Middleton's main achievement is that of a mediator among the disparate worlds of poetry, translation, and academic scholarship. He frequently includes translations in his volumes of poetry and regards the act of translation as a preeminently poetic endeavor, while his critical works appear as the natural by-products of his familiarity with the history and the direct practice of literature.

Middleton has gained wide recognition as a translator, which is to say that he is recognized for his absence, for not being obtrusively present in the works he reproduces in English. Good translators are always difficult to recognize: On the one hand, they are denied the glory of the first creator of the text (after all, the translators' words are not their own), while on the other hand, those bilingual readers best able to appreciate the merits of a translation are precisely the same readers who have no need of one, since they can always read the work in the original. Middleton's many translations, together with his essays on translation, stand as major contributions to a difficult, challenging, and often underestimated art.

Middleton's combined efforts in poetry and translations have attracted much critical attention and honors.

He was awarded the Sir Geoffrey Faber Memorial Prize for Poetry in 1963, and a selection of his works was anthologized that same year in *Penguin Modern Poets Four*. He accepted a Guggenheim Fellowship in 1974-1975, served as a National Endowment for the Humanities fellow in 1980, and won the Schlegel-Tieck Translation Prize in 1986, and the Max-Geilinger-Stiftung Prize for translations in 1987-1988. He was nominated for a Neustadt Prize in 1992.

BIOGRAPHY

John Christopher Middleton was born on June 10, 1926, in Truro, Cornwall, where his father was organist at the cathedral. The family soon moved to Ely, and in 1930, they moved to Cambridge, where Middleton's father later became a senior lecturer in music. Middleton's early childhood atmosphere of cathedrals and music was followed by a series of boarding schools in idyllic pastoral settings, where he took up classical studies. He began to write poems at the age of sixteen. Although he later rebelled against the security of his childhood, he acknowledges that it was "a source for ideas of order." "Ideas of order" became very important for the young Royal Air Force aircraftsman-interpreter (later sergeant-interpreter) arriving among the ruins of Germany just at the end of World War II.

Middleton remained in the Royal Air Force until 1948, then returned by way of southern France to Oxford, where he read German and French and received his B.A. in 1951. He was lecturer in English at the University of Zurich, Switzerland, from 1952 to 1955, during which time he completed his Oxford Ph.D. thesis on the works of Hermann Hesse. In 1953, he married Mary Freer. From 1955 to 1965, he was senior lecturer at King's College, the University of London, except for one year, 1961-1962, when he was visiting professor at the University of Texas at Austin. This brief introduction to the American Southwest marked a crucial turning point in Middleton's career, and Texas joined London and the south of France as a recurring geographical locus for his poems. In 1966, he returned to the University of Texas, where, for more than three decades, he served as professor of German literature, becoming Centennial Professor in Modern Languages. He retired from his academic career in 1998.

ANALYSIS

Christopher Middleton's poems may be understood as poetic tributes to the recurrent possibilities of order. Typically, he subjects an emblem of a conventional and preexistent order (a classical or political theme, a work of art, a still-life on a breakfast table) to linguistic changes that disorder and reorder the given elements in such a way that what emerges is a new and provisional order that contains and signals its own explosive instability. In other words, the poet does not claim to uncover the "real" significance of anything. The uniqueness of Middleton's poetry-of-process lies at least partly in the fact that the changes that take place in his poems always seem somehow slightly accidental, not fully under control, perhaps not even fully the responsibility of the poet. To lay claim to such control and responsibility would be to defeat the very point of the procedure by undermining the surprising freedom that comes with the startling rediscovery of things long thought familiar. This helps to explain Middleton's evident lack of interest in "inspiration," or the creation of order *ex nihilo*; he chooses rather to subject the available material of an imperfectly ordered world to sensational transformations, performing a trick that, as one critic put it, "makes the things hover in the air like a mirage." For Middleton, creation is recreational recreation, and his poems have much in common both with translations and with collages. By merging classical elements (images of order) with modernist techniques (procedures of disorder), Middleton is able to avoid both the chill stasis of a sterile classicism and the self-defeating absurdity of an all-too-radical modernism; in his sensitive hands, old forms of order become as disquieting as the marble torsos of Giorgio de Chirico or René Magritte, or as radiant as Paul Cézanne's weighty apples.

Reviewers are often quick to mention Middleton's open allegiance to the traditions of European modernism, and they often praise his accuracy of detail, together with his "fine sense of the absurd." They frequently notice a certain obliquity—not to say obscurity—in Middleton's approach; one reviewer observed that Middleton "handles his insights with great finesse, but always from a distance as though with tweezers." In a similar vein, others have regretted in his works "the quick change from style to style," "the absence of any unifying personal pressure," and "something constrictingly intellectual." These problems are often regarded as endemic to a self-conscious postmodernism. In fact, these same poetic peccadilloes of flexibility and distance would be praised as virtues in a translator, while "intellectual" references to what one critic called "the *disjecta membra* of a scholar's workshop" can be seen simply as the natural expression of a *modus vivendi* operating between the creative and the professional life. In short, Middleton views poetry as a form of translation, translation as a form of creation, and both as legitimate and important subjects and objects for academic study. In a world plagued with divided loyalties and petty territorial rivalries, this example is indeed a major achievement.

Middleton's modernized classicism is evident even in the titles of most of his volumes of poetry, titles that he always takes care to explain. *Nonsequences/Selfpoems* is chosen for its echoes of nonsenses and consequences, and because "the poems are always consequent-nonsequent." Such self-negating hyphenated compounds are posted in Middleton's explanations like warning signs; he mentions elsewhere the "lucky-unlucky" publication of his first two volumes of poetry, or his preference for a "stark-ambiguous" style. The title of *Pataxanadu, and Other Prose* blends Samuel Taylor Coleridge's exotic dream-poem with Alfred Jarry's "pataphysics," the "science of imaginary solutions." *Carminalenia* merges two words from a line of Propertius to convey both a literal Latin sense of "Softsongs" and, as Middleton notes, a latent suggestion of something "criminal."

The world of Middleton's poems is steeped in a kind of all-pervasive "or-elseness," and his most rewarding works are those in which this quality is directly enlisted in the service of the poem's patterned destruction-and-transfiguration. The latent "or-elseness" of a given work is also opened up by translation, which uncovers new possibilities of order in the mediating language. Middleton has described the task of the poet and translator as a matter of "astonishing speech into incandescence," but it is this same incandescence of unstable matter that also astonishes the poet into speech.

TORSE THREE

The title *Torse Three* refers to one of the meanings of the word "torse," a certain kind of geometrical surface; its etymological cousins include "torsion," "tortuous," and "torture." The final twist in this collection is a poem about order, the fifth and last of "Five Psalms for Common Man," which may be taken as Middleton's most direct statement about the subject. Here the first definitive assertion—"Order imagined against fear is not order"—breaks the logical rule of identity, as "order" quickly becomes plural, a dialectic of order and disorder: "Out of a rumbling of hollows an order is born/ to negate another existing order of fear." A few lines later, the Psalmist sings that "Another order of fear is chaos," while throughout the poem, things either happen or they do not happen: Fear "only negates or does not negate existing order," while "images of chaos . . . accord or do not accord." Out of this logical-sounding but ambiguous tangle emerges the final statement: "The orders revolve as improvisations against fear,/ changed images of chaos. Without fear, nothing." Thus the circle of transformation is complete: Order against fear cannot be order, but without "orders of fear" (or chaos—which has no plural) there can be no order at all. Other writers have described this dilemma in terms of the creator's struggle against entropy; but Middleton seems to suggest that order is only the obverse of entropy, undifferentiation momentarily disguised.

NONSEQUENCES/SELFPOEMS

Nonsequences/Selfpoems introduces the "Texan theme" into Middleton's work, where it immediately takes up permanent residence. Images of politics—of social order—also occupy more territory here than in *Torse Three*, as Middleton develops methods for integrating political material into his vision of the poet's dangerous game. In "Difficulties of a Revisionist," a political extension is added to the notion of the poet as translator or maker of kaleidoscopic collages:

All day fighting for a poem. Fighting against what?
And for what? What? being its own danger, wants
  to get rescued, but from its rescuer?

Which side is the poet to be on in the struggle for a new revisionary vision, if the poem—its own danger—is struggling to be saved from its poet? Danger lurks also in "Dangers of Waking," in which the "reports and messages" brought by children to the recumbent narrator are progressively magnified into the nightmare news of barbed wire, prison cells, and "the killing of this or that/ man, thousand, or million." This poem appears rather late in the volume, and serves as a counterbalance to an earlier description of "Navajo Children" accepting lollipops from tourists in Canyon de Chelly, Arizona.

Repressions past and future stalk the pages of *Nonsequences/Selfpoems*, which shows Middleton at his bleakest. Even the more pastoral and private images of order appear as if at the mercy of angry mobs just over the distant horizon. The natural-unnatural world harbors savages and phantoms: Cats crunch the head bones of mice, the Cyclops's broken eye clings like a slug on a carrot, houses are haunted by shaggy monsters and street-crossings by "this unknown thing." All the poet's combinatory gifts are helpless to rectify or mitigate the horrors of the past; "January 1919" begins with one of Middleton's bitterest lines—"What if I know, Liebknecht, who shot you dead"—and ends with an appeal to "Look upon our children, they are mutilated." In the final poem, "An Englishman in Texas," the poet presents himself as a kind of sky-struck survivor eager to shed the shreds of past identity to exist fully in the present; this last nonsequence voices his wish to "drop character,/ its greed for old presences, its dirt" in order to "move once,/ free, of himself, into some few things."

OUR FLOWERS AND NICE BONES

Our Flowers and Nice Bones, Middleton's next volume of poetry, takes its title from a letter by Kurt Schwitters and represents Middleton's most sustained Dadaistic sortie into such experimental forms as concrete poetry, "found" poems, and works in which sound is invited to take precedence over sense. The poet's quest for order seeks its method either in the visual effect of letters on the page ("Birth of Venus," "Milk Sonnet") or in the shock of finding an unintentional poem ready-made, or a poetic possibility in the merging of two or more such "finds" (such as "Found Poem with Grafts," a true poetic collage). He also organizes poems in terms of sound, either by inventing a mock language of suggestive nonsense (like the Teutonic

Latin Finneganese of "Lausdeo Teutonicus" or the Mexican yodeling of "Armadillo Cello Solo") or by taking existing words through transformations based on their sounds (as in the jazzy bass be-bop of "Ballade in B").

One of the most interesting applications of this technique occurs in "Computer's Karl Marx," since the substitution of sound for sense also serves as a means of parodying the monotonous jargon of Marxist orthodoxy. The poem's epigraph is a quotation from Nikolai Bukharin about "the reorganization of production relations." Taking the words "production relations" as a source of raw sound-material for the manufacture of other words of Latin origin, Middleton reorganizes vowels and consonant clusters to produce such transmogrified tonal echoes as "conscript prostitutes/ rusticate prelates." Another poem in this collection, "Pavlovic Variations," offers additional insight into Middleton's attitude toward translation. As one learns from a postscript, the title of the poem comes not from Pavlov—as readers trained to respond to allusions will immediately have assumed—but from a Yugoslavian poet named Miodrag Pavlović. The opening section of the poem is Middleton's English rendering of a German translation of one of Pavlović's works, whose classical landscapes and political themes are then explored and developed in five subsequent variations. Middleton's poetic techniques have been compared with those of visual artists and with the Impressionists in particular; but in *Our Flowers and Nice Bones*, he borrows systems of order—whether at the level of individual letters, syllables, words, or themes—at least equally from the world of music.

THE LONELY SUPPERS OF W. V. BALLOON

The Lonely Suppers of W. V. Balloon is the most accomplished of Middleton's books of verse, beginning even with the unidentified hovering balloon depicted on the dust jacket, an elaborately equipped bubble of a globe with a suspended Spanish galleon for a gondola, complete with cannon and banners, and dangling ballast of birdcage and wine cask. In this collection, Middleton is at his best, displaying a rare and sensitive mixture of whimsy and provocation, game and threat, entirely accurate as if by accident. One of the most beautiful poems in the volume, "A Cart with Apples," shows Middleton's poetry-of-process at its most masterful. The poem paints a simple still life of an apple cart standing in a field of roses; but through the transforming play of attributes, of fullness and roundness, shadows and primary colors (blue, rose, and yellow), every object—cart, apples, field, and all their interwoven shadows—comes to share in the full, round, colorful reality of every other object until the image achieves a vivid shimmering density worthy of Cézanne.

This is cubist poetry, enriching its objects with layers of perspective while preserving the essence of their unity. Unlike paintings, poems accumulate their being in linear time, but here the quality of the light shifting from stanza to stanza is a poetic reflection of Claude Monet's attempt to capture the shifting colors absorbed and reflected by the facade of the Rouen Cathedral. "A Cart with Apples" offers a vision so much a part of the idea of southern France that one recognizes it without having seen it, just as one knows that the setting is southern France although it is never actually mentioned. Something of the quality of Mediterranean light is captured here with simple words and a lucid technique that clearly reflects Middleton's ideas about the transformational nature of order.

The title poem, "The Lonely Suppers of W. V. Balloon," is another magical still life: a Texas evening, a bottle of wine on the table ("seadark wine," an inversion of the "winedark sea" of Homer's *Odyssey*, c. 725 B.C.E.; English translation, 1614), and a thunderstorm raging outside. It is a poem about, among other things, gratitude: "Thank the thunderstorm," the poet says, because "Here we sit, love . . . and believe/ What floated past the window was Balloon's lasso,/ His anchor was the lightning." Thus, through the intercessionary charm of a word as weird as "balloon," the Englishman conjures up a moment of deep peace with the desert phantoms, so that what passes in the dark is not a noose, but a lasso, and even the flash of lightning can be an image of steadfastness.

However, Balloon's world is not without its dangers, as is suggested by "Briefcase History," a case history of the poet's briefcase done in the style of Guillaume Apollinaire. The briefcase, made from scavenged war materials, is celebrated as a trusted veteran and friend. Nevertheless, the poem ends with an omi-

nous twist—game or threat?—as the poet suddenly tells the travel-worn container of so many mementoes: "you have never contained an explosive device/ never have you contained an explosive device/ yet."

PATAXANADU, AND OTHER PROSE

While both *Our Flowers and Nice Bones* and *The Lonely Suppers of W. V. Balloon* contain examples of prose poetry, Middleton's next collection, *Pataxanadu and Other Prose*, consists entirely of short prose parables, enigmas, and fragments in the tradition of Franz Kafka and Jorge Luis Borges. These prose sketches frequently echo themes from earlier poems, though here newly subjected to the quasi-logical rules of prose and to its mimetic possibilities. Most of the narrators of these prose sketches see themselves as isolated historians writing with a sense of duty and urgency about political or familial situations. The assumptions underlying their specific attitudes are revealed only between the lines, as the dreamlike merges with the matter-of-fact and classical motifs mix with visions of a totalitarian future. The confessional order imposed by eyewitness testimony is here locked in soft-spoken but deadly combat with the disorder of randomness or the false order of political oppression.

Unlike most of the pieces, the five title sketches in *Pataxanadu, and Other Prose* are generated through a system of lexical substitutions originally developed by Raymond Queneau, which Middleton applies to passages from Sir Thomas Malory, Sir Thomas Urquhart's translation of François Rabelais, Jonathan Swift, Herman Melville, and Charles Doughty. In a sense, these are prose equivalents of the "found" poems in *Our Flowers and Nice Bones*, but here their "finding" involves the deliberate systematic distortion of the original text—a method answering Arthur Rimbaud's call for the "systematic disruption of all the senses"—and the results are remarkably droll (Melville's mates, Starbuck, Stubb, and Flask, are "translated" into Stealbudget, Stuff, and Flaunt).

Pataxanadu, and Other Prose also comes with its own key in the form of a review by Middleton's anagrammatical avatar, Doctor Philden Smither, of an imaginary monograph by a certain Professor Erwin Ignaz Steintrommler on the historical significance of short prose. Professor Steintrommler's Germanic pedantry is gently spoofed: He argues, for example, that since all users of language necessarily lie, "the shorter the prose is, the less will be the likelihood of falsification"—a position that leads logically to silence as the supreme form of truth. Steintrommler's examples are all "real," however, ranging from Aesop's fables to Daniil Kharms and Kenneth Patchen, and they offer a valuable reminder of the richness of the tradition of short prose, one which has yet to be fully recognized as a distinct and important genre.

CARMINALENIA

Carminalenia is sparser and sparer than Middleton's previous volumes. Familiar themes recur, and there is also "The Palace of Thunder," a translation of Apollinaire, but the obliquity of many of the poems, the privacy of their references and the mystery of their connections, makes this easily one of the least accessible of all Middleton's works. This privacy extends to the appended notes, where Middleton compares a poem to the experience of diving through a shoal of fish. Middleton's homage to the privacy of his illuminations recalls the style of Wallace Stevens, which finds an obvious echo in the poem titled "A Very Small Hotel Room in the Key of T." Middleton continues to raise questions about the limits of generic frontiers when he titles one blank-verse piece "The Prose of Walking Back to China." In a prose poem titled "Or Else," the poet uses the title phrase as a refrain to retract every statement as soon as it is uttered in favor of an alternative version, itself immediately supplanted by yet another version, and so on. This is another classic example of Middleton's method of composition based on the principle that order is always self-destructing, that it exists only as a perpetual urge to order; once frozen and taken for granted, it becomes a lie, a target.

THE BALCONY TREE

Middleton's characteristic British sensibility and lack of inspirational moments continued to permeate his collection *The Balcony Tree*. His recording of everyday events—a couple parting at a train station, walking the dog, a new neighbor—take on a reserved quality, and his British spellings and uniform-length stanzas keep his poems proper in every sense. The "proper" in these poems thus continues the inaccessibility found in the poems of *Carminalenia*. Old-

fashioned British grammar seems incongruous with the poems' commonplace themes:

> But into you I leaned
> And felt a trembling go
> From all my body out
> Into your sudden sleep

he says, recalling a tender moment.

Nine surreal prose pieces that form the book's final section are more approachable. Intimate and vividly detailed, these ironic accounts seem lifted from a historical chamber of horrors: the funeral of a clown during Russian-Polish strife in 1920, soldiers in 1939 encamped by the sea, the importance that Turkish peasants attach to sleeping on their roofs. Both less formal and more imaginative, these closing works accomplish what the poems of the collection strain to achieve, turning minor events into harbingers.

THE ANTI-BASILISK

The Anti-Basilisk was first published in the United States in 2004 as *Tankard Cat*. This volume contains five sections: "Tableaux I-XX," "The Anti-Basilisk," "Apropos Saul Pinkard," "Twenty Tropes for Doctor Dark," and "Translations." "Tableaux I-XX" consists mainly of poems with historical settings, reminiscent of the old *tableaux vivant*, with parallel episodes and characters from other historical periods overlaid. Middleton's superb grasp of the history of Western civilization is clearly demonstrated here. In "Apropos Saul Pinkard," Middleton adopts an alter ego that is slightly more freewheeling than his usual one.

The main section "The Anti-Basilisk." A basilisk has two quoted meanings: an evil serpent and a destructive piece of artillery. In a sense, Middleton's poetry is the anti-basilisk, the weapon to be used against evil and destruction, of which Western civilization is only too full of examples. In the title poem, the basilisk comes creeping in from the night but cannot enter the house because of the fragile mosquito net, symbolic of Middleton's own poetry. There are many other preoccupations: for example, the decline of Roman civilization and its lessons for today.

In some ways, the poems in the section "Twenty Tropes for Doctor Dark" overshadow those in "The Anti-Basilisk." The poems are classical, sombre, tightly written, and very powerful. Doctor Dark becomes a Mephistopheles figure; the corruption of innocence is a powerful theme as is the desire for a lost paradise. Paradisal scenes are counterbalanced with scenes from Dante's *Inferno* (in *La divina commedia*, c. 1320; *The Divine Comedy*, 1802) and modern warfare. Art exists in the tension of this knowledge of good and evil.

THE TENOR ON HORSEBACK

The Tenor on Horseback contains thirty-five poems, written between 2005 and 2007, in its main section, and eight poems in a subsection titled "Marginala." The poems are more consciously the products of an old man, at a stoic distance from his topics. The title poem is the most significant. Just as a circus horse rides around and around in a circle, so poets, as keepers of wisdom, come round through the ages. Like the Magi, the poet sees himself as a wise man seeking to reinterpret the mystery of suffering and evil to his own generation in terms it can comprehend. Another poem, "Imagine Mallarmé" deals with the continuing frustration of the artist never being able to produce the perfect work of art. However, to practice art is still held a privilege. Some of the poems are more lightly satiric. All are formal, focused and obviously the product of a cultured sensibility only too aware of the fading of civilized values.

COLLECTED POEMS

Poets often collect their works in a single volume at some stage during their careers, often revising and adding to the volume as they continue to produce poetry. Middleton, in comparison to many other poets, left it extraordinarily late in his career—2008, when he was eighty-two years old—to issue such a collection. Middleton's work was largely neglected during the 1980's and 1990's, and before the publication of *Collected Poems*, although a few poems were being anthologized, most of his earlier poetry had gone out of print.

However, Middleton did not publish everything he had ever written in the *Collected Poems*. His first two works, *Poems* and *Nocture in Eden*, were excluded, as were the prose poems of *Pataxanadu, and Other Prose*, *111 Poems* and *Serpentine*. He did include the entire *The Anti-Basilisk*, over half of *The Tenor on Horseback*, and two other poems not published elsewhere.

Such a collection allows some sort of overall assess-

ment to be made of Middleton. Such assessments usually look for development, and where the poet might fit into the streams and schools of a particular age. It also seeks to determine the stature of a poet. However, what strikes a reader most about the *Collected Poems* is not the contents' development, but its consistency, as the poetry follows steadfastly in the modernist footsteps of T. S. Eliot, Ezra Pound, and W. H. Auden. Whereas much British poetry has become either primitivist, as with that of Ted Hughes, or determinedly bourgeois, as with that of the followers of Philip Larkin and the Movement, Middleton remains aristocratic and stoic, intellectually alert and distant. His style seems little touched by postmodernism. His verse forms remain tight and recognizably traditional, ranging from the satiric to the mock heroic to the elegiac.

As an alert and active poet, Middleton continues to engage with the culture of the day. A later poem, for example, features the Spanish tennis ace, Rafael Nadal. Middleton's subject matter changes superficially, but as every modern event is related back either to historical or mythological parallels, its treatment remains the same. His travels have widened, again supplying him with fresh subject matter, but the treatment remains the same. The universality of the human condition, its frailty, its endurance, and its evil continue to be treated as a Roman poet might deal with them. Throughout, he refuses the consolations of religion, and his spirituality thus remains determinedly secular—hence the stoicism.

In these features, he is probably best grouped with American poets such as Anthony Hecht and Galway Kinnell rather than with any British poet. His long sojourn in the United States and his sympathetic acceptance of American culture as an extension of Western civilization has, in fact, made him rather critical of British myopia, even though he maintains a British reserve and dry humor. His long exposure to European literature makes him, above all, the foremost exponent of what it is to be a poet of the West in the twenty-first century.

OTHER MAJOR WORKS
PLAY: *The Metropolitans*, pb. 1964 (libretto).
NONFICTION: *Bolshevism in Art, and Other Exposi-*

tory Writings, 1978; *The Pursuit of the Kingfisher*, 1983; *Serpentine*, 1985; *Jackdaw Jiving: Selected Essays on Poetry and Translation*, 1998; *In the Mirror of the Eighth King*, 1999; *Crypto-Topographia: Stories of Secret Places*, 2002; *Palavers and a Nocturnal Journal*, 2004; *If From the Distance: Two Essays*, 2007 (with Alan Wall); *Depictions of Blaff*, 2008.

TRANSLATIONS: *The Walk, and Other Stories*, 1957 (of Robert Walser); *The Poet's Vocation: Selections from the Letters of Höderlin, Rimbaud, and Hart Crane*, 1967; *Jakob von Gunten*, 1969 (of Walser's novel); *Poems*, 1969 (of Günter Grass); *Selected Letters*, 1969 (of Friedrich Nietzsche); *The Quest for Christa T.*, 1970 (of Christa Wolf's novel); *Selected Poems*, 1972 (of Paul Celan); *Kafka's Other Trial: Or, The Letters to Felice*, 1974 (of Elias Canetti); *In the Egg, and Other Poems*, 1977 (of Grass); *Balzac's Horse, and Other Stories*, 1988; *Andalusian Poems*, 1993 (with Leticia Garza-Falcón); *Institute Benjamenta*, 1995 (of Walser's novel); *Elegies, and Other Poems*, 2000 (of Lars Gustafsson); *Faint Harps and Silver Voices: Selected Translations*, 2000; *Selected Stories*, 2002 (of Walser); *Speaking to the Rose: Writings, 1912-1932*, 2005 (of Walser).

EDITED TEXTS: *No Hatred and No Flag, Twentieth Century War Poems*, 1958 (pb. in German as *Ohne Hass und Fahne*, 1959); *Modern German Poetry, 1910-1960: An Anthology with Verse Translations*, 1962 (with Michael Hamburger); *German Writing Today*, 1967.

BIBLIOGRAPHY

Bête Noire (Spring, 1991). A special issue of this British literary magazine, focusing on Middleton.

Chicago Review 51, nos. 1-2 (Spring, 2005). This issue is devoted to making Middleton better known, through tributes, critical appreciations, portraits, and dialogues. Contains numerous articles, including an interview and portrait by Marius Kociejowski.

McCarey, Peter. "The Wooden Dog Fun Club Presents: Christopher Middleton." *PNReview* 34, no. 1 (September/October, 2007): 34-39. Article introduces Middleton to the new reader from his earliest work through *Woden Dog*.

Mann, John. Review of *Of the Mortal Fire*. *World Literature Today* 79, no. 1 (January-April, 2005): 89-91. Praises the work, calling it "superbly crafted and linguistically demanding."

Young, Alan. "Christopher Middleton." In *Poets of Great Britain and Since 1960*, edited by Vincent B. Sherry, Jr. Vol. 40 in *Dictionary of Literary Biography*. Detroit: Gale Research, 1985. A thorough and sympathetic account by one of Middleton's best critics. Young stresses Middleton's challenge to the reigning assumptions of contemporary British poetry; he sees Romantic as well as high modernist elements in Middleton's work. Includes a primary bibliography and references to secondary sources.

Gene M. Moore
Updated by David Barratt

JOHN MILTON

Born: London, England; December 9, 1608
Died: London, England; November 8, 1674

PRINCIPAL POETRY
Poems of Mr. John Milton, 1645
Paradise Lost, 1667, 1674
Paradise Regained, 1671
Samson Agonistes, 1671
The Poetical Works, 1952-1955

OTHER LITERARY FORMS

Although John Milton's poetry represents only about one-fifth of his total literary production, the prose works are more obscure, largely because he wrote in genres that no longer appeal to a large audience. Milton's prose is usually valued mostly for what it reveals about his biography and his thought. His most prominent theme was liberty—religious, domestic, and civil. The following examples are notable: five antiprelatical tracts (1641-1642); four tracts justifying divorce (1643-1645); and five pamphlets defending the English Puritan cause against the monarchists (1649-1654). The tract *Of Education* (1644) and the classical oration upholding freedom of the press, *Areopagitica* (1644), are the most familiar titles among the prose works. The remaining titles consist largely of academic exercises, letters, additional pamphlets, works of history, and treatises. Milton left in manuscript at his death a Latin treatise on religion, *De doctrina Christiana libri duo Posthumi* (1825), a work that provides valuable clarification of his religious beliefs.

ACHIEVEMENTS

By common agreement, literary historians have ranked John Milton second among English poets. He wrote during the English Renaissance, when authors were attempting to develop a national literature in the vernacular. In this endeavor, they had exceedingly rich sources on which to draw: the classics, many recently translated, which provided both genres and themes; the Judeo-Christian tradition, an area of broad interest and intensive study following the Reformation; and national sources—historical, folk, mythical; and literature from the Continent, particularly Italy and France. By the time Milton began writing, William Shakespeare and his contemporaries had created a national drama that surpassed that of other nations, and Ben Jonson had adapted such classical lyric genres as the ode and the epigram to English verse. As yet no poet had succeeded in creating an epic poem based on a classical model, a task that the age considered the highest achievement of the creative mind.

It remained for Milton to undertake this formidable task, one for which he was well prepared. Among English poets of the first rank, he was the most deeply and broadly learned—in classical languages and literature and in works of the Judeo-Christian tradition. From early life, he considered poetry to be a true vocation, and his development as a poet suggests that he emulated Vergil and Edmund Spenser, beginning with lyric genres and progressing by degrees to the epic. Milton's strongest inclination as a poet was to produce a synthesis of classical and Christian elements, a blend that critics have labeled his Christian humanism.

Milton contributed poems of lasting value and interest to English literature in both major and minor genres. He stressed the importance of the individual will by making his most common theme that of the soul in ethi-

cal conflict—the wayfaring, warfaring Christian. He developed a style peculiarly "Miltonic." In the verses that Milton would have seen as fitting his ideal of "simple, sensuous, passionate," Matthew Arnold discovered "touchstones," or examples of the sublime in poetry. Finally, he adopted the blank verse of English drama as a vehicle for the long poem on a serious theme.

BIOGRAPHY

John Milton was born into an upper-middle-class family in London, his father being a scrivener with real estate interests, sufficiently affluent to assure Milton that he did not have to follow a profession to live. John Milton the elder, who achieved recognition in his own right as a composer and musician, encouraged his son in his studies and enrolled him in St. Paul's School, then a quality day school in London. When he entered Christ's College, Cambridge, at sixteen, Milton had an excellent grounding in Latin and Greek.

Even though he was once suspended from Cambridge, he was a serious and successful student, taking two degrees (B.A., 1629; M.A., 1632). While at Christ's College, he wrote a significant amount of lyric poetry, and he altered his original intention of being ordained. Leaving Cambridge in 1632, he returned to his father's estates at Horton and, later, Hammersmith, remaining there until 1638. Although he continued to write poetry, his essential purpose appears to have been further systematic study of classical and Renaissance literature, history, and philosophy.

Approaching the age of thirty, he set out in 1638 to tour France, Switzerland, and Italy, a journey that lasted fifteen months and enabled him to glean impressions of European nature, art, and architecture that later enriched his poetry. During the tour, he also visited such learned men as Hugo Grotius and Giovanni Diodati and attended the meetings of learned societies.

Returning to England on the outbreak of civil war in 1639, he became engaged in the pamphlet war against the bishops. For a period of about fifteen years, Milton turned his primary attention to the writing of polemic prose, which he regarded as promoting the cause of liberty. His poetic output was small, consisting of a few sonnets and lyrics and translations from the Psalms. For a brief time, he became a schoolmaster, though his school enrolled only a handful of students, two of whom were Milton's nephews. His marriage to Mary Powell in 1642 lasted until her death following childbirth in 1652; a second marriage ended with the poignant death of Katharine Woodcock in 1658. His work as a controversialist brought his merit to the attention of the government of Oliver Cromwell, and he was appointed secretary of foreign tongues to the Council of State in 1649. He was totally blind by 1652 and had to dictate his correspondence and creative work.

By the late 1650's, he began composing *Paradise Lost*; his three major poetic works occupied the remaining years of his life. As the Restoration approached, he tried in vain to stem the tide by writing more antimonarchial and anticlerical pamphlets. During the years following the Restoration, he lived quietly in London with his third wife, Elizabeth Minshull, receiving friends and composing and revising his poems. He was much troubled by gout and died of its complications in 1674.

John Milton (Library of Congress)

ANALYSIS

The greater part of John Milton's lyric poetry was written during his residences at Cambridge (1625-1632) and at Horton-Hammersmith (1632-1638). The work of the Cambridge period includes numerous occasional poems in English and conventionally allusive Latin epigrams and elegies. These early lyrics may owe something to Milton's "Prolusions," which are academic exercises on a set theme with predictable lines of argument, ornamented with numerous classical allusions. Such prose assignments may well have contributed to Milton's rich style and his firm sense of genre.

The poems cover a wide variety of topics: the death of bishops, of an infant, of the university carrier; the anniversary of the Gunpowder Plot; and religious topics. In "At a Vacation Exercise," written before he was twenty, Milton intimates that he will use his native language for "some graver subject" than the one that the hundred-line lyric develops. His lyric "On Shakespeare," included with the commendatory poems in the second folio (1632), had a theme of special interest to the young Milton, the fame that comes to a poet. In this lyric, as in others, the style and diction indicate a debt to Edmund Spenser.

"ON THE MORNING OF CHRIST'S NATIVITY"

Among the poems written during the Cambridge period, the ode "On the Morning of Christ's Nativity" (1629) remains the most significant, perhaps the best nativity hymn in English poetry. The verses depict Christ as a triumphant redeemer—sovereign over nature, baneful to demons, and warmly human. In a rime royal proem (four stanzas), Milton establishes the occasion and setting, and then celebrates the Nativity in thirty-seven stanzas, each being of eight verses, varying in length and rhyming *aabccbdd*. The hymn has three structural divisions: Stanzas 1-7 portray the peace of nature and the civilized world at the time of Christ's birth; stanzas 8-15 celebrate the promise of Christ for the future, with images of music and harmony; stanzas 16-37 foretell the results of Christ's birth for the near future, the cessation of oracles and the collapse of pagan religions. Milton associates Christ with Pan and Hercules, freely drawing on classical mythology and reading it as Christian allegory; at the same time, he follows a different Christian tradition by equating the pagan gods with devils. The ode is remarkable for its exuberant metrical movement and its rich imagery of light and harmony.

"IL PENSEROSO" AND "L'ALLEGRO"

Two of Milton's best-known lyrics, "L'Allegro" and "Il Penseroso," cannot be dated with certainty, though they are usually assigned to the period 1629-1632. "L'Allegro" celebrates the pleasures of the mirthful man, while "Il Penseroso" celebrates those of the contemplative man, whose joyous mood may be tinged with melancholy. These companion poems, both written in iambic tetrameter, employ a similar structure. "L'Allegro" begins in early morning and concludes in the evening; its companion begins in the evening and ends with morning. The speaker in each poem moves through a series of settings, and both poems express the delight and pleasure to be derived from nature and art, their chief appeal being to the senses of sight and sound.

COMUS

The poems of the Horton-Hammersmith period demonstrate the growth of Milton's poetic power and give promise of further development, in *Comus* (1634; pb. as *A Maske Presented at Ludlow Castle*, 1637) and "Lycidas" (1637) being the most notable. A masque is a brief dramatic entertainment, characterized by a simple plot and conflict, usually presented by amateurs and employing elaborate costumes, fanciful situations, song, dance, and highly poetic passages. The poem represents Milton's first important use of blank verse and his first significant work on the theme of temptation. The mythical Comus inhabits a wood and entices travelers there to taste his liquor, which transforms them into monstrous shapes and makes them his followers. Milton's heroine, the Lady, becomes separated from her brothers in this wood and is tempted by Comus but refuses. Although he can force her to sit immobile in a chair, he can attain no power over her mind or will. The brothers, assisted by the guardian spirit Thyrsis, arrive on the scene, drive Comus away, and secure her release through the aid of the water nymph Sabrina. Thereupon the two brothers and the Lady are presented to their parents. The theme of temptation enables Milton to celebrate the power of the human will to resist evil, a central theme of his major poems. In *Comus*, the temptation occurs in a natural setting, almost a pastoral milieu; in later works the setting and character are altered to present the theme in greater complexity.

"LYCIDAS"

The occasion of Milton's pastoral elegy "Lycidas" was the death of Milton's fellow student at Cambridge, Edward King, who drowned in the Irish Sea in 1637. At the time of his death, he had a career as a clergyman open before him. Milton follows the conventions of the pastoral elegy, King being treated as a shepherd whose songs have ended and for whom all nature mourns. The invocation of the muse, rhetorical questions, the fixing of blame, the procession of mourners, the catalog of flowers—all these conventional elements find a place. The traditional elegiac pattern of statement of loss, reconciliation, and looking toward the future is also followed in "Lycidas." Milton uses the convention of allegory in pastoral poetry to meditate on fame and to attack abuses within the Church. The elegy employs a complex rhythm and rhyme pattern that is indebted to the Italian *canzone*.

Over a period of approximately thirty years, Milton wrote twenty-three sonnets, among them some of the most memorable lyrics in English. As with other genres, he made contributions to the form, in this instance both thematic and stylistic. Although the first six sonnets, five of them in Italian, are conventional in style, the English sonnets that follow mark new directions that influenced the history of the sonnet form. The first sonnets were love poems, and most early English sonnets were written in the tradition of Francis Petrarch's sequence to Laura. Shakespeare and John Donne had left influential poems on the themes of friendship and religion. To Milton, the sonnet became a poem written not in sequence but on an occasion of personal or public significance—on his twenty-third birthday, on his blindness, on the death of his wife, on the massacre in Piedmont, on the public reception of his divorce tracts. Although many of the sonnets reflect Milton's strong religious and moral convictions, they are not, strictly speaking, religious poems.

From the standpoint of style, he broke the traditional quatrain division and introduced an inverted Latinate syntax that allowed freedom in the placement of modifiers. The result was numerous enjambments and an alteration of the pauses within the lines of the sonnet. As in his longer poems, Milton juxtaposes Latinate diction and syntax with simple English diction and meter, creating a powerful tension. These stylistic innovations and the rich allusive texture that Milton brings to the sonnet combine to make the sonnets seem more restricted and concentrated than those of the Elizabethan period. When, a century after Milton, the pre-Romantics revived the sonnet as a lyric form, the predecessor whose work they emulated was Milton.

PARADISE LOST

Although he had been planning to write an epic poem for nearly forty years before *Paradise Lost* was published in 1667, Milton did not seriously begin the composition before 1655-1657, when he was approaching fifty years of age. He had thought of an epic based on either British history or a biblical theme; when the time came, he chose the biblical theme and developed it on the grandest scale possible. From a Christian perspective, he set out to narrate all important events in the temporal and spiritual history of humankind, to answer all important questions, to tell what one poet called "the story of all things." Not content to narrate the Fall of Man from grace, Milton included in his statement of the theme, as announced in the prologue to book 1, humankind's restoration and the ability of humans to gain immortality. The theology of *Paradise Lost* is essentially orthodox Protestant, although a few unusual theological views were discovered after students of Milton closely examined the epic in the light of his treatise on theology, *De doctrina Christiana libri duo Posthumi*.

Milton adheres to numerous epic conventions established by Homer and Vergil, his classical predecessors in the form: action set in various realms, divine and human characters, a stated theme, invocation of the muse, epic games, epic similes, warfare, speeches, dreams, catalogs, roll calls, elevated style, and twelve books (or multiples of twelve). A remarkable departure from the practice of earlier epic poets, as T. J. B. Spencer has pointed out, is that numerous minor epic conventions, particularly those concerning warfare and conflict, are more often associated with the demoniac than with the human or the divine. Milton specifically rejects warfare as a subject unworthy of the epic, preferring to celebrate the suffering hero who endures adversity for the sake of conscience and right. In a mythical perspective, Christ represents the hero of Milton's epic, for he is the character who acts, who creates and restores. Yet, Adam receives more attention in the poem and undergoes a change of fortune; for humankind, Milton's readers, he becomes the hero.

As Northrop Frye pointed out, it is instructive to examine *Paradise Lost* as a myth, even though Milton believed that he was narrating events that actually took place—some poetic license and elaboration being permitted. The mythical structure of the epic is cyclic, involving actions primarily of the Deity (constructive) and Satan (destructive). The earliest point in the narrative is the occasion for Satan's revolt, the recognition of Christ as Son of God before the assembled angels in Heaven. Following a three-day war in Heaven, Satan and millions of followers are cast out; and God creates the universe and the human order to restore spiritual beings to vacant places in Heaven. This purpose is challenged by Satan, who journeys to earth to tempt man and bring about his fall. Although Satan achieves his objective, God repairs the loss by giving man the law and redeeming him, enabling man to regain the opportunity of entering Heaven after Judgment Day.

Since Milton follows the epic convention of beginning in medias res, the narrative is not presented chronologically. Instead, after stating the theme, Milton begins the first book with Satan and his followers in the depths of hell. Although the poetic structure of *Paradise Lost* may be approached in various ways, the most common is to divide the epic into three major parts or movements, with four related books in each: 1-4; 5-8; 9-12. Books 1-4 introduce the theme, settings, lines of narrative development, characters (divine, demoniac, human), and motivation. In book 1, Satan and Beëlzebub are found suffering in hell, a place that Milton describes as holding a multitude of torments. They resolve never to submit but to continue their vain attempt against God through guile. Rousing his followers, Satan has them build an enormous palace, Pandemonium, as the site of a council of war. In book 2, after Moloch, Mammon, Belial, and Beëlzebub have proposed plans of action to the council, the plan of Satan, as presented by Beëlzebub, is accepted—that they attempt to thwart God's plan by subverting another world and its beings, a mission that Satan volunteers to perform. He sets out to travel through chaos to earth, while his followers divert themselves with epic games.

In book 3 the setting is changed to Heaven, where another council takes place. God the Father, presiding over the assembled angels, informs them of Satan's mission, predicts its success, explains the necessity for a redeemer, and accepts Christ's voluntary sacrifice to save humankind. The council in Heaven (book 3, vv. 80-415) provides the essential theological basis for the poem, clarifying the redemptive theology of Christianity as Milton understood it. This done, Milton returns to Satan, who deceives the angels stationed by God for man's protection and travels to the peak of Mount Niphates overlooking the Garden of Eden. The fourth book introduces the human characters, Adam and Eve, whom Milton describes as ideal human types, living in an idyllic setting. Even Satan finds the creation of God beautiful, though the beauty does not deter him from his destructive plan. Instead, he approaches Eve in the form of a toad and creates in her mind a troubling dream, until the angels appointed to watch over the Garden discover him and drive him out.

Books 5-8, the middle books of *Paradise Lost*, contribute to the narrative in at least three important ways: They enable Milton to show God's concern for man by sending the angel Raphael to instruct Adam of the danger represented by Satan, the function that George Williamson has described as "the education of Adam." They permit him to provide exposition through an account of the war in Heaven and of the creation. Finally, they enable him to prepare the reader to accept as credible the fall of perfect beings whose only duty was to obey a plain and direct command of God. Book 5 opens with Eve narrating her dream to Adam, the dream cre-

ated by Satan, in which an angel tempts her to disobey God's command and eat of the forbidden tree. The dream follows closely the actual temptation sequence in book 9 and so foreshadows the more complex temptation that follows. Adam reassures her that dreams imply no guilt, and the angel Raphael arrives to begin his explanation of the revolt of Satan. In book 6, the angel narrates the three-day war in Heaven. James H. Hanford has shown that in the narrative Milton describes the types of combat then known—single warriors battling for victory, classic battle formations, artillery, and, finally, an elemental kind of strife like that of the Titans, in which the angels rend up hills to hurl them at their opposition. On the third day, Christ appears to drive Satan and his host out of Heaven.

The seventh book provides an account of the creation of the universe and all living things by Christ, who forms the whole from chaos, bringing order and harmony. To Milton, the creation is consciously and intentionally harmonious and hierarchical. In book 8, Adam explains what he can recall about his own creation and asks Raphael questions about astronomy. When he acknowledges to the angel that he sometimes inclines to Eve's view because her wisdom seems superior, Raphael warns him not to abandon his responsibility as her guide, emphasizing the importance of hierarchy.

The final group of books includes an account of man's fall (9), its immediate aftermath 10), and the long-term consequences (11-12), the final two books representing the education of fallen Adam. In book 9, Satan returns to the Garden under cover of darkness and enters the body of the serpent. The serpent approaches Eve, who has persuaded Adam to let her work apart, and tempts her to disobey God through promises of greater power. When she returns to Adam, he understands what has happened, and at her invitation eats the forbidden fruit, not because he has been deceived but because he wishes to share Eve's fate. The immediate results include inordinate and ungovernable passions in both and disorder in nature. In book 10, Christ appears in the Garden to pass sentence on man, but his words hold out hope of triumph over Satan. As he is returning to hell, Satan meets the allegorical figures Sin and Death, who are paving a broad way to link hell and the earth. His triumph before his followers in hell is eclipsed when they are transformed into serpents that greedily approach apple trees growing outside the great hall, only to discover the fruit to be bitter ashes. Meanwhile, Adam and Eve have understood that God's will must prevail and have begun to take some hope in the promise given them by the Savior.

In book 11, the archangel Michael is sent by God to explain to Adam the effects of sin on his descendants, so that Adam can understand and accept God's plan for humankind. Adam sees the effects of sin, understanding the cause of disease, death, and erroneous choices among men. He witnesses the flood that destroys the world and acknowledges it as just. In book 12, Michael narrates the bringing of the law through Moses, the birth of Christ, the establishment of the Church, and the history of Christianity until Judgment Day. Having understood the entire scope of human history, Adam gratefully accepts God's plan for the restoration of humanity, and he and Eve depart from the Garden, having lost the original paradise but having gained the ability to attain a "paradise within."

For the exalted theme of *Paradise Lost*, Milton achieves an appropriately elevated style that appeals primarily to the ear, creating the "organ tones" for which it is celebrated. He chose blank verse because he believed it to be the closest equivalent in English meter to the epic verse of the classics; yet the stylistic unit is not the line but rather the sentence, and, at times, the verse paragraph. The more prominent stylistic qualities include the following: Latinate diction and syntax ("the vast profundity obscure"), frequent inversions, words either archaic or used in unfamiliar senses, collocations of proper names, epic similes, compound epithets, compression, and, most prominently, the schemes of repetition—the most frequent being polyptoton, antimetabole, and chiasmus.

The style reveals a weaving of related images and a richly allusive texture that can be grasped only after repeated readings. Christopher Ricks has shown, for example, that references to the "hands" of Adam and Eve recur in poignantly significant contexts, creating a cumulative effect with one image. When Milton uses a biblical name, as Ricks notes, he often "transliterates," that is, provides the literal equivalent in English. Thus,

when Satan is named, "adversary" may appear immediately thereafter; "pleasant" occurs in passages that mention Eden—as if to remind readers that names embody meanings of which they are unaware. Further, reading mythology as allegory, Milton freely associates mythical characters with biblical counterparts—Proserpine with Eve, Deucalion with Noah, Ceres with Christ. Finally, the reader learns to interpret biblical characters typologically, as Milton did, where characters in the Old Testament anticipate the New—Adam, Noah, and Moses, for example, all being types of Christ. Through these poetic techniques, Milton achieves a style so complex that its interest and appeal can never be exhausted.

PARADISE REGAINED

Milton's brief epic *Paradise Regained*, written in blank verse and published with *Samson Agonistes* in 1671, represents a sequel to *Paradise Lost*, its hero Christ being a second Adam who overcomes temptation that is much more extensive than that experienced by Adam. Milton makes several assumptions about the temptation of Christ in his source, Luke 4:1-14, an account of events that occurred before the beginning of Christ's ministry: First, Christ does not fully understand either his mission or the role of the Messiah; second, he can be genuinely tempted; third, his withstanding temptation assures his success in the role of redeemer. To Milton, the Book of Job represented the ideal model for the brief epic; it appears that no other poem in English or in the classics influenced the form significantly.

The temptations of Christ, narrated in the four books of the poem, offer easy access to those things that Satan supposes a hero of his kind would want. At the beginning of the narrative, Christ has been fasting in the desert for forty days following his baptism, an event that had attracted Satan's interest. Satan had heard God's recognition of Christ following the ceremony and had supposed that Christ might be the offspring of Adam destined to bruise his head. Resolving to subject Christ to temptations, Satan approaches him in disguise and invites him to turn stones into bread to allay his hunger. After Christ's refusal, Satan next offers a banquet, also refused because Christ recognizes the giver as evil. When Satan realizes that Christ cannot be tempted by ordinary means, he concludes that he is indeed someone extraordinary and appeals to Christ's supposed ambition by offering first wealth, then the Parthian kingdom, then Rome, and, later, all kingdoms of the world in return to fealty to Satan. In rejecting these offers, Christ reveals that his kingdom is not of the world. Undeterred, Satan offers all the learning—philosophy, poetry, history—of Athens, declined by Christ as unnecessary to him and inferior to that of the Hebrews.

Satan raises a storm in the desert in the hope of terrifying Christ and transports him through the air to the pinnacle of the Temple, where he urges Christ to cast himself down and be rescued from death by God. When Christ replies, "Tempt not the Lord thy God," Satan recognizes his divine nature and falls himself, leaving Christ in the protection of angels who minister to him.

Biographer Barbara Lewalski has pointed out that the temptations in *Paradise Regained* are designed to reveal Christ's roles as priest, prophet, and king. The prophet in the wilderness denies himself, the king acknowledges no kingdom of this world, and the priest rejects the false and unnecessary learning for the true.

SAMSON AGONISTES

For his only tragedy, *Samson Agonistes*, Milton adapts a Greek model of the genre to a biblical episode, the story of Samson, as found in Judges 13-16. The title signifies Samson the wrestler or athlete; Milton's hero represents a type of Christ from the Old Testament, though Samson, unlike Christ, falls from favor and undergoes a series of temptations before being restored. Since Milton wrote the tragedy in verse (1,758 lines in blank verse) and since he clearly states that he did not intend the work for the stage, it is usually studied as a dramatic poem.

Samson Agonistes, said to be the English tragedy that most closely follows the Greek model, employs numerous Greek conventions. It takes place on the final day of the hero's life and follows the unities of time, place, and action. Milton divides the major episodes of the play not by acts but by the choral odes, as in Greek drama. The chorus performs its usual functions—providing exposition, advising the hero, announcing arrivals, and interpreting for the audience.

The tragedy opens with a despairing Samson, blind and enslaved to work in a Philistine mill, being visited on a holiday by a group of his countrymen, who form the chorus. Samson blames himself for the loss of God's favor because he revealed the secret of his strength to his wife, Dalila, who betrayed him to the Philistines. The men of Dan announce the arrival of Samson's father Manoa, who is negotiating with the Philistines for his son's release, a prospect that brings Samson little comfort, because he believes that idleness will only increase his sense of guilt. Manoa's effort, however, invites Samson to choose a life of ease and rest much unlike the life he has known, and this he rejects. Dalila arrives and informs Samson that she now wishes that he would return to her and renew their marriage. Her suggestion only arouses his anger, and she leaves, satisfied that she will enjoy fame among her own people. The next visitor is the Philistine champion Harapha, a giant who has come to challenge Samson to prove his strength once again through physical combat, but Harapha discreetly leaves after Samson defies him. This meeting renews Samson's understanding that his strength derives from God, yet it suggests to him that single combat is no longer his role.

A Philistine officer arrives to command Samson to attend the celebration in Dagon's temple to divert the audience with feats of strength. At first, Samson scornfully refuses the command as impious and idolatrous, but, after an inward prompting, changes his mind and accompanies the officer to the temple. As the Chorus and Manoa await Samson's return, they hear a fearful noise, and a messenger arrives to announce that Samson has destroyed the temple and has perished in the destruction, along with thousands of Philistines. The chorus recognizes that Samson has been restored to God's favor and has acted in accordance with divine will.

As in his other major works, Milton in *Samson Agonistes* expands and modifies his source while remaining faithful to its original meaning and spirit. The effort of Manoa to obtain Samson's release, the appearance of Dalila during his imprisonment, and the character of Harapha are all Milton's additions. They enable him to interpret the character of Samson as more complex than the biblical character and to show him undergoing a series of temptations. Although the poetic voice is less intrusive in *Samson Agonistes* than in the epics, Milton, as Hanford has pointed out, identifies rather closely with the blind hero of the tragedy.

MORAL SUBLIMITY

There can be little doubt that religion, as Milton understood it, stands as the major theme of his poetry. The protagonists of his four greatest poetic works—the Lady in *Comus*, Adam in *Paradise Lost*, Christ in *Paradise Regained*, and Samson in *Samson Agonistes*—undergo an elaborate temptation (or a series of temptations) and either triumph or come to terms with failure. Critics recognize that Milton does not excel in characterization, one reason being that his characters are subordinate to his narrative and thematic purposes. Nor does Milton possess a gift for humor or comedy; his infrequent efforts in those directions usually appear heavy-handed.

Milton's religious perspective is Protestant, with greater emphasis on the will than was common for his time. His view of salvation would have been called Arminian during the seventeenth century—that is, Christ provided for the salvation of all who willingly accepted him. To Milton, this assumption takes on classical overtones derived perhaps from Aristotle and Ovid, among others. In kind of Aristotelian teleology, he assumes that one right choice makes a second easier, and thus humankind through the proper exercise of will moves toward the perfection of human nature. Conversely, a wrong choice makes subsequent right choices more difficult and may lead to the degradation of human nature.

In his poetry, Milton seeks to celebrate right choices and to guide readers in their own choices. His poetry of the will and of ethical conflict is expressed in literary genres of lasting interest and in a style so sublime and so rich in poetic meaning that people discover new beauties with each successive reading.

OTHER MAJOR WORKS

PLAY: *Comus*, pr. 1634 (pb. 1637 as *A Maske Presented at Ludlow Castle*).

NONFICTION: *Animadversions upon the Remonstrant's Defence Against Smectymnuus*, 1641; *Of Prelatical Episcopacy*, 1641; *Of Reformation Touching Church Discipline in England*, 1641; *An Apology Against a Pamphlet . . .*, 1642; *The Reason of Church-Government Urg'd Against Prelaty*, 1642; *The Doctrine and Discipline of Divorce*, 1643; *Areopagitica*, 1644; *The Judgement of Martin Bucer Concerning Divorce*, 1644; *Of Education*, 1644; *Colasterion*, 1645; *Tetrachordon*, 1645; *Eikonoklastes*, 1649; *The Tenure of Kings and Magistrates*, 1649; *Pro Populo Anglicano Defensio*, 1651; *Pro Populo Anglicano Defensio Secunda*, 1654; *Pro Se Defensio*, 1655; *Considerations Touching the Likeliest Means to Remove Hirelings Out of the Church*, 1659; *A Treatise of Civil Power in Ecclesiastical Causes*, 1659; *The Readie and Easie Way to Establish a Free Commonwealth*, 1660; *The History of Britain*, 1670; *Of True Religion, Heresy, Schism, and Toleration*, 1673; *De doctrina Christiana libri duo Posthumi*, 1825; *Complete Prose Works of John Milton*, 1953-1982 (8 volumes).

MISCELLANEOUS: *Works*, 1931-1938 (18 volumes).

BIBLIOGRAPHY

Beer, Anna. *Milton: Poet, Pamphleteer, and Patriot.* London: Bloomsbury, 2008. An examination of Milton's life and works that covers his noted poetry and also his pamphlets and political thought.

Bradford, Richard. *The Complete Critical Guide to John Milton.* New York: Routledge, 2001. An accessible, comprehensive guide to Milton for students. Bradford brings Milton to life in an overview of his life and work and provides a summation of the main critical issues surrounding his work. Includes bibliographical references and an index.

Campbell, Gordon. *John Milton.* New York: Oxford University Press, 2007. A biography that covers Milton's entire life, focusing on the development of his political and theological ideas.

Campbell, Gordon, and Thomas N. Corns. *John Milton: Life, Work, and Thought.* New York: Oxford University Press, 2008. Portrays Milton as a flawed human character who became a renowned poet, eloquent polemicist, and major political thinker.

Cummins, Juliet, ed. *Milton and the Ends of Time.* New York: Cambridge University Press, 2003. A collection of essays that examine Milton's focus on the millennium, eternity, and the apocalypse in his works.

Duran, Angelica, ed. *A Concise Companion to Milton.* Malden, Mass.: Blackwell, 2007. This book raises the question of how and why Milton continues to be an important literary figure, while also taking a critical look at his individual texts. Some issues prominent in his writing, such as gender and religion, are examined in this volume's fourteen essays. The writing is basic and easily accessible to readers of all levels. Includes an introduction, chronology, and bibliography.

Fish, Stanley. *How Milton Works.* Cambridge, Mass.: Harvard University Press, 2001. Argues that Milton's work can be seen from the poet's firm belief that the value of his (or any) work lay in its author's commitment to divine truth, not in the tools and devices—plot, narrative, representation—of the author's aesthetic craft.

Jordan, Matthew. *Milton and Modernity: Subjectivity in Paradise Lost.* New York: St. Martin's Press, 2000. Sees Milton's works as essentially revolutionary, necessarily understood in a context of the author's belief in individual human freedom. Includes bibliographical references and an index.

Lewalski, Barbara Kiefer. *The Life of John Milton: A Critical Biography.* Malden, Mass.: Blackwell, 2000. A detailed account of Milton's life and career. Lewalski provides a close analysis of Milton's prose and poetry and shows his development of a revolutionary prophetic voice. Includes bibliographical references and an index.

Silver, Victoria. *Imperfect Sense: The Predicament of Milton's Irony.* Princeton, N.J.: Princeton University Press, 2001. Silver engages the central question of Milton readers: Why do we hate Milton's God? She argues that Milton deliberately presents a repugnant deity, one divided from himself, in an effort to reveal the human experience of a divided or self-contradictory universe driven by our own, ironically limited, vantage.

Stanley Archer

JOHN MONTAGUE

Born: Brooklyn, New York; February 28, 1929

PRINCIPAL POETRY

Forms of Exile, 1958
Poisoned Lands, and Other Poems, 1961 (revised as *Poisoned Lands*, 1977)
A Chosen Light, 1967
Tides, 1970
The Rough Field, 1972, 1989
A Slow Dance, 1975
The Great Cloak, 1978
Selected Poems, 1982
The Dead Kingdom, 1984
Mount Eagle, 1988
New Selected Poems, 1989
About Love, 1993
Time in Armagh, 1993
Collected Poems, 1995
Chain Letter, 1997
Smashing the Piano, 1999
Drunken Sailor, 2004

OTHER LITERARY FORMS

John Montague (MAHNT-uh-gyew) has published short stories, a novella, a memoir, a collection of his essays, several volumes of poems translated into English (some in collaboration with others), and several anthologies of Irish literature.

ACHIEVEMENTS

John Montague is one of the preeminent poets writing in English in the past several decades, perhaps best known for his poems about the Troubles (past and present) in Ireland and about personal relationships. Among his many awards and prizes are the Butler and O'Shaughnessy Awards from the Irish American Cultural Institute (1976), the Marten Toonder Award (1977), the Alice Hunt Bartlett Award from the Poetry Society of Great Britain (1978), a Guggenheim Fellowship (1979-1980), the Hughes Award (1987), the American Ireland Fund Literary Award (1995), a Festschrift, *Hill Field*, in honor of his sixtieth birthday, and the Vincent Buckley Poetry Prize (2000). He received honorary degrees from the State University of New York, Buffalo (1987); University College, Cork; and the University of Ultser, Coleraine (2009). A signal honor was being named, and serving as, the first Ireland Professor of Poetry (1998-2001).

BIOGRAPHY

John Patrick Montague was born in Brooklyn of Irish parents in 1929. His father, James Terence Montague, had gone there for employment in 1925, joining a brother who ran a speakeasy. James's wife, Mary (Molly) Carney, and their two sons joined him in 1928; John, the third son, was produced by this reunion. In 1933, the three brothers were sent to County Tyrone in Northern Ireland, the older two moving in with Carney relatives in Fintona, the youngest staying with two unmarried Montague aunts in Garvaghey. John's mother returned to Ireland in 1936, settling in Fintona (his father did not return until 1952).

Montague was reared apart from his mother and brothers, though he spent some holidays with them. He excelled at local schools, developed a stammer that would persist through his life, and won a scholarship to a boarding school in Armagh. He spent summer holidays during World War II with cousins in the South of Ireland. Having enrolled at University College, Dublin, he received a B.A. in history and English in 1949. He traveled in Austria, Italy, and France; in 1952, he received his M.A. in Anglo-Irish literature.

Montague traveled to the United States in 1953, spending a year at Yale University, a summer at Indiana University, and a year in the University of Iowa Writers' Workshop, where he received a master of fine arts degree in 1955. There he met Madeleine de Brauer. They were married in her native France before returning to Dublin in 1956.

He worked for the Irish tourist board for three years (1956-1959), became associated with Liam Miller's Dolmen Press, helped found Claddagh Records, and published his first book of poems before moving to Paris in 1961, where for two years, he was correspondent for the *Irish Times*. He lived in Paris during most of the 1960's, but also in the United States (teaching during 1964-1965 at the University of California,

Berkeley) and Ireland. His first marriage ended in divorce; in 1972, he was married to Evelyn Robson, a French woman.

They settled in Cork, where Montague taught at University College, Cork (1972-1988) and where they reared their daughters, Oonagh (born 1973) and Sibyl (born 1979). For much of the 1990's, Montague spent a semester each year in residence as distinguished professor in the New York State Writers Institute at Albany. He separated from his second wife. He and his new partner, American-born novelist Elizabeth Wassell, made their home at Ballydehob, County Cork, Ireland.

ANALYSIS

The main subjects of John Montague's poetry are Ireland, his family, and love. He writes about people and places he knew growing up in County Tyrone, about sectarian strife in Ulster and its historical sources, and about relatives, especially his parents, seeking to understand them and his relationships with them. He

John Montague (©John Vickers)

has examined love from all angles: from outside and within, as desired and feared, found and lost, remembered in joy and pain.

FORMS OF EXILE

If Ireland, family, and love are Montague's main subjects, his main theme is loss, a theme clearly seen in his poems about exile, a topic he has explored thoroughly. The title of his first book of poems, *Forms of Exile*, points to this preoccupation. "Emigrants," the shortest of its poems, confronts a major fact of Irish life since the 1840's: economic exile. Its "sad faced" subjects could be Montague's own parents, bound for Brooklyn.

"Soliloquy on a Southern Strand" looks at another sort of exile. After many years in Australia, an Irish priest reflects disconsolately on what has become of his life. He feels cut off from Ireland, alienated from the young people around him on the beach, discouraged about his vocation. In "A Footnote on Monasticism: Dingle Peninsula," Montague thinks about "the hermits, lonely dispossessed ones," who once lived on the peninsula. He feels a degree of kinship with these "people hurt into solitude/ By loss of love." Dispossession, another form of exile, and "loss of love" appear in this early poem to be equivalent.

More than half the poems in *Forms of Exile* allude to religious belief and practice, a subject seldom mentioned in Montague's later books. Clearly, despite his sympathy for the Irish priest in Australian exile and his qualified empathy with the Dingle hermits, Montague is distancing himself from the more parochial aspects of Irish Catholicism. "Rome, Anno Santo" looks unsympathetically at "the ignorant Irish on pilgrimage." "Incantation in Time of Peace" expresses doubt whether prayer can prevent the coming of "a yet more ominous day" in Ireland.

"Cultural Center" (later retitled "Musée Imaginaire") contemplates artworks from different cultures in a museum, each representing a civilization's values. Among them, commanding the speaker's attention and that of a nun in the museum, is a "minatory" Catalan crucifix. The "rigid figure" on the cross, its "sharp body twisted all awry," bespeaks a religion harsh but undeniably real. At the nun's waist swings a miniature crucifix: "a minute harmless god of silver plate," as "inoffensive . . . and mild" as the nun herself. Given these "conflicting

modes" of imaging Catholicism, clearly Montague prefers the strength and authenticity of the "lean, accusing Catalan crucifix"; yet his misgivings about the values it represents are obvious.

Although love would develop into one of Montague's chief subjects, there is more fear than love in *Forms of Exile*. When love does appear, it is merely observed, not actually experienced: in "Irish Street Scene, with Lovers," for example, and "Song of the Lonely Bachelor."

"The Sean Bhean Vocht" introduces an old woman who, symbolically, is Ireland personified, a repository of "local history" and "racial memory." "As a child I was frightened by her," Montague says, but it is not entirely clear what has replaced fear: fascination, respect, perhaps a hint of affection. Montague's ambiguity in this regard suggests that he has only begun to work through his feelings toward Ireland.

POISONED LANDS, AND OTHER POEMS

Poisoned Lands, and Other Poems overlaps with *Forms of Exile*: 40 percent of its poems appeared in the earlier book. In its new poems, Montague continues to write about Ireland, reflecting on his relation to it and its relation to the world. Several of these poems attempt to shape and understand childhood memories. "The Water Carrier" describes the chore of fetching water with precisely rendered details, then stops short. "Recovering the scene," Montague says, "I had hoped to stylize it,/ Like the portrait of an Egyptian water-carrier:/ Yet halt, entranced by slight but memoried life." Realizing that he cannot be that detached from memory, he concludes,

> I sometimes come to take the water there,
> Not as return or refuge, but some pure thing,
> Some living source, half-imagined and half-real
>
> Pulses in the fictive water that I feel.

Memory itself is that "fictive water," a resource on which to draw.

"Like Dolmens Round My Childhood, the Old People" evokes the lives of country neighbors. As megalithic structures dot the Irish countryside, mysterious and yet matter-of-factly present, so these figures populate the landscape of the poet's memory. "For years they trespassed on my dreams," he says, "until once, in a standing circle of stones,/ I felt their shadow pass// Into that dark permanence of ancient forms." He has commemorated the old people without sentimentality and made peace with their memories.

The outside world began to impinge on his local world when he was a schoolboy, as he recalls in "Auschwitz, Mon Amour" (later retitled "A Welcoming Party"). Newsreel images of concentration-camp survivors brought home to him the irrelevance of Ireland's "parochial brand of innocence." Having learned something about evil in the wider world, he has yet to comprehend what he has seen. For now, there is nothing to do but return to school and toss a football. The "Irish dimension" of his childhood, he says, came from being "always at the periphery of incident."

In poems such as "Auschwitz, Mon Amour" and the sarcastic "Regionalism, or Portrait of the Artist as a Model Farmer," Montague's disaffection with Irish provincialism gives him an exile's sensibility, in the tradition of one of his masters, James Joyce. "Prodigal Son" reflects on his annual visits to Ulster: It is a nice place to visit, but he would not want to live there. (Montague is well aware that the self-selected exile of the artist has little in common with exile imposed by economic circumstance, such as he alludes to in the opening poem of *Poisoned Lands, and Other Poems,* "Murphy in Manchester.")

Within the new poems in this collection, the subject of religion all but disappears. Love is alluded to occasionally, mostly in passing; yet the volume does include Montague's first full-fledged love poem, "Pastorals." It is a dialogue between two lovers, a cynic who sees love as but the "movement of unlawful limbs/ In a marriage of two whims" and an idealist who views it as a sanctuary where "hearts long bruised . . . can trace/ Redeeming patterns of experience."

A CHOSEN LIGHT

The first section of *A Chosen Light* is a gathering of love poems. "Country Matters" and "Virgo Hibernica" recall love unspoken; the inhibiting shyness of adolescence. The latter acknowledges "the gravitational pull/ of love," but the former concludes that "the word of love is/ Hardest to say."

"All Legendary Obstacles" memorializes the re-

union of separated lovers. A number of subsequent poems in the section draw on less ecstatic (less "legendary") experiences, including the strains within a marriage. "Loving Reflections," for example, moves in its three parts from tenderness to an angry argument to grim determination to hold on to the relationship.

Montague begins to explore family connections seriously in *A Chosen Light*, particularly in "The Country Fiddler" and "The Cage." His uncle and godfather John Montague, for whom he was named, had been a country fiddler, but his "rural art [was] silenced in the discord of Brooklyn," and he died in American exile. His nephew, born there, became his uncle's "unexpected successor" when sent to Ireland at age four to live. Montague also sees his craft, poetry, as "succession" to his uncle's "rural craft" of music.

In "The Cage," Montague calls his father "the least happy/ man I have known," who drank himself to "brute oblivion." When he finally returned to Ireland in 1952, after twenty-seven years in Brooklyn, he and his son were briefly reunited; by then, however, the son was but an occasional visitor to Tyrone and would soon head for the United States himself. Mingled in the poem are Montague's conflicting feelings toward his father: pity, revulsion, respect, affection.

"The Road's End" grew out of one of Montague's visits home. He retraces childhood steps, noting changes: overgrown thorns, a disused well, abandoned homes. "Like shards/ Of a lost culture," he says, "the slopes/ Are strewn with cabins, emptied/ In my lifetime." His sense of loss is strong.

TIDES

In *Tides,* only two poems allude to Montague's blood kin, "Last Journey" and "Omagh Hospital," and both move from their specific subjects to the larger world of Northern Ireland. The former is subtitled "i.m. James Montague," but salutes Ulster's, as well as his father's, memory, citing the "placenames that sigh/ like a pressed melodeon/ across this forgotten/ Northern landscape." In "Omagh Hospital," Montague's dying Aunt Brigid pleads to be taken home, but he pictures her house, "shaken by traffic/ until a fault runs/ from roof to base." The house that has become uninhabitable is not only the family home but also the whole province, rent by a grievous "fault."

Tides has an increased proportion, and a stunning variety, of love poems. The first two of the book's five sections concentrate on the darker side of love. "Premonition" and "The Pale Light" provide horrific, nightmare images. "Summer Storm" scales down to the more prosaic hell of a couple arguing, Montague returning here to his theme of love gone sour. "Special Delivery," in which "the worm of delight/ . . . turns to/ feed upon itself," reinforces this theme. The two poems in these sections that actually celebrate love are those that, at first glance, might seem least capable of doing so: "The Wild Dog Rose" and "The Hag of Beare." "The Wild Dog Rose" focuses on a haggish woman who has lived a solitary life of few expectations and fewer pleasures. Her one encounter with a man was a terrifying attempted rape. However, love is not absent from this apparently loveless life: The poem ends with a glimpse of transcendent, absolutely selfless love. The poem elicits not pity for the old woman but admiration for her great heart. In "The Hag of Beare," another crone comes to a higher love, at the end of a life utterly different from that briefly sketched in "The Wild Dog Rose." Having known all fleshly pleasures, now denied by age and infirmity, the Hag of Beare expresses her willingness to welcome "the Son of Mary," like so many men before, "under my roof-tree."

The middle section of *Tides* introduces a frankly erotic note into Montague's love poetry. "A Dream of July" celebrates "Ceres, corn goddess," whose "abundant body is/ Compounded of honey/ & gold," and similar imagery of honey and gold can be found in "The Same Gesture" and "Love, a Greeting" (as earlier it was found in "Virgo Hibernica"). Love here is primarily physical, exuberant, largely unassociated with responsibilities, and—as in the title poem, "Tracks"—without commitment.

THE ROUGH FIELD

Poems in Montague's first two books of poems are not randomly arranged, but a greater degree of order obtains in books three and four, which group poems into thematically related sections. Moreover, in *Tides*, the fourth book, sea imagery, often metaphorical, helps unify the volume as a whole. Montague's fifth book, *The Rough Field*, is more highly organized still. Though it contains a number of individual poems capable of standing on their own (eight appeared in previous Montague books), in fact it is one long poem composed of many parts.

Montague began work on *The Rough Field* in the early 1960's, concluding it a decade later, after a new outbreak of sectarian violence struck Ulster. Montague says that he began with "a kind of vision . . . of my home area, the unhappiness of its historical destiny." Violent confrontations in Belfast and Derry gave added point to the project and contributed materials that Montague incorporated into the completed work: "the emerging order/ of the poem invaded," as he says in part 9, "by cries, protestations/ a people's pain."

"Rough Field" translates the name of the townland, Garvaghey, where Montague grew up: "Rough Field in the Gaelic and rightly named/ . . . Harsh landscape that haunts me." He weaves together family stories, incidents from his childhood, and episodes from Irish history since the sixteenth century. The book is populated by members of his family, people from Tyrone whom he knew growing up, and historical figures from Hugh O'Neill (1545-1616) to Bernadette Devlin (born 1947). It evokes the landscape and dwells on the place-names of Tyrone, and of Ulster in general, sites of ancient or recent historical significance. Interspersed among Montague's poems, often with ironic effect, are a variety of "found" texts: excerpts from historical documents, memoirs, letters, newspapers, and the like. The "conversation" among the various voices in *The Rough Field* (Montague's several voices and these "found" voices) contributes to the book's multilayered complexity.

Its complexity notwithstanding, the book is unified by its steady focus on one place (and the continuity of its problems) as well as by recurring images—the rough field, houses, swans—and recurring concerns: home, inheritance, exile; memory; dreams; loneliness; things lost; things broken, shaken, scattered, shattered, including buildings, families, lives, dreams, tradition, a culture, a province. *The Rough Field* is further unified by successfully linking the personal, the familial, the regional, the national, and the global, Montague's Garvaghey becoming a microcosm of "the rough field/ of the universe." Finally, it is unified by successfully linking past and present: generation joined to generation ("This bitterness/ I inherit from my father"), century to century (contemporary exile in the United States and the seventeenth century "Flight of the Earls"). *The Rough Field*, treating a serious theme with artistry and authority, is widely considered Montague's greatest work.

A SLOW DANCE

A Slow Dance is a rich mixture, its five sections linked by recurring images: warmth and cold and, especially, dance. The slow dance, Montague has said, is the "dance of death and life," and this volume reveals a heightened sense of both mortality and vitality.

Section 1 takes the reader "back to our origins"—individually to the womb, collectively to primordial cave—and there the dance of life and death begins. "The humid pull/ of the earth" is immediate; the dance begins "in . . . isolation" but ends in complete identification with the natural world, human "breath mingling with the exhalations of the earth." The section collapses time and dissolves distinctions between civilizations, so that legendary poet-king Sweeny coexists with Saint Patrick, and (in "For the Hillmother") the Christian Litany of the Blessed Virgin provides the form for a pagan invocation to nature as the source of life. The section is about life, with death only hinted at.

Section 2 opens with a birth, but in "Courtyard in Winter," the poet meditates on the suicide of a friend. Montague grieves that he could not "ease the single hurt/ That edged her towards her death," but he does not give in to guilt or despair. Rather, "I still affirm/ That nothing dies, that even from/ Such bitter failure memory grows." Much of the rest of the section consists of lyrical evocations of nature, of which "Windharp" is perhaps the best known.

The opening section collapses time and telescopes civilizations in the service of life; the third does the same in the service of death, "The Cave of Night" substituting for the womb/cave. Ancient Celtic blood sacrifice is juxtaposed to armed struggle in Belfast. Killing with sword and rifle, the slaughtering of a pig in a farmyard and of soldiers on a battlefield, are essentially the same in this hellish section, ruled over by the "Black Widow goddess." The section ends, fittingly, with a poem called "Coldness."

The reader turns with relief in the fourth section to the warmer world of family. Problems here—parents unable to live together, a child denied "the warm circle" of its mother's company—are problems that can be comprehended, sometimes even dealt with. Loneliness is here (it is never far in Montague's poetry), but "human warmth" is, too.

The final section of *A Slow Dance* is Montague's eulogy for his friend the composer Séan Ó Riada. The "slowly failing fire" dies out, and the book ends with a cry of anguish:

> a lament so total
> it mourns no one
> but the globe itself
> turning in the endless halls
>
> of space.

The book, which begins by celebrating "The whole world/ turning in wet/ and silence," thus ends lamenting the same turning world. The "globe itself/ turning" enacts the "slow dance" of life and death.

THE GREAT CLOAK

The Great Cloak focuses on love—no poems here are about growing up, family, or Ireland. Montague examines the breakup of one marriage, the beginning of another, and the interval between. The poems are short (averaging about half the length of those in *A Slow Dance*), uncomplicated, accessible. Their imagery is predominantly visual (attentive to the play of light and shadow) and tactile (hands touching, caressing).

In the first section, sexual encounters are brief respites from loneliness. Loneliness and worse—nothingness, the void—seem implicit in the ominous image that closes the section: "profound night/ like a black swan/ goes pluming past."

The second section, less self-absorbed, sadly sifts through the fragments of a broken marriage. It is an inventory of losses. "Darkness" finds Montague trying to understand his estranged wife's feelings, and in four other poems, he goes so far as to speak with her voice: "I sing your pain/ as best I can," he says, in his own voice. The longest and best poem in the book, "Herbert Street Revisited," returns to the Dublin street where, newly wed, Montague and his wife made their first home. It is a generous-spirited celebration of the love they shared.

"Anchor," title of the last section, expresses a wish; the new relationship Montague explores here seems less fixed, less certain, than the title suggests. "Walking Late," for example, ends with the couple circling "uncertainly/ towards a home." Only in "Protest," which records the birth of their child, and the handful of poems that follow it does the tone of voice become confident enough to warrant the section's title.

SELECTED POEMS

Montague's *Selected Poems* draws from all his previous books of poems and includes a few that would appear later in *The Dead Kingdom* or *Mount Eagle*. Some poems, particularly early ones, show substantive revisions, and the order in which they appear is not always that of the earlier books.

THE DEAD KINGDOM

Like *The Rough Field*, *The Dead Kingdom* is a single long poem—an arrangement of shorter poems, ten of which appeared in previous books. Unlike *The Rough Field*, *The Dead Kingdom* has a narrative line. It begins when news arrives in Cork that Montague's mother has died. "The 'thread' or plot," Montague has written, "is the long drive North" to attend her funeral.

The drive north takes Montague through the Midlands, calling up bittersweet memories of summers in County Longford. More than half the poems in the book's first two (of five) sections connect with "this neutral realm." "Abbeylara" affectionately recalls summers with Carney relatives, but now they are dead, their house abandoned, their carefully tended garden gone wild. The small piece of land to which they gave order is "reverting to first chaos/ as if they had never been."

Two poems in section 1 meditate on transience itself. In "Process," "time's gullet devouring" all that people value becomes an abyss of "fuming oblivion," across which one can but cast "swaying ropeladders" such as "love or friendship,/ an absorbing discipline." "Gone" recalls things great and small that have been "hustled into oblivion" and stoically salutes "the goddess Mutability,/ dark Lady of Process,/ our devouring Queen." Terms such as "chaos," "oblivion," and "the void" spatter the first half of the book, and the metaphor

of "time's gullet" and the "devouring Queen" is reinforced by multiple references to appetite, feeding, and digestive organs.

In section 3, the border of Northern Ireland revives thoughts of violent conflicts there. Weather and mood alike turn cold and dark as the poet returns to the "bloody ground" where he was raised. More despairing than in *The Rough Field*, Montague can but "sing a song for the broken/ towns of old Tyrone" and "for the people,/ so grimly holding on." He calls his wish for "an end to sectarianism" a "forlorn hope."

As in *A Slow Dance*, the almost unrelieved gloom of section 3 gives way to the warmer (even when painful) images of family in section 4. In a series of flashbacks, Montague reviews his parents' lives, together and apart (a photograph of the young couple introduces the section).

Music has woven its way through all of Montague's books, but none of them is as filled with music as *The Dead Kingdom*, which invokes everything from popular songs ("Kathleen Mavourneen," "Paddy Reilly") to Mary Mulvey's music box and "the sound/ of bells in monastic/ sites." Montague himself calls for song in several poems (for example, "sing a song for/ things that are gone"). The principal singer, however, is his father, teaching his son the words to "Ragtime Cowboy Joe"; singing "Molly Bawn" to his own Molly, after his long-delayed return to Ireland; lending his "broken tenor" to Christmas carols in midnight Mass. Montague understands that, back in Brooklyn, his "father's songs/ couldn't sweeten the lack of money" that had contributed to the family's fragmentation. However, Montague recognizes that "the healing harmony/ of music" had been his father's rope ladder across oblivion, and he regrets that his mother's funeral is "without music or song" to "ease the living" and "sweeten our burden."

Montague continues to examine the subject of exile in its various forms, under its various names: "emigration," "transportation," "diaspora," "dispossession." At last, his mother dead, he brings himself to mention the form of exile he himself has experienced most painfully: being rejected by his mother in childhood. "You gave me away," he says to her posthumously ("The Locket"), "to be fostered/ in Garvaghey" ("A Muddy Cup"), "to be fostered/ wherever charity could afford."

This, he says, was the "primal hurt," to be "an unwanted child": "All roads wind backwards to it" ("A Flowering Absence").

"It is hard to work so close to the bone," Montague has said of these poems about his mother. After a lifetime of excavating the strata of his life, Montague has finally reached emotional bedrock. To have been "fostered" is to have been exiled most radically. Nevertheless, "The Locket," "a last song/ for the lady who has gone," ends with a "mysterious blessing": The poet learns, after his mother's death, that the locket she had always worn contained an old photograph of "a child in Brooklyn."

His responsibilities in Tyrone finished, Montague turns his attention to the living woman in his life

> I place my hopes
> beside yours, Evelyn,
> frail rope-ladders
> across fuming oblivion

and heads "back across the/ length of Ireland, home."

MOUNT EAGLE

Mount Eagle is neither arranged as a coherent whole, like *The Rough Field* and *The Dead Kingdom*, nor organized into distinct sections, like *A Chosen Light, Tides, A Slow Dance*, and *The Great Cloak*. Rather, like Montague's first two books, *Forms of Exile* and *Poisoned Lands, and Other Poems*, it is something of a miscellany, though its poems are generally arranged by subject. The volume includes a quartet of poems related to the Troubles in Northern Ireland, each rendering a sharply etched vignette. There is a late harvest of childhood memories, usually recalled, not for their own sake, but for a connection Montague wishes to draw with something in later life. "The Leap," for example, draws an analogy between daring jumps years before across the Garvaghey River and, referring to his second marriage, a new "taking off . . . into the uncertain dark." Four poems are culled from a father's affectionate observation of his young daughter's investigations of their world. Only one poem alludes to Montague's father, and then in passing; none mentions his mother.

Perhaps a third of the poems could be classified under the general heading of "love." "Fair Head" recalls an early, unconsummated love; several other poems, more characteristically, commemorate consummations. "The Well-Beloved" muses on the process by which smitten lovers, each idealizing the other, descend into married life, and wonders what it takes to "redeem the ordinary." The startling "Sheela na Gig," inspired by the grotesquely sexual female figures carved on medieval Irish churches, synopsizes male human behavior in terms of "banishment" from "the first home" at birth and then a lifetime of trying "to return to that [anatomical] first darkness." Birth, too, is banishment: the first experience of exile.

The most interesting development in *Mount Eagle* is its attention to nature. "Springs" expresses the ecologically correct wish to "erase/ from this cluttered earth/ our foul disgrace." "Peninsula" is a much more appealing celebration of "Dame Nature's self-/ delighting richness." Several poems draw on Native American nature myths, including the title poem, wherein an eagle trades its freedom to disappear into, and become "the spirit of," a mountain. The poem seems to encode Montague's own intent to dedicate himself to a new sort of poetry: less subject to the buffeting of life's winds, perhaps less confessional, more abstract. (Montague has privately acknowledged that "Mount Eagle" is a homonym for his own name.) The last seven poems in *Mount Eagle*, which include "Luggala" and "The Hill of Silence," reflect this new direction in his work.

ABOUT LOVE

Montague followed *Mount Eagle* with another collection of selected poems, *New Selected Poems*. Somewhat different selections in this published-in-Ireland volume distinguish it from the 1982 *Selected Poems*, published in the United States. The next collection, *About Love*, is a generous compilation of Montague's love poems, all but three of them previously published (about a third of them drawn from *The Great Cloak*). The variety of the poems is remarkable. They examine love of many kinds, at many stages, and in diverse moods; they examine love coolly and in heat (cerebrally and passionately), with regret and gratitude, bitterness and bemusement, longing and contentment. Mostly, they celebrate love, although that emotion is often shaded with darker feelings: jealousy, guilt, loneliness. The book amounts to a learned treatise on love, Montague's anatomy of love.

TIME IN ARMAGH

Time in Armagh is a small, well-focused collection that recalls its author's years at boarding school (St. Patrick's College, Armagh), from 1941 until 1946. World War II is a presence in five of the volume's twenty-six poems, but its emphasis is on "the harshness of our schooling," as Montague says in the preface. The harshness is evident in the physical violence administered both by the priests who ran the school (seven poems, as well as the book's epigraph from Juvenal, allude to canes or beatings) and by fellow students. The harshness is also evident in the absence of tenderness or love. Although there are moments of humor and even of nostalgia in the volume, the prevailing feelings are anger and bitterness, undimmed after half a century. In his preface, Montague compares his school years with those that Joyce recorded in *A Portrait of the Artist as a Young Man* (1916). When he writes about the beatings administered by the priests at St. Patrick's, most notably in "Guide" and the title poem, "Time in Armagh," Montague's language echoes that of the pandybat scene in Joyce's novel.

COLLECTED POEMS

Collected Poems, a magisterial assemblage, brings together more than three hundred poems, the best work of the first forty years of Montague's output. It is divided into three sections. The first, a bit more than half the book, consists of the three great volumes from the 1970's and 1980's, all symphonically orchestrated (each conceived of as a single, integrated work): *The Rough Field*, *The Great Cloak*, and *The Dead Kingdom*. The second section, constituting nearly 40 percent of the book, contains poems from *Forms of Exile*, *Poisoned Lands, and Other Poems*, *A Chosen Light*, *Tides*, *A Slow Dance*, and *Mount Eagle*. Section 3, less than 10 percent of the book, contains poems from *Time in Armagh* and the previously uncollected long poem "Border Sick Call" (1995). Montague has revised some poems, omitted some poems, and included a few poems translated from the Irish and originally published in *A Fair House: Versions of Irish Poetry* (1973).

SMASHING THE PIANO

Few poets in old age write with undiminished power. William Butler Yeats was one; Montague is another. *Smashing the Piano* is a great follow-up to his *Col-*

lected Poems: not merely a curtain call but a real encore. The collection contains forty-one poems, but since several of these are sequences of lyrics (individually titled and each capable of standing alone), by another way of reckoning the collection contains sixty-five poems.

Unavoidably, many of the poems in this gathering reintroduce themes and characters introduced in earlier books. The opening half dozen poems, for example, recall figures and incidents from a County Tyrone childhood: Aunt Winifred ("Paths"), Aunt Brigid ("Still Life, with Aunt Brigid"), and children who died young ("Kindertotenlieder"). This group segues naturally into a sequence about Montague's own children, "Prayers for My Daughters." The title is deliberately Yeatsian, but the tender domesticity of these poems owes nothing to Yeats.

A sequence of short love poems, "Dark Rooms," recalls many of Montague's earlier love poems, but "Postscript," the sixth of the seven lyrics in the sequence, introduces a new situation: An old poet, having been supplanted by "another, younger man," struggles to contain his rage in the constraining form of a poem—such as this one, more regularly rhymed than most Montague poems. Other poems also demonstrate that this volume is the work of advanced years, most notably "Talking with Victor Hugo in Old Age." The untitled brief poem that serves as the volume's epigraph connects youth and age in a wholly suitable way:

> Fierce lyric truth,
> Sought since youth,
> Grace my ageing
> As you did my growing,
> Till time engraves
> My final face.

A number of poems scattered through *Smashing the Piano* seem to be extensions of the impulse, seen in *Mount Eagle*, to write about nature: "Starspill" even refers to "Mount Eagle." "Between" is a gorgeous meditation on the yin and yang of nature as observed in the Gap, where County Waterford and County Tipperary meet.

The longest sequence in the collection, the eight-part "Civil Wars," reengages political themes that Montague has dealt with memorably before. There are updates here, however: memorializing hunger striker Bobby Sands, excoriating British prime minister Margaret Thatcher, speaking of "the unspeakable" Omagh bombing, respectfully addressing (in conclusion) his own father, once politicized, now dead. "Your faith I envy," he tells his father, though

> Your fierce politics I decry.
> May we sing together
> someday, Sunny Jim,
> over what you might
> still call the final shoot-out:
> for me, saving your absence,
> a healing agreement.

Though in this collection there is the usual great range of subjects and feelings characteristic of Montague's best books of poems, this one is marked with unwonted serenity. This should not be mistaken for a sign of diminished inspiration or power; it is an added, and most welcome, quality: a late blossoming, a late blessing.

OTHER MAJOR WORKS

LONG FICTION: *The Lost Notebook*, 1987.

SHORT FICTION: *Death of a Chieftain, and Other Stories*, 1964 (revised as *An Occasion of Sin*, 1992); *A Love Present, and Other Stories*, 1997; *A Ball of Fire: Collected Stories*, 2009.

NONFICTION: *The Figure in the Cave, and Other Essays*, 1989; *Myth, History, and Literary Tradition*, 1989 (with Thomas Kinsella and Brendan Kennelly); *Company: A Chosen Life*, 2001; *The Pearl Is Ripe: A Memoir*, 2007.

TRANSLATIONS: *A Fair House: Versions of Irish Poetry*, 1973 (from Irish); *November: A Choice of Translations from André Frénaud*, 1977 (with Evelyn Robson); *Selected Poems*, 1994 (of Francis Ponge; with C. K. Williams and Margaret Guiton); *Carnac*, 1999 (of Eugène Guillevic).

EDITED TEXTS: *The Dolmen Miscellany of Irish Writing*, 1962; *The Faber Book of Irish Verse*, 1974 (*The Book of Irish Verse*, 1976); *Bitter Harvest: An Anthology of Contemporary Irish Verse*, 1989.

MISCELLANEOUS: *Born in Brooklyn: John Montague's America*, 1991 (poetry, short fiction, and nonfiction).

BIBLIOGRAPHY

Irish University Review 19 (Spring, 1989). This special issue, edited by Christopher Murray, includes an interview with Montague, seven articles on his work, an autobiographical essay by Montague ("The Figure in the Cave"), and Thomas Dillon Redshaw's checklist of Montague's books.

Kersnowski, Frank. *John Montague*. Lewisburg, Pa.: Bucknell University Press, 1975. The first book-length study of Montague's work (actually a slim monograph), this work surveys his career through *The Rough Field*. Its chief value may be its readings of individual poems and stories.

Montague, John. *Chosen Lights: Poets on Poems by John Montague in Honour of His Eightieth Birthday*. Edited by Peter Fallon. Loughcrew, Oldcastle, Ireland: Gallery Press, 2009. Poets such as Paul Muldoon, Seamus Heaney, Eavan Boland, and Eamon Grennan comment on poems by Montague.

_____. *Company: A Chosen Life*. London: Duckworth, 2001. The first volume of Montague's memoirs, focusing mainly on the 1950's and 1960's. Provides entertaining and often illuminating accounts of his encounters with Samuel Beckett, Brendan Behan, Theodore Roethke, and many others. The book's most memorable portrait, however, is that which emerges indirectly of the author himself. The warmth, wit, intelligence, generosity, and humor of his sensibility inform the book.

_____. *The Pearl Is Ripe: A Memoir*. Chester Springs, Pa.: Dufour Editions, 2007. The second volume of Montague's memoirs, similarly warm and witty, takes up where the author left off in *Company*. Recounts his dealings with Allen Ginsberg, Patrick Kavanagh, and the composer Séan Ó Riada.

Redshaw, Thomas Dillon, ed. *Well Dreams: Essays on John Montague*. Omaha, Nebr.: Creighton University Press, 2004. Eighteen essays examine successive aspects of Montague's career. The most substantial work published on Montague.

Richard Bizot

WILLIAM MORRIS

Born: Walthamstow, near London, England; March
   24, 1834
Died: Hammersmith, near London, England; October
   3, 1896

PRINCIPAL POETRY

The Defence of Guenevere, and Other Poems, 1858
The Life and Death of Jason, 1867
The Earthly Paradise, 1868-1870 (3 volumes)
Love Is Enough: Or, The Freeing of Pharamond,
   1872
*The Story of Sigurd the Volsung and the Fall of the
   Niblungs*, 1876
Chants for Socialists, 1884, 1885
The Pilgrims of Hope, 1885-1886
Poems by the Way, 1891

OTHER LITERARY FORMS

William Morris's first publication was a series of
short prose romances and a review of Robert Browning's *Men and Women* (1855) in *The Oxford and
Cambridge Magazine* (1856). Except for his translations of several Icelandic sagas and his journal of two
expeditions to Iceland (1871, 1873), Morris wrote no
significant prose until 1877, when he began his career
as a public lecturer. Some of his lectures were published as pamphlets; those he considered the more important were collected in *Hopes and Fears for Art*
(1882) and *Signs of Change: Seven Lectures Delivered
on Various Occasions* (1888). Other lectures appear in
The Collected Works of William Morris (1910-1915,
1956; May Morris, editor); *William Morris: Artist,
Writer, Socialist* (1936; May Morris, editor); and *The
Unpublished Lectures of William Morris* (1969; Eugene D. LeMire, editor). During this period he also contributed to the Socialist journal *Commonweal*, which
he edited from 1885 until 1890 and in which he published two utopian dream-visions: *A Dream of John
Ball* (1888) and *News from Nowhere: Or, An Epoch of
Rest, Being Some Chapters from a Utopian Romance*
(1891). *Icelandic Journals by William Morris* (1969)
are an important supplement to the Norse stories in *The

Earthly Paradise* and *The Story of Sigurd the Volsung
and the Fall of the Niblungs* and, less directly, to *Love
Is Enough*, written the year after his first visit to Iceland. His Socialist prose, both fiction and nonfiction,
provides a necessary context for the *Chants for Socialists* and *The Pilgrims of Hope*, and should be of interest
to anyone concerned with the relationship between the
aesthetic earthly paradise of his poetry and the political
earthly paradise of his socialism.

Morris's Utopian fiction is closely related to the series of prose romances he wrote during the last dozen
years of his life: *The House of the Wolfings* (1888), *The
Roots of the Mountains* (1890), *The Story of the Glittering Plain* (1891), *The Wood Beyond the World* (1894),
The Well at the World's End (1896), *The Water of
the Wondrous Isles* (1897), and *The Sundering Flood*
(1897). It is in these works that the thematic concerns of
his earlier poetry reach their final development.

A selection of Morris's letters appears in *The Letters of William Morris to His Family and Friends*
(1950; Philip Henderson, editor). The complete edition
of his letters, edited by Norman Kelvin, has been published under the title *The Collected Letters of William
Morris* (1984-1987).

ACHIEVEMENTS

After the publication of *The Earthly Paradise* in
1868-1870, William Morris was acknowledged as a
major poet and, two decades later, considered the logical successor to Alfred, Lord Tennyson as England's
poet laureate. His strength as a poet lies in his grasp of
human psychology and his inventiveness with narrative forms. The dramatic monologues of *The Defence
of Guenevere, and Other Poems* are remarkable for
their daring psychosexual realism, and both for this
reason and because they are short enough to antholo-
gize, they have come to be the poetry for which Morris
is most widely known. The longer narrative poems that
followed, *The Life and Death of Jason* and *The Earthly
Paradise*, experiment with techniques of distancing
and so forgo the dramatic immediacy of his earliest
work; however, they continue Morris's exploration
of sexuality and broaden it into a profound analysis of
the relationship between erotic desire and the creative
impulse.

The complexly structured *Love Is Enough* and the epic *The Story of Sigurd the Volsung and the Fall of the Niblungs*, which Morris considered his poetic masterpiece, furthered his experiments with narration. Along with his prose fiction, his longer poems constitute a major exploration of narrative technique.

Today, Morris's poetry has been partially overshadowed by his essays and prose fiction and by his accomplishments as a designer, typographer, and political activist. Instead of displacing Morris's achievement as a poet, however, his other work should be judged with it as part of a total effort to transform the thought and lifestyle of Victorian England. Precisely because his interests extended beyond poetry, Morris exemplifies the bond between poetry and other forms of artistic and political expression.

BIOGRAPHY

William Morris was born on March 24, 1834, in the village of Walthamstow, a few miles northeast of London. His father was a well-to-do broker who maintained a household characterized by old-fashioned self-sufficiency. Morris's early life was centered in his family, who encouraged his tastes for literature and the medieval period. At the University of Oxford, which he entered in 1853, he developed close ties with Edward Burne-Jones and a group of friends ("the Brotherhood") who shared these interests. The year after Morris left Oxford, the Brotherhood undertook the publication of *The Oxford and Cambridge Magazine*, which Morris financed and, for a while, edited, and to which he was a regular contributor. In the same year, he apprenticed himself to the architect G. E. Street, but, following the example of Burne-Jones, who was determined to become an artist, he gave up architecture after a few months in Street's office and became a disciple of the Pre-Raphaelite painter Dante Gabriel Rossetti.

Under the spell of Rossetti, Morris joined in the artist's project to paint scenes from Sir Thomas Malory's *Le Morte d'Arthur* (1485) on the interior walls of the Oxford Union. Lingering in the congenial atmosphere of the university, he wrote most of the poems he later published in *The Defence of Guenevere, and Other Poems*, and paid court to Jane Burden, a hauntingly beau-

tiful woman whom Rossetti had persuaded to sit for him as a model. Morris and Burden were married in 1859 and established themselves at Red House, near Upton, ten miles south of London. The house, of considerable architectural interest, had been designed for them by Morris's friend Philip Webb. Morris himself took an active role in planning the interiors of Red House, and this concern led to the establishment of a firm—Morris, Marshall, Faulkner and Company (later, Morris and Company)—dedicated to the improvement of British interior design. The firm produced stained glass, wood carving, metalwork, furniture, wallpaper, fabrics, and carpets, and in time exercised a significant role in modifying Victorian tastes.

The period at Red House, during which Morris's daughters Jane (Jenny) and Mary (May) were born, was the happiest in his married life. In response to the growing business of the firm, however, he moved back to London in 1865, and with this move began Jane Morris's gradual estrangement from her husband and her involvement with Rossetti—a relationship about which

William Morris (Library of Congress)

little is certain but much has been said. Morris's disappointment with his marriage is reflected in *The Earthly Paradise*, which he had begun at Red House but completed in the years after his return to London.

A search for a weekend and vacation home led Morris to Kelmscott Manor in a distant corner of Oxfordshire, a house he leased in 1871 and with which he was soon strongly identified. In the same year, he took the first of his two expeditions to Iceland—an outgrowth of the study of Icelandic language and literature that he had begun in 1868 and that was to exert a formative influence on his subsequent writing.

Although the 1870's saw the publication of *The Story of Sigurd the Volsung and the Fall of the Niblungs* and a major reorganization of the firm, the decade is more strongly marked as the beginning of Morris's political activism. His original concerns were foreign policy and the destruction of historical buildings in the name of "restoration." Soon, though, he had also begun lecturing on the theory of design and manufacture. These efforts to influence public policy confronted Morris with the intransigence of the political and economic establishments, and this experience, along with the influence of John Ruskin, whose writings Morris had admired since his days as an Oxford undergraduate, led him to socialism.

In the 1880's Morris became one of the central figures in the British Socialist movement. He edited the journal *Commonweal* and traveled and lectured up and down the country. He fought, risking his own imprisonment, for the Socialists' freedom of speech, and he set forth his notion of an ideal society in the Marxist romances that remain his most widely read books: *A Dream of John Ball* and *News from Nowhere*.

Ultimately, dissension within the Socialist League and his own general fatigue led to a partial withdrawal from political activities in the 1890's. It was during these last years of his life that Morris established the Kelmscott Press and published a number of books, for which he designed the type, layout, and binding. It was also during this period that he returned to the themes of his earlier writing in a series of prose romances that found a popular audience during the 1970's and 1980's. Morris died on October 3, 1896, and was buried in Kelmscott churchyard.

ANALYSIS

Like other Victorian poets, William Morris is best understood in relationship to the Romantic poets whose work preceded his. Like Tennyson and Browning, he sought an alternative to the Romantic preoccupation with self by writing in literary forms from which the self of the poet was distanced or removed. Unlike Tennyson and Browning, but in part through their example, he had discovered such forms by the time of his first collection of verse. Excluding himself from his poetry, however, was not enough; Morris went on to find and test ways of replacing the self with a collective consciousness. It is this effort that gives shape and purpose to his literary career.

THE DEFENCE OF GUENEVERE, AND OTHER POEMS

Tennyson and Browning had found congenial settings for many of their important poems in classical Greece or Rome, Arthurian England, or the Italian Renaissance. Morris set his earliest poems in the Middle Ages, and this setting freed him, at least partially, from the restraints of his times and allowed him to express emotional and intellectual states for which there were no Victorian equivalents. The violence and sexuality of *The Defence of Guenevere, and Other Poems* would have been difficult or impossible to treat in poems dealing with contemporary England. Moreover, the poems are spoken either by dramatized personas or by the anonymous voice of the traditional song or ballad. Thus, the contemporary poet is excluded from the text and thereby relieved of the need to moralize or interpret its subject by Victorian standards.

The contents of *The Defence of Guenevere, and Other Poems* fall into three categories: poems based on Arthurian materials, poems based on Jean Froissart's *Chroniques de France, d'Engleterre, d'Éscose, de Bretaigne, d'Espaigne, d'Italie, de Flandres et d'Alemaigne* (1373-1410; *The Chronycles of Englande, Fraunce, Spayne . . .* , 1523-1525; better known as *Chronicles*) describing the Anglo-French wars of the fourteenth century, and poems linked not by their common source but by their strong, often hallucinatory symbolism.

The title poem exemplifies the first group. In it, Guenevere uses an extended autobiographical apology to forestall the knights who are about to execute her as an adulteress. Because it is a dramatic monologue, the central ambiguity of the poem remains unresolved: Is Guenevere really a repentant victim of circumstances, or is her speech simply a ploy to gain time? It is, of course, both. If she is a victim—if she allowed herself to be led into marriage with a man she did not love—then her victimization signals the same weakness, the same passive sensuality, that precipitated her infidelity. However, her confession of weakness is itself a seduction of her accusers. In a world determined by sexual desire, her passivity becomes a form of strength. By absenting himself from the poem, Morris allows these contradictory interpretations to interact and thus, in effect, to complicate its meaning. The Guinevere of *Idylls of the King* (1859-1885) is an expression of Tennyson's need to confirm Victorian sexual morality. Morris's Guenevere, in contrast, calls the relevance of moral order itself into question. Ultimately, Lancelot will come to her rescue, and that, in the end, is all that matters.

The Froissartian poems dramatize characters with a real, although usually minor, place in history. They give the lie to the accusation that Morris sentimentalized the Middle Ages. In poems such as "The Haystack in the Floods," "Sir Peter Harpdon's End," and "Concerning Geoffrey Teste Noire," the slow English defeat in the last years of the Hundred Years' War is portrayed with grim realism. In the first and shortest of the three poems, the lovers Jehane and Robert have been taken in ambush and Jehane offered the choice of becoming the lover of an enemy and so saving Robert's life—or at least postponing his death—or refusing and thus bringing about Robert's immediate murder and her own trial by water as a witch. Instead of brooding over her dilemma, she falls asleep, leaning against the wet haystack beside which they had been ambushed. After an hour, she awakens, speaks a quiet "I will not," and sees her lover decapitated and his head beaten to pieces. Again, the power of the poem lies in the absence of authorial comment. Nothing stands between the reader and Jehane's purely instinctual response. Overwhelmed by circumstances, her consciousness is reduced to a sequence of images, culminating in "the long bright blade without a flaw" with which Robert is executed; and the poem is all the more intense for this refusal to verbalize her emotional state.

In the third group of poems, Morris's concentration on imagery results in a poetry comparable to that of the French Symbolists. (Like the Symbolists, Morris at this point in his career was strongly influenced by Edgar Allan Poe.) Poems such as "The Wind" and "The Blue Closet" are richly evocative but elude precise decipherment. The first depicts a speaker who is psychotic; the second, based on a painting by Rossetti, uses deliberate inconclusiveness to suggest a deteriorating consciousness. The longest of the fantasy poems, "Rapunzel," offers a more positive account of the psychosexual development of its protagonist prince from youth to maturity and seems to foreshadow Morris's later concern for the relationship between art and the erotic drives; any interpretation of the poem, however, is bound to be tenuous.

THE LIFE AND DEATH OF JASON AND THE EARTHLY PARADISE

The success of these early poems in confronting the reader with states of passionate intensity has made it difficult for some critics to understand Morris's decision to write in a very different style in the narrative poetry of the 1860's. If the immediacy of *The Defence of Guenevere, and Other Poems* is missing in *The Life and Death of Jason* and *The Earthly Paradise*, though, the shift in style is in no sense a falling off. The manner of the earlier poems would not have worked in a longer narrative. Intensity can be sustained only so long; in time, it becomes unbearable or ludicrous. Moreover, the dramatic monologues and dialogues of *The Defence of Guenevere, and Other Poems*, rich in psychological complexity, limit the role of the reader to that of an observer. The poems that followed reflect Morris's growing concern with the full nature of the experience of art; hence, the storyteller, since his role is now a matter of consequence, must be restored to a position of importance.

The storytellers of *The Life and Death of Jason* and *The Earthly Paradise* are not, however, merely extensions of Morris. Storytelling in *The Earthly Paradise* is complex; the basic assumption of the two works is clear in the simpler narrative of *The Life and Death of Jason*. Morris's subject is classical; his models, however, are not the primary Homeric epic but the imitative secondary epic of Apollonius of Rhodes, his chief source for the materials of the poem, and, explicitly in the invocation to book 17, the medieval poet Geoffrey Chaucer. Thus, *The Life and Death of Jason* is not a direct imitation of a classical narrative, but the imitation of an imitation. The chief result of this device is to distance the storyteller from his story. It is no longer his story; rather, it belongs to tradition. It is his task in the present to retell the tale, not to use it as a mode of self-expression, and given the emphasized distance from the original narrative, the possibility of self-expression is limited. It is the story itself that dictates narrative structure and determines closure—not the narrator's sense that he has had his say. "Another story now my tongue must tell," the poet announces as, having completed his narrative of "the Winning of the Golden Fleece," he undertakes his account of the events that occurred to Jason ten years after his return to Argos. Similarly, when this final episode is completed and capped with the death of Jason, the poem concludes with the assurance that "now is all that ancient story told."

In its original form, *The Life and Death of Jason* was to have been a much shorter poem, "The Deeds of Jason," within the narrative frame of *The Earthly Paradise*. Despite its independent publication, the poem is best understood in that context. *The Earthly Paradise* is an enormous work—more than four times the length of *Idylls of the King* and almost twice as long as Browning's *The Ring and the Book* (1868-1869). The poem consists of a prologue ("The Wanderers") and a related series of narrative interludes framing twenty-four stories drawn from classical and Germanic sources and arranged according to the cycle of the year, from March to February, with two stories for each month. In addition to this narrative frame, the poem begins with an apology and ends with an epilogue, and prefaces each month's storytelling with a twenty-one-line lyric appropriate to the season, all in a first-person voice that may be identified with Morris. If the poet is present in these occasional verses, it is only as an accretion; and this deliberately adventitious role emphasizes his dissociation from the narratives themselves.

The Wanderers are fourteenth century Vikings who flee a plague-stricken Norway in search of a fabled Earthly Paradise—a land of immortal life and happi-

ness—across the Atlantic. After a lifetime of disappointed expectations, they reach an island "midmost the beating of the steely sea," to which long ago Grecian colonists had been sent and where, cut off from the outside world, classical civilization has flourished long into the Christian era. The Wanderers, now old men, decide to remain here and, along with the Greek elders, agree to pass the time telling stories drawn from their two traditions. The obvious lesson of this narrative frame is that the quest for a geographical earthly paradise is vain, and that timelessness and beauty, if they exist at all, are to be found in art. However, the art available to the storytellers, like that of *The Life and Death of Jason*, is carefully limited in its effects. It is not directly self-expressive. It is, at best, a temporary illusion. For the space of the storytelling, its auditors may forget their cares, but the sequence of stories itself—from spring to winter—reminds the reader that they are only a respite, never a real escape from the relentless movement of time and decay. Thus, *The Earthly Paradise* is less a celebration of the power of art than a study of the limits of artistic experience. Its most telling literary analogues are not the medieval frame narratives from which it takes its general structure, but John Keats's "Ode to a Nightingale" and "Ode on a Grecian Urn"—Romantic poems in which the nature of art is probed and tested.

The Wanderers' quest suggests a model of the artist's career. Like the protagonist of another Romantic poem about art, Percy Bysshe Shelley's *Alastor: Or, The Spirit of Solitude, and Other Poems* (1816), they seek a real equivalent to the figments of their imagination—and, since their quest is in part motivated by artistic accounts of an earthly paradise, by the imaginative vision embodied in traditional art and oral storytelling, the failure of this quest teaches them the fundamental irreconcilability of the imagination and the natural world. It is therefore a necessary discipline that prepares them to accept the more limited notion of art that enables them to tell the tales of *The Earthly Paradise*. As such, their geographical quest corresponds to the stage of early Romanticism characteristic of many Victorian writers. (The story of their adventures is, fittingly, Romantic autobiography: The only first-person narrative available to them is the account of their own failure.)

In contrast, the Argonauts of *The Life and Death of Jason*, the classical tale originally to have followed immediately after the Wanderers' prologue, are motivated by two realizable aims—seizing the Golden Fleece and returning safely with it to Argos. The classical counterparts of the Wanderers exemplify, in other words, a classical reasonableness in setting goals for themselves. However, Jason, having accomplished all this, ends his life dissatisfied. His heroic deeds brought to pass, he is left sitting aimlessly on the sand by the rotting hulk of his ship, at length to be crushed in sleep by its falling stem. The Wanderers are able to transform their failure into successful art and so give form and meaning to their lives. Jason, without art, is trapped in memories he is powerless to reshape to the purposes of old age.

This notion of art as strictly limited yet necessary is present in the opening lines of the apology. Morris, referring to himself as "the idle singer of an empty day," compares his work first to the Christmastide illusion of a wizard who made the spring, summer, and fall appear through windows on three sides of a room, "While still, unheard, but in its wonted way,/ Piped the drear wind of that December day"; then, to "a shadowy isle of bliss" like that which the Wanderers come upon "Midmost the beating of the steely sea." These images argue that the full power of art is realized only when its limitations are perceived. The wizard's spell is powerful because his audience never loses awareness of the winter it temporarily displaces; the island is blissful precisely because it holds its own against the sea. The Camelot of Tennyson's *Idylls of the King* is, like the Wanderers' storytelling, a city "built to music." Its relationship to the real world is always ambiguous, however, and it is this ambiguity that spawns the doubt that destroys Arthur's kingdom. For ambiguity, Morris substitutes a tension between the recognized claims of the actual and those of the imaginary, through which each heightens, by contrast, the experience of the other. Art, by giving up its claims to replace actuality, thus subtly pervades and enhances the real world—just as the "lesser arts" of Morris and Company were able to exert an influence over day-to-day life unavailable to the "fine arts" of Victorian England.

In keeping with the project, the twenty-four narra-

tives of *The Earthly Paradise* are generally familiar in subject and simple in narrative style. Certain of the stories, however—in particular, those in the second half of the collection—violate this rule, perhaps reflecting the strains of Morris's personal life or his impatience with simplicity itself. Both in length and in tone, "The Lovers of Gudrun" (November), which Morris based on the Icelandic Laxdaela Saga, seems to break out of its narrative frame.

Two overlapping groups of stories, those dealing with erotic quests and those dealing with artists, appear to have particularly caught Morris's imagination: "The Story of Cupid and Psyche" (May), "Pygmalion and the Image" (August), "The Land East of the Sun and West of the Moon" (September), "The Man Who Never Laughed Again" (October), and "The Hill of Venus" (February). Eros, for Morris, may be sublimated in art or idealized love, but its basic nature as irrational drive is never forgotten. Each of these stories recapitulates, in its own way, the journey and disillusionment of the Wanderers. The protagonists of the first three eventually find fulfillment of their desires, but only after a nadir of despair in which all hope for the recovery of imaginative life is lost. Put to the test, the man who never laughs again is unable to resist the claims of the imagination and is destroyed by the strength of his own desire. In Morris's version of the Tannhäuser legend, Walter's acceptance of the limits of art—here, the erotic fantasy world of the Venusberg—leaves him in a nightmare limbo of "hopeless" joys and "horrors passing hell." Significantly, in this, the final story in the collection, the tension between the imaginary and the actual has itself become a source of frustration. Just as his empathic re-creation of the figures on the Grecian Urn leads Keats to "A burning forehead, and a parching tongue," Morris's storytelling returns full circle to the painful self-consciousness he had originally sought to banish. The earthly paradise afforded by narrative art can, it turns out, provide just the opposite of an escape from the pains of desire.

LOVE IS ENOUGH

This discovery lies behind *Love Is Enough*, the most complex and in some ways most personally revealing of Morris's longer poems. Written after his 1871 journey to Iceland, it is the first of his literary works to reflect his firsthand experience of the scenery and ambience of the North. The core plot is a version of the erotic quests of *The Earthly Paradise*, but carried to an unexpected conclusion. Pharamond deserts his kingdom in search of Azalais, a maiden in a Northern valley about whom he has dreamed obsessively. Years and much hardship later, he finds her and they are united. He then leaves her, however, to return to his old kingdom, now under a new ruler. The poem ends with Pharamond contemplating the changes that have taken place and deciding to return to—yet still apart from—Azalais. This fable is presented as a masque celebrating the wedding of an emperor and empress who, along with the peasant couple Giles and Joan, and the mayor, who functions as a master of ceremonies, comment on the story. Within the masque, Love acts as a commentator on, and at times agent in, the fable; a series of lyric poems ("The Music") add yet another interpretative dimension to Pharamond's quest.

While these framing devices invite comparison with *The Earthly Paradise*, they are not merely a more complicated attempt to distance Morris—and the reader—from his central romantic narrative. Instead, they signal Morris's new concern for the role of the audience. *The Earthly Paradise* deflects attention from the story to the act of storytelling; *Love Is Enough* deflects it from the story to the act of story receiving. The audience witnessing the masque is carefully chosen to represent the nobility, the bourgeoisie, and the working class. Each group's response is different; each uses art for its own purposes; each perceives the story of Pharamond in a somewhat different context. Together, they make up a composite cultural response. Further, it is important to note that this response includes an awareness of the performance of the work. The actor and actress who play the parts of Pharamond and Azalais are the subject of audience discussion. The point, however, is not that the audience is conscious of theatrical artifice—in the way that the listeners to the tales in *The Earthly Paradise* are conscious that what they are hearing is literary artifice. Rather, awareness of the human participants in the masque gives art a grounding in actuality: The story of Pharamond is more "real" because "real" human beings perform it. The truth of art, Morris suggests, lies not in its imitation of

life but in its integration with human experience.

It follows from this view that the artist who seeks this integration must concern himself or herself with the lives of the audience and with the kind of life in which art is most vital. Although the emperor and empress are developed as romantic figures, it is Giles and Joan who are granted the fullest experience of the masque. Their range of response is unhindered by a sense of public role; at the end of the performance, they propose to invite the actor and actress home with them to "crown the joyance of to-day," thus completing the integration of art and life; significantly, they have the last word in the poem. It would seem that the peasant couple represent the consciousness toward which Pharamond himself grows in the course of his life. The subtitle of the poem, "The Freeing of Pharamond," refers to his freedom first from the role of king and, finally, from the role of romantic quester. He must forgo the need for dominance either as a ruler or as a heroic lover if he is to find happiness with Azalais. For this reason, *Love Is Enough* represents an important stage in Morris's development as a social revolutionary, yet it is revolutionary in theme only, not in tone. The dominant feeling of the poem is pain, and the figure of Love who controls the action of the masque is markedly sadistic. Here, more than anywhere else in the longer poems, Morris's own erotic frustration seems to determine the ambience of the narrative.

THE STORY OF SIGURD THE VOLSUNG AND THE FALL OF THE NIBLUNGS

The link between a revolutionary consciousness and eros marks *Love Is Enough* as a turning point in Morris's literary career. It follows from the poem that Morris was beginning to recognize a conflict between his intentions as an artist and the limitations of his bourgeois audience. This conflict is pronounced in *The Story of Sigurd the Volsung and the Fall of the Niblungs*, for Morris's epic is a poem written for a sensibility markedly different from that of the late Victorian reading public.

As early as 1870, Morris had been fascinated by the *Völsunga saga* (c. 1270; *Völsunga Saga: The Story of the Volsungs and the Niblungs, with Certain Songs from the Elder Edda*, 1870), a prose translation of which he had published in that year. What struck him about the Icelandic poem was its artless understatement—"All tenderness is shown without the use of a tender word, all misery and despair without a word of raving, complete beauty without ornament." It is, as a result, "something which is above all art." If the powerful effects that Morris admires in the saga do not have verbal equivalents in the text, then they must be outside it, in the reader's supplying what has gone unsaid. Appropriately, the poet of such work is anonymous—"some twelfth century Icelander, living the hardest and rudest of lives," whose work is more a collection of material than an original composition. Thus, the reader not only is forced to supply the emotional force of the poem but also is given no identifiable narrator on whom to rely.

Further, because Victorian conventions represent an inappropriate supplement to his work, Morris wrote the poem in language that discourages a response based on contemporary assumptions of behavior and morality. He relies heavily on an often archaic Anglo-Saxon vocabulary that forces the reader to perceive the text as embodying an alien mode of expression. The poem makes little effort to engage the modern reader, and for that reason it may seem difficult to read. Only when one has adapted oneself to its style does the poem's power become apparent.

Even its narrative form is not Victorian. If the structure of a novel organized according to the developmental pattern of human life defines what his contemporaries expected from the plot of an extended narrative, then Morris chose a story that ignores this expectation. His central figure, Sigurd, does not appear until the second of the poem's four books and is killed before the end of the third. In the course of the poem various characters—Sigurd, Regin, Brynhild, Gudrun—come into prominence and then pass away. Morris uses imagery and symbolism to suggest organic wholeness, but these devices do not obscure the lack of novelistic unity fundamental to *The Story of Sigurd the Volsung and the Fall of the Niblungs*. Instead of a narrative organized around the development of individual character, it traces the collective fate of a people. The reader, to respond to this subject, must be able to identify structure with a collectivity rather than with an individual life; it is for this reason that the poem is closely related to Morris's later Marxist writings.

Although *The Story of Sigurd the Volsung and the Fall of the Niblungs* effectively ended the major phase of Morris's poetic career, it was not a dead end. After 1876, his chief energies shifted from writing poetry to changing society so that such poems could be read. When he returned to imaginative literature, it was with the recognition that the audience he was seeking could be reached best by prose. The archaic language and collective consciousness of *The Story of Sigurd the Volsung and the Fall of the Niblungs*, however, reappear in *The House of the Wolfings* and the romances that followed.

LATER POETRY

Except for his translations, *The Odyssey of Homer* (1887) and *The Tale of Beowulf* (1895) and for a few of the short pieces collected in *Poems by the Way*, the only verse that Morris published in the last twenty years of his life was directly related to his efforts to popularize socialism. The subject of his *Chants for Socialists*, which appeared in Socialist journals and pamphlets during the mid-1880's, is clear from titles such as "The Voice of Toil," "No Master," "All for the Cause," and "The March of the Workers." The power of such poetry may have passed with its historical occasion; however, that Morris could write verse that caught the imagination of the common man was no mean accomplishment.

The Pilgrims of Hope is a fictional narrative, the concluding sections of which are based on the 1871 Paris Commune. As Karl Marx did, Morris saw the events in France as a stage in the overthrow of bourgeois culture, and for this reason his portrait of the Communards is biased and perhaps sentimentalized. Moreover, the poem, which appeared serially in *Commonweal*, was hastily written, and it was only after Morris was well into it that he seems to have hit on the theme that would bring it to a conclusion. Despite its lapses, however, *The Pilgrims of Hope* is successful in its realistic portrait of working-class London and urban socialism. It also suggests some of Morris's own problems in justifying his status as a businessman with his socioeconomic beliefs. However, just as *Love Is Enough* links eros and revolution, the later poem connects Marxism with a love triangle made up of the protagonist, his wife, and a socialist comrade. Indeed, their decision to go together to Paris and fight for the commune is less strongly felt as a commitment to socialism than as an—explicitly suicidal—resolution of the tensions in their relationship. Not only does the medium of the poem return Morris to the erotic concerns of his earlier poetry, but also that return itself argues that, beneath his commitment to social action, those concerns remained unresolved—a view confirmed by the prose romances of the 1890's, in which he returned to the theme of the erotic quest, now envisioned not simply as an act of the individual protagonist, but as a component of the social history of a people.

Seen in isolation, Morris's career as a poet is inconclusive; seen in terms of his work as a whole, its pattern of development becomes clear. If, like Tennyson and Browning, Morris sought to free his poetry of Romantic self-consciousness, his alternative was more radical than theirs. Typically, the Romantic poem confronts the reader with the self of the poet—in William Wordsworth's terms, "a man speaking to men"—whose presence demands a very personal response. Tennyson, Browning, and the Morris of *The Defence of Guenevere, and Other Poems* replace the self of the poet with a collection of other selves. These alternative figures may no longer speak with the authority of the poet, but the relationship between reader and poem is basically the same: One responds to the poem as one responds to a fellow human being, either directly, in the dramatic monologues, or at second hand, in narrative verse. In the poetry he wrote after *The Defence of Guenevere, and Other Poems*, Morris rejects this model. *The Earthly Paradise* removes even the art of storytelling from the world of the reader. The complicated structure of *Love Is Enough* "frees" not only Pharamond but also the reader from identification with a model of individual development. *The Story of Sigurd the Volsung and the Fall of the Niblungs* replaces individual selves with a collectivity—the language and narrative conventions of Victorian England with alien speech and storytelling. If these poems are difficult to judge by literary standards derived from the work of other poets—if they do not fit the reader's notion of what a Victorian poem is supposed to be—this should remind us that Morris, not only in politics but also in poetry, was a revolutionary.

OTHER MAJOR WORKS

LONG FICTION: *A Dream of John Ball*, 1888; *The House of the Wolfings*, 1888; *News from Nowhere: Or, An Epoch of Rest, Being Some Chapters from a Utopian Romance*, 1890; *The Roots of the Mountains*, 1890; *The Story of the Glittering Plain*, 1890; *The Wood Beyond the World*, 1894; *Child Christopher and Goldilond the Fair*, 1895; *The Well at the World's End*, 1896; *The Sundering Flood*, 1897; *The Water of the Wondrous Isles*, 1897.

NONFICTION: *Hopes and Fears for Art*, 1882; *Chants for Socialists*, 1885; *The Manifesto of the Socialist League*, 1885; *Signs of Change: Seven Lectures Delivered on Various Occasions*, 1888; *Statement of Principles of the Hammersmith Socialist Society*, 1890; *Manifesto of English Socialists*, 1893 (with H. M. Hyndman and George Bernard Shaw); *Socialism: Its Growth and Outcome*, 1893 (with E. Belfort Bax); *William Morris: Artist, Writer, Socialist*, 1936 (May Morris, editor); *The Letters of William Morris to His Family and Friends*, 1950 (Philip Henderson, editor); *Icelandic Journals by William Morris*, 1969; *The Unpublished Lectures of William Morris*, 1969 (Eugene D. LeMire, editor); *William Morris's Socialist Diary*, 1982; *The Collected Letters of William Morris*, 1984-1987 (4 volumes).

TRANSLATIONS: *Three Northern Love Stories, and Other Tales*, 1873 (with Eiríkr Magnússon); *The Aeneids of Virgil*, 1875; *The Odyssey of Homer*, 1887; *The Tale of Beowulf*, 1895.

MISCELLANEOUS: *The Collected Works of William Morris*, 1910-1915, 1966 (24 volumes; May Morris, editor).

BIBLIOGRAPHY

Burdick, John. *William Morris: Redesigning the World*. New York: Todtri, 1997. This biography, illustrated with color and black-and-white photographs, examines the full range of Morris's talents as designer, activist, businessperson, poet, and prose writer.

Helsinger, Elizabeth K. *Poetry and the Pre-Raphaelite Arts: Dante Gabriel Rossetti and William Morris*. New Haven, Conn.: Yale University Press, 2008. Examines the relationship between poetry and visual art and design in the works of Morris and Rossetti. Stresses the importance of Pre-Raphaelitism in literature.

Kirchhoff, Frederick. *William Morris*. Boston: Twayne, 1979. This book provides an overview of Morris's literary achievements, viewing them as "his central mode of self-discovery and expression." Kirchhoff stresses the interdependence of theory, experience, and emotion, and of folk art and sophisticated literary traditions in Morris's work. Includes a chronology, a select bibliography, and an index.

Latham, David, ed. *Writing on the Image: Reading William Morris*. Toronto, Ont.: University of Toronto Press, 2007. A collection of essays on Morris, focusing on all aspects of his life and works.

Le Bourgeois, John V. *Art and Forbidden Fruit: Hidden Passion in the Life of William Morris*. Cambridge, England: Lutterworth Press, 2006. A biography of Morris that examines his marriage to Jane Burden and finds him culpable in part, because of his close attachment to his sister Emma.

LeMire, Eugene D. *A Bibliography of William Morris*. Newcastle, Del.: Oak Knoll Press, 2006. A bibliography of works by and about Morris.

Mahamdallie, Hassan. *Crossing the "River of Fire": The Socialism of William Morris*. London: Redwords, 2008. Examines the political views of Morris and how they affected his writings.

Salmon, Nicholas. *The William Morris Chronology*. Bristol, England: Thoemmes Press, 1996. This substantial reference (292 pages) contains more than two thousand entries, providing a nearly daily account of the life, along with stories and anecdotes told by contemporaries. A unique guide to Morris's life and career. Bibliography.

Tompkins, J. M. S. *William Morris: An Approach to the Poetry*. London: Cecil Woolf, 1988. Tompkins fills in the gaps in previous criticism of Morris's writings by discussing the narrative poems in detail, paying attention to the sources of the tales and the links with Morris's daily life. Includes an index.

Frederick Kirchhoff

EDWIN MUIR

Born: Deerness, Island of Wyre, Orkney, Scotland; May 15, 1887
Died: Swaffham Prior, Cambridgeshire, England; January 3, 1959

PRINCIPAL POETRY

First Poems, 1925
Chorus of the Newly Dead, 1926
Six Poems, 1932
Variations on a Time Theme, 1934
Journeys and Places, 1937
The Narrow Place, 1943
The Voyage, and Other Poems, 1946
The Labyrinth, 1949
Collected Poems, 1921-1951, 1953
Prometheus, 1954
One Foot in Eden, 1956
Collected Poems, 1921-1958, 1960
Selected Poems, 1965, 1974
The Complete Poems of Edwin Muir, 1991

OTHER LITERARY FORMS

Edwin Muir (myoor) is known principally for his poetry, which was compiled near the end of his life into *Collected Poems, 1921-1958*. Muir wrote in other genres, including fiction, biography, and nonfiction, primarily works of literary criticism and theory. Besides his poetry, however, Muir is most remembered for *An Autobiography* (1954) and his translations with his wife, Willa Muir, of the novels and short stories of Franz Kafka.

ACHIEVEMENTS

On the surface, Edwin Muir seems the very image of the erudite and reticent scholar and poet, calling on myth, allusion, and the classical tradition to craft poems that seemed rooted in the English poetic tradition at a time when the modernist poets were taking poetry in a new direction. This picture of Muir, however, is misleading. He came from a rural Scottish family, did not begin writing poetry until he was thirty-five, and endured an impoverished childhood in the harsh environs of Glasgow. Muir distilled his experiences into a powerful, if traditional, poetry and, through his translations, brought the English-speaking world's attention to the work of Kafka. T. S. Eliot speaks admiringly of Muir's "integrity" in his preface to *Selected Poems* (this preface first appeared in *The Listener* in May, 1964, and also in the 1965 edition of *Collected Poems, 1921-1958*), explaining that all of Muir's work and life were of a piece, focused on a single unified expression of his ideas and experience.

In his later life, Muir received many awards and honorary degrees, including the Foyle Prize (1950), the Heinemann Award (1953), membership in the Royal Society of Literature (1953), the Frederick Niven Literary Award (1953), Commander of the Order of the British Empire (1953), and the Russell Loines Award (1957).

BIOGRAPHY

Edwin Muir grew up in the remote Orkney Islands off the northeast coast of Scotland, where he was the youngest child of James Muir and Elizabeth Muir. His father was a tenant farmer, and the family survived under straitened circumstances. In 1901, when Muir was fourteen, the family moved to highly industrialized Glasgow; this marked the end of his formal education and the beginning of a string of menial jobs and personal family misfortunes, including the deaths of Muir's parents and two of his older brothers.

Muir educated himself primarily through reading and began to produce essays and reviews for the weekly journal *New Age* under the mentorship of A. R. Orage. Although raised in a religious Calvinist tradition, in these early years, Muir was influenced by his reading of Friedrich Nietzsche, Carl Jung, and Sigmund Freud. Later in his life, he experienced a revival of interest in traditional Christian ideas, but his writing remained influenced by the reading of his youth.

In 1919, Muir married Willa Anderson, who would become his lifelong partner. As a scholar and teacher of Germanic studies, she worked with him on the translations of Kafka, Hermann Broch, Gerhart Hauptmann, and Lion Feuchtwanger that brought the work of these writers to the attention of the English-speaking world.

These translations were begun while the Muirs were living in Prague and traveling in Europe in the 1920's. Although Muir published several novels during this period, he began to focus more intently on his poetry in the 1930's and 1940's, producing the work for which he would be most well known.

In 1927, the Muirs returned to England and later moved to Scotland; this period was marked by financial hardship and the illnesses of both Edwin and Willa. In 1939, Muir underwent a religious experience that influenced the direction of his poetry for the remainder of his life. The 1940's saw an improvement in the couple's fortunes; in 1942, Muir was appointed to the British Council Staff in Edinburgh and served as director of the British Institute in Prague from 1945 to 1948, allowing the Muirs to return to Europe. From 1949 to 1950, Muir served at the British Institute in Rome, a posting that influenced his awareness of other religious traditions.

Muir increasingly made a name for himself as a poet and critic, delivering the W. P. Ker Memorial lecture in Glasgow (1946) and receiving honorary doctorates from Charles University and the University of Edinburgh. In the remaining ten years of his life, Muir compiled his *Collected Poems, 1921-1951* (1953) and published his well-respected memoir, *An Autobiography*. He spent 1955 as the Charles Eliot Norton Professor of Poetry at Harvard, collecting his series of lectures into *The Estate of Poetry* (published posthumously in 1962). Muir died in a Cambridge nursing home in 1959.

ANALYSIS

From 1937 to 1956, Edwin Muir published six collections of poetry, culminating in the *Collected Poems, 1921-1958* in 1960. Muir's poetry exists on a rather abstract and mythological level. Despite his lack of formal education, his work builds on allusions to biblical, epic, and literary traditions, and his technique is fairly traditional. The recurring themes in his poetry are the relationship of time to eternity, the role of memory in shaping and consolidating experience, and the challenges of inhabiting liminal spaces when moving from life to death, from past to present to future, from dream to waking, and from the personal, individual experience to the world of universal human truth. Muir draws especially on Jung's concept of the collective unconscious, the idea that certain ideas and archetypes inhabit the collective human mind. He also used his early experience of undergoing Freud's new technique of psychoanalysis to explore the significance of dreams. Although Muir never embraced institutionalized religion and was hostile to his early Calvinist upbringing and ideas, in his later life, he moved increasingly toward a Christian worldview, as evidenced by poems in his later collections, *The Labyrinth* and *One Foot in Eden*. Working outside the prevailing modernist and experimental mainstream in poetry at the beginning of the twentieth century, Muir was not as critically heralded as his compatriot Eliot. However, his work contributes a thoughtful, mature, and insightful voice to English poetry of the mid-twentieth century.

JOURNEYS AND PLACES

Muir's first major collection after rededicating himself to poetry was *Journeys and Places*, which explores the motif of the journey. The book is roughly organized into three parts: seven poems dealing with journeys or stages of the journey; seven poems treating mythological, fictional, and historical personages; and ten poems describing places or destinations.

These poems concentrate on one of Muir's most persistent ideas: the role of the imagination in journeying through time. The mind can journey back through memory, although those memories may be lost or distorted in various ways. The tension between the urge to look backward through the history of humankind and the temptation to look forward to some ultimate destiny can at times be paralyzing. Muir's dreamlike and mysterious journeys employ the recurring image of roads circling around hills. In Muir's circular imagery, time becomes timeless and the end of the journey becomes the beginning. In his view, personal history is submerged into the cultural history of the entire human race. Muir traces the journeys or quests of individuals—real or mythic—who have faced loss and connects their stories to the universal experience.

The final group of poems—places—portrays the search for a place of sanctuary. In "The Sufficient Place," the peaceful destination is regarded as a place where people recognize "the Archetypes," another

Jungian concept. The term suggests that personal pain evolves into archetypal pattern, and the individual story becomes the universal story. After a series of questions, the final poem in the collection, "The Dreamt-of Place," ends with the words, "But there was no answer." Muir's final stance seems hopeful but uncertain.

THE LABYRINTH

The Labyrinth is generally regarded as one of Muir's finest works and has received significant critical attention. It shows greater structural unity, more confident technical proficiency, increased maturity, and more influence from his traditional Christian beliefs occasioned by his 1939 religious reawakening. Here, Muir's favorite image of the journey is reformulated as a labyrinth, where the individual must solve the puzzle of the intricate and dangerous maze. These twenty-eight poems begin with the sonnet "Too Much," which describes the narrator on an uncertain and ambiguous quest: "Dark on the highway, groping in the light/ Threading my dazzling way within my night." Humans long for some place of eternal peace, but essential ties keep them linked to Earth and time and the labyrinth.

The Greek myth of Theseus seeking the Minotaur in the labyrinth forms a touchstone for this work. Muir deals with a variety of liminal spaces, spaces on the borders of life/death, time/timelessness, the personal/ the universal, past/present, light/darkness, innocence/ guilt, and dream/reality. He is especially concerned with the points of contact between these liminal spaces and often expresses them as the site of conflict. In one of the few poems in which Muir alludes to contemporary political events, "The Good Town," presumably about the devastation of Prague in World War II, he describes the effects of the war on the citizens of the town.

The Labyrinth builds toward the final poems, particularly "Soliloquy," "The Transfiguration," and "The Toy Horse." Following the poems that explore the tensions of opposites, these final poems attempt to resolve the contradictions into a vision of wisdom built on the consolidation of past experience and the hope of Christ's redemption of humankind. "The Transfiguration" represents a vision, however fleeting, of a world in which all experience unites humankind and Christ appears in a vision of redemption. The final image of the book develops the complex image of the toy horse, which revisits Muir's biblical references to Christ, to life's journey, to real horses, to eternity, and to repose.

ONE FOOT IN EDEN

One Foot in Eden is the last volume of poetry published while Muir was alive and represents one of his most accomplished and mature efforts. The collection contains a frequently anthologized poem, "The Horses," which Eliot described in his preface as "that terrifying poem of the 'atomic age.'" "The Horses" envisions a time after a nuclear cataclysm when the horses arrive in all their strange beauty to replace inoperable machinery. The vision is both apocalyptic in its sense of the end of days and pastoral in its return to the natural world.

Like *The Labyrinth*, *One Foot in Eden* is best read as a structurally unified series of poems. Each of the two parts is introduced by a sonnet ("Milton" and "To Franz Kafka"), in a technique similar to that used in *The Labyrinth*. These sonnets index the concerns and themes of each section.

Muir surveys the history of humankind, from the creation of the world to its final days, a larger pattern paralleling the life span of the individual. The volume reaches its historical conclusion with "The Horses." The final poems following "The Horses" look toward a journey to some other world or state beyond Earth, a world consistent with Christian belief in a spiritual afterlife, but not blatantly so. The final poem, "Song," indirectly alludes both to Persephone and Penelope. Persephone dies to the earth during the winter and then brings back the spring when she returns from the underworld. Penelope, Odysseus's long-suffering wife, weaves all day at her loom while she waits for his return and then tears out what she has done and begins all over again—an image, in Muir's view, of a blend of time and eternity.

OTHER MAJOR WORKS

LONG FICTION: *The Marionette*, 1927; *The Three Brothers*, 1931; *Poor Tom*, 1932.

NONFICTION: *We Moderns*, 1918; *Latitudes*, 1924; *The Structure of the Novel*, 1928; *Scottish Journey*, 1935; *Scott and Scotland*, 1936; *The Story and the Fable*, 1940; *Essays on Literature and Society*, 1949; *An Autobiography*, 1954; *The Estate of Poetry*, 1962.

TRANSLATIONS (WITH WILLA MUIR): *Poetic Dramas*, 1925 (of Gerhart Hauptmann); *Jew Suss*, 1926 (of Lion Feuchtwanger); *The Castle*, 1930 (of Franz Kafka); *The Sleepwalkers*, 1932 (of Hermann Broch); *The Trial*, 1937 (of Kafka); *In the Penal Colony: Tales and Short Pieces*, 1945 (of Kafka).

BIBLIOGRAPHY

Aitchison, James. *The Golden Harvester: The Vision of Edwin Muir*. Aberdeen, Scotland: Aberdeen University Press, 1988. Comprehensive overview and analysis of the entirety of Muir's poetry.

Gairn, Louisa. "Questioning Our Place in the World: The Significance of Pastoral in the Work of Edwin Muir." In *New Versions of Pastoral: Post-Romantic, Modern, and Contemporary Responses to the Tradition*, edited by David James and Philip Tew. Madison, N.J.: Fairleigh Dickinson University Press, 2009. Citing Muir's break with the pastoral in his family's move from the Orkney Islands to Glasgow, Gairn explores Muir's use of pastoral elements and his relationship with technology.

Kinzie, Mary. "Edwin Muir and the Primal World." In *By Herself: Women Reclaim Poetry*, edited by Molly McQuade. St. Paul, Minn.: Graywolf Press, 2000. Kinzie analyzes Muir's poetry and discusses its relationship to *An Autobiography*.

McCulloch, Margery. *Edwin Muir: Poet, Critic and Novelist*. Edinburgh: Edinburgh University Press, 1993. An introduction to the poetry, criticism, and fiction of Muir intended for students and for the general audience.

MacLachlan, C. J. M., and D. S. Robb, eds. *Edwin Muir: Centenary Assessments*. Aberdeen, Scotland: Association for Scottish Literary Studies, 1990. A significant collection of essays on Muir's work. Essayists in the collection consider biographical connections to his work as well as literary analysis of specific works.

Mellown, Elgin W. *Edwin Muir*. Boston: Twayne, 1979. Good basic introduction to the life and work of Muir. Three chapters concentrate on the poetry. Includes chronology, biography, and bibliography.

Whyte, Christopher. *Modern Scottish Poetry*. Edinburgh: Edinburgh University Press, 2004. Examines Muir's work in the context of Scottish poetry from the beginning of World War II until 1999. Muir is one of twenty Scottish poets discussed.

Wiseman, Christopher. *Beyond "The Labyrinth": A Study of Edwin Muir's Poetry*. Victoria, B.C.: Sono Nis Press, 1978. Canadian poet Wiseman offers an in-depth and sometimes critical view of Muir's poetry, examining the structure and development of some of Muir's best-known work.

Ann M. Cameron

PAUL MULDOON

Born: County Armagh, Northern Ireland; June 20, 1951

PRINCIPAL POETRY

Knowing My Place, 1971
New Weather, 1973
Spirit of Dawn, 1975
Mules, 1977
Names and Addresses, 1978
Immram, 1980
Why Brownlee Left, 1980
Out of Siberia, 1982
Quoof, 1983
The Wishbone, 1984
Mules, and Early Poems, 1985
Selected Poems, 1968-1983, 1986
Meeting the British, 1987
Selected Poems, 1968-1986, 1987
Madoc: A Mystery, 1990
The Annals of Chile, 1994
The Prince of the Quotidian, 1994
New Selected Poems, 1968-1994, 1996
Hay, 1998
Kerry Slides, 1998
Poems, 1968-1998, 2001
Moy Sand and Gravel, 2002
General Admission, 2006 (includes song lyrics)
Horse Latitudes, 2006

When the Pie Was Opened, 2008 (illustrations by Lanfranco Quadrio)
Plan B, 2009 (photographs by Norman McBeath)
Maggot, 2010

OTHER LITERARY FORMS

Unlike many other contemporary Irish poets, Paul Muldoon is, generally speaking, content to let his verse speak for him. Hence his production of articles and reviews is small and not very helpful in coming to terms with his poetry. His most notable contribution to Irish literary culture has been his idiosyncratic, and in some quarters controversial, editing of *The Faber Book of Contemporary Irish Verse* (1986). Muldoon has also published translations of a small number of poems by the important contemporary Irish-language poet Nuala Ní Dhomhnaill. The distinctive character of Muldoon's own verse invites the conclusion that translating is much closer to his imaginative inclinations than editing. He has also edited *The Scrake of Dawn: Poems by Young People from Northern Ireland* (1979), *The Essential Byron* (1989), and *Contemporary Irish Poetry* (2006). His lectures of poetry have been collected in *To Ireland, I* (2000) and *The End of the Poem: Oxford Lectures* (2009).

ACHIEVEMENTS

Although Paul Muldoon regularly publishes book-length collections and has become an increasingly familiar presence internationally, particularly in the United States, he remains somewhat overshadowed by older, more celebrated poets from Northern Ireland. Muldoon's fluency and inventiveness have been constants since the publication of his precocious volume *New Weather* in 1973. As a result, it has been easier to take pleasure in his method than to chart the development of his aesthetic and thematic concerns. It is possible that the poet himself has experienced some of this sense of occlusion and that this has accounted, at least in part, for his increasing tendency to write unfashionably long poems. The publication of the book-length poem *Madoc* in 1990—a work that in many senses is a typically quirky yet not wholly unexpected product of the longer poems in *Why Brownlee Left, Quoof*, and *Meeting the British*—provides a pretext for an interim report on the attainments, challenges, and difficulties of the most original Irish poet to emerge since the 1930's.

While the critical jury may still be out as to the overall significance of Muldoon's work, there is no doubt that his poetry signifies an impressive departure from the work of his immediate predecessors among Northern Irish poets (such as Seamus Heaney, John Montague, and Michael Longley) and that Muldoon diverged from the conception of Irish poet as cultural watchdog and keeper of the national conscience, promoted and embodied by the founder of modern Irish poetry, William Butler Yeats.

Certainly the number of awards Muldoon has received suggests a critical acceptance of his work. Some of the accolades he has received include the Eric Gregory Prize (1972), the Sir Geoffrey Faber Memorial Award and the T. S. Eliot Prize for Poetry (both in 1994), the Award in Literature from the American Academy of Arts and Letters and the Bess Hokin Prize from *Poetry* magazine (both in 1996), the *Irish Times* Literature Prize (1997), the Pulitzer Prize and the Griffin Poetry Prize for *Moy Sand and Gravel* (both in 2003), the American Ireland Fund Literary Award and the Shakespeare Prize (both in 2004), the Aspen Prize for Poetry (2005), the European Prize for Poetry (2006), and the John William Corrington Award for Literary Excellence from Centenary College of Louisiana (2009-2010). He has been elected to a Fellowship of the Royal Society of Literature and became a member of the American Academy of Arts and Letters in 2008.

BIOGRAPHY

Paul Muldoon was born on June 20, 1951, in the remote rural community of The Fews, County Armagh, Northern Ireland. Shortly afterward, his family moved to the no less remote area of The Moy, County Tyrone. The poet, therefore, comes from a background that is similar in many external respects to those of Northern Ireland poets such as Seamus Heaney and John Montague, who have done much to put that part of the world on the literary map. This point is relevant because Muldoon's response to his background is very different from that of his illustrious near-contemporaries.

After secondary education at St. Patrick's College, Armagh, Muldoon read English at Queen's University, Belfast, and was graduated with a B.A. in 1971. Like many writers from Northern Ireland, particularly those of an older generation, he worked as a talks producer for the Northern Ireland regional service of the British Broadcasting Corporation in Belfast. He resigned this position in 1986 and began working as a visiting professor in a number of American universities. He has taught at Columbia University, the University of California, Berkeley, and the University of Massachusetts, and in 1990, he began teaching at Princeton University. In 1993, he became director and founding chair of creative writing at Princeton's Lewis Center for the Arts. In 1999, he was elected professor of poetry at Oxford, succeeding James Fenton in this five-year honorary appointment, and he continues at Oxford as fellow of Hertford College. At Princeton, he was elected to the Howard G. B. Clark '21 Professorship and became involved with academic administration as well as teaching. He is a professor emeritus at the University of St. Andrews, Scotland. He has taught on the summer Bread Loaf program of creative writing. In 2007, he became poetry editor for *The New Yorker*.

In his private life, his first marriage to Anne-Marie Conway, an Irish woman, broke up in 1979. After an affair with Mary Ann Powers came to an end with her death, he married the American novelist Jean Hanff Korelitz, a Jewish woman, by whom he has had two children, Dorothy and Asher. The family settled in New Jersey near Princeton. As a hobby, he joined a rock band, Rackett, and has been writing lyrics for its songs.

ANALYSIS

Although direct environmental influences on the growth of the imagination are impossible to prove, it does seem relevant to point out that Paul Muldoon's coming to consciousness coincided with the disintegrative threats to the social fabric of his native province. These threats of violence to civilians and forces of law and order alike, to property and the general communal infrastructure of Northern Ireland, date from 1969, when Muldoon was a freshman at Queen's University, Belfast. The threats have been both carried out and resisted. Disintegration of families, neighborhoods, and institutions has occurred, yet those entities continue to survive. Codes of self-protective speech have arisen, and things are no longer necessarily what they seem on the surface. It would be fanciful to argue that such characteristics of the poet's outer world are precisely what Muldoon's poetry reproduces, since, to begin with, such an argument overlooks the inevitable significance of form in his work. At the same time, however, there is such a degree of unpredictability, play, and opacity in his poetry that it is tempting to consider it an attractive, exuberant, puzzling, and blessedly harmless parallel universe to that of bombers and demagogues.

Paul Muldoon (AP/Wide World Photos)

This does not mean that Muldoon has not addressed poems to the trials and tribulations of the Northern Ireland of his adult life. Poems such as "Anseo" in *Why Brownlee Left* (*anseo* is the Irish word for "here," meaning "present" in the poem), "The Sightseers" in *Quoof*, and the arresting and unnerving title poem of *Meeting the British*—to name well-known instances—confront in ways that are not particularly euphemistic the euphemistically named Troubles. However, it is equally, if not more, revealing of Muldoon that he would name a collection of poems for "our family word/ for the hot water bottle" ("quoof"), particularly since the reader has only the poet's word for it that this is what "quoof" actually means. More than any other Irish poet of his generation, perhaps, Muldoon demands to be taken first and foremost, and if possible, exclusively at his word.

Muldoon's slightly surreal, slightly whimsical, very subjective, and very oblique view of his material—his almost perverse conception of what constitutes "material" itself—sits at a seemingly crazy but refreshing angle to the modern Irish poetic tradition. Muldoon is concerned more with the making of verses than with the making of statements, and his work is airy, reckless, private, and provocative. Many of his poems are as much teases as they are texts in the predictable sense, yet they can also be seen as indebted to a more intriguing tradition of Irish poetry than that inaugurated by Yeats. Muldoon's implicit rejection of the public, vatic role of the poet, his frequent absorption in the minutiae of the natural world, his deployment of fragmented narrative, his use of pastiche, his finding himself equally at ease with foreign or domestic themes, his playfulness, and the challenge of his cunning superficiality have—among numerous other devices and resources—provided a valuable counterpoint to the more solemn, preoccupied, and fundamentally historicist poetry of his Northern Irish elders.

New Weather

New Weather, the title of his early work, has become over time a helpful phrase to describe the surprising novelty of Muldoon's poetry and its place in the canon of modern Irish verse. The poem in which the phrase "new weather" occurs, "Wind and Tree," is in one sense not particularly representative of Muldoon's work, with its talk of love and its unironic, somewhat sheepishly attention-claiming "I." The poem's elaborate metaphorical conceit of lovers being injured as trees are by wind heralds one of the most conspicuous elements in Muldoon's distinctive art, his generally shape-changing propensity, of which metaphor is a primary feature. "Wind and Tree" also provides the revealing lines, "Most of the world is centred/ About ourselves," often availed of by readers struggling for a foothold in some of the poet's less hospitable works.

Much more instructive of things to come in Muldoon's work is "Hedgehog," for the economy and distinctively contemporary quality of its imagery ("The snail moves like a/ Hovercraft, held up by a/ Rubber cushion of itself"), the outrageousness of its conceits (the hedgehog is referred to as "the god/ Under this crown of thorns"), and the possibility that the poem overall is a metaphor for communal and interpersonal division and defensiveness both in Northern Ireland and beyond. As in "Our Lady of Ardboe" (from *Mules*), "Who's to know what's knowable?"

MULES

By the time of the publication of *Mules*, the question of knowability in Muldoon's work was not strictly rhetorical—rather, to be Muldoonish about it, it was strictly rhetorical, meaning that it was built into the nature of the poem, rather than occurring every so often as a detachable line from a given poem. "Lunch with Pancho Villa," with its mysterious quality and the novelty of being written by an Irish poet, is not merely a witty imaginative adventure, expressive of the poet's range and restlessness. The poem interrogates, in a tone that is all the more incisive for lacking solemnity, the consequences of violence, and it questions whether the poet's duty is to respond to what the world contains or to the contents of his own imagination.

"CUBA"

One answer to this question—a question that may be used as a means of investigating Muldoon's increasingly complex mapping of his subjectivity—may be found in "Cuba" (from *Why Brownlee Left*). Here a remembrance of family life and common usages, both domestic (a father's predictable anger) and communal (an erring daughter goes to Confession), is placed in the context of the Cuban missile crisis of 1962, revealing the quirky, intimate, and reassuringly unresolved and unmechanical manner in which personal and public history overlap. This poem, ostensibly a simple narrative elaborating a vignette of memory, is a delicate essay in remoteness and intimacy, last things and initial experiences, innocence and eschatology. The poem's open rhythm (often captured by Muldoon through direct speech) leaves the reader in no doubt that the poet stands for the tender insignificant moments of the human realm rather than a melodramatic characterization of the machinations of history.

"WHY BROWNLEE LEFT"

A comparable sense of openness, of life as new beginnings and deliberately unfinished business, is provided by the title poem of *Why Brownlee Left*, in which the material achieves significance by—as the title implies—being neither a question nor an answer. Who Brownlee is seems irrelevant. The emphasis is on what has remained "a mystery even now." The point is the leaving, the possibility of pastures new, lyrically recapitulated by the absconder's horses at the end of the poem, "gazing into the future."

"IMMRAMA"

Perhaps Brownlee wanted to be able to say, like the narrator in "Immrama" (from *Why Brownlee Left*), "I, too, have trailed my father's spirit"—even if the trail leads to an inconclusive and implausible end for both father and son. Conclusion is less important than continuity. Analogously, Muldoon's work suggests that a poem's happening—the multifarious activities of the words contained by and excited within a prosodic framework (itself various and informal, though necessarily final)—is of more consequence than the poem's meaning. At an elementary level, which the reader dare not overlook, perhaps the happening is more lifelike, by virtue of its free play and variety, its sometimes outrageous rhymes and syncopated rhythms, than the meaning. Though quest as a motif has been present in Muldoon's work from the outset—"Identities" in *New Weather* begins "When I reached the sea/ I fell in with another who had just come/ From the interior"—it becomes more pronounced in the collections after *Why Brownlee Left*. The unusual title "Immrama" draws attention to this fact, as presumably it is meant to. It is the plural form of *immram*, the name in Irish for the genre of medieval Irish romances (including tales of travel to the other world) and a word that in the singular pro-vides the title of Muldoon's first important long poem, which also appears in *Why Brownlee Left*.

In "Immrama," Muldoon releases the possibilities latent or implied not only in the quirky lyrics of *Why Brownlee Left* but also in his overall body of work. Us-ing narrative in order to subvert it—a strategy familiar from, for example, "Good Friday, 1971, Driving West-ward" in *New Weather*—Muldoon brings the reader through a somewhat phantasmagorical, surreal adven-ture that pantomimes the style of hard-boiled detective fiction. Set in Los Angeles, the story itself is too erratic and effervescent to summarize. As the title of the poem is intended to suggest, however, the material maps out a territory that is rich and strange, which may be the land-scape of dream or of vision or the objective manifesta-tion of the psychic character of quest. Lest the reader be merely exhausted by the extent of the poem's literary high jinks—"I shimmied about the cavernous lobby./ Mr. and Mrs. Alfred Tennyson/ Were ahead of me through the revolving door./ She tipped the bell-hop five dollars"—there are important themes, such as identity, fabulation, and rootlessness, and an alert med-itation on the hybrid nature of writing as an imaginative process, of which "Immrama" is a helpful rehearsal.

"THE MORE A MAN HAS THE MORE A MAN WANTS"

Much more allusive, spectacular, and demanding is Muldoon's next adventure in the long poem "The More a Man Has the More a Man Wants" (from *Quoof*). Here, an increasingly prominent interest on the poet's part in the lore and legends of Native American traditional lit-erature comes influentially into play. In particular, the various legends of jokers and shape-changers, particu-larly those of Winnebago literature, are availed of, not in the sense of overt borrowings or new translations but with a respect for and fascination with their spirit. Muldoon is not the first poet to pay homage to these mythical figures. The English poet laureate Ted Hughes employed them in one of his most celebrated works, *Crow: From the Life and Songs of the Crow* (1970, 1972). The results are so different, however, that it is tempting to think of "The More a Man Has the More a Man Wants" as Muldoon's response to the senior poet.

The subject of the poem is change. As in the case of

"Immrama," scenes shift with confusing rapidity, and the inherent transience and adaptability of the persona is once again a central, enabling concern. The thematic mixture is far richer, however, in "The More a Man Has the More a Man Wants." In particular, the nature of change is not confined to Muldoon's familiar deploy-ments, such as travel, quest, and dream. Violence as an agent of change is also explored and its consequences confronted. Here again, a certain amount of frustration will be experienced by the reader, largely because the poem, though promising to be a narrative, becomes a variety of open-minded narrative options, while the in-tegration of the material takes place by virtue of the reader's ability to explore the possibilities of congru-ence within the widely diversified settings and perspec-tives. Sheer verve, inventiveness, unpredictability, and impenitent originality make "The More a Man Has the More a Man Wants" the poem that most fully illustrates the scope of Muldoon's ambitious aesthetic energies, through which all that is solid—including, perhaps par-ticularly, the legacy of history—is transformed into airy, insubstantial, but memorable surfaces.

MADOC

Any claim for the centrality of "The More a Man Has the More a Man Wants" must be made in the awareness of Muldoon's book-length poem *Madoc*. This poem is in effect prefaced by a handful of lyrics recognizably in the mode of, say, those in *Quoof*, among which is the superb elegy "Cauliflowers" (the incongruousness of the title is a typical Muldoon ma-neuver). "Madoc" itself, however, consists of a se-quence of rather impenetrable lyrics, all of which are headed by the name of a philosopher. Subtitled *A Mys-tery*, it is certainly a baffling poem. Once again, the assertion and denial of narrative are fundamental to the poet's procedures.

The source of the poem is a work of the same name written by the English Romantic poet Robert Southey, drawing in a manner vaguely reminiscent of Sir Walter Scott on the heroic legends of one of Great Britain's marginal peoples, in this case the Welsh. Muldoon, without adapting Southey's theme or prosody, seems to have adapted, in a satirical vein, Southey's method. His *Madoc* looks back to an adventure in which Southey was involved—namely, the establishment of a pantisocratic community on the banks of the Susquehanna River in Pennsylvania. The inspiration for this ill-fated scheme was the major English Romantic poet Samuel Taylor Coleridge. Casting his own mind back over the historic, not to mention romantic, dream of community, Muldoon reproduces his own puzzlement with such a project, articulating not the self-deceiving confidence of Coleridge's thought (and, by invoking the names of philosophers, of thought generally) but the fact that so little that is clear remains of what such thought asserted. In turn, or rather concurrently, a disquisition on the knowability of the world, a surreal satire on the inevitable insubstantiality of ideals, and a narrative poem whose most submerged feature is its storytelling, *Madoc* is clearly Muldoon's most sustained and substantial work, though most readers will find it easier to admire than it is to enjoy or decipher.

"INCANTATA"

Muldoon's reputation for mischief making, obfuscation, and intellectual pyrotechnics can lead the reader to forget that he is also a poet of considerable lyric skill and occasionally deep feeling. "Incantata" (from *The Annals of Chile*) is written in memory of Mary Farl Powers, a former lover, who died of cancer in 1992. It is loaded, as usual, with recondite material, but somehow gets out from under its wittiness to reveal, if often in a sideways gesture, his feeling for Powers, often in the context of her work as an artist:

> I saw you again tonight, in your jump-suit, thin as a
>   rake,
> your hand moving in such a deliberate arc
> as you ground a lithographic stone
> that your hand and the stone blurred to one
> and your face blurred into the face of your mother.

The form of the poem (an eight-line stanza) is taken from Abraham Cowley, the seventeenth century Royalist poet. Muldoon quietly traces the history of the affair, sometimes sadly and sometimes with comic gusto, as in their encounter with a priest who objected to their living together outside marriage. "Who came enquiring about our 'status', of the hedge-clippers/ I somehow had to hand, of him running like the clappers." Through the superfluity of references, the feeling rings true:

> . . . the day your father came to call, of your
>   leaving your sick-room
> in what can only have been a state of delirium,
> of how you simply wouldn't relent
> from your vision . . .
> that fate governs everything . . .

It is a poem that disproves the complaint that Muldoon is often "too clever by half" while, at the same time, showing how clever he is.

"ANONYMOUS: MYSELF AND PANGUAR"

"Anonymous: Myself and Panguar" (from *Hay*) shows how relaxed and direct Muldoon can be if the subject is right. In this poem about the poet and his cat, Panguar, the idea is to compare his cat's search for mice with his own search for the right word:

> much as Panguar goes after mice
> I go hunting for the precise
>
> word.

The poem is light, simple, and without show of the virtuoso flashiness that Muldoon possesses:

> Panguar going in for the kill
> with all his customary skill
> while I, sharp-witted, swift and sure,
> shed light on what had seemed obscure.

He may be teasing with the last line, aware, as he is, of the criticism of his sometime obscurity.

POEMS, 1968-1998

Several collections of Muldoon's poems had been published in 1986, 1987, and 1996. However, as some of the earlier volumes went out of print, Muldoon decided to publish a collection including everything he had written through 1998. *Poems, 1968-1998* brought together eight volumes: *New Weather*, *Mules*, *Why Brownlee Left*, *Quoof*, *Meeting the British*, *Madoc*, *The Annals of Chile*, and *Hay*. For the first time, it was possible to trace Muldoon's development clearly and to see some of the particular features that mark his poetry.

This collection highlighted Muldoon's tendency to put a long poem at the end of each volume; his long poems have gradually begun to be seen as his best work. The long poem, generally unpopular in modern poetry, was reinstated by Muldoon as a large canvas on which to explore a number of concurrent themes and motifs that intertwine with each other and gradually come together as the associations become spelled out. In the last poem in the collection, "The Bangle (A Slight Return)," motifs of his father's possible emigration to Australia run alongside a ferry crossing from Ireland to Scotland, to a slap-up meal in Paris (for which there is no hope of payment), to sections of Vergil's *Aeneid* (c. 29-19 B.C.E.; English translation, 1553). There is a postmodernist sense of "all is as the poet wills," and one word or episode can be read instead of another, as if it might somehow be an *erratum* that can be corrected.

The long poems show Muldoon's debt to James Joyce, both as a modernist and as a precursor to postmodernism. At all times, Muldoon engages in free association, backed by his vast and eclectic learning, which, as with Joyce, leaves the reader groping to locate the source and subtext. In terms of other influences, one of the interesting things to see overall in the collection is the way Muldoon marries Irish and American influence. Unlike Heaney, whose American sojourns left almost no dint in his Irishness, Muldoon's *Madoc*, one of his first offerings after his transatlantic translation, suggests a grasping at Americana. His is the new Southey, actually settling in the United States and exploring the landscape. However, what follows is a judicious blend of Irish-themed poetry and a distinctly American poetry. The influence of Robert Frost is obvious, but also the voices of Walt Whitman, Robert Lowell, and John Berryman are discernible.

Perhaps what does become more obvious, and not always for the good, is the influence of creative writing programs, master of fine arts versification, where any associative imagery is rewarded for originality, even genius, regardless of how little relationship to real human value or experience it has. In committing himself to teach courses in creative writing, Muldoon takes a professional risk. However, some of Muldoon's long poems, such as "Incantata," "Yarrow," and "Third Epistle to Timothy," suggest that the associative method allows Muldoon to work out experiences and emotions lodged deep within his psyche, making these poems quite moving and major contributions to the modern long poem.

Perhaps the obvious absence is any sense of the spiritual and a great sense of the more human aspects of sexuality. Muldoon's own experience of Ulster religion seems to have blocked off any ability to explore other forms of spirituality, and he can only recount acts of random violence in some effort to make peace with his past. Thus whole swathes of human experience are excluded from these poems, and the sheer technical brilliance of a poetic mind pouring out startling word associations is never going to compensate for such absence. This, of course, is not to deny Muldoon's achievements, only to suggest that as with the prolific Victorians Elizabeth Barrett Browning or Alfred, Lord Tennyson, a multitude of words in itself does not make for greatness.

MOY SAND AND GRAVEL

After the major collection of poems taking him up to 1998, Muldoon's next volume, *Moy Sand and Gravel*, perhaps might seem a bit of an anticlimax. He gathers poems written between 1998 and 2002, giving the collection the title of one of the very minor poems in it, a sort of Muldoon joke. The Moy, being his childhood village in Ulster, might suggest the poems are reminiscences of childhood memories, and indeed a few, including "The Misfits," "Beagles," "Tell," and "Homesickness," deal with his early life.

Other poems—"Unapproved Road," "Guns and Butter," and "A Brief Discourse on Decommissioning"—also go back to Ireland, but the Northern Ireland of the Troubles. More complex poems return to grapple with the Irish American experience and Muldoon's own uneasy relationship with earlier immigrants. They, like his father, were men of the soil and manual labor: he, by contrast, is part of the "ruling class," the elite and privileged. Thus he writes "outsider" poems such as "The Loaf" (a particularly powerful poem as it touches on past famines), "Summer Coal," "The Stoic," and "As." In "As," everything gives way to something else. Muldoon makes no value judgments as to whether this is a good or a bad thing, but there is, among the joking, a pervasive sense of guilt.

A further complexity has arisen for Muldoon, however, in that his second wife and mother of his son is Jewish. Her family also has experienced immigration, and Muldoon interweaves the Jewish and the Irish experiences to form a new note in this collection, especially in "Cradle Song for Asher," "The Ancestor," and "The Grand Conversation." The collection's high point comes in the one long poem of the collection, "At the Sign of the Black Horse, September 1999." This truly is a great poem, raising the collection into one of significance, and the main reason the collection was awarded a Pulitzer Prize in 2003.

"At the Sign of the Black Horse, September 1999" is written in a series of forty-five eight-line stanzas (a form Muldoon used earlier in "Incantata"), rhyming *aabbcddc*, with line lengths from four to eight feet. Each stanza is run into the next. It can perhaps be best seen as a series of meditations caused by the birth of his son, after the earlier loss of a daughter. It echoes especially Yeats's "Prayer at the Birth of My Daughter," with its echoing of Yeats's phrase "radical innocence" no less than four times. However, it also belongs to a much longer tradition of poems written on the birth of poets' children, going back to William Wordsworth and Coleridge particularly. The occasion makes the poets wonder what sort of world their child is being born into, and for Muldoon, as for Yeats, raises problems of preserving the child's innocence.

The birth shortly preceded Hurricane Floyd, and so flood and deluge imagery becomes significant, as in references to Noah and Ararat, especially as it is shifted to the Holocaust experiences that are part of the child's Jewish heritage. Both Irish and Jewish heritages are fraught, retain a strong identity, and deal with the tragic past with black humor, which runs throughout the poem. In terms of literary tradition, Muldoon's humor is Joycean rather than Yeatsian, with frequent plays on words and, typical of the whole collection, the pursuit of associations caused by rhymes (for example, otter/blotter in "Otter"). While Yeats had his tower, Muldoon only has a "helter-skelter," a fragile, twisted construct.

The poem deals with the hurricane and its aftermath and the context of the child's Irish and Jewish ancestry; however, it also explores modern American and Western culture, especially as reflected in public and road signs, including "No Way Out" and "Please Do Not Leave Window Ajar." The significance of items is often revealed only in the rhyming word. The prohibi-

tions of these signs meld with particular cultural prohibitions, such as Jewish dietary restrictions. The peccary is seen as a case in point: Is it a pig, and therefore forbidden? Muldoon sees it as being sanitized in an autoclave: Does that make it permissible? These are the sort of tensions he is no doubt feeling from interactions with the child's Jewish relatives: Is the boy going to be brought up Jewish or not? Are the religious conflicts that plagued Muldoon's youth going to pursue him in a different form through the child? Is he merely the "goy from the Moy"? In addition, hints of criminality lie in the past of the now respectable Jewish extended family.

Images and themes that run through other poems in the collection are gathered into this poem. Therefore, Tuaregs (African nomads) and signs of the wanderer and exile appear, as do places such as the Bialystock ghetto, Griggstown ("Summer Coal"), Carrickmacross ("John Luke: *The Fox*"), or the Delaware and Raritan Canal ("The Loaf"), which Irish navvies helped build. This melding of past and present, while making statements on an overall culture at a particular moment of history is reminiscent of Robert Lowell's first draft of "The Quaker Graveyard in Nantucket" (from *Lord Weary's Castle*, 1946), and the poem could take on the iconic status for Muldoon that the other poem did for Lowell.

HORSE LATITUDES

Horse Latitudes represents the work done by Muldoon from 2002 to 2006. Most of it appeared first in an impressively wide range of literary magazines and journals. The title derives from one of the major poems of the volume, a long opening poem centered on the persona of Carlotta. At times, she appears to be a conglomerate of all Muldoon's lovers; at other times, she appears to be dying. Her grandfather also figures prominently, suggesting an agrarian ancestry. The horse latitudes are those areas at sea around the tropics where becalmed sailors would throw their horses overboard or eat them, and certainly horses figure prominently in the poems.

The poem is the nearest Muldoon has come to writing a sonnet sequence, each poem being the name of a battle beginning with the letter "B." As in *Madoc*, the poem titles appear to have their own life as part of an independent categorization. The poems are fourteen lines long, but do not rhyme like sonnets and are not formed with iambic pentameters, but rather with tetrameters. However, the overall feel is certainly of a sonnet sequence.

As is typical of Muldoon, the volume ends with a major long poem, "Sillyhow Stride: *In Memory of Warren Zevon*." The whole volume is dedicated to Muldoon's sister Maureen, who died of cancer in 2005, and it is in this poem that the reader is most aware of her presence, even though technically it is the dead Zevon, a fellow musician, who is addressed. The poem is powerful in that the poet's anger at the death of his sister is a predominating force. The other uniting force is Muldoon's focus on the poetry of John Donne, the seventeenth century poet he long admired for his conceits, striking images, and tropes. He quotes Donne's poetry throughout. However, when a poet invites comparison with another poet, this is not always to the advantage of the writer. Donne's poetic strengths are his remorseless logic and control and his passionate writing on love and religion. These are the very qualities that Muldoon lacks. Certainly Muldoon shares with Donne the ability to force quite disparate ideas and themes together, but at times the poem becomes a rant, a verbal performance, in which his sister's death becomes a mere platform. Like Donne, too, Muldoon is able to take contemporary events and meld them into a poetic statement. Here Muldoon deals with ecological issues and the September 11, 2001, terrorist attacks on the United States, and the rhythms are very much those of hip-hop and reggae. In this way, Muldoon is incorporating the performance-art skills gained from his membership in a rock band into mainstream poetry.

The other poems in *Horse Latitudes* seem to be somewhat of a miscellany. Some, like "Soccer Moms" and "Turkey Buzzards," are instantly accessible and typically American, and will no doubt find their way into many anthologies. Others, such as "At Least They Weren't Speaking French" and "The Old Country," are playful, using repetition and popular idioms to make a point. In "The Old Country," Muldoon seems to be dismissing Ireland and nostalgic Irishness as a joke. "Ninety Instant Messages to Tom Moore" (a popular nineteenth century Irish poet) is a bravura sequence of

haiku. Other poems, such as "It Is What It Is" and "Riddle," reflect Muldoon as a family man, living in typical American suburbia. The collection demonstrates that Muldoon is still at the height of his creativity and can turn his hand to whatever form he wishes. It may be that, as some critics claim, that he is freeing modern verse for the twenty-first century; or, it may be that he is just proving that poetry can keep reinventing itself.

OTHER MAJOR WORKS

PLAYS: *Shining Brow*, pr. 1993 (libretto); *Six Honest Serving Men*, pb. 1995; *Vera of Las Vegas: A Nightmare Cabaret Opera in One Act*, pr. 1996 (libretto); *Bandanna*, pb. 1999 (libretto).

NONFICTION: *To Ireland, I*, 2000; *The End of the Poem: Oxford Lectures*, 2009.

TRANSLATIONS: *The Astrakhan Cloak: Poems in Irish by Nuala Ní Dhomhnaill*, 1993; *The Birds*, 1999 (of Aristophanes' play).

CHILDREN'S LITERATURE: *The Last Thesaurus*, 1995; *The Noctuary of Narcissus Batt*, 1997.

EDITED TEXTS: *The Scrake of Dawn: Poems by Young People from Northern Ireland*, 1979; *The Faber Book of Contemporary Irish Verse*, 1986; *The Essential Byron*, 1989; *The Faber Book of Beasts*, 1997; *The Best American Poetry*, 2005 (with David Lehman); *Contemporary Irish Poetry*, 2006.

BIBLIOGRAPHY

Birkets, Sven. "Paul Muldoon." In *The Electric Life: Essays on Modern Poetry*. New York: Morrow, 1989. An assessment of the poet's relationship to his contemporaries on the international scene. Muldoon's originality is identified and appreciated. The provision of a wider context for his work reveals its scope and interest. In particular, Muldoon's distinctive verbal deftness receives attention.

Goodby, John. "'Armageddon, Armagh-geddon': Language and Crisis in the Poetry of Paul Muldoon." In *Anglo-Irish and Irish Literature: Aspects of Language and Culture*, edited by Birgit Bramsback and Martin Croghan. Uppsala, Sweden: Uppsala University Press, 1988. The title comes from Muldoon's poetic sequence "Armageddon." In using the name to pun on the poet's birthplace, the author draws attention to Muldoon's verbal dexterity. His dismantling and reassembling of language is reviewed. These practices are also related to Muldoon's background.

_____. *Irish Poetry Since 1950: From Stillness into History*. New York: Manchester University Press, 2000. Puts Muldoon into the wider context of modern Irish poets. There are three subsections dealing with his development as a poet up until 2000.

Holdridge, Jefferson. *The Poetry of Paul Muldoon*. Dublin: Liffey Press, 2008. Introduces the general reader to some of the main critical discussion around Muldoon's work. Looks particularly at his political stances and the links between suffering and creativity.

Kendall, Tim. *Paul Muldoon*. Bridgend, Wales: Seren, 1996. One of the first full-length studies of Muldoon with individual chapters on all the books up to and including *The Annals of Chile*. A sensible, intelligent reading of the poems in the context of his entire career.

Kendall, Tim, and Peter McDonald, eds. *Paul Muldoon: Critical Essays*. Liverpool, England: Liverpool University Press, 2003. A collection of essays by many experts on contemporary Irish poetry; it gives a rounded picture of Muldoon's achievements.

Osborn, Andrew. "Skirmishes on the Border: The Evolution and Function of Paul Muldoon's Fuzzy Rhyme." *Contemporary Literature* 41 (Summer, 2000): 323-358. A study of Muldoon's rhyme schemes and the semantic and strategic functions in his poetry.

Robinson, Peter. "Muldoon's Humour." In *Politics and the Rhetoric of Poetry: Perspectives on Modern Anglo-Irish Poetry*. Amsterdam: Rodolpi, 1995. The question of how to use humor in serious poems, and otherwise, is examined in the light of Muldoon's reputation for wit.

Wills, Claire. *Reading Paul Muldoon*. Newcastle, England: Bloodaxe Books, 1998. Wills's sensible comments are considerable help in clarifying Muldoon's more difficult texts.

George O'Brien; Charles H. Pullen
Updated by David Barratt

LES A. MURRAY

Born: Nabiac, New South Wales, Australia; October 17, 1938

PRINCIPAL POETRY

The Ilex Tree, 1965 (with Geoffrey Lehmann)
The Weatherboard Cathedral, 1969
Poems Against Economics, 1972
Lunch and Counter Lunch, 1974
The Vernacular Republic: Selected Poems, 1976
Ethnic Radio, 1977
The Boys Who Stole the Funeral, 1980
Equanimities, 1982
The Vernacular Republic: Poems, 1961-1981, 1982
The People's Otherworld, 1983
The Daylight Moon, 1987
The Vernacular Republic: Poems, 1961-1983, 1988
The Idyll Wheel, 1989
Dog Fox Field, 1990
The Rabbiter's Bounty: Collected Poems, 1991
Translations from the Natural World, 1992
Subhuman Redneck Poems, 1996
Fredy Neptune: A Novel in Verse, 1998
Conscious and Verbal, 1999
Learning Human: Selected Poems, 2000
New Collected Poems, 2002
Poems the Size of Photographs, 2002
The Biplane Houses, 2006

OTHER LITERARY FORMS

Les A. Murray has collected several volumes of prose pieces, primarily reviews and articles: *The Peasant Mandarin: Prose Pieces* (1978), *Persistence in Folly* (1984), *Blocks and Tackles: Articles and Essays* (1990), *The Paperbark Tree* (1992), and *A Working Forest: Selected Prose* (1997). Of particular interest in the second book is the essay "The Human Hair-Thread," in which Murray discusses his own thought and the influence Aboriginal culture has had on it.

ACHIEVEMENTS

Les A. Murray is considered not only Australia's major poet but also one of the finest poets of his generation writing in English. His following is an international one, and the uniqueness and power of his poetic voice have caught the ear of many of his fellow poets throughout the world: He has been hailed by Joseph Brodsky, Peter Porter, Mark Strand, and others. He is a prolific and ambitious writer, always willing to try new and unusual techniques but equally at home in the traditional forms of verse, of which he seems to have an easy and lively mastery.

Murray has received numerous awards and prizes, including the Grace Leven Prize (in 1965, with Geoffrey J. Lehmann, and also in 1980 and 1990), the Cook Bi-Centenary Prize for Poetry (1970), Australian National Book Council Award (1974, with others; 1985, 1992), the C. J. Dennis Memorial Prize (1976), the Mattara Prize (with others, 1981), the New South Wales Premier's Prize for the best book of verse (1983-1984), the Australian Literature Society Gold Medal (1984), the Fellowship of Australian Writers Medal (1984), the Canada-Australia Prize (1985), Australian National Poetry Award (1988), the Australian Book Council's Bicentennial Prize for Poetry (1988), the New South Wales Premier's Prize for Poetry (1993), the Victoria Premier's Prize for Poetry (1993), the European Petrarch Award (1995), the United Kingdom's prestigious T. S. Eliot Prize (1996), and the Queen's Gold Medal for Poetry (1999). He was named an Officer in the Order of Australia in 1988. *Learning Human* was shortlisted for the Griffin Poetry Prize in 2001.

BIOGRAPHY

Leslie Allan Murray was born at Nabiac, on the rural north coast of New South Wales, and brought up on a dairy farm in nearby Bunyah, a locale that often figures as the subject or backdrop for his poems. He attended school in the town of Taree and then, in 1957, went to the University of Sydney, where he stayed until 1960. Between 1959 and 1960, he served in the Royal Australian Naval Reserve. He and Valerie Morelli were married in 1962 (they would have several children), and Murray worked as a translator at the Australian National University in Canberra from 1963 to 1967. After a year in Europe, he returned to Sydney, graduated from the University of Sydney in 1969, and worked at a number of transient jobs before going to Canberra

again, where he took a position in the Prime Minister's Department in the Economic Development Branch.

Moving back to Sydney and refusing to work any longer in what he regarded as meaningless employment, Murray, in his own words, "Came Out as a flagrant full-time poet in 1971." He thereafter supported himself solely on the basis of his literary work. In addition to the books he published and those he edited, Murray wrote book reviews, contributed to newspapers and magazines, advised the publishing firm Angus and Robertson, and gave poetry readings throughout Australia and abroad. Between 1973 and 1979, he served as editor of *Poetry Australia*.

Murray lived in Sydney until 1986 and then moved to a farm in Bunyah, near his boyhood home, with Valerie and the youngest of his five children. His celebrity expanded when he became the subject of a televised documentary in 1991, and he continued to win awards. Then, in the mid-1990's, diabetes, depression, and a liver infection led in 1996, to a collapse. After two surgeries and weeks in the hospital, he emerged in time to take note that he had won the United Kingdom's prestigious T. S. Eliot Prize for Poetry, arguably the most important award for poetry that nation bestows. He was too weak to travel to England to accept the award, but he did recover, his literary powers undiminished. His subsequent volumes confirmed his status as the most important voice in Australian poetry.

ANALYSIS

Readers of Les A. Murray's poetry are often attracted by the coherence of the thematic concerns that reappear consistently in his work and that are presented lucidly and imaginatively. Moreover, the stylistic features of his verse, though varied, have themselves cohered into an identifiable style uniquely his own and flexible enough to allow for the wide range of his poetic interests. Broadly, these interests may be grouped under categories of the religious and spiritual, the societal and cultural, the historical and familial, the linguistic and poetic. Murray has strong opinions about many issues facing contemporary society, and his poetry often bespeaks them.

In their most reductive form, these issues would require consideration of such propositions as the following: Western people must rediscover a core of religious values and recover certain traditional modes of being; society should embrace a more democratic egalitarianism, avoiding the twin perils of elitism and false ideology; Aboriginal attitudes regarding nature and the environment need to be better understood by white Australians and to some extent adopted; Australia itself represents an island of hope in the world, as a place where many of the divisive features undermining modern society might be finally reconciled.

"Driving Through Sawmill Towns"

In an early poem, "Driving Through Sawmill Towns," Murray renders the remoteness and tedium of life in the rural towns, those "bare hamlets built of boards," where "nothing happens" and "the houses watch each other." The evocative detail, the careful diction, the sense of quiet control convey both an appreciation of this as a way of life and an acknowledgment that it is a lonely and even desperate existence. A woman gazes at a mountain "in wonderment,/ looking for a city," and men sit by the stove after tea, "rolling a dead match/ between their fingers/ thinking of the future." It is a place one only drives through, not a place in which one wishes to live. In that sense, this poem contrasts with others in which the country life appears more salubrious, as in "Noonday Axeman" or "Spring Hail," where isolation is not necessarily loneliness.

"The Buladelah-Taree Holiday Song Cycle"

Murray's most famous poem of rural Australia is also the one most indebted to Aboriginal sources, "The Buladelah-Taree Holiday Song Cycle." It is a long poem, in thirteen sections, based in part on a translation by R. M. Berndt of "The Moon-Bone Song," a ritual poem of Arnhem Land Aborigines that Murray claims "may well be the greatest poem ever composed in Australia." His poem is an attempt to use an Aboriginal mode and structure to "celebrate my own spirit country," a stretch of land on the north coast between the two towns of Buladelah and Taree, where he grew up and lives as an adult and where many holiday vacationers go in the summer to enjoy the beaches and the countryside.

In the same way that the Aborigines celebrate their unity as a people and their harmony with the land,

Murray sees the returning vacationers, many of whom have family ties to the area, as a cyclic affirmation of ancestral values and a joyous communing with nature. In his vision, each new generation rediscovers the spiritual significance of commonplace things, as people come to possess the land imaginatively. Each section of the poem presents an aspect of this summer ritual, from the preparations made by the local inhabitants to the journey from Sydney along the Pacific Highway (represented as a glowing snake) to all the adventures, experiences, and tensions that go with a summer holiday. The poem ends with a linking of the region with the heavens above, as the Southern Cross constellation looks down on "the Holiday."

The poem is unique in its successful wedding of an Aboriginal poetic structure with the matter of white Australian culture; in particular, Murray's use of placenames and capitalization seems to give mythic status to the events and locations of the poem, analogous to the Aborigine's sense of a "spirit of place."

The Boys Who Stole the Funeral

In 1979, Murray published *The Boys Who Stole the Funeral*, a verse novel consisting of 140 sonnets of considerable variety. This unusual poem picked up many of the concerns and opinions prevalent in the earlier work and fashioned them into a narrative, both effective as poetry and affective as a story. In this work, two young Sydney men, Kevin Forbutt and Cameron Reeby, steal from a funeral parlor the body of Kevin's great-uncle, Clarrie Dunn (a "digger," or World War I veteran), to take him back home to the country where the old man had asked to be buried. Clarrie's relations having refused to pay for or honor this request, the boys have taken it on themselves. In doing this, they set out on a journey of self-discovery as well.

Such familiar Murray themes as the value of community and respect for the ordinary person are underscored repeatedly in the poem, as when the two boys get to Dark's Plain, Clarrie's old home, and are assisted by people there with the burial and with evading the police who have come to arrest them. The novel later culminates with the shooting of Cameron by a police officer. The shocked and distraught Kevin flees into the bush, falls ill, drops into a coma, and has a vision of two figures from Aboriginal legend, Njimbin and Birroogun. In this vision, the central event of the novel, Kevin is put through an initiation where his soul is healed by the symbolic "crystal of Crystals," and where he is instructed by Njimbin and Birroogun (whose name modulates to Berrigan, connoting a blend of white and black Australians) in the mysteries of the spirit. Kevin is offered the Common Dish from which to eat, the vessel of common human joys and sufferings by which most people in the world are nourished. As an act of solidarity with common humanity, Kevin takes it and eats and then wakes from his comatose vision. Having been in effect reborn, he returns to live at Dark's Plain, to "keep faith" with the rural "battlers" who are the spiritual inheritors of the land.

The poem as a whole is a virtuoso performance, displaying Murray's ability to handle the complex interplay of form, narrative, and character. He holds the reader's attention and, once again, interweaves Aboriginal material in a convincing way.

THE VERNACULAR REPUBLIC

One of Murray's preoccupations is with the notion of the vernacular; indeed, when he titles his selected poems *The Vernacular Republic* (three separate collections), he is reflecting on the colloquial nature of his language and simultaneously reflecting a passionate concern that the world of his poems addresses: the need for Australia to fuse its three cultures, urban, rural, and Aboriginal. Murray's vision for Australia is for a culture of convergence, where the sophisticated city dwellers, the more traditional rural folk, and the indigenous blacks can all come together to forge a society in harmony with the continent. In this, he is close to the position of the Jindyworobaks, a literary movement of the 1930's and 1940's that emphasized the uniqueness of the Australian environment and sought to align itself with Aboriginal culture.

Although not as narrowly nationalistic as that earlier group, Murray does see a need to avoid repeating the mistakes of Europe and America and to develop in accordance with the character and values of Australia itself, not in submission to alien and imported fashions or ideologies. For him, Australia has the possibility of becoming truly egalitarian, a place of justice and virtue for the common man, a place where what is traditional is recognizably Australian. This, for Murray, includes a certain dry sense of humor and an appreciation of an unhurried mode of living, which may be primarily a rural manner but nevertheless seems a national characteristic.

"THE QUALITY OF SPRAWL"

His poem "The Quality of Sprawl" is a good example. "Sprawl," in this poem, is defined through the course of eight stanzas as a way of being, at once nonchalant ("the rococo of being your own still centre"), laid-back ("Sprawl leans on things"), generous ("driving a hitchhiker that extra hundred miles home"), unpretentious ("the quality/ of the man who cut down his Rolls-Royce/ into a farm utility truck"), classless (someone "asleep in his neighbours' best bed in spurs and oilskins"), unflappable ("Reprimanded and dismissed/ it listens with a grin and one boot up on the rail/ of possibility"), and so on. It is also defined by what it is not: "It is never lighting cigars with ten-dollar notes"; "Sprawl almost never says Why Not? with palms comically raised"; "nor can it be dressed for." Murray presents it as a very attractive quality indeed, but, characteristically, he is aware of the negative element, the price one sometimes has to pay for independence of mind. "It may have to leave the Earth," he says, but then he gently undercuts his own hyperbole: "Being roughly Christian, it scratches the other cheek/ and thinks it unlikely." While not exactly turning the other cheek in Christian fashion, he does conclude with the mild warning: " . . . people have been shot for sprawl."

Sprawl, then, is the opposite of the uptight, aggressive, overly sophisticated self-consciousness that Murray sees around him and that he considers foreign and inappropriate for Australia—a place, perhaps, where Mark Twain's Huck Finn might have been at home. While "sprawl" may appear a public attitude and manner, it rests on a more essential inward feature, which Murray terms "equanimity," in a poem of that title.

"EQUANIMITY"

"Equanimity" is a poem that draws together several strands of Murray's work: His populist, bardic stance mingles with a more purely prophetic strain. Here, his democratic vistas are underwritten by a transcendental authority, based on a personal and even sacramental experience. That experience, which he calls "equanimity," is like an influx of quiet power, an exaltation of the spirit grounded in love. "There is only love," he says; "human order has at heart/ an equanimity. Quite different from inertia," a place "where all are, in short, off the high comparative horse/ of their identity." This is the place at which people join together in a "people's otherworld," a vernacular republic of the spirit that allows for a "continuous recovering moment." It is an effortless effort, reminiscent of a Buddhist or Kantian disinterestedness: "Through the peace beneath effort/ (even within effort: quiet air between the bars of our attention)/ comes unpurchased lifelong plenishment."

Yet, foremost for Murray, this is a Christian quality; it is at the very heart of Christ's teachings and is the place from which he taught: "Christ spoke to people most often on this level/ especially when they chattered about kingship and the Romans;/ all holiness speaks from it." To experience such equanimity would be tantamount to experiencing holiness itself, and that is precisely the sort of graceful redemption Murray seeks to convey. There can be nothing programmatic about such an attitude, but no program of reform, be it social, political, or cultural, can possibly succeed without it. That, for Murray, is the basis on which all else proceeds, including his own poetry. For Murray, writing is like playing on an instrument, finding out just what it can do and learning how to do it. His poems have an energy and inventiveness that reveal a delight in the resources of language and a conviction that what needs to be said can be communicated through the adequacies of poetry.

BLOCKS AND TACKLES

Murray's faith in the redemptive possibilities of poetry was sorely tested during the 1980's, when it became increasingly clear to him that the production of literature in Australia was tied to a commercial system fundamentally at odds with the spirit of poetry, and that the academic and critical establishment that controlled the terms under which literature was to be studied and understood was itself run by a "cabal" of "elites," notable for their "moral cowardice." In response, there was a discernible retrenchment in Murray's poetry and prose, a willingness to accept his embattled position in the cultural field as a necessary corollary to his role as a virtual poet-prophet to his people. In the essays col-

lected in *Blocks and Tackles*, Murray became more assertive about the sacramental and mysterious qualities of poetry. As he writes in "Poems and Poesies":

> Poetry models the fullness of life, and also gives its objects presence. Like prayer, it pulls all the motions of our life and being into a concentrated true attentiveness to which God might speak. "Here am I, Lord," as Samuel says in his book of the Bible. It is the plane or mirror of intuitions.

DOG FOX FIELD

In the poems published in *Dog Fox Field*, however, the poet attends more often to his function as social critic, particularly in his denunciations of "relegation," the denial of the full humanity of others. In a poem titled "To the Soviet Americans," a working-class man (here the abstract object of much false Marxist piety) ironically declares:

> *Watch out for the ones in jeans*
> *who'll stop you smoking and stop you working:*
> *I call them the Soviet Americans.*

The tone of these poems is often stern and unyielding, written in an age in which one finds "self pity and hard drugs everywhere." Yet, this hardened voice does continue to yield up poems of sympathetic feeling, as if, once protected from the incursions of a hostile world, there is ample room for the common enjoyments of a shared living:

> Never despise those
> who fear an order vaster than reason, more charming
>   than prose:
> surely are those who unknowingly chime with the
>   noblest
> and love and are loved by whom they rhyme with best.
> So let your river be current and torrent and klong
> as far and intricate as your love is long. . . .

SUBHUMAN REDNECK POEMS

The title of this collection, which won for Murray the 1996 T. S. Eliot Prize, indicates Murray's unrepentant determination to diminish the idea of poetry as the exclusive purview of the intellectual elite. The book is as outspokenly angry and tonally excessive as anything he has produced, and, on occasion, goes a bit too far in expressing his disillusion with the new Australia:

Ethnics who praise their home ground
while on it are called jingo chauvinists.
All's permitted, though, when they migrate;
the least adaptable are the purest then,
the narrowest the most multicultural.

His politics swing sometimes crazily into conservatism, and there is a sense that he is not always free of a kind of ungenerous rant.

The book, however, contains several lovely lyrics. Murray's gift for this kind of work is often ignored in the sound and fury of his politically engaged poems. "The Warm Rain" brandishes

palm trees like mops,
its borders swell over the continent . . .
Fruit bumps lawns, and every country dam

brews under bubbles . . .

Murray's eye for detail and witty transformation of such into poetic image is quite charming in "Dead Trees in a Dam":

Castle scaffolding tall in moat,
the dead trees in the dam
flower each morning with birds.

Once away from argument, the poetic juices run magnificently riot:

. . . it may be a misty candelabrum
of egrets lambent . . .

.   .   .   .

Odd mornings, it's been all bloodflag
and rifle green: a stopped-motion shrapnel
of kingparrots. . . .

FREDY NEPTUNE

Murray's *Fredy Neptune*, a "novel in verse," follows the life of an itinerant World War I sailor/soldier of German ancestry across two hundred pages. The narrative, through unlikely adventures and plot twists, follows Fredy's attempts to return home after having been kidnapped and forced onto a German battleship. He experiences both moral outrage and physical disability in response to the atrocities of war—the burning of Armenian women, for example, causes him to lose his sense of touch. The theme of survival in a

chaotic world reaches its climax when, upon finally making his way back home, Fredy discovers that war has destroyed his homeland and he must re-enlist. The language in which Fredy's picaresque experiences are related—full of Australian, blue-collar slang and hit-and-miss rhymes that work to reflect the lunacy of Fredy's experiences—garnered glowing reviews from critics.

CONSCIOUS AND VERBAL

The title of this collection echoes the Australian press reports when the nation's celebrated poet, after three weeks in a coma, awoke. He eventually recovered, and this collection was one of the results. Murray renders his experience here in "Travels with John Hunter," named after the hospital where the poet worked his way back to health. The poems in this collection examine God as a presence in nature, the Australian character, racism and Murray's outraged stance against it, and other typical Murray themes. Also characteristic of Murray are his moral pronouncements, his deploring "that monster called the Twentieth Century," and his didacticism. In "The Instrument," for example, he answers the question of why he writes poetry by stating simply that one must "[work] always beyond/ your own intelligence." Although critics gave the volume mixed reviews, these poems remain a fitting tribute to Murray's reawakening.

OTHER MAJOR WORKS

NONFICTION: *The Peasant Mandarin: Prose Pieces*, 1978; *Persistence in Folly*, 1984; *The Australian Year*, 1985 (photographs by Peter Solness); *Blocks and Tackles: Articles and Essays*, 1990; *The Paperbark Tree*, 1992; *A Working Forest: Selected Prose*, 1997; *The Quality of Sprawl: Thoughts About Australia*, 1999.

EDITED TEXTS: *Anthology of Australian Religious Verse*, 1986; *The New Oxford Book of Australian Verse*, 1986, 1992; *Fivefathers: Five Australian Poets of the Pre-Academic Era*, 1994.

MISCELLANEOUS: *Killing the Black Dog: Essays and Poems*, 1997.

BIBLIOGRAPHY
Alexander, Peter F. *Les Murray: A Life in Progress.* New York: Oxford University Press, 2001. A liter-

ary biography. Well researched, drawing on extensive interviews with Murray.

Birkerts, Sven. "The Rococo of His Own Still Center." *Parnassus* 15, no. 2 (1989): 31-48. A serious and sympathetic appreciation of Murray's poetry by a prominent critic. Birkerts highlights those poems most appropriate for inclusion in the Murray "canon," showing a keen sense of what Murray's poetic project entails. Among the first thorough treatments of Murray's poetry in the United States, this is an accessible and useful introduction.

Bourke, Lawrence. *A Vivid, Steady State: The Poetry of Les A. Murray*. Kensington: New South Wales University Press, 1992. The first full-length academic study of Murray.

Hergenhan, Laurie, and Bruce Clunies Ross, eds. *The Poetry of Les Murray: Critical Essays*. St. Lucia: University of Queensland Press, 2001. Reprints the essays from a special edition of the journal *Australian Literary Studies*, devoted to Murray.

Matthews, Steven. *Les Murray*. New York: Manchester University Press, 2001. A full-length critical study that places Murray in the context of Australian literature and culture.

Murray, Les A. "Les A. Murray." Interview by Barbara William. In *In Other Words: Interviews with Australian Poets*, edited by William. Amsterdam: Rodolpi, 1998. Murray speaks of his interest in less conventional poetry, his depression, and poetry in schools.

Smith, Angela, ed. *Les Murray and Australian Poetry*. London: Menzies Centre for Australian Studies, Kings College London, University of London, 2002. A collection of essays that examine Murray's poetry and how it relates to Australian and other poets from that nation.

Walcott, Derek. "Crocodile Dandy." *The New Republic* 6 (February, 1989): 25-28. This is a generous review by one important poet of another. Walcott makes a case for the international stature of Murray, looking at his extraordinary verbal facility and mastery of form. The sacramental quality of Murray's poetry is noted, and comparisons are made to such authors as Walt Whitman, Dylan Thomas, and Rudyard Kipling.

Wilde, W. H., ed. *The Oxford Companion to Australian Literature*. 2d ed. New York: Oxford University Press, 1995. Includes a lengthy essay on Murray's career and work.

Paul Kane; Christina J. Moose
Updated by Charles H. Pullen

N

THOMAS NASHE

Born: Lowestoft, Suffolk, England; November, 1567
Died: Yarmouth(?), England; c. 1601
Also known as: Thomes Nash

PRINCIPAL POETRY
The Choise of Valentines, 1899

OTHER LITERARY FORMS

Almost all that Thomas Nashe wrote was published in pamphlet form. With the exception of a long poem (*The Choise of Valentines*), several sonnets and songs, and at least two dramas (*Summer's Last Will and Testament*, pr. 1592, and *The Isle of Dogs*, pr. 1597), all his work was prose. His prose works include *The Anatomie of Absurditie* (1589); *An Almond for a Parrat* (1590); a preface to Sir Philip Sidney's *Astrophel and Stella* (1591); *Pierce Penilesse, His Supplication to the Divell* (1592); *Strange News of the Intercepting of Certain Letters* (1592); *Christ's Tears over Jerusalem* (1593); *The Terrors of the Night* (1594); *The Unfortunate Traveller: Or, The Life of Jack Wilton* (1594); *Have with You to Saffron-Walden* (1596); and *Nashe's Lenten Stuffe* (1599).

ACHIEVEMENTS

Thomas Nashe was more a journalist than an artist, if the definition of artist is one who follows the Aristotelian principles of using life as a source from which one creates a story with a beginning, middle, and end. Nashe informed and entertained his sixteenth century audience in the same way that a journalist pleases the public today. He was known in his time not as a poet or a dramatist, although he wrote both poetry and plays. He was known as the worthy opponent of the scholar Gabriel Harvey, as one who with lively rhetoric, biting invective, and soaring wit destroyed every argument the pompous Harvey could muster. He was also known to Elizabethans as the chief defender of the Anglican Church against the attack of the Puritans in the Martin Marprelate controversy. The magnificent invective found in the speeches of William Shakespeare's Falstaff, Prince Hal, and (more especially) Kent was almost certainly derived from the vituperation Nashe hurled at his adversaries.

Among modern students of literature, Nashe is remembered for his most unusual work, the picaresque novel of adventure, *The Unfortunate Traveller*. It is the story of a young page, Jack Wilton, who, after serving in the army of Henry VIII, travels to Europe to find means of earning a living. The underworld realism that Nashe presents in his descriptions of Jack's escapades has earned him a reputation for being something other than a hurler of invective. The book is not a unified work of art; its characters, other than Jack himself, are not particularly memorable. Its descriptions of the harshest elements of human life, such as disease, hunger, torture, rape, and murder, place it in stark contrast to the sweet absurdities of romance; it thus shows the way to the modern novel.

BIOGRAPHY

Thomas Nashe was born in November, 1567, the son of William Nashe, a minister in Lowestoft, Suffolk. Because no record exists of William's being a university graduate, it can be assumed that he was probably a stipendiary curate in Lowestoft, not a vicar. Although the title pages of *Pierce Penilesse, His Supplication to the Divell* and of *Strange News of the Intercepting of Certain Letters* refer to "Thomas Nashe, Gentleman," Nashe himself denied that he was of gentle birth. From his earliest years, indeed, he disliked the propensity he found in middle-class Englishmen to pretend to be something other than what they were.

In 1573, Nashe's father was granted the living in West Harling, Norfolk, where young Thomas probably spent his early years. Nothing is known of Nashe's basic education except that it was sufficient to allow him to enter St. John's College, Cambridge, in October, 1582. In March, 1586, he received his bachelor of arts degree and enrolled immediately to work toward the master of arts degree. In 1588, however, he left Cambridge without the degree. Perhaps financial difficulties forced him to leave the university, for his father had died the year before, in 1587. Without financial support from home, Nashe most likely would not have been able to continue his education; probably his college, dominated as it was by Puritans, would not look with favor in the form of financial assistance on the satirical young Nashe, who supported the pursuit of humanistic studies over the more narrow Puritan theology then in vogue at Cambridge.

Whatever his reasons for leaving Cambridge, Nashe certainly did not have the economic means to remain idle long. He followed the lead of two other Cambridge graduates who, armed with no wealth but their wits, turned to literature as a means of earning a livelihood. Both Robert Greene and Christopher Marlowe had gone to London to write, and both had found moderate success. Nashe may have been acquainted with both men at Cambridge, but he certainly knew them both in London. Like Nashe, both loved poetry and detested Puritans. In the same year that he left Cambridge,

Thomas Nashe (Hulton Archive/Getty Images)

Nashe published *The Anatomie of Absurditie*, a work of inexperience and brashness.

A young writer of pamphlets in London had few opportunities to earn a living by his work. He was generally paid a flat amount for his manuscript, usually two pounds. If a pamphlet were well-received by the public, the patron to whom it was dedicated might be so flattered that he or she might feel disposed to grant the author a stipend to continue his work. Nashe's *The Anatomie of Absurditie*, dedicated to Sir Charles Blount, was, however, of so little literary merit that Nashe probably received no more than his original author's fee.

Nashe dedicated no more works to Sir Charles; but because he did need patrons, he dedicated later works to a variety of people in a position to offer him assistance. Finally, after the dedication of *The Unfortunate Traveller* to Henry Wriothesley, the earl of Southampton, Nashe decided that patrons were more trouble than they were worth. Hating hypocrisy in others and finding himself forced into hypocrisy in order to be paid for his work, Nashe turned to writing only for his readers and depended on them to reward his efforts.

Perhaps what gave Nashe his biggest literary boost was the famous Martin Marprelate controversy. Nashe's part in the verbal battle was limited to the pamphlet *An Almond for a Parrat*, but the style and the vigorous prose of Martin could not help influencing Nashe. Although he was hostile to Martin's Puritanical ideas, Nashe must nevertheless have learned much from the formidable prose of his Puritan adversary, for he attacks Martin with the same devices and force of language that the Puritan propagandist used.

Nashe's entry into the Martin Marprelate controversy brought with it rewards beyond what he might have hoped. Gabriel Harvey wrote disparagingly of Nashe's part in the controversy, thus starting a new fight: the Nashe-Harvey controversy. It was in this battle of wits that Nashe found his place as a writer. Here the verbal streetfighter had the great good fortune to be attacked by a man of reputation who was inferior in wit and writing ability to Nashe. Harvey's reputation never recovered from Nashe's fierce invective. Beginning with a slap at Harvey in his preface to

Greene's *A Quip for an Upstart Courtier* (1592) and ending with *Have with You to Saffron-Walden*, Nashe earned a good reputation and a fair living from his anti-Harvey prose.

All his previous writings were practice for *The Unfortunate Traveller*, published in 1594. A kind of pamphlet itself, but longer and more complex, the work was not particularly popular during his lifetime, but today it is his best-known work.

Nashe was hounded from London in 1597 when the authorities decided that *The Isle of Dogs*, a play he had begun, and which Ben Jonson had finished, was "seditious." Jonson was jailed and Nashe sought, but the famous pamphleteer had fled to Yarmouth, in Norfolk. By 1598, he was back in London, where *Nashe's Lenten Stuffe* was entered in the Stationers' Register.

After *Nashe's Lenten Stuffe*, Nashe wrote no more, and in 1601, history records a reference to his death.

ANALYSIS

Thomas Nashe the satirical pamphleteer, who was wont to use language as a cudgel in a broad prose style, seldom disciplined himself to the more delicate work of writing poetry. Both his temperament and his pocketbook directed him to the freer and more profitable form of pamphlet prose. It is this prose that made his reputation, but Nashe did write poems, mostly lyrical in the manner of his time. No originator in poetic style, Nashe followed the lead of such worthy predecessors as Geoffrey Chaucer, Henry Howard, earl of Surrey, Edmund Spenser, and Christopher Marlowe.

Nashe's interest in poetry was not slight. In typical Renaissance fashion, he believed poetry to be the highest form of moral philosophy. Following Sidney, he insisted that the best poetry is based on scholarship and devotion to detail. Not only does poetry, in his perception, encourage virtue and discourage vice, but also it "cleanses" the language of barbarisms and makes the "vulgar sort" in London adopt a more pleasing manner of speech. Because he loved good poetry and saw the moral and aesthetic value of it, Nashe condemned the "ballad mongers," who abused the ears and sensitivities of the gentlefolk of England. To him, the ballad writers were "common pamfletters" whose lack of learning and lust for money were responsible for littering the streets with the garbage of their ballads—a strange reaction for a man who was himself a notable writer of pamphlets. For the learned poetry of Western culture, Nashe had the highest appreciation.

Nashe's own poetic efforts are often placed in the context of his prose works, as if he were setting jewels among the coarser material, as did George Gascoigne, Thomas Lodge, Robert Greene, Thomas Deloney, and others. *Pierce Penilesse, His Supplication to the Divell*, "The Four Letters Confuted," and *The Unfortunate Traveller* all have poems sprinkled here and there. The play *Summer's Last Will and Testament*, itself written in quite acceptable blank verse, has several lyrics of some interest scattered throughout. Nashe's shorter poetic efforts are almost equally divided between sonnets and lyrical poems. The longer *The Choise of Valentines* is a narrative in the erotic style of Ovid.

SONNETS

Among Nashe's poems are six sonnets, two of which may be said to be parodies of the form. Each is placed within a longer work, where its individual purpose is relevant to the themes of that work. Most of the sonnets are in the English form, containing three quatrains and a concluding couplet. Following the lead of the earl of Surrey (who is, indeed, the putative author of the two sonnets to Geraldine in *The Unfortunate Traveller*), Nashe uses a concluding couplet in each of his sonnets, including "To the Right Honorable the lord S.," which in other respects (as in the division into octave and sestet rhyming *abbaabba, cdcdee*) is closer to the Italian form.

In his first sonnet, "Perusing yesternight, with idle eyes," Nashe pauses at the end of *Pierce Penilesse, His Supplication to the Divell* to praise the lord Amyntas, whom Edmund Spenser had neglected in *The Faerie Queene* (1590, 1596). In "Perusing yesternight, with idle eyes," the famous poem by Spenser, Nashe had turned to the end of the poem to find sonnets addressed to "sundry Nobles." Nashe uses the three quatrains to rehearse the problem: He read the poem, found the sonnets addressed to the nobles, and wondered why Spenser had left out "thy memory." In an excellent use of the concluding couplet in this form, he decides that Spenser must have omitted praise of Amyntas because "few words could not comprise thy fame."

If "Perusing yesternight, with idle eyes" is in the tradition of using the sonnet to praise, Nashe's second sonnet, "Were there no warres," is not. Concluding his prose attack on Gabriel Harvey in "The Four Letters Confuted," this sonnet looks forward to John Milton rather than backward to Petrarch. Here Nashe promises Harvey constant warfare. Harvey had suggested that he would like to call off the battle, but in so doing he had delivered a few verbal blows to Nashe. To the request for a truce, Nashe responds with a poetic "no!" Again using the three quatrains to deliver his message, the poet calls for "Vncessant warres with waspes and droanes," announces that revenge is an endless muse, and says that he will gain his reputation by attacking "this duns." His couplet effectively concludes by promising that his next work will be of an extraordinary type.

The next two sonnets may be thought of as parodies of the Petrarchan style and of the medieval romance generally. Nashe, like his creation Jack Wilton, had little use for the unrealistic in love, war, or any aspect of life. The exaggerated praise of women in the Petrarchan tradition sounded as false to him as it did to Shakespeare and to the later writers of anti-Petrarchan verse. Both "If I must die" and "Faire roome, the presence of sweet beauty's pride," found in *The Unfortunate Traveller*, are supposedly written by the lovesick Surrey to his absent love, Geraldine. Both poems are close enough to the real Surrey's own sonnets to ring true, but just ridiculous enough to be seen clearly as parodies.

The first is addressed to the woman Diamante, whom Surrey mistakes for Geraldine. The dying Surrey requests that his mistress suck out his breath, stab him with her tongue, crush him with her embrace, burn him with her eyes, and strangle him with her hair. In "Faire roome, the presence of sweet beauty's pride," Surrey, having visited Geraldine's room in Florence, addresses the room. He will worship the room, with which neither the chambers of heaven nor lightning can compare. No one, he concludes, can see heaven unless he meditates on the room.

Such romantic nonsense held no attraction for Jack or for Nashe. Jack makes fun of "suchlike rhymes" which lovers use to "assault" women: "A holy requiem to their souls that think to woo women with riddles."

Jack, a much more realistic man, wins the favor of Diamante with a plain table.

The final two sonnets are also anti-Petrarchan in content. Addressed to a would-be patron to whom he dedicated *The Choise of Valentines*, both "To the Right Honorable the lord S." and "Thus hath my penne presum'd to please" ask pardon for presuming to address an overtly pornographic poem to a "sweete flower of matchless poetrie." In the octave of the former, Nashe excuses himself by declaring that he merely writes about what men really do. In the sestet, he proudly asserts that everyone can write Petrarchan love poems, full of "complaints and praises." No one, however, has written successfully of "loves pleasures" in his time—except, the implication is, him.

LYRICS

Nashe's earliest two lyrics, although they are very different in content, are each in four stanzas of six lines of iambic pentameter. The rhyme in each case is *ababcc*. The later songs, those in *Summer's Last Will and Testament*, are in couplets and (in one case) tercets. Except for "Song: Spring, the sweete spring," all the lyrics are laments.

The most personal of the lyrics is "Why ist damnation," printed on the first page of Nashe's famous pamphlet *Pierce Penilesse, His Supplication to the Divell*. Trying to gain prosperity and failing, Nashe "resolved in verse to paint forth my passion." In a logical progression, the poet first considers suicide ("Why ist damnation to dispaire and die") but decides against it for his soul's safety. He then determines that in England wit and scholarship are useless. He asks God's forgiveness for his low mood, but despairs because he has no friends. Finally, he bids adieu to England as "unkinde, where skill is nothing woorth."

"All Soul, no earthly flesh," Nashe's second lyric, is more like the anti-Petrarchan sonnets that Nashe has the earl of Surrey write in *The Unfortunate Traveller* than it is like the other lyrics. Full of exaggerated comparisons (Geraldine is "pure soul," "pure gold"), comic images (his spirit will perch upon "hir silver breasts"), and conventional conceits (stars, sun, and dew take their worth from her), the poem is as far from Nashe as is John Lyly's *Euphues, the Anatomy of Wit* (1579).

In *Summer's Last Will and Testament*, Nashe includes four major lyrics and several minor ones. Some of the lyrics are cheery "Song: Spring, the sweete spring," "Song: Trip and goe," and "Song: Merry, merry, merry," for example. The general mood of the poems is sad, however, as the subject of the whole work would dictate: the death of summer. In watching summer die, readers, like Gerard Manley Hopkins's Margaret, see themselves. "Song: Fayre Summer droops" is a conventional lament on the passing of summer. Written in heroic couplets, the poem uses alliteration successfully in the last stanza to bring the song to a solid conclusion. "Song: Autumn Hath all the Summer's Fruitfull Treasure," also in heroic couplets, continues the theme of lament with lines using effective repetition ("Short dayes, sharpe dayes, long nights come on a pace"). Here, Nashe turns more directly to what was perhaps his central theme in the longer work: man's weakness in face of natural elements. The refrain, repeated at the end of each of the two stanzas, is "From winter, plague, & pestilence, good Lord, deliver us."

It was surely fear of the plague and of humanity's frailty in general that led Nashe to write the best of his lyrics, "Song: Adieu, farewell earths blisse," sung to the dying Summer by Will Summer. Nashe recognizes in the refrain that follows each of the six stanzas that he is sick, he must die, and he prays: "Lord, have mercy on us."

In a logical development, Nashe first introduces the theme of Everyman: "Fond are lifes lustful ioyes." In succeeding stanzas, he develops each of the "lustfull ioyes" in turn. "Rich men" are warned not to trust in their wealth, "Beauty" is revealed as transitory, "Strength" is pictured surrendering to the grave, and "Wit" is useless to dissuade Hell's executioner. In a very specific, orderly manner and in spare iambic trimeter lines, Nashe presents humankind's death-lament and prayer for mercy. One stanza will show the strength of the whole poem:

> Beauty is but a flowre,
> Which wrinckles will deuoure,
> Brightnesse falls from the ayre,
> Queenes have died yong and faire,
> Dust hath closed Helens eye.
> I am sick, I must dye:
>   Lord, have mercy on vs.

THE CHOISE OF VALENTINES

Nashe's last poem is by far his longest. *The Choise of Valentines* is an erotic narrative poem in heroic couplets running to more than three hundred lines. With the kind of specificity that one would expect from the author of *The Unfortunate Traveller*, Nashe tells of the visit of the young man Tomalin to a brothel in search of his valentine, "gentle mistris Francis." Tomalin's detailed exploration of the woman's anatomical charms, his unexpected loss of sexual potency, and her announced preference for a dildo all combine to present an Ovidian erotic-mythological poem of the type popular in Elizabethan England. Nashe's poem must, however, be set off from Shakespeare's *Venus and Adonis* (1593) and Marlowe's *Hero and Leander* (1598), which emphasize the mythological more than the erotic. Nashe clearly emphasizes the erotic, almost to the exclusion of the mythological. Why not? he seems to say in the dedicatory sonnet accompanying the poem: Ovid was his guide, and "Ouids wanton Muse did not offend."

Nowhere, with the exception of the excellent "Song: Adieu, farewell earths blisse," does Nashe rise to the heights of his greatest contemporaries, Spenser, Sidney, Marlowe, and Shakespeare. In that poem, in the sonnet "Were there no warres," and in perhaps one or two other poems his Muse is sufficiently shaken into consciousness by the poet's interest in the subject. The remainder of Nashe's poetry is the work of an excellent craftsperson who is playing with form and language.

OTHER MAJOR WORKS

PLAYS: *Dido, Queen of Carthage*, pr. c. 1586-1587 (with Christopher Marlowe); *Summer's Last Will and Testament*, pr. 1592; *The Isle of Dogs*, pr. 1597 (with Ben Jonson; no longer extant).

NONFICTION: *The Anatomie of Absurditie*, 1589; Preface to Robert Greene's *Menaphon*, 1589; *An Almond for a Parrat*, 1590; Preface to Sir Philip Sidney's *Astrophel and Stella*, 1591; Preface to Robert Greene's *A Quip for an Upstart Courtier*, 1592; *Christ's Tears over Jerusalem*, 1593; *The Terrors of the Night*, 1594; *Have with You to Saffron-Walden*, 1596; *Nashe's Lenten Stuffe*, 1599.

MISCELLANEOUS: *Pierce Penilesse, His Supplication to the Divell*, 1592 (prose and poetry); *Strange*

News of the Intercepting of Certain Letters, 1592 (prose and poetry; also known as *The Four Letters Confuted*); *The Unfortunate Traveller: Or, The Life of Jack Wilton*, 1594 (prose and poetry).

BIBLIOGRAPHY

Crewe, Jonathan V. *Unredeemed Rhetoric: Thomas Nashe and the Scandal of Authorship.* Baltimore: The Johns Hopkins University Press, 1982. A study of the conflict between orthodox values and a cynical perception of society's injustice and exploitation that cuts across Nashe's career, complicating and adding tension to his work.

Helgerson, Richard. *The Elizabethan Prodigals.* Berkeley: University of California Press, 1977. Nashe and his colleagues Christopher Marlowe, Thomas Kyd, George Peele, Robert Greene, and Thomas Lodge, all with university training, formed a group of literary bohemians in London. Helgerson catalogs their escapades and relates them to their lives.

Hilliard, Stephen S. *The Singularity of Thomas Nashe.* Lincoln: University of Nebraska Press, 1986. Hilliard takes a fresh look at Nashe's life and writing, discovering the distinctive qualities of his wit and style and showing how they transformed both poetry and prose.

Holbrook, Peter. *Literature and Degree in Renaissance England: Nashe, Bourgeois Tragedy, Shakespeare.* Cranbury, N.J.: Associated University Presses, 1994. A historical study of political and social views in sixteenth century England.

Hutson, Lorna. *Thomas Nashe in Context.* New York: Oxford University Press, 1997. Considers Thomas Nashe within his social and historical milieu.

McGinn, Donald J. *Thomas Nashe.* Boston: Twayne, 1981. Contains insightful commentary on Nashe's life and works. Focuses on Nashe's works as portrayals of the various types of middle-class Londoners—their appearance, their manners, and their customs.

Nicholl, Charles. *A Cup of News: The Life of Thomas Nashe.* London: Routledge & Kegan Paul, 1984. This scholarly biography sets a high standard. In addition to substantial discussions of Nashe's life and writings, Nicholl includes illustrations of portraits and scenes, as well as reproductions of relevant documents.

Nielson, James. *Unread Herrings: Thomas Nashe and the Prosaics of the Real.* New York: Peter Lang, 1993. This study examines Nashe's use of realism in his works. Bibliography.

Eugene P. Wright

MARGARET CAVENDISH, DUCHESS OF NEWCASTLE

Born: St. Johns Abbey, near Colchester, Essex, England; 1623
Died: Welbeck Abbey, near Nottingham, England; December 15, 1673

PRINCIPAL POETRY

Philosophicall Fancies, 1653 (prose and verse; revised as *Philosophical and Physical Opinions*, 1655)
Poems and Fancies, 1653
Natures Pictures, 1656 (prose and verse)
Plays Never Before Printed, 1668

OTHER LITERARY FORMS

Margaret Cavendish, duchess of Newcastle, left many folio volumes in various prose genres. *Natures Pictures* contains a group of stories in prose and verse told around a winter fire; they are romantic and moralistic (disguises, abductions, wanderings, battles, reunions). The second part, a miscellaneous group of tales, has no framing device. *Grounds of Natural Philosophy* (1668) reworks her views regarding physics and medicine developed in *Philosophicall Fancies*. *Philosophical Letters* (1664) analyzes Thomas Hobbes, René Descartes, and Thomas More. Several romantic comedies, published in *Plays* (1662), have plot elements similar to the tales. The duchess herself appears in such figures as "Lady Contemplation" and "Lady Sanspariel." The duchess's most effective prose, and one of the century's finest biographical works, is *The Life of William Cavendish, Duke of Newcastle* (1667).

Equally lively and clearly written is "A True Relation of the Birth, Breeding and Life of Margaret Cavendish, Duchess of Newcastle, Written by Herself," included in *Natures Pictures*. *The Worlds Olio* (1655) contains epistles on the branches of learning and the pleasures of reading, on the passions, fame, and education. *CCXI Sociable Letters* (1664) contains many interesting observations on manners and literary taste.

ACHIEVEMENTS

As one of the first women who not only composed but also published their verses, Margaret Cavendish, duchess of Newcastle, anticipated the disdain that she would receive and so attempted to create a persona, as did other Cavalier poets, that would help readers understand what she was doing. She developed the concept of "fancy," and the "harmless mirth" it produced, arguing that it was a woman's as much as a man's pursuit. Her poems envision the world as guided by a benevolent goddess, Natura. They movingly express humanitarian sentiments and focus on responses by women to loss of love, misfortune, and death. She used many genres and themes of earlier seventeenth century poetry: the pastoral, the verse treatise, the elegy, and the verse narrative. She is at her best when she is guided by the traditional emblems and images of lyric and narrative verse.

BIOGRAPHY

Margaret Cavendish, duchess of Newcastle, was born Margaret Lucas, one of eight children afforded a privileged upbringing by her mother. Her favorite pastime was writing, for which she neglected her reading, her languages, and her spelling. She also enjoyed designing clothes and was known for her extravagance in dress as well as in her scientific opinions and her poetry. At nineteen, despite her great shyness, she became a maid of honor to Queen Henrietta Maria. In this capacity, she met William Cavendish, then marquis of Newcastle. They married in 1645; he was thirty-three years her senior. The duke was a learned man, a patron of poets, and a virtuoso, a friend of René Descartes and Thomas Hobbes.

The duke and his lady lived happily at Welbeck Abbey after the Restoration, but during the Civil Wars and the Commonwealth the duke was in financial peril. He had left England after the Battle of Marston Moor and spent most of the Interregnum at Antwerp. The duchess, who met her husband at Paris, returned to London in 1652 to attempt the compounding of his estates. It was at that time that she resumed writing poetry. She continued in Holland, where the duke entertained many notable visitors in politics and the arts. The frontispiece of Cavendish's *Natures Pictures* shows her and her husband, crowned with laurel, sitting at a table with the duke's sons and daughters. It provides a fair picture of the congenial literary readings and conversations that they shared.

In 1676, a commemorative volume of *Letters and Poems* in praise of Cavendish was published, with pieces by Thomas Shadwell, Henry More, Sir George Etherege, and Jasper Mayne.

ANALYSIS

Seventeenth century volumes of poetry as diverse as George Herbert's *The Temple* (1633), Mildmay

Margaret Cavendish, duchess of Newcastle (Hulton Archive/ Getty Images)

Fane's *Otia Sacra* (1648), and Robert Herrick's *Hesperides: Or, The Works Both Humane and Divine of Robert Herrick, Esq.* (1648) have general but significant organizing principles. This is quite clearly the case with *Poems and Fancies*, despite its being very poorly printed by a craftsperson who was puzzled by the state of the manuscript and was pressed to get the book out before Margaret Cavendish, duchess of Newcastle, left England to rejoin her exiled husband. Cavendish intersperses, throughout the book, transition pieces called clasps, intended to join one section to the next. As for "Poems," these are verse treatises on the atomistic structure of matter that establish the writer as a female virtuoso (one conversant in a disinterested, amateur way with the sciences and fine arts), followed by moral discourses including complaints about humans' misuse of the world that God has placed under their stewardship, and descriptive pieces on, for example, dispositions to mirth and melancholy. Halfway through the work, the heading "Fancies" ushers in verses on fairies and elegiac pieces. The "claspes" do more than divide the volume into sections. Their main function is to allow the duchess to explain her poetic temperament or cast of mind, her reasons for writing, her disdain for niceties of poetic style, and the primacy of the intellectual content of her own verses.

In her solitary apartment, where few were brave enough, in 1652, to visit the wife of a royalist general, she wrote quickly as the thoughts were generated in her original, thoroughly idiosyncratic, and nimble intellect. Some of her explanations are attempts to justify a woman's audacity in writing poetry. Cavendish is primarily concerned, however, not with what others think of her but with contemporary notions of poetry, particularly philosophical verse, narratives, and lyrics. One must focus not only on her "claspes" but also on the prefatory matter to *Poems and Fancies* to understand the diverse body of poetry that she produced.

Commendatory poems by her husband and his brother Charles Cavendish (her companion in London in 1652) are on the surface fulsome praises but really "harmless mirth": lighthearted punning and sprightly humor. The cavalier and his lady do not take themselves so seriously as to pose as national heroes or great poets. For a fit audience of like-minded readers, affable

modesty and whimsical self-deprecation mark the prefatory verses. In what other spirit could one take the duke's assertion that his wife's writings will set the ghosts of Edmund Spenser, William Shakespeare, and Ben Jonson into fits of jealous weeping? The duchess does indeed lay claim to fame, which she frankly desires for the variety of her fancies, her manifold curiosities about the workings of nature, and the scope of her subject matter. As a female writer, she is very much aware of her uniqueness. She notes that ordering fancies is a similar kind of economy to that which women need to run households, and that verse, being fiction, is recreative to the spirit, wholesomely entertaining, and ingenuous. One part of a poetess's contribution to her readers is in defeating male stereotypes regarding female propensities to idleness, gossip, and slander.

"FANCIES"

"Fancies" is an important word to the duchess; her usage of the word can be understood in relation to the Baconian contrast between imagination and reason. The former produced pleasant delusions, sprightly ingenuity, and alacrity of imaginings. Francis Bacon gave poetry faint praise, and the notion that fancy must be disciplined by judgment was a strong one. Cavendish's own version of this dictum, stated in the "claspes," may be her emphasis on matter as opposed to niceties of style. In general, however, she is content with her fancies as a kind of self-improving, "harmless mirth," a magnanimous way for a studious and shy woman to pass the time. The duchess had a reputation (see Samuel Pepys and Dorothy Osbourne) for eccentricity and arrogance.

The prefatory materials in *Poems and Fancies*, however, suggest a writer who makes no great claims for her own poetic abilities. As with the Cavalier poets whose conventions she borrows and with whom she shares political and social as well as aesthetic values, a mind-muse analogy develops. The poetry provides recreation and reflects the amiable, benevolent disposition of the writer. In this spirit, the duchess follows Herrick and Mildmay Fane with a whimsical allusion to her book as her child. As an introduction, the conceit is in her case as apt as it is conventional.

ATOMISM

The duchess's treatment of atoms is somewhat indebted to Bacon's new rationalism and to the encyclopedic categorizing of the phenomenal world by Guillaume du Bartas and Sir William Davenant. The latter's metaphors from applied and theoretical sciences are similar to some of Cavendish's "similizing." Her diction and iambic pentameter rhymed couplets provide a sensible framework for discursive exposition, but she does not indulge in much analysis. Atomism is merely the trapping for fanciful description, which in itself is similar to du Bartas's quaint and fantastic compilations.

For example, she avers that plants are made up of branched atoms, with hooks that pull the tendrils upward from the roots. Healthy atoms are in tune with one another, like people dancing to harmonious music. Aged atoms slow down and finally move no more; this is the state of death. Sharp, arrow-like atoms make up fire; they can soar upward, while the atoms that cohere to form earth are flat and square, heavy and phlegmatic. Thus the duchess mixes an ancient notion (the four elements) with the modern, empirical one of Hobbes (a personal friend of the Newcastles with whom Sir William held lengthy discussions).

Cavendish lived in the "divided and distinguished worlds" of which Sir Thomas Browne wrote. John Donne and John Milton lived there too, but while their inconsistencies involved seeing God's signatures in the real world (however empirically, up to a point, they were willing to observe it), the duchess's inconsistencies concern not nature and spirit, but nature and fancy. She ingenuously tells the reader that she has not read much Hobbes, Descartes, or Bacon, that her poems were written hastily and not revised to conform with what she read or recalled from her reading. She was fascinated with atomism, however, and was concerned with it throughout *Poems and Fancies*. In one place, she uses a "claspe" to explain that various atoms acting at cross-purposes within the human body are the work of mischievous fairies. The body's animal spirits can be similar tiny creatures working in nerves, muscles, and organs as the various races of humankind do in different parts of the earth, trafficking with one another through veins and arteries.

"A WORLD IN AN EARE-RING"

This leads to the duchess's version of the "metaphysical" metaphor of the body as a map and to other speculations bred of Renaissance skepticism. Her imagination is especially taken with microscopic convolutions of nature and with the perfections attainable within the smallest parameters of nature and art. Jonson and Herrick had similar interests. Although the duchess cannot match their perfections in imagery or verse rhythms, she shares their imaginative empathy. "A World in an Eare-Ring" supposes a universe suspended invisibly from a lady's ear. The poem envisions a grand panorama of mortal existence: great storms and their chaos, mountains, gardens and cities, and an entire cycle of life forms, all revolving around the center or hole in the ring.

PHILOSOPHICALL FANCIES

Cavendish's atomism was undergoing revision as she was writing *Poems and Fancies*. In 1653, she published these revisions, alluded to on the last page of her first book, in a duodecimo volume titled *Philosophicall Fancies*, revised two years later as *Philosophical and Physical Opinions*. Here, in a mixture of prose and verse, she is concerned with matter and motion, the former being infinite while the latter is the agent that changes the form of matter. She also deals with causes of sunlight, diseases, tides, and God as first cause. Extravagant fancies regarding sublunary worlds different from earth and beyond human control predominate. She speculates that rational spirits might so change the laws of physics as to animate trees into deer and make mermaids of water lilies.

MORAL DISCOURSES

Cavendish's moral discourses are dialogues between, for example, nature and humans, wit and beauty, peace and war, and discourses on love, poverty, and humility. Some of her best poetry occurs here, concerned with faculty psychology, humans' stewardship of God's creation, and the humanitarian and compassionate principles that underlie nobility. For the more discursive of these verses, her predecessors would be Samuel Daniel (*Musophilus: Or, A Defence of Poesie*, 1599, 1601, 1602, 1607, 1611, 1623), Fulke Greville's treatises on fame, honor, and war, and George Chapman (*Euthymiae Raptus: Or, The Tears of Peace*, 1609). For the dramatic and narrative efforts, Spenser's didactic fables, Milton's "Il Penseroso" (1629-1632), and perhaps George Wither's and Michael Drayton's works are analogues (not, it should be noted, sources). If indeed the duchess knew the work of these poets, it probably would have been by hearing them read rather than by close study. She was a sporadic reader, and even in childhood, she liked writing not only more than traditional feminine accomplishments such as deportment and snippets of foreign languages but also more than reading. Her widowed mother lovingly indulged these preferences.

"A Dialogue of Birds"

Three of the moral discourses have considerable merit. "A Dialogue of Birds" has an effective dramatic framework: Various species talk of their experiences with humankind. They speak plainly and pathetically of their sufferings brought about by humankind's artful cruelties, not by nature's regime, however harsh. In fact, this poem, the one on the hare, and the fairy verses suggest the folk art which John Broadbent (in *Poets of the Seventeenth Century*, 1980) attributes to her and her husband. The poem is well organized, beginning with the lark's song and ending, after a horrific recital of suffering, with the birds settling their families in their nests, and finally singing a communal hymn, the birdsong softly fading as they fall asleep. The theme of the poem is art's perversion of nature, which is herself benevolent and informed by love. The birds pose the question of the root of humanity's viciousness; they have no answer, but portray—by citing their own mistreatment—human aggression hidden under universally accepted behavior that passes for custom and sport. With that, they turn from what they cannot prevent to practical concerns such as nest building. The rhetorical device at work here, *prosopopoeia*, was brought to perfection by Spenser, and Cavendish uses it well.

"The Hunting of the Hare"

"The Hunting of the Hare" is successful in the same way. It is even more accurate in its detail of the animal's furtive movements and instinctual strategies for self-preservation. The poet's personification of the animal's innocence and despair as the hounds surround him incites pathos. The theme, once again, is people's willful ignorance of the suffering they cause and their prideful desecration of nature. Cavendish's humanitarianism in these and other narratives is as revealing a part of her sensibility as are her introductory verses.

"A Dialogue Between Mirth and Melancholy"

"A Dialogue Between Mirth and Melancholy" was noticed favorably in the eighteenth century (in a witty sketch in *The Connoisseur*, 1774), and in the nineteenth century by Benjamin Disraeli and Leigh Hunt. They appreciated the pastoral descriptions reminiscent of "L'Allegro" (1645) and "Il Penseroso," but the most pervasive feature is the care with which the two states of mind are balanced against each other. Notably, the duchess, who loved retirement, lets melancholy have the last word. It is a "white" melancholy, like that which Herrick sometimes delineates, agreeable and clean. The pleasures of retirement allow sadness to be refined away by the duchess's guiding principle of the good life, fancy. In these verses, she avoids the extravagances that mar so much of her work, including "The Hunting of the Stag," another humanitarian work, which is no sooner under way than a lengthy catalog of trees intrudes.

Fairy poetry

The duchess's fairy poetry constitutes a microcosm of all her concerns. In a prose introduction, she justifies the existence of fairies on the basis of recent scientific discoveries about invisible but potent natural forces. As usual, these speculations resolve themselves into fanciful explanations: If air moves ineluctably through walls, fairies can invisibly go where they will. In "The Fairy Queen," Cavendish spends nearly the entire poem describing the habitat of fairies, which she places in the center of Earth. She brings in the elements, the movements of Earth, and the circulation of the waters. Her humanitarianism is also evident. In the microcosm of the fairies' world, the god of love is not Cupid but the goddess Natura, a female generative principle that gives Queen Mab control over the spirit world and extends motherly beneficence to all creatures. The duchess's interest in folklore and custom can best be seen in "The Pastime of the Queen of Fairies." This rings the changes on Hobgoblin's pranks and is very close to the speeches of Shakespeare's Puck. Throughout all these verses, one senses a preoccupation with miniature gemlike beauties, which only those with refined perceptions and respect for fancy can appreciate. The order of the universe can be seen in the order of minutest nature. The fairy verses in which some anthologists find the most attractive images (because of the succinctness with which they are stated) are in a collection of fragments, *Plays Never Before Printed*.

The sources for all these poems are, in addition to Shakespeare, Drayton and Herrick, writers who use this kind of pastoral without any didactic intentions, but for the ingenious play of the imagination. Cavendish's mushroom table with its dish of ant's eggs is from Herrick, as are the glowworm's eyes, used as lanterns, and snakeskin used as decoration. Mab's chariot made from a nutshell recalls Mercutio's speech in *Romeo and Juliet* (pr. c. 1595-1596). The differences between the duchess's verses and those of her great predecessors lie in their verbal music and their more striking juxtapositions of the familiarity of our world with the mysteriousness of the fairies' world.

ELEGIES AND FEMALE IMAGES

According to the Renaissance definition, an elegy need not be limited to verses on death; it could be any serious meditative poem. A large number of the duchess's poems might be so designated. In Cavendish's elegiac and lyric verses, subjects are female: their beauty, their love, their griefs, their deaths. Some of these are given the general heading of "A Register of Mournful Verses." The two most ambitious deal with a "melting beauty" whose body turns to ice and melts into the funeral urn of her loved one, and with another "mourning beauty" from whose tears flowers with bowed heads grow, and for whom the stars become fellow mourners lighting her way to the grave site. The gods transform her into a comet.

The imagery in the second of these elegies is effectively emblematic, although strained with macrocosm-microcosm analogies. The poem is well unified in its symbolic representation of universal gestures and attitudes of grief, and of grief's fateful consequences. In both poems, one senses woman's isolation, and the psychological effects of the single emotion of black melancholy on the human mind. For this, Seneca is an exemplar, as Ovid is for the mysterious transformations of the women, which suggests in Cavendish's work the principles of natural benevolence set forth in some of the dialogues. These and the duchess's other elegies, especially those for a bereaved mother and for her deceased daughter, would be well complemented by emblems. Her final elegy, on her brother, is in a similar vein, attempting emotional heightening with metaphoric emblems: Her heart is a sacrifice, her sighs are incense, her thoughts mourners. A mythic universality is attempted, or, more accurately, strained after. The opening and closing lines, however, are in an affecting plain style; their commonplaces about honor and fame do not spoil them.

SIMILITUDES

In her short lyrical pieces, Cavendish can focus more exclusively on her "similitudes." The effects are often bizarre; her formlessness and extravagance are all too evident. A sad lover's heart becomes meat for nature's dinner. If Dame Nature has any appetite left, Cavendish presents her with a "bisque" made from a young female's broad forehead, rosy cheeks, white breasts, and swanlike neck. Another conceit involves "Similizing the Heart to a Harp, the Head to an Organ, the Tongue to a Lute, to make a consort of Musique." Another compares the world of the sea to an Arcadia in which the ocean is a country green, the mast a maypole, and the sailors shepherds.

The duchess's conceits often defy classification into Petrarchan, metaphysical, or plain (or eloquent) style. One wishes she were a bit more discreet, less spontaneously prolific, and perhaps a greater reader, like some lettered contemporaries: Lady Bedford; Lady Mary Wroth; Margaret, countess of Cumberland; Lady Falkland, or her daughter-in-law, Letice Morison; or even Dorothy Osbourne, who thought her mad for attempting to write, and especially to publish, poetry. Had she been only a patroness of writers, or a letter writer, however, she would not have been the self-possessed and courageous innovator that she was.

OTHER MAJOR WORKS

PLAY: *Plays*, 1662.

NONFICTION: *The Worlds Olio*, 1655; *CCXI Sociable Letters*, 1664; *Philosophical Letters*, 1664; *The Life of William Cavendish, Duke of Newcastle*, 1667; *Grounds of Natural Philosophy*, 1668.

MISCELLANEOUS: *Paper Bodies: A Margaret Cavendish Reader*, 2000.

BIBLIOGRAPHY

Battigelli, Anna. *Margaret Cavendish and the Exiles of the Mind.* Lexington: University Press of Kentucky, 1998. Battigelli's meticulous scholarship brings Cavendish alive, creating a compelling portrait of her intellectual and creative life. Includes bibliographical references and index.

Clucas, Stephen, ed. *A Princely Brave Woman: Essays on Margaret Cavendish, Duchess of Newcastle.* Burlington, Vt.: Ashgate, 2003. Contains a three-essay section on her poetry, which looks at Hobbesian allegories in her work and *Poems and Fancies.*

Cottegnies, Line, and Nancy Weitz, eds. *Authorial Conquests: Essays on Genre in the Writings of Margaret Cavendish.* Madison, N.J.: Fairleigh Dickinson University Press, 2003. Collection of essays examines Cavendish's use of genre. One essay explores the "poetics of variety."

Mendelson, Sarah Heller. *Margaret Cavendish.* Burlington, Vt.: Ashgate, 2009. Biography of Cavendish that provides substantial critical analysis of her works.

Rees, Emma L. E. *Margaret Cavendish: Gender, Genre, Exile.* New York: St. Martin's Press, 2003. This biography of Cavendish contains an entire chapter on *Poems and Fancies* and examines numerous other works.

Sarasohn, Lisa. *The Natural Philosophy of Margaret Cavendish: Reason and Fancy During the Scientific Revolution.* Baltimore: The Johns Hopkins University Press, 2010. Examines Cavendish's natural philosophy, including atomism, which is featured in some of her poetry.

Whitaker, Katie. *Mad Madge: The Extraordinary Life of Margaret Cavendish, Duchess of Newcastle, the First Woman to Live by Her Pen.* New York: Basic Books, 2003. This biography notes how Cavendish dared to write as a woman despite the resulting scandal. Later generations termed her "Mad Madge," but Whitaker demonstrates Cavendish's merit as a writer.

Jay A. Gertzman

NUALA NÍ DHOMHNAILL

Born: St. Helens, Lancashire, England; February 16, 1952

PRINCIPAL POETRY

An dealg droighin, 1981
Féar suaithinseach, 1984
Rogha dánta, 1984 (*Selected Poems*, 1988)
Pharaoh's Daughter, 1990 (bilingual edition)
Feis, 1991
Leabhar agus caisead du chiud Boyne Vally Honey: Finscealta na hEirann, 1991
The Astrakhan Cloak, 1992 (bilingual edition)
Spíonáin is róiseanna: Compánach don chaiséad CIC L21, 1993
Cead aighnis, 1998
The Water Horse: Poems in Irish, 1999 (bilingual edition)
The Fifty Minute Mermaid, 2007 (bilingual edition)

OTHER LITERARY FORMS

Although known primarily as a poet, Nuala Ní Dhomhnaill (NEE GHON-ahl) has written three plays for children and edited several volumes, including *Jumping off Shadows: Selected Contemporary Irish Poets* (1995; with Greg Delanty). She published several very influential essays, including "Why I Choose to Write in Irish: The Corpse That Sits Up and Talks Back" (published in *Selected Essays*, 2005) which explains and defends her decision to write poetry only in the Irish language (Gaelic).

ACHIEVEMENTS

Nuala Ní Dhomhnaill has developed a distinctive voice as a poet, provided a proto-feminist perspective on every aspect of life in Ireland, and made informative explorations of the cultural ramifications of the suppression of the Irish language. She also has made the interlinkage of language an appropriate focus for poets and contributed to the growing respect for creative translation that has drawn some of the most accomplished poets in the English language to her writing. She has won numerous awards for her work both in the

United Kingdom and the United States, including the O'Shaughnessy Award for Poetry (1988), the American Ireland Fund Literary Award (1991), and the Bess Hokin Prize from *Poetry* magazine (1996).

Biography

Nuala Ní Dhomhnaill was born in England, where her parents, both physicians, were practicing. Her father took a position as surgeon at the hospital in Tipperary when Ní Dhomhnaill was five years old, and the family took up residence in County Kerry, a Gaelic-speaking region—the Gaeltacht—in the west of Ireland. This was Ní Dhomhnaill's introduction to the Irish language, and although the young girl was fascinated by the stories and conversations she heard throughout the community and began to speak Irish as her natural tongue, she wrote only in English. At the age of sixteen, however, it occurred to her that she could more adequately express herself in Irish, and literally in mid-poem, she shifted to that language. The next year, she gave her first poetry reading, an occasion distinguished by the attendance of Caitlín Maude, a poet/singer, who became Ní Dhomhnaill's role model because she was one of the few women included on the reading list for the leaving certificate (a diploma) course. In the early stages of her poetic life, she found that every poem she submitted for publication was "chipped and chopped with no by-your-leave" by editors who had a conception of poetry that nearly completely excluded the subject, style, language, and outlook that Ní Dhomhnaill was developing. She earned a bachelor of arts degree (1972) and a higher diploma education (1973) from the University College Cork. Then in the kind of radical transition that was characteristic of her openness to new experience, she married Dogan Leflef, a Turkish geologist, and she spent the next seven years living in Holland and Turkey. In the 1980's, the family returned to Ireland to raise their four children in the Dingle Gaeltaecht and then in Dublin.

Her first collection of poems, entirely in Irish, *An dealg droighin* (the thorn of the sloe) was published in 1981 by the Mercier Press in Cork, followed by *Féar suaithinseach* (marvelous grass) in 1984. *Rogha dánta* appeared in 1984, and the Raven Arts Press in Dublin published a bilingual version, *Selected Poems*, with

translations by Michael Hartnett, in 1988. The enthusiastic response by both critics and readers on both sides of the Atlantic led to the publication in 1990 of *Pharaoh's Daughter* by the pioneering Wake Forest Press. This bilingual work featured Irish poems with English translations by thirteen poets, including Hartnett, Seamus Heaney, Medbh McGuckian, Ciaran Carson, Eiléan Ní Chuilleanáin, and Paul Muldoon. This volume not only established Ní Dhomhnaill's stature as one of the outstanding poets writing in the United Kingdom, but also brought the Irish language to the attention of the Anglo-American literary community. The publication of Muldoon's translations of her poems in *The Astrakhan Cloak* further elevated Ní Dhomhnaill's reputation. Her work was recognized by several awards and invitations to serve as visiting professor at several American universities. She served as the Ireland Professor of Poetry 2001-2004, spending a year each at Trinity College Dublin, University College Dublin, and Queen's University Belfast.

Analysis

Nuala Ní Dhomhnaill's "Ceist na Teangan" ("The Language Issue"), the last poem in *Pharaoh's Daughter*, expresses her central concern as a writer. She has said that "Irish is a language of enormous elasticity and emotional sensitivity; of quick and hilarious banter and a welter of references both historical and mythological." However, it is also a language that, in spite of its formidable history, had been reduced to the tongue of a small segment of the population of Ireland by the middle of the twentieth century and was in danger of extinction. In the poem, Ní Dhomhnaill writes, "I place my hope on the water/ in this little boat/ of the language," indicating an urgency tempered by an awareness of uncertainty. She likens her poetry to the infant Moses, who is adrift at the mercy of the current and may find refuge "in the lap, perhaps/ of some Pharoah's daughter," and hopes her verses will find an unbiased, sympathetic reader from another culture who will respond with understanding and affection.

Ní Dhomhnaill has linked her sense of the need for cultural preservation to her conviction that "the attitude to the body enshrined in Irish remains extremely open and uncoy" and presents a more honest, humane, and ultimately realistic way to approach the physical nature of humans so that it is "almost impossible to be 'rude' or 'vulgar' in Irish." An adjunct to this is the way in which the Irish folkloric tradition regards beings from "an saol eile" or the "otherworld" to be a subject for easy sentimentalization and infantilization, which "in Irish is a concept of such impeccable intellectual rigor and creditibilty that it is virtually impossible to translate into English," but that can also be "a source of linguistic and imaginative playfulness," a crucial component of her work.

SELECTED POEMS

Selected Poems, a bilingual edition containing Hartnett's translations along with the Irish versions that first appeared in *Rogha dánta*, introduced Ní Dhomhnaill to the English-speaking world. The themes that define her work are already fully explored in this collection and give it a sense of substance as well as a distinctive, singular voice. The candor of her expression of the erotic is beautifully and tastefully conveyed by one of the poems that she herself translated, "Labysheedy" ("The Silken Bed"), in which the landscape is both a setting for and an image of a sexual union. "Féar suaithinseach" ("Marvelous Grass") is a call to the male clergy to offer Ireland the true spirituality that has been missing from a rigid, fossilized, narrowly patriarchial institution. Ní Dhomhnaill has said that she was "pushed into poetry by having to tackle the patriarchy head on," and there are a series of poems addressed to Cú Chulainn, the legendary hero celebrated notably by William Butler Yeats. In "Agallamh Na Mór-Riona Le Cú Chulainn" ("The Great Queen Speaks. Cú Chulainn Listens"), the queen tells the hero "I came to you/ as a queen/ colorfully clothed/ beautifully formed/ to grant you power/ and kingdoms," and calls for the full potential of his wisdom to be employed in the interest of all the Irish. The existence of an "otherworld" resonant in history as well as in the present is depicted in "An Crann" ("The Tree"), in which a "fairy woman" somewhat incongruously appears with "a Black & Decker" to cut down the poet's tree. The consternation at the intrusion expressed by the woman's husband indicates a disjunction, perhaps temporary, between realms that should permit interplay but have been separated by artificial barriers.

PHARAOH'S DAUGHTER

The publication of *Pharoah's Daughter* significantly enhanced Ní Dhomhnaill's stature, as a group of Irish poets provided English translations that displayed the full range of Ní Dhomhnaill's voice. The manner in which poets with their own styles and approaches could find ways to maintain the characteristics of Ní Dhomhnaill's poems suggests the success of her efforts to touch fundamental aspects of Irish culture. Each poet chose and responded to something consonant with his or her own deepest concerns.

Ciaran Carson brought his experience with song and folk motifs to "An tSeanbhean Bhocht" ("The Shan Van Vocht"), in which the Shan Van Vocht (a poor old woman who is identified with self-sacrifice for the sake of Ireland) is seen in a blood-thirsty dotage, still exhorting "stricken youths who took to soldiering" to give their lives for some nebulous idea of patriotism. Carson's use of the vernacular to express Ní Dhomhnaill's exasperated intention to use "anything at all/ To get this old bitch" to finally be silent deftly draws out the tone of the poem.

McGuckian's straight-forward, direct exposition of a card game between a mortal and a woman from another realm in "Geasa" ("The Bond") erases the rational divisions that make other varieties of wisdom suspect. Ní Chuilleanáin continues Ní Dhomhnaill's practice of appreciation for all that is lovely in people with her translation of "Dún" ("Stronghold"). Heaney offers his own reading of "Miraculous Grass," reducing the distance between the speaker and the subject of the poem in comparison with that in the translation by Hartnett. Muldoon offers translations of four poems, including "The Language Issue," which concludes the book and gives it its title.

THE FIFTY MINUTE MERMAID

Playing with the Irish word for translation—*aistriúchán*—in the manner that has come to distinguish his own work, Muldoon employed his mastery of poetic forms to provide supple translations for Ní Dhomhnaill's *The Astrakhan Cloak*, a bilingual edition. The collaboration suited both poets so well that Muldoon worked with Ní Dhomhnaill closely throughout the production of *The Fifty Minute Mermaid*, a collection that includes poems by Ní Dhomhnaill from the preceding decade. The powerful legends of merfolk have fascinated Ní Dhomhnaill from her earliest efforts, including "An Mhaighdean Mhar" ("The Mermaid") from *Selected Poems*, in which the mermaid presents herself: "Though I've got a fish's tail/ I'm not unbeautiful;/ my hair is long and yellow/ and there's a shine from my scale." Ní Dhomhnaill creates an image of an independent woman, a creature from the otherworld, a stranger/other who has made some unconventional choices that are closer to most human impulses than is generally acknowledged.

Ní Dhomhnaill continues her consideration of a species recognizably human in many attributes, but never completely a part of the human universe. The crucial difference is established by the separation of water and dry land, the ocean being the fluid place of origins and the land being the static setting for the development of a stable civilization. The allure of the ocean, its mystery and dangers, is offered in contrast to the certainty, fixity, and stolidity of solid ground. The merfolk are meant to represent those who do not quite fit into an established social order—those who are defined as different because of their ethnicity, gender, religion, or any other quality perceived as an oddity. Every cultural community has individuals who are seen as marching to a different drummer, and Ní Dhomhnaill treasures them, often identifies with them, and while describing a universal condition, implies that they are an analogue for the Irish, an island people on terrain crossed by water courses in a climate where precipitation is often "general all over Ireland."

The poems resemble transcriptions from an oral tradition, with someone who is perhaps a scholar of the species essentially putting a narrative frame around expressions of personal experience by the merfolk. Their words are drawn from deep emotional truths, as if in a fifty-minute counseling session, partially accounting for the title of the book. Ní Dhomhnaill, blending extensive historical research and her own life's encounters with the components of Irish culture that have informed her writing, contributes to the story of her nation in the manner of epic poets from the earliest times.

Other major works

PLAYS: *Jimín*, pr. 1985; *An ollphiast ghranna*, pr. 1987; *Destination Demian*, pb. 1993; *The Wooing of Eadaoin*, 1994 (libretto).

SCREENPLAY: *An goban saor*, 1993.

TELEPLAY: *An t-anam mothála*, 1995.

NONFICTION: *Selected Essays*, 2005.

EDITED TEXT: *Jumping off Shadows: Selected Contemporary Irish Poets*, 1995 (with Greg Delanty); *RTÉ One Hundred Years: Ireland in the Twentieth Century*, 2001; *The Incredible Hides in Every House: A Collection of Short Stories and Poetry in Aid of Habitat for Humanity*, 2005.

Bibliography
Brown, Paul. "Masculine Religion, Feminine Spirituality: The Mythical Landscape in the Poetry of Nuala Ní Dhomhnaill." In *Irish Studies: Geographies and Gender*, edited by Marti D. Lee and Ed Madden. Newcastle, England: Cambridge Scholars, 2008. Looks at how Ní Dhomhnaill uses myth in her poetry and creates a feminine sense of spirituality within the wider, masculine formal structures of religion.

Burke, Margaret Garry. "Framing Masculinity in the Poetry of Nuala Ní Dhomhnaill." *Journal of International Women's Studies* 10, no. 4 (May, 2009): 85-94. A discussion of the ways in which Ní Dhomhnaill's poetry undercuts traditional concepts of masculinity and femininity.

Eamon, Maher, ed. *Liminal Borderlands in Irish Literature and Culture*. New York: Peter Lang, 2008. This collection of essays examining liminality—a concern with borders and being in transition—contains three on Ní Dhomhnaill, looking at female identity, otherworldly figures, and translation issues.

Haberstroh, Patricia Boyle. "Nuala Ní Dhomhnaill." In *Women Creating Women: Contemporary Irish Poets*. Syracuse, N.Y.: Syracuse University Press, 1996. Analyzes Ní Dhomhnaill's work through *The Astrakhan Cloak*, focusing on her portrayals of women, from mythic figures to ordinary women.

McGuckian, Medbh, and Nuala Ní Dhomhnaill. "Comhrá: A Conversation Between Medbh McGuckian and Nuala Ní Dhomhnaill." *Southern Review* 13, no. 3

(Summer, 1995): 581-614. McGuckian and Ní Dhomhnaill have an illuminating and engaging discussion about Irish literature and culture in an issue of *The Southern Review* devoted to Irish poetry. Laura O'Connor provides a foreword and afterword that contain valuable information.

Montague, John, Nuala Ní Dhomhnaill, and Paul Durcan. *The Poet's Chair: The First Nine Years of the Ireland Chair of Poetry*. Dublin: Lilliput Press, 2008. Collects the lectures delivered by Montague, Ní Dhomhnaill, and Durcan during their tenures as the Ireland Professor of Poetry. Contains a foreword by Seamus Heaney.

O'Connor, Mary. "Lashings of Mother Tongue: Nuala Ní Dhomhnaill's Anarchic Laughter." In *The Comic Tradition in Irish Woman Writers*. Gainesville: University Press of Florida, 1996. An incisive consideration of the ways in which Ní Dhomhnaill has used humor, one of the most prominent traditions in Irish literature.

Ó Tuama, Seán. "'The Loving and Terrible Mother' in the Early Poetry of Nuala Ní Dhomhnaill." In *Repossessions: Selected Essays on the Irish Literary Heritage*. Cork, Ireland: Cork University Press, 1995. An informative discussion of the early poetry.

Leon Lewis